THE COMPLETELY ILLUSTRATED
ATLAS
OF REPTILES
AND AMPHIBIANS
FOR THE TERRARIUM

Anolis carolinensis

Lampropeltis triangulum syspila

Distributed in the UNITED STATES by T.F.H. Publications, Inc., One T.F.H. Plaza, Neptune City, NJ 07753; in CANADA to the Pet Trade by H & L Pet Supplies Inc., 27 Kingston Crescent, Kitchener, Ontario N2B 2T6; Rolf C. Hagen Ltd., 3225 Sartelon Street, Montreal 382 Quebec; in CANADA to the Book Trade by Macmillan of Canada (A Division of Canada Publishing Corporation), 164 Commander Boulevard, Agincourt, Ontario M1S 3C7; in ENGLAND by T.F.H. Publications Limited, Cliveden House/Priors Way/Bray, Maidenhead, Berkshire SL6 2HP, England; in AUSTRALIA AND THE SOUTH PACIFIC by T.F.H. (Australia) Pty. Ltd., Box 149, Brookvale 2100 N.S.W., Australia; in NEW ZEALAND by Ross Haines & Son, Ltd., 18 Monmouth Street, Grey Lynn, Auckland 2, New Zealand; in SINGAPORE AND MALAYSIA by MPH Distributors (S) Pte., Ltd., 601 Sims Drive, #03/07/21, Singapore 1438; in the PHILIPPINES by Bio-Research, 5 Lippay Street, San Lorenzo Village, Makati Rizal; in SOUTH AFRICA by Multipet Pty. Ltd., 30 Turners Avenue, Durban 4001. Published by T.F.H. Publications, Inc. Manufactured in the United States of America by T.F.H. Publications, Inc.

THE COMPLETELY ILLUSTRATED
ATLAS
OF REPTILES
AND AMPHIBIANS
FOR THE TERRARIUM

Atelopus varius

Fritz Jürgen Obst
Dr. Klaus Richter
Dr. Udo Jacob

Translated by: U. E. Friese
Editor, English-language edition: Jerry G. Walls

Rhinophrynus dorsalis

The individual authors have worked on the following
topics:
ENGELMANN:
Anatomy and physiology, ethology, genetics
EULENBERGER:
Diseases of amphibians and reptiles
JACOB:
Amphibia, Crocodylia, ecology, zoogeography, taxonomy
KÖHLER:
Terrarium plants
OBST:
Serpentes, Testudines, herpetologists, sociological aspects
RICHTER:
Sauria, Amphisbaenia, Rhynchocephalia, food, terrarium
practice

Reviewed by:
Günther Peters and
Hans–Günther Petzold

Contents

Bufo marinus

Chelus fimbriatus

Keeping terrarium animals has become enormously popular during the last couple of decades or so, and in conjunction with this there has also been a corresponding increase in the availability of popular herpetological publications. The responsible treatment and handling of amphibians and reptiles presuppose an equally high level of knowledge of the biological and ecological relationships involved. In many cases the normal environmental and habitat conditions under which a particular animal lives are not well known, making it difficult to provide the required terrarium conditions. It then requires considerable effort, understanding, and creativity on the part of those wishing to keep some of these animals. Regrettably, regular breeding of terrarium animals over generations is still the exception, in contrast to other areas of pet keeping such as freshwater tropical fish keeping.

We are of the opinion that the popular herpetological literature still lacks a reference that adequately reflects the enormous systematic diversity of amphibians and reptiles, providing at least some basic information about families and genera that normally occur only as names on "checklists," species that, however, can make excellent terrarium animals. This is another point where there is a substantial difference from the aquarium hobby: almost all amphibians and reptiles can be kept under captive conditions. For that reason we have attempted to deal with more or less all genera and have taken into consideration virtually all names from available "checklists." Also, the more important synonyms have been included in this book, attemping to follow modern revisions. On the other hand, our attempt toward completeness of genera has imposed restrictions within species lists, and consequently the species listings often reflect only a representative species selection. Therefore, the experienced terrarium hobbyist may well find certain omissions, particularly within larger genera.

Collecting of wild animals and their trade and captive maintenance have increased on a global scale to such an extent that both national and international protective measures have been enacted. Species that once had been popular among terrarium hobbyist and had been over-collected are now available only as captive-bred progeny. However, there are also many species that are not endangered and that so far have rarely or never been kept in captivity. It is not our intent now to endanger these still abundant species, too, but instead to promote a responsible, controlled removal of wild specimens when stable habitats allow it. This does not relieve the terrarium hobby of its obligation to insist on continuous attempts to breed as many species as possible.

We would like to express our thanks to our collaborators, Dr. Engelmann, Dr. Eulenberger, and Dr. Köhler, who worked on individual subject areas. Our sincere appreciation and gratitude also go out to the numerous photographers and to our artists, Mrs. Britta Matthies and Mrs. Truadl Schneehagen, for their contributions, which so clearly stand out in this book. We would also like to thank the reviewers, Professor Peters and Dr. Petzold, as well as the publisher for their support in helping us realize our goal to produce a truly encyclopedic handbook of reptiles and amphibians that also provides detailed advice on terrarium maintenance and herpetology in general.

Due to the far-reaching comprehensiveness of the theme, it is difficult to eliminate completely all inaccuracies or even true mistakes. Therefore, we would indeed appreciate critical and constructive comments. It is our desire to contribute with this handbook to the further advancement of terrarium science and to provide the user with a reliable and informative reference book.

FRITZ JÜRGEN OBST, KLAUS RICHTER, and UDO JACOB

Interest in the keeping and breeding of terrarium animals is at an all-time high in the United States and England, and there is an urgent need for a reference book that will provide information on virtually all phases of the hobby and on all the animals likely to enter the terrarium. With the current high cost of terrarium animals and the growing assumption of moral responsibility to maintain an animal in the terrarium for as long as possible and even attempt to breed it, hobbyists can no longer afford to just make guesses at the identity of an animal and hope that it can survive in a terrarium set up for an anole or box turtle. The volume by Obst and coworkers is certainly the most comprehensive survey of the terrarium and its animals that I have ever seen, and it cannot fail to be of value to anyone with an interest in herpetology and terrariums.

In working on this edition, I have virtually omitted the cross-references of the original work. Obst, et al., used an elaborate system of arrows to signal references to almost every noun in a discussion, but this made the text virtually unreadable. There are so many entries in this volume that almost any strange word or name can be found as a major entry itself, so the arrows were to a great extent redundant. Generic level synonyms and a few higher level names are still cross-referenced, however, to make using older literature easier. An attempt has been made to check as many of the spellings and citations as possible, but there are sure to still be errors of omission and commission here. Recently described or obscure genera have not been added to this edition. Common names often are not available for foreign herps, but I have attempted to use names already present in the technical and hobbyist herpetological literature as often as possible. Instead of including common names as major entries in the text, an index of common names referenced to genera is provided.

Because the entire book is in alphabetical order, it is especially easy to find information on any specific genus. Entries at the generic level usually are followed by author and date, common name for the genus as a whole, and a short paragraph giving number of species, general distribution, and a few characters that may make the genus easier to recognize. Information on natural history and terrarium care of the genus follows where known. One or several of the more familiar or available species are then listed with common name, range, size, and occasionally more specific terrarium information. Distributions are usually given in a very general way; I have tried (not always successfully) to use the modern names and spellings of countries (i.e., Sulawesi = Celebes, Kalimantan = Borneo). Note that the Portuguese spelling of Brasil is used instead of Brazil, the more familiar American spelling.

I hope that you find this volume as useful and interesting to work with as I have and that it increases your appreciation of the diversity and extent of the terrarium hobby.

JERRY G. WALLS

Triturus cristatus, juvenile

Abdominal cavity: The abdominal cavity (coelom) is lined with peritoneum and contains the internal organs. Only in crocodiles is this cavity subdivided perpendicularly by the *septum posthepaticum*, separating the lungs, heart, and liver from the remaining abdominal organs. In turtles the lungs are separated off dorsally by a horizontal diaphragm.

Ablabes: see *Eurypholis*, genus; *Liopeltis*, genus.

Ablepharus LICHTENSTEIN, 1823. Ocellated Skinks. Genus of Scincidae. Southeastern Europe to western Asia (Pakistan). 4 to 5 species that in a larger sense belong in the *Leiolopisma* Group. Inhabits steppes and open forests. 7 to 12 cm, very slender. Has short, thin, but 5-toed limbs. Lower eyelid joined firmly to the upper one, forming a transparent, snake-like spectacle over the eye. Shiny brown, smooth scales with dark dots or stripes.

These species live among leaves on the ground or underneath rocks; prefer to sun themselves during the early morning hours. Feed on small arthropods. Egg-laying; incubation period about 60 days. The terrarium can be small and should contain a sandy substrate covered with some flat rocks, pieces of tree bark, and some leaves. Temperature during the day from 25 to 30° C.; at night about 20° C. Feed on ant pupae, wingless fruitflies (*Drosophila*), whiteworms, and other small worms. Should have 4 to 8 weeks of winter rest.
- *A. deserti* STRAUCH, 1868. Central Asia.
- *A. kitaibeli* (BIBRON and BORY, 1833). Juniper Skink, Addereye. Hungary, Balkans to western Asia. 12 cm.

Abrana PARKER, 1931. Genus of doutbful status within the Ranidae. Tropical Africa. 2 species. Depending upon individual viewpoints, either a genus, subgenus, or synonym of *Rana*.

Occurs in water holes in dry savannahs and agricultural areas (e. g., flooded rice paddies). Similar to *Ptychadena*, also semiaquatic.
- *A. cotti* PARKER, 1931. Northeastern Cameroons to Mozambique. To 5 cm.
- *A. floweri* (BOULENGER, 1917). Ghana to Sudan. To 4.5 cm.

Abronia GRAY, 1838. Arboreal Alligator Lizards. Genus of Anguidae, subfamily Gerrhonotinae. Central to northeastern South America. At least 10 species. Tropical forests to 3000 m elevation. Sometimes considered a subgenus of *Gerrhonotus*, distinguished externally from that genus primarily by a weaker lateral fold and somewhat shorter limbs. Easily to 30 cm. Prehensile tail. Often bright green, sometimes with dark crossbands.

Almost exclusively arboreal, sometimes up to 40 m high in trees, preferably among bromeliads and other epiphytes. Feeds mainly on arthropods, some snails, and similar prey. Partly ovoviviparous. Requires wet rain-forest terrarium. Between 22 and 28° C., somewhat lower at night especially for species from higher elevations.
- *A. aurita* (COPE, 1868). Central America. Mountain regions between 1000 and 3000 m elevation. 20 to 25 cm. Ovoviviparous.

Abronia taeniata

- *A. taeniata* (WIEGMANN, 1828). Bromeliad Alligator Lizard. Southern Mexico. Subspecies: *A. t. taeniata*, light gray with black crossbands; *A. t. graminea*, bright green.

Abscesses: Localized tissue infections that may lead to variable (partially fluid, partially solid) tissue growths on different parts of the body. In smaller lizards and skinks these occur mainly in the cloacal region, in tortoises around the ears, in other reptiles usually on the head but also on other parts of the body (especially in snakes).

Abscesses develop from infected, often microscopic lesions due to bites from food animals, other terrarium occupants, or ectoparasites. Sterile abscesses, as from an injection, are also possible.

Therapy: Not yet fully developed abscesses can be matured with the aid of astringent ointments. Mature abscesses can be surgically treated through lancing and subsequent cleaning, possibly by flushing with hydrogen

Abronia lythrochila

Acalyptophis peroni

peroxide, and treating with antibiotics or treatment with sulfonamide solutions. For multiple abscesses (pyaemia) or necrosis, bathing in disinfectants is recommended and/or antibiotic treatment.

Abundance: Frequency of occurrence. In ecology this applies to specimen density, less commonly to species density, when referred to a specific area.

Acalyptophis BOULENGER, 1896. Monotypic genus of Hydrophiidae, Hydrophiinae. Occurs from northern Australia to New Guinea. To 1 m, relatively slender. Scales with a short, usually darker keel. Spines projecting from above eyes (supraoculars and postoculars). Head not visually distinct from body. With washed-out brownish white ringed pattern; older specimens become uniformly dark.

Primarily nocturnal venomous snakes found among coral reefs. Appear to feed mainly on fish. The females give birth to up to 10 young. For maintenance see Hydrophiidae.
▪ *A. peroni* (DUMERIL, 1853).

Acanthixalus LAURENT, 1945. Monotypic genus of Rhacophoridae. Tropical West Africa (eastern Nigeria to Congo). In tropical rain forest. Skin covered with warts. Tympanic membrane small, located close behind eye. Distinguishable from closely related genus *Afrixalus* by spines on warts, lower thighs, and along posterior edge of feet, as well as by perpendicular oval adhesive pads. Digits on hands and feet largely interconnected through skin folds. Highly specialized tree dweller. Larvae develop presumably in phytothelms.
▪ *A. spinosus* (BUCHHOLZ and PETERS, 1875). 4 cm.

Acanthocephala: Spiny-headed Worms. Worms that anchor themselves in the digestive tract of a host by means of a hook-equipped proboscis. In reptiles only adults of the genus *Neoechinorhynchus* are regularly found in tortoises, occasionally also *Acanthocephala ranae* in *Natrix*. In rare cases of massive infestations a displacement of the intestinal lumen can occur, leading to possible refusal of food and subsequent starvation.
Therapy: Broad-spectrum anthelmintics in larger dosages.

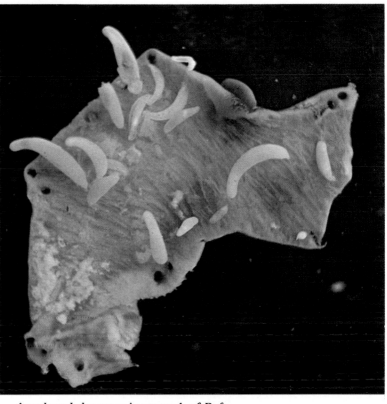

Acanthocephalus ranae in stomach of *Bufo*

Acanthodactylus WIEGMANN, 1834. Fringe-finger Lizards. Genus of Lacertidae. North Africa, Asia Minor; *A. erythrurus* also in southwestern Europe. About 12 species. Occurs in sandy or rocky arid regions with sparse vegetation. 15 to 20 cm. Well-proportioned, with somewhat stout head but pointed snout and a thickened base of the tail. Dorsal scales usually distinctly larger posteriorly than anteriorly and weakly scaled. With characteristically large scale margins on the toes. Similar to genera *Eremias* and *Scapteira*. Primarily tones of brown and gray, frequently in conjunction with whitish or dark brown markings. Juveniles more contrastingly colored; in these as well as in females the underside of the tail is partially brightly colored.

Diurnal, fast. Feeds primarily on arthropods. Egg-laying. For care and maintenance see *Eremias*. However, gen-

Acanthocephalus, proboscis extended

Acanthodactylus erythrurus

erally speaking this genus is less susceptible and hardier. A brief winter rest of 1 to 2 months is recommended, especially for *A. erythrurus*. Has been bred repeatedly.

▪ *A. erythrurus* (SCHINZ, 1833). European Fringe-finger. Northwestern Africa, Iberian Peninsula, southern France. To 20 cm. Tail in juveniles and females ventrally brick red.

▪ *A. boskianus* LICHTENSTEIN, 1856. North Africa to Asia Minor (Mediterranean Region). Easily to 20 cm. Markings less contrasting than in previous species.

Acanthophiops STERNFELD, 1911. Monotypic genus of Scincidae. South Africa. Barely 20 cm, worm-shaped. Similar to *Typhlosaurus*, but with immovable transparent lower eyelid. Without limbs. Lives below ground.

▪ *A. lineatus* STERNFELD, 1911. Yellowish white with dark longitudinal bands.

Acanthosaura armata

Acanthophis antarcticus

Acanthophis DAUDIN, 1803. Death Adders. Genus of the Elapidae. Australia, New Guinea, and adjacent islands. 2 species. Inhabits various arid regions to extreme desert conditions. Usually to 50 cm (lengths to 1 m have been reported). Body flattened dorso-ventrally, with a conspicuously set off head. Characteristically short tail terminating in a conspicuous light-colored horny spine. The tail serves as "bait."

Inactive during the day, often partially buried in soft topsoil or among leaves. Due to its cryptic coloration, it is often seen too late and stepped on (bites are common accidents). Largely nocturnal. Up to 20 young are born.

Should be kept in a well-heated desert terrarium. Often refuses food during acclimation period, but healthy specimens will usually resume feeding after 2 to 4 months. Due to the highly dangerous venom, the basic rules for keeping

venomous snakes must be strictly observed. Has been bred in captivity.

▪ *A. antarcticus* (SHAW, 1794). Death Adder. Occurs over entire generic range except the central and western Australian desert regions. 3 subspecies.

▪ *A. pyrrhus* BOULENGER, 1898. Central and western Australian desert regions.

Acanthosaura GRAY, 1831. Pricklenapes. Genus of Agamidae. Southern China to Sumatra. Used to be included in *Gonocephalus*, but distinguished from it through the absence of a continuous gular fold and the gular pouches in males. 4 species. Occurs in mountain forests. To 30 cm. Weakly laterally compressed. Massive ocular margins, neck with pointed spines, distinct low dorsal crest. Usually brown, in males also shades of green. Able to change colors.

Primarily arboreal, some also occur among fallen leaves. Egg-layers. Terrarium maintenance at high humidity and temperatures from 22 to 28° C.; about 20° C. at night. Has little need to drink; usually regular spraying is sufficient. The species are not particularly aggressive. They feed mainly on arthropods. For species from the more northern latitudes a rest period at 10 to 15° C. is recommended.

▪ *A. capra* GUENTHER, 1861. Green Pricklenape. Southeast Asia. To 30 cm. Primarily green.

▪ *A. lepidogaster* (CUVIER, 1829). Brown Pricklenape. Southern China to Southeast Asia. Mountain forests up to 1000 m elevation. Lives on the ground. Reaches easily 25 cm. Males frequently have green dorsolateral bands. Has lower temperature demands.

Acariasis: Mite and tick infestations. Disease occurring mainly as ectoparasitosis, but also as endoparasitosis. The most dangerous ectoparasitosis in reptiles is caused by the blood-sucking mites of snakes. Freshly caught reptiles, especially tortoises, snakes, and monitor lizards, are often infested by ticks in all developmental stages. Most can be seen with the naked eye or at least with a simple magnifying glass. Restlessness and frequent rubbing along the terrarium walls or substrate are clear indicators of substantial itching caused by these parasites. Massive and/or prolonged infestations can cause chronic skin infections, which can lead to localized hyperkeratosis or to abscesses.

Acanthosaura crucigera

In many cases this also leads to molting difficulties. Preferred parasite locations: Ventral scales, axillae, inside thighs, base of tail, rim of eyes. So far about 250 species of acari have been found on reptiles.

Therapy and Prophylaxis: For details see treatment of ectoparasites. It is recommended that all ticks be manually removed with forceps. Removal requires a left and a right turn in order to loosen the hypostome (mouthparts) of the parasite. However, it is advisable to first kill the parasite with ether or 70% isopropyl alcohol.

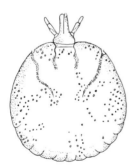

Acariasis, *Amblyomma laticauda*

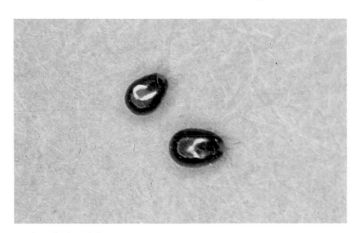

Acariasis, ticks

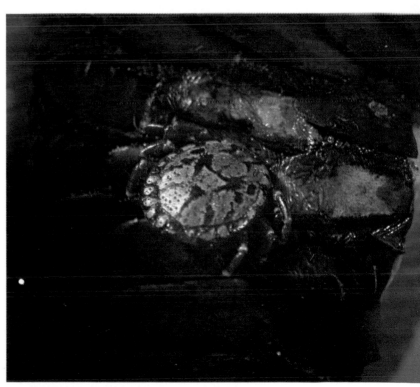

Acariasis, the tick *Amblyomma* on *Dendroaspis*

Acclimation: Adaptation. Reduction of a response following a specific stimulus, which can lead to its complete omission. Through acclimation, for instance, flight or threat behaviors can be largely suppressed or can completely disappear. Similarly, giant snakes and crocodilians used in public demonstrations may become acclimated to their "performances" and therefore do not show a defensive reaction.

Acclimation Period: An acclimation period should be combined with the quarantine period. The animals are gradually introduced to the acceptable microclimate (immediately after transport the animals are often substantially subcooled and MUST NOT be abruptly introduced to a heated terrarium). New arrivals are frequently more or less dehydrated. Drinking water must be offered first. Amphibians in an advanced state of dehydration should be bathed in a physiological salt solution, followed by normal water. A lukewarm bath is also useful to stimulate digestion in reptiles. After the animals have bathed and had water to drink, food is offered, initially only in small amounts in order to start up proper digestion. Large amounts of food taken up immediately after prolonged fasting are usually regurgitated. Force-feeding is used only if an animal continues to refuse food after a prolonged period of time and after different types of food have been offered. Usually if this occurs—and poor environmental conditions are present—one would expect an infection of some sort that must be treated without delay. During the acclimation process the animal should be disturbed as little as possible. Some snakes (e.g., *Coluber*), lizards (*Physignathus, Crotaphytus, Basiliscus*), and frogs (*Rana, Conrauna, Leptodactylus*) are initially so nervous that they can injure themselves when suddenly frightened.

Achalinus PETERS, 1869. Genus of the Colubridae, Xenoderminae. Southeastern Asia (southern China, Japan, Vietnam). 4 to 6 species. Occurs in tropical mountain forests but also found in lowlands. To 50 cm. Head pointed, clearly set off from body, with normal head scales and a slightly subterminal mouth. Dorsal scales strongly keeled. Dorsal region usually monotone gray to reddish brown.

Remains hidden under leaves during the day. Nocturnal ground snakes that prey mainly on earthworms and slugs, possibly also frogs. Egg-laying, 4 to 8 eggs. Should be kept in a tropical rain-forest terrarium with deep substrate layer and many hiding places.
• *A. spinalis* PETERS, 1869. Japan, China. Up to 2000 m elevation.
• *A. rufescens* BOULENGER, 1888. Southern China, Hong Kong to Vietnam, island of Hainan.

Acinixys: see *Pyxis,* genus.

Aclys KLUGE, 1974. Monotypic genus of Pygopodidae. Australian West Coast. 40 cm. Head relatively pointed, smooth scales, ventral and dorsal scales nearly equal in size. Small preanal pores. 5 scales on hind limbs. Natural history virtually unknown.
• *A. concinna* KLUGE, 1974.

Acontias CUVIER, 1817. Lance Skinks. Genus of the Scin-

Acontias sp.

cidae. Southern Africa, Madagascar. 7 species. Sometimes included in subfamily Acontininae, together with similar genera (*Typhlosaurus, Typhlacontias, Nessia,* and others). Occurs in dry, sandy habitats. To 40 cm. Limbless, very short-tailed burrowers with a pointed snout.

Acontias sp.

Surface only after dark. Feed on arthropods. Ovoviviparous, 3 to 6 young.
• *A. holomelas* GUENTHER, 1877. Madagascar.

Acrantophis JAN, 1844. Madagascan Boas. Genus of the Boidae. Madagascar. 2 species. To 4.5 m. Closely resembles the American genus *Boa* in shape and behavior. Lives mainly on the ground, hides during the day, becomes active at dusk. Feeds on small mammals. Juveniles tend to climb more than adults.

Terrarium maintenance as per family description. These species have a greater tendency toward mouth rot than *Boa*. Has been bred in captivity. Raising the young is easier than acclimating newly caught adults.
• *A. dumerili* JAN, 1860. Dumeril's Madagascan Boa. Northern Madagascar. Damp forest regions.
• *A. madagascariensis* (DUMERIL and BIBRON, 1844). Southern Madagascar. Dry forest regions.

Acrantophis dumerili

Acrididae: Family of grasshoppers of the order Caelifera (Saltoria). Worldwide distribution, particularly in dry regions of the tropics and subtropics. About 2 to 10 cm. Most are plant- or grass-feeders. Grasshoppers can be of importance as food animal. They are found in fields and meadows from summer through fall, first as nymphs, which can be distinguished from the adults by their smaller size and the absence of wings. Most lizards feed eagerly on these insects.

Establishing a practical breeding setup is rather difficult, since it is extremely difficult to obtain polyvoltine (several generations per year) stock that does not require a prolonged diapause (resting period) at low temperatures. However, one can store a large egg supply for use during the winter, which then can be hatched as required. For this purpose a number of adults have to be caught during the fall months and be kept in a suitable container with freshly ground grain. A smaller dish with damp sand for the animals to deposit their eggs in is placed inside the container. In order to prevent subsequent drying out, this little dish can—when well sealed—easily be placed inside a

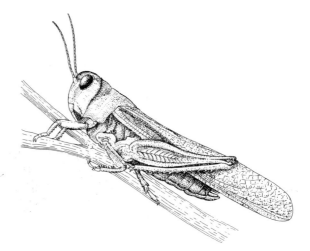

Acrididae, *Locusta migratoria*

Acrididae, colorful Australian grasshopper

refrigerator. As needed, one such dish is then placed inside a container with germinating grain, which serves as food for the newly hatched larvae. The most favorable temperature for this process is from 20 to 25° C. The cooling period for the eggs should not be less than 4 weeks, but can last more than 6 months. Longer periods reduce the hatching rates.

Also belonging to the Acrididae are the locusts (genera *Locusta, Schistocerca, Dociostaurus,* and others), which are easier to breed in captivity. These insects are polyvoltine and their eggs do not require a diapause for their development. The most often cultured species is *Locusta migratoria* from southern Europe, which grows to a length of about 6 cm. A spacious, well-ventilated container is required to breed this species. The box should contain several branches and a heat source (light bulb or floor heating). Most favorable are temperatures around 30° C.; below 20° C. breeding stops almost completely. Various young grasses can serve as food, and germinating grain can be used during the winter months. In addition, oats, bran, fruits, and vegetables can also be offered as food. However, optimal development can only be obtained by feeding at least partially with grass. The eggs are deposited in small dishes placed inside the box and filled about 3 to 5 cm deep with dampened sand. Once sufficient eggs have been deposited

Acrididae, *Locusta migratoria* mating

in such a dish it is replaced with a fresh dish. The egg-filled dish is then transferred to a smaller rearing container. The nymphs hatch after about 15 days; the animals reach sexual maturity after 3 ½ to 4 weeks.

Locusts are eagerly taken by many lizards. Smaller species are given the smaller nymphal stages. However, locusts should not be fed for prolonged periods of time, since they may then be eventually totally rejected.

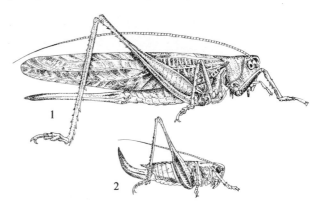

Tettigoniidae: 1 *Tettigonia viridisima,* ♀; 2 *Decticus verrucivoris,* ♀

Acris DUMERIL and BIBRON, 1841. Cricket Frogs. Genus of the Hylidae. Eastern North America. 2 polytypic species. Occurs in shallow, sunny ponds and slow-flowing waters of the lowlands. Fingers free, toes joined along three-fourths of their length by membrane (this characteristic easily distinguishes this genus from *Pseudacris*). Adhesive discs barely wider than tips of fingers and toes. With characteristic triangular or V-shaped dark spot between the eyes and a black stripe or stripes in a light field on the posterior side of the thigh. Dorsally with 4 dark, more or less distinctive longitudinal bands (2 on the back, one on each flank), often partially missing or broken into spots.

Semi-aquatic; does not climb; ecologically comparable to the smaller *Rana* species. The males call from shallow water or sitting on top of floating vegetation, with a prolonged chirping sound. Breeds generally during the spring and summer months. Southern populations breed independently of the seasons during periods of rainfall.

Maintain in an unheated or only barely heated aqua-terrarium. Winter rest not required for southern populations, but the temperature should be reduced.

▪ *A. crepitans* BAIRD, 1854. Great Lakes to northern Mexico east of the Great Plains. To 3.5 cm. Northern populations often with contrasting dark brown pattern against bright green background color. Southern populations often browner, with washed out dark pattern, but highly variable. Rough-edged thigh stripe.

▪ *A. gryllus* (LECONTE, 1825). Southeastern United States between Mississippi River and eastern coast, south of Appalachian area. To 3 cm. Dark pattern against yellow-brown background, variable. Thigh stripe usually smooth-edged, may be double.

Acrochordidae: Wart, Elephant Trunk, or File Snakes. Family of the Henophidia. Southern Asia from India to Indo-China and south through Indo-Australian Archipelago to northern Australia, New Guinea, and Solomon Islands. 2 genera, 3 species: *Acrochordus, Chersydrus*. Found in fresh water, brackish water, and sea water. 1 to 2.5 m, plump to massive, with wrinkled skin appearing to be too large, similar to some Hydrophiinae. Large, flat, wide-mouthed head not set off from trunk. Head and body covered with small granular scales in a mosaic pattern. Only rim of mouth covered with lip plates (labials). Eyes small, directed upward. Apart from eyes, nostrils are highest elevation on head and can be closed under water. Body scales are isolated, non-overlapping, giving skin a very rough surface. Abdominal plates are replaced with 2 to 3 rows of scales forming an abdominal seam that is also reminiscent of Hydrophiinae. *Chersydrus* is considered by several workers to be a synonym of *Acrochordus*.

Rarely or never (*Chersydrus*) hauls out on land, and can remain underwater for several hours. More or less nocturnal. Feed primarily on fish, possibly also frogs, tadpoles, molluscs, crustaceans. All species are viviparous. *Chersydrus* deposits young in water; juveniles of *Acrochordus* presumably live on land (swamps).

Should be kept in spacious warmwater aquariums, with ample hiding places such as submerged tree roots. Juvenile *Acrochordus* require land section that must be easily accessible; adults are less dependent on land. Some salt (NaCl) should be added to provide brackish conditions, especially for *Chersydrus*, less so for *Acrochordus*. Food should be live fish. Adult *Acrochordus* often refuse to take food and may have to be force-fed.

Considered a delicacy in their native lands and marketed extensively as luxury culinary food items, such as Wart Snake livers. Also hunted heavily for leather.

Acrochordus HORNSTEDT, 1787. Java Wart Snakes, File Snakes. Genus of the Acrochordidae. 2 species. Southern Indo-China, Indo-Australian Archipelago, New Guinea, northern Australia. In rivers, lakes, swamps, brackish water (mangrove swamps). Conspicuous size difference between the sexes: males 0.8 to 1.4 m; females in excess of 2.5 m. Characteristic of this genus is its prehensile tail, with which the animals anchor themselves below water on roots and water plants. Dorsally dark brown, ventrally yellowish. Flanks with a row of spots or a more or less defined dark lateral band. Produce 20 to 30 young.
• *A. javanicus* HORNSTEDT, 1787.

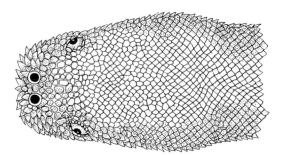

Acrochordus javanicus

Acrodont: see Teeth.

Acrophobia: Innate fear of heights, which are visually recognized as dangerous. Does not seem to occur in most reptile species from the plains, while those from mountain regions instinctively pull back when facing great heights, presumably an innate type of behavior.

Acrostichum L. Mangrove Fern. Genus of the Pteridaceae. Tropics and subtropics. 3 species. Swamp plant closely associated with mangroves. Due to its large size only juvenile plants should be kept in aqua-terrariums or paludariums. Should be given a bright location; summer temperatures 18 to 22° C., winter months 14 to 16° C. sufficient.
• *A. aureum* L.

Activity rhythms: Periodic repetitive pattern in the locomotory activity of animals. These are mostly tied to day/night changes (circadian rhythm) and can occur as endogenous or exogenous rhythms, as well as be composed of various individual activities.

Adelophis DUGES, 1879. Genus of the Colubridae, Natricinae. Mexico. 35 cm. Natural history and care similar to the closely related genus *Storeria*. Has smooth dorsal scales.
• *A. copei* DUGES, 1879.

Adelotus OGILBY, 1907. Tusked Frogs. Monotypic genus of the Leptodactylidae. Coastal regions of southeastern Australia in more or less damp forests or open areas. With broadly rounded snout. Eyes small, pupil horizontal. Tympanic membrane indistinct. Digits without webs and without adhesive discs. Males with 2 large canine-like projections ("tusks") on lower jaw. Dorsal area dark gray or brown, with irregular spotted pattern. Throat and abdomen with white spots against blackish background (males) or distinctly marked with a black and white marbled pattern (females). Groin and hind legs with red spots.

Ground-dweller, hides underneath logs, in burrows, rock crevices, and similar locations close to water (ponds, creeks, puddles). The mating call is mono-syllabic, given off at night, loud and continuous. The females build bubblenests on water (12-15 cm diameter) and guard these. The larvae hatch within a few days after the eggs have been laid and then metamorphose after 3 to 4 weeks. Should be kept in slightly heated, semi-wet terrarium with a separate water section.
• *A. brevis* (GUENTHER, 1863). Tusked Frog. To 4.5 cm, females smaller.

Adelphicos JAN, 1862. Genus of the Colubridae, Lycodontinae. Central America (Mexico and Belize south to Guatemala). 2 species. Closely related to *Atractus* and with similar natural history. About 40 cm. With 4 dark longitudinal bands. Head shields reduced.
• *A. quadrivirgatus* JAN, 1862.

Adenomera STEINDACHNER, 1867. Taxonomic group that includes the *Leptodactylus marmoratus* Group; considered by some systematists a valid genus.

Adenorhinus MARX and RAAB, 1965. Monotypic genus of the Viperidae, Viperinae. East Africa. Tropical mountain

forests. 40 cm. Arboreal venomous snakes. Care similar to *Atheris*.
- *A. barbouri* (LOVERIDGE, 1930). Tanzania.

Adiantum L. Maidenhair Fern. Genus of the Adiantaceae. Tropics and subtropics, primarily in South and Central America, a few species in temperate climates. More than 200 species; some are decorative ferns. Prefers shade and dampness; frequently found growing over calcareous rocks.
- *A. capillus-veneris* L. Leaf stems to 15 cm. Moderate winter hardness.
- *A. caudatum* L. Draping leaves, to 25 cm. Good hanging plant.
- *A. raddianum* K. B. PRESL. Resistant, good grower. Many varieties.
- *A. hispidulum* SW. Very resistant.
- *A. macrophyllum* SW. Rhizome creeping, with large leaves. Leaf stems upright. Decorative.

Adolfus STERNFELD, 1912. Genus of the Lacertidae. Formerly included in *Algyroides*, but without massetericum (temporal scale). Tropical Africa. 3 species. In mountain regions. Barely 20 cm. Inconspicuous. Requires fairly high humidity. Little is known about this genus.
- *A. alleni* BARBOUR, 1914. Eastern Central Africa, on Mount Kenya to 3000 m. Damp mountain meadows. To 18 cm. Snout-vent length 7 cm.

Aechmae RUIZ and PAVON. Genus of the Bromeliaceae. Mexico to Argentina. 150 species. Mostly epiphytic. Only small to medium size plants are suitable for terrariums. Can easily be cultivated in dry air. Summer temperatures 18 to 22° C., 16 to 18° C. in the winter. The soft-leaved species from rain forests require more heat and shade.
- *A. fasciata* (LINDL.) BAKER. Leaves to 50 cm. Can easily be cultivated in a semi-shaded location.
- *A. miniata* hort. var. *discolor*. Grows readily in semi-shaded location.

Aechmae chantinii

- *A. racinae* L. B. SMITH. Leaves to 40 cm. Should be grown at 18° C. Only for larger terrariums.
- *A. recurvata* (KLOTZSCH) L. B. SMITH. Leaves to 30 cm. Hardy. Can endure droughts and direct sunlight. Should be kept in sunny location. Ideally suited for attaching to epiphyte logs.
- *A. weilbachi* DIETR. Is considered to be hardy. Should be kept in semi-shade at 18° C.

Aelurophryne: see *Scutiger*, genus.

Aeluroscalabotes BOULENGER, 1885. Cat Geckos. Monotypic genus of the Gekkonidae, subfamily Eublepharinae (a second doubtful species has been described from Western Australia). Indo-China, Indo-Australian Archipelago. About 15 cm. Without adhesive toe pads; movable lids. Little known in regard to terrarium maintenance. Produces 2 eggs.
- *A. felinus* (GUENTHER, 1864).

Aeromonas colonies

Aeromonas infection: Most important bacterial infection in amphibians and reptiles, especially in aquatic forms. Sometimes appears as a general disease, but at other times quite specific. Affects primarily the digestive tract (diarrhea, stomatitis infectiosa). *Aeromonas* can also cause pneumonia and abscesses.

Relatively specific symptoms in toads and frogs (red-leg): conspicuous reddening of the abdominal skin and along the inside of the upper thigh region. Hemorrhaging areas break open, leading to open wounds. The lymph sacs are filled with serous fluid, causing a bloated appearance. The animals are very apathetic, displaying delayed reactions to external stimuli, and usually die within 10 days due to hemorrhagic septicemia.

Infection occurs via ectoparasites (blood mites in snakes) or directly via minute infected lesions, especially when pathogens are permitted to accumulate in bathing water. Sometimes highly contagious.

Therapy: Apart from symptomatic treatment for specific effects (abscesses, diarrhea, pneumonia), antibiotics, particularly chloramphenicol and tetracycline, are useful.

Prophylaxis: Treatment for ectoparasites, adequate water cleanliness, the drinking and bathing water possibly should be sterilized; remove contaminated animals.

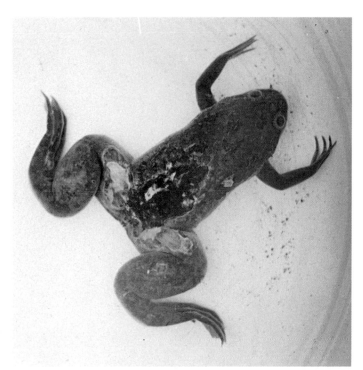

Aeromonas, red-leg in *Xenopus*

Afrixalus LAURENT, 1944. Banana Frogs. Genus of the Rhacophoridae. Tropical Africa, Madagascar. About 20 species, some polytypic. Once included in *Megalixalus*. In tropical rain forests, but species also in open grassland and savannahs, close to water. 2 to 5 cm. Similar to treefrogs in general appearance. Pupil vertical, thus easily distinguishable from *Hyperolius*. Tympanic membrane usually indistinct or covered by skin. Fingers free or with basal membrane only, toes variably webbed depending upon species. Large adhesive discs on tips of fingers and toes. Males with large, unpaired vocal sac. Chirping call. Larvae rather elongated; mouth wide since lower lip is only moderately arched (not indented and V-like).

Nocturnal; during daylight hours found in dark hiding places such as hollow logs, deep in overlapping leaf stem axils, or in banana trees. Climb about in and on swamp plants and other bushes. Eggs are unpigmented, deposited at intervals inside folded up leaves just above water level.

Afrixalus fornasini

The larvae hatch after 10 days and slide into the water below. Metamorphosis occurs after about 2 ½ months.

Forest species should be kept in a tropical rain-forest terrarium with a water section; savannah species are best given a densely planted swamp terrarium at tropical temperatures and high humidity. Sufficient hiding places protected from light must be available. Should be fed during the evening on small flying insects.

Will breed in captivity if suitable leaves are available above a water source. Prior to hatching, funnel-shaped leaves with the eggs inside should be transferred to a separate rearing container. There the leaves are placed in such a way that upon hatching the larvae can slide into the water. After the yolk sac has been absorbed the young can be reared on dried fish food and then on macerated tubifex,

Afrixalus sp.

daphnia, mosquito larvae, and whiteworms; newly metamorphosed young will take *Drosophila* and springtails.

▪ *A. congicus* (LAURENT, 1941). West Africa. 4 subspecies. Tropical rain forests. 3.5 cm. Highly variable in coloration. Dorsum golden, dark spot against brown background.

▪ *A. dorsalis* (PETERS, 1875). West Africa. 3 subspecies. Rain forests and wetlands. 3 cm. Coloration highly variable. Usually brown with golden longitudinal bands.

▪ *A. fornasini* (BIANCONI, 1849). East Africa. Savannahs with tree cover. 4 cm. Dark brown, with 2 rather wide silvery longitudinal bands that can appear fused.

▪ *A. fulvovittatus* (COPE, 1861). West Africa. 3 subspecies. Savannahs and dense forests. 2.5 cm. Dorsum with regular pattern of blackish brown and golden bands.

Afroablepharus GREER, 1974. Genus of the Scincidae. Africa south of the Saharan desert. 6 species. Occurs in sa-

vannah-like areas. In contrast to *Panaspis*, has a solidly attached lid spectacle. Dorsal scales smooth or very weakly keeled. Ground-dweller.
- *A. wahlbergi* (SMITH, 1849).

Afrocaecilia TAYLOR, 1968. Genus of the Caeciliidae. East Africa. 3 species. Used to be included in *Boulengerula*, but distinct from this genus by the presence of 2 rows of teeth in the lower jaw. 20 to 36 cm, slender. Only 128 to 148 primary furrows present, no secondary furrows or scales present. Anal slit perpendicular.
- *A. taitana* (LOVERIDGE, 1935). Kenya, Teifa Mountains. To 36 cm. Glossy black, furrows light bluish gray.

Afroedura LOVERIDGE, 1944. Rock Geckos. Genus of the Gekkonidae, subfamily Gekkoninae. Africa. 7 species. About 10 cm, slender, typical of family in appearance. Adhesive lamellae indistinct.

Nocturnal rock-dweller often occurring at high elevations. Provide rest period during the winter for high altitude species (during the summer in the Northern Hemisphere). No requirement for additional heat. Little known about life in captivity.
- *A. africana* (BOULENGER, 1894). Southwestern Africa.
- *A. nivaria* (BOULENGER, 1894). South Africa. Mountains.

Afronatrix ROSSMAN and EBERLE, 1977. African Water Snakes. Monotypic genus of the Colubridae, Natricinae. West Africa. 75 cm. Primarily aquatic. Biologically, morphologically, and in regard to terrarium care similar to Group 3 of the Natricinae.
- *A. anoscopus* (COPE, 1861). Guinea to Cameroons.

Agalychnis callidryas

Agalychnis annae

Agalychnis COPE, 1864. Red-eyed Treefrogs. Genus of the Hylidae. Central America, nothern South America. 8 species. Occurring in the *selva* and *montana*. Pupil vertical. Upper arms and thighs conspicuously thin. Toes more heavily webbed than fingers. First toe always shorter than the second one, helping to distinguish this genus from the closely related genus *Phyllomedusa*. Dorsum mainly green; most species with conspicuous color pattern on flanks. Ventral region white, yellowish, or orange. Iris yellow or red, covered by transparent, usually net-like upper part of the lower lid when eyes are at rest.

Active at dusk, but primarily a nocturnal tree-dweller. As far as known the eggs (covered in foam) are deposited on the undersides of leaves. A fews days later the eggs slide

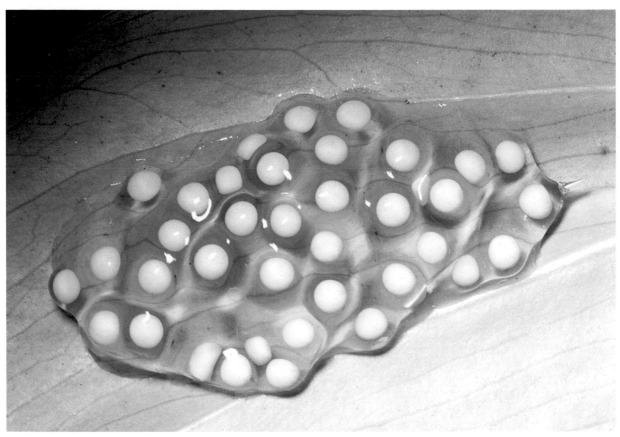

Agalychnis callidryas, egg mass

Agalychnis callidryas, night pattern

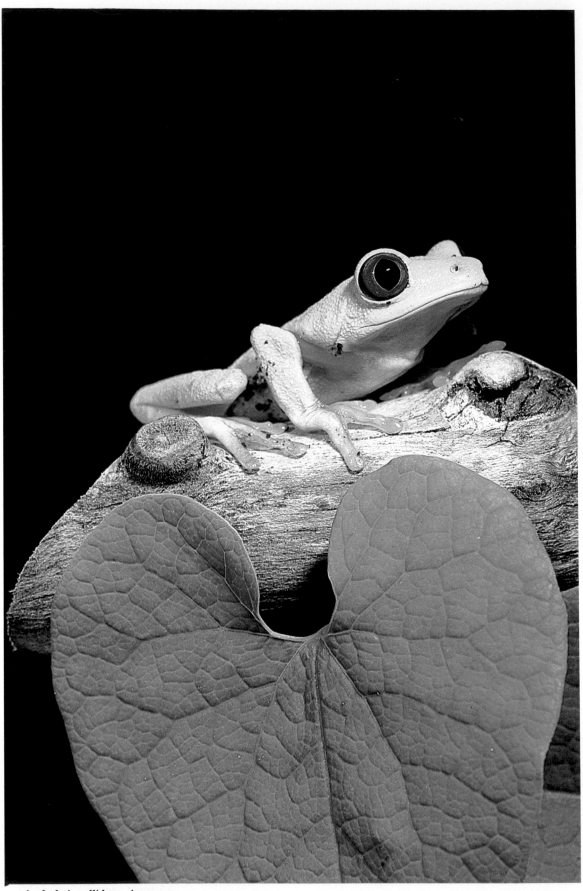

Agalychnis callidryas, immature

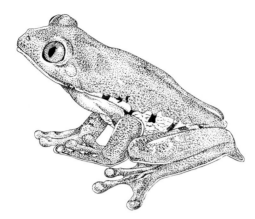

Agalychnis calcarifer

Agalychnis callidryas

off and must fall into water (usually a bromeliad axil funnel or a jungle pool) for further development. Larvae are not very active, mostly resting in a head-up oblique position. 100 to 115 days to metamorphosis.

These are very attractive frogs that are easily kept and even bred in a rain-forest terrarium. Once a particular resting place has been selected it is commonly retained. Should be kept at an even, high humidity with good ventilation. Temperature range 23 to 27° C. The diet consists mainly of large flies, but also takes freshly molted crickets and other soft-skinned insects. The larvae can be reared on dried fish food, some green algae, lettuce leaves, and other vegetable matter. Caution must be taken that the food is not contaminated with herbicides.

▪ *A. calcarifer* BOULENGER, 1902. Colombia, Ecuador. To 8 cm, males smaller. Dorsum olive green. Abdomen orange, flanks and thighs (laterally) with black crossbands. Lower eyelid not reticulated (exceptional within this genus).
▪ *A. callidryas* (COPE, 1862). Red-eyed Treefrog. Central America. To 7 cm, males smaller. Flanks with blue crossbands against cream-colored background. Iris red. Fingers and toes orange. Most frequently imported species.
▪ *A. moreletii* (DUMERIL, 1853). Southern Mexico to Panama. To 8 cm, males smaller. Dorsal area bright green, sometimes sparsely covered with white spots. Ventral area yellow. Flanks without distinctive color pattern.
▪ *A. spurrelli* BOULENGER, 1913. Central America, Colombia. To 8.5 cm, males smaller. Dorsal region with scattered white spots with black margins. Abdomen yellow.

Agalychnis annae

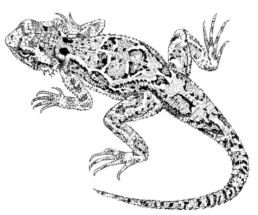

Agama persimilis

Agama DAUDIN, 1802. Typical Agamas. Genus of the Agamidae. Recently split into various independent genera. Africa and southwestern to central Asia; *A. stellio* reaches southeastern Europe. About 60 species and numerous subspecies. Occurs in more or less dry habitats along forest edges, rocky areas to sand deserts; also found in mountain regions. To 40 cm. Head distinctly separated from trunk. Strong limbs. Scales on posterior margins of head and thighs spiny. Dorsal scales either smooth, shingled, or keeled.

Some species with vertically whorled tails and dorsoventrally flattened bodies (e. g., *A. caucasia*, *A. stellio*, *A.*

Agama himalayana

cyanogaster) seem to be opposite—in an evolutionary sense—the presumably more ancient species with shingled tail scales and more laterally compressed bodies (e. g., *A. atra, A. anchietae*). Species like *A. agama* and *A. agilis* seem to occupy an intermediate position.

Outside the mating season the males are usually brown or gray; their breeding colors are bright red, blue, and tones of yellow. Many species can undergo conspicuous color changes. When not in breeding dress, males can be recognized by several rows of anal pores and possibly also on the basis of rows of pores in the center of the abdomen. Also, males have much larger heads than females.

Agamas are primarily ground-dwellers, but a few species (e. g., *A. atricollis*) are semiarboreal. Food consists of arthropods, including aggressive wasps and tough beetles; some species are to a degree even herbivorous. Many species live in colonies and have well-defined territorial behavior (characteristic head nodding). In contrast to many lizards, the females of some agamids play an active part in the reproductive cycle by actively courting males. These are egg-layers, 2 to 20 eggs per clutch, sometimes several clutches in one year. Hatching times vary from 1 ½ to 4 ½ months.

Agamids require a spacious, relatively dry terrarium that can be decorated as a rocky, savannah, or desert terrarium, depending upon the species. The latter requires a thick bottom layer of moderately moist sand. These lizards must have sufficient hiding places, since most species are initially often very shy and frighten easily. Temperatures during the day 25 to 32° C., localized ground temperatures even higher; night temperatures about 10 degrees lower. Species from more northern latitudes require a rest period of about 2 to 3 months during the winter months; montane species should then be kept at about 4° C. The latter species can even be kept in outdoor terrariums during the

summer months. Agamids require little water; regular spraying is sufficient. Ultraviolet radiation is imperative, as are calcium and vitamin supplements. Most males are aggressive, thus keeping only one male per terrarium is advisable. Some species (e. g., *A. stellio*) have been bred in captivity with great regularity.

▪ *A. agama* (LINNAEUS, 1758). Common Agama. Africa. Several subspecies. To 40 cm. Small crest. Grayish brown, but conspicuous color changes to red, yellow, blue, and other markings. 3 to 8 eggs. Aggressive.

▪ *A. agilis* OLIVIER, 1804. Slender Agama. Southwestern to central Asia. Several subspecies. Savannah. To 30 cm. Best known form is *A. a. sanguinolenta* PALLAS, 1844. Up to three clutches with 8 to 10 eggs each per year. Can be given winter rest period. Very susceptible to parasite attacks during acclimation period, but later easy to maintain in terrarium. Has been bred in captivity.

▪ *A. atra* DAUDIN, 1802. Black or Rock Agama. Southern Africa. Rocky habitats. 20 cm. Very dark. Should be kept relatively warm.

Agama agama

Agama lehmanni

Agama nupta fusca

• *A. atricollis* SMITH, 1849. Blue-throated Agama. Kenya. Edge of forest, semiarboreal. 25 cm. Compact, spiny. Grayish brown with white, yellow, or greenish dot pattern. Should be kept relatively moist, but terrarium must not be permitted to cool off too much at night.

• *A. caucasia* EICHWALD, 1833. Caucasian Agama. Caucasus to northern Turkey, Iran, Afghanistan. Up to 2000 m elevation. To 35 cm. Robust, strongly flattened dorso-ventrally. Spiny tail. Brown to olive-gray with reticulated darker pattern. Color changes relatively minor. 6 to 14 eggs. Winter rest period recommended.

Agama a. sanguinolenta

• *A. hispida* (LINNAEUS, 1758). Spiny Agama. Southern Africa. To 30 cm. Relatively conspicuous dorsal spines. Abdominal scales are keeled. Grayish brown to glossy green. 12 to 20 eggs.

• *A. impalearis* BOETTGER, 1874 (= *A. bibroni* DUMERIL, 1851, name not current). Atlas Agama. Northwestern Africa. Mountains. To 30 cm. Gray-brown. Conspicuous color changes. Two clutches of up to 12 eggs each. Terrarium maintenance somewhat difficult; requires significant temperature reduction at night.

• *A. lehmanni* NIKOLSKY, 1896. Turkmenian Agama. Central Asia. Mountain regions up to 3500 m elevation. To 35 cm. Winter rest period important. Easy terrarium maintenance, very hardy. Has been bred repeatedly.

• *A. mutabilis* MERREM, 1820. Desert Agama. North Africa to southwestern Asia. Rocky and sandy deserts. To 25 cm.

Smooth scales. Yellow to reddish brown with spotted pattern. Distinct diurnal rhythm. 5 to 10 eggs. Somewhat sensitive.

• *A. planiceps* PETERS, 1862. Southwestern Africa. Mountain regions. To 35 cm. Nape with spines. Shingled tail. Head and thorax red, rest mainly blackish blue. Substantially herbivorous.

• *A. stellio* (LINNAEUS, 1758). Hardun. Southwestern Asia to northeastern Africa, some parts of Greece. Rocky habitats. In excess of 35 cm. Spiny. Strongly compressed dorso-ventrally. Gray to almost black with light colored spots. Up to three clutches with 8-12 eggs each. Can be kept outdoors. Winter rest period recommended.

Agama caucasia

Agamidae: Agamas. Family of the Squamata, suborder Sauria. Inhabits the entire Old World, except northern Palearctic and Madagascar. Primarily in southern Asia and Australia; in Africa the only genera are *Agama* and *Uromastyx*. 30 genera with more than 300 recent species. Agamidae belongs in the family group Iguanomorpha and presumably forms the sister group of Iguanidae, together with the Chamaeleonidae. There are a number of parallel developments in both families (Agamidae and Iguanidae) as adaptations to particular ecological niches in the Old and New World, respectively. Fossil records exist from the Upper Cretaceous. From tropical rain and mountain forests to steppes and deserts.

Agamids appear to be relatively unspecialized with a usually well-proportioned typical lizard body. The limbs are often strongly developed. The ground-dwelling species are generally dorso-ventrally depressed, those living in trees laterally compressed. Nape, dorsal, and tail crests, gular pouches and folds, helmets, and horns are particularly well developed in males. Some have the ability to produce sounds. Tongue wide, thick, and fleshy. Eyes not particularly large, pupil round. Vertebrae procoelic, without intervertebral discs. Tail without predetermined breakage points (no autotomy), poor regeneration capabilities. Osteoderms absent. Temporal arches complete, lacrimal absent or largely reduced. No pterygoid teeth (important characteristic for distinguishing from Iguanidae). Acrodont jaw teeth, not replaceable, usually differentiated. Most species have the ability for physiological color changes (e. g., *Calotes* species, some *Agama* species).

Some members of *Draco* can perform aerial glides for several meters; other agamids are closely tied to water and will flee by diving into water when threatened (e. g., *Physignathus*, *Hydrosaurus*). The genera *Agama* and *Uromastyx* are found primarily in arid regions in Africa and southwestern Asia to India; *Phrynocephalus* occurs in steppes and deserts in western and central Asia. The Indian area is occupied by the genera *Acanthosaura*, *Calotes*, *Ceratophora*, *Cophotis*, *Japalura*, *Lyriocephalus*, *Oriocalotes*, *Otocryptis*, *Psammophilus*, *Salea*, and *Sitana*. Apart from those genera just mentioned, southeastern Asia (including the Indo-Australian Archipelago) also has the genera *Aphaniotis*, *Draco*, *Gonocephalus*, *Harpesaurus*, *Hydrosaurus*, *Hylagama*, *Leiolepis*, *Lophocalotes*, *Mictopholis*, *Paracalotes*, *Phoxophrys*, *Physignathus*, and *Ptyctolaemus*. Australia is home to the genera *Amphibolurus*, *Chelosania*, *Chlamydosaurus*, *Diporiphora*, *Gonocephalus*, *Moloch*, *Oreodeira*, *Physignathus*, and *Tympanocryptis*.

Threatening, warning, and courtship behavior are strongly developed in males. Head nodding as an expression of different states of excitement is often typical. As far as is known all species in this family (with the exception of *Cophotis* species and some *Phrynocephalus* species) are egg-laying.

Agamodon PETERS, 1882. Genus of the Amphisbaenia, family Trogonophidae. Northeastern Africa, southwestern Arabia. 3 species. In dry regions. Exceeding 10 cm. Head chisel-shaped. Bright yellow to reddish, with dark spots. Sometimes occupies very hard clay ground.
▪ *A. anguliceps* PETERS, 1882. Somalia, Eritrea. 11 cm. Dorsum yellow with dark spots.

Agamura BLANFORD, 1874. Genus of the Gekkonidae. Southwestern Asia. 2 species. In dry, often rocky habitats. About 10 cm. Slender. Tail barely equal to snout-vent length. Limbs very delicate. Mainly brownish. Nocturnal and diurnal ground-dwellers.
▪ *A. persica* (DUMERIL, 1856). Spider Gecko. Afghanistan, Iran, and adjacent areas. 10 cm.

Agassiz, Louis Jean Rodolphe (1807–1873): Swiss-American zoologist and geologist. *Contributions to the Natural History of the USA* (1857).

Agavaceae: Agave plants. Family of the Liliatae. Dry regions of the tropics and subtropics. 18 genera, 560 species. Mostly large, succulent rosette plants, some stem-forming semi-bushes and bushes. Many genera flower only once (e. g., *Agave*)—sometimes only after several years—and then die. *Agave*, *Dracaena*, *Furcraea*, *Sanseveria*, *Yucca*.

Agave L. Agaves. Genus of the Agavaceae. Dry regions of Central America, some species introduced worldwide. About 300 species. Succulent, robust rosette shrubs. Undemanding, decorative, can survive extended droughts, require sunlight and warmth. Should be watered extensively during the summer months, sparingly during the winter. Can be over-wintered in bright, well-ventilated locations at about 5° C. Reproduction is by severing adventive plants formed on short runners. Due to excessive size, suitable in terrariums only as immature plants.
▪ *A. americana* L. Adult plants reach a diameter of 2 to 3 m. Decorative, especially the varieties "marginata" and "striata."

Agkistrodon bilineatus

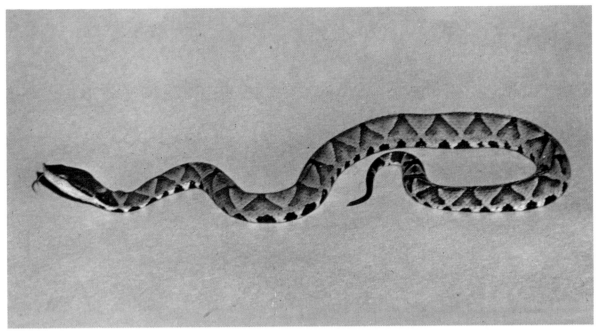

Agkistrodon acutus

- *A. attenuata* SALM-DYCK. Dragon Tree Agave. Stem-forming. Leaves to 20 cm.
- *A. potatorum* ZUCC. Rosette leaves 20 to 30 cm. Most frequently cultivated variety: *verschaffeltii* BERGER.
- *A. stricta* SALM-DYCK. Rosettes to 35 cm diameter.
- *A. univittata* HAW. Rosettes to 85 cm diameter. Leaves to 20 to 30 cm.
- *A. victoria-reginae* T. MOORE. Mexico. Rosettes 50 to 70 cm diameter. Leaves 10 to 15 cm.

Aggregation: Accumulation in a restricted area of several to many individuals of the same species. In amphibians and reptiles this phenomenon occurs in relationship with winter rest (e. g., over-wintering aggregations of garter snakes) or mating (e. g., mating aggregations of common vipers).

Aggression: Types of behavior oriented toward injuring other animals, to driving them away, or defeating them. This includes threatening behavior and ritualistic fighting; it is part of the agonistic behavior that enables animals to cope with conflict (allied to flight behavior and submissive behavior). Apart from interspecific behavior (prey/predator relationship, enemy reaction), the intraspecific behavior is of particular importance. It promotes equal distribution of a particular population within a habitat, provides for a minimum distance between individuals (distance behavior), favors the distribution of a species, and it also helps assure that only the healthiest and strongest of the males survive. The negative influences of intraspecific behavior, such as danger of potential injuries, is mitigated in part by ritualism in fighting, development of a hierarchy, development of fight-inhibiting mechanisms (submissive behavior), and flight behavior. Intraspecific conflicts in amphibians and reptiles are common and of rather variable intensity, and usually are for the purpose of obtaining females willing to mate, suitable egg-laying sites, hiding places, territories, and food organisms. Specific key stimuli act as triggering mechanisms. This is particularly true for

territorial species (territorial behavior), during which some rather differentiated and highly developed types of behavior occur, as among the genera *Agama*, *Anolis*, *Chamaeleo*, and *Amblyrhynchus*. This also includes the ritualistic fighting among male adders, vipers, and pit vipers, where, however, the meaning is still unclear.

Agkistrodon BEAUVOIS, 1799. Copperheads and Moccasins. Genus of the Crotalidae. Asia and North America (into Central America). About 13 species, some polytypic. Length 0.7 to 1.6 m. Top of head with more or less regular large scutes. Currently only three Nearctic species, *A. bilineatus*, *A. contortrix*, and *A. piscivorus*, are included in a restricted genus *Agkistrodon* by some workers. The Oriental species are included in the monotypic genus *Deinagkistrodon* GLOYD, 1978 (containing *acutus*) and in the polytypic genera *Calloselasma* COPE, 1860 (for *annamensis* and *rhodos-*

Agkistrodon acutus

toma) and *Gloydius* HOGE and ROMANO-HOGE, 1978/79 (for, among others, *blomhoffi*, *halys*, *himalayanus*, and *saxatilis*). This classification is not universally accepted. The generic name is spelled *Ancistrodon* in older literature.

Ecological groupings:

1) Semiaquatic species: *A. piscivorus* and *A. bilineatus* and to some degree also *A. blomhoffi*. Prefer warm, dry sunning sites after hunting for fish, frogs, water rats, mice, lizards, and others.

2) Species of temperate regions found along the edges of forests, forest clearings, and to some degree in damp, wooded regions: *A. contortrix*, *A. halys*, *A. saxatilis*. Food mainly small mammals; juveniles will feed on lizards and arthropods.

Agkistrodon acutus

Agkistrodon contortrix

Agkistrodon bilineatus

3) Montane and subalpine mountain-dwellers found in mountain meadows and rocky areas but also in lowland tundras: *A. halys*, *A. monticola*, *A. himalayanus*. Prefer lizards and small mammals.

4) Inhabitants of tropical forests (edges), some also in montane rain forests: *A. acutus*, *A. rhodostoma*. Feed on frogs and small mammals.

Most *Agkistrodon* are ovoviviparous (6 to 20 young), except the egg-laying *A. acutus* (15 to 25 eggs) and *A. rhodostoma* (10 to 35 eggs). Venom effects variable. Primarily hemotoxic venom in *A. piscivorus*, *A. bilineatus*, *A. acutus*, and *A. rhodostoma*, dangerous to man and often lethal without serum therapy. Less dangerous are *A. halys*, *A. blomhoffi*, and *A. contortrix*. Behavior similar to *Crotalus*. When excited, animals will raise end of tail or let it vibrate against the ground, which causes a vibrating ("rattling") sound

Agkistrodon piscivorus

that becomes amplified in contact with leaves on the ground. This serves as a warning sound.

Terrarium maintenance must follow the ecological demands of the respective species. Many species do well in captivity, and bred for several generations. Only those species from high altitudes are problematic; these require annual rest periods. *A. piscivorus, A. halys,* and *A. contortrix* are undemanding, hardy venomous snakes in a terrarium.
▪ *A. acutus* (GUENTHER, 1864). Chinese Copperhead, Sharp-nosed Copperhead. Southern China to northern Vietnam. 1.5 m. Spine-like extended rostral scute.

Agkistrodon contortrix

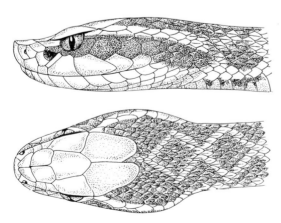

Agkistrodon blomhoffi

▪ *A. bilineatus* GUENTHER, 1863. Cantil, Mexican Moccasin. Southern Mexico to Nicaragua. Several subspecies.
▪ *A. blomhoffi* (BOIE, 1826). Mamushi. Eastern Asia. Several subspecies.
▪ *A. contortrix* (LINNAEUS, 1766). Copperhead. 135 cm. Eastern and central United States. 5 subspecies.
▪ *A. halys* (PALLAS, 1776). Halys's Viper. Siberia, eastern Asia. 3 or 4 subspecies.

Agkistrodon halys

Agkistrodon piscivorus, immature

Agkistrodon rhodostoma

Agkistrodon blomhoffi brevicaudis

Agkistrodon saxatilis

Agkistrodon piscivorus conanti

Aglaonema costatum

- *A. himalayanus* (GUENTHER, 1864). Western Himalayas, 2000 to 5000 m elevation. 70 cm.
- *A. piscivorus* (LACEPEDE, 1789). Water Moccasin, Cottonmouth. Southern United States. 3 subspecies. 180 cm. Adults brownish black, juveniles with light brown crossbands.
- *A. rhodostoma* (BOIE, 1827). Malayan Moccasin. Indo China, Malaya, Sumatra, and Borneo. 100 cm. Highest temperature demands within entire genus.
- *A. saxatilis* EMELJANOV, 1937. Mongolia, USSR (Amur Region).

Aglaonema SCHOTT. Genus of the Araceae. Southeastern Asia, Malaya, Indo-China. About 50 species. Low to medium height shrubs. Will endure temperatures in excess of 25° C.; can be over-wintered as low as 12° C. Direct sun must be avoided! Reproduction is by scissiparity or root formation of cuttings. Well suited as background plants in rain-forest terrarium.
- *A. costatum*. N.E. BR. Low-growing shrub.

Aglyphs: see Teeth.

Aglyptodactylus BOULENGER, 1918. Monotypic genus of the Rhacophoridae. Sometimes also considered as a subgenus of *Mantidactylus*. Madagascar, in forest regions. Slender, long-snouted. Distinguished from *Mantidactylus* by the presence of small, oval-shaped adhesive pads without ventral circular furrow. Fingers free, toes completely webbed. Active during dusk. Ground-dweller, excellent jumpers. Eggs deposited in ponds.
- *A. madagascariensis* (DUMERIL and BIBRON, 1842). 7 cm. Yellowish gray with darker pattern.

Agrionemys CHOSATZKY and MLYNARSKI, 1966. Four-toed or Steppe Tortoises. Monotypic genus of the Testudinidae. Southwestern Asia. On steppes, extending into margins of deserts. To 25 cm. Relatively flat, round carapace. Powerful fossorial feet; anterior feet with only 4 claws.

Agrionemys horsfieldi

Active from April to July; summer drought rest often extends into winter dormancy. Will dig deep burrows. In the wild, eggs will hatch in 80 to 100 days. Terrarium maintenance similar to European *Testudo* species, but more susceptible to damp and cool central European summers. Should then be kept in an indoor terrarium under radiant heat during the day and at slightly lower temperatures at night. Has been bred repeatedly in captivity.
- *A. horsfeldi* (GRAY, 1844). Four-toed Tortoise. Soviet Central Asia, Iran, Pakistan, Afghanistan.

Agrophis F. MUELLER, 1894. Genus of the Colubridae, Calamarinae. Sulawesi (Celebes), Kalimantan. 3 species. 20 to 25 cm. With 15 rows of scales around middle of body. Iridescent dark brown body coloration. Burrowing snakes.
- *A. sarasinorum* F. MUELLER, 1894. Sulawesi. Montane forests up to 1700 m elevation.

Agrionemys horsfeldi

Ahaetulla LINK, 1807. Asian Long-nosed Tree Snakes. Genus of the Colubridae, Boiginae. Southeastern Oriental area. About 8 species. Occurs in upper tree level in tropical monsoon and rain forests; some species also in montane rain forests up to 1800 m elevation. Frequently used synonym: *Dryophis* DALMAN, 1823; some taxonomists prefer to use the name *Dendrelaphis* BOULENGER, 1890, here used for a genus of Colubrinae. 60 cm to nearly 2 m. Very slender, with clearly set off head terminating in a long, extended tip formed by a proboscis-like rostral scale. The large eyes are unmistakably characterized by a pupil shaped like a small figure 8 lying on its side. The body is slightly flattened laterally and is covered with smooth, shingled scales. Dark dorsal area from the tip of the snout

through the eyes and sides of the head and along the flanks clearly set off from the lighter ventral area. Uniformly light green, olive, yellowish, or grayish brown. Sometimes a lighter separating band along the sides.

Active during day and dusk. Feeds on lizards and only occasionally takes frogs or young birds, possibly also eggs and small mammals. Egg-laying, 2 to 12 eggs with well-developed embryos.

Care largely the same as for *Chrysopelea*. Initial adjustment to captivity often difficult, but after that may live for many years; at Leipzig Zoo lived for more than 12 years.
- *A. mycterizans* (LINNAEUS, 1758). Java, possibly also on the Malayan Peninsula. In excess of 1 m. Green or grayish green with a white lateral line.
- *A. nasuta* (LACEPEDE, 1789). India, Sri Lanka, Indo-China south to Thailand. Females nearly 2 m, males 1.3 m. Apart from *A. prasina* the largest and most frequently seen species of this genus. Variable coloration, from green to gray and pink.
- *A. prasina* (BOIE, 1827). Eastern Himalayas, from Indo-China south to Indo-Australian Archipelago. Snout sometimes slightly shorter than in the previous species.

Ailuronyx FITZINGER, 1843. Genus of the Gekkonidae, subfamily Gekkoninae. Madagascar, Mascarenes, Seychelles. 2 species. Rare.
- *A. seychellensis* (DUMERIL and BIBRON, 1836). Seychelles.
- *A. trachygaster* (DUMERIL, 1851). Madagascar and Mascarenes.

Aipysurus LACEPEDE, 1804. Genus of the Hydrophiidae, Hydrophiinae. Coastal areas of Indo-China to Australia, east to New Caledonia. 7 species. 0.5 to 2.0 m. Species-specific coloration subject to substantial individual variations. Most older adults become uniformly dark, but *A.*

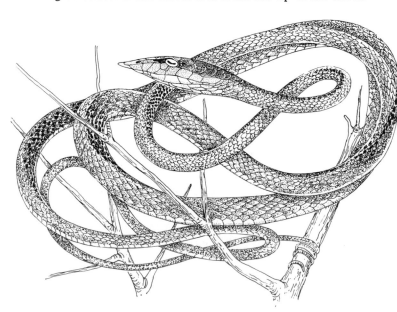

Ahaetulla prasina

Ahaetulla sp.

duboisi and *A. laevis* have light spots or continuous light colored zones along the sides.

Aquatic venomous snakes found primarily on coral reefs, where they hunt for fish. Some species (*A. duboisi, A. euydouxi*) frequently observed at considerable depths (30 to 50 m). Give birth to 2 to 5 young in water.
▪ *A. laevis* LACEPEDE, 1804. Brown Sea Snake. Around the coastline of New Guinea and northern Australia.

Albinism: Partial or complete loss of pigmentation (specifically melanin). Usually occurs as a genetic mutation. Albinos are relatively rare in nature, and because of their lack of concealment coloration usually do not survive very long. Partial as well as complete albinos are known to occur among almost all groups of amphibians and reptiles.

Aipysurus laevis

Aipysurus sp.

Albinism, *Gopherus agassizi*

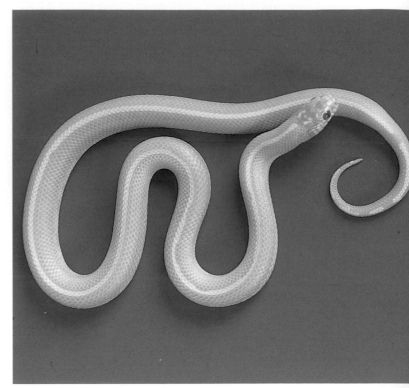

Albinism, *Lampropeltis getulus californiae*

Algyroides BIBRON and BORY, 1833. Keeled Lizards. Genus of the Lacertidae. Southern Europe. Probably closely related to *Lacerta*. Recently the African species formerly referred to *Algyroides* have been established in their own genus, *Adolfus*. Barely 15 cm. Slender, typical representatives of Lacertidae. Dorsal scales large and keeled, while the lateral scales are smaller and smooth. Coloration usually relatively plain, dorsally shades of brown, ventral region lighter.

Lives in semi-shaded habitats that are not too dry, with the exception of *A. nigropunctatus*. Often close to water, oc-

Albinism, *Rana temporaria*

casionally also climbing on walls and bushes. 2 to 6 eggs, 1 or 2 clutches per year.

Care and maintenance similar to *Podarcis*, but keep somewhat more damp. More compatible among each other than many other lacertids. Breeding and rearing fairly easy. Require less ultraviolet radiation than other lacertids.
▪ *A. fitzingeri* (WIEGMANN, 1834). Corsica and Sardinia. To 12 cm.
▪ *A. marchi* VALVERDE, 1958. Spanish Keeled Lizard. Southeastern Spain. About 15 cm.
▪ *A. moreoticus* BIBRON and BORY, 1833. Greek Keeled Lizard. Southern Greece and some of the Ionic Islands. About 15 cm.
▪ *A. nigropunctatus* (DUMERIL and BIBRON, 1839). Bluethroated or Splendid Keeled Lizard. Adriatic east coast. Easily 20 cm. Dorsum chocolate brown with dark dots; males with intensely orange-red abdomen and bright blue throat. The largest, hardiest, and most attractive species of this genus.

Alligator CUVIER, 1807. Alligators. Genus of the Alligatoridae, order Crocodilia. Relictual disjunct distribution in southeastern Nearctic and eastern Palearctic. 2 species. Flat snout broad. In contrast to the caimans, alligators have a bony nasoseptal plate and at the most 6 large adja-

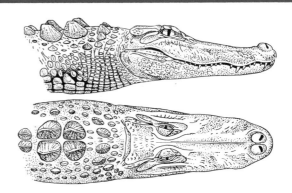

Alligator mississippiensis

cent conical nuchal bucklers. Bony plates of the abdominal armor comparatively weakly developed and not linked through joints.

A. mississippiensis, after large-scale decimation through indiscriminate hunting and habitat destruction, now has its survival assured, and its natural history is today well-known. On the other hand, the survival of *A. sinensis* is indeed threatened in spite of official protective measures by the People's Republic of China. Details of its biology are only sketchy at best. The following discussion of the

Alligator mississippiensis

natural history of alligators refers to *A. mississippiensis*, but to some degree it may also be valid for *A. sinensis*.

Outside the breeding season (April/May) both sexes occupy different habitats. Males are then found in large, open, deep waters, while the females live in smaller, shallower side branches. Males form territories during the breeding season that are marked acoustically (bellowing and slamming head onto water surface) and defended against rivals. The strongest males possess the largest territories and are thus particularly successful in attracting females. Courtship extends over several weeks. The actual mating commences with head-rubbing and coughing sounds. In shallow water the male mounts the female and copulation, lasting only a few minutes, occurs in a lateral position. The eggs are laid at the beginning of June in a mound of plants, twigs, and soil 1 m high and 1.5 to 1.8 wide gathered together by the female. The actual egg chamber is conical and located near the peak of the mound. The clutch consists of 20-35 eggs that are laid at 45-second intervals then caught with the hind legs and carefully manipulated into the nest depression. The female then closes the egg chamber and compacts the nest mate-

Alligator mississippiensis

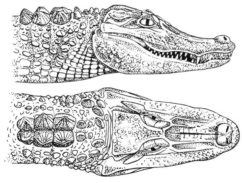

Alligator sinensis

rial on top of the entire nest. Temperature in the egg chamber varies from 26 to 33° C. The female remains close by to guard the eggs against predators such as raccoons and black bears and also keeps the nest mound moist.

Shortly before hatching the young call the female with soft "erk" sounds. Females either carry their young to water or call them into the water. The main predators of young alligators are raccoons, otters, turtles, birds, and large predatory fish. Mortalities during the first 3 years may reach 80 to 90%, despite the fact that the young during this period remain close to the female. After 3 years the maternal ties break down.

Young alligators feed initially on crustaceans, molluscs, small fish, frogs, and large insects. Adults feed mainly on fish (especially gars), snakes, birds, and raccoons, as well as dead animals.

For the care and maintenance of alligators refer to Crocodylia. According to climate-related environmental conditions, these animals should be kept indoors (as in a greenhouse) or, with additional heating, in escape-proof outdoor enclosures with supplementary heating of the water section. *A. sinensis* and the northern populations of *A. mississippiensis* undergo a 2- to 3-month winter dormancy period

spent in burrows in loose soil. This should be allowed in order to stimulate breeding.

A. mississippiensis has been bred in captivity (USA) since at least 1973. An entire clutch is transferred to an incubator, where the young will hatch in 64 days at 33° C. The initial breeding successes made it possible to distribute juvenile alligators to other zoological institutions and to release many back into their natural habitat. Similar efforts are on the way in the United States to save *A. sinensis*. For that purpose all available *A. sinensis* in the USA and in part even from Europe were kept in the southern United States under optimal conditions. *A. sinensis* bred at the Bronx Zoo, New York, in 1979.

Although alligators reared in captivity have the reputation of being hand-tame even as adults, they should not be kept by hobbyists, *A. mississippiensis* because of its size and *A. sinensis* because of its rarity. Even zoological parks no longer have the moral right to keep *A. sinensis* as exhibits due to its precarious status unless there is a chance of breeding this species successfully.

▪ *A. mississippiensis* (DAUDIN, 1802). Mississippi or American Alligator. Southern United States. Maximum size about 6 m, on the average 3 to 4 m.

▪ *A. sinensis* FAUVEL, 1879. Chinese Alligator. Yangtze Kiang Delta. In grassy swamp areas. To 2 m.

Alligatoridae: Alligators and Caimans. Family of the Crocodilia. America, eastern Asia. 4 genera with 7 species. To 6 m. Have relatively short snouts and weak ornamentation. With the mouth closed only the teeth of the upper jaw are clearly visible, since the lower jaw teeth (at least in the anterior snout section) are positioned behind and within the upper jaw teeth relative to the jaw. The fourth lower jaw tooth fits into a corresponding depression in the upper jaw

Alligatoridae: *Alligator* (broad snout) vs. *Crocodylus* (narrow snout)

and is not visible with the mouth closed. Extremities without scale-comb formations. Conical nuchal bucklers usually not separated from dorsal scutes.

Two groups of genera: On one side genus *Alligator*; on the other side the caimans with the genera *Caiman*, *Melanosuchus*, and *Paleosuchus*.

Allochthonous: Having migrated into or been transported or released into an area not normally the natural habitat. For instance, *Bufo marinus* is native to the Neotropics but has been introduced into many other tropical and subtropical regions to feed on sugar cane pests. Thus in Venezuela it would be considered autochthonous (native), but in Florida or Hawaii it would be allochthonous (introduced).

Allopatry, allopatric: Type of distribution of related taxa in which there is no overlap of normal ranges (distribution areas) of 2 or more species or subspecies. If the natural ranges of closely related taxa touch each other and blend into each other via a hybridization zone, these usually are considered to be subspecies. However, if there is an allopatric distribution, the biogeographical situation does not provide a clear indication of the systematic position of the taxa compared—they could be different species or geographical races (subspecies) of the same species. In contrast, see sympatry.

Allophores: see Chromatophores.

Allophryne GAIGE, 1926. Monotypic genus of the Hylidae. South America.
▪ *A. ruthveni* GAIGE, 1926. Guyana.

Alluaudina MOCQUARD, 1894. Genus of the Colubridae, Boiginae. Madagascar. 2 species. 30 to 50 cm. Very large,

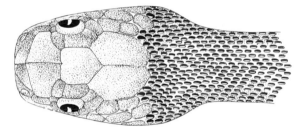

Alluaudina mocquardi

clearly set off head; blunt, wide snout gives impression of being sharply edged. Dorsal scales keeled, the keels isolated in *A. mocquardi* and appearing granular. Uniformly brown to olive or with rows of spots.

Biology and ecology still largely unresearched. Presumably ground-dwelling, nocturnal snakes living in tropical rain forests.
▪ *A. bellyi* MOCQUARD, 1894. Northern Madagascar.
▪ *A. mocquardi* ANGEL, 1939. Northeastern Madagascar.

Aloe L. Genus of the Liliaceae. Primarily in arid regions of South Africa, also in East Africa, Arabia, Madagascar, and introduced into many other tropical and subtropical regions. About 250 species. Succulents. Partially woody, mostly shrubs. Require full sunlight; need little water during the winter months; do not fertilize. Temperature requirements not strictly limited, 10° C. during the winter months sufficient. Reproduction by means of severing adventitious plants.

Low-growing or very short-stemmed species:
▪ *A. brevifolia* MILL. Tufts. Rosettes 10 to 12 cm diameter. Leaves more than 7 cm.

Aloe variegata

▪ *A. humilis* (L.) MILL. Rosette diameter 6 to 7 cm. Leaves 5 to 10 cm.

▪ *A. saponaria* (AJT.) HAW. Leaves 10 to 15 cm. Undemanding. Often found in horticulture.

▪ *A. variegata* L. Forms short underground runners. Rosette up to 30 cm tall.

  Stem-forming, slightly taller species:

▪ *A. ciliaris* HAW. Shoot axis rising to climbing. Leaves up to 15 cm.

Alopoglossus BOULENGER, 1885. Genus of the Teiidae. Northern South America. 5 species. In tropical rain forests. To 20 cm. Lower eyelid with semitransparent window. Dorsal area—and in part also ventral area—strongly keeled. Normal development of limbs. Mainly brown with lighter longitudinal bands.

▪ *A. angulatus* (LINNAEUS, 1758). Northwestern South America. Lowlands of the outer northern Amazon region. Easily 12 cm. Snout-vent length 5 cm, rest tail.

Alsodes BELL, 1843. Genus of the Leptodactylidae. Southern South America. About 5 species, some polytypic. In and near lakes in the Andes and vicinity, Chile and Argentina. Distinguished from the closely related genus *Eupsophus* by often rougher skin and the males possessing areas of mating spines (claspers) on fingers and chest. Largely aquatic or at least remaining close to water.

▪ *A. nodosus* (DUMERIL and BIBRON, 1841). Chile, Argentina. 7 cm and larger. Dark grayish black.

▪ *A. verrucosus* (PHILIPPI, 1902). Northern Argentina. 4.5 cm. Olive, bright yellow dorsal line.

Alsophis COPE, 1862. Genus of the Colubridae, Xenodontinae. Occurs disjunctively in the Caribbean islands, western South America, and on the Galapagos Islands. In secondary forests and rubble fields. Appearance and behavior similar to *Dromicus, Arrhyton*, and *Leimadophis*, but in somewhat drier habitats.

▪ *A. antillensis* (SCHLEGEL, 1837). Lesser Antilles. 6 subspecies.

▪ *A. biserialis* (GUENTHER, 1860). Galapagos Archipelago. 2 subspecies.

▪ *A. cantherigerus* (BIBRON, 1840). Cuba, Cayman Islands. 8 subspecies.

Alsophis sp.

▪ *A. chamissonis* (WIEGMANN, 1835). Central Chile. Original species of the genus.

▪ *A. occidentalis* VAN DENBURGH, 1912. Galapagos Archipelago.

▪ *A. portoricensis* REINHARDT and LUETKEN, 1863. Puerto Rico, adjacent islands. 7 subspecies.

▪ *A. slevini* VAN DENBURGH, 1912. Galapagos Archipelago.

▪ *A. steindachneri* VAN DENBURGH, 1912. Galapagos Archipelago.

▪ *A. vudii* COPE, 1863. Bahamas. 5 subspecies.

Alsophis cantherigerus

Alsophylax FITZINGER, 1843. Even-fingered Geckos. Genus of the Gekkonidae. Northeastern Africa to southwestern Asia and Tibet. 10 species. Occurs in rocky habitats, *A. tibetanus* also at high elevations. 10 cm. Slender. Pupil vertical. Toes extended conspicuously, adhesive pads reduced to tiny tubercles. Dorsum granular, with irregular rows of enlarged scales. Tail about snout-vent length, with scales forming keeled whorls. Overall similar to *Cyrtodacty-*

lus, except lower jaw with only one row of enlarged scales. Sandy colored to light brown with dark spots usually arranged into crossbands. Nocturnal ground-dweller. For care and maintenance refer to *Cyrtodactylus* and Gekkonidae.

- *A. blanfordi* (STRAUCH, 1887). Egypt and Arabia. 8 cm.
- *A. loricatus* STRAUCH, 1887. Central Asia. To 10 cm.
- *A. pipiens* (PALLAS, 1814). Caspian Even-fingered Gecko. Outer Volga region to Afghanistan in the south and to central Mongolia in the east. 8 cm.

Altirana STEJNEGER, 1927. Monotypic genus of the Ranidae. Himalayas. Smooth-skinned. Without tympanic membrane. Fingers free. Toes with webbing over two-thirds of their length. Presumably semiaquatic. For care and maintenance refer to *Nanorana*.

- *A. parkeri* STEJNEGER, 1927. Bhutan, western China (southern Tibet). To 3.5 cm.

Alytes obstetricans

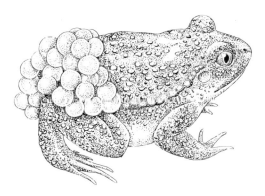

Alytes obstetricans

Alytes WAGLER, 1830. Midwife Toads. Genus of the Discoglossidae. Southwestern Europe. 2 species. Occurs mainly in low to moderate montane regions. Plump, toadlike, with small, dense fields of warts. Protruding eyes, vertical pupil. Tympanum small, clearly visible. Fingers

and toes free, without webbing. Palm of hand with 2 (*A. obstetricans*) or 3 (*A. cisternasii*) tubercles. Front feet are used for burrowing into soft topsoil; no spade on hind feet. No external vocal sacs; call soft; difficult to locate when calling.

Largely nocturnal ground-dwellers that hide during the day, often in the company of others, under rocks, fallen logs, or in the ground. Copulation and laying of eggs on land occur several times a year as in other Discoglossidae. Following rubbing movements by the male in inguinal amplexus, the female produces 40 to 80 large yellow eggs which are extruded in the form of strings. The male fertil-

Alytes obstetricans, male with eggs

Alytes obstetricans

izes the eggs and then slides forward on top of the female, reaches around her throat, and through forward spreading motions of the hind legs wraps the egg strings around his hind legs. The male then hides in a dark, damp burrow until the larvae are ready to hatch (eggs and larvae are light-sensitive!). Increasing movement of the larvae inside the eggs stimulates the male to move briefly into water. This causes spontaneous hatching of the larvae, which then continue to develop in water. Metamorphosis occurs the following summer; the larvae stay for one winter in water.

The terrarium should be kept moderately damp and must contain a thick but loose layer of soil and some flat rocks and stones or pieces of cork or tree bark. Open-air maintenance is allowable during the summer months. The best chances of breeding success are under near-natural conditions as in a spacious outdoor terrarium that is suitably set up.

• *A. cisternasii* BOSCA, 1870. Portugal and western Spain. To 5 cm, usually smaller. Brownish, with more or less darker spots.

• *A. obstetricans* (LAURENTI, 1768). Southwestern Europe, northeastward to Thuringia (eastern Germany). 5 cm. Gray or olive, sometimes with inconspicuous darker spots.

Amastridium COPE, 1861. Monotypic genus of the Colubridae, Natricinae. Southern Mexico to Panama. In tropical rain forests. About 40 cm. Head well set off, with substantially enlarged posterior upper jaw teeth. Ground snakes. Biology unknown.

• *A. veliferum* COPE, 1861.

Amblyodipsas PETERS, 1856. Monotypic genus of the Colubridae, Aparallactinae. Eastern to southeastern Africa. 32 cm. In appearance and mode of life very similar to *Calamelaps*. Dorsally dark brown, ventrally yellow with a median dark band.

• *A. microphthalma* (BIANCONI, 1850). Mozambique to eastern South Africa.

Amblyphrynus COCHRAN and GOIN, 1961. Monotypic genus of the Leptodactylidae. Colombian Andes. Closely related to *Eleutherodactylus*. Very large, broad head reminiscent of *Ceratophrys*. Fingers and toes without webbing. Tympanum clearly visible. Pupil horizontal. Biology unknown.

• *A. ingeri* COCHRAN and GOIN, 1961. To 8 cm.

Amblyrhynchus cristatus

Amblyrhynchus BELL, 1825. Marine Iguanas. Monotypic genus of the Iguanidae. Galapagos Islands. To 1.75 m. Laterally flattened rudder-like tail about twice snout-vent length. Strongly serrated nape and dorsal crests. Dark gray, at times with bright red-spotted courtship coloration.

Food consists of kelp taken mainly underwater. Excess salt is given off via glands in the nasal cavity. Formerly very abundant along shoreline cliffs, now endangered on many islands. Unsuitable for terrarium keeping; also internationally protected as an endangered species.

• *A. cristatus* BELL, 1825. Several subspecies on various islands.

Amblyrhynchus cristatus

Amblyrhynchus cristatus

Amblyrhynchus cristatus

Amblyrhynchus cristatus

Ambystoma TSCHUDI, 1838 (= *Siredon* WAGLER, 1830).
Mole Salamanders. Genus of the Ambystomatidae. Southeastern Alaska and southern Labrador over wide areas of
North America south to the Mexican Highlands (there
with the greatest species diversity). About 26 species, many
polytypic. Rather flattened body; head wide and flattened,
mouth large; skin smooth, with many glands. Distinct costal grooves. Tail roundish or laterally compressed in cross-
section. Males often larger than females, especially with a
longer tail. During the breeding season males have very
swollen cloacas. Often conspicuously marked.

Most species lead a largely cryptic life below logs and
rocks in burrows and other hiding places that are left only
briefly during the breeding season for a few days or on
rainy nights. Mating and egg-laying (up to several thousand eggs per spawning period) usually occur in standing
waters, pools, or even large lakes. (*A. opacum*, the marbled
salamander, lays its eggs each autumn under debris in low-
lying areas along the shoreline and guards the eggs until
they become covered by water during winter or spring
floods, when the larvae hatch.) Most southern species
spawn in winter or they have a fall and spring spawning
period (e. g., *A. mexicanum*); northern species usually
spawn early in spring. Only the very northern montane
populations spawn during the short growing period in
summer, and these populations are strongly inclined toward neoteny. Some species of the Mexican Highlands (especially *A. mexicanum* and *A. dumerili*), also known as axo-
lotls, probably never metamorphose under natural
conditions. Metamorphosis can be artificially induced by
gradual adaptation to terrestrial life, but it succeeds particularly well when administering thyroxin (thyroid gland
hormone). Some species adapt quite well to the prevailing
environmental conditions. This manifests itself not only in

Ambystoma annulatum

Ambystoma jeffersonianum

Ambystoma gracile

a variable reproductive period and facultative neoteny, but also in the appearance of morphological ecotypes such as distinctly cannibalistic larvae that have a particularly large head and long teeth, a weak body, and thin extremities (especially in *A. tigrinum*).

Care and maintenance variable, depending upon the ecological requirements of individual species. Neotenic forms and those larvae capable of metamorphosing are best kept cool (maximum 20° C., preferably 15° C.) in spacious aquariums. Metamorphosed specimens do well in a damp terrarium with a thick substrate layer and adequate hiding places. Feeding is generally easy; will even adjust to strips of lean raw meat. Breeding success, however, requires optimum nutrition. The animals are placed (in pre-estrus) into the winter quarters and are transferred in spring to an aquarium with shallow water. In view of its different biology, *A. opacum* has to be bred differently, since the eggs (usually deposited in fall) have to be flooded after about 80 days by raising the water level (moving the sensitive eggs as little as possible); the larvae will then hatch immediately. The natural reproductive period of *A. mexicanus* is normally the fall, but as food for larvae may be scarce during the winter, most hobbyists keep males and females separate until spring, when breeding is allowed.

Ambystoma gracile

Ambystoma tigrinum

• *A. annulatum* (COPE, 1886). Ringed Salamander. Missouri, Oklahoma, and Arkansas. 20 cm. Dark brown to black with pale yellowish rings.

• *A. maculatum* (SHAW, 1802). Spotted Salamander. Eastern North America with exception of the Gulf Coast and Florida. 20 cm. Blackish with a row of yellow or orange spots on each side of the back, the spots continued on the head.

• *A. mexicanum* (SHAW, 1789). Axolotl. Lake Xochimilco, Mexico. Water temperature in winter 12° C., in summer 20° C. Velvet black, with a more or less bluish sheen. Captive-bred varieties also available: albinos, piebalds, yellows.

Ambystoma tigrinum

Ambystoma maculatum

Ambystoma tigrinum californiense

Once extensively hunted for various reasons (delicacy for natives; alleged healing powers especially against syphilis; scientific interests as research animal). Natural populations are now considered to be extremely endangered and are thus under international protection. Commercially bred stocks widely available.

• *A. opacum* (GRAVENHORST, 1807). Marbled Salamander. Eastern and southeastern United States, with the exception of Florida. 11 cm. Dark brown to black, back with frosted white hourglass-like crossbands.

• *A. talpoideum* (HOLBROOK, 1838). Mole Salamander. Central and southeastern United States. 10 cm. Dark brown with irregular pattern of bluish white spots. Head conspicuously large, body oddly shortened.

• *A. tigrinum* (GREEN, 1825). Tiger Salamander. Eastern and central North America to California and south into Mexico. 21 cm (rarely to 33 cm). Polytypic and highly variable species. Facultatively neotenic. Dark brown to black with light olive to yellow pattern of spots or bars.

Ambystomatidae: Family of the Caudata. Nearctic Region, with greatest species diversity in the Mexican High-

Ambystoma opacum

Ambystoma tigrinum velasci

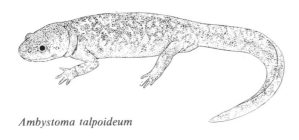

Ambystoma talpoideum

Ambystoma mexicanum

Ambystoma tigrinum

These lizards belong among the genera that have been relatively closely studied in the terrarium. They should be kept in a roomy terrarium with a deep substrate layer, sufficient hiding places, and possibly some low climbing branches. The container should be slightly damp but must never be actually wet. Temperatures: 25 to 30° C. during the day and about 20° C. at night, but never much below this; sensitive to low temperatures. Food consists of various arthropods and newly born pink mice. Occasionally they will also take some fruit. Ultraviolet radiation and reg-

Ambystoma maculatum

lands. Size and shape rather variable, but usually compact, strong body. Distinguished from often externally similar lungless salamanders, family Plethodontidae, by the absence of nasolabial grooves. Palatal teeth present; tongue free only at sides.

Systematic arrangement of the Ambystomatidae:
Subfamily Dicamptodontinae: genus *Dicamptodon*
Subfamily Rhyacotritoninae: genus *Rhyacotriton*
Subfamily Ambystomatinae: genera *Ambystoma* and *Rhyacosiredon*

Ameiva MEYER, 1795, Ameivas, Jungle Runners. Genus of the Teiidae. Southern Mexico south to tropical South America (including Antilles). *A. ameiva* has been introduced into Florida. About 15 species. Frequently in open forests, agricultural land, and similar habitats. 15 to 55 cm. Head relatively pointed. Lower eyelid semitransparent. The rather long tongue is characteristically retractable into a basal tube-like sheath. Very long tail. Dorsal scales granular in appearance; scales of ventral region smooth, in 6 to 16 longitudinal rows. Limbs strong and with long claws. Mainly brown and green, some with very attractive markings consisting of stripes and bright spots; sides often particularly strongly patterned.

Diurnal ground-dwellers, like to dig. Eggs 3 to 5 (usually 4), generally 2 clutches per year.

ular calcium and vitamin supplements should be provided. Most species are rather aggressive, so it is recommended that only one pair be kept in a terrarium.
▪ *A. ameiva* (LINNAEUS, 1758). Southern Mexico to Uruguay; introduced into Florida. Easily 50 cm. Outer forest margins, brushland. Anteriorly green, posteriorly brown. Flanks with white vertical bands. Relatively variable.
▪ *A. chrysolaema* COPE, 1868. Haiti. Dry, rocky coastal areas and steppes. Easily 40 cm. Brown with dark brown and light green longitudinal bands and whitish green dots; tip of snout reddish. Chest and ventral area of tail are black. Difficult to keep in captivity.

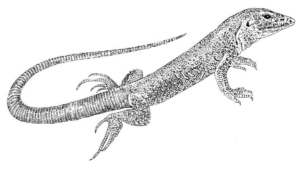

Ameiva ameiva

Ameiva ameiva

▪ *A. lineolata* DUMERIL and BIBRON, 1839. Haiti. Dry steppes. To 20 cm. Conspicuous blue-green tail.

Amniota: Monophyletic group of vertebrates (Vertebrata) characterized by fluid-retaining eggs. Known since the Upper Carboniferous. Independence from open water for reproductive purposes (humidity initially still required) enabled these animals to rapidly become dominant. Originally the Amniota consisted of the various saurians belonging to the paraphyletic groups of the Reptilia, which due to their sometimes gigantic size determined the faunal picture of the Earth at that time. Today the group Amniota includes the birds and mammals as well as the Reptilia.

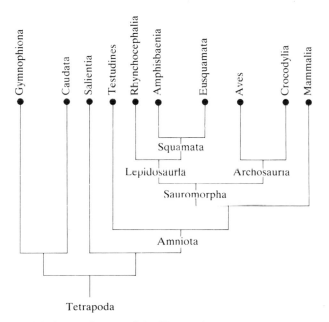

Phylogenetic tree of the Tetrapoda

Among the reptiles there are living today mainly the Squamata, which in more recent times have undergone tremendous diversification, while the remaining 3 Recent orders are represented by only a few species. Among these the turtles represent the most "original" type, so they stand in contrast with all other species in the form of a sister group. Within the Sauromorpha, which contrast with the mammals as a sister group, there are again 2 large monophyletic taxa, the Lepidosauria with the recent Squamata and the Rhynchocephalia, as well as the Archosauria, which includes the Crocodilia and the birds.

Amoebic dysentery: Protozoonosis that occurs especially in snakes (up to 20% mortality) and lizards; also subclinical in turtles. Also called amoebiasis. Ill animals will vomit partially digested food, refuse food, drink more frequently, and rest in an unnaturally extended position; skin turgor reduced; nutritional condition poor. Feces can be slimy to watery, usually containing blood and giving off an unpleasant sweetish odor. Just in front of the cloaca a hard, immovable growth (coprostasis) can be palpated, and the area around the cloaca is strongly edematized. Clinical diagnosis should be confirmed for presence of amoeba, which requires fresh feces put immediately into a special testing apparatus. The pathogen, which can advance from the digestive tract to the liver, can further and decisively increase the effects of the disease through weakening of the host and subsequent infestation by other endoparasites.

Therapy: Administration of preparations based on metronidazole in dosages of 50-60 mg/kg of body weight with simultaneous oral and cloacal application. This medication must NOT be used in pure form. At the same time tetracycline should be given orally (150 mg/kg body weight) to combat possible bacterial pathogens also present. Such treatment should be repeated 7 to 10 times within the course of 2 days, with the entire regimen to be repeated after 2 weeks. If it's expected that the liver or other organs may also be infected, there should be an additional treatment with Chlorochin® (0.5–1 ml/kg body weight, 2–3 times a week for 5 weeks) or with the antibiotic Paromomycinsulfat® (250-750 mg/kg body weight, orally 4 times in one-week intervals) or Emetin® (several times, 40 mg/kg body weight intra-muscular). Treatment combinations with Resochin® and Humatin® are also recommended, particularly in order to reduce the overall treatment time (3 ml/kg + 50 mg/kg). This treatment schedule can be effectively supported by increasing the environmental temperature to 35-37° C. and with simultaneous vitamin supplements.

Prophylaxis: Quarantine of all new animal additions for a period of not less than 3 months; repeated tests of the feces; no random changes of terrarium populations; food animals must NOT be transferred from one container to another; regular and thorough disinfection of all containers, especially after suspicious incidents of disease and mortality.

Amolops COPE, 1865. Genus of the Ranidae. Southern Asia, including Sunda Islands. 15 species. Close to or in flowing waters within lowland and montane rain forests. In the Himalayas as well as on open plateaus (up to 3500 m elevation). To 10 cm. Slender to compact, rather smooth-skinned. Large adhesive discs on fingers and toes; in contrast to closely related genus *Staurois*, adhesive discs without circular furrow around edge. Tympanum small, often barely visible. Fingers free, toes more or less webbed. Adults can easily be mistaken for *Hylarana*. However, the larvae are elongated, with a wide suction mouth and a characteristic gigantic throat disc with adhesive function (effective adaptation to turbulently flowing streams). Adults are often colorful.

Diurnal and crepuscular. Prefer to stay in splash zone of rapidly flowing, cascading rivers, on rocks surrounded by

Amolops loloensis

flowing water, or on rocks along river banks (compare with *Staurois*).

Best kept in large water and rock aquariums with clear water kept in motion with a circulating pump for flowing water effects and high humidity. Temperature flexible according to species and habitat. High mountain species (Himalayas) can be kept in an unheated aqua-terrarium with substantial day-night temperature variations; tropical species should be given about 25° C.

• *A. afghanus* (GUENTHER, 1858). Afghanistan to western China. To 8 cm. Gray-brown with marbled pattern.

• *A. kinabulensis* INGER, 1966. Kalimantan. To 9.5 cm. Dark green, head and neck with light yellow spots, legs brownish.

• *A. loloensis* (LIU, 1950). China: Sikang. To 8 cm. Dark green, with carmine red spots with light margins.

• *A. mantzorum* (DAVID, 1871). Szechwan, China (900-2000 m). To 7 cm. Dorsum reddish brown with dark green spots. Limbs with marbled pattern of green and black.

Amphibia: Frogs, Toads, Salamanders, Caecilians. A grouping (probably artificial) within the Tetrapoda, the four-footed vertebrates, which—according to a widespread opinion—represents a class. However, it actually forms a paraphyletic group and thus within the phylogentic system then becomes dissolved into respective monophyletic subgroups (recent members including only Gymnophiona, Caudata, and Salientia). Yet, for practical reasons the term "Amphibia" continues to be justified, as long as it is not meant to refer to a monophyletic taxon.

Amphibia inhabit all ecological niches, even arid regions such as semideserts and true deserts. They are, however, not found in polar regions or in permanently snow-covered high mountain regions, or in the marine environment (seas, oceans). With the exception of the salamanders (Caudata), which occur primarily in the temperate and subtropical zones of the Northern Hemisphere, the Amphibia are most diversely represented in the tropics.

From less than 1.5 cm to 1.5 m total length. Poikilothermic vertebrates, that—in contrast to other groups of tetrapods—do not have scales (reptiles), feathers (birds), or hairs (mammals) made of a horny (keratinous) substance. However, parts of the skin may be hard, clearly horn-like.

The vast majority of amphibians have 4 limbs (in some specialized forms, such as Amphiumidae and Gymnophiona, these have become partly or completely reduced). Characteristic of almost all Recent Amphibia with limbs are 4-fingered hands and 5-toed feet (even here the number of fingers and toes can be reduced). The jaws and roof of the palate are covered by small, rootless, conical teeth that are constantly replaced. The number of free vertebrae varies from 6 (some Salientia) to about 300 (some Gymnophiona). The heart has two atria and one ventricle. Respiration is via gills, lungs, or through the skin. With the exception of a few live-bearing forms, most amphibians produce a gelatinous spawn (egg mass). From this the larvae hatch and later undergo metamorphosis. However, deposition of the spawn in water has been given up by many forms in all three major groups. In some of the terrestrially spawning species the larvae still have to enter water; in numerous other species embryonic and larval development including metamorphosis take place within the terrestrially deposited eggs. Other amphibians never undergo metamorphosis, instead remaining throughout their life in a larval-like state and also reproducing as larvae (neoteny). Brood care is fairly common in the Amphibia and occurs in various groups (compare Hylidae, Pipidae, and Rhacophoridae). The primitive mode of life is amphibious, but many genera have secondarily gone over to a completely aquatic life, while others have become totally terrestrial.

Phylogenetically the amphibians appear to have been derived from the Rhipidistia that occupied fresh water. They developed during the early Devonian Period and they are the first successful land-dwellers among the vertebrates. The original amphibians were still completely armorplated; some were up to 4 m long and weighed several hundred kilograms. The amphibians reached a tremendous diversity during the Carboniferous and were dominant in fresh water and on land. However, several groups had already become extinct by the Permian.

Amphibious: To occupy two environments. Usually refers to the combination of land and water. Can characterize a predetermined change within an individual's development (e. g., typical of many amphibians), but can also be applied to everyday water—land changes (e. g., applicable to crocodilians, semiaquatic turtles).

Amphibolurus WAGLER, 1830. Bearded Dragons. Genus of the Agamidae. Australia, Tasmania. About 25 species. In rocky semideserts, some also in outer forest areas. 20 to at least 50 cm, dorso-ventrally flattened. Their most obvious feature is a characteristic "beard" on a wide, massive

Amphibolurus pictus

Amphibolurus barbatus

Amphibolurus nobbi

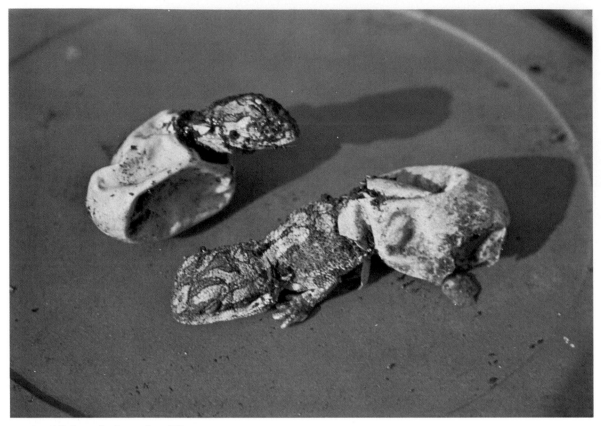

Amphibolurus barbatus, hatchlings

head that for agamids is relatively pointed. The scales on the posterior throat skin and the skin along the sides of the head have spiny extensions. With the aid of the hyoid bone this skin area can be spread in a threat display to increase the apparent size of the head when viewed from in front. Scales along the sides are also in part spiny. Males with femoral and preanal pores. Moderate color changing ability, usually confined to light to dark; weak physiological temperature regulation.

Diurnal ground-dwellers, some semiarboreal. Remain in deep burrows during the heat of the day. When in flight, short distances are run solely on the hind legs with the anterior part of the body erect. *Amphibolurus* feed on arthropods; small species take ants, and occasionally fruit is also taken. Clutches of up to 30 eggs.

Provide temperatures of 25 to 35° C.; the heat source should be localized. Provide a distinct temperature reduction during the night and a 2-month cooler dormancy period (at about 15° C.) during the northern summer if possi-

ble. Moderate requirements for drinking water; regular spraying is generally sufficient. Ultraviolet radiation is important, as are calcium and vitamin supplements. The various species are reasonably peaceful among each other.

▪ *A. barbatus* (CUVIER, 1829). Bearded Dragon. Australia. Easily to 50 cm. Large, with long pointed throat and cheek scales. Coloration varies from nearly black to a mottled pattern of spots and irregular vermiculations.

▪ *A. pictus* PETERS, 1866. Painted Dragon. Central, southern, and western Australia. To 20 cm. Brown with dark pattern. Color changes well-defined.

▪ *A. reticulatus* (GRAY, 1845). Netted Dragon. Southwestern and central Australia. Sandy areas. About 20 cm. Dark, vermiculated pattern. Likes to dig. Requires elevated temperatures, ground temperature during the day about 35° C., localized up to 40° C.

Amphiesma DUMERIL and BIBRON, 1845. Keeled Water

Amphiesma stolata

Amphibolurus barbatus

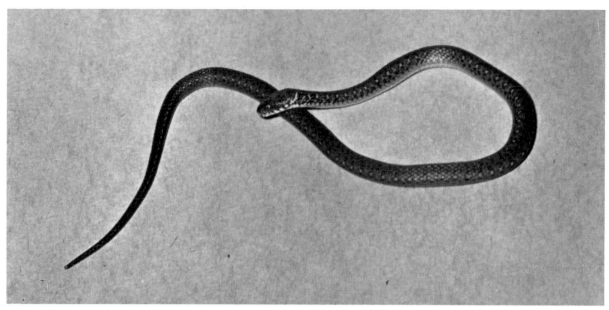

Amphiesma sauteri

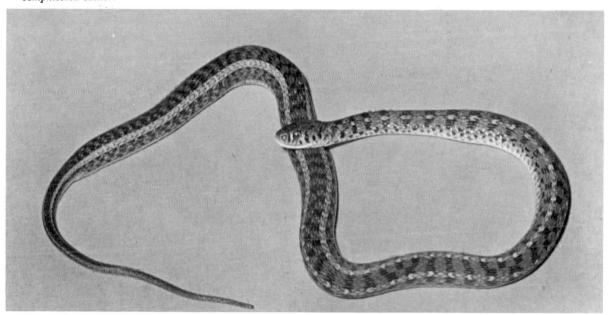

Amphiesma stolata

Amphiesma sauteri

Snakes. Genus of the Colubridae, Natricinae. Eastern and southeastern Asia to New Guinea and northern Australia. About 39 species. In tropical and montane rain forests, also found in brushland and similar habitats up to 2000 m elevation. 0.5 m to 1.0 m. Dentition on upper jaw differentiated, posterior teeth distinctly enlarged. Keeled and partially shingled dorsal scales. Nothing is known about possible venom effects, but often assumed to be potentially dangerous.

Some species terrestrial, others semiaquatic (groups 1 + 2 of the Natricinae). Diet ranges from earthworms to frogs and fishes. Egg-laying, 2 to 6 eggs, maximum of up to 15 eggs in large species.

▪ *A. mairi* (GRAY, 1841) New Guinea, Australia. 2 subspecies. Group 2 of Natricinae.

▪ *A. stolata* (LINNAEUS, 1758). India, Sri Lanka, Indo-China to southern China. 2 subspecies. Rather variable in coloration. Intermediate to groups 1 and 2 of the Natricinae.

• *A. vibakari* (BOIE, 1827). Far eastern USSR, Korea to eastern China, Japan, Hainan. 3 subspecies. Feeds on earthworms. Group 1 of Natricinae.

Amphignathodon BOULENGER, 1882. Monotypic genus of the Hylidae. Ecuador. Slender, with a broad head and a very short, blunt snout. Pupil horizontal. Fingers and toes with large adhesive discs. Fingers free, toes webbed for two-thirds of their length. Long legs. Females with a brood pouch in skin of back (similar to *Nototheca* and *Flectonotus*), opening horseshoe-shaped. Arboreal.
• *A. guntheri* BOULENGER, 1882. 7.5 cm. Olive, upper thighs with contrasting black crossbands.

Amphigonia retarda: Delayed fertilization. In many reptiles and some salamanders the sperm can survive in the female for a long time after copulation, sometimes for years, and remain viable and capable of fertilizing eggs. While the females of lizards and snakes have special enlargements (*receptacula seminis* or seminal receptacles) for holding sperm at various locations along the Muellerian ducts, such structures are unknown in turtles and tortoises. Yet even in these animals there occurs a kind of delayed fertilization. Thus, female diamondback terrapins (*Malaclemys terrapin*) will after separation from a male continue to lay fertile eggs each year for up to 4 years, though in steadily declining numbers. In female snakes it has been shown that sperm can live for up to 5 years.

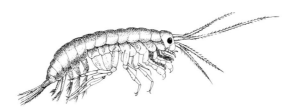

Amphipoda, *Gammarus locusta*

Amphipoda: Order of the Crustacea. Best known genus is the 1 to 2 cm long *Gammarus*, which lives in unpolluted, clean ditches and creeks (additionally, some species are estuarine or marine). Good occasional food for small turtles and is eagerly eaten by aquatic amphibians. A long-lasting supply of live *Gammarus* can be maintained for months in large, cool, shaded containers with a water level at about 15 cm. Provide frequent water changes! They should be given occasional feedings with small amounts of scraped or minced meat (very lean) or even tropical fish foods based on meats. In eastern North America the smaller *Hyalella* may be similarly cultured.

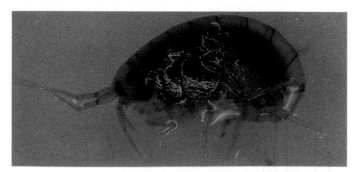

Amphipoda, *Gammarus*

Amphisbaena fuliginosa

Amphisbaena LINNAEUS, 1758. South American Worm Lizards. Genus of the Amphisbaenidae. Tropical South America, northward to Panama, also the Caribbean islands. 45 species. In tropical forests. 20 to almost 60 cm, relatively plump appearance. Exclusively subterranean. Predators; will also accept dead food in a terrarium. Egglaying.
• *A. alba* LINNAEUS, 1758. Red Worm Lizard. South America except extreme south. To 55 cm. Reddish brown.
• *A. fuliginosa* LINNAEUS, 1758. Speckled Worm Lizard. Tropical South America east of the Andes and north to Panama. Barely 40 cm. Black with whitish dots.

Amphisbaenia: Worm Lizards (not to be confused with the Anniellidae). Suborder of Squamata. Tropical and temperate regions of the Old and New World (except Orient and Australia). Easily 20 genera in three families (Bipedidae, Amphisbaenidae, Trogonophidae) and about 130 species. Systematic position doubtful. Usually they are placed in a separate suborder alongside Sauria and Serpentes. There appear to be some characteristics that could indicate that the Amphisbaenia could be the sister group to all other Squamata (Eusquamata). Known since the early Tertiary. 10 to 80 cm, cylindrical. Tail extremely short. Head superbly adapted for burrowing, the skull relatively massive, the temporal arches absent, with mammal-like divided occipital condyles. Lower jaw almost completely included behind upper jaw, thus the small mouth opening is strongly subterminal. The upper jaw contains an uneven number of teeth, of which each tooth fits between the teeth of the lower jaw (even number of teeth). Eyes vestigial, visible only as dark spots underneath the skin; at best they can probably only distinguish differences in brightness. The ears, also hidden underneath the skin, are modified to be particularly sensitive to ground vibrations. In contrast to all other worm-like Squamata, only the left lung is functional in amphisbaenids. Externally visible limbs are completely absent except in *Bipes*; often there are not even remnants of girdle skeletons. Typical squamate scales are found only on the head and in the thoracic region. The entire skin is arranged into more or less complete rings, with 2 rings corresponding to 1 vertebra (except in *Blanus*). Of-

Amphisbaenia, showing the rings

ten there are two lateral folds and in a few cases even a dorsal fold. Osteoderms are absent; preanal pores present in front of cloaca. Primarily reddish, brown, and gray color tones.

As a general rule, amphisbaenids live exclusively underground. Only a few are ever found on the surface at night, most frequently in arid regions under loose rocks. Within their individual burrow systems they manage to be as equally agile moving forward as backward. Prey—mainly insect larvae and earthworms—is perceived mainly by means of ground vibrations caused by the prey animals. A number of species occur in ant and termite nests, which provide food and serve as a place to deposit their eggs. Dead animals are also eaten. The necessary drinking water is sucked with the lips directly out of soil capillaries. Most species are egg-layers. The size of the eggs diminishes significantly from the first to the last eggs. A few species are ovoviviparous.

There have been few terrarium experiences with amphisbaenids, although most species that have been kept seem to do well in captivity. Best known are the genera *Amphisbaena*, *Blanus*, *Bipes*, *Rhineura*, and *Trogonophis*. The prime requisite for keeping these animals in a terrarium is a substrate layer as thick as possible that must be (even for species from relatively dry regions) moderately damp, at least in part. With the exception of that for species from tropical rain forests, the bottom substrate should contain some clay so that the animals can establish a permanent burrow system. Suitable temperatures, depending upon the species, are from 20 to 28° C., slightly less at night. Species from temperate zones should be given a seasonal rhythm with a short winter dormancy period. Soiled bottom substrate should occasionally be replaced. If the area occupied by the substrate along the front window of the

terrarium is covered so it is dark, the animals will establish some of their burrows in this area. Occasional removal of this front cover then enbles adequate viewing of the animals. These animals can also easily be accommodated together with smaller lizards or even frogs, provided the bottom substrate is sufficiently thick. Reptiles and amphibians from arid regions should not be housed with amphisbaenids since they would also tend to burrow and would thus disturb the amphisbaenids.

Amphisbaenidae: Largest family of the Amphisbaenia. 2 subfamilies. Primarily in tropical rain forests, but some also in drier habitats. Distinguished from Trogonophidae by pleurodont dentition (teeth in groove on inner side of jaw) and the less pointed tail that is not turned upward.

Amphisbaeninae: More or less distinctly laterally flattened snout forming a bony parietal crest. Genera *Amphisbaena*, *Ancylocranium*, *Anops*, *Baikia*, *Bronia*, *Cadea*, *Chirindia*, *Cynisca*, *Geocalamus*, *Mesobaena*, *Loveridgea*, and *Zygaspis*.

Rhineurinae: Dorso-ventrally flattened snout edge. Genera *Aulura*, *Leposternon*, *Monopeltis*, *Rhineura*, and *Tomuropeltis*.

Amphiuma GARDEN, 1821. Amphiumas, Congo Eels, Eel Newts. Only Recent genus of the Amphiumidae. Southeastern and southern North America. 3 species. Due to occasional hybridization, *A. means* and *A. tridactylum* are sometimes considered to be conspecific. Occur mainly in standing waters and swamp areas. Head flattened. Mouth with deep cleft. Eyes tiny, lidless, overgrown with skin. Limbs very small, number of fingers and toes 1 to 3, species-specific. Coloration dark.

Hide during the day on the bottom of ditches and ponds, lying in wait for prey (fish, crustaceans, other amphibians) with only the head protruding. During the night they swim about actively with strong side to side movements. Occasionally they will crawl onto land, especially during rainy nights, and then retreat for some time under rocks, logs, and other damp hiding places.

Little is known about reproduction. The females deposit their egg strings in dried up swamp areas and there guard the eggs for the entire (about 5 months) period of embryonic development. The larvae probably hatch during extensive rainfalls in autumn and thus reach water. They have external gills that regress as early as the following spring.

Amphiumas are usually seen in displays in public aquariums since their correct care requires very large containers. The water used in such a tank has to be dechlorinated and unpolluted. A thick, soft substrate layer together with well-leached tree roots and clay pipes provides adequate hiding places. Such an aquarium has to be well covered because these animals are real escape artists. Apart from the natural food items, *Amphiuma* also takes strips of heart and liver (use feeding tongs!). A large specimen can inflict a painful bite.

• *A. means* GARDEN, 1821. Two-toed Amphiuma, Congo

Inguinal amplexus in *Hymenochirus*

Amphiumidae: Family of the Caudata. Southeastern Nearctic. One genus, *Amphiuma*. Eel-like. Body size considerable. Metamorphosis incomplete, adults without external gills but with open gill pore. Lungs present. Legs very small, largely without obvious function. Amphiumas have the largest erythrocytes (red blood cells) among vertebrates (about 10 times as large as those of humans). Aquatic, occasionally venturing onto land. Considered to be dangerous in its native regions since they are capable of administering strong and painful bites; sometimes eaten by humans.

Amphodus: see *Phyllodytes*, genus.

Amplexus: Mating embrace. Typical mating position of frogs and many other amphibians whereby the male embraces the female with his front legs while or preparatory to fertilizing the eggs. Axillary amplexus has the male grasping the female near the front legs; inguinal amplexus has the male grasping above the hind legs.

Amphiuma pholeter

Eel. Southeastern USA. Usually to 75 cm, record length 1.16 m. Dark brown to black above, ventrally dark gray. Legs with 2 digits.
• *A. pholeter* NEILL, 1964. One-toed Amphiuma. Northern Florida and probably adjacent Georgia and Alabama. Maximum size to 33 cm. Monotone darkish. Legs with only 1 digit.
• *A. tridactylum* CUVIER, 1827. Three-toed Amphiuma. Southern USA mostly west of the Mississippi River, Mississippi to Texas. Usually to 75 cm, record size 1.06 m. Dark dorsally, distinctly lighter abdomen. 3 digits.

Axillary amplexus in *Bufo americanus*

Anal spur in *Epicrates striatus*

Amplorhinus A. SMITH, 1847. Monotypic genus of the Colubridae, Boiginae. South Africa. In wet and swampy grasslands. To 60 cm. Head barely set off from trunk. Slightly keeled dorsal scales. Dorsal area uniformly green to olive brown.

Crepuscular ground snakes feeding mainly on frogs, lizards, and small mammals. Live-bearing, 4 to 5 young. Must be given a well-heated terrarium. Keep as Natricinae of Group 1. Hobbyists should be cautious as the bite is venomous and these are very aggressive snakes, but the mouth is quite small.
▪ *A. multimaculatus* A. SMITH, 1847. Cape Many-spotted Snake.

Amyda: see *Trionyx*, genus.

Anadia GRAY, 1845. Genus of the Teiidae. Costa Rica to northern South America. About 10 to 12 species. In tropical rain forests. 20 cm. Elongated, with pointed head. Lower eyelid with window. Tail twice snout-vent length. Weak, short limbs.

Anadia often occurs in epiphytic bromeliads and ferns. They feed primarily on small arthropods.
▪ *A. bitaeniata* BOULENGER, 1903. Venezuela, Colombia, Andes Region. About 15 cm.
▪ *A. metallica* (COPE, 1876). Costa Rica. Montane forests. Barely 20 cm.

Anal plate: A plate covering the cloacal opening; it is enlarged and distinct from the other ventral scales in most snakes and many lizards.

Anal spur or **anal claw:** Externally visible remnant of hind legs near cloaca in the boas and pythons (family Boidae) and Siamese or Oriental pipe snakes (*Cylindrophis*). Substantially larger in males than in females; presumed to participate in courtship, possibly as stimulatory organs. Also called pelvic spurs.

Anarbylus: see *Coleonyx*, genus.

Ancylocranium PARKER, 1942. Genus of the Amphisbaenidae. East Africa. 3 species. Head flattened laterally, pointed, with strong rostral keel. Similar to *Anops*. Burrowing, lives below surface, partially in hard soil. Little known.
▪ *A. somalicum* (SCORTECCI, 1931). Somalia. Easily 20 cm.

Ancylodactylus MUELLER, 1907. Monotypic genus of Gekkonidae. Africa. Little known.
▪ *A. spinicollis* MUELLER, 1907. Cameroons, Ghana.

Andrias TSCHUDI, 1837 (= *Megalobatrachus* TSCHUDI, 1837). Oriental Hellbenders. Genus of the Cryptobranchidae. Japan and China. 1 polytypic species. The better known generic name for these Recent forms is *Megaloba-*

trachus, but there is such little morphological deviation from *Andrias*, described from Miocene fossils, that use of the older *Andrias* appears justified. Aquatic. Largest of the Recent Caudata. Distinguished externally from the Nearctic genus *Cryptobranchus* only by the more massive size and the wart-covered head and throat skin, as well as the completely closed gill openings. After the (incomplete) metamorphosis only 2 gill arches remain. Washed out dark-spotted pattern on a gray-brown body color.

Completely aquatic, on the bottom of cool, rapidly flowing, clear streams. The subspecies *davidianus* also occurs in mountain lakes. During the day these animals remain in dark hiding places. They stalk prey at night (fish, worms, crustaceans). *Andrias* breeds in late summer. Courtship is started by the male building a spawning pit and courting a female. The female produces long egg strings (2 to 18 m) with 400-500 eggs each. These are fertilized and then guarded by the male. The free-swimming larvae hatch after 2 to 3 months. Metamorphosis occurs at a length of about 20 cm.

Andrias species are on the endangered species list. They

Andrias japonicus davidianus

are prized specimens for public institutions (zoos and aquariums), and with the proper care they will live for many years. Suitably large aquarium tanks are required, with cool (about 15° C.), clear, chlorine- and pollutant-free water, preferably running water from a natural spring or passed through a filter. Apparently the only successful breeding in captivity outside Japan was in the Amsterdam Zoo (1902 to 1903) with the nominate form.

▪ *A. japonicus* (TEMMINCK, 1837). Nominate subspecies: *A. j. japonicus*. Japanese Giant Salamander. Southwestern Japan (western Hondo, northern Kyushu). Mountain regions, 300 to 1000 m elevation. 1.0 m (maximum size 1.4 m). Grayish brown with indistinct dark pattern. Head tubercles large.

▪ *A. j. davidianus* (BLANCHARD, 1871). Chinese Giant Salamander. Central China. 1.0 m (maximum size 1.8 m). Head tubercles small.

Aneides BAIRD, 1849. Climbing Salamanders, Tree Salamanders. Genus of the Plethodontidae. North America along Pacific coastal region (4 species) and Appalachians (1

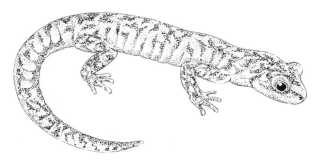

Aneides aeneus

species). Prefers damp conifer forests. 8 to 15 cm. Has heavy jaw and cheek musculature (especially *A. lugubris*) and projecting upper jaw when mouth is closed. Tips of fingers and toes truncated (exception: *A. hardyi*). Tail more or less rounded.

Aneides is totally terrestrial and, because of its good climbing abilities (especially *A. ferreus* and *A. lugubris*), often arboreal. Large aggregations may occur in hollow trees. Other habitats of *Aneides* (especially *A. aeneus*, *A. hardyi*, and *A. flavipunctatus*) are abandoned burrows of small mammals, decaying wood, and rocky crevices. Mating and egg deposition occur during warm, damp periods. A clutch consisting of 9 to 20 stalked eggs is attached to crevice walls by the female and then watched and defended. The completely developed terrestrial young hatch after 3 to 4 months in the fall.

Keep these salamanders in a damp terrarium with climbing branches and hiding places under pieces of tree bark. *A. aeneus* should be given some stacked flat rocks that must be kept wet. For *A. aeneus* a winter dormancy period of several months is recommended. The Pacific species require only a temperature reduction for a few weeks.

▪ *A. aeneus* (COPE and PACKARD, 1881). Green Salamander. Appalachians. 8—13 cm. Green lichen-like pattern against a dark background.

▪ *A. ferreus* COPE, 1869. Clouded Salamander. Western Oregon and northern California. 10 cm. Marbled grayish pattern against dark background.

▪ *A. flavipunctatus* (STRAUCH, 1870). Black Salamander. California and Oregon. Coastal mountains. 13 cm. Black with yellow spots.

▪ *A. hardyi* (TAYLOR, 1941). Sacramento Mountain Salamander. Mountains in New Mexico. 8 cm. Light to dark brown with greenish to bronze-colored dots.

Aneides flavipunctatus

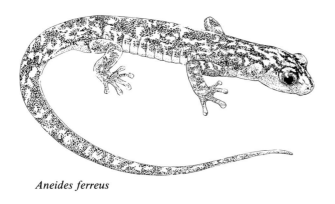

Aneides ferreus

• *A. lugubris* (HALLOWELL, 1849). Alligator Salamander, Arboreal Salamander. California and Baja California. 15 cm. Brown with yellow dots, abdomen white.

Anelytropsidae: American Snake Lizards. Family of the Squamata. Monotypic, for *Anelytropsis* from Mexico. Systematic position unclear. Often considered as part of the basal relict group Scincomorpha in conjunction with Feyliniidae and Dibamidae. In tropical forests. Worm-like, elongated. Massive head; temporal arch completely reduced. Eyes not externally visible or barely visible under skin. External ear openings absent. No osteoderms. Limbs totally absent. Burrowing, subterranean.

Aneides lugubris

Aneides ferrus

Anelytropsis papillosus

Anelytropsis COPE, 1885. American Snake Lizards. Monotypic genus of the Anelytropsidae. Eastern Mexico. In tropical forests. To 25 cm. Has large rostral scale suited for burrowing. Feed presumably mainly on ants. Rarely collected.
• *A. papillosus* COPE, 1885.

Anesthesia: Narcosis. Adequate for minor surgery are local anesthetics such as Lidocain, Chlorprocain, and Tetracain hydrochloride. For major surgery or operations on aggressive patients general anesthesia by means of hypothermy, inhalation narcosis, or injection narcosis is best. Injections based on ketamin hydrochloride in dosages from 20-100 mg/kg body weight have proved to be highly satisfactory. Small animals and unfamiliar species should be given only 20-60 mg/kg. Barbituates in dosages from 15-50 mg/kg are recommended to be administered intraperitoneally.

Angel, Fernand (1881—1950): French herpetologist. Completed Boucourt's illustrations in *Mission Scientifique au Mexique et dan l'Amerique Centrale, Etudes sur les Reptiles et le Batraciens* (1909). Later worked on the amphibians and reptiles in *Faune de France* (1946); *Vie et Moeurs des Amphibiens* (1947); *Vie et Moeurs des Serpents* (1950).

Angolosaurus FITZSIMONS, 1953. Sand Dune Plated Lizards. Monotypic genus of the Cordylidae. Coastal region of southwestern Africa. In dry habitats with lose sand and dunes. Body relatively strongly flattened dorso-ventrally. Head low, with shovel-like snout. Tail long. Weak lateral fold. Toes with lateral scale combs. Able to burrow very fast. Feeds on various insects. Egg-laying. Little known about its natural history.
• *A. skoogi* (ANDERSSON, 1916). Namibia, southern Angola. To 28 cm. Dorsum nearly white with reddish yellow spots. Abdomen nearly black.

Anguidae: Lateral Fold Lizards. Family of the Squamata. Primarily in temperate and subtropical regions of the Northern Hemisphere, some in South America, and a few in southeastern Asia. 3 distinctly separate subfamilies: Diploglossinae, Gerrhonotinae, Anguinae. 60 to 70 species. Within the Anguimorpha the Anguidae belongs to the Diploglossa. Fossil records since the Upper Cretaceous. Head with large, regular scutes. Bones of the lower jaw solidly fused. Massive pleurodont teeth usually blunt and wide, with rows extending far posteriorly; tooth replacement alternating. Tongue at least weakly bilobed, with a narrow anterior section that can be retracted into a broader posterior section. Body with osteoderms. Tail usually longer than body, fragile, with good regenerative properties.

Apart from the basic 4-legged species there are also various specialized forms with reduced limbs all the way to completely limbless species, where there is hardly any remaining evidence of the limb girdles. Primarily ground-dwellers, some species arboreal. No burrowing, subterranean species. All species are carnivorous. Most are egg-layers, but a few are ovoviviparous.
▪ Diploglossinae. Diploglossine Lizards. New World only. Basic group of the family. Normal limbs or rudiments only. Osteoderms well developed, in some cases even shingled. No lateral fold. Genera *Diploglossus, Ophiodes, Sauresia,* and *Wetmorena* (*Celestus* is a synonym of *Diploglossus*).
▪ Gerrhonotinae. Alligator Lizards. Old and New World. With or without limbs. Osteoderms usually well developed. Body with distinctive lateral fold lined with small non-ossified scales (with a substantial gain in elasticity). Genera *Abronia, Gerrhonotus,* and *Ophisaurus.*
▪ Anguinae. Slow Worms. Old World only. Strongly specialized snake-like lizards. Monotypic, genus *Anguis.*

Anniella, the American Legless Lizards, is included by some systematists in the Anguidae and even placed in the subfamily Anguinae, since many of its distinguishing characters are apparently adaptations to its particular mode of life. Here it is considered to be an independent family, Anniellidae.

Anguis LINNAEUS, 1758. Slow Worms. Monotypic genus of the Anguidae belonging to its own subfamily. Distributed throughout most of Europe (Scandinavia up to 64° latitude) to Afghanistan, including the Caucasus region; questionable occurrence in Algeria. Prefers slightly damp

Anguis fragilis

Anguis fragilis

habitats in brushland, forests, and meadows, frequently on agricultural land.

Distinguished from other genera in its family by its pointed teeth and an indication of a hind joint seam in the lower jaw. External ear opening present only in eastern populations. No limbs. Tail fragile, regenerations usually blunt.

Primarily crepuscular. Ovoviviparous.

Anguis should be kept in a semi-damp terrarium and will then do well in captivity (authenticated records in excess of 30 years, allegedly even in excess of 50 years, exist). Temperature, dependent upon origin of specimens, between 20 and 30° C., slightly less at night. Ideally suited for the outdoor terrarium. Winter dormancy of 2 to 4 months important. Feeds on earthworms, slugs, as well as various slow-moving arthropods.

• *A. fragilis* LINNAEUS, 1758. Slow Worm. Europe and Asia Minor. 3 subspecies. To at least 40 cm. Coloration variable, with shades of brown, ventral region darker. *A. f. fragilis* in western and central Europe; *A. f. colchicus* in eastern Europe and Asia Minor (with visible tympanum and light blue spots in the anterior dorsal region); *A. f. peloponnesiaca* on Peloponnesus peninsula, Greece.

Anhydrophryne HEWITT, 1919. Monotypic genus of the Ranidae. Eastern Cape Region, South Africa. In damp montane forests above 1000 m elevation. Rather slender. Wrinkled skin. Snout similar to *Rana*, but males with conspicuous hump on snout. Without vocal sac. Melodic, soft call, repeated 7 to 13 times in rapid succession.

Anhydrophryne lives in damp, cool forest areas on the ground underneath fallen leaves. The food is primarily ground arthropods. Development is totally independent of water (like the closely related genus *Arthroleptella*). The male excavates depressions in the soil into which the female deposits 11-19 large, unpigmented eggs. The entire embryonic and larval development occurs inside the egg. Hatching is in about 4 weeks.

Can be kept in an unheated terrarium with loose, damp forest soil, leaves, moss, and bark, planted with small ferns and similar plants (e. g., *Luzula*).

• *A. rattrayi* HEWITT, 1919. To 2.5 cm. Light gray, coppery, or dark brown, with dark eye band extending to up-

Anguis fragilis, mating and birth

per arm.

Aniliidae: Pipe Snakes. Family of the Henophidia. Relictual distribution in the Orient (2 genera) and Neotropics (1 genus). 3 genera: *Anilius*, *Anomalochilus*, *Cylindrophis*. Found in tropical forests, *Cylindrophis* sometimes among human habitations. Phylogenetics not yet sufficiently researched. In view of its toothed premaxilla, the Neotropical *Anilius* appears to be, on one hand, the most primitive member of the family, but its scale-covered eyes also make it the most specialized burrowing snake within the family. *Cylindrophis* has reached the highest evolutionary level in the family: its premaxilla is toothless and the chin is furrowed, which allows them the characteristic mobility of the mandibles found in higher snakes.

To 90 cm. Round to weakly triangular body. Head weakly set off from body. Dorsal side of the blunt-snouted but somewhat arrow-shaped head is covered in part with small scutes. Body scales relative large and smooth. Tail short. Abdominal scutes narrow and inconspicuous. Anal spurs present, also pelvic girdle remnant. This as well as features of the skull anatomy indicate that these are primitive snakes.

Aniliidae burrow in loose humus soil of tropical forests; *Cylindrophis* also occurs in muddy bottoms of rice paddies in Indo-China. All species are live-bearing. Food consists of various small vertebrates, preferably amphibians and reptiles. *Anilius* appears to be primarily ophiophagous. Behavior when endangered is a family characteristic: they bury their head under their coiled body and offer the often conspicuously colored (on the undersurface) tail. Biology largely unknown.

Should be kept in a well-heated tropical rain-forest terrarium with a deep, well-drained substrate layer or in high glass display terrariums; the latter offer better viewing of specimens. Feed at night. So far rarely imported and only infrequently kept in captivity. Some biological details have been ascertained through terrarium observations. A large water bowl must be provided.

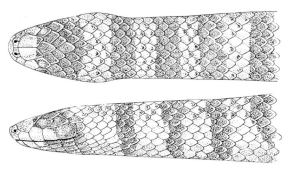

Anilius scytale

Anilius OKEN, 1816. Coral Pipe Snakes. Monotypic genus of the Aniliidae. Northern South America (Amazon and Orinoco Basins, Mato Grosso) in tropical rain forests and dry forests. To 90 cm. Head not set off from body, head scutes small. The very small eyes are each covered by an ocular scute; chin furrow absent. The bright red coloration is characteristic, with black crossbands (incompletely ringed). However, in contrast to *Micrurus* there are no white or yellow rings. Tail very short.

Nocturnal. Hide during the day in the ground, particularly close to water. Feed at night on fish, frogs, snakes, and lizards. Give birth to 8-15 young. The young usually start feeding immediately.

▪ *A. scytale* (LINNAEUS, 1758).

Anisolepis BOULENGER, 1885. Genus of the Iguanidae. Central Brasil to northern Argentina. 2 species. To 25 cm. Heterogenous scale pattern, in part strongly keeled (including ventral scales, tail, and part of gular region). Brown with dark spots and narrow longitudinal lines.

Tree-dweller, little known about mode of life. See *Anolis*.

▪ *A. undulatus* (WIEGMANN, 1834).

Annamemys: see *Mauremys*, genus.

Annelida: Phylum Articulata. Segmented worms. Marine, freshwater, and terrestrial species. From among the three classes (Polychaeta, Oligochaeta, and Hirudinea) only a few families and groups of Oligochaeta have any significance as food organism for terrarium animals, especially the Enchytraeidae, Lumbricina, and Tubificidae (whiteworms, earthworms, and tubificids).

Anniella pulchra pulchra

Anniella GRAY, 1852. Legless Lizards. Sole genus of family Anniellidae. California, Baja California, and some offshore islands, up to 2000 m elevation. 2 species. In slightly damp, sandy areas with sparse cover. To 25 cm. Elongated, worm-like. 6 mm in diameter. Eyes small but fully functional. Limbs and ear openings absent. Tail over ½ snout-vent length. Dorsal region silvery gray with dark longitudinal stripes.

Ground-dweller, burrowing often only a few centimeters below the surface. Allegedly catches prey by thrusting upward. Feeds on small insects and spiders. Ovoviviparous, 1 to 4 young.

Should be kept in a slightly damp, shallow terrarium with thick sandy clay substrate and under tropical conditions. Not a very satisfactory specimen since this animal remains underground most of the time.

▪ *A. pulchra* GRAY, 1852. California Legless Lizard. California, Coronados Islands. Dorsum brownish (one form is brownish black), yellowish, or silver gray with three narrow dark longitudinal stripes. Ventral area lighter.

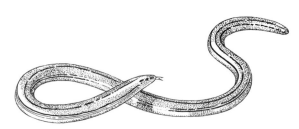

Anniella pulchra

Anniella pulchra nigra

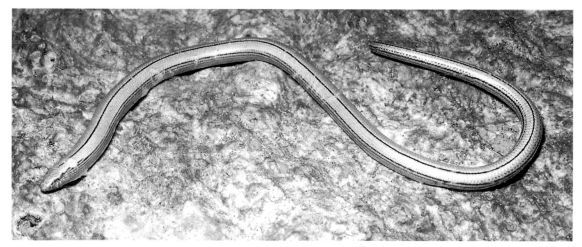

Anniella pulchra pulchra

Anniella pulchra pulchra

Anniellidae: American Legless Lizards. Family of the Squamata, suborder Sauria. Western North America. There are strong ties within the Anguimorpha toward the Anguidae. Some systematists consider these lizards to be merely a subfamily (Anniellinae) of Anguidae, in which case a particularly close relationship to *Anguis fragilis* is assumed and the differences are considered to be largely adaptations to a burrowing mode of life. A relationship to amphisbaenids has also been entertained, but this appears to be unlikely. Body elongated, worm-like. Skull strongly ossified, with a few conical teeth. Tongue forked. Ear openings absent. Tail not longer than body. Legless, shoulder girdle barely indicated in skeleton. Ovoviviparous. The sole genus is *Anniella*.

Anodonthyla MUELLER, 1892. Genus of the Microhylidae. Madagascar. 3 species. Has horizontal pupils. Tympanum sometimes easily visible, sometimes covered. Fingers and toes without webbing, tips with more or less large, wide adhesive discs. Only an internal metatarsal tubercle present.

Terrestrial, a more or less good climber. Lay a few large eggs.
• *A. montana* ANGEL, 1925. Adringitra Mountains. 4 cm. Yellow brown, with variable dark spotted pattern (fused in some specimens).

Anolis DAUDIN, 1802. Anoles, American Chameleons. Genus of the Iguanidae. Southern North America to Bolivia and Paraguay; the Caribbean. About 200 species and 300 subspecies. Here we are considering *Phenacosaurus* as an independent genus, but *Deiroptyx, Audantia, Xiphocercus,*

and some other names are treated as subgenera (also refer to generic overview of Iguanidae). In tropical rain forests, open dry (sclerophyll) forests, savannahs, and steppes, usually close to water; some follow human habitation.

Barely 10 to 60 cm; most species about 20 cm, slender. Shape of head rather variable, pointed to roundish. Tail usually twice snout-vent length. The often very wide adhesive lamellae on the ventral surfaces of toes and fingers are very characteristic. They enable these animals to run along glass and similar smooth surfaces. The large throat sac or gular pouch of males (substantially smaller in females) can be erected by means of the hyoid bone. The degree of erection may indicate different states of excitement. Because of considerable skin tension the brightly colored, sometimes multi-colored, skin between the scales of the pouch becomes visible; this pattern is often a species-specific characteristic. Body color usually green or brown, often with a pattern of darker spots (rarely stripes). A few species, such as *A. carolinensis* and *A. porcatus*, can undergo rapidly progressing physiological color changes. When at ease and during the night they are light green; when excited they become much darker, sometimes even brown or almost black. Some species give off sounds (*A. vermiculatus*). The behavior patterns during courtship and ritualistic fighting are extremely diverse.

The majority of species are more or less strictly arboreal. *A. vermiculatus* (subgenus *Deiroptyx*) lives close to water and flees across the water surface, running or swimming. *A. lucius* prefers darkish crevices or dense root thickets in forests, while many other species can be found in bushes or on walls about human habitation. The diet consists of

Anolis carolinensis

Anolis carolinensis

Anolis equestris

Anolis conspersus

Anolis conspersus

Anolis conspersus

Anolis bimaculatus sabanus, ♂

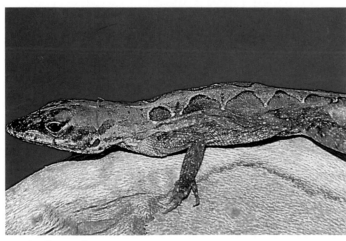

Anolis sagrei

Anolis sagrei

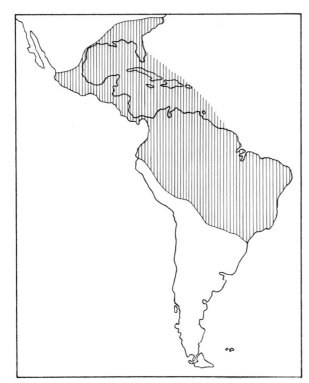

Distribution of *Anolis*

Anolis porcatus, ♂

various arthropods, and larger species will even take small rodents. Egg-layers.

Anoles are perhaps the most popular terrarium animals, since they can be kept in relatively small containers. In contrast to the rather active smaller species, the "giant" species are very quiet. Generally *Anolis* should be kept in slightly damp to damp (NOT wet) terrariums that contain climbing branches and adequate hiding places (c. g., a cork or bark wall). Plants are recommended for esthetic reasons and for their beneficial effect on the humidity. Plants are rarely ever damaged. Peat moss clumps attached to epiphytes are occasionally used as sites to deposit eggs. Temperatures from 25 to 30° C. during the day and about 20° C. at night. Heavy water spraying at night should be used to provide a high humidity; a reduction to 60 or 70% relative humidity during the day is beneficial for many species. Drinking requirements are moderate, and most water is obtained by licking spray off leaves, etc.; in addition, a commercial bird watering container or a drop dispenser can be placed inside the terrarium. Under these conditions even species like *A. carolinensis*, which often lives in relatively dry and hot habitats (agricultural land, cities), can casily be kept. These species are very adaptable; however, in high humidity and only moderate temperatures they rarely show their usual daytime coloration.

The diet must be varied, and large species should also be given newborn mice as well as arthropods. Regular calcium and vitamin supplements and ultraviolet radiation must be given. With the exception of those species from rain forests, most *Anolis* can be kept outdoors during the

Anolis equestris, ♂

Anolis sagrei

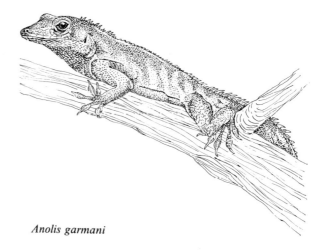

Anolis garmani

Anolis equestris

Anolis garmani

summer months. Males, especially those of closely related species, are often rather aggressive toward each other, so it is recommended that you keep the species separate and in pairs only or one male with several females. The animals should be closely watched so that an aggressive male does not injure any female; if too aggressive, it must be isolated. Species of about the same size but from different habitats can often quite easily be kept together in the same terrarium without any problems.

Many species have been bred in captivity over several generations. As a rule, each female produces several clutches a year, each usually consisting of 2 eggs. The eggs are laid at 3- to 6-week intervals. Damp peat moss or a loose peat moss/sand mixture is suitable for incubation. At temperatures from 28 to 30° C. the young will hatch after 2 or 3 months. With some care and attention and a varied diet the young will reach sexual maturity in a year. However, small species live rarely longer than 3 years, maximally 4 years. In the wild longevity is often substantially less.

• *A. allisoni* BARBOUR, 1928. Cuba. Frequently found in agricultural areas. 20 cm. With pointed head.

• *A. auratus* DAUDIN, 1802. Grass Anole. Panama to northern Brasil. Brushland. 22 cm. Slender, with very long tail. Not an active climber.

• *A. carolinensis* DUMERIL and BIBRON, 1837. Green Anole, Red-throated Anole. Southern United States, Bahamas. Frequently found in agricultural areas. 22 cm. Likes warmth.

• *A. chlorocyanus* DUMERIL and BIBRON, 1837. Leaf Anole. Haiti. 16 cm. Prefers damp habitats.

• *A. cybotes* COPE, 1863. Bigheaded Anole. Haiti. Often found on the ground or on rocks. 20 cm. Very adaptable.

• *A. equestris* MERTENS, 1820. Knight Anole. Cuba. In tree tops. To 55 cm. Not very active. Will occasionally take fruit, lettuce, and similar items, as well as pink mice.

• *A. garmani* STEJNEGER, 1899. Jamaican Crested Anole. Jamaica. Forest dweller. 25 cm. Very attractive, with low dorsal crest.

• *A. lineatopus* GRAY, 1840. Stripe-footed Anole. Jamaica. Lower tree branches, also found on the ground. 20 cm.

• *A. lucius* DUMERIL and BIBRON, 1837. Cave Anole. Cuba. Shady ground, rocky crevices. 18 cm.

• *A. ophiolepis* COPE, 1861. Cuban Grass Anole. Cuba. Grasslands, on plants and low shrubs. 10 cm.

• *A. porcatus* GRAY, 1840. Cuba. 25 cm. Similar to *A. carolinensis*, but stouter.

• *A. ricordi* DUMERIL and BIBRON, 1837. Haitian Giant Anole. In tree tops. 50 cm.

• *A. roquet* (LACEPEDE, 1788). On various Caribbean Islands. Treed savannah. 23 cm. Several subspecies. Best known form is *A. r. extremus* from Barbados.

• *A. sagrei* DUMERIL and BIBRON, 1837. Brown Anole. Florida to Central America, including many islands (Bahamas, Cuba, Jamaica). Several subspecies. Spends much time on the ground among rocks. Agricultural areas. 20 cm. Very adaptable, widely introduced.

• *A. vermiculatus* DUMERIL and BIBRON, 1837. Water Anole. Cuba. In close proximity to water. More than 35 cm.

Anomalepidae: American Blind Snakes. Family of the Scolecophidia. Central and South America. Genera *Anomalepis, Helminthophis, Liotyphlops,* and *Typhlophis,* with collectively about 20 species. Closely related to Typhlopidae, but in contrast to these the Anomalepidae have in some cases (genera *Anomalepis* and *Liotyphlops*) retained a tooth in the lower jaw. The upper jaw has teeth, as in the Typhlopidae. Some systematists consider the Anomalepidae to be merely a subfamily of the Typhlopidae or do not recognize them at all as a valid group. In other anatomical, moprhological, and biological details they resemble the Typhlopidae or in general the Scolecophidia.

Anomalepis JAN, 1860. Genus of the Anomalepidae. Mexico to Peru and Ecuador. 4 species. To 30 cm. Dorsum of head with 3 about equal enlarged scutes; rostral small. Lower jaw with a tooth on each side.

• *A. mexicanus* JAN, 1861. Mexico to Panama.

Anomalochilus VAN LIDTH DE JEUDE, 1890-1891. Monotypic genus of the Aniliidae. Sumatra, in tropical rain forests. 25 cm. Has a cylindrical body, with a small, blunt-snouted head not set off from the trunk. Very short, blunt tail. Maxillary with teeth. Dorsum of head with small scutes. Chin furrow absent. Dorsal region with alternating rows of spots along both sides of the vertebral column. Sides with a continuous white stripe.

Burrowing snakes. Biology and ecology largely unknown.

• *A. weberi* VAN LIDTH DE JEUDE, 1890-1891. Western Sumatra near Kajutanam. Very rare.

Anomalopus DUMERIL, 1851. Genus of the Scincidae. Australia. 6 to 9 species. In relatively damp habitats. 15-25 cm, slender. Eyelids movable, non-transparent. Snout scutes covered by characteristic milky skin. Smooth-scaled. Limbs strongly reduced, with maximum of 3 toes. Dark, frequently with light stripes. Ground-dweller, frequently under rotting wood or rocks. Egg-laying.

• *A. lentiginosus* DE VIS, 1888. Central eastern Australia. Easily 20 cm. Monotone gray to reddish brown. 2 fingers, 1 toe.

• *A. ophioscincus* (BOULENGER, 1885). Central eastern Australia. Barely 20 cm. Dorsal area with black spots amd dark lateral bands. Digits absent.

Anoplohydrus WERNER, 1909. Monotypic genus of the Colubridae of unclear subfamily status, possibly a primitive Asian wolf snake (Lycodontinae). About 45 cm. Presumably a nocturnal ground-dweller in tropical rain forests.

• *A. aemulans* WERNER, 1909. Western Sumatra.

Anops BELL, 1833. Monotypic genus of the Amphisbaenia. South America, in tropical forests. Head clearly laterally compressed with a stout vertical snout edge projecting beyond the lower jaw. Occurs preferably in humus soil underneath decaying tree trunks.

• *A. kingii* BELL, 1833. Southern Brasil, Uruguay to northern Argentina. Easily 25 cm. Brownish.

Anolis gundlachi

Anolis roquet aeneus

Anolis homolechis

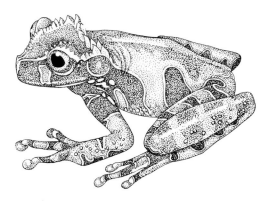

Anotheca spinosa

Anotheca SMITH, 1939. Monotypic genus of the Hylidae. Central America. Montane (1300 to 1800 m). Has very characteristic thorn-like projections on the head that are formed by projections of the dorsal skull bones overgrown by skin. These start to develop in subadult specimens. Pupil horizontally oval, iris bronze-colored. Fingers and toes not distinctly webbed.

Anotheca are active throughout the year. Eggs are deposited in water-filled bromeliad funnels or holes in hollow trees. Larvae feed on mosquito larvae and other frog eggs. Maintenance problems for adult specimens are not yet resolved, only short longevity in captivity, presumably because of nutritional deficiencies due to improper insect foods.
- *A. spinosa* (STEINDACHNER, 1864). Mexico to Panama. To 7.5 cm. Brown with darker pattern.

Anotis BAVAY, 1869. Genus of the Scincidae, *Leiolopisma* Group. Southeastern Australia, New Caledonia. 5 species. In tropical forests. Easily 10 cm. Slender, limbs reduced. Ear openings very small or absent. Brown to shiny black. Cryptic ground-dweller, often in decaying wood.
- *A. maccoyi* LUCAS and FROST, 1894. Southeastern Australia.
- *A. gracilis* BAVAY, 1869. New Caledonia. Lower eyelid transparent, ear opening present.

Anotosaura AMARAL, 1933. Monotypic genus of the Teiidae. Bahia and Pernambuco in Brasil. Similar to *Bachia*. Little known.
- *A. collaris* AMARAL, 1933.

Ansonia STOLICZKA, 1870. Stream Toads. Genus of the Bufonidae. Tropical southern Asia, India to Philippines. 15 species. In rain forests, including cloud forests. 2 to 5 cm. Slender. Characters atypical of family. Skin spiny or wart-covered. Heat flat, snout protruding, some species with 1 to 4 rows of black thorns along the upper jaw. Tympanum usually visible externally (exceptions: *A. mcgregori* and *A. muelleri*). No parotoid glands. Long, thin legs. Fingers free, toes more or less webbed. Extremities with more or less distinct adhesive discs. Males (except *A. guibei*) with unpaired vocal sac. Call cricket-like, chirping. Larva is elongated with long tail and large sucking mouth (adaptation for life in rapidly flowing water).

Ansonia stay on the ground or climb about in bushes. They enter rapidly flowing, even cascading, jungle streams and rivers to breed. The few unpigmented eggs are apparently attached under rocks.

Stream toads should be kept in a rain-forest terrarium. Breeding in captivity is assumed to be difficult in view of the strict ties of these species to fast flowing water. Provide a terrarium with a water section containing clear water at about 20° C. The substrate should be shaded and there should be a water current provided by a circulating pump.
- *A. albomuculata* INGER, 1960. Western Kalimantan. 3 cm. Dark brown with orange-red pattern, white spot below eye.
- *A. fuliginea* (MOCQUARD, 1890). Northern Kalimantan at 1800 to 3000 m elevation. 4 cm. Dorsum brown, flanks and ventral area blackish.
- *A. latidisca* INGER, 1966. Western Kalimantan. Mountains. 6 cm. Brown with red spots. Fingers with large adhesive discs.
- *A. muelleri* (BOULENGER, 1887). Mindanao, Philippines. 3 cm. Black with light pattern, flanks and limbs with white spots.

Antarctic: Faunal region that apart from the continent proper of Antarctica includes the Kerguelen Islands, Falkland Islands, and the southern tip of South America (southern-most Andes, Tierra del Fuego). Only a few species of herptiles (some lizards, Tropidurinae) have penetrated from the Neotropics into Tierra del Fuego. There are no Recent reptiles or amphibians in the Antarctic proper.

Antibiotics: Substances produced by microorganisms that even when vastly diluted are effective in inhibiting the development of or killing other microorganisms. Particularly effective in reptiles are: gentamicin, penicillin, polymyxin, tetracycline (mainly oral), to some degree also carbpenicillin, streptomycin, chloramphenicol (for salmonellosis). For local effects on the digestive tract the hard to absorb neomycin is used. Selection and administration of a particular antibiotic should be specific, preferably after determining the exact pathogen and its antibiotic sensitivity by means of an antibiogram, as well as on the basis of established therapeutic procedures.

Antilles: see Neotropics.

Antillophis MAGLIO, 1970. Genus of the Colubridae, Xenodontinae. Caribbean. Species formerly included under *Leimadophis* or *Dromicus*. Characters, behavior, and care very similar to those two genera.
- *A. andreai* (REINHARDT and LUETKEN, 1863). Cuba. 6 subspecies.
- *A. parvifrons* (COPE, 1863). Haiti and small adjacent islands.

Antivenin: Antiserum produced for the treatment of venomous snake bites. The basis for this is the characteristic of snake venoms to act as antigens and produce specific antibodies in a foreign organism. Horses are usually used for the production of antivenins. Increasing amounts of venom are injected into a horse over a period of days, and after the formation of a sufficiently high antibody-titer (percentage of the blood volume) a large amount of blood is removed that contains the dissolved antibodies. If this is then refined and injected into a human bitten by a venomous snake, the antibodies combine with the proteins of the snake's venom to neutralize its toxic effect.

In practice, the venomous snake sera are available in ampules or freeze-dried as mono- or polyvalent antisera. Monovalent antisera are for the treatment of bites from a particular species; polyvalent antisera can be employed against bites from several different species from a particular geographic region. These are obtained by injecting a horse simultaneously with venoms from the most common venomous snake species in a particular area. These polyvalent antisera are of considerable significant in snake bite therapy, since in areas with several different venomous snake the actual species can often not be identified. The treatment of bites from large specimens may require about 60 ml to 100 ml of antivenin. However, serum treatment of venomous snake bites has some inherent dangers, since the injection of a foreign serum can cause an incompatibility reaction in a patient and thus lead to anaphylactic shock. Antivenin is never given unless the patient has been tested for allergic reactions to horse serum. Such reactions are common and may cause more damage than a mild snakebite.

Ants: see Formicoidea, superfamily.

Anura: see Salientia, order.

Aparallactinae: Ground Vipers. Subfamily of the Colubridae. Africa to Near East (there only genus *Atractaspis*). 10 genera. Formerly mostly included in Boiginae, with *Homorelaps* (syn. *Elaps*) in Elapidae and *Atractaspis* put in the Viperidae. However, recently the genus *Atractaspis* has been removed again from the Aparallactinae and has been established in its own subfamily, Atractaspidinae (monogeneric) in the Colubridae.

Maximum size to 1 m. Head not distinct from body. Head scutes reduced, loreal scute usually absent. Blunt snout, small to very small eyes, short tail. Apical sensory pits absent from body scales. All species have functional venom glands that in some species of *Atractaspis* reach enormous sizes. However, the fangs are rather variably developed. Most genera have rear fangs preceded by 2 to 10 smaller teeth, yet the genera *Homorelaps* and *Atractaspis* have venom fangs at the front of the jaws. In *Homorelaps* the fangs are still relatively small and are proteroglyph; in *Atractaspis* the fangs are solenoglyph and the fang is placed on the maxillary bone so it can be erected and retracted. The effectiveness of the Aparallactinae venom has not yet been comprehensively studied. It is recommended that all species be considered as truly venomous snakes. Usually dark, with little or no markings.

Burrowing snakes. Egg-layers. Most species should be kept in glass terrariums with deep bottom substrates.

The genera are:

(monotypic) *Amblyodipsas* and *Macrelaps*;

(polytypic) *Aparallactus, Atractaspis, Calamelaps, Chilorhynophis, Homorelaps, Micrelaps, Miodon,* and *Polemon.*

Aparallactus lunulatus

Aparallactus A. SMITH, 1849. Centipede-eaters. Genus of the Colubridae, Aparallactinae. Tropical and southern Africa. About 10 species, some polytypic. Formerly included in Boiginae. Primarily in dry habitats (steppes and savannahs to marginal rain forest areas). Blunt-snouted head, not set off from body. 5 to 10 small front teeth in the upper jaw, followed by a relatively short fang at eye level. Smooth scales. Uniformly dark, rarely with longitudinal stripes (*A. lineatus*) or nape bands (*A. capensis, A. lunulatus, A. jacksoni*).

Remain in hiding under rocks during the day or in termite mounds. Main diet consists of centipedes, snails, blind snakes, amphisbaenids.

Glass terrariums are suitable for the care and maintenance of *Aparallactus*. Caution: Bite may be venomous.
- *A. capensis* (A. SMITH, 1849). Black-headed Centipede-eater. Zaire to Republic of South Africa. 5 subspecies.
- *A. lineatus* (PETERS, 1870). West Africa, Guinea to Ghana.

Aparasphenodon MIRANDA-RIBEIRO, 1920. Monotypic (?) genus of the Hylidae. Southeastern Brasil, Venezuela (Orinoco Region). Typical casque-headed treefrog. Head very large, nearly triangular, with long and pointed snout. Mouth cleft subventral. Iris dark brownish red.

Typical nocturnal tree-dwellers that hide during the day in bromeliads and other secluded places that are virtually closed off to the top by the massive, bony skulls of these frogs. Care and maintenance in tropical rain-forest terrariums follow usual procedures.
- *A. brunoi* MIRANDA-RIBEIRO, 1920. Wedged-headed Treefrog. 6 cm. Attractive bronze color with contrasting pattern of black spots during the day; slate gray to grayish brown at night.

Apathya: see *Lacerta*, genus.

Apeltonotus: see *Takydromus*, genus.

Aphantophryne FRY, 1917. Monotypic genus of the Microhylidae. New Guinea. Sometimes considered to be a synonym of *Cophixalus*, but in contrast to this genus it lacks adhesive discs and apparently is a ground-dweller of the grasslands at high altitudes of about 4000 m.
- *A. pansa* FRY, 1917. Mount Scratchley. 3 cm. Dark brown.

Aphelandra R. BR. Genus of the Acanthaceae. Tropical South America. 8 species. Low-growing colorful herbs. Require at least 18° C. during the winter months and need sufficient humidity and semi-shade. Reproduction by means of cuttings.
- *A. goodspeedii* STANDL and BARKL. About 8 cm tall. Undemanding. Red or yellowish spots around the leaf veins.

Aphids and ladybug predator

Aphids: Plant lice. Part of order Homoptera of the class Insecta. Used as food for newly hatched reptiles and amphibians; however, not always taken.

Aplastodiscus LUTZ, 1950. Monotypic genus of the Hylidae. Northeastern Argentina and Brasil. Montane, marginal forest habitats. Ground-dwellers.
▪ *A. perviridis* LUTZ, 1950. To 4.5 cm. Dorsum bright green, abdominal region whitish.

Aporopristis: see *Leiosaurus*, genus.

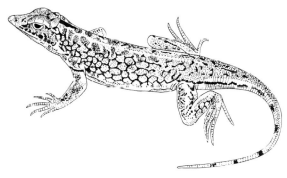

Aporosaura anchietae

Aporosaura BOULENGER, 1887. Monotypic genus of the Lacertidae. Southwestern Africa. In fog-shrouded deserts (the Namib). Body short and wide, flattened dorso-ventrally. Head short, with spade-shaped snout. Base of tail thickened. Limbs long and thin. Femoral pores and enlarged collar scales absent.

These lizards like to burrow and can disappear within seconds in lose sand. General appearance and behavior reminiscent of genus *Phrynocephalus*, and should be kept accordingly in a terrarium as for *Phrynocephalus* and *Eremias*, but without winter dormancy period. Temperature about 30° C. (locally up to 40° C.), somewhat cooler at night. Diet consists of various arthropods, including hard-shelled species.

▪ *A. anchietae* (BOCAGE, 1867). Namib Sanddiver. Angola, Namibia. About 12 cm, snout-vent length about 5 cm. Yellowish brown above with heavy reticulations or spots.

Aporoscelis: see *Uromastyx*, genus.

Apostolepis COPE, 1862. Genus of the Colubridae, Boiginae. South America, from Guyana and Surinam southward to Peru and Argentina. 14 species. In dry areas within tropical forests. 25 to 65 cm. Has reduced head scutes, small eyes, head not set off from body.

Burrowing snakes feeding on worms, insects, and small lizards. Egg-layers. Caution: May have dangerous bite; very large fangs present below eye.
▪ *A. assimilis* (REINHARDT, 1861). Central and southwestern Brasil, Argentina.
▪ *A. flavotorquata* (DUMERIL, DUMERIL, and BIBRON,

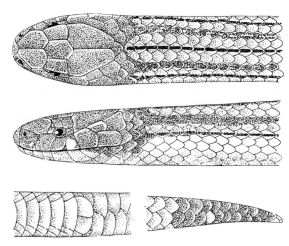

Apostolepis longicaudata

1854). Central Brasil.

Apotype, Apomorph: Derived character state (in contrast to plesiotypic character state) in phylogenetics. While the ending "type" refers to any characteristic, "morph" characterizes anatomical or shape characteristics. Describing simultaneously occurring apotypes nominally as synapotypes facilitates the reconstruction of relationships between organisms.

Appetitive behavior: Specific search behavior for a stimulus situation that triggers a specific terminal response. Expression of an inner readiness to act that is important (but not always essential) for a sequence of various behaviors, such as the directional or non-directional search for prey or the search for a female willing to mate by a sexually stimulated male.

Aprasia GRAY, 1839. Blunt-tailed Scaley-foots. Genus of the Pygopodidae. Southern and western Australia. 9 species. To 14 cm. Worm-like, head rather blunt. Tympanum not visible. Hind limbs extremely reduced, often represented by only a single scale. Scales smooth. Preanal pores absent. Primarily brown with or without additional markings.

Substantially adapted to burrowing mode of life. *Aprasia* species rarely ever leave their hiding place. Diet mainly insects. In the wild, termites provide a substantial part of the diet.

Aporosaura anchietae

Aporosaura anchietae

▪ *A. pulchella* GRAY, 1839. Southwestern Australia. To 12 cm. Brownish gray with indistinct longitudinal stripes dissolved into tiny dots.

Aptycholaemus BOULENGER, 1891. Monotypic genus of the Iguanidae. Northeastern Argentina. Little known. Very similar to and closely related to *Anolis.*
▪ *A. longicauda* BOULENGER, 1891.

Aquarium: Container for keeping live aquatic amphibians and reptiles. Substantial specialized literature is available on aquarium maintenance and technology as applied to tropical fish. In contrast to fish, reptiles do not place stringent demands on water quality (hardness, nitrates, etc.), but attention must be paid to cleanliness due to danger of infections. Turtles are often rather messy, necessitating a daily water change or strong filtration. In such cases it is best to omit a fine-grained bottom substrate; instead, a bottom drain should be installed to facilitate quicker and more effective drainage of the tank and so avoid awkward siphoning. Optimum conditions are provided by a flow-through tank; the continuously added fresh water may have to be pre-heated. Maintenance of aquatic amphibians is essentially the same as that of fish.

Aqua-terrarium: Used for the care and maintenance of aquatic or amphibious reptiles and amphibians. In contrast to a plain aquarium, there is always a small land section in an aqua-terrarium that the animals tend to use for sunning themselves. A radiant heat source should be installed above the land section. For many amphibians the land section should be kept moist. It is important that the animals be able to get in and out of the water without any difficulties. In order to prevent wet animals from becoming too soiled, and also to keep the water from becoming dirty, it is recommended that there be a shallow shore area with flat rocks, gravel, or tree bark.

The water in an aqua-terrarium often becomes badly polluted with feces. Thus a frequent—sometimes daily—water change is essential. For the maintenance of large animals (turtles, giant snakes, crocodiles) there should not be any plants in the water or on the land, except in inaccessible areas of the terrarium. An epiphyte branch suspended from above into an otherwise unplanted aqua-terrarium can be surprisingly decorative. If only small animals are kept there can be ample planting of the water and land sections. Under certain circumstances (no piscivores) fish can even be kept in the water section of an aqua-terrarium. It is imperative that the air temperature above the water surface be higher than that of the water or there will be a danger of respiratory diseases.

Araceae: Arums. Family of the Liliatae. Tropics and subtropics, also temperate zone. 100 genera, about 1800 species. Found primarily in rain forests. Bushes, rhizomatous shrubs, lianas, semi-epiphytes, swamp plants. Flowers usually insignificant, closely crowded against the stem, usually surrounded by a conspicuous spathe. Most important genera:

Acorus L. Sweetflag. Temperate zones of Asia, Europe, North America. 2 species. Swamp plants for outdoor terrariums. *A. calamus* L. and *A. gramineus* SOLANDER, a grass-like slow-growing shrub reaching 20 cm.

Acorus gramineus

Anubias lanceolata

Anubias SCHOTT. West Africa. 12 species. Creeping swamp and shore plants in tropical rain forests. Can endure shade but not winter temperatures below 16° C. Not particularly attractive, but extremely hardy. Reproduces by fission. *A. lanceolota.* N.E. BR., leaves more than 10 cm, and *A. nana* ENGL., leaves about 6 cm.

Other important species and genera include *Calla palus-*

Arachnida, the scorpion *Pandinus imperator*

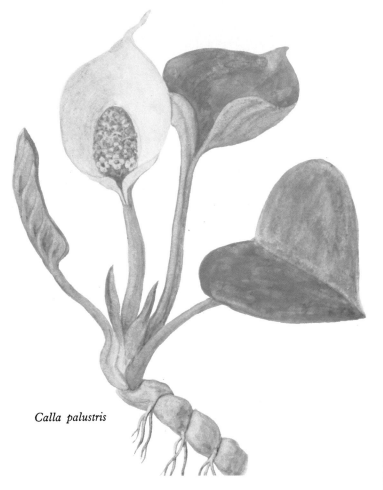

Calla palustris

Arachnida: Spiders and Scorpions. Class of 8-legged Arthropoda with more than 30,000 primarily terrestrial species. Some are used as food organisms for terrarium animals, especially small spiders and occasionally harvestmen. Mites (Acari) are often parasites on terrarium animals as well as in terrarium food breeding operations. Mainly tarantulas, scorpions (Scorpiones), and some wind spiders (Solifugae) are sometimes kept as terrarium animals.

Araliaceae: English Ivys. Family of the Magnoliatae. Primarily in the tropics. 55 genera, about 700 species. Mainly stemmed bushes and shrubs that grow in cool locations. Can be cultured outdoors during the summer months, but require shade from direct sun. *Fatshedera, Fatsia, Hedera.*

tris L., for aqua-terrarium use, a rhizomatous shrub from European sedge swamps and swamp forests; *Cryptocoryne,* a large genus of decorative submersed swamp plants; *Aglaonema; Anthurium; Caladium; Dieffenbachia; Epipremnum; Monstera; Pothos; Scindapsus;* and *Syngonium.*

Cryptocoryne axelrodi

Arachnida, a scorpion, *Diplocentrus*

Arachnida. Solifugae, *Galeodes graecus*

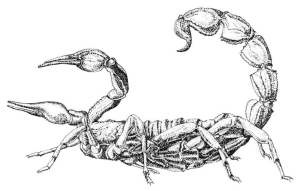

Arachnida. Scorpiones, *Androctonus australis*

Arachnida, a vinegaroon, *Mastigoproctus*

Arachnida, a tailless whipscorpion, *Phrynus*

Arachnida, Solifugae

Araneae. Spiders. Order of the Arachnida. Worldwide distribution with about 25,000 predatory species. Many are eagerly eaten by lizards. Because of their predatory behavior with tendencies toward cannibalism, mass breeding of spiders as reptile food is not really possible. Wolf spiders (family Lycosidae) can be found from spring to fall on the ground, especially close to water. Representatives of the diverse and large family Araneidae are often found in or in close proximity to their webs. Large specimens should have their chelicera removed prior to feeding them to terrarium animals. Young spiders can be caught in large numbers by sweeping in spring and fall. Buildings are frequently occupied by representatives of the genus *Tegenaria*, one of the family of funnel spiders (Agelenidae). Some Araneae are occasionally kept as terrarium animals, especially some of the large bird-eating spiders or tarantu-

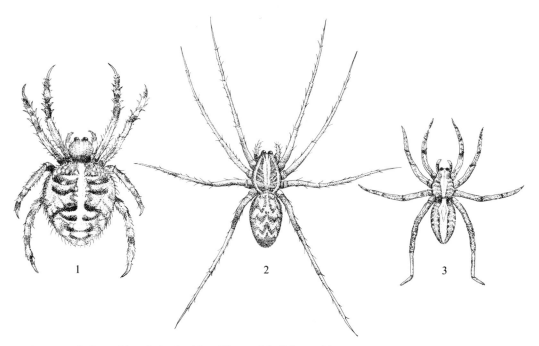

Araneae: 1 Araneidae, 2 Agelenidae (*Tegenaria*), 3 Lycosidae

Araneae, *Avicularia avicularia*

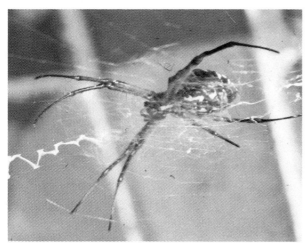

Araneae, *Argiope aurantia*

Araneae, *Latrodectus mactans*

Araneae, *Nephila clavipes*

Araneae, *Pamphobeteus tetracanthus*

Araneae, *Lycosa poliostoma*

Araneae, *Brachypelma smithi*

Araneae, *Phoneutra* sp.

las (Theraphosidae and others) and some of the highly venomous species such as the black widows (*Latrodectus*).

Arboreal: Pertaining to trees, tree-like. Usually applied to animals adapted to living in and moving about in trees.

Arcovomer CARVALHO, 1954. Monotypic genus of the Microhylidae. Brasil. Slender. Round pupil. With broad, truncate finger and toe tips. Natural history unknown.
• *A. passarellii* CARVALHO, 1954. States of Espirito Santo and Rio de Janeiro. 2 cm. Brown with irregular dark dorsal band.

Argalia GRAY, 1846. Monotypic genus of the Teiidae. Northwestern South America. About 10 cm. Inconspicuous ground-dweller. Also refer to *Bachia*.
• *A. marmorata* GRAY, 1846.

Argenteohyla TRUEB, 1970. Monotypic genus of the Hylidae. Uruguay and adjacent areas in Argentina (Parana delta). In swampy shore regions of large rivers.
• *A. siemersi* (MERTENS, 1937). 7 cm and larger. Brown, flanks and sides of limbs with red spots.

Arid: Dry. Refers to overall climate in a particular region. The prevailing annual climate determines the forms of vegetation in the area. Contrasted by humid.

Aristelliger COPE, 1862. Genus of the Gekkonidae. Antilles and Yucatan. 4 to 6 species. Inconspicuous, small, nocturnal lizards. In contrast to similar genera (*Hemidactylus, Thecadactylus*) the well-developed adhesive lamellae of the toes are not separated by a median furrow.
• *A. georgeensis* (BOCOURT, 1870). Yucatan and adjacent islands.
• *A. cochranae* GRANT, 1931. Haiti, Navassa, Inagua.

Arizona KENNICOTT, 1859. Faded Snakes. Monotypic genus of the Colubridae, Colubrinae. Western and central United States southward into Mexico. In different types of dry habitats, in Mexico up to 2000 m elevation. 0.7 to 1.45 m. Head barely set off from body. Dorsal scales very smooth. With variable brown rhomboidal or spotted markings against a light background.

Diurnal and nocturnal ground snakes, found under rocks and in other hiding places; good burrowers. They feed on lizards, smaller snakes, and small mammals. Egg-layers, 8 to 15 eggs. Care similar to *Eryx*, in well-heated arid terrarium (substantially reduced temperatures at night).
• *A. elegans* KENNICOTT, 1859. About 7 subspecies.

Arizona elegans

Arizona elegans

Arrhyton GUENTHER, 1858. Genus of the Colubridae, Xenodontinae. Jamaica, Cuba, Puerto Rico, and smaller islands. 7 species. Used to be included, in part, in *Dromicus*, *Leimadophis*, and *Alsophis*. In appearance, biology, and terrarium care very similar to these.
• *A. exiguum* (COPE, 1863). Puerto Rico and adjacent islands. 3 subspecies.
• *A. funereum* (COPE, 1863). Jamaica.
• *A. vittatum* (GUNDLACH and PETERS, 1862). Cuba and Isle of Pines. 2 subspecies.

Arthroleptella HEWITT, 1926. Genus of the Ranidae. South Africa. 2 species in damp, cool mountain forests. In shape very similar to *Rana*. In contrast to the closely related genus *Anhydrophryne*, males lack a snout hump. No vocal sac; chirping call in rapid succession, repeated 6 to 30 times.

Ground-dweller in shaded forest regions, often close to water. They hide under rocks, fallen leaves, and moss. Embryonic and larval development independent of water. Reproduction occurs during the southern summer, with the eggs are deposited in shallow nest depressions located under moss, rocks, or other protected places. *A. lightfooti* lays only 5 to 8 eggs, *A. hewitti* 20 to 40 eggs. The completely metamorphosed young hatch after about 3 weeks. Care same as for *Anhydrophryne*.
• *A. hewittii* FITZSIMONS, 1947. Natal (above 600 m elevation). To 3 cm. Yellowish to brown, with a dark eyeband.
• *A. lightfooti* (BOULENGER, 1910). Cape Province. To 2.5 cm. Dark brown to blackish, with a dark eyeband.

Arthroleptides NIEDEN, 1910. Genus of the Ranidae. East Africa. 2 species. Closely related to *Petropedetes*. Found in mountain regions. Strongly thickened fingers and toes; well-developed webbing on toes, fingers free. Behavior presumably similar to *Petropedetes*. Survives droughts by burrowing into damp soil.
• *A. martiensseni* NIEDEN, 1910. Usambara Mountains. 6 cm. Gray to yellow-brown.

Arthroleptis SMITH, 1849 (= *Schoutedenella* DEWITTE, 1921). Genus of Ranidae. This genus requires taxonomic revision. Tropical and southern sub-tropical Africa. More than 40 species. Lives in different habitats, such as rain forests, dry sclerophyll forests, savannahs, and grasslands, in lowlands and in mountain regions; abundant in some areas. Also found in cultivated areas. Usually smaller than 3.5 cm. In shape similar to *Rana*. Species of this genus are difficult to distinguish externally from each other and from the related genus *Phrynobatrachus*, therefore some species in this genus have often been referred to *Phrynobatrachus*. Males of some species (e. g., *A. poecilonotus*) have a conspicuously extended third finger (similar to *Cardioglossa*). All species probably have a high, screeching, insect-like chirping call. Vocal sac absent. These species, as do those of *Cardioglossa*, exhibit distinctly different day and night coloration.

Nocturnal ground-dwellers, often burrowers. In contrast to *Phrynobatrachus*, *Arthroleptis* never enters water, since spawning (as far as known) is similar to *Anhydrophryne* and *Arthroleptella* in damp soil. Embryonic and larval development occur inside the egg. In areas with distinctly alternating dry and wet seasons these species survive the dry season by burrowing into the ground.

Arthroleptis should be kept in a tropical terrarium with a thick layer of loose top soil and be provided with artificial wet and dry seasons.

- *A. poecilonotus* PETERS, 1863. Cameroons, Nigeria. Mainly in grasslands. To 3 cm.
- *A. stenodactylus* PFEFFER, 1893. Southern and eastern Africa. Mainly in dry forests. To 3 cm.
- *A. taeniatus* BOULENGER, 1906. Cameroons. To 2 cm.
- *A. variabilis* MATSCHIE, 1893. Cameroons, Nigeria. Varied habitats; follows agricultural development. To 3.5 cm.
- *A. wahlbergi* SMITH, 1849. South Africa. Forests and brushland. To 3 cm.

Arthropoda: Largest phylum of the animal kingdom, containing about three quarters of all recent animal species. Representatives from various classes play important roles as food for terrarium animals: Insecta, Arachnida, and Crustacea. Some are even kept as terrarium animals (scorpions, tarantulas, wolf spiders, land hermit crabs, and others). Recognized by their jointed legs, usually 6 or more in number.

Arthropoda, *Coenobita perlatus,* a land hermit crab

Arthrosaura BOULENGER, 1885. Genus of the Teiidae. Northern South America. 4 species in tropical rain forests. 15 cm. Snout relatively blunt. Tail barely twice snout-vent length. Well-developed limbs. Dorsal scales strongly keeled, ventral scales large and smooth. Strongly enlarged gular folds particularly conspicuous. Primarily brown with lighter vertebral stripes or lateral spots, abdomen yellowish to bright orange. Males more intensively colored.

Ground-dwellers frequently found in sunny areas among fallen leaves. Feed on small arthropods.

- *A. kocki* VAN LIDTH, 1904. Surinam to eastern Brasil. 15 cm. Abdomen orange.
- *A. reticulata* (O'SHAUGHNESSY, 1891). Northwestern Amazon region. Easily 15 cm. More strongly keeled than previous species. Abdomen yellowish.

Arthropoda, *Coenobita clypeata,* a land hermit crab

Arthroseps BOULENGER, 1898. Genus of the Teiidae. Brasil. 2 species. Inconspicuous species on forest floor. Little known.

- *A. werneri* BOULENGER, 1898. Sao Paulo, Santa Catarina.

Ascaphidae: Tailed Toads. Family of the Salientia. Only genus is *Ascaphus.* Considered to be primitive frogs, together with Leiopelmatidae, because their morphology retains many primitive features. The Ascaphidae have essentially the same anatomical characteristics as the Leiopelmatidae and are therefore often included in this family. However, male ascaphids are the only recent frogs with a copulatory organ.

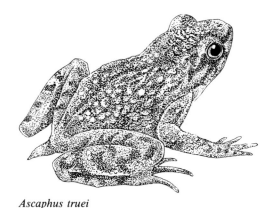

Ascaphus truei

Ascaphus STEJNEGER, 1899. Tailed Toads. Monotypic genus of the Ascaphidae. Pacific North America in and near shady, cool streams in coniferous forests up to 2000 m elevation. Externally rather nondescript, reminiscent of Discoglossidae or even treefrogs (Hylidae). Skin more or less covered with warts. Males with a (for frogs) unique short external, tail-like copulatory organ. Pupil vertical, elliptical. Fingers free; toes with webbing, outer toe conspicuously wider than the other toes. Vocal sac absent; apparently without vocalizing capability.

Spawn is laid underwater in the form of egg strings deposited under rocks. Fertilization is internal. The larvae hatch in August to September and are adapted to flowing water, having a large sucking mouth. Development period of larvae is 2 years.

Maintain in an aqua-terrarium at steady low temperatures. During the summer a semi-sterile resting period in a refrigerator at 10 to 12° C. is recommended with illumination for about 18 hours. A small all-glass tank with a shallow water level and a land section provided with some flat stones is adequate.

• *A. truei* STEJNEGER, 1899. Tailed Toad. Cascade Mountains of British Columbia, Washington, Oregon, and northern California; Rocky Mountains of Montana and Idaho; many local populations. To 5 cm. Olive with dark eyeband and light yellow to greenish spot on top of the head.

Ascaroidea: Roundworms, Nematodes. Found primarily in giant snakes, but also common in lizards. The pathogenic effect of ascaroids comes from mechanical damage (perforation of intestinal lumen; closure of gall and pancreatic ducts and blood vessels until they rupture); their toxic effect that can lead to localized infectious reactions (necrotic and ulcerative enteritis), and can possibly also lead

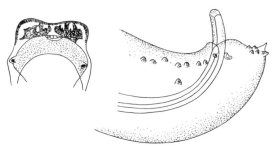

Ascaroidea, *Hexametra sewelli*

to general reactions within the host organism; and the removal of nutrient material from the host. A decisive weakening of the host's resistance probably does not occur until there is a simultaneous bacterial infection or through the effect of amoeba. Ascaroid attacks alone frequently remain unnoticed. The clinical symptoms are non-specific: refusal of food, accelerated loss of condition, possible diarrhea, and constipation.

Therapy: Broad-spectrum anthelminthics, such as piperazine (dosage: 150 mg/kg body weight) repeated three times at weekly intervals given orally via a stomach tube.

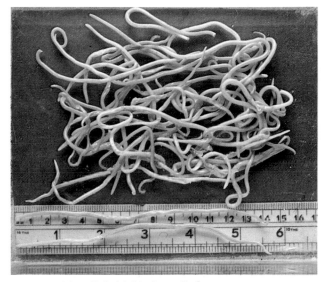

Ascaroidea, *Polydelphis* from *Python*

Asclepiadaceae: Family of the Magnoliatae. Found primarily in tropical Africa, but also in Asia, the Americas, and South Africa. About 250 genera, 2000 species. Most are creeping shrubs, some are succulents that are reminiscent of cacti, and a few are epiphytes. Hanging and climbing plants include *Hoya, Ceropegia*. Succulents include *Caralluma, Huernia, Huerniopsis*, and *Stapelia*.

Aspidelaps FITZINGER, 1843. Shield-nosed Cobras. Genus of the Elapidae. South Africa. 2 species. Found from savannahs to desert-like arid regions. To 80 cm. Characterized by the large rostral scute that is concave below and curves back over the snout. Yellow to deep red-brown with more or less distinct dark spots or crossbands that extend onto the abdominal region. Excited specimens rear up in a cobra-like fashion and flatten the anterior part of the body, making the contrasting stripes of the ventral region become visible. The large rostral is used for burrowing.

Crepuscular and nocturnal. Diet preferably lizards, small snakes, and frogs, also some small mammals and even birds.

Maintenance as for other venomous snakes, in a dry terrarium with heat during the day and cooling off at night. Breeding is probably facilitated by a cooler dry dormant period.

• *A. scutatus* (A. SMITH, 1849). Shield-nosed Cobra. Central South Africa at the level of the Tropic of Capricorn. 2 subspecies.

Aspidistra KER-GAWL. Cast-iron Plants. Genus of the Liliaceae. Eastern Himalayas, China. 8 species. Can take sun and shade, cool or warm site. Reproduces by cutting. *A. elatior* commonly cultured.

Aspidites PETERS, 1864. Black-headed Pythons. Genus of

Terrestrial species, more or less below surface, nocturnal. Biology virtually unknown, but may be comparable to *Micrurus*. Venomous; handle with care.
▪ *A. muelleri* (SCHLEGEL, 1837). New Guinea, New Britain, New Ireland, adjacent islands to d'Entrecasteaux Archipelago. About 4 subspecies.

Aspidites ramsayi

the Boidae. Australia. 2 species in dry forests. Average 2.5 m. Clearly triangular body cross-section. Brownish yellow interrupted by dark brown crossbands. *A. melanocephalus* has a black head and neck; in *A. ramsayi* the head and body are mostly yellowish brown.

Crepuscular ground-dwellers, not active climbers. Feed on small mammals, birds, and reptiles; prefer snakes as prey, including venomous species of family Elapidae.

Should be kept in a well-heated, dry terrarium with water bowl deep enough to permit occasional bathing. Tight hiding places are very important for the well-being of these snakes. Rarely bred. Endangered species.
▪ *A. melanocephalus* (KREFFT, 1864). Black-headed Python. Queensland to northwestern Australia.
▪ *A. ramsayi* (MACLEAY, 1882). Woma or Ramsay's Python. From Queensland to western New South Wales, westward to central and southwestern Australia.

Aspidomorphus FITZINGER, 1843. Genus of the Elapidae. New Guinea and adjacent islands to New Ireland. 3 species. Found at ground level in tropical to montane rain forests. About 65 cm. These snakes have a short, round head and small eyes. The tail is short.

Aspidura WAGLER, 1830. Rough-sided Snakes. Genus of the Colubridae, Lycodontinae. Sri Lanka. 6 species. In mountain forests to more than 2,000 m elevation. About 20 to 40 cm. Head pointed, not set off from body. Head scutes not reduced. Tail short and pointed, terminating in a spur. Spines may be present on the scales in the cloacal region in some species (may be more prominent in males).

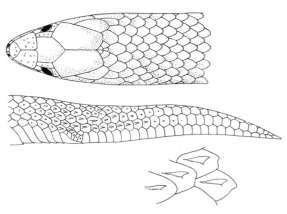

Aspidura trachyprocta

Nocturnal ground-dwellers, burrowing snakes. Feed on worms, insects, and their larvae. Egg-layers, 4 to 21 eggs.
- *A. brachyorrhos* (BOIE, 1827). Sri Lanka. Yellow to reddish brown with four dark longitudinal stripes.
- *A. trachyprocta* COPE, 1860. Sri Lanka. Brown with longitudinal rows of dark spots.

Asplenium L. Spleenworts. Genus of the Filicatae. Worldwide distribution. About 700 species. Epiphytes and ground-dwellers. Habitat highly variable.
- *A. adiantum-nigrum* L. Black-stemmed Spleenwort. 15 to 40 cm tall.
- *A. dimorphum* KUNZE. Leaves to 1 m. Young plants suitable for rain-forest terrariums.

Asplenium nidus

- *A. nidus* L. Birds-nest Fern. Epiphyte. Leaves form a rosette, up to 1 m long. Must be cultivated in nutrient-rich soil. Slow grower. For rain-forest terrariums.
- *A. ruta-muraria* L. Brick-root Spleenwort. 3—15 cm tall. Can tolerate low temperatures. Prefers calcium-rich soil.
- *A. septentrionale* (L.), HOFFM. Northern Spleenwort. On silicate rocks. This species, the two above, and *A. adiatum-nigrum* are particularly suitable for unheated or outdoor terrariums.

Assa TYLER, 1966. Pouched Frogs. Monotypic genus of the Leptodactylidae. Pacific coast of Australia, narrow area of the Queensland-New South Wales border. Perpetually damp coastal forests and adjacent rain forests. Shape compact. Pupil horizontal; tympanum not visible. Fore limbs conspicuously angular. Fingers and toes weakly thickened, without webbing. Males with paired bilateral brood pouches where egg and larval development take place. Metamorphosed juvenile frogs are released.

Ground-dwellers. Should be kept in slightly heated terrarium with adequate hiding places on the ground (rocks, pieces of tree bark).
- *A. darlingtoni* (LOVERIDGE, 1933). To 3 cm. Formerly included in *Crinia*. Dorsal area variably gray, brown, or red, often with dark V-shaped pattern in shoulder region or median longitudinal band. Flanks dark. Abdominal region cream.

Asterochelys GRAY, 1873. Radiated Tortoises. Genus of the Testudinidae. Often considered a subgenus of *Geoche-*

Asterochelys radiata

lone. Madagascar. 2 species. Carapace to 40 cm, highly arched. These are among the most endangered tortoises on earth.
- *A. radiata* (SHAW, 1802). Radiated Tortoise. Southwestern Madagascar. Savannahs and steppes. Constrasting radiating markings. One of the most attractive tortoises. Should be kept in a roomy dry terrarium, and can be kept outdoors in summer during stable weather conditions. Has been bred occasionally. Incubation period 145 to 230 days at 32° C. and 24° C., respectively. Considered to be a delicacy in its native country, so existing populations have become greatly decimated. Usually seen only as a treasured exhibition specimen in public reptile displays.
- *A. yniphora* (VAILLANT, 1885). Angonoka Radiated Tortoise. Northwestern coast of Madagascar. Only in tropical forest regions. An upwardly arched beak-like unpaired gular scute is characteristic of this species. Radiating mark-

Asterochelys radiata, immature

Asterochelys radiata

ings are usually poorly developed, instead with rhomboidal pale brown areas against a dark background. Currently the rarest tortoise species.

Asterophrys TSCHUDI, 1838. Genus of the Microhylidae. Indo-Australian Archipelago, highest species diversity in New Guinea. 17 species in tropical rain forests and fog-shrouded mountain forests. Skin smooth or granular. Basic coloration brown. Pupil horizontal. Tympanum variably visible in different species. Tips of fingers and toes pointed or enlarged into adhesive discs, without webbing.

Occupies bushes and trees, but also a ground-dweller. The clutch of *A. robusta* consists of a few large eggs interconnected by a gelatin thread and attached to a leaf. It is closely guarded by the male. Completely metamorphosed juvenile frogs will hatch from the eggs.

Maintenance and potential breeding are in a rain-forest terrarium at temperatures from 24 to 29° C. Keep high altitude species at about 22° C.

▪ *A. minima* PARKER, 1935. New Guinea. Barely 3 cm. A dark, triangular spot between eye and corner of mouth.

Asterochelys yniphora

▪ *A. robusta* (BOULENGER, 1898). New Guinea and St. Augnan Island. 7 cm.
▪ *A. rufescens* (MACLEAY, 1878). New Guinea. 5.5 cm. Has a dark band from eye to hip.

Astylosternus WERNER, 1898 (= *Gampsosteonyx* BOULENGER, 1900; *Nyctibates* BOULENGER, 1904). Genus of the Ranidae. Tropical western and central Africa. 3 species. Usually found close to flowing waters of tropical mountain regions. Skin smooth. Pupil vertical. Toes clawed and more or less bent (compare with related genera *Scotobleps* and *Trichobatrachus*). Larve to 9 cm, with black tail spots also typical of *Trichobatrachus*; agile swimmers that are nocturnal just as are the adults. They remain in hiding during the day.

Newly caught *Astylosternus* are extremely active, to the point where they can injure themselves with their powerful jumps within the confines of a small transport container. It is often advisable to slightly drug the animals while in transport. Care and maintenance require a roomy aqua-terrarium.

▪ *A. diadematus* WERNER, 1898. Cameroons, Nigeria. Mountain regions between 650 and 1700 m. To 6.5 cm. Blackish brown with light coloration along nape region. Iris reddish golden.
▪ *A. occidentalis* PARKER, 1931. Sierra Leone (Mount Nimba).

Atelopodidae: Atelopidids, Stub-footed Toads. Family of the Salientia, suborder Procoela. Central and South America. 2 genera (*Atelopus* and *Brachycephalus*). Despite the typically frog-like, slender shape, the atelopodids are actually closely related to the true toads (Bufonidae). More or less strong reduction of fingers and toes occurs in most species. The family is characterized by the rigid pectoral girdle, procoelic vertebrae, and enlarged transverse processes on the sacral vertebrae. Amplexus is by means of an axillary grasp. Because of their attractive coloration several species are in demand as terrarium animals. Some of their skin secretions are highly toxic.

Atelopus DUMERIL and BIBRON, 1841. Atelopodids, Stub-footed Toads. Genus of the Atelopodidae. Species uncertain, requiring urgent revision. Central and South America. More than 30 species, many polytypic. Some species have been placed into the bufonid genera *Dendrophryniscus*, *Melanophryniscus*, and *Osornophryne*. Found from lowland to high Andes plateaus (4800 m), in more or less open, treeless and bushless grasslands, such as savannahs and high Andean cloud forests. Also in montane rain forests, for example, *A. boulengeri* and *A. zeteki*. Usually very slender and smooth-skinned, with a small head. Pupil horizontal. Tympanum covered. Limbs long and thin. Fingers free or barely webbed, toes more or less completely webbed. Outer and inner fingers and toes more or less shortened, stubby. Many species are very brightly colored. The skin secretion may be more or less strongly toxic.

Usually diurnal ground-dwellers. Rain water accumulations and flooded areas serve as brood sites. The larvae hatch about 24 hours after spawning and require only a few weeks until metamorphosis. Montane species must not be kept in rain-forest terrariums, which are too warm. Keep-

Atelopus zeteki

ing cloud-forest species without additional heating is best.
Some species can be kept outdoors during summer, but be-
ware of excessive heat. *A. zeteki* is an endangered species.
▪ *A. boulengeri* (COPE, 1862). Ecuador.
▪ *A. elegans* (BOULENGER, 1882). Colombia, Ecuador.
Lower mountain regions. 3.5 cm. Yellow, striped irregu-

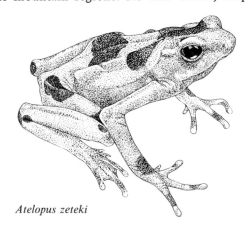

Atelopus zeteki

Atelopus varius

larly with red to reddish brown, with light brown spots. A very slender species.

• *A. ignescens* (CORNALIA, 1849). Colombia, Ecuador. Usually high altitude species. 3 cm. Brownish black; ventral region sharply set off, yellow orange.

• *A. varius* (LICHTENSTEIN and MARTENS, 1856). Central America and Colombia. Savannahs to damp forests. 3.5 cm. Highly variable. Basic coloration usually yellowish with brown vermiculations and red spots, sometimes also

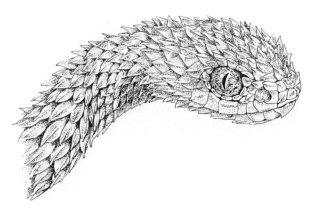

Atheris hispidus

Atelopus sp.

with grayish green dots.

• *A. zeteki* DUNN, 1933. Panama Golden Stub-footed Toad. Panama. 5 cm. Yellow orange, with some shiny black spots. Threatened with extinction.

Atelopus crucigera

Atheris COPE, 1862. Bush Vipers. Genus of the Viperidae, Viperinae. Tropical Africa. 7 to 9 species. To 75 cm. Scales strongly keeled and shingled, in some species almost erect, giving a "rough" appearance (*A. hispidus*, *A. squamiger*). Yellow-brown to green. Superbly adapted to surroundings, they are strongly arboreal and almost invisible in the bushes and trees it inhabits. The only genus of arboreal Viperidae with a prehensile tail.

Atheris is not very active, usually hanging suspended between branches, the head lower than the tail. Prey taken includes treefrogs, lizards, small rodents. Gives birth to up to 20 young. Venom apparently not fatal to humans, though the bite is considered serious.

Provide a relatively small, well-heated terrarium with ample climbing opportunities and high humidity. These snakes seem to do best in a well-planted tropical forest terrarium. Some populations of different species live in montane rain forests and these would require lower nightly temperatures. Knowledge of the origin of specimens to be kept is an essential prerequisite for successful maintenance in captivity. The young can be reared on small crickets, frogs, and pieces of meat offered with long forceps. If need be, force-feed with mashed food injected orally with a large hypodermic and a blunt canula.

• *A. chlorechis* (SCHLEGEL, 1855). Western central Africa. Lowlands. Bright green.

• *A. hispidus* LAURENT, 1955. Congo Basin. Green.

• *A. nitschei* TORNIER, 1902. East Africa. 2 subspecies. Dry brushlands, also in mountain regions.

• *A. squamiger* (HALLOWELL, 1854). Rough-scaled Bush Viper. Western Central Africa. 2 subspecies. Nominate form in lowlands (rain forests in Congo Basin). The other subspecies, *A. s. robustus* LAURENT, 1956, occurs in mountain forests of the Ituri region of the Congo. Blue-green to olive.

Atractaspis SMITH, 1849. Burrowing Vipers, Mole Vipers. Genus of the Aparallactinae. Tropical and southern Africa, Asia Minor, Arabian Peninsula, and Sinai Peninsula northward to Israel. Seldom exceeding 1 m. Head not distinct from body; eyes very small; rostral scale enlarged, often pointed; anal plate sometimes divided; fangs very large. About 16 species, some greatly polytypic.

Found in tropical forest regions and also in dry areas, including deserts, these are burrowing snakes that dig with their shovel-like head, even into hard substrates. Found

Atheris squamiger

out in the open only at night or after heavy rainfall. Their food includes lizards, snakes, and small mammals. When these snakes are uncovered during the day they roll up into a ball and hide their head among the body coils.

Mole vipers are very aggressive at night and are the only representative of the Aparallactinae that has been known to cause fatal bites.

Use of a glass terrarium with a thick substrate is recommended. Species from dry and arid regions require substantial nightly temperature drops, while forest-dwellers need only marginally lowered night temperatures.
- *A. bibroni* SMITH, 1849. Africa south of 5° N. latitude. 2 subspecies. Savannahs.

Atractaspis irregularis

- *A. engaddensis* HAAS, 1950. Israel, Egypt (Sinai). Deserts.
- *A. microlepidota* GUENTHER, 1866. Between Mauretania and Nigeria, eastward to Kenya and northward to Arabian Peninsula. 4 subspecies. Savannahs.

Atractus WAGLER, 1828. Genus of the Colubridae, Lycodontinae. Neotropics from Panama southward to Peru; greatest diversity in the northwestern Amazon Basin and in the montane rain forests of the eastern slope of the Andes. About 70 species. Between 20 and 70 cm. Head not set off from body, blunt-snouted. Rather variable coloration and markings, frequently uniform dark with bright yellow collar.

Nocturnal burrowing ground snakes. Diet consists mainly of earthworms, insect larvae, and small lizards. Egg-layers. Should be kept in glass terrariums with deep substrates.
- *A. major* BOULENGER, 1893. Amazon region of Ecuador, Colombia, Venezuela, and Brasil. Dark spots against a light brown background.
- *A. elaps* (GUENTHER, 1858). Andean slopes from Colombia to Peru. Black and red in incomplete rings.
- *A. occipitoalbus* (JAN, 1862). Andean slopes of Ecuador. Blackish gray with a yellow-white collar.

Atretium COPE, 1861. Genus of the Colubridae, Natricinae. Discontinuous distribution within the Oriental Region. 2 species. 80 to 90 cm. More or less distinct, elongated head. Body covered with strongly keeled scales. Dorsally uniformly olive brown or greenish.

Amphibious, similar to *Natrix*. Diet main fish and frogs. When excited will flatten neck region, without rearing up, similar to *Pseudoxenodon*. Egg-layers, 12 to 30 eggs. Care and maintenance the same as for Natricinae, Group 2.
- *A. schistosum* (DAUDIN, 1803). Southern India, Sri Lanka. Up to 1000 m elevation.
- *A. yunnanensis* ANDERSON, 1879. Western Yunnan, southwestern China. 600 to 1500 m elevation.

Aubria BOULENGER, 1917. Monotypic taxon of doubtful status within the Ranidae. Considered to be either an independent genus or a subgenus or synonym of *Rana*. In rain forests of tropical West Africa. Compact body. Flat-headed, rather long-snouted. Skin wrinkled. Fingers free, toes half webbed. Males with vocal sac. Larvae strongly pigmented, very elongated.

Strictly nocturnal and semi-aquatic in small swamp puddles and forest pools. Larvae form soccerball-size aggregations that slowly roll along the muddy pond bottom. *Aubria* should be kept in a tropical aqua-terrarium with adequate hiding places on land and in the water.
- *A. subsigillata* (DUMERIL, 1856). To 9.5 cm. Dorsum brown with round black, barely visible flecks. Ventrum with brownish violet reticulated markings.

Audantia: see *Anolis*, genus.

Aulura BARBOUR, 1914. Monotypic genus of the Amphisbaenia, family Amphisbaenidae. Tropical South America.
- *A. anomala* BARBOUR, 1914. Brasil. Tropical rain forests. About 20 cm.

Australasian faunal region: Australasia is subdivided into 3 subregions: continental Australian Subregion (including Tasmania); New Zealand Subregion (New Zealand); and Papua-Polynesian Subregion (New Guinea and other South Sea Islands, of which the Solomons and Fiji are of particular herpetological significance).

Australasian faunal region: Jardine River, Australia

Australasian faunal region: Drysdale River, Australia

Australasian faunal region: Termite mounds provide cover and
food for many different animals

The following comments refer to the continental Australian Subregion. The northern half of this subregion is located in the northern marginal tropics, its southern half in the subtropics, and Tasmania in the temperate region. The temperatures are higher than would be expected from the geographical location. Two-thirds of this subregion have average temperatures in excess of 20° C., a tropical climate; in the central Australian desert regions extreme heat prevails, yet slight freezing temperatures occur in the southern part of the continent and in montane regions. The northern coastline has mangrove belts. Grasslands, semideserts, and deserts prevail on the continent due to its arid climate. Forests occur only in the coastal regions, and there only as less than 1% of the entire area. Predominant trees are *Eucalyptus* and *Acacia*, as well as, in the extreme south, *Nothofagus*. Dry forests, monsoon forests, and occasional rain forests occur in the northern and eastern parts of the continent. Subtropical sclerophyll forests of similar development as in the Mediterranean Region and in South Africa, which are followed on by subtropical or temperate (Tasmania) moist forests with *Nothofagus* as in Chile, occur in the

extreme southwest and southeast of the continent. Tasmania has occasional frosts during the southern winter months; this is also the area with the highest precipitation (up to 2800 m elevation) of the entire subregion.

The reptile fauna includes largely families of cosmopolitan distribution, such as Crocodylidae, Boidae, Gekkonidae, Scincidae, Chelidae, and Varanidae. The last three families display their greatest diversity in Australia. Also notable is the diversity of elapid species. Other widely distributed families or subfamilies are completely absent (Testudinidae, Emydidae, Colubrinae). Endemic forms include only two small families: Carettochelyidae and Pygopodidae.

Amphibians are only represented by the Salientia and consist primarily only of Hylidae and two endemic subfamilies of Leptodactylidae. There are also a few Microhylidae and Ranidae that have arrived in the subregion from the north.

Austrelaps WORREL, 1963. Australian Copperheads. Monotypic genus of the Elapidae. Southeastern Australia and Tasamania. Formerly included in *Hoplocephalus* or *Denisonia*. Found in swampy habitats. Reaches 1.7 m. Relatively slender venomous snakes with strongly neurotoxic as well as hemotoxic and cytolytic venom. Adults with large dorsal scales, usually uniformly gray to yellow or reddish brown.

Diurnal and nocturnal (still active at low temperatures). Feeds almost exclusively on frogs. Reproduction ovoviviparous, up to 20 young. Maintenance requires a slightly heated terrarium with a large water or swamp section.
▪ *A. superbus* (GUENTHER, 1858).

Autecology: Subdiscipline of ecology that investigates relationships between individual organisms (as representatives of a species) and their environment.

Autochthonous: Occurrence of an animal or plant species within its natural range. Opposite of allochthonous (introduced or migrant sspecies). For instance, the American bullfrog (*Rana catesbeiana*) is autochthonous in eastern North America, but allochthonous in Cuba and the southern European Alps.

Autotomy: Self-amputation. Ability to drop off individual body parts (usually the tail) as a reaction to a specific stimulus. Some amphibians (such as *Chioglossa*) and numerous lizards have the ability to drop their tail in response to external stimuli (in some species the tail vertebrae have preformed fracture lines). Autotomy is particularly common in skinks and geckos. The lost tail section is usually regenerated more or less completely. Incomplete fractures may lead to the formation of forked or double tails.

Aves: Birds. Birds play a minor role as food animals for some reptiles such as snakes and crocodiles. Day-old chicks obtainable from hatcheries are often utilized, as are sparrows. Pigeons and chickens can be used as food for giant snakes. Wild-caught pigeons should not be used since most are carriers of coccidia and salmonella. Somewhat more difficult is the acquisition of small bird eggs for egg-eating-snakes. Parakeets and similar birds can possibly provide suitable substitutes.

Azemiopinae: Monogeneric subfamily of the Viperidae. Occurs between northern Burma and southern China in damp montane forests of the subtropical Himalayan foothills. The most ancient group within this family. Head covered with large scales; fangs relatively short. Dark gray and orange ringed markings (incomplete).

Ground-dwelling snakes that presumably feed on small mammals. Reproduction details unknown. Maintain in forest terrarium as for *Vipera berus* or *Vipera kaznakovi*.

Azemiops BOULENGER, 1888. Fea's Viper. Monotypic genus of the Azemiopinae. Northern Burma, southeastern Tibet, North Vietnam, and adjacent regions of southern China. At altitudes from 600 to 1500 m.

About 80 cm. Narrow orange crossbands at wide intervals against dark gray to black background; head bright golden orange.
▪ *A. fea* BOULENGER, 1888. Very rarely seen. Very subject to dehydration in captivity.

Autotomy: regenerated tail of *Tarentola mauritanica*

Bachia GRAY, 1845. Genus of the Teiidae. South America (except southern tip). About 20 species. Exact limits of genus uncertain. Today *Anotosaura* and *Heterodactylus* are usually considered independent genera as is *Ophiognomon*. *Scolecosaurus* is here included in *Bachia*. Found in tropical rain forests. To 20 cm, elongated, cylindrical. Tail barely twice the snout-vent length. Limbs sometimes reduced, very thin and short, with variable numbers of toes and claws (often 3). Smooth-scaled. Primarily brown.

Ground-dwellers among fallen leaves or in the upper soil layer. Hardly burrowers, instead these lizards use existing burrow systems. They feed on ants, termites, and other small arthropods; these lizards are often found in ant nests. Can be easily kept together with small arboreal lizards.
• *B. (Scolecosaurus) alleni* BARBOUR, 1914. Trinidad, Grenada, adjacent islands and mainland. To 15 cm.
• *B. lineata* BOULENGER, 1909. Venezuela. Barely 20 cm. Longitudinal stripes.
• *B. monodactylus* DAUDIN, 1802. Guyana, Brasilian Amazon region. Easily 15 cm. Limbs extremely reduced.

Bacterial infections: Bacteria are significant pathogens in some of the most important diseases of reptiles and amphibians, particularly those affecting the respiratory and digestive organs (abscesses, *Aeromonas* infections, diarrhea, pneumonia, *Pseudomonas* infections, colds, stomatitis infectiosa). However, there are only a few primary bacterial infections (salmonellosis, tuberculosis), and even these require some triggering endogenous or exogenous factors (such as stress due to transport, population pressure, unsuitable climatic conditions, endo- or exoparasitic attacks, or vitamin deficiency) in order to produce clinical manifestations.

Therapy: Apart from antibiotic and sulfonamide administration, those factors triggering the clinical manifestations have to be corrected with better husbandry conditions.

Prophylaxis: Optimal husbandry conditions.

Baikia GRAY, 1865. Genus of the Amphibaenidae. West Africa.
• *B. africana* GRAY, 1865. Northern Nigeria. Rare. Poorly known.

Baird, Spencer Fullerton (1823-1887): American naturalist. Founder of the herpetological collection at the Smithonian Institution in Washington, D. C. Co-authored with Girard in 1853 *Catalogue of North American Reptiles.*

Balanophis SMITH, 1938. Monotypic genus of the Colubridae, Natricinae. Sri Lanka. Found in montane rain forests. To 60 cm. Has a triangular, clearly set off head. The posterior part of the upper jaw carries opisthoglyphic fangs. The dorsal region of the body is covered with strongly keeled scales. There is a nuchal gland in the nape region (as in some other Natricinae, *Macropisthodon* and others) that extends to the level of the fifteenth ventral shield. The background color is olive brown with a variable pattern of longitudinal stripes and rows of spots; may be yellowish, reddish, or blackish.

Little is known about the biology of this very rare snake. For details of care and maintenance refer to Group 1 of the Natricinae. Venomous bites.
• *B. ceylonensis* (GUENTHER, 1858).

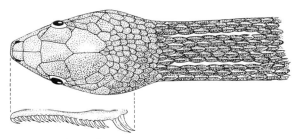

Balanophis ceylonensis

Ball position: The smaller forms among the giant boid species and pipe snakes (genus *Cylindrophis*), among others, tend to defend themselves passively by coiling their body into a ball. The head is then in the center and part

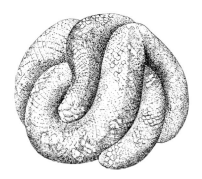

Ball position in *Calabaria*

of the tail is extended to give the impression of being the head or to divert attention through striking coloration.

Baragenys PARKER, 1936. Genus of the Microhylidae. New Guinea and surrounding islands. 4 species. Closely related to *Metopostira*, *Genyophryne*, and *Asterophrys*. Found in tropical rain forests and cloud forests. Smooth-skinned.

Ball position in *Calabaria*

Horizontal pupil. Tympanum clearly visible. Fingers and toes have adhesive discs.

These frogs live among bushes and in trees. Their larvae not aquatic; development of eggs is as in *Asterophrys*.
▪ *B. atra* (GUENTHER, 1896). New Guinea. At 2000 m elevation. 4 cm. Brown, flanks darker.

Barbour, Thomas (1884–1946): American zoologist, director of the Museum of Comparative Zoology, Harvard University. Together with Stejneger inaugurated the *Check List of North American Amphibians and Reptiles*, first edition 1917. Also involved in herpetofauna of Caribbean Region.

Barbourula TAYLOR and NOBLE, 1924. Genus of the Discoglossidae. 2 species. Philippines and Borneo, in slow-flowing jungle streams. In body shape intermediate between *Discoglossus* and *Bombina*. Fingers and toes webbed. Males without vocal sac and without nuptial pads on hands.

Largely aquatic. The unpigmented eggs are attached underneath rocks in the water. These frogs should be kept in a tropical aqua-terrarium with adequate hiding places and clean water kept in motion with a filter or power filter. Feeds on insects. Endangered.
▪ *B. busuangensis* TAYLOR and NOBLE, 1924. Philippines.

Barkudia ANNANDALE, 1917. Monotypic genus of the Scincidae. India. Barely 20 cm. Elongated, with very small ear opening and no limbs. Tail about half snout-vent length. Large scales. Not well known.
▪ *B. insularis* ANNANDALE, 1917. Madras, India. Light brown, back with darker spots.

Barycholos HEYER, 1969. Monotypic genus of the Leptodactylidae. Ecuador, in the coastal lowlands. Related to *Leptodactylus* and *Lithodytes*. Pupil horizontal; tympanum clearly visible. Fingers and toes free, first finger substantially longer than second one.

Natural history unknown, presumably as in *Eleutherodactylus* and the *Leptodactylus marmoratus* Group, which lack a free-swimming larval stage.
▪ *B. pulcher* (BOULENGER, 1898). To 2.5 cm.

Basanita MIRANDA-RIBEIRO, 1923. Genus of the Leptodactylidae. Brasil. 2 species. Considered to be a synonym of *Eleutherodactylus* by some systematists. Flat-headed. Pupil horizontal. Tympanum clearly visible. Fingers and toes free, tips with adhesive discs that are distinctly heart-shaped, except on outer finger and toe. Ground-dwellers.
▪ *B. lactea* MIRANDA-RIBEIRO, 1923. Southeastern Brasil. To 3.5 cm.

Basiliscus LAURENTI, 1768. Basilisks. Genus of the Iguanidae. Southern Mexico to Venezuela and Ecuador. 4 to 5 species that form their own subfamily (Basiliscinae) together with *Laemanctus* and *Corytophanes*. In tropical rain forests. To 80 cm, slender, tail about twice snout-vent length. Dorsal scales granular, ventral scales smooth or keeled. Conspicuously high crests on heads of males. The dorsal crest or helmet is made of skin supported by bony elements and may be up to 6 cm high in *B. plumifrons*, much lower in *B. vittatus*. The helmet and dorsal crest, as well as the dorsal and tail crests, are separated by narrow

Basiliscus plumifrons

gaps. Females have substantially lower crests than males. Toes with webbed margins. Brown or green with variable markings, the abdomen yellowish.

Primarily arboreal, usually in close proximity to water; good swimmers and divers. Due to the webbed margins on the toes these animals can run on the hind legs along a water surface at speeds of up to 12 km/hr. It is alleged that they are able to cross lakes as wide as 400 m in this manner. Predators on small arthropods, snails, frogs, fish, and

Basiliscus plumifrons

small lizards; will occasionally also take some fruit. Egg-layers; nest several times a year, up to 20 eggs per clutch; incubation period about 70—150 days. *B. basiliscus* most likely also occurs in parthenogenic populations.

Should be kept in very spacious, tall rain-forest terrariums. Use only strong plants for decoration. Apart from several climbing branches there must also be a water bowl for swimming. These lizards like to bathe and also often defecate in water; thus absolute cleanliness is of paramount importance. High humidity should be maintained by slight, but constant, heating of the water bowl. The tem-

Basiliscus vittatus

perature should be between 27 and 32° C. (radiant heat is recommended); night temperatures should not drop below 20° C. Occasional ultraviolet radiation is satisfactory. A sufficiently varied diet for adults will not require calcium and vitamin supplements. Pink mice are often refused as food, but crickets are always eagerly eaten.

B. plumifrons has been kept for years in indoor and outdoor cages. Males tend to be rather incompatible. This species should be kept in pairs or one male can be kept with several females. It has been bred in captivity several times.

• *B. basiliscus* (L., 1758). Common Basilisk. Costa Rica to northwestern South America. 80 cm. Brown to olive-green with dark crossbands and a pale lateral stripe. Male with tall dorsal crest, helmet simple but set high. Ventral scales without keels.

• *B. plumifrons* COPE, 1876. Double-crested Basilisk. Guatemala to Costa Rica. To 70 cm. Green with light, often

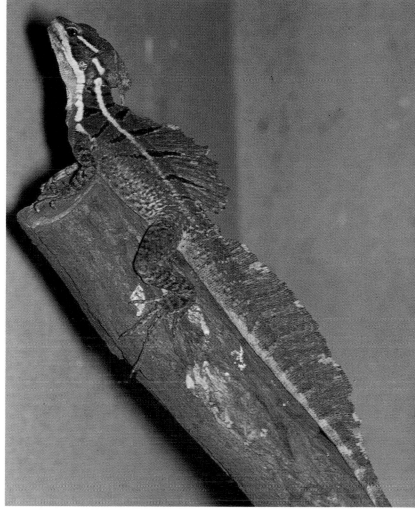

Basiliscus basiliscus

bluish white, spots. Crests particularly high, helmet double. The most attractive species of the genus, but also the most delicate species of basilisk.

• *B. vittatus* WIEGMANN, 1828. Banded Basilisk. Central America. To 75 cm. Coloration similar to *B. basiliscus*. Helmet and crests in males lower. Ventral scales keeled.

Basiliscus basiliscus

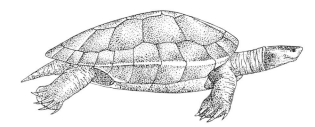

Batagur baska

Batagur GRAY, 1855. Bagatur Turtles. Monotypic genus of the Emydidae. India to Indo-China and Sumatra, in large rivers and lakes. To 60 cm carapace length, one of the largest freshwater turtles in the world. The carapace is streamlined, the extremities flattened, paddle-shaped, and broadly webbed.

Batagur baska

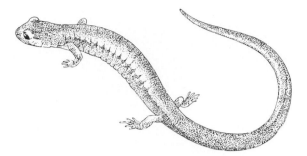

Batrachoseps pacificus

Omnivorous. Hauls out onto sand banks to deposit eggs. Incubation period in the wild is 74 to 122 days. Rarely imported. Suitable only for large display tanks in public aquariums, but can be kept outdoors during the summer months.
▪ *B. baska* (GRAY, 1831). Conspicuously small head. Short tail. Uniformly olive brown. 2 subspecies.

Batrachoseps BONAPARTE, 1839. Slender Salamanders. Genus of the Plethodontidae. Pacific coastal region of North America, where several species occur only in small areas (relict species). 8 species, only 3 well-known. In various habitats (open plains, near desert, forests); *B. pacificus* follows human habitation. Usually not larger than 10 cm, elongated, worm-like. Head small, extremities weak, with 4 digits. Distinct costal grooves.

Batrachoseps displays a fright position in which it coils up and hides its head. Completely terrestrial, without an aquatic larval stage. Lives under tree trunks, tree bark, empty termite mounds, and other hiding places. *B. pacificus* also occurs in suburban gardens, where it likes to hide under flowerpots and shallowly embedded stones. The activity period for coastal populations extends from the rainy fall season (when spawning occurs) to the onset of the dry summer season. In mountain populations (*B. wrighti* and some *B. attenuatus* populations) this activity period is confined to spring.

Specimens from the Pacific coastal region need a summer rest period of several months at slightly elevated temperatures with semi-moist conditions, but hiding places must always contain capillary water. This conforms to the natural ecological conditions.
▪ *B. attenuatus* (ESCHSCHOLTZ, 1839). California Slender Salamander. Southwestern Oregon to northwestern Mexico; also on adjacent islands. 18 to 21 costal grooves. Belly usually black with delicate pattern of white dots.
▪ *B. pacificus* (COPE, 1865). Pacific Slender Salamander. Southwestern California, including adjacent islands, to northwestern Mexico. 2 subspecies. 18 to 21 costal

Batagur baska

Batrachemys: see *Phrynops*.

Batrachophrynus PETERS, 1873. Genus of the Leptodactylidae. Lake Junin, Peru. 2 species. Related to *Telmatobius, Telmatobufo,* and *Caudiverbera*. Smooth-skinned. Pupil horizontal. Tympanum and vocal sac absent. Fingers free, toes webbed. Coloration darkish.

Aquatic. The 2 species live ecologically separated at an elevation of 4100 m in Lake Junin. *B. macrostomus* prefers algal lawn habitats while *B. brachydactylus* occupies the shoreline with its rush belt. Since there are few food organisms of suitable size in these habitats, it is assumed that the metamorphosed frogs feed primarily cannibalistically. For care and maintenance refer to the aquatic *Telmatobius*.
▪ *B. brachydactylus* PETERS, 1873. To 16 cm.
▪ *B. macrostomus* PETERS, 1873. To 30 cm.

Batrachoseps attenuatus

grooves. Belly light with black dots.
- *B. wrighti* (BISHOP, 1937). Oregon Slender Salamander. Mountains of northwestern Oregon. Damp pine forests. Only 16 to 17 costal grooves. Belly black with large white blotches.

Batrachuperus BOULENGER, 1878. Genus of the Hynobidae. Eastern Palearctic west to the Caspian Sea. Greatest diversity (5 species) in China. 7 species. Found in mountain regions from 800 to 4000 m elevation. To 20 cm. Has laterally flattened tail. 4 digits on hands and legs. Larvae with paddle-like tail, a crest that starts at the middle of the back, claw-like horny tips on fingers and toes, thin horny lower jaw edge, and three pairs of long external gills.

Batrachuperus live in close proximity to cold, clear, oxygen-rich and largely fish-free springs and other rapidly flowing waters. Their food consists mainly of amphipods and aquatic insects. Reproduction takes place in spring or (among high montane populations) in summer. As far as is known the spawn contains only a few eggs (7 to 12) and is attached below water to hollow sites below rocks. Outside the breeding season most species live a cryptic terrestrial life. A largely aquatic mode of life has only been reported for *B. musteri* (confirmed by observations in captivity).

Care and maintenance during the aquatic phase is preferably under refrigerated conditions at 10 to 12° C. For the terrestrial phase provide a shaded, moist, cool terrarium with moss-covered rocks.
- *B. karlschmidti* LIU, 1950. Western China at 1800 to 4000 m elevation. 16 to 20 cm. Dorsum uniformly dark olive, abdominal region lighter.
- *B. musteri* SMITH, 1940. Afghanistan west of Kabul, Paghman Mountains at 2400 to 3000 m elevation. 13 cm. Dark olive.
- *B. persicus* EISELT and STEINER, 1970. Northern Iran, Talysh and Elbrus Mountains at 800 to 1200 m elevation. 15 to 20 cm. Grayish yellow with contrasting blackish brown dotted or marbled pattern.
- *B. pinchonii* (DAVID, 1871). Eastern Tibet and Province of Sichuan at 1500 to 4000 m. Fairly common. 13 to 15 cm. Olive with darker spots.

Batrachyla BELL, 1843. Genus of the Leptodactylidae. Southern Chile and western Argentina. 1 to 3 species. Related to *Eusophus*, *Hylorina*, and *Thoropa*. This genus occurs in moist subtropical to subantarctic *Nothofagus* forests. Smooth-skinned, with horizontal pupils and clearly visible tympanum. Fingers and toes free, tips enlarged.

Ground-dwellers that deposit their few large eggs in a damp substrate. The larvae initially remain inside the gelatinous egg capsules, but they become aquatic before metamorphosis.
- *B. leptopus* BELL, 1843. To 3.5 cm. Gray, with washed out blackish spotted pattern.

Batrachylodes BOULENGER, 1887. Genus of the Ranidae. Solomon Islands. 8 species. Primarily in mountain forests up to 1500 m elevation. Fingers and toes free, with more or less wide adhesive discs at their tips. Uniform or patterned dorsal coloration and a blackish lateral band more or less breaking into spots.

Probably more or less bush- or tree-dwellers. Eggs large and unpigmented, presumably deposited outside of water (in *B. trossulus* in damp substrate as in *Platymantis*).
- *B. gigas* BROWN and PARKER, 1970. To 4.5 cm. Wide adhesive discs.
- *B. trossulus* BROWN and MYERS, 1949. To 2 cm. Narrow adhesive discs.
- *B. vertebralis* BOULENGER, 1887. To 3 cm. Wide adhesive discs.

Bavayia ROUX, 1913. Genus of the Gekkonidae. New Caledonia and Loyalty Islands. 2 species. About 10 cm. Nocturnal.
- *B. cyclura* (GUENTHER, 1872). Arboreal. Dorsal area of head normally with small scales. Rather gregarious. Must not be kept too wet.
- *B. sauvagei* (BOULENGER, 1883). Terrestrial in damp habitats. Large, shiny head scales; lateral folds at base of tail reminiscent of *Rhacodactylus*.

Bedriaga, Jakov Vladimirovitch (1854-1906): Russian herpetologist, worked on the herpetofauna of the Mediterranean Region and Mongolia; evaluated the collection of N. M. Przewalski (1898), Russian explorer of Asia. Main work was on the systematics of European amphibians (1879, 1889, 1891, 1896).

Bedriagaia BOULENGER, 1916. Monotypic genus of the Lacertidae. Tropical Africa in tropical forests. Body moderately flattened dorso-ventrally; tail up to 3 times snout-vent length. Dorsal scales large, shingled, and keeled; conspicuously keeled ventral scales. Femoral pores distinct. Olive brown to greenish with 8 longitudinal rows of smaller whitish spots and scattered darker dots. Dendrophyllic. Rare.
- *B. tropidopholis* BOULENGER, 1916. Central Africa (Congo). Easily 30 cm.

Begoniaceae: Family of the Magnoliatae. Begonias. Tropics and subtropics. 5 genera, more than 1000 species. Shrubs, ascendant and climbing semi-shrubs, some epiphytic. In rain forests and montane rain forests. Require semi-shaded positions, sufficient humidity and heat, and nutrient-rich substrate.

Most common genus is *Begonia*, with the following common species: *B. herbacea* VELL.: Epiphytic, leaves 12-20 cm; frequently cultured; *B. imperialis* LEM.: Stem on ground, sensitive to stagnant dampness; *B. glabra* AUBL.: Climbing shrub and decorative hanging plant.

Bell, Thomas (1792-1880): English zoologist. Produced the classic *Monograph of the Testudinata* (1836-1842), which contains the artistic and scientifically valuable plates of James de Carle Sowerby and Edward Lear.

Bibron, Gabriel (1806-1848): French herpetologist. Together with the father and son Dumeril, he authored the 10-volume *Erpetologie Generale ou Histoire Naturelle Complete des Reptiles*.

Billbergia THUNB. Genus of the Bromeliaceae. Mexico to southern Brasil. About 60 species. Primarily runner-producing epiphytes and rock plants, a few growing on the ground. These plants can take dry air and require full light

Billbergia nutans

but not direct sunlight.
- *B. nutans* H. WENDL. Indoor plant. Leaves to 30 cm. Very resistant, frequently cultivated.
- *B. reichardtii* WAWRA. To 20 cm tall.
- *B. saundersii* HORT. Leaves to about 35 cm.

Biocoenosis: Animal community in a particular location (habitat) that in its composition is dependent upon the prevailing ecological factors (biocoenotic laws). Once a biocoenosis has become established in response to a habitat, an ecological balance develops between them.

Biocoenotic laws: Universally valid theorems that express the essential dependency of the organisms on prevailing ecological factors in the ecosystem.
- First Law: The number of species in a particular biocoenosis increases in response to the diversity of abiotic and biotic environmental conditions in a habitat. However, individual species are present in numerically small populations (as in tropical rain forests).
- Second Law: The more abiotic and biotic environmental conditions in a particular habitat deviate from the optimum values for most species, the smaller the species number becomes in the corresponding biocoenosis. However, those few species then occur in large numbers (applicable to, for instance, communities in ponds, high sierras, semideserts).
- Third Law: The species inventory in a biocoenosis depends not only on the ecological structure of the habitat but also upon its longevity. Together with the increase in longevity of a particular habitat there is a corresponding increase in the number of species in the biocoenosis, until finally ecological limiting factors—depending upon the availability of suitable ecologiocal niches—have been reached (e. g., in the settlement of islands and newly established artificial ecosystems).
- Fourth Law: With an increasing intensity of hostile abiotic environmental factors in a particular habitat, the corresponding biocoenosis becomes devoid of species together with declining numbers of specimens.

Biogeocoenosis (geobiocoenosis): Ecological term (incorrect synonym for ecosystem) for a community at a particular geographical location—such as an aggregation of lava lizards (*Tropidurus*), marine iguanas (*Amblyrhynchus*), sea birds, and fiddler crabs along the rocky shoreline of one of the Galapagos Islands—that does not provide the food basis for all members of this community.

Biogeography: Science dealing with the geographical distribution of organisms on the earth, subdivided into plant geography or geobotany and animal geography or zoogeography. Within biogeography the science of chorology deals with the cataloging, description, and comparison of distribution areas. Ecological and historical biogeography uncover causal relationships between distribution and ecology and distribution and geological changes with time such as ice ages, continental drift, and the formation of mountain chains.

Biological clock: Endogenous control of activity periods that are synchronized with environmental conditions only through external triggering mechanisms (e. g., circadian rhythm). In a terrarium one can observe the effects of an internal clock. For instance, tortoises that normally go into a winter dormancy period stop or reduce their food intake in fall for a while although the temperature was not reduced.

Biotope: Specific ecological area where an animal lives.

Bipedidae: Two-legged Worm Lizards. Most primitive family of the Amphisbaenia. Western Mexico. The only genus is *Bipes*. This is the only amphisbaenid with anterior limbs. Pleurodont teeth.

Bipes LATREILLE, 1802. Two-legged Worm Lizards. Genus of the Amphisbaenia. Western Mexico. 3 species.

Bipes biporus

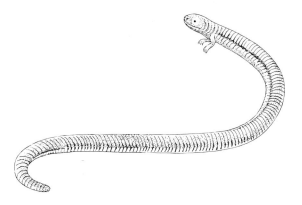

Bipes canaliculatus

About 20 cm. The only amphisbaenids with well-developed anterior limbs. The feet have 3 to 5 toes, some with claws. Brownish to flesh-colored. Found more frequently at the surface than are other amphisbaenids, they are even capable of some climbing. Egg-layers.
• *B. biporus* (COPE, 1894). Baja California. 20 cm. Fifth toe small and without claw.
• *B. canaliculatus* (BONNATERRE, 1789). Western Mexico. About 20 cm. All toes of equal length and with claws.

Bitia GRAY, 1842. Monotypic genus of the Colubridae, Homalopsinae. Southern Burma and Malayan Peninsula to Sumatra. Prefers brackish water region at the mouth of rivers. About 50 cm. The head is small and not set off from the body. Dorsal head scales small. The body has smooth, more or less shingled scales. Body and tail slightly compressed, an atypical subfamily characteristic. The relatively wide abdominal scutes are keeled on both sides. The background color is light gray, traversed by dark broad crossbands. Reminiscent in coloration and shape most strongly of some sea snakes. The main diet consists of fish, and the snakes are frequently caught in fish traps. Females gives birth to only about 3 to 4 young.

Care and maintenance require a brackish water aquarium.
• *B. hydroides* GRAY, 1842.

Bitis GRAY, 1842. Puff Adders, Gaboon Vipers. Genus of the Viperidae. Tropical and southern Africa. About 11 species, some polytypic, occur from extremely sandy deserts to tropical rain forests. 0.3 to 1. 8 m; very stout body. Enlargement of some scales into "horns" above each eye or nostril is characteristic of some species. Dorsal region of

Bipes biporus

Bishop, Sherman C. (1887-1951): American herpetologist. Best known publication is *Handbook of Salamanders* (1943).

Bite inhibition: Complete or graduated inhibition to use teeth during various types of behavior. A complete inhibition occurs in the ritualistic fighting among the males of many snakes, where there are virtually no bite injuries. The characteristic flank or nape bite that is applied by the males to the females in many lizard species during mating also rarely causes serious injuries.

head characterized by the presence of very reduced scales. Coloration and markings highly variable. Species from arid zones have a yellow-brown background coloration with darker spots or a pattern of broken crossbands (with a tendency toward monotone coloration). Jungle species have variably spotted patterns with strong camouflaging effect.

Large species show characteristic caterpillar-crawling, while *B. peringueyi* and other small forms are sidewinders. Most species are crepuscular or nocturnal and not very active. Their prey consists of frogs, small mammals, and

Bitis nasicornis

Bitis peringueyi

Bitis arietans

Bitis arietans

birds; small species prefer lizards and possibly also take arthropods. Puff adders are notorious for their potent venom with strong hematolytic and necrotic effects although primarily a hemotoxic venom. *B. gabonica* has a substantial amount of neurotoxic venom components.

Mating is preceded by ritualistic fights among the males together with characteristic hissing (leading to the common name of this genus) among excited animals. Live-bearers, the recorded maximum births being 157 young in *B. arietans*, but averaging 30 to 40 young. Small species have 4 to 6 young.

Care and maintenance are variably difficult. While *B. arietans* can be easily kept and bred and will live for years in a well-heated dry terrarium, the small species from desert regions (*B. caudalis, B. cornuta, B. peringueyi*) often pose acclimation problems but then often live well in captivity. Jungle and savannah species often do not adapt at all, which is possibly related to incorrect collecting techniques and transport methods. Moreover, species from West Africa often carry amoeba and other internal parasites and then die quickly. Species from high elevations (*B. atropos*)

Bitis nasicornis

Bitis arietans

Bitis gabonica

Bitis gabonica

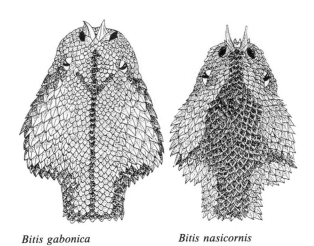

Bitis gabonica   *Bitis nasicornis*

require—just as do desert species—a substantial temperature drop at night, but not such high day temperatures and also somewhat damper hiding places.

- *B. arietans* (MERREM, 1820). Puff Adder. From northern Africa and Arabia to South Africa. Arid regions. To 1.2 m. 2 subspecies.
- *B. atropos* (LINNAEUS, 1758). Mountain Adder. Zimbabwe to South Africa. To 80 cm.

- *B. caudalis* (SMITH, 1839). Horned Puff Adder. Angola to Zimbabwe and Namaqualand, Republic of South Africa. 2 subspecies. About 35 cm. Has several enlarged scales above the eye.
- *B. cornuta* (DAUDIN, 1803). Cape Province. Desert regions. To 40 cm. Only one large horny scale over each eye.
- *B. gabonica* (DUMERIL, DUMERIL, and BIBRON, 1854). Gaboon Viper. Central and eastern Africa. 2 subspecies. Savannahs. Largest species of the genus (1.8 m). *Bitis g. rhinoceros* (SCHLEGEL, 1855) has one large scale over each nostril similar to *B. nasicornis* but has only a thin line on the head.
- *B. nasicornis* (SHAW, 1802). Rhinoceros Viper. Central Africa from west to east in tropical forest areas. To 1.3 m.

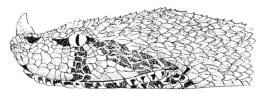

Bitis gabonica gabonica

Bitis gabonica rhinoceros

Bitis gabonica

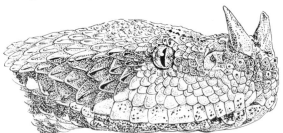

Bitis gabonica rhinoceros

Has an attractive carpet pattern and an enlarged scale over each nostril. Most attractive species, but also the most difficult one to keep in captivity.

▪ *B. peringueyi* (BOULENGER, 1888). Dwarf Puff Adder. Angola and Namibia (Kalahari Desert). Well adapted to its sandy desert environment. About 30 cm.

Blaesodactylus BOETTGER, 1893. Monotypic genus of the Gekkonidae. Madagascar and adjacent islands. Less than 10 cm. Coloration nondescript. Nocturnal.

▪ *B. boivini* (DUMERIL, 1856).

Blanchard, Frank Nelson (1888-1937): American herpetologist at the University of Michigan. Noted for his systematic studies of *Lampropeltis* and *Diadophis* plus many papers on the natural history of the four-toed salamander, garter snakes, and other common North American forms. *A Key to the Snakes of the United States, Canada and Lower California* (1925).

Blanus cinereus

Blanus WAGLER, 1830. Genus of the Amphisbaenia. Africa north of the Sahara and southwestern Europe, also Asia Minor. Several species. Along dry mountain slopes, forest margins, the banks of pools and streams, and in meadows. Snout relatively blunt, the mouth slightly subterminal. A conspicuous lateral line. In contrast to all other members in this group, one body ring corresponds to one vertebra. Yellowish, reddish, or grayish brown.

Can often be found underneath rocks. Egg-layers. A short winter rest period is recommended.

▪ *B. cinereus* (VANDELLI, 1797). Mediterranean Worm Lizard. Iberian Peninsula and northwestern Africa. To 25 cm.

Blind salamanders: Ecological group of more or less closely related North American salamanders. Specifically these include the genera *Haideotriton*, *Typhlomolge*, and *Typhlotriton*, all with greatly reduced eyes, reduced or absent skin pigmentation, and thin legs. Peripherally included in this group are *Eurycea neotenes*, *E. troglodytes*, and *Gyrinophilus palleucus* (among these only *E. neotenes* has well-developed eyes). Analogous to *Proteus*, the olm, they live in subterranean cave systems and usually are aquatic throughout their life (very rarely terrestrial after metamophrosis).

All reach sexual maturity during their larval stage (neoteny), with the exception of *Typhlotriton*, and thus they retain larval characteristics such as external gills and a skinfold around the tail throughout their life; they never leave the water (again except *Typhlotriton*).

These animals are best kept in a darkened aquarium sparsely decorated with gravel and rocks. The water should be shallow, very clean, cool (maximum 15° C.), possibly under refrigeration or in a cool basement. The diet consists primarily of small crustaceans and water insects. This also applies to the larval forms of *Typhlotriton* but metamorphosed animals should be transferred to a terrarium.

Blood: As in all vertebrates, the blood in amphibians and reptiles circulates within a closed circulatory system. It consists of the fluid blood plasma, which contains dissolved salts, proteins, and carbohydrates, as well as different types of blood cells. The composition of blood in the

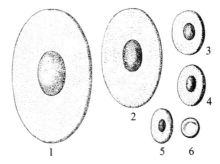

Representative red blood cells: 1 *Amphiuma;* 2 *Proteus;* 3 *Rana;* 4 *Testudo;* 5 *Lacerta;* 6 *Homo*

poikilothermic amphibians and reptiles undergoes considerable variation corresponding to seasonal activity periods. There may also be a correlation between blood composition and the periodic shedding of the skin and reproductive status.

Blythia THEOBALD, 1868. Monotypic genus of Colubridae, Lycodontinae. Assam, Burma. In tropical montane rain forests. About 40 cm. Head not distinct from body. Olive brown to blackish iridescent ground-dwelling snakes.

▪ *B. reticulata* (BLYTH, 1854).

Boa LINNAEUS, 1758. Boa Constrictors. Monotypic genus of the Boidae. Central and South America and southern

Boa constrictor amarali

Boa constrictor occidentalis

Boa constrictor constrictor

Boa constrictor imperator

captive-bred animals. Breeding can be induced by a cool, dry rest period (6 to 12 weeks at 12 to 18° C. and humidities below 70%) and reduced food regimen. Too many guinea pigs quickly lead to obesity; young rabbits and rats are more suitable. Sexual maturity occurs in 3 years.

• *B. c. constrictor* LINNAEUS, 1758. Virtually all of northern and central South America, including Trinidad and Tobago.

• *B. c. occidentalis* PHILIPPI, 1873. Paraguay and Argentina. Most southern form of *Boa*. Easily recognized by rather dark body coloration.

• *B. c. nebulosa* (LAZELL, 1964). Dominica, Lesser Antilles.

• *B. c. imperator* DAUDIN, 1803. Mexico to northwestern South America.

• *B. c. ortoni* COPE, 1878. Northwestern Peru.

Lesser Antilles. Found from dry areas to cloud forests, frequently close to human habitation. 2.5 m (exceptionally to nearly 4 m). Connected rhomboidal dark brown blotches against a paler brown background, tail region often particuarly contrasting. Often called *Constrictor constrictor* in older literature.

Primarily crepuscular or nocturnal. Moderate climbers. Pronounced seasonal activity cycles occur in the northern and southern portions of the range, as well as in the savannah-like dry forests of Central America. Periods of inactivity due to droughts and colds may last for several weeks in these extreme areas, while the rain-forest populations of South America are active throughout the year. The prey consists mainly of mammals. Live-bearers, 15 to 40 young at a time.

Boa constrictors should be kept in a heated terrarium with hiding places as well as climbing facilities made of wood; the substrate should be soft, such as loose peat moss, wood shavings, and moss. These boas like to bathe and are substantial drinkers, so the water container should not be too small and must be kept very clean.

Boa has been bred in captivity for many generations, and hobbyist demands could be completely taken care of with

Boa constrictor imperator

Boa constrictor

Boaedon DUMERIL and BIBRON, 1854. House Snakes. Genus of the Colubridae, Lycodontinae. Arabia to East Africa, southward to the Cape Region. 8 species. Found in arid habitats from outer desert regions to gallery forest; also frequently found in urban areas. 0.5m to 1.0 m. Head more or less clearly set off from body; smooth scales. Either uniformly brownish or with rows of spots (*B. guttatus*) or longitudinal stripes. Considerable variation in colors and markings within all species. See also *Lamprophis*.

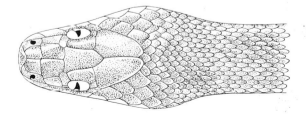

Boaedon fuliginosus

Boaedon fuliginosus

Boaedon fuliginosus

Boaedon fuliginosus

Nocturnal ground snakes that feed mainly on frogs, lizards, small mammals, and birds and their eggs. Egg-layers. Easily kept in captivity much as for *Coluber*.
- *B. fuliginosus* (BOIE, 1827). Central eastern Africa southward to the Cape Region. 2 subspecies. Very common.
- *B. lineatus* DUMERIL and BIBRON, 1864. Sudan and Senegal to Zimbabwe and northern section of Republic of South Africa. 2 subspecies.
- *B. olivaceus* DUMERIL, 1856. Central Africa from west to east. Tropical rain forests up to elevation of 1800 m. Closely associated with wet areas, but feeds mainly on mice.

Bocourt, Marie-Firmin (1819-1904): French herpetologist. Field herpetologist in Thailand (formerly Siam), Mexico, and Central America on behalf of Natural History Museum in Paris. Originally a preparator, but later qualified as scientific illustrator and herpetologist. Contributed to reptile section (together with Auguste Dumeril and Mocquard) of *Mission Scientifique au Mexique et dans l'Amerique Centrale; Etudes sur les Reptiles et les Batrachiens* (1870-1909).

Boettger, Oskar (1833-1910): German herpetologist and malacologist. Worked on herpetological collection of Senckenberg Museum in Frankfurt/Main. Published herpetological excursion findings from Africa, especially from Madagascar, and author of numerous taxa.

Bogertia LOVERIDGE, 1941. Monotypic genus of the Gekkonidae. Brasil.
- *B. lutzae* LOVERIDGE, 1941.

Boidae: Giant Snakes, Boas, Pythons. Family of the Henophidia found in many areas of the tropics and subtropics. 50 cm to 10 m; the majority of species are some 1 m long. Pelvic remnants externally clearly visible as anal spurs. Jaws with large teeth. Many genera with large anterior fangs and smaller teeth behind.
Ecological groups:
1) Aquatic boids: *Eunectes, Liasis amethistinus, Liasis fuscus*, to some degree also *Python reticulatus*.
2) Ground-dwelling boids from dry habitats: *Eryx, Aspidites; Python sebae, Morelia, Lichanura*, and some others prefer similar habitats but like to climb.
3) Ground-dwelling forest boids: *Python curtus, Acrantophis, Casarea, Tropidophis, Ungaliophis. Epicrates angulifer* sometimes is a cave-dweller.
4) Burrowing boids of tropical forests: *Calabaria, Loxocemus*, and *Bolyeria*.
5) Primarily arboreal boids: *Chondropython* and *Corallus*.
6) Cooler tropical montane forests: *Exiliboa, Ungaliophis*, and *Trachyboa*.
4 to 6 subfamilies:
- Loxoceminae: Most primitive group, monogeneric. Central America. Terrestrial burrowing egg-layers. *Loxocemus*.
- Pythoninae (pythons): Africa, Asia, Australia. Distinguished from Boinae by the presence of teeth on the premaxillary (intermaxillary bone), usually 2 rows of subcaudal scales, and (in some some species) well-developed head scales. Most primitive genera: *Liasis, Aspidites*, and *Morelia. Chondropython* is arboreal, *Calabaria* subterranean.

Boidae: Hatching in *Python regius*

Egg-layers, a few species of *Python* incubating the clutch by increasing their body temperature.

• Boinae (boas): Mostly New World snakes, but also found on Madagascar (*Acrantophis, Sanzinia*) and on some Pacific islands (*Candoia*). *Eunectes* is adapted to an aquatic life. *Corallus* is arboreal. *Eryx* and *Charina* are burrowers. More adaptable are *Epicrates* and *Boa*. Burrowing Boinae are sometimes considered to be in the separate subfamily Erycinae. *Candoia* is also sometimes included in the Erycinae. Live-bearers.

• Bolyeriinae (Round Island Boas). Today found only on Round Island, near Mauritius, where almost extinct. No pelvic remnants (a phylogenetically derived characteristic), but large head scales may still be present (primitive characteristic). *Bolyeria, Casarea*.

• Tropidophinae (large-scale boas). New World species resembling more advanced snakes in reduction of scale rows, reduction of lungs, some other characters. *Tropidophis, Ungaliophis, Exiliboa*.

Boids present rather diverse demands in regard to terrarium care. Due to the large size and aggressiveness of some species of *Python, Eunectes*, and *Liasis*, they have only limited use as terrarium specimens. When large species are kept certain precautionary measures must be taken: Have a second person standing by as additional aid; holding boxes that can be securely closed; handle only when snakes are not in their active period (i. e., in the evening and at night). Live prey should only be offered sparingly to prevent snakes from getting too fat. For breeding attempts to be successful they should be correlated with seasonal climatic variations (i. e., dry and rainy periods). For practical reasons these snakes can easily be kept in essentially sterile terrariums. Decorative climbing branches can then replace plants.

Many species of boids have become greatly decimated due to aggressive hunting for leather and the live animal trade. Moreover, substantial habitat alterations (reduction in tropical rain forests and montane forests in Central and South America and Madagascar) are endangering these snakes. Consequently all species are endangered or restricted.

Captive breeding of even some of the more difficult species appears to be on the increase. For some species this is at levels deemed satisfactory to assure survival of the species (e. g., *Boa constrictor, Epicrates cenchria*). For the survival of some endangered species, captive breeding appears to be a realistic survival chance (Round Island boas as well as for some of the dwarf boas and rare *Epicrates* species).

Boiga FITZINGER, 1826. Mangrove Snakes, Tree Snakes. Genus of the Colubridae, Boiginae. Ethiopian and Oriental faunal regions, one species each in the Palearctic and Australia, respectively. About 25 species. In thornbush steppes, dry forests, monsoon forests, tropical rain forests, montane rain forests, and even in mangrove swamps; only *B. trigonata* occurs in dry habitats (marginal desert regions to outer regions of monsoon forests). 0.8 to 2.5 m. Often with distinctly set off head and large eyes. Body more or less laterally compressed. Dorsal scalation in some species distinctly narrowing down the sides and overlapping, shingled (*B. blandingi*). Some *Boiga* species have conspicuous changes in their markings and color patterns as they grow from juveniles to adults. For instance, in *B. blandingi* the juveniles are light brown with dark crossbands, but adults are jet black without markings.

Boiga kraepelini

Boiga dendrophila

All species are nocturnal tree-climbing snakes except *B. trigonata*, which is a ground-dweller. The prey includes frogs, lizards, small mammals, and birds. Egg-layers. The venom is rather potent in some species, thus care must be taken when handling large species (*B. dendrophila, B. blandingi, B. cynodon*).

Care and maintenance must reflect the habitat of the species concerned, with climbing facilities and adequate hiding places. Species from lowlands, rain forests, and mangrove swamps invariably have substantial heat and humidity requirements. However, *B. trigonata* requires a well-heated dry terrarium during the day, which should be permitted to cool down substantially after midnight. In contrast to most arboreal species, *B. trigonata* is also not aggressive.

▪ *B. blandingi* (HALLOWELL, 1844). Central Africa in entire tropical forest zone. To 2.4 m. Adults black. Birds are the preferred prey, but other vertebrates are taken.

▪ *B. ceylonensis* (GUENTHER, 1858). Sri Lanka. To 1.3 m.

▪ *B. cyanea* (DUMERIL and BIBRON, 1854). Green Tree Snake. Found from northern India (Darjeeling) to Indo-China and southern China, southward to Kampuchea and Thailand. To 1.9 m. Uniformly green or with dark green spotted pattern. Preferred prey is snakes, including venomous species.

Boiga dendrophila

Boiga cynodon

Boiga trigonata

Boiga kraepelini

- *B. cynodon* (BOIE, 1827). Dog-toothed Mangrove Snake. From Burma southward to the Indo-Australian Archipelago. Lowland and mountain forests. To 1.7 m. Brown with light brown crossbarred pattern. Feeds mainly on birds.
- *B. dendrophila* (BOIE, 1827). Mangrove Snake. Thailand and Malaysian Peninsula to the Indo-Australian Archipelago and the Philippines. About 6 subspecies. Rain forests and mangrove forests. To 2.5 m. Shiny black with narrow yellow crossbands. Dangerously venomous.
- *B. irregularis* (MERREM, 1802). Indo-Australian Archipelago, New Guinea, and northern Australia. From mangrove forests to montane rain forests up to 1300 m elevation. To 2 m.
- *B. pulverulenta* (FISCHER, 1856). Africa south of the equatorial forest zone. To 1.1 m. Brown with crossbands.
- *B. trigonata* (SCHNEIDER, 1802). Central Asia (USSR) southward to central India. 2 subspecies. The black-headed subspecies, *B. t. melanocephala* (ANNANDALE, 1904), is particularly attractive.

Boiginae: Rear-fanged snakes, a subfamily of the Colubridae. Found primarily in the Neotropics and Ethiopian Region, with a few genera in the Oriental and Holarctic; 1 genus in the Australian region. About 73 genera. Small to mostly medium-sized, with opisthoglyph fangs that are more or less enlarged, with smaller normal teeth in front of the posteriorly located fangs of the upper jaw. However, a similar dentition—especially the existence of posterior fangs—also occurs in some genera of the subfamilies Natricinae and Xenodontinae, as well as in all Homalopsinae, Aparallactinae, and Elachistodontinae.

The venom effect in the Boiginae is rather variable. Bites lethal to humans are documented for *Dispholidus, Thelotornis,* and *Boiga.* The venom in *Malpolon, Psammophis,* and some others is also highly dangerous, plus the fangs are located relatively forward in the upper jaw. Extreme caution must be exercised with these snakes because a South African antivenin is only available for the highly venomous *Dispholidus.*

The Boiginae includes numerous tree snakes with superb adaptations to an arboreal mode of life: *Ahaetulla, Boiga, Chrysopelea, Dispholidus, Thelotornis, Langaha, Oxybelis, Imantodes,* and others. The majority of arboreal Boiginae are diurnal, but a few are nocturnal. The terrestrial species are mainly nocturnal and remain in hiding during the day; only a few are diurnal hunters (*Malpolon, Psammophis,* and others). The terrestrial forms can be found in tropical forests and in warm, dry areas, even deserts. The ground-dwelling forms have given rise to the burrowing species, which are found in variably moist habitats. The only totally amphibious form (genus *Hydrodynastes*) is considered by many systematists not to be a boigid but instead to be a opisthoglyphic natricid.

Many Boiginae feed on other reptiles, a large number being ophiophagous. The arboreal forms feed mainly on frogs, less commonly on birds and small mammals. In all documented cases of reproduction the species concerned were observed to be egg-laying. The Boiginae are probably not monophyletic.

Systematic review by region:

Central and South American genera: *Apostolepis, Clelia, Drepanoides, Elapomojus, Elapomorphus, Enulius, Erythrolamprus, Excelencophis, Gomesophis, Hydrodynastes, Imantodes, Manolepis, Opisthoplus, Oxybelis, Oxyrhopus, Parapostolepis, Phimophis, Procinura, Pseudablabes, Pseudoboa, Pseudoleptodeira, Pseudotomodon, Rachidelus, Rhinobothryum, Scolecophis, Siphlophis, Stenorrhina, Symphimus, Sympholis, Tachymenis, Tantillita, Thamnodynastes, Toluca, Tomodon,* and *Tripanurgos.*

The following genera are North American (many extend into Central America): *Coniophanes, Ficimia, Gyalopion, Hypsiglena, Leptodeira, Sonora, Tantilla,* and *Trimorphodon.*

The following genera are African and Madagascan Boiginae: *Alluaudina, Amplorhinus, Chamaertortus, Choristocalamus, Crotaphopeltis, Dipsadoboa, Dispholidus, Dromophis, Geodipsas, Hemirhagerrhis, Hypoptophis, Ithycyphus, Langaha, Lycodryas, Madagascarophis, Mimophis, Psammophylax, Pythonodipsas, Rhamphiophis, Thelotornis,* and *Xenocalamus.*

Africa as well as Asia are inhabited by *Psammophis, Boiga* (also represented by a single species in Australia), *Macroprotodon, Malpolon,* and *Telescopus.* The latter 3 have advanced all the way to southern Europe, and the latter 2 also are in western Asia.

There are only a few Boiginae that are purely Asian: *Ahaetulla, Chrysopelea, Dryophiops, Hologerrhum,* and *Psammodynastes.*

Bojanus, Ludwig Heinrich (1776–1827): Lithuanian zoologist, University of Vilnius. Classic monograph on the anatomy of *Emys, Anatome Testudinis Europaeae* (1819).

Bolitoglossa DUMERIL and BIBRON, 1854. (*Oedipus* TSCHUDI, 1838, preoccupied; *Magnadigita* TAYLOR, 1944). Tropical Lungless Salamanders. Genus of the Plethodontidae. Northern Neotropic from Mexico to Bolivia and Brasil. 55 species. In varied habitats from cloud forests to arid regions. Body frequently compressed. Males smaller than females. Reminiscent externally of the related genus *Hydromantes.* Generally 13 costal grooves. Extremities slender, fingers and toes flattened, largely or completely webbed. Snout blunt, nasolabial grooves more or less drawn out ventrally into a point (at least in males). Tail base frequently with circular groove representing a predeveloped breakage plane. The tongue is free at all edges and vaguely mushroom-shaped, thus the generic name.

Includes terrestrial, semi-arboreal, and arboreal species, many of the latter typical bromeliad inhabitants, such as *B. macrinii* living in *Aechmea.* Ants form the main diet of many species. Ground-dwellers occupy cracks and crevices below moss or roots. There they may also deposit their few, large eggs. The young will hatch after 4 to 5 months and are completely metamorphosed at hatching. The females stay close to their clutch. Species from arid regions undergo a rest period during the dry season and then reproduce during the rainy season. Reproduction in species from rain forest areas does not appear to be tied to a particular season (as far as has been determined). However, the females require another two years before they are able to produce eggs again.

These salamanders should be kept in a moist tropical terrarium with climbing facilities; cloud-forest species need a moist and cool environment. Caution must be exercised when placing different species together in the same terrarium; many species are incompatible! When breeding any of the species, be sure that the spawn is deposited in sites that are always moist, cool, and protected from light (*B.*

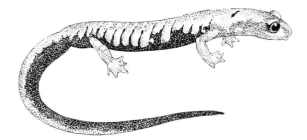

Bolitoglossa subpalmata

Bombina bombina

subpalmata: 10-16° C. spawning site temperature).
▪ *B. adspersa* (PETERS, 1863). Colombia. Savannahs and *paramos*. 8 to 10 cm. Variously colored spotted patterns against a dark background.
▪ *B. altamazonica* (COPE, 1874). Upper reaches of the Amazon, Belem. *Selva*. 8 to 9 cm. Dark gray to brown with dark triangular spot on top of head; flanks and limbs often with whitish spots.
▪ *B. peruviana* (BOULENGER, 1883). Ecuador and Peru. *Selva*. 6 to 8 cm. Yellow to reddish brown with dark brown pattern.
▪ *B. subpalmata* (BOULENGER, 1896). Costa Rica and western Panama. Montane rain forests. To 12 cm. Coloration extremely variable.
▪ *B. yucatana* (PETERS, 1882). Southern Mexico. 14 cm. Dorsal region with light paired longitudinal stripes. Tail conspicuously thickened and long.

Bolyeria GRAY, 1842. Round Island Burrowing Boas. Monotypic genus of the Boidae, subfamily Bolyeriinae. Formerly Mauritius, but now only on nearby Round Island northwest of Mauritius. Found in tropical forests, now largely destroyed. 1 to 1.5 m. The pointed head is not set off from the body and the tail is blunt, remotely reminiscent of *Eryx* species. The head is covered with large symmetrical scales. Usually an irregular, dark, reticulated pattern is present. Ecologically very similar to Central American *Tropidophis*.
    Ground-dwellers and burrowers, prefering moist soil. Apart from small mammals presumably also feeds on lizards and on frogs. Very rare, endangered.
▪ *B. multocarinata* (BOIE, 1827).

Bombina OKEN, 1816 (= *Bombinator* MERREM, 1820). Fire-bellied Toads. Genus of the Discoglossidae. Palearctic. 4 or 5 species, 2 in Europe, 2 or 3 in eastern Asia. Western Palearctic species are usually found in standing waters (*B. bombina* mainly in the lowlands in slow-flowing rivers, *B. variegata* more in highlands in smaller bodies of water, often in the proximity of mountain streams); eastern Palearctic *Bombina* are similar in requirements to *B. variegata* but are found to more than 3000 m elevation. Pupil more or less heart-shaped or triangular. Tympanum barely visible externally. Fingers webbed at base, toes more or less completely webbed. During the breeding season males have

Bombina bombina

Bombina orientalis

Bombina orientalis

Bombina orientalis

Bombina orientalis

black horny nuptial pads on the fingers and lower arms; in *B. maxima* pads are also on the chest, in *B. variegata* on the toes. Males without (*B. bombina*) or with internal vocal sac; calls short and relatively soft, difficult to locate. Ventral surface bright yellow or red and dark blue to black.

Bombina species are both diurnal and nocturnal, live in groups, and are largely aquatic. They like to drift in warm surface water with the legs spread and the body flattened, or they sun themselves in close proximity to their home water. When disturbed they jump into the water and dive to the bottom. When threatened on land they arch their body ventral side upward and thus display the bright warning colors of the ventral region. This reflex action together with a relatively poisonous secretion given off by the skin deters potential enemies from feeding on these toads. However, despite this they are often eaten by large aquatic frogs and snakes. There is also some cannibalism. All species require heat, and they tend to hibernate during the cold winter season in frost-protected hiding places below ground.

Bombina spawns throughout the summer. The eggs are usually attached in small numbers to water plants or they may sink to the bottom. *B. orientalis* attaches its spawn underneath hollowed-out rocks in mountain streams. Generally there are less than 100 eggs per spawning in virtually all species.

Bombina variegata

Bombina species are ideally suited for terrarium care—they are attractive, their behavior is fascinating, and they need only an unheated or only weakly heated aqua-terrarium placed in a sunny position. There must be adequate ventilation. During the summer months they can be kept outdoors. Overcrowding must be avoided in order to prevent aggressive feeding competition that may result in injuries. Insects of suitable size make up the preferred diet, but in captivity *Bombina* will also accept other foods offered with forceps. A winter rest period should be given from the end of October until the end of March. According to available literature, during this period the animals prefer a moderately dampened layer of dead leaves and peat moss. However, for this purpose *Bombina* can also be kept in an essentially sterile environment consisting of a water container (low water level) with some stones placed in a cool, dark spot in the basement.

Since reproduction in *B. bombina* is tied naturally to large bodies of water, this really only succeeds in a captive environment in an outdoor pool. However, the other species will breed in a terrarium, provided it has been set up properly to afford correct care. The water section should contain some water plants and hollowed-out stones as spawning substrates. Correct over-wintering stimulates reproduction in *Bombina*. Raising of the larvae should take place in separate containers due to the cannibalism of the adults.

Bombina variegata

A strange unresolved phenomenon affecting captive care is the fact that captive-bred *B. orientalis* (and also repeatedly captive-bred *B. maxima*), even those bred in outdoor pools, do not develop a red ventral area, but a yellow one instead. However, a supplement of canthaxanthin preparations added to the food and given for several weeks tends to correct this deficiency permanently. However, exact dosages and details of administering these preparations have not yet been determined for *Bombina*. Such miscoloration in *B. variegata* and hybrids of this species and *B. orientalis* can not be corrected by this method, thus one must assume genetic fixing of the yellow coloration has occurred.

• *B. bombina* (LINNAEUS, 1761). Fire-bellied Toad. Central and eastern Europe eastward into Asia. 4.5 cm. Ventral surface more or less orange-red marbled on bluish black. Finger tips without coloration.

• *B. maxima* (BOULENGER, 1905). Giant Fire-bellied Toad. Himalayas into western China (2300 to more than 3000 m elevation). Mainly in small waters with rich aquatic vegetation, rarely in mountain streams. Usually about 6 cm, max-

imum size 7.5 cm. Ventral region with a bright red and black marbled pattern.

• *B. orientalis* (BOULENGER, 1890). Oriental Fire-bellied Toad. Northeastern China, Korea. Highlands along small streams. 4.5 cm. Dorsum light brown to bright emerald green, with shiny black spots; ventral region with marbled red and black pattern.

• *B. variegata* (LINNAEUS, 1758). Yellow-bellied Toad. Central and southeastern Europe. 4 subspecies. 4.5 cm. Dorsum with conspicuous warts, especially in the subspecies *scabra* (KUESTER, 1843). Ventral region yellow to orange, with marbled pattern of bluish gray to black, sometimes with white spots. Finger tips yellow.

Bombinator: see *Bombina*, genus.

Bombycidae: Silk Moths. Family of the Lepidoptera, most species Oriental. The best known species is the silkworm moth, *Bombyx mori* from southeastern Asia. Caterpillars and adults are eagerly eaten by many terrarium animals. Home breeding is somewhat cumbersome, since the natural food (mulberry leaves) of the caterpillars is not available throughout the year and during the winter an artificial substitute food must offered. Several breeding pairs are placed in jars that have the bottom covered with filter paper. The egg masses and newly hatched larvae are transferred to fresh branches. At temperatures of about 25° C. the eggs will hatch in 4 days and the caterpillars will pupate in 25 to 30 days. After another 10 to 14 days the moths will emerge from the pupal cases.

Bonaparte, Charles Lucien Jules Laurent (1803 – 1857): French herpetologist, nephew of French Emperor Napoleon I. Most famous work is the 2-volume *Iconografia della Fauna Italia* (1832-1841).

Bone metabolism disorders: Include *osteoporosis* in adults, *osteodystrophia fibrosa*, *rachitis* in juveniles (most commonly), *scoliosis* (bending of the vertebral column), and the ribs becoming displaced at their bases. The symptoms of bone metabolism disorders usually start with food refusal and an apparent reluctance to move. This is followed by forms of lameness and swelling of the upper arms and upper thighs, occasionally also swelling of the tail (osteodystrophia fibrosa). Turtles are then no longer able to feed sufficiently because it is increasingly difficult for them to move their jaws adequately. Soon thereafter the carapace becomes soft, the growth zone turns into a yellowish white, relatively soft mass, and individual scales become raised; in some animals the carapace begins to lose sections. If ossification resumes these deformations remain. Swollen joints in adult lizards indicate rachitis, whereby bony tissue obtains insufficient amounts of calcium, resulting in an increased flexibility, especially of the extremities. In areas of greatest mechnical stress cartilaginous tissue will develop. Osteoporosis in adults is characterized by an increased brittleness of the bone due to reduced ossification. The causes for these two diseases seem to lie in most cases with a vitamin D deficiency or lack of ultraviolet radiation, which either causes an insufficient amount of calcium to be absorbed from the digestive tract or an insufficient supply of calcium is present in the first instance, resulting in insufficient ossification of the skeleton. Extensive periods of starvation, such as in the case of emaciating diseases (consumption osteoporosis) can produce the same condition. Osteodystrophy occurs primarily in carnivorous turtles and in lizards that are getting an excessive amount of lettuce. It is characterized by osteoclasis and replacement of bone with fibrous tissue. In juveniles there can be a simultaneous occurrence of rachitis and osteodystrophia fibrosa. Causes of osteodystrophy are displacement of the physiological calcium-phosphorus balance from 1-1.5: 1 to 1: 25-40 with a pure meat or fish diet or with an exclusive lettuce diet, or the aftereffect of kidney diseases (increased phosphorus excretion). A simultaneous vitamin D deficiency can further accelerate the disease process. However, high therapeutic dosages of vitamin D can also lead to calcium release from bones and thus could have further detrimental effects on the condition of an animal.

Therapy: Calcium supplements—about 500 mg/kg feed $CaCO_3$ over a 6-week period; 1 ml calcium gluconate 24%/kg body weight subcutaneously twice a week; 1g/kg body weight Rachitis® or Calcipot®; 1000 units per kg body weight vitamin D3 or 1 ml of multivitamin preparation per kg body weight intramuscularly.

Prophylaxis: Maintenance of physiological calcium-phosphorus balance and vitamin A to D3 ratio of at least 5: 1 given in food ration. With a pure meat or fish diet there must be a supplement of 50-100 mg $CaCO_3$ per kg of food offered.

Borborococetes: see *Eupsophus*, genus.

Botanical nomenclature: Scientific assignment of names to plants, blue-green algae, and bacteria that largely corresponds to zoological nomenclature, although both are independent of each other. The most significant difference from zoological nomenclature is the fact that when moving a species from one genus into another, not only is the original author cited within brackets, but his name is followed by that of the revising author. Moreover, most authors' names are conveniently abbreviated and the year of publication is not mentioned. While zoological tautonyms (e. g., *Bufo bufo, Clelia clelia*) are permitted, regulations governing botanical nomenclature prohibit identical genus and species names.

Bothrochilus FITZINGER, 1843. New Guinea Dwarf Pythons. Monotypic genus of the Boidae, subfamily Pythoni-

nae. New Guinea, Bismarck Archipelago, Tokelau Islands. To 1.5 m, cylindrical. Small, pointed head not set off from body. Adult specimens are uniformly light to dark brown or have dark and orange-colored rings. Now often considered a synonym of *Liasis*.

Nocturnal ground-dwellers. Diet consists mainly of small mammals. Should be kept in a damp tropical terrarium with a deep substrate layer of loose peat moss, moss, and wood shavings. Provide adequate hiding places at ground level. Since captive specimens are rare, there are few published terrarium experiences.
▪ *B. boa* (SCHLEGEL, 1837).

Bothrolycus GUENTHER, 1874. Monotypic genus of the Colubridae, Lycodontinae. Tropical Central Africa. Found in tropical gallery forests and rain forests, also in montane rain forests to elevations in excess of 2000 m. About 1.25 m. The light-colored head is clearly set off from the body, with the snout projecting rectangularly. Dorsally the head is light brown with dark scrolls. The neck has a clearly delineated dividing line from the bluish black dorsal body coloration. The body has one dorsal and two lateral bright red longitudinal stripes. The ventral surface is uniformly deep red.

Nocturnal, lives close to ground level. *Bothrolycus* feeds primarily on small mammals. Egg-layers, 4 or 5 eggs.

This rare snake must be kept in a well-heated rain-forest terrarium.
▪ *B. lineatus* (PETERS, 1863). Guinea to Uganda. 2 subspecies.

Bothrops WAGLER, 1824. American Lanceheads. Genus of the Crotalidae. Central and South America. About 50 species. Closely related to the Asiatic *Trimeresurus*. Includes several types of adaptations. 0.6 to 2 m.

Ecological and morphological groups (grossly simplified!):

1) Ground-dwellers in tropical forests, marginal rain forest areas, and in similar habitats (frequently close to human habitations). Robust, usually rather large. Cause serious bites on plantations and in rural settlements. Most species have rhombidal spots, rows of broken spots, or similar markings. Important terrarium animals including numerous attractive species that will readily breed in captivity.

Should be kept in a well-heated dry terrarium with bath-

Bothrops alternatus

Bothrops atrox

Bothrops ammodytoides

Bothrops jararaca

Bothrops godmani

Bothrops jararacussu, immature

ing facilities. Feed primarily on small mammals.

2) Ground-dwellers in dry regions (semideserts, deserts, pampas). Mostly smaller snakes but with very stout bodies. Will strike equally fast as other *Bothrops*. Diet includes lizards and small mammals. *B. ammodytoides* occurs in temperate latitudes in Argentina. Tropical dry regions are occupied by *B. lansbergi*, *B. melanurus*, *B. roedingeri*, and others.

3) Ground-dwellers in montane regions. Small but powerful species found in the outer margins of montane rain forests, highland steppes, or arid rubble fields; also found in moist, treeless high-altitude habitats in the Andes Mountains. All of these species require cool temperatures and demand soil moisture in underground hiding places, but at the same time they also need places to sun themselves. The diet consists mainly of lizards, small mammals, frogs, and similar prey. *B. barbouri*, *B. bicolor*, *B. xanthogrammus*, *B. andianus*, *B. venezuela*, and others.

4) Arboreal (tree-dwellers) species in tropical rain forests and montane rain forests. Medium to small, more slender species that have a more or less well-developed prehensile tail. Coloration mostly uniform green, but also with yellow, reddish, and even black background coloration. Diet is mainly frogs and lizards. *B. bilineatus*, *B. schlegeli*, *B. lateralis*, and others. Venom strongly hemotoxic.

All *Bothrops* have very long fangs and strike with their entire body weight (the common name suggests that these snakes strike their opponents like a lance). Some species raise their body off the ground while striking, such as *B. nummifer*. Despite the availability of antivenin, fatal bites can happen with large *Bothrops*. Successful serum treatment is often followed by extensive tissue destruction.

Bothrops jararacussu

Bothrops lateralis

Bothrops neuwiedi

All *Bothrops* are live-bearers, giving birth to 10 to 60 young.
- *B. alternatus* DUMERIL, BIBRON, and DUMERIL, 1854. Urutu or Halfmoon Lancehead. Southern Brasil to northern Argentina. Nearly 2 m. Group 1.
- *B. ammodytoides* LEYBOLD, 1873. Yararanata. Southern Brasil to Argentina. Head with nasal horn. Group 2.
- *B. andianus* AMARAL, 1923. Peru. Group 3.
- *B. atrox* (LINNAEUS, 1758). Caicaca or Common Lancehead. From Mexico to tropical South America, plus the Lesser Antilles (Trinidad, Tobago, St. Lucia, and Martinique). 2 subspecies. Ecologically very adaptable. Group 1.
- *B. bilineatus* (WIED, 1825). Green Jararaca. Amazon Region. Group 4.
- *B. insularis* (AMARAL, 1921). Island Lancehead. Island of Queimada Grande (Sao Paulo, Brasil). Known for its genetic defect that leads to the development of sterile intersexual animals and thus at least theoretically to the natural extinction of this species. Group 2.
- *B. jararaca* (WIED, 1824). Jararaca. Most frequent *Bo-*

Bothrops nigroviridis

Bothrops neuwiedi pubescens

Boulenger, George Albert (1858-1937): Belgian zoologist working at the British Museum in London. Most significant herpetological publication was the herpetological volumes of the *Catalogue of the British Museum*, which appeared in separate parts from 1882 to 1896. Since the collection of the British Museum contained virtually all forms known at that time, its catalogs were then detailed treatises on the systematics of specific animal groups. As standard publications they also served as a systematic basis for other scientific collections. To this day the British Museum catalogs have not been replaced with a more complete, up-to-date publication. *Monograph of the Lacertidae* (1920-1921) was one of his last works, culminating a publishing history of more than 600 herpetological papers in scientific journals.

throps from Brasil to northern Argentina. Group 1.
- *B. lateralis* (PETERS, 1863). Costa Rica. Green. Group 4.
- *B. nasutus* BOCOURT, 1868. Rhinoceros Lancehead. Veracruz, Mexico to Colombia and Ecuador. Mainly in damp regions of rain forests and montane rain forests. With nasal horn. Group 1.
- *B. neuwiedi* WAGLER, 1824. Jararaca pintada. Bolivia to Brasil and northern Argentina. About 12 subspecies. One of the most frequent and most variably marked *Bothrops*; of considerable ecological plasticity. Group 1.
- *B. schlegeli* (BERTHOLD, 1846). Eyelash Lancehead. Southern Mexico to Venezuela and Ecuador. 2 subspecies. *B. s. superciliaris* has spiny supraorbital scales (the "eyelashes"). Coloration highly variable. Classic representative of Group 4.

Boulengerina DOLLO, 1886. Water Cobras. Genus of the Elapidae. 2 species. Central Africa in standing waters and in rivers. To 1.2 m. The short head is reminiscent of that of true cobras (*Naja*). Body with light and dark crossbands.

Venomous snakes that remain in hiding below the water surface. Assumed to feed exclusively on fish.

Care requires a well-heated aqua-terrarium with dry sites for sunning. Not particularly aggressive, but with extremely potent venom.
- *B. annulata* (BUCHHOLZ and PETERS, 1877). Gabon, Cameroons, Zaire, Lake Tanganyika, Malawi. 2 subspecies.
- *B. christyi* BOULENGER, 1904. Western Congo Basin.

Boulengerula TORNIER, 1896. Monotypic genus of the Caeciliidae. Eastern Africa (Tanzania, possibly also in Kenya). Slender, with 120-131 primary furrows, without secondary furrows. Scales absent. In contrast to the related genus *Afrocaecilia*, only 1 row of teeth in lower jaw. Cloacal opening perpendicular.

Bothrops schlegeli

▪ *B. boulengeri* TORNIER, 1896. Tanzania, Usambara and Magrotto Mountains. To 31 cm. Dorsum bluish gray, ventrum cream.

Bourret, Rene (1884-1950): French herpetologist. Publications on the herpetofauna of Southeast Asia include *La faune de l'Indochine, Reptiles* (1927), *Les serpentes de l'Indochine* (1936), and *Les tortues de l'Indochine* (1941).

Brachycephalus FITZINGER, 1826. Saddle-back Toads. Monotypic genus of the Atelopodidae. Brasil, in montane rain forests. Almost smooth-skinned. A distinctive saddle-like bony plate is embedded in the skin of the back. Pupil horizontal. Tympanum hidden. Fingers and toes not conspicuously webbed and without adhesive discs; only third finger normally developed, all others reduced, stubby; toes with lateral skin folds. Metatarsal projection absent. No external vocal sac. Larvae orange, relatively large (2.5 times adult length).

Not very agile ground-dwellers with reduced jumping ability. Generally found under dead leaves, moss, or decaying wood. The eggs are deposited in water.

Care and maintenance typical of tropical rain forest frogs. Provide a small water section.
▪ *B. ephippium* (SPIX, 1824). Saddle-back Toad. Southeastern Brasil. To 2 cm. Back bright cadmium orange, belly chromium yellow.

Brachylophus fasciatus

Brachylophus WAGLER, 1830. Fiji Iguanas. Genus of the Iguanidae. Fiji and Tonga Islands. 2 species found in tropical forests. To 90 cm, slender. Similar to *Iguana* but with a substantially lower dorsal crest. Tail about 3 times snout-vent length. Females uniformly green, males green with darker and lighter crossbands.

Tree-dwellers that are essentially herbivorous; occasionally crickets are also taken. In captivity these lizards often are rather delicate. *Brachylophus* species are endangered through loss of natural habitats.
▪ *B. fasciatus* (BROYNIART, 1780).

Brachymeles DUMERIL and BIBRON, 1839. Genus of the Scincidae. Philippines. 9 species. 15 to 30 cm, elongated, with short limbs that vary from the normal 5-toed condition through numerous transitional stages to total absence of limbs. Brown with dark markings. Little is known about this genus.
▪ *B. schadenbergi* (FISCHER, 1885). Mindanao. About 20 cm. With 5 toes.

Brachyophidium WALL, 1921. Monotypic genus of the Uropeltidae. Southern India. Closely related to the genus *Teretrurus*. 21 cm long but only 0.7 cm thick. No chin furrow. Tail compressed, the scales along its upper side weak and equipped with 2 or 3 keels. Terminal scale inconspicuous, compressed, terminating in a point. One of the most primitive type of Uropeltidae.

Burrowing snakes in tropical forests.
▪ *B. rhodogaster* WALL, 1921. Palni Mountains in southern India. Dorsally blackish brown, ventrally bright red.

Brachyorrhus BOIE, 1827. Monotypic genus of the Colubridae, Calamarinae. Indo-Australian Archipelago (Java, Moluccas, New Guinea).
▪ *B. albus* (LINNAEUS, 1758). 75 cm, making this the largest species in the subfamily. Uniformly brown above with a darker middorsal band.

Brasilotyphlus TAYLOR, 1968. Monotypic genus of the Caeciliidae. Brasil. Slender. Eyes not visible externally, covered by cranial bones. Tentacles positioned closer to corner of mouth than to nostril. Lower jaw with only 1 row of teeth.
▪ *B. braziliensis* (DUNN, 1945). Brasil, vicinity of Manaus. To 26 cm. Dark gray, lighter ventrally, head whitish.

Brazil, Vital Mineiro da Campanha (1865-1950): Brasilian medical practitioner and herpetologist. Founded snake serum institute at Butantan near Sao Paulo and developed effective antivenins against venomous snake bites.

Breeding range: Areal distribution. Distribution area in the strictest sense, the geographical region where the members of a taxon reproduce. Thus the term does not include the migratory range, which can be substantially larger than the breeding range as such. For instance, some sea turtles may have extremely small breeding ranges but gigantic migratory ranges. Breeding range can be restricted to a specific biogeographical region or to parts of it or extend into other faunal and floral areas. The size of a particular breeding range depends in part on the ecological potency ("vitality") of the organism and distribution barriers.

Brehm, Alfred Edmund (1829-1884): German zoologist, primarily an ornithologist. Produced 6-volume set *Illustriertes Tierleben* (1863-1884), which remains one of the most popular zoological reference works in German (several revisions—most valuable edition 1912-1913, the reptile and amphibian sections revised by F. Werner). Also in zoological park work, from 1863 serving as Director of the Hamburg Zoo and in 1869 founder of the Berlin Aquarium, where he placed an extraordinary emphasis on reptiles and amphibians.

Breviceps MERREM, 1820. Short-headed Frogs. Genus of the Microhylidae. Southern Africa. 13 species, some polytypic. In semideserts, savannahs, dry brushland, and dry forests (*B. sylvestris* and *B. verrucosus* in forests). Body inflated, balloon-like, skin more or less warty. Snout extremely short. Pupil horizontal. Tympanum not visible externally. Limbs weak, upper arms and upper thighs covered by body. Fingers and toes free. Metatarsal projection large, developed into a sharp, shovel-like digging pad.

Breviceps adspersus

Burrowing ground frogs that live below ground during the dry season. The diet consists mainly of termites and ants. Masses of these frogs may appear on the surface during periods of extensive rainfall. Precipitation also seems to induce reproduction. Development of *Breviceps* appears to be direct (as far as is known), without a free-swimming larval stage. The female lays up to 60 very large eggs in an egg chamber that she has dug in the ground. She remains in one of the burrows close to the egg chamber. The eggs can give rise to two types of young: larvae that are without gills, gill clefts, and respiratory openings, and which quickly complete their development inside the cave; or completely metamorphosed juvenile frogs.

These frogs should be kept in a semimoist, very warm and sunny terrarium containing a thick substrate layer.
• *B. adspersus* PETERS, 1882 (= *B. parvus* HEWITT, 1925). Zimbabwe to Cape Province. 6 cm, mostly smaller. Yellow to orange with dark brown spots and a dorsal band.
• *B. mossambicus* PETERS, 1854. Southern Africa north of the Cape Province. 5.5 cm. Uniformly brown.
• *B. verrucosus* RAPP, 1842. Southern Africa. 7 cm. Light brown to dark brown with a washed-out darker longitudinal pattern.

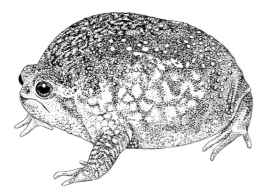

Breviceps verrucosus

Briba AMARAL, 1935. Monotypic genus of the Gekkonidae. Brasil. Only known from its type locality.
• *B. brasiliana* AMARAL, 1935.

British Museum Catalogs: *Catalogue of the (Amphibians and Reptiles) in the Collection of the British Museum.* Edited by G. A. Boulenger from 1882-1896. A series of catalogs of the BM (NH) collection, which due to its comprehensiveness is the only complete summary of amphibians and reptiles (now of course out-dated). Many large museums still arrange their collections based on this catalog. The keys and abridged descriptions serve as important references for the determination of amphibians and reptiles. To this day the British Museum catalogs have not been replaced with a more modern publication of the same content and quality, and thus despite substantial advances in herpetology it is still of considerable importance.

Broad-spectrum anthelminthics: Medications that are effective (usually lethal) simultaneously against worms from different groups, including in part their larval forms. Includes various pharmaceutical versions of the main drugs thiabendazol, tetramisol, mebendazol, and fenbendazol.

Bromeliaceae: Bromeliads. Family of the Liliatae. Subtropics and tropics of South and Central America northward to the southern United States. 46 genera, about 1700 wild species, plus large numbers of commercial varieties. Found in tropical rain forests as well as in dry regions. Rosette plants, epiphytes, rock plants, and ground plants. Bromeliads have special adaptations to collect water (leaf-funnels in so-called cistern plants) and to absorb it (suction scales at leaf base). The roots are often reduced or completely absent, serving only as an attachment mechanism. Primarily epiphytic are *Guzmania, Neoregelia, Nidularium,* and *Tillandsia*. Genera that can tolerate dry climates include *Aechmea* and *Billbergia*. Among the ground- and rock-plants are *Cryptanthus* and *Dyckia*.

When culturing bromeliads, the special ecological requirements of particular genera and species have to be taken into consideration. Hard-leaved species are not sensitive to direct sun. If these species are being kept too wet and in a shady location they tend to lose their condition rapidly and ultimately die. Species with thin, soft leaves require shade, high humidity, and high temperatures (in excess of 20° C.). In leaf-funnel species water should be poured into the funnel, which should always contain clean water; pollution can cause decay of the cistern leaves. As a substrate for the genera *Aechmea, Billbergia, Neoregelia,* and *Nidularium*, as well as for *Cryptanthus* and *Dyckia*, you can use a humus mixture of decaying leaf soil, peat moss, and sphagnum, as well as ground up pieces of fired clay and sand. *Guzmania* and *Vriesea* require a very loose planting medium. *Tillandsia* and all epiphytic species with reduced roots are attached to orchid plant medium or directly onto rough branch sections. Regular spraying is mandatory, as is occasional use of a weak fertilizer solution. Those species that can be cultivated in pots—with the exception of *Cryptanthus* and *Dyckia*—can also be attached to epiphyte logs. For that purpose plant and plant medium are placed inside some gauze-like material such as perlon or nylon stockings, covered on the outside with swamp moss, and then attached to the epiphyte log or branch with non-rusting tie wire. Propagation of bromeliads can be done on a small scale simply by cutting the runners of adventitious plants.

Bronia GRAY, 1865. Monotypic genus of the Amphisbaenidae. Tropical South America.
• *B. brasiliana* GRAY, 1865. Brasil, lower Amazon Region. In tropical forests, often close to water.

Brood care: *Liasis perthensis*

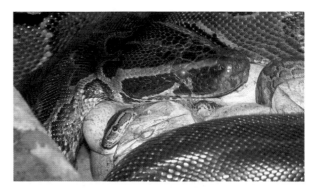

Brood care: *Python molurus bivittatus*

Brood care: Types of behavior that facilitate the protection, care, and viability of the eggs and young. Methods of brood care are rather diversified in amphibians and reptiles. Brood care extends from searching for a suitable site to deposit the eggs (as in turtles) and guarding the clutch (as in crocodiles) to actual brooding of the eggs (as in some pythons). Some frogs have developed remarkable and interesting forms of brood care that make it possible for the spawn to develop at least partially outside the water, as in many genera of the Hylidae, Leptodactylidae, Rhacophoridae, and Ranidae.

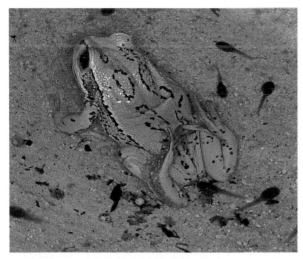

Brood care: *Gastrotheca riobambae*

Brookesia GRAY, 1865. Stub-tailed Chameleons. Genus of the Chamaeleonidae. Africa and Madagascar. About 20 species, including the formerly independent genera *Evolutiocauda* ANGEL, 1942; *Leandria* ANGEL, 1933; and *Rhampholeon* GUENTHER, 1874. In tropical forests. Usually less than 10 cm. Body more or less covered with small nodules and spines, some species with short pointed appendages on the head. Distinct dorsal crests are absent. The tail is very short and non-prehensile. Scales on the soles of the feet have spines, and the claws sometimes are doubled. Color changing ability weakly developed, most species being pri-

marily shades of brown.

Egg-layers, up to 20 eggs per clutch.

Found among low-growing bushes, etc., often close to the ground among leaves or on tree stumps and similar things. For details on care refer to *Chamaeleo*. These little chameleons require high humidity without excessive dampness. They need sites for sunning. A constant supply of very small arthropods as food is essential.

▪ *B. brevicauda* (MATSCHIE, 1892). East Africa. In highland savannahs. To 9 cm. Tail extremely short. Without eye or snout appendages. Individual conical scales on the throat.

▪ *B. perarmata* (ANGEL, 1933). Armored Stub-tailed Chameleon. Western Madagascar. Easily 12 cm. An appendage on the nape and double rows of thorny dorsal spines.

Brookesia spectrum

▪ *B. spectrum* (BUCHHOLZ, 1874). Leaf Chameleon. From Cameroons to East Africa. Easily 10 cm. Snout with an appendage.

▪ *B. stumpfi* BOETTGER, 1893. Spiny Chameleon. Madagascar and adjacent islands. 10 cm. Spines on head and along back. Requires adequate heat.

Bufo LAURENTI, 1768. True Toads. Large genus of the Bufonidae with virtually worldwide distribution, with the exception of Madagascar, Australia (except for the introduced species *B. marinus*), New Zealand, and many Pacific islands. Found in virtually all temperate and tropical latitudes. Most species occur in Central and South America (more than 50), Africa (more than 40), and Asia (about 37 species), with some 17 species in North America and Europe. Species found mainly in dry open areas, cultivated areas, and in semideserts include *B. cognatus, B. punctatus,* and *B. retiformis* in North America; and *B. gariepensis, B.*

Bufo alvarius

Bufo americanus

mauritanicus, and *B. vertebralis* in Africa. Species from tropical rain forests include *B. blombergi*, *B. poeppigi*, and *B. typhonius* in South America; *B. superciliaris* in Africa; and *B. asper* in Southeast Asia. Found in mountains above 4000 m are *B. spinulosus* in South America and *B. tibetanus* on grasslands in the Himalayas.

The body is compact and in most species is wart-covered, partially cornified, and often has bony ridges and parotoid glands in the head region. Conspicuously spiny-skinned species include *B. granulosus* and *B. spinulosus*; nearly smooth-skinned species include *B. blombergi*, *B. guttatus*, and *B. superciliaris*. The pupil is horizontal. The parotoid glands are usually conspicuous and may be quite large. The tympanum usually is clearly visible. The limbs are short and strong. The fingers are free, the toes more or less webbed. Some species have well-developed shovel-like metatarsal projections similar to those of *Pelobates* and *Scaphiopus* that facilitate quick burrowing into the soil. Most *Bufo* have poorly developed jumping capabilities. Males usually are significantly smaller than females. If a vocal sac is present it is usually located under the throat and when inflated during vocalization becomes balloon- or sausage-like. The species-specific call is important for attracting females.

Some *Bufo* give off more or less irritating or poisonous skin secretions from the parotoid glands (in some species this is actually squirted out) that protect them against enemies. The North American *B. alvarius* is considered to be especially poisonous (it has large glands on the legs also). Even the eggs of some toads (e. g., *B. marinus*) can contain poisonous substances.

Nearly all adult *Bufo* are either crepuscular or nocturnal ground-dwellers that hide during the day—protected against light and desiccation—under rocks, logs, and in burrows (*B. quercicus* is active during the day). Newly metamorphosed juveniles are generally active during the day. *Bufo* generally return to water only during the breeding season, since their water requirements are usually adequately met from precipitation and dew. However, *B. hemiophrys* is largely aquatic in swamps and *B. preussi* occurs in creeks.

Reproduction takes place during the spring in temperate latitudes and at the onset of the rainy season in the tropics. The true rain-forest species and those from subtropical and tropical semideserts are not tied to a particular season, but spawn as long as sufficient water is available and can be

Bufo alvarius

Bufo blombergi

utilized (*B. mauritanicus*). Most species spawn in shallow standing water. The African *B. preussi* has a larval type specially adapted for flowing water. Some species can even tolerate salt water—*B. boreas* and *B. raddei* spawn in somewhat saline inland lakes, and *B. viridis* spawns in brackish water of the eastern Baltic Sea. Many species continue to return to the same spawning sites generation after generation, thus transplantations of *Bufo* are most likely to succeed with the transfer of spawn.

At the onset of the breeding season the males appear first at the spawning site and call for the females. The mating drive is very intense at the peak of the breeding season, and unpaired males will often attempt to amplexus with mating pairs, other males, fish, and pieces of driftwood. In fact, toads are notorious for trying to mate with anything that moves, including a collector's foot. The spawn is extruded in strings. The eggs are small and strongly pigmented. Thousands may be present in a single string. Newts tend to prey on toad eggs by carefully peeling the

Bufo boreas

Bufo exsul

Bufo blombergi

Bufo exsul

Bufo calamita

Bufo bufo

Bufo canorus

Bufo carens

Bufo debilis

Bufo carens

Bufo coccifer

embryos out of the capsules. Free-swimming larvae are preyed upon by other frogs, newts, fish, water birds, and predatory water insects. *Bufo* larvae are small and strongly pigmented, with a respiratory opening on the left and the anal opening in a median position. They swim in large schools (swarms) and develop within a few weeks into metamorphosed juvenile toads.

Adult *Bufo* are attacked by various parasites. Some of the European species are parasitized by fly larvae (*Lucilla*) that attack the head of the frog and actually feed on it. Tropical *Bufo* are often infested by nematodes.

Next to treefrogs and *Bombina*, toads are perhaps the most popular group of frogs for the terrarium. This popularity is due to the comparatively easy care of these animals and their attractive characteristics. *Bufo* adapts well to captivity and quickly becomes tame, actually "begging" for food when the hobbyist approaches the terrarium. Food is usually taken directly from the human hand. If allowed to roam in a large room, *Bufo* will often find its own food supply.

The *Bufo* terrarium must be set up with the specific requirements of particular species in mind. For most species a smallish container with a thick layer of damp soil, some dark hiding places such as flowerpots split in half or arched pieces of tree bark, and a shallow water dish is sufficient. Since most *Bufo* species tolerate low humidity, large species, especially the highly adaptable *B. marinus*, are often permitted to roam freely in an apartment. There they will quickly find a suitably dark hiding place (usually under a radiator), where a shallow water bowl should be placed for drinking. This bowl will invariably be used for defecation by the toad, so the apartment is kept clean.

Large *Bufo* species not only require a very spacious terrarium (with an area of 1 m x 0.6 m for a single pair), but they also have an active metabolism that necessitates frequent cleaning of the container. Insufficient attention to this point (recognizable by an obvious ammonia odor) can lead quickly to skin diseases. If well cared for, healthy *Bufo* remain in hiding during the day and appear only during feeding time. Should the animals be restless and attempt to climb out of the container they are either hungry, thirsty, or are being attacked by parasites.

The diet should be varied. Most live terrarium food animals of suitable sizes are taken by toads, which tend to have large appetites. The tropical forms in particular cannot go without food for as long as some other frogs and will quickly lose condition if not fed often. The large toads are most easily fed with mice (freshly killed and/or newborn), locusts, crickets, cockroaches, and earthworms (during the winter mealworms can be given instead).

Captive breeding succeeds only with those species that are not tied to unusual habitats or very large waters, such as *B. blombergi*. High-mountain species such as *B. spinulosus*, which will breed in even the smallest water-filled rocky depression, also have potential for terrarium breeding. The first successful captive breedings of *B. blombergi* (1974/1975) were recorded by zoos in Krefeld, Los Angeles, and Brownsville. Problems that often arise in captive spawnings of toads relate mainly to the enormous number of eggs and embryos, as well as the tremendous sperm masses that decompose and quickly degrade water quality.

Bufo garmani

Bufo marinus

Bufo marinus, 1-month young

Bufo marinus

Bufo melanostictus

- *B. bufo* (LINNAEUS, 1758). Eurasian Common Toad. Europe, North Africa, and Asia to Japan. 13 subspecies, most of them in eastern Asia. Grows to more than 15 cm, but usually smaller. Earth-colored (nominate form); other subspecies may have contrasting yellow and black patterns, especially along the flanks.
- *B. calamita* LAURENTI, 1768. Natterjack Toad. Southwestern and western Europe northeastward to the USSR Baltic republics. To 7 cm. Variably spotted pattern, usually

Bufo peltocephalus

Bufo punctatus

Bufo quercicus

Often this decomposition of excess sperm can be kept in check with strong aeration of the water and by transferring the spawn into a number of separate hatching containers. The larvae can be raised with dried tropical fish food. Triggering of the breeding behavior in temperate species appears to be dependent upon the correct over-wintering period for the species.
- *B. americanus* HOLBROOK, 1836. American Toad. Southeastern Canada and eastern United States. 2 subspecies. Coloration similar to *B. woodhousei*, but with only 1 or 2 warts inside the largest dark dorsal spots.
- *B. angusticeps* SMITH, 1848. Sand Toad, Common Cape Toad. To 7 cm. Light gray to black with lighter and darker markings.
- *B. asper* GRAVENHORST, 1829. Thailand and Burma to Java and Kalimantan. To 12 cm. Dark brown.
- *B. biporcatus* GRAVENHORST, 1829. Philippines and Sundas. 4 subspecies. To 9 cm, mostly smaller. Light to dark brown.
- *B. blombergi* MYERS and FUNKHOUSER, 1951. Colombian Giant Toad. Southwestern Colombia. To 23 cm. Dorsum light golden brown, flanks and legs dark brown to black.
- *B. boreas* BAIRD and GIRARD, 1852. Western Toad. Pacific North America from Alaska to Baja California and to the Rockies. 2-4 subspecies. To 13 cm. Olive green with black spots and a light narrow dorsal stripe.

with a light yellow dorsal stripe.
- *B. carens* SMITH, 1848. Red Toad. Southern Africa northward to Kenya. To 9 cm. Red-brown with darker pattern.
- *B. cognatus* SAY, 1823. Great Plains Toad. Prairies of southern Canada to California and Nevada. To 12 cm. Yellow-gray with large brown spots.
- *B. empusus* (COPE, 1862). Cuban Toad. Cuba. Earth-colored, with conspicuous horny white ring around eye.
- *B. gariepensis* SMITH, 1849. Karroo Toad. Southern Africa. 3 subspecies. To 10 cm. Earth-colored (nominate form); other subspecies may have more contrasting coloration.
- *B. guttatus* SCHNEIDER, 1799. Spotted Toad. Northern South America. To 18 cm. Coloration similar to *B. blombergi*.
- *B. hemiophrys* COPE, 1886. Dakota Toad. Central Canada to Wyoming and the Dakotas. To 7.5 cm. Brown or greenish, with a light dorsal stripe. A hump or boss is present between the eyes.
- *B. marinus* (LINNAEUS, 1758). Giant Toad, Marine Toad. Southern Texas to Argentina. To 23 cm. Earth-colored. Large, nearly triangular parotoid glands. Introduced into many tropical countries to combat insects feeding on cultivated plants (especially sugar cane).
- *B. marmoreus* WIEGMANN, 1833. Marbled Toad. Mexico. To 7 cm. Light brownish black marbled pattern; tips of warts whitish.
- *B. mauritanicus* SCHLEGEL, 1841. Berber Toad. Northwestern Africa. To 15 cm. Light brown with large red and blackish brown spots surrounded by light margins; rarely earth-colored.
- *B. melanostictus* SCHNEIDER, 1799. Black spined Toad. Southern Asia and Sunda Islands. Up to 3000 m elevation in Himalayas. To 9 cm. Variegated brownish, with horny warts tipped with black.
- *B. paracnemis* LUTZ, 1925. Rococo Toad. Central South America. To 25 cm. Similar to *B. marinus*, but with large parotoid glands on the lower thighs.
- *B. peltocephalus* BIBRON, 1838. Cuban Giant Toad. 2 subspecies. To 20 cm. Reddish brown.
- *B. poeppigi* TSCHUDI, 1845. Eastern Peru. To 12 cm. Blackish gray with contrasting lighter pattern.
- *B. preussi* MATSCHIE, 1893. Northwestern Cameroons in mountain streams. To 5 cm. Males black, females with brick-red dorso-lateral band.
- *B. punctatus* BAIRD and GIRARD, 1852. Red-spotted Toad. Southwestern United States into Mexico. To 7.5 cm. Gray to light olive, warts reddish. Parotoid glands small, circular.
- *B. pusillus* MERTENS, 1937. Southern Africa. To 7 cm. Earth-colored. Parotoid glands small, usually indistinct.
- *B. quercicus* HOLBROOK, 1840. Oak Toad. Southeastern United States. To 3 cm. Variable, with black spots and light dorsal stripe.
- *B. rangeri* HEWITT, 1935. Southern Africa. To 11 cm. Coloration similar to *B. regularis*, but usually darker and with black head markings.
- *B. regularis* REUSS, 1834. Panther Toad. Africa south of the Sahara. 4 subspecies. To 11 cm. Sand-colored to dark olive, often with symmetrical dark spots.
- *B. retiformis* SANDERS and SMITH, 1951. Sonoran Green

Bufo retiformis

Bufo spinulosus

Toad, Reticulated Toad. Arizona and Sonora, Mexico. To 6 cm. Black reticulated pattern on yellow to greenish background. Endangered.
- *B. rosei* HEWITT, 1926. Cape Toad. Cape Province. To 4 cm. Dark gray to brownish black; dorsum with 3 light longitudinal stripes and numerous small golden-edged black dots. Skin smooth.
- *B. spinulosus* WIEGMANN, 1834. Spiny Toad. South Amer-

Bufo viridis

Bufo viridis

Bufo vulgaris

ican. 11 subspecies. To 9 cm. Dark spots against cream background. Tips of warts spinous, white.

- *B. superciliaris* BOULENGER, 1887. Cameroons. 20 cm. Dorsum yellow-gray. Upper eyelid extended to a point and attached to overhanging dorso-lateral skin fold. Flanks and legs dark. Endangered.
- *B. tibetanus* ZAREVSKIJ, 1925. Tibetan Toad. Western China. To 7 cm. Olive with irregular black pattern; dorsum with 3 light longitudinal rows of warts.
- *B. typhonius* (LINNAEUS, 1758). Tropical South America. Rain forest. 9 cm.
- *B. vertebralis* SMITH, 1848. Dwarf Toad. Southern Africa. 6 subspecies. To 4 cm, usually smaller. Brown with darker pattern.
- *B. viridis* LAURENTI, 1768. Green Toad. Southern and central Europe, North Africa, and temperate Asia to Himalayas. 3 subspecies. To 15 cm, usually smaller. Green spots and red dots against a light background.
- *B. woodhousei* GIRARD, 1854. Woodhouse's Toad, Fowler's Toad. United States. 3 subspecies. To 10 cm. Yellowish gray or brown with darker pattern; light dorsal stripe.

Bufonidae: True Toads. Family of the Salientia. Worldwide in distribution except for Madagascar, Australia, New Zealand, and many Pacific islands. Heavy but usually compact body. Skin more or less covered with warts. Pupil always horizontally oval. Often with conspicuous parotoid glands behind the head. Males always have a Bidder's organ (a vestigial ovary). Number of trunk vertebrae usually 8, rarely 9 (some *Melanophryniscus*) or 7 (some *Dendrophryniscus* and *Pelophryne*, always 7 in *Mertensophryne*) or 6 (*Oreophrynella, Osornophryne*).

Bufo woodhousei fowleri

Bufo woodhousei woodhousei

Bufo superciliaris

Bufo viridis

Most species are slow-moving animals with limited jumping ability. They are usually burrowing ground-dwellers, though there also are largely aquatic forms (several genera, for instance *Pseudobufo*) and even tree-climbing species. A few are restricted to flowing water, and *Pelophryne* is virtually independent of water. *Nectophrynoides* is the only known bufonid that gives birth to completely metamorphosed young. As far as is known, inguinal amplexus (primitive) occurs only in *Osornophryne*; all other bufonid males grasp the female in the shoulder region or below the arm pits (axillary amplexus). *Bufo* is the genus of greatest terrarium importance within this family.

Systematic summary by region:
- Genus with distribution extending over several faunal regions: *Bufo*.
- Genera of the Neotropics: *Crepidius* (= *Crepidophryne*), *Dendrophryniscus*, *Melanophryniscus*, *Oreophrynella*, *Osornophryne*, *Rhamphophryne*.
- Genera of the Ethiopian Region: *Didynamipus*, *Laurentophryne*, *Mertensophryne*, *Nectophryne*, *Nectophrynoides*, *Wolterstorffia*.
- Genera of the Orient: *Ansonia*, *Cacophryne*, *Ophryophryne*, *Pedostibes*, *Pelophryne*, *Pseudobufo*, *Werneria*.

Bufotoxin: Toxins present in secretions from the parotoids and other glands of toads (especially the genus *Bufo*). These toxins of variable chemical nature serve as defense mechanisms. Bufadienolide (present in bufotoxin from the poisonous secretion given off by the Eurasian common toad, *Bufo bufo*) belongs to the glycosides and increases cardiac activity and at the same time lowers pulse rate.

Bulua: see *Leptodactylodon*, genus.

Bungarus fasciatus

Bungarus DAUDIN, 1803. Kraits. Genus of the Elapidae. Subtropical and tropical Asia to China and the Indo-Australian Archipelago. About 12 species, some polytypic. In savannah-like dry forests (*B. caeruleus*) as well as in foggy montane forests (*B. ceylonicus* and *B. niger*) and in tropical rain forests (*B. fasciatus*, *B. javanicus*). In excess of 2 m. Body characteristically triangular in cross-section or strongly dorso-laterally compressed. Head cobra-like, short, round, slightly set off from body. Most species have a banded pattern of wide light and dark alternating crossbands, but some species are unicolored or nearly so (*B. flaviceps*, *B. lividus*, *B. niger*).

Bungarus multicinctus

Bungarus fasciatus

All *Bungarus* are venomous and nocturnal. During the day these snakes remain in hiding. Specimens disturbed during the day rarely bite, but instead press their head against the ground. The body is then flattened and coiled or tightly rolled up. However, at night these snakes are extremely dangerous and aggressive. Only quick administration of antivenin can prevent human fatalities when bitten by *Bungarus*.

Nearly all species are ophiophagous, though some take lizards, fish, and small mammals. Egg-layers. In some species the female has been observed to guard the clutch.

In captivity *Bungarus* often refuse food for prolonged periods of time. Freshwater fish are often a suitable substitute food that may eventually even be taken voluntarily. Acclimated *Bungarus* tend to be hardy. Some captive breeding has occurred.
- *B. caeruleus* (SCHNEIDER, 1801). Indian Krait. Pakistan and India to Sri Lanka. 2 subspecies.
- *B. fasciatus* (SCHNEIDER, 1801). Banded Krait. Northeastern India, Indo-China, southern China, and the Indo-Australian Archipelago.
- *B. flaviceps* REINHARDT, 1843. Red-headed Krait. Indo-China and large regions of the Indo-Australian Archipelago. Head and tail bright red, body bluish black, sometimes with an orange middorsal stripe.

Bungarus multicinctus

Cabrita GRAY, 1838. Genus of the Lacertidae. India and Sri Lanka. 2 species. Considered by some to be only a subgenus of *Ophisops*. Found in open steppe-like areas. Body more or less flattened dorso-ventrally. Tail long. Dorsal scales large, shingled and strongly keeled, ventral scales smooth. Collar only indicated laterally. Lower eyelid with large window forming almost entire lid; lids not fused. Toes with strongly keeled lamellae. Dorsum brownish to gray with light longitudinal stripes and dark spots. Tail and hind legs usually red or orange.

The diet consists of various arthropods. Egg-layers. For care and maintenance see *Ophisops*, but these species require more minor day/night temperature fluctuations and no cool winter dormancy period.
- *C. leschenaulti* (MILNE-EDWARDS, 1829). India and Sri Lanka. Easily 15 cm. 2 clear white stripes on each side with a black interspace.
- *C. jerdoni* BEDDOME, 1870. India from southwestern Bengal to Tamil Nadu. About 15 cm. Often only with one light lateral stripe. Dorsum with black spots.

Cachexia: Loss of condition and weight.

Cacophis (GUENTHER, 1863). Australian Crowned Snakes. Genus of the Elapidae. Australia. About 3 species, taxonomy still uncertain. Included in the genus *Aspisdomorphus* by some systematists. Found in savannah-like habitats. 0.25 to 1 m. Rounded head, barely or not at all set off from body. Usually blunt-snouted. A characteristic light neckband or a pair of light lateral stripes from the eye to the neck present. Body uniformly brownish to black.

Nocturnal, terrestrial venomous snakes that remain in hiding during the day under rocks, logs, and fallen leaves. They presumably feed on insects and skinks. Reproductive biology uncertain, but available literature reports 2 to 3 large eggs as well as the live-birth of 6 to 10 young for *C. kreffti*; other species give birth to 3 to 6 young.

Venom potency does not appear to be lethal to humans. Moreover, *Cacophis* are not very aggressive and often defend themselves merely with threat displays without biting.

Should be kept in an evenly heated tropical terrarium.
- *C. kreffti* (GUENTHER, 1863). Dwarf Crowned Snake. Coastal Queensland and New South Wales, Australia.
- *C. squamulosus* (DUMERIL, BIBRON, and DUMERIL, 1854). Golden Crowned Snake. Coastal Queensland and New South Wales, Australia.

Cacophryne DAVIS, 1935. Genus of the Bufonidae. Here considered to be monotypic, but some systematists also include *Bufo cruentatus* TSCHUDI, 1838, in this genus. Found in rain forests at altitudes from 600 to 1500 m. Slender. Skin covered with numerous tiny warts. Tympanum small but clearly visible. Legs long; fingers and toes long and not webbed. Ventral surfaces of toes basally with elongated, large tubercles.

Ground-dwellers. Reproductive biology largely unknown.
- *C. borbonica* (TSCHUDI, 1839). Thailand, Malaya, Greater Sunda Islands. 5 cm (female) and 3 cm (male). Brown.

Cacopus: see *Uperon*, genus.

Cacosternum BOULENGER, 1887. Genus of the Ranidae. Southern Africa. 5 species. In open areas close to water.

Head small and snout blunt. Highly variable coloration, but with the exception of *C. capense* all species are very similar.

During the dry season *Cacosternum* leads a very cryptic life, presumably in underground hiding places. However, with the onset of the rainy season these animals often emerge in enormous numbers to form large breeding aggregations in shallow, overgrown waters such as swamps and flooded grasslands. The males produce loud metallic calls in rapid succession while inflating their bodies. The spawn is attached to water plants in large masses, submersed reeds, and similar objects.

Can be kept outdoors during the summer months in an aqua-terrarium, possibly even in a small pool. During the winter they need a warm and relatively dry terrarium with a thick but loose substrate layer and ample hiding places under rocks and among plants. The diet consists of mosquitos and small flies.

• *C. capense* HEWITT, 1925. Cape Province. To 4 cm. Ventrum with large dark spots.
• *C. nanum* BOULENGER, 1887. Southern Africa. To 2.5 cm. Variably green, gray, or brown. Ventrum more or less densely covered with gray dots.

Cactaceae: Cacti. Family of the Magnoliatae. North and South America; genus *Rhipsalis* also in tropical Africa and Sri Lanka. 170 genera, more than 2,000 species. Taxonomically still unstable. Found primarily in semideserts and true deserts, but some in moist habitats. Morphological structure very diverse. Succulents. Caulomes ("stem" axis) columnar, spherical, or disc-like, branched or not branched. Leaves usually completely reduced and nearly always evolved into spines and hairs.

Cacti require lots of sun during the summer and adequate moisture during the vegetative period. Little water is needed during the fall, just enough to avoid desiccation. Since cacti require a winter dormancy period, it is advantageous to remove these plants from the terrarium and store them in a cool (8 to 13° C.) place during the winter.

Epiphytes can be maintained in baskets; they require acid soil (decaying leaf litter and peat moss mixture), a semi-shaded location, and winter moisture. Direct attachment to epiphyte logs is also possible.

Ground-living cacti should be maintained in neutral, permeable soil (decayed leaf litter mixed with coarse sand, vermiculite, and broken flowerpot fragments). Potted cacti can be placed in the terrarium substrate and partially covered with peat moss. Very thorny cactus species with barbed spines should not be used in terrariums to avoid injury to animals.

Cacti are a very diverse group of succulents that have an extensive literature available on their identification and cultivation. Hobbyists interested in these plants should consult the horticultural literature for details.

Cadea GRAY, 1844. Genus of the Amphisbaenidae. Caribbean. 2 species. Little-known burrowers.
• *C. blanoides* STEJNEGER, 1916. Western Cuba and Isle of Pines.

Caecilia LINNAEUS, 1758. Generic type of the Caeciliidae. South and Central America. 26 species. Most species are in excess of 50 cm, with *C. abitaguae* reaching 1.3 m. Tenta-

cles below nostrils on ventral surface of snout and thus not visible from above. 108-283 primary folds, from 0 to 85 secondary folds. Calcareous scales present under skin in some species, absent in others. Head often with light spots.
• *C. gracilis* SHAW, 1802. Tropical South America. To 45 cm. Uniformly lavender blue to lilac.
• *C. nigricans* BOULENGER, 1902. Colombia, Ecuador. To 1.3 m. Slate gray, tip of snout, upper lip, tentacles, and cloacal field whitish.
• *C. tentaculata* LINNAEUS, 1758. Surinam. To 63 cm. Dorsum slate gray, rest of body light brown. Very compressed.
• *C. thompsoni* BOULENGER, 1899. Colombia. To 1.17 m. Back black or blackish brown, sides lighter, abdomen dark. Eyes, tentacles, throat, snout, and cloacal region cream to white.

Caeciliidae: Caecilians. Family of the Gymnophiona. Presumably an artificial group that may have to be split up into several families. Neotropics with 13 genera and more than 60 species; Ethiopian Region with 10 genera and 30 species; Orient with 3 genera and 8 species. Morphology rather variable. Tail present (*Uraeotyphlus, Copeotyphlinus*) or vestigial (remaining genera); cloaca round, longitudinal, or perpendicular; calcareous scales present below skin or absent; tentacles large or small, variable in position; lower jaw with 1 or 2 rows of teeth; penis in *Scolecomorphus* with spines.

Systematic summary by region:
• Neotropical: *Brasilotyphlus, Caecilia, Copeotyphlinus, Cryptosophis, Dermophis, Gymnopis, Luetkenotyphlus, Microcaecilia, Mimosiphonops, Oscaecilia, Parvicaecilia, Pseudosiphonops,* and *Siphonops.*
• Ethiopian: *Afrocaecilia, Boulengerula, Geotrypetes, Grandisonia, Herpele, Hypogeophis, Idiocranium, Praslinia, Schistometopum,* and *Scolecomorphus.*
• Oriental: *Gegeneophis, Indotyphlus,* and *Uraeotyphlus.*

Knowledge of the Caeciliidae is still quite incomplete, and the developmental biology of many genera remains unknown. Egg-laying genera have aquatic larvae and terrestrial adults, while live-bearing genera are always terrestrial.

Few details are available for captive maintenance. Basic care as for Ichthyophiidae, but feeding details available are contradictory. Some species appear at the surface at dusk and also feed there, while others feed exclusively below ground. According to Tanner (as reported for *Hypogeophis rostratus*) the preferred food in captivity seems to be waxmoth larvae and newly metamorphosed aquatic frogs. Insect larvae, waxmoth pupae, earthworms, ant pupae, pieces of raw fish, newborn mice, and processed foods made of shrimp and fish meal are also eaten.

There are no records of successful breeding in captivity.

Caenophidia: Typical Snakes. Central order of the Serpentes. Worldwide in temperate and warmer climates. From 0.2 to 5.5 m; the largest species do not reach the maximum lengths of the giant forms of Henophidia (boids), and certainly not their mass. Primarily slender, relatively fast-moving snakes, but many stout and/or burrowers. Head more or less set off from body and usually covered with large scutes. Most of the Caenophidia have functional, relatively large eyes. Dentition varied; fangs often developed for venom conduction. Reductions in dentition are uncommon exceptions. Eye anatomy is of great significance in the systematics of this group, as is the structure of various maxillary and salivary glands. Within the various families there can be transformations of these glands into venom glands. Dorsal region of body with smooth or keeled scales, these sometimes even more differentiated. Ventral scutes wide. Tail more or less long to very long, may be prehensile (in tree-dwellers) or rudder-like (in sea snakes).

The morphological diversity of the Caenophidia reflects the diversity of their ecology and biology: land-dwellers, amphibious and aquatic freshwater and marine species, burrowers, as well as arboreal forms. This continuum of adaptations makes the systematics of this group difficult. In the largest group, the family Colubridae, research into actual relationships to establish a natural system is still far from conclusive. Consequently, substantial systematic reorganizations can still be expected within the Caenophidia.

Systematic summary:
- Colubridae: 12 subfamilies, more than 300 genera.
- Elapidae: about 50 genera.
- Hydrophiidae: 2 subfamilies, 17 genera.
- Viperidae: 3 subfamilies, 11 genera.
- Crotalidae: 5 genera.

Many of these family groups are certainly artificial, especially the Colubridae. Crotalidae is often considered a subfamily of Viperidae. Hydrophiidae can be treated as a subfamily of Elapidae or more complexly as a separate family including many Australian terrestrial genera.

Caiman SPIX, 1825. Spectacled Caimans. Genus of the Alligatoridae. Tropical and subtropical South America. Systematics uncertain; according to current opinion 2 species, of which *C. crocodilus* is polytypic. Because of apparent allopatry between *C. crocodilus* and *C. latirostris* they could possibly represent one species; this is supported by variation in snout shape relative to the geographical distribution. In slow-flowing and standing inland waters with muddy bottoms, shallow areas, and mud and sand banks. In contrast to the related genera *Melanosuchus* and *Paleosuchus*, which together with *Caiman* form the *Caiman* Group, *Caiman* is characterized by a distinctly raised, arched ridge between the anterior corners of the eyes resembling the bridge of a pair of wire-framed spectacles, thus the common name. Moreover, *Caiman* does not have the longitudinally raised dorsal ridge typical of *Melanosuchus*. *Caiman* is distinguished from *Paleosuchus* by its greenish iris and at the most 3 rows of occipital scutes. The upper eyelid area in *Caiman* is wrinkled to rough. General coloration dark olive; juveniles lighter but with black markings. Juveniles have a conspicuously duckbilled snout. *Caiman* sometimes occurs together with *Melanosuchus niger* at the north of its range, an unusual situation for caimans.

C. crocodilus occurs in the greatest abundance of all South American crocodilians. This species even perseveres in urban areas of the *selva* in Peru and Brasil, but there it leads a reclusive life often unnoticed by people.

In temperament, spectacled caimans display greater vitality than all the other alligatorids, and even *Caiman* babies are aggressive and will bite. For this reason alone these animals should really only be kept in zoological parks.

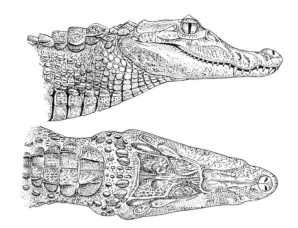

Caiman crocodilus

Caiman crocodilus

Caiman has been bred under farming conditions (e. g., in Colombia), and occasionally also in zoological parks (CSSR, Holland, USA, Japan). Its eggs have an incubation period of 73 to 75 days at 30 to 32° C. and 95% humidity.
- *C. crocodilus* (LINNAEUS, 1758). Narrow-snouted Spectacled Caiman. Southern North America southward to subtropical South America. Polytypic. Length of the snout decreases from north to south. Abdominal scales in 20 to 24 rows.
- *C. c. apaporiensis* MEDEM, 1955. Colombia, upper Rio Apaporis. 2.5 m.

Caiman crocodilus

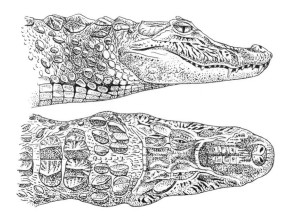

Caiman latirostris

• *C. c. crocodilus* (LINNAEUS, 1758). Northern and northeastern South America to the lower Amazon region. 2.7m.
• *C. c. fuscus* (COPE, 1868). Mexico to Rio Magdalena. To 2 m.
• *C. c. yacare* (DAUDIN, 1802). Central South America to Rio Paraguay and the lower Rio Parana. To 2.5 m.
• *C. latirostris* (DAUDIN, 1802). Broad-snouted Spectacled Caiman. Central South America east of the Andes and south of the Amazon. To 3 m. Particularly short- and broad-snouted; 24 to 28 rows of abdominal scales.

Caimans: Group of related Neotropics crocodilian genera formed of the genera *Caiman*, *Melanosuchus*, and *Paleosuchus*. In contrast to the genus *Alligator*, they do not have a bony nasal septum. This group is also characterized by a larger number (at least 8) of large, interconnected occipital bucklers and well developed bony plates along the abdomen that are connected like hinges (in contrast to the genus *Alligator*).

Calabaria GRAY, 1858. Ball Python. Monotypic genus of the Boidae, subfamily Pythoninae. Tropical western and central Africa. Tropical forests and savannahs. To 1.1 m. The small head is not distinct from the body. The projecting rostral area is used for burrowing in soil. The tail is very short. Brown to reddish brown with irregular reddish spots.
Ecologically and morphologically similar to the boid genus *Eryx*. However, *Calabaria* burrows in soft top-soil as

well as in the harder substrates in savannahs. It remains in its burrow during the day or under roots and decaying logs. Hunts after dark. The preferred diet is small mammals and lizards. Disturbed specimens curl up into a ball, hiding their head in the middle, then the thick tail simulates the head.
Keep in a relatively small tropical terrarium with a deep, soft substrate layer (peat moss, wood shavings, moss). Use only small drinking containers that are anchored so the snake does not dump the water and increase soil moisture. Hardy and undemanding.
• *C. reinhardti* (SCHLEGEL, 1851). Liberia to the Cameroons, Gabon, and the Congo; also on Fernando Poo.

Calamaria BOIE, 1826. Dwarf Snakes. Large genus of the Colubridae, Calamarinae. Ranges over Indo-China from Burma and Assam southward to Malaysia, the Indo-Australian Archipelago, and the Moluccas. About 52 species. 20 to 60 cm. Only 13 rows of scales around middle of body, the lowest number in the subfamily. Coloration usually dark, frequently iridescent, some species spotted, striped, or other individual pattern variations. Burrowing snakes.
These snakes are seldom kept in terrariums. Their natural history is poorly known.
• *C. agamensis* BLEEKER, 1860. Sumatra, Java, Kalimantan.
• *C. leucocephala* DUMERIL and BIBRON, 1854. Malaya, Sumatra, Kalimantan, Java, Bali.
• *C. lumbricoidea* BOIE, 1827. Kalimantan, Java, Sumatra, Sulawesi. 2 subspecies.
• *C. pavimentata* DUMERIL and BIBRON, 1854. Assam and southern China southward to Java. 2 subspecies.
• *C. vermiformis* DUMERIL and BIBRON, 1854. Thailand, Malaya, Sumatra, Kalimantan, Java.

Calamarinae: Dwarf Snakes. Subfamily of the Colubridae. Indo-China, mainly the Indo-Australian Archipelago. 9 genera, about 70 species. Found in monsoon forests, rain forests, and montane rain forests to 1800 m elevation. 20 to 75 cm. Head barely set off from body, pointed or flattened, snout shovel-like; top of head covered by a reduced number of large scales. Rostral frequently projecting so that the mouth becomes subterminal. Skull stout and compact. Body covered by a relatively small number of scale rows (13 to 19 rows). The relatively short tail usually ends

Calabaria reinhardti

Calabaria reinhardti

with a pointed terminal scale that enables the snakes to become anchored inside their burrows.

All Calamarinae are burrowing snakes and lead a strongly subterranean life. They are found outside their burrows only at night or following heavy rains. The diet consists mainly of earthworms and small arthropods and their larvae. Some species have become specialized for a diet of termites. Egg-layers.

Calamarinae are best kept in glass terrariums.

Systematic summary:

▪ 5 monotypic genera: *Brachyorrhus, Padangia, Pseudorhabdion, Rhabdophidium,* and *Typhlogeophis.*
▪ 4 polytypic genera: *Agrophis, Calamaria, Calamorhabdium,* and *Idiopholis.*

Calamelaps GUENTHER, 1866. Genus of the Colubridae, Aparallactinae. Tropical and southern Africa. About 4 species. To 1 m. These snakes have a compact head, subterminal mouth, and small eyes. The rounded snout is flattened and shovel-like. The head is not distinct from the body. Scales smooth, tail short. Uniformly dark. Can sometimes be mistaken for *Atractaspis.*

Calamelaps are burrowing snakes that are largely subterranean. The diet consists mainly of blind worm snakes, amphisbaenids, and skinks. Care similar to other small burrowing snakes. Caution: Venomous bites.
▪ *C. unicolor* GUENTHER, 1888. Tanzania to the Republic of South Africa. 3 subspecies.
▪ *C. ventrimaculatus* ROUX, 1907. Southeastern Africa. 2 subspecies.

Calamodontophis AMARAL 1963. Monotypic genus of the Colubridae, Boiginae. Brasil (Rio Grande do Sul). In tropical forests. 35 cm. Terrestrial.
▪ *C. paucidens* (AMARAL, 1935).

Calamorhabdium BOETTGER, 1898. Genus of the Colubridae, Calamarinae. Sulawesi, Batjan. 2 species. 20 cm. Dark iridescent background coloration. Conspicuous tail spine. Burrowing snakes.
▪ *C. kuekenthali* BOETTHER, 1898. Batjan.

Calathea G. F. W. MEY. Zebra Arrowroots. Genus of the Marantaceae. Tropical America. About 130 species in rain forest areas. Usually bushes with attractively marked leaves. They require high humidity; the leaves roll up in dry air.
▪ *C. makoyana* E. MORR. About 30 to 50 cm tall. Brazil.
▪ *C. undulata* LIND. and ANDRE. To 20 cm tall. Leaves 10 cm.

Callagur GRAY, 1870. Callagur Turtles. Monotypic genus of the Emydidae. Southern India to Sumatra and Kalimantan. In large rivers and lakes; can tolerate brackish water. Carapace rigid, streamlined, with three dark longitudinal bands against a brownish background. Legs flattened, paddle-like, and webbed.

Primarily herbivorous, but also takes small aquatic invertebrates. Because of its large size it is recommended that this species be kept only in large tanks in public aquariums or zoological parks. Because it is a very messy species, it is rarely put on public display.

Callagur borneoensis

Calliophis macclellandi

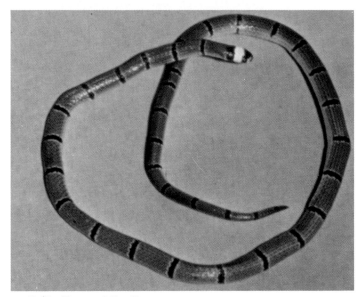

Calliophis macclellandi

• *C. borneoensis* (SCHLEGEL and S. MUELLER, 1844). At 76 cm in carapace length, the largest species (together with *Orlitia*) of the family.

Calliophis GRAY, 1834. Oriental Coral Snakes. Genus of the Elapidae. India, Sri Lanka, Indo-China, southern China, and the Malayan Peninsula, Taiwan, the Ryukyu Islands (Okinawa), the Philippines, and Sumatra. About 13 species, some polytypic, in tropical lowland and highland forests. To 50 cm. Slender, cylindrical glossy snakes, many with more or less contrasty ringed pattern.

Calliophis species are venomous, nocturnal ground-snakes. The diet consists mainly of smaller snakes (blind snakes, *Calamaria*) and lizards (geckos and skinks). Egg-layers.

Provide a well-heated terrarium with a deep layer of loose soil. Caution: Venomous bite.

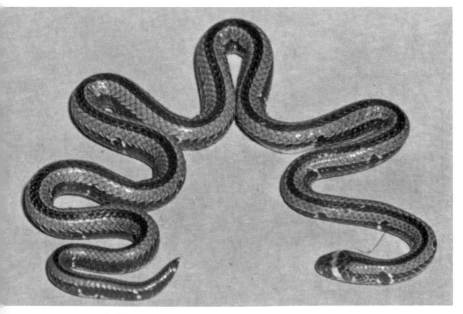

Calliophis sauteri

Calliophis sauteri

- *C. kellogi* (POPE, 1928). Southern China.
- *C. calligaster* (WIEGMANN, 1835). Philippines. 2 or 3 subspecies.
- *C. macclellandi* (REINHARDT, 1844). Nepal, Assam, Southern China, Taiwan. 3 subspecies. Mainly in high montane forests.

Calliphoridae: Flesh Flies. Family of the Diptera (suborder Brachycera). About 1500 species. Usually 8 to 15 mm. The larvae of a number of species live as parasites on insects and vertebrates, such as *Lucilia bufonivora* in toads.

Some species such as blowflies, *Calliphora erythrocephala*, can be bred successfully as food organisms for terrarium animals. The adults are kept in gauze-covered cages and are fed a mixture of honey and powdered milk with some dry yeast added. Liver offered in a plate or dish on a layer of sawdust or the intestines of various small vertebrates or their bodies are offered as egg deposition sites and larval food. At temperatures in excess of 20° C. the larval stage lasts about 1 week and the pupal stage (which takes place in the sawdust) lasts barely 2 weeks. The pupae can easily be stored in a refrigerator. Since the larvae are rather handy, it is advisable to feed only the adult flies in order to avoid parasitic infestations.

A frequent parasite in *Calliphora* cultures is a small wasp that attacks the larvae. Infested cultures should be totally destroyed and new ones started.

Callisaurus BLAINVILLE, 1835. Zebra-tailed Lizards. Monotypic genus of the Iguanidae. Southwestern United States into Mexico. 10 subspecies. In open, dry habitats. About 20 cm, slender. Similar to *Holbrookia*, but ear opening clearly visible. Granular scalation. Light yellow-brown with dark reticulated pattern. Ventral surface of tail with black crossbars continued on the dorsal side. 2 large dark vertical bars within a bluish zone approximately halfway along the side of the body.

Ground-dwellers, sometimes running on the hind legs when fleeing, the tail turned upward to display the black

Callisaurus draconoides

and white banded pattern. They feed on arthropods and sometimes are herbivorous. Egg-layers, up to 5 clutches of 2 to 8 eggs each per year.

Requires dry heat. Rather quarrelsome among each other.
- *C. draconoides* BLAINVILLE, 1835. Zebra-tailed Lizard.

Calliscincopus: see *Tretioscincus*, genus.

Callopistes maculatus

Callopistes GRAVENHORST, 1838. Monitor Tegus. Genus of the Teiidae. Ecuador to central Chile west of the Andes. 2 species; includes *Tejovaranus*. In rocky deserts and steppe regions along the Pacific side of the Andes well into the mountain range. To 1 m. Tail more than twice snout-vent length. Powerful limbs. Dorsal scales small and granular, ventral scales large and flat.

Monitor tegus should be maintained in a spacious, dry terrarium with some large, loosely stacked rocks as hiding places. Day temperatures of 25 to 35° C. with a localized heat source are satisfactory; at night reduce the temperature to about 15 to 20° C.

The diet consists of large arthropods, but large specimens also take young vertebrates. In the wild *C. flavipunctatus* feeds mainly on lizards. Provide regular ultraviolet radiation and vitamin supplements.

C. maculatus goes through a winter dormancy period of several months in the southern part of its range and stores fat in its tail.

Callopistes maculatus

▪ *C. (Tejovaranus) flavipunctatus* (DUMERIL and BIBRON, 1839). Yellow-spotted Monitor Tegu. Ecuador, Peru. Rocky deserts close to the Pacific Ocean. To 1 m.

▪ *C. maculatus* GRAVENHORST, 1838. Spotted Monitor Tegu. Northern and central Chile. Dry regions along the western slopes of the Andes. To 50 cm. Brown to red-brown with dark spots that often have a white margin.

Callopsis: see *Rhinoclemmys*, genus.

Calluella STOLICZKA, 1872 (= *Colpoglossus* BOULENGER, 1904). Genus of the Microhylidae. Ranges from the Himalayan foothills in western China and southern Burma through Indo-China to the Greater Sunda Islands (Sumatra, Kalimantan). 6 species in subtropical and tropical forests, at the northern end of the range also found in agricultural areas (rice paddies). Body squat, toad-like. Pupil round; tympanum covered by skin. Fingers free, in contrast to related genus *Kaloula*; tips not enlarged, but (as in *Kaloula*) with distinct tubercles on fingers and toes. The toes are more or less extensively webbed. As in *Kaloula*, the inner metatarsal tubercle is modified as a burrowing spade.

Found under decaying logs, rocks, and fallen leaves, these are more or less burrowing ground-dwellers. The spawn is deposited in rain water puddles and similar temporary shallow, turbid still-water habitats. The eggs are small and numerous. Care as for *Kaloula*.

▪ *C. brooksi* (BOULENGER, 1904). Kalimantan. To 6 cm. Brown with a dark longitudinal stripe from the upper edge of eye to shoulder, where broken into spots.

▪ *C. guttulata* (BLYTH, 1855). Southern Burma, northern Malaysia. 5 cm. Light brown with darker pattern.

▪ *C. ocellata* LIU, 1950. Eastern Tibet (2400 m). 3.5 cm. Dark gray; 2 conspicuous black eye spots with light margins on lower back.

Callulina NIEDEN, 1910. Monotypic genus of the Microhylidae. East Africa. Closely related to *Breviceps*. Found in damp mountain forests with dense undergrowth. The very depressed body is covered with warts. Pupil horizontal. Tympanum clearly visible. Tips of fingers and toes with large, anteriorly supported adhesive discs. First and second toes opposable. Well-developed tubercles under toes. 2 large, oval, flat metatarsal tubercles.

Ground-dwelling as well as climbing frogs. There is no aquatic larval stage, the embryonic and larval development up to metamorphosis taking place in eggs deposited in dark, damp locations. Should be kept in a rain-forest terrarium at 20 to 24° C.

▪ *C. kreffti* NIEDEN, 1910. Usambara and Uluguru Mountains, Tanzania. 5 cm, males substantially smaller than females. Dark grayish brown to blackish with irregular light and dark pattern.

Calodactylus STRAND, 1926. Genus of the Gekkonidae. India, Sri Lanka. 2 species. Nocturnal ground-dwellers. Natural history details scarce.

▪ *C. aurens* (BEDDOME, 1870). India.

Calotes CUVIER, 1817. Varied Lizards, Blood-suckers. Genus of the Agamidae. Southern and southeastern Asia, from India to New Guinea. About 30 species. 25 to 50 cm,

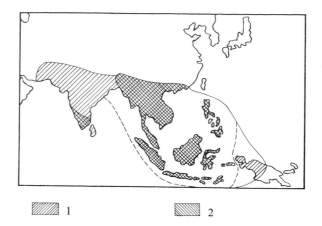

1 ▨ 2

Distribution of: 1 *Calotes*; 2 *Draco*

tail up to three-quarters of total length, slightly compressed laterally. Males have a conspicuous spinous dorsal crest that is highest in its anterior third. Males also often have erectile gular folds or pouches. Dorsal scales large, rectangular, shingled, and clearly keeled, relatively weak and fragile. Mainly shades of brown and green. Physiological color changes strongly developed. Excited animals may display intensive red, blue, iridescent green, and black hues.

All species are arboreal. The diet consists mainly of arthropods and occasional small lizards. Depending upon species, clutches may contain more than 20 eggs. The incubation period is about 2 months.

Calotes require large, well-planted terrariums with high humidities. Temperatures range from 25 to 32° C. (less for montane forms) with only minor reductions at night. A lot of drinking water is required, with a drop dispenser useful.

Calotes calotes

Calotes calotes

Calotes calotes

Calotes versicolor

Calotes has been bred repeatedly, but rearing the young is not easy. Juveniles are susceptible to rickets and need UV radiation and calcium and vitamin supplements.

▪ *C. calotes* (LINNAEUS, 1758). Sawback Agamid. Southern India, Sri Lanka. Open forests. In excess of 50 cm. Extremely long tail. Dorsally emerald green with 5 to 6 light or dark bands. Head yellowish to brownish green. Throat and sometimes entire head red. Flanks with bluish spots. Requires heat.

▪ *C. cristatellus* (KUHL, 1820). Blood-sucker. Indo-China, Philippines, and Indo-Australian Archipelago to New Guinea. Open forests. In excess of 50 cm. Conspicuous dorsal crest. Usually green with red-brown spots, but also may be yellowish, brown, or nearly black. Lips often blood red, thus the common name. Extreme color changes. Few (1-2?) eggs.

▪ *C. mystaceus* DUMERIL and BIBRON, 1837. Indo-China in montane forests. About 40 cm. Substantial color changes, the head, abdomen, and throat in males becoming bright blue when excited. 6 to 10 eggs. Requires temperatures from 20 to 25° C., at night about 15° C.

▪ *C. versicolor* (DAUDIN, 1802). Southwestern Asia from Sri

Calotes emma

Lanka to southern China and Sumatra. To 40 cm. Gular pouch weakly developed. Yellowish gray to brownish yellow. Color changes strongly developed. In excited males the throat and abdomen, sometimes also the flanks, become bright red, the head and nape greenish with red dots and lines, the limbs and tail nearly black. The diet consists mainly of ants (not essential in captivity). 10 to 25 eggs.

Calyptahyla TRUEB and TAYLOR, 1974. Monotypic genus of the Hylidae. Greater Antilles. Arboreal.
• *C. lichenata* (GOSSE, 1851).

Calyptocephalella: see *Caudiverbera*, genus.

Candoia GRAY, 1842. Pacific Island Boas. Genus of the Boidae. Moluccas and New Guinea to Tokelau and Samoas. 3 species. To 1 m; only *C. bibroni* reaches nearly 2 m. Body usually slightly compressed and covered with keeled scales. The clearly set off triangular head terminates in a conspicuously straight snout edge. Brownish with darker spots that can be rather irregular and small (*C. bibroni*) or can be formed into an irregular middorsal band (*C. carinata*) or into a strongly symmetrical row of rhomboids (*C. aspera*).

Semiarboreal to terrestrial; *C. bibroni* and *C. carinata* are better climbers than the smaller, plumpish *C. aspera*. The diet consists of small mammals, birds, lizards, and presumably also frogs.

These boas should be kept in a well-heated tropical terrarium with climbing facilities and a sufficiently deep layer of soft substrate. Bathing facility must be provided since at

Candoia aspera

least *C. aspera* likes to enter water. Newly collected adult specimens often refuse food and may have to be force-fed. Food refusal is probably related to individual imprinting on specific food animals. Occasionally newly imported pregnant females will give birth to young that can be raised in captivity. True captive breeding is so far rare. Often very aggressive!
• *C. aspera* (GUENTHER, 1877). Moluccas, New Guinea, Bismarck Archipelago, Solomons, and Tokelau Islands.
• *C. bibroni* (DUMERIL and BIBRON, 1839). Ceram, Melanesian, and Polynesian Islands. 2 subspecies.
• *C. carinata* (SCHNEIDER, 1801). Celebes to New Guinea and Solomons and Tokelau Islands. 2 subspecies.

Candoia carinata, young

Candoia aspera

Candoia carinata

Cannibalism: Feeding on members of the same species. Usually occurs as a consequence of excessive population density or lack of food and thus serves as a biological population regulation mechanism. A particular form of cannibalism occurs among various frog species (e. g., *Anotheca, Hoplophryne*), where the tapoles live in water with a very limited food supply and the largest number of larvae are eaten by the stronger ones. Cannibalism occurs occasionally among many amphibians and reptiles where the young are considered as prey, e. g., some water frogs (*Phrynobatrachus, Rana*), lizards (*Lacerta, Podarcis*), and ophiophagous snakes (*Ophiophagus, Bungarus*). The confined space of a terrarium may favor cannibalism.

Cantoria GIRARD, 1857. Genus of the Colubridae, Homalopsinae. Burma to the Indo-Australian Archipelago to southern New Guinea. Prefers brackish areas of rivers and mangrove swamp forests in coastal areas. To 1.2 m. White crossbands against black ground on dorsal side. Ventral area whitish. Tail with rings. *Cantoria* resemble some sea snakes.

Nocturnal aquatic snakes. Rare.
- *C. violacea* GIRARD, 1857. Over entire generic range except New Guinea.
- *C. annulata* DE JONG, 1926. Southern New Guinea.

Capillaria: Hair worms. Nematode worms belonging to the Trichocephaloidea that occur as parasites in lizards and snakes; *C. recurva* occurs in crocodiles. *Capillaria* move through the circulatory system from the intestinal tract into other organs, especially the liver, kidneys, and brain, where they can cause severe damage due to blockage of the smallest blood vessels and the kidney ducts.

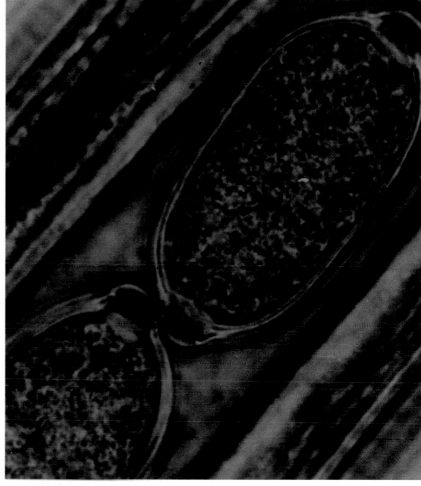

Capillaria, eggs

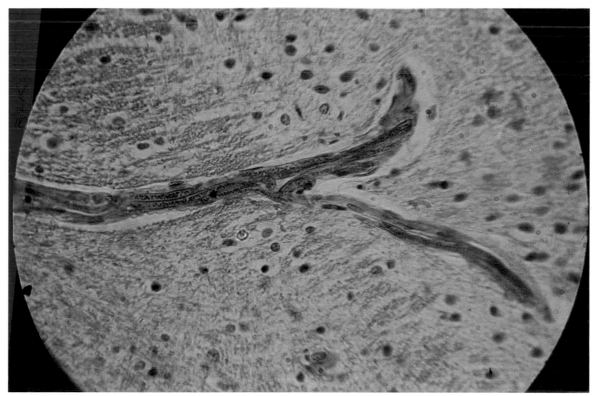

Capillaria in blood vessel

Captive breeding has made available patterns and forms that are otherwise rare: *Elaphe guttata,* albino on top, brilliant young on bottom

Captive breeding: Particular features are outlined under the generic discussions. The following general areas have to be watched for and monitored:
- the onset of mating readiness in males and females;
- care of females during pregnancy;
- incubation of eggs;
- rearing the young.

The main difficulty often is matching a male and female that are ready and willing to mate. Particularly in snakes it can happen that a male may not mate with a certain female. The only way to resolve such an impass is to try out different male/female combinations. In many reptile species this can become forced mating. It is often difficult to ascertain courtship readiness in males and the willingness to mate in females.

If the breeding season is restricted to a particular time of the year (usually during spring), as is the case with nearly all animals from regions with seasonal climatic variations, attempts should be made to simulate this in a terrarium situation (winter dormancy period, dry season). This tends to stimulate courtship readiness. This is often triggered by the change from short to long days. A rather similar effect can sometimes be achieved with ultraviolet radiation. For instance, it has been reported for a particular *Anolis* species that courtship commenced during one short radiation period. Special attention has to be given to providing the correct diet.

If a successful mating has taken place followed by a pregnancy (not every mating must lead to a pregnancy; some reptiles are able to store sperm, so a pregnancy can conceivably be delayed for some time, and possibly in wild-caught specimens mating could have occurred prior to capture), the pregnant females have to be meticulously cared for. This includes:
- sufficient varied and regular feedings, possibly with vitamin supplements;
- disturbances must be kept to a minimum, so other specimens in the same terrarium may have to be removed (if possible always leave the pregnant female in the terrarium she is accustomed to);
- females of ovoviviparous species should be kept individually just prior to birth in order to eliminate any possible cannibalism from animals in the same terrarium;
- calcium supplements should be given to pregnant females, at least for insectivorous and herbivorous species.

If the pregnancy is an unusually long one, consider the possibility of egg binding; this is particularly common among animals caught in a highly pregnant condition.

Special arrangements have to be made for the incubation of eggs. Once the young are born or have hatched they must be reared away from the parents. In most cases they will require somewhat higher temperatures than the adults, and often the young can not yet tolerate substantial nightly temperature reductions (nevertheless, temperatures must not be maintained constant). Young reptiles must always have access to drinking water and should generally be kept somewhat damper than adults (there is a danger of dehydration). The food must be as varied as possible; with insectivorous reptiles there is always the danger of constipation when the diet is too monotonous (especially if it includes mealworms). Young of diurnal open-living species should be given ultraviolet radiation regularly, combined with calcium and vitamin supplements. Young reptiles feeding on vertebrates are less delicate.

Causes for such high UV, calcium, and vitamin requirements appears to be related to high terrarium temperatures and inadequate temperature differences between day and night. It is known that most reptiles reach sexual maturity quicker under terrarium conditions, so with barely justifiable high temperatures and an optimal food supply it is indeed possible to breed many small and medium lizards in less than a year. Therefore, it is understandable that with such hastened growth the risk of deficiency diseases is substantially increased. Young reptiles with normal growth show invariably greater vitality and are hardier and also more colorful. There are, of course, exceptions, whereby for years and over several generations healthy young have been "pushed" to maturity. However, more commonly the situation is such that obtaining progeny from wild-caught parents is relatively easy, only to find that breeding during the F2 or F3 generation then suddenly ceases.

The danger of inbreeding is generally not very great with reptiles, but sibling matings over several generations should be avoided. It goes without saying that only healthy animals and good housing conditions should be used for breeding. On the other hand, under terrarium conditions it is only too common to find that relatively weak progeny are raised (since the available adult material is often severely limited) that in the wild would have no chance of survival. In such cases it is therefore not surprising to find that even after a few generations symptoms of degeneration start to appear.

Caralluma R. BR. Fly Flowers. Genus of the Asclepiadaceae. India, Afghanistan, Arabia, most of Africa, southwestern Mediterranean region. About 105 species. Creeping and erect succulent plants.
- *C. incarnata* (L. f.) N.E. BR. To 30 cm tall. Culture as for *Stapelia*.
- *C. lutea*. N.E. BR. 5 to 10 cm tall.
- *C. mammilaris* (L.) To 15 cm tall.

Carapace: Dorsal shield in turtles and tortoises.

Cardioglossa BOULENGER, 1900. Long-fingered Frogs. Genus of the Ranidae. Western and central Africa. 9 species. Mostly in rain forests and gallery forests, rarely (*C. pulchra*) in montane grasslands. Slender and smooth-skinned. Characterized by the conspicuously long third fingers and fourth toes that are especially well-developed in males (also in some *Arthroleptis* species). Toes and fingers free, but some have laterally serrated skin folds. Adhesive discs more or less well-developed; clearly formed tubercles present. Some species are very attractive. As far as is known they have well-defined day/night coloration changes. In some species the lower section of the iris is black while the upper part is silvery or bronze during the night.

Strictly nocturnal ground-dwellers in dense vegetation. Although the larvae are aquatic, *Cardioglossa* species seem to deviate strongly from typical ranid reproductive biology by their large unpigmented eggs that undergo embryonic development in the oviduct. Except for the purpose of larva (or egg) deposition, *Cardioglossa* species apparently do not enter water and are often found considerable distances from water.

Should be kept in a well-planted terrarium at tropical temperatures and, particularly at night, with high humidity. Can be fed *Drosophila* and whiteworms.

- *C. leucomystax* (BOULENGER, 1903). West Africa. To 3.5 cm. Day coloration silvery gray to grayish brown, with dark pattern. At night brownish black, the upper jaw with contrasting white lips.
- *C. pulchra* SCHIOETZ, 1963. Eastern Nigeria (Obudu Plateau at 1700 m elevation). To 3.5 cm. Black at night with pink dorso-lateral stripes. Limbs spotted with light brown. Belly dark blue with black pattern.

Caretta RAFINESQUE, 1814. Loggerhead Turtles. Monotypic genus of the Cheloniidae. In all temperate and tropical seas, offshore and in coastal waters. Carapace length about 1 m. 5 pairs of costal scutes. Uniformly brown to reddish brown, not very colorful. Meat considered useless.

Primarily carnivorous, mainly on squid, octopus, cuttlefish, crustaceans, some fish. Hauls out on beaches to lay eggs. The same egg-laying sites are used from generation to generation and are repeatedly visited by the same females. Incubation period in the wild is 49 to 67 days.

- *C. caretta* (LINNAEUS, 1758) All tropical and temperate seas.

Carettochelyidae: New Guinea Soft-shelled Turtles. Monogeneric family of the Cryptodira. Southern New Guinea and northern Australia. Fossil records in New Guinea from the Miocene (genus *Carettochelys*), with other genera

Caretta caretta

known from the Cretaceous of Asia and North America. Found in large jungle rivers, but also in brackish water. Carapace length to 50 cm. Head with proboscis-like snout. Shell not covered with horny plates but instead with leathery skin; only early juveniles display scale-like plates on the shell. Carapace strongly arched, with a distinct median

Caretta caretta

Caretta caretta

Carettochelys insculpta, young

ridge that is slightly serrated in juveniles. Anterior limbs with 2 free claws. Despite biological and morphological similarities with Trionychidae there are important anatomical differences, such as the well-developed bony carapace (greatly reduced in true soft-shells).

Aquatic, burying themselves in the soft bottom. Can remain submerged for long periods of time, using supplemental respiration through the oral mucous membranes and water pumps, in the resting animal.

Omnivorous, feeding mainly on small soft-bodied animals such as worms and arthropods. The diet may include fish, but this is not yet substantiated. Much plant matter

(water plants, fruit) is taken. Females will haul out only to lay eggs.

Should be kept in a large, well-heated aquarium. Skin damage must be prevented and treated immediately, possibly by keeping affected animals temporarily out of the water. Substrate should consist of fine-grained sand, NEVER coarse gravel. Considered to be a delicacy by the natives, its survival is endangered. Rarely available commercially.

Carettochelys RAMSAY, 1887. New Guinea Soft-shelled Turtles. Monotypic genus of the Carettochelyidae. Southern New Guinea, northern Australia.

Carettochelys insculpta

Carettochelys insculpta

- *C. insculpta* RAMSAY, 1887.

Carlia GRAY, 1845. Genus of the Scincidae. Australia, New Guinea, and adjacent islands. *Leiolopisma* Group. 20 to 30 species. 10 to 18 cm, slender, appearance similar to *Ablepharus*, but only 4 fingers and movable lower eyelids with transparent window or spectacle, but lids not completely fused (except in *C. burnetti*). Mainly brown, with various patterns.

Diurnal ground-dwellers often found among leaves at the base of trees or among rocks. Egg-layers. For care and

Carettochelys insculpta, young

maintenance see *Ablepharus*; does not require winter domancy period.

- *C. burnetti* (OUDEMANS, 1894). Eastern Australia. 10 cm. Dark dorsal patches and white spots along flanks, tail reddish.
- *C. vivax* (DE VIS, 1894). Northeastern Australia. About 10 cm. Black-bordered spots in rows along body; lighter lateral stripes.

Carphodactylus GUENTHER, 1897. Monotypic genus of the Gekkonidae. Australia. About 10 cm. Nocturnal. Presumably a ground-dweller.

- *C. laevis* (GUENTHER, 1897).

Carphophis GERVAIS, 1849. Worm Snakes. Monotypic genus of the Colubridae of uncertain subfamily status (probably Natricinae). Eastern United States. 30 cm. Scales in 13 rows. Head not distinct from body. Only 5 scales (upper labials) along upper jaw.

Nocturnal burrowing snakes. Found in dry or damp habitats. Diet is mainly earthworms and insects. When picked up will dig the sharp terminal tail scale into the hand. Best kept in a glass terrarium.

- *C. amoenus* (SAY, 1825). Worm Snake. Central to eastern United States, absent in much of Southeast. 3 subspecies. Uniformly brown or black above, pale to bright pink below.

Carphophis amoenus

Casarea GRAY, 1842. Round Island Ground Boas. Monotypic genus of the Boidae, subfamily Bolyeriinae. Mauritius area; only remaining population is on small Round Island northwest of Mauritius, where found in sparse remnants of tropical forests. To 1.5 m. Resembles somewhat *Epicrates* species. Head clearly set off from body. Tail terminates in a point. Mainly brown with remnants of longitudinal markings that are present as a lyre pattern on top of the head and as 2 bands of rhomboids in the tail region.

Nocturnal ground-dwellers. Feeds on small mammals and presumably also frogs and lizards. Although they remain in hiding during the day in burrows with some dampness, in contrast to *Bolyeria* they seem to burrow relatively little. Endangered.

- *C. dussumieri* (SCHLEGEL, 1837).

Casque-headed treefrogs: Grouping of various genera of Hylidae (especially *Aparasphenodon, Osteocephalus, Tetra-*

prion, Trachycephalus, and *Triprion*) that as highly specialized bromeliad inhabitants display strong ossification of the skull. For sleeping and in order to survive the dry season these frogs retreat into bromeliad funnels and close them off by bending their armored heads into the opening.

Castings: Undigested, strongly matted remnants (hairs, feathers, bones, etc.) from food animals that are regurgitated by birds of prey and owls, occasionally also by some giant snakes, monitors, and crocodiles.

Caudacaecilia TAYLOR, 1968. Genus of the Ichthyophiidae. Tropical Southeast Asia, including Indo-Australian Archipelago. 5 species. 20 to 45 cm. Has 350 to more than 430 skin folds. Like *Ichthyophis, Caudacaecilia* has a distinct tail and 3 to 4 secondary folds per primary ring; the secondary and primary folds join at an obtuse angle along the abdomen. The cloacal slit is longitudinal. In contrast to *Ichthyophis, Caudacaecilia* species usually have only 1 (instead of 2) row of teeth on the lower jaw, the inner row absent or modified. Some species are uniformly blue to violet, but others have a conspicuous broad, light lateral stripe.
• *C. nigroflava* (TAYLOR, 1960). Kalimantan, Sumatra, Malaysia. To 45 cm. Dorsal and ventral surfaces black; wide cream lateral stripe present.

Caudata: Also called Urodela. Salamanders, newts, and related forms (a newt is a salamander of the family Salamandridae). Order of the Amphibia. Found almost exclusively in the Northern Hemisphere (only *Bolitoglossa* is found south of the Equator); greatest species concentrations in southern Europe, the southeastern Palearctic, and Mexico. In contrast to Gymnophiona and the Salientia, in adults there is a well-developed, often very long tail that commonly is longer than the body. The front and hind limbs are similar (sometimes the hind limbs are stronger but in a few genera the hind limbs including the pelvic girdle may be reduced or even absent. Hands usually with 4 fingers, the feet usually with 5 toes. Roof of mouth with or without teeth, often a family characteristic (present in Ambystomatidae, Hynobiidae, Salamandridae). Vertebral centra usually amphicoelic. Many species can make squeaks or weak sounds, but this is biologically not as significant as it is in the frogs.

Protection against enemies is through cryptic and nocturnal behavior, excretion of foul-smelling substances (*Neurergus*), and/or poisonous secretions of skin glands, often associated with bright warning coloration (e. g., as in *Ensatina, Salamandra, Salamandrina*) or a breakable tail with preformed fracture point in many genera. Metamorphosed specimens usually lead a sedentary burrowing or cryptic life outside the breeding season, but there are also numerous permanantly aquatic forms in this group, as well as several that keep at least some larval characteristics. Several genera and species are either facultative (may or may not metamorphose depending on local environment) or obligate (unable to metamorphose under natural conditions) neotenics (e. g., *Haideotriton,* many *Eurycea,* and some populations and species of *Ambystoma*). Most species become active at only a few degrees above the freezing point. As cold-adapted, moisture-requiring animals they are exceedingly sensitive to heat and dryness. This also applies to most species in southern and tropical climes, which may undergo a summer dormancy period in cool, damp hiding places or live in higher altitudes or specialized cool microhabitats. Frost and even extreme freezing conditions are survived in decaying mulch, crevices or burrows, or even in mud under water.

Sperm transfer in salamanders is unique among vertebrates (apart from the particularly primitive suborder Cryptobranchoidea) because, in spite of the absence of a

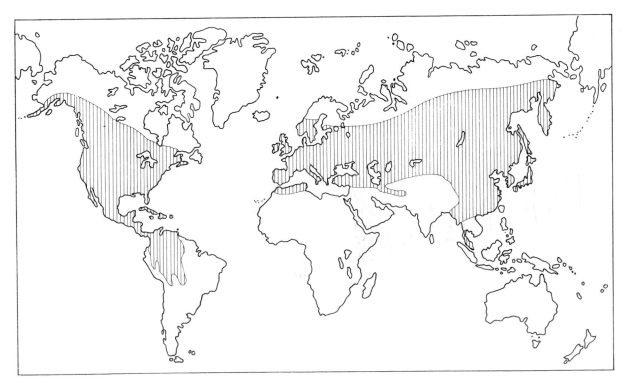

Distribution of the Caudata

copulatory organ, internal fertilization of the eggs occurs. The male deposits a spermatophore (special gelatinous capsule and support containing sperm) that is taken up by the female in her cloaca. Spermatophore exchange is preceded by often elaborate and species-specific courtship behaviors where the male is always the more active partner (a possible exception is *Amphiuma*, where several females may court the same male). Typically a female stores the sperm and may deposit eggs days to months (even years) after mating has been completed. Usually the eggs are deposited in water, but many Plethodontidae have their full development on land. The eggs give rise to more or less elongated larvae with 3 pairs of external gills and a paddle-like tail. In contrast to frog larvae, salamander larvae develop their front limbs first and the hind limbs later. Moreover, they are generally predatory, seldom feeding on plant matter. Adult salamanders that are largely terrestrial tend to reduce the length or presence of the larval stage, with many species laying large eggs that hatch out as adult-like young; *Salamandra* may give live-birth.

Keeping newts and salamanders is now less popular than it once was because many hobbyists have begun to keep tropical frogs. Herpetologists are forever indebted to Wolterstorff for his efforts to propagate newts and salamanders in captivity. His "tradescantia glass"—a glass container with a moist soil layer planted with *Tradescantia* runners and securely covered to create high humidity—still has a use in modern terrarium keeping, especially for rearing newly metamorphosed specimens and for the care of small species that are sensitive to dry air. A modification of his terrarium providing a similar microclimate is the "moss and rock" terrarium, where a gravel layer is barely covered with water upon which moss and rocks are placed. This now conforms largely to current perceptions of correct salamander care, where cluttered natural containers are replaced with clean and simple, controllable small containers. Such terrariums can be located without regard to light conditions as barely any plant growth is present, and can thus be positioned on the basis of thermal conditions, even in cool closets without much light. However, in spring and fall the terrarium should be moved to a location where there is morning sun (but protected against the direct impact of a hot midday sun). Since most Caudata are agile climbers (even the "aquatic" species) the terrarium must be securely covered. Unnecessary handling of these animals should be avoided due to more or less toxic skin secretions that irritate the mucous membranes. Wash your hands carefully after handling any salamander and never put your hand near your eyes, nose, or lips. (This also applies to any other amphibian.) Some of the larger forms can also administer painful bites (*Siren, Amphiuma*).

Many species can be bred easily with considerable predictability in captivity, but this presupposes excellent nutritional conditions and optimal cold winter dormancy. Some forms are difficult to re-adapt to water in spring (e. g., *Taricha*) after spending the winter on land. If the eggs are laid individually they are often difficult to spot with an untrained eye (*Triturus*). Adult salamanders often eat their own eggs (and even aggressively hunt the newly hatched larvae), thus when eggs have been noticed they should immediately be transferred to separate rearing containers. Be cautious scooping out the eggs, especially those adhering to the substrate. Only in forms that brood their eggs (many Plethodontidae, some Ambystomatidae) should the eggs be left with the female until they are hatched.

The larvae and young feed on small animals, including their siblings, and thus they should constantly be sorted into appropriate size groups in order to avoid cannibalism. Various protozoans make an ideal first food for newly hatched aquatic larvae, to be followed by brine shrimp nauplii (carefully washed) and daphnia and cyclops. (Caution: if cyclops are given in large quantities they may attack newly hatched larvae!) Larvae undergoing metamorphosis should be offered floating cork islands or similar objects and the water level should be lowered. From then on the young should be reared in small containers that can be monitored easily. The diet for the young can initially be heavy in whiteworms and fruitflies.

Systematic summary:
- Suborder Cryptobranchoidea: Cryptobranchidae, Hynobiidae.
- Suborder Sirenoidea: Sirenidae.
- Suborder Salamandroidea: Amphiumidae, Proteidae, Salamandridae.
- Suborder Ambystomatoidea: Ambystomatidae, Plethodontidae.

Caudiverbera LAURENTI, 1768 (= *Calyptocephalella* STRAND, 1928). Helmeted Water Toads. Monotypic genus of the Leptodactylidae. Central Chile. Related to *Batrachophrynus, Telmatobufo*, and *Telmatobius*. Found near rivers and lakes. Massive, toad-like frogs, the skin covered with warts. Pupil vertical. Tympanum clearly visible. Fingers free, toes webbed. Inner metatarsal tubercle a large, broadly oval spade; outer tubercle absent. Giant larvae.

Semiaquatic, burrowing during the day; a nocturnal predator. The main diet consists of fish, tadpoles, birds, and small mammals; animals its own body size are eagerly hunted.

Best kept individually in spacious unheated or only moderately heated aqua-terrariums with a thick substrate layer that permits deep burrowing.
- *C. caudiverbera* (LINNAEUS, 1758)(= *geayi* DUMERIL and BIBRON, 1841). Helmeted Water Toad. In excess of 23 cm. Olive with lighter spots. The giant tadpole was originally described as a lizard by Linnaeus.

Causus WAGLER, 1830. Night Adders. Genus of the Viperidae. Africa, except in the Sahara. 4 species. 40 to 80 cm. Body rarely distinct from head, with large scales. Rostral scale well-developed, especially in *C. defilippii*, so that the mouth becomes subterminal. Coloration variable, species-specific.

This genus exhibits warning behavior reminiscent of cobras, widening the neck region but not raising the anterior part of the body. The venom glands of *Causus* are greatly enlarged, extending through the anterior third of the body. However, the bite is relatively mild.

Nocturnal ground snakes found in proximity to water. The life cycle is strongly tied to annual dry and wet seasons. The preferred diet is various frogs. Mating is preceded by ritualistic fighting among males. Egg-layers, 8 to 26 eggs. Sperm storage of up to 5 months has been observed in *C. rhombeatus*.

Care of night adders should be in well-heated dry terrariums with bathing facilities and suitable hiding boxes. Undemanding, durable snakes. Caution: Venomous bite.

▪ *C. defilippii* (JAN, 1862). East Africa, including Zanzibar. Savannahs. Brownish yellow with dark rhomboids with light margins. Best adapted to dry habitats; burrowers.

▪ *C. resimus* (PETERS, 1862). Green Night Adder. East Africa; separated ecologically from *C. defilippii* by strong ties to wetter habitats. Uniformly green or with dark spots.

▪ *C. rhombeatus* (LICHTENSTEIN, 1823). Night Adder, Toad Adder, or Arrow Adder. Africa south of the Sahara, eastward to the Sudan and Somalia. Coloration and markings similar to *C. defilippii*, but with clearer, better defined dark V pointing forward on top of head. Ecologically a most adaptive species.

Cavernicolous: Cave-dwelling. Among herptiles, only some salamanders are truly cavernicolous. Strictly cavernicolous organisms are characterized by the loss of vision and pigmentation, e. g., the olm, *Proteus*, and several *Eurycea*. However, the web-toed salamanders (*Hydromantes*) do not display such extreme adaptations in spite of a more or less cavernicolous mode of life.

Caviidae: Guinea pigs. Breeding guinea pigs (*Cavia aperea porcellus*) for feeding reptiles is possible in principle, but due to the low number of progeny and long gestation period it is economically not very satisfactory. After a 64-day wait the breeder ends up with just 2 young. For best breeding results it is recommended to keep several females with one male. The diet consists primarily of fresh grasses and various vegetables (carrots, hay, lettuce [in moderate quantities], and others). One advantage of raising guinea pigs instead of rats and mice is that if left in the terrarium overnight guinea pigs will not attack any of the terrarium occupants.

Caviidae

Celestus: see *Diploglossus*, genus.

Cemophora COPE, 1860. Scarlet Snakes. Monotypic genus of the Colubridae, Colubrinae. Southeastern United States in dry habitats. To 75 cm. The presence of a red-black-yellow saddled pattern leads to confusion with *Micrurus fulvius* and *Lampropeltis triangulum*.

Nocturnal ground snakes. The diet includes lizards, small snakes, and small mammals; also feeds on lizard and snake eggs. Should be kept in a well-heated dry terrarium with ample hiding places.

▪ *C. coccinea* (BLUMBACH, 1788). Scarlet Snake. Southeastern United States, including Florida.

Cemophora coccinea

Centrolene JIMENEZ DE LA ESPADA, 1872. Giant Glass Frogs. Genus of the Centrolenidae. Pacific Andes. 1 species. The type species, *C. geckoideum*, was reported from the *selva* at Rio Napo (Amazon) but it actually occurs in treeless savannahs and the *paramos* of the high Andes. Appearance similar to treefrogs. Eyes small, the pupil horizontal. Tympanum very small, hardly visible. Vocal sac double, located in corners of mouth. Limbs strong. Large spatulate adhesive discs on tips of fingers and toes. Arms in males hypertrophied. Fingers and toes more or less completely webbed.

Natural history poorly known. Arboreal and terrestrial.

▪ *C. geckoideum* JIMENEZ DE LA ESPADA, 1872. Colombia, Ecuador. 8 cm. Brownish.

Centrolenella NOBLE, 1920 (= *Cochranella* TAYLOR, 1951). Glass Frogs. Genus of the Centrolenidae. Southern Mexico to Argentina. More than 60 species in montane rain forests and tropical rain forests (*selva*). Treefrog-like, delicate, more or less transparent. Pupil horizontal. Iris often silvery. Tympanum very small, often poorly visible. Limbs thin. Fingers basally or up to one-half webbed, toes more or less completely webbed; spatulate suction discs on finger and toe tips. Nearly all species uniformly yellow-green, frequently with white dots. Larvae unpigmented, as far as is known.

Most species are aboreal, crepuscular, night-active animals. Males vocalize with a high, delicate voice close to flowing waters. Spawning occurs above the water level. Hatching larvae slide into the water below and remain there until metamorphosis.

More delicate in captivity than are equal-sized Hylidae. Optimum transport conditions, strict maintenance of the required microclimate in a rain-forest terrarium, and a continuous supply of suitably small arthropods (fruitflies, small spiders) are prerequisites for successful captive maintenance.

- *C. buckleyi* (BOULENGER, 1882). Colombia, Ecuador, Venezuela. Montane rain forests. 3.5 cm.
- *C. euknemos* SAVAGE and STARRET, 1967. Costa Rica to Colombia. Montane. 2.5 cm.
- *C. fleischmanni* (BOETTGER, 1893). Mexico to Ecuador and Surinam. Montane and *selva* forests. 2 cm.
- *C. midas* LYNCH and DUELLMAN, 1973. Eastern Ecuador and northeastern Peru. *selva.* 2.5 cm.
- *C. munozorum* LYNCH and DUELLMAN, 1973. Eastern Ecuador and Peru. *selva.* 2 cm.
- *C. vanzolinii* (TAYLOR and COCHRAN, 1953). Southeastern Brasil to Argentina.

Centrolenella euknemos

Centrolenidae: Glass Frogs. Family of the Salientia, suborder Procoela. Neotropic. 3 genera: *Centrolene, Centrolenella, Teratohyla.* Shape and coloration much like treefrogs. Vertebrae procoelic, pectoral girdle arciferal, calcaneum bone fused and an additional small bone between the last and next-to-last finger and toe joints, terminal toe bone T-shaped. Finger and toe tips enlarged into spatulate suction discs.

Cerastes LAURENTI, 1768. African Horned Vipers. Genus of the Viperidae, Viperinae. North Africa and Arabia in deserts, especially in sand areas. 2 species. To 75 cm. The characteristic, strongly enlarged supraorbital scales ("horns") in *C. cerastes* vary in size between specimens and are population-dependent; they usually are more or less clearly developed but may be totally absent. The sides of the body have obliquely positioned, serrated scales that produce a characteristic scraping warning sound (just as in *Echis*). The dorsal scales are strongly keeled. Sandy brown, sometimes with a pattern of darker spots.

Cerastes cerastes gasparetti

Forward movement is by "side-winding." These snakes are rapid burrowers into loose sand; through lateral shovel-like movements of the flattened flanks, only the eyes and/or horns remain above ground. The diet is mainly lizards (*Acanthodactylus, Scincus*) or small mammals. Egg-layers, 8 to 22 eggs, incubation period 4 to 7 weeks.

These venomous snakes require a well-heated dry terrarium with a substantial temperature drop during the night. They need moist hiding places or a deep sand layer as the substrate. They often are difficult to adapt to captivity because of unsatisfactory collecting and transport conditions,

Cerastes vipera

but after acclimation they become hardy and durable specimens.

• *C. cerastes* (LINNAEUS, 1758). Horned Viper. Morocco to Arabia. 2 subspecies in sandy habitats, rocky deserts, and mountain regions.

• *C. vipera* (LINNAEUS, 1758). Common Sand Viper. Found only in sandy habitats in the Sahara Desert. In contrast to *C. cerastes*, it is always without horns.

Cerathyla: see *Hemiphractus*, genus.

Ceratobatrachus BOULENGER, 1884. Monotypic genus of the Ranidae. Solomon Islands. Closely related to *Batrachylodes* and *Platymantis*. To 8 cm. Head conspicuously flat, triangular. Large adhesive discs on the outer fingers, toes not webbed. Natural history presumably like *Platymantis*.

• *C. guentheri* BOULENGER, 1884. Coloration highly variable.

Ceratophora GRAY, 1834. Horned Agamas. Genus of the Agamidae. Sri Lanka. 3 species. Together with *Lyriocephalus* and *Cophotis*, included in the subfamily Lyriocephaliinae. In highlands close to water. To 25 cm. No gular pouch or folds. Nape crest barely indicated. A horn-like nasal process, larger in males. Tail about ⅔ of total length. Mainly olive-brown with darker spots and lighter lines along sides. Color changes possible.

Lives on or close to the ground, among low bushes.

Normal room temperatures are sufficient for *Ceratophora*, although a low-wattage light for occasional warming up should be present. High humidity necessary; some like to bathe. Diet includes various slow-moving insects, earthworms, and slugs.

Ceratophora tennenti

• *C. aspera* GUENTHER, 1864. Sri Lanka. On the ground among leaves and roots. Easily 12 cm. Nasal projection leaf-like and covered with small scales.

• *C. stoddarti* GRAY, 1834. Horned Agama. Sri Lanka. In mountain regions to more than 2000 m elevation. 25 cm. Nasal projection drawn out into a point, anteriorly without smaller scales.

• *C. tennenti* GUENTHER, 1861. Rhinoceros Agama. In highlands close to water, on the ground and on low bushes. 25 cm. Nasal projection blunt, leaf-like, with small scales. Likes to bathe.

Ceratophrys WIED, 1824. Horned Frogs. Genus of the Leptodactylidae. Tropical and subtropical South America east of the Andes Mountains; some species in the Pacific and Caribbean coastal regions of northern South America. Depending upon taxonomic opinions, 7-14 species. Frequently confused with *Proceratophrys*. In *selva* and *montana*, some species also in dry regions Body plump and

Ceratophrys aurita

massive, the skin covered with warts. Head exceptionally large, the mouth very wide (mouth width sometimes larger than half head/body length). Tongue heart-shaped, free in back. Pupil horizontal. Upper eyelid drawn out into a horn or tubercle in some species, giving rise to the common name. Fingers free, toe webbing variable and species-specific. 2 metatarsal tubercles, the inner one shovel-like. First finger longer than second.

Vocalization in some species reminiscent of bovine-like bellowing. Diurnal or crepuscular ground-dwellers that remain partially buried and lie in wait for prey. They will swallow prey up to their own body size, feeding on frogs, lizards, mice, and large insects. When threatened, the large

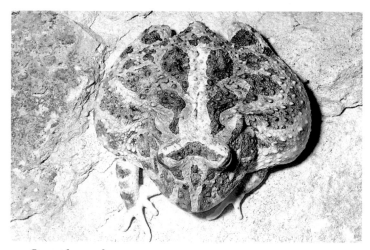

Ceratophrys calcarata

Ceratophrys aurita

Ceratophrys ornata

species are surprisingly fearless and aggressive, even jumping toward the enemy and biting. *Ceratophrys* spawns in standing waters such as jungle pools and small river lagoons.

Because of their grotesque appearance and bright coloration, some species are in great demand as terrarium specimens, although due to their burrowing behavior they are not readily visible in a properly set up terrarium. They should be kept in a rain-forest terrarium with a large bottom area covered with a thick layer of soft, slightly moist soil. Hiding places such as large bark pieces, roots, and similar material must be available; water dish essential. Because of the high metabolic rates of these frogs the substrate should be changed frequently. Only specimens of about the same size should kept together. These are highly predaceous and cannibalistic frogs that really should not be trusted with other animals.

▪ *C. cornuta* (LINNAEUS, 1758). Common Horned Frog. Northeastern Brasil, Guyana, western Ecuador. To 20 cm. Colorful red-brown or dark brown spotted pattern. Bron-

Ceratophrys cornuta

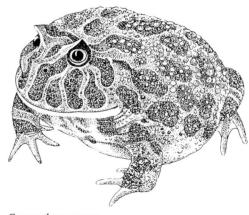

Ceratophrys ornata

Ceratophrys calcarata

Ceratophrys ornata

ze-colored iris with a horizontal red stripe. Eyelid projections long and pointed. Toes with webbing halfway to tips.
▪ *C. ornata* (BELL, 1843). Ornate Horned Frog. Eastern Brasil and eastern Argentina. To 12 cm. Bright green with large reddish black spots with yellow margins. Eyelids with triangular projections, not extended horns.
▪ *C. varia* WIED, 1824. Short-horned Horned Frog. Eastern Brasil. To 18 cm. Shape and coloration as in *C. cornuta*, but toes with webbing only at their origin.

Cerberus CUVIER, 1829. Dog-faced Watersnakes. Genus of the Colubridae, Homalopsinae. Coastal regions of India (Bombay) and Indo-China, throughout the entire Indo-Australian Archipelago to northern Australia. Also found on the Nicobar Islands and along the coast of Sri Lanka. 2 species. (In the Philippines is found only the closely related genus *Hurria*.) Frequently found in brackish water regions of river mouths, but also up to 100 miles offshore. Males to 0.75 cm, females to 1 m. Surface of head covered with relatively small scales; head distinctly set off from body, with strongly protruding, fairly large eyes. Body scales strongly keeled, the keels forming longitudinal rows. Dorsum either uniformly dark or interrupted with darker crossbands. A longitudinal lateral band marks off the whitish abdominal region and a dark band extends from the roundish snout along both sides through the eye region to the sides.

Live-bearers, 8 to 26 young, 17 to 20 cm long. Among the hardiest species of this subfamily. Maintain in a brackish water aquarium.
▪ *C. rhynchops* (SCHNEIDER, 1799).

Cercaspis WAGLER, 1830. Monotypic genus of the Colubridae, Xenoderminae. Sri Lanka. Due to its characteristic vertebral morphology, which resembles strongly that of the Neotropical genus *Xenopholis*, it is included in the subfamily Xenoderminae, but some systematists consider this genus to be a wolf snake (Lycodontinae) on the basis of its dentition. Found up to elevations of 1200 m. About 75 cm. Head longish, normally scaled; strongly keeled dorsal scales. Marked with white to yellowish rings against a black background, the rings becoming narrower with increasing age.

Ground snakes. Little is known about their biology, though they are rather common.
▪ *C. carinatus* (KUHL, 1820).

Cercosaura WAGLER, 1830. Monotypic genus of the Teiidae. Tropical South America. In semi-moist but sunny habitats in dense ground vegetation. To 20 cm. Remiscent of the Old World *Takydromus*. Tail 2.5 times in snout-vent length. Dorsal scales with weak keels. Brown with dark longitudinal stripes that become lighter along the flanks. Sides sometimes also with light spots. Abdominal region white, tail red.

The diet consists of arthropods.
▪ *C. ocellata* WAGLER, 1830.

Cernov, Sergej Alexandrovitch (1903 – 1964): Russian herpetologist working mainly at the Zoological Museum, Academy of Sciences in Leningrad. Worked on the amphibians section for *Animal World of the USSR* (in Russian, 1936 to 1953), *Key to the Soviet Herpetofauna* (1949, together with Terentjew), and herpetofaunal papers on Armenia (1939) and Tadshikistan (1959).

Ceropegia L. Waxflowers. Genus of the Asclepiadaceae. Mainly in Africa, but also Arabia, Asia, Australia, and the Canary Islands. About 200 species. Shrubs and small bushes, recumbent or growing upright. Undemanding, they require moderate moisture and a very bright location. 10-12° C. sufficient for the winter, together with sparing amounts of water. Reproduction is through cuttings or through nodules being formed on the buds of the leaf axis. *Ceropegia* with hanging leaves are ideal as basket plants.
▪ *C. distincta* N. E. BR. Leaves to 4 cm.
▪ *C. radicans* SCHLECHTER. Creeping succulent shrub.
▪ *C. stapeliiformis* HAW. Upright growing shrub.
▪ *C. woodii* SCHLECHTER. Shrub with hanging shoots. Best known species.

Cestoda: Tapeworms. Class of flatworms that are parasitic as adults and larvae in amphibians and reptiles. Determination of cestode infestation in live animals is on the basis of fecal examination for the presence of cestode eggs. Damage to the host usually takes the form of loss of condition and lesions of the intestinal mucosa, which can lead to secondary bacterial infections. Only mass infestation with cestodes leads to more precise clinical manifestations, yet even these are due mainly to secondary infections (amoebic dysentery, stomatitis, *Pseudomonas* diseases). Edemas, especially in giant snakes, skin nodules with exudates showing cestode larval stages, and the frequent discharge of cloacal fluids in snakes are symptomatic. Reinfestation in captivity is impossible due to the absence of intermediate hosts.

Therapy: Niclosamid in dosages of 200 to 400 mg/kg body weight and Praziquantel in dosages of 3 to 5 to 20 to 30 mg (for *Bothridium* and *Duthiersia*) per kg body weight. Fecal samples of new arrivals should always be checked 2 to 3 times and if necessary be treated immediately. 4 to 6 weeks later the success of the therapy should be determined by re-examining another fecal sample.

Cestoda: *Oochoristica parvovaria*

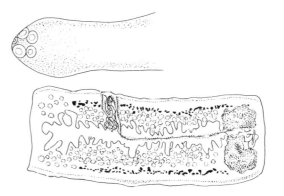

Cestoda: *Ophiotaenia*, head above, proglottid below

Chacophrys REIG and LIMESES, 1963. Genus of Leptodactylidae. Insufficiently differentiated from *Ceratophrys* but considered by some systematists as a monotypic genus. South America, in dry Chacos. Very cannibalistic.
▪ *C. pierotti* (VELLARD, 1948). Argentina. To 5.5 cm. Brown above, olive along the sides, with large, light-bordered spots.

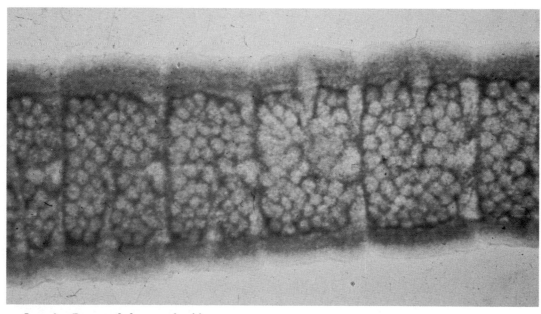

Cestoda: *Proteocephalus*, proglottid

Chalarodon PETERS, 1854. Monotypic genus of the Iguanidae. Madagascar, primarily in steppes. 15 cm, slender. Similar to *Tropidurus*. Dorsal crest present.

A diurnal ground-dweller feeding on arthropods. For details of care and maintenance see *Liolaemus*.

▪ *C. madagascariensis* PETERS, 1854. Southwest Madagascar. To 15 cm.

Chalcides LAURENTI, 1768. Barrel Skinks. Genus of the Scincidae. Mediterranean Region, Africa to Somalia, and western Asia to India. About 10 species in more or less dry habitats, some also in damp meadows. 15 to 40 cm. Slender to extremely elongated, the body cylindrical. Head conical. Tail about equal to snout-vent length. Limbs short and 5-toed or very small and 3-toed, essentially useless for locomotion. Yellowish to brown with variable markings.

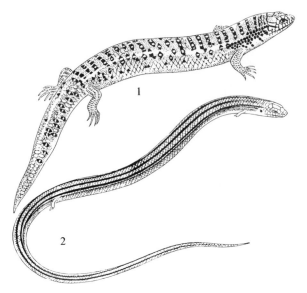

Chalcides ocellatus (1) und *Chalcides chalcides* (2)

Diurnal ground-dwellers. Diet mainly arthropods. Ovoviviparous to viviparous, 4 to 12 young.

Maintain like European lacertids. Climbing facilities not essential. A short winter dormancy period is advisable.

▪ *C. bedriagai* BOSCA, 1880. Spanish Barrel Skink. Spain and Portugal. 15 cm. Similar to *C. ocellatus* but substantially smaller.

▪ *C. chalcides* (L., 1758). Three-toed Skink. Western Mediterranean Region. 40 cm. Grass and brush. Extremely elongated, with very short three-toed limbs. Dark longitudinal stripes.

▪ *C. ocellatus* (FORSKAL, 1775). Ocellated Barrel Skink. Southern Italy and northern Africa to northwestern India. To 30 cm. Dry habitats. Relatively strong, 5-toed limbs.

Chalcides ocellatus

Chalcides sepsoides

Chamaeleo chamaeleon

Chamaeleo hoehneli

Irregular black and white crossbands. Requires much heat. Quarrelsome.

Chamaeleo LAURENTI, 1768. Chameleons. Genus of the Chamaeleonidae (including *Microsaura* GRAY, 1865). Africa and Madagascar; *C. chamaeleon* also in southern Europe, Asia Minor, India, Sri Lanka. About 70 cm. In rain forests to savannahs, some also in mountain regions, rarely in steppe-like habitats. 10 to 60 cm. Often with head appendages, dorsal crests and—less commonly—tail and abdominal crests. Tail long, prehensile. Scales on soles with smooth appearance (spiny in *Brookesia*). Claws always simple.

Strictly arboreal, with the exception of *C. chamaeleon*, which is found mainly on the ground (especially in dry habitats). Only males during courtship and females ready to lay eggs move to the ground. Most species are egg-layers, but some are ovoviviparous. For biological details see Chamaeleonidae.

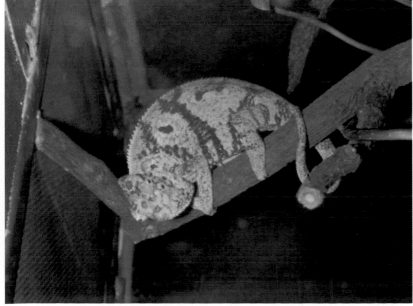

Chamaeleo chamaeleon

Chamaeleo dilepis

Chamaeleo hoehneli

Chamaeleo dilepis

Chamaeleo cristatus

Care and breeding difficult. One of the main problems is obtaining healthy animals. Most imported specimens are heavily parasitized. Long periods in transit and the stress of adjustment to new surroundings favor a rapid increase in the parasite load, thus causing an overall loss of condition. Under these conditions previously non-pathogenic endoparasites can cause diseases or lead to the demise of the animals. The pathogens most frequently involved are *Salmonella, Coccidia, Trichomonas,* and filiaria and other worms. Characteristic symptoms of a deteriorating condition are sunken or closed eyes.

These reptiles should be cared for in reasonably large and not too low terrariums that are equipped with climbing branches and some plants. Many species are most contented in a real plant thicket. Adequate ventilation is essential for species from tropical rain forests, but drafts must be avoided. Accumulating wetness and simultaneous high humidity are incompatible and must be avoided. It is often helpful to pass entering air over a dish with water. Since most species are quarrelsome (although physical aggression is rare, the continuous stress can severely affect weakened animals), it is advisable to use several smaller terrariums rather than a single large one. It is also sometimes easier to keep several females together instead of a pair, but this varies from one situation to the next and thus should be closely monitored.

Chameleons from tropical forests must be given day temperatures between 24 and 28° C. (with a slight reduction at night). Keep montane species between 22 and 25° C. They also require a substantial nocturnal temperature reduction, which is essential for the well-being of these species; the preferred nighttime temperatures are between 10 and 15° C., a range that is tolerable for these species (*C. jacksoni* can even tolerate values around 0° C. without any ill effect and is quite suited for free maintenance in a room with larger plants or with some additional climbing branches). Many chameleons prefer dead branches over live plants. A localized radiant light source must be accessible to the animals because chameleons like to warm up under a lamp

Chamaeleo jacksoni, ♀

Chamaeleo dilepis

Chamaeleo jacksoni, ♂♂

Chamaeleo chamaeleon

Chamaeleo jacksoni

Chamaeleo jacksoni

Chamaeleo jacksoni, 1-day male

during the early morning hours. During the summer months the montane species can be kept in an outdoor enclosure and other species must be given a few hours of ultraviolet radiation. During the colder season occasional ultraviolet radiation together with calcium and vitamin supplements should be provided.

All chameleons require a fair amount of drinking water. In nature these animals receive ample water in the form of dew and precipitation on leaves; they do not learn to drink from a container. The obligatory regular spraying of the plants in a terrarium also is—due to rapid evaporation—rarely sufficient. A drop dispenser is often useful, but even more satisfactory is offering water individually to all animals by means of a pipette. This permits better control of the animals (excessive drinking by individuals often indi-

cates a disease problem) and also affords an opportunity to give regular calcium and vitamin supplements to all animals. Offering drinking water 2 to 3 times a week for adults is sufficient; juveniles should receive water on a daily basis.

The food requirement for smaller, growing animals and pregnant females is substantial. The diet should be as varied as possible. Various arthropods are acceptable. Large chameleon species even take newborn mice. Some species are very fond of snails (with and without shells), which are picked directly off the branches. Sooner or later all chameleons learn to eat from a food dish, but feeding individuals with a feeding stick or by hand affords better diet control. Hobbyists are cautioned against a monotonous diet, such as only mealworms.

Only in recent times has there been any marked success of breeding in captivity, especially among the montane, ovoviviparous species from East Africa, such as *C. bitaeniatus, C. hoehneli,* and *C. jacksoni,* which have been bred over several generations. Longevity records usually refer only to individual specimens, but breeding animals as a rule do not live longer than a few years. The pregnancies of females as well as the continuous unrest among courting males appear to place significant stress on these animals. Imported females that are fully grown are usually pregnant on arrival. Females willing to mate usually fend off an approaching male only for a short period.

Pregnant females must be separated from males in order to eliminate stress. Most of the ovoviviparous species bred in captivity give birth to from 7 to 40 young that burst through the birth membrane immediately after or during

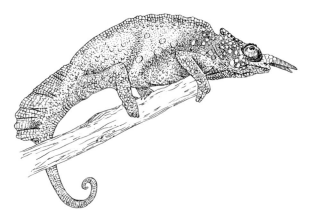

Chamaeleo montium, ♂

Chamaeleo pumilus

birth and then without delay start to actively climb about in the branches. Gestation varies from 3 to 10 months, and appears to be strongly dependent upon maintenance temperatures.

Breeding the oviparous species is more problematic, and most of these species are also more difficult to keep. The females bury their eggs (in excess of 40 eggs in larger species, in some instances more than 70). A flowerpot placed in the terrarium and filled with humus makes an ideal egg-laying site. The incubation period is 3 to 10 months. The

young are fast-growing and will soon feed on aphids and fruitflies. Medium-size species in which the young are about 5 to 6 cm at birth start feeding on these at latest after one week and soon take prey the size of houseflies. Half the adult size is often reached after only 6 months, and many species are sexually mature in less than 1 year.

▪ *C. chamaeleon* (LINNAEUS, 1758). Common Chameleon. North Africa, southern Europe (southern Spain, Crete, Canary Islands), and Asia Minor to India and Sri Lanka. About 4 subspecies in relatively dry habitats. Easily 30 cm. Distinct helmet and low dorsal crest. Egg-layers. Difficult to keep and often susceptible to diseases. Well-defined day-/night rhythm. A cool winter dormancy period (around 10° C.) is required by animals from the northern edge of the range.

▪ *C. bitaeniatus* FISCHER, 1884. Double-banded Chameleon. East Africa. Mountain forests to more than 3000 m. To 20 cm. High helmet and distinct dorsal and throat crests; some with low bony ridge above snout. 1 to 2 rows of large conical scales along sides. Often with a light lateral stripe on a usually blue-green background color. Ovoviviparous. Does well in captivity and has been bred for several generations.

▪ *C. dilepis* LEACH, 1819. Lobed Chameleon. Tropical and

Chamaeleo melleri

Chamaeleo parsoni

Chamaeleo sp.

southern Africa. Prefers savannahs. Easily to 30 cm. Skin folds on the nape. Egg-layer.

▪ *C. fischeri* REICHENOW, 1887. Fischer's Chameleon. East African montane species up to about 3000 m. To 50 cm. 2 membranous large-scaled projections on snout; helmet low. Egg-layer.

▪ *C. jacksoni* BOULENGER, 1896. Three-horned Chameleon. Mountain forests to more than 3000 m in East Africa. To 35 cm. Males with 3 long, forward pointing head horns, these weak or absent in females. Helmet low; a low serrated dorsal crest. Often gray-green with a "lichen-like" pattern. Males may be bright green. Ovoviviparous. Durable and hardy in captivity. Has been bred repeatedly.

▪ *C. hoehneli* STEINDACHNER, 1891. Helmeted Chameleon. East African Highlands. To barely 20 cm. Has a tall helmet and distinct throat and dorsal crests. Very similar to *C. bitaeniatus* and often considered to be a subspecies of this. Ovoviviparous. Adapts well to captivity and is frequently bred.

Chamaeleo (Microsaura) sp.

Chamaeleo (Microsaura) sp.

• *C. melleri* (GRAY, 1865). Meller's Chameleon. East Africa in montane forests. To 60 cm. Large nape folds and a coarsely serrated dorsal crest. Very colorful. An egg-layer.
• *C. montium* BUCHHOLZ, 1874. Mountain Chameleon. Cameroons and adjacent countries in mountain forests. To 35 cm. 2 long rostral horns and a fin-like crest on the back and at the tail base. An egg-layer.
• *C. pumilus* (GMELIN, 1789). Dwarf Chameleon. Southern Africa, in mountains. Easily to 15 cm. Has a low dorsal crest and short throat crest or beard. Hardy and durable. Has been bred repeatedly.

Chamaeleolis BOULENGER, 1885. Crested Anoles. Genus of the Iguanidae. Cuba. 2 species. 30 to 33 cm, laterally compressed. Tail length equal to body length. Head large, with a characteristic low occipital helmet even in females. Very large whitish gray gular pouch.

Arboreal, often remaining motionless for long periods of time. Feed on arthropods. Egg-layers. For details on care refer to *Anolis*.
• *C. chamaeleontides* DUMERIL and BIBRON, 1837. Crested Anole. Grayish with differently colored (black to red) spots.

Chamaeleonidae: Chameleons. Family of the Squamata (also spelled Chamaeleontidae). Africa and Madagascar; *Chamaeleo chamaeleon* is also found in parts of southern Europe, Asia Minor, India, and Sri Lanka. More than 80 living species. In tropical rain forests, savannahs, montane rain forests, and rarely in steppes and semideserts. Fossil records known from the early Tertiary; many authors consider *Mimeosaurus* of the Upper Cretaceous in Mongolia as a true chamaeleonid. The living species are placed in the genera *Chamaeleo* and *Brooksia*.

The chameleons deviate from other lizards in several characteristics related to their mode of life. These differences are so great that for a long time chameleons were placed in their own suborder, Rhiptoglossa ("with a worm-like tongue"), as the opposite all other lizards. The chameleons represent a specialized side branch that can be traced back to the older representatives of the Agamidae, thus they belong in the family series Iguania. This is supported, among other characters, by the non-replaceable acrodont teeth, the absence of pterygoid teeth, fusion of the vomerines, and the surface ornamentation of the hemipenis. Numerous skull and skeletal bones are partially reduced; the clavicles are absent.

Chameleons are more or less laterally compressed. The middorsal line and occasionaly also the midabdominal line may have crests. The dorsal area of the head has 2 lateral ridges leading over the eyes, and at the back of the head there is often an additional median ridge that terminates in a helmet-like structure on the occiput. Occasionally there are wide skin folds on the nape, as in *C. dilepis*. The males of many species have membranous or bony snout projections; in the extreme case there are 4 internally ossified, long horns (*C. quadricornis*).

The large eyes are located in large cavities alongside the head. The lids are fused and leave only the round pupil visible; with closed eyes the lid cleft is vertical. Both eyes can be moved independently of each other (as also is the case in some other lizards), so a chameleon usually perceives two completely different pictures and thus can observe its entire surroundings without having to move the head. Only during the capture of prey are both eyes focused for a brief period upon the prey. The limbs are nearly of equal length. The toes are modified by fusion into grasping claws; the front limbs have 2 outer toes and 3 inner toes, with the reverse arrangement on the hind limbs. Adhesive cilia are present along the insides of the toes. Very similar structures are also found along the ventral side of the tail (at least in *Chamaeleo*), which is prehensile and when not in use is kept coiled up.

Chameleons have developed a unique hunting method. The prey is virtually shot down with the extremely elongated tongue. Young chameleons can reach a distance several times their own body length. Generally the tongue is retracted into the back of the mouth and basally surrounds the extended hyoid bone. The rapid projection of the tongue is achieved through contraction of circular muscles at the base of the tongue and through contraction of the muscles that connect the hyoid bone and thoracic cavity. The tip of the tongue is thickened and at the anterior end is widened and has a depression, so the chameleon can use the tongue to reach with much like an elephant's trunk. In this depression are located glands that make the tip of the tongue sticky.

Also notable is the physiological color change in *Chamaeleo*. More important than mere color adaptation to the surroundings is the fact that the color is an expression of the psychological and physical condition of the animal. Chameleons at rest are generally lighter than those that are excited. Coloration plays an important part in rivalry fights. There are also numerous photoreceptors in the skin. The side in bright light is often darker. Temperature also influences coloration. But there are also persistent reports about attempts to imitate the surroundings, and it is alleged that one particular *C. africanus* imitated the checkerboard pattern of a curtain. A certain camouflage function for the color changes has to be acknowledged. The color scheme (different from species to species) extends from light yellow, green, blue, and brown to jet black, the latter as a fright or submissive coloration. Apart from that there are also different patterns involving yet other shades. Among 1300 *C. chamaeleon* that were examined, scientists

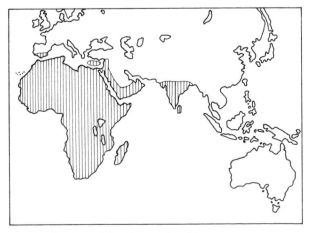

Distribution of the Chamaeleonidae

found no fewer than 104 different variations.

Chameleons are arboreal, but most prefer bushes and shrubs over taller trees. They rarely move down to the ground (exceptions: *C. chamaeleon* and *Brookesia*), except males in search of a female and females preparing to deposit their eggs. Some species will drop to the ground when endangered. Most species sit motionless for hours on a branch; they are rarely active hunters, instead preferring to lie in wait for their prey to pass by. The main diet consists of various arthropods and small vertebrates; snails are also taken.

All chameleons are essentially solitary. A chance encounter of males will inevitably lead to threat displays consisting of head nodding and offering the flattened and thus enlarged broadside to the opponent (chameleons can also inflate themselves, which is frequently done when threatened). These encounters often turn into biting matches or in those species that have horns this can lead to a regular battle. The loser often turns black and moves away. In an encounter among unevenly matched animals, the weaker one will display submissive behavior by lateral body movements (swinging from side to side) together with a change of color. Even females unwilling to mate tend to fend off males with the same side to side swaying motion.

During mating the male climbs onto the back of the female. Generally copulation lasts only a few minutes. The females are capable of storing sperm, so one mating can last for the entire life of the female. It must be remembered that these animals have a fairly short lifespan, although individual animals have been kept in captivity for quite some time. Most species are egg-layers, but those from cooler mountain regions are ovoviviparous.

For care and maintenance see *Chamaeleo*. All species are considered threatened.

Chamaeleontidae: see Chamaeleonidae, family.

Chamaelinorops SCHMIDT, 1919. Genus of the Iguanidae. Hispaniola, highlands. 1 species. Small *Anolis*-like lizards with laterally compressed body (as in *Chamaeleolis*) and compressed toes with lamellae. Arboreal.
• *C. barbouri* SCHMIDT, 1919. Haiti and Dominican Republic. 7.5 cm.

Chamaelycus BOULENGER, 1919. Genus of the Colubridae, Lycodontinae. Tropical central Africa. 2 species. Formerly included in *Lycophidion*. Found in tropical forests. 35 cm. Body stout, head only slightly distinct. Back covered by irregular black crossbands that may break up into large spots against a brownish background.
Burrowing ground snakes. The diet is mainly lizards.
• *C. fasciatum* (GUENTHER, 1858). Sierra Leone to Gabon and the Congo Basin.
• *C. parkeri* (ANGEL, 1934). Congo Basin.

Chamaesaura SCHNEIDER, 1801. South African Snake Lizards. Genus of the Cordylidae. Southern Africa, in montane grasslands. 4 species. 40 to 65 cm. Extremely slender, snake-like. Head pointed, tail usually more than 3 times snout-vent length. Limbs reduced; may have 5 digits on all limbs to limbs absent. Scales large, strongly keeled, arranged in regular longitudinal rows. Primarily brown with (usually) dark longitudinal stripes.

Diurnal. Forward movement snake-like. Do not burrow. The diet includes various arthropods, mainly grasshoppers. Ovoviviparous; 2 to 6, rarely 10, young.

For care and maintenance refer to *Cordylus*, but these lizards need a slighly more moist environment with day/-night temperature variations of at least 10° C. Part of the terrarium should be set up with a dense cover of thin branches or dry grass tufts strewn over the bottom.
• *C. aenea* (FITZINGER, 1843). Transvaal Snake Lizard. South Africa. 40 cm. Limbs with 5 toes.
• *C. anguina* (L., 1758). Cape Snake Lizard. South Africa northward to Angola and Mozambique. Easily to 60 cm. 1 or 2 toes and fingers.
• *C. macrolepis* (COPE, 1862). Large-scale Snake Lizard. Southern Africa. To 65 cm. Front limbs absent or smaller than one body scale.

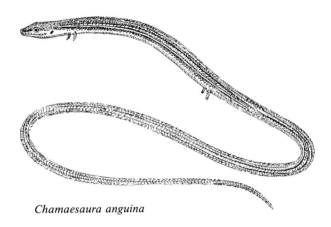

Chamaesaura anguina

Chamaetortus GUENTHER, 1864. Monotypic genus of the Colubridae, Boiginae. Eastern, central, and southern Africa. Sometimes included in the Lycodontinae. Found in damp habitats (gallery forests, wet grassland). To 60 cm. Head distinct; eyes large. Pupil vertical. Smooth dorsal scales. Dorsum brown with small white spots.

Nocturnal, feeding primarily on frogs (*Hyperolius, Arthroleptis*). Maintain in a well-heated forest terrarium. Caution: Venomous bites.
• *C. aulicus* GUENTHER, 1864. Tanzania to Mozambique and the Republic of South Africa. 2 subspecies. Very rare.

Chaperina MOCQUARD, 1892. Monotypic genus of the Microhylidae. Tropical Southeast Asia in tropical rain forests (100 to 1800 m). Slender, smooth-skinned, with horizontal pupils. Tympanum covered by skin and poorly visible. Elbows and heels with distinct thorny points. Long legs. Fingers free, the toes with webbing at base. Tips of digits enlarged into adhesive discs. 1 long inner metatarsal tubercle. Larvae elongated, mouth terminal, without enlarged lips, horny formations, and papillae; anal tube to the right of ventral skin fold.

Adult specimens are largely diurnal and remain on the ground or among dense undergrowth. The larvae develop in shallow water-filled detritus-rich holes on the ground or in plant funnels.

Should be kept in a rain-forest terrarium at temperatures between 25 and 29° C.
• *C. fuscus* MOCQUARD, 1892. Malayan Peninsula, Kali-

Charina bottae

Charina bottae

mantan, southern Philippines. 2 cm (males), 2.5 cm (females). Dorsum yellow with reticulated brown pattern.

Charina GRAY, 1849. Rubber Boas. Monotypic genus of the Boidae. Western North America. Grasslands, outer forest areas, coniferous forests. To 70 cm. Very similar to *Eryx*. Head not set off from body, edge of the snout overhanging the mouth. Tail short and round, giving impression of a second head. Dorsum without markings, medium brown; ventral region lighter, with diffuse spots along sides.

Ground-dweller in coniferous forests, frequently under decaying logs and in grassland under rocks. They are good swimmers and marginal climbers. The main diet is small mammals and lizards. Juveniles also feed on insects.

Rubber boas should be kept in a moderately heated terrarium with a sufficiently deep layer of soft substrate for burrowing. Hiding places and bathing facilities must be provided. Should be given a winter dormancy period for 2 to 3 months. Generally undemanding and hardy. Actual breeding in captivity not yet reported, but there have been repeated rearings of young (2 to 8) from pregnant females collected in the wild.

• *C. bottae* (BLAINVILLE, 1835). Rubber Boa. Found from British Columbia in the north to southern California in the south and Wyoming in the east.

Charina bottae

Checklist: Faunal list for a particular area or taxonomic group or both. May contain important faunistic and/or taxonomic information about the herpetofauna of a particular area or taxonomic group. Frequently supplemented by identification keys and specific remarks. A classic example of a checklist is *An annotated checklist and key to the snakes of Mexico* by H. M. Smith and E. H. Taylor, 1945.

Chelidae: Snake-neck Turtles. Family of the Pleurodira. South America, Australia, New Guinea. Genera include *Chelodina, Chelus, Elseya, Emydura, Hydromedusa, Phrynops, Platemys, Pseudemydura,* and *Rheodytes*. In various freshwater habitats. Carapace fairly typical, but shows some variation from "normal" turtle patterns. Has a tendency toward regression of the neural bones, which are absent in *Platemys* and *Emydura*, while in *Phrynops* only the anterior ones are still present. The scutes of the vertebral series always present, however. The long neck is characteristic and (including the head) can exceed the length of the carapce. In rest the neck is twisted off to one side; in the related Pelomedusidae the anterior section of the neck can still be retracted and only the remainder is twisted against the front edge of the carapace.

The genera *Elseya, Emydura, Phrynops,* and *Rheodytes* live in rivers, but the true snake-neck turtles (*Chelodina* and *Hydromedusa*) frequent small but rather variable bodies of water. Quiet-flowing jungle rivers with ample vegetation are preferred by *Chelus* and *Platemys*. Equally as variable as the habitats frequented by different genera are their requirements for basking. Most Chelidae are carnivorous; only *Emydura* will also take in some supplementary plant matter.

Chelidae must be kept in aqua-terrariums. *Emydura* and *Elseya* require ample swimming room, yet very large *Chelus* do not require much space.

Chelodina FITZINGER, 1826. Australian Snake-neck Turtles. Genus of the Chelidae. Australia and New Guinea. 7 or 8 species in small and large bodies of water. Carapace length to 35 cm, rigid, depressed. Intergular plate of plastron completely enclosed by adjacent plastral plates, not touching carapace edge (except in extremely large speci-

Chelodina longicollis

Chelodina longicollis

mens). Head and neck nearly as long as carapace. The highly flexible neck permits foraging in mud as well as snorkeling.

Carnivorous. Substantial longevity in captivity. Has been bred repeatedly. The incubation period is 75 to 170 days at 23 and 30° C., respectively, in an incubator; for *C. longicollis* under natural conditions the incubation is 118 to 150 days.

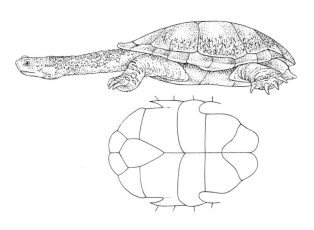

Chelodina longicollis

Chelodina expansa

▪ *C. longicollis* (SHAW, 1802). Smooth Snake-neck Turtle. Eastern Australia. To 30 cm.
▪ *C. novaeguinea* BOULENGER, 1888. New Guinea Snake-neck Turtle. New Guinea and adjacent islands, northeastern Australia. To 20 cm. Carapace plates with furrows. Skin very dark.

Chelonia LATREILLE, 1802. Green Turtles. Genus of the Cheloniidae. Found in all warm seas. 2 species. Carapace length to 1.4 m. Carapace with 4 pairs of costal shields. Bridge between carapace and plastron with 5 plates. Cara-

Chelodina longicollis

Chelonia mydas

pace plates with attractive marbled pattern that can be used as "tortoise shell."

Meat considered to be a delicacy. Threatened with extinction in some areas due to overfishing. Herbivorous, feeding mainly on sea grasses in shallow water.

Behavior and captive maintenance as for other sea turtles. Incubation of eggs takes 48 to 80 days at 32 or 27° C., respectively, in an incubator. In the wild 47 to 80 days are required.

▪ *C. depressa* GARMAN, 1880. Flatback Turtle. Coastal regions of northern and northeastern Australia. Distinguished from *C. mydas* by depressed shell, details of scalation, and distinctive juveniles.

▪ *C. mydas* (LINNAEUS, 1758). Green Turtle. Worldwide in warm seas.

Chelonia mydas, juv.

Chelonia mydas

Chelonia depressa, young

Chelonia mydas agassizi

Chelonia mydas

Chelonia mydas

Cheloniidae: Sea Turtles. Family of the Cryptodira. Very large marine turtles restricted to the seas. Cosmopolitan distribution. The genera are *Caretta*, *Chelonia*, *Eretmochelys*, and *Lepidochelys*. Known as fossils from the Cretaceous. Superficially similar but not directly related to Dermochelyidae.

The characteristic often heart-shaped carapace has a light structure with fontanelles around peripheral bones of carapace visible throughout life and very large in juveniles. The plastron also has large fontanelles and cartilage areas. The genera are distinguished by reduction in numbers of costal, marginal, and bridge scutes plus skull differences related to feeding habits. The limbs are modified into gigantic paddles. The skull is compact, and the neck is only partially retractable.

Mainly herbivorous (*Chelonia*), omnivorous, or mainly carnivorous (*Eretmochelys*). The animal component of the diet is mainly molluscs, echinoderms, crustaceans, and jellyfish, plus an occasional fish.

Sea turtles are extremely site-restricted during mating and subsequent egg deposition, and several thousand of them may gather at a traditional nesting site. While most species have several nesting sites in different regions, *Lepidochelys kempi* has only a single known nesting site along the Mexican Atlantic coast for all individuals of the species. Sea turtles use "sun compass" orientation, using the light intensity of their environment to find the appropriate nesting beaches. Due to excessive egg collecting as well as hunting of egg-laying females for their shells and as food, the Cheloniidae have become endangered. Protection of nesting sites, artificial incubation of eggs, and moving of hatchlings to offshore areas in order to avoid the dangers of maritime traffic and to escape predators are some of the most important conservation steps undertaken for sea turtles along the American and Asiatic coastlines.

Due to these protective measures and because of their considerable demands on aquarium technology these turtles are usually kept only in public aquariums. Hobbyists will need to provide a very large tank and very clean (through high-volume filtration) sea water. The greatest problem is preventing rickets among juveniles. This is only possible with an optimum diet including vitamin and mineral supplements.

Chelonoidis FITZINGER, 1835. American Giant Tortoises. Genus of the Testudinidae, often considered a subgenus of *Geochelone*. South America and the Galapagos Archipelago. 4 species. Tropical forest clearings, thornbush formations, and steppes. Carapace 0.22 to 1.1 m, rigid, domed. Carapace usually dark with light patches on scutes, never with radiating markings. 2 species are often seen in terrariums.

Chelonoidis chilensis

▪ *C. carbonaria* (SPIX, 1824). Red-legged Tortoise. South America east and west of the Andes. Tropical forest regions. 50 cm carapace length. Carapace with a black base coloration with yellow patches. Soft parts with solid orange-red scales. Requires a varied diet (omnivorous) and a well-heated terrarium with bathing facilities. Rearing young without rickets requires a highly varied diet with vi-

Chelonoidis denticulata (top) and *Chelonoidis carbonaria* (bottom)

Chelonoidis carbonaria

Chelonoidis carbonaria

Chelonoidis chilensis

tamin D3 and calcium supplements. Acclimated specimens may live for many years.

- *C. chilensis* (GRAY, 1870). Argentine Tortoise. Argentina and Uruguay, in the *pampas*. 22 cm approximate carapace length, the smallest species in this genus. Uniformly brown-yellow carapace. Likes to dig. Adults can be kept outdoors during the summer. Juveniles more susceptible to rickets than previous species.
- *C. denticulata* (LINNAEUS, 1766). Yellow-footed Tortoise. Distribution and habitat requirements largely identical to

C. carbonaria, but this species does not occur west of the Andes. Similar in appearance, but carapace dark brown and the feet usually have yellow scales.

- *C. elephantopus* (HARLAN, 1827). Galapagos Giant Tortoise. Galapagos Archipelago. Each island has its own geographic subspecies or several subspecies, but some populations are extinct or extremely endangered. To 1.1 m carapace length. Carapace in very large animals and from certain subspecies saddle-shaped. Uniformly dark brown to black. Large populations were decimated from a century

Chelonoidis chilensis

Chelonoidis chilensis

Chelonoidis chilensis

Chelonoidis elephantopus

Chelonoidis denticulata

Chelonoidis chilensis, young

Chelonoidis (chilensis) donosobarrosi

Chelonoidis (chilensis) donosobarrosi

Chelonoidis elephantopus ephippus

Chelonoidis elephantopus abingdoni

Chelonoidis (chilensis) petersi

Chelonoidis elephantopus guntheri

of excessive hunting and because of detrimental influences of feral animals such as goats and pigs. Galapagos giant tortoises are valuable display specimens for zoological parks and live for many years. It has been bred repeatedly. Currently a rehabilitation program is under way at the Darwin Research Station in the Galapagos. Young tortoises have been returned to some of the wild populations and have been transplanated to islands of the archipelago from which the endemic populations had been exterminated. A permanent breeding colony is at the San Diego Zoo. Incubation period 96 to 106 days at 29° C. or 182 days at 28 to 29° C. in an incubator. Eggs in the wild require 120 to 216 days for incubation. Endangered.

Chelonoidis elephantopus porteri

Chelonoidis elephantopus elephantopus

Chelonoidis elephantopus darwini

Chelonoidis elephantopus, hatchling

Chelonoidis (chilensis) petersi

Chelonoidis elephantopus hoodensis

Chelonoidis (chilensis) petersi

Chelonoidis (chilensis) petersi

Chelonoidis (chilensis) petersi

Chelosania GRAY, 1845. Monotypic genus of the Agamidae. Western Australia in arid regions with thornbush vegetation. Somewhat arboreal. Small species with a low dorsal crest.

Diet mainly arthropods. Egg-layers. So far only a few specimens have been found.

▪ *C. brunnea* GRAY, 1845. About 15 cm. Rare.

Chelus DUMERIL, 1806. Matamata. Monotypic genus of the Chelidae. Northern and central South America in slow-flowing or standing jungle waters. Carapace to 40 cm, depressed, with 3 keeled ridges, rigid. Head flat, with conspicuous proboscis and skin fringes on the chin and neck. Plastron relatively small. Juveniles have contrasting colors, including red and black neck stripes; colors darkening with increasing age.

Matamatas lie in wait for prey. By suddenly opening the mouth and dropping the floor of the mouth they create a

Chelus fimbriatus

sudden strong suction that actually pulls small fish into the mouth.

Acclimated specimens generally do well in captivity. In spite of their size they do not require excessive space. It has been bred repeatedly. The incubation period is 208 days at 28 to 29° C. in an incubator. Long-lived.

▪ *C. fimbriatus* (SCHNEIDER, 1783). Eastern Peru to Venezuela, Guyana, and Surinam, south through northern and central Brasil.

Chelydra SCHWEIGGER, 1812. Snapping Turtles. Monotypic genus of the Chelydridae. North and South America

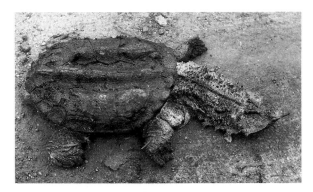

Chelus fimbriatus

Chelus fimbriatus

Chelus fimbriatus

Chelus fimbriatus

Chelus fimbriatus

Chelus fimbriatus

Chelydra serpentina osceola

Chelydra serpentina, hatchling

in large to small bodies of water. To 50 cm. Head very large, with a strongly hooked beak. Carapace with 3 keeled ridges; plastron cross-shaped, rigid and very small, so that the legs can not be retracted. Tail about as long as carapace, covered with large coarse pointed scales.

Aquatic, feeding mainly on molluscs, fish, amphibians, and even water birds. Large prey is torn apart.

Snapping turtles should be kept in large aquariums with moderate heat. They are quite rapid growers. Depending upon origin, specimens can be kept out doors part of the year or throughout the year (winter protection must be provided). Bred on farms in the United States. The incubation period is 60 to 140 days at 30° C. and 20° C., respectively, in an incubator; in the wild 48 to 125 days. Caution: Bites and often very aggressive; head capable of broad swings.

▪ *C. serpentina* (LINNAEUS, 1758). Southern Canada

Chelydra serpentina rossignoni

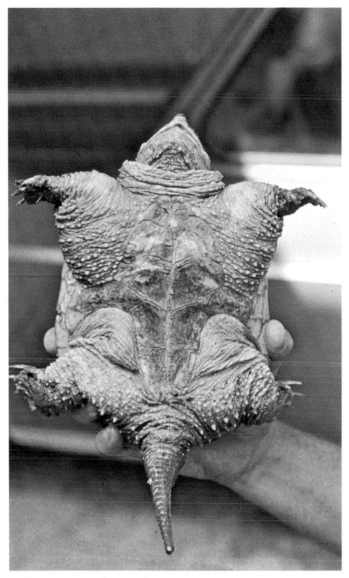

Chelydra serpentina acutirostris

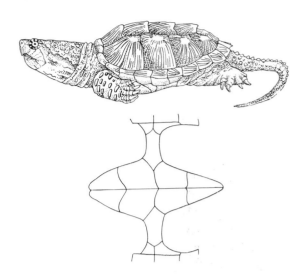

Chelydra serpentina

Chelydra serpentina acutirostris

through the central and eastern USA to Florida, Central America, and northwestern South America (Ecuador). 4 subspecies.

Chelydridae: Snapping Turtles. Family of the Cryptodira. Americas. 2 monotypic genera, *Chelydra* and *Macroclemys*. Fossil records also from Europe. Found in fresh water. Carapace length to 70 cm. Head massive, large, neck covered with large spiny tubercles. Beak is very powerful and distinctly hooked. Plastron small, cross-shaped. The conspicuously long tail is covered with large, rough scales.

Strongly aquatic, the snapping turtles like to hide in soft bottoms, lying in wait for prey. Crepuscular and nocturnal, but they like to bask regularly.

Snapping turtles should be kept in an aquarium with a land section. Heat is required, especially for *Macroclemys*, while *Chelydra* is less sensitive (northern populations can survive at room temperature and can even be kept outdoors). They grow rapidly (often too rapidly) on a varied carnivorous diet with calcium supplements. Adult specimens often are quarrelsome, so they should be kept indi-

Chersina angulata

Chersina angulata

Chersina angulata

vidually, especially *Macroclemys*, if the tank is not large enough to provide ample hiding places. Snapping turtles have strong bites and a temperament to match. They have been known to "attack" swimmers. Best handled by the tail. These bizarre turtles, despite some reservations, can be recommended for the beginning hobbyist.

Chersina GRAY, 1831. Bow-sprit Tortoises. (Also spelled *Chersine*.) Monotypic genus of the Testudinidae. Southern Africa in savannahs and along outer desert areas. The elongated domed carapace has a characteristic unpaired projecting gular plate. The carapace scutes have distinct light areas with wide dark margins.

Mainly herbivorous, depending upon seasonal availability of food items. Biology largely unknown, but the incubation period for eggs in the wild is 180 to 420 days, ex-

tremely long. Numbers reduced recently. For terrarium maintenance refer to *Agrionemys*. Not quite as delicate as *Psammobates* or *Homopus*.

▪ *C. angulata* (SCHWEIGGER, 1812). Bow-sprit Tortoise. South-West Africa to Cape Province. 15 to 25 cm.

Chersodromus REINHARDT, 1860. Monotypic genus of the Colubridae of uncertain subfamily (possibly Natricinae). Mexico to Guatemala. About 35 cm. Strongly keeled dorsal scales. Ground snakes. Biology little known.
▪ *C. liebmanni* REINHARDT, 1860.

Chersydrus CUVIER, 1817. Indian Wart Snakes. Monotypic genus of the Acrochordidae. Southern India, Sri Lanka, Indo-China, and the Indo-Australian Archipelago to New Guinea, the Philippines and the Solomon Islands. Included in *Acrochordus* by many systematists. Mainly in brackish or sea water. To 1.2 m. Head and tail flattened. Markings consist of light and dark crossbands.

These wart snakes prefer mangrove forests and inshore coral reefs, where they hunt for fish at night. Sometimes these snakes can even be found offshore. 6 to 10 young.
▪ *C. granulatus* (SCHNEIDER, 1799).

Chiasmocleis MEHELY, 1904. Genus of the Microhylidae. Central and tropical South America. About 12 species in dry forests and rain forests. Relatively slender, smooth skinned, with small head and small eyes typical of family, but without occipital fold. Pupil round or oval-horizontal. Tympanum covered. Fingers free, sometimes with lateral skin folds; toes variously webbed (more or less completely in *C. anatipes*, only basally in *C. ventrimaculata*). Adhesive discs absent or only indicated. Outer metatarsal tubercle absent.

Nocturnal ground-dwellers that climb among low bushes close to their spawning pond. More or less specialized for feeding on ants. During the mating season the males call the females with short, delicate humming tones from shallow areas of standing waters.

▪ *C. albopunctata* (BOETTGER, 1885). Brasilian States of Mato Grosso and Gojas, Paraguay. 2.5 cm. Brown with a few white spots.

▪ *C. anatipes* WALKER and DUELLMAN, 1974. Eastern Ecuador, *selva*. 2.5 cm. Dark olive-green to brown with metallic green and golden spots. Upper arm yellow-orange. Abdomen white with brownish black spots.

▪ *C. ventrimaculata* (ANDERSSON, 1945). Eastern Ecuador, *selva*. 2.5 cm. Dark olive-brown with small golden spots. Ventrally bluish white with contrasting pattern of black spots.

Chilomeniscus COPE, 1860. Banded Sand Snakes. Genus of the Colubridae of uncertain subfamily status (Colubrinae or Boiginae). Southwestern United States and northwestern Mexico. 2 species. Highland deserts to 1000 m. 20 to 25 cm. Shovel-like head, not set off from body. Black crossbands on an orange background, sometimes nearly plain tan or orangish or weakly spotted.

Subterranean in sandy deserts, active on surface only at night. These little snakes are able to "swim" in loose sand. They feed on millipedes and insects and their larvae. Should be kept in glass containers.

▪ *C. cinctus* COPE, 1861. Banded Sand Snake. 25 cm. Southwestern United States into Mexico on both sides of the Gulf of California.

▪ *C. stramineus* COPE, 1860. Spotted Sand Snake. Only at southern tip of Baja California.

Chilorhinophis WERNER, 1907. Genus of the Colubridae, Aparallactinae (formerly included in the Boiginae). Tropical Africa. 3 species. 40 cm. Head not set off from body, head scales reduced. Fangs relatively far forward, preceded by only 3 or 4 rudimentary upper jaw teeth. In that respect *Chilorhinophis* together with *Aparallactus* represent the most primitive type within this subfamily. Dorsally dark brown to black with rows of light spots and stripes.

When disturbed, *Chilorhinophis* will often hide its head under body coils and display the short, blunt tail. These snakes are assumed to feed mainly on arthropods, especially insects; they occasionally also take amphisbaenids and small lizards. Caution: Venomous bites.

▪ *C. gerardi* (BOULENGER, 1913). Zaire and Zimbabwe to Republic of South Africa. 2 subspecies.

Chinemys SMITH, 1931. Chinese Swamp Turtles. Genus of the Emydidae. China, Korea, Japan, Taiwan, and Vietnam. 3 species in various types of water, including small ponds and pools as well as rice paddies. Dully colored. Carapace usually with 1 to 3 longitudinal keels.

Almost exclusively carnivorous. Hardy and suited for beginning hobbyists. Should be kept outdoors during the summer months; *C. reevesi* can possibly remain outside throughout the entire year if given protection in winter.

▪ *C. kwangtungensis* (POPE, 1934). Chinese Redneck Turtle. Vietnam and southern China. Only 1 carapace keel developed.

▪ *C. megalocephala* FANG, 1934. Area around Nanjing, China. Carapace with 3 dark longitudinal stripes (no keels); distinctively large head.

▪ *C. reevesi* (GRAY, 1831). Reeves's Turtle. Central and eastern China, Japan, and Korea (possibly all populations outside China are introduced). Has been bred in captivity

Chinemys reevesi

Chinemys kwangtungensis

Chinemys reevesi

Chinemys reevesi

Chinemys reevesi

over several generations and is the only species ever imported regularly. 10 cm, occasionally 35 cm. Carapace with 3 strong keels.

Chioglossa BOCAGE, 1864. Gold-striped Salamanders. Monotypic genus of the Salamandridae. Northwestern Iberian Peninsula; localized distribution in damp, broadleaved montane forests to 1300 m elevation with springs and creeks. Graceful. Tongue very long and can be "shot" from mouth to capture prey. 10 or 11 costal grooves. The tail is very long, fragile, and has a predetermined fracture line. Similar to the related genus *Mertensiella* in appear-

ance, very agile and fast on land and in water. Larvae elongated, with conspicuously small legs and gills.

Adults are crepuscular and nocturnal ground-dwellers that hide during the day under moss, rocks, logs, etc. Little is known about their mating behavior, which occurs on land or in shallow water during the early spring. The female attaches the eggs individually to rocks in moderately flowing water. A winter dormancy period extends from December through January and a summer rest period occurs during the warm period of the year, thus this salamander is only active during spring and late fall.

Chioglossa lusitanica

Care and maintenance are not easy. Provide an aqua-terrarium with a small water section at a temperature of from 10 to 22° C. Requires high humidity that can be produced by aerating the water section. The terrarium must be tightly covered since these animals can escape through the smallest gap! The main diet is live flies, especially gnats, which are easily caught with the tongue in the narrow confines of the terrarium. The rest periods must be strictly maintained in captivity.
▪ *C. lusitanica* BOCAGE, 1864. Gold-striped Salamander. 15 cm. Brown, the back with 2 copper-colored shiny longitudinal stripes that glisten like gold after shedding of the skin; the stripes fuse on the tail.

Chionactis COPE, 1860. Shovelnosed Snakes. Genus of the Colubridae of uncertain subfamily status (Colubrinae or Lycodontinae). Southwestern United States and northwestern Mexico. 2 species found in variably dry habitats including sandy deserts. 25 to 40 cm. Shovel-shaped snout overhanging a subterminal mouth. Banded or ringed in red, black, and white.

Burrowing ground snakes that "swim" in loose sand and surface only at night. The diet includes millipedes, scorpions, and insects. They should be kept in glass terrariums and allowed a substantial temperature drop at night.
▪ *C. occipitalis* (HALLOWELL, 1854). Western Shovelnosed Snake. 45 cm. Southwestern United States. 4 or 5 subspecies.
▪ *C. palarostris* (KLAUBER, 1937). Sonoran Shovelnosed Snake. 40 cm. Northwestern Mexico to U.S. border. 2 subspecies.

Chirindia BOULENGER, 1907. Genus of the Amphisbaenidae. Southern Africa. 5 species. About 15 cm. Poorly known burrowers.
▪ *C. swynnertoni* BOULENGER, 1907. Mozambique, Zimbabwe.

Chirixalus: see *Philautus*, genus.

Chiroleptes: see *Cyclorana*, genus.

Chiromantis PETERS, 1855. African Foam-nest Treefrogs. Genus of the Rhacophoridae. Tropical and southern subtropical Africa. 3 species. In West Africa found in rain forests; in eastern and southern Africa found in savannahs. Robust, long-legged frogs with granular skin or small warts. Pupil horizontal. Tympanum distinctly visible. Tongue with a deep furrow in back. Fingers and toes with adhesive discs. Fingers webbed only at base, toes com-

Chionactis palarostris

pletely webbed; inner finger opposing outer one to form a grasping hand. Males without visible vocal sacs. Larvae have a comparatively short body and tall, lance-shaped tail terminating in a point.

Treefrogs living among bushes and in trees. Breedings occurs during the rainy season. These frogs build large white foam nests above water (often over muddy, temporary puddles) at 1 to 2 m in height (rarely to 15 m). About 150 eggs are deposited in these nests. The larvae hatch in

Chiromantis petersi

Chiromantis xerampelina

about 2 days and remain in the nest for another 4 days, when they fall into the water below and remain there until metamorphosis.

Hardy captive specimens that will quickly become tame. *C. rufescens* should be housed in a tall, humid tropical terrarium that must be equipped with branches. The other species can be kept in similar terrariums but should be given alternating simulated dry and wet seasons; bathing facilities must always be present. The main diet consists especially of large insetcs.

Chiromantis xerampelina

Chironius fuscus

• *C. petersi* BOULENGER, 1882. East Africa. 2 subspecies. Savannahs. 8 cm. Gray with dark markings.

• *C. rufescens* (GUENTHER, 1868). Rough-skinned Foam-nest Treefrog. Tropical West Africa. Rain forests and brushland. 9 cm. Gray-green with dark markings.

• *C. xerampelina* PETERS, 1854. Gray Foam-nest Treefrog. Bark-colored, gray with darker markings. Has the ability to change colors quickly. Southern and eastern Africa.

Chironius FITZINGER, 1826. Sipos. Genus of the Colubridae, Colubrinae. Neotropics between Nicaragua and southern Brasil and Argentina. About 14 to 18 species in tropical rain forests and montane forests. 1 to 2.3 m, very slender. Head characteristically set off from laterally slightly flat-

Chironius fuscus

tened body. Conspicuously large eyes. Uniformly brown to greenish or with spots and crossbands; variable. Scales very large, in 12 or fewer rows.

More or less nocturnal tree snakes that feed on frogs. Egg-layers, 10 to 15 eggs. Should be given a rain-forest terrarium.

• *C. carinatus* (LINNAEUS, 1758). Central America into tropical South America.

• *C. fuscus* (LINNAEUS, 1758). Panama to central Brasil, eastward to French Guiana and westward to Peru. 1.2 m.

• *C. scurulus* (WAGLER, 1824). Amazon Basin. Largest species in this genus, 2.3 m.

Chironomidae: Bloodworms. Family of midges (Nematocera), order Diptera. Larvae of most species are found in fresh or brackish water and are known as bloodworms to aquarists. They are widely distributed and suitable as food for many aquatic amphibians. The adults are 2 to 14 mm long, look a bit like mosquitoes, but do not bite. When resting they can be recognized by a characteristic twitching of the raised front legs and the "bottlebrush" antennae of the males. The adults sometimes occur in huge swarms and can also be used as food for amphibians. The red larvae are usually available commercially living or frozen.

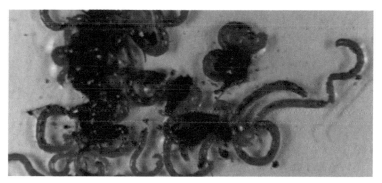

Chironomidae

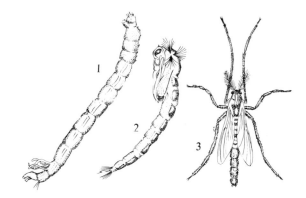

Chironomidae: 1 Larva; 2 pupa; 3 imago or adult

Chironomidae

Chironomidae

Chiropterotriton TAYLOR, 1944. Genus of the Plethodontidae. Central America southward to Costa Rica, with the center of abundance in Mexico. Found in subtropical evergreen forests, cloud forests, and damp mountain forests. Some 20 species, about half recently moved to the genera or subgenera *Dendrotriton* and *Nototriton*. Closely related to *Bolitoglossa* and *Pseudoeurycea* and externally indistinguishable from these, also comparable in terms of natural history—partially terrestrial and also arboreal, often in bromeliads.

Should be maintained cool (below 20° C.).
- *C. arboreus* (TAYLOR, 1941). Mexico.
- *C. bromeliacea* (SCHMIDT, 1936). Guatemala.
- *C. chiropterus* (COPE, 1863). Mexico.
- *C. nasalis* (DUNN, 1924). Honduras.

Chirotes: see *Bipes*, genus.

Chitra GRAY, 1844. Narrow-headed Soft-shell Turtles. Monotypic genus of the Trionychidae. India and western

Indo-China in larger rivers. To 1.15 m carapace length. Head narrow and short, on short, thick neck with distinctive longitudinal stripes. Oval leathery carapace is nearly circular in juveniles and has dark-bordered scribbled markings. 4 callosities on plastron.

Carnivorous, prefers fish and molluscs.
- *C. indica* (GRAY, 1831). Narrow-headed Soft-shell Turtle. Pakistan, northern India, western Indo-China from Burma to Malaya Peninsula. Old reports of specimens 2 m long.

Chlamydosaurus GRAY, 1825. Frilled Lizards. Monotypic genus of the Agamidae. Australia and southern New Guinea in open dry forests and tree-covered steppes. To 90 cm. With characteristic extremely wide neck frill (in males to 30 cm) that can be erected by equally well-developed hyoid bones in a threat display. Low dorsal crest. Femoral and preanal pores present in males.

Primarily arboreal. When fleeing on the ground it tends

Chlamydosaurus kingi

Chitra indica

Chlamydosaurus kingi

Chlamydosaurus kingi

Chlamydosaurus kingi

to run on its hind legs only. The diet includes arthropods and smaller lizards, plus eggs. Totally protected.

▪ *C. kingi* GRAY, 1825. Frilled Lizard. In excess of 90 cm. Different shades of brown, but when excited changes colors; red, yellow, white, and black spots on the frill.

Chlorophis: see *Philothamnus*, genus.

Chlorophytum KER-GAWL. Grass Lily, Bride's Veil. Genus of the Liliaceae. Tropics. More than 100 species. Shrubs. Most frequently cultivated form is *C. cosmosum* (THUNB.) JACQ. "Variegatum." Undemanding. Can also be used in baskets.

Chondrodactylus PETERS, 1870. Sand Geckos. Monotypic genus of the Gekkonidae. Southern and southwestern Africa in deserts and semideserts. 15 cm. Slender, tail about equal to snout-vent length. Very long, thin limbs; toes stumpy, without adhesive lamellae, ideally suited for digging.

Nocturnal. Captive maintenance probably similar to *Teratoscincus*, but without winter dormancy period.

▪ *C. angulifer* PETERS, 1870. Sand Gecko. Light brown.

Chondropython MEYER, 1874. Tree Pythons. Monotypic genus of the Boidae, subfamily Pythoninae. New Guinea, northern Australia, and some adjacent island groups (Aru, Schouten, and Solomon islands). To 1.8 m. Body triangular in cross-section. Head clearly set off from body, with long fang-like teeth. Very similar externally to the South American tree boas, but distinguished (among other ways) by lacking pits on upper lip. Prehensile tail. Adults mainly green, rarely bluish or brownish violet; juveniles yellow, orange, brownish, or reddish with white scales arranged in

Chondrodactylus angulifer

Chondropython viridis

Chondropython viridis

Chondropython viridis

Chondropython viridis

Chondropython viridis, young

Chondropython viridis

a diffuse rhombic pattern (particularly along vertebral column).

Largely arboreal. They lie in wait in a characteristic flat-coiled resting position on branches, waiting for unsuspecting prey (frogs, lizards, small mammals, birds). The clutch is incubated on the ground.

Tree pythons should be kept in a well-heated rain-forest terrarium with climbing branches, a basking spot, and hiding places. It should include sturdy terrarium plants that must be sprayed regularly, a moderately damp substrate (peat moss), and a water bowl. *Chondropython* have been bred in captivity but are difficult. Brooding animals must be protected against any disturbance. The young can be reared on frogs, lizards, and young mice.

Endangered, so only captive-bred progeny should be purchased. Considered a delicacy in New Guinea.
• *C. viridis* (SCHLEGEL, 1872). Green Tree Python. This python has a reputation for extremely aggressive behavior.

Chondropython viridis

Choristocalamus WITTE and LAURENT, 1947. Monotypic genus of the Colubridae, Boiginae. Southern Africa. To 33 cm. In appearance and mode of life similar to *Calamelaps*, but with the rostrum not projecting. Uniformly dark.
• *C. concolor* (A. SMITH, 1849). Natal, northern Transvaal.

Chromatophores: Color cells. Special body cells containing the pigments that largely determine the coloration of an animal. They are found particularly in the integument, in the iris of the eye, in the epithelium of the abdominal cavity, and in various organs. The most frequently observed type of chromatophore is the melanophore, containing brownish black melanins, with its branched cell processes. The lipophores possess alcohol-soluble red and yellow lipid color pigments, while the red pigments of the allophores are not soluble in alcohol. The chromatophores also include the guanophores or iridocytes, which contain colorless guanine crystals and similar compounds that produce colors by light reflection and light scattering.

Chromosomes: Thread-like or rod-like structures in the cell nucleus that can be made visble under the microscope during cell division by means of special staining techniques. Their main component is desoxyribonucleic acid (DNA), the carrier of genetic information. Each body cell contains 2 identical sets of chromosomes (2N or diploid number); the sex cells or gametes contain—due to a special division process—only 1 set of chromosomes each (N or haploid number). During the fertilization process a diploid embryo is reestablished, so that a paternal set and a maternal set of chromosomes with their genetic factors are then combined.

The chromosome number and form of a cell produce the species-characteristic karyotype, which by means of comparisons provides information about genetic relationships. In amphibians and reptiles there are, apart from the large I- and V-shaped macro-chromosomes, frequently also more or less numerous dot-shaped micro-chromosomes. This differentiation is not very clear in salamanders and related forms and is further distorted due to transitional forms. The same applies to turtles and crocodiles. Since it is further assumed that both arms of a V-shaped chromosome have been formed through the fusion of 2 rod-shaped chromosomes, so these are then counted double for the determination of the basic number of chromosomes for a species. Thus, one obtains the N. F. Value ('nombre fondamental'), which shows a surprising conformity for certain related groups of animals with a variable number of chromosomes. The chromosome formula for the tuatara (*Sphenodon punctatus*), for instance, contains the following data: 2n = 36, V = 12 (V-shaped chromosomes), I = 18 (rod-shaped chromosomes), m = 6 (dot-shaped micro-chromosomes), N. F. = 48. This N. F. value is also characteristic for most saurians.

The sex in many animals is determined by special sex chromosomes. These are frequently distinguishable morphologically. Through the meeting of two identical (isogamy) or different (heterogamy) sex chromosomes within the fertilized egg cells, the sex of that animal is determined. However, in amphibians morphologically distinguishable sex chromosomes are generally not visible. In some instances, however, heterogamy can happen in the male and female sex in salamanders and related forms, while in frogs this only occurs in females. Various reptiles, e. g., crocodiles and turtles, do not display sex-related differences in their chromosome sets, while in other groups heterogamy is found in the female sex, rarely in the male sex.

Chrysemys GRAY, 1844. Painted Turtles and Sliders. Genus of the Emydide. North America to South America. Some 14 species and over 35 subspecies found in large lakes, rivers, and smaller bodies of water. 20 to 40 cm carapace length. Males usually substantially smaller than females and with conspicuously elongated claws on front legs used in courtship dances. Carapace usually moderately domed to quite flat. Side of head and neck with yellow stripes. American herpetologists recognize 3 genera or subgenera: *Chrysemys* for *C. picta*; *Trachemys* for *C. scripta* and allies; and *Pseudemys* for the other sliders.

Chrysemys picta dorsalis

Chrysemys floridana hoyi

Chrysemys nelsoni

Chrysemys dorbigni

Chrysemys decorata

Chrysemys picta picta, ♀

Chrysemys alabamensis

Chrysemys picta belli

Chrysemys concinna

Chrysemys picta picta

Chrysemys rubriventris

Chrysemys scripta elegans

Chrysemys scripta cataspila

Chrysemys scripta elegans

Chrysemys nelsoni

Chrysemys scripta elegans

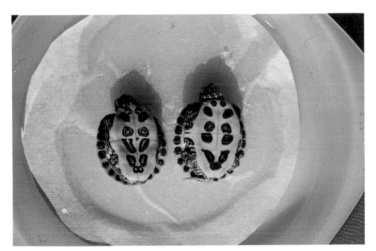

Chrysemys scripta elegans

Chrysemys scripta elegans

Chrysemys scripta venusta

Chrysemys scripta elegans

Sun-loving, very active turtles. Juveniles were once readily available terrarium animals. Rearing of rachitis-free animals requires strict compliance with correct nutritional requirements (mainly carnivorous, with increasing plant component as size increases) and vitamin and calcium requirements. Juveniles should be given an aqua-terrarium with a dry and sunny land section (not an aquarium), ultraviolet radiation together with regular vitamin D3 and mineral supplements, together with a varied diet to effectively counteract any nutritional deficiency diseases. Bred in commercial farms in the United States. Due to their rapid growth, large size as adults, and related space requirements, maintenance in an indoor aqua-terrarium quickly becomes a problem. Species from North America can be kept in an outdoor pool if precautions are taken to avoid cold damage.

▪ *C. concinna* (LE CONTE, 1830). River Cooter. Eastern

Chrysemys terrapen

Chrysopelea ornata

United States into northeastern Mexico. 5 doubtful subspecies that are hard to distinguish from each other. Incubation takes 66 to 114 days at 30° C. and 23° C., respectively. 41 cm.

• *C. dorbigni* (DUMERIL and BIBRON, 1835). Tropical Slider. Southeastern Brasil and northeastern Argentina. Very similar to *C. scripta*.

• *C. floridana* (LE CONTE, 1830). Cooter. Southeastern and central United States. 3 subspecies. Incubation takes 49 to 102 days at 30° C. and 25° C., respectively. 40 cm.

• *C. picta* (SCHNEIDER, 1783). Painted Turtle. Southern Canada and virtually entire USA. 4 subspecies. 25 cm. Most attractive, flattest, and smallest species of genus. Incubation takes from 48 to 95 days at 30° C. and 22° C. respectively.

• *C. rubriventris* (LE CONTE, 1830). Red-bellied Turtle. Central Atlantic Seaboard of USA. Related to *C. nelsoni* of Florida. 40 cm.

• *C. scripta* (SCHOEPFF, 1792). Slider. Eastern USA to northern South America. 13 to 15 subspecies, the tropical subspecies *ornata* and *callirostris* and others here included in *C. scripta*. Incubation takes 59 to 93 days at 30° C. and 25° C., respectively. Best known and most popular species among hobbyists. 28 cm. The red-eared slider, *C. scripta elegans*, is still bred in the thousands for export to Europe and Japan.

• *C. terrapen* ((LACEPEDE, 1788). Antillean Slider. Antilles and Bahamas. About 9 subspecies.

Chrysopelea BOIE, 1826. Flying Tree Snakes. Genus of the Colubridae, Boiginae. Southern Asia from India and Sri Lanka through Indo-China to southern China and the Indo-Australian Archipelago, southward to the Aru Islands; not found in New Guinea. 5 partially polytypic species. Found in the upper tree regions in tropical monsoon forests and rain forests. 0.9 to 1.5 m. Slender, with elongated, somewhat blunt-snouted, head and large eyes. Long

tail. Dorsally spotted or banded, in some forms the crossbands modified into either a uniform coloration or a reticulated pattern of light scales with dark margins. Coloration and markings can vary substantially from juveniles to adults, and there are also considerable individual variations not based on geographic distribution. Dorsal scales usually rather small and smooth, only the central rows keeled.

Diurnal, sun-loving tree snakes. They hunt for lizards in sunny tree tops and occasionally take frogs. They can move with great rapidity among the branches, going from one tree to the next by jumping and gliding with the body distinctly flattened. This behavior has given rise to the popular name "flying snakes," although it would be more ap-

Chrysopelea ornata

propriate to think of this as a highly developed broad jump technique. Egg-layers, the eggs deposited by the females in the substrate in tropical forests.

Maintenance in a tropical rain-forest terrarium has some problems since replication of the rain-forest atmosphere with its high humidity in the lower section and simultaneous sunny upper region poses some technical difficulties. These can really only be overcome through the installation of a reliable ventilation system and weak ultraviolet lights that must be able to radiate continously for long periods of time without causing burns to animals and plants. Obtaining an adequate supply of lizards can also be a problem. Sometimes captive specimens can be acclimated to accept substitute foods such as mice.
• *C. ornata* (SHAW, 1802). Ornate Flying Snake. India and

Chrysopelea ornata

Sri Lanka through Indo-China eastward to southern China, southward to Malayan Peninsula.
• *C. paradisi* BOIE, 1827. Paradise Flying Snake. Indo-China and Indo-Australian Archipelago to Java and Kalimantan, Sulawesi, and the Philippines.
• *C. pelias* (LINNAEUS, 1758). Malayan Peninsula, Sumatra, and Kalimantan including the smaller adjacent islands; not found on Java.
• *C. rhodopleuron* (BOIE, 1827). Moluccas and adjacent islands, Sangi.
• *C. taprobanica* M. SMITH, 1943. Southern India and Sri Lanka.

Chthonerpeton PETERS, 1879. Genus of the Typhlonectidae. Tropical South America. 6 species. 30 to 60 cm. Worm-like. without a median skin fold, and with 68 to more than 170 primary folds. Tentacle organ about equal distance from nasal opening and eye or somewhat closer to the nose. Tones of gray, purple, or blue.
• *C. viviparum* PARKER and WETTSTEIN, 1929. Brasil. To 60 cm, but only 1 cm thick. Uniformly bluish gray.

Circadian rhythm: Day and night rhythm or 24-hour rhythm in behavior and physiological body functions of an animal that is usually guided by internal "clocks" but is synchronized by time-related stimuli from the environment. Many amphibians and reptiles display a well-defined circadian rhythm, so typically day-active species (e. g., many frogs and lizards) and night-active species (e. g., many toads and most geckos) can be distinguished.

Circulatory system: Closed system of vessels present in all vertebrates for the purpose of circulating blood. Consists of the heart as the motor organ, the arteries (efferent blood vessels), and veins (afferent blood vessels). Between the arteries and veins, which split into a multitude of smaller vessels, there is a fine capillary network that surrounds the tissues and facilitates internal gas exchange.

Fish have a simple circulatory system where the blood flows from the heart through the gills into the body and then returns to the heart. With the development of lungs as respiratory organs in terrestrial vertebrates a double circulation has evolved where the blood is first pumped to the lungs to obtain oxygen and then returns to the heart to commence its course through the body. The separation of the two circulatory systems is rather variably developed in amphibians and reptiles. The most primitive condition is found in the salamanders and newts and the caecilians, which retain throughout their life the 4 posterior-most gill arches of the 6 found embryonically in all vertebrates. A further reduction of the arteries and the disappearance of the *Ductus arteriosus Botalli* during metamorphosis in frogs leads to an ultimate separation of lung and body circulation within the arterial system. However, in the simple ventricle (divided only by numerous septa, net-like in salamanders and related forms and folded in frogs) there is still ex-

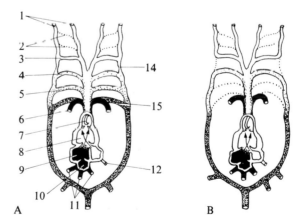

Circulatory system, comparing the relationships of the heart and branchial (efferent) arteries

A. SALAMANDERS AND NEWTS
Partially separated auricles, undivided ventricle; connections between pulmonary arteries and body arteries as *ductus arteriosus* and between third and fourth branchial arteries as *ductus caroticus* are present; fifth branchial artery reduced

B. FROGS (after metamorphosis)
Separated auricles, undivided ventricle; no connections between third and fourth branchial arteries or between lungs and body arteries; fifth branchial artery absent

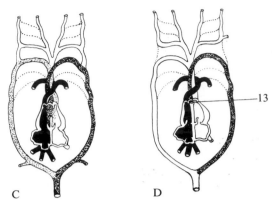

C   D

C. REPTILES (except crocodilians)
Separated auricles, partially separated ventricles; left root of aorta carries richly oxygenated blood and supplies body arteries; right root of aorta carries mostly poorly oxygenated blood that mixes in the heart with the richly oxygenated blood; sixth branchial artery becomes the pulmonary artery

D. CROCODILIANS
Separated auricles and ventricles; at the root of the aorta through the *foramen panizzae*, transfer of richly oxygenated blood and poorly oxygenated blood between the left and right aortic arteries is possible

1 Internal and external cephalic arteries; 2 First and second branchial arteries absent; 3 Third branchial arteries; 4 Fourth branchial artery becomes aortic arch and unites below heart as dorsal artery; 5 Fifth branchial arteries, absent except in salamanders; 6 Pulmonary arteries; 7 Bulbus arteriosus with valve; 8 Ventricle(s); 9 Auricle(s); 10 Sinus venosus; 11 Body cavity veins; 12 Pulmonary vein; 13 *Foramen panizzae*; 14 *Ductus caroticus*; 15 *Ductus arteriosus Botalli*

Richly oxygenated blood shown without shading; poorly oxygenated blood shaded; mixed blood stippled

tensive mixing of oxygenated and deoxygenated blood. Only in frogs are the two atrial chambers completely separate; in all other amphibians the dividing wall remains perforated.

The development of a partial septum in the ventricle and a triple separation of the efferent vessels in reptiles facilitates maintaining a larger volume of deoxygenated blood in the lung circulatory system and oxygenated blood in the body. This development is most advanced in crocodilians, where both heart chambers are completely separated. Only at the base of the two aortic arches is there (via the *foramen panizzae*) a connection that permits oxygenated blood from the right aortic arch to move to the left and also in reverse.

Circumtropical: Widely distributed throughout the tropics.

Cissus DC. Grape Ivys. Genus of the Vitaceae. Tropics, rarely in subtropics. About 350 species. Primarily climbing shrubs with runners; also succulents without runners.
   Non-succulent, climbing species:
▪ *C. antarctica* VENT. Kangeroo Ivy. Evergreen climbing shrub. Very robust, can grow at 5° C. as well as at 18° C. Can be reared as hanging or climbing plant.
▪ *C. discolor* BL. Climbing Ivy. Demanding, decorative, requires high humidity and ample water.

Cissus antarctica

Succulent, climbing species:
▪ *C. quadrangula* L. Liana with cactus-like spikes. For semidesert terrariums with African or Asiatic animals.

Claudius COPE, 1865. Big-headed Mud Turtles. Monotypic genus of the Kinosternidae. Eastern Mexico to Belize. About 10 cm carapace length. Head conspicuously large, only partially retractable. Carapace with 3 weak keels; the rigid plastron is loosely connected to the carapace by means of connective tissue. Uniformly dark brown.

Claudius angustatus

Claudius angustatus

Crepuscular and mainly aquatic. Carnivorous, preying mainly on molluscs, worms, and similar items. Has been bred in captivity. Incubation period is 150 days at 28° C. Ideal for aquariums with a land section. Very aggressive—will bite.

▪ *C. angustatus* COPE, 1865. Eastern Mexico and Belize.

Clelia FITZINGER, 1826. Mussuranas. Genus of the Colubridae, Boiginae. Neotropics from Mexico southward to Argentina, in South America east of the Andes. 6 species. Some systematists include *Clelia* in *Pseudoboa*. In outer

Clelia rustica

Clelia occipitolutea

forest areas, gallery forests, and similar habitats. To 2.5 m. Head more or less distinctly set off. Juvenile *C. clelia* have a black head and yellow neckband followed by a black neckband, the body red-brown. With increasing age the coloration darkens and becomes more uniform, so that adults are uniformly bluish black. Due to these color changes juveniles are often mistaken for *Drepanoides anomalus*, *Pseudoboa coronata*, or *Oxyrhopus formosus*, while adults are similar to *Drymoluber dichrous*.

Nocturnal ground snakes that feed on lizards and snakes, mainly venomous snakes (*Bothrops*). They bite into

Clelia rustica

the neck of the prey and wind themselves around it; they appear to be somewhat immune to the venoms of crotalids. Egg-layers, 40 eggs.

Must be kept in a well-heated dry terrarium. Rarely aggressive, yet caution is advised due to the possibility of venomous bites.

▪ *C. clelia* (DAUDIN, 1803). From Belize and Guatemala southward to Argentina. 2 subspecies.

Clemmys insculpta

Clelia clelia

Clemmys insculpta

Clelia clelia

Clemmys RITGEN, 1828. Pond Turtles. Genus of the Emydidae. North America. 4 species. 12 to 25 cm. Although all the species make hardy terrarium animals, all are considered locally threatened or endangered.

Feed heavily on earthworms and other invertebrates.

▪ *C. guttata* (SCHNEIDER, 1792). Spotted Turtle. Northeastern and eastern USA in small lakes, pools, ponds, ditches. 12 cm carapace length. Irregular yellow spots against

Clemmys marmorata

blackish brown carapace color. Suited for year-round outdoor maintenance, but its small size makes it ideal for the indoor aquarium. Incubation takes 45 to 70 days at 30° C. or 25° C. in an incubator, under natural conditions 70 to 83 days.

• *C. insculpta* (LE CONTE, 1830). Wood Turtle. Northeastern United States. Amphibious mode of life. Prefers small bodies of water in broad-leaf or mixed forest habitats. Recognized by strong radial furrowing of the brown carapace scutes and low carapace keels. Plastron light with dark spots. Mainly carnivorous, primarily on snails and worms, but also eats fruits and other plants. An excellent climber, so requires an adequate fence if kept outdoors. Eggs hatch

Clemmys muhlenbergi

in 40 to 67 days at 30° C. and 25° C. in an incubator, under natural conditions 60 to 77 days.

• *C. marmorata* (BAIRD and GIRARD, 1852). Western Pond Turtle. Coastal North America from Canadian border to northwestern Mexico. 2 subspecies. Prefers larger water bodies than the other species. To 17 cm carapace length. Inconspicuous marbled pattern on carapace. Ideally suited for outdoor pools, where with adequate protection it can be kept outdoors throughout the year.

• *C. muhlenbergi* (SCHOEPFF, 1801). Bog Turtle or Muhlenberg's Turtle. Northeastern and eastern USA in

Clemmys guttata

Clemmys insculpta

Clemmys muhlenbergi

Clemmys guttata

Clemmys marmorata

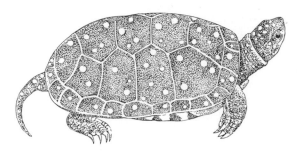

Clemmys guttata

swamps and peat bogs. With a carapace length of only 11 cm, it is the smallest species of the genus. Incubation takes 43 to 62 days at 30° C. and 25° C., respectively. In nature prefers very shallow water. Endangered.

Climatic diagram: Schematic depiction of ecologically significant climatic factors at a particular location based on long-term observations. In the usual climatic diagrams, the top left has the name of location together with its elevation in parentheses and the number of observation years in square brackets. The abscissa shows the months Jan. to Dec. in the Northern Hemisphere or July through June in the Southern Hemisphere, thus providing a comparable representation. The left ordinate axis has a temperature scale, the upper value the annual mean temperature, the lower value the lowest temperature ever measured. A thin black curve marks the progression of monthly mean temperatures. The right ordinate axis has the precipitation scale (10° C. to correspond to 20 mm precipitation), the upper numerical value the mean annual precipitation. A heavy black curve marks the progression of monthly mean precipitation.

If the precipitation curve is above the temperature curve there is a humid climate (shown as a vertically hashed area); if the situation is the reverse the climate is arid (shown as a dotted area). If the monthly precipitation is higher than 100 mm, the scale is reduced by a factor of 10.

Black bars below the abscissa indicate frost periods, and oblique hashed bars indicate the possible occurrence of frost.

Cloaca: Termination of the digestive tract in some invertebrates and vertebrates (cartilaginous fishes, lungfishes, amphibians, reptiles, birds, monotremes) that also receives the efferent ends of the urinary and sex ducts. In amphibians and reptiles the cloaca consists of three parts more or less clearly separated by mucous membranes: an anterior section (proctodeum) where feces is stored; a center section (urodeum) where the urinary and sex ducts enter; and a posterior section that leads to the outside through the vent slit. A urinary bladder may be present in the form of a ventral protrusion from the central segment opposite the urinary ducts, but this is absent in snakes and crocodiles. In the males of Gymnophiona the entire proctodeum can be extruded during copulation, and the copulatory organs in reptiles are special modifications of this section of the cloaca. Cloacal glands can also discharge secretions into the cloaca that play a role in the search for a partner and stimulate reproduction.

Cnemaspis STRAUCH, 1887. Genus of the Gekkonidae. Tropical Africa to southeastern Asia and the Indo-Austra-

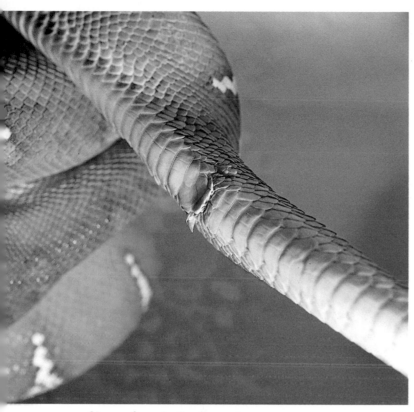

Cloaca of a male *Corallus caninus*

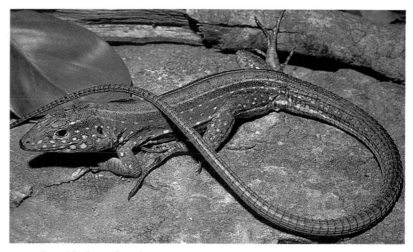

Cnemidophorus lemniscatus

lian Archipelago. Easily 20 species. 8 to barely 15 cm. Slender. Pupil round. Toes not enlarged (except in *C. littoralis*); rows of lamellae under 2 distal joints. In appearance and mode of life reminiscent of *Gonatodes*.
- *C. ornata* (BEDDOME, 1870). Southern India. Dry forests. About 12 cm. Brown with black and white markings.
- *C. littoralis* (JERDON, 1853). India. Dry forests. 8 cm.

Cnemidophorus WAGLER, 1830. Whiptails or Racerunners. Genus of the Teiidae. USA to northern Argentina. About 40 species. Typically in grasslands, prairies, semideserts, and deserts. To 35 cm. Slender, in appearance and behavior similar to Lacertidae. Head relatively long. Tail more than twice snout-vent length. Dorsal scales small, granular, often abruptly changing to large, rough, keeled tail scales. Ventral scales large, smooth, generally in 8 longitudinal rows. Sexes recognizable mainly by the presence of preanal pores in males and larger femoral pores. Mainly brownish or grayish, usually with light longitudinal stripes, sometimes with spotted markings.

Agile diurnal ground-dwellers. Feed on arthropods, mainly grasshoppers and spiders. Apart from normal bisexual species such as *C. sexlineatus*, *C. inornatus*, *C. tigris*, *C. deppei*, and others, there are forms where part of the population is parthenogenic (*C. tesselatus*) and those were males are completely unknown. These parthenogenic species can be allodiploid (*C. neomexicanus*, *C. cozumelus*) or allotriploid (*C. exanguis*, *C. flagellicaudus*, *C. uniparus*, *C. velox*, and others). Generally 4 to 6 eggs are laid, the young hatching in 8 to 10 weeks.

Whiptails require large, spacious terrariums with sufficient hiding places (rocks, dry roots, driftwood, etc.); some of the substrate must be kept slightly moist. Provide day temperatures between 25 and 30° C. and a warmer basking spot. Northern species may tolerate temperatures about 10 degrees cooler. Specimens from the United States should be given a winter dormancy period for about 2 to 3 months at about 10° C. These species can also be kept in outdoor terrariums during the summer months. A varied diet of arthropods and a drinking bowl are required. Give regular ultraviolet radiation as well as calcium and vitamin supplements. Difficult to keep in captivity, often prone to disease.
- *C. deppei* WIEGMANN, 1830. Seven-striped Racerunner. Mexico to Costa Rica. 24 cm.

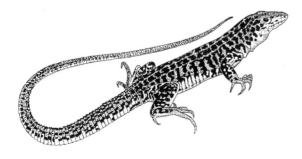

Cnemidophorus tesselatus

Cnemidophorus exsanguis

Cnemidophorus gularis

rator of amphibians and reptiles at the U.S. National Museum in Washington, D.C. *Living Amphibians of the World* (1961); *The New Field Book of Reptiles and Amphibians* (1970) and *The Frogs of Colombia* (1970) (both with C.J. Goin).

Cockroaches: Members of the insect class Blattaria. About 3000 species found primarily in warmer climatic zones around the world. Some are of importance as pests, others as potential disease carriers.

Roaches are eagerly eaten by most terrarium animals. They are commonly found under debris, especially along

Cnemidophorus lemniscatus

• *C. lemniscatus* (LINNAEUS, 1758). Dotted Racerunner. Honduras to Guyana. 30 cm.
• *C. sacki* WIEGMANN, 1834. Spotted Racerunner. Central America. 25 cm.
• *C. sexlineatus* (LINNAEUS, 1758). Six-lined Racerunner. Eastern and central United States. Barely 27 cm.
• *C. tesselatus* (SAY, 1823). Colorado Checkered Whiptail. Southwestern United States, northern Mexico. To 40 cm.

Coccidiosis: Protozoan disease caused by organisms called coccidia affecting blood cells and cells of the digestive tract, mainly in juvenile animals. Snakes and chameleons seem to be more frequently affected than most other reptiles. Specific organs are affected only with massive infestations, so clear-cut clinical symptoms rarely occur. Diarrhea can conceivably be expected with intestinal parasites, which can be fatal in juveniles.

In principle coccidia must be considered as potential pathogens since there is a biological balance between host and parasite that can at any time suddenly be disturbed through exogenous factors.

Therapy: Coccidiostats (sulfonamide).

Prophylaxis: Fecal examinations, especially during quarantine period, and treatment for ectoparasitic intermediate hosts.

Cochran, Doris (1898–1968): American herpetologist, cu-

outer forest edges. Several species can easily be bred. Depending upon the size of the terrarium animals either the nymphs or the adults are fed. When breeding temperate species special precautions have to be taken to prevent inadvertent escapes of cockroaches that can then form the nucleus of a breeding population in home or apartment. Tropical species, as a rule, do not breed readily in human habitations.

Cockroaches are usually bred in glass, plastic or metal containers that are tightly covered with a gauze lid. Covering the upper inner rim of the container with petroleum jelly also prevents cockroaches from escaping. The preferred temperature is between 25 and 30° C. Rat and mouse food pellets, bread, oatmeal, ground chicken meal, dog biscuits, and similar items can be used as food. Water must also be available; it is usually supplied in a test tube plugged with cotton. The substrate should consist of a thin layer of sawdust covered with a layer of corrugated cardboard.

Best known are the Oriental kitchen coackroach, *Blatta orientalis*, with a developmental cycle of 6 months, and the German cockroach, *Blatella germanica*, with a developmental period of about 3 months. The American cockroach, *Periplaneta americana*, reaches a size of more than 5 cm and has a development period of about 6 months. Occasionally some very large tropical and subtropical species are bred,

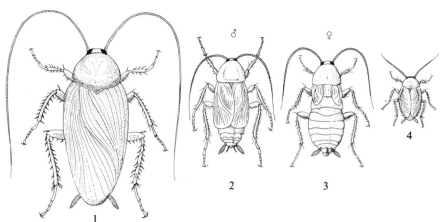

Cockroaches: 1 *Periplaneta americana;* 2 and 3: *Blatella orientalis;*
4 *Ectobius* sp.

such as the giant cockroach, *Blaberus sp.*; the Australian
cockroach, *Periplaneta australesiae*; and the Madeira cockroach, *Leucophaea madeirae*.

Codiaeum A. JUSS. Wonderbush. Genus of the Euphorbiaceae. Southeast Asia. 14 species. Evergreen bushes. Today
widely distributed throughout the tropics as decorative
plants. Require adequate moisture and warmth, but do not
require shade. If too shaded, leaf coloration becomes less
intense. Temperatures not below 18° C. Many varieties of
C. variegatum (L.)A. JUSS. in horticulture.

Coleodactylus PARKER, 1926. Genus of the Gekkonidae.
Brasil, Guyana. 4 species in tropical forests. To 5 cm. Slender, tail and limbs short. Pupil round. Toes only slightly
widened. Dorsal scales weakly overlapping, smooth or
slightly keeled. Claws retractile. Brown with variable lighter markings.

In part diurnal ground-dwellers, often among leaves or
under decaying branches and logs. Natural diet mainly
springtails (Collembola). Females deposit 1-egg clutches
several times a year.
▪ *C. amazonicus* (ANDERSSON, 1918).

Coleonyx GRAY, 1845. Banded Geckos, Clawed Geckos.
Genus of the Gekkonidae. Southwestern United States to
Central America. 5 species in arid and semi-arid habitats.

To 20 cm, slender. Eyelids freely movable. The thick tail
serves as a water storage organ and is about equal to snout-
vent length. Males have strong spurs at sides of tail base.
The relatively delicate limbs lack adhesive lamellae. Light
yellowish brown with variable dark brown spots or irregular crossbands. *Anarbylus switaki* from Baja California and
southern California is very closely related.

Nocturnal ground-dwellers requiring relatively high heat
(preferred temperature is 28° C.). Substrate should be partially damp. At least *Coleonyx variegatus* in the wild requires a winter dormancy period of several months at
about 10° C. 3 to 4 clutches (mostly of 2 eggs each) per
year. Incubation period at 20° C. is about 2 months.
▪ *C. elegans* GRAY, 1845. Mexico, Honduras, Guatemala.
▪ *C. variegatus* (BAIRD, 1859). Western Banded Gecko.
Southwestern United States and northern Mexico. Perhaps
the best known species.

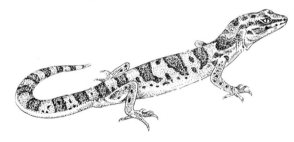

Coleonyx variegatus

Coleonyx variegatus

Coleonyx variegatus

Coleonyx variegatus

Coleonyx variegatus

Coleoptera: Beetles. Largest order of the Insecta, with more than 350,000 species (some estimates exceed 700,000). Many beetles can serve as food for terrarium animals. Of particular importance is the family Tenebrionidae, which among others includes the flour beetle (*Tenebrio molitor*), whose larva is the mealworm. Also eagerly eaten are adults and larvae of many Scarabaeidae, as well as leaf beetles (Chrysomelidae) and weevils (Curculionidae), Elateridae, and Cerambycidae. On the other hand, the commonly caught ladybug beetles (Coccinellidae) are nearly always refused.

Adults and many different larvae are commonly found under loose tree bark, in decaying wood, and underneath rocks. The larvae are often more suitable as food than are the adults, especially the Staphylinidae, Cerambycidae, Silphidae, and Carabidae, which are all occasionally taken, es-

pecially by larger lizards. Also eaten are scarabs (June beetles, etc.).

Only under exceptional circumstances are adult carabids eaten; in fact, these beetles often attack smaller terrarium animals. On the other hand, most large beetles can be left in a terrarium together with amphibians and reptiles for some time without bothering the terrarium occupants.

Collar: Neckband. Perpendicular skin fold below the neck in many lizard species; often called a gular fold. In snakes the word is used for a colored band on the nape.

Collecting: Collecting large and potentially dangerous animals (crocodiles, monitors, giant snakes) as well as venomous snakes should be left to experienced specialists and professional collectors. Any hobbyist collecting animals has to inform himself of any prevailing local, national, and in-

Coleoptera: A giant mealworm beetle

ternational conservation laws and regulations. Collecting methods vary substantially depending upon the species concerned. Amphibians and reptiles often live in specially restricted areas, but may occur in fairly large numbers.

The most favorable time to collect reptiles is during the early morning hours. They are not that fast then and they are often reluctant to leave their sunning locations, so they can often be approached fairly closely before they flee. The evening hours are also suitable, because at that time crepuscular and nocturnal species can be encountered. There are only few amphibians that are actual sun bathers. Most amphibians can be caught with nets in spring during their courtship and mating activities in the water. Larvae are particularly easily caught, and rearing them is often quite feasible. Nocturnal amphibians can often be collected during the day in their hiding places or, if they occupy deep burrows, at night with a flashlight. Those animals following human habitation often tend to congregate around lights, which attract food organisms.

Many amphibians and turtles as well as many lizards and snakes are best caught by hand. Reaching rapidly is often required after large rocks and logs are turned over or after bark has been peeled off (CAUTION: There can also be venomous snakes, scorpions, centipedes, and spiders under rocks and bark!). It is advisable that collecting be done by two people—one who turns over the logs while the other (on the other side) reaches for the animals. Small, fast lizards as well as some snakes are best collected with snares, others in traps. A simple trap is a smooth-walled bucket embedded up to its rim in the ground. In addition, such traps are often even more effective when baited with food. Toads are particularly easy to catch in such traps. It goes without saying that only the healthiest specimens are taken home, while the rest are released unharmed. Obvious ectoparasites (such as ticks) should be removed immediately. Pregnant late-term females should be released (even careful handling and transport often lead to difficulties such as egg-binding and premature births). Special care has to be taken to avoid loss of the tail in lizards.

Colobodactylus AMARAL, 1933. Monotypic genus of the Teiidae. Southeastern Brasil. Small ground-dwelling lizards commonly found in forests. Limbs poorly developed. Few biological details available.
▪ *C. taunayi* AMARAL, 1933.

Colobosaura BOULENGER, 1887. Genus of Teiidae. Brasil, Paraguay. 3 species. Poorly known ground-dwellers. 2 species are known only from their type localities.
▪ *C. modesta* REINHARDT and LUETKEN, 1862. Bahia, Brasil.

Colopus PETERS, 1869. Monotypic geneus of the Gekkonidae. Southern Africa. Presumably nocturnal grounddwellers.
▪ *C. wahlbergi* PETERS, 1869.

Coloration: In animals, coloration is determined primarily by chromatophores embedded in the skin. A variable distribution of these color cells leads to the formation of color patterns and markings that are genetically fixed within a certain range of variability. Amphibians and reptiles usually possess only brown-black, yellow, and red color pigments. Through layering and in conjunction with structural colors (occurring through light refraction and light scattering off the guanine crystals in the guanophores) blue and green color shades are created. Apart from the speciesspecific variability there is also sexual and age-related coloration variation. Occasionally there are also more or less well-defined physiological color changes.

Coloration of an animal provides protection against dangerous ultraviolet radiation from the sun. It also often serves as camouflage by breaking up a body's contours (somatolysis), e. g., in the horned frogs (*Ceratophrys*), and as a disguise (cryptic coloration), e. g., in leaf-tailed geckos (*Phyllurus*) and the flying geckos (*Ptychozoon*), which—aided by their body shape—are virtually unrecognizable against the tree bark.

Particularly conspicuous (phaneric) coloration or coloration elements (warning coloration) are found in many poisonous amphibians (e. g., family Dendrobatidae) and in some venomous snakes (e. g., spectacle markings on the hood of the Indian cobra, *Naja naja naja*), which thus serves to drive off enemies. Certain types of coloration or parts of color patterns are of considerable significance for courtship behavior and related display behavior in many lizards.

Color changes: The ability of an animal to change its body coloration. In certain lizards and snakes color changes are facilitated by the spreading of portions of the skin, suddenly revealing normally hidden colors (e. g., gular pouches in *Anolis*; the bright blue skin between scales on the neck of the bronze tree snake *Dendrelaphis pictus*). These color changes play important roles in courtship as well as serving in threatening and warning behavior.

Physiological color changes are more complicated, since these are determined by external factors (light, temperature, and humidity) and internal factors (excitement, condition of health). Such color changes are initiated through hormonal or neurophysiological changes of the melanin distribution in the melanophores (chromatophores). Color changes are known to occur to some degree in Caudata as well as in Salientia, where it is especially well-defined in the genera *Hyla*, *Cardioglossa*, and *Arthroleptis*.

Among the reptilians it is mainly the chameleons (family Chamaeleonidae) as well as some agamids (family Agamidae), anoles (family Iguanidae), and geckos (family Gekkonidae) that are capable of color changes. Color changes

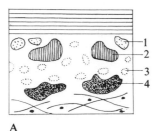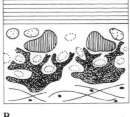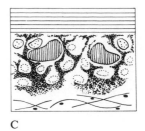

A　　　　　　　　B　　　　　　　　C

Color change mechanisms of *Agama agama:* A Orange; B red-brown; C chocolate brown; 1 yellow lipophores; 2 red lipophores; 3 guanophores; 4 melanophores

for the purpose of camouflage are of considerable importance, and often the coloration (or at least tone) of the surroundings is assumed. Color changes also seem to play a role in body temperature regulation, since with its support a certain degree of heat absorption or loss is possible (*Phrynosoma*).

Colostethus COPE, 1866. Genus of the Dendrobatidae. Central America and tropical South America (southward to the Brasilian state of Gojas). More than 40 species. Length only a few cm. In contrast to *Dendrobates*, lacking warning colors and with maxillary dentition. Webbing and skin folds on fingers and toes variably developed. Camouflage colors (brown and cream) are typical for this genus. The back in most species is brown or olive with whitish dorso-lateral longitudinal stripes, the sides are black, sometimes with white dots or patches, and the abdomen is pale.

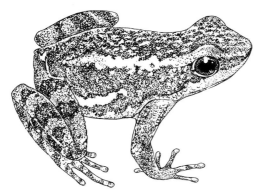

Colostethus inguinalis

For details on natural history refer to Dendrobatidae. However, the males of *Colostethus* carry substantially more larvae on their backs (often more than 20, more or less arranged in 2 rows) than *Dendrobates* and *Phyllobates*. The larvae are nearly always in flowing waters. Care and breeding as for *Dendrobates*.
- *C. inguinalis* (COPE, 1868). Panama, western Colombia (100 to 850 m elevation). 3 cm. Flanks black, interrupted in the pelvic region by a white longitudinal stripe.
- *C. marchesianus* (MELIN, 1941). Eastern Ecuador, *selva* often a long distance from flowing water. Atypically for this genus, the larvae are deposited in the bases of bromeliads and other epiphytes.
- *C. nubicola* (DUNN, 1924). Costa Rica and Panama, up to 1800 m elevation. 2.2 cm. The light dorso-lateral stripe is narrow and clearly delineated above a black lateral band.
- *C. pratti* (BOULENGER, 1899). Costa Rica, Panama, and Colombia, up to 1200 m elevation. 2.4 cm.

- *C. taeniatus* (ANDERSON, 1945). Ecuador, montane forests at 1500-2900 m elevation. 2 cm. Dorsum bronze-green, with more or less defined longitudinal stripes.

Colpoglossus: see *Calluella,* genus.

Coluber LINNAEUS, 1758. Racers. Genus of the Colubridae, Colubrinae. Mainly Holarctic, a few species in adjacent Neotropic, Ethiopian, and Oriental Regions. About 30 species. Probably an artificial assemblage. Found in diverse dry lowland habitats but also in montane regions to 2500 m elevation (steppe valleys, rubble slopes, rocky slopes with brush). 0.6 to 2.5 m. More or less slender. Head more or less set off, the eyes large. Smooth dorsal scales. Many species have attractive markings and bright coloration as juveniles, but gradually assume a uniform, often dark adult coloration with a tendency toward melanism. There is substantial individual variation in some species (*C. ravergieri, C. rhodorhachis,* and others).

Coluber constrictor constrictor, young

Coluber constrictor constrictor

Coluber jugularis

Coluber jugularis

Coluber constrictor foxi

Diurnal ground snakes that are fast movers and also capable climbers. The diet is mainly small mammals, also birds and their eggs, lizards, and other snakes. Juveniles will also feed on insects (especially grasshoppers) and lizards. Some of the smaller, more slender species are lizard-feeders (among others *C. karelini, C. spinalis, C. najadum*); in captivity these are often difficult to acclimate to a diet of mice. Egg-layers, up to 45 eggs per clutch in large species.

Racers should be provided with a well-heated, sunny, dry terrarium with adequate hiding places. Most species are suited for secure outdoor enclosures or an outdoor terrarium with supplementary heating and can (with proper protection) even be over-wintered outdoors. These conditions are more conducive for breeding. Most species are extremely aggressive but often calm down with time; others retain their aggressiveness throughout their life.

Coluber spinalis

Coluber ravergieri

• *C. constrictor* (LINNAEUS, 1758). American Racer. From southwestern Canada over almost all the USA to northeastern Mexico. About 10 subspecies. To 2 m. Adults vary from black to green, some with pale flecks; juveniles have spots and crossbands.

• *C. hippocrepis* LINNAEUS, 1758. Horseshoe Snake. Iberian Peninsula, Sardinia, northwestern Africa. To 1.5 m. Dark brown with black-bordered rhombic pattern against lighter background. Stout body.

• *C. jugularis* GMELIN, 1789. Caspian Whip Snake. Balkan

Coluber karelini

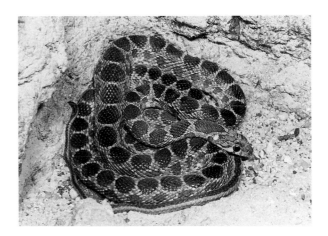

Coluber hippocrepis

Coluber hippocrepis

Coluber viridiflavus

Peninsula throughout Caucasus countries to Asia Minor. 4 subspecies. To almost 2 m. Adults uniformly brown. *C. j. schmidti* NIKOLSKY, 1909, is reddish with bright red ventral region. Stout body.

▪ *C. najadum* (EICHWALD, 1831). Slender Racer. Balkans to Caucasus eastward to northwestern Iran and south to Syria. 2 subspecies. To 1 m. Very slender. Two rows of dots along neck, remainder of body uniformly olive. Likes to climb.

▪ *C. karelini* BRANDT, 1838. Near East and central Asia. 2 subspecies. Variable, similar to sympatric *C. rhodorhachis* (JAN, 1865) and to allopatric *C. florulentus* GEOFFROY, 1827, northeastern Africa; *C. algirus* (WERNER, 1894),

Coluber ravergieri

Coluber ravergieri, young

Coluber ravergieri

Coluber viridiflavus

Coluber rubriceps

Malta and northwestern Africa; *C. rogersi* (ANDERSON, 1893), Libya to Arabia; and others. To 1 m. Very slender. Excellent rock climbers.

• *C. ravergieri* MENETRIES, 1832. Variegated Racer. Caucasus, Near East to Soviet Asia. 3 subspecies. To 1.2 m. Stout.

• *C. viridiflavus* LACEPEDE, 1789. Yellow-green Racer. Western and southern Europe. 2 subspecies. To 2 m. Adults with black and yellow crossbands or uniformly black. Stout body.

Colubridae: Colubrid or typical snakes. Family of the Caenophidia. Largest and most diverse snake group. Separated from other families primarily on the basis of dentition, the teeth aglyphic or opisthoglyphic. The colubrids are generally referred to as "non-venomous" snakes as opposed to the four families of venomous snakes, but with the restriction that some subfamilies of the Colubridae also include species with fangs located far forward in the upper jaw and having highly potent venoms (some Natricinae, Boiginae, Homalopsinae, Aparallactinae). Found in diverse habitats. 20 cm to nearly 4 m long. Head usually with large and regular scales, reduced among the various burrowing species.

Colubrids are diurnal to nocturnal snakes found on the ground, in trees, and in water as well as burrowers. Apart from generalized carnivores there are also some highly specialized feeders. There are no unifying characteristics in the mode of reproduction in this family. They range from egg-layers (with clutches ranging from 1 to more than 100 eggs, depending upon species) to viviparous species.

The great variability of this family makes it hard to define, and the numerous subfamilies are equally hard to define.

The following 14 subfamilies are recognized here:
Xenoderminae, 7 genera; Sibynophinae, 3 genera; Xenodontinae, 28 genera; Calamarinae, 9 genera; Colubrinae, 50 genera; Dasypeltinae, monogeneric; Lycodontinae, 52 genera; Natricinae, 37 genera; Homalopsinae, 11 genera; Boiginae, 73 genera; Dipsadinae, 3 genera; Pareinae, 2 genera; Elachistodontinae, monogeneric; Aparallactinae, 10 genera.

Many genera are doubtfully assigned to subfamilies.

Colubrinae: Subfamily of the Colubridae. A very diverse group with representatives in Asia, Europe, Africa, and the Americas; Australia with only 1 genus. About 50 genera. From 20 cm to more than 3 m. Generally with only a few roughly similar teeth in upper jaw. Fangs always absent. Many Colubrinae are very aggressive and will bite. The following is an attempt at an ecological and morphological summary:

1) Land snakes preferring drier habitats. Diurnal, sun-loving, fast-moving. Diet is mainly lizards, small mammals, and ground birds. *Coluber, Ptyas, Zaocys, Coronella, Masticophis, Mastigodryas, Spalerosophis, Drymarchon, Pseustes,* and others.

2) More or less nocturnal land snakes also preferring dry habitats. Often more or less specialized feeders. *Eirenis* feeds on arthropods; *Lampropeltis* feeds on snakes; *Duberria* feeds on snails; *Pituophis* feeds on mammals.

3) Climbing snakes, frequently found in somewhat more moist habitats and forests. Primarily crepuscular. Diet includes lizards, small mammals, birds and their eggs, frogs (especially arboreal forms). This includes, among others: many species of *Elaphe, Dendrelaphis, Philothamnus, Thrasops, Opheodrys, Dendrophidion, Gastropyxis, Hapsidophrys, Chironius, Leptophis.*

4) Burrowing nocturnal snakes that inhabit variably firm substrates (from loose sand to firm, clay-like steppe soil), preferably in dry areas; rarely found in forests. *Lytorhynchus, Pseudaspis, Chilomeniscus, Chionactis, Phyllorhynchus, Salvadora, Prosymna, Scaphiophis.*

True water snakes and true tree snakes are absent. There are some exceptions, such as certain species of some genera that are somewhat amphibious (e. g., *Elaphe rufodorsata*), while many genera from drier habitats are actually agile swimmer and sometimes flee into water (e. g., *Spilotes, Zaocys,* and others).

Relationships of genera within this subfamily are insufficiently known.

Systematic-zoogeographic review:

Europe: *Coluber* (also occurring in North Africa, northern Asia, North America); *Elaphe* (with similar distribution except not in Africa); *Coronella* (occurs in Europe as well as in North Africa and western Asia); *Eirenis* (in eastern Europe and western Asia).

Asia: *Dendrelaphis* (which has penetrated into Australia); *Eurypholis; Gonyophis; Hydrablabes; Iguanognathus; Liopeltis; Ptyas; Rhynchophis; Zaocys; Lytorhynchus* and *Spalerosophis* (also occur in North Africa).

Africa: *Duberria; Gastropyxis; Hapsidophrys; Meizodon; Philothamnus; Prosymna; Pseudaspis; Scaphiophis; Thrasops.*

North America: *Cemophora; Contia; Opheodrys; Stilosoma.* The genera *Arizona, Chilomeniscus, Chionactis, Drymarchon, Drymobius, Lampropeltis, Masticophis, Phyllorhynchus, Pituophis, Rhinocheilus,* and *Salvadora* also live in Central and/or South America.

Neotropics: *Chironius; Conopsis; Dendrophidion; Drymoluber; Leptodrymus; Leptophis; Mastigodryas; Pseudoficimia; Pseustes; Simophis; Spilotes.*

Comfort behavior: Type of behavior related to body care (removal of ectoparasites and other particulate matter, care of body surfaces or skin derivatives). Body care can be administered to the animal's own body or to other individuals. Such behavior is relatively little developed among am-

Comfort behavior: Licking of the eye by the gecko *Cyrtodactylus pulchellus*

phibians and reptiles and is usually confined to occasional scratching and rubbing against solid objects or by using the extremities. If such behavior is frequently observed for a particular specimen it may be a clear indication of the presence of ectoparasites. Comfort behavior also includes the wiping of the eye reflex in geckos, as well as the licking of the lips after feeding that is particularly typical for monitors and lizards. A special case of comfort behavior is represented by cleaning symbiosis.

Commelinaceae: Spideworts. Family of the Liliatae. Tropics and subtropics. 40 genera, about 600 species. Usually upright shrubs or creepers, somewhat succulent. *Cyanotis, Dichorisandra, Tradescantia, Zebrina.*

Commensalism: Association between different animals for the purpose of mutual utilization of a food source. True commensalism rarely occurs among amphibians and reptiles (e. g., congregations of termite-feeding frogs and lizards at termite mounds). Under terrarium conditions where an unnatural "forced commensalism" can occur due to similar food spectrums of the various inhabitants, the problems of competition for food must not be ignored.

Commensalism: Termites draw large numbers of reptiles and amphibians to their mounds for feeding purposes

Communication: Prerequisite for social behavior. Includes signal transfer and the exchange of information for the purpose of intra- as well as interspecific communication. Communication media include chemical stimuli (e. g., secretions from the cloacal glands in salamanders and related forms during courtship), optical stimuli (e. g., display of erectile gular pouches in *Anolis*), acoustical stimuli

(e. g., vocalization of frogs during the mating season, squeaking of young crocodiles still inside the egg just before hatching), and tactile stimuli (e. g., ramming of male land tortoises before mating).

Community terrarium: Terrarium containing different species; in an extreme case, species of different taxonomic levels. It is important that a community terrarium meets the ecological requirements of the species being cared for. The simplest form of community terrarium is one where closely related species from similar habitats are kept together. However, all animals must be compatible, something which must be determined before they are introduced. For instance, the males of *Anolis carolinensis* and *A. porcatus* are incomptable, while keeping either one of these together with *A. lucius* or *A. sabanus* is quite possible. Various turtles or different smaller frogs can also be kept together. Another form of community terrarium is one where different genera, orders, or families are kept together. Large arboreal lizards (iguanids, basiliscs) are often kept together with small crocodilians.

Competition: May occur between individuals of the same species (intraspecific competition) or among different species (interspecific competition) in order to satisfy their natural requirements, particularly in regard to habitat and food. In interspecific competition one distinguishes more and less competitive species. For instance, the small montane *Lacerta vivipara* is displaced by the larger sand-dwelling *Lacerta agilis*, which is turn is driven out of the habitat by the emerald lizard, *Lacerta viridis*. The possibility of competition always has to be considered when stocking an outdoor terrarium or a community indoor terrarium. Ignoring this can lead to the loss of valuable animals unless competition is eliminated with sparse specimen density, suitable coinhabitants, adequate provision for hiding places, and monitoring of food intake (if need be, individual hand-feeding).

Compsophis MOCQUARD, 1894. Monotypic genus of the Colubridae, Lycodontinae. Northern Madagascar. 17 cm. Head large, clearly distinct from body, with large eyes with round pupils. Dorsal scales smooth, shingled. Uniformly brown, with darker vertebral markings.

Biology and ecology not yet researched. Probably ground snakes in montane forests.
▪ *C. albiventris* MOCQUARD, 1894.

Conflict behavior: During simultaneous activation of different, more or less opposing types of behavior (e. g., attack and flight) a conflict occurs that is solved by a compromise, diverted by a supplementary object, or leads to a displacement activity.

Coniophanes HALLOWELL, 1860. Genus of the Colubridae, Boiginae. Southern USA (Texas) through Central America southward to Ecuador and Peru. 12 species. In dry and moist habitats (gallery forests, outer jungle zones, but also in semideserts). 50 to 75 cm. Head slightly off set. Most species with a more or less distinct light and dark longitudinal striped pattern and a light band through the eye.

Ground snakes. Diet includes frogs, toads, lizards, and small mammals. Should be kept in a well-heated dry terrarium. Danger: Venomous bites possible.

• *C. imperialis* (BAIRD, 1859). Black-striped Snake. Southern Texas and northeastern Mexico to Honduras. 3 subspecies.

• *C. fissidens* (GUENTHER, 1858). Mexico to Ecuador. 6 subspecies.

Conolophus GRAY, 1831. Galapagos Land Iguanas. Genus of the Iguanidae. Galapagos Islands. 1 or 2 species in rocky dry regions. More than 1 m. Body compressed. Large occipital crest and smaller dorsal crest. Yellowish brown.

Herbivorous, including cacti. Egg-layers. Endangered.

• *C. subcristatus* GRAY, 1831. To 1.1 m.

Conophis PETERS, 1860. Genus of the Colubridae, Xenodontinae. Southern Mexico to Costa Rica. 4 species in dry habitats to semideserts. About 70 cm. Dorsal region with longitudinal striped pattern or uniformly dark.

Prey mainly on lizards. Keep in a dry terrarium.

• *C. lineatus* (DUMERIL, DUMERIL, and BIBRON, 1854). Veracruz and Yucatan to Costa Rica. 3 subspecies.

Conopsis GUENTHER, 1858. Genus of the Colubridae, Colubrinae. Central Mexico. 2 species. About 35 cm. Snout pointed. Gray-brown with dark spots and/or ocelli (eye spots).

Ground snakes; litte known about their biology.

• *C. nasutus* GUENTHER, 1858. Highlands of Mexico.

Conrana: see *Conraua*, genus.

Conraua NIEDEN, 1908 (includes *Gigantorana* NOBLE, 1931). Often wrongly spelled *Conrana*. The name is derived not from *Rana*, but instead from the African explorer CONRAU. Genus of doubtful status within the Ranidae. Tropical Africa. 4 or more species in flowing waters, mainly in mountain creeks; *C. goliath* in jungle streams. To 40 cm, including the largest frogs. Often considered a subgenus or synonym of *Rana*, but distinguished from *Rana* by primitive shoulder girdle characteristics, posteriorly completely rounded tongue, and other features. Males larger than females, compact. Head flat, broad. Skin very slippery. Strong legs; toes completely webbed. Dark.

Excellent swimmers and divers that are more or less nocturnal and almost completely aquatic. If they leave their streams at all, they sit on rocks surrounded by water or on the bank, but always very close to water. When disturbed they flee immediately back into the water. Collecting these frogs is extremely difficult, although *C. goliath* can be caught with a cast net. Predatory, mainly on vertebrates. The prey is always eaten under water.

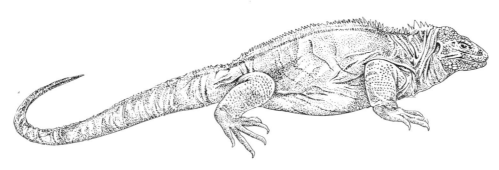

Conolophus subcristatus

Conolophus subcristatus

Large specimens should be kept in spacious aquariums with a small land section. The tank must be covered with a cloth during the acclimation period in order to avoid injuries from fright reactions. Long-term food acquisition often difficult, therefore these animals are mainly kept in public institutions.

- *C. beccarii* (BOULENGER, 1911). Northeastern Africa, Ethiopia. Highland streams. To 16 cm.
- *C. crassipes* (BUCHHOLTZ and PETERS, 1875). West Africa. Montane forest streams. To 9 cm.
- *C. goliath* (BOULENGER, 1906). Goliath Frog, Giant African Frog. Cameroons, Equatorial Guinea. Usually to 30 cm but maximum length 40 cm; largest of the recent frogs.
- *C. robusta* NIEDEN, 1908. Cameroons. Montane forest streams. To 14 cm.

Conspecific: Belonging to the same species.

Constipation: Obstruction of intestine by thickened, hardened feces or (intestinal blockage) by various foreign objects. Animals that are constipated refuse to feed, do not pass any feces, and frequently vomit. In snakes one can palpate a movable swelling along the abdomen and notice flatulence. In herbivorous animals constipation is often caused by too much roughage (excess fiber, rough-stemmed plants), aluminum foil wrappers, plastic bags, and similar items. Carnivorous animals can suffer constipation from a diet that contains too many feathers or rough materials. Endogenous causes for constipation include amoebic dysentery, gout, worm infestations, insufficient intestinal motility due to metabolic disturbances (e. g., calcium deficiency), excessive periods of time in transit, and hardening of feces following the winter dormancy period.

Therapy: Paraffin oil, which can be administered via stomach pump and simultaneously also as an enema (check with your veternarian first). Glauber's salt (sodium sulfate) or Karlsbad salt is recommended for use with larger animals. If an animal pushes hard or even shows a trend toward cloacal prolapse an antispasmodic should be administered by your veterinarian.

Prophylaxis: Watch for regular bowel movements, especially following prolonged transport, after a winter dormancy period, and subsequent to disease problems. Before animals are transferred to winter quarters, if possible the intestine should be emptied by giving a lukewarm bath.

Contia BAIRD and GIRARD, 1853. Sharptail Snakes. Monotypic genus of the Colubridae, Colubrinae. Western United States in coniferous forests to 2000 m. To 48 cm. With very pointed terminal tail scale. Reddish to pinkish brown with a dark eye stripe.

Nocturnal ground snakes found under tree stumps and rocks. Often out in the open after warm rain. Care and maintenance as for Natricinae of Group 1.

- *C. tenuis* (BAIRD and GIRARD, 1852). Sharptail Snake. Washington to California. Each ventral scale has a dark bar on its anterior edge.

Cope, Edward Drinker (1840–1897): American herpetologist and ichthyologist, publishing largely through the Academy of Natural Science, Philadelphia, and the U.S. National Museum. More than 1300 publications, the most important papers being *The Batrachia of North America* (1889), *Classification of the Ophidia* (1895), and *The Crocodilians, Lizards and Snakes of North America* (1900). In honor of his excellent contributions the American Society of Ichthyologists and Herpetologists gave its journal the name *Copeia*.

Copeotyphlinus TAYLOR, 1968. Monotypic genus of the order Gymnophiona of uncertain family membership, usually included in Caeciliidae, but possibly a representative of

Contia tenuis

Typhlonectidae. Honduras. Body with short, pointed, flattened tail. Very small eyes. Tentacle position as in *Typhlonectes* and *Chthonerpeton*. 130 primary folds, 40 secondary folds.

▪ *C. syntremus* (COPE, 1866). Dark leaden gray; head yellow-brown; furrows narrowly yellow.

Copepoda: Copepods or "oar-footed" crustaceans. Order of the Crustacea. Worldwide distribution. Many types are suitable for feeding to predatory amphibian larvae and small amphibians. Usually caught together with water fleas (daphnia) in standing waters. Small copepod larvae (nauplii) are also suitable as food for newly hatched amphibian larvae.

Copepoda: *Cyclops*

Copepoda: *Canthocampus*

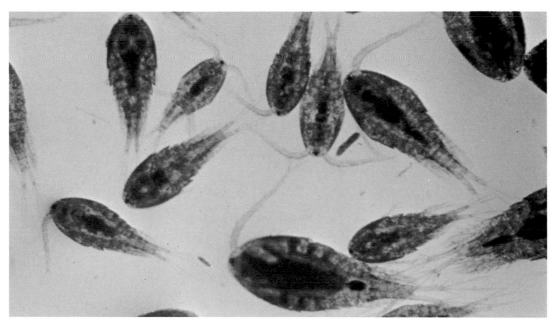

Copepoda: *Cyclops*

Cophixalus BOETTGER, 1892. Genus of the Microhylidae. 20 species (here excluding *Aphantophryne*). Mainly in New Guinea, but 3 species in northeastern Australia. Found in damp coastal forests, rain forests, and cloud forests. Not readily distinguishable from closely related genera (*Oreophryne*, *Sphenophryne*) on the basis of external characteristics. Mostly smooth-skinned. Pupil horizontal. Fingers (and to a large extent also the toes) without webbing. Tips of fingers and toes enlarged. Brown.

Mostly in bushes and on trees. No free-swimming aquatic larvae, embryonic and larval development occurring within the eggs, which are deposited on land.
- *C. ornatus* (FRY, 1912). Northeastern Australia. Coastal forests. 2.5 cm. Dark band from eye to corner of mouth.
- *C. verrucosus* (BOULENGER, 1898). Southern New Guinea, Ferguson Island. 3.5 cm. Skin covered with warts.

Cophophryne: see *Scutiger*, genus.

Cophoscincopus MERTENS, 1934. Monotypic genus of the Scincidae (*Leiolopisma* Group). West Africa. Snout-vent length about 5 cm. Related to *Panaspis*, but with strongly keeled body scales.

Close to water; semi-aquatic. For details of care and maintenance see *Tropidophorus*.
- *C. durus* (COPE, 1862).

Cophotis PETERS, 1861. Earless Agamas. Genus of the Agamidae. Sri Lanka and Sumatra. 2 species. Together with *Ceratophora* and *Lyriocephalus*, it is included in the subfamily Lyriocephalinae. In mountain forests to 2,000 m. Barely 20 cm. Strong occipital, dorsal, and caudal crests and small gular pouch. 2 humps on nose. The prehensile tail has more or less large, spiny scales. Mainly brown.

Diurnal, on or below fallen trees. For details on care see *Ceratophora*.
- *C. ceylanica* PETERS, 1861. Earless Agama. Sri Lanka. To 20 cm. 4 to 5 young.

Cophyla BOETTGER, 1880. Monotypic genus of the Microhylidae. Madagascar. Compact *Rana*-like body. Horizontal pupil. Tympanum not visible. Strong legs, the fingers free and thick, the toes webbed only at the base. Large adhesive discs. Probably arboreal.
- *C. phyllodactyla* BOETTGER, 1880. Nossi-Be, Nossi-Komba, Montagne d'Ambre. 3 cm. Variably gray-brown with darker pattern.

Corallus DAUDIN, 1803. Tree Boas. Genus of the Boidae. Central America into much of South America. 3 species. To 2 m. Body compressed and triangular in cross-section. Large head distinctly set off from body. Large fang-like teeth in anterior upper jaw. Deep pits in upper lip scales. Prehensile tail.

The arboreal *C. caninus* leaves its hiding place in trees less frequently than do the other two species, which are more frequently encountered on the ground. *C. caninus* is a specialized feeder on birds and small mammals, while *C. annulatus* and *C. enydris* also take lizards and frogs as food.

Due to its rigid prey imprinting, *C. caninus* often has greater difficulty in adjusting to captivity than the other two species. However, acclimated specimens are often quite hardy. Keep in a well-heated, tall tropical terrarium with climbing branches. Terrarium plants are recommended for *C. caninus*. Imported females of all species may give birth to rather small young that can be reared on insects, frog meat, and young mice. *C. enydris* has been bred in captivity over several generations.

Cophotis ceylanica

- *C. annulatus* (COPE, 1876). Ringed Tree Boa. Nicaragua to Colombia. 3 subspecies. Follows human habitation. To 1.3 m. Brownish olive.
- *C. caninus* (LINNAEUS, 1758). Emerald Tree Boa. Amazon Basin from Peru to Bolivia and Guyana to Brasil. Tropical rain forest. To 2.2 m. Green with white spots above, yellow below. Young reddish.
- *C. enydris* (LINNAEUS, 1758). Garden Tree Boa. Nicaragua to Peru and Guyana; not in central Amazon Basin. To 2 m. Brownish.

Corallus caninus

Corallus enydris

Corallus caninus

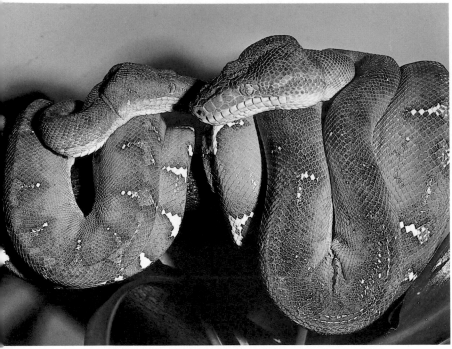

Corallus caninus

Corallus caninus, young

Corallus caninus

Corallus enydris

Corallus caninus

Corallus caninus, young

Corallus enydris cooki, young

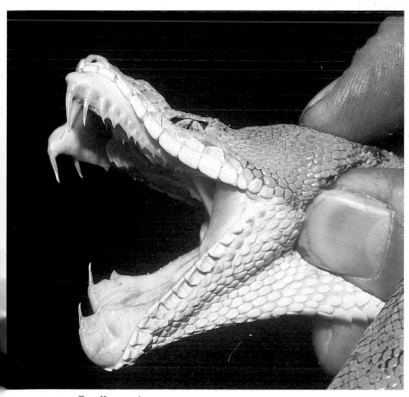

Corallus caninus

Corallus enydris cooki

Corallus enydris

Coral snakes: Collective term for venomous snakes with brightly ringed patterns. Includes the following elapid genera: America: *Micrurus, Micruroides,* and *Leptomicrurus;* Africa: *Homorelaps, Aspidelaps,* and some *Elapsoidea;* Southeast Asia: some *Bungarus, Calliophis;* Australia: *Simoselaps* and others.

Coral snake markings are colorful, consisting of at least yellow (or white) and black alternating crossbands that either extend around the entire body or are restricted to the dorsal side. More completely developed patterns consist of yellow (or white), black, and red bands. All species are more or less dangerous venomous snakes with a highly potent neurotoxin. The facts that the coral snakes have small heads with often tiny fangs and that they are nocturnal and during the day are clearly reluctant to bite make them somewhat less dangerous, although human fatalities are not unknown.

Numerous nonvenomous or only marginally venomous snakes (subfamilies Colubrinae and Boiginae) also have similar banded patterns and in a sympatric situation they are often hard to distinguish from coral snakes (e. g., *Lampropeltis, Boiga, Erythrolamprus, Chionactis*). There are various opinions about the significance of this phenomenon, called mimicry or "Mertensian mimicry."

Coral snake: *Micrurus frontalis*

Cordylosaurus subtesselatus

Cordylidae: Girdle-tailed Lizards. Family of the Squamata (Scincomorpha), suborder Sauria. Southern Africa; *Tracheloptychus* and *Zonosaurus* on Madagascar. 2 subfamilies, 10 genera, fewer than 50 species. Primarily of medium size, with more or less strongly dorso-ventrally flattened body and normally developed limbs; *Chamaesaura* and *Tetradactylus* have extremeley slender bodies and variously reduced limbs. Mostly with large rhombic scales that are frequently arranged in obvious rows; dorsal scales strongly keeled (with few exceptions), some even spiny. Osteoderms present. Head scales firmly fused with roof of skull. Tongue fleshy, slightly furrowed. Nearly always with femoral pores, which are more strongly developed in males.

Some authors give family status to the subfamilies listed here:
- Gerrhosaurinae: Body moderately flattened. Head large, slightly set off. Tail fragile, frequently reminiscent of that of skinks. Large scales in regular longitudinal and transverse rows, sometimes keeled but never spiny. A distinctive deep lateral fold is covered with only granular scales, which permits substantial expansion of body; in *Tracheloptychus* the fold is restricted to the neck region. Egg-layers, as far as is known. Genera: *Angolosaurus, Cordylosaurus, Gerrhosaurus, Tetradactylus, Tracheloptychus,* and *Zonosaurus.*
- Cordylinae: Relatively flattened, with the exception of *Chamaesaura.* Tympanal region laterally widened, thus head clearly set off from neck, triangular when viewed from above. Tail not fragile. Lateral fold absent. Scales often strongly keeled or spiny, with heavily spinous tail whorls. *Platysaurus* is relatively smooth-scaled. Ovoviviparous with the exception of some egg-laying *Platysaurus* spe-

cies. Genera: *Chamaesaura, Cordylus, Platysaurus,* and *Pseudocordylus.*

Cordylosaurus GRAY, 1865. Monotypic genus of the Cordylidae. Southern Africa in open, dry, and sandy habitats. Similar to *Gerrhosaurus,* but substantially smaller and more agile. 15 cm. Prefrontal scales absent. Lower eyelid with a window. Scales underneath toes keeled.

Cordylosaurus likes to dig. It requires elevated temperatures during the day, slightly reduced at night.
- *C. subtesselatus* (SMITH, 1844). Blue-black Plated Lizard. Southern Angola to Cape Province. 15 cm. Dark brown to black with light longitudinal stripes. Tail often blue.

Cordylus LAURENTI, 1768. Girdle-tailed Lizards, Sungazers. Genus of the Cordylidae. Southern Africa, *C. cordylus* to East Africa. Nearly 20 species in rocky, dry regions. From 15 to 40 cm. Large head, triangular when viewed from above. Body strong, more or less flattened dorso-ventrally, with large, keeled scales that are in part spinous, especially behind the head and along the flanks. Tail with spinous scales arranged in whorls. Mainly brown to nearly black, some with lighter spotted pattern. Males with large femoral pores.

When endangered, *Cordylus* will flee into cracks and crevices and there will jam their spinous scales so solidly that the lizards can not be pulled out. They take various arthropods, mainly hard-shelled beetles; larger forms will also take an occasional smaller vertebrate. Although *Cordylus* can handle an extended mealworm diet better than many other lizards, variation is desirable. Larger species will also take newborn mice and even the occasional piece

Cordylus cataphractus

Cordylus warreni depressus

of meat. Ovoviviparous, usually 1 to 6 young per year.

These lizards adapt well to captivity, are relatively peaceful, and are compatible. The terrarium should contain a thick sand layer and a large loosely stacked rock pile, possibly also a branch flat on the ground and some aloe. It is important to provide enough hiding places. A drinking dish is not absolutely necessary, since *Cordylus* can take up sufficient water through the skin, so occasional spraying is sufficient. The substrate should have at least one area that never dries out completely. Day temperatures should be around 30° C. A localized heat source is not really required (but will definitely be used if available). Preferred ground temperature is around 45° C., but a nightly reduction of air temperature to 18 to 20° C., sometimes even lower, is best. Regular ultraviolet radiation and calcium and vitamin supplements should be available. Maintenance in an outdoor terrarium during the summer months is preferred (but be careful of excess humidity).

There are numerous observations on the intelligence and learning capability of *Cordylus*, mainly for the purpose of obtaining food. Various species have been bred in captivity (especially *C. cordylus* and *C. jonesi*), but they are not easy. A cool period of 4 to 8 weeks is recommended as a triggering mechanism for breeding. Rearing the relatively large young (about a quarter of adult size), which barely show an indication of the spinous scales, does not present any problems.

▪ *C. cataphractus* BOIE, 1828. Armadillo Lizard. Southwestern Africa. To 21 cm. Yellow-brown with dark dots. Rather spinuous; rolls up when in danger, taking the tail in the mouth.

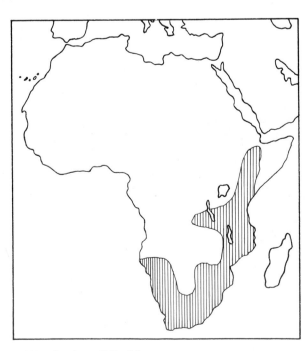

Distribution of *Cordylus*

Cordylus cataphractus

Cordylus giganteus

Cordylus giganteus

Cordylus giganteus

Cordylus cordylus

• *C. cordylus* (L., 1758). Common Girdled Lizard. Southern Africa northward to southern Ethiopia. Several subspecies. Moderately rocky habitats, but also in brushy steppes, under branches and tree stumps. To 18 cm. Ranging in color from black to orange-brown. Greatly reduced spination.

• *C. giganteus* SMITH, 1844. Sun-gazer. Southern Africa. To 40 cm. Brown, with many long spines. Usually 2 young.

• *C. jonesi* (BOULENGER, 1891). Southern Africa. Very similar to *C. cordylus*, often considered to be merely a subspecies.

• *C. warreni* (BOULENGER, 1908). Warren's Girdled Lizard. Southern Africa. Several subspecies. 30 cm. Moderately spiny, strongly flattened. Usually dark brown with lighter spots.

Cornufer: see *Platymantis*, genus.

Cordylus warreni depressus

Coronella girondica

Coronella LAURENTI, 1768. Smooth Snakes. Genus of the Colubridae, Colubrinae. Europe, northwestern Africa, and western Asia. 2 species found on dry mountain slopes up to 3,000 m, as well as in dry lowland habitats such as heath, dry grassland, and evergreen forests. 70 cm. Head barely set off, with small eyes. Smooth dorsal scales. Yellow-brown to gray-brown with indistinct dark brown markings (spots and longitudinal stripes; the latter considered a rare mutant).

Coronella austriaca

Coronella austriaca

Coronella girondica

Lizards are preferred food (*Lacerta, Anguis*), but smooth snakes will also feed on venomous snakes (*Vipera*), small mammals, and birds. When handled, *Coronella* will often bite aggressively and also empty the anal glands.

In a suitably heated terrarium, breeding is possible if a winter dormancy period has been provided. The young can be reared on crickets but should quickly become imprinted on mice as the main diet. Newly collected adults often do not adapt to captive conditions.

- *C. austriaca* LAURENTI, 1768. Smooth Snake. Central and southern Europe to Asia Minor and the Caucasus. 2 subspecies. Live-bearer, up to 15 young.
- *C. girondica* (DAUDIN, 1803). Gironde Smooth Snake. Italy, southern France, Iberian Peninsula. Not as aggressive

Corucia zebrata

Coronella austriaca

as *C. austriaca*. Egg-layer.

Corucia GRAY, 1855. Tree Skinks. Monotypic genus of the Scincidae. Solomon Islands in tropical forests; also follows human habitation. To 65 cm. Stout, with a short, wide head and blunt snout. Scales smooth, conspicuously large, particularly on the long, prehensile tail. Well-developed clawed limbs.

Crepuscular to nocturnal herbivorous tree-dwellers. During the day they hang suspended from branches or hide in tree hollows. Feed mainly on *Piper* and *Epipremnum*. Ovoviviparous (apparently only 1 young).

Need a damp terrarium with climbing branches. Provide a day temperature of 25 to 30° C., dropping during the night to 20° C. Suitable foods include fruit (especially apples) and vegetables mixed with a boiled egg and meat

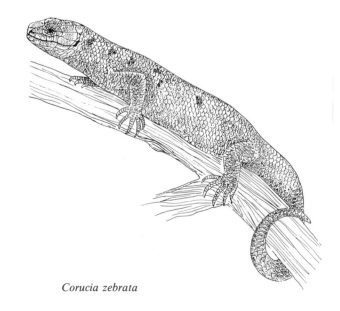

Corucia zebrata

Corucia zebrata

scrapings, also *Monstera* and *Scindapsus*, possibly large insects. Feeding on their own feces (coprophagy) has been observed repeatedly.

• *C. zebrata* GRAY, 1855. Solomons Tree Skink. Greenish white with brownish, often indistinctly banded.

Corytophanes BOIE, 1827. Helmeted Iguanas. Genus of the Iguanidae. Southern Mexico through Central America to northeastern Colombia. 3 species in tropical rain forests. To 35 cm. Slender, laterally compressed. Tail about twice snout-vent length. Limbs long. High helmet on nape fol-

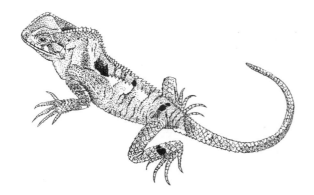

Corytophanes cristatus

Corytophanes cristatus

Corytophanes cristatus

lowed by an occipital crest and a serrated low dorsal crest. When excited not only is the occipital crest raised, but also a moderately developed, also serrated, gular pouch. Dorsal and ventral scales granular with intermixed larger roughened scales. Ventral and lower caudal scales strongly keeled. Mainly brown with some darker spots or bands.

Arboreal, feeding on arthropods. Reproduction apparently occurs throughout the year, with 6 to 11 eggs per clutch. For details on care refer to *Basiliscus*, but not as restricted to water. Males—recognizable by the substantially larger helmet—are rather quarrelsome among themselves.
▪ *C. cristatus* (MERREM, 1821). Smooth-headed Helmeted Iguana. Mexico to Colombia.

Cosmopolitan: Distributed worldwide.

Cosymbotus FITZINGER, 1843. Genus of the Gekkonidae. Southern Asia and the Indo-Australian Archipelago. 2 species. In various habitats that are not too dry; originally on trees and on mountains, but today typically follow human

habitation in and on houses. To 12 cm. Slender, tail about snout-vent length, flattened. Well-developed digital adhesive lamellae. Pupil vertical. Mainly brown.

Diurnal and nocturnal. Partially herbivorous, it does well in captivity and has been bred successfully.
▪ *C. platyurus* (SCHNEIDER, 1792).

Courtship behavior: Type of behavior that is largely genetically fixed, including signals that precede the actual mating and which facilitate the meeting of sexual partners and bond formation. It serves to distinguish and recognize species and individuals and stimulate and synchronize willingness to copulate, as well as serving to dismantle any contact shyness present. This type of behavior is extremely diverse in reptiles and amphibians and includes specialized and also ritualized behaviors related to particular courtship coloration and body appendages (optical stimuli), as well as the use of acoustic, chemical, and tactile stimuli.

Craspedoglossa MUELLER, 1922. Taxon of unclear status within the Leptodactylidae. Considered to be either a genus or a synonym of *Zachaenus*.

Crassula L. Genus of the Crassulaceae. Mainly in southern Africa. About 300 species. Mostly succulent bushes, shrubs, and annual plants. Undemanding and can be easily

Cosymbotus platyurus

Crassula falcata

cultivated. Over-wintering should be dry and light at about 8° C. Excessive fertilization and moisture produce atypical plants. Reproduction in most species is by means of root-forming cuttings.
▪ *C. arborescens* (MILL.) WILLD. False Monkey Bread Tree. Frequently cultivated species. Only smaller plants useful for normal size terrariums.
▪ *C. falcata* (DC. H. WENDL.).
▪ *C. lactea* SOLAND. ex. AIT. Bush. To 30 cm tall.
▪ *C. lycopodioides* LAM. Low semi-bush.
▪ *C. socialis* SCHOENL. Low cushion plant.

Crassulaceae: Family of the Magnoliatae. Predominantly Mediterranean Region, Mexico, and South Africa. About 30 genera, 1400 species. In dry regions. Do not require high temperatures and grow well in dry air. Frost-free overwintering sufficient for non-cold-resistant species.
   Crassula, Echeveria (incl. *Dudleya*), *Kalanchoe* (incl. *Bryophyllum*).

Crenadactylus DIXON and KLUGE, 1964. Monotypic genus of the Gekkonidae. Western Australia. Close to *Diplodactylus*. About 10 cm, with short tail. Ground-dweller.
▪ *C. ocellatus* (GRAY, 1844).

Crepidophryne COPE, 1889 (= *Crepidius*). Monotypic genus of the Bufonidae. Central America. Compressed body, with short legs. Skin covered by numerous tiny warts.

Courtship behavior in the salamander *Mertensiella caucasica;* the spur on the tail base of the male stimulates the female

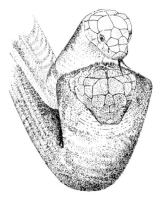

Courtship behavior in the snake *Ophiophagus hannah;* the chin and tongue of the male stroke the head of the female

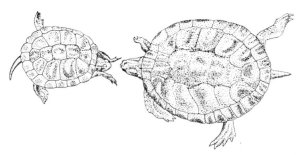

Courtship behavior in the turtle *Chrysemys scripta elegans;* the long claws of the male stroke the face of the female

Without tympanum. Parotoid glands small, roundish. Fingers and toes short, the inner ones largely regressed. Metatarsal tubercles absent.
   Probably ground-dwellers in tropical rain forests. Should be accommodated in a rain-forest terrarium.
▪ *C. epioticus* (COPE, 1876). Costa Rica and Panama. Dark blackish.

Cricetidae: New World rats and mice, true hamsters, lemmings. The Syrian golden hamster as well as some of the other smaller hamsters can be bred with good success as food animals for reptiles. Care and maintenance similar to Muridae, but long-fibered nesting material will have to be provided. The diet should be varied, consisting of different grains, cereals, bread, vegetables, and similar items. Additional drinking water usually is not required. The gestation period is 16 days. There are about 5 litters per year, each

Cricetidae: Hamsters

with 6 to 12 young per litter. It is advisable to keep pregnant and nursing females individually.

Cricosaura GUNDLACH and PETERS, 1863. Cuban Night Lizards. Monotypic genus of the Xanthusiidae. Cuba in tropical forests. 12 cm. Presence of two frontonasals, a simple frontal, and the complete absence of parietals were the reasons used to establish *Cricosaura* in its own subfamily, Cricosaurinae.

Nocturnal, hides during the day under rocks and feeds mainly on various small arthropods. In captivity whiteworms are also accepted. Must be kept in a moderately moist terrarium at temperatures from 25 to 30° C., with a slightly lower temperature at night. Remains buried in loose soil during the day. Drinking water must be available. Occasionally these night lizards will bathe, especially if the humidity is too low.

• *C. typica* GUNDLACH and PETERS, 1863. Cuban Night Lizard. Cuba, Oriente Province. Snout-vent length 3 to 4 cm, tail length 6 to 8 cm. Uniformly brown, the sides darker and the abdomen lighter; a characteristic light postorbital or lateral stripe is present. Very rare.

Crinia TSCHUDI, 1838. Australian Froglets. Genus of the Leptodactylidae. New Guinea, Australia, and Tasmania. Here *Geocrinia* BLAKE is considered to be a synonym of *Crinia*. About 17 species, including some sibling species that are very similar to each other and very hard to distinguish morphologically, being recognized best by the species-specific calls of the males. Froglets occur in a wide range of habitats (with the exception of extremely dry areas) usually in the proximity of water. Many *Crinia* have conspicuously small ranges, but they sometimes occur locally in substantial numbers. Females are larger than males. 2.5-4 cm. Shape and coloration similar to toadlets (*Bufo*). Abdominal skin granular. Pupil horizontal. Tympanum indistinct or not visible. Toes and fingers without webbing; tips of fingers and toes only slightly enlarged or not at all.

Some *Crinia* are semi-aquatic. Largely terrestrial species survive extensive dry periods in subterranean hiding places. In these forms the activity or reproductive period is usually triggered by rainfall. *C. laevis* deposits its spawn in moist burrows and the larvae reach their aquatic environment by being carried along with floods. As far as is known, the other *Crinia* species attach their eggs in clumps to plants or rocks. Some species are dependent on flowing water for their development and have larvae with large suction-cup mouths to prevent drifting.

Crinia should be kept in an unheated or only weakly heated semidamp terrarium with a water section. Should be kept outdoors during the summer months.

• *C. laevis* (GUENTHER, 1864). Coastal area of southeastern Australia, Tasmania. To 3.5 cm. Gray or brown with reddish black-bordered dots, sometimes with an irregular darker pattern.

• *C. parinsignifera* MAIN, 1957. Southeastern Australia, except coastal regions. To 2 cm. Very similar to *C. signifera*, but females without contrasting black and white abdominal pattern.

• *C. signifera* GIRARD, 1853. Common Eastern Froglet. Southeastern Australia, Tasmania. To 3 cm. Coloration extremely variable, even within the same population.

• *C. tasmaniensis* (GUENTHER, 1864). Tasmania above 600 m elevation. 3 cm. Brown or gray, with large, irregular dark spots, often also with orange to dark brown lateral band. Largely aquatic.

Crocodilurus SPIX, 1825. Crocodile Tegus. Monotypic genus of the Teiidae. Northern South America in swampy habitats of the *selva*. Easily 50 cm. Slender with a long, laterally compressed tail with a double keel. Body scales small, granular, dark.

The terrarium must have a spacious water bowl with water temperatures from 24 to 28° C.; provide an air temperature of about 28° C., dropping at night to 20 to 22° C. The natural diet consists mainly of fish and frogs; in captivity pieces of meat, larger arthropods, and occasionally pieces of fruit are also taken. *Crocodilurus* often spends the entire day in shallow water. In a terrarium the water has to be changed frequently, since the feces are deposited there. Not recommended for inexperienced hobbyists.
▪ *C. lacertinus* (DAUDIN, 1802). Crocodile Tegu. Amazon Basin. 50 cm. Makes squeaking sounds.

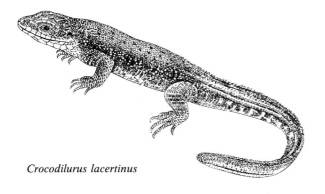
Crocodilurus lacertinus

Crocodylia: Crocodiles, Caimans, and Alligators. Order of the Archosauria in the Reptilia. Circumtropical and subtropical distribution. More closely related to birds than to any other Recent reptiles or amphibians. In existence since the Triassic, with about 14 known fossil families. Recent forms are in 3 families (Alligatoridae, Crocodylidae, Gavialidae).

From about 2 m to 7 m, exceptionally to 10 m (*Crocodylus porosus* and *C. niloticus madagascariensis*). Some of the crocodiles are the largest, heaviest, strongest, and most capable of defending themselves living reptiles. Crocodiles in excess of 3 m have—apart from humans—no enemies. The more or less strictly allopatric distribution of the crocodilians is based essentially on eliminating competition between the large species for comparable requirements for space and food. There was a larger diversity of forms during the Cretaceous and Tertiary, iincluding true land and marine forms.

The body of a crocodilian is superbly anatomically and physiologically adapted to the amphibious mode of life. Eyes, ears, and nostrils are located in elevated positions on the head so that their functions are not impaired even when the animal's body is below the water. In this position crocodiles can also breathe with their mouth open without water entering into the respiratory passage. The choanae enter into the pharyngeal cavity far posteriorly, and a skin valve assures closure of the air passage from the oral cavity. The eyes are closable by means of movable lower lids (the upper lids are more or less ossified) and a semitransparent nictitating membrane. The external auditory meatus (absent in other reptiles) and the nose can also be closed off

with skin folds. Voluminous lungs together with a reduced metabolism and a perforation within the aortic arch allowing equalization of pressure between the lung and body circulations permit crocodiles to submerge for in excess of an hour. The very large, muscular tail serves as an effective propulsion organ for rapid swimming and diving. All crocodilians are agile, tenacious swimmers. The limbs are relatively small, especially the front limbs (with 4 fingers), when compared to the massive body. The hind limbs have 5 toes that are nearly always webbed. The inner 3 toes are equipped with strong claws. Movement on land appears clumsy, but in most species it is rapid and nimble. With the exception of *Gavialis*, crocodiles can elevate their body above the ground and run on extended limbs. Some crocodilians (savannah inhabitants) undertake extensive land migrations in order to look for new suitable habitats.

The large-scaled skin of the crocodilians is—especially on the back—strongly cornified and lies on top of underlying bony plates, thus producing a virtual armor plating. On the other hand, the abdominal region is much more flexible and only contains osseous formations below the skin in the genera *Caiman*, *Paleosuchus*, *Osteolaemus*, and in 3 *Crocodylus* species. Arrangement and number of scales are used as diagnostic characters. Of particular significance are the postoccipitals and nuchals. The last dorsal scale is that one that terminates at the posterior margin of the upper thigh. The scales of the tail are similar to those on the back. The 2 crests along the upper edges—consisting of triangular scales—become fused at about the middle of the tail into a single longitudinal crest.

The jaws in all crocodilians have strong dentition, with teeth that are angled horizontally as well as vertically. The tall, conical teeth, which are open at their base and project from sockets (alveoli), are used for grasping food, but not for chewing and macerating of large food items. Since the dentition is functional throughout the life of the animals, old teeth have to be replaced by new ones. The dentition plays an important part in crocodile systematics.

The crocodile stomach is two-chambered. Food is mechanically prepared in the anterior chamber with aid of strong musculature and grinding plates, aided by rocks (gastroliths) consumed by the crocodilian. However, opinions are divided over the function of these gastroliths. Some scientists consider them to be only a diving aid by increasing the body weight (crocodile stomachs can contain a great number of gastroliths, corresponding to 1% of the body weight). Crocodilians have ribs on the trunk, lumbar, pelvic, and the first 5 to 10 caudal vertebrae, as well as on the first 2 neck vertebrae. Furthermore, they possess abdominal ribs (7 or 8 pairs), which lie unattached in the musculature up to the midline of the abdomen.

There are only assumptions about the maximum age of crocodilians based on the growth rate in relation to body length. Crocodilians never stop growing. Males are generally larger than females. Growth is particularly rapid up to sexual maturity (about 30 cm annually) and then slows down considerably (only a few cm per year). Crocodilians may reach a natural age of about 100 years (proven longevity in captivity is 56 years). Length and width in crocodiles are not always in the same proportions. The snout in young crocodiles is, for instance, relatively short; at the onset of sexual maturity it is elongated; and then it becomes broad in older specimens due to growth in width.

Paired musk glands along the inner jaw and in the cloaca give off secretions during the mating season that serve to stimulate sexual activity. Males have an extrusable, unpaired penis that is inserted into the female's cloacal slit (which in crocodilians is always longitudinally oriented) during mating, which takes place in water. All crocodilians are egg-layers with clutch sizes of about 15 to 100 eggs. As far as is known incubation lasts 64 to 115 days at more or less constant temperatures of 29 and 34° C. and a humidity close to 100%. Females engage in active brood care (nest building, guarding the clutch, coaxing or transporting the young to water). According to nest type, one distinguishes "sand pit diggers" (*Gavialis, Crocodylus acutus, C. intermedius, C. rhombifer, C. niloticus, C. palustris, C. johnstoni, C. siamensis*) and "nest pile builders" (*C. cataphractus, C. novaeguineae, C. porosus, Tomistoma*; all genera of the Alligatoridae).

After they have separated from the mother, young crocodilians in the wild never live together in the same area with sexually mature animals as a biological safety mechanism to avoid cannibalism. Therefore, on crocodiles farms the young are always segregated into size groups. This also facilitates feeding the same size of food items to particular size groups. All crocodilians prey on other animals. The long-snouted ones (*Gavialis, Tomistoma*) are specialized to feed on fish. In the wild prey is apparently taken only in the water, while crocodiles on farms and in zoos also take food on land. Food pieces that are too large to be gulped down are seized with the jaws and then torn apart with the hind legs; frequently this is accompanied by spinning around in the water. Even humans are occasionally attacked by crocodiles, but the widespread fear and dislike of these animals is invariably based on unrealistic impressions. The food demand is not very large since crocodilians are cold-blooded and thus do not require much energy to maintain a constant body temperature. However, they are capable of a certain degree of body heat regulation.

All species are now vastly decimated or nearly extinct due to excessive hunting and the lucrative skin trade. Between 1930 and 1948 more than 250,000 skins of *C. intermedius* were taken in Colombia and 12,509 skins of *C. niloticus* came from Tanzania in 1950. Due to excessive hunting by humans, crocodilians—especially large specimens—have become extremely cryptic except in certain wildlife reserves. Often the animals are even afraid to haul out for sunbathing. Only during the last decade has the concept of crocodile protection been accepted in certain parts of the world. The transport of (and thus the trade) in crocodilian products has become subject to strict international regulations. Independent of this, some countries are protecting their crocodilian populations with their own national legislation.

Today attempts are being made to reconcile crocodile protection and economic interests in crocodile leather. In one method crocodile egg clutches are collected in the wild under government supervision and are then incubated on rearing farms. A certain number of the young raised under these conditions are returned to the wild at an age of about 3 years (usually about 5%; under natural conditions no more than 1 to 2% would have survived. The rest are marketed as leather. Zimbabwe uses this method with *C. niloti-*

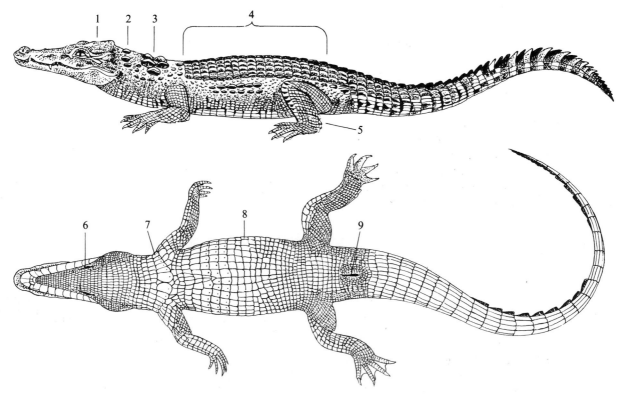

Crocodylia: 1 Occipital shelf; 2 postoccipitals; 3 nuchals; 4 dorsal plates; 5 comb scales; 6 musk glands; 7 collar scales; 8 ventral plates; 9 vent or cloacal opening

cus. In another method, sexually mature animals are kept on farms and are bred there. The young are handled the same as in the first method (e. g., in Cuba with *Crocodylus rhombifer* and Thailand with *C. porosus* and *C. siamensis*). Breeding in zoos is also on the increase in recent years.

Due to the size, dangers involved, and value of the animals, crocodilians should really only be kept on farms or in zoos or similar institutions. Juveniles generally grow quickly, so that after about 2 to 3 years providing proper accommodations becomes increasingly difficult. Moreover, to transfer specimens that have grown too large in private ownership to a suitable institution is often very difficult due to an acute shortage of space there also. Thus hobbyist should restrict their interest to small species from the genera *Osteolaemus*, *Paleosuchus*, and *Alligator*. Unfortunately, however, these species are particularly endangered due to their insufficient reproduction in captivity, and even own-

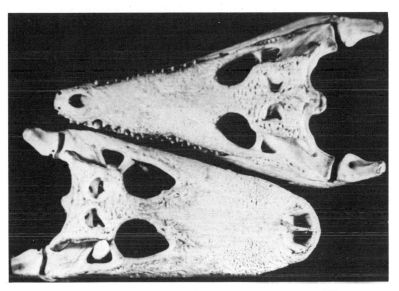

Comparison of the skulls of *Crocodylus* (above) and *Alligator* (below)

ership of these species in public institutions should be criticized. Fortunately, current trends in zoos involve specialization to a few crocodile species and then initiating a breeding program, rather than a random collection of a number of different species that the uninitiated find hard to distinguish anyway.

If properly kept and cared for, crocodilians are usually very hardy. Specimens in excess of 80 cm must be kept in secure enclosures of bolted or welded framework with security glass or heavy wire mesh; the enclosure must be at least 3 times the length of the animal. The enclosure must be set up as an aqua-terrarium with a large water section and a small land section. The water must be sufficiently deep (i. e., about 1 m) if breeding is to be attempted (to permit mating in water). In this case the land area also has to be large enough to permit nest-building and provide either a deep sand layer or nesting materials such as damp straw. Decorative elements such as rocks and logs have to be firmly cemented in. Decorative plants must be out of reach for the crocodilians.

The water section must have a drain that can be serviced from the outside so that feces and leftover food can be re-

moved without danger. Water and air temperatures have to be adjusted in accordance with the country of origin of particular species (in general, a good air temperature is 27 to 30° C., water 25° C.). Clean, hygienic, and odor-free maintenance of crocodilians is only possible with rapid water changes following defecation.

Working inside the terrarium, even with presumably tame animals, has to be done with great caution in order to avoid serious accidents. Dead food must be given by either throwing it toward the animal or by means of a food stick. Caution: all crocodilians will initially remain motionless and then suddenly make a lightning-fast snap at the food, even off to one side! Food should be offered sparingly, about twice a week is adequate, because in captivity crocodilians have a tendency to become fat. If a lot of lean meat or marine fish is given, calcium and vitamin supplements are essential. A lack of vitamin E has detrimental effects on embryonic development resulting in poor hatching. All crocodiles require ultraviolet radiation, even those that are essentially crepuscular in their activities. Long-snouted species damage themselves easily in containers that are too narrow, especially when snapping at food and during their nightly activity phase. Even short-snouted species sometimes incur malformations of the snout in containers that are too small.

Dormancy periods for savannah species and winter dormancies for subtropical crocodilians have seldom been imitated under captive conditions, although it should have positive effects on health and provide stimuli for captive breeding. Good results in this area have been obtained in the USA.

Crocodylidae: Family of the Crocodylia. Circumtropical to subtropical, in Africa and southern Florida entering the temperate zone. Genera: *Crocodylus*, *Osteolaemus*, *Tomistoma*.

The dentition is characteristic: the fourth lower jaw tooth fits into a corresponding pit that is open to the outside and thus remains visible even when the mouth is closed. All the teeth are more or less vertically oriented and bite between each other. The snout (except in *Osteolaemus*) is long and flat, sometimes extremely elongated and thus reminiscent of *Gavialis* (*Tomistoma*, *Crocodylus cataphractus*, *C. johnstoni*). The eyes are clearly smaller than in the Alligatoridae, closer together, less raised, and oriented obliquely, which gives the crocodiles their typical "cross-eyed" facial expression (exception: *Osteolaemus*). The limbs mostly have distinct longitudinal scale combs, the fingers are hardly webbed, and the toes are more or less completely webbed.

Crocodylus LAURENTI, 1768. Crocodiles. Genus of the Crocodylidae. Circumtropical, the largest genus of the recent Crocodylia. 11 species found mainly in freshwater habitats but also in brackish water (*C. acutus*) or more or less regularly in marine situations (*C. porosus*, less frequently *C. niloticus*), thus allowing large distribution areas including islands. All species are closely related and not always easily distinguishable from each other. Hybridization occurs occasionally, but as a rule this is effectively inhibited through geographic or ecological isolation among individual species (e. g., on Cuba *C. rhombifer* occurs in fresh water and *C. acutus* lives in brackish water habitats).

Snout more or less elongated. Dentition typical of family (in contrast to *Tomistoma*), never more than 19 teeth in each side of upper jaw. Elevated ornamentation on the head is in the form of paired ridges converging toward the snout (*C. novaeguineae, C. porosus*), bumps (*C. acutus, C. moreletii*), or triangles (*C. rhombifer, C. siamensis*) between eyes and nose; all other species lack such head ornamentation. Ornamentation along snout margins is more or less distinct and only absent in species with elongated gavial-like snouts (*C. cataphractus, C. johnstoni*). The iris is greenish or yellowish (excellent diagnostic characteristic to distinguish from *Osteolaemus*). Occipital, nuchal, and dorsal

Crocodylus niloticus, young

bucklers well-developed. Posterior margins of limbs equipped with scale combs; fingers usually only webbed at base; toes mostly totally webbed.

Most biological data about *Crocodylus* was obtained from the Nile crocodile, *C. niloticus*. This species occupies various types of habitat in the African savannah and avoids waters in closed forest regions. During the breeding season the males form territories that are marked acoustically by roaring and by patrolling the area by constantly swimming along the territory perimeter. Intruding males are driven off, which can lead to rivalry fights. The females do not prefer the strongest males, but instead those that occupy the areas with the best sunning and nesting sites. The breeding period depends upon the general climate and usually takes place during the dry season (December/January), a period during which the clutches are safe from heavy rainfall and flooding. Only in areas where the dry season coincides with low temperatures do the Nile crocodile populations prefer the warmer, although also wetter, seasons.

Mating actually occurs months before the eggs are laid and takes place in the water. The male pushes himself onto the back of the female and holds on with his claws. Copu-

lation lasts 30 to 120 seconds. Nesting sites are in those areas along sandy river banks without many rocks. If such places are difficult to find it can lead to the establishment of nest colonies with densities of up to 24 nests being counted in an area of 62 square meters. The female digs a pit that is usually 20 to 50 cm deep and is invariably located 2 m above the water line and about 5 to 30 m away from it. Egg-laying occurs at night or during the early morning hours. Usually some 50 eggs are laid and arranged in 3 layers that are then covered over with sand. If the nest is in a sunny location the female also piles grass on top of the nest to provide shade. The temperature in the egg chamber is 30 to 35° C. and never varies more than 3° C. The female guards her nest and leaves it only for short periods of time to cool off in the water. Crocodile nests are frequently raided by Nile monitors, marabous, baboons, hyenas, and other predators.

Incubation lasts for about 11 weeks. The young signal their imminent hatching with squeaking sounds. This is a biological safety mechanism to alert the female of the correct time to remove the compacted top layer of the nest; the newly hatched young would not be strong enough to penetrate this layer on their own. The female then carries the young in her mouth to water or calls them into the water. The nest is not used again.

The maternal family stays together only for a short period of time, and soon the young move away, keeping away from larger specimens and leading a cryptic life as protection against cannibalism. Unfavorable weather conditions are passed in self-dug burrows or caves. Often several juveniles of the same size jointly make a cave and then use it together. About 98% of the young perish during the first year of their life, preyed upon mainly by birds of prey, marabous, soft-shell turtles, and large fish. Only at a size of about 2.5 m (i. e., at an age of 9 to 12 years, representing sexual maturity) do they start living together with other large crocodiles.

The food of Nile crocodiles was investigated (among other places) at the Kruger National Park in South Africa. There crocodiles fed mainly on turtles, antelopes, occasional young giraffes, buffalos, young hippopotamuses, hyenas, and lions. Sometimes dead animals are also eaten.

Other crocodile species deviate more or less in their mode of life from *C. niloticus*. The South American *C. intermedius*, also an occupant of waters in open areas, is a typical crocodile of the *llanos*. It also builds sand pit nests—just as *C. niloticus*—but stays with its young much longer, for several breeding periods. In some areas of its range large specimens of this species may burrow and pass through droughts by means of a summer dormancy period.

C. porosus, the saltwater crocodile that occupies wide areas throughout tropical Asia, builds nest mounds made of plant material and keeps these damp by regularly spraying water on it from a self-dug water pit.

Because these animals are protected by international conservation laws, they are essentially inaccessible to terrarium hobbyists. Moreover, even juveniles have to be handled with extreme care due to their foul temperament and fierce aggression. In spite of activity phases occurring mainly during dusk and dawn, some *Crocodylus* species give—in comparison to *Tomistoma* and some genera of the

Crocodylus niloticus

Alligatoridae—a most alert impression that is combined with—for reptiles—surprising intelligence and memory. The food spectrum offered should be as diversified as possible and consist of live and dead whole animals, mainly fish, birds, and small mammals. Feed sparingly . . . crocodiles have a tendency to grow too fat!

Some species are being systematically bred in outdoor farms (e. g., in Cuba *C. rhombifer* and in Thailand *C. siamensis* and *C. porosus*), but some zoological parks have also had some breeding successes: *C. niloticus* (zoos in Berlin, Cologne, and Nigeria), *C. palustris* (India), *C. acutus* (Santo Domingo), *C. johnstoni* (Melbourne), *C. moreletii* (USA, Mexico). Generally, in zoos and also in some out-

Crocodylus intermedius

• *C. cataphractus* CUVIER, 1824. Panzer Crocodile. Tropical western and central Africa, also eastern Africa in Lake Tanganyika. Polytypic. Freshwater and brackish water habitats. To 4.2 m. Adults dorsally blackish. 4 nuchal bucklers. Endangered.

• *C. intermedius* GRAVES, 1819. Orinoco Crocodile. Upper reaches of the Orinoco, primarily in rivers of the *llanos*. Usually to 4 m (maximum size 7 m). Natural populations severely endangered.

• *C. johnstoni* KREFFT, 1873. Australian Crocodile. Northern Australia. Freshwater habitats. To 3.2 m. 6 nuchal bucklers.

• *C. moreletii* DUMERIL and DUMERIL, 1851. Morelet's Crocodile. Atlantic slope of Central America (Honduras, Guatemala). To 2.5 m. Dorsum of adults nearly black. Natural populations severely endangered.

Crocodylus niloticus

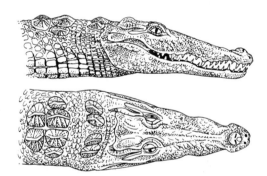

Crocodylus niloticus

door crocodile farms the clutches are transferred to an incubator where through the maintenance of suitable temperatures (about 29 to 34° C.) and a high humidity (about 95%) excellent hatching results are obtained. However, on a crocodile farm in Bangkok, Thailand, the eggs are left in grass nests built by the females themselves, and only the incubation conditions in the nests are monitored.

• *C. acutus* CUVIER, 1807. American Crocodile. Southern Florida through Central America, including some Antillean islands, to Colombia, Peru, and Venezuela. Freshwater, brackish, and seawater habitats. Usually to 3.8 m (maximum length 7.6 m). Natural populations severely endangered.

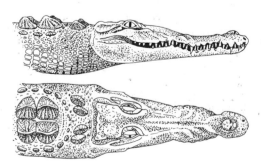

Crocodylus acutus

• *C. niloticus* LAURENTI, 1768. Nile Crocodile. Originally Africa from the Sahara to Cape Province, plus Madagascar, the Seychelles, and the Comoros. Now extinct in many areas, including the last two island groups. Polytypic. To 7 m (maximum size of some races to 10 m). Head in older specimens with strongly bulging lateral margins. Endangered.

• *C. novaeguineae* SCHMIDT, 1928 (including *mindorensis* SCHMIDT, 1935). New Guinea Crocodile. New Guinea and Sulu Archipelago of Philippines. To 5 m, but usually under 3 m. 4 occipital bucklers arranged in one row.

• *C. palustris* LESSON, 1834. Swamp Crocodile. India, Indo-China, Sunda Archipelago. Polytypic. To 5.8 m. Endangered.

• *C. porosus* SCHNEIDER, 1801. Saltwater Crocodile. Orient to northern Australia. Brackish and marine habitats. To 7 m (maximum size 10 m). In contrast to *C. novaeguineae*,

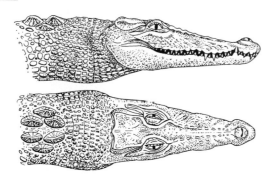

Crocodylus porosus

Crocodylus johnstoni

usually without occipital bucklers. Populations severely endangered, but farm breeding has prevented extinction.

▪ *C. rhombifer* CUVIER, 1807. Cuban Crocodile. Cuba and Isle of Pines. Fresh water. To 4 m. Dorsum in adults black, with contrasting yellow dots. Endangered.

▪ *C. siamensis* SCHNEIDER, 1801. Siamese Crocodile. Indo-China, Java, Kalimantan. Fresh water. To 3.8 m. Populations severely endangered, but extinction prevented through farm breeding.

Crossobamon eversmanni

Crossobamon BOETTGER, 1888. Monotypic genus of the Gekkonidae found from Iran to central Asia in deserts and semideserts. Easily 15 cm. Slender, tail about 1.5 times snout-vent length. Toes without adhesive lamellae. Pupil vertical. Brownish.

Crepuscular and nocturnal ground-dwellers, occasionally moderate climbers. For details on care refer to *Teratoscincus*.

▪ *C. eversmanni* (WIEGMANN, 1834).

Crossodactylodes COCHRAN, 1938. Monotypic genus of the Leptodactylidae. Southeastern Brasil. Stout, oval. Similar to *Zachaenus*, but with broader finger and toe tips.

Terrestrial. The few large eggs are deposited in bromeliads, where the larvae develop under semi-aquatic conditions.

▪ *C. pintoi* COCHRAN, 1938. To 1.7 cm. Brown.

Crossodactylus DUMERIL and BIBRON, 1841. Genus of the Leptodactylidae. Southeastern Brasil and northern Argentina. 6 species. Pupil horizontal. Clearly visible tympanum. Free fingers and toes with enlarged tips; males with

species-specific number of spines on thumb. Ground-dwellers.

▪ *C. gaudichaudi* DUMERIL and BIBRON, 1841. Vicinity of Rio de Janeiro. To 3 cm. Olive with white glandular stripe behind tympanum. Up to 6 thumb spines.

▪ *C. aeneus* MUELLER, 1924. Similar to *C. gaudichaudi*. Up to 5 thumb spines.

Crotalidae: Pit Vipers. Family of the Caenophidia (often considered a subfamily of Viperidae). Nearctic and Neotropical, with a few representatives also in the eastern Palearctic and Orient. 12 genera: *Agkistrodon* (with *Calloselasma, Deinagkistrodon, Gloydius*), *Crotalus, Sistrurus, Lachesis, Bothrops, Trimeresurus* (with *Ovophis* and *Tropidolaemus*), *Hypnale*. In temperate and cool climates (Canada, Siberia, mountainous central Asia, and much of America) as well as in dry and hot desert areas, steppes, thornbush regions, and various types of tropical forests. 0.6 m to 3.5 m. Massive in build. Head in many species nearly triangular, clearly set off from body. In primitive forms the top of the head has large regular scales (*Agkistrodon, Sistrurus*); specialized genera have small, irregular head scales. Between the nostril and eye on each side is a conspicuous pit (thus "pit vipers") that can be compared in function to the labial pits in some Boidae. The pit organs can detect temperature variations of as low as .003° C. and play an important part in the search for food and orientation in darkness. At the front of the upper jaw are the solenoglyphic fangs that can be fully erected by means of ligaments in the mov-

Crotalidae: 1 Nostril; 2 pit organ

able upper jaw. They are folded back and protected inside
a skin fold when the mouth is closed. The relative and absolute size of the fangs is considerable. The tail is short.
Arboreal species have a prehensile tail (*Trimeresurus*, *Bothrops schlegeli*). The rattles at the end of the tail in the genera *Crotalus* and *Sistrurus* are unique. The venom is
strongly hemotoxic, with some additional neurotoxic components in a few species (e. g., *Crotalus durissus terrificus*).
Extensive necrosis that can lead to amputation is often the
after-effect of non-lethal bites, especially from *Bothrops*
species.

Crepuscular and nocturnal. Mostly terrestrial, but the
genus *Agkistrodon* has some amphibious species and the
genera *Bothrops* and *Trimeresurus* have arboreal species. *Agkistrodon*, *Sistrurus*, and *Crotalus* have species superbly ad-
apated to cool climates, but there are also tropical crotalid
species that prefer moderate temperatures (e. g., *Lachesis*,
various montane species of *Trimeresurus*). Many species are
adapted to more or less dry habitats (e. g., *Crotalus cerastes*).

Crotalids feed mainly on vertebrates, usually small mammals. Food specialists include *Agkistrodon piscivorus*, a fish-
eater, and some *Trimeresurus* that feed on lizards or frogs.
Many juvenile crotalids feed on arthropods.

Ritualistic fighting is common among males, especially
among *Crotalus*. Most crotalids are live-bearers. Some *Agkistrodon* species, *Lachesis*, *Trimeresurus monticola*, *T. kaulbacki*, and *T. mucrosquamatus* are egg-layers.

Many species do well in captivity, live long lives, and
have been bred. Rearing the extremely small juveniles of
Agkistrodon contortrix and some *Trimeresurus* and *Bothrops*
species is complicated.

Crotalus LINNAEUS, 1758. Rattlesnakes. Genus of the
Crotalidae. Americas, with the greatest diversity in the
southwestern USA and Mexico; only *C. durissus* and *C. vegrandis* occur in South America. About 27 species, many
polytypic. Found in many habitats but seem to prefer outer
forest regions, prairies, rocky and sandy deserts; few species in humid forests. The rattle is distinctive and causes a
rattling warning sound. The rattle is completely lost in *C.
catalinensis*. The dorsal surface of the head is covered with
small scales, except the large supraorbital scales (in con-

Crotalus adamanteus

trast to *Sistrurus*). There are uniformly colored species as
well as those marked with rows of rhomboids or crossbands. The dominant colors are shades of brown.

Crepuscular and nocturnal ground snakes. Prey consists
mainly of mammals and ground birds. Smaller species,
such as *C. lepidus*, *C. pricei*, *C. transversa*, and others, feed
mainly on lizards.

Crotalus cerastes

Crotalus atrox

Mating, which can last up to 20 hours, is preceded by impressive ritualistic fights among males. Live-bearers, 6 to 60 young. Sperm storage is frequently observed among *Crotalus* females.

The venom in most *Crotalus* is hemotoxic; only in *C. durissus* is there also a large neurotoxic component. Because of the length of their fangs and the amount of venom present, the large *Crotalus* species are extremely dangerous. Polyvalent and monovalent antiserums are available.

Crotalus atrox

Many species, especially *C. atrox*, *C. adamanteus*, and *C. durissus*, have substantial longevities in well-heated dry terrariums. Some of these have been bred for generations. Species from northern latitudes and high elevations require a winter dormancy period, an important prerequisite for captive breeding of *C. viridis*, *C. horridus*, and *C. lepidus*. Some species, such as *C. horridus* and *C. durissus*, prefer more moisture and should be given bathing facilities as well as hiding places. For desert species that also like to bathe (*C. atrox*, *C. basiliscus*, *C. cerastes*), a nocturnal temperature reduction and increase in humdity are essential.

- *C. adamanteus* BEAUVOIS, 1799. Eastern Diamondback Rattlesnake. Southeastern USA. Warm coastal lowlands. Largest species of this genus, to 2.5 m and 10 kg in weight. Frequently bred in captivity. Extremely dangerous.
- *C. atrox* BAIRD and GIRARD, 1853. Western Diamondback Rattlesnake. Southwestern USA to Mexico. 1.5 m, rarely more than 2 m. Most commonly kept species; ecologically very adaptable. Frequently bred. Causes the most snake bites in USA. Very dangerous.
- *C. basiliscus* (COPE, 1864). Basilisk Rattlesnake. Mexico. 2 subspecies. Dry forest habitats along the western coast. Medium size. Extremely dangerous venom.

Crotalus cerastes

- *C. catalinensis* CLIFF, 1954. Catalina Rattlesnake. Found only on Catalina Island, Gulf of California. Only species without a rattle. Medium size.
- *C. cerastes* HALLOWELL, 1854. Sidewinder. Southwestern USA and northwestern Mexico. 3 subspecies. Deserts. Small. Feeds on lizards.
- *C. durissus* LINNAEUS, 1758. Cascaval or South American Rattlesnake. Southern Mexico to Brasil and northern Argentina. 6 subspecies. The most widely distributed South American rattlesnake. In dry habitats (savannahs, outer forest regions). To 1.8 m. Despite serum therapy, 10% of

Crotalus durissus cascavella

Crotalus durissus terrificus

Crotalus horridus

Crotalus horridus

Crotalus horridus

Crotalus durissus terrificus

Crotalus lepidus klauberi

bites are lethal. Durable and hardy in captivity; can be bred.

▪ *C. vegrandis* KLABER, 1941. Venezuela.

▪ *C. horridus* LINNAEUS, 1758. Timber Rattlesnake. Eastern United States. Forest and swamps, mountains to bottomlands. Requires winter dormancy period. 1.9 m.

▪ *C. lepidus* (KENNICOTT, 1861). Rock Rattlesnake. Southwestern United States to central Mexico. 3 subspecies. 82 cm.

Crotalus lepidus lepidus

Crotalus lepidus klauberi

Crotalus molossus nigrescens

Crotalus molossus

▪ *C. molossus* (BAIRD and GIRARD, 1853). Blacktail Rattlesnake. Arizona and Texas to Mexico. 3 subspecies. Medium size, 82 cm.

▪ *C. viridis* (RAFINESQUE, 1818). Prairie Rattlesnake, Western Rattlesnake. Southwestern Canada (northernmost *Crotalus* species) to northwestern Mexico, also at higher elevations. About 9 subspecies. 1.6 m. Winter dormancy period strongly recommended.

Crotalus scutellatus

Crotalus viridis

Crotalus viridis nuntius

Crotalus viridis viridis

Crotalus viridis

Crotaphopeltis hotamboeia

Diurnal ground-dwellers. Excellent jumpers with powerful hind legs; will flee when threatened, sometimes running rapidly on hind legs. The diet is mainly arthropods, but young lizards, snakes, and occasionally plant matter are taken. Egg-layers, 2 to 24 eggs. Frequently 2 clutches in brief succession. For care and maintenance see *Sceloporus*. Require a spacious terrarium. Collared lizards often do not adapt well to captivity and can be rather delicate at

Crotaphytus collaris

times. Require a lot of heat; can endure up to 45° C., preferred temperatures between 37 and 39° C. A well-defined day-night temperature cycle is important.
▪ *C. collaris* (SAY, 1823). Collared Lizard. Central USA to Mexico. To 35 cm. Greenish, yellowish, or brownish with

Crotaphytus collaris

Crotaphopeltis FITZINGER, 1843. Genus of the Colubridae, Boiginae. Tropical and southern Africa. 3 species. To 70 cm. Very similar to *Telescopus*.

2 species inhabitat different types of dry habitats and 1 species is amphibious. Nocturnal, feeding mainly on Salientia (especially toads), lizards, and small mammals. Egg-layers, 6 to 12 eggs. Must be kept in a well-heated, dry terrarium similar to *Coluber*.
▪ *C. degeni* (BOULENGER, 1898). Central eastern Africa. Amphibious. Feeds on frogs. For details on care refer to Natricinae, Group 2.
▪ *C. hotamboeia* (LAURENTI, 1768). White-lipped Snake. East to South Africa. Dry habitats.

Crotaphytus HOLBROOK, 1842. Collared Lizards. Genus of the Iguanidae. Central USA to Mexico. Closely related to *Gambelia*. 4 species in rocky, open areas. To 40 cm. Stout, massive body with large, broad head. Tail about twice snout-vent length. Markings and coloration highly variable. Collar of 2 black bands with white interspace in *C. collaris*, reduced in other species.

Crotaphytus bicinctores

Crotaphytus collaris

Crustacea: *Gecarcinus,* a land crab

lighter spotted pattern. Distinct double neck collar. Egg-bearing females have deep red lateral spots.
▪ *C. reticulatus* BAIRD, 1858. Reticulate Collared Lizard. Southwestern Texas and adjacent northern Mexico. 42 cm. Collar absent. Several cross rows of black spots with light edges.

Crustacea: Largest and most diverse class of Arthropoda. Copepods, daphnia, brine shrimp, isopods, amphipods, shrimp, crawfish, crabs. The crustaceans provide good food for some of the aquatic amphibians and their larvae, while some snakes and turtles feed heavily on shrimp and crawfish. Land-dwelling isopods are also eaten by terrestrial amphibians and many lizards.

Crustacea: *Pacifastacus leniusculus,* a crawfish

Crustacea: *Procambarus alleni,* a crawfish

Crustacea: *Porcellio scaber,* a terrestrial isopod or sowbug

Crustacea: *Coenobita perlatus,* a land hermit crab

• *C. acaulis* (LINDL) BEER. Can take sunny locations and temperatures below 18° C.
• *C. beuckeri* E. MORR.
• *C. bivittatus* (HOOK.) REGEL. Easy to cultivate.
• *C. bromeloides* OTTO and A. DIETR. About 30 to 40 cm tall.
• *C. fosterianus* L. B. SMITH. Leaves to 30 cm. Reproduction through shoots.
• *C. zonatus* (VIS.) BEER. Leaves to 20 cm.

Cryptobatrachus RUTHVEN, 1916. Genus of the Hylidae. Colombia. About 3 species, insufficiently defined. In more or less damp montane rain forests. Fingers free, toes webbed from ⅔ to ¾ of their length. Brown base coloration with lighter thigh markings, somtimes also body markings.

As far as is known *Cryptobatrachus* has a rather specialized mode of reproduction. Eggs and larvae develop into fully metamorphosed juvenile frogs on the back of the female.
• *C. fuhrmanni* (PERACCA, 1914). To 6 cm (males smaller).

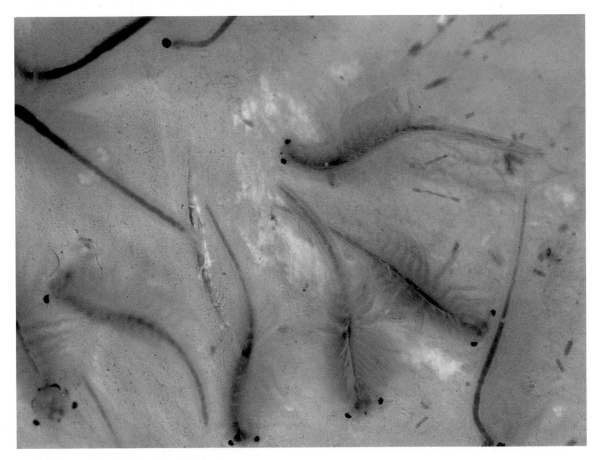

Crustacea: *Artemia,* the brine shrimp

Cryptanthus OTTO and A. DIETR. Genus of the Bromeliaceae. Brasil, Surinam. 20 species in dry forests. Require temperature of 20° C. and a light but not necessarily sunny location with adequate moisture. Should be cultured on humus-rich, loose soil; will also survive as epiphytes. Reproduction by means of new shoots rising abundantly from axis of the rosette leaves.

Cryptoblepharus WIEGMANN, 1834. Genus of the Scincidae (*Leiolopisma* Group). Southeast Africa, the Indo-Pacific islands, Australia, Hawaii, and the western coast of Peru, widely introduced. Currently thought to be a monotypic species with many subspecies. Found in various habitats. About 10 cm. Slender. Fused eyelid spectacle. Well-developed 5-toed limbs. Brown, gray, or black, often with light

Cryptoblepharus boutoni poecilopleurus

longitudinal stripes.

Equally as agile on the ground as in trees, on islands frequently found among mangroves or in the littoral zone. Like sun. Feed on small arthropods. Clutches consist of 1 or 2 eggs.
▪ *C. boutoni* (DESJARDIN, 1831).

Cryptobranchidae: Giant Salamanders, Hellbenders. Family of the Caudata. Southeastern Palearctic (genus *Andrias*) and eastern Nearctic (genus *Cryptobranchus*). *Andrias* was also represented in Europe (Alps, Pyrenees) during the Miocene. To 1.8 m. Massive. Head and body flattened dor-

Cryptoblepharus boutoni

so-ventrally. Head large, mouth deeply cleft, eyes tiny Hands with 4 fingers. Sides with pleated skin folds. Tail shorter than body, strongly compressed. Skin slimy. Metamorphosis incomplete. Although the external gills are reduced in adults, the eyes always remain lidless, the arrangement of teeth is identical for larvae and adults, and there is an external gill slit.

Aquatic. Eggs are fertilized externally, as in the related family Hynobiidae. Development progresses slowly, the larval period lasting about 2 years, and sexual maturity occurring after 5 years at the earliest. Although totally harmless, they are considered to be dangerous by fishermen.

Cryptobranchus LEUCKART, 1821. Hellbenders. Monotypic genus of the Cryptobranchidae. Eastern North America. Prefers fast-flowing rivers and streams of 25 to 75 cm water depth. Externally very similar to eastern Palearctic genus *Andrias*, but after metamorphosis usually 1 pair of open gill slits remain (sometimes closed on one side) and longitudinal furrows are present on the throat that fuse toward the chin. 4 gill arches are maintained internally.

During the day *Cryptobranchus* remains at the bottom, hiding under large rocks, sunken driftwood, and similar places.

If correctly kept, *Cryptobranchus* can be quite hardy in captivity. They require spacious aquariums with clean, chlorine-free, well aerated, preferably filtered water. Keep in a dark location. Aquatic insect larvae, earthworms, newly molted crawfish, and fish are eaten; will often adapt to strips of lean meat. Apparently have rarely been bred in captivity.

Cryptobranchus alleganiensis

▪ *C. alleganiensis* (DAUDIN, 1802). Hellbender. Polytypic species. Nominate form widely distributed in northeastern USA especially Susquehanna River system; subspecies *bishopi* GROBMAN, 1942, restricted to Ozarks. 28 to 57 cm (record length, male 69 cm, female 74 cm). Mainly gray but also yellow-brown to black, often with washed-out spotted pattern.

Cryptodelma: see *Pygopus*, genus.

Cryptodira: Suborder of the Testudinata. Worldwide distribution. 10 families: Chelydridae, Kinosternidae, Dermatemyidae, Platysternidae, Emydidae, Testudinidae, Cheloniidae, Dermochelyidae, Trionychidae, and Carettochelyidae. These typical turtles are capable of retracting the head into the carapace by means of an S-shaped bend in the vertebral column. Reduction of transverse processes of neck vertebrae facilitates the strong bending of the neck section of the vertebral column. However, in some groups of the Cryptodira the ability to retract the head has been greatly restricted (Cheloniidae, Dermochelyidae). Another anatomical characteristic of the Cryptodira is that the pelvis is freely suspended inside the carapace. The plastron usually consists of 6 pairs of scutes, the most anterior ones fused into a single plate. The intergular plate is always absent.

Cryptolycus BROADLEY, 1968. Monotypic genus of the Colubridae, Lycodontinae. Southeastern Africa (Mozambique) in dry habitats. Ground snakes.
▪ *C. nanus* BROADLEY, 1968.

Cryptophis WORRELL, 1961. Small-eyed Snakes. Genus of the Elapidae. Eastern and northern Australia. 2 species in dry to wet tropical forests. About 50 cm, sometimes up to a maximum size of 1.2 m. Head slightly but still clearly set off from body. Usually dark brown to blackish.

Terrestrial, nocturnal venomous snakes. Feeds on frogs and lizards. Live-bearers, about 2 to 6 young. Keep in a well-heated forest terrarium with hiding places and a large water bowl. Caution: Dangerous bites.
▪ *C. nigrescens* (GUENTHER, 186__). Eastern Small-eyed Snake. Eastern Australia in coastal regions.

Cryptosophis BOULENGER, 1883. Monotypic genus of the Caeciliidae. Central America. Eyes covered by skull bones. Lower jaw with only one row of teeth. Tentacle apparatus tiny, situated closer to eye than to nostril. 117 to 126 primary folds, 97 to 106 secondary folds; tiny scales. Cloacal slot perpendicular.
▪ *C. simus* (COPE, 1877). Nicaragua, Costa Rica. To 47 cm. Dark brown, ventral region slightly lighter (in preservative).

Cryptothylax LAURENT and COMBAZ, 1950. Monotypic genus of the Rhacophoridae. Zaire. In tropical rain forests. Pupil vertical. Tympanum clearly visible. Distinguished from related genus *Kassina* by the presence of completely webbed toes. Adhesive discs large. Tree-dwellers.
▪ *C. greshoffi* (SCHILTHUIS, 1889). Light rust brown with strong, wax-like gloss. Fingers orange, red throat, abdomen yellowish white, iris emerald green.

Ctenoblepharis TSCHUDI, 1845. Genus of the Iguanidae. From Peru and Chile to Bolivia and Argentina. 6 species. Found in open, relatively dry habitats. Easily 15 cm. Moderately flattened.

Tree-dwellers. Similar in appearance and related to *Tropidurus*. Not kept as terrarium specimens.
• *C. adspersus* TSCHUDI, 1845. Peruvian coastal deserts.
• *C. janesi* BOULENGER, 1891. Chile, in the Andes to elevations in excess of 3000 m.

Ctenodon: see *Tupinambis*, genus.

Ctenophryne MOCQUARD, 1904. Monotypic genus of the Microhylidae. Tropical South America in *selva*. Robust, compact, smooth-skinned. Head relatively large and wide, with a pointed snout. Tympanum not visible. Body wide and egg-shaped when viewed from above. Fingers short, with lateral skin seams. Toes mostly webbed. Vocalizes with a continuous trill.
• *C. geayi* MOCQUARD, 1904. Colombia, Ecuador, Peru, Guyana, Brasil. 5.5 cm. Light brown with whitish yellow dorsal stripe. Abdomen dark, with creamy spots.

Ctenosaura pectinata

Ctenosaura hemilopha

Ctenosaura WIEGMANN, 1828. Black Iguanas, Spiny-tailed Iguanas. Genus of the Iguanidae. Mexico, large areas of Central America and adjacent islands to Panama. 4 or 5 species in open forests along rocky slopes. 0.8 to 1 m. Strongly built. The tail serves as a defensive weapon and is equipped with whorls of very large, strongly spined scales; located between the whorls are one or several rows of granular scales. Low dorsal crest present. Juveniles mainly green; adults dark brown to black with light or dark crossbands.

Found on rocks, on walls, or high in trees, usually in groups dominated by a major male. Clutches of 20 to 30 eggs; incubation period about 3 months.

Ctenosaura pectinata

Must be given relatively high heat in captivity and a moderate nightly reduction to about 20° C. These iguanas do not require much water, yet a water dish must be available. Apart from various plants, mainly fruit, the diet includes arthropods, young mice, and lean meat. Males tend to fight among themselves.

▪ *C. acanthura* (SHAW, 1802). Mainly along the Atlantic side of Mexico. Only a few tail whorls; more than one row of granular scales between the whorled scales.

▪ *C. similis* (GRAY, 1831). Mexico to Panama. Most frequently imported species. More than one row of granular scales between tail whorls.

Ctenotus STORR, 1964. Genus of the Scincidae. Australia and New Guinea (1 species). Over 40 species. Closely related to *Sphenomorphus*. In dry, desert-like habitats. To 30 cm. Slender, with long tail. Lower eyelid movable, without window. Ear opening distinct. Well-developed 5-toed limbs. Dorsal scales smooth to weakly keeled. Have bright longitudinal stripes and sometimes spots.

Diurnal ground-dwellers with very high activity temperatures. Egg-layers. Best kept in desert or steppe terrariums at temperatures about 30° C., with localized radiant heat; at night drop the temperature to about 15 to 20° C. Should be given a varied diet of arthropods.

▪ *C. pantherinus* (PETERS, 1869). Central and western Australia. 25 cm. Grasslands. Light spots with dark edges arranged in longitudinal rows.

▪ *C. taeniolatus* (SHAW, 1802). Copper-tailed Skink. Eastern Australia. 25 cm. Shiny brown with numerous light longitudinal stripes. Tail copper-colored.

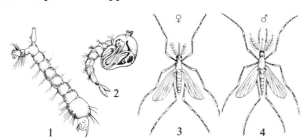

Culicidae: 1 Larva; 2 pupa; 3 imagos or adults

Culicidae: Mosquitos. Family of Diptera. Larvae and pupae often found in large numbers in small, often heavily, polluted waters. Useful as food for aquatic amphibians. Best known genera are *Culex*, *Anopheles*, and *Aedes*.

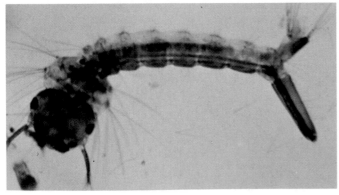

Culicidae: Mosquito larva

Cuora amboinensis

Cuora GRAY, 1855. Asian Box Turtles. Genus of the Emydidae. Southeast Asia. 5 species found mainly in swamps and smaller waters. Carapace to 20 cm, with 1 to 3 more or less well-defined longitudinal keels. Plastron with a median hinge.

Mainly carnivorous. Hardy. Good inhabitants for moderately heated aqua-terrariums.

▪ *C. amboinensis* (DAUDIN, 1802). Malayan Box Turtle. Indo-China, Sunda Archipelago, Philippines. Carapace highly arched, with only one longitudinal keel. A distinc-

Cuora amboinensis

Cuora trifasciata

Cuora amboinensis

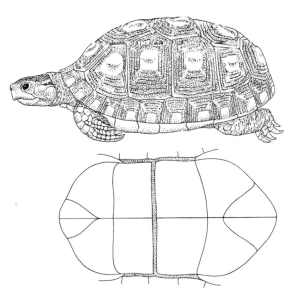

Cuora flavomarginata

tive bright yellow band along the neck to eye region. Most frequently imported species of the genus.

▪ *C. flavomarginata* (GRAY, 1863). Yellow-margined Box Turtle. Southern China, Taiwan, and Ryukyu Islands (Okinawa). The dark plastron has a yellow edge. The carapace shape is very similar to *C. amboinensis*. Lives more on land and often is a poor swimmer. More carnivorous (snails, worms) than the previous species.

▪ *C. galbinifrons* BOURRET, 1939. White-fronted Box Turtle. North Vietnam, southern China. Strongly terrestrial.

▪ *C. trifasciata* (BELL, 1825). Three-keeled Box Turtle. Southern China, northeastern Indo-China, Hainan. To 20

cm. Carapace with three dark keels. Eyeband dark, in contrast to light band of *C. amboinensis*. Amphibious swamp turtle that requires more sun or ultraviolet radiation than the previous species.

Cuora flavomarginata

Cuora amboinensis

Cyclagras gigas

Cupriguanus GALLARDO, 1964. Genus of the Iguanidae. Northern and central Argentina. 4 species. Formerly included in *Leiosaurus*.
▪ *C. scapulatus* (BURMEISTER, 1861).

Cuvier, Georges Leopold Chretien Frederic Dagobert (1769-1832): French zoologist. *Regne Animal* (1829).

Cyclagras COPE, 1885 (= *Hydrodynastes*). Brasilian Water-cobras. Monotypic genus of the Colubridae, Xenodontinae. Eastern Bolivia and Brasil to northern Argentina. Aquatic, near secondary forests, plantations, and urban developments. More than 2 m. Strongly built. Head clearly set off. Adult males yellow-brown with blackish brown irregular crossbands; adult females light brown with paler markings.

Excited specimens will flatten their neck (as in *Xenodon*), raise the front of the body, and emit threatening hisses. Ground snakes found in and close to water. They feed on fish, frogs, small mammals, and birds. Egg-layers, to 36 eggs per clutch. Should be kept in a spacious, well-heated tropical terrarium with a large water section. Excellent display specimens for public institutions.
▪ *C. gigas* (DUMERIL, DUMERIL, and BIBRON, 1854).

Cyclanorbis GRAY, 1854. African Flap-shell Soft-shells. Genus of the Trionychidae. Central Africa. 2 species in large rivers. Oval-shaped, leathery carapace. To 60 cm. Plastron with skin-like flaps posteriorly and 9 or more callosities recognizable.

Purely carnivorous. For details on care and maintenance refer to *Trionyx*. Rarely imported.
▪ *C. senegalensis* (DUMERIL and BIBRON, 1835). Senegal Soft-shell Turtle. Central Africa from Senegal to Sudan. Older specimens with uniformly dark carapace and 4 or

Cyclagras gigas

Cyclanorbis senegalensis

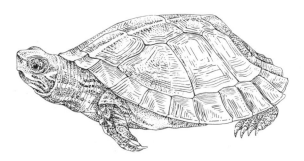

Cyclemys dentata

Cyclemys BELL, 1834. Asian Leaf Turtles. Monotypic genus of the Emydidae. Southeast Asia and the Philippines. To 24 cm carapace length. Carapace with a median longitudinal keel, uniformly dark brown; plastron with radiating markings that darken with increasing age but always remains visible. A plastral hinge develops in adulthood.

Ecologically very adaptable. Mainly carnivorous. Hardy in an aqua-terrarium with little heat and some sun, and suitable for outdoor enclosures during the summer months.

▪ *C. dentata* (GRAY, 1831). Asian Leaf Turtle. Burma through western and central Indo-China to Malaysian Peninsula, Western Sunda Islands, and Philippines.

Cyclanorbis senegalensis

Cycloderma frenatum

more callosities in jugular region of plastron. Juveniles with pattern of small dark spots.

▪ *C. elegans* (GRAY, 1869). Nubian Soft-shell Turtle. Central Africa from Nigeria to Sudan. Large light-colored dorsal spots; callosities absent from jugular region.

Cycloderma PETERS, 1854. Dotted African Soft-shell Turtles. Genus of the Trionychidae. Africa south of the Equator. 2 species in large rivers and lakes. 55 cm. Plastron with skin-like flaps over posterior limbs. Similar to genus *Cyclanorbis*, but eyes more anteriorly located.

Cyclemys dentata

Cycloderma frenatum

Mainly carnivorous, they prefer fish. For details on care and maintenance refer to *Trionyx*. Rarely imported.
- *C. aubryi* (DUMERIL, 1856). Aubry's Soft-shell. Western equatorial Africa. Characterized by the presence of a continuous dark band along both sides of the neck and through the eye.
- *C. frenatum* PETERS, 1854. Bridled Soft-shell. East Africa from Tanzania to Mozambique. Upper side of neck with 5 dark continuous lines.

Cyclorana STEINDACHNER, 1867 (= *Chiroleptes* GUENTHER). Water-holding Frogs. Genus of the Leptodactylidae. Australia. 7 species. *Rana*-like, more or less inflated. Tympanum well developed. Pupil horizontal. Thumb opposable to remaining fingers. Fingers free, but toes more or less completely webbed. Strong metatarsal tubercles present, often spade-like to facilitate digging.

Burrowing ground-dwellers that can survive prolonged drought below the ground and with water stored in the abdominal cavity, urinary bladder, and below the skin. The water storage capacity of *C. platycephalus* is well known; Aborigines dig up specimens to get drinking water. Larvae develop in temporary ponds that are formed during the rainy season.

Care and maintenance of *C. cultripes* and *C. platycephalus*, which inhabit extremely arid regions in the interior of the continent, should be in a well-drained desert terrarium with a thick substrate. It is best to simulate the long drought periods at tropical temperatures (about 28° C.), interrupting them for some weeks by a simulated rainy season with considerable moisture and a temperature reduction. Food should be offered then along with a water bowl for breeding. All other species can be kept without seasonal variations in semi-dry terrariums with increased humidity during the night.
- *C. australis* (GRAY, 1842). Northern Australia. Deserts, savannahs, dry brushland, forests. 10 cm. Sandy brown with conspicuous dorso-lateral skinfolds. Juveniles sometimes bright green.

- *C. cultripes* PARKER, 1940. Central Australia. To 5 cm. Variably gray, brown, or green, with irregular pattern of dark spots; usually with a light-colored median dorsal stripe.
- *C. platycephalus* (GUENTHER, 1873). Water-holding Frog. Central Australia. To 6 cm. Olive-green, often with lighter median dorsal line. Dorsal skinfold absent. Best known species.

Cyclorhamphus TSCHUDI, 1838. Genus of the Leptodactylidae. South America. 7 to 9 species. Related to *Crossodactylodes* and *Zachaenus*. Found in mountain forests. Body egg-shaped. Skin smooth or granular. The slightly protruding eyes have horizontal pupils. Tympanum not visible. The fingers are free, the toes variously webbed (species-specific). The tips of the fingers and toes are enlarged, button-shaped. Darkish.

Ground-dwellers. The few large eggs are deposited in a moist substrate. The larvae complete their development under aquatic conditions.
- *C. asper* WERNER, 1899. Southeastern Brasil. 3.5 cm. Toes webbed at base only.
- *C. fuliginosus* TSCHUDI, 1838. Southeastern Brasil. 4.5 cm. Toes webbed for ⅔ of their length. *C. neglectus* LUTZ, 1928, is a very similar species.
- *C. granulosus* LUTZ, 1929. Southeastern Brasil. 4.5 cm. Toes free. Skin warty.

Cyclorus DUMERIL and BIBRON, 1854. Monotypic genus of the Colubridae, Lycodontinae, included in the Natricinae by some systematists. Philipines in tropical rain forests. To about 50 cm. Head barely set off from body. Eyes small. Dorsum brownish with three darker longitudinal lines to tip of tail.

Nocturnal ground snakes that feed mainly on other small snakes (*Calamaria* and similar forms). For care and maintenance see Natricinae Group 1.
- *C. lineatus* (REINHARDT, 1843).

Cyclura HARLAN, 1824. Rhinoceros Iguanas, Island Iguanas. Genus of the Iguanidae. Antilles. Many forms of uncertain systematic level, but commonly 6 species are recognized. Found in rocky areas and brushlands. In excess of 1.2 m, very strong. Body weakly compressed laterally. Large head. Tail barely 1 ½ times snout-vent length. Dorsum with moderately developed crest; distinctly developed gular sac (these characteristics are more strongly pronounced in males). In older males the occiput is substantially widened, forming two large bony humps above and behind the eyes. Uniformly dark gray to olive, darker crossbands often vaguely indicated.

Diurnal ground-dwellers that have hiding places in the ground or in hollow trees. Apart from fruit, these lizards also feed on small to medium-size vertebrates. In captivity they take strips of lean meat, boiled rice or semolina, soaked white bread and similar items (to be fed sparingly—easily become obese). 15 to 20 eggs per clutch. They require a spacious dry terrarium with climbing branches. Temperatures between 28 and 35° C. are good, along with a localized heat source; at night drop the temperature to about 20° C.

Populations seriously endangered. Should only be on display in public institutions.

Cyclura baelopha

Cyclura carinata

Cyclura cornuta

▪ *C. cornuta* (BONNATERRE, 1780). Rhinoceros Iguana. Haiti, Puerto Rico. Easily 1 m. Males with three short, conical horns on snout, these only indicated in females.
▪ *C. ricordi* (DUMERIL and BIBRON, 1839). Haiti. 1.2 m. Without horns.

Cylindrophis WAGLER, 1828. Oriental Pipe Snakes. Genus of the Aniliidae. Sri Lanka and Southeast Asia to the Indo-Australian Archipelago and Aru Islands. About 8 species. In rain forests or montane rain forests; *C. rufus* follows human habitation, especially in rice paddies. To 75 cm. Head not set off, covered with large scales; eyes are free. Below the head is a distinct chin furrow. The premaxillaries are toothless, in contrast to the other family mem-

Cyclura macleayi

Cyclura cornuta

bers; considered to be a derived characteristic. When threatened, head is covered under body coils, as is common to all family members. Body covered with large, smooth scales. Ventral scutes small. Tail flattened, broad (genus characteristic), raised when alarmed. Dark background color with white, yellow, or reddish spots or irregular crossbands. Below the tail are alternating black and white or black and red stripes that become visible when the tail is raised.

Pipe snakes live damp to wet ground, some even in muddy swamps. They feed on frogs and presumably also on worms and insect larvae. In captivity fish and strips of lean meat are also taken.

• *C. aruensis* BOULENGER, 1820. Aru Islands near New Guinea. Most southeasterly species of this genus.
• *C. maculatus* (LINNAEUS, 1758). Ceylonese Pipe Snake. Sri Lanka. Montane forests. Common.
• *C. rufus* (LAURENTI, 1768). Red Pipe Snake. Burma and throughout Indo-China and large areas of the Indo-Australian Archipelago. 2 subspecies.

Cynisca GRAY, 1844. Genus of the Amphisbaenidae. West Africa. 12 species in tropical forests. Not very specialized species. They have with round head and large nuchal scutes. The tail is relatively long, similar to *Amphisbaena*.
• *C. leucura* (DUMERIL and BIBRON, 1839). Liberia to Nigeria. About 30 cm.

Cynops TSCHUDI, 1839. Fire-bellied Newts. Genus of the Salamandridae. Southeastern Palearctic, extending into tropical latitudes. 8 forms, of which usually 4 or 5 are given species status, the remainder generally given subspecies status. In standing waters. Closely related to *Triturus*. Tail laterally compressed, often terminating in a thread. Without dorsal crests. Darkish with orange, yellow, or reddish ventral area with a few black spots.

Most forms are largely aquatic throughout the year. The southern forms are found either at higher latitudes and in relatively cool water or in warm water (*C. ensicauda*).

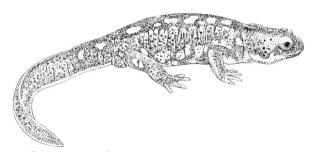

Cynops ensicauda

These newts are best kept in an aquarium with floating cork islands at water temperatures between 12 and 15° C. For *C. ensicauda* provide an aqua-terrarium during the summer at 25 to 26° C., about 15° C. during the winter. If kept in accordance with ecological requirements these animals usually live for many years and can also be bred easily. The female attaches the eggs individually onto floating plants (*Salvinia*) at the water surface or onto suitable wet substrates above the water surface. Depending upon the temperature, the larvae will hatch in 2 to 4 weeks. Duration of the larval stage is 90 to 120 days.

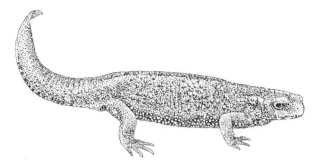

Cynops pyrrhogaster

• *C. ensicauda* (HALLOWELL, 1860). Swordtail Newt. Southern Japan and Ryukyu Islands. Probably only a subspecies of *C. pyrrhogaster*. 11-14 cm. Ventrum yellow or orange.
• *C. orientalis* (DAVID, 1873). Chinese Dwarf Newt. Yangtse River delta. 7 to 9 cm. Ventrum red.
• *C. pyrrhogaster* (BOIE, 1826). Japanese Fire-bellied Newt. Hondo, Shikoku, Kyushu. 9 to 12 cm. Ventral area light red to carmine red. Tip of tail with well-developed thread.

Cyperaceae: Rushes, Reeds. Family of the Liliatae. Worldwide, primarily in temperate climatic zones. About 70 genera, more than 3700 species. Almost exclusively shrubs or grass-like in appearance. Mainly in damp locations.
• *Carex* L. Reeds. About 1100 species.
• *Cyperus* L. Rushes. About 600 species. Most frequently cultured species is *C. alternifolius* L. Up to 1 m tall. *C. haspan* L. is very similar in appearance. 30 to 50 cm tall. Grows in a temperature range between 10 and 25° C.

Cynops pyrrhogaster

Cynops pyrrhogaster

Cyrtodactylus GRAY, 1827. Naked-finger Geckos, Bow-finger Geckos. Genus of the Gekkonidae. Tropics and subtropics of the Old World. About 70 species. Formerly included in *Gymnodactylus*. Found in more or less dry habitats. 10 to 20 cm. Slender. Tail easily equal to snout-vent length. Pupils vertical. Toes not enlarged, basally with some small adhesive lamellae, vertically compressed distally, bent upward at an angle, returning to the ground again at the strongest claw. Dorsal scales granular, interspersed with irregular longitudinal rows of tubercles that change almost into spines on the tail where they form little whorls. Coloration and markings variable, base color usually greenish, light gray, or brown.

Primarily crepuscular to nocturnal, these geckos like to sunbathe occasionally during the day. They can be found under rocks, behind the bark of fallen trees, on rocks, and among human habitation. The diet consists mainly of various arthropods. In the terrarium they must be provided with sufficient damp hiding places. The terrarium should

have some rocky structures and/or large pieces of tree bark. A weak radiant heat source is commonly frequented during the day. Recommended temperatures are around

Cyrtodactylus pulchellus

Cyrtodactylus caspius

25° C. during the day and 20° C. at night (for subtropical species down to 15° C.; these also require a winter dormancy period of 6 to 8 weeks at 6 to 10° C.). Rather quarrelsome, as are all geckos. Several species have been bred in captivity. Juveniles are rather sensitive and not very easy to rear. They must not be kept too dry.

• *C. caspius* (EICHWALD, 1831). Caspian Naked-finger Gecko. Altai to Iran, Afghanistan, introduced into Trans-Caucasus. Rocky habitats. To 15 cm.

• *C. fedtschenkoi* (STRAUCH, 1887). Soviet Central Asia, Iran, Afghanistan. Open habitats. To 18 cm. Very slender and with large tubercles. Gray-brown.

• *C. kotschyi* (STEINDACHNER, 1870). European Naked-finger Gecko. Southern Italy to southwestern Asia. Numerous subspecies. 10 cm.

• *C. pulchellus* GRAY, 1928. Near East to Southeast Asia. 12 cm. Tan with bright yellow-bordered dark crossbands. Should be kept damper than the previous species.

Cyrtomium

Cyrtomium K. B. PRESL. Genus of the Filicatae. Asia, Africa, North and South America. Ground-dwellers. Durable, undemanding ferns with few temperature demands. Can take shade.

Cystopteris BERNH. Blister Ferns. Genus of the Filicatae. Worldwide distribution. 18 species. Rhizomes short.

• *C. fragilis* (L.) BERNH. Rock Blister Fern. In shaded locations on drip-moistened limestone rocks and also on the ground. Usually up to 20 cm tall. Winter-resistant. A rock fern for outdoor and unheated terrariums.

Daboia lebetina obtusa

Daboia GRAY, 1842. Oriental Adders. Genus of the Viperidae. Southeastern Palearctic and adjacent Oriental region. At least 6 species. Formerly included in *Vipera*, and still considered a subgenus by some workers. 0.8 to 2 m. Head elongated, triangular, clearly set off from body, covered with small keeled scales, except for the usually large supraocular scutes. Body with 23 to 27 rows of scales around the middle. Markings consist of a band of rhomboids that sometimes break into individual spots; rarely with longitudinal stripes (*D. raddei latifii*).

3 ecological groups can be recognized.

1) Mountain-dwellers that occupy dry, warm slopes with substantial temperature reductions at night. Includes *D. xanthina*, *D. raddei*, and some subspecies of *D. lebetina*.

2) Occupants of montane steppes and rocky deserts that require more heat. Some *D. lebetina*, *D. mauretanica*.

3) Occupants of subtropical to tropical lowlands, from dry forests to the edge of tropical rain forests. *D. palaestinae*, *D. russelli*.

Lizards, small mammals, and birds are eaten. Reproduction is usually ovoviviparous; only in *D. lebetina* do most subspecies still lay eggs.

The venom is dangerous, and *D. russelli* is one of the venomous snakes that cause most of the world's fatal snake bites.

Maintain in a spacious, well-heated dry terrarium with a water bowl (although *Daboia* species come from dry habi-

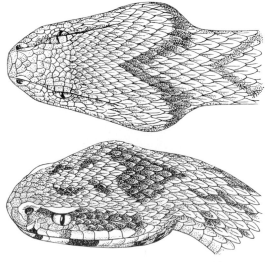

Daboia lebetina (above) and *Daboia xanthina* (below)

Daboia lebetina obtusa

Daboia lebetina turanica

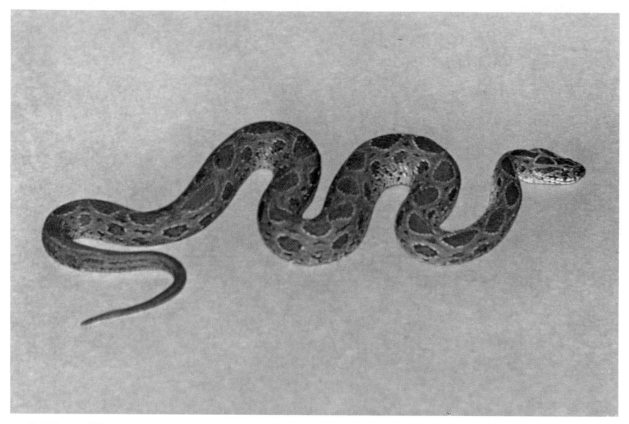

Daboia russelli

Daboia lebetina schweizeri

Daboia russelli

Daboia raddei

tats). North African species and those from Asia Minor and the Caucasus should be given a cooler winter dormancy period of 2 to 3 months. This is important for breeding attempts. In captivity Oriental adders will take small mammals and chickens, sometimes imprinting onto particular food items (e. g., *D. lebetina* on chicks).

Breeding of *D. russelli*, *D. xanthina*, and *D. palaestinae* is relatively easy; *D. mauretanica* and *D. lebetina* are difficult.
▪ *D. lebetina* (LINNAEUS, 1758). Levantine Adder, Bluntnosed Viper. Cyclades of Greece (there *D. l. schweizeri* WERNER, 1935) and Cyprus (nominate form), Asia Minor and Caucasus (*D. l. obtusa* DWIGUBSKIJ, 1832) to Central Asia (*D. l. turanica* CERNOV, 1940, most attractively colored subspecies). About 5 subspecies. Incubation period about 40 days.

Daboia lebetina turanica

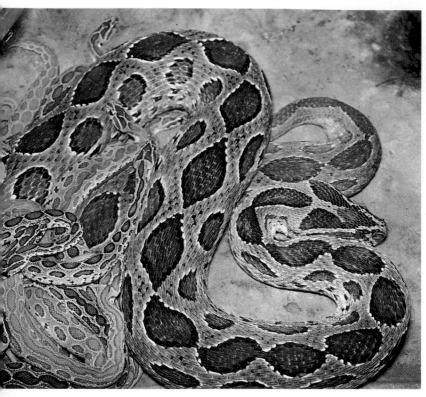

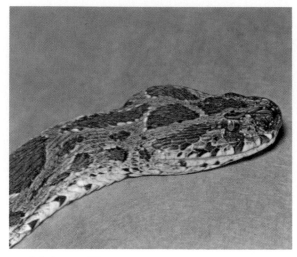

Daboia russelli

Daboia russelli

• *D. mauretanica* (GRAY, 1849). Northwestern Africa to Libya. 2 subspecies.

• *D. palaestinae* WERNER, 1938. Palestinian Viper. From Syria to Jordan to Israel. Very attractive markings reminiscent of *D. russelli*.

• *D. raddei* (BOETTGER, 1890). Caucasus Adder. 2 to 3 subspecies: nominate form in Armenia (USSR) and northeastern Turkey; *D. r. latifii* (MERTENS, DAREVSKY, and KLEMMER, 1967) in northern Iran; *D. r. bornmuelleri* WERNER, 1898, in Lebanon Mountains, Lebanon, Israel, and Jordan. All these taxa are considered to be valid species by many systematists.

Daboia russelli

▪ *D. russelli* (SHAW, 1802). Russell's Viper, Seven-Pacer. Pakistan through India and Sri Lanka to southern China, Taiwan, and Indonesia. 5 subspecies. Spectacular markings. Exceedingly dangerous species.
▪ *D. xanthina* (GRAY, 1849). Mountain Adder. Turkey.

Damage fights: In contrast to a ritualistic fight, the damage fight leads to more or less severe injuries or even to the death of one animal. Within a terrarium situation there can be damaging fights as a consequence of courtship or territory formation or defense, which can easily lead to the demise of one of the combatants, since the loser can not get away within the confines of the terrarium. Such incompatibilities have to be given special consideration when placing together crocodiles, many lizards, and also turtles.

Daphnids: see Phyllopoda, order.

Darlingtonia COCHRAN, 1935. Monotypic genus of the Colubridae, Xenodontinae. Haiti. 30 cm. Head distinctly set off from body. Ground-dwelling snakes. Biology virtually unknown, probably very similar to *Dromicus*.
▪ *D. haetiana* COCHRAN, 1935.

Dasia GRAY, 1839. Tree Skinks. Genus of the Scincidae, subfamily Lygosominae; formerly included in *Lygosoma*. Southern and southeastern Asia. 16 species. In tropical forests. 20 to 30 cm. Cylindrical, snout pointed. Movable eyelids without windows. Ear opening distinct. Tail long.

Dasia smaragdina

Limbs well developed, with enlarged platelets under the toes to facilitate climbing. Often attractively colored, including bright green.

Tree-dwellers that rarely move down to the ground. The diet consists mostly of arthropods, occasionally sweet fruit. Clutches of 2 to (mostly) 6 eggs are deposited under tree bark.

Dasia should be kept in rain-forest terrariums with sufficient climbing branches at day temperatures of 25 to 28° C. and moderate localized radiant heat (to 35° C.), with only marginal reduction at night. They do not require much drinking water, and regular spraying is sufficient. Provide occasional ultraviolet radiation and calcium and vitamin supplements. High intra-specific compatibility.
▪ *D. smaragdina* (LESSON, 1830). Emerald Skink. Philippines, New Guinea, smaller islands. 25 cm. Emerald green anteriorly, posterior part of body sometimes brown.
▪ *D. haliana* NEVILL, 1887. Ceylonese Tree Skink. Sri Lanka. 25 cm. Banded with black and lilac. Only 2 eggs.
▪ *D. vittata* EDERLING, 1864. Banded Tree Skink. Kalimantan. 25 cm. Anteriorly black.

Dasypeltinae: African Egg-eating Snakes. Monogeneric subfamily of the Colubridae. Africa, except central northern area. About 6 species found in savannahs to semideserts. Very similar to the Oriental subfamily Elachistodontinae, and many systematists incorporate both names under Dasypeltinae. However, the different evolutionary origin of both groups is more probable, thus both are listed here separately. To 80 cm. Head clearly set off from body, short, with relatively large eyes. The extreme mobility of the lower jaw and the absence of dentition on the anterior section of upper and lower jaws and on the sphenoid are important characters. Weak, tiny teeth are present only on the posterior part of the mandibles. The function of the teeth has been taken over by processes of the neck vertebrae (hypapophyses) that extend into the esophagus. They have sharp edges and are covered by tooth enamel. After an egg is swallowed it is cut open lengthwise by the processes and crushed in the esophagus. Only the contents are digested, the shell being regurgitated.

The dorsal scales are shingled, with distinct keels forming continuous longitudinal rows. Smaller, obliquely positioned scales are along the sides, with rough or serrated keels. This scale arrangement is similar to that of the venomous *Echis* and together with similarities in shape and markings sometimes give rise to dangerous misidentifications.

More or less nocturnal ground snakes that hide during the day under stones and similar objects. Egg-layers.

African egg-eating snakes should be kept in a well-heated dry terrarium with a substantial temperature reduction at night. A constant supply of fresh eggs of suitable size is essential. Those of parakeets, quail, and pigeons, depending upon the size of the snake, are usually necessary.

Dasypeltis WAGLER, 1830. African Egg-eating Snakes. Genus of the Colubridae, Dasypeltinae. About 6 species. In savannahs, thornbush steppes, semideserts, and mountains to 2000 m, but will not avoid more moist habitats. Excellent swimmers. They recognize and search for eggs by means of highly developed senses of smell and taste (tongue flicking). Egg-layers, 10 to 15 eggs. Incubation period about 3 ½ months.

Disturbed specimens imitate the warning sound of *Echis*, and *D. scabra* even resembles *Echis* in its markings.

Dasypeltis scabra

Newly collected *Dasypeltis* often refuse food for a long time and may have to be force-fed with fresh eggs through a hypodermic with a rubber or plastic hose. Acclimated specimens usually do well in captivity and have substantial life spans.

▪ *D. scabra* (LINNAEUS, 1758). Common Egg-eating Snake. Southwestern Arabia, Egypt, all of eastern Africa, south to Republic of South Africa. 2 subspecies.

▪ *D. inornata* (A. SMITH, 1849). Southeastern Republic of South Africa.

▪ *D. fasciata* (A. SMITH, 1849). Central African Egg-eating Snake. Central Africa from west to east (Gambia, Cameroons, Zaire to Uganda). Dry forests to outer jungle areas.

Dasypops MIRANDA-RIBEIRO, 1924. Monotypic genus of the Microhylidae. Brasil. Snout-vent length a few cm. Similar to *Myersiella*, but toes webbed at base.

▪ *D. schirki* MIRANDA-RIBEIRO, 1924.

Daudin, Francois Marie (1774-1804): French ornithologist and herpetologist. Cooperated with Buffon and Lacepede on *Historie Naturelle des Reptiles* (1802).

Deciduous forests: Summer-green broad-leaf forests in the temperate zone, especially in North America, central Europe, and eastern Asia; in the Southern Hemisphere only in central Chile (forests of *Nothofagus*) and in small areas in New Zealand and Tasmania. In contrast to coniferous forests the periodic leaf renewal is not caused by periods without precipitation but instead by annual temperature fluctuations (cold winters).

Decorations: Used for the improvement of the esthetic value of the terrarium, subject to the requirements of the species concerned and to be selected accordingly. They also have to satisfy functional requirements, such as providing sufficient hiding places or climbing facilities. Terrarium plants often contribute to the improvement of the microclimate.

Deirochelys AGASSIZ, 1857. Chicken Turtles. Monotypic genus of the Emydidae. Southeastern USA in standing and flowing waters. Carapace length to 26 cm. Head and neck very long for an emydid turtle. Carapace with characteristic narrow yellow to orange reticulated pattern.

Omnivorous; older specimens prefer plants as food. Best suited for outdoor maintenance, it can be kept there year-round with proper winter protection (origin of specimens has to be taken into consideration).

▪ *D. reticularia* (LATREILLE, 1801). North Carolina to Florida, west to Oklahoma and eastern Texas. 3 subspecies.

Deirochelys reticularia

Deirochelys reticularia

Deirochelys reticularia

Deiroptyx: see *Anolis*, genus.

Delayed Fertilization: see *Amphigonia retarda*.

Delma GRAY, 1831. Smooth-scaled Scaleyfoots. Genus of the Pygopodidae. Australia. About 12 species. To more than 50 cm. Slender, head relatively pointed. Tympanum externally visible. Tail about 3 times snout-vent length. Hind limb vestiges distinct. Smooth scales. Preanal pores absent. Mostly tones of brown above, some species with attractive head markings.

Primarily found on the ground, though some species will occasionally climb. For more on mode of life and care refer to *Pygopus*.

▪ *D. fraseri* GRAY, 1831. Fraser's Scaleyfoot. Western Australia. To about 50 cm. Dorsally uniformly olive-brown, head usually black with narrow yellowish crossbands.

▪ *D. tincta* DE VIS, 1888. Northern half of Australia. About 50 cm.

Demansia GRAY, 1842. Australian Whip Snakes. Genus of the Elapidae. Australia, New Guinea. About 7 species. Steppes and savannahs, various dry habitats. 0.5 to 1 m. Slender, the small head more or less distinctly set off from body, with conspicuously large eyes. While the body is nearly uniformly colored in most species, there is usually a dark stripe running from the snout to the eye and then sharply backward. *D. torquata* has a double dark neckband, while *D. psammophis* may be covered with a light and dark braided pattern.

Demansia species are extremely fast diurnal terrestrial venomous snakes. They prey on lizards, frogs, and possibly also small mammals and birds. Egg-layers, 4 to 13 eggs, incubation period only 14 days.

These whip snakes can be kept in well-heated dry terrariums. The venom of *D. atra, D. psammophis,* and *D. olivacea* is potentially dangerous to humans.
- *D. olivacea* (GRAY, 1842). Central northern and northwestern Australia and southeastern New Guinea. 2 subspecies.
- *D. psammophis* (SCHLEGEL, 1837). Yellow-faced Whip Snake. Australia, except in the north. 2 subspecies.

Dendrelaphis BOULENGER, 1890. Bronzy Tree Snakes. Genus of the Colubridae, Colubrinae. Southeast Asia. Formerly called *Dendrophis* (a synonym) and *Ahaetulla* (a different genus considered to apply to boigine tree snakes). About 12 species, some polytypic. In monsoon forests, rain forests, and montane rain forests, as well as in bamboo forests. Some species (*D. pictus,* among others) follow human habitation (rice paddies, sugar plantations, and others); other species live at considerable elevations (*D. tristis* to 2700 m in the eastern Himalayas). 0.65 to 1.3 m, very slender. Head distinctly set off from body, with very large eyes. Dorsal scales differentiated, the middle dorsal row enlarged and trapezoidal, the sides with the scales clearly narrowed and obliquely arranged (similar to *Thrasops, Boiga, Dispholidus,* and a few others). Abdominal scutes very wide to facilitate climbing. Tail long. Iridescent brown to olive tones. Most species have a few to many light and dark longitudinal stripes that give them an even longer and more slender appearance.

The diet includes frogs and lizards. Egg-layers, 3 to 5 large, elongated eggs containing advanced embryos.

These tree snakes should be kept in well-heated tropical forest terrariums with many plants, climbing branches, and bathing facilities.

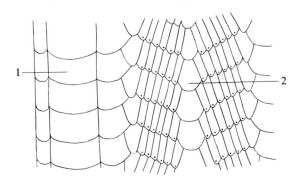

Dendrelaphis scalation: 1 Ventral scale; 2 enlarged middorsal scale row

- *D. calligaster* (GUENTHER, 1867). New Guinea and adjacent islands to northern Australia. 3 subspecies.
- *D. caudolineata* (GRAY, 1834). Malaysia through large parts of the Indo-Australian Archipelago, eastward to the Philippines. 3 subspecies.
- *D. picta* (GMELIN, 1789). Himalayas throughout Indo-China, eastward to southern China, Hainan, and Philippines, southward to Timor. 4 subspecies.
- *D. punctulata* (JACQUINOT and GUICHENOT, 1842). New Guinea and adjacent islands to northern Australia. 2 subspecies.
- *D. tristis* (DAUDIN, 1803). India.

Dendroaspis angusticeps

Dendroaspis SCHLEGEL, 1848. Mambas. Genus of the Elapidae. Central and southern Africa except Cape Province. 4 species in tropical forests and montane forests; *D. polylepis* also in dry savannahs. 2.5 to 4 m. Slender, with a long, narrow head with large eyes. Large dorsal scales. Depending upon species and age, green (*D. angusticeps, D. viridis,* but also juvenile *D. polylepis*) or dark brown to black (adult *D. polylepis*). *Dendroaspis* species can—in contrast to most other elapids—erect the fangs by means of movable maxillary bones.

Arboreal, very agile venomous snakes. Their diet consists of mammals, birds, and reptiles. Egg-layers, 10 to 25 eggs.

Should be kept in a tropical terrarium with climbing and bathing facilities. Caution: Highly venomous; even with

Dendroaspis angusticeps

Dendroaspis angusticeps

Dendroaspis angusticeps

immediate serum treatment a large number of bites are still quickly fatal due to respiratory paralysis. Initially mambas are very aggressive. They have been bred in captivity, some species over several generations.

• *D. angusticeps* (A. SMITH, 1849). Common Mamba. Eastern Africa from Kenya to Natal.

• *D. polylepis* GUENTHER, 1864. Black Mamba. Somalia and Ethiopia to Natal, westward to Namibia. 2 subspecies. To 4 m, the largest species of the genus. Well adapted to dry forests and a terrestrial mode of life.

• *D. viridis* (HALLOWELL, 1844). Green Mamba. West Africa. Tropical forests.

Dendrobates WAGLER 1830. Poison Arrow (or Dart) Frogs. Genus of the Dendrobatidae. Central America and tropical South America. More than 20 species. Together with the related genus *Phyllobates* these are the little frogs famous for their poisonous skin secretions used to treat arrows. Generic differences from *Phyllobates* are problematic, and we here follow recent work by Silverstone and Savage. Small, rarely to 5 cm. Distinguished from *Phyllobates* by the absence of dentition on the upper jaw, the thickened (about twice normal) second and third fingers (thicker in males than in females), and in the larvae by the median location of the vent. Skin secretions poisonous. Often with bright, contrasting warning colors.

Dendrobates histrionicus

Dendrobates histrionicus

Dendrobates auratus

Dendrobates histrionicus

Dendrobates leucomelas

Dendrobates granuliferus

Dendrobates pumilio

Dendrobates auratus

Dendrobates pumilio

Dendrobates (histrionicus) lehmanni

The diet consists mainly of ants, termites, and other small insects and small spiders. The male (more rarely the female) transports the small number of larvae to water accumulations (as in *Phyllobates*) such as phytothelms or small puddles. For details of the mode of life, behavior, and reproduction see Dendrobatidae.

Species from the *selva* and *montana* should be kept in tropical rain-forest terrariums with high humidity and temperatures between 20 and 29° C. Where these conditions can be maintained on a larger scale such as a large room or tropical greenhouse, these frogs can be kept unconfined and can even be bred under such conditions.

Breeding attempts should only be made with animals kept under optimum conditions and fed a varied, nutritious diet. Courtship is frequently initiated with vocalizations (a prolonged trilling sound) and stimulation of the partner by touching, shoving, tapping, and attempts to mount, the male being the active partner. This is followed by the pair searching for a suitable spawning site. The incubation period is about 2 to 4 weeks, when the tadpoles emerge. Under less than natural maintenance conditions the normal reproductive behavior in caring for the eggs and transporting the young to water can become more or less impaired, resulting in parental eating of eggs, negligent brood care, and loss of the urge to transport the young to water. Often under captive conditions the larvae will fall into the water on their own. For proper rearing, the tadpoles should be transferred into separate containers with shallow water; overcrowding must be avoided to inhibit aggressive behavior and cannibalism. Commercially available dry fish foods are useful as rearing food. The natural diet of the tadpoles consists of protozoans and tiny crustaceans.

• *D. auratus* (GIRARD, 1854). Green Poison Arrow Frog. Panama and northwestern Colombia. 4 cm. Black and green or light blue; very variable, but usually the black in spots or broken bands.

• *D. azureus* HOOGMOED, 1969. Border region of Brasil and Guyana and Surinam. 4.5 cm. Metallic blue with black spots. In damp, wooded areas in the *llanos*.

• *D. granuliferus* TAYLOR, 1958. Panama (sea level to 700

Dendrobates histrionicus

m). 2 cm. Red with pale yellow dots; legs and abdomen with blue and black marbled pattern.

▪ *D. histrionicus* BERTHOLD, 1843. Western Colombia and northwestern Ecuador (sea level to 1100 m). 3.5 cm. Highly variable, brown and black with round spots of blue, green, yellow, or red, sometimes vermiculated or banded.

▪ *D. lehmanni* MYERS and DALY, 1976. Colombia. *Montana* (between 850 and 1200 m). 3.5 cm. Wide red and black crossbands; probably a variant to *D. histrionicus*.

▪ *D. leucomelas* STEINDACHNER, 1864. Northeastern Brasil, Venezuela, Guyana, Surinam (50 to 800 m). 3.5 cm. Black with broad yellow crossbands, black spots in the yellow zones.

Dendrobates quinquevittatus

Dendrobates quinquevittatus with tadpole

▪ *D. pumilio* SCHMIDT, 1858. Strawberry Poison Arrow Frog. Nicaragua, Costa Rica, and Panama (sea level to 1000 m). 2.4 cm. Red with sparse black dots or vermiculation; hind limbs and hands with marbled pattern of dark blue and black.

▪ *D. speciosus* SCHMIDT, 1858. Northwestern Colombia (1100 to 1600 m) and Panama. 3 cm. Uniformly red.

▪ *D. tinctorius* (SCHNEIDER, 1799). French Guiana and northeastern Brasil. *Selva.* 5 cm (largest *Dendrobates* species). Black with wide yellow stripes; legs blue with black spots. Stripes often variably fused.

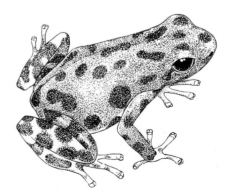

Dendrobates pumilio

Female

Male and female before mating

Male calling to female

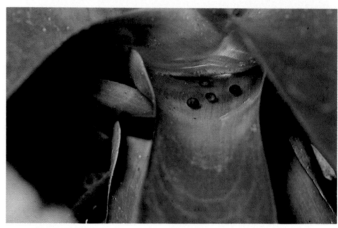

Eggs at 3 to 4 days

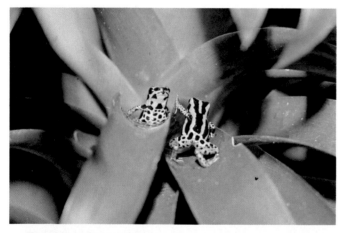

Female coming to male

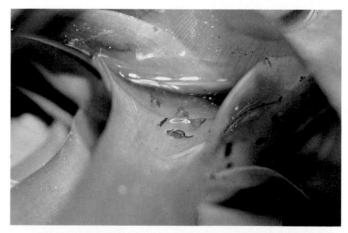

Eggs at 7 to 8 days

Female circling male

Detail of eggs

Dendrobates quinquevittatus

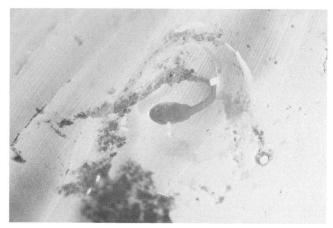

Egg just before hatching

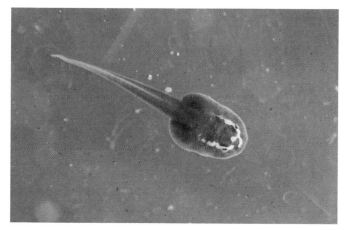

Tadpole with early color pattern

Male carrying two tadpoles

Tadpole just before metamorphosis

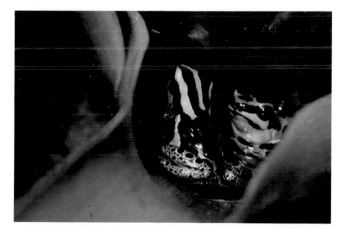

Male with tadpoles

Dendrobates reticulatus: Compare with *D. quinquevittatus* below

Male putting tadpoles in water

Dendrobates quinquevittatus

Dendrobatidae: Family of the Salientia. Strictly Neo-tropic, the greatest species density in central South American and Colombia, but extending north over Central America. More than 80 species in 3 genera (*Colostethus, Dendrobates,* and *Phyllobates*). Found in evergreen forests and tropical rain forests (*selva* and *montana*), but also in more or less open areas such as savannahs and *paramos*. Intra- and inter-family relationships are doubtful. Usually the Dendrobatidae are considered to be closely related to the true frogs (Ranidae), often even treated as a subfamily of the Ranidae. However, according to work by Lynch the Dendrobatidae are derived from the Elosiinae within the Leptodactylidae. The generic limits have also not been uni-formly treated. Some systematists place morphological cri-teria (especially maxillary dentition, development of adhe-sive discs on tips of fingers and toes) in the forefront, while others give greater credence to behavioral patterns, voice structures, and skin poison composition. Skin poisons oc-cur in the poison arrow frogs (genera *Dendrobates* and *Phy-llobates*). They are in part highly potent nerve toxins (ba-trachotoxin, pumiliotoxin, histrionicotoxin) with a steroid structure and are used by the Amerindians as an arrow poi-son to kill birds and monkeys.

All dendrobatids are diurnal and live on or close to the ground. Few are even 5 cm long. The finger and toe tips have glandular muscular adhesive pads. Webbing and lat-eral skin folds are absent from the fingers and toes in many species, but they can be well-developed, especially in *Col-ostethus*. Males have two vocal slits and an unpaired jugular vocal sac. They give off humming, trilling, or chirping sounds. The territory is optically (through warning color-ation) and vocally (special "territoral calls") defended, usu-ally from an exposed location (rock or tree stump). There can be intraspecific ritualistic fighting (shoving, jumping, pushing, biting). In *D. azureus* the females can be aggres-sive toward each other. As far as known, all dendrobatids deposit only a few large eggs on leaves or on the ground close to water. If amplexus actually occurs (in many species the male ejaculates the sperm directly over the eggs) it is always on land, never in water. The eggs are guarded and kept wet by the male. He carries the newly hatched tad-poles on his back to water (sometimes with the help of the female). There tends to be considerable sibling aggression among the larvae.

Due to their attractive markings and coloration and their fascinating behavior, these frogs play an important part in the modern terrarium hobby. Although several spe-cies have been bred over several generations, there usually are sooner or later symptoms of degeneration that may be due to nutritional deficiencies or genetic in origin due to inadequate population size. Continuous imports from the wild will inevitably lead to serious depletion of some den-drobatid species in the wild unless there is greater success in keeping these frogs. There must be planned breeding and selection programs to reduce the reliance on import-ations.

Dendrobatorana AHL, 1927. Monotypic genus of the Ranidae. Nigeria. Similar to *Cardioglossa*, but toes webbed about halfway. Natural history unknown. Should be kept much as *Cardioglossa*.

▪ *D. dorsali* (PETERS, 1875). Southwestern Nigeria. To 2.5 cm.

Dendrolycus LAURENT, 1956. Monotypic genus of the Colubridae, Lycodontinae. Tropical Africa in tropical rain forests. Closely related to and very similar to *Lycophidion*. About 50 cm. Slender, laterally compressed. Dark widely spaced crossbands against a light background.

Tree snakes. Should be kept in a well-heated and ade-quately planted rain-forest terrarium. The diet consists of frogs and lizards.
▪ *D. elapoides* (GUENTHER, 1874). Cameroons.

Dendrophidion FITZINGER, 1843. Genus of the Colubri-dae, Colubrinae. Mexico south to northern South America. 8 species. In tropical forests. 0.7 to 1.1 m. Extremely slen-der, with a very long fragile tail.

Diurnal and crepuscular, terrestrial or semiarboreal. The main diet consists of frogs. Egg-layers, 12 to 15 eggs. Often very aggressive.
▪ *D. dendrophis* (SCHLEGEL, 1837). Found from Guatemala to Ecuador. Olive with dark brown spots.

Dendrophis: see *Dendrelaphis,* genus.

Dendrophryniscus JIMENEZ DE LA ESPADA, 1871. Genus of the Bufonidae. South and Central America. 4 species. Systematics uncertain; some species were moved here from the family Atelopidae. *D. brevipollicatus* in *montana, D. mi-nutus* in *selva*. Small, slender, flattened, with thin limbs. Granular skin. Superficially like treefrogs but with similar-ities to toads. Snout pointed. Pupil horizontal (contrary to some literature references). Tympanum not visible. Paro-toid glands absent. Fingers and toes webbed at base and equipped with adhesive discs (but in some species the fin-gers and toes are free and without adhesive discs).

D. brevipollicatus is arboreal. It inhabits bromeliads, at-taching its few eggs to the underside of a leaf. *D. minutus* lives on the jungle floor and in plants close to the ground. Up to 245 eggs are present in females, deposited presuma-bly in water.
▪ *D. brevipollicatus* JIMENEZ DE LA ESPADA, 1871. Central America to Brasil. 2.5 cm. Brown.
▪ *D. minutus* (MELIN, 1941). Brasil, eastern Ecuador. 2.5 cm. Light brown, sides reddish yellow, with tiny light blue spots.

Dendrovaranus: see *Varanus,* genus.

Denisonia KREFFT, 1869. Genus of the Elapidae. Aus-tralia. About 5 species. In savannahs or steppes. About 50 cm. Relatively compact, more or less flattened dorso-ven-trally. Head distinctly set off from body, short-snouted. Tail short. Either with irregular crossbands (*D. devisii, D. fasciata*) or uniformly dark except for markings on head.

Nocturnal venomous snakes that hide under rocks, logs, and similar items during the day. Presumably feed on liz-ards and small mammals. *D. maculata* is a live-bearer, up to 8 young; other species have unknown reproductive biology.

Need well-heated dry terrariums. Venom is considered to be relatively dangerous.
▪ *D. devisii* WAITE and LONGMAN, 1920. De Vis's Banded

Snake. Eastern Australia. Mountains.

• *D. maculata* (STEINDACHNER, 1869). Ornamental Snake. Coastal Queensland. Bite potentially dangerous.

Dentition: see Teeth.

Dermaptera: Earwigs. Relatively small order of Insecta recognized by the heavy forceps at the end of the abdomen. Best known species is the brown, 1.5 cm common earwig, *Forficula auricularia*. Eaten by many lizards.

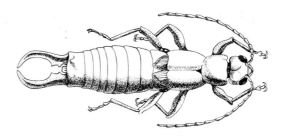

Dermaptera, *Forficula auricularia*

Dermatemys mawi

Dermatemydidae: Central American River Turtles. Monogeneric family of the Cryptodira. Central America. Fossil records from the Cretaceous frequent in the Americas and in Asia. Herbivorous, fairly large turtles with a shallow, heavily fused carapace. The complete row of 4 inframarginals on the bridge between carapace and plastron is characteristic.

Dermatemys GRAY, 1847. Central American River Turtles. Monotypic genus of the Dermatemydidae. Veracruz to Guatemala in large rivers and lakes. Carapace length to 50 cm. Rigid carapace streamlined. Scutes greatly fused in large adults. Head small. Feet fully webbed. Brownish.

Agile swimmers. Adults often have difficulty adjusting to captivity, and juveniles are rarely commercially available and are difficult to keep. They require much swimming space.

• *D. mawi* GRAY, 1847. Eastern Mexico to Yucatan, Guatemala, Belize. Vegetarian. Almost totally aquatic.

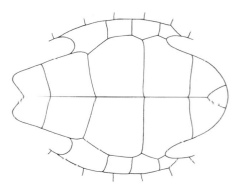

Dermatemys mawi, plastron showing bridge with 4 inframarginals

Dermatemys mawi

Dermatonotus MEHELY, 1904. Monotypic genus of the Microhylidae. Central South America in dry regions. Body almost spherical. Head very small, with pointed snout. Limbs fragile. External metatarsal tubercle absent.

Ground-dwelling termite and ant feeder. Spawn in ponds during the rainy season.

▪ *D. muelleri* (BOETTGER, 1885). Northern Argentina, southeastern Bolivia, Paraguay, Brasil. To 5 cm, rarely larger. Dirty olive-green, limbs with black and white marbled pattern.

Dermestidae: Skin or Fur Beetles, Dermestids. Family of the Coleoptera. Barely 1000 species. Worldwide in distribution. *Dermestes vulpinus* is 7 to 9 mm long, with hairy larvae that are twice this size. They feed on dead, dry animal matter and can be raised artifically on semolina. At temperatures between 25° C. and 30° C. a complete reproductive cycle takes about 40 to 50 days. The soft larvae are eagerly eaten by many lizards. When breeding, extreme caution has to be exercised to avoid the escape of these beetles that can attack carpets, dried foods, and clothing.

Dermochelyidae: Leatherback Turtles. Monogeneric family of the Cryptodira found in all tropical and subtropical seas. Fossil records date back to the Miocene. The largest of the living turtle species, reaching 2 m in carapace length and 600 kg in weight. The carapace is spindle-shaped and has 7 longitudinal keels. Juveniles have mosaic-like covering consisting of small bony elements that are lost with growth. In adults the shell is leathery, without any visible scutes. Underneath the leathery skin there are strongly reduced remnants of the osseous carapace. Due to their long evolutionary isolation and primitive characters of the skull, the Dermochelyidae forms a separate branch of sea turtles that is not directly related to the Cheloniidae. Although these turtles as well as the Cheloniidae can not retract their head, they belong on the basis of skull structure in the suborder Cryptodira. Conspicuous are the enormous size of the head and the anterior indentation of the upper jaw where the strongly bent hook-like lower jaw fits

Dermochelys coriacea

in. All the legs are flippers.

Carnivorous, feeding mainly on jellyfishes and other soft, gelatinous prey. These turtles move to tropical coastal waters to mate and lay eggs. Incubation in nature takes 60 to 68 days.

Rarely kept in captivity, even in public aquariums. Leatherbacks have never been reared to sexual maturity and adaptation to captivity of stranded specimens has never been successful.

Dermochelys BLAINVILLE, 1816. Leatherback Turtles. Monotypic genus of the Dermochelyidae. In all tropical and subtropical seas. To 2 m and 600 kg. Characteristic spindle-shaped leathery carapace with 7 longitudinal keels.

▪ *D. coriacea* (LINNAEUS, 1766).

Dermochelys coriacea, juvenile

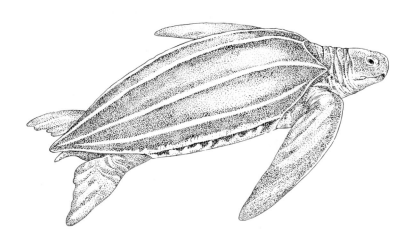

Dermochelys coriacea

Dermochelys coriacea

Dermochelys coriacea

Dermophis PETERS, 1879. Genus of the Caeciliidae found from Mexico through Central America to northern South America. 10 species, in part polytypic. 18 to 60 cm, conspicuously compact. 89 to 135 primary folds, 13 to 133 secondary folds. Eyes in some species not visible. Tentacle located closer to eye than to nostril. Lower jaw with 1 row of teeth. As fas as known, ovoviviparous.

• *D. gracilior* (GUENTHER, 1902). Panama, Costa Rica. To 35 cm. Dorsally lead-gray, ventrally light gray to whitish. Areas around snout, tentacles, eyes, and cloaca particularly light.

• *D. mexicanus* (DUMERIL and BIBRON, 1841). Mexico and Central America. Polytypic. To 60 cm. Dorsum gray to brown-olive. Abdomen yellowish, furrows black.

• *D. oaxacae* (MERTENS, 1930). Mexico. To 45 cm. Brownish, abdomen much lighter, each furrow dark anteriorly and light posteriorly.

Dermophis mexicanus

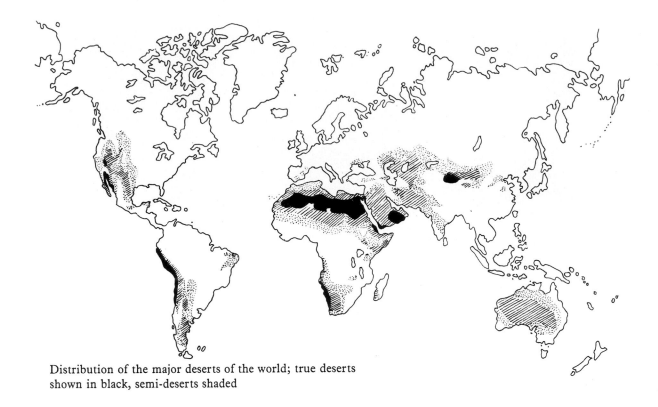

Distribution of the major deserts of the world; true deserts shown in black, semi-deserts shaded

Deserts: Due to constantly arid climates where there is only sporadic rainfall at intervals of years, deserts are nearly vegetation-free areas of the eremial. They occur where there is strong solar radiation exposure (except in fog deserts) and it is therefore extremely hot during the day (up to 60° C.) and rather cold at night (down to a few degrees above freezing). Apart from subtropical hot deserts (e. g., central Sahara), there are also true deserts in freezing regions (Gobi) and cold deserts at high altitudes within mountain chains (Pamir, Tibet). All deserts have a tendency toward more or less pronounced salinization due to rising underground water, which also has an inhibiting influence on the establishment of plants and animals. In deserts, in contrast to many other ecosystems, the most moist locations are sand and the driest are clays. The sparse and species-poor vegetation consists mostly of deep-rooting plants or those that grow along rocky crevices and are thus able to utilize capillary water. The fauna in extreme deserts is also very sparse, although several reptiles and even some anurans are true desert-dwellers. Most references to "deserts" probably apply more appropriately to semideserts.

Desert terrarium: The climatic conditions of a desert are often very difficult to duplicate in a terrarium. In an indoor terrarium the main problem is that of great nocturnal cooling. Nearly all true desert animals spend the night, as well as the hot midday hours, in deep burrows where there are relatively balanced temperature conditions as well as a certain perpetual remnant dampness. It is of paramount importance that these factors be accounted for in a desert terrarium. The substrate should be as deep as possible (not less than 10-15 cm thick even for small animals) and the lowest layers must always be slightly damp. If egg-laying is to be expected there must also be a dish or other shallow

Adrar (313 m)

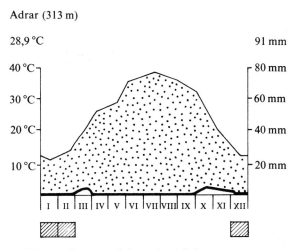

Climate diagram of the central Sahara

container with a moist substrate. All diurnal desert animals require a lot of light and ultraviolet radiation. Another problem is providing drinking water. In a true desert terrarium one can do without plants. Most animals described as desert inhabitants are more likely to be inhabitants of semideserts or steppes. There are different requirements for inhabitants of coastal or fog deserts such as the Namib.

Desmognathus BAIRD, 1850. Dusky Salamanders. Genus of the Plethodontidae. Eastern North America, with greatest diversity in the Appalachian Mountains. 7 to 10 species, several polytypic; systematic status of several forms not yet decided. Together with *Leurognathus* and *Phaeognathus* these salamanders form the subfamily Desmognathinae of the Plethodontidae. Mostly in or close to small flowing waters (small creeks) in highland areas, but some in swampy lowlands. Tiny to medium size, 5 to 19 cm. Moderately stout, 13 to 15 costal grooves. Lower jaw rigid, the mouth

Desmognathus fuscus

Desmognathus ochrophaeus

Desmognathus monticola

opened by raising the upper jaw (subfamily character). Hind legs heavier than front legs. Coloration dependent upon species, race, age, and individual variability, usually brown with a brighter middorsal stripe. Most species have an oblique light band from the eye to the corner of the mouth. Often very agile swimmers.

The individual forms vary substantially in their mode of life and ecological requirements. Many forms are largely aquatic as adults, such as *D. brimleyorum* and *D. quadramaculatus*. Closely tied to water but with a semiaquatic mode of life are *D. fuscus*, *D. monticola* (both found close to small flowing waters), and *D. auriculatus* (close to stagnant waters rich in humic and tannic acids). Terrestrial forms are *D. aeneus*, *D. wrighti*, and *D. ochrophaeus*, *D. aeneus* and

D. wrighti lacking an aquatic larval stage.

The breeding season extends generally from late summer into early fall. Normally the females attach their unpigmented eggs (mostly less than 20) to the substrate in or directly adjacent to water and guard the clutch.

Care and breeding requirements must agree with the ecological requirements of the species. Semiaquatic, flowing water species should be kept in an aqua-terrarium with cool, always clean, fresh water with ample hiding places under flat stones and patches of moss. Aquatic forms should be kept like *Leurognathus*. Terrestrial forms can be kept in a humid terrarium with moss and many hiding places. Forms from nothern latitudes require a winter dormancy period in water. With the exception of the terrestrial forms, specimens from more southern latitudes should be kept for about 8 weeks at reduced temperatures (10 to 15° C.).

▪ *D. aeneus* BROWN and BISHOP, 1947. Seepage Salamander. North Carolina to Alabama. Semiterrestrial. 4 to 6 cm. Slender. Light brown, flanks darker than back, which may show dark longitudinal stripe in a broad tan dorsal strips.

▪ *D. fuscus* (RAFINESQUE, 1820). Northern Dusky Salamander. Southeastern Canada to Florida. 12 cm, rarely to 18 cm. Highly variable in coloration. Tail keeled. Brownish with a broad, wavy dorsal stripe made from fused light spots. Abdomen only slightly lighter than back. Older specimens more or less uniformly darkish.

▪ *D. monticola* DUNN, 1916. Seal Salamander. Appalachian Mountains, Pennsylvania to Alabama. 2 subspecies. To 12 cm. Dorsally dark with vermiform dark markings. Abdomen light.

▪ *D. ochrophaeus* COPE, 1859. Mountain Dusky Salamander. Northeastern USA and Appalachian Mountains. 2 subspecies. To 10 cm. Highly variable coloration. Dorsal light band delineated by a pair of dark lateral longitudinal bands. Often brightly colored.

▪ *D. quadramaculatus* (HOLBROOK, 1840). Black-bellied Salamander. Appalachian Mountains. 17 cm, rarely to 21 cm.

Sides with 2 longitudinal rows of white dots, abdomen black.

- *D. wrighti* KING, 1936. Pygmy Salamander. Border region of Virginia/Tennessee/North Carolina. 4-5 cm. Light bronzy brown, with a dark herringbone dorsal pattern.

Diadophis BAIRD and GIRARD, 1853. Ringnecked Snakes. Genus of the Colubridae, Natricinae. USA except in central northwest, southward to Mexico. As many as 3 species, although most workers recognize 1 species with about a dozen subspecies. In damp habitats at elevations of up to 2500 m. To 75 cm. Slender. Uniformly darkish above, belly yellow to orange or red; a narrow yellowish or reddish neckband present.

Nocturnal ground snakes found under rocks, logs, and in similar hiding places. The diet consists of earthworms, salamanders, smaller snakes. When excited they hide the head under the body coils, presenting the spirally coiled tail and end of the body, which are often red underneath. Care and maintenance as for Natricinae, Group I.

- *D. punctatus* (LINNAEUS, 1766). Eastern Ringnecked Snake. Ventral color not extending onto scales of sides. Great Plains east.

Diadophis punctatus regalis

Diadophis punctatus amabilis

Diadophis punctatus

Diadophis punctatus regalis

Diadophis punctatus edwardsi

Diaglena: see *Triprion*, genus.

Diaphorolepis JAN, 1863. Monotypic genus of the Colubridae, uncertain subfamily status (Xenoderminae, Xenodontinae, or Natricinae). Panama to Ecuador in tropical lowlands and mountain forests. 70 cm. Head distinctly set off, with very large eyes. Enlarged row of vertebral scales with double keels, the other dorsal scales with a single keel. Dorsally uniform brown.

Ground snakes that appear to feed on frogs. For details on care refer to Natricinae, Group I.
• *D. wagneri* JAN, 1863.

Diarrhea: Change in consistency, form, color, and odor of feces. Due to increased intestinal motility and impaired resorption, the feces turn greenish to bloody red and are given off more frequently and take on a liquid consistency. The presence of mucus indicates more profound, long-standing changes in the intestinal mucous membrane. Often diarrhea coincides with the refusal to feed or regurgitation of partially digested food. Only rarely can an exact cause be determined on the basis of changes in the feces, except possibly for amoebic dysentery. Diarrhea can also occur as side-effects of infectious diseases, endoparasitosis, and be triggered by fright reactions. Infections and endoparasitosis are primarily caused by inadequate conditions (specimens kept too cool, incorrect diet, vitamin deficiency).

Therapy: Apart from antibiotics, sulfonamides, and vitamin supplements, successful treatment of diarrhea lies in symptomatic therapy. The environmental temperature should be increased (with additional basking lamps); and the drinking water can be supplemented with astringent agents and a dash of salt. In order to avoid dehydration of the animal's body, it is advisable to administer isotonic electrolyte solutions and adsorbent agents (animal charcoal) with a stomach tube or (for herbivores) with the food. Antispasmodics and analgesics may be recommended by a veterinarian to decrease intestinal motility.

Dibamidae: Dibamids. Family of the Squamata. Southeast Asia and the Indo-Australian Archipelago to the Philippines and New Guinea. Genus *Dibamus* is the only living genus. Systematic position unclear, often considered in conjunction with Anelytropsidae and Feyliniidae to be closely related to   skinks, but other characters suggest relationships to the geckos. Found in tropical forests. Body worm-like, elongated. Skull massive, elements rigidly fused, temporal arch completely reduced. Pterygoid teeth absent. Eyes regressed. No external ear openings. Limbs absent except small fin-like rudiments of the hind limbs in males that function during mating. Osteoderms absent. Caudal vertebrae with preformed fracture line for autotomy.

Subterrestrial ground-dwellers. Eggs have a calcium shell.

Dibamus DUMERIL and BIBRON, 1839. Dibamids. Genus of the Dibamidae. Southeast Asia to Indonesia, the Philippines and New Guinea. 3 species. Tropical forests. To 30 cm. Head scutes fused into large plates. Tail with fracture lines from fifth vertebrae on. Primarily brown.

Lives below ground. Egg-layers.
• *D. novaeguineae* DUMERIL and BIBRON, 1839. New Guinea, Sunda Islands.

Dicamptodon STRAUCH, 1870. Giant Salamanders. Genus

of the Ambystomatidae. USA and Canada, Pacific Northwest. 2 species. Close to and in clear, cool flowing waters and mountain lakes. To 30 cm, robust, compact. Head large, broad, flat, temporal region appearing inflated. Legs stout, hind legs longer than front legs, tips of fingers and toes thickened and knob-like. In contrast to *Ambystoma*, fourth toes with only 3 segments, palmar foot tubercles absent. Tail muscular, laterally compressed, keeled on top and rounded below. Body with about 12 very indistinct costal grooves.

Dicamptodon ensatus

Dicamptodon ensatus

Dicamptodon ensatus

Dicamptodon species occupy cool, damp evergreen forests of the plains and montane regions to about 1750 m, where they are semiaquatic. On land these animals occupy hiding places under rocks, logs, and bark, but also climb about among bushes and in trees. Spawning occurs in early spring immediately after the snow has melted. The eggs are stalked and are attached individually to the solid substrate, which is invariably in flowing water. Depending upon the water temperature, the larvae will hatch the following winter or even later. Metamorphosis occurs at the earliest during the second summer. Neoteny sometimes occurs. Sexually mature larvae may reach a maximum size of 33 cm.

Giant salamanders should be kept in a cool, sufficiently large aqua-terrarium at high humidity and with ample hiding places such as tree bark, decorative cork pieces, and flat rocks positioned to provide a cave. During the hot summer months a location in a refrigator or in a basement is recommended. The diet includes earthworms, small frogs, and medium size slugs. Provide a winter dormancy period from at least November to February. Larvae and neotenic adults must be kept in an aquarium.

• *D. ensatus* (ESCHSCHOLTZ, 1833). Pacific Giant Salamander. Coastal region of British Columbia to California, also in the Rocky Mountains (Idaho, Montana). 30 cm. Brown with a dark marbled pattern. Metamorphosed adults common, but often neotenic. The very similar *D. copei* of the Cascades is always neotenic, seldom exceeds 17 cm.

Dicrodon DUMERIL and BIBRON, 1839. Desert Tegus. Genus of the Teiidae. Coastal areas in Peru and Ecuador. 3 species. In coastal steppes and semideserts. To about 40 cm. Reminiscent of some Lacertidae.

Diurnal ground-dwellers. For details on care refer to *Cnemidophorus*.

• *D. heterolepis* (TSCHUDI, 1845). Peru and southern Ecuador. Easily 35 cm. Insect feeders.

• *D. guttulatum* DUMERIL and BIBRON, 1839. Peru. Easily 40 cm. Herbivorous.

Dicroglossus GUENTHER, 1858. Monotypic genus of doubtful status within the Ranidae. Considered by different workers to be either an independent genus or a subgenus or synonym of *Rana*. Africa. Skin covered with warts. Eyes conspicuously close to each other, pointed obliquely upward, protruding and ball-like.

Largely aquatic, but not tied to a particular habitat. Should be accommodated in a tropical aqua-terrarium.

• *D. occipitalis* (GUENTHER, 1848). To 13.5 cm. Dorsum more or less distinctly spotted, with a characteristic light occipital crossband.

Didynamipus ANDERSSON, 1903. Genus of the Bufonidae. Tropical West Africa. 2 species. Tympanum hidden. Fingers and toes free; only 4 toes. Skin without distinct warts.

• *D. sjoestedti* ANDERSSON, 1903. Cameroons. 2 cm. Yellow-brown with small dark spots.

Dieffenbachia SCHOTT. Genus of the Araceae. Tropical America. About 40 species. Shrubs with strong stems. High humidity required, 20 to 25° C., semishaded location. Reproduction through cuttings. Most frequently cultured form is *Dieffenbachia bausei* hort.

Digestive system: All organs associated with food intake, digestion, and excretion of food remnants. The digestive system is formed by the intestinal tract with its various segments and the glands associated with digestion, especially the liver and pancreas. In the mouth regions of amphibians and reptiles there usually are teeth as well as a variably formed tongue sometimes modified as a thrust mechanism for prey capture (*Chioglossa, Hydromantes, Bufo,* Chamaeleonidae) or for olfactory perception (tongue flicking in snakes). Also leading into the oral cavity are various (in snakes particularly strongly developed) salivary glands that give off secretions that moisten the food. Following the short pharynx is the esophagus (short in amphibians, substantially longer in reptiles), which ends in a muscular sac, the stomach. In crocodilians, as in birds, the stomach is divided into an anterior glandular stomach and a posterior muscular stomach. The intestine is of rather variable length. It receives at its anterior end ducts from the liver (a gall bladder also is usually present) and pancreas. In algae-eating tadpoles the intestine is particularly long in relationship to the size of the body and usually contains many loops. Appendices can occur at the transition from mid-gut to hind-gut. The last section of the intestine is the cloaca, which usually has associated with it 1 or 2 urinary bladders and opens to the outside via a perpendicular or longitudinal cloacal slit.

Maceration of food in the oral cavity is not possible for many amphibians and reptiles or is achieved only to a limited degree (e. g., the crushing of prey animals by the jaws of many lizards). In snakes this leads to the formation of large amounts of gas, which can substantially bloat the body. Many amphibians and reptiles can survive relatively long periods without food (extreme cases in snakes of more than 2 years) and replenish their energy requirements from body reserves such as fat bodies. Food intake and rate of digestion are strongly dependent upon the temperature. Animals kept too cold in a terrarium will usually stop feeding. If amphibians and reptiles are to be overwintered at low temperatures it is therefore important that the food taken in last is completely digested and the intestinal tract has been completely emptied.

Dimorphognathus BOULENGER, 1906. Monotypic genus of the Ranidae. Western Africa in tropical rain forests. Externally similar to *Phrynobatrachus*. Males, like *Phrynodon*, have a pair of long, hook-like, tooth-shaped processes on the upper jaw. They occupy muddy, swampy habitats.
▪ *D. africanus* (HALLOWELL, 1857). Cameroons and Gabon. To 3 cm.

Dinodon DUMERIL and BIBRON, 1853. Big-tooth Snakes. Genus of the Colubridae, Lycodontinae. Eastern Himalayas eastward to China, Japan, and Indo-China. 8 or 9 species. Closely related to *Lycodon*. In damp, overgrown habitats. 0.7 to 1.4 m. Head oval, well demarked. Smooth or slightly keeled dorsal scales. Most species have simple color markings such as dark bands against a light background; frequently there is a light neckband.

Nocturnal ground snakes. Some species (e. g., *D. rufozonatum*) also enter water. The food includes fish, frogs, toads, lizards, and snakes. If threatened, *D. rufozonatum* (and possibly all species) coil up into a ball.

Dinodon rufozonatum

Dinodon septentrionalis

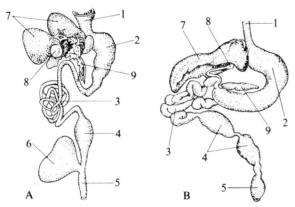

Digestive systems of: A Amphibia *(Rana)*, B Reptilia *(Phrynosoma)*.

1 Esophagus; 2 stomach; 3 small intestine; 4 large intestine; 5 cloaca; 6 urinary bladder; 7 liver; 8 gall bladder; 9 pancreas

Dinodon rufozonatum

Dinodon septentrionalis

For details on care refer to Natricinae, Group 1. Should be given a well-planted, moderately heated terrarium with a large water bowl.

- *D. orientale* HILGENDORF, 1880. Japan. 70 cm.
- *D. septentrionalis* (GUENTHER, 1875). Eastern Himalayas to China, Taiwan, and North Vietnam. 1.2 m.
- *D. rufozonatum* (CANTOR, 1842). Red Banded Snake. China and Korea to the USSR border; Taiwan. Barely 1 m.
- *D. flavozonatus* POPE, 1928. From Burma to western China. 1.4 m, largest species of the genus.

Diplodactylus GRAY, 1832. Genus of Gekkonidae. Australia. About 20 species in dry forests and dry grasslands. 7 to 15 cm. Tail usually distinctly shorter than snout-vent length; substantially thickened in some species (serving as a storage organ), in other species with spinous processes. Toes with distinct adhesive lamellae. Some species excrete a toxic, viscous substance from tail pores as a defense. Coloration highly variable, with distinct color changes.

Crepuscular to nocturnal ground-dwellers; some species are arboreal. During the day they usually shelter under tree bark. The diet consists mainly of small, soft arthropods. Clutch is 2 eggs with soft shells.

- *D. stenodactylus* BOULENGER, 1896. Northern and central Australia. Grasslands. To 7 cm. Tail short and slightly thickened. Brown with a reticulated pattern and light spots; variable.
- *D. vittatus* GRAY, 1832. Wood Gecko. Southern Australia in dry open country. To 8 cm. Extremely short, thickened tail (about 3.5 cm). Usually brown with yellow-brown serrated median band. Found under rocks, sometimes buried in soft sand.

Diploglossus WIEGMANN, 1834. Galliwasps. Genus of the Anguidae. Southern Mexico through Central America (in-

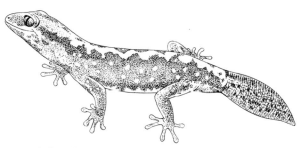

Diplodactylus vittatus

cluding the Antilles) to South America. 20 to 30 species. *Celestus* GRAY, 1839, with non-retractile claws, is closely related and here considered a synonym. In tropical forests. 20 to 30 cm. Short limbs but with 5 elongated toes; claws retractile into sheaths (*Diploglossus* proper) or not (*Celestus*). Lateral fold missing. Scales relatively small, at the most weakly keeled. Tail long. Primarily brownish, frequently with darker narrow crossbands. Juveniles often darker, with light-colored bands. Some species black and red or black and yellow when young.

Diploglossus monotropis

Diplodactylus vittatus

Crepuscular ground-dwellers frequently found under fallen leaves; some species like to dig. They feed on small worms, snails, and arthropods. Egg-layers or ovoviviparous.

Galliwasps do well in semi-moist terrariums but are very shy. One *D. costatus* specimen lived for 10 years in a greenhouse but was only seen 3 times in that period.
▪ *D. lessonae* PERACCA, 1890 (= *D. tenuifasciatus* PARKER, 1924). Brasil.
▪ *D. montanus* (SCHMIDT, 1933). Central America.

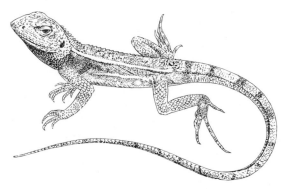

Diporiphora bilineata

Diploglossus fasciatus

Diplolaemus BELL, 1843. Genus of the Iguanidae. Patagonia to Straits of Magellan. 3 species found in rocky habitats. About 20 cm. Compact.

Diurnal ground-dwellers that should be kept in a moderately damp terrarium at room temperatures with localized radiant heat and a large temperature drop at night. A winter dormancy period for 2 to 3 months is essential.
▪ *D. darwini* BELL, 1843. Darwin's Iguana. Gray-brown with irregular black crossbands that posteriorly have partially yellow edges.

Diplometopon NIKOLSKY, 1905. Monotypic genus of the Amphisbaenia, family Trogonophidae. In dry regions.
▪ *D. zarudnyi* NIKOLSKY, 1905. Arabia to southern Iran. Easily to 10 cm. Brown with small darker dots.

Diporiphora GRAY, 1842. One-lined Dragons. Genus of the Agamidae. Australia and New Guinea. 6 species. To 25 cm. Slender, tail about twice snout-vent length. Low, serrated nuchal and dorsal crests present. Usually with a narrow light line high on the side. In appearance somewhat reminiscent of *Calotes*, but much less arboreal and found in drier habitats.
▪ *D. bilineatus* GRAY, 1842. Northern Australia and New Guinea. To 25 cm. Males light olive-green with a yellow longitudinal stripe on each side and a washed-out black

shoulder spot. Females and juveniles red-brown with dark crossbands.

Dipsadinae: Subfamily of the Colubridae. Neotropics. 3 genera: *Dipsas*, *Sibon*, and *Sibynomorphus*, about 48 species. Close to Oriental subfamily Pareinae. There appears to some uncertainty about the actual relationships of the two groups, whether this is a case of parallel evolution of different origins or whether they are actually of similar origin. Found in rain forests and montane rain forests. 25 to 75 cm. Slender, the body more or less laterally compressed. The head is conspicuously set off from the body and very short. The eyes are very large. Lower jaws more rigid (less movable) than in other snakes, especially in *Dipsas*, where a chin furrow is absent. This genus has reached the highest degree of specialization within its family. In contrast to most other colubrid snakes, the anterior teeth are heavy fangs.

Nocturnal ground snakes. They feed mostly on snails, which are pulled out of their shells and are then eaten. Due to the great amount of slime given off by the snails, respiration of the snakes is restricted while they are feeding and they thus have to rely on air stored in the lungs.

Should be kept in a rain-forest terrarium with high humidity and a radiant heat source. The diet can consist of local snails. A winter food supply will have to be stored (about 3 to 8 medium snails per snake per week). Slugs, due to the extremely great amount of mucus given off, are less suitable as food.

Dipsadoboa GUENTHER, 1858. Genus of the Colubridae, Boiginae. Tropical Africa. 4 species. In tropical rain forests and gallery forests. 0.9 to 1.1 m. Slender, laterally compressed body. Head distinctly set off from body, with very large eyes with vertical pupils. Uniformly brown or olive to light green.

Nocturnal tree snakes. Their main diet consists of frogs (*Phrynobatrachus*, *Arthroleptis*, and *Wolterstorffina*). Egg-layers, 6 eggs. Should be maintained in a well-heated and properly planted rain-forest terrarium. Caution: Venomous bites.
▪ *D. unicolor* GUENTHER, 1858. Guinea eastward to Uganda. 2 subspecies. Dorsum uniformly grass-green, rarely brown to olive with dark scale interspaces. Nominate subspecies yellow to yellow-green ventrally, tail region clearly demarked, blackish blue. Subspecies *D. u. viridiventris* LAURENT, 1956, has the belly uniform pale green.
▪ *D. duchesni* (BOULENGER, 1901). Guinea to Ghana. 2 sub-

species. Light brown to greenish.

Dipsas LAURENTI, 1768. American Snail-suckers. Largest genus of the Dipsadinae. Neotropics between Mexico and Paraguay. About 33 species. Tropical rain forests (Amazon Basin), montane rain forests, and cloud forests. To 90 cm. Distinctly laterally compressed body with a conspicuously short, stout head. Large eyes. Lower jaws with large anterior fangs; relatively immovable anteriorly, connected with firm skin, no chin furrow. Usually marked with reddish and yellowish rhomboidal or trapezoidal spots or broken crossbands against a dark background.

Nocturnal tree snakes.

• *D. bicolor* (GUENTHER, 1895). Pacific slopes from southern Nicaragua to northern Costa Rica. Montane rain forest.

• *D. indica* LAURENTI, 1768. South America to Paraguay, the southernmost species. 4 subspecies. A lowland species.

• *D. oreas* (COPE, 1868). Western slopes of the Ecuadorian Andes. Montane rain forests.

• *D. pratti* (BOULENGER, 1897). Central Cordilleras of Colombia. Montane rain forests.

Dipsas indica

Dipsosaurus HALLOWELL, 1854. Desert Iguanas. Genus of the Iguanidae. Southwestern United States, northern Mexico, small islands in the Gulf of California. 3 species. In dry, semidesert habitats. About 35 cm. Dorso-ventrally flattened, stout. Head small and round. Tail fragile, about equal to snout-vent length. Body with small scales, but tail with large, keeled whorls of scales. Very low dorsal crest. Light grayish brown with dark crossbands and longitudinal lines partially broken into spots and forming a reticulated

Dipsosaurus dorsalis

Dipsosaurus dorsalis

pattern. Ventral area light.

Diurnal ground-dwellers. When endangered they flee by running in part on the hind legs only. They require much heat during the day. Egg-layers, 1 or 2 clutches per year, each with 3 to 10 eggs. For details on care refer to *Uromastyx*. Apart from plants, will also feed on larger arthropods and pieces of lean meat.

• *D. dorsalis* (BAIRD and GIRARD, 1852). Desert Iguana. Southwestern USA and northwestern Mexico.

Dipsosaurus dorsalis

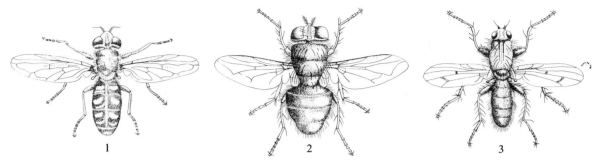

Diptera: 1 Syrphidae *(Lasiophthicus pyrastri),* 2 Calliphoridae *(Lucilia sericata),* 3 Scatophagidae *(Scatophaga stercoraria)*

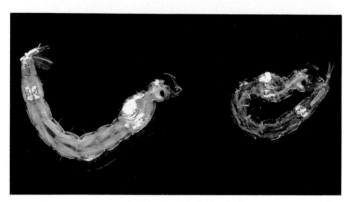

Diptera: Glassworms, larvae of *Chaoborus*

Discoglossidae: Fire-bellied Toads, Midwife Toads, and allies. Family of the Salientia. Mainly in the Palearctic (genera *Alytes, Bombina, Discoglossus),* with 1 genus, *Barbourula,* in the Philippines and Borneo. 4 genera. Of rather variable shape (e. g., *Alytes* is a "toad" and *Discoglossus* is *Rana*-like) and coloration. Pupil circular, heart-shaped, or triangular (never horizontal). Tympanum usually indistinct. Tongue disc-shaped, atttached by wide base to mouth floor and not projectile. Adult specimens have true ribs. The tadpoles have the spiracle opening along the abdominal line. Amplexus inguinal. Most of these characters are primitive or unspecialized.

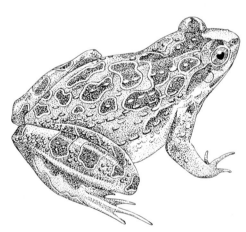

Discoglossus pictus

Diptera: Flies. Order of Insecta. More than 90,000 species. Some play a role as parasites and potential disease vectors, while some are important as food animals. During the summer months flies are the main component of meadow plankton. Many species can be collected in fly traps that are baited with cheese, meat, or fish. Terrariums located close to a window can use fly traps that have an entrance funnel right into the terrarium. In outdoor enclosures flies can be attracted in large numbers simply by placing bait at various locations (inaccessible to the reptiles, of course).

The larvae of various mosquitos and midges (suborder Nematocera, Culicidae, Chironomidae) serve as food for aquatic amphibians. Some Diptera can also be produced through continuous breeding setups. Among the other important food flies are representatives of the families Drosophilidae (fruitflies), Muscidae (houseflies), and Calliphoridae (bluebottle flies).

Discodeles BOULENGER, 1918. Genus of the Ranidae. Solomon Islands and New Britain. 4 species. Closely related to *Batrachylodes, Ceratobatrachus,* and *Platymantis.* Close to or in montane creeks in tropical regions. Head broad and flat. Skin covered with warts. Webbing on toes well developed (except in *D. malukuna).* Adhesive discs more or less distinct (particularly large in *D. guppyi).* Brownish.

Mode of life usually semiaquatic. The eggs are laid out of water and the larvae also develop out of water as in *Platymantis.* For details on care refer to *Petropedetes.* Need a spacious terrarium.
- *D. guppyi* BOULENGER, 1918. To 20 cm.
- *D. malukuna* BROWN and WEBSTER, 1969. To 7 cm.
- *D. opisthodon* (BOULENGER, 1884). To 15 cm.

Discoglossus OTTH, 1837. Painted Frogs. Genus of the Discoglossidae. Mediterranean countries. 2 species. Most frequently found in open, sunny swamp waters, but also found in mountain streams as well as in brackish water. Similar to *Rana,* but with round or heart-shaped pupil and poorly visible tympanum. Skin relatively smooth, only the flanks and thighs with small conical warts or dermal ridges; females with rougher skin than males. Fingers free, toes extensively webbed. Males without vocal sac, mating calls consist of repeated short, metallic sounds. At peak of mating season males have black nuptial pads on fingers, toes, and along the abdomen. Larvae adapted to standing waters, with a short and high tail.

Diurnal and nocturnal, largely aquatic. The diet consists mainly of young fish, tadpoles, earthworms, and large insects; cannibalism is common. These frogs spawn up to 4 times per year. During inguinal amplexus each pair produ-

Discoglossus pictus

ces up to 1000 eggs that sink to the bottom. Depending upon the water temperature, the larvae will hatch in 2 to 10 days, metamorphosis occurs in 30 to 60 days.

Painted frogs should be kept in unheated, sunny, spacious aqua-terrariums; they also can be kept outdoors during the summer. A cool winter dormancy period of several weeks as in *Bombina* may stimulate seasonal breeding activities. Can readily be bred in captivity.

• *D. nigriventer* MENDELSSOHN and STEINITZ, 1943. Israel. Ventrum dark. Very small area of distribution and endangered, possibly extinct.

• *D. pictus* OTTH, 1837. Painted Frog. Mediterranean countries. 2 subspecies. To 7.5 cm. Nominate subspecies with 3 types of markings; uniformly gray-brown, greenish, or reddish; with an ornamental pattern of dark brown spots; or with 3 light yellow longitudinal bands. Subspecies *D. p. sardus* TSCHUDI, 1837, restricted to islands of the western Mediterranean Sea, is larger and never striped.

Discophus: Incorrect spelling of *Dyscophus*.

Disinfection: Elimination of the dangers of infection through the destruction of disease pathogens on dead or living matter by means of physical and chemical procedures. This refers mainly to the disinfection of terrariums and decorations, ideally without removing the occupants. Each disinfection must be preceded by a thorough cleaning. The decorations should be completely replaced periodically, or cleaned outside the terrarium and sterilized with boiling water.

The most important disinfectants are phenols and their derivatives (3 to 5% solutions), formaldehyde (2 to 5 %), and quaternary ammonium compounds (0.5 to 2 %). Dis-

infectants generally require at least 4 hours of exposure for maximum effective action.

Disjunct distribution: Division of a taxon's distribution range into 2 or more parts that are separated from each other by zones where the taxon is absent. It is thus impossible for specimens from one area of the range to mate with those in the other area. Discontinuities of distribution are common in biogeography and can only be explained by geological changes, such as the South American—African disjunction of the Pipidae and the South American—African—Southern Asian disjunction of the Gymnophiona through continental drift, or the disjunction within the newt genus *Neurergus* by climatic and vegetational changes in the Near East.

Dispersion: Distribution of individual members of a population in a given space. This can be random, regular (normal), or in groups. Random dispersion occurs only rarely because it presupposes a (under natural conditions) never-occuring homogeneity of the environment and non-recognition of individuals among population members, e. g., distribution of mealworms in bran medium or frogs buried in a semidesert in order to survive drought conditions. Regular (normal) distribution depends on the homogeneity in the environment and the territorial behavior of population members toward each other (e. g., territorial lizards). Natural conditions of dispersion are usually based on a group distribution pattern, such as increased frequency of individuals at certain locations (e. g., *Mauremys caspica* tends to occupy mainly thermal spring effluents along its northwestern distribution border; congregations of salamanders in winter quarters). Knowledge of dispersion patterns is a prerequisite for a reasonably accurate determination of population size and is as an essential factor for establishing utilization, protection, and eradication measures for wild populations of plants and animals.

Dispholidus DUVERNOY, 1832. Boomslangs. Monotypic genus of the Colubridae, Boiginae. Africa from Senegal and Eritrea southward to Cape Province. In savannahs. To 1.7 m. Slender, with weakly set off head that appears high and short. Conspicuously large eyes with round pupils. Opisthoglyphic, relatively large fangs at eye level. Body scales strongly keeled and shingled, becoming markedly

Dispholidus typus

Dispholidus typus with *Chamaeleo* prey

Dispholidus typus, young

narrower along the sides. Uniformly green, brown, or black, sometimes with black edges around scales with a green base coloration (*D. t. kivuensis* LAURENT, 1956). Juveniles are lighter, usually brown to yellowish.

Diurnal tree-dwellers, rarely on the ground except when laying eggs. Predators of lizards (mainly chameleons), tree-frogs, birds, and small mammals, sometimes also snakes. In its native habitat it is frequently mistaken for *Dendroaspis*. When frightened it substantially inflates its neck region, making the snake appear dorso-laterally much broader.

Should be kept in a well-heated tropical terrarium with climbing facilities. Boomslangs lose their aggressiveness rapidly in captivity and become "tame," which has led to fatal accidents. Venom has been lethal to humans. South African antivenin available and must be kept in store when this snake is kept. Has been bred repeatedly in captivity, 8 to 24 eggs.

• *D. typus* (A. SMITH, 1829). 2 subspecies.

Display behavior: Innate type of behavior used in order to impress a rival or sex partner. Display behavior is usually part of any threatening behavior or courtship behavior, as well as mating behavior, and it also serves in species recognition. Thus, for instance, a male green iguana (*Iguana iguana*) displays toward a female as well as toward another male by rapidly nodding his head and spreading the gular pouch. Structures of varied sorts are often included in display behavior and used as optical signals: erectile skin folds in frilled lizards, *Chlamydosaurus*; gular pouches in *Anolis*; the hood in cobras, *Naja*.

Disteira LACEPEDE, 1804. Genus of the Hydrophiidae, Hydrophiinae. Persian Gulf to Indo-Australian waters. 3 or 4 species. 1.5 m. Resembles the closely related *Hydrophis*.
• *D. stokesi* (GRAY, 1846). India to Australia.

Dispholidus typus

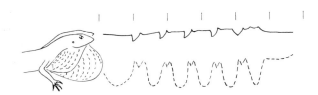

Display behavior of grass anoles, *Anolis auratus*, showing the typical sequence of head bobbing and rhythmic spreading of the gular pouch

Display behavior: By spreading the gular pouch, inflating the body, and standing high on the legs, the size of the grass anole is greatly exaggerated

Distributional barriers: Generally insurmountable geographical or ecological barriers for particular taxa that prohibit the enlargement of the distributional area. For instance, oceans can act as distributional barriers for terrestrial organisms that can not fly and are poor swimmers, thus islands that are geologically young and are located far out in the ocean have fewer species than the adjacent land mass. Also, high mountain chains and deserts act as distributional barriers, thus the Sahara Desert and Himalayan Mountains more or less separate entire faunal regions. In many instances only the existence of such distributional barriers can effectively explain the fact that some organisms are restricted to certain lakes, river systems, or mountain chains.

Distribution center: Geographical region with a particularly large number of species, which decreases more and more away from such a center. Such particular species aggregations in faunal and floral elements, including endemic forms, can possibly be based on the fact that the distribution center is at the same time a center of evolutionary processes. However, distribution centers often become primarily refuges during periods of particularly unfavorable climate. Once the climate improves, species will begin to radiate from such a distribution center again. Due to the abundance and diversity of species at distribution centers they become popular excursion, collecting, and research areas: for instance, in Europe the Iberian, Appeninian, and Balkan Peninsulas; in eastern Asia the Amur Region, southern China, and southern Japan; in North America areas such as Florida, Mexico, and California.

Disturbances: Physical and psychological disturbances of a terrarium animal can be directly contributed to specific captive conditions. A typical example is the frequent refusal to feed by newly caught snakes, which first have to overcome psychological shock and then have to adapt to the terrarium. Some species such as the blood python (*Python curtus*) or *Acrochordus javanicus* are known to accept food only with difficulty or not at all when first in captivity. Other disturbances include stunted growth and vitamin deficiency diseases that often lead to soft carapaces or carapace deformations in young turtles.

Ditaxodon HOGE, 1958. Monotypic genus of the Colubridae, Xenodontinae. Southeastern Brasil. Formerly included in *Philodryas* and biologically similar.
▪ *D. taeniatus* (HENSEL, 1868).

Ditmars, Raymond Lee (1876–1942): American zoologist and herpetologist who worked in zoological parks. Curator of mammals and reptiles at the Bronx Zoo, New York. Collected animals on many expeditions and successfully kept and bred them. One of the first and greatest popularizers of herpetology in North America. *The Reptiles of North America* (1936), *Snakes of the World* (1931), *Field Book of North American Snakes* (1939).

Dogania: see *Trionyx*, genus.

Dominance: In ecology, the relative (i. e., percentage) frequency of a species in reference to all other species examined at the same time and in the same sample area. Also refers to the social standing of an individual in a species hierarchy.

Dracaena DAUDIN, 1802. Caiman Lizards. Genus of the Teiidae. Tropical South America. 2 species found mainly close to water in the *selva*. Up to 1 m. Stout. The large, heavy teeth have blunt crushing and grinding surfaces. The tail is laterally flattened. Dorsal scales consist of very large raised and keeled plates surrounded by granular scales. Plate-like scales on the upper surface of the tail form two longitudinal serrated keels similar to those in caimans. Dark olive to dark brown.

Caiman lizards are semiaquatic in boggy swamps, climbing onto bushes along banks mainly for the purpose of sleeping. The diet consists almost exclusively of large snails, whose hard shells are cracked open effortlessly and are then spat out. The eggs are laid in termite nests.

Requires spacious, heated aqua-terrariums with large water bowls (25 to 28° C.) and sturdy climbing branches. They will eagerly feed on various snails. Caution: When handling adult specimens, remember that the lashing tail can cause painful welts.
▪ *D. guianensis* (LACEPEDE, 1788). Caiman Lizard, Jacuruxy. Northeastern South America. Easily to 1 m.

Dracaena VAND ex L. Dragon Trees. Genus of the Agavaceae. Tropics and subtropics of the Old World. About 80 species. Woody plants. Require high temperatures, humidity, and shade. Only young plants are suitable for terrarium use.
▪ *D. marginata* LAM. Leaves to 30 cm.
▪ *D. deremensis* ENGLER. Frequently cultivated are the varieties "Bausei" and "Warneckii."
▪ *D. surculosa* LINDL. Densely branched, bush-like. Leaves to 10 cm.

Dracaena guianensis

Dracaena paraguayensis

Dracaena guianensis

Draco volans

Draco LINNAEUS, 1758. Flying Dragons. Genus of the Agamidae. Southeast Asia, Philippines, and Indo-Australian Archipelago. 20 species. In damp, warm tropical forests. To 30 cm, usually smaller. Recognized by the characteristic, semicircular skin folds along the sides that are supported by 5 or 6 false ribs; these "wings" are folded fan-like against the body when at rest. Males have large gular pouches and lateral throat folds. The tail is as long as the body, with shingled scales. Mostly shades of brown. The "wings" (gliding membranes) and gular pouches are often bright red or yellow spotted with black.

Generally arboreal at heights between 3 and 10 m. The spread gliding membranes enable these lizards to glide over distances of up to 30 m, the flight terminating on other trees or branches. The diet consists mainly of arthropods, especially ants. Egg-layers, 3 to 10 eggs. Incubation period 1 to 3 months.

Flying dragons must be given a spacious, well-planted terrarium with high humidity and day temperatures from 28 to 32° C., with minimal nocturnal reduction. At lower temperatures the animals become sluggish, and at temperatures over 34° C. they seem to have respiratory difficulties. They require adequate drinking water delivered with a drop dispenser and regular spraying. Rearing the young is extremely difficult and apparently has never been accomplished successfully. Captive maintenance is rather problematic.

- *D. fimbriatus* KUHL, 1820. Indo-Australian Archipelago. To 30 cm. Relatively robust.
- *D. volans* LINNAEUS, 1758. Common Flying Dragon. Indo-China, Sumatra, Java, Kalimantan. About 20 cm. Males with low dorsal crest. Wings orange and black. Throat folds in males orange, in females small and blue. 2 to 5 eggs.

Dravidogecko SMITH, 1933. Monotypic genus of the Gekkonidae, subfamily Gekkoninae. Southern India, in highlands. Nocturnal.
- *D. anomallensis* (GUENTHER, 1875).

Drepanoides DUNN, 1928. Monotypic genus of the Colubridae, Boiginae; sometimes also included in the Natricinae. Andean slopes of southern Colombia to central Bolivia. About 35 cm. Only 15 rows of scales. Head barely set off, tip of snout black, top of head white, head separated from body by a black collar. Uniformly red-brown above. Burrowing ground snakes.
- *D. anomalus* (JAN, 1863).

Drinking: The taking up of liquids occurs in aquatic amphibians over the entire body surface and through the clo-

Draco lineatus

aca when they lie in water. Their mode of life in water or in more or less moist habitats leads to only minor water losses that are usually replaced with water taken in with the food.

Reptiles and to some extent more terrestrial amphibians of dry habitats have strongly keratinized skin that provides excellent protection against dehydration. Desert reptiles can quite often meet their entire water demand from the food organisms taken in. Most reptiles drink by dipping their snout into water, accompanied by swallowing movements of the throat (turtles, tortoises, snakes) or licking movements of the tongue (lizards). For the purpose of terrarium maintenance it has to be remembered that many arboreal rain-forest species are used to taking water drop by drop. Sea turtles, sea snakes, marine iguanas, and brackish water filesnakes will drink seawater; these animals possess special salt glands for the excretion of excess salts.

Dromicodryas BOULENGER, 1893. Genus of the Colubridae, Lycodontinae. Madagascar. 2 species. To 1.2 m. Morphologically and biologically very similar to *Boaedon* with attractive patterns of light and dark lines. Ground-dwelling snakes.
- *D. bernieri* (DUMERIL and BIBRON, 1854). Western, southern, and southeastern Madagascar.
- *D. quadrilineatus* (DUMERIL and BIBRON, 1854). Eastern and northeastern Madagascar.

Dromicus BIBRON, 1843. Genus of the Colubridae, Xenodontinae. Neotropics. About 12 species in various types of habitats. Some systematists include the large genus *Leimadophis* as a synonym in *Dromicus*, while the Galapagos species are placed in the genus *Alsophis*. The Antillean species placed in *Antillophis* and *Arrhyton* are considered to be independent genera. To 50 cm.

Diurnal ground snakes preferring the proximity of water. The diet consists mainly of frogs. For details of care refer to Natricinae, between Groups 1 and 2.
- *D. melanotus* (SHAW, 1802). Colombia, Venezuela, Trinidad and Tobago, Grenada.

Dromicus sagittifer

Dromophis PETERS, 1869. Genus of the Colubridae, Boiginae. Tropical Africa. 2 species. Close to rivers and in swamp regions. To 1 m. Morphologically similar to *Psammophis*, but with amphibious mode of life. Olive-green, with lighter or darker greenish to yellow longitudinal stripes.

The preferred diet is frogs. Egg-layers. For details of care refer to Natricinae, Group 2.
- *D. lineatus* (DUMERIL and BIBRON, 1854). Sudan and Guinea-Bisseu to Zimbabwe and northern sections of the Republic of South Africa.

Drosophilidae: Dewflies, Vinegarflies, and Fruitflies. Family of Diptera. About 750 species from 2 to 6 mm long. Best known species is *Drosophila melanogaster*, the common fruitfly. Somewhat larger (to 4.5 mm) is *D. funebris*. Breeding is simple. Use of a "wingless" variety is recommended. The larvae of most species feed on fermenting plant matter. The most useful breeding setup is a glass jar or similar container into which a layer (1-2 cm) of food medium is placed. The top must be sealed with gauze or fine porous cloth. The generation time is about 2 weeks at temperatures of about 25° C. A simple, useful food medium is made from 10 g of agar dissolved in 700 ml water; mix 60 g raw sugar, 120 g corn semolina, and 10 g dried

Dromicus typhlus

Drosophilidae: Normal fruitflies, *Drosophila melanogaster*

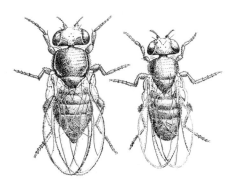

Drosophilidae, *Drosophila melanogaster*

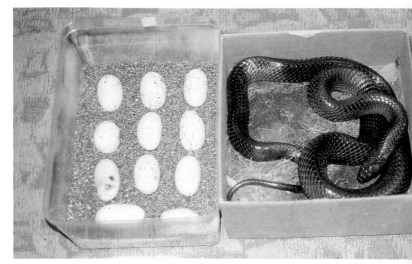

Drymarchon corais couperi with eggs

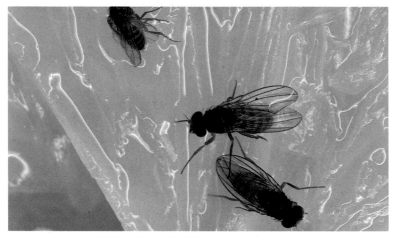

Drosophilidae: Giant fruitflies

Drymarchon corais couperi

yeast with 160 ml water and add to the agar mixture; bring to a boil and put into jars while hot. Even more simple is the use of commercially available baby food fruit mixtures to which a small amount of yeast is added. The addition of a fungi-inhibiting food additive prevents the formation of fungus. It is also advisable to place a tongue depressor or similar item (popsicle sticks, etc.) upright in the medium in order to facilitate pupation outside the food medium (the sides of the glass jar are also used for that purpose) and to offer additional resting areas for the flies.

Drymarchon FITZINGER, 1843. Indigo Snakes. Monotypic genus of the Colubridae, Colubrinae. Found from southern USA (Florida and Texas) southward to Argentina

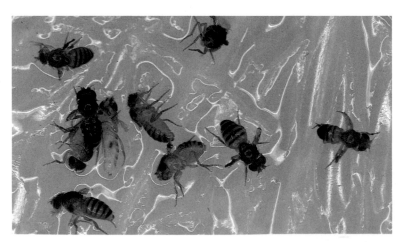

Drosophilidae: Vestigial-winged fruitflies, *Drosophila melanogaster*

Drymarchon corais couperi

Drymarchon corais couperi

in diverse habitats; prefer proximity to water. To 2.3 m. Strongly built, with a slightly triangular body cross-section. Older specimens are usually uniform blue-black or brown; the juveniles have washed-out crossbars.

The diet consists mainly of frogs, toads, small mammals, birds, lizards, and snakes, the latter including rattlesnakes and other Crotalidae. Excited specimens simulate the warning behavior of *Crotalus* by vibrating the tip of the tail. Egg-layers, 8 to 12 eggs. For details on care refer to *Coluber*, but climbing facilities have to be included. Hardy in captivity and often bred.

▪ *D. corais* (BOIE, 1827). 8 subspecies.

Drymobius FITZINGER, 1843. Tropical Racers. Genus of the Colubridae, Colubrinae. From Texas southward to

Peru. 4 species in different types of habitats. To 1.3 m. Fast-moving snakes. Head markedly set off from body, with large eyes.

Diurnal ground snakes often found close to water. At least *D. rhombifer* appears to sleep among bushes at night, an unusual type of behavior for terrestrial snakes. The main diet consists of frogs. Should be kept in a well-heated terrarium, as for Natricinae, Group 2.

▪ *D. margaritiferus* (SCHLEGEL, 1837). Speckled Racer. Texas to northern South America. 4 subspecies.

▪ *D. rhombifer* (GUENTHER, 1860). Nicaragua to Peru.

Drymobius margaritiferus occidentalis

Drymarchon corais melanurus

Drymobius margaritiferus

Drymobius margaritiferus

Drymoluber AMARAL, 1929. Genus of the Colubridae, Colubrinae. Tropical South America east of the Andes. 2 species. In tropical forest regions of a dry nature. About 1 m. Very slender. Head small, little set off, with large eyes.

Diurnal tree snakes that sleep at night among the branches of low bushes. The diet consists mainly of lizards (teiids and *Anolis*). Should be kept in a well-heated dry terrarium with climbing and bathing facilities.

▪ *D. dichrous* (PETERS, 1863). Upper Amazon Region, Colombia, eastern Ecuador, eastern Peru, northern Brasil, and southern Venezuela. Great differences between juvenile and adult colorations.

Dryocalamus GUENTHER, 1858. Genus of the Colubridae, Lycodontinae. Malayan Peninsula, Sumatra, Kalimantan, Philippines, India, and Sri Lanka. 5 species. Closely related to *Lycodon*. In monsoon forests and rain forests. 35 to 90 cm.

Nocturnal climbing snakes. Diet: arthropods, small lizards, and frogs.

▪ *D. subannulatus* (DUMERIL and BIBRON, 1854). From Malaysia to Sumatra. Alternating black spots against a light brown background dorsally.

▪ *D. tristrigatus* GUENTHER, 1858. Kalimantan and surrounding islands in montane rain forests to 600 m. Dark brown with three white longitudinal stripes.

Dryophiops BOULENGER, 1896. Monotypic genus of the Colubridae, Boiginae. Malayan Peninsula and large areas of the Indo-Australian Archipelago. About 75 cm. Slender, with a laterally compressed body and large, elongated head clearly set off by a thin neck. Eyes horizontally elongated, vaguely reminiscent of those in *Ahaetulla*, but the pupil (shaped like a horizontal figure 8) substantially wider. Body covered with smooth scales. The large ventral scales are rounded off on both sides (characteristic of climbing snakes). Very long tail. Dorsally reddish brown with small black dots.

No details available on food preferences and reproductive biology. For details on care refer to *Chrysopelea*.

▪ *D. rubescens* (GRAY, 1834).

Drysdalia WORRELL, 1961. Australian Crowned Snakes. Genus of the Elapidae. Southern Australia. 3 species. Formerly included in closely related genus *Denisonia*. To 40 cm. More or less slender. Head clearly set off from body. Variably uniform in coloration; a dark or light collar may be present (*D. coronata* and *D. mastersi*), but without other markings.

Nocturnal venomous snakes that feed on arthropods, frogs, and lizards. Give birth to 5 to 15 young at a time. Should be kept in well-heated dry terrarium. Venom not considered to be very dangerous.

▪ *D. coronoides* (GUENTHER, 1858). White-lipped Snake. Tasmania and southeastern Australia. Does not require much heat.

Duberria FITZINGER, 1826. African Slug-eaters. Genus of the Colubridae, systematic position uncertain. Eastern Africa from Ethiopia to Cape Province. 2 species on steppes and montane rubble slopes to elevations in excess of 3000 m. 30 to 45 cm. Head small, with rounded snout, barely set off from body. Smooth dorsal scales. Tail short, terminating in a blunt point. Background color uniformly reddish brown to blackish or covered with irregular spots and dots.

Nocturnal, hiding under rocks during the day. Prefers slugs and snails, the latter being pulled out of their shells. Occasionally lizards and even small snakes are taken. Egg-layers. Best kept in a well-heated dry terrarium with a substantial nocturnal temperature reduction.

▪ *D. lutrix* (LINNAEUS, 1758). Ethiopia to Cape Province. 3 subspecies. Highly variable in coloration and markings.

Duerigen, Bruno (1853-1930): German zoologist and herpetologist. Published the standard treatise *Deutschlands Amphibien und Reptilien* (1897) with the cooperation of numerous amateur herpetologists supplying information.

Dumeril, Andre Marie Constant (1764–1860): French anatomist and herpetologist. Together with Bibron (and after his death with his son, Auguste H. A. Dumeril), publisher of the 10-volume *Erpetologie Generale ou Histoire Naturelle Complete des Reptiles*. This was the first comprehensive treatise on the amphibians and reptiles. A large number of the 121 turtle, 468 lizard, 586 snake, and

218 amphibian species recognized by Dumeril and Bibron were illustrated on 120 colored plates.

Dumeril, Auguste H. A. (1812–1870): Son of Andre M. C. Dumeril. Coauthor of *Erpetologie Generale ou Histoire Naturelle Complete des Reptiles* begun by his father and Bibron. Together with Bocourt, Brocchi, and Mocquard, worked on the 17-volume treatise *Mission Scientifique au Mexique et dans l'Amerique Centrale; Etudes sur les Reptiles et les Batraciens* (appeared from 1870 to 1909), which became the basis for Central American herpetology.

Dunn, Emmet Reid (1894–1956): American herpetologist, professor at Haverford College. *Salamanders of the Family Plethodontidae* (1926), *American Caecilians* (1942), *American Frogs of the Family Pipidae* (1948).

Dyckia SCHULT. Genus of the Bromeliaceae. Mainly in Brasil. About 80 species. Ground-dwelling xerophytes on *campos* and rocky heather plateaus. Usually low-growing rosette plants. Leaves about 20 cm long, spinous. Undemanding, can be cultivated like succulents. Full exposure to sun and air essential.

Dyckia spec.

Dyscophus GRANDIDIER, 1872. Tomato Frogs. Genus of the Microhylidae. Madagascar. Depending upon prevailing systematic views, from 3 to 6 species. Head flat, pupil horizontal (Boulenger indicates erroneously a vertical pupil). Tympanum variably visible or not (in *D. insularis* tympanum not visible). Fingers free, toes webbed halfway, adhesive discs absent. Metatarsal tubercle a more or less shovel-like spade. Found in various types of habitats.
• *D. antongili* GRANDIDIER, 1877. Tomato Frog. Tropical

Dyscophus antongili

Dyscophus antongili

northwestern Madagascar. In coastal areas (only during the breeding season?) in ditches. 11 cm. Red.
• *D. insularis* GRANDIDIER, 1872. 5 cm. Reddish brown with dark vermiculate pattern.

Ear: Sensory organ in terrestrial vertebrates where the senses of equilibrium and hearing are combined. The ear is phylogentically very old and is constructed similarly in the various vertebrate classes. It registers the position relationships and turning movements of the head. The rather variably developed hearing function perceives sound waves and vibrations. The ear includes the inner ear with its bony and membranous labyrinth, which contains several sacs and canals (utriculus, sacculus, 3 semi-circular canals, saccus endolymphaticus, and lagena or cochlea) and the corresponding sensory cells; the middle ear cavity with tympanum and auditory ossicles; and the outer ear (in mammals).

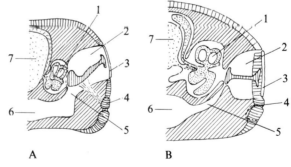

Ear: A Frog; B Reptile
1 Inner ear with membranous labyrinth; 2 middle ear with columella; 3 eardrum; 4 quadrate bone of jaw with ligament connecting to columella; 5 Eustachian tube; 6 pharynx; 7 brain

The hearing organ in amphibians seems very simple but is also somewhat specialized and degenerate. Most frogs have a well-developed tympanum and a middle ear with 1 or 2 auditory ossicles (stapes or columella and operculum). Hearing ability in frogs is also relatively well developed. For instance, *Rana* can distinguish vibrations of from 100 to more than 1500 Hz. The middle ear cavity and tympanum are absent in salamanders, the caecilians, and in some frogs; the auditory ossicles can also be reduced or completely absent. These animals perceive vibrations by means of a ligamentous or muscular connection from the base of the skull or the pectoral girdle to the ear, so that ground vibrations are detected.

The hearing organ in reptiles also shows variable development among the various orders and reaches its highest development in the crocodilians, where the lagena starts to coil into a snail-like cochlea. Crocodilians are the only reptiles with an externally closable ear. Among the lizards, geckos have excellent hearing (some are also able to vocalize quite well); optimal sensitivity lies between 300 and 1000 Hz, and some species still react to vibrations of 10,000 Hz. Snakes have lost the tympanum, middle ear cavity, and the connection to the oral cavity (Eustachian tube). Their hearing ability, if present at all, is only minimally developed. Since an auditory ossicle (the stapes) is connected to the quadrate of the lower jaw, ground vibrations are easily perceived by the middle ear. Tendencies toward the reduction of the middle ear and the connection of the stapes to the quadrate are also found among various lizards with different modes of life (e. g., Chamaeleonidae, Amphisbaenidae, Lanthanotidae). Turtles have relatively nonsensitive hearing that is only adequate in the lower range of tones of about 500 Hz, but they are very sensitive to ground vibrations. Generally, it appears that the ability to perceive sound waves is of relatively low significance in amphibians and reptiles when compared to other senses, especially that of smell.

Earthworms: Group of families of the Annelida, class Oligochaeta. Includes especially Lumbricidae, Glossoscolecidae, Ocnerodrilidae, and Megascolecidae. Worldwide. Many species are suitable as food for amphibians, some lizards, and small snakes. They are also often eagerly eaten by turtles. Some lizards will feed on earthworms only after their mucus has been removed.

The best-known earthworms include the 30 cm nightcrawler (*Lumbricus terrestris*) and various smaller forms of the genera *Lumbricus* and *Allobophora*. Members of *Eisenia* (dungworms) are infamous for giving off foul-smelling secretions and should not be fed in large quantities; however, a few now and then will do no harm. These particular species usually are purplish red and have yellow rings.

In order to have a supply of earthworms on hand for the winter it is advisable to set up a box filled with layers of

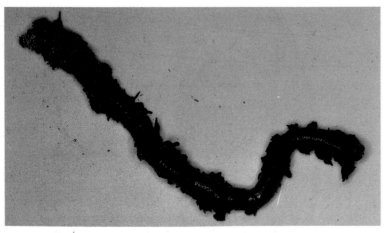

Earthworm

Earthworm

leaves covered with humus. Styrofoam containers are useful, as are wooden boxes with tight-fitting lids or large porous earthenware containers. Occasionally some food is placed inside the container; vegetable leftovers, oatmeal, boiled potatoes, and similar items are suitable as food. Actually breeding earthworms under similar conditions is quite possible. Sometimes it is useful to roll earthworms in calcium and vitamin preparations or inject them with supplements just before feeding them to terrarium animals.

Ebenevia BOETTGER, 1878. Genus of the Gekkonidae. Madagascar and Mascarene Islands. 2 species. Under 10 cm. Slender. Head deep, with protruding eyes. Tail spinous. Slender toes with simple lamellae, without claws. Appearance and mode of life strongly reminiscent of *Phyllodactylus*.
• *E. inunguis* BOETTGER, 1878. Madagascar. Dark olive-brown with dark brown lateral stripe and indistinct dorsal lines.

Echeveria DC. (including *Dudleya* BRITT. and ROSE). Genus of the Crassulaceae. Found mainly in Mexico north to Texas and southward to Peru. More than 150 species. Succulent, stemless shrubs or short-stemmed semi-bushes with spirally arranged leaves. Undemanding. For semi-desert terrariums.
• *E. agavoides* LEM. Lawn-forming. Stemless. Very resistant.
• *E. purpusii* K. SCHUM. Stemless. Rosettes with diameter of 10 cm.

Echinosaura BOULENGER, 1890. Rough Teiids. Monotypic genus of the Teiidae. Panama to Ecuador. Easily to 15 cm. Slender, with a pointed head and a weakly compressed tail. Limbs normally developed. Large, relatively pointed rough scales forming more or less distinct cross rows and surrounded by small granular scales.

Nocturnal, slow-moving ground-dwellers that feed on small arthropods. They fake death when threatened.
• *E. horrida* BOULENGER. 1890. Rough Teiid. Ecuador to Panama. To 15 cm. Brown with indistinct yellowish spots.

Echiopsis FITZINGER, 1843 (incl. *Brachyapsis* BOU-LENGER, 1896). Bardicks. Monotypic genus of the Elapidae. Southern Australia. In deserts on different substrates. To 60 cm. Heavy, short head. Usually uniformly brown without markings.

Nocturnal venomous snakes that feed on lizards, frogs, and insects. Live-bearers, up to 10 young. Venom not lethal to humans. Keep in a well-heated dry terrarium with a substantial temperature reduction at night.
• *E. curta* (SCHLEGEL, 1837).

Echis MERREM, 1820. Saw-scaled Vipers. Genus of the Viperidae, Viperinae. Africa north of the equatorial rain forest zone to the Near East and central Asia; also to India and Sri Lanka. 6 species, in part polytypic. In sand and rubble deserts, also in steppes, savannahs, and in outer forest areas. 70 to 90 cm. Head with very large eyes with vertical pupils. Dorsal scales differentiated: median rows straight, strongly keeled; sides with obliquely running rows of scales that have serrated keels. These side rows when rubbed along each other cause a scraping, rattling noise. Markings consist of rhomboid to round spots in rows, sometimes broken into an irregular crossbanded pattern.

Primarily nocturnal. Venomous. The prey consists of small mammals and lizards; juveniles will also take arthropods. Locomotion in part is through sidewinding. Live-bearers, 6 to 15 young. Venom extremely potent, often fatal despite antivenin treatment. Keep in well-heated dry terrariums with a nocturnal temperature reduction. Has been bred repeatedly. Feeding the young is often difficult if crickets, young lizards, and newborn mice are not taken. Force-feeding with a paste food mixture presents considerable risk due to the agility of these snakes.

Echis coloratus

• *E. carinatus* (SCHNEIDER, 1801). Saw-scaled Viper. 3 or 4 subspecies: *E. c. carinatus* (SCHNEIDER, 1801), southern India, Sri Lanka; *E. c. leakeyi* STEMMLER and SOCHUREK, 1971, East Africa; *E. c. pyramidum* (GEOFFROY-ST. HILAIRE, 1827), Egypt, Near East; *E. c. sochureki* STEMMLER, 1969, Pakistan.
• *E. coloratus* GUENTHER, 1878. Arabian Saw-scaled Viper. Southeastern Egypt, Arabian Peninsula, in the north to southern Israel. Largest species of the genus.
• *E. multisquamatus* CHERLIN, 1981. Soviet Central Asia, northern Iran.

Echis coloratus

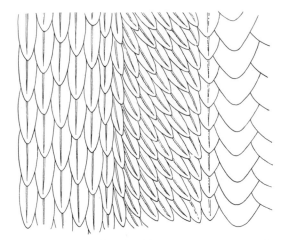

Differentiated lateral scales of *Echis*

Echis carinatus

Ecological balance: The dynamic balance that exists based on the reciprocal actions between the habitat and the living things in each ecosystem. The changes of one component also affect changes in other components. Diversely structured ecosystems have a balanced regulatory ability, whereby the ecological balance over long periods of time is not significantly displaced. In contrast, in simply structured ecosystems even minor changes are sufficient to strongly upset the ecological balance so that irreversible damage may occur; i. e., the system collapses.

Simulated ecosystems in a terrarium have—due to the unavoidable paucity of components and the relative overcrowding—no possibility at all for self-regulation. They are ecologically not balanced at all, and therefore without continuous external influence they are unstable. It would be wrong here to talk about an ecological balance or even to attempt to achieve one.

Only under near-natural conditions such as in a very large, diversely structured outdoor terrarium or a greenhouse can simple regulatory mechanisms occur. These reg-

ulatory mechanisms can be of great significance for the reproduction of ecologically particularly demanding species.

Ecological factors: Those components of the environment that affect organisms. Since an active environment consists of animate and inanimate components, one distinguishes between abiotic and biotic ecological factors. Abiotic factors important for amphibians and reptiles include for instance temperature, humidity, and water radiation intensity; biotic factors of significance are food organisms, competitors, enemies, and parasites.

Abiotic factors have a favorable effect on an organism only within a certain area; that is, they have a certain value (ecological valence) toward organisms. In reverse, the ability of an organism to utilize ecological factors is referred to as ecological potency.

Ecological niche: Often used erroneously in the sense of ecological position, when indeed it actually applies to proper utilization—not the "position" as such but instead the "working relationship" within the ecosystem.

Ecological position: A permanent position (of an organism) within the competitive structure and food chain of an ecosystem. For instance, in tropical rain forests the position of an insect-feeder on the leaves (which is occupied in South America by treefrogs, in tropical Asia by flying frogs), in an arid sand and rock desert the position of a ground-dwelling small predator that feeds mainly on insects and spiders (in Africa and Asia occupied by agamids, in America by *Cnemidophorus*). It is ecologically irrelevant which species uses the ecological position; what is important (in the sense of regulating ecosystems) is that they are being utilized.

Ecological potential: Differentially developed ability in a particular species to exist in a more or less wide spectrum of one or more ecological factors. The ecological potential can be depicted graphically as a potential curve, a wide amplitude indicating eurypotentials and narrow amplitude indicating stenopotentials. Stenopotential species are tied to a particular habitat and in their distribution therefore are more readily endangered than are eurypotential species, such as those following human habitation.

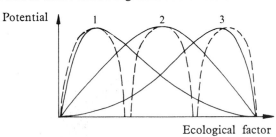

Ecological potential: Graphic representation of stenopotential species (1), mesopotential species (2), and eurypotential species (3) in relation to ecological factors

Ecological valence: Value of an ecological factor for a species; easily depictable graphically as a valence curve. For an organism the most favorable portion of a factor is the optimum, the barely acceptable values are the minimum and maximum. Between the extreme values and the

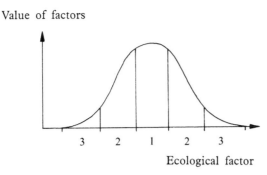

Value of factors

Ecological factor

Ecological valence: Graphic representation showing the optimal region (1), suboptimal region (2), and extremes (3) with minima and maxima

optimum lies the suboptimal region. Usually the "ecological optimum" and "physiological optimum" (that is, the actual) do not coincide under natural conditions, since one species is often pushed into the suboptimal region by more competitive species. Therefore, it is basically wrong—in terms of terrarium management—to attempt to duplicate in a terrarium exactly the environmental conditions found at a particular location. The physiological optimum of a species can only be experimentally determined by the exclusion of all competition from other species.

Ecology: Study of the reciprocal relationships between organisms and their environment; its structure, dynamics, and economy of nature. The extremely multilayered questions and problems posed within ecological research can be arranged into 4 plateaus or levels: an individual organism; a population; a collection of organisms (biocoenosis) composed of several individual species; and an ecosystem.

Apart from pure basic natural science research, ecology has to cope with increasingly practical questions and applied problem-solving. Thus ecology deals with utilization potentials as well as with regulatory mechanisms of natural and artificial ecosystems, has its role in environmental research, and provides the necessary scientific basis for nature and environmental protection.

Ecosystem: Usually a very complexly structured unit of habitat within the corresponding environment, more or less clearly delineated from other similar units; e. g., a mixed mountain forest, a lake, or a semidesert with all its characteristic organisms. In each ecosystem there is a continuous cycle between organisms and their environment. On the other hand, energy flow (via photosynthesis converting solar energy) through an ecosystem is always in one direction: producers to consumers to destroyers (converters).

Within the consumers of an ecosystem, amphibians and reptiles occupy different positions. Consumers of the first level are plant-eating tortoises and lizards; the second and third levels are occupied by the vast majority of carnivorous amphibians and reptiles and their enemies. The consumers at the top are the crocodiles and giant snakes.

Ecpleopus DUMERIL and BIBRON, 1837. Genus of the Teiidae. Ecuador, western Brasil. 2 species. Small ground-dwellers.
• *E. affinis* PETERS, 1862. Ecuador. About 15 cm. Andean valleys.

Ectoparasitosis: Disease symptoms caused by parasites that live in or on the outer skin embed their mouth parts in the skin and in order to reach blood vessels. As such they damage the subcutaneous tissue and thus function as transmittors of other disease organisms. In reptiles the most important ectoparasites are mites and ticks. Occasionally leeches (e. g., *Haementeria costata*) have been known to attack amphibians, aquatic turtles, and crocodiles.

Therapy: Spraying or bathing with Trichlorphon (0.1—

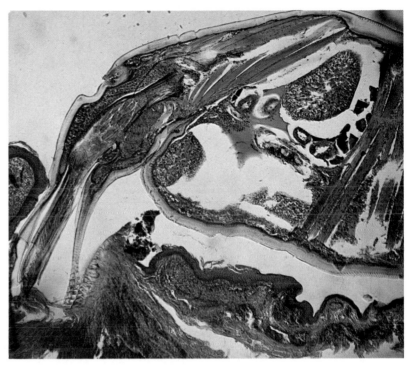

Ectoparasitosis: Cross-section of the tick *Ornithodoras tholuzari*

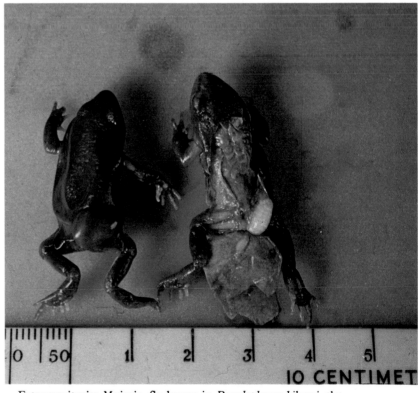

Ectoparasitosis: Myiasis, fly larvae in *Pseudophryne bibroni*, the larva exposed in the right specimen

Ectoparasitosis: Ticks on *Lacerta viridis*

0.2% solution) is the most effective procedure. However, there are considerable differences in the susceptibility of the various ectoparasites. Chlorinated hydrocarbons are very toxic to reptiles!

Since the bite wounds from parasites and their sites of attachment are often prone to secondary bacterial infections, there must also be localized antibiotic or sulfonamide treatment with a spray or powder. A vitamin A-enriched ointment speeds up the healing of local lesions.

Prophylaxis: All newly acquired animals must be thoroughly checked for the presence of ectoparasites and if need be should also be treated accordingly. If necessary, all the terrarium decorations should also be sprayed or, better yet, be replaced. Peat moss should be sterilized before it is placed inside a terrarium.

Edalorhina JIMENEZ DE LA ESPADA, 1870. Genus of the Leptodactylidae. Upper Amazon Basin of Ecuador, Peru, and western Brasil. 2 species. Related to *Lithodytes* and *Physalaemus*. Lives in the *selva*. Slender, with conspicuous tubercular projections on the upper eyelids and snout. Pupil horizontal. Tympanum visible externally. Tips of fingers and toes enlarged, not webbed. Body with dorso-lateral skin folds.

Diurnal ground-dwellers. Larvae aquatic. Should be accommodated in a tropical rain-forest terrarium with small water bowl.

▪ *E. perezi* JIMENEZ DE LA ESPADA, 1870. 3.5 cm. Dorsum chromium yellow, flanks black. Belly clearly set off, lacquer-white.

Edaphic: Referring to the ground. Edaphic factors such as composition and structure of the ground, its moisture content, and temperature gradients are of considerable importance to reptiles and amphibians, which—due to their particular mode of life—have more or less close contact to the ground, and are also important for the development of eggs deposited in or on the ground. Thus for species-cor-

rect maintenance natural conditions have to be provided in captivity. However, in most cases it is irrelevant whether the substrate is of natural or artificial origin.

Egernia GRAY, 1838. Spiny-tailed Skinks. Genus of the Scincidae. Australia. About 20 species. Mostly in dry, open, rocky habitats. 15 to 55 cm. Appearance variable; some smooth-scaled species (*E. inornata, E. saxatilis*) are reminiscent of *Lacerta*; others are similar to *Tiliqua*, but with keeled to spinous scales and a body-long tail. *E. depressa* and *E. stokesii* are depressed, with a short, particularly spinous tail. Various shades of brown with variably spotted and lineate patterns.

Diurnal, in part gregarious. Ovoviviparous, generally 4 to 10 young. For details on care refer to *Tiliqua*. These skinks do not need a large water bowl, but provide some

Egernia depressa

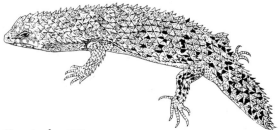

Egernia depressa

Egernia depressa

Egernia striolata

Egernia stokesi

Egernia whiti

Egernia cunninghami

binding are less specific: refusal to feed, apathy, and particularly respiratory difficulties should lead to a suspicion of egg-binding, a diagnosis that can really only be confirmed with an X-ray examination.

Egg-binding can be caused by a change of habitat just before the eggs are to be laid, by temperatures that are too low, by inflammation of the cloacal and oviduct mucous membranes, by the oviduct being twisted, or by traumatic damage to eggs in the oviduct.

Therapy: Optimal temperature and humidity, localized warming of the abdomen by means of wet compresses, application of some drops of DMSO preparation, injection of 1-5 Int. Units Oxytocin subcutaneously. If proper equipment is on hand, surgical removal of eggs and remnants is possible, even in turtles.

Egg callus: Corneous thickening along the edge of the snout in embryos of turtles, crocodilians, and tuataras that aids in opening the eggshell. Drops off after hatching. Also refer to egg tooth.

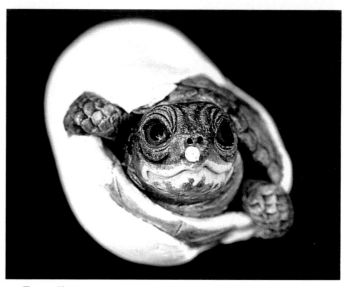

Egg callus

rocks instead. A winter dormancy period for 2 to 3 months at 10 to 15° C. is frequently recommended. Will change over to the seasonal rhythm of the Northern Hemisphere with difficulty. Mainly carnivorous. Digestion and emptying of digestive tract presumed to be facilitated by the addition of 5 to 10% glucose to the drinking water.

- *E. cunninghami* (GRAY, 1845). Cunningham's Skink. Southwestern and South Australia. Rocky areas. Easily to 35 cm. Males dark brown with light dots, females with salmon-colored dorsum.
- *E. depressa* (GUENTHER, 1875). Pygmy Spiny-tailed Skink. Southwestern Australia. Steppes. 15 cm. Body and tail covered with spines. Short tail. Reddish brown with sprinkling of black dots.
- *E. stokesii* (GRAY, 1845). Gidgee Skink. Central Australia. Tail heavily spinous. Darker than preceding species.
- *E. striata* STERNFELD, 1919. Night Skink. Central Australia. Sandy semideserts. 30 cm. Vertical pupil. Dark brown to yellowish red, some with two longitudinal stripes.
- *E. striolata* (PETERS, 1870). Spiny Tree Skink. Eastern and central Australia. Open forests. 20 cm. Relatively smooth. Brown with dark longitudinal lines interrupted by light dots. To some degree arboreal. Only 1 to 3 young. Must not be kept too dry!
- *E. whiti* LACEPEDE, 1804. White's Skink. Coastal southeastern Australia, Tasmania. Rocky areas. To 35 cm. Smooth. Brown with dark longitudinal bands with white dots and rows of spots. Quarrelsome!

Egg-binding: Failure of the egg to move completely through the oviduct. An increase in size in the abdominal and cloacal regions in snakes is often a clear indication that egg-binding has occurred. In turtles the symptoms of egg-

Eggs: Female sex cells (oocytes, gametes). Zygotes (fertilized egg cells) are generally also referred to as eggs.

Amphibian eggs: Most are moderately yolk-rich. In the order Caudata they are usually fertilized in the oviduct; in order Salientia usually after they have been laid. Glandular cells in the oviduct wall secrete a series of membranes around the egg (in salamanders and newts 3 to 6, and in frogs 1 to 5) that strongly swell up in water and form a gelatinous or slimy protective mass (the spawn). The elastic egg membranes are sufficiently permeable for the dissolved oxygen in the water to penetrate. The innermost layer liquifies quickly so that the embryo can develop inside a small, closed off space.

Reptile eggs: Yolk-rich. Following fertilization in the oviduct the eggs are surrounded with a firm but permeable eggshell (which can be parchment-like or solid with calcium deposits) by glandular cells in the uterus wall. In live-bearing species the eggshell remains membrane-like. Reptilian eggs are, like those of birds and mammals, typical amniote eggs, where the developing embryo produces embryonic membranes.

Egg tooth: Forward-pointing tooth on premaxillary with which embryos of the order Squamata cut open the eggshell. Falls off a few days after hatching. As an exception, the gekkonids (family Gekkonidae) have paired egg teeth.

Eichwald, Karl Eduard von (1795-1876): German-Russian naturalist and medical practitioner in St. Petersburg (Leningrad). Author of *Fauna Caspio-Caucasia* (1841) and various herpetological taxa from that region.

Eirenis JAN, 1863. Dwarf Snakes. Genus of the Colubridae, Colubrinae. Northeastern Africa and some islands in the Aegean Sea northward to the Caucasus countries and Turkmenia, eastward to northwestern India. 14 species found in variable dry habitats. 30 to 60 cm. Very slender. Usually brown to gray, often completely without markings, especially adult specimens.

Egg tooth cuts from hatching *Elaphe guttata*

Crepuscular, hiding under rocks during the day. *Eirenis* species feed on arthropods (crickets, scorpions, and others) and lizards, especially small skinks (*Ablepharus*) and gekkonids. Egg-layers, 2 to 8 eggs that are very large and cylindrical.

Should be kept in a moderately heated dry terrarium with ample hiding places (stone structures, caves, etc.). Ideally suited for small terrariums, as they will not even disturb succulents since they seldom burrow.

- *E. collaris* (MENETRIES, 1832). Collared Dwarf Snake. Caucasus and Near East. 32 cm. Distinct collar.
- *E. modestus* (MARTIN, 1838). Headband Dwarf Snake. From Aegean Islands to the Near East eastward to Iran, north to the Caucasus and south to Syria. 2 subspecies. To 60 cm. Juveniles with 2 dark headbands.
- *E. persicus* (ANDERSON, 1872). Turkey to northwestern India. 3 subspecies. 40 cm. Dark head and neck with a light crossband.
- *E. punctatolineatus* (BOETTGER, 1892). Southern Lesser Caucasus, Turkey, Iran, Iraq. 2 subspecies. To 50 cm. Rows of spots dorsally.

Eggs of *Chelonia mydas*

Eirenis collaris

Eirenis collaris

Elaphe climacophora

Elachiglossa ANDERSSON, 1916. Monotypic genus of the Ranidae. Thailand.
- *E. gyldenstolpei* ANDERSSON, 1916.

Elachistocleis PARKER, 1927. Genus of the Microhylidae. Central and South America. 2 species. Mainly in semidry grasslands (*llanos*). Plump. Very small head with a pointed, conical snout, head separated from egg-shaped body by nuchal fold. Eyes tiny. Tympanum not visible. Fingers and toes free. Close to and in small water accumulations (swamps, rain puddles).
- *E. ovalis* (SCHNEIDER, 1799). Colombia, Venezuela, Trinidad, Brasil, Paraguay. 6.5 cm. Olive-green, sides and abdomen black with yellow dots.

Elaphe carinata

Elachistodon REINHARDT, 1863. Indian Egg-eating Snakes. Monotypic genus of the Colubridae, Elachistodontinae. Northern Bengal. 80 cm. Dark olive-brown to blackish above with yellowish white spots and 2 white stripes from rostral scale along the lip plates and above the eyes. Whitish below with brown spots along the outer edges of the abdominal scales. Very rare!
- *E. westermanni* REINHARDT, 1863.

Elachistodontinae: Indian Egg-eating Snakes. Monogeneric subfamily of the Colubridae. Northern Bengal. 1 monotypic genus. Similarly modified as is the Ethiopian subfamily Dasypeltinae, without being closely related to it. Head not distinct from body as in the Dasypeltinae. Skull with strongly reduced dentition, only the posterior part of the upper jaw still with teeth; two small opisthoglyphic fangs on the upper jaw. The hypapophyses of the neck vertebrae are modified into an egg-cutting apparatus, just as in the Dasypeltinae. In contrast to the Dasypeltinae the dorsal scales are smooth and the central row of scales along the vertebral column is somewhat enlarged.

Ecology and biology largely unknown. Care and maintenance presumably as in Dasypeltinae, but actual experience is not yet available since these snakes are extremely rare (less than 10 specimens in museums).

Elaphe FITZINGER, 1833. Rat Snakes. Genus of the Colubridae, Colubrinae. Mainly Holarctic and in the adjacent Neotropical and Oriental regions. More than 50 species. Usually in damper habitats such as field margins with bushes, deciduous forests, bamboo forests, and similar

Elaphe dione

Elaphe guttata

habitats; some species most common in farm areas (e. g., *E. dione, E. guttata, E. obsoleta,* and others). 60 cm to more than 2 m. Head more or less distinctly set off, with large eyes and nearly evenly large teeth. Dorsal scales smooth or weakly keeled. Abdominal scales often clearly rounded and very flexible (climbing adaptation). Coloration and markings variable, even within the same species; striped and spotted patterns as well uniform coloration occur among various species. Different coloration between juveniles and adults obvious in many species.

Primarily crepuscular and nocturnal ground-dwellers or more or less arboreal. *E. rufodorsata*—in contrast to other *Elaphe*—is amphibious and feeds on fish. Other *Elaphe* occur in damp areas (e. g., *E. quadrivirgata, E. japonica*) and prefer frogs as their main diet, while the majority of species feed mainly on small mammals. The prey is killed by constriction. Some *Elaphe* also feed on birds and their eggs (*E. quatuorlineata, E. schrencki,* and others). Most *Elaphe* are egg-layers, and only a few species are live-bearing (e. g., *E. rufodorsata*).

Rat snakes are popular as terrarium animals. They can—depending upon ecological requirements—be kept more or less dry, but bathing facilities as well as climbing branches, hiding places, and sunning places have to be provided. Breeding requires a cool winter dormancy period (at least 4 to 6 weeks). The young can be raised initially on crickets and later with newborn mice. However, some *Elaphe* are difficult to acclimate and are often specialized feeders (e.

Elaphe guttata, albino

Elaphe guttata

Elaphe moellendorffi

g., *E. longissima*, *E. situla*, and some Chinese species).

▪ *E. climacophora* (BOIE, 1826). Japan. 2 subspecies. Feeds on mice. Sometimes aggressive.

▪ *E. dione* (PALLAS, 1773). Steppe Rat Snake. Ukraine (USSR) eastward to Korea and northeastern China. Easy to keep, barely aggressive.

▪ *E. guttata* (LINNAEUS, 1766). Corn Snake. Much of USA to northern Mexico. Often very colorful. Easy to keep, frequently bred, many color varieties available.

▪ *E. longissima* (LAURENTI, 1768). Aesculapian Snake. Central and southern Europe to western Asia. 3 subspecies. Can be difficult, sometimes aggressive.

▪ *E. mandarinus* (CANTOR, 1842). Mandarin Rat Snake. Western China to Burma. Very attractive. Difficult.

▪ *E. moellendorffi* (BOETTGER, 1886). Flower Snake. Southern China. Prefers heat.

▪ *E. obsoleta* (SAY, 1823). Rat Snake. Eastern North America to northeastern Mexico. About 9 subspecies. Extremely variable in markings and coloration. *E. o. quadrivittata*

Elaphe carinata

Elaphe mandarinus

Elaphe guttata, young

Elaphe helena

Elaphe longissima

Elaphe obsoleta quadrivittata

Elaphe guttata, albino

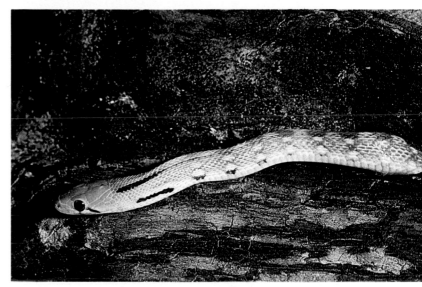

Elaphe helena

Elaphe longissima

Elaphe moellendorffi

Elaphe obsoleta quadrivittata

Elaphe obsoleta spiloides

Elaphe mandarinus

Elaphe porphyracea

Elaphe obsoleta rossalleni, young

Elaphe obsoleta quadrivittata

Elaphe obsoleta rossalleni

Elaphe obsoleta rossalleni

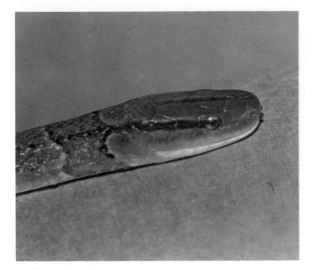

Elaphe porphyracea

Elaphe quatuorlineata sauromates

Elaphe quaturolineata, striped form

Elaphe quadrivirgata

Elaphe quaturolineata sauromates

Elaphe scalaris

(HOLBROOK, 1836) is superficially similar to *E. qu. quatuor-lineata*. Easy to keep, frequently bred. Ecologically very adaptable. May be aggressive.

▪ *E. quadrivirgata* (BOIE, 1826). Japan, Kurile Islands. Feeds on frogs.

▪ *E. quatuorlineata* (LACEPEDE, 1789). Four-lined Rat Snake. A spotted subspecies, *E. q. sauromates* (PALLAS, 1814) occurs from eastern Europe throughout the Caucasus to Iran. 3 subspecies in Italy, the western Balkan Peninsula, and Aegean have more or less distinct longitudinal stripes. Easy to keep, barely aggressive.

▪ *E. radiata* (SCHLEGEL, 1837). Burma eastward to southern China and southward to the Indo-Australian Archipelago.

▪ *E. rufodorsata* (CANTOR, 1842). Korea, adjacent USSR, China. Amphibious. Care as for Natricinae, Group 2.

▪ *E. scalaris* (SCHINZ, 1822). Ladder Snake. Southwestern

Elaphe schrencki

Elaphe rufodorsata

Elaphe rosaliae

Elaphe vulpina gloydi

Elaphe taeniura

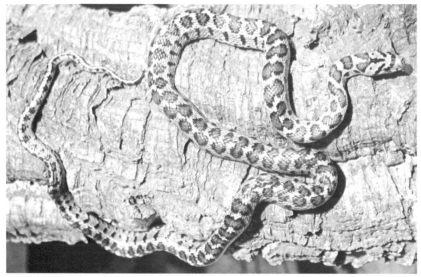

Elaphe situla

Elaphe subocularis

Elaphe schrencki

Elaphe scalaris

Elaphe triaspis intermedia

Europe. Very aggressive! Somewhat problematic to keep (can be kept as *Coluber*).

▪ *E. schrencki* (STRAUCH, 1873). Amur Rat Snake. Northeastern China, Korea, to eastern USSR. 2 subspecies. Easy to keep, not aggressive.

▪ *E. situla* (LINNAEUS, 1758). Leopard Snake. Southern Italy eastward through the Balkans to Asia Minor. Often feeds only on lizards.

▪ *E. subocularis* (BROWN, 1901). Trans-Pecos Snake. Southern Texas and northern Mexico. Semideserts. Care and maintenance as for *Coluber*.

▪ *E. taeniura* COPE, 1860. Assam eastward to northern China, southward to the Indo-Australian Archipelago. 2 subspecies [*E. t. grabowsky* (FISCHER, 1885)]. Easy to keep.

▪ *E. vulpina* (BAIRD and GIRARD, 1853). Fox Snake. North America near the Great Lakes. 2 subspecies.

Elapidae: Cobras and allies. Family of the Caenophidia. Worldwide distribution except Holarctic, only touching its

Elaphe taeniura

Elaphe subocularis

southern borders. Center of abundance and diversity Australia, where it is the dominant group of snakes. More than 50 genera and about 200 species. Closely related to Hydrophiidae. Some recent workers have repartitioned these two families, assigning many Australian terrestrial genera to a redefined Hydrophiidae.

Mainly 0.3 to 1 m; exceptions are *Ophiophagus* (record size 5.6 m) and *Oxyuranus* (record size easily 4 m), 2 of the 3 largest recent venomous snakes (the third is *Lachesis*). Usually slender, only a few genera adder-like, plump (*Acanthophis*). Head not or only weakly set off from body, covered with the normal large plates. Loreal scale absent. Proteroglyphic fangs present far forward in upper jaw, short in comparison to those of the Viperidae and Crotalidae. Maxillary bone still movable only in a few genera (*Dendroaspis, Oxyuranus*). Elapid venom is mostly neurotoxic, though hemotoxic venom components are present rarely.

The Elapidae can be conveniently arranged into fairly well-defined ecological and morphological groups:

1) Ground-dwellers that hide in the substrate or burrow. Usually small, with short tails, small narrow mouths, frequently with ringed markings. Strictly nocturnal; usually slow-moving and reluctant to strike. Seldom kept by terrarium hobbyists. *Micrurus*, etc.

2) Ground-dwellers that are large and slender. Diurnal or crepuscular. Fast, frequently aggressive, usually with threat postures (e. g., *Naja, Ophiophagus, Hemachatus*, and others). Of significance to terrarium hobbyists.

3) Tree-dwellers. Small to rather large, slender, with long tails and large eyes. Diurnal. *Dendroaspis, Paranaja, Pseudohaje, Hoplocephalus*.

4) Only species of the genus *Boulengerina* are amphibious.

There are many genera in which the biology remains yet to be investigated in detail. Small species feed primarily on arthropods and reptiles, especially geckos and blind snakes; larger species will frequently take frogs and toads (mainly Bufonidae), small mammals, and ground birds. Ophiophagous genera include (among others) *Ophiophagus* and *Bungarus*. Either egg-layers or live-bearers. The short incubation period in many Elapidae indicates a smooth transition between oviparity and ovoviviparity.

Care and maintenance: The ground rules for the care of venomous snakes must be strictly adhered to. Due to their agility and the frequently rapid effect of their neurotoxins, many elapids are extremely dangerous (*Naja, Dendroaspis, Oxyuranus, Parademansia, Pseudechis, Notechis, Ophiophagus, Acanthophis*, and others). Some Elapidae are able to spray their venom into the face of an enemy using the aerosol principle ("spitting cobras" of the genera *Naja* and *Hemachatus*). Other highly venomous elapids are at least during the day reluctant to bite and are thus less dangerous (*Bungarus, Micrurus*, many members of Group 1), while others are considered to be unpredictably aggressive and extremely fast in striking (*Naja, Ophiophagus, Notechis, Pseudechis, Dendroaspis*, and in a way also the slow *Acanthophis*). Some species have been bred over several generations. Numerous species are endangered through human interference in their native countries, thus captive breeding programs and nature reserves and habitat protection in general are becoming increasingly important.

The evolution and the resultant systematics of the elapids have so far been insufficiently researched. According to the latest opinions, the elapids should be arranged vastly different than presented here and be placed in a different relationship to the Hydrophiinae. For the moment, we will use the old system recognizing a simple family Elapidae. For simplicity, the genera can be arranged zoogeographically:

- North America: *Micrurus, Micruroides*.
- Central and South America: *Micrurus, Micruroides, Leptomicrurus*.
- Africa: *Aspidelaps, Hemachatus, Boulengerina, Elapsoidea, Dendroaspis, Paranaja, Pseudohaje, Naja*.
- Asia: *Naja, Bungarus, Calliophis, Maticora, Ophiophagus, Walterinnesia*.
- Australia (including New Guinea): *Acanthopis, Aspidomorphus, Austrelaps, Demansia, Denisonia, Drysdalia, Glyphodon, Hoplocephalus, Neelaps, Notechis, Parademansia, Pseudechis, Pseudonaja, Oxyuranus, Tropidechis, Vermicella, Suta, Toxicocalamus, Unechis*, and many more.

Elapognathus BOULENGER, 1896. Monotypic genus of the Elapidae. Lower southwestern corner of Australia. In desert-like dry landscapes. 40 cm. Mostly uniform brown, but juveniles and some adults with a collar band.

Rare venomous snakes. Biology almost unknown. Venom probably not very potent. Desert terrarium.
- *E. minor* (GUENTHER, 1863). Little Brown Snake. Vicinity of Albany.

Elapoides BOIE, 1827. Monotypic genus of the Colubridae, Lycodontinae. Sumatra, Java, Kalimantan. In tropical montane rain forests at elevations from 1000 to 1800 m. Barely 50 cm. Head not set off; rather small eyes. Dorsum dark brown with yellow spots or yellow brown with a dark middorsal stripe.

Burrowing ground snakes. Little known about their mode of life. Should be kept in glass terrariums.
- *E. fuscus* BOIE, 1827.

Elapomojus JAN, 1862. Monotypic genus of the Colubridae, Boiginae. Brasil.
- *E. dimidiatus* JAN, 1862.

Elapomorphus WIEGMANN, 1843. Genus of the Colubridae, Boiginae. South America, northeastern Brasil to Argentina. 8 species in tropical rain forests. 20 to 30 cm. Round head not set off from smooth body, eyes very small.

Burrowing ground snakes, best kept in glass containers. The diet consists of insects, worms, small lizards, and snakes.
- *E. bilineatus* DUMERIL, DUMERIL, and BIBRON, 1854. Southern Brasil, Uruguay, Paraguay, and Argentina. With 2 dark longitudinal stripes.
- *E. quinquelineatus* (RADDI, 1820). Eastern and central Brasil. With 5 dark longitudinal stripes.

Elaps: see *Homorelaps*, genus.

Elapsoidea BOCAGE, 1866. Monotypic genus of the Elapidae. Tropical and southern Africa. To 1 m. Body cylindrical; inconspicuous barely distinct head. Either plain gray-brown or with light and dark crossbanded pattern.

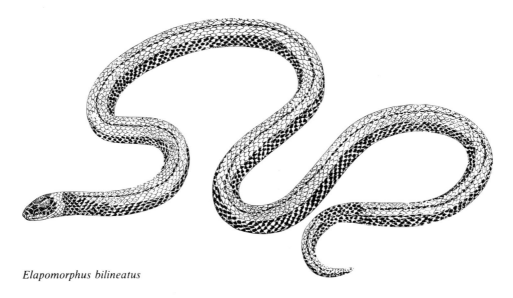

Elapomorphus bilineatus

Elapomorphus bilineatus

Venomous nocturnal snakes that hide during the day, frequently inside termite nests. Presumed to feed mainly on lizard eggs, especially those of geckos; it is assumed that lizards are also taken. Egg-layers, 8 to 12 eggs. The terrarium must have ample hiding places. The humidity should be between savannah and desert conditions, depending upon the origin of the specimen.

▪ *E. sundevalli* (A. SMITH, 1848). Venomous Garter Snake. Tropical Africa, southward from 15° North throughout entire southern Africa except Cape Province. 11 subspecies. Depending upon individual systematists, the various subspecies may be considered to be as many as 6 independent species.

Eleutherodactylus DUMERIL and BIBRON, 1841 (= *Noblella* BARBOUR, 1930; *Phrynanodus* AHL, 1933; *Trachyphrynus* GOIN and COCHRAN, 1963). Dwarf Barking Frogs. Largest genus of the Leptodactylidae. From Mexico through Central America, including the Antilles, to northern Argentina and southern Brasil. About 400 species, plus many that have not yet been described. Found in various types of habitats from plains and mountains up to about 4000 m. 1.2 to 10 cm. Pupil horizontal. Other than that,

Eleutherodactylus chiastonotus

no distinctive external characteristics. Fingers free, toes variously webbed. Tips of fingers and toes more or less enlarged through presence of a very small T-shaped terminal bone. Vocal sac, if present, is an unpaired sac.

Usually nocturnal ground-dwellers that hide during the day. Without an aquatic larval stage. The few large eggs (deposited in a moist substrate) develop within 2 to 3 weeks into completely metamorphosed juvenile frogs that hatch with egg-tooth-like structures. They thus are not tied to the proximity of water, so large areas only marginally suitable to frogs can be occupied by these frogs. Some species live on trees and bushes and deposit their eggs in epiphytes (e. g., *E. diadematus* and *E. nasutus*).

The terrarium should be kept semimoist, with ample hiding places (under pieces of tree bark, plants, crevices); provide a temperature appropriate to the origin of the species. Outdoor maintenance is recommended during the summer. A water bowl is not necessary.
▪ *E. binotatus* (SPIX, 1824). Peru, Bolivia. 5.5 cm. Clay colored.
▪ *E. bufoniformis* (BOULENGER, 1896). Costa Rica, Panama, Colombia, Ecuador. 8 cm. Red-brown with a variable darker pattern.
▪ *E. diadematus* (JIMENEZ DE LA ESPADA, 1875). Ecuador, *selva*. 4.5 cm. Dark brown or black pattern on whitish yellow background.
▪ *E. guentheri* (STEINDACHNER, 1864). Brasil. 5 cm. Brown.
▪ *E. latidiscus* (BOULENGER, 1898). Panama, Colombia, Ecuador. 5.5 cm. Brown with a darker pattern. Large adhesive discs.
▪ *E. longirostris* (BOULENGER, 1898). Southern Central American and northern South America. 5.5 cm. Brown with a darker pattern. Snout long and pointed.
▪ *E. nasutus* (LUTZ, 1925). Southeastern Brasil. 3.5 cm. Brown. Snout long and pointed.

Elgaria: see *Gerrhonotus*, genus.

Elosia: see *Hylodes*, genus.

Elseya GRAY, 1867. Austral River Turtles. Genus of the Chelidae. Australia and New Guinea. 3 species. Primarily in rivers. Carapace length 22-30 cm. Carapace flat, a dorsal keel more or less well developed. Head with chin barbels; neck warty.

Primarily aquatic. Carnivorous, aggressive predators. Acclimating adult specimens not easy; they are excessively restless and frequently aggressive and quarrelsome.
▪ *E. dentata* (GRAY, 1863). River Snapper. Northern and northeastern Australia. Carapace clearly keeled, posterior margin serrated. Incubation period 160 days at 28° C. in an incubator.
▪ *E. latisternum* GRAY, 1867. Saw-shelled Snapper. Eastern Australia. Carapace similar to *E. dentata*, but there is a conspicuously large intragular plate (as large as the paired gular plates) on the plastron. Incubation is 54 days at 29° C. in an incubator.
▪ *E. novaeguineae* (MEYER, 1874). New Guinea Snapper. New Guinea. Carapace with dark spot on each vertebral and costal scute.

Elseya novaeguineae

Emaciation: Symptomatic of inadequate metabolism or elevated energy drain due to poor environmental conditions or as a consequence of disease trauma. Manifests itself in weight loss and increase of skin folds in conjunction with insufficient skin (cutaneous) turgor, together with a reluctance to feed or total refusal of food and increasing loss of overall condition. Continous maintenance below optimum temperature range can be a significant factor in leading to this condition. Vitamin and mineral deficiencies as well as bone metabolism disturbances also play an important part in this condition. It may also occur in conjunction with some chronic or sub-acute diseases (amoebic dysentery, acariasis, pneumonia, stomatitis infectiosa, helminths).

Eleutherodactylus sp.

Elseya latisternum

Therapy: Temperature adjustment, vitamin supplements, specific treatment of infectious diseases.

Embryonic development: Development of the embryo from fertilization of the egg cell to birth or hatching. Embryonic development commences with cell cleavage. Initially this involves synchronous divisions causing an increase in cell numbers without an increase in overall volume. Through various shifting of these cells there are at first 2 cell layers and then 3 cell layers (the germ layers—(ectoderm, endoderm, and mesoderm), which during subsequent growth give rise to the individual organ buds of the embryo.

Eggs with a moderate amount of yolk (i. e., those of most amphibians) display an uneven but complete cleavage. The yolk supply that nourishes the growing embryo is taken up into the embryonic digestive tract during subsequent development. This is not possible in the yolk-rich eggs of the reptiles (as well as in some amphibians, e. g., order Gymnophiona). There cleavage extends only to the small, yolk deficient section of the egg, so that a blastodisc (germinal disc) is formed. The yolk supply will then be overgrown by an extraembryonic envelope, the yolk sac, formed by the embryo. The embryo itself will then be located on the outside of the yolk sac.

As an adaptation to independence from water, the terrestrial reptilian embryo forms two additional membranes: the amnion, which surrounds the embryo floating in a liquid inside; and the serosa or chorion, which is located immediately adjacent to the egg shell and its membranes, enclosing the yolk sac and the amnion. An evagination of the archenteron (primitive gut), the allantois, pushes between amnion and serosa. It is in the form of a membranous bladder that serves initially to store various metabolic waste products. Later the allantois becomes partially fused with the chorion to form the chorio-allantois, which is heavily

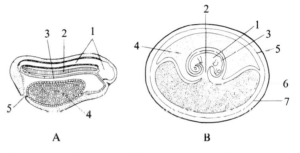

Embryonic development: A Frog embryo: 1 Dorsal nerve tube and fore-brain; 2 Notochord; 3 intestine; 4 yolk; 5 anus

B Reptile embryo and membranes: 1 Embryo; 2 yolk stalk; 3 amnion; 4 allantois; 5 chorion; 6 yolk; 7 yolk sac;

vascularized and takes over the task of gas exchange. In live-bearing reptiles the chorio-allantois, as well as the yolk sac, can participate in the formation of a placenta-like structure.

Emoia GRAY, 1845. Coastal Slender Skinks. Genus of the Scincidae, *Leiolopisma* Group. Islands of the Indo-Pacific region. More than 40 species. In tropical forests. Barely 10-30 cm. Slender. Large window in movable lower eyelid. Well-developed 5-toed limbs. Coloration highly variable. Tails of juveniles bright blue or red.

Diurnal, in part arboreal, frequently in mangroves or in the littoral zone; *E. atrocostata* is alleged to dive into the sea and catch small fish and crustaceans. 2 eggs per clutch, several clutches a year.
• *E. atrocostata* (LESSON, 1830). Mangrove Skink. Singapore and numerous islands to northern Australia. 25 cm.
• *E. cyanura* (LESSON, 1830). Blue-tailed Slender Skink. Similar distribution. Blue tail. Dark brown dorsally with lighter longitudinal stripes.
• *E. samoensis* (DUMERIL, 1851). Numerous islands. Green.

Empagusia, subgenus: see *Varanus*, genus.

Emydidae: Freshwater Turtles. Family of the Cryptodira. Primarily in the Americas and Asia; not in tropical Africa and Australasia. Carapace rather variable. Two intermediate scates missing from bridge between carapace and plastron; only pectoral and abdominal scutes present. Both carapace halves can be connected rigidly or be pliably connected by connective tissue. Hinges sometimes divide the plastron into movable flaps. The limbs usually have free fingers and webbed toes.

According to McDowell (1964), the Emydidae are divided into the mainly Asiatic subfamily Batagurinae, with the genera *Batagur, Callagur, Chinemys, Cuora, Cyclemys, Geoclemys, Geoemyda, Hardella, Heosemys, Hieremys, Kachuga, Malayemys, Mauremys, Melanochelys, Morenia, Notochelys, Ocacia, Orlitia, Pyxidea, Rhinoclemmys* (in America), *Sacalia,* and *Siebenrockiella;* and the primarily American subfamily Emydinae, with the genera *Chrysemys* (including *Pseudemys), Clemmys, Deirochelys, Emydoidea, Emys* (in Europe), *Graptemys, Malaclemys,* and *Terrapene.* Most emydids are more or less tied to water except *Pyxidea, Terrapene,* and in part *Geoemyda* and *Heosemys.* They should be kept in spacious aqua-terrariums with swimming and diving facilities. The land section must include absolutely dry sunning places (natural sunlight or artificial light, i. e., ultraviolet lamps and spotlights) from which the animals can have quick and easy access to water.

Emydids are usually omnivorous. A suitable diet can include earthworms, arthropods, molluscs, freshwater fish, shrimp meal (coarse), lean beef, and daphnia. Most will also take water plants, dandelion leaves, and leafy vegetables. Water cleanliness is essential—these are messy turtles that need large-volume filtration with powerful pumps PLUS frequent water changes for proper health and growth of the animals. Proper heating plus calcium and vitamin supplements are also essential.

Emydocephalus KREFFT, 1869. Turtle-headed Sea Snakes. Genus of the Hydrophiidae, Hydrophiinae. In tropical waters of Australia (*E. annulatus*) and southern China to the Ryukyu Islands (*E. ijimae*); disjunct distribution. 2 species. 75 cm. Characteristic rostral plate like a sea turtle beak in older males. Other generic characteristics include reduction of the dentition, including the fangs, in terms of both size and numbers. Coloration and markings highly variable, from conspicuous light and dark banding to uniform coloration.

Aquatic venomous snakes. Food specialists: feed exclusively on fish eggs picked off the sea floor.
• *E. annulatus* KREFFT, 1869. Indonesia.
• *E. ijimae* STEJNEGER, 1898. China and Japan.

Emydoidea GRAY, 1870. Blanding's Turtles. Monotypic genus of the Emydidae. North America. Formerly included in the Eurasian genus *Emys,* but more closely related to the genera *Deirochelys* and *Terrapene.* In larger, mainly standing waters. Carapace length to 25 cm, elongated. Plastron divided into two movable flaps. Marginal black spot on each plastron scute.

Carnivorous; prefer small crustaceans (daphnia and others) in large quantities. Require more heat than *Emys.* Out-

Emydoidea blandingi

Emydoidea blandingi

door maintenance during the summer or even all year is possible with adequate winter protection. Incubation takes 48 to 82 days in an incubator, in the wild about 77 to 88 days.
• *E. blandingi* (HOLBROOK, 1838). Blanding's Turtle. Southern Canada (southeastern Ontario) to Nebraska and Pennsylvania.

Emydura BONAPARTE, 1836. Australian Short-necked Turtles. Genus of the Chelidae. Australia and New Guinea. 5 species. Closely related to *Elseya.* Mainly in rivers. Carapace to 40 cm, shallow, with a relatively small plastron. Neck length conspicuously short for the family.

Primarily aquatic. Tenacious swimmers. Mainly carnivorous, although some plant matter is taken. Captive maintenance difficult due to large size and large swimming space requirements. *E. albertisi* has been bred for generations. Species numbers and status as well as distribution so far insufficiently investigated.

- *E. albertisi* BOULENGER, 1888. New Guinea Short-necked Turtle. Southeastern New Guinea. Small. Characteristic red temporal band. Can be recommended for beginners.
- *E. kreffti* (GRAY, 1831). Eastern Australia, possibly also in New Guinea. Temporal band always yellow. Plastron horn-colored to greenish.
- *E. macquarrii* (GRAY, 1831). Murray River Turtle. Eastern Australia. 2 subspecies. Yellow temporal band. Carapace wider and flatter than in *E. kreffti*. Incubation is 45 days at 29° C. in an incubator; under natural conditions in 66 to 85 days.

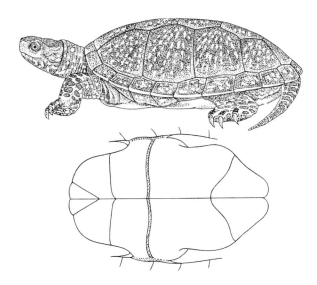

Emys orbicularis

Emydura macquarrii

Emys orbicularis

Emydura australis

Emys DUMERIL, 1806. European Pond Turtles. Monotypic genus of the Emydidae. Europe, northwestern Africa, and southwestern Asia. Mainly in standing waters, from ponds to large lakes. Carapace and plastron joined movably at bridge by means of connective tissue. Plastron divided into 2 sections by central cross joint. Tail relatively long.

Carnivorous, not choosy. Can be kept outdoors through all seasons. Incubation in 55 to 82 days at 30° C. or 25° C. in an incubator; observed under natural conditions to be 93 to 101 days. Regular breeding not uncommon.

Only isolated populations occur in northern and central Europe, where they are totally protected; in southern Eu-

Emys orbicularis

Emys orbicularis

Emys orbicularis

rope and the Near East pond turtles are still very common. There has been considerable reduction in numbers due to the unfortunate coincidence of climatic factors (low temperatures making incubation of eggs impossible) and excessive hunting by humans; they were caught in large numbers as fasting food in central Europe, particularly during the 17th and 18th centuries.

▪ *E. orbicularis* (LINNAEUS, 1758). European Pond Turtle. Europe (except the North) and western Asia to Lake Aral, northern Iran; in northwestern Africa from Morocco to Algiers. Subspecies systematics insufficiently researched.

Enchytraeids: see Whiteworms.

Enclave: Specially limited occurrence outside the main

area of distribution. For instance, *Natrix tesselata*, *Emys orbicularis*, and *Lacerta viridis* have their main areas of distribution in southern central Europe, but also occur in enclaves in northern central Europe.

Endemics: Taxa with a distribution confined to a single biogeographic region or part of it, in contrast to a distribution over a larger area. Thus, one speaks for instance about endemics of the Neotropics or that a certain species is endemic to the Seychelles, the Sonoran Desert, or the Usambara Mountains.

Endoparasitosis: Disease of the internal organs caused by parasitic protozoans, helminths, and various arthropods.

Therapy: Broad-spectrum anthelminthics, specific medications. Treatment of endoparasitosis involves primarily prophylactic measures (quarantine, fecal examinations, and regular cleaning and disinfecting measures).

Enemy reaction: Defense reactions. Stimulus given off by an enemy that triggers a specific reaction in the flight behavior, or it may lead to a species-specific threat behavior. The rearing up and spreading of the neck region (hood) in cobras and the "toad reflex" are typical enemy reactions.

Engystomatidae: Synonym for Microhylidae. No longer in use.

Engystomops: see *Physalaemus*, genus.

Enhydrina GRAY, 1849. Monotypic genus of the Hydrophiidae, Hydrophiinae. Persian Gulf and Madagascar to Australia and New Guinea. Included in *Disteira* by some systematists. Found in both brackish and sea water. To 1.6 m. The conspicuously wrinkled and loose skin appears to be too large when taken out of water. The shingled dorsal scales carry a short keel. Juveniles have distinct light and dark crossbands that fade with increasing age.

Nothing is known about food specialization. The meat and leather are considered to be worthless, so they are not commercially exploited.

Captive *Enhydrina* are more aggressive than other sea snakes and their venom is more potent than that of *Naja*. • *E. schistosa* (DAUDIN, 1803). Persian Gulf to Australia; also in rivers and freshwater lakes, e. g., Toute-Jap in Kampuchea.

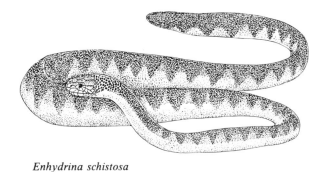

Enhydrina schistosa

Enhydris LATREILLE, 1802. False Water Snakes. Largest genus of the Homalopsinae, Colubridae. Northern India eastward through Indo-China to southern China, southward through the Malayan Peninsula and through the Indo-Australian Archipelago to New Guinea and northern

Enhydris bocourti

Enhydris chinensis

Enhydris plumbea

Australia. About 16 species. These snakes are far more closely tied to fresh water than most of the other Homalopsinae. They are sometimes found on land and tend to follow human habitation, being found frequently in rice paddies and their irrigation channels. They also occur in natural standing or flowing freshwater habitats. Several species can frequently be found in brackish water regions (river mouths) and in mangrove forests. Between 50 cm and 1.5 m. Massive, plump, head more or less clearly set off. Relatively short tail. Dorsal scales smooth and sometimes shingled. Coloration and markings vary from unico-

Enhydris plumbea

Enhydris chinensis

lored olive-brown (*E. longicauda* and others) to forms with a pattern of light and dark crossbands or rhomboidal spots down the back. *E. bocourti* is one of the most attractively marked species and is reminiscent of the beautifully marked *Homalopsis*.

More diurnal than other subfamily members. The diet consists mainly of fish and frogs. Live-bearers, 8 to 28 young. Many species are distinctly aggressive. For details on care refer to aquatic tropical Natricinae.

• *E. bocourti* (JAN, 1865). Thailand and Kampuchea to Malaysia. Males to 70 cm, females to 1.4 m. Largest species

of the genus.

• *E. chinensis* (GRAY, 1842). Southern China, Taiwan, Hainan, North Vietnam. Follows human habitation. Common. Gray with small black spots.

• *E. enhydris* (SCHNEIDER, 1799). From northern India through all of Indo-China to Malaysia. Follows human habitation. Common. Feeds mainly on fish and frogs, some lizards.

• *E. plumbea* (BOIE, 1827). From Burma eastward to southern China, Hainan, Taiwan, south through the Indo-Australian Archipelago at elevations to more than 1000 m in canals, ponds, and rice paddies, as well as in mangrove forests along coastal regions. Very aggressive.

▪ *E. polylepis* (FISCHER, 1886). New Guinea and northern Australia. 2 subspecies.

Ensatina GRAY, 1850. Ensatina Salamanders. Monotypic genus of the Plethodontidae. Pacific coastal region of North America in evergreen forests up to about 2500 m elevation. Skin smooth. Head long, with grooves from nostrils to upper lip. Tail roundish, conspicuously thickened, with poison glands on top. Base of tail constricted at preformed fracture line. Males have longer tail than females and during mating season the males also have a distinctly thickened lower lip. Bright yellow or red spots or bands against dark brown background; sometimes all brown above; belly pale.

Ensatinas prefer areas close to flowing water but lead a completely terrestrial life. Found among fallen leaves, below tree bark, rocks, logs, in burrows, and in other hiding places. The activity phase, including a mating period, is triggered in southern populations by autumn rainfalls and

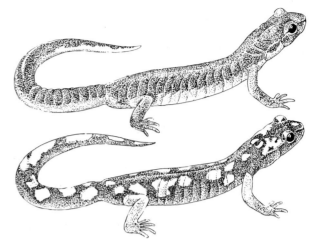

Ensatina eschscholtzi

Ensatina eschscholtzi xanthopicta

Ensatina eschscholtzi xanthopicta

Ensatina eschscholtzi klauberi

then extends throughout the winter to the end of April. Northern populations and those in high mountain regions are active only in fall and spring, with summer and winter dormancy periods. Females deposit a few relatively large eggs in a moist substrate and curl themselves around the clutch. Completely metamorphosed juvenile salamanders hatch from the eggs.

• *E. eschscholtzi* GRAY, 1850. Ensatina. Southwestern California northward along the coast to southwestern British Columbia. 7 subspecies. To 15 cm.

Entechinus: see *Eurypholis, Opheodrys.*

Enulius COPE, 1871. Genus of the Colubridae, Boiginae. Southwestern Mexico southward to Colombia. 3 species in tropical forests. 30 to 40 cm. Head not set off from body. Snout flattened, shovel-like, and projecting.

Burrowing ground snakes. Biology virtually unknown.

• *E. flavitorques* (COPE, 1869). Southern Mexico to Colombia. 3 subspecies.

Environment: The totality of all objects, appearances, and energies to which an organism is exposed. However, since not all factors acting on an organism are significant for its survival or well-being, one distinguishes between total environment and effective environment. The effective environment is the totality of the ecological factors to which any organism responds and is thus variable and species-specific.

When setting up an artificial environment in a terrarium it ultimately depends on whether it is intended to duplicate the total environment on a reduced scale or whether it is accepted that the essential components of the effective environment for a species are sufficient. For instance, it does not matter at all for a burrowing species whether the essential body contact with the substrate, its temperature and moisture, is provided by "natural" substrate or by synthetic materials. A nature-imitating setup of the terrarium is particularly useful where the abstract formation of an effective environment would technically be even more expensive or the damands of a species on its environment are extremely diversified and to a degree still unknown. Regular breeding of some tropical rain-forest species succeeds only in sufficiently spacious surroundings closely imitating their natural habitat (e. g., in a greenhouse).

Enyalioides BOULENGER, 1885. Genus of the Iguanidae. Southern Central America to northwestern South America. 7 species. Small, similar to *Enyalius*, but not closely related to it. Belongs to the Tropidurinae.

• *E. laticeps* (GUICHENOT, 1855). Colombia, Ecuador, Brasilian Amazon Basin.

Enyaliosaurus GRAY, 1845. Spiny-tailed Swifts. Genus of the Iguanidae. Mexico to Guatemala. 4 or 5 species. To 40 cm. Reminiscent of *Ctenosaura* but smaller; recently synonymized with that genus. Tail often flattened and widened at base, with whorls of spiny scales usually alternating with rows of granular scales. Captive data scarce; see *Ctenosaura*.

• *E. defensor* (COPE, 1866). Northern Yucatan. Without granular scales between spinous whorled scales.

Enyaliosaurus sp.

Enyaliosaurus clarki

• *E. quinquecarinatus* (GRAY, 1842). Southern Mexico (Oaxaca). With granular scales between whorled scales.

Enyalius WAGLER, 1830. Fat-headed Anoles. Genus of the Iguanidae. South America. 8 species. In tropical forests. About 30 cm. Body slightly laterally compressed, head short and wide. Tail about twice snout-vent length. Very low simple dorsal crest. Capable of rapid physiological color changes. When at rest mainly brown; excited males become bright green.

Relatively slow tree-dwellers that feed on arthropods. Egg-layers. For details on care refer to *Anolis*. Require lots of drinking water. *E. catenatus* is sensitive to temperatures in excess of 30° C., although a nocturnal reduction to 15° C. is very favorable.

• *E. catenatus* (WIED, 1821). Brasilian Chameleon. Southeastern Brasil in coastal mountains. Usually found about 2 m off the ground among branches. Blue-green, green, or with reddish brown longitudinal stripes or spots on green. Rarely available through commercial channels.

Enzymes: Large molecule proteins occurring in all organisms that act as biocatalysts to reduce the energy of activation in metabolic reactions without undergoing any change themselves. Numerous enzymes have been shown to be present in snake venoms. They have digestive functions or they can also be related directly to the venom effect.

Ephalophis SMITH, 1931. Monotypic genus of the Hydrophiidae, Hydrophiinae. Coastal regions of northern Australia. Head small, not set off from the slender neck region. Body deep and massive, with center of gravity in the posterior half. Rhomboidal spots or crossbands that are dark against a gray-green or blue-green background.

Venomous aquatic snakes. Little is known about their ecology and biology.

• *E. grayi* SMITH, 1931. Northwestern coastal region of Australia.

Epicrates WAGLER, 1830. Slender Boas. Genus of the Boidae, subfamily Boinae. Central and South America (except southernmost region) and Caribbean islands. 7 species. Usually close to water; in part follow human habitation. 0.75 to 4.5 m (*E. angulifer*). Head distinctly set off from body. Coloration and markings highly variable both within and between species.

Crepuscular. On or close to the ground, feeding mostly on birds and mammals. *E. angulifer* in Cuba frequents caves, where the diet consists mainly of bats. *E. inornatus* is difficult to keep since the food requirements are similar to *Tropidophis,* mostly frogs and lizards.

A few species have been bred over several generations.

Epicrates angulifer

Epicrates angulifer

Epicrates cenchria

Epicrates cenchria cenchria

Epicrates cenchria crassus

Epicrates cenchria cenchria

Epicrates cenchria cenchria

Epicrates cenchria maurus

Epicrates cenchria alvarezi

Epicrates fordi fordi

Epicrates cenchria maurus

Epicrates striatus

Epicrates inornatus

Epicrates striatus striatus

Epicrates striatus

E. cenchria unfortunately has been maintained as intergrades of various subspecies. Occasionally newly captured imports will give birth upon arrival (*E. angulifer, E. striatus*, and recently *E. subflavus*).

• *E. angulifer* BIBRON, 1843. Cuban Boa. 4.5 m.

• *E. cenchria* (LINNAEUS, 1758). Rainbow Boa. Costa Rica to northeastern Argentina and Paraguay. 10 subspecies.

• *E. inornatus* (REINHARDT, 1843). Puerto Rican Boa. 75 cm.

• *E. striatus* (FISCHER, 1856). Fischer's Boa. Haiti, Bahamas. About 5 subspecies.

Epicrionops BOULENGER, 1883. Genus of the Ichthyophidae. Northern and northeastern South America, southward to Peru. 8 species, in part polytypic. 15 cm to more than 30 cm. 240 to 410 circular furrows that just about meet along the abdomen. The tiny tentacles are located directly in front of the eye as in *Rhinatrema*. Mostly uniformly darkish, but may have light lateral bands or a marbled pattern.

• *E. bicolor* BOULENGER, 1883. Ecuador, Peru. To 27 cm. Dorsum brownish lilac, with a wide yellow band along each side.

Epipremnum aureum (LIND. and ANDRE) BUNTING (= *Rhaphidophora*). Very similar to *Scindapsus*. Grows well under optimum conditions of even humidity, shade, and temperature about 20° C.

Episcia MART. Genus of the Gesneriaceae. Mexico to Brasil. 35 species. In rain forests. Delicate plants with short, creeping stems producing runners. Require lots of heat, high humidity, and a shaded location. Used as a ground cover or in hanging arrangements. Reproduction through cuttings.

Epicrates striatus

Episcia cupreata

▪ *E. cupreata* (HOOK.) HANST. Colombia. Shrub producing numerous runners. Used in hanging plant arrangements. Leaves about 8 cm.

▪ *E. dianthiflora* H. E. MOORE and R. G. WILS. Leaves about 3 cm.

Eremial: Regions on the Earth where prevailing climatic conditions, especially lack of precipitation and unfavorable wind conditions, prohibit the development of continuous brush or tree formations. Typical eremial areas are grasslands (steppes, prairies, savannahs, *llanos*, pampas), sandy or rocky deserts, and semideserts, provided these do not occur at high montane elevations or close to the poles. Eremial areas provide an environment for numerous reptiles as well as for some amphibians.

Eremias WIEGMANN, 1834. Old World Racerunners, Desert Lacertids. Genus of the Lacertidae. Africa to southeastern Europe and Near East to Manchuria. About 50 species in semideserts or deserts. Included here is the former genera *Scapteira* WIEGMANN, 1834 (= *Scaptira* WIEG.), from north of the Equator; the South African species are put in their own genus, *Meroles* GRAY, 1838. Typical lacer-

Eremias velox

Eremias grammica

tids. Nostril scale with raised areas, not in contact with supralabial (in contrast to *Acanthodactylus*). Dorsal scales small, usually granular; rows of ventral scales extend obliquely toward the middle. Collar more or less distinct. Toes sometimes with fringes. Some species with indications of eyelid windows. Dorsally mostly brownish to gray with highly variable markings, including longitudinal stripes (most clearly defined in juvenile specimens) and light and dark spots and dots. Abdominal region white to cream-colored; ventral surface of tail often yellow, red, or blue, especially in juveniles.

Ground-dwellers that like to burrow and usually spend the night (as well as the hot midday hours) in self-dug burrows. *Eremias* species are predators feeding on a variety of sometimes hard-shelled arthropods. Short-lived, the smaller species rarely living more than 2 to 3 years in the wild. Sexual maturity is reached at the end of the first year. *E. przewalskii* and *E. multiocellata* from the semideserts of Mongolia are ovoviviparous; all other species produce 2 to 4 clutches of eggs per year, each with 2 to 6 (rarely 10) eggs. The young hatch in 2 to 3 months.

These racerunners require spacious, dry terrariums, but a section of the terrarium — or better yet the lower layers of the sand or clay substrate (at least 10 cm thick)—should always be moderately moist. Day temperatures should be 25 to 35° C.; localized overhead basking light is important (floor heat is less desirable). The lizards should have an opportunity to move to cooler areas by burrowing into the substrate. Terrarium decorations should include some stones or rocks, a branch along the ground, and some semi-arid plants. A drinking dish is important, especially when subterranean moisture is not available; otherwise regular spraying with water is sufficient. A nocturnal temperature reduction to about 15 to 20° C. is essential for the well-being of the animals. They should also be given a winter dormancy period of about 4 to 8 weeks at 8 to 10° C., particularly if breeding is intended. Most species are also suitable for keeping outdoors in the summer if humidity requirements are met. Regular ultraviolet radiation and

Eremias nitida

vitamin and calcium supplements should be available.

Feed on small insects (fruitflies, meadow plankton); some ants may also be taken. Relatively compatible even in small groups, they can also be kept together, for instance, with *Phrynocephalus*.

Some species, especially those from southern Europe and the Transcaucasus, have been bred repeatedly. Juveniles are even more sensitive than adults and can only be reared with some difficulty and great attention to detail (here again a constant temperature must be avoided).

- *E. arguta* (PALLAS, 1771). Eremias, Racerunner. Romania to southwestern USSR. Steppe regions. 20 cm.
- *E. grammica* (LICHTENSTEIN, 1823). Central Asia. Open sand, shifting dunes in deserts. Barely 30 cm. Well-developed toe fringes. Largest species of the genus.
- *E. lineolata* (NIKOLSKY, 1897). Central Asia. Grass and brush steppes. 15 cm.
- *E. multiocellata* GUENTHER, 1872. Mongolia. Semideserts. Easily 15 cm. Ovoviviparous.
- *E. pleskei* BEDRIAGA, 1907. Transcaucasus. Often in rocky deserts. Less than 15 cm.
- *E. scripta* (STRAUCH, 1867). Central Asia southwestward to Iran. Steppe regions. 15 cm.
- *E. strauchi* KESSLER, 1876. Near East, Transcaucasus. Sandy as well as rocky semideserts and steppes. Easily 20 cm.
- *E. velox* (PALLAS, 1771). Near East to western Mongolia. Sandy and rocky semideserts and steppes. Easily to 20 cm.

Eretmochelys FITZINGER, 1843. Hawksbill Turtles. Monotypic genus of the Cheloniidae. In tropical and subtropical seas. Carapace length to 90 cm. In juveniles, the carapace shields are shingled posteriorly. Always with 4 pairs of costals. Carapace shields translucent brown, marbled or flamed with yellow ("tortoise-shell").

Incubation in nature takes 52 to 74 days.
- *E. imbricata* (LINNAEUS, 1766). Hawksbill. Atlantic and Indo-Pacific in tropical and subtropical waters.

Eretmochelys imbricata

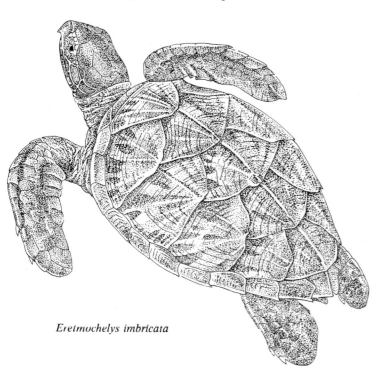

Eretmochelys imbricata

Eretmochelys imbricata

Eretmochelys imbricata

Ericaceae: Heather plants. Family of the Magnoliatae. Worldwide. 82 genera, about 2500 species. Bushes and semibushes with evergreen, often needle-like leaves. Nearly all ericas live symbiotically with fungi (mycorrhiza) and occupy almost exclusively acid soils. Indispensable for terrarium maintenance, where used for planting for outdoor terrariums in conjunction with moor or heath landscapes.

• *Arctostaphylos* ADANS. Bear Berry. About 50 species. Low-growing shrubs. For heath and rocky habitats.

• *Czalluna* SALISB. Heather. Evergreen miniature shrub. Single species, *C. vulgaris* (L.) HULL. Can only be grown on lime-free sandy peat moss substrate.

• *Erica* L. Heaths. *E. tetralix* L.

• *Oxycoccus* HILL. Moss Berry. Low miniature bush with thin, thread-like runners that grow over moss pads.

• *Vaccinium* L. Bilberry, Huckleberry. About 150 species.

Eristicophis ALCOCK and FINN, 1897. McMahon's Vipers. Monotypic genus of the Viperidae, Viperinae. Deserts. Afghanistan and Pakistan. 60 cm. The tip of the snout is oddly formed; on each side of the wide rostral are two wing-like enlarged scales. Dorsally uniformly sandbrown, darker along sides; light-bordered middorsal spots.

McMahon's vipers are sidewinders like *Cerastes* and *Echis*. In contrast to those, it is found only in sandy areas. The activity period is confined to a short season (April-August). Nocturnal. Feeds on lizards and small mammals. Venom highly dangerous, hemotoxic.

Keep in a well-heated desert terrarium with a thick substrate layer of fine-grained sand. Should have a nocturnal temperature reduction. Often has difficulty adapting to captivity because of improper collecting and shipping methods subjecting it to considerable stress. Occasional breeding successes occur. Long-lived.

• *E. macmahoni* ALCOCK and FINN, 1897.

Eristicophis macmahoni

Erpeton LACEPEDE, 1800 (also spelled *Herpeton*). Tentacled Snakes. Monotypic genus of the Colubridae, Homalopsinae. Southeast Asia. 70 to 90 cm. Head distinctly set off from body, forming a trapezoid when viewed from above. Normal large head scales plus numerous small scales between. Projecting laterally from each nostril there

Erpeton tentaculatum

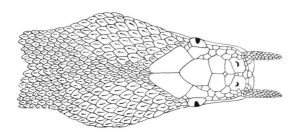

Erpeton tentaculatum

is a 6 to 7 mm scaled "tentacle" that is not actively movable. Presumably they serve as sensory organs to recognize prey in turbid water, but their function is unproved. Chin furrow weakly indicated, thus lower jaws relatively rigid. Body with keeled scales. Abdominal scales reduced, narrow, double-keeled.

Erpeton tentaculatum is by far the most aquatic species of the subfamily. The rigid body posture of *Erpeton* is reminiscent of that of fishes. Females give birth to 9 to 13 young.

Keeping healthy imported specimens in a spacious, well-planted, heated aquarium rarely presents any problems. They feed on freshwater fish and will live many years. Young born in captivity can normally be raised without difficulty. The aquarium must be tightly covered.
▪ *E. tentaculatum* LACEPEDE, 1800.

Erymnochelys BAUR, 1888. Madagascar River Turtles. Monotypic genus of the Pelomedusidae. Madagascar, in rivers and sometimes also in smaller waters. To 43 cm. Rigid, elongated carapace, streamlined. Anterior feet with 5 claws, posterior feet with 4 claws, as in *Podocnemis*. Distinguished from *Podocnemis* by internal characters.

Omnivorous, with a strong plant component in diet. Should be kept in spacious aquariums (needs much swimming space) with a suspended land section. Rarely kept in captivity.
▪ *E. madagascariensis* (GRANDIDIER, 1867).

Erymnochelys madagascariensis

Erythrolamprus WAGLER, 1830. False Coral Snakes. Genus of the Colubridae, Boiginae. Neotropics, from Nicaragua to southern Brasil, northwestern Ecuador, and along the western Andean slopes. 6 species. In different types of tropical forests. 0.6 to 1 m. Resembles in coloration the venomous *Micrurus* species; *E. aesculapii* is strongly reminiscent of *Micrurus lemniscatus*.

Nocturnal ground snakes. The diet is mainly reptiles, especially snakes, including venomous species.

These attractively colored but aggressive snakes should be kept in a well-heated rain-forest or dry forest terrarium. Caution: Venomous bites are possible.
▪ *E. aesculapii* (LINNAEUS, 1766). Amazon Region and Tobago Island. 5 subspecies.
▪ *E. mimus* (COPE, 1868). Honduras and Nicaragua to Peru. 3 subspecies.

Erymnochelys madagascariensis

Erythrolamprus aesculapii

Erythrolamprus aesculapii

Erythrolamprus mimus

Erythrolamprus aesculapii

Eryx DAUDIN, 1803. Sand Boas. Genus of the Boidae, subfamily Boinae. Southeastern Europe to central Asia and India, also northern to central Africa. About 10 species. Primarily in steppes and rocky and clay deserts. 0.5 to 1 m. Head not set off from body, with subterminal mouth, strong, protruding rostral scales, and small eyes. Tail short and usually blunt.

Burrowing, crepuscular ground-dwellers found under rocks or in rodent burrows. Only *E. miliaris* is a true sand snake. The diet comprises lizards, small mammals, and birds. *E. tataricus* also preys on ground squirrels and marmots. Live-bearers.

Can be kept in relatively small terrariums, but must have an adequately deep substrate and ample hiding places. Climbing facilities are not required. Heat should be provided by means of a basking lamp; provide a substantial nightly temperature reduction. All species should be given

a winter dormancy period of 2 to 3 months, except *E. colubrinus*, *E. muelleri*, *E. conicus*, and *E. johni*. The latter species require a dry dormancy period of several weeks to stimulate breeding. *E. johni*, *E. conicus*, and *E. miliaris* have been bred repeatedly. Identification of individual species is often difficult due to the occurrence of natural hybrids (*E. tataricus* X *E. miliaris*).

- *E. conicus* (SCHNEIDER, 1801). Rough Sand Boa. Pakistan and India to Sri Lanka. 2 subspecies. 1 m. Most colorful species of the genus.
- *E. jaculus* (LINNAEUS, 1758). Javelin Sand Boa. Balkans to Asia Minor and North Africa to Morocco. 3 subspecies. About 70 cm.
- *E. johni* (RUSSELL, 1801). Brown Sand Boa. Iran to West Bengal. About 1 m. Tail ends abruptly in a simulated head. Brown.
- *E. miliaris* (PALLAS, 1873). Desert Boa. Central Asia to Mongolia.
- *E. tataricus* (LICHTENSTEIN, 1823). Tartar Sand Boa. East coast of the Caspian Sea to western China. 2 or 3 subspecies. Ecologically the most adaptable species.

Eryx conicus

Eryx colubrinus loveridgei

Eryx conicus

Eryx colubrinus loveridgei

Eryx conicus, juvenile

Eryx johni, juvenile

Eryx jaculus

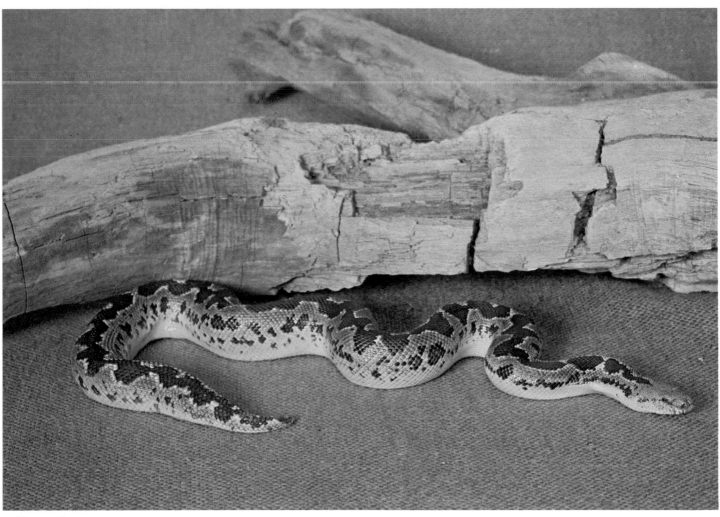

Eryx conicus

Eryx johni johni

Eryx johni

Eryx tataricus

Eryx tataricus

Eryx tataricus

Eryx miliaris

Ethiopian Faunal Region: Includes Africa south of the Sahara (which acts as a distribution barrier to the Palearctic fauna), the southern tip of the Arabian Peninsula, and the Madagascan subregion with Madagascar, the Seychelle Islands, and the Mascarenes. The Ethiopian Region is located totally within the tropics and subtropics (frost occurs only in high-altitude mountain regions) and thus wet and dry seasons are of greater importance than thermal seasons. In view of the considerable precipitation variations and their seasonal distribution, rain forests, dry sclerophyll forests, savannahs, grasslands, semideserts (Karroo, Kalahari), and true deserts (Namib) are all significant tropical to subtropical types of vegetation that are represented. However, deciduous forests dependent on winter rains developed only in the Cape Region. The Cape represents its own floral kingdom, but it is not zoogeographically separated from the Ethiopian. However, the herpetofauna of the Cape is distinctive in many ways, including its multitude of tortoises and the endemic frog group Heleophryninae.

The Ethiopian—as part of Gondwana—had ancient land contact with South America and the Indian subcontinent, which is still reflected to this day in disjunct distributions, such as the Neotropic-Ethiopic distribution of the Pipidae and the Amphisbaenidae; the Ethiopic-Oriental distribution of the Melanobatrachinae, Rhacophoridae, Platymantinae, and Aparallactinae; and the Neotropic-Ethiopic-Oriental distribution of the Caeciliidae, Leptotyphlopidae, and Boiginae.

The herpetofauna of the Ethiopian Region consists predominantly of widely distributed families and subfamilies. Only a few endemic: Phrynomeridae, Hemisinae, Petropedetinae, Heleophryninae, Arthroleptinae, Astylosterninae, Brevicipitinae, Cordylidae, Feyliniidae, and Dasypeltinae. Almost completely restricted to the Ethiopian is the Chamaeleonidae. Great diversity of species has been reached by the Testudinidae, Trogonophidae, Typhlopidae, and Lycodontinae. On the other hand, absent from the Ethiopian are otherwise widely distributed families and subfamilies such as Emydidae, Crotalidae, Hylidae, and Ichthyophiidae.

Eublepharis macularius

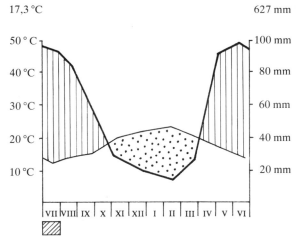
Climate diagram of the Cape region of Africa

Eublepharis macularius

Ethogram: Behavioral inventory, behavioral repertoire. Description and recording of all behavioral characteristics, including vocalization, peculiar to a particular animal species. The ethogram forms the basis for later ethological investigations. The publication of behavioral observations based on terrarium specimens and those by hobbyists engaging in herpetological fieldwork are of considerable importance for further adding to the behavioral inventory of amphibians and reptiles.

Ethospecies: Cryptic species. Species that are morphologically hardly distinguishable from each other but which are clearly separated on the basis of genetically fixed different types of behavior. Examples of ethospecies can be found in the genus *Hyperolius* and in the other genera of the family Rhacophoridae, which in part can only be distinguished by their different vocalization. In the USA a familiar example is the greater and lesser gray treefrogs (*Hyla versicolor* and *H. chrysocelis*), which are externally identical but have different male calls.

Eublepharids: Group name for geckos with movable eyelids and toes that have claws but no lamellae. Subfamily Eublepharinae.

Eublepharis GRAY, 1827. Fat-tailed Geckos. Genus of the Gekkonidae. Eastern and southwestern Asia. 4 species. In arid and semiarid habitats. To 30 cm. Sturdily built. Tail shorter than snout-vent length. Eyelids freely movable. Body with numerous wart-like bumps. Toes without adhesive lamellae.

Nocturnal or crepuscular ground-dwellers that require relatively great heat and like to sunbathe occasionally. The eggs are relatively soft-shelled. These geckos require sub-

stantial day/night temperature fluctuations (day 25-30° C., locally to 35° C.; night 20° C. or less). Part of the substrate should be kept damp. At least *E. macularius* needs about a 2-month winter dormancy period (without food) at 10 to 15° C. Have been bred in captivity over several generations. Recommended as hardy terrarium animals.

• *E. macularius* (BLYTH, 1854). Leopard Gecko. Asia Minor, Turkmenia to northwestern India. Easily to 25 cm. Dirty white to yellowish with numerous blackish brown spots; juveniles with crossbands.

Eugongylus FITZINGER, 1843. Genus of the Scincidae, *Leiolopisma* Group. About 6 species. In tropical forests of New Guinea and Australia. Taxonomic status rather uncertain. 20 to 60 cm. The relatively large head has clearly visible ear openings and movable opaque eyelids. The scales are smooth or weakly keeled. Limbs short. Brown to

Eublepharis macularius

but they avoid tropical forests as well as extremely arid regions (exception: *E. schneideri*). The main diet is arthropods; some species also take snails. Primarily egg-layers; a few species in North America are ovoviviparous. Females provide brood care (e. g., *E. obsoletus*) by guarding the eggs, turning them, and also providing adequate moisture by burying the eggs deeper and urinating over the eggs.

For details on care and maintenance refer to *Lacerta*, but only a few species are occasional climbers. The terrarium must provide some moderately damp hiding places under rocks, tree bark, and similar items. Intraspecific aggression may be severe.

- *E. fasciatus* (L., 1758). Blue-tailed Skink, Five-lined Skink. Eastern United States. Open forests. 22 cm.
- *E. obsoletus* (BAIRD and GIRARD, 1852). Great Plains Skink. Great Plains of USA into northern Mexico. 35 cm. Prairies to forests. Very adaptable.
- *E. laticeps* (SCHNEIDER, 1801). Broad-headed Skink. Eastern USA. Agricultural areas. 30 cm. Occasionally climbs trees.
- *E. schneideri* (DAUDIN, 1802). Schneider's Skink, Dotted Skink. Northwestern Africa to western Asia. Dry brushy

Eublepharis macularius, young

black, in part iridescent. Crepuscular ground-dwellers.
- *E. rufescens* (SHAW, 1802). New Guinea to extreme northern Australia. Snout-vent length 15 cm.

Eumeces WIEGMANN, 1834. Genus of the Scincidae. Southern Asia, northern Africa, and North and Central America. To 45 cm. In appearance vaguely similar to *Lacerta*, but much smoother and the limbs somewhat shorter. Ear openings distinct; eyelids movable, without window. Usually brown to greenish with various markings, especially longitudinal stripes; head often with bright colors. Juveniles are particularly contrastingly colored, often with blue or red tails.

Mainly ground-dwellers in habitats that are not too dry,

Eumeces laticeps

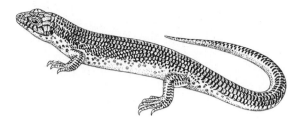

Eumeces obsoletus

Eumeces fasciatus

Eumeces laticeps

and rocky steppes. To 32 cm. The best-known form is the northwest African subspecies *E. s. algeriensis* (PETERS, 1864), called the Berber Skink, a strikingly colored skink with orange spots (considered to be a valid species by some systematists).

Eumeces taeniolatus

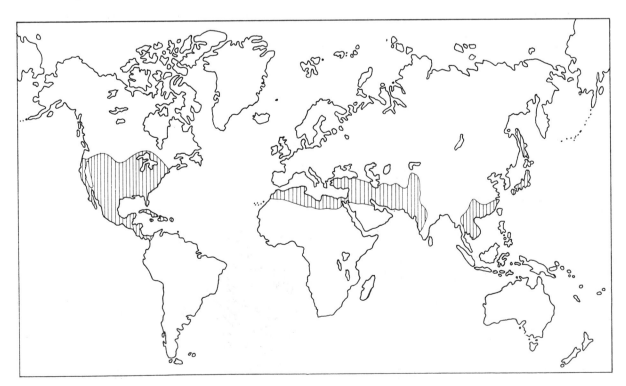

Distribution of *Eumeces*

Eumeces schneideri algeriensis

Eumeces skiltonianus

Eumeces schneideri

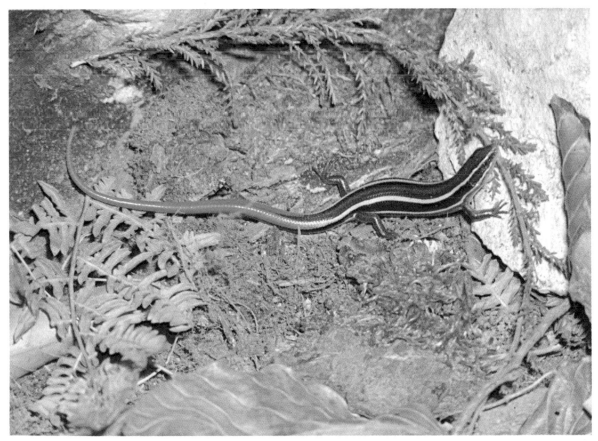

Eumeces skiltonianus

Eumecia BOCAGE, 1870. Genus of the Scincidae. Africa. 2 species. Closely related to *Mabuya*. Body strongly elongated, limbs very small, useless for locomotion. Little known.

Eunectes WAGLER, 1830. Anacondas. Genus of the Boidae, subfamily Boinae. South America except in the extreme south. 4 species. 2 to 9 m. The nostrils are located dorsally and the body scales are small and crowded.

E. murinus, next to *Python reticulatus*, is the largest of the Recent snakes; although its length is contested (the 9-m records are often doubted), it is definitely the heaviest snake known. Anacondas are tied very closely to water, and they

Eunectes murinus

Eunectes murinus

Eunectes murinus

Eunectes notaeus

Eunectes notaeus

Eunectes murinus

are excellent swimmers and divers. Resting and sunning places are preferably in trees extending over water along river banks, so the animals can flee into water below. The diet consists primarily of fish, but mammals and reptiles (mainly young caimans and crocodiles) are taken. Livebearers.

Anacondas must be kept in a well-heated aqua-terrarium with a large water section and dry, warm sunning sites. Large specimens should only be kept in zoos. As a precautionary measure with such large snakes there should always be a second person present when a terrarium with these snakes is being serviced. Most suitable for hobbyists is the relatively small *E. notatus*. Since feces are usually deposited in water, frequent water changes are required, thus permanent installation of adequate drainage and refilling pipes makes servicing the terrarium easier. Some anacondas have become notorious for their aggressiveness. There is no doubt that a large anaconda can kill an adult human, so be very careful.

• *E. barbouri* DUNN and CONANT, 1936.

• *E. deschauenseei* DUNN and CONANT, 1936. Both these uncommon species are known mainly from the Amazonian Marajo, but recently reported from the Guianas. Some authorities question their status.

• *E. murinus* (LINNAEUS, 1758). Anaconda. Amazon and Orinoco rivers system, Trinidad. 2 subspecies. 7 m (recorded to more than 9 m). With a weight of about 200 kg, this is the most massive of the giant snakes. Large dark dorsal spots; small lateral spots with lighter centers. Older specimens have washed-out colors, becoming darkish and unattractive. Has been bred over several generations.

• *E. notaeus* COPE, 1862. Yellow Anaconda, Paraguay Anaconda. Northern Argentina to southern Brasil. Mature at 2 m, largest specimen to nearly 3.5 m. Even older specimens are still attractive, with paired dark dorsal spots, frequently joined together; lateral spots always without light centers. Has been bred over several generations.

Euparkerella GRIFFITHS, 1959. Monotypic genus of the Leptodactylidae. Brasil. Related to *Eleutherodactylus*. Externally very similar to *Zachaenus parvulus* (both species also occur together), but with stubby first, second, and fourth fingers. Toes not webbed. Tips of fingers slightly enlarged. Pupil horizontal. Tympanum not visible.

Terrestrial. Presumably the eggs are deposited in damp substrate and develop there without a free-swimming larval stage.

▪ *E. brasiliensis* (PARKER, 1926). Guanabara (Serra dos Orgaos). To 2 cm.

Eupemphix: see *Physalaemus*, genus.

Euphorbia L. Spurges. Genus of the Euphorbiaceae. Primarily southern and eastern Africa, also India, Madagascar, America, and Europe. 200 species. Woody shrubs and herbs, many succulent. They give the landscape of southern and eastern Africa a distinctive look. Can take high temperatures, and in winter will survive to 10° C. Water and nutritional requirements similar to cacti. The latex may be dangerous.

Richly branched, succulent, bushy species without spines:

▪ *E. aphylla* BROUS and WILD.

▪ *E. mauretanica* L.

Ball-shaped species without spines:

▪ *E. globosa* (HAW.) SIMS. Undemanding. Vegetative reproduction is by means of rooting cuttings.

▪ *E. meloformis* AIT. Branched from ground up, individual ball-shaped shoots less than 10 cm in diameter. Winter-resistant, somewhat succulent southern European species.

▪ *E. myrsinites* L. Shrub with shoots close to the ground.

Winter-resistant central European species:

▪ *E. cyparissias* L. Cypress Spurge. In dry lawns and dry heath regions.

Euphorbiaceae: Spurges. Family of the Magnoliatae. Primarily tropical America and dry regions in Africa and Asia; few species in temperate zones. 290 genera, about 7500 species. Mostly succulent woody plants; shrubs, rarely annuals. Suitable for rain-forest, semidesert, stepped and general terrariums that copy the dry vegetation of America and Africa. Poisonous latex: be careful if used with herbivorous herps. *Codiaeum, Euphorbia,* and *Phyllanthus* are common genera.

Euproctus GENE, 1838. European Mountain or Brook Salamanders. Genus of the Salamandridae. Southwestern Europe (Pyrenees, Corsica, Sardinia). 3 species in mountain regions. The skin in *E. asper* is conspicuously rough; smoother in the other species. Head flattened, broad. Tail laterally compressed, pointed. The parotoid glands are more or less distinct. Brownish with varied patterns. The larvae have elongated bodies, small gills, and legs and tails adapted to flowing waters. The dorsal crest of the tail commences over the hind legs.

Euproctus species are sluggish, not very agile, and found only in regions that are frost-free and snow-free for about 4 to 5 months. They survive the winter buried deep in the ground. During their activity period they stay close to or in cold (5 to 15° C.), clear, oxygen-saturated streams and alpine lakes. These newts absorb oxygen through the skin and their lungs are small. The reproductive period extends

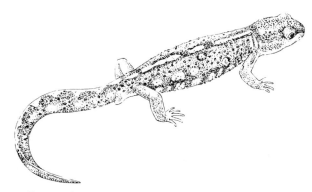

Euproctus asper

Euproctus montanus

throughout the entire summer. Mating occurs in the water. The male wraps his tail around the pelvic region of the female. This mating posture is sometimes maintained for hours until—with cloacal contact—the spermatophore is transferred. The female attaches her eggs individually to rocks in the water. The larvae hatch in about 4 weeks. Metamorphosis occurs after 12 months.

Euproctus should be kept at low summer temperatures (possibly under refrigeration or in a cool basement). For the largely aquatic species *E. asper*, a nearly sterile aquarium with a few rocks and low water level (10 cm) is sufficient. The other species are better kept in a moss and rock aqua-terrarium at a water level of about 5 cm. If *E. asper* is kept together with other species it has to be remembered that the courting males will also grasp females of other species if not enough *E. asper* females are available. This can seriously endanger the other females, preventing them from surfacing for breathing. Over-winter terrestrially.

• *E. asper* (DUGES, 1852). Pyrenees Mountain or Brook Salamander. Iberian Peninsula, mainly in central and eastern sections. 2 subspecies. Found at elevations from 200 to 3000 m, particularly common at 2000 m. 16 cm, rarely larger. Brown with a bright yellow, more or less interrupted longitudinal dorsal stripe and some yellow spots on the sides. Cloaca in males round, in females elongated toward one end.

• *E. montanus* (SAVI, 1838). Corsican Mountain Salamander. Corsica. Most frequently at elevations from 600 to 1500 m. 10 cm. Brown.

• *E. platycephalus* (GRAVENHORST, 1829). Sardinian Mountain Salamander. Sardinia. Most frequently at elevations from 1500 to 1800 m. 14 cm. Brown with a dark marbled pattern and light dorsal stripe. Abdomen yellowish with brown spots.

Eupsophus FITZINGER, 1843 (= *Borborocoetes* BELL, 1843). Genus of the Leptodactylidae. South America, Andean Region. 7 to 15 species mostly in damp, subtropical forests with dense undergrowth. Smooth-skinned. Pupil horizontal. Tympanum indistinct. Fingers free. Toes variably webbed (⅔ to absent). In contrast to *Alsodes*, males

have flattened nuptial pads.

Ground-dwellers. The larvae develop in standing waters.
• *E. roseus* (DUMERIL and BIBRON, 1854). Chile, Argentina. To 7 cm. Compact. Brown with a darker pattern.
• *E. taeniatus* (GIRARD, 1854). Chile, Argentina. To 4 cm. Slender. Gray or ochre with a wide brown dorsal band and thin interrupted dorso-lateral black stripes.

Eurycea RAFINESQUE, 1822 (including *Manculus* COPE, 1869). American Brook Salamanders. Genus of the Plethodontidae. Eastern North America to central Texas, greatest diversity in the Appalachian Mountains. About 10 to 12 species. Relationship to *Typhlomolge* problematic. Slender, with a small head. Tail often very long. Nasolabial grooves often extended downward, cirrus-like (especially in males). 14-20 costal grooves. Mostly yellow ventrally, with blackish dorso-lateral and middorsal stripes on a tan background.

Eurycea exhibits several different modes of life. Typical brook salamanders such as *E. bislineata* and *E. multiplicata* are largely aquatic both as larvae and adults. *E. (Manculus) quadridigitata* is found in swampy areas and moist litter sometimes far from water. Most species become at least partially terrestrial after metamorphosis, including *E. longicauda* and *E. lucifuga*. *E. nana* and *E. neotenes* are surface-dwelling aquatic, obligatorily neotenic forms. Subterranean waters of central Texas and inhabited by *E. latitans* and *E. troglodytes*, the latter very similar to *Typhlomolge*.

Care and maintenance of the cold-water brook salamanders and the surface neotenic species are much as for *Leurognathus*. The subterranean neotenic forms can be treated like *Haideotriton wallacei*. *E. (Manculus) quadridigitata* can be kept like *Plethodon*.
• *E. bislineata* (GREEN, 1818). Two-lined Salamander. Southern Canada to northern Florida. 3 or 4 subspecies (status doubtful). 12 cm. Light brown with dark dorso-lateral stripes and often a middorsal row of irregular dark spots. Abdomen yellow.
• *E. longicauda* (GREEN, 1818). Long-tailed Salamander. Central and eastern USA south to northern Florida. 3 subspecies. 18 cm. Bright tan, the sides densely covered with black dots (often fused); usually a strong middorsal stripe. Abdomen white.
• *E. lucifuga* RAFINESQUE, 1822. Cave Salamander. Virginia to Oklahoma. 18 cm. Large black spots on an orange to reddish background, belly unmarked.
• *E. multiplicata* (COPE, 1869). Many-ribbed Salamander. Ozark and Ouachita Mountains of Arkansas, Oklahoma, and Missouri. 2 subspecies. 10 cm. Light to dark brown,

Eurycea longicauda longicauda

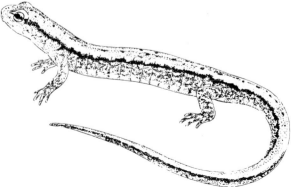
Eurycea bislineata

Eurycea longicauda guttolineata

Eurycea lucifuga

Eurycea longicauda

dark dorso-lateral stripes interrupted by light dots.
• *E. neotenes* BISHOP and WRIGHT, 1937. Texas. 10 cm. Yellowish gray with longitudinal rows of white dots. External gills always present, eyes distinct.
• *E. (Manculus) quadridigitata* (HOLBROOK, 1842). Dwarf Salamander. Southern United States. 9 cm. Dorsally dark or light brown; wide lateral blackish band. Hind feet with only 4 toes.
• *E. troglodytes* BAKER, 1957. Sinkholes in central Texas. 8 cm. Gray-white. External gills always present. Eyes rudimentary.

Eurypholis major

Eurydactylodes WERMUTH, 1965. Genus of the Gekkonidae. New Caledonia. 2 species. About 12 cm. Tail strong, prehensile, as long as body. Toes with wide lamellae. Body weakly laterally compressed (not in *E. vieillardi*). Biology barely known. Rare.
• *E. vieillardi* (BAVAY, 1869).

Eurydactylus: see *Eurydactylodes*, genus.

Eurypholis HALLOWELL, 1860. Genus of the Colubridae, Colubrinae. Southern Indo-China and Japan. 8 species. Similar to *Liopeltis* and *Opheodrys*. Many authors consider this generic name to be invalid (preoccupied by a fossil fish) and refer the species to *Entechinus* and/or *Opheodrys*. Found mainly in damp montane bamboo forests. A common synonym for *Eurypholis*: *Ablabes*. 0.8 to 1.2 m. Slender. Head distinctly set off, with large eyes. Most species are green.

Diurnal snakes, terrestrial, to some degree arboreal. The diet is mainly earthworms, insects, and frogs. Egg-layers, 6 to 13 eggs. For details of care refer to Natricinae, Group 1.
• *E. major* (GUENTHER, 1858). Southern China, Taiwan, North Vietnam. Now thought to belong to the genus *Entechinus* Cope.
• *E. multicinctus* (ROUX, 1907). Northern Indo-China, southern China. Now thought to belong to the genus *Entechinus* Cope.

Euspondylus TSCHUDI, 1845. Genus of the Teiidae. Northwestern South America south to Peru and Bolivia. 10 species. In forests, partially montane. To 20 cm. Strongly elongated. Head deep. 5-toed, but limbs weakly developed. Primarily brown.

Ground-dwellers found close to sunny forest clearings, along river banks, and in similar habitats. Feeds on small arthropods.

Should be kept in a semimoist terrarium at a temperature of 25 to 30° C., reduced at night by about 5° C. Quite suitable for keeping together with small *Anolis*.

Eurypholis major

• *E. brevifrontalis* BOULENGER, 1903. Venezuela. To 20 cm. At elevations above 300 m. Vaguely similar to *Lacerta vivipara*.

• *E. maculatus* TSCHUDI, 1845. Southern Ecuador and northern Peru. Coastal regions.

Evolutiocauda: see *Brookesia*, genus.

Excelencophis SMITH, 1942. Monotypic genus of the Colubridae, Boiginae. Island of Maria Madre, Tres Marias Islands, off the Pacific coast of Mexico. Closely related to *Tantilla*.

• *E. nelsoni* (SLEVIN, 1926).

Excretory organs: Organ systems to enable excretion of metabolic waste products and related products, water, and salts. In reptiles and amphibians (as in virtually all vertebrates) excretory systems consist of paired kidneys, the urinary ducts, and the urinary bladder. The urinary bladder, however, is absent in amphisbaenids, monitors, snakes, and crocodiles. In frogs and turtles the urinary bladder can also serve as a water storage organ.

The primitive vertebrate kidney (holonephros) is still present in the Gymnophiona. Its anterior section, the primordial kidney or pronephros, is always present in the embryo but then regresses or is changed into a lymphoid organ and remains nonfunctional, serving only as a head kidney in some amphibian larvae. In the course of evolutionary development the posterior kidney section (opisthonephros) loses its open connection to the abdominal cavity. However, some frogs still have open kidney ducts with ciliary funnels.

In amphibians (as well as in cartilaginous fishes) the anterior section of the opisthonephros connects in males with the testes. There can then be one or more new urinary ducts (ureters) growing toward the cloaca, which can lead under certain circumstances to a complete separation of both systems. These structural and morphological relationships can be highly variable among the salamanders and newts as well as among the frogs. The amphibian kidney is thus correspondingly variable in shape and form. It is elongated in salamanders, newts, and related forms, with a tendency toward great expansion of the posterior section with a simultaneous reduction of the anterior section into a shortened, compactly developed organ in frogs.

According to modern views the reptilian kidney is also considered to be a particularly specialized form of the opisthonephros, whereby the development of a new efferent duct system in the form of independent ureters is completed. These are located in the posterior body section and are compact or elongated, with smooth or notched edges, but they can also be segmented into small folds or be shaped like a roll of coins.

An important excretory product of the reptilian kidney is the hard to dissolve uric acid, which contains primarily poisonous ammonia as a product of protein metabolism. Through resorption of water in the cloaca and urinary bladder, uric acid is given off in the form of a whitish to yellowish mass. In contrast to this, the amphibians excrete primarily more soluble, but also nitrogenous, urea.

Exiliboa BOGERT, 1968. Mexican Dwarf Boas. Monotypic genus of the Boidae, subfamily Tropidophiinae. Oaxaca, Mexico, in cloud forests up to 2500 m. Less than 50 cm. Head moderately distinct. Body black dorsally and ventrally. Tail short, prehensile.

Nocturnal ground-dwellers that hide during the day under rocks, logs, and other places. Feed mainly on frogs. So far only a few specimens have been found.

• *E. placata* BOGERT, 1968. The type fed on juvenile *Eleutherodactylus* (dwarf barking frogs) only in the dark.

Eye diseases: Nubecula disease, keratitis, conjunctivitis, and lid swelling are most frequent. The most frequent eye disease in turtles of the genera *Clemmys, Emys, Chinemys, Chrysemys, Pseudemys, Pelomedusa,* and others are diseases of the tear or Harderian glands that are accompanied by swelling and protrusion of the eyelids (lid edema) and inflammation of the cornea (keratitis) and conjunctiva (conjunctivitis). The glands produce yellowish white secretions below the eyelids, especially under the severely swollen nictitating membrane. The cornea appears matte, occasionally with a shriveled surface. The animals display pain reactions, refuse food, and finally die after a prolonged pe-

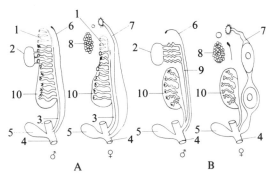

Excretory and reproductive organs: A Amphibians; B reptiles. 1 Pronephros; 2 testis; 3 urinary duct; 4 cloaca; 5 urinary bladder; 6 Bidder's organ, rudimentary ovary; 7 oviduct; 8 ovary; 9 urethra; 10 opisthonephros

Eye diseases: Abscess of lacrimal gland in *Mauremys leprosa*

Eye diseases: Exophthalmos in *Gekko gecko*

Eyes: Light sensory organs constructed with a variable degree of complexity, occurring in different phyla. Amphibians and reptiles have typical vertebrate eyes that enable the perception of images. Various changes take place in amphibian eyes as these undergo the transition from an aquatic existence to terrestrial life These affect the eye diameter and curvature of the retina in relationship to the different refractive indexes of water and air. A group of muscles raise the eyes above the head surface in order to increase the field of vision. Accommodation of the eye in amphibians to different distances is facilitated by means of a special muscle ring that enables the position of the lens—which can not change its shape—to be changed. In frogs and salamanders there is an additional muscle at the posterior lens margin that facilitates the inclination of the lens. Since amphibians do not possess foveal pits (*foveae centrales*) on their retina, required for special visual acuity, visual acuity is the same over the entire retina. Amphibians can perceive shapes and movements. In frogs it has been demonstrated that there may also be color discrimination for blue.

In reptilian eyes accommodation is accomplished through deformation of the lens, the ciliary muscles pressing against the lens through the ciliary body, which causes the lens to bulge forward. The arrangement is somewhat different in snakes: here ciliary muscles put pressure on the vitreous body, which is avoided by the lens through moving forward. This vastly different mechanism is interpreted to mean that the snakes have evolved from ancestral forms that lived underground and were largely blind; they later had to redevelop functional eyes and did it in a different way. Visual ability is rather well developed in most reptiles. Even the ability to distinguish between different colors has been demonstrated for many groups. The eyes are largely reduced in primitive burrowing snakes.

Accessory organs in the form of protective eyelids occur in amphibians as well as in reptiles. Among the latter the lids have become fused into a transparent pair of spectacles in groups with different relationships (e. g., in most Gekkonidae, family Pygopodidae, family Xantusiidae, family Amphisbaenidae, some species of Scincidae and Lacertidae, and all Serpentes). Specialized eyelids exist in the family Chamaeleonidae.

Lacrimal glands are located at the posterior eye angle and give off their secretion under the eyelids. These glands are absent in frogs and salamanders and in most snakes.

riod. This sort of disease can affect several animals simultaneously. The fundamental cause is presumed to be a vitamin A deficiency. This affects the natural resistance of the eye surface, including the conjunctiva, which then leads to secondary bacterial infections. However, primary bacterial infections in connection with pneumonia as a cause of conjunctivitis and keratitis are also possible. With pneumonia in turtles there are occasionally pus accumulations in the anterior eye chamber. Eye diseases can also be caused by endoparasites such as filaria.

Therapy: a) Inflammatory eye diseases: Vitamin supplements to battle vitamin deficiency and antibacterial treatment. The diseased animals have to be isolated. After the eyes have been cleaned out with boric acid solution and possibly with 2% hydrogen peroxide, an antibacterial preparation—possibly with glucocorticoid added—is applied to the eye. b) Purulent conjunctivitis: 0.6% neomycin solution. Treatment of pus in the hypopyon (anterior eye chamber) requires general therapy with an antibiotic.

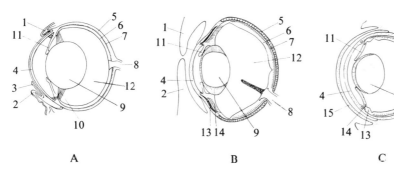

    A   B   C

Eyes: A Amphibian; B lizard; C snake. 1 Upper eyelid; 2 lower eyelid; 3 nictitating membrane; 4 cornea; 5 sclera; 6 retina; 7 chorioid membrane; 8 optical tract or nerve; 9 lens; 10 lens muscle; 11 iris; 12 vitreous body; 13 ciliary body; 14 ciliary muscle; 15 brille or spectacle

Pupil shape is rather variable. As a rule, diurnal species often have round pupils, while the nocturnal species have vertical, more or less slotted pupils. Horizontally slotted pupils (e. g., in genus *Ahaetulla*) occur rather infrequently and may function as an aiming mechanism in some snakes.

Farancia GRAY, 1842. Mud Snakes. Genus of the Colubridae, Lycodontinae. Southern USA. 2 species. Very smooth, iridescent dorsal scales. When attacked, the snake presents the ventral side of the brightly colored tail as a warning gesture. The tail terminates in a sharp scale that the snake thrusts at the enemy (or a human hand that picks up the snake). Although harmless, the spine is thought to be a "stinger" by many people, who consider mud snakes (erroneously) to be venomous.

More or less nocturnal, strongly aquatic snakes. Underwater burrowers. Sometimes found in floating water hyacinth carpets. The diet consists mainly of fish, aquatic salamanders (*Siren, Pseudobranchus, Amphiuma*), and frogs. Egg-layers. Record (probably communal) clutch (*F. abacura*) 104 eggs. For details on care and maintenance refer to Natricinae, Groups 2 and 3.

▪ *F. abacura* (HOLBROOK, 1836). Mud Snake. 2 subspecies. Dorsum blackish blue; belly with alternating red and black bands that may extend up the sides. 200 cm. Texas to Illinois and Virginia.

▪ *F. erytrogramma* (LATREILLE, 1802). Rainbow Snake. Dorsum black with three red stripes; sides yellow; ventrally red with 2 rows of black spots. Highly iridescent. Formerly considered to be monotypic genus, *Abastor*. 170 cm. Maryland to Louisiana on the Coastal Plain.

Farancia abacura reinwardti

Farancia abacura

Fatbodies: Paired organs located in the abdominal cavity; of variable form and extent. Serve to store energy reserves in the form of fat to be used during the formation of sexual products and during periods of insufficient food supply.

Fatshedera GUILLAUM. Cross between *Fatsia japonica* and *Hedera helix*. For details on culturing and use refer to *Fatsia*.

Farancia erytrogramma

Fatshedera lizei

Fatsia DECNE and PLANCH. Angelica. Genus of the Araliaceae. *F. japonica* (THUNB.) DECNE and PLANCH is the
only species. Japan. Unbranched, evergreen bush. Undemanding. Can be kept in outdoor terrariums during the
summer but must be protected against draught. During
the winter takes 6 to 10° C.

Faunal elements: Animal species that have developed in
a particular zoogeographic region and thus have become a
characteristic of it. For instance, anacondas (*Eunectes*) are
a faunal element of the Neotropics, and the land tortoises
Testudo graeca and *T. hermanni* are Mediterranean faunal
elements.

Feeding: With the exception of food specialists, most terrarium animals should be given a highly diversified diet.
Juveniles of insect-feeding species often have to be "kept
in food"; adults should be fed only 2 or 3 times a week,
except small species and those feeding on plants. Snakes
should be fed at longer intervals (depending upon their
size, every 1 to 4 weeks). An occasional feeding pause of
about 2 to 4 weeks will not harm the animals (except rain-
forest dwellers and very small species). The many insect-
feeders among the reptiles (mainly lizards) should be given
additional calcium and vitamin supplements in order to
avoid nutritional deficiencies. Hobbyists often have a tendency to feed too much, leading to obesity and making
breeding success difficult. Most herbivorous species also
occasionally require some meat. If there is a well-defined
social hierarchy in a terrarium, special attention has to be

Feeding: A constrictor, *Epicrates striatus*

given so that all specimens get sufficient food. Any uneaten
live rodents must be removed, since they will gnaw on
wooden parts, gauze, and even some of the reptiles.

Feeding behavior: Types of behavior associated with
food acquisition and intake. It is often preceded by a
search for food. Amphibians and reptiles feed actively;
most frog larvae feed initially as passive filter-feeders.

Feeding: A cruncher, *Eublepharis macularius*

Feeding: A grabber, *Mastigodryas bifossatus*

While the amphibians are essentially predators, there are among the reptiles—especially in turtles, but also some lizard families (e. g., Iguanidae, Lacertidae)—true plant-feeders. Depending upon mode of life and types of food, the feeding behavior can vary substantially among different groups.

Upon occurrence of an internal feeding willingness, the specific, innate feeding behavior is then initiated by optical, chemical, warmth, and/or tactile stimuli emanating from the food. Assuming the correct maintenance conditions are provided, then for normal feeding behavior to take place in a terrarium situation it is important that the correct food or its equivalent substitute be provided. This is particularly important for food specialists (e. g., egg-eaters, snake-eaters). Sometimes food preferences can be changed (e. g., from lizards to mice) if the new food is initially rubbed with the normal food in order to transfer aromatic substances to the substitute food. Newborn or newly hatched snakes often refuse to feed, since they are not being offered the type of food that would trigger normal feeding behavior. In these instances one has to resort to force-feeding.

Femoral pores: Glands on the underside of the upper thighs found in several lizard families. Usually they are arranged in a single row and better developed in males. Particularly during the breeding season these glands give off a viscous yellowish secretion that forms plugs. The exact purpose of these glands is uncertain.

Feylinia GRAY, 1845. African Snake Skinks. Genus of the family Feyliniidae (or subfamily Feyliniinae of the Scincidae according to many authorities). Tropical Africa. 4 species. To 35 cm. Limbless. Head slightly flattened, covered with hexagonal plates. Tail about ⅓ of total length.

Subterranean. Known to feed on termites found in decaying wood. Several fully developed juveniles are delivered.
• *F. currori* GRAY, 1845. To 35 cm.

Feyliniidae: African Snake Skinks. Family of the Squamata. Tropical Africa. Systematic position uncertain; often considered—in conjunction with Dibamidae and Anelytropsidae—to be closely related to the Scincomorpha. In fact, Feyliniidae is considered a subfamily of Scincidae by many workers. In tropical forests. Body elongated, worm-like, the eyes very small and covered by a transparent scale. Skull massive, somewhat flattened. External ear openings completely absent. No osteoderms. Only one genus, *Feylinia*.

Ficimia GRAY, 1849. Mexican Hook-nosed Snakes. Genus of the Colubridae of uncertain systematic status (Colubrinae or Boiginae). Extreme southern Texas through eastern Mexico into Honduras. 6 species. Closely related to *Gyalopion*. Found in dry habitats. 30 to 45 cm. Tip of snout turned up. Dorsal pattern of washed-out dark crossbands against a light background. Easily distinguishable from *Heterodon* by the presence of smooth scales.

Nocturnal, subterranean, often found in the proximity of water and most likely to be found on the surface following rains. The diet consists of large spiders and millipedes.

The females of some species have small hemipenes and/or hemipene retractor muscles.
• *F. olivacea* GRAY, 1849. Extreme southern Texas and eastern Mexico.
• *F. publia* COPE, 1866. Mexico to Honduras.

Ficus L. Fig Trees, Rubber Trees. Genus of the Moraceae. Primarily tropical. About 1000 species. Trees, epiphytes, lianas, and strangling vines. Leaves evergreen. Apart from small specimens of the rubber tree, *F. elastica* ROXB., only low-growing small-leaved or creeping species are suitable for terrarium purposes.
• *F. deltiodea* JACK (= *F. diversicolor*). Mistletoe Fig Tree. A heavily branched bush about 50 cm tall. Very slow grower. High humidity and 18 to 20° C. are required for adequate growth in horticulture.
• *F. pumila* L. Climbing Fig Tree. Branches with anchoring roots, climbs just like *Hedera*. Temperature range 5 to 25° C.; requires adequate humidity. Very hardy. Suitable for background decoration in terrariums, as a hanging plant, or as a ground cover. Reproduces by cuttings.
• *F. benjamina* L. Richly branched bush of delicate appearance. Leaves 5 to 12 cm.
• *F. rubiginosa* DESF. Low, richly branched shrub. Leaves 7 to 10 cm. Grows well at 10 to 12° C.

Fiji Islands: Melanesian island group (322 islands of which 106 are inhabited) in the tropical Pacific, part of the Papuan-Polynesian subregion of the Australasian, together with the Solomon Islands, New Guinea, and other South Seas Islands. Numerous volcanos (to 1390 m); rain forests only in the east; extensive savannahs in the northwest. Of herpetological significance only due to the occurrence of the otherwise Neotropic-Madagascan Iguanidae (*Brachylophus*). Since *Gonocephalus* of the Agamidae also occurs there, the Fiji Islands represent the only meeting point of these otherwise allopatrically distributed families.

Filaria: Filaroidea. Thread-like worms of the Nematoda. A few occur in snakes and lizards (mainly in chameleons) and in crocodilians. They enter through blood vessels as

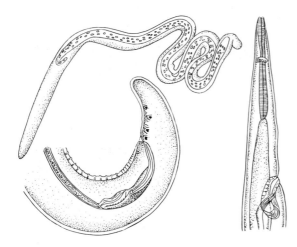

Filaria: *Macdonaldius oschei*

microfilaria as well as adults (usually spread by insect bites), and spread through the entire body, especially in highly vascularized organs (lungs, kidneys, and brain), where inflammatory reactions occur. Filaria and their larvae can cause blockages in blood vessels that can lead to the complete or partial destruction of those organs. Perforation of larger blood vessels can also lead to extensive internal bleeding. Adult filaria are often found in large clumps in the abdominal cavity. Microfilaria occur in the subcutaneous tissues, causing tissue reactions. In snakes this leads initially to the raising of individual scales followed by dermal inflammations.

Adult filaria are about 20 to 60 mm long; microfilaria are about 0.2 mm long. The diagnosis of filaria can be made microscopically by means of the suspended blood drop method, the blood being taken from the pharyngeal cavity.

Massive infestation with Filaroidea can lead to death, particularly since the various traumatic symptoms are in many cases irreversible.

Therapy: Diethylcarbamin preparations. Caution: Toxic; extreme care required; see your veterinarian.

Fimbrios SMITH. 1920. Bearded Snakes. Monotypic genus of the Colubridae, Xenoderminae. Southeast Asia from South Vietnam to Kampuchea in mountain forests between 1000 and 1800 m elevation. It is also supposed to be found not too infrequently in the Elephant Mountains of Kampuchea near Bogor. 40 cm. Head weakly set off from body, with normal head scales. The lower lip scales are conspicuously modified: they possess posterior edges that protrude strongly, so that the edge of the snout has almost a "bearded" appearance. There is nothing known about the function of this unusual structure. The dorsal scales are strongly keeled and shingled. Ventral surface of tail with only a single row of scales.

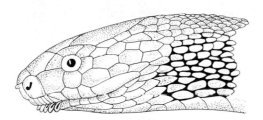

Fimbrios klossi

Ground snakes, the mode of life largely unknown, but presumably nocturnal. Should be housed in a rain-forest terrarium with ample hiding places. The food includes earthworms, slugs, and frogs.
▪ *F. klossi* SMITH, 1920. Dorsum uniformly olive to dark gray, ventrally whitish.

Fittonia COEM. Genus of the Acanthaceae. Tropical South America. Small ground plants with colorful leaves and low stems. Prefer shade; can tolerate condensation, but sensitive to drafts. High temperatures are required, never below 16° C. Reproduction is by means of cuttings.
▪ *F. verschaffeltii* COEM. Peru. Leaves 7 to 10 cm. Variety "Argyroneura" is available.

Fittonia argyroneura

Fitzinger, Leopold (1802-1884): Austrian zoologist and herpetologist at the Imperial Natural History Museum in Vienna; also zoo director in Munich and Budapest. Made a considerable contribution to herpetology with his *Neuen Classification der Reptilien und ihren natuerlichen Verwandschaften* (1826), *Systema Reptilium* (1843), as well as the popular illustrated *Bilder-Atlas* (1850). Author of many taxa.

FitzSimon, Vivian Frederick Maynard (1901-1975): South African zoologist, director of the Transvaal Museum in Pretoria. Produced the standard faunistic works *The Lizards of South Africa* (1943) and *The Snakes of Southern Africa* (1962). His father, Fredrick William FitzSimon (1870-1951) was an important specialist in South African snakes.

Flectonotus MIRANDA-RIBEIRO, 1926. Monotypic genus of the Hylidae. Southeastern Brasil. Similar to *Nototheca,* but skin of head fused with skull.
▪ *F. ulei* MIRANDA-RIBEIRO, 1926.

Flight behavior: Retreat from enemies, intruders, and rivals after the flight distance has been transgressed. Differs from species to species, and also with considerable intraspecific variation. The flight behavior of the amphibians and reptiles is genetically fixed within a certain degree of variability, and it can be significantly influenced by temperature and time of day. Diurnal active predators generally display a well-developed flight behavior together with a large flight distance, while well-camouflaged predators that lie in wait have a less developed flight behavior or none at all. Many lizards can easily be caught with a long-handled noose because if the handle is sufficiently long the flight behavior is not triggered. In captivity the flight behavior can be largely or completely suppressed by the herptile becoming accustomed to people. If an animal is prevented from fleeing after the flight distance has been transgressed past a critical point, the animal will then attack. This critical distance has to be carefully kept in mind for safety reasons when working with dangerous venomous snakes, giant snakes, large monitors, and crocodilians.

Fog deserts: Deserts along the southwestern coast of Africa (the Namib) and the southwestern coast of South America (the Atacama) that due to their leeward position get virtually no precipitation but instead are shrouded in fog for most of the year due to cold sea currents. Because of this fog cover the nightly temperatures are higher than would be typical for desert regions, a point that must be taken into consideration when amphibians and reptiles from fog deserts are being kept.

Food fish: Goldfish, *Carassius auratus*

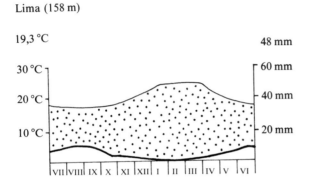

Food fish: Feeder guppies, *Poecilia reticulata*

View of the Chilean-Peruvian fog desert with clumps of *Tillandsia*

Food fish: Exclusively representatives of the class Osteichthys. There are numerous fish-feeders among terrarium animals—some snakes, turtles, crocodilians, and various amphibians—which are given small fish or pieces of fish. Catching small fish is not easy. Some of the small minnows are the most suitable. These can be caught or purchased at bait shops in numbers and kept alive in an aquarium.

Actual breeding of food fish is rarely a worthwhile exercise, but various live-bearers (Poeciliidae) can always be produced in reasonable numbers, e. g., guppies (*Poecilia reticulata*), platies (*Xiphophorus maculatus*), and swordtails (*X. helleri*). Unfortunately, however, these are not eaten by all fish-eating terrarium animals. Another fish easy to produce in numbers is the egg-laying White Cloud Mountain minnow (*Tanichthys albonubes*).

Turtles and some snakes can be fed with strips of muscle meat from larger fish or fish fillets that are commercially available and can be kept frozen. Oily fish should be avoided, all frozen fish must be fully thawed before feeding, and in most cases feeding frozen fish should be a last resort in emergencies.

Food fish: Golden shiner, *Notemigonus*

Food plants: Plants that are used by amphibians or reptiles as part of their diet. Most frog tadpoles feed exclusively or primarily in plant material. This includes mainly algae, delicate water plants, and possibly also new shoots of various terrestrial plants such as dandelions and green lettuce. For herbivorous and partly herbivorous turtles and lizards there are a multitude of wild plants available: dandelions (*Taraxacum officinale*), coltsfoot blossoms (*Tussilago farfara*), plantain (*Plantago*), *Chenopodium* sp., chickweed (*Stellaria media*), clover (*Trifolium* sp.), and others. Vegetables and fruits (particularly banana) are also often eagerly eaten. For specific food requirements refer to the species concerned.

Food refusal: Although amphibians and reptiles can fast relatively longer than can warm-blooded animals, any long-term refusal to feed must be viewed with concern. It must be pointed out that reptiles especially sometimes cease feeding for a period of time for no apparent reason, and when in new surroundings they will often only start to feed with great reluctance. The causes of refusing to feed can often be found in improper maintenance conditions or unsuitable food and can thus be easily corrected. However, if these check out as being adequate and the animal continues to refuse to feed, one should suspect a disease problem or deficiency of some sort (e. g., vitamin deficiency, acariasis, amoebic dysentery, bacterial infections, endoparasites, constipation, stomatitis). In cases of persistent refusal to feed without visible causes, force feeding sometimes leads to a normal resumption of proper feeding. There can also be problems with food specialists (e. g., termite-feeders), which have to be changed over gradually to a substitute food.

Foot stomping: Submissive behavior in lizards. Following a rivalry fight the loser presses his body flat to the ground and stomps his feet in place. He is then no longer attacked and can flee. This is interpreted as ritualized flight.

Force-feeding: Applied in the case of persistent refusal to feed and possibly also during medical treatment. Force-feeding is an emergency solution and must never become a permanent situation. Initially the mouth of the animal must be opened. Some large lizards and many snakes will open their mouth automatically when handled, otherwise it

Force-feeding: Grasp the snake securely behind the head

Force-feeding: Insert a smooth wedge at the front of the jaws

Force-feeding: Shift the wedge to the angles of the jaws

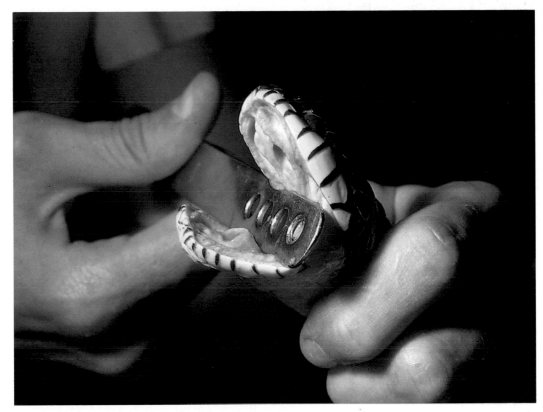

Force-feeding: This metal wedge has special openings to aid in
putting the force-feeding tube down the throat

Force-feeding: After feeding, massage the throat

Force-feeding: A large hypodermic syringe and blunt canula can be used

requires a slight bilateral pressure on the posterior jaw angles. If this does not cause the mouth to open, it can sometimes be achieved by a slight pull on the jaw skin or by means of a soft wooden stick (tongue depressor) or a piece of hard rubber wedged between the tooth rows. Small lizards should be held lengthwise in the palm of the hand, confining one front leg between the fingers. Snakes will often coil around the hand and forearm, so in order to be able to work properly it is advisable to have the help of a second person. Sometimes a trick can be used, having the snake crawl through a pipe or tube and reaching for the head and neck as soon as they protrude from the other end. Force-feeding large animals (giant snakes, monitors, crocodiles) always requires several persons.

If the animal to be force-fed is not yet severely weakened and if there are no medical contraindications, at first the normal food should be fed. In easy cases (occasionally in lizards) it may be sufficient to slide the food slightly between the teeth in order to trigger a chewing reflex. If it is possible to move the food further into the pharynx this will invariably trigger a swallowing reflex. Only extremely sick animals can not be persuaded to swallow on their own. In most cases a single force-feeding will stimulate normal food intake again. Under no circumstances must large amounts of food be force-fed. Snakes are given small prey animals (if normally one adult mouse is consumed, the animal should be force-fed with 1 or 2 pink mice).

If an animal is seriously ill, force-feeding can be done by using an artificial semiliquid mixture. This requires a small-diameter soft rubber tube that is inserted as far back as possible into the pharynx. Small amounts of the food mixture (e. g., egg yolk with some glucose) are then given. By this method one can also administer at the same time medication as well as vitamin preparations. For such serious cases it is advisable to consult a veterinarian.

Fordonia GRAY, 1842. White-bellied Water Snakes. Monotypic genus of the Colubridae, Homalopsinae. Ranges from Bangladesh to Burma, along the entire coast of Southeast Asia, the Nicobar Islands, and the Indo-Australian Archipelago to the coast of northern Australia. In brackish water, marine areas, and mangrove forests, but also far out in the open sea. Males about 70 cm, females to 95 cm. Small head not set off from the plump body. Smooth scales. Tail relatively short. Dorsum uniformly yellow, reddish, brownish, or blackish; ventrum always yellowish white.

Mainly nocturnal, usually hiding during the day, preferably in crab burrows and similar places. The diet consists mainly of fish and crabs, which appear to be severely affected by *Fordonia* venom.
• *F. leucobalia* (SCHLEGEL, 1837).

Forest terrarium: A cool terrarium mainly for amphibians from temperate latitudes. Characterized by a high humidity and soil/substrate dampness with no accumulated wetness. Temperatures seldom exceed 20° C. This type of terrarium should be located in a cool place during the summer so there is relatively minor temperature variations during the day and little if any direct sun exposure.

Suitable plants include: *Adiantum, ·Cyrtomium, Nephrolepis, Polypodium, Acorus, Aspidistra, Aucuba, Chlorophytum, Cissus, Coleus, Ficus pumila, Ophiopogon, Reineckea, Saxifraga stolonifea, Soleirolia, Stenotaphrum*, Poaceae, *Tradescantia*.

Formicoidea: Ants. Superfamily of the Hymenoptera. Worldwide. Ants form an important food item for many reptiles and some amphibians in the wild. They are absolutely essential for captive maintenance of many desert lizards (e. g., *Phrynosoma, Moloch, Phrynocephalus*).

Live ant pupae are also eagerly eaten by many terrarium animals.

The reader's attention should be drawn to the pharaoh ant (*Monomorium pharaonis*), which was introduced worldwide during the last 100 years and has become an univited,

Formicoidea: Ants

Formicoidea: Ants

unpleasant guest in many large terrarium displays. It has not yet been completely determined to what degree this ant is actually a disease vector.

Fractures: Bone fractures, carapace fractures. Fractures of extremities are invariably shown in lameness or non-usage of the affected limb. The fracture is often indicated by swelling. Moving the fractured segments often creates a grinding noise (crepitation). In snakes new and old fractures are often indicated by vertebral deformations or swellings in the rib region. Turtles often suffer carapace fractures.

Most fractures are due to mechanical causes, such as bites or general trauma caused by other terrarium inhabitats (monitors, crocodilians), animals falling off rocky decorations or off tables, as well as incorrect forceful handling. Spontaneous fractures can occur from metabolic disturbances affecting bone structures.

Therapy: Standard application of plaster cast for about 12 weeks (monitors) or bone pegs, metal wires, or other methods, possibly in conjunction with fiberglass resins. Any operation should be followed by antibiotic treatment and vitamin supplements to hasten healing processes. Healing can be anticipated to be complete after 14 weeks, but ossification of the fractured surfaces will start after about 6 weeks. After 12 weeks the affected limb can be used again. Carapace fractures usually heal only in tortoises; in aquatic turtles infections will usually set in.

Fritzia: see *Fritziana*, genus.

Fritziana MELLO-LEITAO, 1937 (= *Fritzia* MIRANDA-RIBEIRO, 1920). Dish-backed Treefrogs. Monotypic genus of the Hylidae. Short-snouted; the eyes point forward and protrude; pupil horizontal. Fingers and toes webbed at base only.

Tree-dwellers. Reproductive biology highly specialized (similar to *Gastrotheca* and *Nototheca*). The few large eggs develop inside thin paired skin sacs on the dorso-lateral regions of the female. The newly hatched larvae are transferred to water-filled bromeliad funnels, where they remain until they metamorphose. For details on care and maintenance refer to arboreal, tropical *Hyla*.
▪ *F. goeldi* (BOULENGER, 1895). 3.3 cm. Reddish yellow, with dark, Y-shaped head markings and sepia dots on back and legs, but may also be more or less uniformly brown.

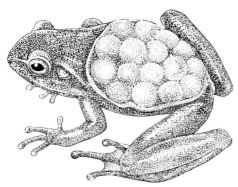

Fritziana goeldi

Frog toxins: Poisonous substances occurring in the skin secretions of many frogs (e. g., family Bufonidae, family Dendrobatidae, family Hylidae, family Ranidae). Those substances so far closely examined for their chemical composition and efficacy include the bufotoxins and the poisonous secretions occurring in the family Dendrobatidae.

Furcraea VENT. (= *Fourcraea*). Genus of the Agavaceae. America. 25 species. Stemless and stem-forming shrubs similar to *Agave*. Small specimens are suitable for unheated, dry terrariums.

Furcraea gigantea

Furina DUMERIL, 1854. Red-naped Snakes. Monotypic genus of the Elapidae. Most of Australia, except in the South. Found in dry regions. Included in *Aspidomorpha* by some systematists. 40 cm. Slender. Head and neck black, interrupted by a reddish crossband immediately following the head plates.

Venomous snakes. Nocturnal, hiding during the day below ground, often in termite nests. They prey on lizards (skinks) and insects. Ovoviviparous, 8 to 10 eggs per clutch. The venom is not very potent. Moreover, excited specimens often strike with a closed mouth.

Should be kept in a dry terrarium with substantial nighttime temperature reduction.
▪ *F. diadema* (SCHLEGEL, 1837).

Galapagos Islands: Rocky island group of volcanic origin (volcanos up to 18000 m high, in part still active) in the tropical eastern Pacific Ocean, 900 km northwest of South America, politically affiliated with Ecuador. 12 main islands and several hundred smaller ones, that have—in spite of their equatorial location—a comparatively cool climate due to the discharge of the Humboldt Current close by.

Little precipitation and strong wind exposure only permit cacti and thornbush vegetation; there are some forests at higher elevation. Zoogeographically the Galapagos Islands belong to the Neotropics and are distinguished by a fauna that is not only rich in endemic forms but also has a relict character. The famous herpetofauna includes giant tortoises and the iguanid genera *Conolophus* and *Amblyrhynchus*.

Due to excessive collecting for food and zoos and the detrimental influences of civilization (including introduction of domesticated animals and rats), the fauna and flora of the Galapagos Islands have been in part severely damaged and to some degree have even become extinct. Today the government of Ecuador and various private and governmental organizations watch over the islands; large areas of the Galapagos have been declared a national park.

Gallery forests: Forests along river banks. Not dependent upon the prevailing general climate but on the water table.

Gallotia BOULENGER, 1916. Canary Island Lizards. Genus of the Lacertidae. Canary Islands. 3 species. Characteristically large number of ventral scales, in 10 to 20 longitudinal rows. The neck bite of the males during courtship and the ability to emit grating and squeaking sounds are also peculiar to these lizards. Coloration is generally rather dark. Adult males have a more or less dark throat, sometimes with blue lateral spots in the anterior of half of the body. Females sometimes retain the striped juvenile markings, while in males the stripes either disappear entirely or are changed into narrow bands.

Gallotia atlantica

Gallotia galloti galloti

The diet consists of various arthropods and also young mice. Adults also take some plant matter (e. g., fruits, vegetables, dandelions). Some like to feed on fruit yogurt! Large species may produce in excess of 20 eggs per clutch. Males are particularly quarrelsome in a terrarium situation. They require lots of heat (locally up to 40° C.) with a nighttime reduction to about 20° C. A winter dormancy period of 4 to 6 weeks is recommended. Has been bred repeatedly (after a cool winter domancy period!).

• *G. atlantica* (PETERS and DORIA, 1882). Eastern Canary Islands. To at least 20 cm. Smallest species of the genus.

• *G. galloti* (DUMERIL and BIBRON, 1839). Western Canary Islands. Several subspecies. 15 to 35 cm. Males often have blue lateral or cheek spots or patches.

• *G. simonyi* (STEINDACHNER, 1889). Western Canary Islands. To 60 cm. Apart from *Lacerta lepida*, the largest species in this family. According to the latest information the nominate form appears to be still in existence. The subspecies *G. s. stehlini* from Grand Canary is more common, but is substantially smaller. Lately it has been considered to be a valid species.

Gambelia BAIRD, 1859. Leopard Lizards. Monotypic genus of the Iguanidae. Southwestern USA and northern Mexico. *Gambelia* was included until lately in *Crotaphytus* as a subgenus. Very similar to that genus, but much more slender. Light brown with numerous black-brown spots and broad light, occasionally reddish, crossbands. Distinct light to dark color changes possible.

Egg-layers, usually two clutches with 2 to 20 eggs each. Mode of life similar to *Crotaphytus*.

• *G. wislizeni* (BAIRD and GIRARD, 1852). Longnosed Leopard Lizard. To 38 cm. Fertilized females have red abdomens and spots along the sides. Much of southwestern USA and northern Mexico. *G. w. silus* (Stejneger, 1890), the Bluntnosed Leopard Lizard of central California, is often considered a full species; endangered.

Gampsosteonyx: see *Astylosternus*, genus.

Gambelia wislizeni

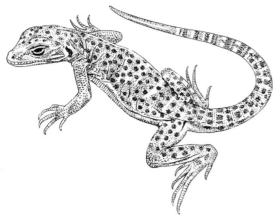

Gambelia wislizeni

Garbesaura AMARAL, 1933. Monotypic genus of the Iguanidae. Para, Brasil. Known only from type locality.
▪ *G. garbei* AMARAL, 1933.

Garthia DONOSO-BARROS and VANZOLINI, 1965. Genus of the Gekkonidae. 2 species. Similar to *Homonota*. Little known.
▪ *G. gaudichaudii* (DUMERIL and BIBRON, 1836). Western coastal Chile.
▪ *G. penai* DONOSO-BARROS, 1966. Coquimbo, Chile, 1500 m.

Gasteria DUVAL. Genus of the Liliaceae. South and South-west Africa. About 75 species. In dry regions. Mostly stemless or short-stemmed succulent shrubs, often with white-spotted or wart-like leaves. Often with a carpet-like growth form through runners. Undemanding in regard to temperature and humidity. Reproduction is by means of cuttings and the rearing of adventitious plants.
▪ *G. armstrongii* SCHOENL. Remains small. Leaves to 6 cm, very thick.
▪ *G. liliputana* v. POELLNER. Carpet-forming; remains small. Leaves to 6 cm.
▪ *G. verrucosa* (MILL.) DUVAL. Carpet-forming; leaves 10 to 15 cm. Very frequently cultivated. Robust.

Gasteria spec.

Gastralia: Abdominal ribs. Common in crocodilians and *Sphenodon*. Rib-like ossifications (osteodermata) located in the abdominal musculature without connection to the vertebral column. Also occur in some lizards.

Gastropholis FISCHER, 1886. Monotypic genus of the Lacertidae. Tropical East Africa. Body and head flattened

dorso-ventrally. Tail more than twice body length. Dorsal scales small and only weakly keeled, the most lateral scales are the largest. Ventral scales strongly keeled. Collar and femoral pores well developed.

Trees and bushes. Little known. Captive maintenance probably similar to *Lacerta echidna*.
▪ *G. vittata* FISCHER, 1886. Tropical East Africa. More than 30 cm. Males greenish blue, females brownish with wide, light-colored dorso-lateral stripes.

Gastrophryne FITZINGER, 1843. Narrow-mouthed Toads. Genus of the Microhylidae. North and Central America. 5 species, in part polytypic. In open, semiarid regions such as prairies and semideserts. Similar to *Hypopachus*, but without external metatarsal tubercle and webbing. Larvae strongly pigmented.

Nocturnal, hiding in burrows under logs and rocks during the day. Reproductive period initiated by extended rainfall. Male vocalization like the bleat of a lamb or calf. Eggs are laid in small numbers in rain puddles, ponds, and swamps. The larvae develop quickly. For details of care refer to *Hypopachus*.
▪ *G. carolinensis* (HOLBROOK, 1836). Eastern Narrow-mouthed Toad. Southern USA. 3.5 cm. Olive to brown. Dorsum usually darker in the middle than on the sides; belly dark, vermiculated.
▪ *G. olivacea* (HALLOWELL, 1856). Western Narrow-mouthed Toad. Southwestern USA into Mexico. 4 cm. Olive, sparingly covered with black dots; belly pale, almost unmarked.

Gastrophrynoides NOBLE, 1926. Monotypic genus of the Microhylidae. Kalimantan (possibly also on Sumatra). In tropical rain forests at 200 to 1000 m. Compact, with smooth skin and conical snout. Pupil round; tympanum not visible. Distinct skin fold from eye to shoulder. Short limbs. Fingers free, toes webbed at base only. Outer fingers and toes clearly enlarged, with adhesive discs; 1 (inner) oval metatarsal tubercle.

Ground-dwellers. Should be kept in suitably decorated damp rain-forest terrarium at temperatures from 25 to 28° C.
▪ *G. borneensis* (BOULENGER, 1897). 4 cm. Dark brown, with fine white dots.

Gastropoda: Banana slug, *Ariolimax columbianus*

Gastropoda: Snails and slugs. Largest class of the Mollusca. The shell-less slugs are especially suitable as food for many amphibians, although a number of lizards and turtles will also eat them. The large common garden slugs more than 10 cm length such as the genus *Arion* are generally refused. Some terrarium animals, e. g., the sheltopusik (*Ophisaurus*) and Dipsadinae, will also eat large snails. Other animals may eat snails if the shell has been smashed with a hammer first. This is one way of administering large amounts of calcium. Slugs and snails sometimes become more acceptable if lightly boiled and the mucus removed.

Gastropoda: *Limax maximus*

Gastropoda: *Ariolimax columbianus*

Gastropoda: *Haplotrema minimum*

Gastropoda: *Ariolimax columbianus*

Gastropoda: *Limax flavus*

Gastropoda: *Pomacea bridgesii*

Gastropoda: *Glyptostoma newberryanum*

Gastrotheca riobambae

Gastropyxis COPE, 1860. Monotypic genus of the Colubridae, Colubrinae. Tropical Africa from Guinea to Angola, eastward to Uganda. Closely related to *Hapsidophrys*. Tropical rain forests and gallery forests. To 1.2 m. Very slender, head distinctly set off from body, with very large eyes with round pupils. Dorsal scales with continuous longitudinal rows of keels. Dorsally uniformly green; abdomen yellowish.

Diurnal and crepuscular tree snakes that feed primarily on frogs (mainly *Hyperolius*) and lizards (Gekkonidae and Agamidae). Egg-layers, 3 or 4 eggs. Should be kept in a well-heated tropical forest terrarium.

• *G. smaragdina* (SCHLEGEL, 1837).

Gastrotheca FITZINGER, 1843. Marsupial Frogs. Genus of the Hylidae. Central and South America, with greatest species diversity in Colombia. About 40 species, to some degree not clearly delineated. In rain forests (*selva*) but also in montane rain and cloud forests as well as in Andean high-altitude grass plateaus (*puna, paramo*). The head in most species is wide, in some with projections from the upper eyelid (*G. bufona, G. cornuta*). The fingers are unwebbed or webbed only at the base; toes are more or less completely webbed. Females have a brood pouch (marsupium) formed from the skin of the back, with a round or oblong opening above the cloaca. In males the brood pouch is only indicated.

Treefrogs and ground-dwellers, the latter usually hiding under rocks and in burrows during the day and during drought periods, sometimes together with other frogs (*Bufo, Pleurodema*). Spawning occurs on land after a 24-hour amplexus, as far as is known. During egg-laying the female either raises her hind legs so that the eggs slide under the abdomen of the male to be fertilized and then into the female's brood pouch, or she may depress her back (dish-like) so that the eggs are fertilized by the male and then "shovelled" with the hind legs into the brood pouch (*G. marsupiata*). The eggs remain in the brood pouch until free-swimming larvae are fully developed (*G. marsupiata*) or until fully metamorphosed juveniles frogs have developed (*G. ovifera*).

Gastrotheca marsupiata

Gastrotheca marsupiata

Gastrotheca riobambae

Gastrotheca riobambae showing pouch

Species from high Andean altitudes can be kept without additional heating and climbing facilities in semi-moist terrariums. Species from rain forests and cloud forests can be kept in saturated terrariums at temperatures from 23 to 27° C. Adequate ventilation and nighttime temperature reductions are recommended. Ample hiding places must be provided; e. g., tree bark, rocks, halved flowerpots, and bromeliads. *G. marsupiata* and other high-altitude species can be kept successfully in an open-air terrarium during the summer months. Apart from insects, the frogs also feed on earthworms, centipedes, and other live foods.

Breeding *Gastrotheca* requires a water bowl for most species. Here the female places the free-swimming larvae after a development period of 40 to 50 days. The larvae can be reared with dry fish food plus occasionally a yeast suspension and some finely ground tender liver.

▪ *G. cornuta* (BOULENGER, 1898) (= *G. ceratophrys* (STEJNEGER, 1911)). Panama, Colombia, Ecuador (to 1500 m). Rain and cloud forests. To 8 cm, males smaller. Mainly brown, upper eyelid with a tubercle.

▪ *G. marsupiata* (DUMERIL and BIBRON, 1841). Ecuador. To 6 cm, males smaller. Irregular elongated green spots on gray-yellow background. Frequently bred.

▪ *G. ovifera* (LICHTENSTEIN and WEINLAND, 1854). Giant Marsupial Frog. Ecuador, Venezuela (cloud forest of Rancho Grande). To 10 cm, males smaller.

▪ *G. peruana* (BOULENGER, 1900). Peru. Andes Mountains in excess of 4000 m. 6 cm, males smaller. Gray with irregular elongated green spots.

Gavialidae: Gavials. Family of the Crocodylia. Orient. The only recent genus is *Gavialis*. Of all living crocodilians, this one is tied most closely to water. The head is extremely elongated, the snout very narrow and without ornamentation. The teeth are mostly similar, the fourth lower tooth not (as in other crocodilian families) fitting into a furrow (Alligatoridae) or into a socket (Crocodilidae). All the teeth insert between each other and are pointed slightly outward. The posterior edges of the limbs have elevated scale combs.

Gavialis OPPEL, 1811. Gavials, Gharials. Monotypic genus of the family Gavialidae, order Crocodilia. Orient. In large, deep rivers, especially in the Indus, Ganges, Brahmaputra, Kolawadi, and Irrawaddy. Males to more than 7 m, females to 5 m. Extremely long, narrow, snout with even dentition. Only one pair of occipital bucklers. Nuchal bucklers not separated from occipital bucklers. Limbs relatively weak. Hauls out onto land only for sunning and laying eggs using a clumsy forward pushing of the heavy body. Dorsum with crests. Tail flat, with conspicuously high crest that is a double row to the 18th or 20th caudal vertebra. Sexually mature males have a bulbous nose, the so-called ghara (Hindi: soup pot), of uncertain function.

Due to excessive hunting (it provides a valuable leather and is a predator on fish used for human consumption) and flood control measures, now nearly extinct. According to estimates by the Zoological Society of India, in 1968 there were only about 300 specimens in 3 branches of the Ganges (Chambal, Girwa, and Narayani), plus about 100 speci-

Gavialis gangeticus

Gavialis gangeticus

mens in Nepal. Protected in India, Pakistan, Nepal, and Bangladesh.

The diet consists mainly of fish. Females reach sexual maturity in their eleventh year and then join a harem of 4 to 6 females and one adult male. Copulation occurs in November or December. In March the female begins to built several nests on sand banks above flood level. One will be used in April for depositing her 9-cm-long eggs. During the 60 to 80 days of incubation, the female remains close to the nest and drives off any egg predators such as jackals. Due to nests being plundered and the effects of flooding, clutches laid in the wild rarely get a chance to hatch. Therefore, attempts are being made to increase the gavial's numbers through artificial rearing of eggs collected in the wild and taken to special breeding farms. If these animals are kept in captivity it should only be in public institutions.
- *G. gangeticus* (GMELIN, 1789). Gavial, Gharial. Juveniles with dark spots and crossbands against a light background. Adults uniformly dark olive-gray.

Geagras COPE, 1876. Monotypic genus of the Colubridae, Boiginae, very close to *Tantilla*. Mexico (Isthmus of Tehuantepec). In dry forest regions to semideserts. Barely 20 cm. Head not set off from body, with flattened, shovel-like, projecting rostrum. Eyes very small. Tail short.

Subterranean nocturnal burrowing snakes. Food mainly arthropods.
- *G. redimitus* COPE, 1876.

Geatractus DUGES, 1898. Monotypic genus of the Colubridae, Lycodontinae. Mexico (State of Guerrero on the Pacific coast). Closely related to and similar to *Geophis*.
- *G. tecpanecus* (DUGES, 1896).

Geckolepis GRANDIDIER, 1867. Genus of the Gekkonidae. Madagascar and Nossi Be. 5 species. In tropical forests. About 15 cm. Robust. Toes with adhesive lamellae. Body with conspicuously large (to 4 mm), delicate scales that easily come off when the animals are handled. Nocturnal.
- *G. typica* GRANDIDIER, 1867.

Geckonia MOQUARD, 1895. Monotypic genus of the Gek-

konidae. Northwestern Africa. In dry, often sandy habitats. Barely 10 cm. Compact. Head very large and high, helmet-like, wide, dorsally well set off from neck. Tail easily equal to snout-vent length. Limbs long, thin. Dorsal scales granular, with wide longtidunal rows of enlarged tubercles. Light gray brown.

Nocturnal ground-dwellers. Relatively slow. Not aggressive.
- *G. chazaliae* MOQUARD, 1895. Helmet-headed Gecko.

Geckonidae: see Gekkonidae, family

Gegeneophis PETERS, 1879. Genus of the Caeciliidae. India. 3 species. To 34 cm. Eyes covered by orbital bones. Inner tooth row of lower jaw with 2 to 8 teeth. 90 to 112 primary folds, 7-14 secondary folds. Small scales present only toward posterior part of body. Tentacles spherical, obliquely behind or below the nostril.
- *G. carnosus* (BEDDOME, 1870). India, State of Karnataka. To 17 cm. Flesh-colored to pink.

Gehyra GRAY, 1834. Genus of the Gekkonidae. Madagascar to southern and Southeast Asia to Australia and Occania; introduced into Mexico. Almost 20 species. Here considered to include *Peropus*. Found in different types of

Gehyra australis

habitats, some species following human habitation. 10-15 cm. Tail about length of body, only slightly enlarged. Adhesive lamellae very well developed, distal half enlarged. Strong claws. Skin with tiny scales, delicate, will come off easily when handled roughly. Coloration mainly brown to yellowish.

Crepuscular and nocturnal semiarboreal or ground-dwelling species that like to sun themselves occasionally. 1 to 2 eggs. Provide day temperatures around 25° C., at night about 20° C. Do not keep too dry. At least *G. mutilata* likes to feed on sweet, fermenting fruit. *Gehyra* species do well in captivity and have been bred over several generations.

▪ *G. australis* GRAY, 1842. Australian House Gecko, Northern Dtella. Australia. Follows human habitation. To 12 cm. Sandy colored with washed out darker spots.

Gehyra australis

Gehyra mutilata

Gehyra mutilata

• *G. mutilata* (WIEGMANN, 1835). Pacific Gecko. Distribution as for the genus, except Australia. 12 cm. Often placed in a separate genus, *Peropus*.

• *G. variegata* (DUMERIL and BIBRON, 1836). New Guinea, Australia, Oceania. 10 cm. Yellow-brown with irregular dark spots or marbled pattern.

Gekko LAURENTI, 1768. Tokay ·Geckos. Genus of the Gekkonidae. Southeast Asia, including the Indo-Australian Archipelago, and north to Korea and Japan. 20 species. To 35 cm. Rather heavily built. Pupil vertical, with indentations. Tail about snout-vent length. Toes with well-developed adhesive lamellae. Dorsal scales granular, sometimes with tubercles.

Crepuscular and nocturnal (exception: the diurnal *G. smaragdinus*) tree-dwellers; *G. gecko* is a typical follower of human habitation. Feed on a variety of arthropods, but also small vertebrates; *G. japonicus* also feeds on some plant material. Males produce distinct sounds (a loud barking in *G. gecko*).

Tokay geckos should be given day temperatures of 25 to 30° C., reduced at night to 20° C. (not much less). Provide a relatively high humidity and ample climbing facilities. There is considerable intraspecific and interspecific aggression, so they should be kept only in pairs. Have been bred over several generations, especially *G. gecko*.

• *G. gecko* L. 1758. Tokay Gecko. Southeast Asia. To 35

Gekko gecko

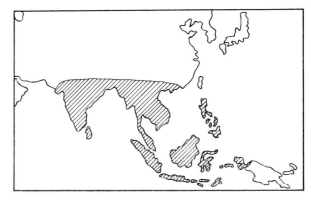

Distribution of *Gekko gecko*

Gekko gecko

cm. Blue-gray to brownish gray with numerous deep blue and orange-red spots.

- *G. japonicus* (DUMERIL and BIBRON, 1836). Japanese Gecko. Eastern China, Korea, Japan, Ryukyu Islands. 25 cm. Keep somewhat cooler than indicated for the genus.
- *G. smaragdinus* TAYLOR, 1922. Emerald Gecko. Philippines. 25 cm. Green.
- *G. monarchus* (DUMERIL and BIBRON, 1836). Indo-China, Indo-Australian Archipelago, Philippines. 35 cm. Similar to *G. gecko*, but more brownish and with more distinct markings.
- *G. vittatus* HOUTTUYN, 1782. From Java eastward to Oceania. 20 cm.

Gekkonidae: Geckos. Family of the Squamata. Tropics and warm temperate regions. More than 80 genera and in excess of 670 species. Together with Pygopodidae and (according to some authors) Xanthusiidae as well as the Dibamidae, forming the family series Gekkota. In various habitats from deserts to rain forests as well as following human habitation. On the basis of vertebral structure, hyoid bone, fleshy tongue, and scale patterns, geckos are considered to be a relatively primitive group that occurs as fossil from the Eocene. From barely 5 cm to a maximum of 40 cm. The body is more or less flattened dorso-ventrally or is cylindrical. The head usually is large and distinctly set off from the neck, with very large protruding eyes that

Hatching of *Gekko gecko*

Gekko gecko

Gekkonidae: Detail of the lamellae and preanal pores of *Gekko gecko*

Gekkonidae: Detail of the complex pupil of *Gekko gecko*

usually are covered by a transparent spectacle (exception: Eublepharinae) that is fused with the lids and which is regularly cleaned with the fleshy tongue. The pupil is slit-like in nocturnal and crepuscular species, becoming substantially enlarged in darkness. Tail relatively short, limbs always well-developed. Skin thin, velvety to the human touch. With few exceptions, the dorsal and ventral scales are granular, not overlapping, the ventral scales larger than the dorsals. The enlarged adhesive lamellae or pads underneath the toes are characteristic of the Gekkonidae (though occasionally absent). They consist of rows of microscopically small hook cells that enable these lizards to adhere to even relatively smooth surfaces such as glass and ceilings. This mechanism is absent in some tree-dwellers and the entire subfamily Eublepharinae. The claws in some genera are retractable (e. g., *Ptyodactylus, Phyllodactylus*) and are completely absent in other genera (*Pachydactylus, Phelsuma*). Additional clinging (*Rhacodactylus*) and adhesive (*Lygodactylus, Phyllodactylus*) organs occur on the tail in some genera. Also on the tail are located several other modifications, such as extreme enlargements (thickening with a fat or water storage function) (*Nephrurus, Oedura*) and broadening with skin folds that in part may surround the entire body (*Ptychozoon, Uroplatus*). Many species—especially the diurnal ones—are capable of physiological color changes. Coloration of the Gekkonidae is mainly brown, yellowish, or gray with variable markings. Many are capable of vocalization.

The diet consists of a wide range of arthropods, but some will also take some plant material occasionally. The old skin is shed in large pieces and then usually eaten.

Most gekkonids are egg-layers, except the ovoviviparous New Zealand genera *Heteropholis, Naultinus*, and *Hoplo-*

dactylus, as well as one *Rhacodactylus* species. Usually 2, rarely 3, eggs are laid several times a year (small species usually lay only 1 egg). These eggs are initially soft and rather sticky. They are often attached to tree bark or in crevices, where they soon harden. Gekkonid eggs are more resistant to temperature and humidity fluctuations than are the majority of all other squamate eggs. The young hatch in 2 to 6 months. Eggs laid in captivity should—if possible—be transferred (including the substrate they are attached to) into an incubator. Removing the eggs from a smooth substrate is sometimes possible if done with great care. The eggs can also be left in the terrarium, but they must be protected against cannibalistic parents or other animals by placing a small gauze cover over them. Parthenogenesis is known for individual species from among the genera *Hemidactylus, Lepidodactylus*, and *Gehyra*.

Due to their small size and adaptability to captive conditions, many geckos are among the most popular terrarium animals. The majority of species will modify their crepuscular or nocturnal behavior when fed regularly during the evening hours, so there can be ample opportunities to observe the animals. One can also reverse the day/night cycle by providing illumination during the night and partially darkening the terrarium during the day. Geckos require a weak basking light that gives the animals the opportunity to sun themselves during the morning or afternoon hours. Their ultraviolet requirements are modest, and generally they can do without additional lighting (exception: diurnal genera such as *Phelsuma*). The temperature should be between 25 and 30° C. during the day, and 15 to 20° C. at night for animals from dry regions. There should be little variation, if any at all, for animals from rain forests. A diversified, nutritious diet is very important.

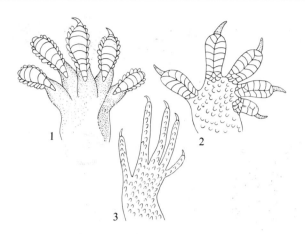

Gekkonidae: Feet of: 1 *Tarentola*; 2 *Hemidactylus*; 3 *Cyrtodactylus*

The systematics of the family have not yet been completely defined and are often treated variably by different authors. Some even elevate the subfamilies to family status and/or establish further subfamilies (*Uroplatus* and *Rhacodactylus*, for instance, are relatively isolated from each other). Here we distinguish 3 subfamilies: the primitive Eublepharinae, the Sphaerodactylinae, and the Gekkoninae (genera known mainly from type specimens and thus of uncertain category are included here):
• Eublepharinae: *Aeluroscalabotes, Coleonyx, Eublepharis, Hemitheconyx, Holodactylus*
• Sphaerodactylinae: *Coleodactylus, Gonatodes, Lepidoblepharis, Pseudogonatodes, Sphaerodactylus*
• Gekkoninae: *Afroedura, Agamura, Ailuronyx, Alsophylax, Ancylodactylus, Aristelliger, Bavayia, Blaesodactylus, Bogertia, Briba, Calodactylus, Carphodactylus, Chondrodactylus, Cnemaspis, Colopus, Cosymbotus, Crenadactylus, Crossobamon, Diplodactylus, Dravidogecko, Ebenavia, Cyrtodactylus, Eurydactylodes, Garthia, Geckolepis, Geckonia, Gehyra, Gekko, Gymnodactylus, Hemidactylus, Hemiphyllodactylus, Heteronotia, Heteropholis, Homonota, Homopholis, Hoplodactylus, Kaokogecko, Lepidodactylus, Lucasium, Luperosaurus, Lygodactylus, Millotisaurus, Narudasia, Naultinus, Nephrurus, Oedura, Pachydactylus, Palmatogecko, Paragehyra, Perochirus, Phelsuma, Phyllodactylus, Phyllopezus, Phyllurus, Pristurus, Pseudoceramodactylus, Pseudogekko, Pseudothecadactylus, Ptenopus, Ptychozoon, Ptyodactylus, Quedenfeldtia, Rhacodactylus, Rhoptropella, Rhotropus, Rhynchoedura, Saurodactylus, Stenodactylus, Tarentola, Teratolepis, Teratoscincus, Thecadactylus, Trachydactylus, Trigonodactylus, Tropiocolotes, Uroplatus, Underwoodisaurus,* and *Wallsaurus.*

Gelechiidae: Grain Moths. Family of the Lepidoptera. Breeding the grain or corn moth (*Sitotroga cerealella*) can be done according to the technique described for the waxmoths (Pyralidae). Untreated winter wheat is best suited as food. Generation time is 5 to 6 weeks. Larvae and adults are suitable as food for terrarium animals.

Gentamycin: Broad-spectrum antibiotic effective primarily against Gram-negative bacteria. Significant as an antibiotic against serious bacterial diseases in reptiles, and frequently the only effective treatment for pseudomonad infections. Has dosage-dependent kidney toxicity (leading to gout, kidney diseases). Ideally administered at 2- or 3-day intervals; maintain temperature at 15 to 20° C.

Genyophryne BOULENGER, 1890. Monotypic genus of the Microhylidae. New Guinea. Closely related to *Asterophrys*. In montane rain forests (2000 m). Head broad, flat, jaws without teeth. Pupil horizontal. Tympanum small and more or less hidden. Fingers and toes short, free, without distinct adhesive discs or tubercles.
Presumed to be ground-dwellers. Embryonic and larval development occur in the few large, terrestrially deposited eggs.
• *G. thomsoni* BOULENGER, 1890. 3.5 cm. Light yellow-brown, with dark brown pattern. Dorsum with paired longitudinal skin folds.

Geobatrachus RUTHVEN, 1915. Monotypic genus of doubtful family; usually included in the Leptodactylidae as a relative of *Eleutherodactylus*, but possibly belonging in the Microhylidae. Colombia.
• *G. walkeri* RUTHVEN, 1915. Sierra Santa Marta. 2 cm. Brown.

Geocalamus GUENTHER, 1880. Genus of the Amphisbaenidae. Kenya and Tanzania. 2 species. Subterranean. Little known.
• *G. acutus* STERNFELD, 1912. About 25 cm.

Geochelone FITZINGER, 1835. Genus of the Testudinidae. In the restricted sense used here, found only in Africa and southern Asia. 4 species in steppes, savannahs, and dry forest areas. Carapace length 70 cm. Most species (at least as juveniles) have radiating markings. Primarily herbivorous, but also require some animal products as supplements. (For the other species of *Geochelone* in the broad sense, see *Asterochelys, Chelonoidis, Indotestudo, Manouria,* and *Megalochelys,* often considered subgenera.)
• *G. elegans* (SCHOEPFF, 1795). Indian Star Tortoise. India, Sri Lanka. Carapace length 25 cm, smallest species of the genus. Apart from *Asterochelys* species, one of the most at-

Geochelone elegans

Geochelone elegans

Geochelone elegans

tractive tortoises. Carapace elongated, with strongly elevated or smooth carapace plates. Specimens from tropical forest regions are more susceptible to respiratory diseases than those from dry regions. Likes water more than any other species of this genus. Has been bred occasionally. Populations endangered in many areas.

▪ *G. pardalis* (BELL, 1828). Leopard Tortoise. Central and South Africa. 2 subspecies. In variably dry regions. Carapace length to 70 cm. Radiating markings in adults more or less broken into spots ("leopard-like" appearance); juve-

niles with dark-edged scutes. Should be kept in a well-heated dry terrarium, and can also be kept outdoors during warm weather periods. Has become rather rare in large areas of its range. Egg incubation takes 132 to 230 days at 30° C. and 24° C., respectively. In the wild, extreme incubation periods of 189 and 440 days have been recorded.

▪ *G. platynota* (BLYTH, 1863). Burmese Tortoise. Indo-China. In size and shape similar to *G. elegans*, but carapace plates always smooth. Details on biology scanty. Incubation takes 110 days at 27-30° C. For details of care see *G.*

Geochelone elegans

Geodipsas BOULENGER, 1896. Genus of the Colubridae, Boiginae. Central Africa and Madagascar. 6 species in tropical dry forests and rain forests. 35 to 80 cm. Head clearly set off from body, with large eyes and round pupils.

Nocturnal ground snakes. The preferred food is frogs. They should be kept in well-heated tropical terrariums with moderate humidity. Caution: Venomous bites are possible.

• *G. boulengeri* (PERACCA, 1892). Madagascar. Brown with light spots along the sides.
• *G. depressiceps* (WERNER, 1897). Cameroons to Uganda. 2 subspecies. Light head and dark body.
• *G. infralineata* (GUENTHER, 1882). Eastern Madagascar. Brown with dark longitudinal stripes.

Geoemyda GRAY, 1834. Monotypic genus of the family Emydidae. Southeast Asia. Close to small waters, but sometimes substantial distances from water in tropical forests. Carapace length to 14 cm. Carapace with characteristic vertebral keel and two shorter lateral keels. Posterior marginal plates deeply serrated.

Geoemyda spengleri

Geoemyda spengleri

Usually terrestrial. Omnivorous, different specimens often with individual food preferences. Should be kept in a rain-forest terrarium with substantial nighttime temperature reduction. Has occasionally been bred.
• *G. spengleri* (GMELIN, 1789). Black-bellied Notched Turtle. Southeast Asia, southern China, Ryukyu Islands, parts of the Indo-Australian Archipelago (Sumatra, Kalimantan, Batu Islands). 2 subspecies.

Geomyersia GREER and PARKER, 1968. Monotypic genus of the Scincidae (*Leiolopisma* Group). Solomon Islands. Related to *Carlia*. Barely 10 cm. Ground-dwellers.
• *G. glabra* GREER and PARKER, 1968.

Geophis WAGLER, 1830. Genus of the Colubridae, Lycodontinae. From Mexico to northwestern Colombia. Greatest species diversity occurs in Nearctic Mexico, with two-thirds of species. 34 species, many species with severely restricted ranges or known only from the type locality. In dry regions (especially in cacti deserts), in part also in dry secondary forests. 25 to 40 cm. Head hardly set off; small eyes. Dorsal scales either completely smooth or keeled only on the posterior part of the body. Usually with irregular dark spots or crossbands against a lighter brownish background. Nocturnal ground snakes.
• *G. bicolor* GUENTHER, 1868. Near Mexico City.
• *G. championi* BOULENGER, 1894. Panama.
• *G. dubius* (PETERS, 1861). Mexican Highlands.
• *G. hoffmanni* (PETERS, 1859). From Honduras southward to Panama. A common species.
• *G. nasalis* (COPE, 1886). Highlands of Guatemala (600 to 1500 m, the "coffee bean zone"). Found frequently on plantations.
• *G. semidoliatus* (DUMERIL, DUMERIL, and BIBRON, 1854). Central eastern Mexico.

Geotrypetes PETERS, 1880. Genus of the Caeciliidae. Tropical Africa. 4 species. 24 to 36 cm. 81 to 103 primary folds, 28 to 56 secondary folds; tiny scales present. Tentacles located obliquely behind and below nostril. Dorsum brown to blue-violet, the furrows usually lighter.
• *G. congoensis* TAYLOR, 1968. To 23 cm. Dark violet with yellowish white lateral furrows and a lighter jugular band.
• *G. seraphini* (DUMERIL, 1859). Tropical West Africa. 2 subspecies. To 36 cm. Dorsum dark gray to violet, with narrow creamy white lateral furrows.

Gephyromantis METHUEN, 1919. Genus of the Rhacophoridae. Madagascar. 12 species. Mainly in montane forests. Similar to *Rana*. Pupil horizontal. Fingers free, toes only basally webbed, with large adhesive discs. Light background color, with more or less contrasting sharply defined dark patterns.

Arboreal. Larvae develop in phytothelms.
• *G. bertini* GUIBE, 1947. 2.5 to 3 cm. With spectacle markings between the eyes. Dark crossbands on upper sides of thighs.
• *G. boulengeri* METHLIEN, 1919. Eastern Madagascar. In forest regions, widely distributed. 2.5 to 3 cm. Highly variable in coloration and markings.
• *G. deckaryi* ANGEL, 1930. Mountains of eastern Madagascar. Slightly over 2 cm.
• *G. pulcher* (BOULENGER, 1882). Forest regions, fre-

quently on pandanus trees. 3 cm. Light green, with violet-red spots.

Gerardia GRAY, 1849. Monotypic genus of the Colubridae, Homalopsinae. In coastal regions (river mouths) of India (Bombay and Malabar Coast), Sri Lanka, Burma, and along the coast of Indo-China, southward to the Malayan Peninsula. Brackish regions of river mouths. 60 cm. Smooth body scales. Dark gray to brown, uniform above; ventrally whitish with darker spots.
- *G. prevostiana* (EYDOUX and GERVAIS, 1837).

Gerrhonotus WIEGMANN, 1828 (here including *Elgaria* GRAY, 1838). Alligator Lizards. Genus of the Anguidae. Western North America from southern Canada to Central America. About 15 species. Distinguished externally from *Abronia* by the deeper lateral fold (but *Abronia* is sometimes included in *Gerrhonotus*). Typically in habitats that are open but not too dry. To easily 50 cm. Head flat, wedge-shaped; teeth conical. Four well-developed yet relatively thin 5-toed limbs. Tail longer than body length, sometimes used as prehensile organ while climbing. Body scales large, plate-like, shingled, except in lateral fold, where granular. Mainly shades of brown with contrasting crossbands often

Gerrhonotus multicarinata

Gerrhonotus multicarinata

particularly obvious along the sides.

Primarily ground-dwellers, although some like to climb. The diet consists mainly of various arthropods, snails, and occasionally also eggs. Most are egg-layers; *G. coeruleus* and some montane species are ovoviviparous. The females of some species guard their clutches.

Alligator lizards should be kept in semimoist terrariums with climbing facilities and ample hiding places. They will

Gerrhonotus multicarinata

Gerrhonotus kingi

Gerrhonotus multicarinata

• *G. multicarinata* (BLAINVILLE, 1835). Southern Alligator Lizard. Coastal western North America, Washington to Baja California. 3 subspecies. 50 cm. Usually brown, the sides with black, posteriorly white-edged, crossbands. Ventral scales with indistinct dark lines on the scale rows. Egg-layer.

Gerrhosaurus WIEGMANN, 1828. Plated Lizards. Genus of the Cordylidae. Southern and eastern Africa. 6 species in dry, often rocky, semi-open habitats. 40 to 70 cm. The powerfully built body is only moderately flattened. The limbs are relatively delicate. The head and neck are barely set off from the body. The tail is about twice the body length. The scales are placed in regular longitudinal and lateral rows and are usually quite large. Dorsal scales are regularly keeled, while the ventral scales are smooth,

Gerrhonotus multicarinata

do well under such conditions. Few temperature demands—an activity temperature of 11 to 33° C., on the average about 20° C., slightly lower at night, is fine. Need to drink. They take occasional sunbaths and should be given ultraviolet radiation, as well as calcium and vitamin supplements. There often is intraspecific aggression between males. Some species have been bred repeatedly.

• *G. coeruleus* WIEGMANN, 1828. Northern Alligator Lizard. Northwestern USA to southwestern Canada. 4 subspecies. To 35 cm. Tail nearly twice as long as the body. Usually olive-brown with numerous dark spots that are barely recognizable as broken bands. Abdomen with indistinct dark longitudinal stripes between scales. Ovoviviparous, 2 to 15 young.

• *G. kingi* (GRAY, 1831). King's Alligator Lizard. Arizona to northern Mexico. 45 cm. Gray to olive with wide brown, posteriorly black-edged, crossbands. Egg-layer.

barely overlapping. A deep, fine-scaled lateral fold is characteristic and permits considerable body extension. Most species are various shades of brown, frequently with lighter longitudinal stripes.

Gerrhosaurus major

Gerrhosaurus species like to dig and are also capable swimmers and divers. They are frequently found in termite mounds. Apart from various small animals (including lizards, newborn rodents, and termites), this genus also eats various plant materials, preferably sweet fruit. Egg-layers, only 2 to 6 leathery eggs per clutch.

Because of their size, these lizards require spacious, dry terrariums with hiding places. The decorations need consist of only some larger rocks and possibly a sizable branch. A water dish must be present, although drinking requirements are modest. Provide day temperatures around 30° C., higher under localized heat lamps, with an evening reduction to about 20° C. Ultraviolet radiation should be given. A winter dormancy period of 4 to 6 weeks without illumination at 15 to 20° C. has a beneficial effect on breeding, although actual breeding rarely ever succeeds.

Plated lizards will become tame fairly quickly. They often appear cumbersome and slow, but acclimated specimens feed well, are not choosey, and may even take some canned dog food.

Gerrhosaurus major

Gerrhosaurus flavigularis

• *G. flavigularis* WIEGMANN, 1828. Yellow-throated Plated Lizard. Southern and eastern Africa. 45 cm. Dorsum brown with 2 lighter black-edged longitudinal stripes above sides. Ventrally white; throat, chest, neck, and sides of head yellow to orange when in breeding condition.
• *G. major* DUMERIL, 1851. Tawny Plated Lizard. Eastern and southeastern Africa. In excess of 50 cm. Yellow to dark-brown with or without black longitudinal stripes. Large component of the diet can be plants. Usually only 2 eggs are laid.

• *G. validus* SMITH, 1849. Giant Plated Lizard. Southern Africa north to Angola and Mozambique. Almost 70 cm. Blackish brown with narrow, light yellow vertical stripes. Takes a large amount of plant material. The largest species of the genus.
▪ *G. nigrolineatus* HALLOWELL, 1857. Black-lined Plated Lizard. Central to southern Africa. 45 cm. Dark brown to black with light longitudinal stripes. More agile than the other species; likes to dig.

Gesner, Conrad von (1516-1565): Swiss natural history researcher and medical practitioner. Published the first comprehensive treatise of the animal kindom, the *Historia Animalum* (1559-1586) The "herpetological" sections (Gesner did not provide an exact separation of the vertebrate classes in the modern sense) appeared separately later as *De quadrupedibus oviparis* (1617) and *De Serpentium natura* (1621). Up to Linneus's times these publications provided much of the general zoological knowledge of European scholars.

Gigantorana: see *Conraua,* genus.

Girard, Charles Frederic (1822-1895): Swiss zoologist who worked together with Baird at the Smithonian Institution in Washington, D. C. Numerous joint publications with Baird.

Glands: Cells, either within special organs or individually in the epithelium, that produce and give off certain secretions. The exocrine glands give off their secretions either directly or via special ducts to the body surface or into body cavities. This type of gland includes those belonging to the digestive system, including the venom glands of many amphibians, venomous lizards (family Helodermatidae), and numerous snakes (modified salivary glands). The skin of many amphibians is also conspicuously gland-rich; numerous mucous glands keep the surface constantly moist and (among other functions) facilitate respiration via the skin. However, the cornified skin of reptiles has hardly any glands.

The endocrine glands produce hormones that are given off directly into the circulatory or lymph system. These important glands include the hypophysis, thyroid, thymus, adrenal, and parathyroid glands. The endocrine glands play an important role in the control of the most diverse life functions. The sex glands (gonads) include both endocrine and exocrine functions.

Glauertia LOVERIDGE, 1933. Genus of the Leptodactylidae. Tropical northern and northwesten Australia. 3 species. Stout, short-limbed, toad-like. Skin with warts. Pupil horizontal. Tympanum not visible. 2 long metatarsal tubercles. Fingers free, toes webbed basally only. Dark.

Burrowing, nocturnal ground-dwellers found during the rainy season in ponds, flooded swamps, etc., where they sometimes spawn in massive aggregations.
• *G. orientalis* PARKER, 1940. Arnhem Land, northern Australia. 3 cm. Unicolored light to dark brown, the raised glandular regions somewhat lighter.

Glossostoma GUENTHER, 1901. Genus of the Microhylidae. Central and South America. 2 species. Head large, snout rounded when viewed from above. Limbs relatively strong. Skin smooth. Eyes small. Tympanum not visible. Fingers free, toes webbed more than halfway. Metatarsal tubercles and vocal sac absent.

▪ *G. aterrimum* GUENTHER, 1901. Costa Rica, Colombia. 6.5 cm. Brown.

Glyphodon GUENTHER, 1858. Genus of the Elapidae. Australia, New Guinea. About 3 species in tropical forests. 0.5 to 1 m. Relatively slender. Head large, more or less set off from body. Uniformly dark; *G. tristis* has a light collar.

Terrestrial, nocturnal ground snakes that hide during the day under logs and in similar places. Very aggressive when disturbed, but bite thought not to be lethal to humans. Biology virtually unknown. Provide a well-heated tropical forest terrarium.

▪ *G. tristis* GUENTHER, 1858. Australian Brown-headed Snake. Northeastern Australia, New Guinea.

Glyphoglossus GUENTHER, 1868. Monotypic genus of the Microhylidae. Tropical southeastern Asia. Closely related to *Uperodon*. Head rather small when compared to the bloated body, blunt-nosed. Mouth small. Pupil triangular (pointing downward). Tympanum not visible. Fingers free, short, toes largely webbed. Inner metatarsal tubercle developed into very large, sharp-edged digging pad. The mode of life and care are similar to *Uperodon*.

▪ *G. molossus* GUENTHER, 1868. Burma, Thailand. 7 cm. Reddish brown, laterally with white dots.

Glypholycus GUENTHER, 1893. Monotypic genus of the Colubridae, Lycodontinae. Tropical central Africa. To 60 cm. In shape of head and body similar to *Boaedon*.

Amphibious, in part nearly aquatic, ground snakes. The diet consists of fish (mainly cichlids). For details on care refer to Natricinae, Group 2.

▪ *G. bicolor* GUENTHER, 1893. Most frequent around Lake Tanganyika. Dorsum dark brown, whitish below.

Gmelin, Johann Friedrich (1748-1804): German zoologist. Edited the 13th edition of Linnaeus's *Systema Naturae* (1789-1796). *Gemeinnuetzige systematische Naturgeschichte des Amphibien* (1815).

Gomesophis HOGE and MERTENS, 1959. Monotypic genus of the Colubridae, Boiginae. Eastern Brasil from Minas Gerais to Rio Grande do Sul. Closely related to *Tachymenis* and *Coniophanes*. In tropical forests. To 70 cm. Compact, head not set off from body. Probably a burrower.

▪ *G. brasiliensis* (GOMES, 1918).

Gonatodes FITZINGER, 1843. Genus of the Gekkonidae. Central and South America, introduced into Florida. About 20 species. Found in various habitats, often in forests; some follow human habitation. About 10 cm. Slender, with round pupil. Tail about snout-vent length. Limbs well developed. Toes without adhesive pads, slightly enlarged. Claws not retractile (in contrast to *Coleodactylus* and *Pseudogonatodes*). Coloration mainly brown with varied markings. Conspicuous sexual dimorphism present, males sometimes with light yellow to orange heads.

Gonatodes fuscus, juv.

Gonatodes cecilia

Gonatodes fuscus, ♂

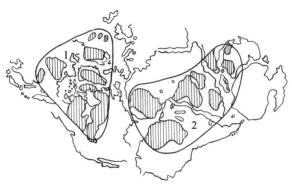

Gondwana: The earth about 1.7 million years ago, with Gondwana (2) and Laurasia (1) marked

Gonatodes fuscus

Gondwana: The earth during the Mesozoic

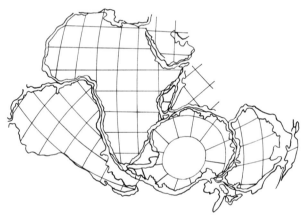

Gondwana: The southern continents placed to reconstruct the form of Gondwana before it split

Diurnal to crepuscular ground-dwellers; some are semi-arboreal and like to sun themselves occasionally. Clutches of 1 egg laid several times a year. Incubation times vary from 50 to 110 days.

- *G. albogularis* (DUMERIL and BIBRON, 1836). White-throated Gecko. Northeastern South America, Central America. To 12 cm. Males without markings.
- *G. fuscus* (HALLOWELL, 1855). Yellow-headed Gecko. To 10 cm. Males with yellow head. Cuba, southern Florida; possibly only a subspecies of *G. albogularis*.
- *G. annularis* BOULENGER, 1887. Venezuela, Guyana, Surinam, northern Brasil. 10 cm. Highly variable; males sometimes with orange abdomen.

Gondwana: Giant southern continent of the Paleozoic that included large sections of South America, Africa, Madagascar, the Indian subcontinent together with Ceylon (Sri Lanka), western Australia, and parts of Antarctica. It disintegrated during the Mesozoic and its pieces have since drifted apart. Remnants of the Gondwana fauna, also referred to as the "southern fauna," have in the meantime evolved and could include from among herpetotaxa the Gymnophiona, Pipidae, Pleurodira, Iguanidae, and Boidae.

Pendant to Gondwana was the northern ancient continent Laurasia, which included large sections of the Holarctic and also Southeast Asia. Its Laurasian fauna ("northern fauna") could have given rise to the Caudata, Pelobatidae, Xenosauridae, Alligatoridae, and others.

Goniochersus: see *Chersina*, genus.

Gonionotophis BOULENGER, 1889. Genus of the Colubridae, Lycodontinae. West Africa. 3 or 4 species. In tropical forests. 45 to 50 cm. Head trapezoidal, markedly set off, in appearance similar to the closely related *Boaedon*. Dorsal scales distinctly keeled. Dorsum brownish.

Ground snakes that hunt at night for small ground frogs, lizards, and possibly other snakes.

- *G. brussauxi* MOCQUARD, 1889. From Guinea-Bisseu to the Congo Basin.

Gonocephalus KAUP, 1825. Hump-headed Dragons. Genus of the Agamidae. Southern Indo-China to northern Australia. About 36 species (formerly including *Acanthosaura*). In tropical rain forests and montane forests. 30 cm to 1 m. Slightly compressed laterally. The high occipital and dorsal crests as well as a gular pouch are typical of males. Mainly shades of brown and green.

Arboreal. Feeds mainly on arthropods, but larger species will also take small vertebrates. 2-6 eggs, sometimes laid on the ground in the open. Incubation period to 4 months. Lowland species breed throughout the year. Provide day temperatures of 25 to 30° C., slightly less at night; keep montane species somewhat cooler. Must have drinking water. Relatively hardy.

▪ *G. abbotti* COCHRAN, 1922. Thailand.

▪ *G. boydi* (MACLEAY, 1884). Northeastern Queensland, Australia. 45 cm, snout-vent length 15 cm.

▪ *G. grandis* GRAY, 1845. Southern Indo-China, Sunda Archipelago.

Gonocephalus abbotti

Gonocephalus grandis, ♂

Gonocephalus abbotti

Gonyosoma oxycephala

Gonocephalus boydi

Gonyophis BOULENGER, 1891. Monotypic genus of the Colubridae, Colubrinae. Malayan Peninsula and Kalimantan, in the mountains of Kalimantan to 900 m elevation. To 1.6 m. Head slender, with large eyes. Reminiscent of the related genus *Zaocys*. The weakly keeled dorsal scales have a wide, black-edged yellow-green center. Posterior part of body and tail with orange rings.

Ground snakes that prefer the vicinity of water (similar to *Zaocys*). The main diet includes frogs. Must be kept in well-heated terrarium with a large water bowl, as for Natricinae, Group 2.
- *G. margeritatus* (PETERS, 1871).

Gonyosoma WAGLER, 1828. Climbing Rat Snakes. Genus of the Colubridae of uncertain subfamily membership, Colubrinae or Natricinae. Southeast Asia. 3 species. In tropical monsoon forests and rain forests. *G. prasina* lives in montane rain forests to 1800 m elevation; *G. oxycephala* in lowlands and also in mangrove forests with brackish water or in bamboo forests. 1 to 2.1 m. Slender but strong. Body compressed laterally and covered with smooth or minimally keeled scales. Abdominal scales wide and strong, rounded off on both sides to facilitate climbing. Adult specimens usually uniformly green, juveniles with blackish spots. The tail in *G. oxycephala* is reddish brown, and sometimes the black juvenile spots are also maintained; this distinguishes this species from others.

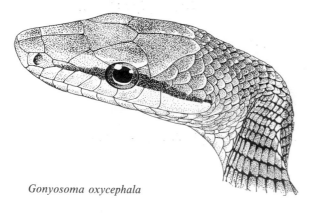

Gonyosoma oxycephala

Gonyosoma oxycephala

Arboreal snakes that feed mainly on frogs, lizards, and small mammals. Egg-layers.

Newly captured specimens are extremely aggressive, but they adjust to a well-heated terrarium (see Natricinae, Group 2) equipped with adequate climbing facilities, similar to *Elaphe*, and usually settle down quickly and change their behavior. Have been bred repeatedly.

• *G. prasina* (BLYTH, 1854). From Darjeeling to the Malayan Peninsula. Uniformly green.

• *G. oxycephala* (BOIE, 1827). Red-tailed Rat Snake. Found from Thailand and Kampuchea throughout large areas of the Indo-Australian Archipelago and Philippines.

Gopherus RAFINESQUE, 1832. Gopher Tortoises. Genus of the Testudinidae. Southern USA and northern Mexico. 4 species in dry regions from dry forests to marginal desert regions. Usually to 40 cm carapace length. Front limbs flattened for digging.

Gopherus berlandieri

Gopherus agassizi, albino

Primarily crepuscular. They dig deep burrows that are also used by other animals (e. g., gopher frog, burrowing owl, gopher snake, many insects). The males use the anterior section of the plastron, which is modified into a ramrod, in rivalry fights. Egg incubation in the wild takes 84 to 120 days; in an incubator 110 days at 27° C.

For details on care refer to *Agrionemys*. Has been bred repeatedly. Acclimated adult specimens have lived in captivity for decades. All species are now considered threatened or endangered and they are strongly protected in several states of the USA.

• *G. agassizi* (COOPER, 1863). Desert Tortoise. Southwest-

Gopherus agassizi

Gopherus polyphemus

Gopherus agassizi

Gopherus polyphemus, hatchling

Gopherus polyphemus

Gopherus flavomarginatus

ern USA to northwestern Mexico. 37 cm. Carapace narrow and elongated. Coloration dark brown to blackish.

▪ *G. berlandieri* (AGASSIZ, 1857). Texas Tortoise. Texas and northeastern Mexico. 22 cm. Carapace higher than in previous species. Coloration consists of variable light and dark brown patches.

▪ *G. flavomarginatus* LEGLER, 1959. Bolson Tortoise. Northern Mexico. 65 cm; largest species of the genus. Yellow-brown, lighter toward the marginal plates. Each marginal plate contains a clearly delineated dark spot.

▪ *G. polyphemus* (DAUDIN, 1802). Gopher Tortoise. Southeastern USA. 37 cm. Carapace coloration dark brown without lighter areas or markings on the marginal plates.

Gout: Accumulation of uric acid in the blood and deposition of its salts (urea) in serous tissue and internal organs (intestinal gout, kidney gout) as well as in joints (uratic arthritis). When an animal does not appear to be well (refusal to feed, reluctance to move, impaired body posture) and has difficulties in shedding its skin as well as having an appearance of constipation, gout may be implicated. Uratic arthritis or joint gout may be indicated in the case of swollen joints and/or their immediate vicinity as well as by impaired movements.

Gout is caused by impaired function of the kidney epithelium, possibly arising from environmental temperatures being too high or the humidity too low, protein-rich diet, irregular drinking water availability, as well as kidney damage caused by various substances such as drugs (gentamycin). Due to mechanical irritation caused by the urea deposits, local inflammations and connective tissue damage may occur, leading to a further reduction in kidney function and thus further impairing the function of other organs. A lack of vitamin A may intensify a predisposition to gout.

When gout is shown to be present, the prognosis for a successful therapy is doubtful but should be attempted. It is suggested that an injection be made of the following mixture: 0.3 ml Ursovit A, D3, E, C, and 0.2 ml vitamin B-complex, 10 ml physiological salt solution, and 10 ml glucose solution (20%) per kg bodyweight, given 3 times at weekly intervals. In addition, antibiotics can be administered to combat any simultaneously occurring bacterial infection. Other animals cared for under the same conditions as those that may have died of gout should have the protein content in their diet reduced and the feeding intensity lowered, the water intake should be monitored, and vitamin A treatment initiated.

Grandidier, Alfred (1836-1921): French zoologist and herpetologist. Explored Madagascar and described many Madagascan amphibian and reptile taxa.

Grandisonia TAYLOR, 1968. Genus of the Caeciliidae. Seychelle Islands. 5 species. 10 to 33 cm. Tentacle pit horseshoe-shaped, as in *Hypogeophis*, located closer to nostril than to eye. At the most 88 primary furrows. Small calcareous scales in the skin. Larvae with paired gill openings dorso-laterally in second furrow. Adults more or less uniformly reddish, violet, or brown-black. Presumably aquatic.
• *G. alternans* (STEJNEGER, 1893). Seychelles. To 33 cm. Black-brown to violet.

Graptemys AGASSIZ, 1857. Map Turtles. Genus of the Emydidae. North America. 9 or 10 species. In larger waters (lakes and slow-flowing large rivers) and streams with ample vegetation. Carapace length 12 to 32 cm in females; males substantially smaller than females, 9 to 15 cm. Carapace with raised, knobby dorsal keel, the second and third vertebral scales often particularly high. Only in large females of *G. geographica* and *G. kohni* is the keel nearly smooth. Usually a yellow spot or crescent behind the eye.

Omnivorous, females feeding heavily on plants. Likes heat and needs sunning that give easy access to water, similar to *Chrysemys*. N asy to raise rachitis-free juveniles, but some species (especially *G. kohni* and *G. geographica*) can be kept easily as adults. Depending upon ori-

Graptemys barbouri

Graptemys barbouri

Graptemys caglei

Graptemys caglei

Graptemys barbouri, male

Graptemys flavimaculata

Graptemys geographica

Graptemys geographica

Graptemys kohni

Graptemys kohni

Graptemys kohni

Graptemys kohni

Graptemys flavimaculata, male

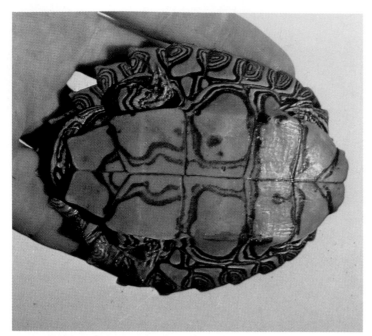

Graptemys nigrinoda

Graptemys pseudogeographica

Graptemys nigrinoda

Graptemys ouachitensis

Graptemys versa

Graptemys pulchra

Graptemys oculifera

Graptemys pulchra

Graptemys pseudogeographica

gin·of the particular species, they can be kept outdoors during the summer or possibly throughout the year. Have been bred in captivity.

• *G. geographica* (LE SUER, 1817). Map Turtle. Southeastern Canada and Maine in the north to Kansas and Tennessee. Carapace keel comparatively smooth. Incubation in 51 to 83 days at 30 or 25° C., respectively.

• *G. kohni* (BAUR, 1890). Mississippi Map Turtle. Central and southern USA. Carapace keel distinctly rough. A yellow crescent behind the eye. Incubation takes 86 days at 25° C. Most frequently kept species. Now often considered a subspecies of *G. pseudogeographica*.

• *G. oculifera* (BAUR, 1890). Ringed Map Turtle. Pearl River, Mississippi and Louisiana. Very distinct knobs on carapace and characteristic yellow or orange rings on marginal and lateral scutes. Incubation period 63 days at 25° C.

• *G. pseudogeographica* (GRAY, 1831). False Map Turtle. Central USA. Carapace keel with only few low humps. Reticulated markings on carapace similar to *G. geographica*. Incubation takes 53 to 93 days at 30° C. or 22-25° C. in an incubator; under natural conditions eggs hatch in 76 to 82 days.

Grasshoppers: see Saltatoria, Acrididae.

Gray, John Edward (1800–1875): British zoologist at the British Museum, London. Published several catalogs of the Museum collections that included comprehensive discussions of the groups as well as numerous descriptions of new species. *Catalogue of Shield Reptiles* (1855 and 1870).

Grayia GUENTHER, 1858. African Water Snakes. Genus of the Colubridae, Natricinae. Tropical Africa. 2 species. 0.8 to 2.5 m. Head more or less clearly set off. Dorsal scales smooth, not overlapping, each scale nearly isolated. Dark olive-brown background coloration with more or less obvious rhomboids or crossbands. Ventrally light without markings.

Aquatic snakes living in or near large rivers and lakes, similar to *Natrix tesselata*. Prey mainly on fish, aquatic frogs (*Xenopus, Hymenochirus*, and their larvae). For details on care refer to Natricinae, Group 2.

• *G. smithi* (LEACH, 1818). Sudan to southern Tanzania, westward to Senegal and southward to Angola. Very heavily built. 0.8 to 2.5 m.

• *G. tholloni* MOCQUARD, 1906. Nigeria eastward to Tanzania. Slender. 1.2 m.

Greenhouse terrarium: Suitably constructed greenhouses of variable size for the maintenance of many animals. The same prerequisites in regard to heating, ventilation, and soil moisture apply as for indoor terrariums. During the summer season at least the roof of such a terrarium should be replaced with gauze inserts in order to permit penetration of ultraviolet radiation and to provide protection against overheating. Shade has to be provided. A combination with an outdoor terrarium during the summer is quite suitable, except for rain-forest species.

Group effect: Transfer of mood(s) that leads to an adaptation of actions and synchronization among the individuals of a group. For instance, the mutually stimulating effect of frogs croaking ("frog concert") can be interpreted as a group effect.

Gryllidae: Crickets. Family of the order Ensifera (Saltoria) of worldwide distribution. Most of the more than 2000 species are found in the tropics and subtropics. A characteristic of crickets is the vocalizing ability of the males that is often hard to endure when these animals are bred in captivity. This sound is created through the rubbing together of the wing covers.

Many of the omnivorous cricket species are an excellent food for terrarium animals, particularly since they can be readily bred in large numbers. This is easily done in gauze-covered glass containers (not too small) at temperatures from 25 to 30° C. Corrugated cardboard is placed inside the container (to provide hiding places) as well as a small dish filled with a 5 to 8 cm layer of a damp sand-soil mixture for the crickets to deposit their eggs in. Drinking water is most suitably offered in a test tube plugged with cotton or in a shallow dish containing a sponge. Crickets are generally omnivorous, so the food can be items like poultry meal, dog kibble, crushed rat/mouse pellets, and occasionally some fish or dried and macerated beef. Green food should be given at intervals in the form of grass or vegetables. However, the moisture in plant products creates a risk of mite infestations that could destroy the entire culture. Another suitable food consists of a mixture of whole wheat or oatmeal, powdered milk, and some dietary yeast.

The house cricket (*Acheta domesticus*) is the best-known species. Maximum size is about 25 mm. It is frequently found in crushed rock fills, rubble piles, and similar habitats. The young hatch (under favorable conditions) from

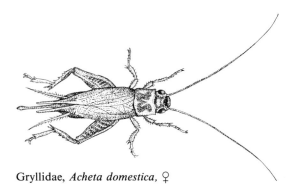

Gryllidae, *Acheta domestica*, ♀

Gryllidae: *Gryllus*

Gryllidae: *Acheta domestica*

the eggs after 10 days. The eggs must be transferred from the spawning dish to a separate rearing container. Sexual maturity is reached in about 7 weeks. One female can lay up to about 800 eggs.

The field crickets (*Gryllus*) can be bred under the same conditions. They are slightly larger than the house cricket and have a longer development cycle. Found on meadows and along the periphery of forests, they prefer a moister environment and feed mainly on green food. Some of the tropical and subtropical species are easy to breed, e. g., *Gryllus bimaculatus*, which is also larger than the house cricket. Some of these species are much less noisy and not

as cannibalistic. The nutritional value of crickets can be further enhanced when they are given calcium and vitamin supplements in their diet.

Guenther, Albert Carl Ludwig Gotthelf (1830–1914): German ichthyologist and herpetologist at the British Museum in London. Originally a medical practitioner, he later turned to zoology. Apart from his publications on fish, he continued Gray's catalog publications with a treatise on the frogs and colubrid snakes. *Reptiles of British India* (1864). Amphibian and reptile sections of *Biologia Centrali Americana* (1885 to 1902). In 1867 Guenther recognized the special position of the tuataras and their membership in the Rhynchocephalia.

Guzmania RUIZ and PAV. Genus of the Bromiliaceae. Central America to Peru. About 120 species in tropical rain forests. Epiphytes or ground plants. Require high humidity, 18-22° C. Must not be exposed to direct sunlight. Small-leaved species are suitable for terrariums.
- *G. angustifolia* (BAK.) WITTM. Leaves to about 15 cm.
- *G. minor* MEZ. Leaves to about 20 cm, arranged in delicate rosettes.
- *G. sanguinea* ANDRE and MEZ. Rosettes to 30 cm tall. Leaves with reddish stripes.

Gyalopion COPE, 1860. Western Hook-nosed Snakes. Genus of the Colubridae of uncertain subfamily status (Boiginae). Southern USA and Mexico. 3 species. Closely related to *Ficimia* and formerly included in that genus. 30-40 cm.

Gyalopion quadrangularis

Tip of snout pointing upward. Bu rowing ground snakes.
• *G. canum* COPE, 1860. Western I ok-nosed Snake. Texas south into central Mexico. 36 cm Pops" the cloaca when threatened.

Gymnodactylus SPIX, 1825. Genus of the Gekkonidae, subfamily Gekkoninae. In all tropical and subtropical regions. Today this genus includes only a few (3 ?) New World species with vertical, non-? pupils. Neotropic species with lobed pupils are now genus *Wallsaurus* (2 species), which of late is being d in *Homonota*. The genus *Underwoodisaurus* c Australian and New Guinean species that are clc rus. More than 70 Old World species with a ver pupil are now placed in the genus *Cyrtodactylus* ely correspond in mode of life and required ter e to those few species retained in *Gymnodactylu* o *Cyrtodactylus* for maintenance requirements.
• *G. antillensis* LIDT DE JEUDE, 188 thern Venezuela and adjacent offshore islands. Dry, habitats. Barely 10 cm. To some degree also diurna Males with yellow heads.
• *G. geckoides* SPIX, 1825. Brasil. Several subspecies. About 12 cm.

Gymnophiona: Caecilians. Order of the Amphibia (also called Apodes). The families are uncertain, but include Caeciliidae, Ichthyophiidae, and Typhlonectidae. Tropics and subtropics of America, Africa, and Southeast Asia, including offshore islands. The smallest amphibian order in terms of family, genus, and species numbers, and at the same time also one of the least known and understood vertebrate groups. Found in various sufficiently moist bottom substrates; e. g., soil, humus piles, abandoned termite mounds, frequently also under decaying material and underneath rocks. 7 cm to 135 cm, a few millimeters to 3 cm thick. Limbless, earthworm-like. Skin naked (but in some species with tiny calcareous scales buried below the surface). Characteristically ringed with primary and secondary grooves or furrows. Tail very short or absent, either terminal or, due to the position of the cloaca, subterminal. Head flattened, eyes regressed and covered by skin, hidden under bones of the massive skull. Eyes apparent only in Typhlonectidae, where still used as light sensory organs. Hearing organs also regressed. Orientation mainly by means of smell and with (characteristic for Gymnophiona) paired retractile tentacle organ that rests inside a closable pit in the animal's cheek region between the eye and nostril. The position of the tentacle is an important systematic characteristic. Mouth deeply cleft. Upper jaw with 2 rows of pointed teeth that are bent backward. Lower jaw commonly with 2 rows of teeth, but the interior one can be reduced or even be absent. The dentition is also of importance in systematics. Tongue not protrusible, completely fused with bottom of oral cavity.

During development there are 3 pairs of gill tufts or (in *Typhlonectes*) 2 giant lobate gills. Generally the gills will be reduced prior to hatching. Aquatic larvae then have only 1 or 2 gill apertures through which respiratory water, taken in through the mouth, is expelled again. However, even these gill opening can be closed (Typhlonectidae). Adult specimens are without gills or gill openings, depending on lung respiration (only the right lung is developed) and also respiration through the skin and the oral cavity. Tail short during the larval stage, surrounded by a median skin seam, usually completely reduced in metamorphosing specimens (exceptions: Ichthyophiidae, *Uraeotyphlus, Copeotyphlinus*). Usually dark brown to bluish black.

Except for the amphibious Typhlonectidae, all Gymnophiona lead a burrowing mode of life. Terrestrial species are not capable of swimming. Movements in self-dug tunnels are fast, both forward and backward. They will surface after dark in search for food and (according to terrarium observations) in order to mate. These animals are predators, feeding mainly on arthropods, earthworms, millipedes, cockroaches, and other invertebrates. There can also be cannibalism among these animals. Their natural enemies include snakes, especially coral snakes, and birds.

Males have a protrusible, very large and complicated penis (the only copulation organ among amphibians, except in Ascaphidae). In ovoviviparous forms (e. g., Typhlonectidae) the eggs are regularly arranged inside the oviduct; upon resorption of the yolk the embryos are fed with socalled uterine milk, oil droplets and cell material given off by the oviduct. In egg-laying species (e. g., Ichthyophiidae) the clutch consists of about 30 conspicuously large, yolk-rich eggs that are attached string-like to each other; the female curls around this string of eggs. Clutches removed from a female apparently do not develop normally.

Up to now these animals have played no significant part in terrarium keeping, and in fact, there is not much captive data for these animals at all. However, according to the little available information the Gymnophiona are indeed suitable terrarium animals (having been kept for more than 9 years). Attempted matings have also been observed. For details on care and maintenance refer to the particular family.

Gymnophthalamus MERREM, 1820. Spectacled Tegus. Genus of the Teiidae. Southern Mexico to northern Argentina, including some Caribbean islands. 6 species. In relatively dry habitats and also following human habitation. To 15 cm. Slender. Lower eyelid transparent, solidly fused with upper eyelid. Short limbs with 4 toes. Large, very smooth scales. Strongly reminiscent of small skinks such as *Ablepharus kitaibelli*.

Ground-dwellers found among fallen leaves, grass, and under rocks, occasionally in houses. Feed on small arthropods. 2-3 eggs in crevices in the ground. *G. underwoodi* presumably is parthenogenic.
• *G. speciosus* (HALLOWELL, 1861). Northern Brasil. 15 cm. Tail about 4 times snout-vent length. Shiny graybrown with blue head stripes. Orange tail.
• *G. underwoodi* GRANT, 1958. Guyana, Surinam, Trinidad, and neighboring islands. Easily to 12 cm. Bronze-brown with lighter longitudinal stripes. Flanks black.

Gymnopis PETERS, 1874. Genus of the Caeciliidae. Central America. 3 species. Compact. 102-133 primary folds, 64-117 secondary folds. Eyes covered by orbital bones. Tentacles just below the eye level, located close to eye and far from nostril. Tiny scales present.
• *G. proxima* (COPE, 1875). Atlantic region of Nicaragua, Costa Rica, and Panama. To 47 cm. Dorsum violet, abdo-

men cream-colored; eyes, tentacle field, nostrils, and cloaca whitish.

Gyrinophilus COPE, 1869. Spring Salamanders. Genus of the Plethodontidae. Eastern North America. 2 polytypic species. 20 cm. Robust, with short legs. Tail laterally compressed. *G. palleucus* retains larval characteristics (external gills, tail with tall skin fold, lidless rudimentary eyes) and is subterranean. *G. porphyriticus* is similar to *Pseudotriton* but lighter, in some subspecies with a black-edged line from eye to nostril.

• *G. palleucus* MCCRADY, 1954. Tennessee Cave Salamander. Cave waters in Tennessee and adjacent regions of Alabama and Georgia. 3 subspecies. 20 cm. Nominate form largely without pigments, the other subspecies brown to dark brown-red, with dark spots and stripes. Same care as for other neotenic blind salamanders (see *Eurycea*).

• *G. porphyriticus* (GREEN, 1827). Spring Salamander. Southern Canada to Mississippi and Alabama, largely absent from Atlantic coastal region. 4 subspecies. In and

Gyrinophilus palleucus palleucus

close to mountain creeks and streams. 22 cm. Orange to salmon-colored, dorsum and flanks with variable pattern of black dots or reticulations. Ventral region often sprinkled with silver-white. Semiaquatic. Courtship and mating occur in fall, spawning in spring to summer. The larval stage lasts 3 years; neoteny sometimes occurs. Same care as for semiaquatic *Desmognathus* species.

Habitat: More or less well delineated area for an animal community (biocoenosis), such as a swamp pond, peat bog, montane rain forest, grassland at high altitudes, or a semidesert. Habitat and the respective biocoenosis form an ecosystem.

Habitat terrarium: Specially set up terrarium where, in addition to compliance with the correct husbandry procedures, there is also emphasis on geographically correct decorations, especially as far as the selection of plants and animals is concerned. Habitat terrariums have great educational merits and should be used for special teaching and display purposes. However, generally such efforts have little bearing on the well-being of the animals, which invariably do not care whether the plants used in a particular terrarium come from a South American, African, or Asiatic rain forest.

Habrahyla GOIN, 1961. Described as a monotypic genus (*H. eiselti*) of the Hylidae from Brasil, this taxon was later placed in the synonymy of the African *Leptopelis notatus* (Rhacophoridae), being based on a mislabeled specimen.

Haideotriton CARR, 1939. Monotypic genus of the Plethodontidae. Very small area of distribution in the southeastern USA. Albinistic, obligate neotenic form with conspicuously long, wide, flattened head; slender long red external

Haideotriton wallacei

gills; and extremely thin limbs. Juveniles have tiny, skin-covered eye remnants; adults are without eyes. Mode of life and care same as other blind salamanders.

▪ *H. wallacei* CARR, 1939. Georgia Blind Salamander. Northern Florida and southern Georgia in perpetually dark, cool cave waters and deep springs. 8 cm. Colorless opalescent white.

Haldea: see *Virginia*, genus.

Hamptophryna CARVALHO, 1954. Monotypic genus of the Microhylidae. Tropical South America, *selva*. Smooth skin. Head small, with pointed snout. Tympanum not visible. Fingers and toes long and free, tips with small adhesive discs. Call consists of long, loud "baah."

Nocturnal ground-dwellers. Feed mainly on ants and spawn in jungle ponds and pools.

▪ *H. boliviana* (PARKER, 1927). Western Amazon Basin from Ecuador to Bolivia. 4 cm. Attractive; dorsum yellow-brown with fine lighter median line; cheeks and flanks dark brown; ventrum whitish yellow with brown-black pattern.

Haplocercus GUENTHER, 1858. Monotypic genus of the Colubridae, Lycodontinae. Sri Lanka. In montane forests to 1800 m elevation. 45 cm. Head not set off from body, head scales reduced. Brown with a black median line.

Ground snakes, possibly burrowers.

▪ *H. ceylonensis* GUENTHER, 1858.

Haplodon GRIFFIN, 1910. Monotypic genus of the Colubridae, Lycodontinae. Philippines. In tropical lowland forests. To 80 cm. Rhomboidal head distinctly set off from body. Eye with vertical pupil. Dorsal pattern consisting of narrow white and wide dark brown crossbands.

Nocturnal ground snakes. Biology so far unknown.

▪ *H. philippinensis* GRIFFIN, 1910.

Haplopeltura DUMERIL and BIBRON, 1853. Monotypic genus of the Colubridae, Pareinae. Malaysia and southern Thailand through the Indo-Australian Archipelago to the Philippines. To 85 cm. Distinguished from the closely related genus *Pareas* by the presence of a single row of plates along the ventral side of the tail. Background color yellow-brown, with 3 dark stripes in the head region. Body unicolored or with dark spots.

Egg-layer, 4 eggs.

▪ *H. boa* (BOIE, 1828).

Hapsidophrys FISCHER, 1856. Monotypic genus of the Colubridae, Colubrinae. Tropical Africa, from Guinea to Angola, eastward to Tanzania, Kenya, and Uganda. Closely related to *Gastropyxis*. In tropical gallery forests, rain forests, and montane rain forests to 2000 m elevation. To 1.1 m. Very slender. Conspicuously set off head with very large eyes. Dorsum covered with keeled scales. Green with narrow black longitudinal stripes, edges of ventral scales with wide pale green bands.

Tree snakes that feed mainly on frogs. Must be housed in a well-heated and properly planted tropical rain-forest terrarium.

▪ *H. lineata* FISCHER, 1856.

Hardella GRAY, 1870. Brahminy River Turtles. Monotypic genus of the Emydidae. Indian region in large flow-

Haplopeltura boa

ing waters. Carapace to 50 cm, males smaller. A slightly bumpy, indistinct keel present on carapace. Characteristic light longitudinal band between costal and marginal plates.

Excellent swimmers and divers. Omnivorous, with a large plant component to the diet. Adults suitable only for large aqua-terrariums in public zoos.

▪ *H. thurji* (GRAY, 1831). River systems of the Ganges and Brahmaputra. 2 subspecies; *H. t. indi* (GRAY, 1870) occurs in the Indus system.

Hardella thurji

Hardella thurji

Harpesaurus BOULENGER, 1885. Genus of the Agamidae. Indo-Australian Archipelago. 5 species, most of them known only from the type locality. To 20 cm. A characteristic large horn (bent backward) on the snout, formed by a single scale.

Arboreal. Behavior and captive requirements probably similar to *Calotes*.

▪ *H. beccari* DORIA, 1888. Sumatra.

Hatteria: see *Sphenodon*, genus.

Haworthia DUVAL. Genus of the Liliaceae. Southwestern and southern Africa, mainly in Cape Province. More than 80 species. Low-growing succulent shrubs with rosette leaves. Undemanding, growing well even at low temperatures; about 10° C. is sufficient for over-wintering. For semidesert terrariums.

Stem-forming species with hard leaves:

▪ *H. reinwardtii* (SALM-DYCK) HAW. Dense spirally leafed stem. Many subspecies in horticulture.

▪ *H. rigida* (LAM.) HAW. Carpet-forming.

▪ *H. tortuosa* HAW.

▪ *H. viscosa* (L.) HAW.

Stemless, thick-leaved, rosette-forming species:

▪ *H. fasciata* (WILLD) HAW.

▪ *H. margaritifera* (L.) HAW. Frequently cultivated.

▪ *H. papillosa* (SALM-DYCK) HAW.

▪ *H. radula* (JACQ.) HAW. Delicate, carpet-forming. Leaves 6-8 cm.

Haworthia fasciata

Haworthia sp.

Heating: Most indoor terrariums require some sort of heating. Except for a few strictly nocturnal reptiles and amphibians, this also applies where the entire room is heated, since nearly all herptiles require a particularly warm sun-bathing place. Fundamentally, one has to distinguish between air, substrate, and basking heating.

Air heating for amphibians, including nocturnal forms, may call for a very large temperature gradient between the terrarium and the room. Adjustable, thermostatically controlled room air heaters can be used for very large containers. In smaller terrariums fresh air can be channeled through a space containing a heat source either below or behind the terrarium.

Substrate heating involves the use of various heating cables and heating plates. Plastic-coated heating cables are particularly popular beause they can be shaped into any arrangement and placed in the substrate, a water basin, or attached to thick branches. When embedded in the substrate the material has to be taken into consideration (cables must not be placed into peat moss) and the cables have to be protected against being uncovered by burrowing animals, displaced, or even damaged. 100 watts per square meter is considered to be a baseline value. If a small area is to be heated, low-wattage aquarium heaters may be used (maximum 30 watts), but they must be surrounded by an aluminium cover to conduct the heat. When using substrate heating special attention has to be paid to the fact that the entire bottom is not heated uniformly, forming a temperature gradient. Substrate heating is an unatural heat source for most animals but is still highly effective and useful ecologically for large terrariums. Natural conditions are approximated most closely if the heating coil is placed not only into the ground but also along branches and under a basking spot.

When using fluorescent lights, the starter units can be used as weak substrate heaters. They are placed (well insulated) either directly into the substrate or are used as bottom heaters for containers placed on top. Substrate heating is most effective for nocturnal specimens.

Radiant heat is without doubt the most important type of heating. It provides both air and substrate heating and thus approximates natural sun heating. Radiant heat can be provided by various types of lamps, from normal incandescent light bulbs with a reflector, incandescent bulbs with internal silver reflector coating, carbon arc lights, and mercury vapor lamps. About 15 to 25 watts are generally sufficient for very small terrariums; larger ones require 40 to 100 watts (the former for forest animals and the latter for steppe and desert animals). Incandescent lighting used primarily for terrariums can also provide sufficient basking heat for forest-dwelling animals. The heat source is best mounted inside the terrarium, except in very small ones. Special care has to be taken that the animals can not jump or climb directly onto the lamps.

Hedera L. Ivy. Genus of the Araliaceae. Europe, Asia. 7 species. Evergreen, climbing or ground-creeping shrubs with hard leave. Resistant, multi-purpose climbing or hanging plants. Develops larger leaves at elevated temperatures (undesirable for terrarium use). The multicolored varieties are not all winter resistant.
• *H. colchica* K. KOCH. Caucasian Ivy. High climber. Leaves 10-20 cm.
• *H. helix* L. Common Ivy. Ground-creeping or climbing shrub.

Heleioporus GRAY, 1841. Moaning Frogs. Genus of the Leptodactylidae. Subtropical Australia. About 5 species. Body more or less spherical, plump. Skin granular. Large protruding eyes, the pupils vertical. Tympanum usually not clearly visible. The limbs are short, the anterior ones in males particularly strong. Fingers free, toes webbed at base only. Metatarsal with large, unpigmented inner tubercle. During the breeding season males have conical spurs on fingers 1 to 3.

Ground-dwellers that rarely leave their hiding places (self-dug burrows, rocky crevices, wells). They presumably deposit their spawn in burrows, some inside a large foam nest (*H. australiacus*) along river banks. Must be given a spacious, semimoist, unheated, or weakly heated terrarium with a deep substrate layer. Should be kept outdoors during the summer.
• *H. albopunctatus* GRAY, 1841. Southwestern Australia. 8 cm. Gray, back and sides with scattered white spots.
• *H. australiacus* (SHAW, 1795). Giant Burrowing Frog. Coastal region of southeastern Australia. 9.5 cm. Dorsum chocolate brown, flanks with white dots.

Heleophryne SCLATER, 1898. African Ghost Frogs. Genus of the Leptodactylidae. Southern Africa from the Cape to Natal and eastern and northeastern Transvaal. 3 species, 1 polytypic. In and near clear, fast-flowing, shaded mountain streams. The only species of the Leptodactylidae in Africa, representing their own subfamily (Heleophryninae). Bulging eyes, vertical pupils, and clearly visible tympanum. Tips of fingers and toes with well-developed adhesive discs; fingers free, toes webbed halfway up.

Crepuscular and nocturnal; semiaquatic, excellent swim-

mers, sometimes also found long distances away from water. Eggs not yet found, but presumably deposited close to river banks in damp substrate underneath rocks and similar places. Larvae extremely well adapted to fast-flowing waters. They feed on epiphytic algae and undergo a developmental period of up to 2 years.
• *H. natalensis* HEWITT, 1926. 6.5 cm. Blue-black or dark brown with a light green pattern.
• *H. rosei* HEWITT, 1925. 6.5 cm. Dark green, with red reticulation.

Helicops WAGLER, 1830. South American Water Snakes. Genus of the Colubridae, Natricinae (subfamily sometimes considered to be uncertain). South America, from Colombia to Argentina. About 14 species. To 1 m. Head small, roundish, the nostrils and eyes dorsal, elevated. Body covered with strongly keeled and shingled scales. Uniformly grayish blue or brownish, sometimes with longitudinal stripes or a spotted pattern.

Helicops angulatus

Helicops carinicaudus

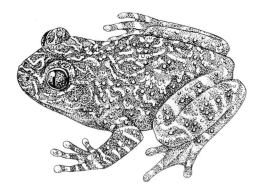
Heleophryne natalensis

Helicops leopardinus

Helicops leopardinus

Helicops carinicaudus

The diet consists mainly of fish and frogs. These are the most strongly aquatic Natricinae. Should be cared for as Group 3 Natricinae. All species are very aggressive. Egg-layers, but some with a short incubation period and possibly becoming ovoviviparous.
• *H. angulatus* (LINNAEUS, 1758). From Venezuela and Colombia to Ecuador, Bolivia and Peru.
• *H. carinicaudus* (WIED, 1825). Southeastern Brasil and

Uruguay to Argentina. 2 subspecies. Longitudinally striped or uniformly brown. Dorsal scales very strongly keeled.
• *H. leopardinus* (SCHLEGEL, 1837). From Guyana and Surinam to Brasil and northern Argentina. 2 alternating rows of spots on back.
• *H. polylepis* GUENTHER, 1861. Amazon Basin.

Helminthophis PETERS, 1860. Genus of the Anomalepidae. Central America to northern South America. 3 species. To 25 cm. Dorsal region of head with scales of equal size except the large rostral. Lower jaw toothless.
• *H. frontalis* (PETERS, 1860). Costa Rica.

Helminths: Collective grouping for all parasitic intestinal worms of the Acanthocephala, Cestoda, Nematoda, and Trematoda. Tongueworms (Pentastomida) are not considered helminths.

Heloderma WIEGMANN, 1829. Gila Monsters, Beaded Lizards. Genus of the Helodermatidae. Southwestern USA and Mexico. 2 species, *H. suspectum* in desert-like habitats,

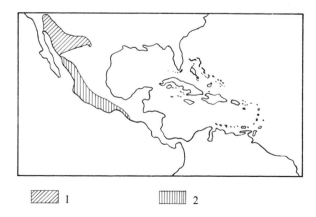

Distribution of: 1 *Heloderma horridum;* 2 *Heloderma suspectum*

Heloderma suspectum

Heloderma suspectum

H. horridum more in dry, open forests. 50 to 80 cm. Heavily built, plump, cylindrical. Head broad, flat, and with a blunt, rounded snout. Limbs short and powerful, with strong claws. Tail rounded, very thick; serves as a fat reservoir. Eyes small. External ear openings slot-like. Tongue fleshy but deeply cleft. The small, hemispherical body scales are arranged so an impression of oblique rows is conveyed; they are supported by osteoderms.

Heloderma species are the only Recent venomous lizards. The venom glands (up to 4 cm long) are located at the posterior margin of the lower jaw. The venom reaches the teeth via a groove between the jaw and lip; the multiple fangs are grooved anteriorly and usually also posteriorly. Some upper jaw teeth also have grooves. The teeth are located deep inside the gums, which are pushed back during the bite so that the teeth can penetrate 9 to 10 mm deep. These lizards must chew to inject the venom. The venom affects mainly the central nervous system and can, through paralysis of the respiratory centers, be lethal in certain cases (particularly in conjunction with alcohol).

Nocturnal ground-dwellers. The activity period of *H. suspectum* is very short, restricted to the breeding period in spring and the rainy season in July and August. The remainder of the time is spent using up the fat reserves in their tail while resting in self-dug burrows. The diet of these usually awkward and slow animals consists mainly of eggs of reptiles and ground-nesting birds, as well as young rodents; dead animals are also eaten. When in good health and warm, Gila monsters can be surprisingly active and quick, so be very careful. The venom appears to serve mainly as a defensive mechanism. The sometimes bright colors of these animals have to be viewed in conjunction

Heloderma suspectum

Heloderma horridum

Heloderma horridum

sometimes lay for hours in water in captivity and drink a lot. Suitable food in captivity consists of raw, cracked chicken eggs and occasionally some scraped meat or heart. Newborn mice are sometimes also accepted. *H. suspectum* has been bred regularly in the USA.

Although these animals are relatively slow and "reluctant to bite," they have to be handled with extreme caution. Their venom paralyzes the respiratory centers and thus can be fatal. It is very difficult to obtain legally collected specimens.

• *H. suspectum* COPE, 1869. Gila Monster. Southwestern USA and northern Mexico. To 60 cm. Tail only about ⅔ of body length. Body covered extensively by orange-yellow to flesh-colored spots. Longevity in captivity is up to 20 years.

• *H. horridum* (WIEGMANN, 1829). Mexican Beaded Lizard. Western Mexico. To 80 cm. Tail same length as body or slightly longer. The pattern consists of pale yellow dots, less extensive than in the above species, on a blackish background.

Helodermatidae: Beaded Lizards. Family of the Platynota, Sauria. 2 recent species in one genus. Fossil records from the Oligocene in North America and Europe. The only Recent venomous lizards. For details see *Heloderma*.

Hemachatus FLEMING, 1822. Spitting or Ringed Cobras, Ringhals. Monotypic genus of the Elapidae. Southern and southeastern Africa in dry habitats (savannahs, covered mountain slopes, steppes, and similar regions) of variable character. To 1.2 m. Distinguishable from the closely related genus *Naja* by the presence of keeled dorsal scales

with their venomous characteristics. The colors consist of an irregular number of variably sized bright yellow to red spots (in a more or less oblique arrangement) against a dark brown or black background. The tail may have 4 to 7 crossbands.

A clutch consists of 3 to 13 eggs. The young hatch after 30 days and are up to 20 cm long. Possibly there are several clutches per year, since oviducts of females have shown up to 30 eggs.

Beaded lizards adjust well to captivity and have substantial longevities, although maintenance is not without problems. The terrarium must have a deep substrate to accommodate the animal's burrowing activities. Day temperatures can vary from 25 to 30° C., and directly below the basking light it can be 35° C.; provide a nocturnal reduction to about 20° C. A large water bowl must be available (water temperature about 25° C.), since the animals

Hemachatus haemachatus feigning death

and viviparity. Variably brown with darker crossbands, changing to uniform coloration toward the head. Ventral region of the throat with 2 conspicuous dirty white crossbands, the upper one 1-2 ventral scales wide and the lower up to 7 ventrals wide. Ringed cobras (ringhals) are capable of "spitting" their venom (usually directed toward the eyes of an enemy) from the relatively short fangs through the slightly opened mouth.

Gives birth to from 15 to 60 young. Must be kept in well-heated dry terrarium. Small mammals, toads, lizards, and snakes are eaten. They will often take dead prey, even fish or pieces of meat. Wearing protective heavy-duty glasses is absolutely mandatory when handling spitting cobras. If the venom should enter the eyes it must immediately be flushed out under running water and with a weak potassium permanganate solution.
▪ *H. haemachatus* (LACEPEDE, 1790).

Hemiaspis FITZINGER, 1843. Genus of the Elapidae. Eastern Australia. 2 species. Sometimes included in *Denisonia*. Found in variable habitats, *H. signata* often in the vicinity of standing or flowing waters. 50 cm. Relatively slender, more or less uniformly gray-brown; *H. damelii* has a dark collar.

More or less diurnal and crepuscular venomous snakes. They feed on frogs and lizards. Live-bearers; *H. damelii* has 6-12 young, *H. signata* 4-20 young at a time. Venom not fatal to humans, but a bite from *H. signata* is very painful. Keep in a well-heated terrarium with a large water bowl and hiding places.
▪ *H. damelii* (GUENTHER, 1876). Central western Queensland and New South Wales.

Hemidactylium TSCHUDI, 1838. Four-toed Salamanders. Monotypic genus of the Plethodontidae. Eastern North America in forests with mossy patches (*Sphagnum*) or meadows and swampy regions. Hind feet 4-toed. A circular furrow at the base of the tail, the preformed fracture line. Abdomen enamel white with black spots; reddish brown above.

Mode of life similar to *Plethodon*. Mate during late summer and fall. Immediately after leaving their winter quarters the females move to their spawning grounds. About 30 eggs are deposited individually either into water or in the close proximity of creeks, springs, and small streams. Usually the female remains with her clutch until the larvae hatch. Metamorphosis of the aquatic larvae occurs in about 6 weeks.

Four-toed salamanders should be kept in a moist terrarium with moss. If the animals are paired off they are transferred immediately after their winter domancy period into an aqua-terrarium with clear, cool water.
▪ *H. scutatum* (SCHLEGEL, 1838). Four-toed Salamander. From Nova Scotia to Wisconsin and Alabama. 5 to 9 cm.

Hemidactylus OKEN, 1817. Leaf-toed Geckos. Genus of the Gekkonidae. Southern Europe, through Africa and Asia to Oceania; some cosmopolitan forms introduced into America (*H. mabouia*, *H. frenatus*, *H. turcicus*). About 65 species. Great habitat diversity. 10-20 cm. Tail about equal to snout-vent length. Pupil vertical, mostly lobate. Toes with well-developed adhesive lamellae in basal region, not widened distally, cylindrical. Dorsal scales granular, some species with several longitudinal rows of enlarged tubercles. Mostly brown or gray with various dark or light spotted patterns, the spots often arranged into irregular crossbands or rows of spots.

Primarily crepuscular or nocturnal. For details on care refer to *Cyrtodactylus*. Some damp patches in the terrarium

▨ 1　　　　　▧ 2　　　　　■ 3

Distribution of: 1 *Hemidactylus mabouia*; 2 *Gehyra mutilata*; 3 *Cyrtodactylus kotschyi*

Hemidactylus garnotti

Hemidactylus frenatus

Hemidactylus triedrus

are absolutely essential. Several species have been bred in captivity.

• *H. flaviviridis* RUEPPEL, 1835. Yellow-green Leaf-toed Gecko. Sudan through Arabia northeastward to India. To 19 cm. Light yellow to greenish gray with light and dark spots. Pupil not lobed.

• *H. frenatus* DUMERIL and BIBRON, 1836. Virtually around the entire Indo-Pacific in warmer regions; introduced into many areas. To 15 cm. Spotted brown and gray. Scales granular.

• *H. mabouia* (MOREAU DE JONNES, 1818). Tropical Gecko, House Gecko. Southern Africa; introduced into Central America including the Antilles, also eastern South America. To 20 cm. Gray to gray-brown with indistinct darker markings.

• *H. turcicus* (L., 1758). Mediterranean Gecko, Turkish Gecko. Mediterranean Region; in Africa southward to Kenya, eastward to India; introduced into North America and Mexico. 12 cm. Reddish to yellow brown with dark brown spots or crossbands and whitish spots.

Hemidactylus garnoti

Hemidactylus frenatus

Hemidactylus persicus

Hemidactylus turcicus

Hemiergis WAGLER, 1830. Genus of the Scincidae. Australia. About 8 species of uncertain status. In forests, some in highlands. Easily 10 cm. Slender. Lower eyelid movable, with window. Ear openings absent, except in one species. Limbs small, 2- to 5-toed.

Cryptic ground-dwellers. Ovoviviparous, 2 young.
▪ *H. decresiensis* (FITZINGER, 1826). Southeastern Australia. 12 cm. 3 toes and fingers. Brown with dark stripes, flanks gray with spots.

Hemigraphis NEES emend. T. ANDERS. Genus of the Acanthaceae. Tropical and subtropical Asia. 20 species. Durable, low-lying, soft-leaved shrubs. Used as ground cover like *Ruellia* and *Aphelandra*, also as hanging plants.

Reproduction by means of cuttings; with soil temperatures of 20-22° C. the roots grow rapidly. Most frequently cultivated form is *H. alternata* (BURM. F.) T. ANDERS.

Hemipenis: see Sex Organs.

Hemiphractus WAGLER, 1828 (including *Cerathyla* JIMENEZ DE LA ESPADA, 1871). Casque-headed Horned Treefrogs. Genus of the Hylidae. Central and South America. About 9 species in tropical montane rain forests and cloud forests. Head very large, triangular, extended posteriorly, helmet-like, the posterior corners drawn out to points. Upper eyelids and tip of snout with tubercles. Mainly brown with a darker pattern.

Nocturnal ground-dwellers that feed on other frogs, among other things. The 8 to 14 conspicuously large eggs develop while in the honeycomb-like maternal dorsal skin. They emerge as fully metamorphosed juvenile frogs.

These bizarre frogs should be cared for in a tropical rainforest terrarium with a deep, suitably structured substrate, a mixture of soil and peat moss and fresh moss. Provide hiding places under tree bark and plants. Aggressive, even

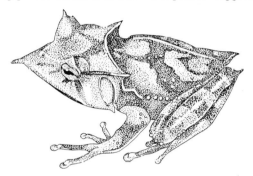

Hemiphractus panamensis

in a terrarium.
▪ *H. bubalus* (ESPADA, 1870) (− *H. johnsoni* (NOBLE, 1917)). Colombia. To 5 cm.
▪ *H. panamensis* (STEJNEGER, 1917). Panama. To 6 cm.

Hemiphyllodactylus BLEEKER, 1860. Genus of the Gekkonidae. India to Oceania. 3 species in variable habitats,

Hemiphyllodactylus typus

but not too dry; some follow human habitation. Easily to 10 cm. Slender. Pupil vertical. The adhesive lamellae on the toes are distally well-developed. Nocturnal.

▪ *H. typus* BLEEKER, 1860. Gypsy Gecko.

Hemipipa: see *Pipa*, genus.

Hemiptera: Superorder of Insecta containing the true bugs (Heteroptera) and the leafhoppers, aphids, and cicadas (Homoptera).

Hemirhagerrhis BOETTGER, 1896. Bark Snakes. Genus of the Colubridae, Boiginae. Eastern and southern Africa. 2 species in savannahs and in mountain regions to 1800 m elevation. Barely 40 cm. Slender. Head barely set off, narrow. Smooth dorsal scales. Indistinct dark middorsal zigzag band against brownish background.

The preferred food is lizards (geckos, skinks) and frogs. Egg-layer, 2-4 small eggs. For details on care refer to *Psammophis*. Caution: Possibly venomous bites, although seemingly inoffensive.

▪ *H. nototaenia* (GUENTHER, 1864). Bark Snake. Central and South Africa. 2 subspecies.

Hemisphaeriodon PETERS, 1867. Genus of the Scincidae. Little known.

Hemisus GUENTHER, 1858. Shovel-nosed Frogs. Genus of the Ranidae. Tropical and subtropical Africa. 5 species. In dry regions (savannahs, grasslands) close to water. Males much smaller than females. The body appears bloated and balloon-like; by comparison the head is tiny, triangular. Similar in appearance to Microhylidae. Snout hardened, used for digging. Legs short.

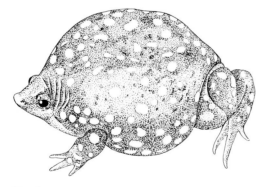

Hemisus guttatus

These frogs are rarely collected, since they live hidden below ground. The food probably consists of ants and termites. The female lays up to 2000 unpigmented eggs in a self-dug, smooth-walled, spherical hole 8-15 cm below the surface and 10 cm to 1 m away from water and guards the clutch. When the larvae are hatched the female digs a passage to the water; there the larvae become free-swimming and remain until metamorphosis.

Since these frogs are highly specialized feeders and lead a cryptic life they can be recommended only for advanced hobbyists. They require a very moist (but not waterlogged) substrate.

▪ *H. guttatus* (RAPP, 1842). Spotted Shovel-nosed Frog. Southern Africa. To 8 cm. Olive brown with light yellow spots.

▪ *H. marmoratus* (PETERS, 1854). Marbled Shovel-nosed

Frog. Africa south of the Sahara. 2 subspecies. To 4 cm. Brown with a greenish or yellowish marbled pattern.

Hemitheconyx STEJNEGER, 1893. Fat-tailed Geckos. Genus of the Gekkonidae. Eastern and western Africa. 2 species in relatively dry habitats. About 20 cm. Lids freely movable. Toes without adhesive lamellae.
Ground-dwellers. See *Eublepharis*.

▪ *H. caudicinctus* (DUMERIL, 1851). West Africa.

▪ *H. taylori* PARKER, 1930. Somalia.

Hemitheconyx caudocinctus

Hemitheconyx caudicinctus

Henophidia: Boas and allies. Central order of the Serpentes. Circumtropical. 5 families: Aniliidae, with 3 genera and about 10 species; Acrochordidae, with 2 monotypic genera and 3 species; Boidae, with 4-6 subfamilies, 25 genera, and about 78 species; Uropeltidae, with 8 genera and about 44 species; and Xenopeltide, a monogeneric and monotypic family. From 40 cm to 10 m, with highly variable shapes and diversified modes of life. Most have more or less well-defined pelvic rudiments, and in several families there still are visible external anal spurs. Most families have muscular bodies that are circular in cross-section.

Features of the skull identify these snakes as primitive ones in snake evolution. However, the 5 Recent families represent in part highly specialized relics of various evolutionary pathways. According to current research, however, these 5 families can be sufficiently delineated from the Scolecophidia and from the further developed "modern" Caenophidia as being from the more primitive original central order.

Heosemys STEJNEGER, 1902. Cogwheel Turtles, Spiny Turtles. Genus of the Emydidae. Southeast Asia. 5 species. In small bodies of water in tropical mountain forests or lowland rain forests. Carapace length 20 to 40 cm. 1-3 carapace keels, the carapace conspicuously flat. Some species undergo a profound change in shape from juveniles to adults (most obvious in *H. spinosa*).

Crepuscular and omnivorous, presumably with species-specific or individual feeding specializations. Biology not well known. Should be kept in spacious aqua-terrarium only marginally heated.

▪ *H. depressa* (ANDERSON, 1875). Indo-China. Carapace length to 25 cm. Characteristic longitudinal keel and very shallow carapace.

▪ *H. grandis* (GRAY, 1860). Southern Indo-China, Malayan Peninsula. With 40 cm carapace length, the largest species of the genus. Posterior edge of carapace clearly serrated, dorsal keel very low.

Heosemys grandis

Heosemys grandis

Heosemys grandis

Heosemys grandis

Heosemys spinosa

Heosemys spinosa

Heosemys spinosa

Heosemys spinosa

▪ *H. spinosa* (GRAY, 1831). Cogwheel Turtle. Southern Indo-China, Malayan Peninsula and Sunda Archipelago. Carapace to 22 cm, with distinctly lighter longitudinal keel. All marginal keels extended, spine-like, extremely so in juveniles. Even the areoles of the costal scutes extend into elevated spines that become smoother with increasing age. Plastron with characteristic radiating pattern. Very docile. Crepuscular. More terrestrial than amphibious.

Herpele PETERS, 1879. Genus of the Caeciliidae. Central Africa. 2 species. Eyes covered by orbital bone. Tentacle obliquely below and behind nostril. Tiny scales and secondary folds present; some folds present posterior to cloaca.
▪ *H. squalostoma* (STUTCHBURY, 1834). To 56 cm. Pale gray.

Herpes: Gray spot disease of turtles. A virus infection found mainly in young freshwater turtles; occurs also as iguana, sea turtle, and snake herpes viruses in other reptiles, but without causing pathological changes. It is also assumed that in freshwater turtles these infections can be latent and only manifest themselves clinically due to detrimental external factors. Herpes virus infection appears in young turtles about 60 to 80 days after hatching. Apart from general disturbances there are either extensive gray patches on the skin or sore-like pustules together with necrosis of the epidermis. Herpes virus infections are highly contagious (90-100% of specimens housed together will contract the disease); with an acute infection the mortality may be 5-20%.

Therapy and prophylaxis: refer to virus infections.

Herpetoseps: see *Scelotes*, genus.

Heterodactylus SPIX, 1825. Genus of the Teiidae. Brasil. 2 species. Small, slender ground-dwellers. Little known.
▪ *H. imbricatus* SPIX, 1825. Rio de Janeiro, Minas Gerais.

Heterodon LATREILLE, 1800. Hog-nosed Snakes. Genus of the Colubridae, Xenodontinae. Eastern and central USA southward to northeastern Mexico. 3 species. Prairies, sand dunes, grasslands, swampy areas, and river banks. In Mexico found in montane regions up to almost 3000 m ele-

Heterodon nasicus

Heterodon hatching

Heterodon platyrhinos

Heterodon platyrhinos

Heterodon platyrhinos

Heterodon platyrhinos

vation. 0.4 to 1.1 m. Compactly built. Tip of snout turned upward. Head large, not strongly set off from body. Dorsal scales keeled.

Hog-nosed snakes feed mainly on toads (*Bufo, Scaphiopus*). When excited they flatten the neck like cobras and emit a strong hissing sound. If the disturbance persists they turn over on their back and fake death. Egg-layers, 5 to 40 eggs.

Should be kept in a well-heated dry terrarium with adequate bathing facilities. Will adapt quickly to captive conditions and are long-lived if enough food can be provided.
▪ *H. nasicus* BAIRD and GIRARD, 1852. Western Hog-nosed

Heterodon nasicus nasicus

Heterodon nasicus nasicus

Heterodon simus

Heterodon nasicus kennerlyi

Snake. Southern Canada throughout central USA to eastern Mexico. 3 subspecies. More likely to take lizards and *Rana*, thus more keepable.

▪ *H. platyrhinos* (LATREILLE, 1801). Eastern Hog-nosed Snake. Throughout eastern USA south of the Great Lakes. An almost exclusive toad-eater.

Heteroliodon BOETTGER, 1933. Monotypic genus of the Colubridae, Lycodontinae. Eastern Madagascar. 32 cm. Ecologically and biologically hardly known.
▪ *H. torquatus* BOETTGER, 1913.

Heteronota: see *Heteronotia*, genus.

Heteronotia WERMUTH, 1965. Genus of the Gekkonidae. Australia. 2 species in open forests that are not too dry; in part follows human habitation. Easily 10 cm. Slender. Tail easily snout-vent length. Adhesive lamellae inconspicuous. Skin rough, with a scattering of small wart-like scales. Nocturnal ground-dwellers.
▪ *H. binoei* (GRAY, 1845). Bynoe's Gecko. 11 cm. Variable coloration; some very bright reddish brown with irregular black-edged pale gray crossbands. Very common. Does well in captivity. Lays 2 eggs.

Heteropholis FISCHER, 1882. Genus of the Gekkonidae. New Zealand (South Island). 6 species. About 15 cm. Mainly green (at higher elevations also brown), with light markings along the sides.
    Diurnal tree-dwellers. Ovoviviparous, 2 young. Does not require much heat, but a weak basking light is essential for sunning. Provide a short winter dormancy period at 10 to 15° C. For details on care refer to *Naultinus*.
▪ *H. stellatus* (HUTTON, 1872).

Heteroptera: True Bugs. Order of the Insecta (often considered a suborder of Hemiptera). Hardly suitable for breeding as food organisms, but some plant-sucking species are of importance due to their common occurrence in meadow plankton during late fall, especially the 5 to 10 mm cinch bugs (Miridae), which are eaten by many terrarium animals. The larger and better known stink bugs (Pentatomidae) and the very common stainers (*Pyrrhocoris*) are usually refused.

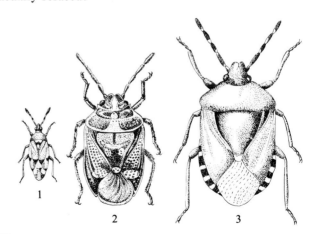

Heteroptera: 1 *Lygus*, Miridae; 2 and 3: *Eurydera oleracea* and *Dolycoris baccarum*, Pentatomidae

Heurnia DE JONG, 1926. Monotypic genus of the Colubridae, Homalopsinae. New Guinea, Mamberamo River delta.
▪ *H. ventromaculatus* DE JONG, 1926.

Hierarchy: Upon triggering a particular behavioral pattern (e. g., courtship behavior, aggressive behavior) by means of a key stimulus, the individual behavioral elements proceed according to a fixed sequence; that is, they are structured in a hierarchy. Therefore, the "wedding dance" of true newts (*Triturus*) is based on a essentially uniform behavioral scheme: After the male has searched for and found a partner recognized as a female, he rubs his snout against the female's body and rams her. This is followed by intense tail waving by the male perpendicularly in front of the female, whereby aromatic substances are apparently transferred through the water. The male finally swims forward followed closely by the female. A spermatophore is then deposited and picked up by the still following female with her cloaca.

In more normal usage the term hierarchy also refers to the place of an individual within a social structure—thus a dominant male (or female) is at the top of the hierarchy in many lizard colonies and their behavior controls all behavior by subordinate animals.

A social hierarchy developed usually through ritualistic fighting among animals living in social groups. Within certain limits such an hierarchy remains stable and serves to maintain the social organization. The animal highest in rank is called the alpha animal, the lowest animals the omega animals. Such hierarchies often occur only among sexes of the same species. Complicated hierarchies as they are known among birds and mammals, or even fish, do not occur among amphibians and reptiles.

An example of a simple rank hierarchy can be seen among black iguanas (*Ctenosaura*), where one male is the alpha male of a colony and can enter and remain in the territories of any of the other males. Within the limited space available in a terrarium it usually happens that even among animals with territory formation but without a natural hierarchy (e. g., geckos, *Anolis*), in a short period of time one of the several males kept together will become the dominant alpha male and will suppress all other males. There is some evidence that a hierarchy may also occur among some tortoises.

Hieremys SMITH, 1916. Temple Turtles. Monotypic genus of the Emydidae. Indo-China in large standing waters. Carapace about 50 cm, smooth.

Omnivorous. Requires a suitably large aquarium with

Hieremys annandalei

Hieremys annandalei

Hieremys annandalei

adequate filtration and some heating. Worshipped as a sacred animal in the ponds of Buddhist temples. Becomes tame quickly, even exhibiting begging behavior.
• *H. annandalei* (BOULENGER, 1903). Temple Turtle. Thailand, Kampuchea to Malayan Peninsula.

Hildebrandtia NIEDEN, 1907. Ornate Frogs. Taxon of doubtful taxonomic level within the Ranidae; considered either as an independent genus or as a subgenus of *Rana*. Tropical and subtropical Africa. Compact, egg-shaped (similar to *Pyxicephalus*). Larve to 9.5 cm, the tail long and pointed, the upper jaw without teeth.

For biological details refer to *Pyxicephalus*. Comes to the surface only after rainfall, when it breeds.
• *H. ornata* (PETERS, 1878). Ornate Frog. East and South Africa. To 5.5 cm. Dark brown with green and light brown stripes and spots. Belly shiny white, with 3 brown longitudinal stripes along the throat.

Hispaniolus: see *Chamaelinorops*, genus.

Holarchus: see *Oligodon*, genus.

Holarctic: The largest faunal kingdom in terms of area. It comprises most of the Northern Hemisphere, including areas from the subtropical to Arctic climatic zones. The Holarctic is divided into the Palearctic (Old World) and Nearctic (New World), with faunal groups that in Arctic latitudes are largely identical (holarctic), but southward they become increasingly different. There is not one species of reptile or amphibian with a holarctic distribution (i. e., found in both regions), but at the genus level there are several holarctic taxa, such as *Hydromantes*, *Bufo*, *Rana*, *Coluber*, and *Alligator*. Only the salamanders have endemic families which occur in both Old and New World Holarctic (Proteidae, Cryptobranchidae); other mainly holarctic families penetrate either into the Neotropic (Plethodontidae, Xenosauridae), the Orient (Salamandridae), or into the Neotropics as well as into the Orient (Anguidae). Such widely distributed families as Bufonidae, Hylidae, Ranidae, Emydidae, Testudinidae, Gekkonidae, Scincidae, Typhlopidae, Boidae, Colubridae, Crotalidae, and others have representatives in both Old and New Worlds. From among the largest and most advanced herpetotaxa only the Gymnophiona are completely absent from the Holarctic.

Holaspis GRAY, 1863. Sawtailed Lizards. Monotypic genus of the Lacertidae. Tropical Africa. In forests. Body strongly flattened. The broad tail has a row of sawtoothed scales on each side. Spiny scales are also present on the ventral sides of the toes. Lid windows indicated.

Dendrophilic, often behind loose tree bark. Feeds on various small arthropods. 2 eggs per clutch.

Should be kept in a rain-forest terrarium in which slightly larger temperature variations than normal prevail.
• *H. guentheri* (BOULENGER, 1887). Sawtailed Lizard. About 15 cm. Dorsum striped with black and yellow-green; belly orange; tail blue.

Holbrook, John Edward (1794-1871): American herpetologist, ichthyologist, and medical practitioner. *North American Herpetology* (3 volumes, 1836-1838); the second edition in 5 volumes was published in 1842 and forms the basis of North American herpetology.

Holbrookia GIRARD, 1851. Earless Lizards. Genus of the Iguanidae. Southwestern USA and Mexico. 4 species with numerous subspecies. Mainly in steppes. To 20 cm. Slender. Found in habitats similar to those occupied by *Callisaurus* and *Uma*. External ear openings absent (covered

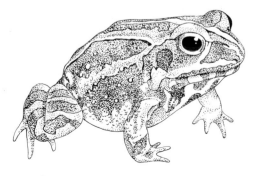

Hildebrandtia ornata

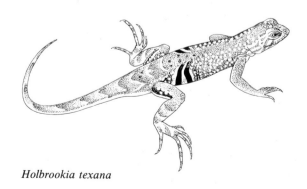

Holbrookia texana

Holbrookia maculata

with scales). Variably brown with numerous lighter dots and regularly spaced dark chevrons or bands. Two large, blue-black, white-edged vertical or oblique spots along middle of sides.

Diurnal ground-dwellers that feed mainly on arthropods. Egg-layers, up to 5 clutches (2-10 eggs) per year. For details on care refer to *Sceloporus*.

• *H. maculata* GIRARD, 1851. Lesser Earless Lizard. To 19 cm. Lower surface of tail without markings. Abdominal spots surrounded by bright blue in males. Smooth scales.

• *H. texana* (TROSCHEL, 1850). Greater Earless Lizard. To 20 cm. Ventral surface of tail with black crossbands. Abdominal spots just in front of hind legs long. Often placed in a separate genus or subgenus, *Cophosaurus*.

Holoaden MIRANDA-RIBEIRO, 1920. Genus of the Leptodactylidae. Coastal region of southeastern Brasil. 2 species. Related to *Eleutherodactylus*. In ·highlands. Externally very similar to *Zachaenus stejnegeri*. Pupil horizontal. Tympanum externally not visible. Fingers and toes free. Vocal sac absent.

Terrestrial. Eggs are deposited in damp substrate.

• *H. bradei* LUTZ, 1959
• *H. luederwaldti* MIRANDA-RIBEIRO, 1920.

Holodactylus BOETTGER, 1893. Genus of the Gekkonidae. Eastern Africa. 2 species in dry habitats. About 20 cm. Lids free. No adhesive lamellae. Ground-dwellers. Little known. See *Eublepharis*.

• *H. africanus* BOETTGER, 1893. Eastern Ethiopia to Kenya.

Hologerrhum GUENTHER, 1858. Monotypic genus of the Colubridae, Boiginae. Philippines. 36 cm. Burrowing ground snakes. Biology still unknown.

• *H. philippinum* GUENTHER, 1858. Brownish above, pink to red below; head with a yellow to salmon stripe along the lip and sometimes a black pattern.

Homalopsinae: Subfamily of the Colubridae. India through Indo-China and the Indo-Australian Archipelago to the coastal region of northern Australia; also southern China and the Philippines. 11 genera, about 35 species. In fresh water (rivers, lakes); follows human habitation (in rice paddies, cotton fields, and associated irrigation systems); also in brackish water such as river mouths and mangrove forests along coasts. Some genera (*Cerberus*, *Fordonia*) are also found in marine habitats along coastal regions as well as offshore. Related to Boiginae, but in contrast adapted to an aquatic mode of life. Possess open-grooved venom teeth of the opisthoglyphic type located in the posterior section of the upper jaw. Apparently the venom of these snakes is not particularly dangerous to humans, but it appears to be highly effective and specific for fish and crustaceans.

The majority of species are heavy-bodied. Some genera, e. g., *Enhydris*, *Cerberus*, and *Bitia*, are reminiscent of Hydrophiinae, particularly because of the thick head not clearly set off from the body. The head has tube-like nostrils that are located on top. They can be closed off by valves when diving, an adaptation to an aquatic mode of life. The small eyes also point upward. Usually plainly colored or with light and dark crossbands. The ventral scales and head scales correspond with typical Colubridae, except *Erpeton*, in which the ventral scales are reduced to dorsal scale size and are difficult to recognize due to their double keels. Tail round, except in *Bitia*.

Only a few species of *Enhydris* and *Homalopsis* ever haul out on to land to sun themselves, and locomotion out of the water is relatively awkward. Some genera, such as *Bitia*, *Fordonia*, and especially *Erpeton*, apparently never leave the water on their own. Crepuscular and nocturnal, feeding mainly on fish; *Enhydris* also takes frogs, while *Fordonia* and *Cerberus* also feed heavily on crustaceans. Live-bearers; give birth in water to 6-20 relatively large young.

Can be kept in an aqua-terrarium with large swamp or water sections or directly in an aquarium (*Erpeton*) with swamp and water plants as hiding places. Sea water—or at least additions of salt—is suggested for *Cerberus*, *Fordonia*, and other marine or brackish water species; the salt promotes proper health and reduces the risk of skin and metabolic diseases.

Due to its attractive coloration and ease of maintenance, *Homalopsis* is very popular, as is *Erpeton* because this genus is totally aquatic and has a peculiar shape. These two and a few others have been bred repeatedly.

Homalopsis KUHL, 1822. Asian False Water Boa. Monotypic genus of the Colubridae, Homalopsinae. Southern Burma throughout Indo-China and the Indo-Australian Archipelago (not to New Guinea). Frequently found in fresh water (irrigation systems, follows human habitation), but also do not avoid brackish mangrove forests. To 1.3 m. Massive head clearly set off from body, with normal head scutes. Dorsum covered with keeled scales. Back dark

Homalopsis buccata

brown, sharply delineated along sides from whitish yellow ventral area. More or less complete crossbands extend over the back and correspond in color to the abdominal region. The neck has a white band that is interrupted with a black patch over the vertebral column. The neckband can also be shaped like an inverted "V".

Homalopsis, more so than any other Homalopsinae, will sometimes haul out on land. The diet consists mainly of fish and frogs. Females give birth to 9-21 young.

These snakes should be housed in aqua-terrariums with large, well-planted water sections. If these snakes are to be kept in an aquarium, there must be a suspended easily accessible land section, proper ventilation, and a tight-fitting, sturdy cover of fine welded mesh for ventilation. Has been bred repeatedly. A hardy, durable terrarium animal with substantial longevity.
• *H. buccata* (LINNAEUS, 1758).

Home range: Area or areas occupied by an animal in the course of its life. This includes seasonal territories and permanent territories as well as the pathways used. In contrast to a territory, this region is not defended. However, in territorial species the home range is in fact part of the territory as such. For specimens in a terrarium the surrounding container forms the home range, which thus requires consideration of the environmental conditions needed by a particular species.

Homoiothermic: Maintaining the body temperature at a constant level. Birds and mammals are homoiothermic (endothermic or warm-blooded) since they produce body heat and possess temperature regulating mechanisms that enable these animals to maintain their body temperature more or less constant within narrow limits. Among the reptiles, the extinct Pterosauria were presumably homoiothermic (as has been suggested for dinosaurs), but all Recent

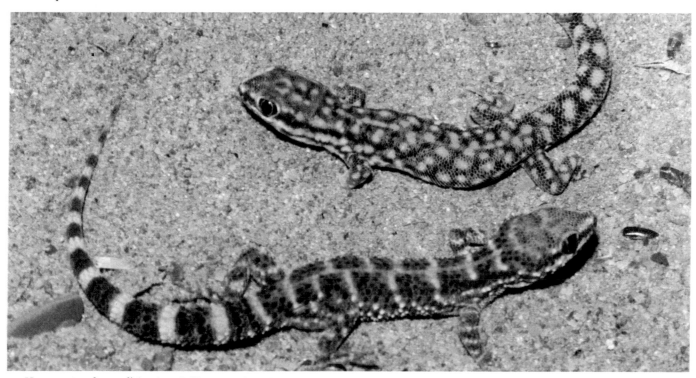

Homonota underwoodi (top) and *Homonota horrida* (bottom)

reptiles and amphibians are cold-blooded or poikilo-thermic.

Homonota GRAY, 1845. Genus of the Gekkonidae. South America. Now with about 10 species (originally only 2; some *Gymnodactylus* and *Wallsaurus* species now have been added). In relatively dry habitats. 5-10 cm. Gray-brown or brownish with dark markings. Tail barely snout-vent length, relatively thick.

Nocturnal ground-dwellers. For maintenance details refer to *Cyrtodactylus*.
▪ *H. darwini* BOULENGER, 1885. Uruguay, Argentina.

Homonym: Exact identity of scientific names for different taxa. Homonyms are not permitted under the rules of nomenclature and must be replaced.

Within the realm of the species a name is a homonym if the same name occurs more than once within the same genus. For instance, within the newt genus *Triturus* only one species can have the species name *vulgaris*.

There must be no identical names at the generic level. The introduction of a new genus requires a detailed search to determine whether the intended name has ever been used before for a Recent or fossil animal genus. The removal of homonyms is subject to the nomenclatural rule of priority. For instance, the name *Triton* was chosen by LAURENTI, 1768, for a newt genus, but it had earlier been used for a mollusc, so the new replacement name *Triturus* RAFINESQUE, 1815, is now being used. *Triturus* is the oldest available name, *Triton* LAURENTI being considered preoccupied and thus unavailable.

Since zoological and botanical nomenclature are independent of each other, the same name used for a genus of animal and a plant genus is not a homonym. Thus, *Dracaena* is valid for both animal and plant genera.

Homonyms also are not permitted among families, but the status of homonyms at higher taxonomic levels is still uncertain.

Homopholis BOULENGER, 1885. Velvety Geckos. Monotypic genus of the Gekkonidae. Southern Africa (according to some authors there is a second species on Madagascar). In dry habitats, often close to rivers. Barely 20 cm. Relatively strongly built. Pupils vertical. Scales small and smooth. Toes short and wide, with undivided adhesive lamellae. Inner toes without claw, other claws retractile.
▪ *H. wahlbergi* (SMITH, 1849). Wahlberg's Velvety Gecko. Gray to gray-brown, unicolored or with a dark reticulated pattern and usually with 6 light dorsal spots.

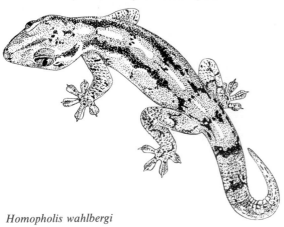

Homopholis wahlbergi

Homopus DUMERIL and BIBRON, 1835. Parrot-beaked Tortoises. Genus of the Testudinidae. Southern Africa. 4 species. Found in savannahs, steppes, and marginal desert regions. Carapace length to 16 cm. Carapace relatively flat, plastron rigid. The gular plates are wider than long. The upper jaw is often strongly bent and hook-like.

Activities are strongly dependent upon season and probably related to growth of certain succulent food plants. 1 or 2 eggs, incubation taking 210-240 days.

As for virtually all reptiles from dry habitats, they require heat, basking areas of adequate warmth, and a nocturnal temperature reduction. The substrate must be deep enough to permit burrowing. Longevity in captivity by and large limited, and there is virtually no data on captive reproduction. All species are endangered due to habitat destruction.

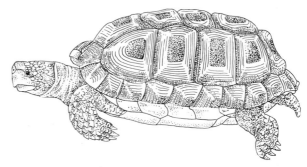

Homopus areolatus

Homopus areolatus

▪ *H. areolatus* (THUNBERG, 1887). Parrot-beaked Tortoise. Southeastern Cape Province. Forelimbs with 4 claws. Characteristic hook-like beak. Centers of dorsal scutes (areoles) light brown with dark to black margins.
▪ *H. boulengeri* (DUERDEN, 1906). Donner-weer Tortoise. Karroo Desert of Cape Province to Namaqualand. Forelimbs with 5 claws. Posterior margin of carapace smooth.
▪ *H. femoralis* (BOULENGER, 1888). Karroo Tortoise. Southeastern Cape Province. Forelimbs with 4 claws. Beak seldom hooked. Dorsally olive, scutes often with dark edges (as in *H. areolatus*). A large, sharp thorn on each upper thigh.
▪ *H. signatus* (SCHOEPFF, 1782). Speckled Tortoise. Cape Province and Namaqualand. Forelimbs with 5 claws. Pos-

terior margin of carapace markedly bent upward and serrated.

Homorelaps JAN. 1858. African Dwarf Garter Snakes. Genus of the Colubridae, Aparallactinae. More familiar as *Elaps*, an unavailable name. Formerly included in Elapidae. In desert-like, dry habitats. To 50 cm. Cylindrical, head not set off. Recognized by the characteristic dorsal stripe, yellowish in *H. dorsalis*, orange-red in *H. lacteus*. With (*H. lacteus*) or without (*H. dorsalis*) a variable yellow and black crossband pattern. *H. lacteus* juveniles are similar to adult *H. dorsalis*.

Mainly subterranean and nocturnal. Venomous. They often select termite mounds as hiding places. The diet consists of small lizards (geckos) and small snakes (*Leptotyphlops* and *Typhlops*). Egg-layers, 2 to 6 eggs laid in December.

They should be housed in a dry terrarium with a deep substrate layer. Provide a strong day/night temperature gradient and a cooler dormancy period according to native climatic conditions.
- *H. dorsalis* A. SMITH, 1849. South Africa, from the Transvaal to Natal and the Orange Free State. Blackish with a yellow dorsal stripe.
- *H. lacteus* (LINNAEUS, 1758). Cape Province and adjacent territories of South Africa. Banded with black and yellow, the stripe orange-red.

Hoplocephalus WAGLER, 1830. Genus of the Elapidae. Eastern Australia. 3 species. In savannahs (*H. bungaroides* in rocky areas with some shrubs). Head large, wide-mouthed, markedly set off from body. With a more or less distinctive crossband pattern (*H. bungaroides*, *H. stephensi*) or without markings except for head and neck (*H. bitorquatus*).

Arboreal, crepuscular and nocturnal venomous snakes. Excellent climbers. The diet consists mainly of frogs and lizards, plus some small mammals and birds. Live-bearers, 8-20 young.

Need a well-heated terrarium with ample climbing and bathing facilities. For details on care refer to the genus *Dendroaspis*. The venomous bite of these aggressive and fast snakes is very painful and can sometimes be fatal.
- *H. bitorquatus* (JAN, 1859). Pale-headed Snake. Queensland and New South Wales. Coastal region.

Hoplocercus FITZINGER, 1843. Prickle-tail Iguanas. Monotypic genus of the Iguanidae. Southern Brasil. In dry savannahs. To 15 cm. Compact. Reminiscent of *Uracentron*, but with unequal dorsal scales. Tail only about half snout-vent length, as wide as the body and with very strong, spiny, whorled scales. The only genus of the subfamily Tropidurinae where males have femoral pores.

Crepuscular ground-dwellers that dig their own tube-like burrows under bushes. The food is mainly arthropods, especially termites as well as some plant matter. Egg-layers.

Should be kept in a dry terrarium with a deep substrate layer (the lower layers should be damp) at day temperatures from 25 to 35° C. Basking lights are rarely used by these animals. Drop the nighttime temperature to about 20° C. Often reluctant to feed in captivity.
- *H. spinosus* FITZINGER, 1843. Dark brown with irregular laterally widened, dirty white crossbands.

Hoplodactylus FITZINGER, 1843. Genus of the Gekkonidae. New Zealand. 4 species in various habitats. 15-25 cm. Tail about equal to snout-vent length. Limbs in some species with conspicuously wide adhesive lamellae. Mainly brown with rather variable markings. Well-defined light and dark color changes.

Nocturnal. Ovoviviparous, 2 young. Heat requirements are relatively low. Apart from insects these geckos should also be given honey water.
- *H. granulatus* (GRAY, 1845). Brushland and forests. To 18 cm. Arboreal.
- *H. pacificus* (GRAY, 1842). Rocky areas, follows human habitation. The most common species of the genus. To 15 cm. Adaptable. Generally does well in captivity.

Hoplophryne BARBOUR and LOVERIDGE, 1928. Genus of the Microhylidae. East Africa. 2 species in perpetually damp mountain forests. Strongly flattened. Skin granular. Pupil horizontal. Fingers and toes free; fingertips slightly enlarged. Males with spinous nuptial pads on fingers, sides of chest, lower thighs, and feet. Males have excellent vocalizing and hearing abilities. Dark brown.

Lives among bushes and in trees. The large, unpigmented eggs are attached individually to phytothelms such as the axis of large leaves and hollow bamboo above small water accumulations. The larvae hatch at an advanced stage, fall into the water below, feed mainly carnivorously, and metamorphose shortly thereafter. For maintenance and possible breeding attempts these frogs should be kept in a densely planted montane rain-forest terrarium at temperatures from 20 to 24° C.
- *H. uluguruensis* BARBOUR and LOVERIDGE, 1928. Uluguru Mountains of Tanzania. 2.5 cm. Abdomen silvery.
- *H. rogersi* BARBOUR and LOVERIDGE, 1928. Usambara Mountains. 2.5 cm. Abdomen reticulated with brown and white.

Hoplurus: see *Oplurus*, genus.

Hormones: Various organic compounds that are formed in minute quantities in animals and plants. They are active substances controlling numerous metabolic processes and life functions. Central in importance in the hormone system is the hypophysis, where various hormones are formed and stored. Some of these control the hormone production in other endocrine glands, such as the thyroid gland producing thyroxin, which initiates metamorphosis in amphibians.

Hormonotus HALLOWELL, 1857. Monotypic genus of the Colubridae, Lycodontinae. Tropical Africa from Guinea eastward to Uganda. In tropical forests. 85 cm. Conspicuously set off trapezoidal head. Dorsum sandy yellow; abdomen whitish.

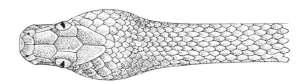

Hormonotus modestus

Nocturnal ground snakes that prey on small mammals and lizards, especially geckos. Maintain in a well-heated rain-forest terrarium.
- *H. modestus* (DUMERIL and BIBRON, 1854).

Hoya R. BR. Wax Flowers. Genus of the Asclepiadaceae. Southeast Asia, Australia. 200 species. Mostly climbing or hanging creeping plants. Evergreen, with tough leaves. 2.5 cm. Winter temperatures of 12° C., summer temperatures of 20° C. required. Reproduction by means of cuttings.
- *H. bella* HOOK. Non-twining, branched shrub. Recommended for hanging arrangements. Suitable for the rain-forest terrarium.
- *H. carnosa* (L.) R. BR. Wax Flower. A twining plant that requires less heat than the other species and is suitable for temperate terrariums. Robust, suitable for terrariums with larger climbing animals. Herbivorous species apparently avoid the hard leaves of this plant.

Hoya carnosa

Humidity: An essential factor in the terrarium's climate, closely related to soil humidity. The humidity should be higher at night (together with a temperature reduction) than during the day. For desert terrariums or animals from a steppe-like environment it is usually sufficient to keep a section of the substrate damp. After the illumination and the heating have been turned off, there is a resultant moderate increase in the humidity. Animals that originate from fog-shrouded deserts (e. g., the Namib) require a higher humidity since they are strongly adapted to frequent saturating dew and fog conditions. In the various types of rain-forest terrariums the humidity should be between 60% and 90% and even higher during the night. There must be regular spraying.

Electric air humidifiers can be employed in very large terrariums; they are operated briefly in the morning before the illumination is turned on. Also useful are small ventilators (fixed in such a position that they blow across a rather wet, porous substrate) or rain simulating devices (in the form of a perforated pipe or sprinkler system attached to the roof of the terrarium and connected to a freshwater faucet). Ideally such systems should be operated by an automatic timing device.

Heating the water is sufficient for aqua-terrariums or terrariums with a large water section. In centrally heated apartments the fresh air should be passed through water in order to avoid rapid desiccation of the container. Some-

times a heated water bowl placed underneath the terrarium can be effectively used to humidify the air around the terrarium.

Humidifying devices can also be coupled to a hygrostat in order to maintain a roughly constant humidity, but retaining a nocturnal increase in humidity.

Hurria DAUDIN, 1803. Monotypic genus of the Colubridae, Homalopsinae. Coastal regions of the Philippines. Very similar to the closely related genus *Cerberus* that is often considered to be synonymous.
- *H. microlepis* (BOULENGER, 1896). Rare.

Hybridization: Cross-breeding of taxa that differ genetically at least in one characteristic. Such cross-bred products (the hybrid) contain the combined genetic material from both parents. In appearance it can either be intermediate to both parents or be similar to one parent if a particular characteristic inherited is either dominant or recessive.

Hybridization occurs regularly under natural conditions between some taxa in those areas where their ranges overlap (called an intergradation zone) so that their systematic status as subspecies then becomes rather obvious. On the other hand, hybridization between different species is, as a rule, generally precluded due to differentially effective isolating mechanisms, such as different reproductive behaviors, different reproductive organ structures, and sterility and non-viability of hybrids. Nevertheless, natural hybrids are known to occur among amphibians and reptiles, including such combinations as crosses between certain toads, puff adders and Gaboon vapers, and between species in the genus *Clemmys*. Other hybrids are related to a special reproductive mechanism (as in the genera *Ambystoma*, *Rana*, and *Cnemidophorus*) where the occurrence of polyploidy is observed.

Hybridization attempts made with terrarium animals can often provide indications of relationships when the viability and fertility of hybrid generations are studied.

Hydrablabes BOULENGER, 1891. Genus of the Colubridae, Colubrinae. Kalimantan. 2 species in tropical rain forests. About 50 cm. Head not set off from body, with round snout and small eyes. Distinctly blunt tail end.

Burrowing ground snakes. Biology unknown. Should be kept in glass terrariums.
- *H. periops* (GUENTHER, 1872). Brownish olive with a yellow longitudinal stripe along each side.

Hydrelaps BOULENGER, 1896. Monotypic genus of the Hydrophiidae, Hydrophiinae. In waters between New Guinea and northern Australia, mainly in mangrove forests in coastal regions. To 50 cm. Yellow background color interrupted by dark rings or bands. Biology virtually unknown.
- *H. darwiniensis* BOULENGER, 1896.

Hydrodynastes FITZINGER, 1843. Monotypic genus of the Colubridae, Boiginae. Amazon Basin, Guyana, Surinam, and French Guiana. In tropical lowland forests. About 2 m. Back covered with smooth scales. Red-brown, covered with yellow-edged black rings arranged in pairs.

Ground snakes found close to water. The diet consists

Hydrodynastes bicinctus

mainly of frogs. Maintenance as for Natricinae, Group 2; use a well-heated terrarium.
• *H. bicinctus* (HERRMANN, 1804).

Hydrolaetare GALLARDO, 1963. Monotypic genus of the Leptodactylidae. Amazon Basin. Related to *Leptodactylus* and *Limnomedusa*. In rain forests (*selva*). Pupil vertical. Tympanum clearly visible. Fingers webbed at base, toes completely webbed.
   Ground-dwellers, presumably at times aquatic.
• *H. schmidti* (COCHRAN and GOIN, 1959). Colombia, near Leticia. To 10.5 cm. Gray-black.

Hydromantes GISTEL, 1848. Web-toed Salamanders, Grotto Salamanders. Genus of the Plethodontidae. California, USA (3 species) and Mediterranean Europe (2 species). 5 species total. In mountains. To 11 cm. Slender, with short snout; fingers and toes are webbed. The tongue is very long and can be suddenly thrust out up to ⅓ of the body length to catch prey. Males have slightly protruding upper jaw teeth. Yellow-brown to blackish, with metallic sprinkles or lichenose blotches.

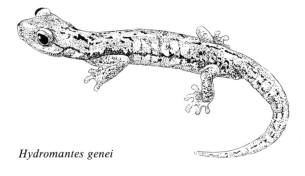

Hydromantes genei

The 3 American species have been placed in the genus *Hydromantoides* LANZA and VANNI, 1981, not yet accepted by most authorities.
   Mostly nocturnal ground-dwellers that lead a largely cryptic life in perpetually moist, cool, dark rocky crevices and caves. They are excellent climbers and can easily and quickly pursue their prey (spiders, small insects, centipedes, and small slugs) along smooth vertical walls. The European species are live-bearers; the American species lay eggs on land that develop directly into young (no aquatic larval stage).
   Must be kept at evenly low temperatures with very high humidity on nearly sterile substrates. A thin layer of gravel is barely covered with water and some flat stones are piled up in such a way as to form several dark caves. At the back of these caves sand is placed so that the caves are constantly wet and highly humid due to the capillary action of the water. The terrarium has to have a tightly fitting cover since these animals will escape through even the narrowest gap. The entire container is placed in a suitable refrigerator or in the basement at temperatures of up to 15° C. According to the origin of the particular specimens, the animals should be given a winter as well as a summer dormancy period. Strict compliance with this enhances breeding possibilities. The American species are protected.
• *H. genei* (SCHLEGEL, 1838). Sardinia.
• *H. italicus* DUNN, 1923. Southeastern France to Italian Adriatic coast, southward to Tuscany. 4 subspecies.
• *H. platycephalus* (CAMP, 1916). Mount Lyell Salamander. Sierra Nevada and Sequoia National Park, California. 1600 to 4400 m elevation.

Hydromantoides: see *Hydromantes*, genus.

Hydromedusa WAGLER, 1830. South American Snake-neck Turtles. Genus of the Chelidae. South America. 2 species. In various types of water. Carapace to 25 cm, flat, more or less keeled (especially in juveniles). Distinguished from *Chelodina* by nuchal scute being pushed back completely behind the marginal plates into the row of vertebral plates. The anterior edge of the intragular scute always reaches the anterior edge of the plastron.

The snake-like neck is used for snorkling and dabbling in the bottom or in mud. Carnivorous. Specimens should be kept in marginally heated aqua-terrariums or aquariums with land sections.

• *H. maximilianus* (MIKAN, 1820). Brasilian Snake-neck Turtle. Southeastern Brasil. Carapace smooth, a low keel present only in juveniles.

• *H. tectifera* COPE, 1869. Argentine Snake-neck Turtle. Southeastern Brasil, Paraguay, Uruguay, Argentina. Carapace in juveniles strongly keeled and with rough vertebral and costal scutes, becoming smoother with age. Head and neck with a light dark-edged longitudinal band.

Hydromedusa tectifera

Hydromedusa tectifera, male

Hydromedusa tectifera, female

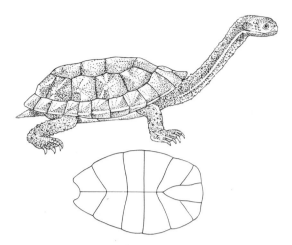

Hydromedusa tectifera

Hydromorphus PETERS, 1859. Genus of the Colubridae, Natricinae. Honduras to Costa Rica and Panama. 3 species. In waters of tropical lowland forests. Barely 1 m. Head fairly distinct, the eyes very small, and the nostrils pointing upward. Dorsal scales smooth. Brownish above.

Mainly aquatic. The principal diet is fish and frogs. Maintenance same as for Natricinae, Group 3, in a well-heated aqua-terrarium.
• *H. concolor* PETERS, 1859. Honduras and Costa Rica.

Hydrophiidae: Sea Snakes. Family of the Caenophidia. Subfamily Laticaudinae, 1 genus; subfamily Hydrophiinae, 14 genera with about 50 species. Indo-Pacific and adjacent tropical and subtropical seas; not native to the Atlantic. Only as strays in temperate waters. Maximum size 2.75 m. More or less strongly adapted to life in water, especially to the marine environment. Body cylindrical or substantially compressed, but always terminating in a rudder-like tail in the Hydrophiinae. All species have the ventral scales more or less reduced in size and approaching the size of the dorsal scales. A salt gland is present in the jaws and facilitates salt excretion.

The majority of the sea snakes have great difficulty moving on land, and some can no longer move on land at all. The diet consists mainly of fish, but there are also several food specialists feeding on particular fish species or on their eggs. Only the Laticaudinae have to move onto land to deposit their eggs; all Hydrophiinae give birth to live young in the water.

Sea snakes have proteroglyphic fangs. Their venom is mainly neurotoxic and is highly potent. Rare but fatal bites are quite possible. A polyvalent antiserum has been developed in Australia. Experiences vary on the lack of aggression and reluctance to bite among sea snakes hauled out onto land. It should be assumed that these snakes can use their fangs far more often than they really do, so they should not be handled. They are offered as food at local markets and the skin from many species is desired as leather.

When keeping these snakes in captivity, learning the proper food and feeding requirements and assuring a regular food supply present by far the greatest problems. Housing sea snakes in a spacious seawater aquarium is relatively simple in view of the advanced technology available to aquarists, yet sea snakes are rarely kept, since collecting

and transporting these snakes cause considerable trauma and mechanical damage leading rapidly to secondary infections. The highly specialized sea snakes of the subfamily Hydrophiinae can suffer severe internal injuries due to collapse of their abdominal cavity just by being hauled onto land. Because the abdominal muscles are reduced and weak, respiration becomes impaired when on land and they often simply suffocate. The somewhat less specialized species of the subfamily Laticaudinae are more likely to survive such stress and more often end up in the hands of hobbyists. Longevities in excess of 5 years are so far unknown. Based on experiences gained by marine biological laboratories, the chances of keeping Hydrophiidae for prolonged periods of time should be better.

Hydrophiinae: Rudder-tailed Sea Snakes. Subfamily of the Hydrophiidae. Mainly in coastal regions, and frequently in surf zones with possibilities of getting washed on shore. Sometimes found in brackish water, they even enter the lower reaches of rivers. *Hydrophis* is to some degree found in fresh water. *Pelamis* is found only on the high seas. Size and shape of the head are rather variable among the genera, as indeed is the overall appearance of many genera within this subfamily. The nostrils are located dorsally to facilitate breathing at the surface. The fangs of these snakes are behind smaller teeth that are arranged in one row. In most species the center of gravity is in the posterior half of the body, so swimming or resting motionless in water can be done effortlessly with the head erect. The body musculature has regressed to such an extent that most species can no longer crawl or breathe comfortably on land. Reduction of the ventral scales to a row of scales that

Hydrophiinae: Sea snake showing valvular nostrils

at best are only minimally wider (if at all) than the remaining body scales occurs in all genera except *Aipysurus* and *Emydocephalus*. The body scales are smooth or keeled to spinous; there are some very rough-skinned Hydrophiinae.

These aquatic, venomous snakes feed primarily on fish. The prey is paralyzed and killed by means of the extremely potent venom. They give birth in water to a few (2-6) rather large (half adult size), fully developed juveniles.

Most systematists recognize 14 genera: *Acalyptophis, Aipysurus, Disteira, Emydocephalus, Enhydrina, Ephalophis, Hydrophis, Hydrelaps, Kerilia, Kolpophis, Lapemis, Parahydrophis, Pelamis,* and *Thalassophis.*

Hydrophis LATREILLE, 1802. Banded Sea Snakes. Genus of the Hydrophiidae, Hydrophiinae. From India to China and Japan, southward to Australia. About 25 species, some polytypic. The largest genus of sea snakes. Found in coastal areas as well as on coral reefs and in mangrove forests. Some species (*H. obscurus* and others) are also found in brackish water and even in freshwater river deltas; *H. semperi* is the only hydrophiid found only in fresh water. 50 cm to 2.75 m (*H. spiralis* is the largest species of the Hydrophiidae). The small, indistinct head is followed by a slender neck section that gradually merges into the massive posterior part of the body. Most species have a more or less conspicuous crossbanded pattern against a lighter background.

The venom is highly potent; fatal bites by *H. ornatus* are documented.

• *H. cyanocinctus* DAUDIN, 1803. Blue-banded Sea Snake. Persian Gulf to Japan.

• *H. fasciatus* (SCHNEIDER, 1799). Banded Sea Snake. Indian Ocean and Indo-Australian waters. 2 subspecies.

• *H. semperi* GARMAN, 1881. Fresh water; Lake Taal in Luzon, Philippines. Possibly only a subspecies of *H. cyanocinctus.*

Hydrops WAGLER, 1830. Genus of the Colubridae, Natricinae. Amazon Basin. 2 subspecies. 0.5 to 1.15 m; females of *H. marti* are twice the size of the males. Head small, not set off from body. Nostrils and small eyes point upward. Smooth dorsal scales. Dorsum brown to reddish with black crossbands.

Hydrophis cyanocinctus

Hydrophis klossi

Hydrophis cyanocinctus

Aquatic, inhabiting densely overgrown waters. The diet consists mainly of fish, frogs, and aquatic caecilians. For details on care refer to Natricinae, Group 3. Keep in well-heated and planted aqua-terrariums.

• *H. marti* (WAGLER, 1824). Upper Amazon region (Peru, Colombia, and northwestern Brasil). 2 subspecies.

• *H. triangularis* (WAGLER, 1824). Eastern Peru to French Guiana and Trinidad. 6 subspecies.

Hydrosaurus KAUP, 1828. Sailfin Dragons. Genus of the Agamidae. Indonesia, New Guinea. 3 species of doubtful validity. To more than 1 m. Slightly compressed, with a long tail. High occipital and dorsal crests as well as a very high crest supported by vertebral processes on the anterior portion of the tail. Males have femoral and preanal pores. The toes have lobate skin folds.

Hydrosaurus live close to water and when threatened will flee into water. The diet consists mainly of arthropods and small vertebrates. Egg-layers.

These large lizards require very large, damp terrariums with a large water bowl and climbing facilities. Day temperatures can vary from 25 to 30° C., with only a slight nighttime reduction. They will take pieces of meat or raw fish, as well as eggs and sometimes also plant material (lettuce, fruit, and similar items).

• *H. amboinensis* (SCHLOSSER, 1788). Sailfin Dragon, Soa Soa. Indonesian islands to New Guinea. Easily to 1 m.

Hygiene: Feces, shed skin, dead plant leaves, and similar items must be removed regularly from a terrarium. Only in well-planted terrariums with only a few small specimens can feces be biologically reduced on the ground. Food and water containers must be kept clean. Diseased animals must be removed immediately and transferred into quarantine. Frequent transfers of animals between terrariums

Hydrosaurus amboinensis

should be avoided. Diseases can also be transferred by the keeper or through escaped food animals. Mite infestations have to be eradicated without delay, even if it is only a marginal infestation (mites are disease vectors), so all new arrivals must be treated for mites.

Personal hygiene must also prevail at all times, although the dangers of infections from reptiles or amphibians to humans are far less than from warm-blooded animals.

Hydrosaurus amboinensis

Hyla LAURENTI, 1768. Treefrogs. Genus of the Hylidae.
Highest concentration of species is mainly in the Neotropics of Central and South America east of the Andes; there
are about 20 species in the Nearctic, plus a few species in
Eurasia. If the Australasian *Litoria* (often included in *Hyla*)
is removed, there are still more than 230 species in *Hyla*.
Many unusual or atypical species have been placed in
smaller genera, and it is likely that the species remaining
in *Hyla* are not all closely related. The size is highly variable. The skin is smooth or (especially in the abdominal region) granular. Pupil horizontal. Iris usually copper or
bronze colored, in the *erythromma* and *uranochroa* com-
plexes bright red, in *H. crepitans* emerald green. The fingers usually are webbed about halfway up; in the *eximia*
Group the fingers are free, while in the *boans* and *miliaris*
Groups the fingers are completely webbed. Toes in all species are webbed at least halfway up from the base. Adhesive discs on tips of fingers and toes always well-developed.

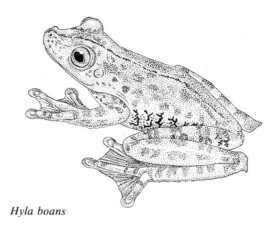

Hyla boans

Hyla cinerea

Hyla arenicolor

Vocal sac usually unpaired and large; absent only in species
that breed in flowing waters (*bistincta, mixomaculata*, and
taeniopus Groups). Mostly yellow, green, or brown above.

Predominantly crepuscular and nocturnal tree-dwellers
that stay close to water. Some specialized forms utilize very
small water accumulations in bromeliads and hollow logs
and branches as habitats for their larvae (*bromeliacia* and
zeteki Groups). On the other hand, species from treeless
and brushless regions lead a more diurnal and crepuscular,
palustral, or even semiaquatic life (*H. albomarginata, H. la-*

Hyla arborea

Hyla cinerea

Hyla crepitans

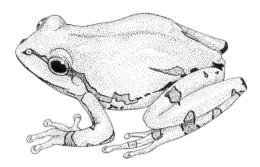

Hyla eximia

Hyla gratiosa

Hyla cipoensis

Hyla crucifer

Hyla lanciformis

bialis) or even are active in bright sunlight (*H. arenicolor* likes to bask on hot, completely dry rocks).

As far as known, all *Hyla* have free-swimming larvae. In about half of the species the larvae develop in standing waters; the others develop in cooler, nutrient-poor, oxygen-rich flowing waters. *H. boans* and *H. faber* engage in brood care by digging crater-like, water-filled spawning pits 20-30 cm in diameter and 10 cm deep at the edge of standing water.

Arboreal species are best kept in well-planted tall terrari-

Hyla gratiosa

Hyla microcephala

ums with ample dark hiding places. There must be adequate ventilation. Species from cloud forests require a constantly high humidity that can be achieved by spraying with rain water and placing shallow, water-filled containers inside the terrarium. Inhabitants of the *selva* are used to humidity gradients and will select a place in the terrarium that suits them. Palustral species require semi-moist terrariums with a large water section and climbing facilities such

Hyla meridionalis

Hyla punctata

Hyla regilla

Hyla regilla

Hyla punctata

Hyla (Osteopilus) septentrionalis

Hyla pulchella

as dead branches and robust swamp plants. *Hyla* species from semiarid regions are most suitably kept in an almost dry terrarium in a sunny location with a shallow water bowl.

Most *Hyla* species feed on dry insects and their larvae, the greatest feeding stimulus coming from flies. Mealworms, waxmoth larvae, and similar items should be given on the end of a thin, flexible wire or in a suspended con-

Hyla (Osteopilus) septentrionalis

Hyla smithi

Hyla (Osteopilus) septentrionalis

tainer with a climbing pole for the food animals. Most specimens will also quickly learn to search along the bottom for food. Robust predatory species such as *H. boans*, *H. crepitans*, and *H. septentrionalis* may display cannibalistic tendencies toward smaller specimens.

The males of many *Hyla* species can be a nuisance because of their loud, prolonged calls during the evening and night hours.

Be careful when touching these frogs, because the skin secretions of many species cause skin irritations of the mucous membranes. Never pass your hand near your eyes, nose, or mouth after handling a treefrog.

Breeding requires spacious terrariums with a near-natural setup. Most suitable are greenhouses or outdoor enclosures with screen covers. More difficult is the rearing of larvae adapted to flowing water, which require particularly oxygen-rich water. *Hyla* larvae feed on detritus and plank-

Hyla rosenbergi

tonic and attached microscopic plants and animals, thus they do not require supplementary food if they are in a sufficiently brightly lighted location. If the larvae are to be reared indoors an artificial diet can be offered consisting of powdered milk, wheat bran, ground-up wheat germ, and dried yeast, mixed together with cod liver oil and slightly diluted with water. Newly metamorphosed frogs can initially take only fruitflies, aphids, and springtails, which may be difficult to provide in sufficiently large quantities.

H. boans, H. cinerea, H. crepitans, H. dominicensis, H. pulchella, H. regilla, and numerous other species have been bred.

▪ *H. andersoni* BAIRD, 1854. Pine Barrens Treefrog. Eastern USA, disjunct distribution. 5 cm. Bright green, flanks purplish brown, set off from back by a cream stripe.

▪ *H. arborea* (LINNAEUS, 1758). European Treefrog. Palearctic. Polytypic. Variable, mostly green, black stripe through eye, abdomen white.

▪ *H. arenicolor* COPE, 1866. Canyon Treefrog. Southwestern USA and western Mexico. 6 cm. Dorsally brownish, with dark brown spots.

▪ *H. boans* (LINNAEUS, 1758). Central and South America, *selva*. 13 cm. Reddish to dark brown.

▪ *H. bromeliacia* SCHMIDT, 1933. Atlantic region of southern Mexico to Honduras, mountains. 3 cm. Light brown.

▪ *H. chinensis* GUENTHER, 1858. Southeastern China. 4 cm. Flanks and thighs with dark spots. Tympanum within a triangular dark patch. Common.

▪ *H. cinerea* (SCHNEIDER, 1799). Green Treefrog. Southern USA. 6.5 cm. Bright green with a white band along the sides.

▪ *H. crepitans* WIED, 1824. Central and South America, *selva* and *montana*. 7 cm. Light brown, gray-white when at rest. Iris bright emerald green.

Hyla vasta

▪ *H. crucifer* WIED, 1838. Spring Peeper. Eastern North America. 3.5 cm. Brown with a large dark brown X-shaped dorsal marking.

▪ *H. eximia* BAIRD, 1854. Mountain Treefrog. Central Mexican mountains to southwestern USA. 4 cm. Bright olive green with dark brown spots; flanks brown. Common.

Hyla (Osteopilus) septentrionalis

Hyla vasta

• *H. septentrionalis* BOULENGER, 1882. Cuban Treefrog. Cuba, Bahamas, Cayman Islands, southern Florida (introduced). 9 cm. Olive-brown to green. Skin of head fused to skull. Often put in genus *Osteopilus*.

• *H. taeniopus* GUENTHER, 1901. Atlantic region of Mexico, mountains. 7 cm. Variably olive green or brown with irregular dark spots; legs with dark crossbands.

• *H. uranochroa* COPE, 1876. Costa Rica and Panama. Montane rain forests. 4 cm. Olive, abdomen yellow orange, thin white line along flanks. Iris bright red.

• *H. zeteki* GAIGE, 1929. Central America, *montana*. 2.5 cm. Golden. Iris red brown. Head broad and snout blunt.

• *H. faber* WIED, 1821. Brasil, Argentina. 9 cm. Brownish with a dark median stripe and some spots along back. Arms and legs with cross stripes.

• *H. labialis* PETERS, 1863. Colombia. 4.5 cm. Bright green, sparingly covered with black dots. Ventral area conspicuously granular.

• *H. meridionalis* BOETTGER, 1874. Mediterranean countries. In contrast to *H. arborea*, without a dark stripe on the sides.

• *H. miliaria* (COPE, 1886). Central America to Colombia. 10.5 cm. Brown, with an inconspicuous dark pattern. Fingers and toes completely webbed.

• *H. regilla* BAIRD and GIRARD, 1852. Pacific Treefrog. Southwestern Canada, western USA to Baja California. 5 cm. Variably green or brown, sometimes with darker spots. Dark stripe through eye.

• *H. rubra* LAURENTI, 1768. Amazon Basin, *selva*. 4 cm. Silver-gray with fine dark dots. Common.

Hyla (Ololygon) sp.

Hyla versicolor

Hylactophryne LYNCH, 1968. Barking Toads. Genus of the Leptodactylidae. Southwestern USA and Mexico. 2 species, in part polytypic. Related to *Ischnocnema* and *Eleutherodactylus*. Toad-like in shape but with smooth skin. Mouth large. Pupil horizontal. Tympanum clearly visible. A dorso-lateral skin fold that also connects the tympanums. Forelimbs conspicuously long. Fingers and toes free, first finger longer than second. Loud barking voice.

If threatened they will inflate the body. These are predatory terrestrial frogs that rarely leave their hiding places (caves, crevices). The eggs are deposited in damp soil and development proceeds without a free-swimming larval stage.
• *H. augusti* (DUGES, 1879). To 9.5 cm. Brown with dark spots.

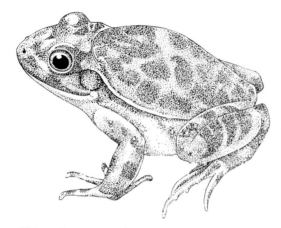

Hylactophryne augusti

Hylagama MERTENS, 1924. Monotypic genus of the Agamidae. Kalimantan. Known only from the type locality.
• *H. borneensis* MERTENS, 1924.

Hylambates: see *Kassina*, genus.

Hylarana TSCHUDI, 1838. Taxon of disputed systematic level within the Ranidae. Considered either as an independent genus or a subgenus of *Rana*. Africa (type species: *R. erythraea*) to tropical Asia, 80 species or more. In rain forests, montane rain forests, and wet savannahs. Pointed snout; usually with dorso-lateral skin folds. Clearly visible tympanum. Large adhesive discs on tips of fingers and toes, so strongly reminiscent of *Amolops;* in contrast to that genus, males have upper arm glands and the larvae have several conspicuous glandular areas in different parts of the body and a fringed lower lip.

Forest-dwellers are more or less good climbers and often remain in the proximity of flowing waters. The savannah-dwellers lead a semiaquatic life in ponds and swamps.

Forest species should be kept in a rain-forest terrarium with a water section (use a pump to achieve adequate water circulation). The savannah species can be kept in tropical aqua-terrariums. Also refer to *Rana*.
• *H. albolabris* (HALLOWELL, 1856). Rain forests in western and central Africa. To 7.5 cm. White upper lip.
• *H. chalconota* (SCHLEGEL, 1837). Tropical southeastern Asia and offshore islands. 2 subspecies. In rain forests and montane rain forests; prefers splash zone of mountain streams, water falls. To 7.5 cm. Bronze colored. White up-

per lip.
• *H. lepus* (ANDERSSON, 1903). Western and central Africa. Rain forests and gallery forests near rivers. To 10 cm. Skin granular; without dorso-lateral skin fold.

Hylidae: Treefrogs. Family of the Salientia, suborder Procoela. Neotropics (31 genera and more than 300 species), Australasia (genera *Litoria*, *Nyctimystes*, etc., with about 100 species), Nearctic (genera *Acris*, *Pseudacris*, *Limnaoedus* with 10 species), and Palearctic (only genus *Hyla* with about 6 species). Hylids are absent from Africa (except North Africa) and from India to southeast Asia. There are a total of about 37 genera (many split off from *Hyla*), with an estimated 450 species, of which *Hyla* (without *Litoria*) includes more than 230 species. The taxonomy is very complex and far from being settled.

The hylids are characterized by the presence of procoelic vertebrae, a disc-like intermediate joint (intercalary plate) in fingers and toes between the last and the penultimate joint, as well as by a modified pectoral girdle. The tips of the fingers and toes have more or less obvious adhesive discs, and the fingers and toes are more or less webbed. Most hylids have horizontal pupils (vertical in the genera *Agalychnis*, *Nyctimystes*, *Pachymedusa*, and *Phyllomedusa*). The tympanum in the majority of species is externally distinctly set off and clearly visible. The vocal sac as a rule is unpaired. However, in some species it is in two parts, and it is absent in a few species.

Most hylids are arboreal, including those that are specialized to live on epiphytic bromeliads. However, there are also terrestrial, palustral, and semiaquatic species among the hylids. As far as known, the hylids (except *Cryptobatrachus*, *Hemiphractus*, some *Gastrotheca*, and a few others) have free-swimming larvae that develop in water. Some genera (*Anotheca*, *Fritziana*, *Nyctimantis*) and those *Hyla* species of the *bromeliacia* and *zeteki* Groups are specialized to use water accumulated in bromeliads, hollow trees and branches, bamboo stumps, and similar locations.

Virtually all *Hyla* are ideally suited for terrarium care. Numerous species are bred regularly.

The hylid genera are arranged into the following subfamilies:
• Phyllomedusinae: *Agalychnis*, *Pachymedusa*, *Phyllomedusa*.
• Hemiphractinae: *Hemiphractus*.
• Amphignathodontine: *Amphignathodon*, *Anotheca*, *Cryptobatrachus*, *Flectonotus*, *Fritziana*, *Gastrotheca*, *Nototheca*, *Nyctimantis*, *Stephania*.
• Hylinae: *Acris*, *Allophryne*, *Aparashenodon*, *Aplostodiscus*, *Argenteohyla*, *Calyptahyla*, *Corythomantis*, *Hyla*, *Hylopsis*, *Limnaoedus*, *Litoria*, *Nyctimystes*, *Osteocephalus*, *Phrynohyas*, *Phyllodytes*, *Plectrohyla*, *Pseudacris*, *Pternohyla*, *Ptychohyla*, *Smilisca*, *Sphaenorhynchus*, *Trachycephalus*, *Triprion*.

Hylodes FITZINGER, 1826 (= *Elosia* TSCHUDI, 1838). Genus of the Leptodactylidae. Venezuela (*H. duidensis*) and southeastern Brasil. About 9 species. Related to *Megaelosia* and *Crossodactylus*. 3 to 4.5 cm. Skin in most species smooth, some with warts. Tympanum clearly visible. Fingers and toes free but with skin folds, tips enlarged. Males of nearly all species with paired vocal sacs.

▪ *H. aspera* (MUELLER, 1924). 4.2 cm. Skin with warts.

▪ *H. lateristrigata* (BAUMANN, 1912). 4 cm. Skin granular, with conspicuous light-colored dorso-lateral longitudinal folds.

Hylopsis WERNER, 1894. Described as a monotypic genus from South America, this taxon is now considered to be a *Centrolenella* and is involved in a nomenclatural tangle of priority with that name. Will eventually be suppressed or will replace *Centrolenella*.

Hylorina BELL, 1843. Monotypic genus of the Leptodactylidae. Southern Chile. Related to *Batrachyla*, *Eupsophus*, and *Thoropa*, but externally more reminiscent of the hylid genus *Phyllomedusa*. Inhabits moist subtropical forests. Pupil vertical. Fingers and toes extremely long and thin, tips not enlarged, without webbing. Tympanum clearly visible.

Ground-dwellers. Biology still largely unknown.

▪ *H. sylvatica* BELL, 1843. Chile southward to Valdivia. To 6 cm. Emerald green with dorso-lateral bronze-colored longitudinal stripes.

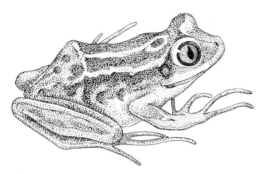

Hylorina sylvatica

Hyloscirtus PETERS, 1882. Monotypic genus of the Hylidae. Colombia. Presumably inhabits bromeliads in the *montana*. Without distinct tympanum. Fingers and toes short, fingers webbed at base only, toes up to ⅔ of their length. No natural history data available.

▪ *H. bogotensis* (PETERS, 1882). Vicinity of Bogota and Province of Cauca, Colombia. 5 cm. Dorsum with black dots against a yellow-brown background.

Hymenochirus BOULENGER, 1896. Dwarf African Clawed Frogs. Genus of the Pipidae. Tropical West Africa, Zaire to Nigeria and Cameroons. 4 species, in part polytypic. To 4 cm. Flattened. Skin granular. Head small and

pointed. Inner three toes with claws. Fingers and toes webbed. In contrast to *Pseudhymenochirus*, eyelids absent. As a significant exception among frogs, *Hymenochirus* (also *Pseudhymenochirus*) possesses a hyoid bone. Teeth are absent. Males are easily recognized by the well-developed postaxillary gland immediately behind the forelegs. During the breeding season they also give off clicking sounds. Dorsum gray-brown with irregular light sprinkles and dark spots. Abdomen whitish. Larvae chunky, with a dorsal mouth. Adults and larvae aquatic. The male clasps the female in her pelvic region; the sex products are given off by the animals while lying on their backs at the surface.

Must be kept in aquariums with a low water level at temperatures between 22 and 27° C. Small tanks are sufficient. Aeration is not required, since these frogs breathe atmospheric air. Usually they remain close to the bottom but do not stir up the substrate and are suitable for planted

Hymenochirus curtipes

Hymenochirus curtipes

Hymenochirus curtipes

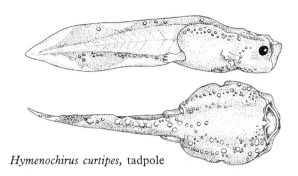

Hymenochirus curtipes, tadpole

tanks and even community aquariums. Ample hiding places should be available in the form of flowerpot halves, well-soaked and leached roots, and rocks. The diet should consist of tubifex worms, mosquito larvae, water fleas (daphnia), whiteworms, and small earthworms.

These little frogs will readily breed in captivity, particularly when stimulated with cool (15° C.) fresh water. Keep the water temperature after spawning at 25 to 27° C. Since the adults will eat their own eggs and young, the spawning pair will have to be removed immediately after spawning. Usually only those eggs floating on the surface will develop normally. The larvae hatch on the second or third day; they will immediately swim to the surface and hang there on water plants and the sides of the aquarium for about 6 days. Once the larvae start to swim freely they become predators, initially taking only the smallest food items, but these have to be offered in large quantities. On the first to fifth days offer ciliates, followed by rotifers, *Artemia* nauplii, and finally cyclops. Metamorphosis occurs in 60 to 75 days, depending upon water temperatures.

▪ *H. boettgeri* (TORNIER, 1896). Nigeria and Cameroons to Zaire.

▪ *H. curtipes* NOBLE, 1924. Lower Congo Basin. Skin finely granular.

Hymenoptera: Order of the Insecta. The bees, wasps, and ants. Often one of the major components among the insects caught as meadow plankton. The larger wasps, bumblebees, and bees are eaten without problems by some of the larger agamids. Honey bees (*Apis mellifica*) should not be caught. However, if honey bees should be available from a bee keeper they are excellent food for many lizards

Hymenoptera: A wasp, *Vespula*

Hymenoptera: Bee pupae

and large amphibians if they are first permitted to sting into a soft cloth to remove the spine. Drone larvae are also very good food for many reptiles. Ants are of importance to some highly specialized feeders among terrarium animals.

Hynobiidae: Hynobid Salamanders. Family of the Caudata. Eastern Palearctic; largest diversity in China and Japan. Together with Cryptobranchidae the most primitive of recent salamanders and newts. The teeth are in an obvious V-position in the roof of the mouth. Fertilization, in contrast to nearly all other Caudata (except Cryptobranchidae), is external, the female depositing 2 egg clusters in the water that are then fertilized by the male (except genus *Ranodon*).

The larval stages are aquatic, and neoteny occurs more or less regularly. Metamorphosed animals are largely terrestrial, except during the often very short breeding period. They are rapid, eager feeders. Most species live long and well in captivity and will also breed with some degree of regularity.

Systematic arrangement of Hynobiidae:

▪ Subfamily Hynobiinae, with the genera *Batrachuperus, Hynobius, Onychodactylus,* and *Pachypalaminus.*

▪ Subfamily Ranodontinae, with only the genus *Ranodon.*

Recently several other genera of uncertain status have been described: *Liuia, Pachyhynobius, Paradactylon.*

Hynobius TSCHUDI, 1838. Genus of the Hynobiidae. Eastern Palearctic; greatest species diversity in Japan (12 species). 18 mostly monotypic species. 4 fingers, 5 (rarely 4) toes. Larvae morphologically of still-water type (high, relatively short tail). Dorsal crest of tail extending onto anterior dorsal region. 3 pairs of well-developed external gills.

5 species groups can be distinguished within the genus on the basis of the shape of the metamorphosed animals, habitat occupied, and distribution:

▪ *nebulosus* Group (with *H. abei, H. dunni, H. nebulosus, H.*

tsuensis). Southern Japan. Long tail that is laterally flattened, with a more or less high dorso-ventral skin fold. Breeds only in still water.

• *lichenatus* Group (with *H. lichenatus, H. nigrescens, H. retardus, H. sadoensis*). Central and northern Japan. Tail long, laterally flattened. Reproduces in creeks, natural springs, ponds, lakes. Egg clusters very large, with longitudinal grooves.

• *naevius* Group (with *H. kimurai, H. naevius, H. okiensis, H. sonani, H. stejnegeri*). Southern Japan, Taiwan. Tail short and rounded. Reproduces only in flowing water over a gravel and rubble substrate.

• *chinensis* Group (with *H. chinensis, H. leechi, H. shihi*). China. Not very specialized. A tendency toward neoteny. Horny claws on fingers and toes. Reproduction occurs in different types of aquatic habitats.

• *keyserlingi* Group (only *H. keyserlingi*). From Ural Mountains to Siberia and northern Japan. Only 4 toes. Deviates also in coloration from all other species and often considered as representative of a separate genus, *Salamandrella* DYBOWSKI, 1870. Reproduces in still waters.

As a rule these animals move toward the spawning waters immediately after the snow has melted. Spawning and fertilization occur during more or less close cloacal contact of the partners. Each of the 2 egg clusters (tubes) can contain up to 60 eggs, but usually less. Soon after the sex products have been given off the animals return to a largely terrestrial life, but remain close to water.

Hynobius species become active at a few degrees above freezing, but also survive without problems in summer heat to 25° C. Many *Hynobius* species attain considerable longevities in captivity (*H. naevius*, 17 years). Ideally they should be kept in a damp moss and rock terrarium (the bottom barely covered with water) in a location that is not too bright (morning and late afternoon sun excellent). *Hynobius* species have been bred repeatedly, but to develop a full complement of eggs they need a varied diet and a cold winter dormancy period (1-5° C.).

• *H. keyserlingi* (DYBOWSKI, 1870). 12 cm. Dorsum bronze-colored, laterally with a black marbled pattern over a light brown background. A typical, common *taiga* species.

• *H. lichenatus* BOULENGER, 1883. Northern Honshu, Japan. 11 cm. Blackish, with a net-like gray-green pattern.

• *H. naevius* (TEMMINCK and SCHLEGEL, 1838). Southern Japan, disjunct distribution at 500 to 1000 m elevation. 14 cm. Black some with small bluish spots.

• *H. nebulosus* (TEMMINCK and SCHLEGEL, 1838). Central and southern Japan. 2 subspecies. Lowlands and foothills. 10 cm. Yellow-brown.

• *H. nigrescens* STEJNEGER, 1907. Central Japan, from lowlands to 2500 m elevation. 15 cm. Dark brown or bluish.

• *H. retardatus* DUNN, 1923. Hokkaido, Japan, at 0 to 1000 m elevation. 14 cm (rarely to 18.5 cm). Dark olive.

Hyophryne CARVALHO, 1954. Monotypic genus of the Microhylidae. Brasil. Related to *Stereocyclops*. Compact, strongly flattened. Natural history unknown.

• *H. histrio* CARVALHO, 1954. Bahia. Dorsum yellow with a dark pattern; ventrum black with light spots.

Hyperoliidae: see Rhacophoridae, family.

Hyperolius RAPP, 1842. Reed Frogs. Genus of the Rhacophoridae. Sometimes considered as representative of a separate family, Hyperoliidae. Africa south of the Sahara, Madagascar. More than 140 species, many poorly understood because of their great variability, often with several color phases dependent upon age and sex. In more or less open areas, such as brushland, wet and dry savannahs, and also found in rain forests and agricultural land. Snout-vent length only a few cm. Pupil horizontal (in contrast to the related genus *Afrixalus*). Fingers and toes webbed, with adhesive discs at their tips. Males have strongly inflatable unpaired vocal sacs (visible as a gular "plate" when at rest). The call consists of a metallic short and sharp sound given

Hyperolius marmoratus taeniatus

Hyperolius fusciventris burtoni

Hyperolius marmoratus

Hyperolius marmoratus taeniatus

erilinguis) or on submerged water plant leaves facing the surface (e. g., *H. nasutus, H. marmoratus, H. viridiflavus*). *H. pusillus* deposits its eggs between waterlily leaves pushed over each other. In those species that attach their eggs above water, the newly hatched larvae will then fall into the water below while eggs that have fallen into the water before the larvae have hatched are inhibited from further development. Most *Hyperolius* species are easily kept in captivity and will breed regularly. *H. nasutus* is a specialized mosquito feeder and thus somewhat difficult to keep.

They should be housed in a densely planted tropical swamp terrarium with some submerged water plants in the water section. The best food includes small insects such as fruitflies and springtails. The diet should be supplemented occasionally with some fruit. Breeding attempts initially are sometimes difficult since potential partners are sometimes not recognized as belonging to the same species due to their highly variable coloration. Before breeding is attempted the animals should be kept somewhat drier for awhile (water drained and bathing dish removed), then to trigger breeding behavior the rainy season is imitated. A popular spawning site is *Pistia stratiotes* (water lettuce). After the yolk sac has been absorbed the larvae are fed as suggested for *Afrixalus*. During metamorphosis provide a low water level (only a few mm). Since some species have been bred in captivity for several generations, certain genetic degeneration symptoms (probably as a manifestion of deficiencies while in captivity) have appeared, e. g., retarded growth, crippling, changes in behavior patterns, and increased mortalities among eggs and larvae.

• *H. argus* PETERS, 1854. East Africa. 3 cm. Males green with light dorso-lateral stripe; females gray-brown with

Hyperolius sp.

off in rapid succession (often deafening when in unison with other specimens). Males of many species retain juvenile coloration, often with characteristic bright yellow or white dorso-lateral stripes. Females and some males are substantially different in coloration, usually with a conspicuously patterned dorsal area. Larve elongated. Tail delicate, terminating in a point, posteriorly highly pigmented in some species. Lower lip flat, V-shaped (in contrast to *Afrixalus*).

Most species inhabit shore vegetation in the shallow regions of lakes and river. If these areas dry up the animals withdraw into their hiding places. Although they often occur in large number, each male requires his own little territory that is acoustically and optically marked and if need be is defended against intruders. During the day these animals may sit for hours in the sun, but the main activity periods fall in the hours of dusk and darkness. *H. horstocki* is known for the fact that it moves to *Zantedeschia* blossoms (arum plants), takes on the coloration of its surroundings, and catches the small insects that are attracted to the flower for pollination.

Hyperolius species do not build bubblenests as do many of the other Rhacophoridae. They attach their eggs either above water on a solid substrate (e. g., *H. concolor, H. tub-*

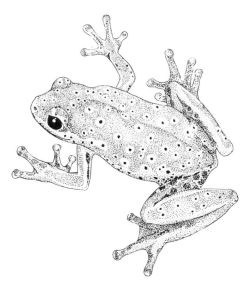

Hyperolius marmoratus marginatus

Hyperolius sp.

large black-edged spots.

• *H. concolor* (HALLOWELL, 1844). 3 subspecies. Tropical western and central Africa. 4 cm. Variable. Yellow-brown with dark dorsal spot or dark longitudinal bands, also unicolored green.

• *H. fusciventris* PETERS, 1876. West Africa. 3 subspecies. In rain forest clearings. 2.5 cm. Transparent light green with light dorso-lateral stripes or green with white flanks covered by a black pattern.

• *H. guttulatus* GUENTHER, 1858. West Africa. In rain forest clearings. 3.5 cm. Either green or yellow-green with black dots, also orange spots or light dots on a brown background.

• *H. hieroglyphicus* AHL, 1931. Eastern Nigeria and western Cameroons. Highlands. 4 cm. Male green, with lighter dorso-lateral stripes; females attractive glossy black with a yellow vermiform pattern.

• *H. horstocki* (SCHLEGEL, 1837). Arum Reed Frog. South Africa. 4 cm. Brown with creamy white dorso-lateral stripe; in *Zantedeschia* blossoms becomes off-white.

• *H. marmoratus* RAPP, 1842. Central, eastern, and southern Africa. A superspecies with 23 subspecies. 3 to 4 cm. Highly variable, often with light and dark marbled pattern or with longitudinal bands.

Hyperolius viridiflavus

• *H. nasutus* GUENTHER, 1864. Long-nosed Reed Frog. Tropical Africa. 5 subspecies. 2.5 cm. Nasal region pointed. Light green to brown, males with light dorso-lateral stripe.

• *H. nitidulus* PETERS, 1875. Tropical West Africa. 3 subspecies. 3.5 cm. Two color phases with intermediate forms: dorsum uniformly brown, dorso-lateral stripe dark on top and whitish below; or dorsum and flanks unicolored gray-brown.

• *H. pusillus* (COPE, 1862). Dwarf Reed Frog. East Africa. Lowlands. 2 cm. Transparent green, sometimes with black dots.

• *H. quinquevittatus* BOCAGE, 1866. Tropical central and eastern Africa. 2.5 cm. Green to golden brown with dark longitudinal stripes.

• *H. rubrovermicularis* SCHIOETZ, 1975. Eastern Kenya. Forest regions. 3 cm. Glossy black with bright red spots and a whitish dorso-lateral stripe.

• *H. tuberilinguis* SMITH, 1849. East Africa. Brushland. 3 cm. Green, sometimes with large, constricted, washed-out dorsal spot.

• *H. viridiflavus* (DUMERIL and BIBRON, 1841). Tropical Africa. Savannahs and rain forest. A superspecies with numerous subspecies. 2-4 cm. Highly variable, often with dark spotted or striped pattern.

Hypnale FITZINGER, 1843. Hump-nosed Vipers. Genus of the Crotalidae. Sri Lanka and southern India. 3 species. In tropical forests and also in montane rain forests. To 50 cm. Similar to *Agkistrodon*, but with only irregular large scale remnants on top of the head. Tip of snout clearly bent upward, humped.

Hypnale nepa

Terrestrial to semiarboreal. Frogs, lizards, and small mammals are eaten. Live-bearers, 4-10 young. Keep in a tropical forest terrarium with damp patches and dry and warm basking sites. Caution: Venom highly potent.
- *H. hypnale* (MERREM, 1820). Indian Hump-nosed Viper. India south of 10° C. North, Sri Lanka.
- *H. nepa* (LAURENTI, 1768). Ceylonese Hump-nosed Viper. Sri Lanka.

Hypogeophis PETERS, 1879. Genus of the Caeciliidae. Seychelles. 3 species, partly polytypic. Tentacle pit horseshoe-shaped, located about the same as in *Grandisonia*; distinguished from that genus by the larger number of primary furrows (96 or more). Skin with very small scales. More or less uniformly dark purple, violet, or brownish black.
- *H. rostratus* (CUVIER, 1829). Several subspecies. To 37 cm. Dark purple to brownish violet.

Hypopachus KEFERSTEIN, 1867. Sheep Toads. Genus of the Microhylidae. Southwestern USA to Costa Rica. 2 species. Prefer semiarid regions. Plump, short-legged. Head small, separated from more or less balloon-like inflated body by an occipital fold. Pupil round or elongated oval. Tympanum hidden. Fingers and toes without adhesive discs; webbing only weakly developed or absent. Both metatarsal tubercles present and large.

Burrowing ground-dwellers that leave their hiding places (burrows, crevices, decaying wood piles, etc.) only rarely during the dry season, and then only at night. The diet includes mainly termites, ants, and tiny flies. Rainy seasons and floods trigger activity phases and reproduction. Males—drifting in water—vocalize with a sheep-like bleating sound.

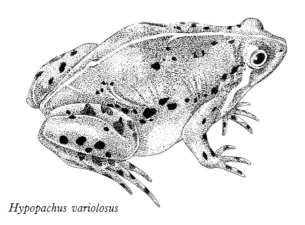

Hypopachus variolosus

Sheep toads should be housed in a semimoist to nearly dry terrarium with a deep substrate layer and ample hiding places. For breeding purposes the animals should be transferred to an aqua-terrarium or to an aquarium with very shallow water levels. Species from the subtropics can be kept in an open-air terrarium during the summer.
- *H. variolosus* (COPE, 1866). Sheep Toad. Southern Texas to Costa Rica. 4 cm. Olive above, sides lighter; a narrow yellow line in the middle of the back and also the belly.

Hypotophis BOULENGER, 1908. Monotypic genus of the Colubridae of uncertain subfamily affinities (Boiginae or Aparallactinae). Tropical Africa (Congo Basin). Small,

with a clearly set off, wide, triangular head, adder-like stout body and tail. Ground snakes. Biology virtually unknown.
- *H. wilsoni* BOULENGER, 1908. Zaire to Zambia.

Hypselotriton WOLTERSTORFF, 1934. Chinese Crested Newts. Monotypic genus of the Salamandridae. Often synonymized with *Cynops*. Western China in mountain lakes and streams at about 1800 m elevation. Robust, similar to large *Triturus*. Body relatively deep, compressed, with a long, paddle-like tail, the upper tail crest continuing as a ridge over the entire body. Back legs distinctly stronger than anterior ones. Cloaca in male circular, in female oval with papillae present in cloacal slot.

Presumably largely or completely aquatic. Mode of reproduction unknown, but some *Hypselotriton* populations have a clear tendency toward neoteny.
- *H. wolterstorffi* (BOULENGER, 1905). Yunnan. To 16 cm. Dark olive to black, dorsal crest and ventral region orange-red. Sides, legs, and tail sparingly covered with orange-red dots.

Hypsiglena COPE, 1860. Night Snakes. Genus of the Colubridae, Boiginae. Western USA and Mexico southward to Central America. 3 to 5 species. In various dry habitats and also at higher elevations. To 60 cm. Head very distinct, the eyes with vertical pupils. Light brown with dark brown spots; a lyre-shaped blackish brown collar in *H. torquata*.

Strictly nocturnal. Frogs and lizards are eaten. Egg-layers. Should be kept in a well-heated dry terrarium with nighttime temperature reductions. Caution: Theoretically dangerous, although human bites have had little effect.
- *H. torquata* (GUENTHER, 1860). Western USA to Costa Rica. Number of subspecies uncertain.

Hypsiglena torquata

Hypsiglena torquata

Hypsirhynchus GUENTHER, 1858. Monotypic genus of the Colubridae, Xenodontinae. Haiti and small adjacent islands. 1 m. Resemble *Arrhyton* and *Antillophis*, but distinguished from these by a vertical pupil. Natural history virtually unknown.
- *H. ferox* GUENTHER, 1858.

Ialtris COPE, 1862. Genus of the Colubridae, Xenodontinae. Haiti and small adjacent islands. 2 species. To about 75 cm. Well-developed opisthoglyphic fangs. Biology barely known. Ground snakes.
- *I. dorsalis* (GUENTHER, 1858). W-shaped markings on back of head. Dorsum brown with darker spots.

Ichnotropis PETERS, 1854. Rough-scaled Sand Lizards. Genus of the Lacertidae. Southern Africa. About 6 species. In open landscapes with some vegetation. Typical lacertids in shape but with characteristically very large, shingled, and strongly keeled dorsal scales. Tail often more than twice the body length. Mainly shades of brown.

Usually found on sandy substrate, less often in rocky areas. Feed on termites and similar foods. Egg-layers. Few specimens have been kept in captivity, but they probably can be kept like *Eremias*, but without winter dormancy.

- *I. capensis* (SMITH, 1838). Rough-scaled Sand Lizard. Northern Africa to southern Zaire. About 20 cm. Dorsally light brown, flanks dark brown, sometimes with some white; males with orange-red longitudinal band. 6 eggs per clutch.

Ichthyophiidae: Family of the Gymnophiona. Tropical South America and Southeast Asia, including the Indo-Australian islands. Genera include *Caudacaecilia, Epicrionops, Ichthyophis,* and *Rhinatrema.* Possibly *Uraeotyphlus* should be removed from the Caeciliidae and also to be included in the Ichthyophiidae.

In contrast to the Caeciliidae and Typhlonectidae, there is a clearly developed tail. Apart from primary furrows there are also 2-4 secondary furrows per body segment. In Neotropical genera the furrows come together straight, in Oriental genera they meet in a blunt angle. The lower jaw usually has 2 rows of teeth, except *Caudacaecilia.* The anal opening is usually developed as a longitudinal slit, but is oblique in *Rhinatrema.*

As far as is known the larvae are aquatic and the adults terrestrial. Egg-layers. Eggs are deposited either in burrows or underneath rocks, but always close to water, where the larvae become free-swimming. Metamorphosis can take place within a few weeks to several years. During the transition to a life on land the gills slits are closed. Transformed specimens will drown when in water. There have been few observations made in captivity, but based on data from the wild, adult animals should be kept at tropical temperatures (about 25° C.) in spacious terrariums with a 30 cm layer of loose substrate, where they like to remain burrowed during the day. The condition of the substrate must permit adequate air circulation in order to avoid soil toxification due to an accumulation of carbon dioxide, methane, and other suffocating gases. Ideally one uses a mixture of garden soil, sand, peat moss, and coarse unsifted properly decomposed compost, which should be kept constantly damp without accumulating excess water. The latter condition can be avoided by installing a drainage systen (a layer of coarse gravel, perforated concrete, a ceramic plate, or similar items) for water runoff to the outside. However, since the caecilians under these conditions are hard to monitor and control, a more "sterile" maintenance in, for instance, damp foam rubber cubes is also feasible.

There is little nutritional data available, and much of what there is is contradictory. Apparently there are species-specific or genus-specific differences. One thus has to ascertain whether the animals take their food at night at the surface or feed in their burrows. Earthworms seem to be particularly well suited as food. They are grabbed inside the burrow, then disoriented through a body rotation by the ichthyophiid and then gradually swallowed (according to TANNER for *Ichthyophis glutinosus*). Insect larvae also appear to be suitable as food.

Ichthyophis FITZINGER, 1826. Largest genus of the Ichthyophiidae. Tropical Asia and adjacent islands. 27 species, some to more than 50 cm. Body with 259 to 430 furrows; primary and secondary furrows similar, furrows meet along abdomen at blunt angles (except: *I. orthoplicatus*). Tentacles small, often directly above mouth, usually closer to eye than to nostril, but in *I. beddomei* an equal distance between both. Very small calcareous scales may be embedded below the skin; variously developed, absent in

Ichthyophis kohtaoensis

Ichthyophis kohtaoensis

some species, in others with up to 2000 rows. Tail often very short.

Uniformly dark, usually bluish or with conspicuous light lateral bands.
▪ *I. glutinosus* (LINNAEUS, 1758). Sri Lanka. To more than 40 cm. Unicolored chocolate brown with bluish sheen.
▪ *I. hypocyaneus* (VAN HASSELT, 1827). Java. To more than 25 cm. Dorsum dark olive, abdomen steel blue.
▪ *I. monochrous* (BLEEKER, 1879). Kalimantan. To 23 cm. Uniformly violet brown.
▪ *I. tricolor* (ANNANDALE, 1909). India. About 30 cm. Dorsally violet brown; laterally with a wide yellow band with dark edge below; ventrally white.

Idiocranium PARKER, 1936. Monotypic genus of the Caeciliidae. West Africa. At 12 cm maximum length this is one of the smallest representative of the caecilians. 80 to 87 primary folds, 23 to 27 secondary folds. Very small scales present only along posterior part of body. Tentacle organ vertical, below nostril. Inner tooth row on lower jaw with only 4 teeth. Egg-layers.
▪ *I. russeli* PARKER, 1936. Cameroons, Nigeria. To 12 cm, 4.5 mm wide. Dorsum blue-gray, ventrum lighter.

Idiopholis MOCQUARD, 1892. Genus of the Colubridae, Calamarinae. Kalimantan. 2 species. 15-19 cm. Smallest taxa in the subfamily. Dark with a wide light colored collar or light head and neck.
▪ *I. collaris* MOCQUARD, 1892. Northeastern Kalimantan.

Iguana LAURENTI, 1768. Iguanas. Genus of the Iguanidae. Central Mexico to central South America, *I. delicatissima* also on some Caribbean islands. 2 species, mainly in rain forests. To 2 m. Slender, body slightly laterally compressed, the head large. Snout-vent length 50 cm, the tail much longer than the body. Strong limbs. Characteristic large gular pouch with a serrated crest under the chin. A tall dorsal crest continues to the first third of the tail. The crests are better developed in males than in females. Green; with age there is an increasing intensity of the dark crossbands on the body and tail, darkest over the vertebral column. Often temporarily becoming grayish or bluish green.

Arboreal, in the proximity of large bodies of water (individual populations of substantially smaller animals occur in dry habitats). Iguanas are excellent swimmers. Juveniles

Iguana iguana

feed almost exclusively on arthropods, while adults are almost completely herbivorous. Egg-layers.

Iguanas are among the most popular and attractive terrarium animals, with only fully grown adults somewhat difficult to house in an indoor terrarium. Generally they require a spacious tank or screened enclosure with adequate climbing branches. A bottom substrate is not essential, which facilitates cleaning out of feces. Plants should be

Iguana iguana

avoided with adult (herbivorous) iguanas, but juveniles can be kept in a planted terrarium. Day temperatures from 25 to 30° C. are satisfactory, with an incandescent lamp for sunbathing; provide a nocturnal temperature reduction to 20 to 24° C. Iguanas like to bathe, thus a large water bowl is required. Alternatively, the humidity must be kept high by regular spraying. The most suitable food items include mainly bananas, dandelions, clover, and occasionally some lettuce. In addition, juveniles should be given mealworms, grasshoppers, and scraped lean meat to which some calcium is added. The diet should be varied, as each animal's taste may be different. During the summer months adult specimens can easily be kept in partially roofed over outdoor enclosures, but they should get at least some sun exposure and supplemental ultraviolet radiation during the winter months. Larger animals kept in an indoor terrarium should be given an outside run in the room. They need exercise to prevent the dangers of obesity. Animals raised in captivity tend to become very tame and used to people, but beware of tail lashes.

To this day successful breeding of iguanas is considered to be a remarkable event, although copulation and eggs being laid (20-40 per clutch) are not too rare. The main problem appears to be the egg incubation. The most important factors are relatively constant temperatures of 28 to 32° C. and an evenly high humidity of 80-100%, although successful broods (definitely exceptions) have been obtained under less favorable conditions. The incubation period is 65-115 days. At hatching the young are about 20 cm long. Under ideal conditions they can reach sexual maturity in 3 years. Iguanas can be kept together with swamp turtles and tortoises and other large lizards.

▪ *I. iguana* (L. , 1758). Green Iguana, Common Iguana. Mainland Central and South America. Large scale below tympanum behind angle of jaw.

▪ *I. delicatissima* LAURENTI, 1768. Southern Caribbean Islands. Rare. No large scale below tympanum.

Iguanidae: Iguanas, Anoles, Swifts, etc. Family of the Sauria. Southwestern Canada to Tierra del Fuego. *Amblyrhynchus*, *Conolophus*, and *Tropidurus* on Galapagos Islands; *Chalarodon* and *Oplurus* on Madagascar; *Brachylophus* on Tonga and Fiji. 5 subfamilies, more than 50 genera, and in excess of 700 species. Placed in the family series Iguania together with the Old World Agamidae and Chamaeleonidae. Found in all habitats from tropical forests to deserts and along the seashore. 10 cm to more than 2 m. Well-proportioned, most typically "lizard-like," but a few bizarre genera (*Phrynosoma*). Tail usually longer than body, fragile in many genera (unlike the Agamidae). Easy and certain external distinction from the Agamidae is not possible, the best character being the pleurodont teeth (on sides of jaws) in Iguanidae (acrodont in Agamidae), which in addition are also replacable. Usually there are also some pterygoid teeth present.

Scales highly variable. The head scales are relatively small and irregular, the only scales supported by osteoderms. Dorsal scales are usually small, the ventral scales larger, but seldom in regular rows (exceptions: some genera from dry regions, e. g., *Sceloporus*). Crests, helmets, and gular pouches occur in a variety of forms, usually more strongly developed in males than in females and playing a

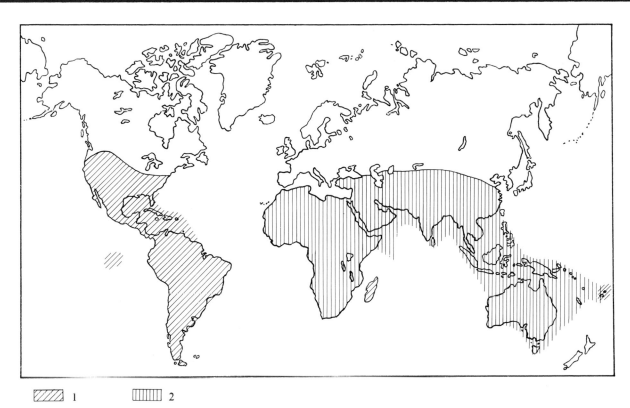

Distribution of the Iguanidae (1) and Agamidae (2)

significant part during courtship and in rivalry fighting. These activities are invariably associated with strong lateral flattening and thus an increase in profile, together with active head nodding. The ability to display physiological color changes is in some iguanids (e. g., *Anolis*) as well developed as in the Chamaeleonidae.

The mode of life is highly variable. In contrast to the related agamids, the iguanids do not have any gliding or subterranean forms; some of the large species have gone over to a herbivorous diet. Mating is usually associated with a neck bite. The majority of iguanids is egg-layers, but some are ovoviviparous.

Within the family Iguanidae there are 5 subfamilies made up of the following genera.
• Iguaninae; more or less large species. *Amblyrhynchus, Brachylophus, Conolophus, Ctenosaura, Cyclura, Dipsosaurus, Enyaliosaurus. Iguana, Sauromalus.*
• Basiliscinae: *Basiliscus, Corytophanes,* and *Laemanctus.*
• Anolinae: *Anolis* (about 300 species), *Anisolepis, Aptycholaemus, Chamaeleolis, Chamaelinorops, Cupriguanus, Diplolaemus, Enyalius, Leiosaurus, Phenacosaurus, Phrynosaura, Polychroides, Polychrus, Tropidodactylus, Urostrophus,* and *Xiphocercus.*
• Sceloporinae: relatively primitive, primarily ground-dwellers with femoral pores in males and females. *Callisaurus, Crotaphytus, Gambelia, Holbrookia, Phrynosoma, Petrosaurus, Sator, Sceloporus, Uma, Urosaurus,* and *Uta.*
• Tropidurinae: rather heterogenous, femoral pores absent. *Ctenoblepharis, Enyalioides, Garbesaura, Hoplocercus, Leiocephalus, Liolaemus, Morunasaurus, Ophryoessoides, Plica, Phymaturus, Proctotretus, Stenocercus, Strobilurus, Tropidurus, Uracentron,* and *Uranoscodon.* The genera *Chalarodon* and *Oplurus* from Madagascar are somewhat isolated.

Iguanognathus BOULENGER, 1898. Monotypic genus of the Colubridae of uncertain subfamily relationship. 30 cm. Sumatra. Teeth of an even size, characteristically spatula-shaped (very unusual for a snake). Biology and ecology unknown. Probably burrowing snakes in tropical rain forests.
• *I. werneri* BOULENGER, 1898.

Illumination: In terrariums illumination is used to assure adequate light levels, except for nocturnal or burrowing species. Most suitable are fluorescent light tubes located inside a reflector. A terrarium 70 x 40 x 75 cm should be illuminated with 4 to 6 fluorescent tubes. Such a light level is not really required for the animals but is essential for optimal plant growth. Mercury vapor lamps are also suitable for terrarium illumination. Preferably white or daylight tubes are used, but in order to achieve optimum plant growth special plant tubes can be used. Such a tube invariably provides a somewhat uncomfortable (to us) light color, but this is usually compensated for by using other "normal tubes." Growth-enhancing plant fluorescent tubes are said not to pose a danger to the animals. When several light tubes are used adequate ventilation must be provided to avoid a heat buildup.

For specimens requiring localized radiant heat (sunning spots), it is recommended that an additional radiant light source be added that apart from light provides mainly heat (incandescent bulbs with reflectors are usually used).

The use of ultraviolet lights often poses problems when in operation continuously. The intensity is invariably too high, so that these light can only be used for short periods.

Imantodes DUMERIL and BIBRON, 1853. Blunt-headed Tree Snakes. Genus of the Colubridae, Boiginae. Mexico and Central and South America, east of the Andes (Paraguay, Argentina). 5 species. Tropical rain forests and montane rain forests (canopy level). In excess of 1 m. Ex-

Imantodes cenchoa

tremely slender, especially anteriorly, strongly laterally compressed. Head large, blunt, almost square, markedly set off from slender neck, with enormously large eyes. Tail long, as thin as neck. Similar in appearance to *Dipsas*, but much more slender and with 15-17 rows of dorsal scales (*Dipsas* has only 13 rows). The markings consist of dark spots and bands on a light background.

Nocturnal and arboreal, feeding mainly either on lizards (*I. cenchoa*) or frogs (*I. lentiferus*), which favors the joint occurrence of several species in the same habitat. Egg-layers, 2-4 eggs. Should be kept in a well-heated rain-forest terrarium with a slight nocturnal temperature reduction and many climbing branches. Caution: Venomous bites are possible.

▪ *I. cenchoa* (LINNAEUS, 1758). Tropical Mexico southward to Paraguay and Bolivia. 3 subspecies.
▪ *I. lentiferus* (COPE, 1894). Amazon Basin.

Incubation: The duration of incubation varies from species to species. It usually lasts from 2 to 4 months, but in tuataras and some tortoises it can last up to 12 or 13 months. Incubation is very much temperature-dependent. For instance, *Sceloporus undulatus* young will hatch on the average after 60 to 70 days at 25° C., in about 40 days at 30° C., and in 30 days at 35° C.; however, the number of young that actually hatched decreased with increasing temperature. Recently it has been observed in turtles that the sex of the young may be temperature-dependent. At very high temperatures the young are usually not very vital and therefore not strong enough to free themselves from the

Imantodes cenchoa

Incubation of snake eggs on vermiculite

eggshell. The cause of this phenomenon may also lie in an inadequate diet of the mother during the time the eggs were developing before laying. The most favorable temperatures appear to be around 25 to 30° C.; substantially higher temperatures lead to the death of the embryos. A nocturnal reduction of the temperature to about 20° C. is usually not detrimental to most eggs (except rain-forest dwellers). Temperature control by means of a thermostat is certainly advisable.

The eggs are placed in an incubator either individually or attached to some of the substrate (see Gekkonidae). When eggs are transferred special attention has to be given those eggs that are a few days old: these should be turned as little as possible. To this day there is no universally valid recommendation for an incubator. It is particularly important that the substrate is sufficiently loose for adequate ventilation, always damp, and as germ-free as possible. Depending upon the particular situation, the most useful substrates are peat moss, sand (without clay), sand and peat moss mixture, fresh moss (sphagnum), and the now increasingly popular small foam rubber cubes. Peat moss and sphagnum offer the advantage that an experienced hobbyist can recognize the degree of dampness by their color; moreover, these two substances remain acid and thus stay relatively germ-free.

Utilization of foam rubber cubes as a substrate facilitates a rather simple regulation of the degree of dampness: a container is filled about ⅔ with foam rubber cubes (each side about 0.5-1 cm), the eggs are placed on top in a small depression and are then covered by a 1-cm thick foam rubber sheet. The bottom of the container should have about 1 cm of water, which guarantees an even dampness in the upper layers and can be replenished as required.

It must be remembered that most reptile eggs are soft-shelled (snakes, many lizards) and take up a lot of water, therefore increasing in size quite substantially after laying and later in development. Under no circumstances must the eggs be kept too wet. Apart from increased dangers of decay and fungus formation due to lack of ventilation, there can also be excessive water intake under such circumstances.

It is advisable to place the incubating container (e. g., a porous flowerpot or a plastic container with holes) on a pedestal in a heated aquarium with a very low water level, which maintains an even temperature and provides a high humidity. Much more expensive (although more professional and with mechnical safeguards to prevent breakdowns) are commercial incubators where only the humidity will have to be monitored and maintained.

It is difficult to determine the degree of development inside the eggs. Using the transmitted light technique (candling) gives the best indication but also places the eggs at risk due to excessive manipulation. The simplest method is to place the egg on top of a hole punched into a piece of cardboard that is then held above a light source. Actually opening an egg can only be justified with very large clutches. If one has had some experience with this with a particular species, an overdue clutch can be tested by opening an egg (variations of a few days are quite normal) and so possibly saving some of the young, which are unable to free themselves. The same applies if only some of the young have hatched from a clutch and there are no additional hatchlings within a few days. Here too there are sometimes exceptions where the hatching time within a clutch can be highly variable. Manual assistance is always indicated when there are cracks in an eggshell but the young has been unable to leave the shell on its own after a reasonable period of time.

During incubation the clutch is inspected regularly and decaying eggs are promptly removed. Unfertilized eggs usually collapse after a short period of time, but others can remain firm for weeks. A few days before the anticipated hatching date the incubator is checked daily to remove any hatched juveniles and transfer these to a rearing terrarium.

Indotestudo LINDHOLM, 1929. Genus of the Testudinidae. Southeast Asia. 2 or 3 species. Often treated as part of *Geochelone*. In dry forests up to the outer areas of rain forests. Carapace length to 28 cm. Carapace elongated, typically with light areoles and an incomplete dark margin around the plates.

Indotestudo travancorica (left) and *Indotestudo elongata* (right)

Indotestudo elongata

Mainly herbivorous, with some animal protein in the form of insects and worms. Biology little known.
▪ *I. elongata* (BLYTH, 1853). Yellow-headed Tortoise, Elongate Tortoise. Eastern India through Indo-China to the Malayan Peninsula and Sulawesi. Characteristic white to yellow head and rather light base coloration of carapace. Skin of nose and around eyes turns pink in breeding specimens. Should be kept in a well-heated dry terrarium with

Indotestudo travancorica

a large water bowl. Grows rapidly to a considerable size. Has been bred in captivity. Most frequently imported species of this genus.
▪ *I. travancorica* (BOULENGER, 1907). Travancore Tortoise. Southwestern India. Similar to *I. elongata*, but with a somewhat flatter and wider carapace and darker brown color. Probably only a subspecies of *I. elongata*.

Indotyphlus TAYLOR, 1960. Monotypic genus of the Caeciliidae. India. 133-141 primary folds, secondary folds and tiny scales present. Inner tooth row in lower jaw with 4 teeth. Tentacle located closer to nostril than to eye, on a line between nostril and eye. Cloacal slit perpendicular.
▪ *I. battersbyi* Taylor, 1960. Poona, India. Over 20 cm. Uniformly lavender-brown, paler below.

Indovaranus: see *Varanus*, genus.

Inhibition: In ethology, a blockage of types of behavior due to certain internal and external stimuli or due to superceding or opposing behavior patterns. A reciprocal inhibition of types of behavior can lead to conflicts and displacement activities. For instance, it is known that the highly venomous kraits (*Bungarus*) are under striking inhibition during the day and so can usually be handled without the danger of being attacked. These are nocturnal snakes and will only attack in darkness.

Insecta: Insects. Class of Arthropoda. More than 1 million species. Worldwide distribution. Important in terrarium maintenance mainly as food organisms. Insects are the largest component in meadow plankton. Of particular significance are the representatives of the Saltoria, Blattaria, Hymenoptera, Coleoptera, Lepidoptera, and Diptera. Many can be easily bred as a year-round food supply. Some insects are known as parasites and disease carriers, especially certain flies and midges. Some insects species are particularly attractive or have an interesting biology and are sometimes kept in terrariums, especially walkingstick insects and praying mantids.

Insect traps: Employed to catch food organisms for terrarium animals. Best known are fly traps. Flies are attracted

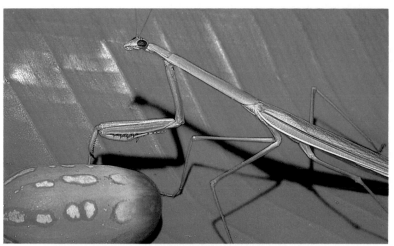

Insecta: A praying mantis

Insecta: Meal moth larvae

Insecta: A dragonfly

by means of strong-smelling bait (meat, cheese) and are then trapped when leaving the bait. Such a trap is best deployed outside about 1 m above the ground.

Light traps are also a well-known technique. The simplest involves placing a powerful light in an elevated position in front of a white cloth. This is best done on a dark, still night. Bright moonlit nights are not particularly productive.

Ground traps are used mainly for catching various beetles that are eaten by relatively few insects.

Instinct: The ability of animals to react with genetically fixed, species-specific types of behavior in response to internal and external stimuli. Such learning-independent, innate behavior patterns are described as instinct movements or genetic coordination and are of considerable significance in the lives of amphibians and reptiles since they largely determine their behavior (e. g., reproduction, food intake).

Integument: Also referred to as cutis or skin. Tissue forming the outer body delineation, serving to protect against external influences and picking up environmental stimuli (touch, pressure, and temperature stimuli) by sensory cells, and also involved in excretion, water and salt regulation, thermoregulation, and respiration. It is a car-

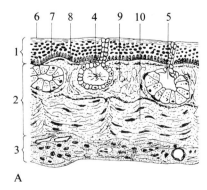

A

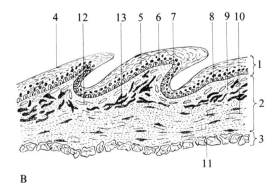

B

Integument: A) Amphibian after metamorphosis: 1 Epidermis; 2 cutis or corium; 3 subcutis; 4 mucous gland; 5 secretory (poison) gland; 6 stratum corneum; 7 stratum germinativum; 8 basal membrane; 9 stratum spongiosum; 10 stratum compactum with muscle bundles

Integument: B) Reptile: 1 Epidermis; 2 cutis or corium; 3 subcutis; 4 keratinous scale; 5 stratum corneum; 6 stratum intermedium; 7 stratum germinativum; 8 basal membrane; 9 stratum laxum; 10 stratum compactum; 11 musculature; 12 guanophore layer; 13 pigment layer

rier of color pigments and so is substantially responsible for the characteristic body coloration.

The integument in vertebrates consists of a multiple-layered outer skin (epidermis) and the dermis (corium) underneath made up of connective tissue with its inclusions of embedded collagens and elastic fibers, blood vessels, nerves with sensory cells, skin muscles, and color cells (chromatophores). Connective-tissue-like fat cells forming the subcutis connect the integument to the musculature.

The lowest layer of the epidermis (stratum germinativum, stratum basale) continuously forms new cells through cell division; these cells are then pushed upward. Through the inclusion of keratinous or corneous (stratum corneum) layers (to protect against desiccation), a tough skin is developed in amphibians and reptiles, as well as in birds and mammals. This corneous layer is constantly being worn out or shed periodically. The degree of cornification is generally rather limited in amphibians. It is also characterized by the presence of numerous skin glands in the corium that give off mucus and secretions to keep the skin moist. On the other hand, the nearly glandless integument of reptiles displays a significant degree of cornification, which as a special formation also includes the production of scales, where strongly cornified layers are pushed over less cornified sections. Moreover, in many reptiles the integument also forms dermal bones (osteodermata) that can become fused.

Intention movements: An incomplete sequence of behavior that serves as preparation for the entire action, but which can also be of new significance as a signal. Intention movements indicate the readiness for a specific action and reflect the mood of the animal. A ritualistic intention movement is, for instance, gular pouch spreading in chameleons, which has evolved from threatening mouth opening.

Intention movements: Gular pouch spreading in *Chamaeleo pumilus*

Intergradation zone: Overlapping or adjacent portion of the range of subspecies where the formation of mixed populations (intergrades) occurs. Existence of intergrades is evidence that there are no reproductive barriers between the respective taxa. Also compare with allopatry and sympatry.

Iphisa GRAY, 1851. Monotypic genus of the Teiidae. Amazon Basin, in the *selva*. To 15 cm. Slender. Lower eyelid with a large window. The weakly developed limbs have a short fifth toe that is clawless. The scales are conspicuously enlarged and smooth, with 2 rows of extremely large dorsal

scales and ventral scales, with a total of only 12 rows around midbody. Brown.
▪ *I. elegans* GRAY, 1851.

Iridocytes: see Chromatophores.

Ischnocnema REINHARDT and LUETKEN, 1862. Genus of the Leptodactylidae. Tropical South America. 2 species. Related to *Eleutherodactylus*. In *selva*. Externally hard to distinguish from *Hylactophryne*. Robust. Head and dorsal skin with warts, head large. Horizontal pupil. Clearly visible tympanum. Fingers and toes free.

Ground-dwellers. Larval development presumably takes place in a damp substrate.
▪ *I. quixensis* (JIMENEZ DE LA ESPADA, 1872). Northeastern Amazon Basin. 6 cm. Olive with a dark brown to red-brown pattern. Iris bronze-colored.

Island tameness: Can be frequently observed on islands without human inflence, where the animals do not display any fear toward humans. The appearance of humans does not trigger flight behavior. Such tameness has contributed greatly to the decimation of such species as Galapagos land iguanas and marine iguanas by humans.

Isopoda: Isopods. Order of the Crustacea. Various land isopods (pillbugs, sowbugs) are eaten by many terrarium animals, especially by amphibians. However, sometimes they are refused after 1 feeding. Isopods are found under rocks, behind loose tree bark, along damp walls, and in similar places. They feed on decaying plant matter and can be bred in containers filled with leaves and vegetable remains that should be kept moderately damp (but not fungusy).

Isopoda: *Asellus*, a freshwater genus

Ithycyphus GUENTHER, 1873. Genus of the Colubridae, Boiginae. Madagascar. 2 species. In tropical dry forests and rain forests. Maximum size about 1 m. Clearly set off head with relatively large eyes and round pupils. Opisthoglyphic fangs that are rather large; nothing is known about their venom potency. Either uniformly brown to gray or with V-shaped crossbars.

Nocturnal ground snakes. The diet presumably consists of lizards and frogs. Should be kept in well-heated, moderately damp forest terrarium. Caution: Venomous bites possible.

• *I. goudoti* (SCHLEGEL, 1854). With crossbands. 90 cm.
• *I. miniatus* (SCHLEGEL, 1837). More than 1 m.

IUCN: International Union of Conservation of Nature and Natural Resources. Special organization of UNESCO (umbrella organization formed by the UN) that brings together specialists from national zoological and nature conservation research institutes as well as accomplished scientists. Headquarters located in Switzerland. Best known publication is the international *Red Book*. Herpetological matters are dealt with by the IUCN within 3 working parties: general amphibians and reptiles, sea turtles, and crocodilians. Cooperates with the WWF (World Wildlife Fund).

Ixalus: see *Philautus*, genus.

Jacobson's Organ: Paired organ lined with olfactory epithelium that in amphibians consists of only a ventral blind sac in the nasal cavity. The J. O. is absent from turtles, crocodilians, and birds. However, it does exist in the Lepidosauria and in various forms in mammals as two cavities completely separate from the nose (except in tuataras) that are connected to the oral cavity by the Stenson's Canal. The greatest significance of the J. O. is in the Squamata, where it exceeds by a large margin the olfactory capability of the nose. However, it has regressed in some of the agamids, iguanids, and chamaeleonids, or it may even be completely absent. The sensory epithelium resembles that of the nasal cavity and is neurologically connected to the

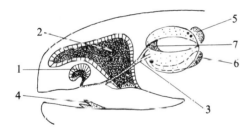

Jacobson's organ and associated glands of a lizard: 1 Jacobson's Organ; 2 nostril; 3 tear duct; 4 tongue; 5 lacrimal gland; 6 Harderian gland; 7 nictitating membrane

bulbus olfactorius accessorius. Tongue-flicking transfers scent substances to the J. O. from the tip of the tongue, to which (in some species) openings of the Stenson's Canal are connected. In addition, tear secretions also have some importance in transporting scents to the olfactory epithelium, being transferred via the tear ducts to the Stenson's Canal and moved along by ciliary cells. In many lizards and snakes the J. O. also plays a role in searching for and recognizing a partner, prey, or enemies. For instance, rattlesnakes recognize their enemies the kingsnakes (genus *Lampropeltis*) with the aid of the J. O. and react with a characteristic defensive behavior.

Jan, George (1791-1866): Italian zoologist, director of the museum in Milan. Authored 3-volume *Iconographie Generale des Ophidiens* (1860-1881), which depicted (with illustrations by Sordelli) all snakes known at that time, and to this day is still an extremely valuable identification aid for snakes.

Japalura GRAY, 1853. Mountain Lizards. Genus of the Agamidae. Himalayas, China, Indo-China, parts of the Indo-Australian Archipelago. About 20 species. In montane rain forests. 15 to 40 cm. Slightly compressed laterally. Tail about twice snout-vent length. Low occipital, dorsal, and caudal crests. Dorsal scales variably large, shingled, and keeled. Ventral scales also keeled. Mainly shades of brown and green.

Ground-dwellers to semiarboreal on rocks, tree stumps, and low bushes. The diet consists mainly of small arthropods. Egg-layers. They require relatively large amounts of drinking water. Temperature requirements are moderate (room temperature).
• *J. tricarinata* (BLYTH, 1853). Cloud-forest Agamid. Himalayas. Fog-shrouded mountains to 3000 m. To 18 cm, snout-vent length 6 cm. Females brown with lighter markings. Males when excited become green with a black stripe from eye to shoulder. Color changes. Semiarboreal.

Kachuga GRAY, 1855. Roof Turtles. Genus of the Emydidae. India and northern Indo-China. 6 species in rivers. Carapace 22-60 cm, males of most species substantially smaller than females. Carapace with distinct keel that can be more or less broken into individual humps, the keel on the second and third vertebrals often particularly conspicuous.

Kachuga tecta circumdata

Kachuga smithi

Excellent swimmers and divers that like to take sunbaths within flight distance from deep water. Omnivorous, with substantial plant component in the diet; often displays individual feeding preferences, some being completely herbivorous (which causes substantial water pollution). A temperate water flow-through system is recommended rather than filtration. Growth is very slow. Imported specimens often have substantial carapace defects that under hygienic care and optimum maintenance conditions will completely heal after some years. Threatened, seldom imported. Some species have seldom been kept in captivity.

• *K. dhongoka* (GRAY, 1834). Ganges and Brahmaputra systems to Assam. Carapace flat, keel broken into humps. Olive brown with a characteristic light stripe on the head extending from the eye.

• *K. smithi* (GRAY, 1863). Pakistan and northern India. Carapace keel weakly developed.

• *K. tecta* (GRAY, 1831). Indian Roof Turtle. Pakistan to northern India, southward into river systems of the Mahanadi, Godavari, and Krishna. 3 subspecies that are not clearly distinguished. The characteristically high carapace has markedly increasing keel sizes on the first to third vertebrals. The most colorful species and the most often kept.

Kachuga tecta

Kalanchoe ADANS. Genus of the Crassulaceae. Primarily in Africa and Madagascar, also in tropical Asia and 1 species in tropical America. More than 200 species. Mostly nearly bare succulent bushes and shrubs, some of which are annuals or biennials. Leaves may have brood buds (formerly genus *Bryophyllum*). They require even humidity during the summer at a bright location and should be kept dry during the winter.

• *K. blossfeldiana* v. POELLN. Flaming Kathrine. To 30 cm high. Multipurpose plant useful for dry terrariums.

• *K. laxiflora* BAK. To 50 cm. Brood buds.

• *K. pinnata* (LAM) PERS. Tall-growing plant. Adventive plants are formed in the leaf axis.

• *K. tomentosa* BAK. Leaves 5-6 cm. Whitish.

• *K. tubiflora* (HARV) R. HAMET. Brood buds in leaf axis.

• *K. uniflora* (STAPF). R. HAMET. Epiphytic hanging or basket plant.

Kachuga tecta circumdata

Kalimantan: Borneo.

Kalophrynus TSCHUDI, 1838. Genus of the Microhylidae. Tropical Southeast Asia, with largest species diversity in Kalimantan. 7 species in tropical lowland and montane rain forests. More or less compact, snout-vent length only a few centimeters. Skin more or less granular. Snout short, eyes far apart and relatively small, pupil horizontal. Tympanum clearly visible, in contrast to the related genus *Microhyla*. Fingers free, toes usually webbed at base only (rarely to two-thirds of their length); tips not enlarged; fourth finger conspicuously short. Most species have 2 tubercles underneath the fourth finger. External sexual characteristics develop during courtship in males in the form of finger spines, upper arm spines, dorsal spines, and upper arm glands; rarely without any characteristic. Larvae compact; respiratory opening and anal tube median; without enlarged lips, teeth, or papillae on terminal mouth.

Diurnal and nocturnal ground-dwellers. Spawning waters are invariably small, shallow, temporary rain-water accumulations. The larval period is short, about 2 weeks from spawning to metamorphosis.

Should be kept in a tropical rain-forest terrarium at temperatures from 24 to 29° C.

• *K. heterochirus* (BOULENGER, 1900). Kalimantan. To 3 cm. Red-brown with light dorso-lateral longitudinal bands and light-colored spots along the sides.

• *K. pleurostigma* TSCHUDI, 1838. Southern Malaysia, Sumatra, Kalimantan, Philippines, and Java. To 6 cm. Pointed snout. Dorsum reddish brown, clearly set off from black sides.

Kaloula GRAY, 1831. Malayan Narrow-mouthed Toads. Genus of the Microhylidae. Tropical and subtropical southeast Asia. 10 species. In various habitats, including agricultural areas and even urban areas. Plump. Skin smooth or granular. Broad head and short snout. Pupil round. Tympanum not visible. Short limbs. Fingers free, tips more or less enlarged into blunt adhesive discs (a distinguishing feature from the closely related genus *Calluella*). Toes more or less extensively webbed. Only one

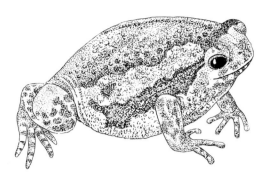

Kaloula pulchra

metatarsal tubercle present, longish oval in shape, developed as a digging spade. Males have dark throats and are capable of loud vocalizing. When threatened they inflate their bodies tremendously. Larvae have a terminal mouth without horny teeth and papillae; the respiratory opening is in the posterior ventral region of the body.

Nocturnal; mostly ground-dwellers, some will climb into trees. They live in self-dug burrows sometimes several meters long or other suitable hiding places during droughts; heavy rainfall will trigger courtship, independent of season. The males then congregate in temporary rain-water puddles, vocalize at night to attract females, and then mate. The eggs are small and float as a thin layer on the surface. Only 15 days pass from spawning to metamorphosis, an adaptation to the temporary nature of the spawning pool.

These frogs can easily be kept and bred in captivity. *K. pulchra* is of particular importance to terrarium hobbyists. When keeping these animals attmepts will to have to be made to simulate dry and rainy seasons. Provide a slightly damp substrate during the dry period and a warm, murky

(possibly required to stimulate breeding) water section. *Kaloula* species are heavy feeders with correspondingly substantial metabolic waste product accumulation, so the substrate must be replaced frequently. The small mouth dictates small insects or small worms as food. Rearing the larvae can be done with dry fish food flakes.

- *K. baleata* (MUELLER, 1836). Malaya, Sunda Islands. 3 subspecies. To 6.5 cm. Brown or olive, the bases of the limbs with yellow, orange, or red marks.
- *K. picta* (DUMERIL and BIBRON, 1841). Philippines. 4.5 cm. Coloration similar to *K. pulchra*.
- *K. pulchra* GRAY, 1831. Malayan Narrow-mouthed Toad, Indian Bullfrog. 4 subspecies. India and tropical Southeast Asia, including Sunda Islands and Sulawesi. To 7.5 cm. Earth-brown, pinkish, or dark brown, with a very large purplish dorsal spot.
- *K. rugifera* STEJNEGER, 1924. Western China. To 5 cm. Variable olive-green, with light-colored shoulder markings.

Kaokogecko STEYN and HAACKE, 1966. Monotypic genus of the Gekkonidae. Northwestern Namibia. Similar to *Palmatogecko*. First to fourth toes webbed; tips with adhesive lamellae. Desert-dwellers. Little known.
- *K. vanzyli* STEYN and HAACKE, 1966.

Karyotype: see Chromosomes.

Kassina GIRARD, 1853 (= *Hylambates* DUMERIL, 1853). African Striped Frogs, Running Frogs. Genus of the Rhacophoridae. Africa south of the Sahara. About 20 species.

Kassina maculata

Kaloula pulchra

Kassina weallii

Kassina cochranae

Kassina senegalensis

Closely related to *Phlyctimantis*. Mostly in open savannahs. Conspicuously short-legged. Skin smooth. Pupil vertical. Fingers and toes webbed at base only, if at all; tips in some species distinctly enlarged into adhesive discs (these forms are often separated into the genus *Hylambates*). Males have a distinct vocal sac that becomes substantially extended when vocalizing. They have a loud call in the form of multiple claps. Adults have a more or less well defined pattern of black longitudinal stripes or spots against a silvery gray background. The larvae are large (in *K. maculata* up to 16 cm), the tail short but high and terminating in a point. The corneous upper and lower lips form a circular figure. When grazing on the surface film, the body is suspended vertically.

Nocturnal ground-dwellers. These frogs rarely ever jump, but instead run. Most species remain in burrows during the dry season. Shallow, flooded grasslands, swamps, and bogs that form during the rainy season in the savannah are the preferred habitats and breeding waters for most of these frogs. In contrast to this, *K. maculata* is a bush- or tree-dwelling species in tropical rain forests.

Small terrariums are sufficient for *Kassina*, with the required temperature range during the day of 24 to 30° C., at night somewhat cooler. Also required are a loose, slightly damp, sufficiently deep substrate layer as well as bathing facilities. *Kassina* species are largely unspecialized feeders. When kept in a community terrarium, care must be taken to provide sufficient food. Females often become prey to the more aggressive males! Cannibalistic tendencies can be inhibited by placing only animals of equal size together.

Breeding attempts require a spacious terrarium with good drainage and a shallow, heated water section. The rainy season should be simulated with regular spraying and only slightly varying temperatures. *K. maculata* and other arboreal forms should be kept in a tall, damp, tropical rainforest terrarium.

- *K. cassinoides* (BOULENGER, 1903). West Africa. Savannahs. 4. 5 cm. Silvery gray with black longitudinal stripes or spots.
- *K. fusca* SCHIOETZ, 1967. West Africa. Savannahs. 3 cm. Yellow-brown with dark spots.
- *K. maculata* (DUMERIL, 1853). West Africa and coastal areas of East Africa. Rain forests. 6.5 cm. Gray with oval black spots with light margins.
- *K. senegalensis* (DUMERIL and BIBRON, 1841). Senegal Running Frog, Senegal Kassina. Eastern and southeastern Africa. 4 cm. Highly variable. Several differently marked types occur, such as one with 5 longitudinal stripes partially broken into spots against a silvery base coloration.
- *K. wittei* (LAURENT, 1940). Zaire and Gambia. Mountains. 2 cm. Lance-like dark elongated spots against a silvery gray background.

Kentropyx SPIX, 1825. Keeled Tegus. Genus of the Teiidae. South America east of the Andes. 9 species. In the *selva* and savannahs. To 35 cm. In shape and pattern reminiscent of *Ameiva* and *Cnemidophorus*. Head pointed. Dorsal, tail, and large abdominal scales sharply keeled. Lateral scales conspicuously smaller. Mainly shades of brown with greenish areas on the anterior half of the body and with varied yellowish and black stripes and spots.

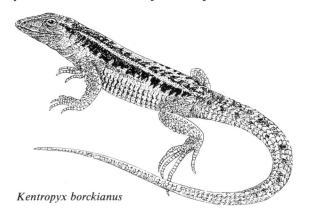

Kentropyx borckianus

Diurnal ground-dwellers found in open, sunny areas. *K. borckianus* appears to be parthenogenic. For details on mode of life and maintenance refer to *Ameiva*.
- *K. borckianus* PETERS, 1869. Guyana, Venezuela, Trinidad, and adjacent islands. Easily to 30 cm. Tail twice snout-vent length. So far only females have been found.
- *K. calcaratus* SPIX, 1825. Northern South America to

Peru, central Brasil. 30 cm.
- *K. striatus* (DAUDIN, 1802). Northern South America. 35 cm.

Keratophagy: The eating of keratinous (horny) substances. Most amphibians and some reptiles (mostly geckos) eat the skin shed during the process of molting. This shed skin consists of the upper skin layer made up of dead, cornified cells and is eaten whole or in pieces. This supports the molting process and provides valuable proteins to the organism.

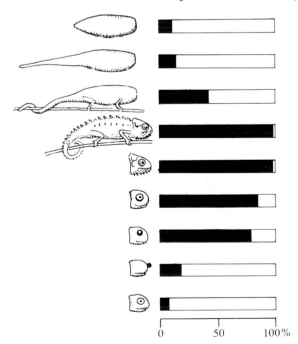

Keratophagy: *Gastrotheca riobambae* eating its shed skin

Kerilia GRAY, 1849. Monotypic genus of the Hydrophiidae, Hydrophiinae. East Indies and Sri Lanka to Kalimantan. About 1 m. Head short, distinctly set off from laterally compressed body. Unlike most sea snakes that increase greatly in diameter in the last third of the body, *Kerilia* is slender. The markings consist of either a row of dorsal spots or rhomboids that are complete crossbands in juve-

Key stimulus: Effectiveness of various models in promoting head-shaking behavior in *Chamaeleo pumilus*. Note that the head silhouette is almost as effective as the full animal.

niles and then break up with increasing age. *Kerilia*, together with *Thalassophis*, is one of the most primitive of the Hydrophiinae.

Aquatic venomous snakes. Biology and ecology barely known.
- *K. jerdoni* GRAY, 1849.

Key stimulus: A signal stimulus that initiates through an innate trigger mechanism a species-specific instinct reaction. Key (or sign) stimuli can be of various natures. Optical sign stimuli can be distinguished with the aid of tests utilizing dummies. This has been shown in chameleons, where a chameleon head silhouette is sufficient to trigger the head-shaking part of the display behavior.

Kidney diseases: Diseases of the urinary organs, especially the kidneys, can be of non-infectious (nephrosis) or infectious (nephritis) origin. The first symptoms are an increased desire to drink and diseases of the skin and mucous membranes that are caused secondarily by urinary substances in the blood.

Causes of kidney diseases include *Pseudomonas* infections, parasite infections (filaria, oxyuroids), vitamin deficiency. The important kidney disease in reptiles is gout.

Kidney diseases: Dehydration in *Lichanura trivirgata*.

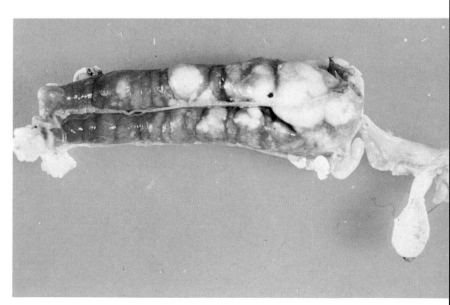

Kidney diseases: Carcinoma in *Xenopus*.

Killing of prey: Those amphibians that are exclusively predatory swallow their prey live or crush the prey first with their jaws. Reptiles employ a wide range of methods to kill their prey. Many of the aquatic snakes swallow their prey (fish, frogs, worms) alive, the prey then dying in the stomach under the influence of the digestive fluids. However, most of the reptiles kill their prey before actually swallowing it. Most predatory turtles and lizards crush their prey in their powerful jaws. Crocodiles pull large prey animals under water in order to drown them. Many lizards will literally shake their prey to death with lateral head movements, often slamming the prey against rocks or the ground. Boids and some other snakes coil themselves around their prey and thus strangle (or constrict) it to death. This procedure is a reflex action that follows immediately after the attacking bite. The most effective method to kill prey is employed by venomous snakes and lizards, where a venomous bite kills the animal.

Killing of prey by a constrictor, *Epicrates cenchria*.

Kinixys BELL, 1827. Hinge-back Tortoises. Genus of the Testudinidae. Tropical Africa. 3 species. 32 cm. Carapace elongated, with a characteristic movable hinge across the

Kinixys belliana

Kinixys homeana

posterior dorsal section in adults. Plastron not hinged.

Herbivorous, but with a strong carnivorous tendency. Sometime difficult feeders when in captivity. *K. belliana* apparently is quite suitable for captive maintenance, but *K. erosa* is difficult to keep.

▪ *K. belliana* GRAY, 1831. Bell's Hinged Tortoise. Central and southern Africa and northern Madagascar. 20 cm. Dry regions to desert margins. Subspecies: *K. b. belliana* GRAY, 1831, central and southern Africa; *K. b. mertensi* LAURENTI, 1956, central Africa; *K. b. nogueyi* (LATASTE, 1886), West Africa. Coloration and markings highly variable, shape of the carapace changing with age. Identification of subspecies depends on the availability of juveniles, and specimens without indication of origin are problematic. The most widely distributed species.

Kinixys belliana

▪ *K. erosa* (SCHWEIGGER, 1812). Schweigger's Hinge-back Tortoise. West Africa. Savannahs to rain forest. Largest species of the genus, with a carapace length in excess of 30 cm. Posterior margin of carapace strongly serrated and evenly arched upward. Prefers fruit, some animal matter

Kinixys homeana

Kinosternon bauri

(such as fish). Likes to bathe. Does not do well in captivity and not long-lived.

• *K. homeana* BELL, 1827. Home's Hinged Tortoise. West Africa. In forests. Carapace to more than 20 cm, with an extremely steep posterior slope. Carapace dark brown, often with light yellow stripes. Soft parts dark or light, sometimes with rich yellow or orange tones. Needs lots of water and likes to bathe.

Kinosternon SPIX, 1824. Mud Turtles. Genus of the Kinosternidae. Americas. About 15 species. Found in different types of water, including temporary pools and ditches. Carapace length 12 to 20 cm. Frequently keeled. The plastron has 2 hinges that allow anterior and posterior sections to be movable yet linked to a rigid center section, thus providing the perfect closing device for the carapace.

Kinosternon acutum

Kinosternon angustipons

Kinosternon flavescens

Kinosternon herrerai

Kinosternon cruentatum

Kinosternon hirtipes

Kinosternon cruentatum

Kinosternon sonoriense

Aquatic. Mainly crepuscular, but sometimes like to bask. Carnivorous, not particularly selective.

Undemanding. Mud turtles should be kept in large aquariums with land sections. Several species have been bred over several generations.

• *K. acutum* GRAY, 1831. Sharp-nosed Mud Turtle. Eastern Mexico, Belize, and Guatemala. Carapace length about 10 cm.

• *K. bauri* GARMAN, 1891. Striped Mud Turtle. Florida to South Carolina. 12 cm. Incubation 94-124 days at 30° C. or

Kinosternon leucostomum

Kinosternon subrubrum subrubrum

25° C. Does not do well in captivity for unknown reasons.

▪ *K. cruentatum* DUMERIL, BIBRON, and DUMERIL, 1851. Red-cheeked Mud Turtle. Southern Mexico to Guatemala, El Salvador. 15 cm.

▪ *K. flavescens* (AGASSIZ, 1857). Yellow Mud Turtle. Central USA to northeastern Mexico. About 15 cm. Incubation 94 to 108 days at 26-30° C.

▪ *K. leucostomum* DUMERIL, BIBRON, and DUMERIL, 1851. White-lipped Mud Turtle. Eastern Mexico and Central America to northern South America. About 15 cm carapace length. Incubation 148 to 174 days at 30° C. or 25° C.

▪ *K. scorpioides* (L., 1766). Scorpion Mud Turtle. Western and southeastern Mexico to northern Argentina. At 20 cm carapace length, the largest species of the genus. Incubation takes 90 to 176 days at 30° C. or 25° C.

▪ *K. subrubrum* (LACEPEDE, 1788). Eastern Mud Turtle. Eastern USA. Incubation 71 to 114 days at 32° C. or 25° C.

Klauber, Laurence Monroe (1883-1968): American engineer and herpetologist. One of the first herpetologists to collect large series of American desert snakes and lizards by road-cruising at night. Numerous taxonomic papers on southwestern reptiles, but most noted for his extensive studies of the rattlesnakes, resulting in the fundamental 2-volume treatise *Rattlesnakes: their habits, life histories and influences on mankind* (1956).

Klauberina SAVAGE, 1957. Monotypic genus of the Xanthusiidae. Found only on some southern California offshore islands. Grassland and rubble slopes. Relatively large for the family, 20 cm. 16 longitudinal rows of ventral scales (other genera with less) and 2 rows of supraocular scales.

Nocturnal, occasionally diurnal. Apart from arthropods, also feeds on some plant matter, as indicated by the teeth, which are typically notched along the outer margin. Livebearers, 4 to 9 young.

Kinosternon scorpioides

▪ *K. riversiana* (COPE, 1883). Island Night Lizard. San Clemente, Santa Barbara, and San Nicholas Islands off the southern California coast. Snout-vent length to 10 cm. Dorsum ash-gray to yellow-brown with numerous dark specks or (rarely) stripes.

Klingelhoeffer, Wilhelm (1871-1953): German medical practitioner and herpetologist. Worked intensively with habitat-correct captive maintenance of terrarium animals, especially the planning of terrariums and the methods of outdoor terrarium maintenance. Standard publications *Einrichtung von Zimmer-und Freiland-Aquarien und Terrarien* (1928) and *Terrarienkunde* (1931), re-published as a 4-volume new edition (1955-1958). Numerous articles in German language hobbyist journals.

Kolpophis SMITH, 1926. Monotypic genus of the Hydrophiidae, Hydrophiinae. Coastal areas of Indo-China to Java. Prefer mangrove swamps and also like to migrate into freshwater areas of river deltas. About 1 m. Short, blunt head not set off from evenly strong, deep body. Dorsum olive-green with dark crossbands. Ventrum whitish.
▪ *K. annandalei* (LAIDLAW, 1901).

Krefft, Paul (1872-1945): German terrarium hobbyist. Co-authored *Das Terrarium, Handbuch der haueslichen Reptiliennpflege*, as well as instructions for identifying terrarium animals (revised by Werner), the first major German terrarium handbook.

Kyarranus: see *Philoria*, genus.

Labial pits: Cavities in various upper and lower lip shields (labials) in many giant snakes (family Boidae) and a few other snakes. They may be of different sizes and arranged into constant patterns that vary from genus to genus. Well supplied with blood vessels and nerves, they serve to detect temperature gradients and are capable of distinguishing differences of as low as 0.026° C. Just as the loreal pits in pit vipers (family Crotalidae), the labial pits also enable locating of warm-blooded prey.

Lacepede, Bernard (1756-1825): French zoologist. Maintained and continued the 44-volume (started by Buffon and co-workers) *Histoire Naturelle* under the title *Histoire de Quadrupedes Ovipares et des Serpents* (1789). Numerous amphibian and reptile species were first described by Lacepede.

Lacerta LINNAEUS, 1768. Common Eurasian Lizards, Green Lizards. Genus of the Lacertidae. Europe, western Asia, and Africa. More than 30 species. The systematics continue to be unclear. *Podarcis* and *Gallotia* formerly were included here. Subdivision into several subgenera is in part artificial. Found in brush, steppes, dry outer forest regions, and in stony to rocky habitats. The body structure is that of a "typical" lizard. Collar always distinct, consisting of enlarged scales. Anal scale enlarged. The small dorsal scales are only marginally shingled or not at all. The ventral scales are large, rectangular, in more or less distinct longitudinal rows (6-8), always substantially overlapping.

Only two groups can be clearly distinguished: *Lacerta* s. str., "emerald lizards," with the typical species *agilis, viridis, trilineata, schreiberi*, and *strigata* as well as the deviant *lepida* and *princeps*; primarily large, massively built species with snout-vent lengths from 7 to 20 cm; and *Zootoca* WAGLER, 1830, "forest lizards," which includes most of the remaining species, but also some that are strongly deviant and whose exact relationships have not yet been determined. Between the often used names *Zootoca* (in the current sense) and *Archaelacerta* MERTENS, 1921 (rock lizards) there are no clear differences. Most species included in

Labial pits plainly visible in upper labials of *Corallus caninus*

Lacerta danfordi anatolica

Lacerta princeps kurdistanica

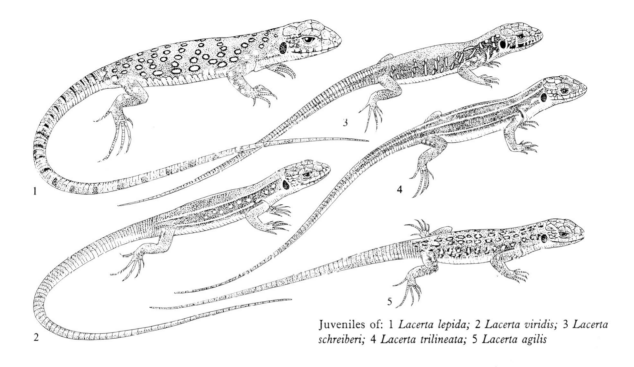

Juveniles of: 1 *Lacerta lepida;* 2 *Lacerta viridis;* 3 *Lacerta schreiberi;* 4 *Lacerta trilineata;* 5 *Lacerta agilis*

Lacerta jayakari

Zootoca are relatively small (snout-vent length under 10 cm), and the skull is comparatively weakly ossified. In contrast to *Lacerta* s. str., shades of green are rare, being found at most in males only during the breeding season, when the abdomens frequently have shades of bright yellow, red, or blue. Blue to blue-green spots at the transition zone from ventral scales to dorsal scales are often typical. Sexual dimorphism is only weakly expressed in markings. Juveniles often have bright blue or green tails. In contrast, females in *Lacerta* s. str. in part maintain the characteristic light dorsal stripes of juveniles, while these disappear completely in males. The males in *Lacerta* s. str. are also distinctly green, a color shade restricted to them (often also in *agilis* and *schreiberi*).

Parthenogenic species occur among the rock lizards from the Caucasus, although this phenomenon also occurs in various other lizards, e. g., *Cnemidophorus*. The best known parthenogenic species are *L. armenica* and *L. unisexualis*, which are diploid. Crosses with adjacent bisexual populations produce triploid progeny (also males) that, however, are not viable or are unable to reproduce.

All *Lacerta* are excellent climbers. They require more moisture than *Podarcis*. When both occur side by side in mountain valleys, *Lacerta* usually occupies the ground and *Podarcis* the elevated rocky slopes and walls. They prey on various arthropods, in late summer mainly on grasshop-

Lacerta lepida

pers. Large lacertids may even eat small mammals. Even snails and earthworms are occasionally eaten. Some emerald lizards show individual food preferences and may even nibble on sweet fruit and honey.

All species are egg-layers except the ovoviviparous *L. vi-*

Lacerta agilis

Lacerta raddei

vipara. There is a strong correlation between body size and clutch size, ranging from more than 20 eggs in *L. lepida* to 2-6 eggs among the smaller species. 1 or 2 clutches are laid per year, rarely 3. Incubation takes 2 to 4 months. Sexual maturity occurs in 2 to 4 years, in captivity often earlier.

Successful permanent maintenance over several generations requires large, spacious terrariums with a sandy, slightly damp substrate, large rocks, climbing branches, and if possible a rock or cork back wall. Suitable plants include, for instance, bromeliads and ivy. They must have a drinking container. Daytime temperatures from 25 to 30° C. with a substantial nocturnal reduction, if possible down to 10° C., are fine. A warmer basking area is necessary. Provide a varied diet. During the summer give lots of meadow plankton and for larger species occasionally newborn mice or rats (excellent to meet calcium requirements). For permanent indoor maintenance regular ultraviolet radiation and calcium and vitamin supplements are required.

Outdoor or open-air maintenance is optimal for all *Lacerta*, which even in central Europe can be kept outside throughout the entire year for nearly all species, particularly when part of the area is roofed over with glass and frost-free over-wintering sites are available. Winter dormancy is recommended and will stimulate breeding activity even in southern forms. Such a dormancy period should last for 4 to 6 weeks in subtropical species and 2 to 4 months for species from temperate regions. Just turning off the heat with a simultaneous increase in humidity for 4 to 6 weeks is sufficient for all species from the Near East. A common mistake when keeping *Lacerta* is to maintain a more or less even temperature in the terrarium day and night throughout the year.

Many species have been bred over several generations. A prerequisite for healthy, strong progeny is the optimum condition of the female. Be sure to give calcium supplements. The incubation temperature must not be above 30° C., otherwise the young are often weak and in poor condition. Rearing newborn *Lacerta* requires considerable patience and attention, a varied diet, ultraviolet radiation, and calcium and vitamin supplements.

▪ *L. agilis* LINNAEUS, 1758. Sand Lizard. Western Europe to central Asia. 9 subspecies. Easily to 20 cm; eastern subspecies almost 30 cm. Compact, head blunt and short. Coloration variable. In the central European nominate subspecies mainly the flanks of the males are green, but in eastern forms the whole back is almost completely green. Must not be kept too dry. Winter dormancy important.

▪ *L. armeniaca* MEHELY, 1909. Armenian Lizard. Caucasus. Mountain valleys and slopes. Barely 20 cm. Most robust form of the parthenogenic rock lizards.

▪ *L. bedriagae* CAMERANO, 1885. Tyrrhenian Mountain Lizard, Bedriaga's Rock Lizard. Corsica, Sardinia. Mountains. To easily 20 cm. Dorsally greenish to brown, often with wide, dark reticulated pattern. Requires lots of moisture.

▪ *L. danfordi* (GUENTHER, 1876). Danford's or Anatolian Lizard. Southern and western Turkey. Rocky areas. Rather dry habitats, often among old ruins (walls, etc.). Easily to 20 cm. For mode of life refer to *Podarcis muralis*. Robust.

▪ *L. echinata* BOULENGER, 1887. Spiny-tailed Lizard. West Africa. In forests and treed savannahs. To 35 cm. Tail more than ⅔ of snout-vent length, with very large spinous scales. Dorsally green, throat orange; abdomen yellow; tail brown. Isolated within the genus and apparently not

Lacerta viridis

closely related to any of the other species. Should be kept in a moderately damp terrarium with climbing branches and with only slight temperature gradient between day and night (max. 5° C.).

• *L. graeca* BEDRIAGA, 1886. Greek Rock Lizard. Southern Greece. Often in rocky but level habitats. Barely 25 cm.

• *L. laevis* GRAY, 1838. Eastern Mediterranean Region. 25 cm. Dorsum usually unicolored rust-brown, flanks dark brown; throat and abdomen in males greenish, yellowish in females. Requires a fair amount of heat and a short winter dormancy at about 10° C.

• *L. lepida* DAUDIN, 1802. Ocellated, Jeweled, or Eyed Lizard. Southern France to northwestern Africa. More than 60 cm. Mainly green with blue ocelli and dark vermiform markings.

• *L. oxycephalus* DUMERIL and BIBRON, 1839. Sharp-snouted Rock Lizard, Dalmatian Lance-headed Lizard. Southwestern Yugoslavia. Rocky habitats, often close to water. Barely 20 cm. Mostly blue-green with a dark reticulated pattern, but melanistic specimens also occur.

• *L. parva* BOULENGER, 1887. Dwarf Lizard. Caucasus, Turkey. Rocky steppes to 2000 m elevation. Barely 15 cm. Appearance and markings similar to *L. agilis*.

• *L. pater* LATASTE, 1880. Northwestern Africa. 45 cm. Green with blue flank spots. Females often brownish. The first reptile to develop melanistic progeny in captivity. More delicate and requires more heat than closely related *L. lepida*.

• *L. praticola* EVERSMANN, 1834. Meadow Lizard. Caucasus and northern Balkan Peninsula. Relatively damp habitats with dense vegetation. About 15 cm. Must not be kept too hot and dry. Similar to *L. vivipara*.

• *L. saxicola* EVERSMANN, 1834. Caucasus Rock Lizard. Crimea to Caucasus and Iran. Rocky habitats that are not too dry. Easily to 20 cm. Males may have bright green dorsal coloration.

• *L. schreiberi* BEDRIAGA, 1878. Iberian Emerald Lizard, Schreiber's Green Lizard. Southern, western, and central sections of the Iberian Peninsula. To 30 cm. Most males green, females brown or green, often with white spots on sides. Requires more moisture than *L. viridis* and is somewhat more sensitive, but can easily be kept in captivity.

• *L. strigata* EICHWALD, 1831. Caucasus Emerald Lizard. Caucasus to Iran. Bushy steppes to mountain chains. Barely 40 cm. Light dorsal stripes with dark spots between. Males usually almost without markings, green. Winter dormancy important.

• *L. trilineata* BEDRIAGA, 1886. Giant, Three-lined, or Balkan Emerald Lizard. Southeastern Europe and southwestern Asia. Drier and somewhat more open habitats than *L. viridis*. To 50 cm. Cheeks and lateral neck region blue during breeding season; sometimes with 8 longitudinal rows of ventral scales. Often delicate in captivity and prone to diseases.

• *L. unisexualis* DAREVSKY, 1966. Caucasus. Relatively wet mountain valleys. Barely 20 cm. Parthenogenic.

• *L. viridis* (LAURENTI, 1768). Green or Emerald Lizard. Southern and central Europe to Asia Minor. 40 cm. Males during the mating season have blue throats (see *L. trilineata*). Relatively adaptable. Does well in captivity and breeds easily.

• *L. vivipara* JAQUIN, 1787. Viviparous Lizard. Temperate and cool (in Scandinavia beyond the Polar Circle) Palearctic from northwestern Spain to Siberia. Outer forest regions, forest clearings, and in swamps. 15-18 cm. Brown, males with orange-yellow to red abdomen. Ovoviviparous, usually 2 to 6 young. Hardy, but often prone to diseases in an indoor terrarium. Must not be kept too hot and dry. Winter dormancy beneficial to the animals.

Lacertidae: Lacertids. Family of the Squamata. Mainly in subtropical and temperate zone of the Palearctic and in Africa, with some species extending to southwestern Asia. About 22 genera, more than 200 Recent species. Lacertidae belongs to the family series Scincomorpha and together with Teiidae and some smaller families is opposite the Scincidae. Found in deserts, steppes, open forests, rocky areas, and (rarely) in tropical rain forests. Invariably the body is slender, the tail relatively long, and the limbs well developed (some exceptions). The upper temporal arch is completely ossified. The dentition is rather homogenous, pleurodont. Osteoderms are present only on the head, fused with the skull bones of the roof. Dorsal area of head with enlarged and often paired shields. Ventral scales large, mostly in distinct longitudinal rows. Caudal scales spinous. A collar is characteristic of this family and consists of large scales between throat and thoracic scales; it is indistinct (or completely absent) in only a few species. Femoral pores are almost always present on the ventral side of the thighs. These are glandular scales that give off a wax-like secretion and are particularly well developed in males. They appear to have a function in reproduction and territory marking. They can also be used to distinguish the sexes in many species; in females they are small and apparently without function. The tail is very fragile and can be thrown off when in danger. Preformed fracture lines for autotomy are present from the 6th tail vertebra onward. Lacertidae have an excellent regeneration capability, but the new tail never reaches the full length of the original one.

The ability for quick physiological color changes is not or only poorly developed, and then is restricted to quite weak lightening or darkening of colors. The males of some species are brightly colored during the mating season. Juvenile coloration and markings are usually more contrasting than those of adults; very brightly colored tails are quite common. All species are diurnal and love to sunbathe (with the possible exception of some little known cryptic tropical forest species).

The territorial behavior of virtually all species with the exception of some desert species is of importance in terrarium management. The males of many *Lacerta* species are so incompatible among each other that usually only one male can be kept with several females in one terrarium. Before the fight the males threaten each other by flattening their bodies laterally and by simultaneously rising up on their forelegs. The following biting usually remains within tolerable levels, certainly with smaller species, but the constant repetition of this under confined terrarium conditions sooner or later leads to the demise of defeated males. For the purpose of mating the male follows the female, which will always attempt to flee. In most species the male secures a characteristic flank bite laterally and just in front

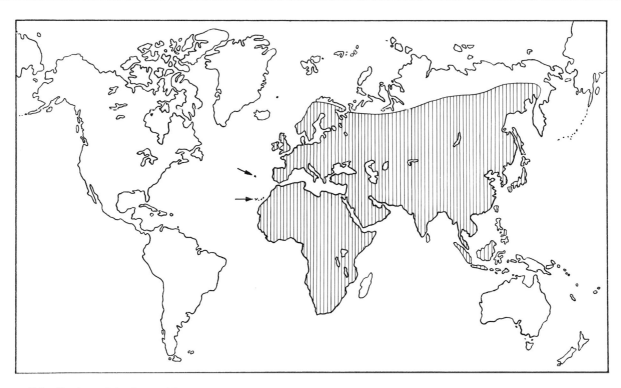

Distribution of the Lacertidae

of the hind legs, and by bending his body under that of the female inserts both hemipenes into the cloaca of the female, the male often being dragged along by the evasive female. The neck bite, widely occurring among lizards, is only seen in a few of the more primitive genera, such as *Gallotia* and *Psammodromus*. A characteristic movement of the females is kicking: When a male approaches the female she raises her forelegs and executes walking movements in the air. "Kicking" females are often more or less ready to mate. This type of behavior is particularly well defined in, for instance, species of *Lacerta*. With the exception of *Lacerta vivipara* and some *Eremias* species that are ovoviviparous, most species are egg-layers.

The systematics of this family has yet to be satisfactorily resolved. The following genera occupy primarily subtropical regions of the Palearctic: *Acanthodactylus*, *Algyroides*, *Eremias*, *Gallotia*, *Lacerta*, *Latastia*, *Ophisops*, *Philochortus*, *Podarcis*, and *Psammodromus*. Numerous genera, mostly with only a few species, inhabit Africa: *Adolfus*, *Aporosaura*, *Bedriagaia*, *Gastropholis*, *Holaspis*, *Ichnotropis*, *Meroles*, *Nucras*, *Poromera*, and *Tropidosaura*. The genera *Cabrita* and *Takydromus* are confined to the Orient.

Lachesis DAUDIN, 1803. Bushmasters. Monotypic genus of the Crotalidae. Nicaragua to northern South America and on Trinidad. Found in cooler microhabitats of the tropical rain forest, especially in mountains. To 3.75 m, the largest of the Recent venomous snakes (together with *Ophiophagus* and *Oxyuranus*). Dorsal surface of head covered with small scales. Tail without rattle, but with horny spines. When excited, the tail end will also vibrate as in *Agkistrodon*, *Crotalus*, and *Sistrurus*. Body with dark rhomboidal spots with light edges.

Nocturnal, usually rare snakes that prey mainly on small mammals. The venom is not very potent, but the dosage injected with each bite is very large and the long fangs in-

Lachesis muta

Lachesis muta

ject the venom deeply, so bites can easily be fatal. Egg-layers.

Maintenance is difficult, since newly collected animals often refuse to feed (presumably due to inappropriate collecting methods, stress, and incorrect maintenance). They should be given a rain-forest terrarium with constantly high humidity (70%) and relatively low temperatures (18-22° C.). Basking spots must be provided. These snakes require adequate hiding places. Breeding has succeeded under such conditions. Incubation takes 76-79 days.
• *L. mutus* (LINNAEUS, 1766). Bushmaster, Surucucu. 2 subspecies.

Laemanctus WIEGMANN, 1834. Casque-headed Iguanas. Genus of the Iguanidae. Central America from southern Mexico to Honduras. 2 species (4 species according to some authors) in tropical rain forests. To 70 cm. Very slender, tail about 3 times snout-vent length. Limbs long. An obliquely backward pointing helmet present, substantially more strongly developed in males; sometimes also a simple serrated dorsal crest. Green or brown with dark crossbands and sometimes with lighter longitudinal stripes. Distinct physiological color changes.

Ideally adapted to an arboreal life, rarely leaving the trees. Egg-layers, 3-5 eggs per clutch. Maintenance similar to *Basiliscus*. Require lots of heat, day temperatures to 35° C. They should be given water, but they rarely bathe. Males incompatible.
• *L. longipes* WIEGMANN, 1834. Helmet without a serrated crown. Dorsal crest absent.
• *L. serratus* COPE, 1864. Helmet with distinctly serrated crown. Low, serrated dorsal crest.

Laemanctus longipes

Lampropeltis FITZINGER, 1843. Kingsnakes. Genus of the Colubridae, Colubrinae. Southwestern Canada southward to northern South America, most diverse in the USA and Mexico. About 7 species and many subspecies whose systematic status is still doubtful. Found in many types of habitats from swamps and forests to savannahs and semi-deserts. 35 cm to almost 2 m. Many species are coral snake "mimics" (*L. pyromelana*, *L. zonata*, *L. triangulum*) and are commonly called tricolored kings. *L. getulus* and its subspecies have incomplete black and white or yellow rings that can vary quite substantially from a sprinkling of spots to uniform coloration or even longitudinal stripes.

Primarily crepuscular and nocturnal ground snakes that feed mainly on earthworms and amphibians (*L. triangulum*), lizards, snakes (including crotalids!), small mammals,

Laemanctus longipes

Lampropeltis alterna

Lampropeltis getulus californiae

Lampropeltis getulus californiae

Lampropeltis calligaster rhombomaculata

birds and their eggs, and reptilian eggs. The large species (especially *L. getulus*) have gained a reputation as venomous snake exterminators. Egg-layers, 6-25 eggs per clutch. Must be kept in a well-heated dry terrarium with sufficient hiding places. Most species do well in captivity, although the tricolors can be very delicate and difficult to feed. Bathing facilities should be available for at least *L. getulus* and *L. triangulum*.

▪ *L. getulus* (LINNAEUS, 1766). Eastern Kingsnake. USA east of the Rocky Mountains and in the Southwest to

Lampropeltis getulus floridana

Lampropeltis getulus californiae

Lampropeltis getulus floridana

Lampropeltis getulus californiae

Lampropeltis mexicana

Lampropeltis getulus holbrooki

Lampropeltis mexicana

Lampropeltis getulus splendida

Lampropeltis getulus getulus

Lampropeltis pyromelana pyromelana

Lampropeltis triangulum triangulum

Lampropeltis triangulum elapsoides

Lampropeltis triangulum sinaloae

Lampropeltis zonata pulchra

northern Mexico. About 7 or 8 subspecies.
- *L. pyromelana* (COPE, 1866). Sonoran Mountain Kingsnake. From northern Utah to southeast Arizona and Sonora and Chihuahua, Mexico.
- *L. triangulum* (LACEPEDE, 1788). Milk Snake. From the eastern USA to central Mexico and Yucatan, and then through Central America to Ecuador. Well over 20 recognized subspecies.
- *L. zonata* (LOCKINGTON, 1876). California Mountain

Lampropeltis zonata parvirubra

Kingsnake. California and Baja California. About 5 subspecies.

Lamprophis FITZINGER, 1843. South African House Snakes. Genus of the Colubridae, Lycodontinae. Eastern and southern Africa. About 5 species in dry habitats (savannahs), also entering urban areas (*L. aurora*). 40 cm to 1.1 m. See also *Boaedon*.

Lampropeltis triangulum annulata

Lampropeltis zonata multifasciata

Nocturnal ground snakes that feed mainly on lizards (skinks and geckos). Egg-layers, 8-10 eggs. Should be kept in a well-heated dry terrarium with ample hiding places.
• *L. aurora* (LINNAEUS, 1754). Aurora House Snake. Southern and southeastern Republic of South Africa. Olive brown with a very attractive red dorsal stripe.

Lampropholis FITZINGER, 1843. Genus of the Scincidae (*Leiolopisma* Group). Australia, Tasmania. 5 species. Related to *Notoscincus* and *Carlia*. To 15 cm. Distinguished from the above two genera by movable eyelid. Limbs with 5 toes. Egg-layers.
• *L. delicata* (DE VIS, 1888). Eastern Australia. 12 cm. Rain forest. Light and dark bands. Ground-dweller.

Langaha BRUGNIERE, 1784. Leafnose Snakes. Genus of the Colubridae, Boiginae. Madagascar. 2 species in tropical dry forests and rain forests. About 1 m. Readily recognized by the peculiar snout extension whose function is still unknown. In males the protrusion is cylindrical and termi-

Lampropholis delicata

Robert Sprackland

This is the 1878 illustration of the earless monitor from Steindachner's original description. A photograph of the holotype in Vienna is shown for comparison. Tom Harrison, one of the first scientists to see a live specimen, claimed that the original illustration of this lizard, depicting it with a "piggy little eye" was misleading. Judge for yourself.

Sarawak's Earless Monitor Lizard

(Lanthanotus borneensis)

One of the world's rarest and most evolutionarily intriguing reptiles becomes a little better known.

Louis Porras

by Robert George Sprackland, Ph.D.

Herpetology has come a long way since Francois Daudin wrote the first purely herpetological text in 1802. Reptiles and amphibians have proven to be excellent model animals for studying most aspects of general zoology, from reproduction and development to anatomy and behavior.

Published information about herpetology has grown, and pertinent papers now find copious avenues for publication in hundreds of journals, newsletters, yearbooks and magazines.

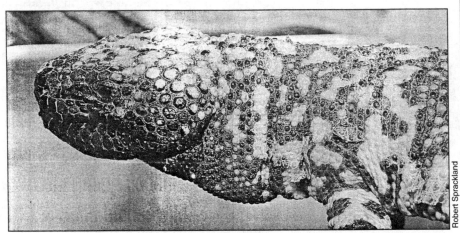

Because of superficial anatomical similarities between the American beaded lizards and the Bornean earless monitor, all were long considered members of the same family, the Helodermatidae. This is a Gila monster, *Heloderma suspectum*.

Additionally, hundreds of books are available, with dozens of new titles coming out each year.

This information deluge has forced herpetologists to become specialists, if for no other reason because it is humanly impossible to keep up with all the literature and still have time to conduct research (and teach, and write for grants and talk to your spouse...). Despite this information saturation, relatively few syntheses are published for given species (though for excellent examples, see any of Auffenberg's works on Komodo, Gray's and Bengal monitor lizards), leaving a considerable chore for the person trying to get solid data when, for example, a rare species turns up after a long hiatus. In some cases, as when the first live specimen of the rare Sumatran tree agama, *Harpesallrus* (=*Harpesaurus*) *becarrii*, was discovered in the 1980s, no prior literature record existed; the species had been known for about 100 years from just a handful of preserved specimens. On the other hand, some species leave a record based on the spotty observations made now and again over a great span of time, in which case the literature may be obscure and out of print, leaving modern researchers scrambling to find clues to the nature of the animal.

A case in point is the earless monitor lizard from Borneo. *Lanthanotus borneensis* ("hidden ear from Borneo") was described in 1878 by Austrian zoologist Franz Steindachner based on a single large specimen that remains remarkably well preserved at the Naturhistorisches Museum in Vienna. In the intervening years, we have learned a considerable amount of detail about the anatomy of *Lanthanotus*, a bit about its captive husbandry and far less about its natural history.

For many years, *Lanthanotus* was considered an odd relative of the Gila monster, and later was believed a primitive ancestor to snakes. Its apparent rarity makes the availability of even small tissue samples, for molecular analysis, difficult. Recently, new specimens have begun to show up in collections, but with exorbitant price tags that make private ownership very difficult. Earless monitors are seen as difficult to maintain in captivity, yet specimens collected in the 1960s lived for nearly 18 years under crude conditions.

In this article, *Lanthanotus borneensis* will be examined in light of the past 127 years of observation.

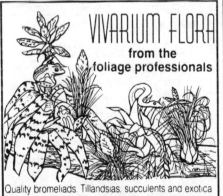

Discovery and Description

Steindachner immediately recognized his new species as being quite different from any other known Bornean lizard—in fact, he was sure that *Lanthanotus* was distinct enough from any lizard to justify placing it in its own family, the Lanthanotidae. The body and tail are subcylindrical, covered with a heterogeneous mix of large and small scaly tubercles. The larger tubercles form longitudinal rows that begin on the neck and extend the length of the tail. Four or five large tubercles run along the temples. The head is flat, blunt and covered with tiny scales. Their tiny eyelids have translucent white "windows," and the tinier nostrils are directed dorsally. The tongue is forked, as it is in monitors and tegus, and the single specimen was preserved with the mouth forming a wry smile. There is no sign of an external ear opening, and Steindachner used this character to give his new genus its name. The legs of *Lanthanotus* are short and stocky, but each terminates in five well-developed and clawed digits. The holotype measures about 17 inches (435 millimeters) overall, but a record specimen measuring 20 inches was collected in the mid-1960s. We have since learned that a broken tail does not regenerate.

In color, *Lanthanotus* is orange-brown dorsally and beneath the head, lacking any pattern of spots or bands. The belly is mottled with rusty orange and ochre. Overall, the average person would probably see an earless monitor, shrug, and move on, for it is not what one would normally consider an impressive animal.

Despite intense interest in *Lanthanotus*, it remains a poorly understood species. It is not, however, as rare as some accounts suggest, for most major natural history museums have specimens. Nevertheless, it is a hard animal to find, and the frustration of several generations of seekers has added to the lizard's mystique.

Relationships: Fossils and Snakes

Ever since "biodiversity" replaced "ecology" as the new life-science buzzword, there have been many questions about the value of making inventories of living things and studying rare or obscure creatures. However, such basic research is the foundation upon which other studies must be built, for applied sciences often are inspired by incidental observations made by scientists who are interested in nature for its own sake. Thus, the basic science of taxonomy lead pharmacists from a rare California tree that possesses a chemical that treats some cancers to a distant, but related tree in Europe, which is more common and contains much higher quantities of the life-saving substance. We don't always know where "mere" observation

nized, or was there an existing family more similar to *Lanthanotus* that would suffice? He chose the latter, and included the Bornean lizard with America's beaded lizards in the Helodermatidae. The generally similar body forms, beaded scales, forked tongues and short limbs were considered features of relatedness, not convergence. Shortly after the catalogue was published, Boulenger managed to borrow a specimen of *Lanthanotus* from the Sarawak Museum, with the object of examining the dentition to see if the two groups were actually related. His resulting

WHAT IS A FAMILY?

A family represents a cluster of similar genera, which in turn represent clusters of closely related species. However, biologists are far from concordant about what a species is, so the subject of families becomes rather ethereal. A major point of confusion (and antipathy) revolves around the difference between a phylogeny (q.v.) and a classification.

A phylogeny attempts to show the pattern of relationships between and among living things, and as such is really a chart of the origins of species. In contrast, a classification is an attempt to organize such data so that it is retrievable for further study. Ideally, the classification reflects phylogeny, so that as species clusters become larger new "files" are invented to collect them together. There is no such thing in nature as a genus or family, but they serve as sophisticated call numbers for the library of living things.

Is *Lanthanotus* to be included in the Varanidae or the Lanthanotidae? It really doesn't matter. Its phylogenetic position places it between beaded lizards and monitors, so wherever it is placed, it should be with its closest relatives (it is generally held to be a bit more monitorlike than beaded lizardlike). The hierarchical system of family and higher names is often so subjective that many biologists are suggesting they be discarded altogether.

and luck will bring us. In some cases, they may lead to a better understanding of ancestors.

Steindachner's prize did not become an obscure footnote like many other species named from a lone specimen. A few years after the Austrian description of the lizard, Belgian herpetologist George Albert Boulenger began working on a catalogue of lizards for the British Museum (Natural History). The publication was intended to update earlier works listing the museum's holdings, but Boulenger decided to list all the known species in the world, with the request that species listed but not represented in the museum should be considered on the museum's "wish list." Boulenger hoped that travelers and museum colleagues would send specimens to fill in the gaps.

When Boulenger had to catalogue *Lanthanotus*, he was unsure how to include it. Was Steindachner's family to be recog-

paper was ambiguous, and he left *Lanthanotus* with *Heloderma*. A generation of zoogeographers would use this odd example of Asian-American distribution to support and refute theories of land bridges and drifting continents. As recently as 1946, Hobart Smith would note that a third venomous lizard species might inhabit Borneo.

The picture changed drastically in 1954 when Samuel McDowell and Charles Bogert dissected the only American (known at the time) specimen of *Lanthanotus* and compared its anatomy with a wide variety of other lizards. Bogert had been working on a major study of beaded lizards (published in 1960 with R.M. del Campo as *The Gila Monster and its Allies*, reprinted by the Society for the Study of Amphibians and Reptiles), and resolving the relationships of *Heloderma* with *Lanthanotus* was an important part of that work. The footnote study became a major mono-

Say you saw it in REPTILES!

graph leading to several astonishing conclusions.

Lanthanotus, it was quickly demonstrated, lacked grooved teeth or venom glands. It was superficially beaded-lizardlike, but this was due to evolutionary convergence. In fact, the two genera lived in quite different habitats, and the convergence was shown to be less remarkable than anticipated. The Bornean enigma was compared with the other lizard families, but obviously belonged within the Anguimorphan lineage, the group that includes beaded lizards, monitors, alligator lizards, xenosaurs and California legless lizards.

Furthermore, its anatomy placed *Lanthanotus* square between beaded lizards and monitors (the Platynota, now called Varanoidea), and McDowell and Bogert suggested that it just might be a survivor of the otherwise extinct Aigia-losaur group (an idea later discarded). The real innovation, however, was the suggestion that *Lanthanotus* possessed the various features necessary for a modified subterranean existence, including reduced

family, Lanthanotidae, as proposed by its describer in 1878.

Lanthanotus had been thrust into the limelight of evolutionary biology's search for the origins of snakes, and the Bornean lizard would be fixed in that role for decades. The biggest problem for students of snake origins is that snakes make lousy fossils. The few decent fossils are relatively recent Tertiary specimens less than 40 million years old, but snakes are known to have lived side-by-side with Mesozoic animals at least 80 million years ago. Those older fossils are fragmentary and lack the telltale bones that would help answer evolutionary questions. Deprived of such direct evidence, scientists turn to available materials to look for probable (or at least possible) ancestors. By 1954, the earless monitor seemed to answer the job description for such a relative. Consequently, the subsequent fame, interest and research into *Lanthanotus* since then has largely revolved around the presumed snake-earless monitor relationship.

PHYLOGENETIC METHODS

A phylogeny is really nothing more frightening than a genealogy of species, purporting to show the relationships between ancestors and descendants. In reality, we cannot be certain of most ancestors, though we can closely predict the group that is most likely ancestral to another, later species (and we do know that descendants did have ancestors).

To do this, evolutionary biologists employ a comparative method that examines individual characters, such as anatomy, genetics or DNA sequences, that are most likely part of an ancestor-descendant sequence. Such shared characters are called homologies, or synapomorphies. The wings of birds and bats are homologous, being formed from the same embryonic tissues of bones (five fingers) and muscles; the bee's wing is not homologous, however, as it derives from quite different back tissues (a situation called analogy).

It is never simple to determine if characters are homologous. Consider the reptilian forked tongue. Monitors, earless monitors, beaded lizards, tegus and snakes all possess this character, but only the first three seem to share it from a common ancestor, while tegus and snakes may have "invented" their tongues independently.

As zoologists learn more about developmental biology, new homologies are discovered, analogies discarded and phylogenies will improve. With each new breakthrough, we get a better view of the history of life through time.

eyes, no external ear, recurved teeth, a forked tongue and elongated body, that seemed to be indicative of an ancestor to snakes. The *Lanthanotus*-snake link replaced the heloderm link, and has predominated in earless monitor studies to this day (with, not surprisingly, little consensus at this time). The unusual position of *Lanthanotus* warranted its own

The bulk of those ensuing studies corroborated both the unique familial status and snakelike morphology of *Lanthanotus*. But in the late 1970s, herpetology was embracing a new tool for studying relationships among organisms, a method called phylogenetic systematics, or cladistics. The method had been proposed by German entomologist Willi Hennig in the 1950s and began to catch on after his book was translated into English in the 1960s (although Hennig established himself as an entomologist and founder of a new school of taxonomy, one of his earliest works was a review of the flying dragons, genus Draco).

In short, Hennig stated that overall similarity was not enough data to base a classification, rather, one must be sure to

Some contemporary herpetologists have cited the many evolutionarily related similarities (synapomorphies) between the earless monitor and true monitors (*Varanus*) and combined the lizards together into the family Varanidae. Others maintain that the Lanthanotidae remains justified. So long as the relationships are understood, agreement on family rank is really of minor importance.

The island of Borneo is divided among four nations, Sabah, Brunei, Indonesian Kalimantan and Malaysian Sarawak. The only confirmed locality records for *Lanthanotus* are from riverine areas of Sarawak (lightened area on map), though recent reports have claimed specimens originating from Kalimantan. The latter reports, concerning specimens collected by an Indonesian animal dealer and subsequently sold to an American zoo, have yet to be confirmed.

Area of confirmed reports of *Lanthanotus*.

Brunei

Sabah

Sarawak (Malaysia)

Kalimantan (Indonesia)

BORNEO

Source: Robert Sprackland

compare features for which evolutionary relatedness can be reasonably assured. Many of the features that made *Lanthanotus* seem snakelike (reduced eyes and limbs, elongated body, bifid tongue, loss of upper temporal arch of skull and external ear openings, etc.) were also found in many other lizards. When new characters were examined for which relatedness could be reasonably assumed, *Lanthanotus* no longer seemed a reasonable snake ancestor. For now, the origin of snakes is again an open issue. Meanwhile, the true relatives of *Lanthanotus* were being recognized.

For more than 100 years, *Lanthanotus* sat alone on the western half of Borneo, with no close relations in sight. This changed as the result of joint Mongolian-Polish palaeontological expeditions into the Gobi desert, where Magdelena Borsuk-Bialynicka discovered fossil remains of a Cretaceous (about 75 million years old) lanthanotid which she dubbed *Cherminotus*. From this fossil, we have learned that the lanthanotid line has remained little modified over the vast time involved, and that fossil lanthanotids were no more monitorlike or beaded lizardlike than modern species.

Life History

Lanthanotus borneensis, the only known living species in its group, is widely distributed in Sarawak along the northwest third of Borneo, and all museum records for the lizard come from Sarawak. More recently, reports have come from Indonesia that specimens are being found in the border country of Kalimantan (the Indonesian bulk of Borneo) near Sarawak. These reports have not been confirmed, but they are not improbable. *Lanthanotus* is probably not rare, just rarely collected. Most major museums have at least one specimen, while many have three or more, and "new" specimens are still being discovered.

While examining lizards at the Royal Museum of Scotland in Edinburgh in 1994, I chanced upon such a lizard on display in the reptile gallery. It had been purchased some 90 years ago from a London animal dealer and had long been thought to be only a cast! It seems that rare specimens are still likely to turn up in the most unexpected places.

At times, such as during periodic spring floods, several specimens may turn up in traps in a single village. The relative rarity of the species probably

Learn as much as you can about a reptile *before* you purchase it.

reflects three causes. The first is lack of economic importance. An earless monitor doesn't provide much of a meal, nor are they plentiful enough to be a reliable food source. They are useless for fashioning leather goods. Consequently, they may go unnoticed even where they might be common. Despite large rewards for the capture of specimens, western researchers often reported that they had failed to find a local who had even seen a specimen. One herpetologist suggested that earless monitors had not been brought in to the Sarawak Museum because the illustration with the reward-for-capture notice, a copy of Steindachner's 1878 illustration, did not resemble the lizard closely enough for local people to recognize it. Actually, Steindachner's artist did an excellent job; the preparator, however, may have posed the specimen in a more dynamic pose than ever seen in a live specimen.

Second, they are fossorial and semi-aquatic, habits that make any search laborious, and incidental discovery unlikely. Most of the roughly 100 known specimens were collected serendipitously during seasonal flooding, when lizards would be washed out of the ground and caught in baskets and fish traps. During the rest of the time, they are probably deep underground in burrows, for they are rarely turned over when gardens are tilled. So far as I can tell, no one has succeeded in deliberately searching for and finding a live *Lanthanotus*.

Finally, Sarawak is not a country that permits commercial export of live animals. For most of this century, limited scientific collecting has been permitted, but not the broader, economy-linked collecting that would make hunting and selling of the lizards valuable to local people. Commercial collecting would probably have resulted in the discovery of many more specimens over the years, and would most likely be the only way to motivate a lot of people to seek an otherwise valueless animal. Fortunately for Sarawak's unusual fauna, such collecting virtually ceased by the start of World War I. Were it not for the voluminous logging currently deforesting Sarawak, its protection and research policy over wildlife would be most admirable.

The life of *Lanthanotus* is generally well known, but many details are still missing. Once basic details of husbandry were worked out (around 1963), subsequent captives in competent hands seemed to thrive. It is known that the lizard is a burrower that prefers moist soil near river banks. The blunt snout is a functional digging tool, and the tiny legs fold against the body, providing little resistance. The lizard also

Gender can be determined by the shape of the jaw. Males have blunt, rectangular jaws (as viewed ventrally), while females have acute, pointed jaws. Males are also thicker at the tail base, while in females the tail becomes distinctly narrower just posterior to the hips.

Reproduction of earless monitors may involve copulation while in the water and may last for an hour or more.

Lanthanotus borneensis remains an enigmatic species about which most normal questions go unanswered. Is it rare or just rarely seen? When is egg-laying done? What is the incubation time? Are the lizards really lethargic or is that a result of captivity? What is their natural diet, their natural range? Are earless monitors ancestrally related to snakes or not? Someday, perhaps we shall be lucky enough to know the answers.

RIGHT: The earless monitor is a burrowing species that inhabits moist environments, which may be part of the reason it is so elusive to humans.

Robert Sprackland

LEFT: *Lanthanotus borneensis* is a drab lizard that would easily escape the notice of anyone but a specialist.

Louis Porras

can swim, and may remain submerged for at least an hour, during which time the eyes are covered by the translucent lower lid, and valves tightly constrict to shut the nostrils. Specimens have been observed to initiate a kind of metabolic reduction, in which breathing and movement cease for as long as a day. To the uninitiated, this state may be taken for coma or death. A similar ability has been observed in the Chinese crocodile lizard, *Shinisaurus crocodilurus*, which is similar in appearance and, to the degree that it is also semiaquatic, habits. Such an ability is beneficial to an animal that lives in burrows that can occasionally flood with water. Reduced breathing and heartbeat can make it possible to survive until waters recede or escape is possible. Earless monitors have been induced to climb, aided by a highly prehensile tail, but have not been observed to do so voluntarily.

The natural diet is unknown. Captives readily accept fish filets, earthworms and an occasional beaten egg, and have been known to subsist on this diet, with no ill effects, for more than a decade.

Eggs, which were reported as early as 1912, have not been laid by captives, but have been taken from preserved specimens and number three or four. They are medium-sized (1.25 inches long), oval and leathery-shelled.

Captive earless monitors require little leg room, because they are rarely active. Robert Mertens kept a pair of these lizards for many years in a terrarium about the size of a 10-gallon aquarium. The lizards prefer a deep substrate of moist (not wet) potting soil and soft moss in a consistency that allows burrowing. A large dish of water is essential, and the lizards regularly swim, or remain quietly submerged. Daytime air temperature should be kept between 78 and 85 degrees Fahrenheit, dropping to 70 to 75 degrees at night. Indirect, full-spectrum lighting is recommended, with a fluorescent tube kept over the area with the water dish. Animals typically refuse food the first month or so, but once they begin feeding should be offered food three times per week. There is no report of problems keeping several specimens together.

Acknowledgements

My research into the natural history of this unusual lizard would have been impossible without the help of three curators of the Sarawak Museum, the late Tom Harrisson, the late Benedict Sandin and Lucas Chin. The late Robert Mertens also corroborated hypotheses from his observations of captive *Lanthanotus*. This article is dedicated to the memory of my father, Joseph Francis Smith (1919-1994), in recognition for his continued support and encouragement of my study of this enigmatic animal. ✤

Dr. Robert George Sprackland, a longtime contributor to REPTILES, is a systematic herpetologist who has studied monitors and earless monitors since 1967. He is a Research Associate of the National Museums of Scotland, and is co-founder of Young Forest Company, an applied taxonomy CD-ROM publisher. Dr. Sprackland has just completed the first volume in The CURATOR Project, titled "Sharks and Rays of the World," and is resuming work on a comprehensive book about monitors.

requisite is an adequate supply of eels (specialized feeders). The snakes must also be able to haul out onto a dry land section since they molt and rest on land. Provide hiding places and a basking spot.

- *L. colubrina* (SCHNEIDER, 1799). Yellow-lipped Sea Krait.
- *L. laticauda* (LINNAEUS, 1758). Black-banded Sea Krait.

Laticaudinae: Sea Kraits. Monogeneric subfamily of the Hydrophiidae. Typically in coastal regions. Venomous snakes with many primitive features in contrast to the subfamily Hydrophiinae. Body normal, oval in cross-section, the tail flattened laterally. Scales of the body are still differentiated into smaller, shingled dorsal scales and relatively wide ventral scales. The head also displays primitive features, and the structure of the upper jaw is more like that of the closely related Elapidae than the Hydrophiinae; the fangs are located anteriorly.

These snakes leave the water occasionally and may live on the beach. Their movements on land are still agile, but feeding is always done in water. Egg-layers.

Latreille, Pierre Andre (1762-1833): French entomologist and herpetologist. Author of various forms of North American herpetofauna.

Laurasia: see Gondwana.

Laurenti, Joseph Nikolaus. Austrian physician and herpetologist of the 18th Century. Author of numerous taxa in *Synopsis Reptilium,* which was published in 1768. The author's name, "Laurenti," is an incorrectly formed Latin genitive. However, the manuscript (submitted as a medical dissertation) was not written by Laurenti but instead by his student (and later chemist), Winterl from Budapest, who worked anonymously for the wealthy and egotistical Laurenti. This plagiarism was discovered by Fitzinger in 1832. Laurenti must not be confused with the Belgian herpetologist R. Laurent, author of numerous herpetological taxa from central Africa.

Laurentophryne TIHEN, 1960. Monotypic genus of the Bufonidae. Tropical Africa. Related to *Nectophryne* and *Wolterstorffina.*
- *L. parkeri* (LAURENT, 1950).

Leandria: see *Brookesia,* genus.

Learning: Information gained from an individual's experiences are absorbed and stored during the learning process so that they can be retrieved for proper action as needed. There is no comprehensive knowledge about learning capabilities of amphibians and reptiles. However, individual investigations (using labyrinths as well as color and shape discrimination) have shown that reptiles have a very poorly developed visual learning ability when compared to fish, birds, and mammals.

Lechriodus BOULENGER, 1882. Genus of the Leptodactylidae. New Guinea (3 species) and Australia (1 species). Found in various types of forests (rain forests, dry forests). Rather slender. Externally somewhat reminiscent of *Platymantis,* but in contrast has a smooth skin. The tympanum is clearly visible. Pupil horizontal. Narrow adhesive disks on tips of fingers and toes.

Lechriodus species breed in ponds and pools as well as in flowing waters, but never in large aggregations (maximum 6 to 12 pairs). The eggs are deposited in the form of sticky clumps in shallow water. The larvae are carnivorous. Cannibalism is common.
- *L. fletcheri* (BOULENGER, 1890). Fletcher's Frog. Australia, Pacific coast. 5 cm. Light gray to reddish brown with dark spots. Frequently with dark crossbands between the eyes.
- *L. melanopyga* (DORIA, 1875). New Guinea. Common. 5 cm. Light olive, sparingly covered with a black pattern consisting of a double dorsal band, dorsal and flank spots, and double crossbands on the thighs.

Leimadophis FITZINGER, 1843. Genus of the Colubridae, Xenodontinae. Southern Central America southward to Argentina. About 30 species. Very confused; some species of *Dromicus, Alsophis, Antillophis,* and *Arrhyton* were formerly included in *Leimadophis.* Outer tropical forests and steppes. 25 to 50 cm.

Diurnal ground snakes. The diet consists of frogs, lizards, and mice. For care see Natricinae, Group 1, but these snakes also require dry areas.
- *L. reginae* (LINNAEUS, 1758). Northern South America.
- *L. poecilogyrus* (WIED, 1823). Amazon Basin to Argentina.

Leimadophis reginae

Leimadophis poecilogyras

Leiocephalus GRAY, 1827. Curly-tailed Lizards. Genus of the Iguanidae. Antilles from Cuba to Trinidad. About 12 species. Similar mainland forms are now placed in a separate genus (*Ophryoessoides*). Typically in open forests, rocky steppes, and on sandy beaches. 15 to 35 cm. Strongly built. Tail longer than snout-vent length. Dorsal scales large, shingled, and strongly keeled. There may be low dorsal and caudal crests. Lateral scales are variable, either similar to the dorsal scales (e. g., *L. carinatus*, *L. personatus*) or small and then with a distinct lateral fold (*L. schreiberi*, *L. melanochlorus*). Often attractively colored. Particularly conspicuous are the reddish tail in *L. personatus* that is operated like a whip when threatened and the black and white banded tail in *L. carinatus* that is rolled vertically up and down when excited.

Leiocephalus personatus

Leiocephalus carinatus

Leiocephalus carinatus

Diurnal ground-dwellers that feed mainly on arthropods. Egg-layers. For details on care refer to *Liolaemus* and *Tropidurus*. Nighttime temperatures should not drop much below 20° C. Males are rather incompatible among each other. Has been bred occasionally.
• *L. carinatus* GRAY, 1827. Cuban Curly-tail. Cuba. Rocky deserts, often close to shore. To 25 cm. Very large scales.
• *L. personatus* COPE, 1862. Masked Curly-tail. Haiti. Several subspecies. Sandy beaches to open forests. 25 cm. Males very attractively colored; highly variable.
• *L. schreibersi* (GRAVENHORST, 1838). Red-sided Curly-tail. Haiti. Dry, hot habitats. 22 cm. A distinct lateral fold is present.

Leiolepis CUVIER, 1829. Butterfly Lizards, Butterfly Runners. Genus of the Agamidae. Southern China through Indo-China to Sumatra. In relatively dry, open habitats. 5 species. To 50 cm, slightly flattened dorso-ventrally. Head rounded. Tail long, the caudal scales slightly keeled. Dorsal scales small, granular. Crests and gular pouch absent, but a wide gular fold present. Males have femoral pores but are without preanal pores.

Ground-dwellers that dig deep burrows. The diet consists mainly of arthropods, occasionally also some young plant shoots. Generally speaking, they are strictly monogamous. Egg-layers. One species is triploid and parthenogenic.

They should be given a dry terrarium with a deep sub-strate layer (the lowest layer must always be slightly damp). Day temperatures can range from 30 to 35° C., at night about 10° C. lower. Require lots of drinking water.
• *L. belliana* (GRAY, 1827). Butterfly Lizard. Several subspecies. Gray to olive above, sides yellow to red with black stripes.

Leiolopisma DUMERIL and BIBRON, 1839. Genus of the Scincidae. Southern Australia, Tasmania, New Zealand, New Caledonia, and some other islands. 35-40 species. 10 to 40 cm. Slender. With the exception of *L. pseudoornatum*, the lower eyelid has a transparent window and is freely movable. Ear opening large. The tail is long. The well-developed limbs are 5-toed (with one exception). Primarily shades of brown, often with darker spots; some species with light longitudinal stripes. Juveniles have brightly colored tails.

Ground-dwellers, some frequently in agricultural areas. They may like to sunbathe and be diurnal (*L. austrocaledonicum*, *L. metallicum*); others live cryptically along the ground in tropical rain forests or in montane forests (*L. tricolor*, *L. spenceri*); still others occupy trees and bushes (*L. nigrofasciolatum*). The diet consists mainly of arthropods, but large specimens will also take small lizards. Egg-layers, clutches with up to 9 eggs. Captivity data scarce. Refer to *Mabuya*.
• *L. austrocaledonicum* BAVAY, 1869. New Caledonia. 15 cm.
• *L. metallicum* O'SHAUGNESSY, 1874. Southeastern Australia; introduced into Hawaii. 20 cm.
• *L. spenceri* LUCAS and FROST, 1894. Southeastern Aus-

Leiolepis belliana

Leiolopisma telfairii

tralia. Montane regions.

Leiopelma FITZINGER, 1861. New Zealand Frogs. Genus of the Leiopelmatidae. New Zealand. 3 species, the only native amphibians of New Zealand. *L. hochstetteri* lives in montane streams, while the other two species occur in cool, humid areas. No tympanum. Pupil horizontal. Fingers free, toes webbed to about half their length (*L. hochstetteri*) or webbing largely reduced (*L. archeyi* and *L. hamiltoni*). The latter species have conspicuous large glands behind the eyes that give off a white secretion of unknown function.

Semiaquatic (*L. hochstetteri*) or terrestrial (other species). *L. archeyi* and *L. hochstetteri* deposit a few (up to 10) very large (5 mm diameter) eggs on land in burrows or under rocks. These eggs are surrounded by a gelatinous layer and contain—apart from the actual germ layer and yolk material—a lot of water, in which the entire larval development takes place. The larvae inside the eggs deviate in several characteristics from free-swimming frog larvae; they lack a respiratory opening and keratinous structures (jaws, teeth)

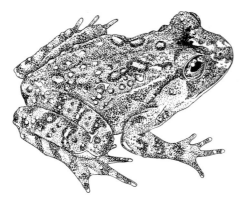

Leiopelma archeyi

in the mouth. The young frogs, still carrying a tail, hatch as largely metamorphosed specimens after about 40 days. These animals occur in only a very few places and are strictly protected. Not significant in the terrarium hobby.
• *L. archeyi* TURBOTT, 1942. Coromandel Peninsula, above 250 m elevation. To 4 cm. Variable, black pattern against green to brown background. Has been bred in captivity.
• *L. hamiltoni* McCULLOCH, 1919. Stephens Island, Maud Island, South Island. Coastal forests above 150 m elevation. To 5 cm. Light to dark brown, legs and flanks with darker pattern. Rarest species.
• *L. hochstetteri* FITZINGER, 1861. Warkworth, Waitakeri Ranges, Coromandel Peninsula, southward along coastal regions. To 5 cm. Brown with darker pattern. Compact. Skin with warts.

Leiopelmatidae: Family of Salientia. New Zealand; only one genus, *Leiopelma*. Together with the Nearctic family Ascaphidae considered as ancestral frogs since these are the most primitive of the Recent frogs. Primitive characters include amphicoelic vertebrae, the largest number (9) of free vertebrae in frogs, flexible pectoral girdle, free bony ribs, remnants of abdominal ribs, and a rudimentary tail musculature.

Leiosaurus DUMERIL and BIBRON, 1837. Genus of the Iguanidae, subfamily Anolinae. Argentina, southern Brasil.

5 species of uncertain status. A little known genus.
• *L. belli* DUMERIL and BIBRON, 1837.

Lepidobatrachus BUDGETT, 1899. Genus of the Leptodactylidae. South America, Gran Chaco Region. 3 species. Related to *Ceratophrys*, but in contrast the metatarsal tubercle is absent in *Lepidobatrachus*. More than 12 cm. Pupil vertical. Extremely aggressive.
• *L. asper* BUDGETT, 1899. Argentina. Males 7 cm, females 9 cm. Brownish.

Lepidoblepharis PERACCA, 1897. Genus of the Gekkonidae. Central America and northern South America. 7 species.
    Small ground-dwellers, little known. See *Sphaerodactylus*.
• *L. festae* PERACCA, 1897. Brasil.

Lepidochelys FITZINGER, 1843. Ridley Turtles. Genus of the Cheloniidae. Found in tropical and subtropical seas, absent from the Mediterranean Sea. 2 species. Carapace length to 75 cm. Carapace with 5-9 pairs of costal shields. Bridge between carapace and plastron on both sides with 4 large inframarginal shields. Carapace brownish to olive, without a marbled pattern, thus not desirable commercially as tortoise shell.
    Incubation in the wild takes 49-70 days.
• *L. kempi* (GARMAN, 1880). Atlantic or Kemp's Ridley. Mainly in Gulf of Mexico, straying north to New England and Canada. Seriously endangered since this species has only one known site where all females to deposit their eggs (Mexican coast near Rancho Nuevo). Feed on crustaceans, molluscs, fish.
• *L. olivacea* (ESCHSCHOLTZ, 1829). Pacific Ridley, Olive Ridley. Indo-Pacific and South Atlantic.

Lepidochelys olivacea

Lepidochelys kempi

America, restricted to small areas. 7 often rare species predominantly in rocky habitats. The absence of supraocular scales and the variable size of the dorsal scales are characteristic. In some species the sides have vertical rows of clearly enlarged, keeled scales, but the dorsal scales are always small and smooth. Mainly shades of brown and gray, often with round yellow spots.

▪ *L. flavimaculatus* DUMERIL, 1851. Mexico to Panama. Easily to 10 cm. Rows of distinctly keeled lateral scales.

▪ *L. gaigeae* MOSAUER, 1936. Southern Mexico. Very rare. About 10 cm. Lateral scales not conspicuously enlarged.

Lepidophyma flavimaculata

Lepidophyma nr. *flavimaculata*

Lepidodactylus FITZINGER, 1843. Genus of the Gekkonidae. Southern and southeastern Asia through the Indo-Australian Archipelago to Oceania. 16 species. Close to *Hemidactylus*. Found in various types of habitat and follows human habitation. Barely more than 10 cm. Toes with indistinct adhesive lamellae.

Crepuscular to nocturnal. For maintenance see *Hemidactylus*, but should be kept slightly warmer and possibly damper.

▪ *L. lugubris* (DUMERIL and BIBRON, 1836). Mourning Gecko. Distribution as above; introduced into New Zealand and Panama. Barely 10 cm. Mainly brown, with highly variable markings. Parthenogenic, reproducing without males.

Lepidophyma DUMERIL, 1851. Central American Night Lizards, Bark Lizards. Genus of the Xanthusiidae. Central

Lepidodactylus lugubris

Lepidophyma gaigeae

Lepidoptera: Butterflies and moths. Order of Insecta. About 150,000 species. The larvae (caterpillars) of many Lepidoptera make excellent food for terrarium animals if they are not too hairy. They can sometimes be collected in huge numbers off plants or bushes. Nocturnal moths and related forms often make excellent food for large amphibians and many lizards. These insects can easily be attracted with a strong light source. A number of Lepidoptera can easily be bred and are among the most popular food organisms.

Lepidoptera: Moths are eaten by many lizards and frogs

Lepidosauria: see Amniota.

Leposoma SPIX, 1825. Genus of the Teiidae. Costa Rica southward to northern South America. 7 species in tropical rain forests. To 10 cm. Slender. Snout-vent length barely 4 cm. Lower eyelid with a semitransparent window. Well-developed limbs. Large, keeled scales. Mainly brown with light longitudinal stripes and a yellowish to orange belly.

Ground-dwellers. Diet mainly small arthropods. *L. per-*

carinatum is parthenogenic.
- *L. percarinatum* (MUELLER, 1923). Venezuela, Guyana, and northern Brasil. To 10 cm.

Leposternon WAGLER, 1830. Genus of the Amphisbaenia. Tropical South America. 6 species. In forests. 20 to 30 cm. Slender. Head with a dorso-ventrally flattened snout.

Ground-dwellers. Some species are supposed to feed mainly on earthworms.
- *L. microcephalum* WAGLER, 1824. Small-headed Worm Lizard. Amazon Basin to northern Argentina.

Leptobrachella: see *Nesobia*, genus.

Leptobrachium TSCHUDI, 1838. Asian Spadefoots. Genus of the Pelobatidae. Subtropical and tropical eastern Asia. 5 species in tropical rain forests in lowlands and mountains; the northernmost form (*L. oshanensis*) is found under rocks along dry, cultivated mountain slopes. 3 to 9 cm. Skin smooth. Externally distinguishable from the closely related genus *Megophrys* by the rounded inner metatarsal tubercle that does not extend onto the first toe. Pupil vertical. Tympanum distinct or partially covered by skin. Fingers free, toes free or webbed at base only. Larvae elongated, with a subterminal mouth and the respiratory aperture on the left side.

Nocturnal ground-dwellers. The larvae live in slight currents in clear creeks and small streams among rocks and plants (bamboo, free-floating roots, etc.).

Tropical species should be kept in a rain-forest terrarium with a diversely structured bottom layer. *L. oshanensis* must be provided with a slightly heated, semimoist steppe terrarium.
- *L. gracilis* GUENTHER, 1872. Malaya and Kalimantan. Males 3 cm, females 5 cm. Brown with darker pattern.
- *L. hasselti* TSCHUDI, 1838. Burma and Malaya to Java, Kalimantan, Bali, and the Philippines. 3 subspecies. 6.5 cm (males) and 9 cm (females). Brown with darker spots, limbs with dark crossbands.
- *L. oshanensis* (LIU, 1950). Western China, Sichuan (1,000 m). 3 cm. Red brown with sparse black pattern.

Leptodactylidae: Family of the Salientia. Mainly in Neotropics (subfamilies Ceratophryninae, Telmatobiinae, Elosiinae, and Leptodactylinae) and Australia (subfamilies Cycloraninae and Myobatrachinae), also in South Africa (subfamily Heleophryninae). Probably a paraphyletic group, since they do not include the Dendrobatidae, which were derived from the Elosiinae. The Australasian forms are often put in a separate family, Myobatrachidae. Presently with 57 genera and about 650 species. The Leptodactylidae include such diverse forms that recognition based on external features seems hardly possible; however, in these frogs the fingers are always free (no webbing). Apart from amphibious species there are also completely aquatic ones (extreme development in *Batrachophrynus* and some *Telmatobius*) as well as terrestrial species without a free-swimming larval stage (*Eleutherodactylus* and related genera of the *Leptodactylus marmoratus* Group). Therefore, this family is in a good position to utilize large lakes as well as areas with little open water.

The subfamilies contain the following genera:
- Cycloraninae: *Adelotus, Cyclorana, Heleioporus, Lechrio-*

dus, Limnodynastes, Mixophyes, Neobatrachus, Notaden, Philoria.

- Myobatrachinae: *Crinia, Glauertia, Metacrinia, Myobatra-chus, Pseudophryne, Taudactylus, Uperoleia.*
- Heleophryninae: *Heleophryne.*
- Ceratophryninae: *Ceratophrys, Cacophrys, Lepidoba-trachus.*
- Telmatobiinae: *Amblyphrynus, Batrachyla, Batrachophry-nus, Caudiverbera, Crossodactylodes, Cyclorhamphus, Eleuth-erodactylus, Euparkerella, Eupsophus, Holoaden, Hylacto-phryne, Hylorina, Ischnocnema, Niceforonia, Odontophrynus, Proceratophrynus, Scythrophrys, Sminthillus, Syrrhophus, Tel-matobius, Telmatobufo, Thoropa, Tomodactylus, Zachaenus.*
- Elosiinae: *Crossodactylus, Hylodes, Megaelosia.*
- Leptodactylinae: *Barycholos, Edalorhina, Hydrolaetare, Leptodactylus, Limnomedusa, Lithodytes, Paratelmatobius, Pleurodema, Pseudopaludicola.*

Leptodactylodon ANDERSSON, 1903 (= *Bulua* BOULENGER, 1904). Genus of the Ranidae. Tropical West Africa. 5 species. In mountain streams. To 4 cm. Compact when viewed from above, egg-shaped and flattened. Skin smooth. Limbs short, stout. Tympanum difficult to see. Toes webbed at base only. Males with more or less paired gular vocal sacs.

- *L. albiventris* (BOULENGER, 1905). Cameroons, Nigeria. To 2.5 cm. Dorsum dark brown, abdomen whitish.
- *L. ovatus* ANDERSSON, 1903. Cameroons, Nigeria. To 4 cm. Light yellowish red, the thighs with dark crossbands; ventral region black with a lighter marbled pattern.

Leptodactylus FITZINGER, 1826. Tropical Bullfrogs, White-lipped Frogs. Genus of the Leptodactylidae. From Texas through Central America, including the Antilles, to Ecuador and east of the Andes south the Argentina. Between 30 and 60 species; the genus needs to be revised.

Leptodactylus pentadactylus

Primarily in lowlands (plains), montane forms not found in excess of 1200 m elevation. Body size highly variable (2 to more than 20 cm). Externally similar to *Rana*, but toes without webbing. Pupil horizontal. Dorso-lateral skin folds present or absent. Vocal sac unpaired, paired, or absent. Tympanum clearly visible or hidden. Lateral skin folds present or absent on toes.

More or less semiaquatic, preferring to remain close to water. Species occupying arid regions tend to survive the dry periods in hiding and then congregate in pools, ponds, and puddles during the rainy season. The males of most species are able to vocalize loudly to attract females. At that time some species also develop secondary sex characteristics, e. g., nuptial pads on the hands and extraordinarily swollen arms (*L. pentadactylus*, *L. ocellatus*). Species of the *melanotus*, *ocellatus*, and *pentadactylus* Groups deposit

Leptodactylus fallax

numerous small eggs in floating bubblenests. In contrast to this, species of the *fuscus* Group establish their bubblenests on damp ground in self-dug pits that may even be surrounded by an earthen wall or be largely covered with soil as protection against desiccation. At high water the larvae can then reach the the pool or pond, or get washed into it through run-off. The *L. marmoratus* Group does not have a free-swimming larval stage, but instead fully metamorphosed juvenile frogs hatch directly from the few large eggs deposited on the damp ground; they therefore are sometimes placed in a separate genus (*Adenomera*).

Leptodactylus species should be kept in a damp terrarium with a small water section (palustral species) or in an aquaterrarium (semiaquatic species). Large species (e. g., *L. ocellatus*, *L. pentadactylus*) should only be kept together with specimens of equal size or, better yet, should be kept individually because of cannibalism.

▪ *L. labialis* (COPE, 1877). Mexican White-lipped Frog. Texas to Venezuela. 5 cm. Brown with dark spots, the upper lip white, delineated by black below. Palustral. Has been bred in captivity in terrariums with a deep substrate.

▪ *L. marmoratus* (STEINDACHNER, 1867). Colombia to Brasil. 3 cm. Brown with orange markings. Terrestrial.

▪ *L. melanotus* (HALLOWELL, 1860). Black-backed Whistling Frog. Mexico to Central America. 5 cm. Semiaquatic.

▪ *L. mystaceus* (SPIX, 1824). Amazon Basin, *selva*. 6 cm. Gray-olive with a dark eyeband and a white upper lip. Terrestrial.

▪ *L. ocellatus* (LINNAEUS, 1758). Ocellated Bullfrog. Venezuela to Argentina. To 13 cm. Olive-green with irregular dark spots. Semiaquatic.

▪ *L. pentadactylus* (LAURENTI, 1768). South American Bullfrog. Central America to Brasil. In excess of 20 cm. Highly variable. Dorsum with wide red-brown crossbanded pattern against a yellow-brown background. Semiaquatic.

Leptodeira FITZINGER, 1843. Cat-eyed Snakes. Genus of the Colubridae, Boiginae. From southern Texas to northern Argentina and Paraguay, absent at higher elevations in the Andes and from the dry regions of western South America. 9 partly polytypic species. At median levels in tropical forests, frequently in agricultural areas (especially on banana plantations). 0.75 to 1.1 m, very slender. Head clearly set off from thin neck. Conspicuously large eyes with vertical pupils. Body laterally compressed. Tail long. Can be mistaken for *Dipsas* or *Imantodes* as well as *Tripanurgos*. Markings usually consist of dark rhomboids against a light background.

Nocturnal, arboreal. They like to bathe in standing water and may even hunt there for frogs, as well as among

Leptodeira annulata

Leptodeira annulata pulchriceps

bushes. Should be kept in a well-heated tropical forest terrarium. Caution: Venomous (painful but not deadly) bites possible.

▪ *L. annulata* (LINNAEUS, 1758). Mexico to Argentina. 6 subspecies. Sometimes more terrestrial than other species in this genus.

▪ *L. septentrionalis* (KENNICOTT, 1859). Cat-eyed Snake. Texas to Peru.

Leptodrymus AMARAL, 1927. Monotypic genus of the Colubridae, Colubrinae. In lowlands of Central America from Honduras and Guatemala to Nicaragua and Costa Rica. Closely related to *Masticophis* and *Coluber*. Found in dry forest regions, in secondary forests, and thornbush vegetation. To 1.2 m. Head slender, elongated. 2-4 black longitudinal stripes against an olive-brown dorsal coloration.

Ground snakes. Maintenance as for *Coluber*.

▪ *L. pulcherrimus* (COPE, 1874).

Leptomicrurus SCHMIDT, 1937. Slender Coral Snakes. Genus of the Elapidae. Northern South America. 3 species. To 60 cm. Banded like other coral snakes, but the rings not completely encircling body. For details on ecology, biology, and maintenance refer to *Micrurus*. This is a very doubtful genus that probably is best considered part of *Micrurus*.

▪ *L. collaris* (SCHLEGEL, 1837). Guyana, Surinam, French Guiana.

Leptopelis GUENTHER, 1858. Forest Treefrogs. Genus of the Rhacophoridae. Tropical and subtropical Africa. More than 30 species, but needs revision. Mainly in tropical forests of the plains and mountains, but also found on savannahs. 6 to 8 cm. Compact. Skin granular. Head large and broad, the snout short and blunt. Very large protruding eyes, the pupils vertical. Tympanum clearly visible. Fingers and toes more or less webbed, tips usually with large adhesive discs. Inner metatarsal tubercle large, the outer one usually very small or absent. Females often twice the size of males. Frequently with species-specific juvenile coloration. Larvae very elongated and heavily pigmented.

Leptopelis bocagei

Predominantly bush- and tree-dwellers found close to water. Nocturnal. Typical forest species move to the ground for reproduction. As far as is known, a pair while in amplexus burrows backward into damp soil of the banks along water and there deposit a small number of large eggs. There are no large breeding congregations. Embryonic and larval development are slow. When hatched, the larvae wriggle into the water close by, often into jungle streams, but also into any small waterhole. Another ecological type

Leptopelis argenteus concolor

is represented by *L. argenteus, bocagei, bufonides, cinnamoneus, oryi,* and *viridis*, which occupy savannahs. They are characterized morphologically by more or less distinct adhesive discs and very poorly developed webbing on the feet. They climb just like forest-dwellers among bushes, on trees, and in tall grass, but during the dry season they burrow into the ground. *L. bocagei* has lost all climbing abilities and is a ground-dweller.

These frogs should be kept in a spacious tropical rainforest terrarium or in a savannah terrarium with normally damp soil and a small water section, which will be used only occasionally. Robust plants and thick branches have to be available, since the frogs often like to sleep at the highest possible location in the terrarium. The diet should consist primarily of large insects. Caution: *Leptopelis* will swallow any animals, including lizards and other frogs, that fit into their mouth. Outside the breeding season the smaller males should be kept apart from the very much larger females. A rainy season must be simulated and water with suitable banks must be present. Due to the great metabolic activity of these frogs, the terrarium becomes dirty quickly and must be cleaned often. These frogs become tame fairly quickly.

▪ *L. argenteus concolor* AHL, 1929. Kenya and Tanzania. Coastal region. 3.5 cm. Light brown, with diffuse darker pattern.

▪ *L. bocagei* (GUENTHER, 1864). East Africa. 6 cm. Brown, dorsum with horseshoe-shaped darker markings.

▪ *L. flavomaculatus* (GUENTHER, 1864). Eastern and southern Africa. 7 cm. Dorsally either uniform green or with a triangular or horseshoe-shaped figure against brown background.

▪ *L. macrotis* SCHIOETZ, 1967. Sierra Leone to Ghana. Montane rain forests. In excess of 8 cm. Reddish brown with irregular dark crossbands and spots that are sometimes fused.

▪ *L. vermicularis* (BOULENGER, 1909). Tanzania (Usambara and Rungwege Mountains). 7 cm. Several color varieties. Dorsum bright green or brown with thin black vermiform lines.

▪ *L. viridis* (GUENTHER, 1868). Tropical West Africa to Cameroons. 5 cm. Reddish brown with a dark brown pattern. Abdominal region white.

Leptophis BELL, 1825. Parrot Snakes. Genus of the Colubridae, Colubrinae. Mexico southward to central Argentina. 7 species in dry tropical forests and brushlands. To

Leptophis occidentalis

Leptophis ahaetulla

Leptophis ahaetulla

1.4 m. Very slender, with a large, elongated head. Body covered by large scales in only 15 rows, which can be either smooth or keeled and are shingled. Green to blue-green.

Diurnal ground snakes. The diet includes frogs, birds, and lizards. Egg-layers, to 15 eggs per clutch. They should be kept in a well-heated dry forest terrarium. Newly collected specimens are very aggressive.

• *L. ahaetulla* (LINNAEUS, 1758). Mexico to Argentina. 12 subspecies.

• *L. mexicanus* DUMERIL, DUMERIL, and BIBRON, 1854. Southern Mexico and Yucatan to Costa Rica. 2 subspecies.

Leptotyphlopidae: Slender Blind Snakes. Family of the Scolecophidia. America, Africa, Asia (Indian eastern border); not in Madagascar, Southeast Asia, Australia, or Europe. Most systematists include the about 40 species in the genus *Leptotyphlops*, although on zoogeographical grounds alone further genera could be justified, e. g., *Rhinoleptus* in Africa. Found in dry regions as well as in rain forests and montane forests. 8-30 cm. Evenly cylindrical, many species only to 3 mm in thickness. In contrast to the Typhlopidae, the tail in these snakes is always longer than wide. The top of the head is covered with large scales; the rostral is the largest scale and is often projecting, covering the subterminal mouth. In contrast to the Typhlopidae, there are no teeth in upper jaw, but instead there are teeth in the lower jaw. Rudiments of the pelvis and upper leg bones are present; in some species these are visible as anal spurs on either side of the cloaca. Body scales are few and large (up to 14 rows around middle of body). The median abdominal scales are somewhat larger than the remaining body scales. Mostly uniform brown, but some species have yellow longitudinal stripes.

These snakes live underground in ant nests and termite mounds. Species from rain forests are frequently found in the root tangles of epiphytes. The diet consists of ant and termite larvae; frequently only the fluids are sucked out. These snakes may be active outside their hiding places following heavy rain and after dark. Reproduction is by means of few, but very large eggs. Feeding may be difficult since these snakes appear to be food specialists.

Leptotyphlops FITZINGER, 1843. Slender Blind Snakes. Genus of the Leptotyphlopidae. About 40 species. For details on biology and maintenance refer to family description.

• *L. dulcis* (BAIRD and GIRARD, 1853). Texas Blind Snake. Kansas to Mexico. Dry regions. Apart from *L. humilis*, the northernmost species of the family.

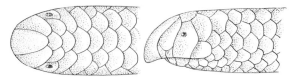

Leptotyphlops macrorhynchus

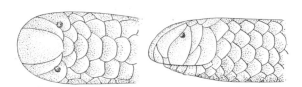

Leptotyphlops narirostris

Leptotyphlops weyrauchi

• *L. humilis* (BAIRD and GIRARD, 1853). Western Blind Snake. California to Texas and into Mexico. Dry regions.
• *L. sundevalli* (JAN, 1862). Ghana, Togo. Tropical forests. 10 cm, the smallest species of this family in Africa.
• *L. macrorhynchus* (JAN, 1862). Turkey, Iran, Arabia, Pakistan. Dry regions. To 17 cm.
• *L. tesselatus* (TSCHUDI, 1845). Peru. Montane rain forests. To 8 cm. Found in epiphyte root stocks. Longitudinal stripes. Among the smallest species of the genus.

Leptotyphlops humilis

Lepturophis BOULENGER, 1900. Monotypic genus of the Colubridae, Lycodontinae. Kalimantan. To 1.4 m, slender. Head large, clearly set off. Dorsal scales strongly keeled. Uniform brown.

These appear to be nocturnal, arboreal snakes in tropical rain forests. Little is known about their biology.
• *L. borneensis* BOULENGER, 1900.

Lerista BELL, 1833. Genus of the Scincidae. Australia. About 35 species found in open, dry habitats. To 15 cm. Slender, elongated. Lower lid with window, movable or partially fused. Ear opening small. Scales smooth. Front feet 5-toed to completely reduced.

Diurnal ground-dwellers frequently found in loose sand. The diet includes ants and termites. Egg-layers.
• *L. labialis* STORR, 1971. Arid Central Australia. 15 cm. Similar to *L. bipes*, but only one supraocular in contact with frontal.
• *L. bipes* (FISCHER, 1882). Northwestern Australia. 15 cm. Eyelid movable. Anterior limbs absent, hind limbs with 2 toes. Reddish brown with dark spots or longitudinal lines.

Leurognathus MOORE, 1899. Shovel-nosed Salamanders. Monotypic genus of the Plethodontidae. USA. Found in clear, cool flowing waters largely free of predators, at elevations from 300 to 1700 m. To 14 cm. Heavily built. Head flat, with small eyes. Tail keeled above. Hind legs better developed than front legs. Distinguished from *Desmognathus* by the internal nasal openings in the roof of the mouth; in *Desmognathus* they are clearly visible holes, while in *Leurognathus* they are poorly visible slits.

Completely aquatic, preferring sandy or gravel bottoms with ample hiding places, mainly under rocks. Due to their inconspicuous marbled camouflage coloration, they barely stand out against the surroundings.

Can be kept and bred in aquariums with cool, oxygen-rich, always clean water, preferably in a cool location (refrigerator or basement). Small crustaceans (amphipods) as well as aquatic insects are eaten.

• *L. marmoratus* MOORE, 1899. Shovel-nosed Salamander. Borders area of Virginia, North and South Carolina, and Georgia.

Lialis GRAY, 1835. Long-headed Scaley-foots. Genus of the Pygopodidae. Australia and New Guinea. Semideserts

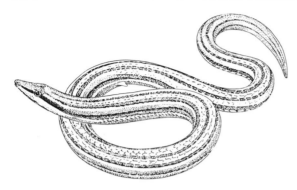

Lialis burtonis

to rain forest. 2 species. To 75 cm. Elongated, the tail as long as the body. The head is pointed and covered with small scales, the mouth slightly subterminal, with numerous large, backward-pointing, sharp teeth. Tympanum visible. Hind limb rudiments about 5 mm long. Smooth scales. Preanal pores present. Yellowish, reddish, gray, or brown, mostly with a striped pattern.

Ground-dwellers, partly diurnal. They feed on arthropods and small lizards.

• *L. burtonis* GRAY 1835. Burton's Snake-lizard. Virtually all of Australia plus New Guinea. To 60 cm. Markings

variable, usually dark brown longitudinal stripes on the body and white lines on the head.

• *L. jicari* BOULENGER, 1897. New Guinea Snake-lizard. New Guinea. To 75 cm.

Liasis GRAY, 1842. Indo-Australian Rock Pythons. Genus of the Boidae, subfamily Pythoninae. Indonesian Islands to New Guinea and Australia. Taxonomy unstable. About 7 to 10 species. Variable; *L. childreni* to 1.5 m, *L. amethistinus* in excess of 6 m (some data suggest to 8 m). Slender, with slender head clearly set off from body and covered with large symmetrical head shields. *Liasis*, together with *Aspidites*, are among the most primitive pythons. Mainly shades of brown. Without markings are *L. fuscus*, *L. olivaceus*; minimally spotted are *L. amethistinus*, *L. mackloti*; spots and rhomboid bands are found in *L. childreni*. Some species are closely tied to the proximity of water; *L. ameth-*

Liasis olivaceus

Lialis burtonis

Liasis mackloti

Liasis albertisi

Liasis amethistinus

Liasis perthensis

istinus and *L. fuscus* occur in mangrove forests; *L. childreni* is found in various habitats close to water; *L. mackloti* and *L. albertisi* are forest-dwellers; *L. olivaceus* is also found in dry montane limestone rock areas. All species are good climbers and swimmers. The diet is dependent upon the habitat; *L. fuscus* prefers young crocodiles.

These pythons should be kept in spacious, well-heated terrariums with climbing and bathing facilities. They often are long-lived but are always aggressive. The following species have occasionally been bred in captivity: *L. amethistinus, L. albertisi, L. childreni, L. fuscus,* and *L. mackloti*.

• *L. albertisi* PETERS and DORIA, 1878. White-lipped or D'Albert's Python. New Guinea and the Bismarck Archipelago. To 3 m. Often considered a subspecies of *L. fuscus* by systematists.

• *L. amethistinus* (SCHNEIDER, 1801). Amethyst Python. Moluccas and Timor to New Guinea, the Solomon Islands, and northern Australia (Queensland). Largest species in this genus. Now often placed in the genus *Python*.

• *L. fuscus* PETERS, 1878. Brown Water Python. Timor to eastern New Guinea and northern Australia. To 3 m.

• *L. olivaceus* GRAY, 1842. Olive Python. New Guinea and northern Australia.

Lichanura COPE, 1861. Rosy Boas. Genus of the Boidae. Western North America. 1 (possibly 2) species. In dry habitats, including oases in western American deserts. To 80 cm. Head only marginally set off from body. Tail short and not terminating in a blunt end as in *Charina*, some *Eryx*, or *Calabaria*. Coloration variable, from an irregular light and dark mosaic pattern to longitudinal stripes in shades of blue gray to reddish brown. Juveniles lighter.

Ground-dwellers preferring areas with little plant

Lichanura trivirgata gracia

growth. Mainly nocturnal. Like to climb about in bushes. They rarely burrow, like *Epicrates* and *Tropidophis*, and feed mainly on small mammals and birds. 3 to 10 young.

Should be kept in moderately heated terrariums with climbing facilities and hiding places. Depending upon the origin of the animals, a short winter dormancy may be recommended.

Some specialists recognize only *L. trivirgata* with several subspecies, while others distinguish 2 species:
▪ *L. roseofusca* COPE, 1868. Coastal Rosy Boa. Southern California to northern Baja California.
▪ *L. trivirgata* COPE, 1861. Mexican Rosy Boa. Baja California and northwestern Sonora into Arizona.

Light: Sufficient light is essential for the well-being of terrarium animals, except for strictly nocturnal or subterranean species. Usually the illumination also serves to heat a basking rock. See Illumination.

Liliaceae: Lilies. Family of the Liliatae. Worldwide distribution. 220 genera with 3500 species. Hardy shrubs with bulbs, tubers, or rhizomes, rarely woody plants. *Aloe, Gasteria, Haworthia, Aspidistra, Chlorophytum, Ophiopogon, Reineckea, Ruscus*.

Limnaoedus MITTLEMAN and LIST, 1953. Least Grass-frogs. Monotypic genus of the Hylidae. Southeastern USA in lowland swamps. Fingers free, toes webbed only at base.

Lichanura trivirgata gracia

Small toe discs. Dorsally brown with characteristic dark brown lateral stripe against cream-colored flanks, brown dorsal stripe, and a triangular spot between the eyes.

These little frogs live among grasses and reeds close to water in pine flatlands. The call of males is an insect-like chirp that is high-pitched, the higher sounds sometimes beyond the human hearing range. Reproduction of Florida populations is not tied to seasons, but northern populations breed from January to September. They should be

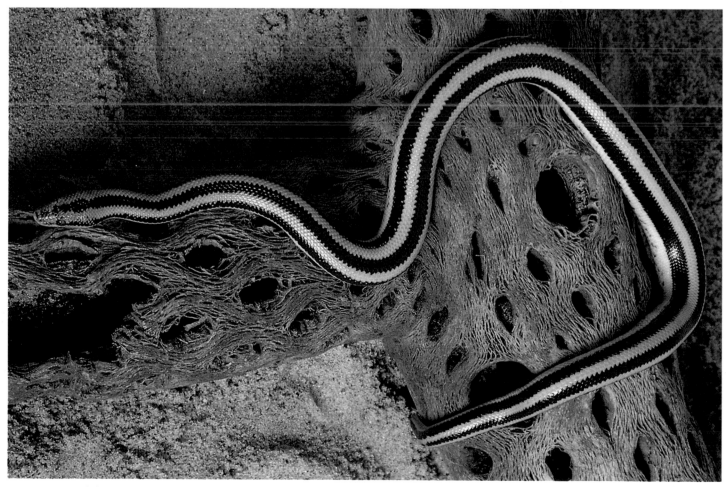

Lichanura trivirgata trivirgata

kept in unheated or only marginally heated aqua-terrariums with large land sections. The diet should consist of very small insects such as fruitflies and springtails.
▪ *L. ocularis* (BOSC and DAUDIN, 1801). Southern Virginia to Florida and adjacent Alabama. About 1.5 cm. The smallest of the North American frogs.

Limnodynastes FITZINGER, 1843. Australian Swamp Frogs. Genus of the Leptodactylidae. Australia (except central arid regions) and New Guinea. About 10 species in various habitats. Mostly about 5 cm, rarely to 9 cm. *Rana*-like, but more spherical. Large head. Pupil horizontal. Tympanum barely visible or not at all. Limbs strong. Fingers free, toes webbed at base only.

Limnodynastes species survive droughts buried in the ground and appear at the surface only on very humid nights. Reproduction occurs during the rainy season in standing or flowing waters. The females transform the egg masses into foamy, floating clumps with their forelimbs. Males are able to vocalize under water.

These frogs should be kept in semimoist terrariums with deep bottom layers and a small water section at tropical or subtropical temperatures (depending upon the origin of the specimens). Small containers are sufficient. Open-air maintenance is recommended during the summer months. *L. peroni* and *L. tasmaniensis* have been bred over several generations.
▪ *L. dorsalis* (GRAY, 1841). Western Banjo Frog. Southwestern Australia. To 7 cm. Gray or brown with an irregular black pattern and a white or yellow narrow dorsal median stripe. Pelvic region red.
▪ *L. ornatus* (GRAY 1842). Ornate Burrowing Frog. Northern and eastern Australia. To 4.5 cm. Highly variable, uniformly dark gray or brown, also light gray or brown with irregular dark spots.
▪ *L. peroni* (DUMERIL and BIBRON, 1841). Brown-striped Frog. East coast of Australia to northern Tasmania. To 6.5 cm. Light gray-brown with an irregular dark brown pattern and often with a wide dorsal band.
▪ *L. tasmaniensis* GUENTHER, 1858. Spotted Grass Frog. Eastern and southeastern Australia and Tasmania. To 4.5 cm. Light brown or olive green with dark brown spots and often with a light median dorsal stripe. Small head.

Limnomedusa FITZINGER, 1843. Genus of the Leptodactylidae. Southern Brasil, Uruguay, and northern Argentina. 2 species on the coastal plain. Externally similar to the related genus *Leptodactylus*, but distinguishable from it by the vertical pupil (also see *Hydrolaetare*). Tympanum externally visible. Toes with lateral skin folds, webbed at base.
▪ *L. macroglossa* (DUMERIL and BIBRON, 1841). To 6 cm.

Limnophis GUENTHER, 1865. Monotypic genus of the Colubridae, Natricinae. Angola to Zimbabwe. Closely related to *Natriciteres*. In flowing waters. 60 cm. Dorsal scales smooth. Alternating light and dark brown longitudinal stripes on the back.

Water snakes that feed on fish and frogs. Egg-layers, about 4 eggs. Maintenance as for Natricinae, Group 2.
▪ *L. bicolor* GUENTHER, 1865.

Lineatriton TANNER, 1950. Monotypic genus of the

Plethodontidae. Mexico. Close to *Bolitoglossa*. Mode of life and reproduction presumably as for other tropical plethodontids.
▪ *L. lineolata* (COPE, 1865). Veracruz.

Linne, Carl von (Latinized as Carolus Linnaeus) (1708-1778): Swedish physician, zoologist, and botanist. Founder of the Stockholm Academy of Sciences and a university professor at Uppsala. Started a comprehensive natural history collection that was the basis for the *Systema naturae*, first published in 1735. In the 10th edition of this book (1758) he presented for the first time a universal system of scientific names of all animals and plants using a two-part name in Latin (binominal nomenclature). He also established the systematic categories of species, genus, order, and class. Numerous amphibians and reptiles still carry the name with his authorship (usually abbreviated by L.).

Lioheterodon DUMERIL and BIBRON, 1854. Genus of the Colubridae, Lycodontinae. Madagascar. 3 species in tropical rain forests. 1.2 to 1.4 m. Compact, with a broad, flat head more or less clearly set off from the body and with large eyes protected by the supraorbitals. Body with smooth, shingled scales. Dorsum dark brown, sometimes with a longitudinal zig-zag band (*L. madagascariensis*).

Ground-dwelling snakes that prey predominantly on frogs. Should be kept in a well-heated, moderately damp rain-forest terrarium with ample hiding places.

Lioheterodon modestus

▪ *L. madagascariensis* DUMERIL and BIBRON, 1854. One of the most common snakes in Madagascar.
▪ *L. modestus* (GUENTHER, 1863). Western Madagascar.

Lioheterophis AMARAL, 1935. Monotypic genus of the Colubridae, Xenodontinae. Paraiba, northeastern Brasil. Closely related to *Leimadophis, Dromicus, Liophis*, and similar genera in this subfamily. In tropical lowland forests. About 40 cm.
▪ *L. iheringi* AMARAL, 1935.

Liolaemus WIEGMANN, 1834. South American Swifts, Smooth-throated Swifts. Genus of the Iguanidae. South America. 45-50 species in various types of habitats but nearly always in dense forests in dry areas. They are found in coastal desert regions as well as in clearings in damp montane forests or in the Andean *puna*. *L. multiformis* is found in the Andes up to 5000 m elevation, often close to the snow line; *L. magellanicus* of Tierra del Fuego is the southernmost reptile species. To 25 cm. Slender to moderately compact, with a blunt head. Tail about twice snout-vent length. Dorsal scales large, shingled, and in some species strongly keeled. Dorsal crest absent. Usually brown, rarely green or gray, with varied markings. Usually with light longitudinal stripes and dark spots.

Distribution of *Liolaemus*

The diet consists mainly of arthropods (especially ants), but occasionally some plant matter is also taken. Predominantly egg-layers, except the ovoviviparous *L. multiformis*, *L. altissimus*, and a few other species. These lizards should be kept in steppe terrariums with a thick bottom layer of sand; the lowest layer must always be kept slightly damp. There should also be some rock piles and possibly some dry roots. Provide day temperatures from 25 to 35° C., slightly higher under a local radiant heat source. High-altitude forms should be kept slightly cooler, but even these forms like to sunbathe in temperatures of up to 30° C. The

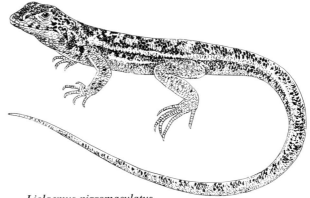

Liolaemus nigromaculatus

temperature should be reduced to 15-20° C. (lowland species) or to about 10° C. (for high altitude species). A small drinking container should be available. Desert species should be sprayed occasionally, montane forms daily. Ultraviolet radiation and calcium and vitamin supplements may be necessary.
▪ *L. altissimus* MUELLER and HELLMICH, 1932. Southern Chile, Argentina (Patagonia). In the Andes up to the snow line.
▪ *L. chilensis* (LESSON, 1830). Central Chile, adjacent regions of Argentina. Bushy regions in lowlands.
▪ *L. fuscus* BOULENGER, 1885. Southern Chile, Argentina (Patagonia). Lowlands.
▪ *L. magellanicus* (HOMBROM and JACQUINOT, 1847). Southern tip of South America.
▪ *L. monticola* MUELLER and HELLMICH, 1932. Central Chile. Andean region.
▪ *L. multiformis* (COPE, 1876). Peru, Bolivia, northern Chile, and Argentina. Andean region to 5,000 m elevation.
▪ *L. nigromaculatus* (WIEGMANN, 1835). Northern Chile. Coastal lowlands.
▪ *L. nitidus* (WIEGMANN, 1835). Northern and central Chile. Rocky deserts and steppes in lowlands and at medium elevations.
▪ *L. occipitalis* BOULENGER, 1885. Southern Brasil, Uruguay. Coastal dunes.

Liolepis: see *Leiolepis*, genus.

Liopeltis FITZINGER, 1843 (= *Ablabes* DUMERIL, 1853). Genus of the Colubridae, Colubrinae. Southern slopes of the Himalayas eastward through Burma and large sections of Indo-China and southward to the large islands of the Indo-Australian Archipelago; also Sri Lanka and the Nicobar Islands. About 9 species. Closely related to the Japanese-Chinese genus *Eurypholis* and the Near East genus *Eirenis*, as well as to *Opheodrys*. In monsoon forests and rain forests; *L. frenatus, stoliczkae, calamaria*, and others occur in mountain ranges up to 2,000 m elevation. To 80 cm. Head barely set off from body. Some species are uniformly brown, others have longitudinal stripes (*L. frenatus, calamaria, longicauda, scriptus, tricolor*) or crossbars (*L. baliodirus* and *rappi*). *L. scriptus* has a collar.

Ground snakes that feed on small lizards and various arthropods. Little is known about their mode of life. They should be provided with well-heated damp terrariums with ample hiding places, similar to Natricine, Group 1. However, there must also be some completely dry, warm areas in the terrarium.

- *L. baliodirus* (BOIE, 1827). From Malaya to Java, Sumatra, Kalimantan.
- *L. calamaria* (GUENTHER, 1858). Mountain regions of Sri Lanka.
- *L. frenatus* (GUENTHER, 1858). From Assam and Burma to Laos. Mountains.
- *L. rappi* (GUENTHER, 1860). Himalayan slopes from Simla through Nepal to Darjeeling, where quite common.
- *L. tricolor* (SCHLEGEL, 1837). From Malaya to Java, Sumatra, Kalimantan. Mountains to 1200 m.

Liophidium BOULENGER, 1896. Genus of the Colubridae, Sibynophinae. Madagascar, Comores, Reunion. 5 species. In tropical rain forests and dry forests. 30 to 50 cm. Head barely set off from body. Frequently with dorsal as well as ventral longitudinal markings. Nocturnal, rather cryptic ground snakes.

- *L. mayottensis* (PETERS, 1873). Mayotte, Comores. Rain forests.
- *L. torquatus* (BOULENGER, 1888). Eastern Madagascar. Rain forests.
- *L. vaillanti* (MOCQUARD, 1901). Madagascar and Reunion.

Liophis WAGLER, 1830. Genus of the Colubridae, Xenodontinae. South America. About 25 species. 60 to 80 cm.

Nocturnal ground snakes. with a clear preference for the proximity of water (swamps, gallery forests, and similar locations); good swimmers. The diet consists mainly of frogs plus some fish and insects. Egg-layers, up to 8 eggs. Main-

Liophis anomalus

Liophis miliaris

Liophis jaegeri

tenance as for Natricinae, Group 2, in a well-heated terrarium.

• *L. cobella* (LINNAEUS, 1758). South America east of the Andes.

• *L. miliaris* (LINNAEUS, 1758). Amazon Region southward to Argentina.

Liophis elegantissima

Liopholidophis MOCQUARD, 1904. Genus of the Colubridae, Lycodontinae. Madagascar. 5 species. 0.6 to 1.0 m. With more or less distinctly set off, narrow head and conspicuously large eyes. Most species are marked with brownish yellow longitudinal bands. Ecology and biology virtually unknown.

• *L. lateralis* (DUMERIL and BIBRON, 1854). Common.

• *L. sexlineatus* (GUENTHER, 1882). Central Madagascar. Largest species of the genus.

Liotyphlops PETERS, 1857. Genus of the Anomalepidae.

Costa Rica to Paraguay. 12 species. To 35 cm. Head with projecting rostral scale that is larger than any of the other head scales. Lower jaws with one tooth each.

• *L. albirostris* (PETERS, 1857). Costa Rica to southern Brasil and Paraguay.

Lipinia GRAY, 1845. Genus of the Scincidae. Southeast Asia to the Philippines, and New Guinea to Oceania. About 20 species. Related to *Scincella*. To 15 cm. Slender. External ear openings absent. Limbs small, 5-toed. Distinct light and dark longitudinal markings.

Tree-dwellers. Ovoviviparous.

• *L. vittigera* BOULENGER, 1895. Southeast Asia.

Lissemys M. A. SMITH, 1931. Indian Flap-shelled Turtles. Monotypic genus of the Trionychidae. India, Sri Lanka, northern Indo-China. In different types of water, sometimes in temporary pools. The oval, leathery carapace reaches 30 cm. The plastron has 7 callosities and leathery flaps under the posterior legs. The posterior margin of the carapace has embedded plates.

During the dry season these turtles burrow in sandy gravel substrate. Carnivorous. For details on maintenance refer to *Trionyx*. Breeding appears to be facilitated by a dry summer dormancy period, which may be a stimulant for mating.

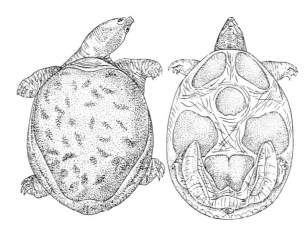

Lissemys punctata

Lipinia noctua

Lissemys punctata

• *L. punctata* (LACEPEDE, 1788). Western Pakistan to northern Tenasserim and Sri Lanka. 3 subspecies. Carapace dark olive with yellow spots and scribbled lines.

Lithodytes FITZINGER, 1843. Monotypic genus of the Leptodactylidae. Outer regions of Amazon Basin, from Guyana to Ecuador and Bolivia, in *selva*. Externally very similar to some Dendrobatidae (*Dendrobates, Phyllobates*), but clearly distinguishable by the large red spots on the upper thighs and pelvis. Pupil horizontal. Tympanum externally not visible. Fingers and toes free.

Diurnal and nocturnal ground-dwellers. Breeding biology unknown. Should be kept in a tropical rain-forest terrarium with a small water section.

• *L. lineatus* (SCHNEIDER, 1799). To 5.5 cm. Dorsum and sides black, sharply divided by a golden stripe. Legs yellow-brown with a black pattern, the upper thighs in pelvic region with large red spots.

Litoria TSCHUDI, 1838. Australasian Treefrogs. Genus of the Hylidae. Formerly considered to be a subgenus or synonym of *Hyla*, and now sometimes considered a separate family, Pelodryadidae. Australia, Tasmania, New Guinea. A large, diverse genus, certainly not monophyletic. Insufficiently delineated from *Hyla* and characterized essentially by the Australian distribution and to some extent by chromosome numbers (*Hyla* mostly n = 12, rarely n = 15; *Litoria* n = 13). Easily distinguishable from the second Australian genus of the Hylidae, *Nyctimystes*, by the horizontal pupil in *Litoria*.

Litoria infrafrenata

There are arboreal *Litoria* species recognizable by the presence of large adhesive discs on the tips of the fingers and toes, as well as terrestrial and semiaquatic forms. Some species follow human habitation, living in buildings (*L. caerulea, L. infrafrenata*) or in garden ponds, city water reservoirs, and similar places (*L. aurea*). Nearly all species spawn in water, and often the eggs float on the surface. In contrast, *L. iris* attaches its few large eggs to plants above the water surface. There is always a free-swimming larval stage. In species that are ecologically tied to flowing water the larvae have a large, wide, oval sucking mouth as protection against drifting.

Captive maintenance depends on the ecological requirements of the respective species. *L. caerulea* is suitable for keeping free indoors; it only requires a shallow water dish. Arboreal species prefer to rest in an elevated position, a fact that has to be taken into consideration when a terrarium is set up. Feeding is best done with insects (grasshoppers, mealworms) or newborn mice pierced by the end of a long wire and then dangled in front of the frogs.

• *L. aurea* (LESSON, 1830). Green and Gold Bell Frog. Southeastern Australia; introduced in New Zealand. To 8.5 cm. *Rana*-like. Dorsally mainly green with irregular large brown or bronze spots. Skin along flanks granular, skin protrusions cream. Semiaquatic, aggressive feeders; cannibalistic.

Litoria caerulea

• *L. bicolor* (GRAY, 1842). Northern Dwarf Treefrog. Northern Australia and southern New Guinea. Subhumid tropical climates with a dry season during the southern winter; open grasslands. To 3 cm. Light green dorsal region separated from yellow ventral region by a wide brown longitudinal stripe.

• *L. caerulea* (SHAW, 1790). White's Treefrog. Northern and eastern Australia. Arboreal in different habitats; tends to follow human habitation. To 10 cm. Plump. Green. Also active during the dry season (crepuscular). Attractive and frequently imported.

• *L. chloris* (BOULENGER, 1839). Red-eyed Australian Treefrog. Australia, eastern coast. Brush and trees in various habitats. To 6.5 cm. Dorsally bright green, iris red. Active after heavy rainfall.

• *L. congenita* (PETERS and DORIA, 1878). Southern New Guinea in more or less dry forests. To 4 cm. Dorsum brown, frequently with yellow longitudinal stripes. Active

Litoria caerulea

following rainfall.

- *L. dentata* (KEFERSTEIN, 1868). Bleating Treefrog. Southeastern Australia along coast. To 4.5 cm. Dorsally brown, dorso-laterally with an irregularly delineated cream-colored longitudinal band. Iris bronze red. Calls are protracted and penetrating.
- *L. dorsalis* (MACLEAY, 1878). Dwarf Rocket Frog. Northern Australia and New Guinea. Open range. To 2 cm. One of the smallest *Litoria* species. Gray or brown, often with irregular dark spots. Penetrating chirping call. Very active.
- *L. inermis* (PETERS, 1867). Northern Australia. 3.5 cm. Brownish with a dark pattern. Pointed snout. Ground-dweller. Active following rainfall.
- *L. infrafrenatus* (GUENTHER, 1867). Giant Treefrog. New Guinea and northeastern Australia (Cape York Peninsula). Various habitats; tends to follow human habitation. To 11 cm. Plump. Green to brown with conspicuous white stripes on the lower lip and posterior part of the hind limbs.

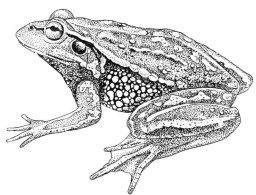

Litoria aurea

- *L. iris* (TYLER, 1962). New Guinea. To 3.5 cm. Dorsum green with a dense pattern of black dots.
- *L. latopalmata* GUENTHER, 1867. Northern and eastern Australia. To 4 cm. Variable, light to dark brown with a dark interrupted lateral stripe. Ground-dweller often found large distances from water.
- *L. nasuta* (GRAY, 1842). Rocket Frog. Northern and eastern Australia, also in New Guinea. To 5 cm. Highly variable, but mostly with large, clearly delineated dark brown spots. Snout conspicuously long and pointed. Nocturnal ground-dweller.
- *L. nigropunctata* (MEYER, 1874). New Guinea, not above

1,500 m elevation. To 4 cm. Gray with black dots. Arboreal.

- *L. peroni* (TSCHUDI, 1838). Peron's Treefrog. Southeastern Australia. Variable habitats often considerable distances from water. To 6 cm. Highly variable gray or brown with irregular dark dots or a reticulated pattern. Call loud, penetrating, a continuous rattling sound.
- *L. rubella* (GRAY, 1842). Desert Treefrog. Southern New Guinea and Australia except southern coastal region. In damp and dry climates. Bushes and trees close to water.

Littoral: Shallow water region adjacent to shore in freshwater (limnological littoral) and marine environments (marine littoral). Here there is high light penetration and thus good habitat for submersed water plants. Toward the shore the littoral is succeeded by the supralittoral (splash zone) and epilittoral (dry shore region). The limnological littoral is occupied by many amphibians and reptiles. The only Recent forms of herptiles that have managed to invade the marine littoral include *Amblyrhynchus*, many Hydrophiidae, *Malaclemys*, and various mangrove inhabitants.

Liver diseases: Diseases caused by nutritional deficiencies as well as by numerous toxic, infectious, and parasitic diseases and occurring in various forms, most commonly as hepatitis (icterus) and fatty degeneration. While icterus can be diagnosed in live animals by yellow discoloration, especially of the mucous membranes, other liver diseases can be determined on the basis of general symptoms (apathy, refusal to feed, loss of condition, dehydration). Even if liver diseases are just suspected, any causal therapy should be supplemented with the following "liver support therapy": 10 ml glucose 5% and/or 2 ml calcium gluconate 24%; 1 ml amino acid infusion solution; 0.5 ml vitamin B

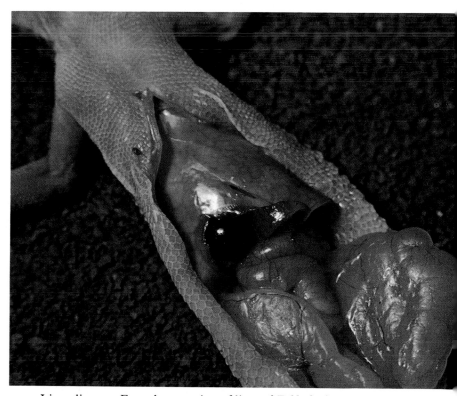

Liver diseases: Fatty degeneration of liver of *Eublepharis*

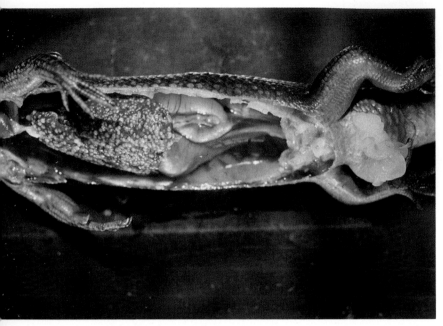

Liver diseases: Pseudotuberculosis of liver of *Egernia*

Locomotion: A: Creeping and lateral motion in tailed amphibians and lizards

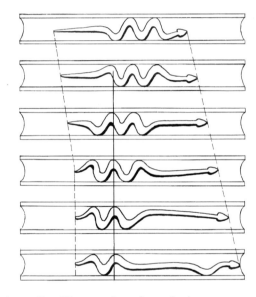

B: Accordion-like creeping of a snake in a narrow tube

complex; 0.1 ml vitamin combination AD3EC aqueous (about 1000 units vitamin A)—per kg of body weight.

This can be administered via stomach tube or subcutaneously. For strongly dehydrated animals it is recommended that an additional 10-20 ml of physiological saline solution be given.

Llanos: Form of savannah covering wide areas in eastern Colombia and Venezuela. Completely dried out grasslands with intermittent palm stands and other evergreen trees during the dry season; widely covered by water during the rainy season.

Lobulia GREER, 1974. Genus of the Scincidae. New Guinea. 5 species. Related to *Scincella* and *Ablepharus* and similar to these but body more robust. Barely 20 cm. Ground- and tree-dwellers.
▪ *L. elegans* BOULENGER, 1897. Tree-dweller.
▪ *L. stanleyana* BOULENGER, 1897. Ground-dweller in forests.

Locomotion: The aquatic larvae of amphibians move by means of lateral movements of the rudder-like tail that often has crests above and/or below. In salamanders adapted for a terrestrial life the legs are often weakly developed. In the frogs the hind limbs have become substantially enlarged so that a simultaneous extension of the legs facilitates jumping as well as swimming. Many reptiles (turtles, lizards, crocodiles) utilize their extremities to an increasing degree for locomotion, although even here locomotion is to some extent more or less supported by lateral body motions. Some long-legged lizards are capable of running in a trotting gait, while others can run on their hind legs (e. g., *Chlamydosaurus, Amphibolurus, Basiliscus*). Crocodiles can also gallop.

Variable habitats and different modes of life have led to special adaptations in the development of the legs. Numerous amphibians and aquatic turtles have webbed feet, and lizards living on sandy ground have widened fingers and toes. The limbs of sea turtles have become modified into elongate, extremely strong flippers. Some tree-dwelling frogs have adhesive discs on the tips of their fingers and toes, and the geckos and some anoles have developed pads under the toes covered with tiny hairs that act as adhesive lamellae. Chameleons have hands and feet that work like pliers and are ideally suited for climbing. A tendency toward a complete reduction of legs occurs to a variable degree in many lizard families and several salamanders, culminating in the limbless snakes and the caecilians. These animals move with lateral sinusoidal motions. Apart from

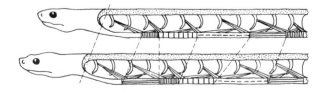

C: Caterpillar-like creeping of a snake, a straight linear forward movement produced by alternate contractions and relaxations of abdominal muscles in waves from front to rear

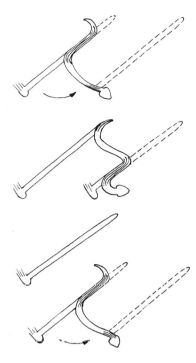

D: Sidewinding in snakes, produced by the body unrolling in single steps so the body touches the ground only at 2 or 3 points at a time

these wave-like motions, the snakes have also developed other forms of locomotion; accordion-like crawling, an alternate stretching and lateral bending of the body; caterpillar-like crawling, straight forward movement created by waves of muscle contractions and relexations; and sidewinding, where the snake's body touches the ground only at two or three points and thus the body moves laterally, obliquely to the actual direction of travel.

Longevity: Time interval between the hatching or birth of an organism and its natural death. Amphibians and reptiles have longevities that can vary from one or two years to far in excess of 100 years. Documented longevities are obtained mostly from terrarium and zoo observations that reflect natural conditions only to a limited extent. Natural longevities have seldom been established with any degree of accuracy. One method to determine the age of a specimen is by counting growth rings on bones if they are produced in reptiles that display periodic (winter/summer) growth.

Representative Longevities in Years

AMPHIBIANS

Sirenidae (*Siren lacertina*)	25
Cryptobranchidae (*Andrias japonicus*)	70
Salamandridae (*Salamandra salamandra*)	50
Proteidae (*Proteus anguineus*)	15
Discoglossidae (*Bombina bombina*)	20
Bufonidae (*Bufo bufo*)	36
Hylidae (*Litoria caerulea*)	16

REPTILES

Chelydridae (*Macroclemys temmincki*)	59
Testudinidae (*Megalochelys gigantea*)	152
Testudinidae (*Testudo hermanni*)	115
Emydidae (*Emys orbicularis*)	70
Sphenodontidae (*Sphenodon punctatus*)	77
Gekkonidae (*Tarentola mauritanica*)	7
Anguidae (*Anguis fragilis*)	54
Helodermatidae (*Heloderma suspectum*)	20
Boidae (*Boa constrictor*)	40
Colubridae (*Elaphe situla*)	23
Elapidae (*Naja melanoleuca*)	29
Hydrophiidae (*Laticauda laticauda*)	5
Viperidae (*Vipera ammodytes*)	22
Crotalidae (*Crotalus horridus*)	28
Alligatoridae (*Alligator mississippiensis*)	56

Lophocalotes GUENTHER, 1872. Monotypic genus of the Agamidae. Sumatra. Similar to *Calotes*.
▪ *L. ludehingi* (BLEEKER, 1860).

Loreal pits: Pit organs characteristic of all pit vipers (family Crotalidae) that are located on either side of the head between the nostril and eye. They serve as highly sensitive heat sensory organs that can detect directional temperature gradients as low as 0.003° C.

Loreal pit in *Agkistrodon contortrix*

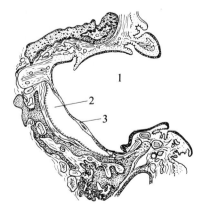

Microscopic cross-section through a loreal pit. 1 Outer pit; 2 inner pit; 3 pit membrane

Loveridgea VANZOLINI, 1951. Genus of the Amphisbaenidae. Tanzania. 2 species. Similar to the better known *Amphisbaena* and *Zygaspis*.
▪ *L. phylofiniens* (TORNIER, 1899).

Loveridgelaps McDOWELL, 1969. Monotypic genus of the Elapidae. Solomon Islands, in tropical forests. 0.8 to 1.0 m. Rounded head barely set off from body, blunt-snouted. Head white with a black rostral area, rest of body with orange and black bands.

Nocturnal venomous snakes that remain underground during the day. The diet consists mainly of frogs, lizards, and worm snakes (*Typhlina*). Like *Bungarus*, it seldom attacks during the day. For breeding and maintenance see *Micrurus*. Potency of venom still unknown.
▪ *L. elapoides* (BOULENGER, 1890).

Loxocemus COPE, 1861. Mexican Burrowing Pythons. Monotypic genus of the Boidae, subfamily Loxoceminae. Southern Mexico to northern Costa Rica. Found in relatively dry, rocky areas to moderately damp tropical forests. To 1.2 m. The head is covered with the normal head scales, the rostral enlarged and projecting. Dark brown, somewhat iridescent, sometimes with a few scattered dark and light spots.

with a delicate dark marbled pattern and a wide light band in the middle of the dorsal region and light lateral spots. Central desert of Australia.

Lucasius: see *Lucasium*, genus.

Luetkenotyphlus TAYLOR, 1968. Monotypic genus of the Caeciliidae. Brasil. Body rather elongated. 131 primary folds in the type specimen. Secondary folds and scales absent. The lower jaw has only one row of teeth. The tentacle is closer to the eye than to the nostril. Cloacal field large, without furrows.
▪ *L. brasiliensis* (LUETKEN, 1851). Brasil. To more than 50 cm. Coloration of preserved specimen more or less uniformly gray.

Lungworms: Nematode worms, especially species of *Rhabdias*, that affect mainly amphibians, snakes, and chameleons. An infection with lungworms can be indicated by reduced and eventually no food intake, loss of condition, respiratory difficulties, nasal discharge, and flow of mucus from the trachea. The presence of lungworm eggs and larval stages can be determined through fecal examinations.

Therapy: Administration of broad-spectrum anthelminthics, combined with symptomatic measures (such as treat-

Loxocemus bicolor

A burrowing snake that is seldom seen except when crossing roads at night and after heavy rains. In captivity it feeds mainly on small mammals. Care similar to *Calabaria*.
▪ *L. bicolor* COPE, 1861.

Lucasium WERMUTH, 1965. Beaded Geckos. Monotypic genus of the Gekkonidae. Australia in arid regions. 10 cm. Slender. Toes with indistinct adhesive lamellae.

Nocturnal ground-dweller that needs relatively large temperature variations. Refer to *Diplodactylus*.
▪ *L. damaeum* (LUCAS and FROST, 1895). Reddish brown

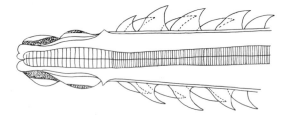

Anterior end of a lungworm, *Pneumonema tiliquae*

ing for pneumonia). Animals remaining untreated have only a slight chance of survival.

Prophylaxis: Proper hygiene.

Luperosaurus GRAY, 1845. Genus of the Gekkonidae. Philippines. 4 species known almost only from their type localities.

▪ *L. cumingi* GRAY, 1845.

Lutremys: see *Emys*, genus.

Lycodon BOIE, 1826. Asian Wolf Snakes. Genus of the Colubridae, Lycodontinae. Throughout wide sections of the Orient. About 15 or 16 species found in various types of dry habitats from steppes to outer rain forest areas and also in rocky mountain ranges in excess of 2,000 m elevation. 0.4 to 1 m. The head is short, more or less distinctly set off, and round-snouted. The dorsal scales are smooth and shingled. Usually dark brown or black, frequently with bright neckbands and light and dark crossbands.

Nocturnal ground snakes that hide during the day under rocks and logs. They prey on lizards (geckos and skinks), but also take large arthropods and small snakes. Egg-layers, 2-8 very large eggs. Should be maintained in a well-heated dry terrarium with ample hiding places and a nocturnal temperature reduction.

▪ *L. aulicus* (LINNAEUS, 1754). India and Sri Lanka

Lycodon striatus bicolor

through Indo-China and southward to the Indo-Australian Archipelago and the Philippines. Introduced on Mauritius. 2 subspecies. 80 cm.

▪ *L. striatus* (SHAW, 1802). Soviet Central Asia southward to central India. 2 subspecies. 40 cm. *L. s. bicolor* NIKOLSKY, 1903, from Soviet Central Asia and Pakistan, has very attractive golden yellow markings.

▪ *L. subcinctus* BOIE, 1827. Southern China, Hainan, and Indo-China southward to the Indo-Australian Archipelago. The largest species, to more than 1 m maximum length.

Lycodonomorphus FITZINGER, 1843. White-lipped Water Snakes. Genus of the Colubridae, Lycodontinae. Africa south of the Equator. About 3 species. To 1.1 m. Slender, with a distinctly set off head, large eyes, and smooth scales. The lips are often white.

Amphibious, so treat as Natricinae, Group 2. Feed predominantly on frogs and fish. Egg-layers.

▪ *L. rufulus* (LICHTENSTEIN, 1823). Brown Water Snake. Southeastern and southern Africa. 2 subspecies. Uniformly brown.

Lycodontinae: Wolf Snakes. Subfamily of the Colubridae. Essentially restricted to the Orient and African regions, with the center of diversity in tropical Southeast Asia and Africa, including Madagascar. Only a few species in the Neotropics, 2 genera in the Nearctic region, and 1 or 2 genera in the Palearctic; completely absent from Australia. About 52 genera. Mainly small to medium-size snakes. The colloquial name is based on differentiation of the teeth into large fangs that are located in an anterior and a posterior group in the upper jaw and an anterior group in the lower jaw. In addition, there are also numerous small grasping teeth. Venom teeth are absent.

The largest number of genera within this subfamily fall into 2 ecological groups:

1) Ground-dwelling, medium-size terrestrial snakes with a large, sometimes trapezoidal head that is markedly set off from the body. Primarily nocturnal. *Lamprophis, Oligodon, Boaedon, Bothrophthalmus, Lycophidion,* and others. Some diurnal genera from Madagascar and the Seychelles (*Lioheterodon, Liopholidophis, Lycognathophis,* and others) can be put here.

2) Small burrowing snakes with a typically small head not set off from the body, small eyes, strongly reduced head scales, smooth body scales, and a short tail, often with a terminal spine. *Aspidura, Blythia, Chamaelycus, Atractus, Geophis, Ninia, Lycodon,* and others. A few exceptions are mainly nocturnal, arboreal snakes: *Lepturophis, Dendrolycus, Mehelya.*

Some more or less nocturnal species prefer damp habitats (swamps, rain forests) and thus provide a transition to an aquatic mode of life (*Dinodon* and several African genera). Other genera are amphibious (*Farancia, Stegonotus, Glypholycus, Lycodonomorphus, Pseudoxyrhopus*) in standing or slowly flowing waters. They fish and hunt for frogs. The Oriental genus *Opisthotropis* is specialized for life in cool mountain streams in montane rain forests.

Systematic-zoogeographic summary:

▪ Orient: *Anoplohydrus, Aspidura, Blythia, Cyclorus, Dinodon, Dryocalamus, Elapoides, Haplocercus, Haplonodon, Lepturophis, Lycodon, Oligodon, Opisthotropis, Oreocalamus, Plagiopholis, Rhabdops, Rhynchocalamus, Stegonothus, Tetralepis, Trachischium,* and *Xylophis.*

▪ Africa: *Boaedon, Bothrolycus, Bothrophthalmus, Chamaelycus, Compsophis, Cryptolycus, Dendrolycus, Dromicodryas, Glypholycus, Gonionotophis, Heteroliodon, Hormonotus, Lamprophis, Lioheterodon, Liopholidophis, Lycodonomorphus, Lycophidion, Meelya, Micropisthodon, Pararhadinaea,* and *Pseudoxyrhopus.*

▪ Neotropics: *Adelphicos, Atractus, Geagras, Geatractus, Geophis, Ninia,* and *Tropidodipsas* (some have penetrated the Nearctic regions of the Mexican Highlands). The genus *Farancia* is a Nearctic endemic in southeastern North America (its relationship to Lycodontinae is doubtful).

Lycodryas GUENTHER, 1879. Genus of the Colubridae, Boiginae. Madagascar and Comores Islands. 8 species in tropical dry forests to rain forests. 40 cm to 1.1 m. Slender, with a markedly set off, adder-like short head. Very large eyes with vertical pupils. Body compressed.

Tree snakes. In regard to food (frogs and lizards), ecology, and maintenance, refer to the Neotropical *Imantodes.*

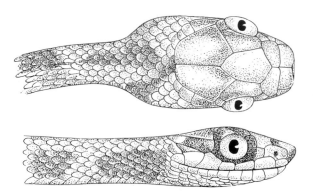

Lycodryas betsileanus

Caution: Venomous bites possible.
- *L. variabilis* (BOULENGER, 1896). Maximum size 1.1 m, largest species of the genus.
- *L. arctifasciatus* (DUMERIL and BIBRON, 1854). Northern and central Madagascar, Nossi-Be.
- *L. gaimardi* (SCHLEGEL, 1837). Madagascar, Comores Islands. 2 subspecies.

Lycognathophis BOULENGER, 1893. Monotypic genus of the Colubridae, Lycodontinae. Seychelles. About 1 m. Head distinctly set off from body. Keeled dorsal scales. Uniformly gray-brown with a conspicuous dark band through the eyes and above the temporal region. Sometimes with rows of dark spots on the back.
   Probably diurnal ground snakes in dry habitats.
- *L. seychellensis* (SCHLEGEL, 1837).

Lycophidion FITZINGER, 1843. Wolf Snakes. Genus of the Colubridae, Lycodontinae. Tropical and southern Africa. About 6 species. In savannahs and mountains to 3,000 m. 25 to 70 cm. Distinctly set off, trapezoidal, blunt-snouted head similar to the closely related *Boaedon*. Has extraordinarily large fangs in the upper and lower jaws with which they can grasp smooth-scaled skinks (*Mabuya*, *Riopa*, and others).
   Nocturnal ground snakes. Egg-layers, 6-8 eggs.
- *L. capense* (A. SMITH, 1831). From Ethiopia southward to Cape Province, westward to the Congo basin. 2 subspecies. Uniform brown to reddish brown, often covered with small silvery spots.

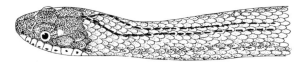

Lycophidion rhodogaster

Lycophidion semicinctum

Lygodactylus GRAY, 1864. Dwarf Geckos. Genus of the Gekkonidae. Tropical Africa and Madagascar. About 30 species. In open, dry forests and rocky mountains, some following human habitation. 6-10 cm. Tail easily snout-vent length, typically the ventral surface with additional adhesive pads. Toes with distinct, well-developed adhesive lamellae that are distally substantially enlarged. Mainly shades of brown and gray, but males of some species have bright colors.
   These geckos are agile climbers. Some are more or less diurnal. Terrarium maintenance must include basking light. The terrarium should not be kept too dry. Has been bred occasionally.
- *L. capensis* (SMITH, 1849). Common Dwarf Gecko. Southern and southwestern Africa. 8 cm. Crepuscular.
- *L. picturatus* (PETERS, 1868). Painted Dwarf Gecko. Southern Tanzania to Zambia, west to eastern Zaire. To 9 cm. Head and forebody in males attractive yellow with dark brown stripes and spots. Throat black. Females inconspicuous. Diurnal and crepuscular.

Lygodactylus picturatus

Lygophis FITZINGER, 1843. Genus of the Colubridae, Xenodontinae. South America. 8 species. In tropical forests and also in damp habitats. 35 to 75 cm. Slender, the head elongated and slightly set off.
   These little snakes live close to the ground near water, but also like to climb the lower branches of trees. The main diet is frogs and lizards. For maintenance see Natrici-

Lygophis lineatus

nae, Group 1. A source of basking heat is absolutely essential.

▪ *L. coralliventris* (BOULENGER, 1894). Southeastern Brasil, Paraguay. Dorsum olive-green to blue-gray, abdomen whitish; undertail coral red with black spots.

▪ *L. lineatus* (LINNAEUS, 1758). Panama southward to northern Argentina. 3 subspecies. Dorsum yellowish to olive with light and dark interrupted longitudinal dorsal bands and continuous lateral bands.

Lygosoma GRAY, 1827. Genus of the Scincidae. Southeastern Asia to Australia. 7 species as now restricted. Formerly several hundred species were included here, but they have now been placed into numerous other genera. Elongated. Tiny limbs with reduced toes. Cryptic; some are burrowers.

▪ *L. novaeguineae* MEYER, 1875. New Guinea.

Lymphatic system: An efferent (one-way) drainage system that collects tissue fluid (lymph, containing white blood cells) and discharges into the venous system, to which it is connected at various points in the body. Particularly well developed in amphibians, frogs possess numerous lymph sacs underneath their skin, with only a few larger lymphatic canals and usually only with 4 lymph hearts. However, the lymphatic system in salamanders and related forms and caecilians is extensively branched out and equipped with numerous paired lymph hearts (up to 100 pairs) that support the movement of lymph with their contractions. The lymphatic system in reptiles is also well developed, but it has only 2 lymph hearts in the pelvic region.

Lyriocephalus MERREM, 1820. Lyre-headed Agamids. Monotypic genus of the Agamidae. Sri Lanka, in montane forests. Easily to 30 cm. Slightly compressed laterally, the tip of the nose with a scaly hump. Bony ridges run from the snout over the eyes to the back of the head, there terminating in blunt horns. There is a short, strong occipital crest. All the crests are larger in males, and males also have a gular pouch. The ventral scales are large and distinctly keeled, especially under the tail. Well-defined color changes.

Ground-dwellers. The diet consists mainly of arthropods, but occasionally tender plant shoots are also taken. Egg-layers. Should be kept at room temperature with a basking light and high humidity.

▪ *L. scutatus* (LINNAEUS, 1758). Lyre-headed Agamid. Dorsum greenish, ventrally lighter. Gular pouch yellow with black spots.

Lysapsus COPE, 1862. Genus of frogs of the Pseudidae. Subtropical South America. 2 species in standing waters with a cover of floating plants. 2-5 cm. Distinguished from related genus *Pseudis* by its rougher skin, adhesive discs at the enlarged tips of the fingers and toes, and by the palatal teeth located obliquely behind the posterior nares.

Maintenance as for *Pseudis*, in an aquarium that does not need to be heated. Open-air maintenance is recommended for the summer months. *Lysapsus* feed on insects, mealworms, and pieces of meat dangled in front of them.

▪ *L. limellus* COPE, 1862. Bolivia, Paraguay, Argentina. 4 subspecies. To 2 cm. Olive with 2 light stripes along the flanks.

▪ *L. mantidactylus* (COPE, 1862). Southern Brasil, Uruguay, Argentina. To 5 cm (females) or 4 cm (males). Olive, ventrally with dark dots on a light background.

Lystrophis COPE, 1885. South American Hog-nosed Snakes. Genus of the Colubridae, Xenodontinae. Southern South America. 3 species. In outer tropical forests, also in savannahs and pampas. 30 to 75 cm. Somewhat compact, heavily built, the head barely set off from the body. The short snout terminates in an upturned rostral shield similar to the possibly related genus *Heterodon*.

Nocturnal ground-dwellers. Specialized feeders on toads and frogs. Maintenance as for *Heterodon*.

▪ *L. dorbignyi* (DUMERIL, DUMERIL, and BIBRON, 1854).

Lyriocephalus scutatus

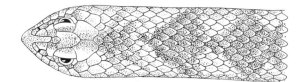

Lystrophis dorbignyi

Lystrophis dorbignyi

Lystrophis dorbignyi

Southeastern Brasil, southern Paraguay, central Argentina, Uruguay.

▪ *L. semicinctus* (DUMERIL, DUMERIL, and BIBRON, 1854). From northern Argentina and southwestern Brasil to southern Bolivia and Paraguay.

Lytorhynchus PETERS, 1862. Long-nosed Sand Snakes. Genus of the Colubridae, Colubrinae. Algeria eastward to Paksitan and central Asia northeastward to Turkmenia (USSR). 3 species. Found in dry habitats, from steppes to the edge of deserts, in mountain regions up to 2,000 m elevation. 35-45 cm. Head pointed, the rostral forming a distinct swelling, so the mouth is subterminal. Body slender, covered with smooth scales. Light brown to yellowish with spots and rhomboidal markings sometimes confluent in rows. Top of head with a crossband at eye level that can extend to the occipital region (*L. diadema, L. ridgewayi*).

Crepuscular and nocturnal snakes preying upon lizards (*Phrynocephalus*, geckos) as well as on their eggs, also on some arthropods. Egg-layers, 3-4 eggs.

Should be kept in a well-heated dry terrarium with a nighttime temperature reduction. Must have ample hiding places.

▪ *L. diadema* (DUMERIL and BIBRON, 1854). From Algeria eastward through the Arabian Peninsula northeastward to Iran.

▪ *L. ridgewayi* BOULENGER, 1887. Iran, Turkmenia (USSR), and Afghanistan to southwestern Pakistan.

Lystrophis semicinctus

Mabuya FITZINGER, 1826. Mabuyas. Genus of the Scincidae. Southeast Asia, Africa, tropical America. More than 80 species found in varied habitats, except not in deserts or shaded forests. To 30 cm. Slender, body cylindrical or moderately flattened dorso-ventrally. Head relatively pointed, barely set off. Lower eyelid movable, in some species with a window. Ear opening distinct. Tail long. The limbs are well developed and have 5 toes. Markings and coloration are highly variable, but are mostly shades of brown, frequently with brightly colored areas and longitudinal stripes.

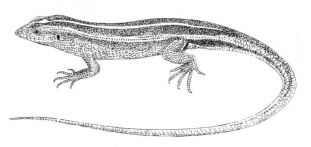

Mabuya quinquetaeniata

Mabuya septemtaeniata

Primarily ground-dwellers, but some climb rocks, walls, fences, or even trees. Forest species occur only where there are ample sunbathing opportunities. During the activity period the body temperature is about 3 to 10° C. higher than ambient temperatures. The diet consists mainly of arthropods, but they will also occasionally take some sweet fruit. Mainly egg-layers, but some species ovoviviparous.

Mabuya species should be kept in spacious terrariums equipped with some rocks, pieces of tree bark, roots, and branches. A section of the substrate must be kept damp, and there must always be sufficient sunning sites with a radiant heat source. Day temperatures of 25 to 30° C., somewhat higher under a basking light, with nocturnal reductions to about 20° C. (but not below) are fine. A drinking bowl must be accessible to the animals. Regular ultraviolet radiation and calcium and vitamin supplements are suggested. Usually they are relatively compatible with each other and with specimens of equal size, but males can be aggressive toward each other. Many species are somewhat difficult in captivity, particularly those with fragile tails.

▪ *M. capensis* (GRAY, 1830). Southern Africa. Grasslands. 25 cm. 10-15 young.

▪ *M. carinata* (SCHNEIDER, 1801). Shiny Skink. India and Sri Lanka. Forest regions. To 30 cm. Egg-layer.

▪ *M. mabouya* (LACEPEDE, 1804). American Shiny Skink. Central and South America. 25 cm. Ecologically quite adaptable.

▪ *M. multifasciata* (KUHL, 1887). Many-striped Mabuya. Southeast Asia, including Indonesia and the Philippines. Relatively dry brushland. Easily to 20 cm. Burrowing. Ovoviviparous.

Mabuya quinquetaeniata

Mabuya striata

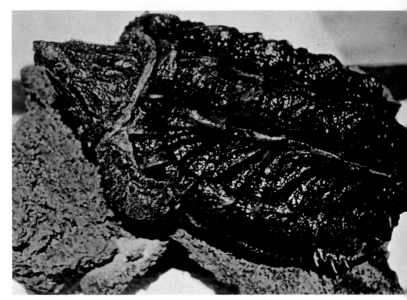

Macroclemys temmincki

- *M. quinquetaeniata* (LICHTENSTEIN, 1823). Rainbow Rock Skink, Five-striped Mabuya. Northeastern to southeastern Africa. Savannahs to steppes; some follow human habitation. To 25 cm. Egg-layer.
- *M. striata* (PETERS, 1844). African Striped Skink, House Skink. Eastern and southern Africa. Various habitats; may follow human habitation. To 20 cm. Ovoviviparous.
- *M. septemtaeniata* (LINNE , 1758) (= *M. aurata*) Northeastern Africa to southwestern Asia. Dry, often rocky habitats. Easily to 20 cm. Ovoviviparous.
- *M. vittata* (GMELIN, 1789). Northeastern Africa to Asia Minor. Grassland and brush. 18 cm. Ovoviviparous.

Macrelaps BOULENGER, 1896. Natal Black Snakes. Monotypic genus of the Colubridae, Apallactinae. Extreme southeastern Africa in damp habitats (swamps, banks of ponds, pools). To 1 m. Similar to *Choristocalamus* and *Atractaspis bibroni*. Uniformly dark.

Burrowing snakes, excellent swimmers. Feed mainly on frogs. Maintenance as for Natricinae, Group 1. Caution: Venomous bites possible.
- *M. microlepidotus* (GUENTHER, 1860).

Macroclemys GRAY, 1855. Alligator Snapping Turtles. Monotypic genus of the Chelydridae. South-central USA. In calm, large waters. One of the largest freshwater turtles. Carapace length to 70 cm. The massive head has a powerful, hooked beak. Carapace with 3 rows of knobby, keeled scutes. Plastron narrow, rigid, cross-like. Characteristic of the genus is a row of scutes between the costals and marginals of the carapace. Tail conspicuously long, covered with large rough scales.

Aquatic. They lie in wait underwater for unsuspecting prey to pass by. Inside the open mouth there is a red, mo-

tile worm-like projection from the tongue that acts as bait to attract small fish. Should be kept in moderately heated aquariums. The young are easily reared in captivity. Alligator snappers have been bred regularly in the USA. Incubation takes 82 to 114 days at 29 or 25° C. in an incubator. Under natural conditions hatching usually occurs within 100 to 108 days. They should be kept outdoors during the summer months. Caution: Capable of serious bites and often aggressive.

Macroclemys temmincki

• *M. temmincki* (TROOST, 1835). Alligator Snapping Turtle. Southeastern Kansas to southwestern Indiana, south to southeastern Texas and northern Florida and Georgia.

Macropholidus NOBLE, 1921. Genus of the Teiidae. Peru and Ecuador. 2 species in mountain valleys. Ground-dwellers. Rare.
• *M. annectens* PARKER, 1930. Ecuador.

Macropisthodon BOULENGER, 1893. Hooded Keelbacks. Genus of the Colubridae, Natricinae. Southern Asia (India, Sri Lanka, Indo-China, Indo-Australian Archipelago, and southern China). 4 species. Predominantly in montane forests to 2,500 m elevation. To 1 m. Distinguished from the closely related *Pseudoxenodon* by its more massive, compact body structure. Head distinctly set off from body. Dentition corresponds largely to that of *Pseudoxenodon* and *Rhabdophis*. The strong, heavily built body is covered with keeled and shingled scales. Green (*M. plumbicolor*) to brown (*M. rudis*), frequently with wide interrupted crossbands or rhomboidal spots. They hunt at night for toads and fish and are capable of handling very large prey. Egg-layers, up to 25 eggs. These keelbacks have a characteristic defense behavior: They flatten almost the entire body and erect it like a cobra. At the same time the mouth is opened

Macropisthodon rhodomelas

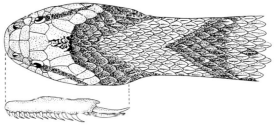
Macropisthodon plumbicolor

Macropisthodon rudis

Macropisthodon rudis

and a vicious bite follows. Nothing is known about possible venom effects, but caution is advised. They should be kept in a forest terrarium with moderate heat (Natricinae, Group 1).

- *M. rudis* BOULENGER, 1906. Southeastern China, Taiwan.
- *M. plumbicolor* (CANTOR, 1839). India and Sri Lanka. To 2,500 m elevation, very rare in lowlands. Green with black and yellow to orange markings.
- *M. rhodomelas* (BOIE, 1827). Malayan Peninsula and Indo-Australian Archipelago to Sulawesi.

Macropophis BOULENGER, 1893. Genus of the Colubridae, Natricinae. Southeast Asia. About 5 species. Closely related to *Rhabdophis*, *Pseudoxenodon*, and *Macropisthodon*. *Macropophis* is often listed under *Natrix* in older literature. Their biology and captive maintenance are similar to these genera.

- *M. maculata* (EDELING, 1864). Malaya, Sumatra, Kalimantan.
- *M. hypomelas* (GUENTHER, 1877). New Guinea (York Island).

Macroprotodon GUICHENOT, 1850. False Smooth Snakes, Hooded Snakes. Monotypic genus of the Colubridae, Boiginae. Southern Iberian Peninsula and North Africa from Morocco to Egypt. 50 cm. An iridescent dark area on the head is markedly set off from the light brown body.

Ground snakes. Ecology, biology and maintenance largely the same as for *Telescopus*, but more likely to take lizards as food.

- *M. cucullatus* (GEOFFROY, 1827). 2 subspecies.

Macroscincus BOGAGE, 1873. Monotypic genus of the Scincidae. Cape Verde Islands of Razo and Branco. In dry habitats. To 50 cm. Heavily built, with powerful limbs.

Predominantly nocturnal ground-dwellers. Herbivorous. In captivity they will accept fruit, cabbage, lettuce, and similar items, occasionally some meat and eggs. Formerly common in terrariums, but now threatened with extinction or may already be extinct.

- *M. cocteaui* (GRAY, 1845). Cape Verde Giant Skink. Gray-brown with dark and light spots.

Madagascar: Island located off southeastern Africa that—together with the Seychelles and Mascarenes—forms the Madagascan subregion of the Ethiopian. It lies within subtropical latitudes and is similar to eastern Africa in terms of its vegetation. The windward (east) coast with its mountains exposed to the moist tradewinds has permanently wet, subtropical rain forests. On the leeward side are the central and western dry forests, savannahs, and grasslands. Semideserts exist in the southwestern region of the island. Today the natural vegetation of Madagascar has been largely destroyed.

The herpetofauna is closely related to that of Africa but far less diverse. For instance, the Bufonidae, Pipidae, Agamidae, Lacertidae, Varanidae, and Elapidae are completely absent from Madagascar. On the other hand, Mantellinae and Cophylinae are endemic on the island. Former land contact (through Gondwana) with South America is indicated by the presence of some genera of otherwise predominantly Neotropic groups (Pelomedusidae, Iguanidae). There are similar connections to the Orient (Madagascan-

Oriental distribution of Dyscophinae, as well as genus *Rhacophorus*).

Madagascarophis MERTENS, 1952. Monotypic genus of the Colubridae, Boiginae. Madagascar in dry forests and rain forests. About 1 m. Body oval, head markedly set off from body, blunt-snouted, with large eyes. The brown body is covered with 3 or 4 rows of spots. A short dark temporal band extends from the eye to the end of mouth.

The diet includes frogs and lizards as well as small mammals. Frogs are swallowed alive in natricine fashion, while mice and lizards are constricted. The venom of these snakes probably is not very potent. They should be kept in a well-heated terrarium with climbing facilities and ample hiding places.

- *M. colubrina* (SCHLEGEL, 1837). One of the most common snakes on Madagascar.

Madagascarophis colubrina

Madakinixys: see *Kinixys*, genus.

Madecassophryna GUIBE, 1974. Monotypic genus of the Microhylidae. Madagascar. Flattened, the snout long and pointed. Pupil horizontal. Tympanum clearly visible. Fingers and toes free and without adhesive discs. Ground-dwellers that lay a few large eggs.

- *M. truebae* GUIBE, 1974. 2.3 cm. Dark, abdomen light, with sparing pattern of dark spots.

Magnadigita: see *Bolitoglossa*, genus.

Malaclemys GRAY, 1844. Diamondback Terrapins. Monotypic genus of the Emydidae. Atlantic coast of North America from Massachusetts southward to the Yucatan Peninsula. Found in brackish coastal waters. Length to 25 cm. Carapace with an indistinct keel, broken into individual blunt knobs. Scutes deeply sculptured.

Continuous maintenance in freshwater leads to skin diseases and metabolic disturbances. They must be kept in

Malaclemys terrapin macrospilota

Malaclemys terrapin

Malaclemys terrapin tequesta

brackish water. However, there are individual records of specimens having been successfully very slowly acclimated to fresh water. They have been bred repeatedly by terrarium hobbyists in Europe and were once bred commercially in the USA. Once highly desired for food on the American market, they were virtually exterminated over wide areas of the range. Incubation takes 61 to 68 days at 30° C. in an incubator, 60 to 90 days under natural conditions.

▪ *M. terrapin* (SCHOEPFF, 1793). 7 subspecies, often poorly defined. Carapace varies from almost smooth to conspicuous grooves surrounding the areoles to irregular buckling of individual shields. The soft, silvery gray skin on the head and neck has a dark dotted pattern; often a dark moustache over the upper jaw.

Malacochersus LINDHOLM, 1929. Pancake Tortoises. Monotypic genus of the Testudinidae. Eastern Africa in moderate mountain ranges, where they hide in rocky crevices. Carapace distinctly flat and pliable, the bone elements very thin and separated by large, secondarily developed fontanelles. Juveniles have a normally arched carapace with the osseous elements still close together.

The diet consists mainly of shrubs and succulent plants. They appear to maintain a dry season dormancy. These are very active turtles running quite fast and climbing well. 1 to 4 eggs are laid.

Maintenance requires a moderately heated (cool at night), spacious terrarium with sufficient running space as

Malacochersus tornieri

Malacochersus tornieri

well as climbing facilities and ample hiding places. Can be kept outdoors during the summer months.

Pancake tortoises have repeatedly been observed in captivity to lay eggs followed by successful incubation (178 days at 29° C.). Individual specimens have been kept in terrariums for decades. Endangered.

▪ *M. tornieri* (SIEBENROCK, 1903). Carapace length about 15 cm. More or less distinct radiating lines on carapace.

Malayemys LINDHOLM, 1931. Malayan Snail-eating Turtles. Monotypic genus of the Emydidae. Indo-China and also on Java. Prefers standing or small waters. To 20 cm. Carapace with 3 moderate keels. Characteristic light longitudinal stripes on head and side of neck. Snout area marked like a mask. Marginal scutes with characteristic black spot or stripe along outer posterior section of each scute.

Carnivorous, with a strong preference for molluscs. Captive maintenance difficult, seldom long-lived. The animals die suddenly while apparently doing well.

▪ *M. subtrijuga* (SCHLEGEL and S. MUELLER, 1844). Thailand and Kampuchea southward through the Malayan Peninsula to Java.

Malayemys subtrijuga

Malayemys subtrijuga

Malpolon FITZINGER, 1826. Montpellier Snakes. Genus of the Colubridae, Boiginae. Southern Europe, North Africa, and the Near East. 2 species in varied habitats, especially brushland (*macchias*). To 1.7 m. Slender, head set off. The large eyes are protected by well-developed roof-like supraorbital scales. Juvenile coloration is brownish with light and dark spots and vermiform lines on the head. The coloration becomes paler with increasing age, adults being uniformly gray-brown to steel-blue. The opisthoglyph fangs are rather large.

Malpolon monspessulanus

Malpolon nr. *moilensis*

Diurnal ground snakes. They feed on snakes, lizards, small mammals, and ground birds, slightly raising the anterior part of the body while hunting to increase the field of vision. Egg-layers, about 20 eggs. Should be kept in a well-heated dry terrarium with a nighttime temperature reduction, much as for *Coluber*. Caution: Venomous bites possible.

▪ *M. monspessulanus* (HERMANN, 1804). Coastal southern Europe (not Italy) to the Near East and North Africa.

▪ *M. moilensis* (REUSS, 1834). From Morocco southward to the Atlas Mountains and eastward to Egypt.

Mammalia: Mammals. The mammalian order Rodentia provides several rodent species that are used regularly as food for terrarium animals, most notably the common

Malpolon monspessulanus

house mouse (*Mus musculus*), Norwegian rat (*Rattus norvegicus*), golden hamster (*Mesocricetus auratus*), and Guinea pig (*Cavia aperea*). Occasionally large snakes and crocodiles can also be given any of a number of other small mammals such as rabbits. Some larger reptiles and amphibians will also take pieces of lean meat, heart, or liver.

Manculus: see *Eurycea*, genus.

Mangrove swamps: Dense tangles of vegetation in the tidal regions of tropical and (less commonly) subtropical coasts in surf-protected muddy areas, often with some freshwater run-off (lagoons, river deltas). Often they support a very diverse group of animals. Mangrove stands consist mainly of trees and large bushes with stilt roots (an adaptation for variable water levels) and asparagus-like upwardly pointing respiratory roots (an adaptation for an oxygen-deficient substrate). The most diverse mangrove swamps occur in tropical Southeast Asia (up to 26 woody plant species), while the simplest mangrove tangles are found in tropical Central and South America (maximum of 4 woody species). Among the herpetologically more significant species that regularly inhabit mangrove swamps are *Crocodylus* species, see snakes, amphibious *Varanus* species (e. g., *V. mertensi*), and aquatic snakes of various groups (e. g., *Acrochordus*).

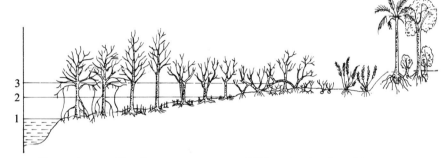

Vegetation profile of a mangove swamp: 1 Water level at low tide; 2 high tide; 3 highest water level

An Australian mangove swamp

Mangrove swamp with *Rhizophora*
coast

Manouria emys

Manouria impressa

Manolepis COPE, 1885. Monotypic genus of the Colubridae, Boiginae. Pacific highlands of Mexico from Nayarit to the Isthmus of Tehuantepec. In different dry habitats up to 2,800 m elevation. To 60 cm. Head clearly set off. Eyes with vertical pupils.

Nocturnal ground snakes that prey mainly on lizards. Should be kept in a dry terrarium that is well-heated and has a nocturnal temperature reduction. The opisthoglyph fangs are very large, so venomous bites may be possible. Poorly known.
• *M. putnami* (JAN, 1863). Light brown with a darker dorsal band.

Manouria GRAY, 1852. Indo-Chinese Tortoises. Genus of the Testudinidae. Indo-China. 2 species. In tropical forests. Carapace length 30-60 cm. Often considered a subgenus of *Geochelone*. Carapace flattened.

Mainly carnivorous (fish, worms, snails, insects) as well as plants, particularly fruit. Crepuscular, not very active. Should be kept under tropical temperature conditions and high humidity. Bathing facilities are required.
• *M. emys* (SCHLEGEL and S. MUELLER, 1844). Brown Tortoise. India (Assam) and Indo-China to Sunda Archipelago (Sumatra and Kalimantan). 60 cm carapace length, the largest tortoise in Asia.
• *M. impressa* (GUENTHER, 1882). Indo-China to Malayan Peninsula. Carapace length to 30 cm. Yellow head with intensely orange-yellow colored edges along vertebral plates and remnants of radiating lines on costal plates.

Mantella BOULENGER, 1882. Golden Frogs. Genus of the Rhacophoridae. Madagascar. 4 species in tropical montane rain forests. Externally resembling Dendrobatidae, with horizontal pupil and clearly visible tympanum. Fingers and toes free, with distinct adhesive discs. Males produce a chirping call. Often brilliantly colored.

Diurnal ground-dwellers with small home ranges, but often socially in small groups along jungle floor among leaves, under decaying trees and branches, or climbing about among branches close to ground. Fertilization internal, copulation occurring some time before spawning occurs on damp bottom substrate. Apparently the newly hatched larvae reach water in run-off discharging into jun-

Mantella aurantiaca

gle pools, where they remain until metamorphosis (about 3 months).

Should be kept in a moderately warm tropical rain-forest terrarium. Occasional temperature reductions to 10° C. are tolerated without harm.

▪ *M. aurantiaca* MOCQUARD, 1901. Golden Frog. 3 cm. Bright orange.

▪ *M. cowani* BOULENGER, 1882. 2.5 cm. Black with a variable pattern of yellow to deep orange spots.

Mantidactylus BOULENGER, 1895. Genus of the Rhacophoridae. Madagascar. 32 species (that require revision). Externally and anatomically highly diverse. Pupil horizontal. Fingers free, webbing between toes variable. Adhesive discs variably developed in size, but always with a circular groove on their ventral surface.

Mode of life diverse, from semiaquatic to arboreal. Eggs are deposited outside of water, either on the ground or on leaves above water (similar to *Rhacophorus*). Larval development usually occurs in water, but possibly is direct in some species. Larvae in phytothelms (*M. pulcher* Group) in arboreal species.

▪ *M. elegans* (GUIBE, 1974). Eastern Madagascar (Andringitra and Tsarantana Mountains). 6 cm. Reddish brown with large dark brown, whited-edged spots.

▪ *M. femoralis* (BOULENGER, 1882). Eastern Madagascar. 6.5 cm. Dark brown with a black pattern.

▪ *M. guttulatus* (BOULENGER, 1881). Eastern Madagascar. 12.5 cm, robust, compact. Gray-brown.

Mantipus PETERS, 1883. Genus of the Microhylidae. Madagascar. 6 species. 2 to 9 cm. Legs short. Pupil horizontal. Tympanum variably visible, depending upon species concerned. The fingers and toes are free, with distinct adhesive discs. They appear to be terrestrial.
- *M. inguinalis* (BOULENGER, 1882). Eastern Madagascar, Andringitra Mountains. 9 cm. Gray brown with black, light-edged spot in pelvic region. Thighs with dark crossbands.
- *M. serratopalpebrosus* GUIBE, 1975. 3 cm. Brown with a dark pattern. Upper eyelid with a protruding tubercle.

Maranta L. Arrow Root. Genus of the Marantaceae. Tropical America. 30 species. Upright or creeping plants with conspicuously colored leaves.
- *M. leuconeura* E. MORR. 30 cm. Suitable for the rain-forest terrarium.

Marantaceae: Arrowroot plants. Family of the Liliatae. Tropical America. 32 genera, about 350 species. Long-lasting shrubs in rain forests under subdued light. Shade plants. *Calathea, Maranta*.

Mariguana: see *Anolis*, genus.

Mascarenes: Island group in the Indian Ocean 700 km east of Madagascar. They belong zoogeographically to the Madagascan subregion of the Ethiopian and are notable herpetologically for the endemic subfamily Bolyeriinae of Boidae and fossil giant tortoises of the genus *Cylindraspis*. Best known individual island is Mauritius.

Masticophis BAIRD and GIRARD, 1853. Coachwhips and Whipsnakes. Genus of the Colubridae, Colubrinae. Northwestern and southern USA, throughout Central America to

Maranta bicolor (var. kerchoveana)

Masticophis flagellum piceus

Masticophis flagellum piceus, juvenile

Masticophis flagellum testaceus

Masticophis taeniatus taeniatus

Masticophis lateralis

northern South America. 8 species. In mountains to more than 3,000 m elevation. 0.75 to 2.3 m. Slender, similar to *Coluber*. Behavior also largely identical. Mainly longitudinally striped patterns; a few species have rows of rhomboids or spots.

Ground snakes. Maintenance as for *Coluber*. Very nervous, active snakes.

• *M. flagellum* (SHAW, 1802). Coachwhip. Southern USA and Mexico.

• *M. mentovarius* (DUMERIL, DUMERIL, and BIBRON, 1854). Mexico to Colombia and Venezuela.

Mastigodryas AMARAL, 1935. Tropical Racers. Genus of the Colubridae, Colubrinae. From Mexico to Argentina. 11 species found in different dry habitats from semideserts to outer rain forest areas. 1 m to 1.8 m. Appearance and biology rather close to the genus *Coluber*. Markings frequently consist of interrupted crossbands that are contrasting yellow and black. Such striking markings and coloration appear to have a strong camouflage function in the habitat of these snakes.

Ground snakes that feed mainly on small mammals, lizards, and birds and their eggs. Egg-layers, 8-12 eggs. Should be maintained in well-heated, sunny, dry terrariums with climbing and bathing facilities.

• *M. bifossatus* (RADDI, 1820). Venezuela and Colombia southward to northern Argentina.

• *M. boddaerti* (SENTZEN, 1796). Colombia and Venezuela to western Brasil.

• *M. melanolomus* (COPE, 1868). Mexico southward to Panama.

Mastigodryas bifossatus

Mastigodryas bifossatus

Maticora GRAY, 1834. Long-glanded Coral Snakes. Genus of the Elapidae. Indo-China to Sulawesi and Philippines. 2 polytypic species. In tropical and montane rain forests. 0.6 to 1.5 m. The round head is barely set off from the body, short, and with a rounded snout. The generic character is an enormous enlargement of the venom glands, which extend through the anterior third of the body and cause a displacement of the internal organs. Dark with more or less well-defined light longitudinal stripes. Intraspecific variations in markings is high. When excited, *Maticora* species raise their tail to display red bars underneath.

Terrestrial, nocturnal venomous snakes. The diet appears to consist mainly of lizards and other snakes. Details of the life history are largely unknown. For maintenance refer to *Micrurus*.

- *M. bivirgata* (BOIE, 1827). Indo-China amd large areas of the Indo-Australian Archipelago.
- *M. intestinalis* (LAURENTI, 1768). Southern Indo-China, Indo-Australian Archipelago, Philippines.

Mating behavior: Meeting of the sexes for the purpose of joining their gametes, which usually is tied to a complicated, mutually reciprocal type of behavior of both partners and which follows the courting behavior. Mating behavior is often species-specific or genus-specific and therefore forms an effective hybridization barrier. For instance, when lizards of the genera *Lacerta* and *Podarcis* mate the male secures a firm bite into the flank of the female. However, in the related genus *Gallotia* mating is ac-

Mating behavior: *Coleonyx variegatus*

Mating behavior: *Bombina variegata*

Mating behavior: *Epicrates cenchria*

companied by a neck bite. Mating behavior can be accompanied by vocalization (mating calls, as in most frog species, crocodilians, and some tortoises). Amplexus is the typical mating position in frogs and many salamanders. Reptile males (except tuataras) have special sex organs (penes and hemipenes) that are inserted into the cloaca of the female for copulation.

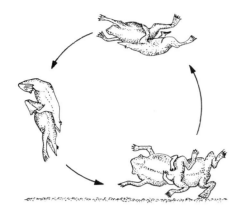

Mating behavior: *Pipa pipa*

Mauremys (Annamemys) annamensis

Mating behavior: *Gopherus polyphemus*

Mauremys GRAY, 1869. Eurasian Pond Turtles. Genus of the Emydidae. Europe and northwestern Africa to eastern Asia. 5 species. Formerly included in the genus *Clemmys*. Found in small waters but also in large lakes and rivers. To 20 cm.

- *M. caspica* (GMELIN, 1774). Caspian Pond Turtle. Eastern Mediterranean Region from the Balkans to Asia Minor, the Caucasus to Iran. 2 subspecies. Head narrow, pointed, the neck with light longitudinal stripes. At the northern limits

Mauremys nigricans

Mauremys leprosa

Mauremys nigricans

of the the range (Balkans) it is found in thermal springs, while at the southern edge of range it occurs in brackish water. Omnivorous, with a substantial animal component. Incubation takes 95 to 101 days in the wild. Depending upon the origin, it can be kept outdoors throughout the year or only during the summer months. Protection against winter cold must be provided.

• *M. japonica* (TEMMINCK and SCHLEGEL, 1833). Japanese Pond Turtle. Japanese islands, from Tokyo southward. Carapace length to 15 cm; the scutes distinctly sculptured and somewhat rough. Rarely imported. Very hardy.

• *M. nigricans* (GRAY, 1834). Three-keeled Pond Turtle. From southern China to central Vietnam and also on Taiwan and Hainan. To 20 cm. Carapace with 3 low longitudinal keels; plastron with a large dark spot on each shield. A distinct yellow temporal band runs back from the eye. Incubation period 65 to 95 days at 30 and 25° C.

• *M. leprosa* (SCHWEIGGER, 1812). Iberian Pond Turtle. Iberian Peninsula and North Africa. Formerly considered a subspecies of *M. caspica*. Frequently in water holes in oases in the Sahara region. Omnivorous. Hardy, can be kept outdoors during the summer.

Mauremys caspica

Meadow plankton: Common designation for a mixture of various arthropods that can be caught from spring through fall by sweeping a large insect net through grass of meadows, fields, along forest margins, and in similar places. After several sweeps the contents of the net are emptied into a glass jar or plastic bag. The composition of such an arthropod mixture changes with the season, the prevailing forms being Diptera, Hymenoptera, Heteroptera, Homoptera, Coleoptera, and Araneae. Often large numbers of grasshoppers are also caught in this manner, but then usually only juvenile stages. Before feeding meadow plankton it is recommended that it be sorted according to the size of the terrarium animals that are to be fed. Undesired insects should be thrown away (the common lady beetles are often collected in large numbers and are nearly always not eaten). Before collecting commences it has to be ascertained that there has not been a recent spraying with insecticide or herbicides, which are potentially damaging to terrarium animals.

Mealworms: See Tenebrionidae.

Mediterranean Region: Those countries of southern Europe, northern Africa, and Asia Minor located around the Mediterranean Sea. Characterized climatically by warm, dry, sunny summers and cool, rainy winters. This has led to the large-scale development of evergreen sclerophyll vegetation, which, however, has been severely depleted by man during recent historic times. Similar vegetation also occurs in other winter-rain regions (California, central Chile, Cape Province, South Australia). The Mediterranean is herpetologically of considerable significance since it contains numerous refuges and distribution centers of the western Palearctic and is still characterized by the immense diversity of its herpetotaxa.

Megaelosia MIRANDA-RIBEIRO, 1923. Monotypic genus of the Leptodactylidae. Southeastern Brasil. Related to *Elosia* and *Hylodes*. Found in fast-flowing, rocky mountain streams. The head is wide, the eyes large and protruding. Tympanum small. Upper jaw teeth conspicuously large, curved, fang-like. Long, powerful hind legs. Fingers free, with narrow skin folds; toes webbed only at base. Tips of fingers and toes slightly broadened. Males without vocal sac. Cryptic frogs that are difficult to collect.

• *M. goeldi* (BAUMANN, 1912). Males to 7 cm, females to 12 cm.

Megalixalus GUENTHER, 1868. Monotypic genus of the Rhacophoridae. (Some species formerly in *Megalixalus* are now in *Afrixalus*.) Seychelles. To 6.5 cm. Pupil vertical. Tympanum clearly visible (?). Fingers webbed for about 50% of their length, toes almost completely webbed. Tips of extremities enlarged into adhesive discs.

Presumably nocturnal bush- and tree-dwellers. Maintenance as for forest-dwelling *Afrixalus* species

• *M. seychellensis* (TSCHUDI, 1838).

Megalobatrachus: see *Andrias*, genus.

Megalochelys FITZINGER, 1843. Seychelles Giant Tortoises. Monotypic genus of the Testudinidae. Formerly considered a subgenus of *Geochelone*. Seychelles. In dry regions. Maximum carapace length 1.23 m, the largest

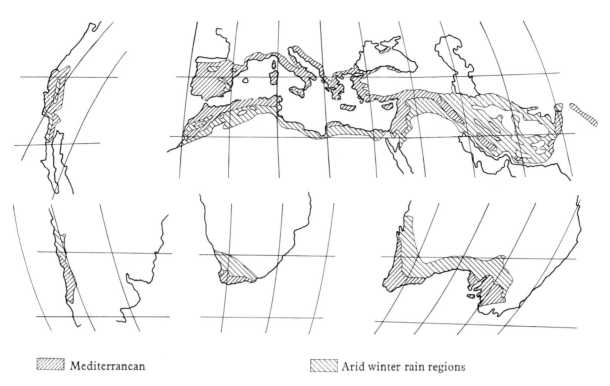

░▒▓ Mediterranean   ░▒▓ Arid winter rain regions

Mediterranean and winter-rain regions of the earth

species of Recent tortoise. Unicolored dark carapace. In contrast to *Chelonoidis elephantopus*, the nuchal scute is present. Continous growth to an advanced age (officially recorded age 152 years) results in peculiar saddle-shaped depressions in the neck region and the posterior carapace margin that are not seen in juveniles.

The diet consists of seasonal plants and fruits. Severely endangered by feral domestic animals and increased hunting by humans for food. They are impressive display speci-

mens in zoological parks and have been bred repeatedly.
• *M. gigantea* (SCHWEIGGER, 1812). Aldabra Giant Tortoise. Seychelles and Aldabra. The form from Mahe, Seychelles (*sumeirei*) is probably extinct. Populations of the other subspecies (*gigantea*) on Aldabra are not endangered. Established on Zanzibar.

Megalophrys: see *Megophrys*, genus.

Megophrys KUHL and VAN HASSELT, 1822 (= *Megalo-*

Megalochelys gigantea

Megalochelys gigantea

phrys KUHL, 1830). Asian Spadefoots. Genus of the Pelobatidae. Southeast Asia from the foot of the Himalayas to the Indo-Australian Archipelago. Over 20 species. Species native to the Himalayas inhabit open, steppe-like landscapes (also on agricultural land); tropical species occur in rain forests of the lowlands or in cool mountain regions. 3-17 cm, toad-like. Plump, males often substantially smaller than females. Mostly with smooth skin and a short snout projection. A skin fold from above the eye to the tympanum and shoulder; rarely also dorsal ridges. Coloration cryptic; *M. monticola* looks like dry leaves. Distinguished externally from the closely related genus *Leptobrachium* by the presence in *Megophrys* of an oval inner metatarsal tubercle that extends onto the first finger. Fingers free, toes free or webbed at base only. Only inner metatarsal tubercle present, large and oval. The larvae are elongated, with a very large, funnel-shaped mouth (specialized feeder on microorganisms at the surface); the larvae cling with their mouth at the surface while their body hangs down vertically.

Light-sensitive nocturnal ground-dwellers. The eggs are unpigmented and are deposited at night underneath rocks and in other dark areas in gently flowing or standing water.

The most important terrarium species is *M. monticola nasuta* (often considered a full species), which requires a spacious, permanently damp and relatively cool (22-24° C.) rain-forest terrarium. This species will also breed quite easily if the water section is freshwater and has suitable areas for depositing the eggs, such as floating cork pieces or hollow stacked rocks. The larvae feed only off the surface on tiny food particles, such as commercial fish foods of suitably fine grade. Juveniles grow rapidly in captivity.

▪ *M. baluensis* (BOULENGER, 1899). Kalimantan. To 7 cm. Dark brown, the sides sharply set off with yellow.

▪ *M. carinensis* (BOULENGER, 1889). Yunnan, Thailand, Burma. To 17 cm. Yellow-brown with a black pattern.

▪ *M. feae* (BOULENGER, 1887). Burma. To 15 cm. Olive brown, the sides darker.

▪ *M. minor* (STEJNEGER, 1926). China (eastern Tibet, Si-

chuan) above 1000 m. To 4.5 cm. Dark brown.

▪ *M. monticola* KUHL and VAN HASSELT, 1822. Asian Horned Frog. Southeast Asia. The subspecies *nasuta* (SCHLEGEL, 1837), with long snout and upper eyelid projections, occurs on Kalimantan and is usually considered a full species. To 14 cm. Variegated brown. 2 skin folds on the back.

Megophrys monticola nasuta

Mehely, Ludwig von (1862-1952): Hungarian herpetologist. Worked mainly with the amphibians of Hungary and Romania and on the systematics and phylogeny of the genus *Lacerta*.

Mehelya CSIKI, 1903. File Snakes. Genus of the Colubridae, Lycodontinae. Tropical and southern Africa. 8 species. 35 cm to 1.6 m. The head is often trapezoidal and is moderately set off from the body, similar to *Boaedon*. The body is triangular in cross-section and has an enlarged row of vertebral scales that carry very sharp keels. The lateral dorsal scales are also strongly keeled. Usually brownish olive, the keels sometimes distinctly lighter (*M. capensis*).

Nocturnal, sluggish snakes. The diet consists primarily of frogs, lizards, and to a great extent other snakes, includ-

Mehelya capensis

ing venomous ones (*Causus, Atheris, Dispholidus,* and others). Cannibalism is not too infrequent, so they must be kept individually in the terrarium. Egg-layers.

File snakes require well-heated, moderately damp tropical forest terrariums with climbing facilities and hiding places. Substantial longevities are recorded in captivity (in excess of 10 years).

▪ *M. capensis* (A. SMITH, 1847). Cape File Snake. From Tanzania to the South African Republic.

Meizodon FISCHER, 1856. Bush Snakes. Genus of the Colubridae, Colubrinae. Tropical Africa. 4 species. Formerly included in *Coronella* (and closely related). In savannahs and thornbush steppes. 60 to 80 cm. Uniformly darkish olive to black; juveniles of most species have 3 or 4 light crossbands behind the eye, on the back of the head, and on the neck. Smooth dorsal scales.

More or less nocturnal ground snakes hiding during the day under tree stumps, dead bushes, and similar places. The diet consists mainly of lizards (skinks and geckos), sometimes also small mammals. Egg-layers, 2 eggs. Should be kept in a well-heated dry terrarium.

▪ *M. semiornatus* (PETERS, 1854). Senegal eastward to Uganda, Kenya, and Tanzania, southward to Mozambique and Zimbabwe. 2 subspecies. Blackish, without markings.

▪ *M. coronatus* (SCHLEGEL, 1837). From Senegal eastward to the southern Sudan and Kenya. With 3 or 4 light crossbands.

Melanin: Complex nitrogenous compound, the brown to blackish natural color pigments that occur in special cells, the melanophores (melanocytes, chromatophores), usually combined with proteins as melanoproteins. Melanins are important in the development of body colors in animals. Physiological color changes in various amphibians and reptiles are due to a changing distribution of melanins under hormonal control.

Melanism: Increased deposition of melanins that leads to a dark to black body coloration. "Melanos," as such black animals have been called, occur among many species and are especially common in snakes.

Melanism: Melanistic *Thamnophis elegans vagrans*

Melanobatrachus BEDDOME, 1878. Monotypic genus of the Microhylidae. Southern India. Closely related to the African genera *Hoplophryne* and *Parhoplophryne*. Skin granular. Snout blunt. Round pupil. Tympanum and middle ear absent. Males without vocal sac. Fingers free, the toes webbed at the base only, without distinct metatarsal tubercles. Adhesive discs are absent.

Terrestrial mountain-dwellers (900-1400 m). Mating, spawning, and larval development occur on land.

▪ *M. indicus* BEDDOME, 1878. 4 cm. Dark brown to black, with white pustules.

Melanochelys GRAY, 1869. Indian Terrapins. Genus of the Emydidae. India, Sri Lanka, and Burma, plus adjacent areas. 2 species. Semiaquatic. From 16 to 30 cm. 3 well developed longitudinal keels on carapace. In *M. trijuga* the males are substantially larger than the females (unusual for turtles).

Primarily carnivorous, with small plant component to the diet. Should be kept in a heated aqua-terrarium. Has been bred. Hardy.

▪ *M. tricarinata* (BLYTH, 1856). Three-keeled Indian Terra-

Melanism: Normal appearance of *Thamnophis elegans vagrans*

Melanochelys trijuga trijuga

Melanochelys trijuga

pin. India and Bangladesh. To 16 cm. Biology little known.
▪ *M. trijuga* (SCHWEIGGER, 1812). Black-bellied Terrapin. India, Sri Lanka, Burma. 6 subspecies. Incubation in the wild took less than 60 days. Suitable for large aqua-terrariums and can be kept outdoors during the summer months.

Melanophidium GUENTHER, 1864. Genus of the Uropeltidae. Southern India. 3 species in mountain regions between 900 and 1500 m. 56 cm, 10-14 mm thick. The only genus of the family with a mental groove (between the scales under the chin). Tail distinctly compressed, the scales smooth, the enlarged terminal scale with 2 serrated keels that terminate in low spines. Iridescent black with light spots or longitudinal stripes. Very rare.
▪ *M. wynaudense* (BEDDOME, 1863). Southern India.

Melanophryniscus GALLARDO, 1961. Genus of the Bufonidae. South America. 5 species (some of these were formerly included in Atelopidae). In grasslands, pampas. Compact, with short legs. Pupil horizontal. Without visible tympanum and parotoid glands. Fingers and toes webbed at base and with lateral skin folds. Adhesive discs absent. Very dark background coloration with conspicuously bright markings that are presented to potential enemies in the form of the "toad reflex," the back strongly depressed. The skin secretions are more or less poisonous.

Mostly diurnal. Spawning occurs in puddles during the rainy season. The males perform ritual fights. These little toads should be kept in a semimoist, sunny terrarium. Open-air maintenance is recommended for the summer months.
▪ *M. moreirae* (MIRANDA-RIBEIRO, 1920). Eastern Brasil. Mountains. 2.5 cm. Brownish black with bright yellow spots; abdomen yellow. Metatarsal tubercles indistinct.
▪ *M. stelzneri* (WEYENBERGH, 1875). Paraguay, Uruguay, Argentina. 3.5 cm. Coloration similar to *M. moreirae*, but with both metatarsal tubercles well-developed.

Melanoseps BOULENGER, 1887. Genus of the Scincidae. East Africa. Legless. Little known.

▪ *M. ater* (GUENTHER, 1873). Malawi.

Melanosuchus GRAY, 1825. Black Caimans. Monotypic genus of the Alligatoridae. Tropical South America in standing and flowing waters, mainly in the *selva*, sometimes together with *Caiman crocodilus*. The largest species of the *Caiman* Group, on the average 3 to 4.5 m, rarely to 6 m. Both sides of jaws with 5 intermaxillary teeth on either side. Iris greenish (as in *Caiman*). In contrast to *Caiman*, the bony eye sockets are conspicuously extended toward the nose. Surface of upper lid with only fine lines, never wrinkled. Snout moderately long, flat and wide; the median longitudinal pair of ridges on the dorsal surface form a wide, elevated ridge. Occipital bucklers in 4 or 5 rows, followed closely by at least 4 rows of nuchal bucklers.

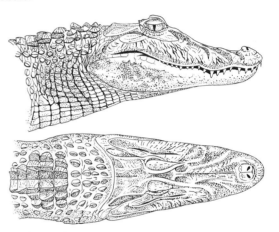

Melanosuchus niger

▪ *M. niger* (SPIX, 1825). Black Caiman. Found predominantly in the river systems of the Orinoco and Amazon, but today largely decimated or seriously endangered by excessive hunting. Depending upon prevailing climatic conditions, the animal is active either throughout the year or remains buried in mud during the dry season. The dorsal region in adults is jet black, the abdomen light; juveniles are yellowish with dark crossbands.

Menetia GRAY, 1845. Monotypic genus of the Scincidae. Australia. In open forests and grasslands. Closely related to *Carlia*. 10 cm. Slender. A lid spectacle present, as are tiny ear openings. Preanal scales little enlarged. 4 fingers, 5 toes. Brown with dark lateral stripes. Ground-dwellers.
▪ *M. greyi* GRAY, 1845. Virtually all of Australia except the northern and southeastern coasts.

Meroles GRAY, 1838. South African Sand Lizards. Genus of the Lacertidae. 6 species. South Africa. Formerly included in *Scapteira*. Found in semideserts and deserts. Similar to *Eremias*, but ventral scales in straight lines or oblique; supralabial region angular, projecting. Fringes on toes usually well developed.

For details on maintenance refer to *Eremias*, but these lizards need to be kept somewhat warmer and without cool winter dormancy period. Egg-layers.
▪ *M. cuneirostris* (STRAUCH, 1867). Coastal regions of Southwest Africa. Easily to 15 cm. Sand dunes.
▪ *M. reticulatus* (BOCAGE, 1867). Coastal regions of Southwest Africa to Angola. Barely 15 cm. Mainly among sand dunes.

Merrem, Blasius (1761-1824): German zoologist. The first scientist to separate precisely the amphibians and reptiles, in *Versuch eines Systems der Amphibien* (1820).

Mertens, Robert (1894-1975): German zoologist and herpetologist, Director of the Senckenberg Museum, Frankfurt/Main. More than 600 publications, including *Die Amphibien und Reptilien Europas*, 3 editions—1st (1928), 2nd with Mueller (1940), and 3rd with Wermuth (1960). Monographs: *Die Warn- und Drohreaktion der Reptilien*, (1946); *Die Familie der Warane*, 3 parts (1942). Coauthored with Wermuth the classic checklists and identification keys for the recent turtles, crocodiles, and tuataras (1955 and 1961). Numerous other papers describing many taxa.

Mertensian Mimicry: Theory proposed by R. Mertens to explain the presence of coral snake patterns (alternating black, yellow, and red or white rings) that occur in various unrelated snakes. Ringed coloration is considered to be a warning coloration that is supposed to have originated initially among relatively non-dangerous but rather aggressive species (e. g., genera *Erythrolamprus*, *Rhinobothryum*). These snakes were able to convey negative experiences to their enemies and therefore by means of their coloration they had a deterrent effect.

Mertensiella WOLTERSTORFF, 1934. Spine-tail Salamanders. Genus of the Salamandridae. Relict forms in extreme southeastern Europe, Asia Minor, and the western Trans-Caucasus. 2 species (of these *M. luschani* occasionally is placed in the closely related genus *Salamandra*). Found in damp montane forest and brush regions. 12 to 20 cm. Very elongated (*M. caucasica*) or more compact (*M. luschani*). Males, in contrast to *Chioglossa* and *Salamandra*, have a distinct thorn-like protuberance at the base of the tail. The tail in cross-section is more or less round. There is a predetermined fracture line where the fragile tail may break off. Large protruding eyes. Parotoid glands in *M. caucasica* are indistinct, in *M. luschani* conspicuous, long, and narrow.

Like *Chioglossa*, these are remarkably agile and fast salamanders. Largely terrestrial, they have a cryptic, crepuscular, or nocturnal mode of life. Larval development occurs in small, rocky, clear, cool, flowing waters, especially in those with rapids that are largely fish-free.

Mating behavior is similar to *Pleurodeles*. The tail thorn is positioned exactly underneath the cloaca of the female

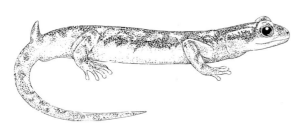

Mertensiella luschani

and there causes tactile stimulation. The larvae of *M. caucasica* remain in very small, shallow, moving springs among moss and rocks. They metamorphose at a length of about 7.5 cm. Newly metamorphosed specimens remain in the splash zone, while adults may move away from water for considerable distances. Activity phases are confined to spring and fall. These salamanders become dormant during the winter as well as during the summer, and they are then extremely difficult to find.

These rarely seen salamanders should be kept in damp terrariums with a bottom layer of clean, coarse gravel that is barely covered with water, with shallow rocks and moss pads on top. Preferred temperatures are from 9 to 15° C.; the summer dormancy period may be slightly warmer (to 20° C.). Winter dormancy must be passed under frost-free conditions. They will feed on various amphipods, aquatic insect larvae (which are picked up out of very shallow water), small worms, waxmoth larvae, and flies. They apparently have not yet been bred in captivity.

▪ *M. caucasica* (WAGA, 1876). Caucasus Salamander. Southwestern extensions of the Caucasus, mostly among *Fagus orientalis* stands from 600 to 1,000 m. 18 to 20 cm. Brown and black with 2 longitudinal rows of small orange-red spots.

▪ *M. luschani* (STEINDACHNER, 1891). Luschan's Salamander. The nominate form occurs in southern Anatolia; *M. l. helverseni* lives on the Aegean island of Karpathos. 12 cm. Brownish with a pattern of yellow dots.

Mertensophryne TIHEN, 1960. Genus of the Bufonidae. Tropical central and eastern Africa. 3 species. Toad-like, compact. Skin of dorsum covered with conical warts, ventral skin granular. No tympanum, middle ear, or vocal sac (no hearing and vocalizing ability). Snout projecting. Legs short. Fingers and toes free. 2 distinct metatarsal tubercles. Ground-dwellers. Maintain as for *Bufo*.

▪ *M. micranotis* (LOVERIDGE, 1925). 2 subspecies. Kenya and Tanzania.

▪ *M. schmidti* GRANDISON, 1972. Congo. 2.5 cm.

▪ *M. ushanorus* (LOVERIDGE, 1932).

Mesobaena MERTENS, 1925. Monotypic genus of the Amphisbaenidae. Northern South America. Slightly flattened snout.

▪ *M. huebneri* MERTENS, 1925. Upper Amazon Region, Colombia and Venezuela. Tropical rain forest.

Mesoclemmys: see *Phrynops*, genus.

Metacrinia PARKER, 1940. Monotypic genus of the Leptodactylidae. Southwestern tip of Australia in damp forests. Compact, toad-like. Skin covered with warts, granular on abdomen. Snout short, limbs weak. Pupil horizontal. Tympanum indistinct or not visible. Fingers and toes free. Ground-dwellers with a cryptic mode of life.

▪ *M. nichollsi* (HARRISON, 1927). Nicholl's Toadlet. 2.5 cm. Dorsum dark brown to black. Ventrum gray, bluish, or black, with white dots and spots. Base of forelimbs and underneath hind limbs with conspicuous orange spots.

Metamorphosis: Transformation of a larval form into a sexual animal. All amphibians with a free-living larval stage undergo metamorphosis, far-reaching changes in body structure, physiology, and mode of life occurring (except in those that are neotenous). Amphibian metamorphosis is triggered by thyroid hormone (thyroxin), which in turn is controlled by thyreotropin produced by the anterior pituitary lobe.

Among the earliest changes in the progression of metamorphosis—which can last from a few weeks to several

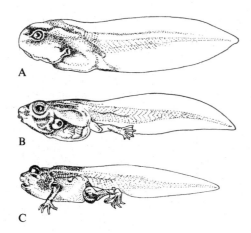

Metamorphosis of a frog tadpole. A: Early stage larva; B: early metamorphosis, with head beginning to change and hind legs well developed; C: nearing transformation, all four legs well developed, head frog-like, skin changing, tail smaller

months—is the formation of lungs, which take over respiration from the gills through a connection established from the nasal opening to the oral cavity. At the same time the simple larval blood circulatory system gives rise to a partially independent lung circulation. Formation of the extremities (in salamanders first the front legs; in frogs first the hind legs) enables eventual locomotion on land.

Changes in the skin affect among other things the development of multicellular skin glands and the disappearance in salamanders and related forms of the Leydig's Cells, whose function is not yet clearly established. The lateral line organ, a sensory organ to register current gradients, is lost in most species.

Particularly obvious are the morphological changes during metamorphosis of tadpoles into juvenile frogs. With the establishment of the front limbs the tail becomes shortened until only a small stump is left. The oval body becomes more angular, the eyes move dorsally, and a hearing organ with an external tympanum develops. In conjunction

Metamorphosis of *Gastrotheca riobambae*

with an altered feeding mode (filter-feeding or plant-eating larvae are turned into predatory juvenile frogs) there are far-reaching changes to the entire digestive tract, including the mouth and jaws, which lead to a temporary halt in food intake. The extremely long digestive tract of tadpoles becomes only twice the body length of the young frog. A larynx, together with the ability to produce sound, usually develops.

Metamorphosis in salamanders and related forms is less obvious, since the elongated body form and the tail remain more or less constant. The dorsal and/or ventral crests on the tail may regress. Due to their predatory habits, the larval salamander head has strong similarities with the head of the metamorphosed sexual animal.

Metaphrynella PARKER, 1934. Genus of the Microhylidae. Tropical Southeast Asia. 2 species in tropical lowlands and montane rain forests. Compact. Skin granular. Short-snouted. Pupil horizontal. The small tympanum may be partially covered by a skin fold that extends in an arch from the eye to the shoulder. Limbs short. Fingers webbed at base, the toes mostly webbed. Tips of fingers and toes conical, some distinctly widened and with adhesive discs. Insides of hands at bases of fingers with conspicuously large, wide, adhesive pads.

Arboreal, living in hollow logs and branches and presumably spawning in phytothelms. Maintain them in a tropical rain-forest terrarium with small water dishes among the branches (e. g., half coconut shells) and temperatures from 25 to 29° C.
- *M. pollicaris* (BOULENGER, 1890). Malayan Peninsula (900-1800 m) and Sumatra. 4 cm. Olive-brown, sides with a yellow pattern.
- *M. sundana* (PETERS, 1867). Kalimantan. 2 cm (males), 2.5 cm (females). Brown with an irregular darker pattern.

Metatarsal tubercle: Usually refers to one or more tubercles lying at the base of the underside of the foot in frogs and used by some as an implement for burrowing (e. g., *Pelobates*, *Scaphiopus*).

Metopostira MEHELY, 1901. Monotypic genus of the Microhylidae (formerly *Metopostira* species were referred to *Baragenys*). New Guinea. Related to *Asterophrys* and *Genyophryne*. Slender. Skin smooth. Pupil horizontal. A skin fold about the tympanum; tympanum in juveniles not visble, but in adults clearly visible. Fingers and toes free, the tips enlarged into adhesive discs (larger on toes). The tubercles of the fingers and undersides of the toes have an adhesive function. 1 inner metatarsal tubercle.

Presumably more or less arboreal, rain-forest dwellers without an aquatic larval stage.
- *M. ocellata* MEHELY, 1901. 4.5 cm. Greenish brown with dark brown dots and with a dark, light-edged paired eye spot (ocellus) in the sacral region.

Micrablepharus BOETTGER, 1885. Genus of the Teiidae. Southern Brasil, Paraguay. 2 species. 15 cm. Elongated, with weakly developed limbs. Large, smooth scales. Mode of life presumably as in *Gymnophthalamus*.
- *M. maximiliani* (REINHARDT and LUETKEN, 1862).

Micrelaps BOETTGER, 1879-1880. Genus of the Colubridae, Aparallactinae. Eastern Africa from Somalia and the Sudan and Kenya. 2 or 3 species in thornbush steppes to semideserts and in montane regions up to 2,000 m. To 40 cm. Head rounded, clearly set off. Body with smooth scales.

Nocturnal ground snakes. Biology largely unknown. Caution: Venomous bites possible.
- *M. boettgeri* (BOULENGER, 1901). Sudan to Kenya.
- *M. vaillanti* (MOCQUARD, 1888). Somalia.

Micrixalus BOULENGER, 1888. Genus of the Ranidae. Tropical southern Asia. About 10 species. Adhesive discs on the tips of the fingers and toes are well developed. The fingers are free, the toes webbed. The tympanum is indistinct or not visible at all and is always small. No pharyngeal teeth. Often olive to brown with an indistinct darker pattern, the thighs with dark crossbands.

Mode of life and maintenance similar to *Amolops* and *Staurois*.
- *M. baluensis* (BOULENGER, 1896). Kalimantan.
- *M. opisthorhodus* (GUENTHER, 1868). Southwestern India.
- *M. saxicola* (JERDON, 1853). Southwestern India.

Microbatrachella HEWITT, 1926. Monotypic genus of the Ranidae. Cape Province. Primarily in dry grassy steppes (*Restio* stands). Fingers free, toes webbed. Males produce a sharp chirping call and in doing so inflate their vocal sac to about the size of the entire body. Highly variable in coloration.

Spawning takes place during the rainy southern winter (June/July) in shallow water.
- *M. capensis* (BOULENGER, 1910). To 1.7 cm.

Microbatrachus: see *Sphenophryne*, genus.

Microcaecilia TAYLOR, 1968. Genus of the Ceciliidae. Northern South America. 3 species. To 23 cm. Eyes covered by orbital bone and more or less invisible. Tentacle close to eye. Lower jaw with only 1 row of teeth.
- *M. albiceps* (BOULENGER, 1882). Ecuador. To 23 cm. Gray-brown, ventrally lighter, the head, neck, and posterior part of body yellowish.

Microgecko: see *Tropiocolotes*, genus.

Microhyla TSCHUDI, 1838. Asian Narrow-mouthed Toads. Genus of the Microhylidae. Tropical to subtropical Asia, India to Japan, southward to the Sunda Islands. 18 species in rain forests but also in open cultivated areas. Snout-vent length a few centimeters. More or less compact. Skin usually smooth. In contrast to the related Asiatic genus *Kalophrynus* the tympanum is not visible externally. Pupil round. Fingers free, with more or less distinct adhesive discs; first finger very short. Toes with more or less developed webbing. 1 or 2 metatarsal tubercles, the inner one in some species developed into a digging spade. Males have a large vocal sac and good vocalizing ability. Larvae in some species have a dish-like enlarged lower lip, the respiratory aperture covered by a fringed skin fold.

Ground-dwellers. Spawning takes place in shallow, murky puddles, as in rice paddies. Due to the temporary nature of these waters the development of embryos and larvae takes place quickly.

Species from agricultural areas, especially those from

populations at the northern end of the generic range, must be kept under alternating dry and damp conditions; sudden exposure to wet conditions (together with a heated water bowl and fresh but turbid water and a few roots or water plants) will often stimulate breeding. More southern species should be kept in a rain-forest terarrium with diversely structured bottom.
- *M. berdmorei* (BLYTH, 1856). Tropical Southeast Asia from Burma and Thailand to Sumatra and Kalimantan. 3 cm. Pink to brown with large light-edged dark dorsal spots that narrow toward the center.
- *M. okinavensis* STEJNEGER, 1901. Ryukyus. 3 cm. Gray or reddish, the back with a large characteristically shaped parallel-bordered patch.
- *M. ornata* (DUMERIL and BIBRON, 1897). India (Malabar) to China. 2 cm. Light olive-brown with pink stripes.
- *M. palmipes* BOULENGER, 1897. Malaya, Sumatra, Java, Bali. Dorsum light brown with dark gray spots with white margins.
- *M. pulchra* (HALLOWELL, 1860). Orange-thighed Narrow-mouthed Toad. Southern China, Kampuchea, Vietnam. Dorsum variable, but with distinct triangular marking. Ventrum yellow, the thighs bright yellow to orange.

Microhylidae: Narrow-mouthed Toads. Very large and diverse family of frogs. Mainly in tropical Southeast Asia, including the Indo-Australian Archipelago (21 genera, some very large), Central and South America (18 genera), Madagascar (13 genera), and eastern and southern Africa (7 genera). Closely related to Ranidae and Rhacophoridae, but distinguished from these two families by the conspicuously small mouth and more or less widened transverse processes of the sacral vertebrae.

Burrowing ground-dwellers as well as tree-dwellers. Often larval development takes place independent of water. Most species lack teeth and are specialized to feed mostly on termites as well as on ants. A good substitute food in captivity is wingless fruitflies. Cannibalism is virtually nonexistent due to the necessity to feed on small food organisms. Beyond that, there is insufficient information about the biology of most species; this deficiency can be made up to some extent by adequate terrarium observations.

Systematic review:
- Subfamily Dyscophinae: Teeth present; diplasiocoelic vertebrae; larvae aquatic; developmental biology largely unknown. Madagascar and Southeast Asia.
Genera *Dyscophus, Calluella*.
- Subfamily Cophylinae: Teeth usually present; procoelic vertebrae; developmental biology largely unknown. Madagascar.
Genera *Anodonthyla, Cophyla, Madecassophryne, Mantipus, Paracophyla, Platyhyla, Paltypelis, Plethodonthyla, Pseudohemisus, Rhombophryne, Scaphiophryne, Stumpffia*.
- Subfamily Asterophryninae: Toothless; vertebrae mostly diplasiocoelic, rarely procoelic; larval development within terrestrially deposited eggs. New Guinea.
Genera *Asterophrys, Baragenys, Genyophryne, Metopostira, Xenobatrachus*.
- Subfamily Microhylinae: Toothless; vertebrae mostly diplasiocoelic, rarely procoelic; larvae aquatic.
Genera from tropical Southeast Asia: *Chaperina, Gastro-*

phrynoides, Glyphoglossus, Kalophrynus, Kaloula, Metaphrynella, Microhyla, Phrynella, Ramanella, Uperodon.
Genera from tropical and suptropical America: *Arcovomer, Chiasmocleis, Ctenophryne, Dasypops, Dermatonotus, Elachistocleis, Gastrophryne, Geobatrachus, Glossostoma, Hamptophryne, Hyophryne, Hypopachus, Myersiella, Otophryne, Relictivomer, Stereocyclops, Synapturanus, Syncope.*
▪ Subfamily Sphenophryninae: Toothless or with minute teeth; procoelic vertebrae; larval development within terrestrially deposited eggs. New Guinea and northeastern Australia.
Genera *Aphantophryne, Cophixalus, Microbatrachus, Oreophryne, Sphenophryne.*
▪ Subfamily Brevicipitinae: Toothless; diplasiocoelic vertebrae; larval development within terrestrially deposited eggs. Africa.
Genera *Breviceps, Callulina, Probreviceps, Sphelaeophryne.*
▪ Subfamily Melanobatrachinae: Toothless; procoelic vertebrae; tympanum and middle ear completely reduced; eggs deposited on land, larval development outside of egg. Africa and tropical Southeast Asia.
Genera *Hoplophryne, Melanobatrchus, Parhoplophryne.*

Micropechis BOULENGER, 1896. Pacific Coral Snakes. Monotypic genus of the Elapidae. New Guinea and adjacent islands in tropical forests. To 1.5 m. Stout, with a large cobra-like head distinctly set off from the body and with small eyes. Tail short. Usually dark brown with more or less distinct yellowish crossbands.
Terrestrial, predominantly nocturnal venomous snakes. When disturbed these snakes will slightly raise the anterior part of the body as a threat posture. Biology and effect of venom on humans largely unknown; at least one human fatality recorded.
▪ *M. ikaheka* (LESSON, 1830). Ikaheka Snake. New Guinea and adjacent islands, also on Aru. Several subspecies.

Micropisthodon MOCQUARD, 1894. Monotypic genus of the Colubridae, Lycodontinae. Northern Madagascar (island of Nossi-Be). About 70 cm. Head only slightly set off from the body, which is slightly compressed. A dark V-shaped mark on the neck points toward the head against a light brown background.
Ecology and biology unknown.
▪ *M. ochraceus* MOCQUARD, 1894.

Microsaura: see *Chamaeleo,* genus.

Micruroides SCHMIDT, 1928. Arizona Coral Snakes. Monotypic genus of the Elapidae. Northern Mexico to southwestern USA in steppe-like dry regions. To 55 cm. Cylindrical, with a short, blunt-snouted head. Typical coral snake coloration of black, white, and red (wider than all other colors) bands.
Nocturnal venomous snakes that hide during the day under rocks and similar places. The diet consists mainly of arthropods, lizards, and sometimes newborn small mammals. *Micruroides* venom is very dangerous, but these snakes will rarely bite unless mishandled. Maintain in a heated dry terrarium. A short winter dormancy period is essential for breeding.
▪ *M. euryxanthus* (KENNICOTT, 1860). 2 subspecies.

Micruroides euryxanthus

Micrurus WAGLER, 1824. American Coral Snakes. Genus of the Elapidae. Southern USA to northern Argentina. About 50 species, some polytypic. Taxonomy still badly confused. In tropical rain forests and montane rain forests; only *M. fulvius* is found in temperate areas (in the USA).
From 40 cm to 1.5 m. Body more or less round (tail sometimes flattened), with a short, rounded head. Typical red, yellow (or white), and black rings (one color may be missing in some species). Distinguishing the individual species is often rather difficult.
Nocturnal, terrestrial venomous snakes. Disturbed specimens often raise their tails a few centimeters off the ground and move it rapidly back and forth, while the head is being kept still and pressed against the ground or hidden under the coiled body. These snakes rarely bite during the day. Their venom is very potent; 10% of bites that are not treated are fatal.
The diet includes arthropods, frogs, lizards, newborn small mammals, and ground-nesting birds. Examination of

Micrurus corallinus corallinus

coral snake stomachs has produced specimens of very rarely seen snakes and lizards.

Maintenance of *Micrurus* depends upon the species and its origin. Usually a humid, heated forest terrarium and ample hiding places are necessary. If the substrate is thin (to prevent the snakes from burrowing out of sight), shallow hiding boxes can also be provided for pressure contact and can be filled with foam rubber kept damp. The snakes will feel more secure with such provisions.

Specimens collected roughly often have neck damage and refuse to feed. Small, slender freshwater fish are sometimes a suitable substitute food if more normal prey is unavailable.

▪ *M. corallinus* (WIED, 1820). Eastern Brasil southward to the Mato Grosso. Venom very dangerous.

▪ *M. frontalis* (DUMERIL, DUMERIL, and BIBRON, 1854). Southwestern Brasil, Uruguay, Paraguay, northern Argen-

Micrurus fulvius

Micrurus frontalis frontalis

Micrurus lemniscatus carvalhoi

tine. One of the most dangerous and the southernmost species within this genus.
- *M. fulvius* (LINNAEUS, 1766). Northern Coral Snake. Southeastern USA to northern Mexico.
- *M. lemniscatus* (LINNAEUS, 1758). Ibiboboca. Northeastern South America, Trinidad.
- *M. spixi* WAGLER, 1824. Giant Coral Snake. Amazon Basin.

Mictopholis SMITH, 1935. Monotypic genus of the Agamidae. Known only from the type locality in Assam. Closely related to *Salea* and often included in it.
- *M. austeniana* (ANNANDALE, 1908).

Migration: Periodic and non-periodic movements of animals over sometimes very long distances. Often they gather (aggregation) for such a purpose. Some amphibian species migrate in spring to their spawning waters, and certain reptiles in temperate zones migrate to specific over-wintering quarters. Massive migrations can also be observed in sea turtles, which generally return to the same beach where they were hatched to lay their eggs. An important prerequisite for such specific directional migration is to have the ability for exact orientation.

Millotisaurus PASTEUR, 1962. Monotypic genus of the Gekkonidae. Madagascar. Known only from the type locality.
- *M. mirabilis* PASTEUR, 1962.

Mimophis GUENTHER, 1868. Monotypic genus of the Colubridae, Boiginae. Madagascar. Related to *Psammophis*. In dry habitats (grasslands, dry forests to outer jungle areas). About 1 m. The head is long and narrow and clearly set off from the body. The large eyes are protected by supraorbital scales. A dark brown middorsal band.

Fast, agile, diurnal ground snakes that feed mainly on lizards, less often on small mammals. Maintenance similar to *Coluber*. Caution: Venomous bites possible.
- *M. mahafalensis* (GRANDIDIER, 1867). One of the most common snakes on the island.

Mimosiphonops TAYLOR, 1968. Monotypic genus of the Caeciliidae. Eastern Brasil. Cylindrical body. 87 primary folds (in the type specimen), no secondary folds. Scales absent. Tentacle slightly closer to nostril than to eye. Lower jaw with only 1 row of teeth. Similar to *Luetkenotyphlus*, with clearly unfurrowed cloacal field. Cloacal slit perpendicular.
- *M. vermiculatus* TAYLOR, 1968. Brasil. 19 cm.

Miodon DUMERIL, 1859. Genus of the Colubridae, Aparallactinae. Tropical Africa. 3 or 4 species. Closely related to *Polemon*. In diverse tropical forests in mountain ranges up to 2,000 m elevation. To 85 cm. The small, round-snouted head is not set off from the body. Smooth dorsal scales. Uniformly dark.

Nocturnal ground snakes that prey mainly on smaller snakes, especially worm snakes. They should be kept in a rain-forest terrarium or a glass terrarium. Caution: Venomous bites possible.
- *M. collaris* (PETERS, 1881). Nigeria and Cameroons throughout Congo Basin eastward to Uganda. Blackish with a narrow light neckband.

Mixophyes GUENTHER, 1864. Australian Barred Frogs. Genus of the Leptodactylidae. Australia. 4 species along the eastern coast in subtropical and tropical rain forests and deciduous forests. Females larger than males. *Rana*-like. Head large. Strong, long hind legs. Pupil vertical. Tympanum clearly visible. Fingers free, toes webbed.

Ground-dwellers. Predatory, feeding mainly on insects and other frogs.
- *M. fasciolatus* GUENTHER, 1864. Great Barred Frog. Central eastern coast. To 8 cm. Dark gray or brown, covered sparingly with dark spots with light edges. Limbs with crossbands narrower than interspaces.
- *M. iteratus* STRAUGHAN, 1968. Giant Barred Frog. Extreme southern Queensland and New South Wales. To 11.5 cm. Dark olive with darker spots or uniformly black. Crossbands on limbs slightly narrower than interspaces. Skin granular.

Mocquard, Francois (1834–1917): French herpetologist. Coauthored with Auguste Dumeril, Bocourt, and Brocchi the 17-volume *Mission Scientifique au Mexique et dans l'Amerique Centrale; Etudes sur les Reptiles et les Batraciens* (1870-1909).

Moloch GRAY, 1841. Moloch, Thorny Devil. Monotypic genus of the Agamidae. Australia in semideserts and deserts. About 20 cm. Strongly flattened. Mouth small, the lateral lower jaw teeth pointing inward horizontally. Tail

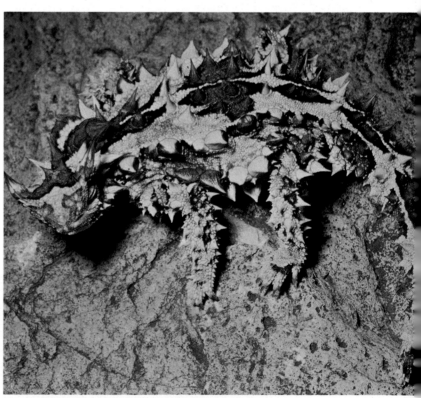

Moloch horridus

and legs short. Entire body surface more or less covered with long, symmetrically arranged thorny scales, 2 particularly long ones on the back of the head. Spiny fat storage organs are present on the neck. Between the scales are minute canals that collect water (from dew) and funnel it to the corners of the mouth. Can change colors. Egg-lay-

Moloch horridus

ers, 6-8 eggs per clutch.

Should be kept in a sandy container with a deep substrate that must always be slightly damp in its lower layers. Satisfactory day temperatures are 30 to 35° C., the basking area on the ground about 40° C.; provide a substantial temperature reduction at night by at least 10° C. During the Australian winter (= European and North American summer) keep the terrarium generally somewhat cooler. Should be sprayed occasionally and allowed regular access to ultraviolet radiation.

Specialized to feed on ants and termites, which are essential for long-term survival in captivity. Substitutes using the acid from ants as an additive are unsatisfactory. It has been calculated that *Moloch* will take up to 1800 small ants per day. Apart from these various other arthropods are also taken to a lesser extent. Virtually unavailable today.

• *M. horridus* GRAY, 1841. Moloch, Thorny Devil. Southern, western, and especially the central regions of Australia. Brown with yellow and reddish markings.

Molting: Periodic shedding of the outer skin layer, which consists of dead, keratinized cells. Amphibians, which have a very thin corneous layer, shed their skin in its entirety (e. g., *Bufo*) or in sections (e. g., *Rana*). This veil-like layer often is immediately eaten (ceratophagy). In crocodilians and turtles corneous sections of scutes at various body sites are being replaced constantly. Lizards and snakes have regular molting periods when the outermost skin layer is stripped off in large sections (in most lizards) or in its entirety (in most snakes). In snakes the onset of this period can be recognized by a gradual clouding of the eyes, which will clear up again 2 to 3 days before the actual

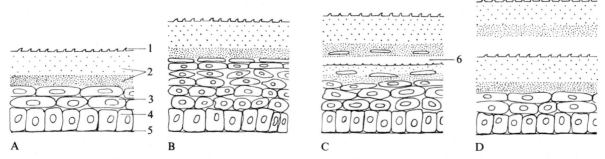

Schematic representation of molting in a snake. A: Resting stage; B: increase of basal cells to generate a new epidermis; C: development of a splitting zone between the old and new epidermis; D: shedding of the old skin. 1 Scales; 2 stratum corneum; 3 stratum intermedium; 4 stratum germinativum or stratum basale; 5 basal membrane; 6 splitting zone

Shed skin of *Elaphe obsoleta*

shedding process.

Molting is controlled by internal factors (hormones produced by the thyroid gland and thymus gland) that in turn are influenced by environmental factors (temperature, humidity, food availability). The general health of a specimen plays an important part in this. Snakes or lizards that are kept under less than ideal conditions or are diseased usually have molting problems (skin only partially shed or not at all, although the molting process has commenced). Should this happen, hobbyists are advised to give such animals a forced bath for several hours. Thereafter, the skin

Molting in *Lampropeltis getulus getulus*

can usually be manually removed with the aid of forceps (caution obviously required with venomous snakes!).

In field herpetology the presence of shed snake skins can give an indication about the snake fauna in a particular area, since the species sometimes can be determined on the basis of scale patterns.

Molting problems: Deviations from the normal molting process in the form of delayed or (more commonly) incomplete molting. In salamanders the skin takes on a milky-yellow appearance and usually gives off a watery or less frequently puss-like secretion. Delayed and incomplete moltings are caused primarily by unfavorable biophysical environmental conditions (temperatures too high, humidity too low) or dietary deficiencies (vitamin deficieny). They can also be caused by mite infestations. Excessive amounts of vitamins given to snakes can lead to repeated moltings at very short intervals and thus cause the death of the animal due to exhaustion.

Therapy: Increased humidity, bathing or spraying with warm water, vitamin B-complex injections or in the form of water-soluble vitamin preparations over or in food animals. With simultaneous mite treatment it is recommended that the skin be painted with an oily vitamin preparation.

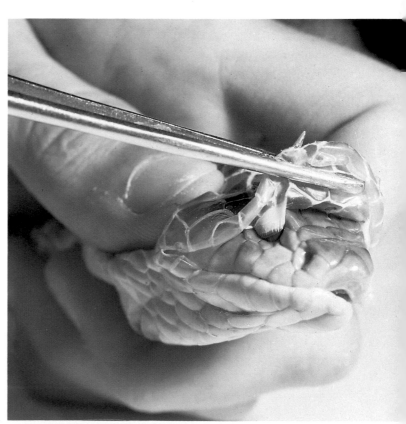

Molting problems: Helping remove skin adherent to eye

Monopeltis SMITH, 1848. Wedge-snouted Amphisbaenids. Genus of the Amphisbaenia. Tropical and southern Africa. In forest regions. To 70 cm. Slender, with a shovel-like, dorso-ventrally flattened snout equipped with 1 or 2 heavy scutes resembling a fingernail.

Subterranean. Supposed to feed in part on dead animals. Egg-layers.

• *M. capensis* SMITH, 1848. Southern Africa. Several subspecies. To 30 cm. Flesh tones to pink.

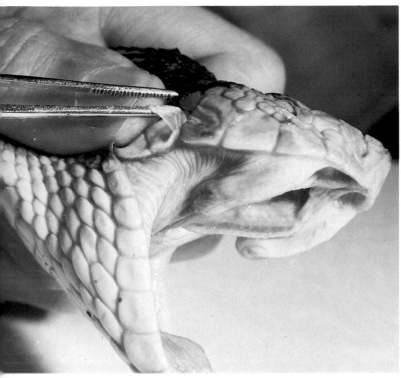

Molting problems: Helping remove adherent skin

Monophyletic: Group of organisms all derived from a single original species and at the same time including all species derived from this species. In the cladistic philosophy of systematics, phylogenetic systems are based exclusively on monophyletic groups, while paraphyletic and polyphyletic groups are not allowed.

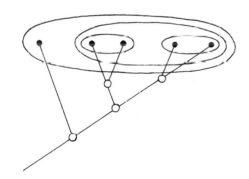

Schematic representation of a monophyletic group

Monotypic: Including only a single taxon. Refers to a species that has no subspecies or to a genus containing only a single species (which, however, can be polytypic).

Monsoon forests: Deciduous forests occurring in regions with well-defined monsoon climate. During the summer half of the year on-shore winds carry in large amounts of precipitation; during the winter half of the year there are only dry off-shore winds). Typical of eastern and southeastern Asia. Development of agricultural lands has destroyed much of the original monsoon forests.

Monstera ADANS. Genus of the Araceae. Tropics of the Americas. About 30 species. Large-leaved climbing, ground-dwelling, or semiepiphytic plants that send aerial roots to the ground.

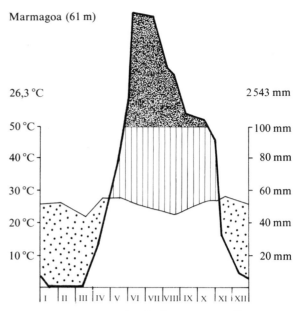

Marmagoa (61 m)

26,3 °C   2 543 mm

Climatic diagram of an Indian monsoon forest

▪ *M. deliciosa* LIEBM. Hardy if cultured like *Philodendron*. Can take temperatures from 8 to 25° C. Suitable for large rain-forest terrariums.
▪ *M. obliqua* L, Brasil.

Montana: Also called *yunga*. Montane rain forests occurring in the tropics of Central and South America, especially along the eastern slopes of the Andes, the central American Cordilleras, Jamaica, and Haiti, at elevations from about 1300 m to 3000 m. In contrast to the *selva* it is perpetually wet and rich in epiphytes.

Montane rain forests: Forests that occur in permanently wet, relatively cool (19 to 23° C.) regions of tropical mountains and mountain chains at elevations between 1300 and 3000 m. If these forests occur within cloud belts (above 1800 m) where the air is supersaturated with water and light intensity is largely reduced, one refers to these as cloud forests.Montane rain forests are distinguished from rain forests of the lowlands by lower tree heights and a conspicuous diversity of epiphytes (including mosses, lichens, ferns, orchids, Araceae, Bromeliaceae) and tree ferns. Montane rain forests occur primarily in the northern Neotropics, in the southern Orient, and on New Guinea.

Morelia GRAY, 1842. Carpet and Diamond Pythons. Monotypic genus of the Boidae, subfamily Pythoninae. (Now often included in *Python*.) Australia and New Guinea. In dry forest regions and steppes. About 3 m. Slender, the head distinctly set off from the body and with large fang-like teeth. There are 2 color patterns that are different in their markings: diamond pythons have irregular to strongly symmetrical (vaguely diamond-like) yellow spots about 1 scale in size surrounded by black scales; carpet pythons have blackish blotches or crossbands on pale tan.

These are good climbers that feed on birds and small mammals. They should be kept in a well-heated and ventilated terrarium with strong climbing facilities. Sometimes they like to bathe when in captivity. For unknown reasons longevity is generally short in captivity, although individual specimens have lived for more than 10 years.

Morelia spilotes variegata

Morelia spilotes spilotes

• *M. spilotes* (LACEPEDE, 1804). Virtually all of Australia except the west.

Morenia GRAY, 1870. Peacock Turtles. Genus of the Emydidae. India and Indo-China. 2 species. Mainly in standing waters. To 21 cm. Characteristic yellow eye spots (ocelli) on each carapace scute. Longitudinal stripes on head and neck, one stripe extending from tip of snout through the eye.

Mainly herbivorous, only a few animals taken (small crustaceans, molluscs). Maintenance generally similar to other herbivorous tropical turtles (*Kachuga, Ocadia, Callagur*). An open water system is recommended.

• *M. ocellata* (DUMERIL and BIBRON, 1835). Ocellated Peacock Turtle. Southern Burma, including Tenasserim. Only a single ocellus on each scute, the center darker than the rest of carapace.

• *M. petersi* (ANDERSON, 1879). Peter's Peacock Turtle. Bengal. 1 to 3 ocelli on each scute, the center of eye spot not darker than the background color.

Morenia ocellata

Morenia ocellata

Morethia GRAY, 1845. Genus of the Scincidae. Australia. 6 species in dry to very dry habitats. To 15 cm. Slender. A transparent lid spectacle. 5-toed limbs. Smooth scales.

Ground-dwellers that feed mainly on arthropods. Up to 6 eggs. They require high daytime temperatures and low night temperatures.

• *M. taeniopleura* PETERS, 1874. Firetail Skink. Northern and central Australia. 10 cm. Brown to black with light longitudinal stripes and a red to orange tail.

Morunasaurus DUNN, 1933. Genus of the Iguanidae. Ecuador to Panama. 2 species. Small ground-dwellers that are reminiscent of *Hoplocercus* because of their heavily spinous tails; they were formerly included in that genus.

• *M. annularis* (O'SHAUGHNESSY, 1881). Amazon Region of Ecuador.

Mueller, Lorenz (1868-1953): Painter and herpetologist in Munich. Coauthored with Mertens the checklist *Die Amphibien und Reptilien Europas* in 1928 and 1940. Published many articles on herpetological systematics.

Muridae: Mice. Of all the mammals, the Muridae play by far the most important role as terrarium food animals as well as laboratory animals. There are numerous special laboratory strains of mice (*Mus musculus*) and rats (*Rattus norvegicus*). Apart from the well-known white forms there are also many pigmented forms that are sometimes more eagerly eaten by snakes than are the white ones.

Mice (and rats) can easily be bred in plastic boxes with wire mesh lids (they must not be kept in wood) kept at 18-22° C. Harem breeding (several females and one or two males) is the most productive method. With new animals cannibalism is possible. In order to minimize the offensive urine odor, bedding is placed inside the breeding container (wood shavings, sawdust). Food should be offered in the form of commercially prepared mouse and rat diets (pellets, cubes) and water must be offered from a drinking bottle suspended inside or on the box. If commercial feed is not available these rodents will also eat grain, dry bread, vegetables, and similar items.

Muridae: *Mus musculus*

The gestation period is 20-21 days for mice and 22-24 days for rats. Each litter consists of 6-12 young (in rats rarely up to 20). Under favorable conditions a colony can produce 7 rat litters and 9 mice litters per year. Mice reach sexual maturity in about 2 months, rats in 3 months.

Less odorous than the house mouse is the African mouse *Mastomys coucha*, which can give birth to litters of up to 18 or 19 young every 4 weeks.

Muscidae: Houseflies. Family of the Diptera. About 4000 species. From 3 to 15 mm. These flies often can be caught in large numbers in fly traps. The common housefly (*Musca domestica*) and the small housefly (*Fannia canicularis*) are best suited for breeding as food for amphibians and reptiles. However, sometimes they are eaten only for short periods. The larvae (maggots) are extremely resilient and can sometimes cause damage to the digestive tract of smaller animals or are simply excreted completely undigested. The adults are best kept in mesh cages, and the larvae are hatched in a large bowl tightly covered with gauze. To obtain eggs, dishes of food are placed inside the fly cage or out in the open in suitable locations. Larval food can be prepared by mixing flour, wheat bran, yeast, and water at 1 : 1 : 0.2 : 5. Before use this mixture should be left to ferment for a few days. The flour is left out of other mixtures or replaced by skimmed milk cheese. Another food mix consists of about 200 g bran, 1 tablespoon sugar, 1 teaspoon powdered milk, 100 ml water, and some baker's yeast. Used up food is continuously replenished. The larvae will turn into pupae in about 2 weeks at 25° C. The

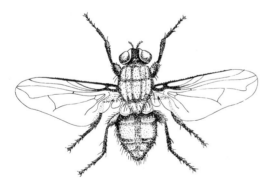

Muscidae, *Musca domestica*

Muscidae: Maggots

pupae are initially red and turn dark red within 2 days. The flies emerge after 4 or 5 days and are then fed with powdered milk, glucose, and powdered eggs. The fly cage must be equipped with a drinking facility. The nutritional value of the flies can be enhanced if a multivitamin preparation is added to the food mixture. Fly pupae can readily be stored at temperatures of about 4° C. Small amounts can be removed and brought to hatching as need be. The unavoidable fermentation odor when breeding flies is often unpleasant.

Mushroom-tongued salamanders: Generic grouping in the Plethodontidae. In a strict sense this includes the following genera: *Bolitoglossa*, *Chiropterotriton*, *Lineatriton*, *Oedipina*, *Parvimolge*, *Pseudoeurycea*, and *Thorius* (plus a few close relatives). In a wider sense it includes also *Batrachoseps* and *Hydromantes*. Predominantly in Central America. All of these salamanders have very long, free tongues that can be thrust out chameleon-like and used to capture prey. The tongue bears a fancied resemblance to a miniature mushroom.

Some species are ground-dwellers, others are arboreal in bromeliads. As far as known, all species are oviparous, but without an aquatic larval stage. Fully metamorphosed juvenile salamanders hatch from the eggs. The females practice more or less well-defined brood care.

Mycetophilidae: Fungus Gnats. Family of the Diptera. From 3 to 12 mm. Some can be bred in large petri dishes. The bottom should be covered with humus and a few lumps of soya mush added. Development takes 20 to 30 days. Adults as well as larvae are suitable as food for small frogs.

Mycoses: Fungus diseases. Diseases caused by parasitic fungi affect particularly the mucous membranes in the digestive tract, the respiratory organs, and the skin or carapace. Mycoses of the skin are characterized by chronic, in part necrotic, inflammations as well as lesions of the carapace. Occasionally it can also be diagnosed by the presence of nodules in the organs of the live animal. Mycoses in snakes are indicated by raised brownish, discolored scales and in aquatic turtles by a dirty-white film over the skin. It is possible that the proliferation of the fungi is actually increased by administering antibiotics.

Therapy: Trypaflavin or potassium permanganate solution (1: 100,000). For mycotic stomatitis infectiosa, a twice daily application (over 15 days) locally of 200 I. U. Nystatin® suspension can be used. For endomycoses the antibiotic Miconazol (20 mg/kg body weight) can be tried experimentally.

Myersiella CARVALHO, 1954. Monotypic genus of the Microhylidae. Southeastern Brasil. Elongated-oval, flattened. Skin smooth. Long, pointed snout. Pupil round. Tympanum not visible. Fingers and toes free, but with lateral skin folds.
▪ *M. subnigra* (MIRANDA-RIBEIRO, 1920). 2 cm. Brown.

Myobatrachus SCHLEGEL, 1850. Monotypic genus of the Leptodactylidae. Extreme southwestern Australia. Flat and round, the head small. Pupil horizontal or round. Tympanum not visible. Limbs very short and thick, fingers and toes stubby, without webbing.

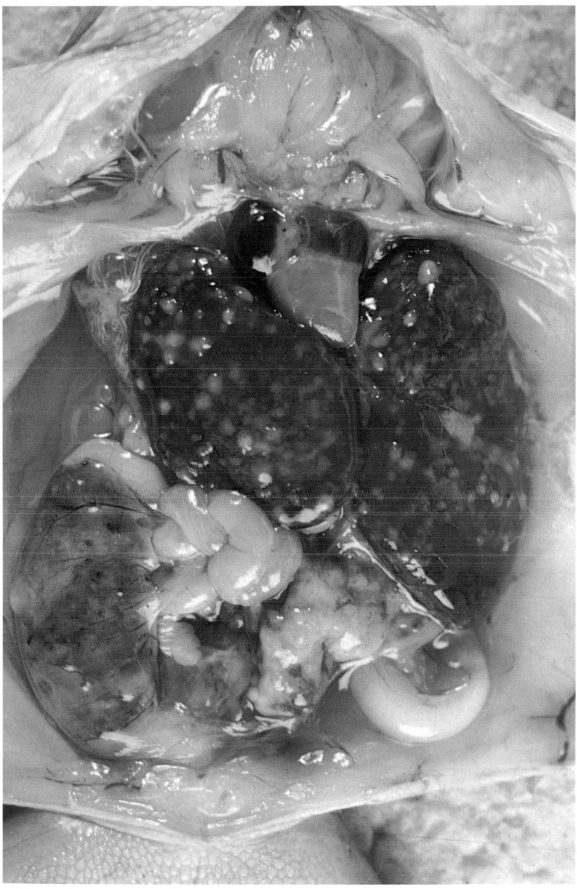

Mycoses: Fungal infection of the liver of *Litoria caerulea*

These little frogs usually burrow into the ground, feeding on termites. Development is terrestrial, without a free-living larval stage.

• *M. gouldii* (GRAY, 1841). Turtle Frog. 6 cm. Gray or brown.

Myriapoda: Millipedes and centipedes.   Class of the Arthropoda. Seldom used as food organisms for terrarium animals, though centipedes are eagerly eaten by many lizards. Many types of centipedes barely 5 cm long and often found under rocks and behind tree bark can be collected almost anywhere.

Myriapoda: A centipede, *Scolopendra viridicornis*

Myriapoda: A colorful eastern American millipede, *Apheloria corrugata*

Myron GRAY, 1849. Monotypic genus of the Colubridae, Homalopsinae. Coastal areas of New Guinea, Aru Islands, and Australia in mangrove swamps. 40 to 60 cm. Dorsal scales keeled. Dark crossbands on a lighter background.

Nocturnal. Feeds mainly on fish and possibly also on crustaceans.

• *M. richardsoni* GRAY, 1849.

Naja LAURENTI, 1768. Cobras. Genus of the Elapidae. African-Oriental distribution. 6 to 8 partly polytypic species, the taxonomy still in some doubt. Found from peripheral zones of tropical rain forests to thornbush steppes. 1.4 to 2.5 m. Raising of the anterior quarter or third of the body together with spreading of the ribs in the neck region into a hood is characteristic of this genus when excited or disturbed; the head is pointed horizontally at the enemy. The back of the hood displays in some species light-colored

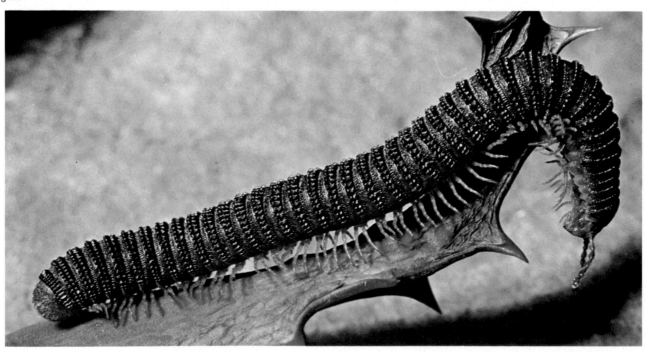

Myriapoda: A giant African millipede, *Lophostreptus*

Naja melanoleuca

snakes. In Indian and Egyptian mythology various *Naja* species have great significance as holy animals.

• *N. haje* (LINNAEUS, 1758). Egyptian Cobra. Africa except Cape Province, also the Arabian Peninsula. About 3 subspecies. Dry regions.

• *N. melanoleuca* HALLOWELL, 1858. Black-lipped Cobra. Africa south of 15° N. 2 subspecies. Savannahs.

• *N. naja* (LINNAEUS, 1758). Asian or Indian Cobra. Southern Asia and Indo-Australian Archipelago. Numerous subspecies, including *N. n. naja* (LINNAEUS, 1758), the spectacled cobra of India; *N. n. kaouthia* LESSON, 1831, the monocled cobra; and *N. n. sputatrix* BOIE, 1827, the Indonesian spitting cobra.

"spectacles" or "monocles."

Venomous snakes often found close to water. Usually many types of food are eaten, although some are food specialists (e. g., *Naja melanoleuca* and *Naja oxiana* feed on toads). Egg-layers, 8 to 25 eggs. Incubation 14 to 21 days. Bites are fatal without rapid administration of antiscrum. Some species and subspecies (*Naja naja sputatrix, N. nigricollis, N. mossambica,* and sometimes also *Naja naja naja*) spray or spit their venom over several meters at their attacker.

Cobras should be kept in a well-heated dry terrarium with bathing facilities. Strict compliance with the requirements for venomous snake care is essential. Well acclimated and settled specimens become tame and often live for many years (in excess of 15 years). Some species are regularly bred in captivity. Oriental fakirs often use *Naja* species in public performances to display their "charming" abilities, although cobras are virtually deaf like all other

Naja mossambica pallida

Naja haje

Naja naja

▪ *N. nigricollis* REINHARDT, 1843. Spitting Cobra. Africa south of 25° C. Savannahs.
▪ *N. nivea* (LINNAEUS, 1758). Cape Cobra. Republic of South Africa and Namibia. Bright yellow or dark brown.
▪ *N. oxiana* (EICHWALD, 1831). Central Asian Cobra. Soviet Central Asia northward to Kasachstan. A 2 to 3 months winter domancy period is needed for specimens from northern populations. The most northern cobra species.

Naja naja

Naja nigricollis

Naja nivea

Naja oxiana

Nannobatrachus BOULENGER, 1882. Genus of the Ranidae. Southern India. 3 species in rain forests. Snout-vent length a few centimeters. Compact. Pupil vertical. Tympanum not visible. Small adhesive discs on fingers and toes. Externally distinguishable from the closely related genus *Nyctibatrachus* only by the toes lacking webbing. Mainly ground-dwellers.
• *N. beddomei* BOULENGER, 1882. Southwestern India. 2 cm. Brown with an indistinct darker pattern.

Nannophrys GUENTHER, 1868. Genus of the Ranidae. Sri Lanka. 2 species. Compact but streamlined, the snout short and conspicuously broad. Skin granular. Tympanum more or less clearly visible. Fingers and toes free or toes webbed at the base only, the tips not enlarged into adhesive discs. Males have paired vocal sacs. Brown.
Terrestrial outside of breeding season. They should be kept in a tropical, damp terrarium with a small shallow water section.
• *N. ceylonensis* GUENTHER, 1868. 2 subspecies. To 4.5 cm.
• *N. guentheri* BOULENGER, 1888. To 3 cm.

Nanorana GUENTHER, 1896. Monotypic genus of the Ranidae. High plateaus of the eastern Himalayas (3,000 to 4,000 m). Flattened. Skin smooth. Legs short for family. Tympanum small, covered by skin, but clearly developed (in contrast to *Altirana*). Fingers webbed at base, the toes webbed to more than 50% of their length.
Slow, awkward, poor swimmers and divers. Semi-aquatic, found mainly in standing waters but also in mountain rivers. They should be kept in an unheated aqua-terrarium with day and night temperature variations. A winter dormancy is required.
• *N. pleskei* GUENTHER, 1896. Western China. 4 cm. Variable, the dorsum light green to olive with sharply deline-

ated dark brown spots.

Narudasia METHUEN and HEWITT, 1914. Monotypic genus of the Gekkonidae. Southwestern Africa in dry habitats. Small, nocturnal, poorly known ground-dwellers.
• *N. festiva* METHUEN and HEWITT, 1914.

Natalobatrachus HEWITT and METHUEN, 1913. Monotypic genus of the Ranidae. South Africa in splash zone of cool, shaded streams and river rapids. Slender, with a pointed snout. Fingers and toes long and thin, their tips with well-developed adhesive discs. Fingers free, toes webbed at base. No vocal sac.
Agile; excellent jumpers and good swimmers and divers that remain close to water among the rocks and similar perpetually wet habitats. The eggs are deposited in clumps (75-100 eggs), always above the water level on overhanging rocks, branches, or leaves so that hatching larvae fall into the water below.
• *N. boneberge* HEWITT and METHUEN, 1913. Coastal region of Natal. 4 cm. Dark to light or greenish brown.

Natricinae: Water Snakes and Allies. Subfamily of the Colubridae. Worldwide. About 37 genera. 50 cm to 2 m. This subfamily is in many respects not uniform and is poorly defined. The head and body scales (predominantly keeled body scales) conform to the general family characteristics, while the dentition is extremely variable. Some species possess opisthoglyphic fangs similar to the Boiginae and have indeed caused some fatalities (*Rhabdophis tigrina*), while others are completely harmless (*Natrix natrix*, all *Thamnophis* species), except perhaps in the case of allergic reactions.
For terrarium purposes it may be best to arrange the Natricinae according to their ecology into the following groups:
1) More or less terrestrial, sometimes burrowing species, always found in damp habitats (meadows, swamps, forest valleys), but never tied to open water. They also occupy montane forest regions. The diet of smaller species consists mainly of earthworms and large frogs. The terrarium should contain moss and a deep substrate.
2) Amphibious species that hunt in water for fish and frogs. They are excellent swimmers and divers, but always require dry, warm basking places. These points must be kept in mind when setting up the terrarium, otherwise these forms are prone to blister-like bacterial skin diseases. They are easily kept in a simple terrarium with a large water bowl.
3) More aquatic species that also like to bask on dry land but may stay in water for very long periods (up to several days). They should be kept in aqua-terrariums.
When discussing terrarium requirements, reference is made to these 3 groups. The geographical origin then determines the specific temperature requirements for a particular species of this subfamily.
Feeding natricins does not provide any problems, but due to their rapid digestion the fish feeders must be fed frequently. The terrarium, and especially the water bowl, has to be cleaned very often. Most species become tame quickly and accept defrosted food fish offered with forceps. Strict frog-feeders are sometimes difficult to accommodate due to their solid imprinting on this type of food.

On the other hand, earthworm-feeders are easy to look after, since they will also take strips of lean meat (heart, kidney, liver).

Natricinae are egg-laying or live-bearing. Many species are among those easily bred in a terrarium (*Thamnophis, Nerodia,* and others). Many species out of Group 2 are suitable for beginners. However, a word of caution against careless handling of any of the rear-fanged genera (*Rhabdophis, Pseudoxenodon, Macropisthodon, Macrophis, Balanophis*) is necessary.

Systematic-zoogeographic review:
- North America: *Carphophis, Diadophis, Nerodia, Seminatrix, Regina, Storeria, Tropidoclonion, Virgina.*
- North and Central America: *Thamnophis.*
- Central and South America: *Adelophis, Amastridium, Chersodromus, Diaphorolepis, Helicops, Hydromorphus, Hydrops, Paraptychophis, Pliocercus, Pseudoeryx, Ptychophis, Trimetopon.* (The relationship of several of these genera to Natricinae is highly doubtful.)
- Africa: *Afronatrix, Grayia, Limnophis, Natriciteres, Natrix.*
- Asia: *Atretium, Balanophis, Gonyosoma, Macropisthodon, Macrophis, Oxyrhabdium, Pararhabdophis, Pseudoxenodon, Rhabdophis, Sinonatrix, Xenelaphis,* and *Xenochrophis.*
- Asia to Australia: *Amphiesma.*

Natriciteres LOVERIDGE, 1953. Genus of the Colubridae, Natricinae. Tropical Africa. 3 species. 40 to 60 cm. Smooth, shingled dorsal scales.

Amphibious water snakes that prey mainly on frogs and toads. The mode of life and maintenance are as for Natricinae, Group 2.
- *N. olivacea* (PETERS, 1854). Sudan westward to Ghana and southward to the Republic of South Africa. 2 subspecies. Olive-green and brown. Defensive behavior includes emptying the intestinal tract and anal glands, as in *Natrix.*

Natrix LAURENTI, 1768. Eurasian Grass or Water Snakes. Genus of the Colubridae, Natricinae. Palearctic. 3 species. 80 cm to nearly 1.5 m. Head relatively distinct, with large eyes and nearly evenly large teeth. Although the secretion from the salivary glands is strongly toxic, there are no efferent ducts into the mouth and grooved or enlarged teeth are absent. The body is covered by strongly keeled, often shingled, scales. Coloration and markings extremely variable, especially in the polytypic species.

Amphibious water snakes, excellent swimmers and divers, that prey on fish and amphibians. These snakes require dry, warm basking places and dry sites for depositing

Natrix natrix helvetica

Natrix natrix

their eggs, often a long way from water. Egg-layers, to 35 eggs. These water snakes rarely bite in defense, instead splashing about feces and foul-smelling anal gland secretions. They may fake death (akinesis) if under strong pressure.

Water or grass snakes are simple to look after and are hardy if ecological requirements are met (Natricinae, Group 2). Frequent water changes and strong ventilation of the terrarium are required. They must have dry basking places warmed by radiant heat. If these are absent and the snakes are kept in humid air, skin diseases are likely to occur ("pox") and so is mouth rot. These snakes will quickly become tame. Some species have been bred over generations.

The genus *Natrix* formerly included many more species (frequently under the synonym *Tropidonotus*). Today most of these former species are now included in other genera (*Afronatrix, Amphiesma, Nerodia, Rhabdophis, Regina, Seminatrix, Sinonatrix, Xenochrophis,* and others).

▪ *N. natrix* (LINNAEUS, 1758). Ringed Snake, Grass Snake. Europe, northwestern Africa, and western Asia. 8 subspecies. Mostly with a separate yellow neckband on a dark background. Often terrestrial. Feeds on frogs. The subspecies *N. n. schweizeri* (L. MUELLER, 1932), on Miloas and Kimolos, Cyclade Archipelago, is specialized to feed on lizards and mice as the main diet.

▪ *N. tesselata* (LAURENTI, 1768). Dice Snake. Central Eu-

Natrix maura

rope (CSSR, West Germany) and Italy eastward to central Asia. Number of subspecies uncertain. Dorsally darkish, ventrally with irregular checkerboard markings. Amphibious. Feeds on fish.

▪ *N. maura* (LINNAEUS, 1758). Viperine Water Snake. Western and southwestern Europe and northwestern Africa. A zig-zag dark middorsal band makes it resemble the vipers. Amphibious, prefers fish as food.

Naultinus GRAY, 1842. Genus of the Gekkonidae. Northern New Zealand. 2 species. To 18 cm. Tail about equal to snout-vent length and used as supplementary prehensile grasping organ. Bright green, often with a light lateral stripe or series of spots; sometimes entirely sulphur yellow. Tongue violet, the oral mucous membranes deep blue.

Diurnal brush inhabitants, agile climbers. Ovoviviparous; 2 young about 7 cm long. These odd geckos require terrarium temperatures of about 25° C. and a weak radiant heat source; the air must not be too dry. The diet consists mainly of various arthropods; in addition, these geckos like honey water and even take small pieces of sweet fruit.

▪ *N. elegans* GRAY, 1842. Green Tree Gecko. Rare.

Natrix tesselata

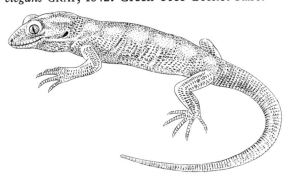

Naultinus elegans

Nearctic Region: Zoogeographic region, belonging to the Holarctic, including the whole of North America and connected to the adjacent northern Neotropics by a more or less wide mixing zone. The rather arbitrarily drawn border between the Nearctic and Neotropics extends along the Mexican Highlands, which (in contrast to Mexican coastal regions and southern Mexico) belong to the Nearctic. According to the geographic and climatic diversity, the Nearctic contains nearly all types of vegetation (other than tropical): forests, steppes (not true deserts), and tundra. Typically large, spacious ecosystems in the Nearctic are (among others) the taiga, various types of forests, prairies, and semideserts. One of the best known and herpetologically most significant Nearctic semideserts is the Sonoran. Important refuges or distribution centers with diverse herpetofaunas extend in a wide belt through the southern part of the USA and northern Mexico; additional diversity centers occur in Oregon and south of 50° latitude along the Pacific and Atlantic coasts.

The Nearctic herpetofauna is—in comparison to the Palearctic—quite large outside the extreme south. On the other hand, the species are not as widely distributed to the north. Turtles and lizards barely reach 51° N (*Chrysemys picta, Phrynosoma douglassi, Eumeces skiltonianus, Gerrhonotus coeruleus*); snakes to just about 52° N (except *Thamnophis sirtalis*, which extends to 61° N); salamanders reach about 58° or 60° N (*Ambystoma macrodactylum, Taricha granulosa*); and the frog genera *Rana, Hyla, Pseudacris,* and *Bufo* reach to just about the Polar Circle; the northernmost Nearctic herptile is *Rana sylvatica*.

Endemic herptile families of the Nearctic (including the Mexican mixing zone) include Ambystomatidae, Amphiumidae, Sirenidae, Ascaphidae, Bipedidae, Anelytropsidae, Helodermatidae, and Anniellidae. Dermatemydidae, Chelydridae, Sceloporinae, and Xanthusiidae penetrate more or less into the Neotropics. Great diversity is reached by the Plethodontidae and Crotalidae.

Nearctic Region: A typical stream in northeastern North America

Nectocaecilia TAYLOR, 1968. Genus of the Typhlonectidae. Tropical and subtropical South America. 4 species. 35
to 60 cm. Worm-like, with 76 to 142 primary furrows and
without a median skin fold along the posterior part of the
body. Tentacle small, located immediately behind nasal
opening. Anal region in males creamy white, radially furrowed. Usually dark, often with blue or violet tones.
• *N. petersi* (BOULENGER, 1882). Upper Amazon region. In
excess of 60 cm. Dark olive-gray.

Nectophryne BUCHHOLZ and PETERS, 1875. African Tree
Toads, Leaf Toads. Genus of the Bufonidae. Tropical Africa. 2 species in tropical rain forests. Snout-vent length a
few centimeters. Relatively slender. Skin with warts. Similar to the closely related Asiatic genus *Pedostibes*, with
wide adhesive discs on the tips of the fingers and toes.

Good climbers and jumpers that inhabit the ground,
bushes, and trees. They presumably spawn outside of the
water, but the larval stages are aquatic. Maintain and
breed in a tropical rain-forest terrarium with a small water
section. The diet consists mainly of Drosophilidae and
springtails.
• *N. afra* BUCHHOLZ and PETERS, 1875. Cameroons, Nigeria. 2.5 cm. Dorsum gray-brown, posteriorly green, often
with 3 large dark gray spots.
• *N. batesi* BOULENGER, 1913.

Nectophrynoides NOBLE, 1926. Livebearing Toads. Genus of Bufonidae. Africa. 3 species, 2 in East Africa and 1
in Guinea with a very small range. Conspicuously large
glands on legs.

Famous for their unusual (for Salientia) mode of reproduction, these toads give birth to fully metamorphosed
young. Through cloacal contact during amplexus the male
transfers sperm, but a special copulatory organ (as to *Ascaphus*) is absent. In the female the lower oviducts are fused
and have taken over the functions of the uterus and the
placenta, housing the larvae. Oxygen is supplied through
diffusion, probably through contact of the larval tail with
the oviduct walls. Food is supplied through oviduct secretions taken in by the atypical, unkeratinized mouth of the
larvae. The development period is about 9 months. During
birth the female inflates herself with air and pushes the
young out in groups. The total number of young is species-
specific (2-16 in *N. occidentalis*, 35 in *N. tornieri*, up to 135
in *N. vivipara*).

N. occidentalis occupies seasonally wet grasslands at an
elevation of 1300 to 1600 m on Mount Nimba. This species
survives the extended dry period of many months in rocky
crevices. The activity phase is confined to the rainy season
from May to August, when the females give birth and mating occurs. The East African species are rain-forest dwellers with excellent climbing abilities and profound color
adaptability to changing habitats.

All species are protected.
• *N. occidentalis* ANGEL, 1943. Guinea. 2 cm.
• *N. tornieri* (ROUX, 1906). Tanzania. 3 cm.
• *N. vivipara* (TORNIER, 1905). Tanzania. 6 cm.

Necturus RAFINESQUE, 1819. Waterdogs, Mudpuppies.
Genus of the Proteidae. Eastern North America, with
greatest diversity in the south. About 5 species, but taxon-

Necturus maculosus

omy confused. Found in lakes and flowing waters. 18 to 23
cm, *N. maculosus* to 49 cm. Strongly built. Head short and
wide, flattened. Permanent external gills and a high tail
crest are present. Eyes small. Body cylindrical or depressed, with costal grooves. Legs small, the hands and
feet with 4 digits. Usually brown to gray above with darker
spots and reticulations; belly white or spotted brown.

Aquatic, crepuscular and nocturnal salamanders found
in clear water; may be active throughout the day in turbid
water. A wide food spectrum is taken, including fish, fish
eggs, small crustaceans, aquatic insects, and molluscs.
Must not be kept in a brightly lit aquarium and should be
given ample hiding places. Water temperature 10 to 20° C.
The water must be chlorine-free.
• *N. beyeri* VIOSCA, 1937. Gulf Coast Waterdog. South-central USA (southern Louisiana to northern Georgia). Flowing water. 15-22 cm. Variable, but mostly brown with dark
brown to black spots.
• *N. maculosus* (RAFINESQUE, 1818). Northern Mudpuppy
or Waterdog. Eastern North America from southern Canada to south-central USA in lakes and flowing waters. 20
to 33 cm (maximum length 49 cm). Usually gray, with a
sparse pattern of blue-black spots.
• *N. punctatus* (GIBBES, 1850). Dwarf Waterdog. Southeastern USA (Virginia to Georgia). Rivers. 11-16 cm (maximum length 19 cm). Gray to blackish, the throat and central abdomen whitish, without large spots.

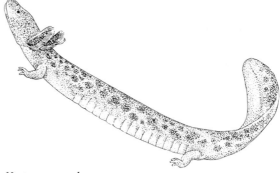

Necturus maculosus

Neelaps GUENTHER, 1858. Australian Black-naped
Snakes. Genus of the Elapidae. Southwestern Australia. 2
species related to *Vermicella* and *Simoselaps*. 25 to 50 cm.
Venomous. Biology hardly known.

• *N. bimaculatus* (DUMERIL, DUMERIL, and BIBRON, 1854).

Nematoda: Roundworms. Widely occurring parasites of amphibians and reptiles that infest various organs, primarily the digestive tract and the lung. Disease symptoms may be apparent only with massive infestations. Juvenile animals are more susceptible. Blood filaria can lead to dangerous thromboses even in small numbers. Most nematodes actually are free-living in the soil, and a few are of value in feeding larval salamanders (vinegar eels).

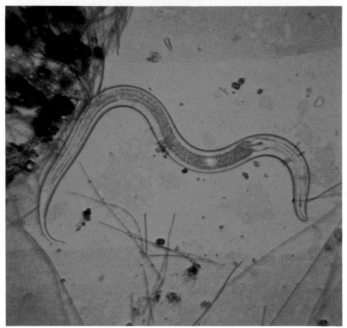

Nematoda: A free-living species of roundworm

Neobatrachus PETERS, 1863. Genus of the Leptodactylidae. Southern Australia. 5 species in arid regions. Plump, externally reminiscent of Pelobatidae. Pupil vertical. Tympanum barely visible. Limbs short, the fingers free and the toes more or less webbed. A large black or dark brown metatarsal spade is present.

These frogs survive dry periods burrowed in the ground, and will then surface only on humid nights. Reproduction is triggered by the onset of the rainy season. Breeding waters are usually shallow clay pans filled with rain water in the savannah. They should be kept in semimoist, unheated, or only slightly heated terrariums. Open-air keeping is recommended for the summer months. Breeding requires a water section in the terrarium.
• *N. centralis* (PARKER, 1940). Trilling Frog. Western and south-central Australia. 5.5 cm. Light brown or yellow with small irregular spots; often with a light median dorsal line.
• *N. pictus* PETERS, 1863. Southeastern Australia. 5 cm. Gray, yellow, or light brown with large irregular dark brown or olive-green patches; usually with a light median line.

Neoregelia L. B. SMITH (= *Aregalia*). Genus of the Bromeliaceae. Brasil, Peru, Surinam. 34 species. Epiphytes or rock plants. They require a bright location and temperatures in excess of 22° C. Due to their high light requirements, they are ideally suited for use as epiphytic backgrounds.

Neoregelia princeps

• *N. ampullacea* (E. MORR.) L. B. SMITH. Leaf rosette 10 cm high.
• *N. chlorosticta* (BAK.) L. B. SMITH. Small species.
• *N. cyanaea* L. B. SMITH. Leaves to about 20 cm.
• *N. pineliana* L. B. SMITH. Leaves to more than 40 cm.
• *N. princeps* (BAK.) L. B. SMITH. Thick rosette.
• *N. spectabilis* (T. MOORE) L. B. SMITH. Leaves to 40 cm.
• *N. tristis* (BEER) L. B. SMITH. Leaves to 15 to 20 cm.

Neoseps STEJNEGER, 1910. Monotypic genus of the Scincidae. Florida, in dry, sandy habitats. To 13 cm. Worm-like. Lower eyelid with window. Ear opening absent. Front limbs very small, 1-toed, can be hidden in a body fold. Hind limbs also strongly reduced, 2-toed. Dirty white to brown.

Burrowing ground-dwellers that feed mainly on ants and termites. Egg-layers, usually 2 eggs. Difficult to keep.
• *N. reynoldsi* STEJNEGER, 1910. Florida Sand Skink.

Neoteny: Continuation of the larval stage in certain animals, especially salamanders that reach sexual maturity in this stage. Metamorphosis may be completely omitted, as in the axolotl (*Ambystoma*) and the olm (*Proteus*) or occur only partially, as in *Andrias*. Metamorphosis usually can be initiated artifically in neotenic species by administering thyroid hormones or by an enforced terrestrial residence.

Neotropic: Zoogeographic region extending from Baja California and Mexico (except the Mexican Highlands), the Antilles, Central America, and South America to the Straits of Magellan. It is bordered on the north on the Nearctic, on the south by the Antarctic. Geographically, climatically, and in terms of vegetation the Neotropic is one of the most diverse regions, with vast rain forests (*selva*), montane rain forests (*montana*), high Andean grasslands (*puna, paramo*), dry forests, savannahs (*llanos*), semi-deserts, and deserts (*atacama*), also with mangrove swamps and, in the South, with temperate wet forests and winter-rain dependent sclerophyll vegetation. There is particularly heavy precipitation along the windward ranges (eastern slopes) of the Andes Mountains, where the rain-bringing tradewinds build up. In contrast, some of the leeward zones on the Pacific coast have some of the lowest precipitation levels on Earth. Regular night frosts (or above 5,500 m even permafrost and snow) occur in the high Andes even at equatorial latitudes. The potential for frost also exists throughout the subtropical area of Argentina, Uruguay, and Paraguay, and at higher elevations in southern Brasil. Due to the extent of the Neotropics toward subantarctic

Neoseps reynoldsi

Neotropics: Contrasts in Mexico

Neotropics: The Rio Negro floodplain in Brasil

latitudes there is a well-defined species gradient. For instance, in Argentina the number of snake species decreases from 55 in the north to zero in the south. The most southern form is here *Bothrops ammodytoides*. Among the frogs, *Pleurodema bufonina* extends southward to the Straits of Magellan at the southern border of the Neotropic (52° S). Only lizards reach the Antarctic region, *Tropidurus* species.

In terms of plants the Neotropics are well characterized by (apart from many endemic families) the important terrarium families Agavaceae, Bromeliaceae, Cactaceae, and Marantaceae. From a herpetological point of view the Neotropic fauna is notably less characteristic than its mammal, bird, and fish faunas. Due to the absence of distribution barriers there is a wide mixing zone toward the Nearctic that has been penetrated by such Neotropical faunal elements as Kinosternidae, Teiidae, Iguanidae, Boinae, and Xenodontinae.

Endemic herptile families and subfamilies include the Typhlonectidae, Atelopodidae, Centrolenidae Dendrobatidae, Pseudidae, Rhynophrynidae, Sphaerodactylinae, Basiliscinae, Anomalepidae, Loxoceminae, and Dipsadinae. The greatest species diversity within several widely distributed families and subfamilies is reached in the Neotropics by Caeciliidae, Leptodactylidae, Hylidae, Pelomedusidae, Tropidurinae, Boinae, and Alligatoridae. Neotropic-African distributions (Amphisbaenidae, Pipidae) and Neotropic-Madagascan distributions (Pelomedusidae, Tropidurinae) indicate former land contacts with Africa; Neotropic-Australian distributions (Leptodactylidae, Hylidae, Chelidae), indicate attachment to the ancestral southern continent (Gondwana). The Ichthyophiidae, Microhylinae, and Aniliidae have a Neotropic-Oriental distribution.

Nephrolepis SCHOTT. Sword Ferns. Genus of the Filicatae. Tropics and subtropics. 30 species. Epiphytic and ground-dwellers. The rhizomes produce runners. Undemanding and can take some sun.
▪ *N. exaltata* (L.) SCHOTT. Cultivated in several varieties. Reproduction is by cutting of runners.

Nephrurus GUENTHER, 1867. Knob-tail Geckos. Genus of the Gekkonidae. Australia. 6 species in deserts and semideserts. 8-10 cm snout-vent, 15 cm total length. Short-bodied, the head conspicuously large. The tail is little more than half the snout-vent length, thickened, flattened dorsoventrally, usually distinctly warty or spinous, ending in a characteristic small knob.

Nocturnal ground-dwellers. In the characteristic defensive behavior the lizards raise their body on all four limbs and leap at their enemy with a wide-open mouth. Day temperatures of 25 to 30° C., at night from 18 to 20° C., are satisfactory. Lower substrate layers must be kept slightly damp.

Nephrurus laevis

▪ *N. laevis* DE VIS, 1886. Smooth Knob-tail Gecko. Central and western Australia. To 8 cm snout-vent. Reddish brown with a few white tubercles and short stripes. Head and back at level of hind legs often with violet-brown markings.

Nerodia BAIRD and GIRARD, 1853. American Water Snakes. Genus of the Colubridae, Natricinae. Nearctic

(North America east of the Rock Mountains and northern Mexico). 8 to 10 species. 80 cm to almost 2 m.

Aquatic snakes that correspond morphologically, biologically, and in terms of husbandry to the Palearctic *Natrix* (refer to Natricinae, Group 2), but are ovoviviparous.

▪ *N. cyclopion* (DUMERIL and BIBRON, 1854). Green Water Snake. Southern USA. Maximum number of young 110.

▪ *N. erythrogaster* (FORSTER, 1771). Red-bellied Water Snake. North America from the Great Lakes southward to northeastern Mexico. Up to 20 juveniles per birth.

▪ *N. rhombifera* (HALLOWELL, 1852). Diamond-back Water Snake. Central USA and northeastern Mexico. About 18-62 young per birth.

▪ *N. sipedon* (LINNAEUS, 1758). Common Water Snake. Eastern USA. About 9-70 young per birth (99 maximum observed number). One of the hardiest snakes in a terrarium.

Nerodia sipedon

Nerodia sipedon, juvenile

Nerodia rhombifera

Nerodia (Clonophis) kirtlandi

Nerodia fasciata

Nervous system: Organ system consisting of specialized cells that regulate and coordinate numerous body functions on a bioelectric and biochemical basis. In vertebrates it is arranged into the central nervous system (brain and spinal cord) and the peripheral nervous system (all nerve cords leading to and away from the central nervous system).

The main organ in the central nervous system is the brain, located in and protected by the cranial chamber. Its five segments—forebrain (telencephalon), interbrain (diencephalon), midbrain (mesencephalon), hindbrain (metencephalon), and medulla oblongata (myelencephalon)—are still mostly sequentially arranged in amphibians and reptiles. The two hemispheres of the forebrain are mainly involved in olfaction (sense of smell). In their anterior sections (in amphibians more or less fused) they form the olfactory bulbs (Bulbi olfactorii); these are located more toward the nose in reptiles and connected to the hemisphere via a long Tractus olfactorius. In reptiles with an acute olfactory sense (e. g., turtles) the Bulbi olfactorii are extremely large; in species with this sense less developed (e. g., *Anolis, Chamaeleon*) they are very small. Frequently present is a small swelling behind the olfactory bulb, the Bulbus olfactorius accessorius, which receives the nerves from Jacobson's Organ. Similar relationships to variously developed visual capabilities exist in the vision centers

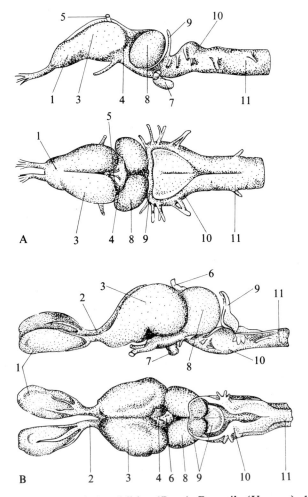

Nervous system: A Amphibian (*Rana*); B reptile (*Varanus*). 1 Bulbus olfactorius; 2 tractus olfactorius; 3 anterior hemisphere; 4 diencephalon; 5 epiphysis; 6 parietal lobe; 7 hypophysis; 8 lobus opticus; 9 cerebellum; 10 myelencephalon; 11 spinal cord

(Lobi optici) in the midbrain, which in reptiles and amphibians receive most of the nerve endings from the Nervus opticus. In forms with rudimentary eyes (olm, blind snakes) they are only of limited development.

The medulla oblongata and the cerebellum form the roof of the hindbrain and control the most important motorcenters of the amphibian and reptile brain. Here significant regulatory centers are localized, such as the respiratory center, and nerves of the auditory and equilibrium senses also terminate here. Muscle movements controlled from the spinal cord in these vertebrates are not subject to continuous control by the brain. Thus, following experimental surgical removal of the brain the body is still capable for some time of executing coordinated independent movements.

Nesobia VAN KAMPEN, 1923 (= *Leptobrachella* SMITH, 1925). Genus of the Pelobatidae. Indo-Australian Archipelago. 2 species. In tropical rain forests. Snout-vent length only a few centimeters. Skin smooth. Fingers and toes free, tips with small conical adhesive discs. Carpal projection large and high. Inner metatarsal tubercle indistinct, flat and oval.

Nesobia species are found less commonly on the ground than are those of the related genera *Leptobrachium* and *Megophrys* and tend to climb about low bushes surrounding the water where the larvae developed and metamorphosed (jungle streams, etc.). Males vocalize at night. The eggs are unpigmented and are presumably deposited under rocks in a creek or stream. These frogs should be maintained in an amply structured tropical rain-forest terrarium at temperatures from 24 to 29° C.
- *N. mjobergi* (SMITH, 1925) (= *N. baluensis* (SMITH, 1931)). Northern Kalimantan (200 to 2200 m). To 2 cm (males), 2.5 cm (females). Brown, with a dark brown crossband between the eyes.
- *N. natunae* (GUENTHER, 1895). Great Natuna Island, Malaysia.

Nesomantis BOULENGER, 1908. Monotypic genus of the Ranidae. Seychelles. Mode of life as in the related *Sooglossus*. Because of its extremely small range it is considered endangered.
- *N. thomasseti* BOULENGER, 1908. To 4.5 cm. Body toadlike in appearance.

Nessia GRAY, 1839. Singalese Skinks. Genus of the Scincidae. Sri Lanka. 8 species related to *Acontias*. Small, elongated. Degenerate eyes. Ear openings tiny or absent. Pointed, wedge-shaped snout. Teeth pointing inward. Limbs largely or completely reduced. The diet is mainly earthworms. Egg-layers.
- *N. burtoni* GRAY, 1839.

Neurergus COPE, 1862. Near Eastern Newts. Genus of the Salamandridae. Southwestern Asia (Turkey, Iraq, Iran). Formerly considered a monotypic genus, today many systematists recognize at least 3 species. In arid, now largely deforested grasslands and semideserts close to or in (even in summer) cool (10-13° C.) montain streams that always carry water at from 500 to 1750 m elevation. 11 to 17 cm, somewhat flattened. Hardly distinguishable anatomically from *Triturus*, but males in courtship coloration never have

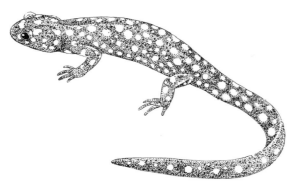

Neurergus strauchi

Neusticurus ecpleopus

dorsal crests and have at the most a low skin fold on the tail. If disturbed they produce a bitter odor. A yellow or orange pattern on a dark background, considered to be warning colors.

During the activity period *Neurergus* remains exclusively in water; in contrast, the winter dormancy period is spent above the high-water mark under rocks in the ground. Courtship activities are unusual for salamandrids tied to flowing water, and in fact they are similar to those of *Triturus* in still water. The male in tail-waving posture courts the female, but there is no body contact. The larvae are adapted to flowing water habitats (conspicuously long tail) and require about a year before metamorphosis; the first winter is spent in water.

These newts should be kept in an aqua-terrarium with a large water section and low water level (10 cm) at temperatures below 15° C. (possibly in a refrigerator or in a basement location). They are shy animals and will even hide among rocks, driftwood, etc., when under water. Not such aggressive feeders as *Triturus* and *Pleurodeles*.
• *N. crocatus* COPE, 1862. Northern Iraq, western Iran. 17 cm. Yellow spots.
• *N. kaiseri* SCHMIDT, 1952. Southwestern Iran. 11-13 cm. With a yellow wavy dorsal band.
• *N. strauchi* (STEINDACHNER, 1887). Southeastern Anatolia. 16 cm (rarely larger). Coloration similar to *N. crocatus*, but the abdomen is largely dark (including the throat and feet) except for a light central zone. In courtship coloration the cloaca of the female is hardly protruding; the male has silver-blue tail spots.

Neusticurus DUMERIL and BIBRON, 1839. Water Tegus. Genus of the Teiidae. Costa Rica to the Amazon Region. 7 species in tropical rain forests. To easily 30 cm. Slender, with a laterally compressed tail and well-developed limbs. Numerous longitudinal rows of enlarged, rough, keeled scales; two longitudinal keels on the tail. Primarily brown, some species with indistinct light lateral spots.

Semiaquatic (except *N. cochranae*). At night they rest in burrows along the banks or on branches above water. When threatened they let themselves simply drop into the water below. The diet consists mainly of water insects, tadpoles, small fish, and terrestrial arthropods. Usually only 2 eggs are deposited in decaying plant material.

These interesting teiids should be kept in spacious, heated aqua-terrariums equipped with some branches suspended above water. Day temperatures between 25 and 30° C., slightly reduced at night, are satisfactory.

• *N. bicarinatus* (LINNAEUS, 1758). Northern South America. To 30 cm. Close to waters in the *selva*.
• *N. cochranae* BURT and BURT, 1931. Ecuador. To 18 cm. Medium size mountains. Not closely tied to water.

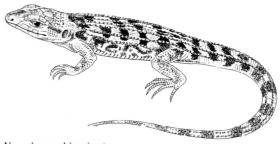

Neusticurus bicarinatus

New Guinea: Second largest island on earth, located off the coast of northern Australia in the tropical Pacific. Politically two countries (New Guinea and Irian Jaya), it forms the Papuan-Polynesian subregion of the Australasian together with the Southsea islands to the east. It is also the center of species diversity in this subregion. New Guinea is

New Guinea: Wagau Valley

subdivided by mountain chains that reach an elevation of 5030 m and so produce a characteristic gradation of vegetation. High precipitation (up to 5,000 mm) has led to vast development of montane rain forests from 900 m upward that grade into cloud forests with numerous ferns and in part also pine forests. The snow line is at 4,300 m. Lush mangrove swamps surround New Guinea, and on the south these are followed inland by vast swamps and floodlands with bamboo jungles. Along the leeward side of the mountains with little precipitation there are even savannahs in areas with low ground-water levels.

The herpetofauna in New Guinea at the family or subfamily level is not very distinctive. Endemic are only the Asterophryninae, while great diversity is shown by the Platymantinae. There are especially close ties to the continental fauna of Australia, which at the generic level includes the Sphenophryninae, Carettochelyidae, and Pygopodidae. On the other hand, many groups penetrate from the Orient into New Guinea (and even into Australia), such as the Ranidae, Dibamidae, Anguidae, Boidae, Natricinae, Homalopsinae, and Boiginae, so that New Guinea accommodates a zoogeographically mixed fauna.

Newt plague: A primarily non-infectious, epidemic-like, fatal disease of newts. Incomplete molting sometimes has been observed as a starting symptom for this disease. After feeding stops the animals still become heavier and soon appear bloated, especially in the throat region. They display respiratory difficulties and attempt to leave the water. The animals and the water give off a "parsley-like" foul odor. Characteristic symptoms include changes in the skin, including the appearance of gray dots 1 to 2 mm in diameter; cracked, watering sores; development of fungus; and flaking skin. During the terminal stage thick mucus may emerge from the mouth.

Causes: A complex of inadequate maintenance conditions, especially temperatures too high, excessive humidities, and vitamin deficiency. Bacterial infections or fungi develop secondarily.

Therapy: Proper care.

Prophylaxis: Through cleaning and disinfection of container, equipment, etc.

New Zealand: Island group southeast of Australia. As the New Zealand subregion it belongs zoogeographically with Australia and is located in subtropical and temperate climatic regions. In contrast to Australia, the surface area of New Zealand is strongly broken up by mountains (the central mountains up to 3700 m elevation) and thus it is climatically rather diversified. The windward regions along the western coast have high precipitation levels and thus give rise to damp forests. The vegetation is dominated by many endemic forms analogous to those of Tasmania and southern Chile, as well as many ferns.

In contrast to Australia, New Zealand's herpetofauna is characterized by omission of many groups, such as crocodiles, turtles, and snakes. Apart from some Gekkonidae and Scincidae, the reptiles are mainly represented by the endemic Rhynchocephalia (one recent species) and the amphibians by the endemic Leiopelmatidae (3 recent species). Some species have been introduced (e. g., *Litoria aurea*).

N. F.: Nombre fondamental. See Chromosomes.

Niceforonia GOIN and COCHRAN, 1963. Genus of the Leptodactylidae. Colombia to Bolivia. About 8 species. High Andes (*paramo, puna*). Snout-vent length only a few cm. Pupil horizontal. Fingers free, toes free or webbed at base only. Tympanum variably developed, absent in some species.

Ground-dwellers. The eggs are deposited in a damp substrate, and there is no free-swimming larval stage. They can be kept in small terrariums equipped with moss and low-growing grass species that are kept semimoist. Open-air maintenance is recommended during the summer months.

• *N. nana* GOIN and COCHRAN, 1963. Colombia. To 2 cm.

Nidularium LEM. Genus of the Bromeliaceae. Eastern Brasil. 23 species. In rain forests. Most are epiphytes. The leaves are in a tight rosette. Although they require sufficient light, they should be protected from direct exposure. Temperatures 22-25° C. during the day, 18-20° C. at night.

• *N. fulgens* LEM. Leaves to 30 cm, marbled.

• *N. innocenti* LEM. Leaves to 25 cm. Many varieties.

• *N. microps* E. MORR. Leaves to 40 cm.

• *N. purpureum* BEER. Leaves to 30 cm. Not very spinous.

Nidularium

Nikolsky, Alexander Michailovitch (1858-1942): Russian herpetologist at the St. Petersburg (now Leningrad) museum. *Herpetologia rossica* (1905) plus descriptions of numerous new forms from Russia and adjacent countries.

Ninia BAIRD and GIRARD, 1853. Ringnecked Coffee Snakes. Genus of the Colubridae, Lycodontinae. From Mexico southward to Venezuela, Colombia, and Ecuador. 8 species. 40 to 60 cm. Cryptic coloration.

Biology virtually unknown. Probably nocturnal ground-dwelling snakes. Egg-layers, 2-4 eggs.

• *N. atrata* (HALLOWELL, 1845). From Costa Rica to Ecuador. Uniformly black or with a pale neckband.

• *N. diademata* BAIRD and GIRARD, 1853. From Mexico to Guatemala. Brown with pale nape markings.

Noble, Gladwyn Kingsley (1894-1940): American herpetologist, Curator of Herpetology at the American Museum of Natural History, New York. *The Biology of the Amphibia* (1931) belongs among the classic herpetological works.

Noblella: see *Eleutherodactylus*, genus.

Nomenclature: Scientific naming of all Recent and fossil organisms that is subject to internationally binding regulations and recommendations. It is important to assure consistency in the naming of organisms and groups of organisms and so to enable communication between all biologically oriented branches of science. Taxonomy and systematics deal with nomenclature.

Norops, subgenus: see *Anolis*, genus.

Nose: Originally in fish the nose served as a chemical sensory organ. In land vertebrates the nose, in conjunction with respiration, is connected to the mouth cavity. In amphibians there is a simple nasal cavity located under the nasal opening, which in part is lined with olfactory epithelium and leads into the mouth through the choana (posterior nostril) in the anterior palatal roof. The nasal cavity in reptiles is more elaborately constructed. A small nasal area is delineated where cartilaginous and bony plates fuse to enlarge the outer surface area dorsal to the olfactory epithelium-lined cavity. Nasal glands keep the mucous membrane of the nose lubricated. Because of the formation of a secondary palate in turtles and crocodiles, the inner nasal opening is pushed back (see Jacobson's Organ). The olfactory sense localized in the nose plays a particularly important role in salamanders in their search for food and during mating and is also of great importance for many reptiles (e. g., turtles). However, in snakes the nose seems to be less important when compared to the efficiency of the Jacobson's Organ.

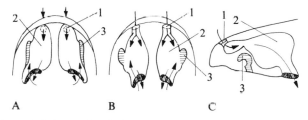

Nose: A Salamander; B frog; C reptile. 1 Nostril; 2 nasal cavity; 3 Jacobson's Organ

Notaden GUENTHER, 1873. Crucifix Toads. Genus of the Leptodactylidae. Australia. 3 species in arid regions. 5-6.5 cm. Spherical, toad-like, the skin with warts. The snout is very blunt, the pupil horizontal, the tympanum not visible. The limbs are thin and short, the fingers free and the toes webbed at the base only, but with lateral folds. Some species very brightly colored. They may give off a viscous, white, foul-smelling, venomous secretion when excited.

Notaden species survive dry periods buried in the ground and surface only following heavy rainfall. The diet consists mainly of ants and termites. Usually the eggs are laid in temporary ponds in savannahs and dry forests. Due to their food specialization and the skin secretions they are not suitable as terrarium animals.
- *N. bennettii* GUENTHER, 1873. Crucifix Toad. Southeastern Australia. Dry regions, especially in river valleys. 5 cm. Lemon yellow to green, with a cross-like pattern of black warts and white and red tubercles.

Notechis BOULENGER, 1896. Tiger Snakes. Genus of the Elapidae. Australia. 2 species. Found in dry, rocky habitats and also in grasslands, thornbush steppes, and swamp areas. To 1.5 m. Head cobra-like, short, the body heavily built and strong. Adults tend to become darker grayish to uniform black-brown. There is a strong tendency toward melanism among snakes from island populations.

Notechis scutatus

Primarily nocturnal venomous snakes that feed on frogs, lizards, snakes, small mammals, and birds. Island populations may specialize in seasonal colonial seabirds and their young; outside the seabird breeding season, *Notechis* on small islands are largely cannibalistic. Live-bearers, usually 15 to 20 young (maximum 109 young).

The venom of these very aggressive snakes is very potent and is often fatal despite serum treatment.

The southernmost populations (on Tasmania and other islands) and those from mountains are adapted to cold climates resulting in a serious potential danger when specimens escape to the outside from a terrarium. They must be kept—if they are kept at all—in strict compliance with all requirements for venomous snake care. Has been bred in captivity.
- *N. ater* (KREFFT, 1866). Black Tiger Snake. Southwestern Australia plus isolated mainland (far south) and island populations (Kangaroo, King, Tasmania). Several subspecies in part seriously endangered.
- *N. scutatus* (PETERS, 1862). Mainland Tiger Snake. Victoria and New South Wales. Widely distributed.

Nothophryne POYNTON, 1963. Monotypic genus of the Ranidae. Africa.
- *N. broadleyi* POYNTON, 1963.

Nothopsis COPE, 1871. Monotypic genus of the Colubridae, Xenoderminae. Found along the Atlantic coast of Central America from Nicaragua to Panama and along the Pacific coast of Colombia and Ecuador. In tropical rain forests. 70 cm. Distinctly rough-scaled, similar to the partially sympatric *Trachyboa*. Ground snakes. Ecology and biology nearly unknown.
- *N. rugosus* COPE, 1871.

Notochelys GRAY, 1863. Flat-back Turtles. Monotypic genus of the Emydidae. Indo-China to Sumatra. Prefers flowing water but is also found in small ponds and rice paddies. Carapace to 30 cm. Flat above with a distinct keel. Always with 6 vertebral scutes rather than the normal 5. Back of carapace slopes suddenly downward at the

Notochelys platynota

fourth to fifth vertebral. Plastron in adults clearly de-pressed along bridge and joined movably to carapace. Juve-nile carapace yellowish green to olive green with 1 or 2 dis-tinct black spots on each vertebral scute. The base coloration becomes darker with increasing age, so that these spots become less distinct in adults. Posterior margin of carapace very roughly serrated.

Mainly herbivorous (leaves, fruit). Sometimes it refuses to feed, but this can sometimes be overcome by a highly varied plant diet. Not hardy.
▪ *N. platynota* (GRAY, 1834).

Notophthalmus RAFINESQUE, 1820 (= *Diemictylus* RAF-INESQUE, 1820). Red-spotted Newts. Genus of the Sala-mandridae. Eastern North America southward to north-eastern Mexico. 4 partly polytypic species. Generally similar to *Triturus*. Hind legs substantially stronger than front legs, in males with black nuptial pads during the breeding season. No dorsal crest, at the most a low dorsal

Notophthalmus viridescens viridescens, eft

Notophthalmus viridescens dorsalis

ridge. Both sexes have 3 or 4 pairs of large temporal pores. The cloaca in males is hemispherical, in females bluntly conical and projecting. Yellow, red, and black spots on brown back and flanks; belly yellow to orange, finely dot-ted with black.

The common red-spotted newts mate in small pools and

ponds in autumn and spring. During amplexus the male grasps the female around the throat or chest region from above and remains there for hours, dismounting only just prior to the extrusion of the spermatophore. Spawning oc-curs in spring, the female attaching about 200-300 eggs in-dividually on water plants. The larvae hatch in 20-35 days and usually metamorphose after some 2 to 3 months. Some newts retain rudimentary gills throughout life and seldom leave the water. Newly metamorphosed newts leave the water to spend 1-3 years on land before becoming sexually mature. They are bright red, have rough skin, and are called efts. After mating, adults usually also return to the land.

For details on care and maintenance refer to *Triturus*. One can attempt to prolong the aquatic phase by keeping the newts throughout the summer in an aqua-terrarium with a very low water level and a small land section. Northern populations require a winter dormancy period of several months that can take place in water (refrigerate at close to 0° C.), but specimens from the southern end of the range need only a temperature reduction to 10-15° C. for about 8 weeks.

• *N. meridionalis* (COPE, 1880). Mexican Newt, Black-spotted Newt. Southern Texas and coastal northeastern Mexico. 8-11 cm. Black spots on yellow-green background, irregular yellow stripes. Abdomen orange. *N. m. kallerti* (WOLTERSTORFF, 1930) is the southern subspecies.

• *N. perstriatus* (BISHOP, 1941). Striped Newt. Southern Georgia and northern Florida. 5-10.5 cm. Dorsum with continuous red stripes on a brown background. Abdomen yellow.

• *N. viridescens* (RAFINESQUE, 1820). Eastern Newt. Eastern North America from southern Canada to Florida and Texas. 4 subspecies. Dorsum dark brown, with red dots that may be encircled by black or interrupted red stripes. Abdomen yellow to orange.

Notoscincus FUHN, 1969. Genus of the Scincidae. Australia. 2 species of uncertain taxonomic status (and 2 former species transferred to *Proablepharus*). In grasslands. Barely 10 cm. Slender. Lids with spectacles, but lids not fully fused. Ear opening tiny. Short limbs with 5 toes. Ground-dwellers. Egg-layers.

• *N. ornatus* (BROOM), 1896. Northern central Australia.

Banksisus BOKERMANN, 1950. Genus of the Hylidae, sometimes considered to be a synonym of *Flectonotus*. Tropical South America. 3 species. Slender. Pupil horizontal. Webbing poorly developed. Skin of head not fused with skull (in contrast to *Flectonotus*). Female with 2-chambered brood sac on back, with an opening in the shape of a forked longitudinal slit. Tree-dwellers.

• *N. fissilis* (MIRANDO-RIBEIRO, 1920). Southeastern Brasil. 3 cm. Yellow-brown with longitudinal rows of dark spots.

Nuchodorsal glands: Skin glands of uncertain function located below the nape or anterior dorsal scales in some water snakes (*Natrix* and related genera).

Nucras GRAY, 1838. Tiger Lizards. Genus of the Lacertidae. Southern and southeastern Africa, northward to about Kenya. About 6 species in steppes. Typical lacertid in appearance, much like *Lacerta* but the nostril not in contact with the supralabials. Body only slightly flattened. Tail twice snout-vent length. Dorsal scales small, not keeled. Ventral scales only weakly shingled. Collar well-developed. Femoral pores present. Often very attractively marked.

Diurnal predators on various arthropods. Egg-layers, mostly 2-6 eggs per clutch. Maintenance much as for *Ere-*

mias, but should preferably be kept slightly more damp. A winter dormancy period is not required. Seldom kept in terrariums.

• *N. delalandi* (MILNE-EDWARDS, 1829). Southern Africa. To 30 cm. Pale brown with 8-10 longitudinal rows of white ocelli with black margins. Head and sides of neck with black and white vertical bars. Hind limbs and tail orange to red. Adults have more black with increasing age, often with black crossbars over the entire body.

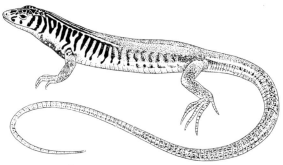

Nucras tessellata

• *N. intertexta* (SMITH, 1838). Southern Africa, not extending to Cape Province. To 30 cm. Markings highly variable, ocelli usually less numerous than in previous species, but light longitudinal markings are well-defined.

• *N. tessellata* (SMITH, 1838). Southern Africa (Namaqualand, Zambesi to Natal). To 23 cm. Red-brown, lighter posteriorly, with light longitudinal stripes along the back in variable numbers and arrangement. Black and white vertical bars along the neck and on the chest. Tail red at least in juveniles.

Nuptial pads. Male accessory organs present in most frog species and in some salamanders. They facilitate grasping the female during amplexus and consist of horny lumps, pads, or spines, usually black or dark brown, that are sometimes supported by bony projections. They are connected with glandular areas.

Nuptial pads in *Xenopus laevis*

Nyctibates: see *Astylosternus*, genus.

Nyctibatrachus BOULENGER, 1882. Genus of the Ranidae. Southern India. 5 species. 2-6 cm. Streamlined. Pupil vertical. Tympanum hidden. Legs relatively short and stout, with small adhesive discs on the tips of the fingers and toes. Fingers free, the toes more or less broadly webbed.

Largely nocturnal. Should be kept in tropical aqua-terrarium.
• *N. major* BOULENGER, 1882. To 6 cm. Brown with an indistinct pattern of light and dark markings.
• *N. pygmaeus* (GUENTHER, 1875). To 3 cm. Dark brown with a blackish pattern.

Nyctimantis BOULENGER, 1882. Monotypic genus of the Hylidae. Ecuador, in *selva*. Tympanum clearly visible. Iris dark brown. Fingers free, the toes webbed about halfway up their length. Large adhesive discs. Dorsum light, ventrum dark ("reverse coloration").

Nocturnal tree-dwellers, preferably in cane. Eggs are deposited in water-filled stems and hollow logs. Maintenance as for the arboreal tropical *Hyla* species.
• *N. rugiceps* BOULENGER, 1882. To 6.5 cm. Dorsally light yellow-brown; flanks sharply delimited, dark brown with large yellow spots. Abdomen also dark brown.

Nyctimystes STEJNEGER, 1916. Genus of the Hylidae. Primarily in New Guinea. 3 species with very limited distribution in northeastern Australia, about 23 species total. Found in montane rain forests of the New Guinea Highlands (about 1200 to 3000 m elevation). Easily distinguishable from the other Australian hylid genus, *Litoria*, by the vertical pupil and golden or black reticulated lower eyelid. 4 to 10 cm. Some species (e. g., *N. papua* and *N. disrupta*) are without vocal sacs.

Crepuscular or nocturnal tree-dwellers. Spawning is much as in *Litoria* and larval development occurs in water. Larvae tied to flowing water have a large, wide-oval suction mouth.

Maintain in a rain-forest terrarium with high temperatures (25-30° C.), high humidity, and adequate air circulation. A water section is required for breeding.
• *N. humeralis* (BOULENGER, 1912). Central District of New Guinea at 1200 to 2500 m elevation. At more than 10 cm, it is one of the largest species in the genus. Green above, sides with yellow spots.
• *N. kubori* ZWEIFEL, 1958. Central Highlands of New Guinea in open, wide river valleys at 1500 to 2000 m elevation. To 6 cm (females), 4.5 cm (males). Sandy brown with an irregular pattern of white and black dots. Frequent.
• *N. papua* (BOULENGER, 1897). Southeastern New Guinea, not below 1500 m elevation. To 6 cm (females), 5 cm (males). Olive-brown above with white spots and very irregular, sometimes confluent black spots. Development occurs in flowing water.
• *N. pulchra* (WANDOLLEK, 1911). Northwestern New Guinea at 1500 m elevation in the proximity of small rivers. To 8 cm (females), 6.5 cm (males). Brown. Long heel spur.
• *N. vestigia* TYLER, 1964. Northeastern Australia, York Peninsula near Cooktown. To 5 cm. Dorsum brownish, often with dark-bordered light spots.

Observations: In captivity close observation is valuable for determining the biology of a particular species and in many instances is the only way to obtain information about, e. g., certain types of behavior. On the other hand, observations in captivity should not necessarily be interpreted as replications of natural behavior, since natural relationships with the environment can not be completely duplicated in a terrarium. One has to also consider disturbances that can occur as a consequence of being kept in a terrarium and thus affect the value of captive observations. Nevertheless, all interesting observations of captive behavior made by serious terrarium hobbyists should be recorded and if possible published.

Ocadia GRAY, 1870. Chinese Striped Turtles. Monotypic genus of the Emydidae. Northern Vietnam, southwestern China, also Hainan and Taiwan. In standing water. To 22 cm. The evenly arched carapace has 3 low carapace keels. Distinct round dark blotches on each yellow plastral scute (weak in Taiwanese specimens). The head has delicate light and dark stripes.

Ocadia sinensis

Ocadia sinensis

Primarily herbivorous, but will also take some animals (small crustaceans, molluscs). Maintain in an aqua-terrarium that is slightly heated. Suitable for outdoor maintenance during the summer months.
• *O. sinensis* (GRAY, 1834). Although common in Taiwan, it seems to be uncommon or rare elsewhere.

Odatria, subgenus: see *Varanus*, genus.

Odontophrys REINHARDT and LUETKEN, 1862. Genus of the Leptodactylidae. South America. 5 species. Related to *Proceratophrys*. In open, more or less arid regions. To 6 cm. Externally reminiscent of *Ceratophrys* in shape. Skin with warts. Short but very wide snout. Pupil horizontal. Tympanum not visible. Parotoid glands more or less distinct. Fingers free, toes webbed to about half of their length, the tips not enlarged.

During the dry season *Odontophrys* species rarely leave their underground burrows. They surface during the rainy season to deposit their numerous small eggs in ponds. Should be kept in a weakly heated, semimoist terrarium with a thick bottom layer. Open-air maintenance is recommended for the summer months.
• *O. americanus* (DUMERIL and BIBRON, 1841). Southeastern Brasil, Argentina, Bolivia, Uruguay. Parotoid glands small.
• *O. cultripes* REINHARDT and LUETKEN, 1862. Southeastern Brasil. To 6 cm. Parotoid glands large.

Oedipina KEFERSTEIN, 1868. Tropical Worm Salamanders. Genus of the Plethodontidae. Neotropics, from southern Mexico through Central America to western Colombia and northwestern Ecuador, with the greatest species diversity in Costa Rica. 15 to 20 species. Related to *Bolitoglossa* and other tropical free-tongue salamanders. Found in wooded lowland regions and foothills (only 2 species extend to 2300 m elevation). 12-25 cm. Extremely elongated, with a very long tail. Head small, the snout usually truncated. Eyes tiny. Legs short, with flattened, webbed fingers and toes. Costal grooves very numerous, 17 to 22. Usually dark brown to blackish.

These salamanders inhabit very damp areas immediately adjacent to creeks and streams, hiding underneath damp moss and decaying wood. Some species burrow in wet sand or gravel along creek beds just above the water line. The main food (as in *Bolitoglossa*) is presumably ants. Reproduction is probably also similar to *Bolitoglossa*, eggs laid on land, without an aquatic larval stage. Maintenance requires a very damp tropical terrarium. Temperature 23 to 27° C.

O. parviceps Group: 17 to 18 costal grooves; usually with white head markings.
• *O. complex* (DUNN, 1824). Panama to northwestern Ecuador. 11.5 cm.
• *O. elongata* (SCHMIDT, 1936). Mexico to Belize. 16 cm.
• *O. parviceps* (PETERS, 1879). Costa Rica to southwestern Colombia. 15 cm.
O. uniformis Group: 19 to 22 costal grooves; mostly without light head markings.
• *O. collaris* (STEJNEGER, 1907). Costa Rica, Panama. 25 cm.
• *O. taylori* (STUART, 1952). Guatemala, El Salvador. 18 cm.

• *O. uniformis* KEFERSTEIN, 1868. Costa Rica, Panama. 18 cm.

Oedipus: see *Bolitoglossa*, genus.

Oedura GRAY, 1842. Velvet Geckos. Genus of the Gekkonidae. Australia. 9 species in more or less dry habitats. To 18 cm. Slender, the head relatively pointed. Tail less than ½ snout-vent length, usually thickened. Toes with well-developed adhesive lamellae and, with the exception of the protruding claws, rather truncated in appearance. Scales very small, velvet-like.

Crepuscular to nocturnal ground-dwellers or semiarboreal. They hide during the day under rocks, loose tree bark, etc. Eggs are relatively soft-shelled. For details on maintenance refer to Gekkonidae. Has been bred frequently.
• *O. lesueuri* (DUMERIL and BIBRON, 1836). Lesueur's Velvet Gecko. Coastal southeastern Australia. 10 cm. Gray-brown with a dark marbled pattern. Tail thick.
• *O. marmorata* GRAY, 1842. Marbled Velvet Gecko. Northern and central Australia. To 18 cm. Blue-gray with yellowish crossbands; older speicmens have indistinct markings. Will feed on smaller lizards. Tail only moderately thickened.

Oedura marmorata

Oeser, Richard (1891-1974): German physician and terrarium hobbyist. Oeser worked for many years as a ship's doctor, which gave him opportunities to make collecting excursions for fish, amphibians, reptiles, and plants, especially bromeliads. His main interest was tropical frogs, and he bred about 35 species (mostly for the first time and for several generations).

Ogmodon PETERS, 1864. Fijian Snakes. Monotypic genus of the Elapidae. Fiji Islands. To 40 cm. Head small, pointed, with small eyes. Tail short. Dark brown with lighter spots; juveniles with a light spot on the head and a dark spotted pattern on the body.

Terrestrial burrowing venomous snakes. The preferred food is arthropods. Little is known about their biology. Maintain like *Micrurus*.
• *O. vitianus* PETERS, 1864.

Okada, Yaichiro (1892-1976): Japanese herpetologist and ichthyologist. Published numerous studies on the herpetofauna of Japan, including *The Tailless Batrachians of the Japanese Empire* (1931). Considered to be the founder of the Japanese herpetological school.

Oligodon BOIE, 1827. Genus of the Colubridae, Lycodontinae. Asia, from southwestern Turkmenia (USSR) and

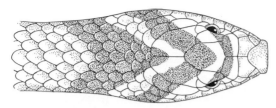

Oligodon taeniolatus

mainly of lizards and their eggs. Egg-layers, 3-6 eggs; *O. cyclurus* lays up to 16 eggs.

Maintain these snakes in well-heated dry terrariums with ample hiding places. A nocturnal temperature reduction is required for high-altitude species and those from extremely arid regions.

▪ *O. bitorquatus* BOIE, 1827. East Indies. The southernmost species of the genus.

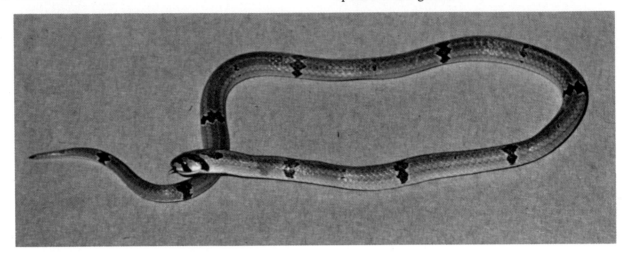

Oligodon ornatus

Iran eastward to China and southward to the Indo-Australian Archipelago, but not in New Guinea. About 56 species in diverse habitats from desert margins to outer rain forest areas. 30 cm to nearly 1 m. Head barely set off and terminating with a distinctly truncated, wide rostral scale that may be turned back over the snout. Smooth dorsal scales. Gray, olive-brown, yellow, and reddish color tones are predominant, often covered by black or light dots, spots, or longitudinal lines. Frequently with conspicuous head and neck markings.

Crepuscular and nocturnal ground snakes that hide during the day under rocks, plants, etc. The diet consists

▪ *O. calamarius* (LINNAEUS, 1758). Sri Lanka. 1000 to 1300 m elevation. 25 cm. The smallest species of the genus.
▪ *O. cyclurus* (CANTOR, 1839). From Assam southeastward to Thailand. Nearly 1 m. The largest species of the genus.
▪ *O. taeniolatus* (JERDON, 1853). From Turkmenia (USSR) southward to Sri Lanka. The northernmost species of the genus.
▪ *O. venustus* (JERDON, 1853). Southern India. To 2,000 m in the Nilgiri and Palni Mountains.

Onychodactylus TSCHUDI, 1839. Clawed Salamanders. Genus of the Hynobiidae. Eastern Palearctic. 2 species. In

Oligodon formosanus

fog-shrouded, high precipitation regions that at the northern end of the range are in lowlands and in the south in mountainous regions up to 2,200 m elevation. 16 cm. Elongated. Head relatively small. Larval forms and adults both have sharp, black keratinous claws on the tips of the fingers and toes. Males larger than females, tip of tail blunter, hind legs much stronger than fore legs. Nuptial pads are rough during the mating season and the outline of the male cloaca forms an acute angle when viewed from above (horseshoe-shaped in females). Larvae have a high crest on the tail that does not extend onto the body.

Largely aquatic, these salamanders are found in cold creeks and mountain lakes where the summer temperatures do not exceed 15° C. The breeding period is May to June. The female deposits two egg strings with relatively few (about 9 per string) large, unpigmented eggs below rocks in water. The larval period lasts for 2 years.

These primitive salamanders should be kept in semisterile aqua-terrariums with water and an air temperature below 15° C. (in a refrigerator or basement). A suitable diet will include small insects and their larvae, slugs, worms, and millipedes.

Dried specimens are used officially in Japan as a vermicide.

- *O. fischeri* (BOULENGER, 1886). Eastern Asia from Siberia southward to South Korea. 16 cm. Yellow dorsal markings indistinct. 14-16 costal grooves.
- *O. japonicus* (HOUTTUYN, 1782). Central Japan. 16 cm. A distinctive, more or less zigzag dark-edged dorsal band. 13-14 costal grooves.

Onychodactylus fischeri

Ooeidozyga KUHL and VAN HASSELT, 1822 (= *Oxydozygota* KUHL, 1938). Paddy Frogs. Genus of the Ranidae. Tropical Southeast Asia, including the Sunda Islands, Sulawesi and Philippines. 9 species. Found in diverse types of water. Compact and stream-lined, the legs short and conspicuously heavy. Fingers free, toes more or less completely webbed. Adhesive discs small if present. Tympanum not visible. Palatine teeth absent. Males substantially smaller than females. Vocal sac paired (*O. baluensis*) or single (*O. laevis*, *O. lima*, probably also *O. floresiana*). Olive to gray-brown, with a dark pattern.

More or less aquatic, predominantly crepuscular and nocturnal. *O. laevis* lives in flooded rice paddies, slow-flowing waters, and small rain puddles. Other species are tied to particular types of water (e. g., *O. floresiana* lives in

small mountain creeks). Maintain in a tropical-warm aqua-terrarium with a small land section.

- *O. baluensis* (BOULENGER, 1896). Kalimantan. 3.5 cm.
- *O. floresiana* (MERTENS, 1927). Flores. 5.5 cm.
- *O. laevis* (GUENTHER, 1858). Paddy Frog. Tropical Southeast Asia, except Java. 2 subspecies. 4.5 cm.
- *O. lima* (GRAVENHORST, 1829). South China to Java.

Oophilositum: see *Chamaelycus*, genus.

Open-air terrarium: An intermediate form between the indoor or typical terrarium and the outdoor terrarium. The simplest example is a "normal" indoor terrarium moved outdoors, as onto a balcony, in order to supply more fresh air and—most importantly—to obtain unobstructed access to ultraviolet radiation. Most suitable for this purpose is a cage where large areas are made of gauze. Such a terrarium must never be placed in a drafty location. With prolonged exposure to sunlight there must also be adequate shaded places in the terrarium. An inherent danger exists in the fact that such open-air terrariums when placed in a sunny location can quickly reach lethal temperature levels for the animals unless at least 2 sides and the lid are made of gauze. An improvisation for temporary sun exposure can be provided by screened cages. Arboreal species can be placed outdoors by surrounding entire bushes or shrubs with gauze or other fine-meshed material in order to prevent the animals from escaping. Usually open-air terrariums are used only on a temporary basis.

Opheodrys FITZINGER, 1843. American Green Snakes. Genus of the Colubridae, Colubrinae. Eastern North America from the Great Lakes southward to eastern Mexico and Yucatan. 3 species. In grasslands and mountains to more than 3,000 m elevation. 30 cm to 1.1 m. Very slender, head only slightly set off, the upper and lower lips white. *O. aestivus* has keeled scales, *O. vernalis* and *O. mayae* have smooth dorsal scales. Dorsum uniformly grass-green.

Asian species previously referred to *Opheodrys* are now variously referred to *Liopeltis*, *Eurypholis*, or *Entechinus*.

These are diurnal snakes. *O. aestivus* is arboreal, moving about among bushes; the other species prefer damper habi-

Opheodrys aestivus

tats on the ground close to water. The diet consists mainly of insects (soft larvae, crickets) and spiders.

They should be kept in a well-heated dry terrarium with green plants for climbing as well as a dish with water for bathing. Often delicate and hard to feed (baby crickets may work).

• *O. aestivus* (LINNAEUS, 1766). Rough Green Snake. Southeastern USA to northeastern Mexico.

• *O. maya* (GAIGE, 1936). Northern part of the Yucatan Peninsula. This species probably does not belong in *Opheodrys*, instead belonging to *Symphimus*.

• *O. vernalis* (HARLAN, 1827). Smooth Green Snake. Southeastern Canada, northeastern USA, central prairies to Texas. 2 subspecies.

Opheodrys vernalis

Ophidiocephalus LUCAS and FROST, 1827. Monotypic genus of the Pygopodidae. Central Australia. Large head plates. Scales smooth. Eye conspicuous. Presumably largely subterranean in sandy areas.

• *O. taeniatus* LUCAS and FROST, 1897. Known only from the holotype. Snout-vent length 10.2 cm.

Ophiodes WAGLER, 1828. South American Worm Lizards. Genus of the Anguidae, subfamily Diploglossinae. Brasil to southern Argentina. 4 species found in relatively dry habitats that are not too open. Easily to 20 cm. Elongated, the head small and inconspicuous. Tiny but movable hind limb rudiments are present, the front legs absent.

These burrowers feed on small arthropods and similar organisms. At least some are ovoviviparous.

• *O. striatus* (SPIX, 1824). Brasil to northern Argentina.

Ophiognomon COPE, 1868. Snake Teiids. Genus of the Teiidae. Upper Amazon, Ecuador, Peru. 3 species. Lately often included in *Bachia*. 15-20 cm. Elongated, cylindrical. Limbs strongly reduced.

• *O. vermiformis* (COPE, 1874).

Ophiomorus DUMERIL and BIBRON, 1839. Snake Skinks. Genus of the Scincidae. Greece and Asia Minor to Pakistan. 6-10 species. To 20 cm. Slender, worm-like, the head wedge-shaped with angular sides. Lateral ridges present on abdomen. Limbs very small or absent; if present they can be pulled into body folds and are useless for locomotion. Brownish to yellowish with dark longitudinal stripes or rows of dots.

Mode of life same as *Scincus*, usually on or in loose sand. Ovoviviparous.

• *O. punctatissimus* (BIBRON and BORY, 1833). Greek Snake Skink. Greece and Asia Minor. Without limbs. Lives under rocks.

• *O. tridactylus* (BLYTH, 1855). Three-toed Snake Skink. Iran to Pakistan. Tiny, 3-toed limbs. A sand-dweller.

Ophiophagous: Animals that feed preferentially on snakes. This is particularly common among snakes themselves, such as the king cobra (*Ophiophagus hannah*), kraits (*Bungarus*), mussurana (*Clelia clelia*), and kingsnakes (*Lampropeltis*).

Ophiophagus (GUENTHER, 1864). King Cobras, Hamadryads. Monotypic genus of the Elapidae. India and Indo-China to southern China and the Indo-Australian Archipelago, Bali, and the Philippines. In tropical forests and montane rain forests. Average length to 4 m, the recorded max-

Ophiodes sp.

Ophiophagus hannah

Ophisaurus apodus

imum length in excess of 5.5 m. Closely related to true cobras (*Naja*) and formerly included in *Naja*. Adult specimens are medium to dark brown with washed-out light and dark crossbands along the body. Juveniles are black with rows of light spots in place of crossbands. A king cobra erect in display shows on the light anterior abdominal surface 3 dark crossbands each 2-5 scale rows wide. The hood is very pronounced. When in a threat display these snakes can raise the anterior part of their body about 1 m off the ground, and in contrast to *Naja* these snakes are able to follow their enemy in this position over considerable distances.

King cobras prefer the proximity of water (they are good swimmers and divers). They feed primarily on other snakes, including venomous snakes (*Naja* and *Bungarus*). To what degree there is cannibalism has not yet been determined.

Egg-layers, to 40 eggs. They provide brood care, which is most unusual in snakes. The females push leaves and branches into a nest pile where the eggs are incubated by the elevated decomposition temperatures. The female remains on top of the nest to guard the eggs and the male also remains close by. During the brood care period *Ophiophagus* tends to be aggressive toward approaching humans.

The extreme danger of a bite from this snake lies in the gigantic size of the fangs and the very large amount of venom injected. Even in elephants the bite from this snake can penetrate the skin of the trunk or the foot and thus cause death within a few hours.

King cobras are among the most attractive highlights in large display terrariums at zoos. Wherever this snake is kept there must be strict compliance with the prerequisites for venomous snake care. If force-feeding becomes necessary (substitute foods include freshwater fish, especially eels) it is best to have several animal keepers assisting. Once substitute food is accepted, king cobras have obtained considerable ages in captivity. They must be given a large water bowl, a hiding box with a sliding door (for safety), and adequate heating. They have been bred in captivity. King cobras have gained a reputation for "intelligent" behavior among their keepers.

▪ *O. hannah* (CANTOR, 1836). King Cobra or Hamadryad.

Ophiopogon KER-GAWL. Snakebeard. Genus of the Liliaceae. Eastern Asia, Japan to Himalayas region. 8 species. Grass-like, lawn-forming shrubs about 15-20 cm tall with evergreen leaves close to the ground. Extremely adaptable, they can take shade, can be cultivated in wet and dry environments, and can take temperatures down to almost 0° C. but are not totally frost-resistant. The most frequently cultured species is *O. japonicus* (L. F.) KER-GAWL; varieties of this species have yellowish leaves. For similar uses as indicated for *Reineckia* and *Liriope*.

Ophioscincus PETERS, 1873. Indonesian Snake Skinks. Genus of the Scincidae. Indonesia. 3 species. Limbs completely reduced. Probably should be included in *Anomalopus*. Ovoviviparous.

Ophioseps BOCAGE, 1873: see *Aprasia*, genus.

Ophisaurus DAUDIN, 1803. Glass Lizards. Genus of the Anguidae, subfamily Gerrhonotinae. Indonesia, southern Asia and the Near East, southeastern Europe, North Africa, and North America. About 10 species in stony steppes and more or less damp forests. Some species to more than 100 cm. With the exception of tiny rudiments of the hind legs in a few species, limbs are essentially absent. The body is elongated, snake-like, but with its large scales and strong osteoderms it appears relatively rigid. Head rather blunt, the large teeth conical. Lateral fold well developed. Adult coloration usually rather plain, mainly shades of brown or green. Juveniles may have more contrasting markings.

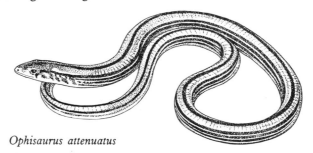

Ophisaurus attenuatus

Mainly crepuscular and nocturnal ground-dwellers that occasionally also burrow. Predators that feed on arthropods and (sometimes predominantly) on snails; the large teeth can easily handle even larger snail shells. Large specimens may also take the occasional small mammal.

Egg-layers. In the Eurasian *O. apodus* the development of the relatively soft-shelled, elongated eggs takes at least 6 weeks. Females of the American glass "snakes" (so-called because of the shape and fragile tail) guard their eggs by coiling around the clutch. Their body temperature is then about 0.3 to 0.4° C. higher than normal.

These are very hardy, durable terrarium animals (although there is no experience at hand with the Southeast Asian species) that should be kept in a spacious, slightly heated terrarium (activity temperature for *O. ventralis* is 18-30° C.). In addition to ample hiding places there must also be climbing branches and a water bowl (absolutely essential since these lizards tend to drink a lot). A nocturnal temperature reduction of 5-10° C. is desirable. Some specimens will feed occasionally on lean meat and eggs as well as arthropods, snails, and an occasional pink mouse. Sunbathing and ultraviolet radiation are important. Most of the commonly available subtropical species can be kept in an outdoor terrarium during the summer months. A brief over-wintering period at about 10° C. is recommended.

Ophisaurus ventralis

▪ *O. apodus* (PALLAS, 1775). Sheltopusik. Balkan Peninsula through Turkey, Syria, and the Caucasus to central Asia. Brush steppes to open forests. To 1.4 m. Tail equal to body. Back in adults dark brown to straw yellow; juveniles light gray with dark crossband. Hindlimb remnants about 2 mm long are found lateral to the cloaca. Sheltopusiks take an occasional bath, lay 6 -12 eggs, and may live in excess of 20 years in captivity.
▪ *O. attenatus* BAIRD, 1880. Slender Glass Lizard. Southern

Ophisaurus compressus

and central USA. Brown, sometimes with darker stripes. 1 m (29 cm snout-vent).
▪ *O. koellikeri* (GUENTHER, 1873). Koelliker's Glass Lizard. Northwestern Africa. To easily 40 cm. Olive brown with shiny green dots. Damp habitats with dense vegetation.
▪ *O. ventralis* (LINNAEUS, 1766). Eastern Glass Lizard. Southeastern USA in damp forests and meadows. To 1 m. Usually appears greenish, with white bars on the neck. Prefers semishade.

Ophisops MENETRIES, 1832. Snake-eyed Lacertids. Genus of the Lacertidae. North Africa to the Near East and India. About 6 species in relatively dry, often rocky steppe regions. Body relatively round, the tail about twice the body length. Dorsal scales large, shingled, and strongly keeled. The toes have keeled lamellae. The collar is weakly developed and in some species is absent in the center. The most conspicuous characteristic is the "spectacles": the eyelids have become fused and the lower one has a very large transparent window, yet the lids remain movable (the eyes can be closed, the lower lid being pushed into a fold for cleaning of the spectacle). Similar to *Cabrita*. Mainly brown to olive-gray with light lateral stripes and dark spots, the tail in some species reddish.

Diurnal, feeding on a variety of arthropods. Egg-layers. Maintenance requirements similar to *Acanthodactylus* and *Eremias*, but require a bit more dampness. Fairly compatible among each other. Somewhat delicate, thus keeping and breeding are usually problematic.

Ophisops elegans

▪ *O. elegans* MENETRIES, 1832. European Snake-eye. Extreme southeastern Europe to western regions of the Near East and the Caucasus. To 15 cm.
▪ *O. occidentalis* BOULENGER, 1887. Western Snake-eye. Libya to Morocco. About 15 cm. Very similar to the above species.

Ophryoessoides DUMERIL, 1851. Genus of the Iguanidae. Andean South America to Brasil and Paraguay. About 14 species in rocky dry regions in mountain ranges above 2,000 m. Formerly included in *Leiocephalus* and very similar to this genus. About 20 cm. Slender, with a conspicuously smooth head and keeled dorsal scales. Maintenance as for *Liolaemus*.
▪ *O. aculeatus* (O'SHAUGHNESSY, 1879). Peru, Ecuador, slopes of the Andes. About 20 cm.
▪ *O. ornatus* (GRAY, 1845). Ecuador and northern Peru. Coastal regions. Barely 20 cm.

Ophryophryne BOULENGER, 1903. Genus of the Bufonidae. Southeast Asia. 2 species. In mountain ranges. Tym-

Ophryoessoides trachycephalus

panum clearly visible. Fingers free, toes webbed at base only.
• *O. microstoma* BOULENGER, 1903. Vietnam, Man-Son Mountains. 5.5 cm. Gray with symmetrical dark markings. Sides and limbs with black dots.

Opipeuter UZZELL, 1969. Monotypic genus of the Teiidae. Bolivia, eastern Andean slopes from 1,000 to 3,000 m. Small, slender, ground-dwellers often found close to rivers and streams.
• *O. xestus* UZZELL, 1969.

Opisthodont: see Teeth.

Opisthoglyph: see Teeth.

Opisthoplus PETERS, 1882. Monotypic genus of the Colubridae, Boiginae. Brasil (Rio Grande do Sul). Closely related to and similar to *Tomodon*. About 65 cm. Caution: Venomous bites possible.
• *O. degener* PETERS, 1882.

Opisthothylax PERRET, 1962. Monotypic genus of the Rhacophoridae. Central Africa in tropical rain forests close to flowing waters. Numerous small warts evenly distributed on the skin. Head wide. Pupil vertical. Tympanum very small, barely visible. Males have a conspicuously large throat disc. The fingers are webbed at their bases, the toes webbed to about ⅔ of their length. Tips with adhesive discs.
• *O. immaculatus* (BOULENGER, 1903). Nigeria, Gabon, Cameroons. 3.5 cm. Dorsally uniformly yellow brown, the abdomen light yellow; iris light gray golden.

Opisthotropis GUENTHER, 1872. Genus of the Colubridae, Lycodontinae. Indo-China northeastward to southwestern China and Hainan, southward to Kalimantan and Sumatra. About 11 species. 25 to 80 cm. The trapezoidal head is distinctly set off. Dorsal scales smooth or keeled.

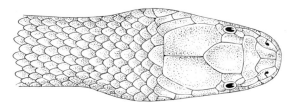

Opisthotropis andersoni

Dorsum uniformly colored or with light and dark crossbands.

All species are amphibious, in part corresponding to the Natricinae, Group 2. Some species have become adapted to inhabit montane streams in rain forests or monsoon forests where they hide under rocks or water plants. Nocturnal, they will also pursue prey out of water (crustaceans, fish, frogs, and earthworms). Captured specimens empty their foul-smelling anal gland secretions similar to *Natrix*.

Maintenance as for Natricinae, Groups 1 and 2 combined. Clean fresh water, preferably in a flow-through open system, is very important.
• *O. balteatus* (COPE, 1895). From Kampuchea northeastward to southern China and Hainan. The largest species of the genus. Banded.
• *O. jacobi* ANGEL and BOURRET, 1933. North Vietnam (Tam Dao).
• *O. latouchi* (BOULENGER, 1899). Southern China. Striped.
• *O. rugosa* (LIDTH DE JEUDE, 1890-1891). Sumatra. Uniformly olive brown.
• *O. typica* (MOCQUARD, 1890). Northern Kalimantan (Kinabalu). Uniformly olive.

Oplurus (CUVIER, 1829). Madagascan Swifts. Genus of the Iguanidae. Madagascar. 6 species in rocky dry regions. To 25 cm. Similar in appearance and mode of life to *Tropidurus*. The large, rough, spinous scales on the tail are conspicuous; a dorsal crest is absent (in contrast to *Chalarodon*).

Some species are tree-dwellers (e. g., *O. cyclurus*), but most are ground-dwellers. They feed on arthropods. For maintenance see *Liolaemus*.
• *O. cyclurus* (GRAY, 1845). Treed steppes and open forests. About 15 cm, 7 cm of this body. A black neckband with a white border.
• *O. sebae* DUMERIL and BIBRON, 1837. Rocky areas. About 25 cm. Brown with several dark crossbands and light spots, especially distinct anteriorly.

Oplurus grandidieri

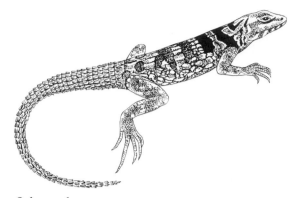

Oplurus sebae

Maxillaria punctata

Oplurus cyclurus

Opuntia MILL. Prickly Pear Cacti, Chollas. Genus of the Cactaceae. American, introduced into other regions of the world. More than 200 species. Bizarre branching plants with disc-like enlarged shoots covered with stiff spines and bristles. Some species are frost-resistant. Suitable for semi-desert terrariums are:
• *O. robusta* WENDL. Without spines or with only a few strong (5 cm long) yellow thorns.
• *O. leucotricha* DC. With white, hair-like thorns.
• *O. pilifera* WEB.

Orchidaceae: Orchids. Family of the Liliatae. Worldwide, primarily in tropics and subtropics. About 700 genera and approximately 25,000 species. Shrubs and herbs preferring humus soil; many are epiphytes; in Europe and most of North America they are terrestrial herbs, many symbiotic with soil fungi (mycorrhiza). Orchidaceae can be moss-like and minute, but can also reach diameters of several meters. They hybridize easily so that a multitude of forms, even intergeneric hybrids, have been propagated. When culturing orchids it has to be kept in mind that epithytic species require a medium consisting of osmunda (royal fern) and polypodium as a water-repellent substrate and sphagnum

as a water-retaining substrate. Also included should be some beech tree leaves. Terrestrial species should be given some additional lawn soil or coarse sand. Fertilizing must be done sparingly, preferably with an organic liquid fertilizer in a weak concentration. Heat requirements vary substantially. Species from tropical rain forests require an even heat and high humidity. Day and night variations are usually advantageous, and as a general rule the night temperature must be lower than the day temperature. Epiphytic species attached to a log or some other base must be given adequate moisture by spraying, optimally with pure rain water. Species with fleshy leaves or storage organs require little moisture after their growth period. Often orchid hybrids are easier to keep than the pure wild forms. Common forms include:

Cattleya bowringiana

• *Apasia lunata* LINDL. A small epiphyte.
• *Cattleya* LINDL. 40 species. Require ample light and usually do not do well in a terrarium with an even climate. *C. citrina* LINDL is recommended as being hardy; a hanging plant.
• *Coelogyne* LINDL. 130 species. Epiphytic and terrestrial. *C. speciosa* LINDL can take heat and is considered hardy.
• *Dendrobium* SW. About 1,000 species.
• *Maxillaria* RUIZ and PAV. 250 species. Temperature tolerant but not very attractive.
• *Phalaenopsis* BL. About 40 species. Many hybrids, but due to their small size the wild forms, such as *P. luddemanniana* RCHB. f., or *P. parishii* RCHB. f., should be given preference for use in a terrarium.

Brassocattleya cliftoni var. *albens*

Oreal: Climatically related, open, high-mountain plateaus (in temperate zone above about 2,300 m to 3,500 m, in the tropics from about 3,300 to 5,500 m), usually grassland or shrubs (e. g., *puna*, *paramo*), or rocky deserts. The oreal is characterized by extreme day/night temperature gradients (up to 50° C.) and high solar radiation. Those amphibians and reptiles that occur in these regions survive the cold nights (or winter) by living buried in the ground where there is less thermal fluctuation.

Oreocalamus BOULENGER, 1899. Monotypic genus of the Colubridae of uncertain taxonomic status, probably belonging to the Lycodontinae. Kalimantan. In tropical montane rain forests. Barely 40 cm. Head flattened, somewhat pointed, not set off from body. Eyes relatively small. Body covered with smooth scales. Tail very short. Uniformly black-brown above.

Burrowing snakes, rare, the biology unknown.
• *O. hanitschi* BOULENGER, 1899. Northern Kalimantan, Mt. Kinabalu to 1,400 m.

Oreodeira GIRARD, 1858. Monotypic genus of the Agamidae. Known only from the type specimens from southeastern Australia. Very similar to *Amphibolurus*.
• *O. gracilipes* GIRARD, 1858.

Oreolalax MYERS and LEVITON, 1962. Genus of the Pelobatidae. Himalayas. 4 species. In mountains between 1,000 and 3,400 m. Formerly included in *Scutiger*, but in contrast to *Scutiger* teeth are present and there is a notched posterior tongue margin. Despite the toad-like appearance, relatively slender. Skin granular or covered with warts. Pupil vertical. Tympanum not visible. Fingers free, with 2 distinct metatarsal tubercles. Toes free or webbed at base only, with 1 inner oval metatarsal tubercle. Courting males with oval, rough nuptial patch on each side of the chest.

Larvae similar to *Pelobates*, but not as large.

Sluggish frogs that tend to stay in or close to water, usually in calm, shallow areas of mountain streams or lakes. *Oreolalax* spawn in very slow-flowing water, where the eggs are deposited in clumps (protected from light) under rocks. The larvae remain in hiding under rocks, although they are agile swimmers.

Should be kept in a semisterile aqua-terrarium (only water and rocks) in a cool location (ideally an old refrigerator or in the basement).
• *O. popei* (LIU, 1947). Western China. To 6.5 cm. Reticulated dark brown pattern over a yellow-brown base color. Limbs with dark brown crossbands.

Oreophryne BOETTGER, 1895. Genus of the Microhylidae. Indo-Australian Archipelago to the Sundas, Philippines, Sulawesi, New Guinea. 23 species. In tropical rain forests and cloud forests. Snout-vent length only a few cm. Skin usually smooth. Pupil horizontal. On the basis of external characteristics hard to distinguish from the related genera *Cophixalus* and *Sphenophryne*. Fingers free; toes free or webbed at base only. Tips of digits with distinct adhesive discs. Often with a dark W- or X-pattern on the shoulder region.

Usually bush- or tree-dwellers. No free-living larval stage. The eggs are deposited in damp holes or hollows in plants or the ground (light protected), which also become the hiding places for the frogs. Completely metamorphosed juvenile frogs hatch from the eggs and often remain with the adults. No cannibalism; they appear to be specialized feeders on small insects.
• *O. celebensis* (MUELLER, 1894). Sulawesi, New Guinea. 3 cm.
• *O. monticola* (BOULENGER, 1897). Lombok, Bali (1200 to 2500 m). 3 cm.
• *O. variabilis* (BOULENGER, 1896). Sulawesi. 3 cm.

Oreophrynella BOULENGER, 1895. Genus of the Bufonidae. 1 or 2 species. Related to and similar in appearance to *Dendrophryniscus*, *Melanophryniscus*, and *Osornophryne*.

Presumably a bush- and tree-dweller. Maintenance as for *Osornophryne*, but with climbing facilities and an epiphyte log.
• *O. quelchii* (BOULENGER, 1895). Mt. Roraima, between Venezuela and Guyana.

Oriental Region: Zoogeographic area including tropical Asia from India and Sri Lanka to the Sundas, Bali, Lombok, and the Philippines. Delineation from the Palearctic along the southern slopes of the Himalayas is rather abrupt with the start of tropical vegetation, but borders rather problematic in southern China, since the Palearctic and Oriental faunal elements are widely intermixed in this region. Delineation is similarly difficult in the southeast, where there exists a distinct mixing region with the Australian that is referred to as Wallacea. In terms of the Earth's history, the Orient has been formed from two different components. The Indian subcontinent was formerly connected to Madagascar and Africa (and through Africa with South America) as part of the southern continent Gondwana, while the Malayan region always belonged to the northern continent (Laurasia). This explains the African-Oriental types of distribution of the southern fauna and the Holarc-

Oriental Region: Lake Lanao, Philippines

tic-Oriental distribution of the northern fauna.

The climate of the Orient is truly tropical and is largely determined by the monsoons with their seasonal direction changes. Summer monsoon precipitation is sufficient for at least savannahs to become established, if not monsoon forests or even true rain forests. Therefore, treeless areas are present—at the most—in small areas only.

The herpetofauna of the Orient is extremely rich due to its diverse origin, the close contact to the Australian fauna, the absence of extended distribution barriers toward the Palearctic, and the tropical climate. It includes, apart from widely distributed families, the following endemic families or subfamilies: Megophryninae, Nyctibatrachinae, Platysternidae, Lanthanotidae, Paraeinae, Xenoderminae, Xenopeltidae, Uropeltidae, Elachistodontinae, Calamarinae, and Gavialidae. Primarily Oriental (but penetrating into the northern Australian) are Dibamidae, Acrochordidae, and Homalopsinae. The Hydrophiidae appear have an Oriental-Australian distribution center. Great diversity is reached by the Emydidae, Trionychidae, Testudinidae, Crotalidae, Natricinae, and Lycodontinae in the Orient. A few salamanders enter the Oriental region from the north, so that this faunal kingdom contains (just like the Neotropics) all the orders of amphibians.

Orientation. Ability of an animal to adjust its body and its behavior relative to time and space. Space orientation utilizes special reference stimuli and time orientation time-related stimuli. Time orientation is, for instance, when many lizards and snakes can be observed to move to basking sites at certain times of the day. Within the concept of space orientation one distinguishes between local and distant orientation. Local orientation is, for instance, object orientation during prey capture for many salamanders, frogs, toads, and chameleons that have to orient themselves toward the prey in respect to direction and distance to initiate the capture action by their flicking or thrusting tongue. Space orientation relates to territorial orientation behavior and presupposes recognition of familiar surroundings. It is associated with memory and learning capabilities. For instance, it enables the animal's return to a particular hiding place (homing capability). Space orientation can also last over longer periods of time, thus amphibians usually can find the pond where they underwent their own larval stage. Orientation toward polarizing light on the pineal organ and according to the magnetic field have been shown for salamanders and frogs.

Distant orientation frequently utilizes the sun as a fixed reference point. During such solar orientation the animals respond according to the angle of the sun's rays (sun compass orientation). Such complicated orientation mechanisms are found, for instance, in sea turtles, which sometimes migrate across the oceans for thousands of kilometers.

Oriocalotes GUENTHER, 1864. Monotypic genus of the Agamidae. Eastern Himalayas. Related to *Calotes*, so mode of life possibly similar. Little known.
▪ *O. paulus* SMITH, 1935.

Orlitia GRAY, 1873. Bornean River Turtles. Monotypic genus of the Emydidae. Malayan Peninsula, Sumatra, Kalimantan. In large waters, mainly in rivers. Amphibious to aquatic. To 76 cm. Carapace with a keel. Front limbs with 5 claws, the hind limbs with 4. Brown.

Omnivorous. Very rarely seen even in zoos. Maintenance requires a flow-through open–water system.
▪ *O. borneensis* GRAY, 1873.

Orlitia borneensis, juv.

Oscaecilia TAYLOR, 1968. Genus of the Caeciliidae. Central and South America. 6 species. To 1 m. Very elongated. Eyes covered by skull bones. Tentacle located below nostril. 146-280 primary furrows, 0-54 secondary furrows. Either more or less uniformly colored or two-toned.
• *O. bassleri* (DUNN, 1942). Ecuador, Colombia, Peru. To 1 m. Uniformly slate to lavender blue-gray.
• *O. ochrocephala* (COPE, 1866). Panama and northwestern Colombia. To 62 cm. Dorsum gray to olive, separated from white abdomen by a dark stripe.

Osornophryne RUIS and HERNANDEZ, 1976. Genus of the Bufonidae. Northwestern South America. 2 species in the perpetually wet, cool high Andes. *O. percrassa* prefers cloud forests above 2700 m; *O. bufoniformis* is characteristic of the higher elevations of the *paramos*. Plump. The skin has warts. Snout blunt. Tympanum poorly visible. No distinct parotoid glands. Fingers and toes short, stubby, barely protruding. Amplexus inguinal. Brown.

Slow-moving ground-dwellers. Should be kept in an unheated terrarium equipped with mosses, grasses, dwarf ferns, bark, and rocks. High humidity essential. Open-air or outdoor keeping in a shaded location is recommended during the summer months.
• *O. bufoniformis* (PERACCA, 1904). Southern Colombia, northern Ecuador. 3.5 cm (females), 2 cm (males).
• *O. percrassa* RUIZ and HERNANDEZ, 1976. Colombia. 4 cm (females), 3 cm (males). Legs very frail.

Osteocephalus STEINDACHNER, 1862. Genus of the Hylidae. Tropical South America. About 5 species in *selva*. Some species have a conspicuously rough skin (*O. orcesi, O. taurinus*). Hind limbs slender. The fingers are webbed at the base and the toes are almost completely webbed. Paired vocal sacs located behind the corner of the mouth. Dark brown.
• *O. leprieuri* (DUMERIL and BIBRON, 1841). Tropical South America east of the Andes (Colombia to Brasil). To 5.5 cm. The thighs have wide dark crossbands.

Osteoderms: Bony plates, scutes, and bucklers formed in the skin. These occur in many reptiles, such as Scincidae and Anguidae, and can essentially enclose the body in dermal armor. The abdominal ridges in crocodilians and the carapace of turtles (where, however, parts of the skeleton also become involved) are usually ossifications of the skin.

Osteolaemus COPE, 1861. African Dwarf Crocodiles. Monotypic genus of the Crocodylidae. Tropical western and central Africa, in part sympatric with *Crocodylus niloticus* and *C. cataphractus*, but generally inhabiting smaller, slow-flowing jungle streams. Lives individually, sometimes at considerable distances from water. 1.3 to 1.6 m (maximum 2 m). Morphologically more reminiscent of Alligatoridae than of Crocodylidae, mainly due to the short snout and the absence of scale combs on the digits. Iris dark brown, the upper eyelid almost completely ossified, smooth. Occipital bucklers small, arranged in an irregular cross row, and followed by 4 large trapezoidal nuchal bucklers that are in contact with each other, and separated from the dorsal scales by a wide space. Juveniles with light spots; adults uniformly blackish.

For general maintenance see Crocodylia. These animals

Osteolaemus tetraspis

require water and air temperatures from 28 to 30° C. The diet must be varied, including fish, molluscs, crustaceans, frogs, and others. Due to their relatively small size, peaceful, curious, and largely diurnal behavior and their attractive "good natured" appearance, *Osteolaemus* could be suitable for hobbyists. However, since these animals are endangered, private ownership can really not be justified. It has only occasionally been bred in captivity in zoos in the USA and Japan. The clutches of 16-31 eggs were transfered to incubators and required temperatures between 25 and 32° C. to hatch in 84-105 days.
• *O. tetraspis* COPE, 1861. African Dwarf Crocodile. The nominate subspecies comes from Sierra Leone, Guinea, Ghana, Togo, Nigeria, Cameroons, Gabon, Angola, and Liberia. *O. t. osborni* (SCHMIDT, 1919) occurs in northeastern Zaire.

Otocryptis WAGLER, 1830. Genus of the Agamidae. Southern India and Sri Lanka. 2 species. Together with *Sitana* included in the subfamily Sitaninae. Found in wooded river valleys of the lowlands and hill country. To 25 cm. Slightly compressed laterally. Tympanum not visible. Males with or without a large gular pouch. Tail ⅔ to ¾ of total length. A low nuchal crest. Mainly brown.

Diurnal and semiarboreal. When in retreat it sometimes runs on the hind legs only. Egg-layers, 3-4 eggs per clutch; will breed throughout the year. Provide daytime temperatures of 25 to 28° C., dropping at night to not much below 20° C. High humidity and large drinking requirements. Feeds on arthropods and some delicate, tender plant shoots.
• *O. wiegmanni* WAGLER, 1830. Sri Lanka. 25 cm. Snout-vent length about 7 cm. Males with a large orange-red, green-edged gular pouch that extends to the base of the abdomen. Neck green when excited.
• *O. beddomi* BOULENGER, 1885. Southern India. No gular pouch.

Otophryne BOULENGER, 1900. Monotypic genus of the Microhylidae. Northern Amazon Basin in *selva*. Flattened. Tympanum clearly visible. Legs short. Fingers free, the toes webbed at the base only; no metatarsal tubercles.

Ground-dwellers, uncommon. Development presumably without a free-swimming larval stage.
- *O. robusta* BOULENGER, 1900. Venezuela and Colombia. 5 cm. Brown with a pale lateral stripe.

Otosaurus GRAY, 1845. Monotypic genus of the Scincidae. Philippines. Easily to 30 cm. Similar to *Lygosoma*. Little known.
- *O. cumingi* GRAY, 1845.

Outdoor terrarium: Suitable for most animals from temperate zones during the summer months and also for subtropical and many tropical species. In contrast to open-air terrariums, an outdoor terrarium is larger, usually obtained by walling-off a section of backyard or garden. There are no specific recommendatioins in regard to maximum size, but enclosures of less than 3 to 4 sq. m. are hardly functional; most of the outdoor terrariums incorporate an area between 10 and 50 sq. m. Selection of the site depends upon the species to be accommodated. Reptiles require generally more sun than amphibians; in any event, shaded areas should be available in any outdoor terrarium. The walls can consists of a variety of materials, but it is important that the surrounding wall penetrates at least 40 cm deep into the ground in order to contain burrowing animals and to keep out rodents. Small outdoor terrariums can be protected by burying a rust-proof fine wire mesh

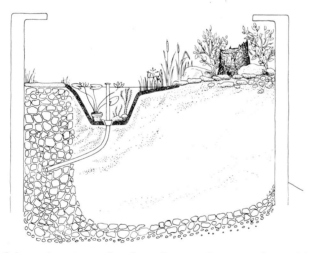

Schematic cross-section through an outdoor terrarium, with representative plantings

covering under the entire area. The wall, which should generally be 0.5 to 1 m high (a lower wall is suitable for turtles), should have built in at or near its top and at an angle a continuous piece of hard plastic, glass, or rust-proof sheet metal as a final barrier. Sometimes a protruding layer of bricks can also to the same job. These barrier are NOT suitable for geckos, anoles, amphibians, and snakes, which can climb smooth horizontal barriers. For these animals a complete fine wire mesh cover must be installed. Frequently such high barriers are visually not very appealing and are often distracting, especially in smaller outdoor terrariums. This can be overcome by lowering the level of the terrarium by 0.5 to 1 m so that one looks at the terrarium virtually from above. Another variation of a barrier is a moat about 50 cm wide and 20 to 30 cm deep

that is followed on the outside by a low 30 to 40 cm partition of glass or acrylic. Here it has to be rememebered that many amphibians when wet can possibly climb such an obstacle. Such a barrier is also unsuitable for snakes, yet it works well with many lizards and turtles. Finally, there should also be additional protection against cats and birds of prey (the latter not necessary in densely built-up urban areas), in the form of large-meshed nets.

Animals from warmer regions should be able to find some shelter against the rain. Even specialized lizards such as *Uromastyx* and *Phrynosoma* have been kept for years (during the summer months) in such enclosures.

Should a greenhouse be available, one can possibly combine this with an outdoor enclosure and give the animals a choice between outdoors and indoors. Animals from temperate and subtropical regions can even over-winter in larger enclosures, but this requires some protected, frost-free areas. The simplest type to provide is a pit containing slowly decaying leaves, wood shavings, and similar material. The distance from the surface to the center of the pit should be at least 1 m. During the winter a solid cover should be placed over the pit.

Most animals will breed in an outdoor terrarium, but it is often difficult to find the eggs in a large enclosure. This means that the animals must be closely watched. Even in very large enclosures the animals will usually continue to lay their eggs in a few favorable sites (e. g., under flat rocks in a sunny location). The eggs should always be removed and incubated separately. Natural foods such as flying insects are a welcome additional food supply, but supplementary feeding will always be required.

The animals to be kept determine whether such an outdoor terrarium should reflect steppes, forest, rocky, heath, moor, or riverbank habitat. There are many suitable plants for the various types of habitats required. For instance, for:

Rocky (mountain) habitats: *Alyssum, Draba*, Brassicaceae, *Festuca*, Poaceae, *Saxifraga, Sedum, Sempervivum*.

Dry, steppe-like habitats, semi-dry lawns and fields: *Coronilla, Euphorbia, Festuca, Fumana, Helianthemum, Hippocrepis, Thymus, Yucca*, turf-forming grasses of different genera.

Low-growing coniferous trees: *Juniperus, Pinus*.

Swamp and moor habitats: *Calla palustris*, Araceae, Cyperaceae, *Hydrocotyle, Menyanthes, Oxycoccus*, Ericaceae, *Sphagnum*.

Heath habitats: *Armeria maritima, Calluna*, Ericaceae, *Euphorbia cyparissias, Festuca, Genista, Polypodium vulgare*.

Damp forest habitats: *Ajuga, Asarum europaeum, Galeobdolon, Glechoma*. *Hedera, Sagina, Primula, Oxalis acetosella, Waldsteinia*.

Ferns: *Asplenium, Athyrium, Cystopteris, Dryopteris, Polypodium, Pteris*, and others.

Oviparity: Form of reproduction where the female produces eggs that develop outside the body. Egg-layers.

Ovoviviparity: Form of reproduction where the young hatch just before, while, or shortly after the eggs are laid. Differs from viviparity (live-birth) in that the young are not nourished by the parent while inside the body. Recently the value of this concept has been questioned as distinct from viviparity.

Oxybelis WAGLER, 1830. Vine Snakes. Genus of the Colubridae, Boiginae. Southern Arizona in the USA, southward to Brasil, Peru, and Bolivia. 4 species in tropical forests, mainly in secondary growth, and also following human habitation. To 1.3 m, exceedingly slender. Head usually very elongated and pointed. Body round, with an extremely long tail. Green, gray, brown, or yellowish, often with stripes.

Diurnal and arboreal snakes that feed mainly on lizards and frogs. Egg-layers, 4-6 eggs. Maintenance requires a well-heated rain-forest terarrium. Caution: Venomous bites possible.
- *O. aeneus* (WAGLER, 1824). Mexican Vine Snake. Enters Arizona from Mexico and Central and South America.
- *O. fulgidus* (DAUDIN, 1803). Green Vine Snake. Mexico to South America.

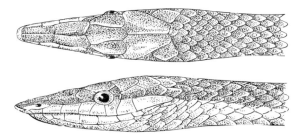

Oxybelis aeneus

Oxybelis fulgidus (green) and *Oxybelis aeneus* (brown)

Oxydozygota: see *Ooeidozyga*, genus.

Oxyrhabdium BOULENGER, 1893. Genus of the Colubridae, Natricinae. Philippines. 2 species in tropical lowlands and montane rain forests to 2,000 m elevation. 60 to 80 cm.

Ground snakes that prefer to stay under shrubs, fallen branches, and similar cover. They tend to burrow using

Oxybelis fulgidus

the pointed head, which is not set off from the body. The diet presumably consists of worms, insects, and frogs. Care as indicated for Natricinae, Group 1, in a well-planted forest terrarium.
- *O. modestum* (DUMERIL and BIBRON, 1854).
- *O. leporinum* (GUENTHER, 1858).

Oxyrhopus WAGLER, 1830. Genus of the Colubridae, Boiginae. Southern Mexico southward to the Amazon Basin and west of the Andes in Peru. 11 species in tropical lowland forests. 80 cm to 1 m. Large grooved fangs positioned relatively far forward below the eye. Head clearly set off from the body. Most species are banded with red—white (or yellow)—black and look like coral snakes.

Diurnal and nocturnal ground snakes that prey mainly on lizards. Egg-layers, to 18 eggs per clutch. Maintain in an evenly heated rain-forest terrarium. Caution: Venomous bites possible.
- *O. petola* (LINNAEUS, 1758). Mexico to Amazon Basin.
- *O. rhombifer* DUMERIL, DUMERIL, and BIBRON, 1854. Amazon Basin to Argentina.
- *O. trigeminus* DUMERIL, DUMERIL, and BIBRON, 1854. Amazon Basin and Mato Grosso, Brasil.

Oxyrhopus trigeminus

Oxyrhopus rhombifer

Oxyuranus KINGHORN, 1923. Taipan. Monotypic genus of the Elapidae. Northeastern Australia and New Guinea. In various types of habitat from thornbush steppes across savannahs and into tropical forests. 2.4 to 4 m. Slender, one of the longest venomous snakes. The large, narrow head is clearly set off from the body. Dark brown with lighter sides, markings absent.

Terrestrial, diurnal and nocturnal venomous snakes that feed primarily on rat-size small mammals. Egg-layers, to 20 eggs. Accidental bites are rare since this snake is not too often kept in captivity. However, there is an 80% fatality rate without quick serum treatment.

Taipans should be kept in a well-heated, large terrarium with a large water bowl and a solidly built box (with sliding doors) as the only available place to hide. This snake rarely loses its aggressiveness.
▪ *O. scutellatus* (PETERS, 1868). Taipan. The nominate subspecies is from Australia and is 2-3.2 m long. *O. s. canni*

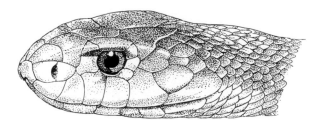

Oxyuranus scutellatus

SLATER, 1956, from eastern New Guinea, reaches 4 m.

Oxyuroidea: Pinworms. Significant nematode parasites in reptiles (about 150 species). They are particularly common in tortoises. These worms attach themselves to the intestinal mucous membrane and there cause irritation and superficial lesions that in heavy infestations can also lead to necrosis and inflammation of the intestinal serosa (exudative peritonitis). This is indicated by swelling of the abdominal region, reluctance to move, refusal to feed, and loss of condition. Constipation can then become the ultimate cause of death. Common are also mixed infections (amoebic dysentery, ascarids, cestodes) and simultaneous bacterial infections.

Therapy: Broad-spectrum anthelminthics.

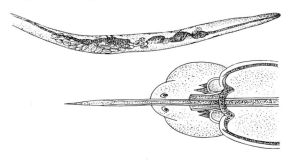

Oxyuroidea *(Ozolaimus cirratus, Macracis papillosa)*

Pachycalamus GUENTHER, 1881. Monotypic genus of the Amphisbaenia, family Trogonophidae. Island of Socotra in the Gulf of Aden. Rocky dry regions. Burrower.
▪ *P. brevis* GUENTHER, 1881. About 15 cm.

Pachydactylus WIEGMANN, 1834. Thick-toed Geckos. Genus of the Gekkonidae. Africa south of the Sahara. 25 species in various damp habitats, some following human habitation. To 20 cm. Compact, the tail barely equal to snout-vent length. The toes have well-developed adhesive lamellae and are without claws. Pupil vertical. Dorsal scales granular, in numerous dense rows, much coarser on the tail. Mainly brown or gray with various markings.

Pachydactylus capensis tigrinus

Pachydactylus bibroni

These geckos are active mainly during the early morning hours and early evening hours, but sometimes they are also found out of their hiding places during the middle of the day. Fairly social. For details on maintenance refer to *Cyrtodactylus*. Keep the day temperatures slightly higher and provide ample climbing facilities. Has been bred successfully.
• *P. bibroni* (SMITH, 1846). Southern Africa. 18 cm. Numerous white and dark brown spots.
• *P. capensis* (SMITH, 1845). South Africa. Easily to 15 cm.
• *P. maculatus* GRAY, 1845. Eastern South Africa. 12 cm. Contrasting light and dark spots.

Pachymedusa DUELLMAN, 1968. Monotypic genus of the Hylidae. Western Mexico in savannahs to 1000 m elevation. Plump. The golden iris is covered with black reticulations; an elliptically vertical pupil. Webbing between the fingers and toes poorly developed.

Bush- and tree-dwellers. Active throughout the year, without a dormancy period during the 7-9 months of the dry season. The eggs are attached to plant leaves in ponds

Pachymedusa dacnicolor

and slow-flowing waters. Larval development occurs in water. The swimming position of larvae is obliquely upward, and they presumably are surface feeders on microorganisms.
• *P. dacnicolor* (COPE, 1864). To 10 cm. Green above, whitish yellow below.

Pachypalaminus THOMPSON, 1912. Taxon of doubtful level within the Hynobiidae, either a monotypic genus or a synonym or subgenus of *Hynobius*. Southern Japan at 1000 to 1500 m elevation. Compact. Head very large, wide, and flat. Distinct parotoid glands.

These animals live near mountain streams but enter water only during the breeding season. Reproduction occurs in May. Two strands of eggs, each 15-18 cm long and with about 15 eggs, are attached under rocks and logs. The larvae hatch in about 3-4 weeks, and metamorphosis occurs in the fall of the same year. Rarely kept in Europe. Maintenance as for *Hynobius*.
• *P. boulengeri* THOMPSON, 1912. Osaka, Shikoku, and Ky-

Pachymedusa dacnicolor

ushu. 16 cm. Dorsum uniformly black-brown, ventrum lighter.

Pachytriton BOULENGER, 1878. Monotypic genus of the Salamandridae. Southeastern China. In small flowing waters of foothills and mountains (100 to more than 800 m elevation). Eyes small. Distinct upper lib lobes. Tail compressed, paddle-like, rounded at the tip. Legs short, with stubby fingers and toes. A distinct gular fold.

Largely aquatic and somewhat comparable to the related genus *Euproctus*. Mating behavior is unknown. The spawning season is in late summer, when about 40-72 eggs per female are laid.

These newts should be kept in a semisterile aquarium decorated with rocks and with a shallow water level. Temperatures around 15° C. are satisfactory.
▪ *P. breviceps* (SAUVAGE, 1876). 14-18 cm. Brown-black above, ventrally yellow to orange-red with an irregular pattern of black spots usually forming an interrupted median stripe.

Padangia WERNER, 1924. Monotypic genus of the Colubridae, Calamarinae. Sumatra.
▪ *P. pulchra* WERNER, 1924.

Pair-bonding: Permanent monogamy between two organisms, which presupposes individual recognition and contact maintenance between both partners. Such firm pair-bonding is unknown among amphibians and reptiles. However, sometimes they may live together for long periods (e. g., *Lacerta*) and jointly occupy a territory. Usually partner relationships are very loose and are limited to direct involvement in activities related to reproduction.

Palearctic: Zoogeographic region that belongs to the Holarctic and includes all of Europe, North Africa to the southern edge of the Sahara, the entire Near East, and Asia except the tropical southern portion. It is bordered to the southwest by the Ethiopian and to the southeast by the Oriental, with which it forms a mixing zone—especially in southern China—with this purely tropical region.

Corresponding to the enormous size and the large climatic differences (Arctic to subtropic, marine climate to continental climate, variable amounts and distribution of precipitation), there are numerous types of vegetation pres-

Palearctic: Amur Basin, U.S.S.R.

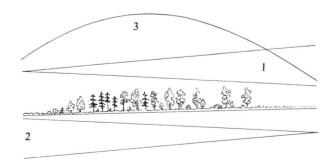

Palearctic: Schematic North-South profile through eastern Europe. Left to right: tundra, wooded tundra, taiga, mixed forest, deciduous forest, wooded steppe, steppe, desert.
1 Increase in evaporation rate, vegetation size, sunlight, and mid-year temperature; 2 decrease in groundwater available for vegetation; 3 amount of precipitation (maximum in mixed forest zone)

ent. Non-tropic forms of the arboreal, eremial, and tundral are prominent, including the taiga, steppes, deciduous forests, semideserts, and deserts. A more or less well-defined temperature-dependent seasonal climate is typical (in contrast to seasons in the tropics that are detemined by amounts of precipitation). Seasonal temperature differences are particularly pronounced in the continental climate region; winters are generally so cold that all herptiles from the Palearctic should preferably be given or must have a winter dormancy period.

The herpetofauna is mainly concentrated in the southern regions of the Palearctic. Important refuges and distribution centers of great species diversity are, among others, the Mediterranean, Sahara, Caucasus and Caspian regions, Iranian and Turkestanian regions, Mongolia, the Himalayas, Manchuria, western China, eastern China, and southern Japan. The number of species strongly declines northward and away from these nuclear areas. The northernmost reptile species are *Emys orbicularis* at 57° N., *Lacerta agilis* (62° N.), *Anguis fragilis* (64° N.), *Natrix natrix* (65° N.); the Polar Circle is transgressed by *Vipera berus* (67° N.) and *Lacerta vivipara* (70° N.). Among the amphibians that have moved across the Polar Circle are *Hynobius keyserlingi* (winter temperatures down to -66° C.) and *Rana temporaria* (71° N., which—on the world scale—make this species the northernmost herptile).

Among the endemic families and subfamilies the Palearctic contains only the Pelodytidae (family status rather doubtful) and the Hynobiidae. Almost endemic are the

Discoglossidae, which outside the Palearctic occur only as one genus in the Philippines and Borneo (Kalimantan). Great diversity is reached by the Salamandridae and Lacertidae in the Palearctic.

Paleosuchus GRAY, 1862. Smooth-fronted Caimans. Genus of the Alligatoridae. Tropical South America. 2 species. Smallest of the living crocodilians, maximum length 1.5 m. In contrast to the related genera *Caiman* and *Melanosuchus*, there are only 4 teeth on each side of the premaxilla. Snout relatively long, wedge-shaped. Iris chocolate brown (unique in family). The forehead lacks ridges. Occipital bucklers are in 1-2 cross rows, the nuchal bucklers usually arranged in 5 rows. Abdominal plates are large, strongly keratinized, and in 17-19 rows, the central cross row with 10-12 scales. Dorsally dark brown, the abdomen more or less covered with dark spots.

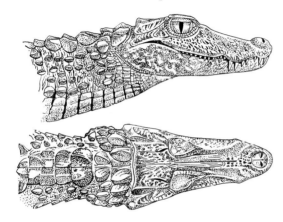

Paleosuchus palpebrosus

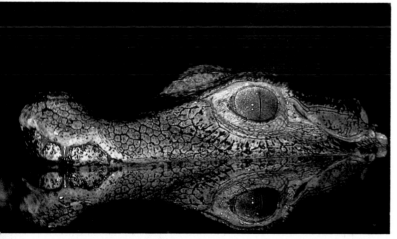

Paleosuchus palpebrosus

Exact distribution and biology are insufficiently known, but they are mainly crepuscular and nocturnal. The diet consists mainly of aquatic molluscs, crustaceans, and fish.

Endangered. There have been a few successful captive breedings. *P. trigonatus* has an incubation period of 115 days at 28-32° C.
- *P. palpebrosus* (CUVIER, 1807). Dwarf Caiman. Orinoco and Amazon Basin, southward to 20° S. To 1.5 m. Head with distinct eyebrow-like ridges and a sharp cheek ridge; usually with 2 rows of occipital bucklers.
- *P. trigonotus* (SCHNEIDER, 1801). Smooth-fronted Caiman. Orinoco and Amazon Basin, southward to 10° S. To

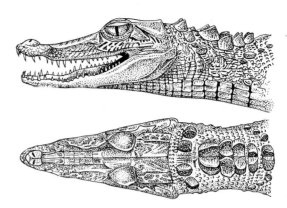

Paleosuchus trigonatus

1.25 m. Head without distinct cheek ridges, the occipital bucklers usually only in 1 row.

Pallas, Peter Simon (1741-1811): German zoologist and physician to the Russian Imperial court. His *Journey through various Provinces of the Russian Empire* (3 volumes, 1771-1776) and his *Zoographia Rosso-Asiatica* (1811) form the basis for the later herpetological work by Strauch and Nikolsky on Russian herpetology.

Palmatogecko ANDERSSON, 1908. Monotypic genus of the Gekkonidae. Southwest Africa in fog-shrouded deserts (Namib). 12 cm. Slender, the tail less than snout-vent

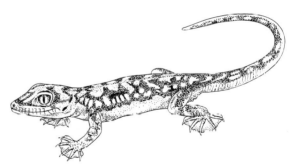

Palmatogecko rangei

length. Toes webbed (for "sand swimming"?). Pupil vertical. Skin very delicate, transparent.

Nocturnal ground-dwellers in loose sand. The diet consists mainly of termites.

Maintenance is somewhat problematic. It is essential to keep in mind that temperature differences in coastal deserts are relatively small and there is massive dew formation. Refer to *Teratoscincus*.
- *P. rangei* ANDERSSON, 1908. Namib Sand Gecko. Reddish brown with light spots.

Palmatorappia AHL, 1927. Monotypic genus of the Ranidae. Solomon Islands. Head broad. The fingers and toes are strongly flattened, broad, with large adhesive discs and well developed webbing.

Mode of life unknown. Presumably deposits eggs under rocks in mountain streams. For details on maintenance refer to *Petropedetes*.
- *P. salomonis* (STERNFELD, 1920). To 3 cm. Gray-green, the ventral area creamy, the hands and feet yellow.

Paludarium: Sometimes also used for a rain-forest terrarium, but here applied to vivariums that are simultaneously aquariums and terrariums, the terrarium section depicting a densely planted rain-forest habitat. Paludariums have a very high esthetic display value, but their maintenance is often expensive. Only very large terrariums can be used as paludariums. Generally the front for its entire length is used as the aquarium part, changing into the land section toward the back. Densely planted epiphyte logs can be suspended above the water.

In regard to ventilation and heating, the same prerequistes as outlined for rain-forest terrariums are also applicable here. Due to the large open water surface in a paludarium there are rarely any problems with maintaining an adequate humidity level. If there is a steep temperature gradient between the paludarium and the ambient room temperature, fresh air should be directed along the front glass, thus preventing condensation. For tall paludariums with a deep water section simple illumination from above is no longer sufficient and an additional fluorescent tube must be suspended directly above the water.

Paludariums are not particularly well-suited for turtles, crocodilians, giant snakes, and large lizards; simple aqua-terrariums are more suitable for these animals.

Large paludariums generally offer optimal environmental conditions for many small rain-forest animals. However, breeding is often problematic under such conditions because the eggs often can not be found. Smaller terrariums with less decorative material are often more useful for that purpose.

Plants suitable for aqua-terrariums and paludariums:
Water plants: *Pistia.*

Swamp and shore plants: *Acorus, Acrostichum, Anubias, Hygrophila, Lasia, Ophiopogon, Reineckea.*

The actual land section of the paludarium can be planted with plants listed for the rain-forest terrarium.

Paludicola: see *Physalaemus,* genus.

Palustrial: Inhabiting swamps.

Panaspis COPE, 1868. Genus of the Scincidae (*Leiolopisma* Group). Africa south of the Sahara. About 25 species. In tropical rain forests and damp savannahs. 10 to 20 cm. In appearance similar to *Ablepharus,* but with movable or only incompletely fused lower eyelids, with a window.

Ground-dwellers. Maintenance as for *Ablepharus,* but damper and without substantial temperature reduction at night.
▪ *P. cabindae* (BOCAGE, 1966).

Pandanaceae: Screw Pines. Family of the Liliatae. West Africa to Southeast Asia. 3 genera, about 880 species. In forests and coastal regions in wet or damp locations. Trees, bushes, or lianas. Only small specimens are useful for terrarium purposes.
▪ *Freycinetia* GAUD. Tall climber, richly branched. Formerly a popular terrarium plant, today only rarely cultivated.
▪ *Pandanus* SOLAND. ex PARKINS. Screw Pines. More than 250 species. Recommended. Upright, non-climbing woody plants. *P. pygmaeus* THOU is low and richly branched; height 60 cm; Madagascar. *P. stenophyllus* KURZ is from Java.

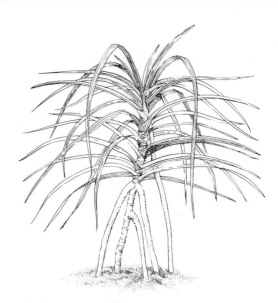

Pandanus graminifolia

Pantodactylus DUMERIL and BIBRON, 1839. Genus of the Teiidae. 2 species. Lowlands of central South America east of the Andes to northern Argentina. To 10 cm. Slender. Brown. Mode of life like *Bachia.*
▪ *P. schreibersi* (WIEGMANN, 1834).

Papusaurus, subgenus: see *Varanus*, genus.

Paracalotes BOURRET, 1939. Monotypic genus of the Agamidae. Known only from the type locality in Southeast Asia. Similar to *Calotes.*
▪ *P. boilani* BOURRET, 1939.

Paracophyla MILLOT and GUIBE, 1951. Monotypic genus of the Microhylidae. Madagascar. Can be distinguished from *Cophyla* only on the basis of dentition (*Paracophyla* lacks vomerine teeth). It has been found in the leaf axis of *Pandanus* and *Crinum.*
▪ *P. tuberculata* MILLOT and GUIBE, 1951. Perinet Forest, Madagascar. 1.7 cm. Brown-black with darker crossbands.

Paradelma KINGHORN, 1926. Monotypic genus of the Pygopodidae. Northeastern Australia. Blunt head. Tympanum visible. Smooth scales.
Biology virtually unknown.
▪ *P. orientalis* (GUENTHER, 1876). 30-40 cm. A light crossband followed by a dark one immediately behind the head.

Parademansia KINGHORN, 1955. Monotypic genus of the Elapidae. Australia. Closely related to *Oxyuranus.* 2.5 m. Slender. Brown with an irregular pattern of spots.

A rare diurnal venomous snake. Biology virtually unknown. According to the latest pharmacological evaluation the venom of this snake is the most effective terrestrial snake venom known to science.
▪ *P. microlepidota* (McCOY, 1879). Fierce Snake. Arid southwestern Queensland to western New South Wales. Dangerously venomous.

Paragehyra ANGEL. 1929. Monotypic genus of the Gekkonidae. Madagascar. Little known.
▪ *P. petiti* ANGEL, 1929.

Parahydrophis BURGER and NATSUNO, 1975. Monotypic

genus of the Hydrophiidae, Hydrophiinae. Gulf of Carpentaria, New Guinea and Australia. Closely related to *Ephalophis* and formerly in that genus.
- *P. mertoni* (ROUX, 1910). 50 cm. 40-50 crossbands, black or grayish.

Paramesotriton CHIANG, 1935. Warty Newts. Genus of the Salamandridae. Border region of the southeastern Palearctic and northeastern Orient in North Vietnam and China. About 5 species. Found in flowing waters. Similar to a large *Triturus*, but without a dorsal crest. Skin very rough. The tail is long and laterally compressed. Bright and contrasting ventral colors. Males in courtship coloration have a distinctive whitish or bluish band in the tail.

Largely aquatic, *P. deloustali* prefers cold (11° C.) mountain streams. *P. chinensis* lives in turbulently flowing small rivers and also is tied to cool water. In contrast, *P. hongkongensis* is an aquatic form of small, densely overgrown flowing water at 17 to 20° C.; reproduction occurs during the cool season. Little is known about reproduction in the other species. Mating behavior is largely similar to *Triturus*.

For maintenance of the coldwater species see *Euproctus asper*. *P. hongkongensis* can be kept like *Cynops ensicauda* in a well-planted warm-water aquarium.
- *P. chinensis* (GRAY, 1859). Chinese Warty Newt. Delta region of the Yangtze. To 15 cm. Olive to dark brown, the ventral region bluish black with orange dots.
- *P. deloustali* (BOURRET, 1934). Vietnamese Warty Newt. Known only from the type locality near Hanoi. 20 cm.

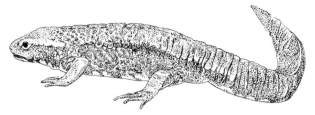

Paramesotriton deloustali

Dark olive above, orange-red below with an irregular black reticulated pattern.
- *P. hongkongensis* (MYERS and LEVITON, 1962). Hong Kong Warty Newt. Hong Kong. 14 cm. Olive to chocolate brown, ventrally black or bluish black, with large orange spots.

Paramo: Type of vegetation of the equatorial permanently wet high Andes above 3,500 m. Rich with grasses and tufted shrubs. A large number of foggy days (in excess of 300 per year) on which the midday temperatures do not rise significantly above 10° C. Light frosts are common at night. The *paramo* is inhabited by significantly more animal species than in the adjacent southern *puna*, for instance frogs of the families Bufonidae, Atelopidae, Dendrobatidae, Hylidae, Leptodactylidae, *Bolitoglossa* salamanders, as well as iguanids and several teiid species.

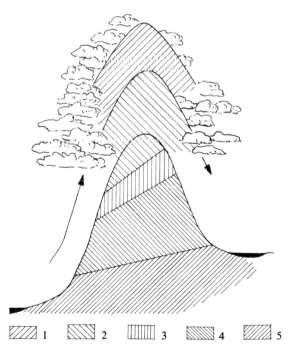

Schematic vegetational profile of the equatorial Andes. 1 *Paramo;* 2 cold *montana;* 3 warm *montana;* 4 dry forest; 5 cactus and thorn-bush savannah

Paramesotriton hongkongensis

Paranaja LOVERIDGE, 1944. Monotypic genus of the Elapidae. Tropical West Africa. To 1.55 m. Similar to the genus *Pseudohaje*, characterized by the few large dorsal scales and large eyes. Brown with oblique dark crossbands.

Venomous snakes, more or less arboreal. Biology and venom potency hardly known. Maintain in a tropical forest terrarium similar to *Dendroaspis*.
- *P. multifasciata* (WERNER, 1902).

Venom effects unknown. Maintenance as for *Micrurus*.
- *P. hedigeri* ROUX, 1934. Hediger's Snake. Known from Bougainville Island, Solomon Islands.

Parapostolepis LEMA, 1967. Monotypic genus of the Colubridae, Natricinae. Brasil, Rio Grande do Sul. Closely related to *Ptychophis*. Found in slow-flowing and standing waters. About 60 cm. Head distinctly set off, with large opisthoglyphic fangs. Dorsal scales keeled and shingled.

Mainly aquatic, predators on frogs and fish. Maintenance as for Natricinae, Group 3. Caution: Venomous bites possible.
- *P. meyersi* LEMA, 1967.

Pararhabdophis BOURRET, 1934. Monotypic genus of the Colubridae, Natricinae. Indo-China. Closely related to *Rhabdophis* and *Pseudoxenodon*. About 90 cm.
- *P. chapaensis* BOURRET, 1934.

Pararhadinea BOETTGER, 1898. Monotypic genus of the Colubridae, Lycodontinae. Madagascar in tropical rain forest. 25 cm. The head has a projecting rostral scale and small eyes. Burrowing snakes.
- *P. melanogaster* BOETTGER, 1898. Nossi-Be Island, northern Madagascar.

Parasitism: Type of relationship in which one animal lives by feeding at the expense of another organism that serves as the host. Massive parasite infestations may cause diseases in the host and may lead to the death of the host.

Paratelmatobius LUTZ and CARVALHO, 1958. Genus of the Leptodactylidae. Coastal region of the state of Rio de Janeiro, Brasil. 2 species. Pupil horizontal. Tympanum not visible. Legs short. Toes completely webbed. Vocal sac absent. Mode of life and developmental biology unknown.
- *P. gaigeae* (COCHRAN, 1938) (= *pictiventris* LUTZ and CARVALHO, 1958). 2 cm.
- *P. lutzi* LUTZ and CARVALHO, 1958. 3 cm.

Pareas WAGLER, 1830. Asian Snail-eating Snakes. Genus of the Colubridae, Pareinae. Southeast Asia (southern Himalayan slopes through Indo-China to the Indo-Australian Archipelago. About 12 to 15 species, some polytypic. To 90 cm. Dinstinguished from the closely related *Hoplopeltura* by the presence of paired subcaudal scales. The body in *P. margeritophorus* and *P. macularius* is not as distinctly later-

Paramo with *Espeletia*

Paraphyletic: Group of taxa derived from a single original species but not including all species derived from the orginal form. Thus, a paraphyletic group does not exactly reflect the genealogical relationships of the taxa and therefore is not allowed in the cladistic system of systematics. Amphibia and Reptilia are paraphyletic groups.

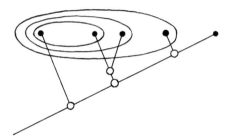

Schematic diagram of a paraphyletic group

Parapistocalamus ROUX, 1934. Monotypic genus of the Elapidae. In tropical forests to 600 m elevation. To 60 cm. Head with a blunt, short snout and small eyes. Dorsum dark, iridescent, the sides and belly whitish.

Nocturnal venomous burrowing snakes. They seem to be specialized to feed on snail eggs, which is reflected in the reduced number of teeth (as in other egg-eating snakes. However, stomach samples have shown only soil particles.

Pareas formosensis

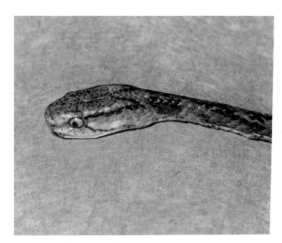

Pareas formosensis

ally compressed as in other species. Coloration and markings are mainly shades of brown; some species have distinct neck markings in the shape of an X (*P. monticola, P. carinatus*).

Egg-layers, 2 to 9 eggs. Feed largely on land snails.
• *P. carinatus* WAGLER, 1830. Thailand southward to the Indo-Australian Archipelago (Lombok). 2 subspecies. Lowland rain forests.
• *P. margeritophorus* (JAN, 1866). Southern China, Hainan, and Indo-China to Malaya. Monsoon forests as well as montane forests to 1,500 m. In contrast to the other species mentioned, the dorsal scales lack keels.
• *P. monticola* (CANTOR, 1839). Eastern Himalayas. Montane rain forests. The most frequent species in the area.

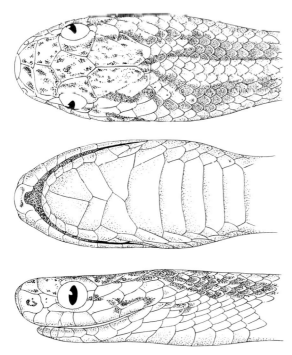

Pareas boulengeri

Pareinae: Asian Snail-eating Snakes. Subfamily of the Colubridae. Southeast Asia. 2 genera: *Pareas* with 12-15 species and the monotypic *Haplopeltura*. Morphologically and biologically similar to the Neotropical subfamily Dipsadinae. Found in monsoon forests, montane forests, and rain forests. To 80 cm. More or less laterally compressed.

The short, blunt head is markedly set off from the body and has very large eyes with vertical pupils. The lower jaws are firmly attached and have large fangs at the front. Due to the absence of the chin furrow and the presence of large fused scales on the ventral side of the head, the rigid jaws are superbly adapted to feeding on snails, which the snakes can readily extract from their shells. Nocturnal tree snakes. Egg-layers. Maintenance as for Dipsadinae.

Parhoplophryne BARBOUR and LOVERIDGE, 1928. Monotypic genus of the Microhylidae. East Africa in perpetually damp montane forests. Related to *Hoplophryne*, but without hearing and vocalization ability. Feet not webbed and without adhesive discs. Undersides of toes with distinct tubercles; 2 metatarsal tubercles.

Presumed to be largely ground-dwelling, possibly climbing about in bushes. Larval development occurs in wet locations or in tiny water accumulations such as a leaf axis. For details on care refer to *Hoplophryne*.
• *P. usambaricus* BARBOUR and LOVERIDGE, 1928. Usambara Mountains. 2.5 cm. Purplish gray, darker along the sides, the limbs with deep purple spots. A white band from the eyes to the base of the arm.

Parietal organ: Parapineal organ, parietal eye, third eye. A dorsal protrusion of the diencephalon, an unpaired organ that is capable—to a limited extent—of perceiving light. It occurs in tuataras and in lizards of various families. The parietal organ has a cup-shaped retina with a lens-shaped structure; the cavity is filled with a gelatinous substance. Light can penetrate through an opening in the roof of the skull (foramen parietale) and a pigmentless window in the interparietal scale to the sensory cells, which in many cases are connected to the diencephalon by a fine nerve.

Behind the parietal organ is a further protrusion of the diencephalon, the pineal organ (also originally capable of perceiving light), which becomes the epiphysis in amphibians, reptiles, birds, and mammals. Crocodilians do not have a parietal organ, and the epiphysis is also absent. Turtles and snakes possess only the epiphysis.

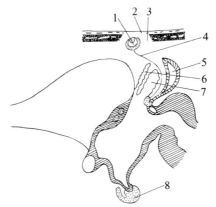

Parietal organ: Longitudinal section through the parietal complex of a lizard. 1 Parietal organ; 2 window in interparietal shield; 3 foramen parietale; 4 nerve of parietal organ; 5 epiphysis; 6 paraphysis; 7 dorsal sac; 8 hypophysis

Parker, Hampton Wilder (1891-1968): British herpetologist at the British Museum, London. *A monograph of the frogs of the family Microhylidae* (1934), *Snakes* (1965), and, jointly with Alice Grandison, *Snakes—a natural history* (1977).

Paroxyrhopus SCHENKEL, 1900. Genus of the Colubridae, Xenodontinae. South America, from the Amazon Basin to Mato Grosso and Paraguay. 3 species. Included in the Natricinae by some systematists. In tropical forests of different types. To 75 cm. Enlarged posterior teeth are in the upper jaw.

Ground snakes. Little is known about their biology, which could resemble that of *Oxyrhopus*.
- *P. atropunctatus* AMARAL, 1923. Minas Gerais, Brasil.
- *P. reticulatus* SCHENKEL, 1900. Paraguay.
- *P. undulatus* (JENSEN, 1900). Amazon Basin and Mato Grosso.

Parthenogenesis: Form of reproduction whereby an egg cell starts to develop without previous fertilization by a sperm cell; virgin birth. Within the reptiles there are several parthenogenetic forms among Caucasus rock lizards (genus *Lacerta*) and among the North American race runners (genus *Cnemidophorus*). In these species males do not occur or are very rare. The occurrence of natural parthenogenesis is also found in the following genera: *Gymnophthalmus, Leposoma* (family Teiidae); *Hemidactylus, Lepidodactylus, Gehyra* (family Gekkonidae); *Leiolepis* (family Agamidae); *Brookesia* (family Chamaeleonidae); *Lepidophyma* (family Xantusiidae); *Basiliscus* (family Iguanidae); and others. Parthenogenetic populations have also been observed among some forms of the salamander genus *Ambystoma*.

Parvicaecilia TAYLOR, 1968. Genus of the Caeciliidae. Colombia. 2 species. To 27 cm. 106-157 primary folds, numerous secondary folds. Very tiny scales. Tentacle close to eye. Only 1 row of teeth in the lower jaw.
- *P. nicefori* (BARBOUR, 1925). Colombia (Caribbean region). To 27 cm. Gray to gray-brown, the head and anterior abdominal region yellowish brown (when preserved).

Parvimolge TAYLOR, 1944. Genus of the Plethodontidae. Referred to as a dwarf salamander, together with *Thorius*. Mexico. To 5 cm. Terrestrial or arboreal, in Bromeliaceae. Hands and feet nearly completely webbed. The status of this genus is confused. 3 species have normally been assigned to it, but it has recently been restricted to its type species.
- *P. praecellens* RAAB, 1955. Veracruz. To 6 cm. Brown. (Now is *Pseudoeurycea*.)
- *P. richardi* TAYLOR, 1949. Costa Rica. (Now in *Nototriton*, a genus made from part of *Chiropterotriton*.)
- *P. townsendi* (DUNN, 1922). Veracruz. To 5 cm. Lacquer black, with large paired green spots.

Pedostibes GUENTHER, 1875. Asian Tree Toads. Genus of the Bufonidae. Tropical Southeast Asia. 6 species in tropical rain forests. Toad-like, the skin covered with warts and spines. Wide, worn-looking adhesive discs on the tips of the fingers and toes. Tympanum and parotoid glands usually present (absent in *P. maculatus*). Larvae with a wide subterminal suction mouth.

Good climbers that live along the banks of small rivers, partially on the ground and also in the lower reaches of the surrounding vegetation. The diet consists mainly of ants.

Pedostibes hosei

The egg masses—similar to *Bufo*—consist of strands with numerous small, strongly pigmented eggs and are deposited in moderately flowing sections of a stream or river.

They should be kept in a tropical rain-forest terrarium with a water bowl, at temperatures from 25 to 29° C. The diet should consist of ants, but various other small insects are taken.
- *P. hosei* (BOULENGER, 1892). Southern Thailand, Sumatra, Kalimantan lowlands. 10 cm (females), 5-8 cm (males). Dark brown to blackish above, females often with shades of purple and with yellow vermiform spots.
- *P. rugosus* INGER, 1958. Kalimantan, to 1000 m elevation. 9.5 cm (females), 5-8 cm (males). Brownish with a darker pattern.

Pelagic: Inhabiting the open waters of the ocean or large lakes. Truly pelagic animals live above the bottom and are free-swimming. The sea turtles and some sea snakes (*Pelamis*) are marine pelagics. There are no known freshwater pelagic herptiles.

Pelamis DAUDIN, 1803. Pelagic Sea Snakes. Monotypic genus of the Hydrophiidae, Hydrophiinae. Eastern coast of Africa to the western coast of tropical America, throughout the warm Indo-Pacific. Although *Pelamis* has been reported in the Panama Canal, there have been no observations in the Atlantic. To 1 m. These sea snakes deviate substantially in appearance and mode of life from all other sea snakes. The head is characteristically large, narrow, and distinctly elongated. This genus can open its mouth far wider than other sea snakes. The body is covered with hexagonal or rhomboidal scales that are not shingled. Black above, yellow below, the colors distinctly delineated along the flanks by a horizontal line. This pattern disappears on the paddle-shaped tail, where the yellow ventral coloration extends onto the dorsal side and is covered by spots arranged in wavy lines. Many variants of this pattern are known.

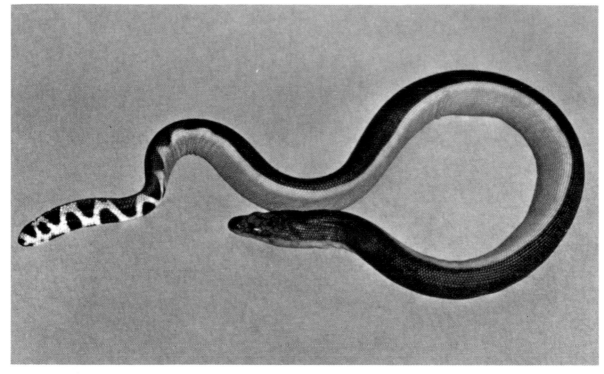

Pelamis platurus

Pelamis on the high seas drifts at the surface in a characteristic resting position with the head and tail hanging downward. If suitable prey (fish) approaches, it is suddenly lunged at. The venom is a highly potent neurotoxin and fatal bites have occurred. Captured specimens handled carefully in transit have survived in large marine aquariums for several months.
▪ *P. platurus* (LINNAEUS, 1766). Yellow-bellied Sea Snake.

Pellaea LINK. Genus of the Filicatae. A fern from non-tropical regions of South America, South Africa, and New Zealand. Can survive droughts but is susceptible to excess wetness.
▪ *P. atropurpurea* (L.) LINK. On limestone. To 25 cm. With proper winter protection it can be cultivated in an open-air terrarium.
▪ *P. falcata* (R. BR.) FEE. New Zealand. Leaves to 3 cm.
▪ *P. rotundifolia* (G. FORST.) HOOK. New Zealand. Leaves 20 to 30 cm.

Pellaea rotundifolia

Pellionia GAUD. Genus of the Urticaceae, the nettles. Tropical Asia. About 30 species. Creeping shrubs that require sufficient moisture and warmth, temperatures not below 18° C. Can be cultured as hanging plants or as creepers. Reproduction is by means of cuttings.
▪ *P. repens* (LOUR.) MERR. Close to the ground. Leaves 3 to 5 cm, olive-green.
▪ *P. pulchra* BR. Leaves blackish brown.

Pelobates WAGLER, 1830. Eurasian Spadefoot Toads, Garlic Toads. Genus of the Pelobatidae. Western Palearctic. 4 species. Compact. Small warts in the middle of patches of smooth skin. Eyes large and protruding, the pupils vertical. Tympanum barely visible or completely covered over. No protruding parotoid glands. Fingers free, the toes completely webbed. Only the inner metatarsal tubercles are present, developed as keratinous sharp-edged spades. Excited specimens can give off a garlic odor. Variably spotted with green to brown on a light tan background. Larvae large, reaching 18 cm during over-wintering, but shrinking considerably during metamorphosis. Anal opening median in larvae; respiratory aperture on the left, pointing obliquely upward and posteriorly.

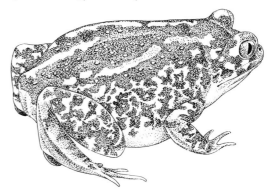

Pelobates cultripes

Outside of the brief breeding period these toads are nocturnal ground-dwellers that require lots of heat. During the day they hide in self-dug burrows that are often nearly vertical, extending down to a meter or so. Not territorial, individual specimens will burrow where they find themselves at dawn. These toads move about only on warm nights. They are only found in areas where there are large areas of loose, sandy, easily warmed up substrate. Breeding usually occurs during early spring. The eggs are released during inguinal amplexus by the partners in shallow water. The eggs are small, up to 1000 per mating. The larvae hatch after barely a week, initially forming swarms but later becoming more solitary.

Due to the largely cryptic mode of life, they really are

Pelobates fuscus

only suitable for specialist hobbyists. These spadefoots should be kept in slightly damp terrariums with a loose substrate at least 10 cm deep. There should be moderate humdity and a temperature gradient to give the animals the opportunity to find the most suitable location in the terrarium. These toads will become tame quickly. The garlic odor will subside and the animals will emerge from their burrows even during the day to take food.
• *P. cultripes* (CUVIER, 1829). Western Spadefoot. Southwestern Europe. To 10 cm. Spade black.
• *P. fuscus* (LAURENTI, 1768). Common Spadefoot, Garlic Toad. Temperate Europe and western Asia. 2 subspecies. To 8 cm, usually smaller. Spade pale. A distinct swelling just behind the eyes.
• *P. syriacus* BOETTGER, 1889. Eastern Spadefoot, Syrian Spadefoot. 3 subspecies. *P. s. balcanicus* KARAMAN, 1928, occurs in the eastern Balkan Peninsula; the others are found in Asia Minor and the southern Caspian Sea region. Spade pale, with a black edge.
• *P. varaldi* PASTEUR, 1959. Moroccan Spadefoot. Northwestern Morocco. 7 cm. Spade as in *P. syriacus*.

Pelobatidae: Spadefoot Toads. Family of the Salientia. Considered here in the strictest sense, without *Pelodytes*. Usually toad-like and compact. Pupil vertical. Tympanum poorly visible or not (except possibly *Nesobia*, allegedly with a horizontal pupil and distinctly visible tympanum). Fingers always free, the toes more or less extensively webbed. Inner metatarsal tubercle often developed into a digging spade. Spadefoots are burrowers, except *Nesobia*, which deviates from all other genera by its more or less arboreal behavior.

The Pelobatidae are usually nocturnal, light-shy frogs.

Many breed at night and deposit their spawn in dark areas under rocks and driftwood. Amplexus is inguinal, a primitive character. The larvae of some species often are of enormous size (*Pelobates*) or have very large funnel mouths (*Megophrys*).

Systematic review:
• Subfamily Pelobatinae (procoelic vertebrae; Holarctic): *Pelobates* and *Scaphiopus*.
• Subfamily Megophryninae (amphicoelic vertebrae, free intervertebral discs; Oriental): *Leptobrachium*, *Megophrys*, *Nesobia*, *Oreolalax*, *Scutiger*, and *Vibrissaphora*.

Pelochelys GRAY, 1864. Giant Soft-shell Turtles. Monotypic genus of the Trionychidae. Eastern India, Indo-China to southern China, Hainan, Sundas, Philippines, and New Guinea. In large rivers, also appearing in the brackish water regions of river deltas. Leathery carapace oval, to 1.3 m. Plastron with 4 large callosities. Head very short and rounded.

Hardly any captive maintenance data are available, but probably as for *Trionyx*.
• *P. bibroni* (OWEN, 1853).

Pelochelys bibroni

Pelodytes BONAPARTE, 1838. Parsley Frogs. Genus of doubtful family membership; here considered Pelodytidae, but often put in Pelobatidae. Southwestern Europe, Caucasus. 2 species. 5 cm. Relatively slender. Skin with warts. Snout flat, long. Eyes protruding. Pupil vertical. Tympanum hidden or poorly visible. Palatine teeth arranged in 2 separate groups. Courting males with dark nuptial pads on

Pelodytes punctatus

the first and second fingers, lower and upper arm, chin, chest, abdomen, and toes. Soft vocalizing ability, even under water, but no external vocal sac. Throat dark. Larvae similar to *Pelobates*, sometimes of giant size.

Largely nocturnal outside the breeding season (despite frequent reports to the contrary). Good jumpers and climbers, but essentially ground-dwellers that hide during the day in burrows, under rocks, and similar places. Individuals ready to mate enter water for a short period of time—they are good swimmers and divers—but the breeding period of one population can extend from spring to fall. Spawning habitats include standing, densely overgrown waters with muddy bottoms. The larvae hatching at the end of spring metamorphose in summer; the fall hatch overwinters in the water.

Pelodytes should be kept in an unheated, damp terrarium with bathing facilities. Breeding can be attempted in a spacious aqua-terrarium or under open-air outdoor conditions. The diet should consist mainly of insects, especially flies. A winter dormancy period is not necessary; cool maintenance (10 to 15° C.) for several weeks is adequate.
- *P. caucasicus* BOULENGER, 1896. Caucasus Parsley Frog, Caucasus Mud Diver. Northern Caucasus and western Transcaucasus. 5 cm.
- *P. punctatus* (DAUDIN, 1803). Common Parsley Frog, Western Mud Diver. Southwestern Europe northward to Belgium and eastward to northwestern Italy. 5 cm. Ash gray to olive with delicate green spots, abdomen whitish.

Pelodytidae: Family of the Salientia. Southwestern Palearctic. One genus, *Pelodytes*. In contrast to the closely related family Pelobatidae, more slender and smaller, without spades, the toes not distinctly webbed but with fused astragalus and calcaneus, and with modified inguinal amplexus (clasping grip only with front legs, hind legs of male parallel to each other on the abdomen of the female, pointing forward). These differences are not acceptable as family characteristics by many systematists who instead place *Pelodytes* in the Pelobatidae.

Pelomedusa WAGLER, 1830. Helmeted Terrapins. Monotypic genus of the Pelomedusidae. Central and South Africa and Madagascar in all types of fresh water. To 25 cm. A flat, unicolored carapace and a relatively small, rigid plastron.

When temporary bodies of water dry out the animals migrate overland in search of water or they simply burrow

Pelomedusa subrufa

into the ground. Undemanding and easy to keep. Can be kept outdoors during the summer months.
- *P. subrufa* (LACEPEDE, 1788). Helmeted Terrapin. Apart from *Pelusios*, the most widely distributed freshwater turtle in Africa.

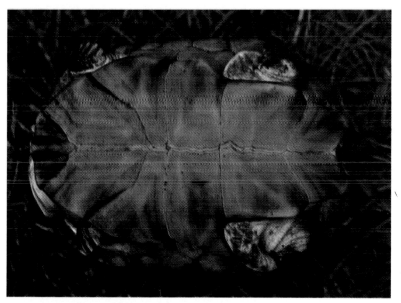

Pelomedusa subrufa

Pelomedusidae: Helmeted Side-necks. Family of the Pleurodira. Africa, Madagascar, and South America. Genera: *Erymnochelys, Pelomedusa, Pelusios, Peltocephalus, Podocnemis*. Found from very small bodies of water to jungle streams and large rivers. Fossil records dating back to the Cretaceous in Africa, Americas, Europe, and Asia. Small to large freshwater turtles. The plastron has an additional median pair of bones, the mesoplastrals. In *Pelusios* the plastron has a movable anterior flap. The nuchal scute is absent in all species.

Some genera include typical river turtles (*Peltocephalus, Podocnemis, Erymnochelys*) that haul-out only on sandbars or river banks in order to sunbathe or lay their eggs. These particular species are mainly herbivorous. The species of the other genera live in various bodies of water, including temporary ones (*Pelomedusa, Pelusios*) and are mainly carnivorous. When the water dries up they either burrow and estivate or they migrate—predominantly at night—to other bodies of water.

Maintenance of the first group of Pelomedusidae requires a spacious aquarium with ample swimming room. For large species (as of *Podocnemis*) this can really only be satisfactorily accomplished in zoo aquariums or in tropical outdoor enclosures. *Pelomedusa* and *Pelusios* are undemanding and hardy and can be recommended to hobbyists.

Pelophryne BARBOUR, 1938. Genus of the Bufonidae. Tropical Southeast Asia. 6 species, some difficult to distinguish from each other. In tropical rain forests and cloud forests. At the most to 4 cm, usually smaller. Slender. Skin rough or covered with small warts. Head flat and with a long snout. Tympanum usually distinctly visible (exception: *P. breviceps*). Fingers and toes short and thick, more or less joined by fleshy skin. Some species have well-developed, anteriorly truncated adhesive discs. Larvae, as far as known, have a greatly reduced feeding tract, especially the mouthparts, and the intestines hardly spiral.

Ground-dwellers or climbers in low vegetation. In respect to their developmental biology they are independent of water and thus deviate in this respect quite substantially from typical toads. Only a few, but very large eggs (up to 20) per clutch are deposited in small rainwater accumulations (e. g., in puddles and in phytothelms) where the larvae feed exclusively on their yolk. Development is very rapid.

Maintenance and attempted breeding can be tried in a rain-forest terrarium at temperatures of about 26° C. for lowland forms and 22° C. for mountain-dwellers.

▪ *P. breviceps* (PETERS, 1867). Moluccas, Sumatra, and Kalimantan to the Philippines. Elevations to more than 2,000 m. 2.5 cm. Variably brown, back usually lighter than flanks.

▪ *P. misera* (MOCQUARD, 1890). Kalimantan, usually at elevations from 2,000 to 3,000 m. 2 cm. Deep blackish, sometimes with white spots.

Peltocephalus DUMERIL and BIBRON, 1835. Dumeril's Helmeted Turtles. Monotypic genus of the Pelomedusidae. Northeastern South America in large rivers. To 50 cm. No longitudinal groove between the eyes as in *Podocnemis*. Forefeet with 5 claws, hind feet with 4 claws.

Predominantly aquatic. Omnivorous, with a substantial amount of plants. Only juveniles are suitable for aquariums; adults can only be kept in large display facilities at zoos or public aquariums. Must be given a basking site.

▪ *P. dumeriliana* (SCHWEIGGER, 1812).

Pelusios WAGLER, 1830. African Black Turtles. Genus of the Pelomedusidae. South Africa, Madagascar, Mauritius, and Seychelles. About 8 species; systematics insufficiently researched. Found in different types of water. To 45 cm. Carapace evenly arched, usually blackish. Plastron with central hinge.

These very adaptable side-necks burrow into the substrate when the water dries up. They are very hardy when kept in an aqua-terrarium and can be maintained outdoors during the summer.

▪ *P. niger* (DUMERIL and BIBRON, 1835). West African Black Turtle. West Africa.

▪ *P. subniger* (LACEPEDE, 1788). East African Black Turtle. East Africa and offshore islands. Incubation takes 58 days at 28-30° C.

Peltocephalus dumeriliana

Pelusios subniger

Pelusios gabonensis

Pelusios adansoni

the large blood vessels (including the heart) in snakes and lizards. By feeding on prey containing the larvae (fish, amphibians, lizards, birds) and through cannibalism, the larvae reach the host bronchi, where they develop to sexual maturity. In other organs and to some degree in the lung, the larvae become encysted. Pneumonia occurs after secondary bacterial infections because the bacteria can find particularly suitable developmental conditions where the worms have caused tissue damage with their head hooks or mouthparts. The parasites alone apparently cause very little tissue reaction in the host, although their heads are solidly anchored into the tissue.

The relationships of the tongueworms is uncertain, although they are normally thought to be very degraded arthropods. They are not related to the helminth parasites.

Pelusios castaneus

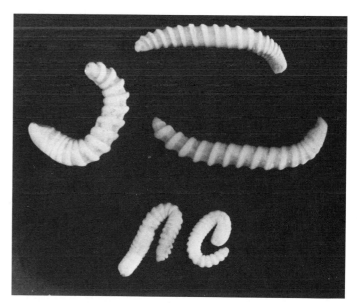

Pentastomida: 2 larvae of *Armillifer grandis* and 3 larvae of *A. armillatus*

▪ *P. sinuatus* (A. SMITH, 1838). Serrated Turtle. Eastern and southeastern Africa. 45 cm, the largest species of the genus. Posterior margin of carapace serrated.

Pentastomida: Linguatulids, Tongueworms. Worm-like parasites that—either as larvae or as 15 cm adult worms—live primarily in respiratory organs and less commonly in

Peperomia RUIZ and PAV. Dwarf Peppers. Genus of the Piperaceae. South America. Between 600 and 1000 species in rain forests. Low bushes, shrubs, or epiphytes with somewhat succulent shoot axis and leaves. They require ample light but must be protected against direct solar radiation. Temperature in excess of 18° C. Less demanding in

Peperomia rotundifolia

respect to humidity, so brief dry periods can be endured. Reproduction is by means of rooted cuttings.

• *P. argyreia* (MIQ.) E. MORR. Leaves 8-12 cm.

• *P. clusiaefolia* (JACQ.) HOOK. Grows upward. Thick, stiff leaves.

• *P. incana* (HAW.) A. DIETR. Thick wooly white leaves.

• *P. rubella* (HAW.) HOOK. Leaves about 1 cm, red underneath.

• *P. rotundifolia* (L.) DAHLST. Hanging plant with round leaves and thread-like shoots.

Perilepta BREMEK. (= *Strobilanthes*). Genus of the Acanthaceae. Southeast Asia. 8 species. Low bushes and shrubs. Repeated trimming assures richly branched plants.

• *P. dyerana* (MAST.) BREMEK. Leaves with a metallic sheen. Only young plants are decorative (cuttings will grow roots quickly with substrate heat). A shady location is essential for optimum leaf coloration.

Perochirus BOULENGER, 1885. Genus of the Gekkonidae. Philippines. 5 species in tropical forests. About 15 cm. Head barely set off. Pupil vertical. Toes short, with wide lamellae; inner finger rudimentary and clawless. Tail flattened, the margin finely serrated. Gray-brown.

Nocturnal. Little known.

• *P. ateles* (DUMERIL, 1856).

Peropus: see *Gehyra*, genus.

Peters, James A. (1922-1973): American herpetologist, curator of the herpetological section of the U.S. National Museum. *Dictionary of Herpetology* (1964); with Donoso-Barros, *Catalogue of the Neotropical Squamata. Part I, Snakes; Part II, Lizards and Amphisbaenians* (1970).

Peters, Wilhelm Carl Hartwig (1815-1883): German zoologist and physician, director of the Museum for Natural History, Berlin, and university professor. Worked on the herpetological results of the German Africa Expeditions in the 5 volumes of *Journey to Mozambique* (1852-1883). Author of numerous species.

Petropedetes REICHENOW, 1874. Genus of the Ranidae. Tropical western and central Africa. 6 species found primarily along flowing waters in mountain rain forests. Skin smooth to warty. Large adhesive discs on fingers and toes. Fingers free, the toes of most species with well-developed

webbing. Tympanum small, in *P. cameronensis*, *P. johnstoni*, and *P. newtoni* with bumps. Larvae have a very long tail (with barely noticeable crest) and inhabit flowing water only as early larvae that have a large suction mouth; after the development of legs they live on rocks even out of water.

Nocturnal, very shy. Excellent jumpers and climbers. Species with well-developed webbing lead a largely aquatic life. They prefer to remain along rocks on the banks or on rocks in flowing water. In contrast, *P. johnstoni* and *P. newtoni* prefer to remain on damp jungle floors.

Despite more or less strong ties to mountain streams, keeping these animals is relatively easy when they are kept in a planted water and rock terrarium with tropical temperatures and high humidity. Frequent spraying with water simulates the preferred locations of some species in the splash zone near waterfalls.

• *P. cameronensis* REICHENOW, 1874. Nigeria, Cameroons. To 5 cm. Dark.

• *P. johnstoni* (BOULENGER, 1887). Cameroons. To 7.5 cm.

• *P. palmipes* BOULENGER, 1905. Cameroons. To 5 cm.

Petrosaurus BOULENGER, 1885. Baja Rock Lizards. Genus of the Iguanidae. Lower California and adjacent islands. 2 species. Closely related to *Streptosaurus*, and that genus is sometimes considered a subgenus. Rocky dry regions. Easily to 20 cm. Slender, flattened. 3 or 4 black collar bands behind head. Distinguished from *Uta* primarily by small, unkeeled scales even in the middle of the dorsal region.

Diurnal ground-dwellers. For maintenance see *Sceloporus*.

• *P. repens* (VAN DENBURGH, 1895). Short-nosed Rock Lizard. Southern Baja California except in the Cape region. 20 cm.

Petrosaurus thalassinus

Phaeognathus HIGHTON, 1961. Red Hills Salamanders. Monotypic genus of the Plethodontidae. Alabama, USA. In cool, damp ravines. Elongated, with 20-22 costal grooves, the tail long. Uniformly brown. The largest woodland salamander.

A strict burrower hiding during the day and appearing near the surface at night in the burrow opening but retreating quickly when disturbed. Treat much as *Desmognathus*, but not aquatic at any stage.

■ *P. hubrichti* HIGHTON, 1961. Red Hills Salamander. Red Hills region in southern Alabama. To 25 cm. Rarely collected, poorly known, and threatened because of the extremely small range of only a few square kilometers. The first specimen was taken by accident by Hubricht while collecting land snails and caused a furor in American herpetology.

Phelsuma GRAY, 1825. Phelsumas, Madagascar Day Geckos. Genus of the Gekkonidae. Madagascar, various neighboring island groups (Mascarenes, Seychelles, Comores, Andamans, Amirantes), and the coast of East Africa. About 25 species in tropical forests and coconut plantations, some following human habitation. To more than 25 cm. Usually relatively strongly built. Tail easily equal to snout-vent length. Toes with well-developed, broad adhesive lamellae, without claws. Eyes large, the pupil round. Dorsal scales granular. Most *Phelsuma* species are a very attractive green color with red spots; some species are inconspicuous dark olive to gray-brown.

Phelsuma laticauda

Phelsuma cepediana

These geckos are diurnal and arboreal. The diet consists mainly of various arthropods and occasionally some sweet fruit; they also like to lick honey. Phelsumas require spacious terrariums with ample climbing facilities; they tend to prefer relatively smooth areas to rest and sunbathe. Adequate planting contributes to a balanced humidity (about 60-80%) and thus to the well-being of the animals. A weak radiant heat source should be present and occasionally some ultraviolet radiation should be provided. Day temperatures should be 25 to 30° C., at night about 20° C. The diet should be as varied as possible, including regular vitamin and large calcium supplements. Drinking containers and regular spraying of the plants are essential.

Most species are rather quarrelsome among each other. Large species can have the run of the apartment, but water and a basking spot must be available. Some species have been bred over several generations, and usually only captive-bred specimens are commercially available because the species are all protected. The females lay 2 eggs several times a year that require an incubation period of 2 to 3 months at a temperature of about 28° C. With proper care

Phelsuma guentheri

Phelsuma lineata

and attention the young reach sexual maturity in about 1 year. Males can be recognized by their distinctly broader head; females have calcium deposits on each side of the neck.

▪ *P. abbotti* STEJNEGER, 1893. Aldabra Day Gecko. Northwestern Madagascar and offshore islands. 14 cm. Olivegray to blue-gray with reddish brown spots.

▪ *P. cepediana* (MERREM, 1820). Blue-tailed Day Gecko. Mauritius and Reunion. Easily to 15 cm. Dark green to blue-green with attractive red spots. Quarrelsome.

Phelsuma madagascariensis

▪ *P. dubia* (BOETTGER, 1881). Zanzibar Day Gecko. Madagascar, Comores, Zanzibar, and coastal regions of Tanzania. 15 cm. Olive with dark yellow or reddish brown spots.

▪ *P. laticauda* (BOETTGER, 1880). Golddust Day Gecko. Eastern Madagascar, Comores. 12 cm. Light green with golden yellow dotted pattern. Can survive prolonged dry periods.

▪ *P. lineata* GRAY, 1842. Striped Day Gecko. Madagascar. To 12 cm. Light green with red dorsal spots and with a brown and white lateral band.

▪ *P. madagascariensis* (GRAY, 1831). Common Madagascar Day Gecko. Madagascar, Seychelles, and some smaller islands. Several subspecies often hybridized in captivity. 25 cm. Green with a red-spotted pattern that can be highly variable. The largest species of the genus.

▪ *P. mutabilis* (GRANDIDIER, 1869). Madagascar. About 10 cm. Gray-brown with darker spots. Tail conspicuously thick.

▪ *P. quadriocellata* (PETERS, 1883). Peacock Day Gecko. Central and southern Madagascar. 12 cm. Bright green with inconspicuous red dorsal markings and large black ocelli with narrow light blue margins on each side behind the front legs.

Phenacosaurus BARBOUR, 1920. Andean Anoles. Genus of the Iguanidae. Colombian Andes. 3 or 4 species in the Andes Mountains between 1800 and 3700 m; *paramos*. To easily 20 cm. Slender. Formerly included in *Anolis* and very similar to that genus. The tail serves as a prehensile organ. An occipital helmet and heterogenous scale patterns are characteristics for this genus. Green to light brown, some with a dark striped pattern.

Slow-moving brush inhabitants. Egg-layers. They should be kept in a damp terrarium with a day temperature from 20 to 25° C. and occasional sun. Night temperatures can drop to about 15° C. Small arthropods are eaten.

▪ *P. heterodermus* (DUMERIL, 1851). The head shape, compressed body, and rows of enlarged tuberculate scales make this species look like an Old World chameleon.

Philautus GISTEL, 1848 (= *Ixalus* DUMERIL and BIBRON, 1841, *Chirixalus* BOULENGER, 1893). Genus of the Rhacophoridae. The similar *Theloderma* is here considered distinct. Tropical southern and southeastern Asia, including the Greater Sunda Islands. About 60 species in tropical rain forests and cloud forests. Treefrog-like. Skin smooth or with small spines. Palatine teeth absent, in contrast to the related genus *Rhacophorus*. Pupil horizontal. Tympanum variably visible. Fingers and toes with adhesive discs. Fingers either free or webbed at base only; toes more or less completely webbed. In most species fingers 1 and 2 are opposable with fingers 3 and 4 to form a grasping hand.

Brush and tree inhabitants. Reproduction similar to *Rhacophorus* and *Theloderma*. Several species lack a free-living larval stage, development occurring to metamorphosis in a bubblenest out of water. Maintenance as for tree-dwelling *Rhacophorus*.

▪ *P. aurifasciatus* (SCHLEGEL, 1837) (= *acutirostris* PETERS, 1867, *longicrus* BOULENGER, 1894). Thailand and Kampuchea to Java and Kalimantan and the Philippines. 3 cm. Highly variable.

▪ *P. bimaculatus* (PETERS, 1867). Moluccas, Kalimantan.

3.5 cm. Brown with a darker pattern, the flanks with light blue dots.

- *P. pictus* (PETERS, 1871). Malaya, Singapore, Sumatra, Kalimantan. 3.5 cm. Dark brown with white dots.
- *P. variabilis* (GUENTHER, 1858) (= *femoralis* GUENTHER, 1864). Southern India and Sri Lanka. 3.5 cm. Highly variable.
- *P. spinosus* (TAYLOR, 1920). Philippines. 4 cm. Skin spinous. Brown with a sparse pattern of lemon yellow to orange spots. Diet consists mainly of ants.
- *P. vittatus* (BOULENGER, 1887). Burma, Thailand, Vietnam. In bushes along standing waters. Light brown with dark brown and golden spots. A yellowish white eyeband.

Philippinosaurus, subgenus: see *Varanus*, genus.

Philochortus MATSCHIE, 1893. Genus of the Lacertidae. Southern Arabia to northeastern Africa. 6 species of uncertain taxonomic status. Closely related to *Latastia* and *Eremias*. Body weakly flattened dorso-ventrally. Lower eyelid frequently with a transparent lid window. Tail generally more than twice snout-vent length. Dorsal scales more or less strongly keeled. 2-6 characteristic longitudinal rows of very large, plate-like dorsal scales. Tail whorls distinctly keeled, alternately long and short. Toes with lamellae. Collar well developed. Dorsally brown to black with 5 or 6 light longitudinal stripes; ventrally light, sometimes spotted. Underside of tail—at least in juveniles—orange to deep red.

Mode of life like *Eremias*.

- *P. spinalis* (PETERS, 1874). Eritrea. To 20 cm. 6 light stripes that sometimes break up in adult specimens.
- *P. neumanni* MATSCHIE, 1893. Southwestern Arabia. Barely 30 cm. 6 light longitudinal stripes and light spots along the middle of the back.

Philodendron SCHOTT. Genus of the Araceae. Tropical America. 250 species in rain forests. Mostly shrubs, climbing plants, or semiepiphytes that require constant moisture, warmth, and shade. Winter temperatures not below 15° C. They require occasional fertilization. Reproduction is by means of root formation on cuttings with aerial roots. Due to their large size, nearly all species can be used for terrarium planting only when young.

- *P. elegans* KRAUSE. Stem climber.
- *P. erubescens* K. KOCH and AUG. Young leaves brown-red.
- *P. laciniatum* (VELL.) ENGL. Leaves with deep cleavage.
- *P. scandens* K. KOCH and SHELLO. Climber. Undemanding, with reduced light requirements.

Philodryas WAGLER, 1830. South American Green Snakes. Genus of the Colubridae, Xenodontinae. South America. 15 species. Barely 1 to 1.4 m. Slender, head distinctly set off from body, which in turn is distinctly laterally compressed and covered with smooth or slightly keeled scales. Tail very long. Usually uniform green (*P. aestivus*, *P. baroni*, *P. olfersi*, *P. viridissimus*), but ecologically more adaptable species are olive-brown to gray with patterns of dark spots or lateral stripes (*P. psammophideus*, *P. natteri*, *P. burmeisteri*, and others).

Predominantly tree snakes that prey on lizards and frogs captured mainly during the day. They should be housed in well-planted and heated rain-forest terrariums with climbing facilities and a dry, warm, sunbathing site.

- *P. aestivus* (DUMERIL, DUMERIL, and BIBRON, 1854). Brasilian Mato Grosso and adjacent regions. 2 subspecies.
- *P. olfersi* (LICHTENSTEIN, 1823). Eastern Peru, western Brasil, southward to Argentina.
- *P. psammophideus* GUENTHER, 1872. Eastern Bolivia, southwestern Brasil to Argentina. Semiarboreal to ter-

Philodryas baroni fuscoflavescens

Philodryas aestivus

Philodryas patagoniensis

Philodryas olfersi

Philodryas psammophideus

Philodryas baroni

Philodryas burmeisteri

restrial.
▪ *P. viridissimus* (LINNAEUS, 1758). Amazon Region and its tributaries in gallery forests.

Philoria SPENCER, 1901 (= *Kyarranus* MOORE, 1958). Genus of the Leptodactylidae. Scattered distribution in southeastern Australia. 4 species in perpetually wet montane habitats (river banks, rain forests, sphagnum swamps). Moderately stout but *Rana*-like. Pupil horizontal. Tympanum indistinct or not visible. Limbs relatively short. Fingers and toes free. *P. frosti* has distinct parotoid glands.

Reproduction highly specialized. Only a few large eggs are deposited in wet soil or mossy depressions. The entire larval development occurs inside the eggs, and fully metamorphosed juvenile frogs hatch from the eggs.
▪ *P. loveridgei* PARKER, 1940. Queensland and New South Wales border near the coast. 3 cm. Uniformly brown with a dark snout band and a dark band from eye to axilla.

Philothamnus A. SMITH, 1840. Green Bush Snakes. Genus of the Colubridae, Colubrinae. Africa south of the Sahara. 7 species in rain forests, gallery forests, savannahs,

Philothamnus semivariegatus

Philothamnus sp.

and marshes. 80 cm to 1.3 m. Very slender. The head is oval, distinctly set off, with large eyes. Smooth dorsal scales. Ventral scales often keeled. Usually green, but sometimes spotted.

Diurnal and crepuscular brush inhabitants. Excellent swimmers, frequently found close to water. They prey on frogs, lizards, even other snakes. Hunting for frogs usually takes place on land.

For details on care and maintenance refer to Natricinae, Group 2. Keep in a tropical terrarium with lots of plants and sufficient climbing facilities.
▪ *P. irregularis* (LEACH, 1819). Senegal to the Sudan and southward to the Republic of South Africa. 3 subspecies. Mostly uniform green above.
▪ *P. semivariegatus* (A. SMITH, 1840). Eritrea and the Sudan southward to the Cape region. 2 subspecies. Dorsally green to gray with dark spots.

Phimophis COPE, 1860. Genus of the Colubridae, Boiginae. Neotropics from Panama southward to Argentina. 4 species. In savannahs and grasslands (pampas) to semideserts. 60 cm to 1 m. Head distinctly set off, with a large, pointed rostral plate. Eyes with vertical pupils. Body covered with smooth scales. Frequently with dark longitudinal stripes (*P. vittatus, P. guerini*).

Ground snakes that prey mainly on lizards during the night and hide during the day. Maintain in a well-heated dry terrarium with sufficient hiding places and nocturnal temperature reduction. Caution: Venomous bites possible.
▪ *P. guerini* (DUMERIL, DUMERIL, and BIBRON, 1854). Southeastern Brasil to Argentina.

Phlyctimantis LAURENT and COMPAZ, 1958. Genus of the Rhacophoridae. Tropical Africa. 3 species. Morphologically, anatomically, and biologically hardly distinct from *Kassina*, so the status of *Phlyctimantis* as a genus is questionable. In tropical rain forests. To 5 cm. Pupil vertical. Small but distinct adhesive discs present on fingers and toes. Fingers free, the toes webbed at the base only.

Brush and tree inhabitants. Larval development occurs in small, stagnant, usually temporary jungle waters. Care as for *Kassina maculata*.
• *P. leonardi* (BOULENGER, 1906). West Africa. 4.5 cm. Gray to olive-green, the limbs black with red stripes.
• *P. verrucosus* (BOULENGER, 1912). Uganda to eastern Zaire. 5 cm. Uniformly dark above. Skin with warts.

Phoboscincus GREER, 1974. Genus of the Scincidae, *Leiolopisma* Group. Formerly part of *Eugongylus*. 2 species, one known only from the type specimen.
• *P. garnieri* (BAVAY, 1869). New Caledonia. 55 cm.

Pholidobolus PETERS, 1862. Genus of the Teiidae. Ecuador, Peru. 2 species. Andes Mountains. Ground inhabitants. Similar to *Ecpleopus*.
• *P. montium* (PETERS, 1862). Ecuador.

Pholidosis: Relationships of the scales in reptiles. Species and group characteristics of scalation fall within certain variation limits, so that they are easily accessible features for use in systematics and identification. One distinguishes small scales laying side by side from shingled, overlapping scales that can be smooth or keeled, and granular scales from larger shields. On the body the dorsal scales usually are most clearly differentiated from the ventral scales. Their numbers and shapes are of systematic significance, as are the numbers and development of the caudal scales.

Phoxophrys HUBRECHT, 1881. Genus of the Agamidae. Kalimantan and Sumatra. 5 species. Hardly known.
• *P. cephalum* (MOCQUARD, 1890). Northern Kalimantan. About 20 cm.

Phrynanodus: see *Eleutherodactylus*, genus.

Phrynella BOULENGER, 1887. Monotypic genus of the Microhylidae. Tropical Southeast Asia. In rain forests. Skin smooth. Pupil horizontal. Tympanum disguised. Fingers webbed at base, the toes webbed for ¾ of their length. Tips of fingers widened into large, triangular adhesive discs, tips of toes smaller. An adhesive function is also exercised by the large tubercles along the undersides of the fingers and toes. Only small inner metatarsal tubercles are present. Males during the breeding season have dark nuptial pads on the inner hand surface and dorsally on the first and second fingers.

Presumably arboreal. They will spawn in small rainwater accumulations such as phytothelms and puddles.
• *P. pulchra* BOULENGER, 1887. Malayan Peninsula, Sumatra, Mentawai Islands. 4 cm. Brown with a regular pattern of dark dots.

Phrynobatrachus GUENTHER, 1862. Genus of Ranidae. Africa south of the Sahara. More than 50 species, but needs to be revised. In various habitats, from tropical rain forests to savannahs and grasslands. Similar to *Rana*. Often compact. Some species difficult to distinguish from the related genus *Arthroleptis*, which in the literature is sometimes included in this genus; other references use *Phrynobatrachus*. Skin smooth, rarely with warts. More or less well-developed webbing between toes. Males have an unpaired vocal sac, which in some species can be inflated to equal the size of the entire body. Coloration highly variable in most species.

Diurnal and nocturnal, mostly ground-dwellers found close to or in water. In contrast to many other frog species, *Phrynobatrachus* species vocalize during the day, usually from river banks. When disturbed they will flee into the water. Species with distinct adhesive discs (e. g., *P. plicatus*) climb about in bushes and on trees. In contrast to *Arthroleptis*, *Phrynobatrachus* species spawn in water; the eggs are small, numerous, and float individually on the surface.

They should be kept in accordance with relevant habitat details for particular species, usually in a tropical terrarium with a water section.
• *P. albolabris* (AHL, 1923). Cameroons, Nigeria. Rain forests. Throat of males bright yellow (dark in all other species).
• *P. calcaratus* (PETERS, 1863). Nigeria, Cameroons. Tropical forests and savannahs. To 2.5 cm.
• *P. natalensis* (SMITH, 1849). Southern edge of the Sahara to southern Africa. Savannahs. To 4 cm. Skin with warts.
• *P. plicatus* (GUENTHER, 1858). Tropical West Africa, close to the coast. Rain forest. To 4 cm.

Phrynocephalus KAUP, 1825. Toad-headed Agamids. Genus of the Agamidae. Asia from Arabia to Manchuria. About 40 species in dry regions. *P. theobaldi* occurs above

Phrynocephalus luteoguttatus

5,000 m in the Himalayas, the highest elevation for any reptile. To 25 cm. Flattened dorso-ventrally, the head large, distinctly set off, rounded. Tympanum covered by scales. Nostrils small, often slot-shaped. Swollen, keratinous eyelids. Tail about equal to snout-vent length. Body scales are predominantly small. Underneath individual large scales there are species- and sex-specific glands. The toe scales are in part fringe-like and widened. Femoral and preanal pores are absent. Shades of gray and brown prevail, frequently with attractive markings.

Diurnal ground-dweller found on loose sand as well as on rocky ground. At least the larger species are incompatible with each other. These agamids will defend themselves bravely against other lizards and even against snakes. Many dig deep burrows where they spend the hottest hours of the day and cool hours of the night. When digging both limbs on the same side are used simultaneously. Characteristic vertical tail rolling occurs when excited, exposing the black and white striped pattern on the underside of the tail.

Most species are egg-layers, producing several clutches each with 1-6 eggs. Species from the northern limits of the range and some of those from high elevations (e. g., *P. theobaldi*) are ovoviviparous.

Phrynocephalus mystaceus

Provide a spacious, dry terrarium with a deep sand layer and some rocks. The lowest substrate layer should always be kept slightly damp, as the animals like to bury themselves there. Day temperatures should be between 30 and 35° C., locally on the ground up to 40° C. (a warm basking site); substantial temperature reduction is suggested at night, to about 20° C. Animals from the northern edge of the range and those from higher elevations should be given an over-wintering period of 2 to 4 months at about 10-15° C. The diet should consist of arthropods. Many species prefer small spiders and ants, but ants do not appear to be essential in captivity. Occasional spraying is necessary since these animals do not use open water containers and they should not be used. Provide regular ultraviolet radiation and calcium and vitamin supplements. Difficult to keep.

• *P. guttatus* (GMELIN, 1789). Tail Roller. Western Asia to the extreme southeastern section of European USSR. On sand. 13 cm.

• *P. helioscopus* (PALLAS, 1771). Sun-gazing Agamid. Trans-Caucasus to Mongolia. Mainly on rocky steppes. 12 cm. Head conspicuously round, the snout slightly turned up. Most likely species to survive for any length of time in captivity.

Phrynocephalus raddei boettgeri

• *P. interscapularis* LICHTENSTEIN, 1856. Spiny Toad-head. Asia. Dune regions with some growth. 10 cm. Difficult to keep.

• *P. mystaceus* (PALLAS, 1776). Bearded Toad-head. Central Asia, northern Iran, Afghanistan. Steppes and deserts. 25 cm. Spines at the corners of the mouth can be erected when threatened, this enlarging the mouth to about 3 times its actual size. Toes with distinct fringed scales. Compared with other species of the genus, this one does relatively well in captivity.

Phrynodon PARKER, 1935. Monotypic genus of the Ranidae. Southwestern Cameroons. Closely related to *Petropedetes*. Found along streams in montane rain forests. Males, as in *Dimorphognathus*, have a pair of hook-shaped tooth-like odontodes in the upper jaw. Mode of life and care similar to *Petropedetes*.

• *P. sandersoni* PARKER, 1935. To 2.5 cm. Yellow-brown above, lemon-yellow below.

Phrynohyas FITZINGER, 1843. Genus of the Hylidae. Tropical and subtropical Central and South America. 5 species. Conspicuous warty protruding skin glands. Head with a short snout. Iris golden to brownish with black reticulation. Fingers webbed for about ⅓ of their length, the toes webbed for about ⅔ of their length. Paired vocal sacs are located immediately behind the corners of the mouth. Coloration highly variable.

Nocturnal tree-dwellers. During the dry season they are found in bromeliad funnels, hollow trees and branches, and similar hiding places. Heavy rainfall triggers mating behavior. The eggs float in a single layer on the surface in

Phrynohyas venulosa

order to assure adequate oxygen supply. The larvae develop in shallow pools.

Secretions given off by these frogs tend to cause acute mucous membrane irritations in humans and can lead to temporary blindness if the eyes are affected. There is a divergence of opinions as to the function of the skin secretions. They may be for protection against enemies, protection against desiccation, or to aid skin respiration.

▪ *P. venulosa* (LAURENTI, 1768). Poisonous Treefrog. Central America and tropical South America east of the Andes. To 11.5 cm (females) or 10 cm (males). Rather variable olive-brown with an irregular pattern of dark spots.

Phrynomeridae: Snake-necked Frogs. Family of the Salientia, suborder Diplasiocoela. Often considered a subfamily (Phrynomerinae) of the Microhylidae. Ethiopian. One genus: *Phrynomerus*. Similar to Microhylidae, but distinguished by the presence of an inserted supplementary bone between the last and the penultimate bones of the digits, just as in Rhacophoridae, Pseudidae, Centrolenidae, and Hylidae. The colloquial name refers to their ability to turn their head slightly sideways, a characteristic also found in some of the Hylidae.

Phrynomerus NOBLE, 1926. Snake-necked Frogs, Creeping Frogs. The only Recent genus of the Phrynomeridae. Africa south of the Sahara to the Cape. 3 partially polytypic species found in semiarid and arid open areas. Flattened and compact, the head and snout small. Pupil vertical, the tympanum hidden. Fingers and toes free, but with more or less distinct adhesive discs (except in a few populations of *P. affinis*). Hind legs very short. Usually a conspicuous color pattern is present. Larvae have a very pointed tail. The mouth lacks any horny structures (no teeth) and is wide.

Nocturnal ground-dweller without jumping ability. Often found long distances from water. During the cooler seasons (southern populations) they are found in hiding places (self-dug holes) in the ground and under rocks and wood. The diet consists mainly of ants and termites. During the breeding season the males congregate in shallow waters and vocalize loudly. Amplexus is axillary. Spawning

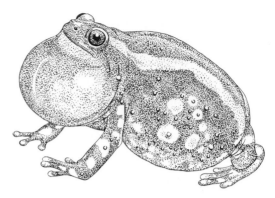

Phrynomerus bifasciatus

occurs in shallow water among plants. The egg masses number about 600 eggs that float on the surface. The larvae hatch after about 4 days and feed on microorganisms. At a size of barely 4 cm, about one month after hatching, metamorphosis occurs. The *Phrynomerus* terrarium should be kept warm, sunny, and semimoist. It should have a deep substrate layer and additional hiding places. Open-air maintenance is recommended for the summer months. For animals from southern populations a winter resting period of 1 to 2 months at low temperatures is advisable.

▪ *P. annectens* (WERNER, 1910). Angola to southern Africa. 3.5 cm. Gray to dark brown with oval black, red-brown, and yellow-green spots.

▪ *P. bifasciatus* (SMITH, 1842). Red-banded Crevice Creeper. Tropical and southern Africa. Polytypic, cream to orange dorso-lateral stripes and spots on the arms, legs, and body.

Phrynops WAGLER, 1830. Toad-headed Turtles. Genus of the Chelidae. South America. About 7 species. In many types of waters. Carapace 35 to 40 cm, rather flat. The wide, short head is on a short neck (for a side-necked turtle).

Strongly aquatic. Carnivorous. Hardy terrarium specimens with modest space requirements and quiet behavior. Exact relationships and distribution of the species uncertain.

▪ *P. geoffroanus* (SCHWEIGGER, 1812). Dark Toad-headed

Phrynomerus annectens

Turtle. South America from Guyana in the north to southern Paraguay. 2 subspecies. The carapace is more or less strongly keeled. The neck has a dark longitudinal stripe leading through the eye. Juveniles are brightly patterned, with a red and black plastron and contrasting light and dark markings on all skin areas. Occasionally bred.

• *P. gibbus* (SCHWEIGGER, 1812). Humpback Toad-headed Turtle. Northeastern to central South America and Trinidad. The brown carapace has yellow outer margins. Has been bred occasionally. Incubation takes 152 days at 28 to 32° C. in an incubator.

• *P. nasutus* (SCHWEIGGER, 1812). Frog-headed Turtle. Northern to central South America. 3 subspecies.

Phrynosaura WERNER, 1907. Genus of the Iguanidae. Northern Chile and western Argentina. 3 species. In dry regions. Easily to 15 cm. Moderately flattened.

Ground-dwellers. Appearance and possibly mode of life

Phrynops geoffroanus, juv.

Phrynops geoffroanus geoffroanus

Phrynops hilarii

Phrynops wermuthi

Phrynops gibbus

Phrynops nasuta nasuta

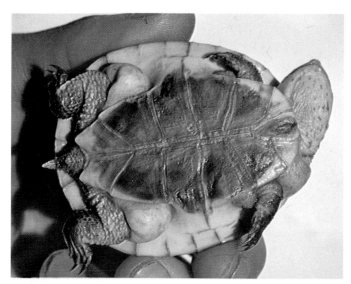

Phrynops gibbus

Phrynops tuberculatus

Phrynops rufipes

Phrynops rufipes

similar to *Tropidurus* and *Liolaemus*.
▪ *P. marmoratus* (BURMEISTER, 1861).

Phrynosoma WIEGMANN, 1828. Horned Lizards, Horned "Toads." Genus of the Iguanidae. Southwestern Canada, over wide areas of the western and central United States to Guatemala. About 15 species. In sandy deserts, semideserts, grasslands, and open forests. 10 to 20 cm. Extremely flattened dorso-ventrally, the body of some species nearly round when viewed from above. Head short and wide, posteriorly with large, often very long spinous "horns." Tail usually less than ½ snout-vent length. Body scales granular, interspersed with larger tubercles or spines. Along the sides there is usually a distinct fringe of enlarged, pointed scales. Primarily shades of brown with light and dark spots and blotches. Often a middorsal pale stripe. These lizards are capable of distinct light and dark color changes.

The diet consists mainly of arthropods. An important role is played by ants, which apparently serve to acidify the digestive tract. When endangered these lizards may "play dead." Some are able to eject drops of blood from their

Phrynosoma cornutum

eyes over a distance of more than 1 m. (A similar type of behavior is also know for *Sceloporus occidentalis* populations in the same area.)

Mating occurs during spring and early summer. Mostly egg-layers, 5 to more than 30 eggs per clutch; *P. douglassi*, which extends all the way to Canada in the north, is ovoviviparous, 6-36 young. Many species undergo a rest period

Phrynosoma douglassi, 2 days old

Phrynosoma asio

Phrynosoma coronatum

Phrynosoma cornutum after squirting blood from eye

for several months—northern animals a winter dormancy period, southern specimens estivation during the practically rainless dry season (for *P. asio*, from September to April).

Keeping these lizards requires considerable experience, and they are not recommended for beginners. They require spacious, dry terrariums with a thick sandy bottom substrate where the lower layers are kept damp, some rocks and dry pieces of wood. Day temperatures can reach between 30 and 40° C., with warmer basking sites; at night the temperature should be reduced to about 15-20° C. Northern specimens should be given a winter dormancy period of about 2 months at about 10° C., other species possibly a dry rest period. Drinking needs can be satisfied by regular spraying or individually via pipette. The diet should consist of small, soft arthropods and must be varied; include ants on a regular basis. Fruitflies are particularly eagerly taken; feed the wingless mutants. Regular ultraviolet radiation is very important, as are calcium and vitamin supplements.

Some species have occasionally been bred, but rearing the young is extremely difficult and requires meticulous

Phrynosoma douglassi

care. Juvenile specimens require more moisture than adults.

During the summer months these lizards should be given an outdoor or at least open-air enclosure. Specimens from the central and northern USA have been kept the entire year in suitably protected enclosures in central Europe. Several states prohibit collecting, selling, and keeping *Phrynosoma*.

• *P. asio* COPE, 1864. Mexican Horned Lizard. Mexico to Guatemala. Grassland and brush. To 20 cm. Head spines long. Very long spines along the flanks and 2 series of large, pointed dorsal scales.

• *P. cornutum* (HARLAN, 1825). Texas Horned Lizard. South-central to southwestern USA into Mexico. Deserts and steppes. To 14 cm. Central head spines long. Dark stripes radiate from eye.

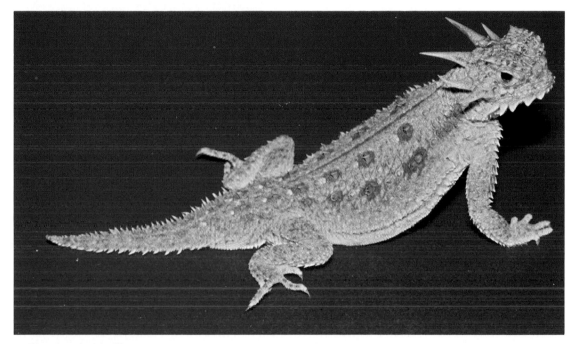
Phrynosoma m'calli

Phrynosoma douglassi brevirostre

Phrynosoma modestum

Phrynosoma orbiculare orientalis

• *P. coronatum* (BLAINVILLE, 1835). Coast Horned Lizard. California to northern Baja California. Deserts and semideserts with open vegetation, in part rocky, but intermittently with open sandy areas. To 15 cm. Long occipital spines.

• *P. douglassi* (BELL, 1833). Short-horned Lizard. Southwestern Canada to Mexico. Highlands. Usually in cool and relatively damp valleys, Easily to 10 cm. Occipital spines very short. Must not be kept too dry and hot. Ovoviviparous (at least the northern populations).

• *P. modestum* GIRARD, 1852. Roundtailed Horned Lizard. Texas to Arizona and central Mexico. Partial to rocky deserts and semideserts with sparse vegetation. Easily to 10 cm. Head with short spines, otherwise nearly smooth, the lateral seam of spines absent.

Phyllobates DUMERIL and BIBRON, 1841. Poison Arrow Frogs. Genus of the Dendrobatidae. Central America and tropical South America. About 20 species. *Phyllobates* is closely related to *Dendrobates*, and generic distinctions are

Phrynosoma solare

unstable. Here we follow the recent research of Silverstone and Savage. 2-5 cm. Distinguished from *Dendrobates* by the presence of maxillary teeth and small finger and toe discs; during the larval stage the anal opening is located on the right. From *Colosthethus* it is distinguished by the presence of skin poisons. Coloration often very bright and contrasting (warning coloration), sometimes cryptic.

Mode of life, behavior, and reproduction as typical of the family. Some species are active only during the rainy season and go into hiding during the dry periods (*P. lugubris* in the Peruvian *selva*). The male usually carries only a few larvae on its back to the water, mostly in phytothelms or small water accumulations on the ground. Care and breeding as for *Dendrobates*.

▪ *P. bicolor* DUMERIL and BIBRON, 1841. Western Andes of Colombia. 3 cm. Reddish yellow above, brown-black below.

▪ *P. femoralis* (BOULENGER, 1884). Eastern Ecuador, nor-

Phyllobates tricolor

Phyllobates lugubris

Phyllobates terribilis

theastern Peru. Similar to *Colostethus*. Abdomen black with blue spots.

• *P. lugubris* (SCHMIDT, 1858). Colombia, Ecuador, Peru. 3.3 cm. Black with 2 dorso-lateral golden stripes, the flanks and legs with emerald green spots.

• *P. parvulus* (BOULENGER, 1882). Ecuador. 2.2 cm. Reddish brown above, abdomen blue with black spots. Pectoral and pelvic regions yellow.

• *P. pictus* (DUMERIL and BIBRON, 1841). Ecuador, Peru, Colombia. 2.4 cm. Similar to *Colostethus*, belly with light blue spots.

• *P. tricolor* (BOULENGER, 1899). Southwestern Ecuador. Western slopes of the Andes Mountains, 1250 to 1800 m. 2.5 cm. Brown-black, ventrally yellow or white.

• *P. trivittatus* (SPIX, 1824). Peru, Venezuela, Guyana, Surinam. 3 cm. Black above, with three whitish longitudinal stripes, abdomen black.

Phyllodactylus GRAY, 1828. Leaf-fingered Geckos. Genus of the Gekkonidae. Tropics and subtropics, nearly worldwide distribution. More than 60 species in various habitats. About 10 cm. Relatively strongly built. Tail slightly less than snout-vent length, cylindrical, relatively thick, in some species with a moderate constriction at the base. Pupil vertical. Toes with well-developed, enlarged adhesive lamellae. Upper sides of toes with 2 strongly enlarged nearly triangular scales distally, into which the claws can be retracted. Coloration and markings highly variable, mainly shades of brown.

Crepuscular to nocturnal. At least the hiding places must be kept slightly damp. See *Cyrtodactylus*, but keep preferably somewhat moister.

• *P. europaeus* GENE, 1838. European Leaf-finger. Southern Europe (Mediterranean Region). To 9 cm. Males velvet black with grayish white dots, females gray to gray-brown. Winter dormancy period of 6-8 weeks.

• *P. marmoratus* (GRAY, 1844). South Australia and neighboring islands. 11 cm. Sandy colored with darker marbled pattern.

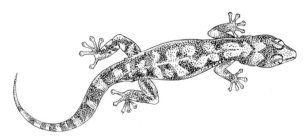

Phyllodactylus europaeus

Phyllodactylus pictus

Phyllodytes WAGLER, 1830 (Syn. *Amphodus* PETERS, 1872). Genus of the Hylidae. Tropical South America. About 5 species. Slender. Horizontal pupil, distinctly visible tympanum, and a heart-shaped tongue. Fingers free, toes with webbing at base only, adhesive discs well developed.

• *P. luteolus* (WIED, 1824). Southeastern Brasil. 2.2 cm. Yellowish red with brown spots.

Phyllomedusa WAGLER, 1830 (= *Pithecopus* COPE, 1866). Grasping Frogs, Monkey Frogs. Genus of the Hylidae. Central and South America southward to Paraguay and Argentina. About 30 species. First finger and toe opposable to remaining digits; these frogs can grasp thin branches, along which they move about slowly, chameleon-like. Pupil vertical (unique within the South American Hylidae other than in *Agalychnis*). Upper part of the lower green eyelid transparent, but never reticulated (in contrast to *Agalychnis*). Eyes large, iris whitish. Limbs very thin. Fingers and toes free, not webbed. First finger and toe in nearly all species except *P. bicolor* longer than the second (also a distinguishing characteristic from *Agalychnis*). Dorsum green, flanks and inside of legs (not visible when resting) bright orange, red, or even with a violet pattern.

Phyllomedusa lemur

Predominantly nocturnal bush- and tree-dwellers. As far as is known, the monkey frogs stick together leaves into a funnel where they deposit their gelatin-covered egg mass, which is later surrounded by foam. The newly hatched larvae have to reach water in bromeliad funnels or jungle pools in order to be able to develop further.

These frogs should be kept in a densely planted tropical rain-forest terrarium at 23 to 27° C., with high humidity and adequate ventilation. The diet should consist of live insects. The larvae can be raised on a suspension of tropical fish food and yeast.

• *P. burmeisteri* BOULENGER, 1882. Brasil. To 8 cm. Dorsally green, abdomen yellow.

• *P. lemur* BURMEISTER, 1882. Lemur Frog. Costa Rica, Panama. Montane. To 6 cm (females) or 4 cm (males). Daytime coloration light green, insides of thighs orange.

• *P. rohdei* MERTENS, 1926. Eastern Brasil, Paraguay. To 4 cm. Dorsally green, flanks orange-yellow with black markings.

• *P. venusta* DUELLMAN and TRUEB, 1967. Eastern Panama. To 10 cm (female) or 9 cm (males). Dorsally green, abdomen orange.

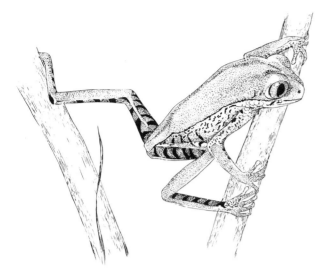

Phyllomedusa hypochondrialis

Phyllomedusa rohdei

Phyllopezus PETERS, 1877. Monotypic genus of the Gekkonidae. Central South America. Little known.
▪ *P. pollicaris* (SPIX, 1825).

Phyllopoda: Water Fleas and allies. Order of the Crustacea that includes, among others the water fleas (Cladocera) with the well-known genus *Daphnia*. They are found in large masses in nearly all standing waters. They are excellent food for smaller aquatic amphibians and amphibian larvae.

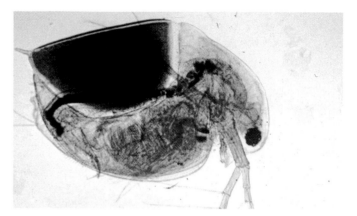

Phyllopoda: A daphnid

Phyllorhynchus STEJNEGER, 1890. Leafnosed Snakes. Genus of the Colubridae, Colubrinae. Southwestern USA and northwestern Mexico (Baja California and Sonora). 2 species in dry regions and deserts. To 50 cm. Small head not set off from the body. Digging and burrowing is supported by the very large leaf-like, compressed, projecting, vertical rostral scale. Either with a spotted pattern (*P. decuratus*) or incomplete bands (*P. browni*) of brown on pale grayish tan.

Nocturnal burrowing ground snakes. They can be found in the open on wet, warm nights. The diet consists mainly of gekkonids (*Coleonyx*) and other small lizards and their eggs. Egg-layers.
▪ *P. browni* STEJNEGER, 1890.
▪ *P. decurtatus* (COPE, 1868).

Phyllorhynchus browni

Phyllorhynchus browni browni

Phyllurus SCHINZ, 1822. Leaf-tailed Geckos. Genus of the Gekkonide. Australia. 3 species. Close to the *Gymnodactylus* Group and in part also to *Underwoodisaurus*. To 25 cm. Characterized externally mainly by the short (half snout-vent length), flattened, and substantially widened tail. The vertical pupil is lobate. The body has numerous small, wart-like protruding scales.

Require little heat. Arboreal or living on rocks. Nocturnal geckos. Room temperature is sufficient in the terrarium. Should not be kept too dry.

• *P. cornutus* (OGILBY, 1892). Northern Leaf-tailed Gecko. Eastern Australia. Rain forests. To 25 cm. Brownish with irregular markings. Tail with spinous scales. Arboreal, hiding under tree bark during the day.

• *P. platurus* (SHAW, 1790). Southern Leaf-tailed Gecko. Eastern New South Wales. Rough mountain regions close to the coast, also following human habitation. To 18 cm. Gray-brown marbled pattern, tail without distinct spines.

Phyllurus cornutus

Phymaturus GRAVENHORST, 1838. Monotypic genus of the Iguanidae. Chile, in the high Andes to 3,000 m. 20 cm. Compact, flattened dorso-ventrally. The thorny tail is about ½ snout-vent length. Dorsal scales granular.

Ground-dwellers. Primarily carnivorous. Keep in a slightly damp terrarium with extreme nocturnal temperature reduction and localized radiant heat. Feeding in captivity is difficult. It will possibly take dandelions, soft lettuce leaves, and similar items, occasionally a few insects. Ovoviviparous, 4 young. Maintenance in captivity difficult.

• *P. palluma* (MOLINA, 1782). High-mountain Lizard. Chilean Andes to Patagonia. 20 cm. Gray-brown, somewhat greenish or reddish after molting.

Physalaemus FITZINGER, 1826 (= *Paludicola* WAGLER, 1830, *Eupemphix* STEINDACHNER, 1863, *Engystomops* JIMENEZ DE LA ESPADA, 1872). Genus of the Leptodactylidae. Southern Mexico to Argentina. About 34 species. Mostly in semiarid, more or less open areas, also in secondary and rarely in primary rain forests. Shape more or less toad-like. Pupil horizontal. Tympanum mostly disguised (except in *P. pustulatus*). Fingers and toes free and without lateral skin folds. Vocal sac very large, with a tendency toward paired development. Parotoid glands present in some species, absent in others.

Ground-dwellers. Numerous small eggs are deposited in foam nests that float on stagnant water. Maintain in a semimoist terrarium. An aqua-terrarium is required for breeding attempts.

• *P. cuvieri* FITZINGER, 1826. Bolivia, Brasil, Paraguay. 3 cm.

Physalaemus nattereri

• *P. gracilis* (BOULENGER, 1883). Brasil, Uruguay. 2.5 cm.

• *P. petersi* (JIMENEZ DE LA ESPADA, 1872). Ecuador. 3 cm. Dark brown with numerous orange or red pustules.

• *P. signiferus* (GIRARD, 1853). Brasil. 2 cm. Very attractive; red brown, with sepia spots surrounded by a yellowish white margin.

Physignathus CUVIER, 1829. Water Dragons. Genus of the Agamidae. Indo-Australian Archipelago to northern Australia; 1 species on Southeast Asian mainland. 8 species. In tropical rain forests. To 1 m. Laterally compressed. Head relatively massive, jaws and teeth strong. Tail about twice snout-vent length. Strongly serrated high nuchal, dorsal, and partial caudal crests. Gular pouch absent, but a well-defined gular fold is present.

Physignathus cocincinus

Predominantly arboreal, close to water; good swimmers and divers that will flee into water when disturbed. The diet consists of arthropods, frogs, small lizards, and bird, occasionally some fruit. Egg-layers, 8-12 eggs per clutch, incubation period about 3 months.

Water dragons should be kept in a spacious terrarium with a large water bowl and temperatures from 24 to 30°

Physignathus cocincinus

Physignathus lesueuri

C., with a slight reduction at night. Specimens caught as adults often do not become tame and may suffer head injuries while trying to escape.

▪ *P. lesueuri* (GRAY, 1831). Brown Water Dragon. Eastern and northeastern Australia, New Guinea. To barely 1 m; of this about 60 cm is tail. A continuous crest, highest in occipital and nuchal region, reaches nearly to the tip of the tail. Grayish brown to olive-brown with light crossbars.

▪ *P. cocincinus* CUVIER, 1829. Green Water Dragon. Southeast Asian mainland and the Indo-Australian Archipelago. Smaller than the preceding species. Dorsal crest higher, extending only to the first third of the tail. Relatively rare, but has been bred repeatedly in captivity.

Phytothelms: Small rainwater accumulations on or in plants, such as in bromeliad funnels, branch forks, hollow trees and branches, and bamboo stalks. Utilized by many arboreal species for drinking water and used by many frogs as development water for their larvae. When arboreal animals are kept there should always be a few phytothelms in the terrarium.

Physignathus cocincinus

Physignathus lesueuri

Physignathus cocincinus, juv.

Pilea LINDL. Canoneer Flowers. Genus of the Urticaceae. Tropics, except in Australia. About 200 species. Low, lawn-forming plants. Fast growers that like shade and moisture. The preferred temperature range is between 15

Pilea cadieri

Pilea nummularifolia

and 25° C. Reproduction is by means of cuttings. Can be used as ground-cover.

▪ *P. cadieri* GAGNEP and GUIL. 15-20 cm tall. Frequent trimming of the shoots makes for full plants.

▪ *P. microphylla* (L.) LIEB. Equally suited for warm and cool locations.

▪ *P. spruceana* WEDD. Peru. A runner-producing shrub.

Pipa LAURENTI, 1768. Surinam Toads. Genus of the Pipidae. Here includes *Hemipipa* MIRANDA-RIBEIRO, 1937, and *Protopipa* NOBLE, 1925, as synonyms. Neotropics. 5 species in oxygen-deficient, muddy, turbid, and sometimes even heavily polluted standing and flowing waters. 5 to 20 cm, more or less rectangular in shape, the pelvic region barely indicated. Head more or less triangular in outline, some species with tentacle-like or lobate projections at tip of snout and at corners of the mouth. Fingers free, with a characteristic tactile organ in the shape of a rayed star on their tips. Toes are completely webbed and either clawless (*P. pipa*, *P. snethlageae*), 2 claws more or less indicated (*P. aspera*, *P. parva*), or with 3 distinct claws (*P. carvalhoi*). Males with protruding vocal sac producing a metallic, trilling sound. Darkish gray black, the abdomen lighter.

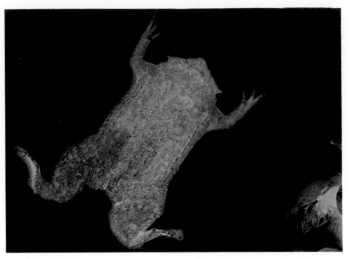

Pipa pipa

Pipa pipa

Pipa carvalhoi

Some species probably never leave the water (*P. pipa*) or only during the rainy season (*P. carvalhoi*). They live mainly along the bottom, swimming about with jerky swimming motions, surfacing only for air. The female lies on her back near the surface to deposit the eggs individually close to her back with a protruding, tube-like cloaca. There they are fertilized by the male and then distributed over the back of the female. The eggs adhere and then sink into the sponge-like dorsal skin, forming more or less distinct "honey combs." The eggs stay there until free-swimming larvae emerge from the eggs (*P. carvalhoi* and *P. parva*) or fully metamorphosed frogs (*P. pipa*).

Collecting *Pipa* is best done by means of a baited underwater trap net. These animals should be kept in aquariums with a large bottom area and a relatively low water level. The recommended temperature range is from 23 to 28° C., but they can also tolerate substantially lower temperatures; temporary cooling down may even stimulate reproduction by simulation of the rainy season. The substrate should consist of dark, coarse, washed sand or gravel. Hiding places can be provided by placing halved flowerpots, rocky caves, and well-soaked driftwood. Even small species will damage water plants; for *P. pipa* and *P. snethlageae* one could at best use some highly robust potted water or swamp plants. A whole range of items are eaten, as long as the food can be swallowed; this includes tubifex, earthworms, small fish, amphibian larvae, scraped lean meat, and small dead animals. Due to their high metabolic rate the water is quickly polluted, therefore filtration and frequent water changes are highly recommended.

A breeding group should consist of 1 male and 1 or 2 females. Spawning occurs regularly. Since there is considerable cannibalism among *Pipa*, the young should be removed from the dorsal skin of the female and raised separately. Depending upon the water temperature, metamorphosis is usually completed after 60 to 75 days (*P. carvalhoi*).

▪ *P. carvalhoi* (MIRANDA-RIBEIRO, 1937). Eastern Brasil. To 8 cm. The most frequently bred species.

▪ *P. parva* RUTHVEN and GAIGE, 1923. Colombia, Venezuela. To 4 cm. Forelegs conspicuously thin and short. Head egg-shaped, elongated.

Pipa pipa

Pipa pipa

- *P. pipa* (LINNAEUS, 1758). Surinam Toad. Peru, Guyana, Surinam, Brasil. Amazon Region. To 20 cm.

Piper L. Peppers. Genus of the Piperaceae. Tropics. Between 700 and 2000 species. Upright or climbing shrubs, hanging or crawling plants. To be cultured in moist and shaded surroundings. See *Philodendron*.
- *P. nigrum* L. Climber. Can take shade and not very temperature-sensitive.
- *P. ornatum* N. E. BR. Leaves with pink spots in juvenile plants.

Piper ornatum

Pipidae: Clawed Frogs, Tongueless Frogs. Family of the Salientia, suborder Aglossa. 4 genera: in South America, *Pipa*; in Africa, *Hymenochirus*, *Pseudhemynochirus*, and *Xenopus*. This Neotropic-Ethiopian distribution indicates a great age for the Pipidae. Indeed, these few Recent species are the remnants of a family widely distributed during the Cretaceous. Family characteristics include—among others—lateral organs in the form of skin papillae (particularly distinct in *Xenopus*), opisthocoelic vertebrae, reduced number (5-8) of free vertebrae due to fusion, and strongly enlarged processes on the sacral vertebrae. Skeleton

Pipidae: Spawning behavior

strongly ossified. Larvae, in contrast to other frog larvae, have paired respiratory apertures. Tongue and horny teeth absent. *Xenopus* larvae filter very small plankton; all other genera are predators.

More or less completely aquatic. Although the Pipidae show many primitive characteristics, the aquatic mode of life was obtained secondarily. Correlated with this is the regression of the tongue and the small lidless eyes (except in *Pseudhymenochirus*).

Reproduction contains primitive and highly specialized elements. During mating the male grasps the female in the pelvic region. The sex products are given off during looplike swimming (the animals alternately on their backs) close to the surface.

All species should be kept in an aquarium. Some species are easily bred laboratory animals.

Pituophis HOLBROOK, 1842. Pine Snakes, Bull Snakes, Gopher Snakes. Genus of the Colubridae, Colubrinae. North America from southern Canada southward to Guatemala. About 3 to 5 species, some polytypic. Taxonomic status of many forms in doubt. In pine forests (pine snakes) as well as in treeless prairies; in the Highlands of Mexico found in rocky deserts up to 3,000 m elevation. Frequently follows human habitation (agricultural land and urban developments). 90 cm to 2.3 m. Strongly built. The head is short, distinctly set off, and may have 4 internasal scales. *Pituophis* species have keeled dorsal scales. Markings are usually dark rhomboids on uniform blackish. Spots often form stripes anteriorly on the body.

Some species are semiarboreal but most are ground-

Pituophis melanoleucus melanoleucus

Pituophis melanoleucus deserticola

Pituophis melanoleucus melanoleucus

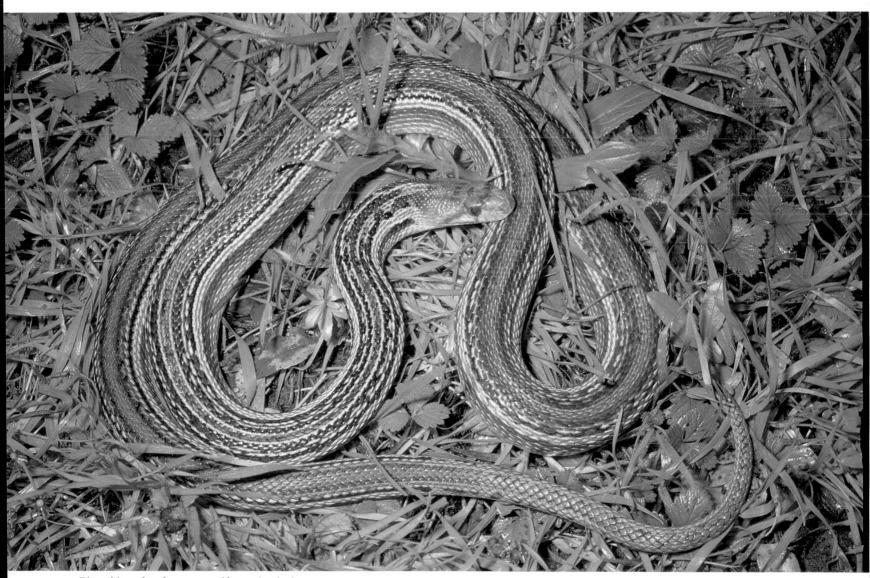

Pituophis melanoleucus catenifer, striped phase

Pituophis melanoleucus catenifer

Pituophis melanoleucus lodingi

Pituophis melanoleucus affinis

dwellers. The diet consists mainly of small mammals, and birds and their eggs. Egg-layers. Should be maintained in a dry, warm terrarium, similar to *Coluber* or *Elaphe*. They have been bred repeatedly.

▪ *P. lineaticollis* (COPE, 1861). Mexico to Guatemala. 2 subspecies.

▪ *P. melanoleucus* (DAUDIN, 1803). Pine Snake. USA and Mexico. About 8 subspecies, 2 or 3 of which may be full species.

Placosoma TSCHUDI, 1847. Genus of the Teiidae. Southeastern Brasil. 2 or 3 species. Small, slender, ground-

Pituophis melanoleucus

dwellers. Little known.
• *P. gordylinum* TSCHUDI, 1847.

Plagiopholis BOULENGER, 1893. Genus of the Colubridae, Lycodontinae. Northern Indo-China to southern China. 3 species in mountain forests. *Plagiopholis* is here taken to include *Trirhinopholis* BOULENGER, 1893. About 40 cm. Shape, sexual differences, body scales, and mode of life similar to *Trachischium*. For details on care refer to Natricinae, Group 1.
• *P. blakewayi* BOULENGER, 1893. Burma.
• *P. nuchalis* (BOULENGER, 1893). Burma, northern Thailand. Between 600 and 1200 m elevation.

Plastron: Abdominal carapace in turtles.

Platemys WAGLER, 1830. Twist-neck Turtles. Genus of the Chelidae. South America. 4 species in small and large waters of tropical rain forests. Carapace to 20 cm, flat, rigid, elongated, with a distinctly flat-bottomed and elongated depression along the vertebral column. Neck relatively short.

These common side-necks have a calm disposition and are carnivorous. They should be kept in a slightly heated aqua-terrarium (to 25° C.) and are sensitive to sudden temperature drops.
• *P. platycephala* (SCHNEIDER, 1792). Twist-neck Turtle. Eastern Peru to northern Brasil and Guyana and Surinam. Longitudinal carapace furrow located between 2 keels.

Platemys platycephala

Platemys platycephala

Platemys radiolata spixii

Carapace solid brown with lighter edges. Plastron black-brown surrounded by a yellow edge. Upper side of head red brown.

• *P. pallidipectoris* FREIBERG, 1945. Chaco Twist-neck Turtle. Chaco Region of Argentina. Longitudinal carapace furrow only weakly developed. On the outside of the upper thighs is a group of large, rough scales, the largest one developed as a spur.

Platycerium DESV. Elkhorn Ferns. Genus of the Filicatae. Australia, southern India, Africa, 1 species in South America. 17 species in rain forests. Epiphytes that are cultivated in loose permeable plant material (peat moss, decomposing leaf soil) on pieces of tree bark, on epiphyte logs, or in wooden baskets. An occasional addition of fertilizer solution is advantageous. Winter temperatures 16-18° C.; during the summer 18-20° C. is essential. Place in a bright location, but no direct sun; high humidity.

• *P. bifurcatum* (CAV.) C. CHR. Relatively undemanding. Many varieties.

Platyhyla BOULENGER, 1889. Genus of the Microhylidae. Often considered to be a synonym for *Platypelis*. Madagascar. In mountain ranges. Skin with warts. Pupil horizontal. Tympanum not visible. Fingers free, with large and very wide adhesive discs. Toes webbed at base only, with small adhesive discs. Presumably arboreal.

• *P. grandis* BOULENGER, 1889. 10.5 cm. Highly variable. Brown, tips of the warts light.

Platymantis GUENTHER, 1858 (= *Cornufer* TSCHUDI, 1838). Wrinkled Ground Frogs. Genus of the Ranidae. Philippines, Solomon Islands, New Britain, Fiji Islands, and New Guinea. More than 30 species. Closely related to *Batrachylodes*. Found mainly in tropical forests (rain, monsoon, and montane forests). Conspicuously slender and flat-headed, similar to *Hyla*; some species stout. Skin often appearing shriveled. Tympanum large, always clearly visible. Fingers and toes free or webbed at base only, with

Platymantis vitiensis, eggs

Platymantis vitiensis

more or less well-developed adhesive discs on the tips (particularly large on the outer fingers in *P. dorsalis* and *P. guentheri*).

Some species are ground-dwellers, but others are virtually arboreal; *P. guentheri* prefers to live in tree ferns. Reproduction is not dependent upon water. These frogs deposit a few large, yolk-rich eggs in damp substrate, and the entire larval development takes place inside the egg. They should be kept in rain-forest or montane rain-forest terrariums. A water section is not essential. A few species have occasionally been bred in captivity.

• *P. boulengeri* (BOETTGER, 1892). New Guinea. Light gray, the cheeks dark brown.

• *P. corrugatus* (DUMERIL, 1853). Philippines. To 4 cm. Reddish brown, with regular dark spots. Adhesive discs absent.

• *P. dorsalis* (DUMERIL, 1853). Fiji Islands. Gray to reddish brown with a darker pattern.

• *P. guentheri* (BOULENGER, 1882). Philippines. To 4.5 cm. Brown with an irregular pattern of black spots.

• *P. papuensis* MEYER, 1874. 3 subspecies. New Guinea. To 5.5 cm. Usually violet gray with round blackish spots.

Platynion AMARAL, 1923. Monotypic genus of the Colubridae, Xenodontinae. Mato Grosso and southeastern Brasil. Closely related to *Conophis*. Tropical forests. About 75 cm. Head short, not set off from the body. Teeth in the upper jaw reduced to just 5 anterior teeth, followed immediately below the eye by a large opisthoglyphic fang.

Burrowing ground snakes. Biology virtually unknown.

• *P. lividum* AMARAL, 1923. Blue gray above with black spots.

Platypelis BOULENGER, 1882. Genus of the Microhylidae. Madagascar. 8 species. Snout short. Pupil horizontal. Tympanum more or less disguised. Fingers free, the toes webbed at the base only. Large, wide adhesive discs present.

Arboreal. *P. milloti* has been found in the leaf axis of *Typhonodorum*.

• *P. cowani* BOULENGER, 1882. 2 cm. Olive-brown with

dark spots.
▪ *P. tubifera* (METHUEN, 1919). 4 cm. Light brown with an indistinct dark pattern and a light longitudinal stripe on the back.

Platyplacopus, subgenus: see *Takydromus*, genus.

Platyplectrurus GUENTHER, 1868. Genus of the Uropeltidae. Southern India and Sri Lanka. 2 species. To 44 cm, only 1.1 to 1.3 cm thick. The head has a rounded snout and normal large head scales. In contrast to all other genera in this family, the eyes are not covered by ocular shields. Chin furrows absent. Tail compressed, covered by smooth scales. Terminal scale also compressed, warty, ending in a thorn. Burrowing snakes.
▪ *P. trilineatus* BEDDOME, 1867. Anamalai Hills, Travancore, southern India. Red-brown with 3 darker longitudinal stripes.
▪ *P. madurensis* BEDDOME, 1877. Travancore Hills, southern India, also southern Sri Lanka. 1,800 m elevation. 2 subspecies.

Platysaurus SMITH, 1844. Flat Lizards. Genus of the Cordylidae, subfamily Cordylinae. Southern Africa. About 10 species in rocky dry regions (granite, sandstone, and other crevice-forming rocks). In appearance somewhat similar to Lacertidae. From barely 20 cm to more than 35 cm. Strongly depressed dorso-ventrally. Head large and flat. Tail barely twice snout-vent length. Limbs well-developed. Body scales small, almost granular; tiny spines present only in the shoulder region. Caudal scales large, keeled, in regular whorls. Often strikingly colored, the males green to blue-green with brown to red tails, the sides orange; lighter spots or longitudinal stripes often present on the back. Markings of the substantially smaller females are similar, but the background coloration is mostly brown.

Platysaurus sp.

Platysaurus guttatus rhodesianus

Platysaurus sp.

Diurnal. Excellent climbers that live almost exclusively along vertical rock faces. The diet consists mainly of small arthropods. Ovoviviparous or egg-layers, only 1-2 young or usually 2 eggs. In the native habitat the eggs are deposited in rocky crevices from November to January.

Under captive conditions, *Platysaurus* has the same requirements as *Cordylus*. They are generally compatible except for males during the breeding season. When setting up a terrarium for these animals special efforts have to be made to provide vertical planes, such as a rock wall, with ample hiding places. Even food and drink containers should be at the base of such a rock wall, since some animals are extremely reluctant to move onto horizontal planes.
▪ *P. capensis* (SMITH, 1844). Southern and southwestern Africa. Barely to 30 cm.
▪ *P. intermedius* MATSCHIE, 1891. Greater Flat Lizard. Southern Africa. 7 subspecies. 32 cm.
▪ *P. guttatus* SMITH, 1849. Small Flat Lizard. Southern Africa. Several subspecies. Between 16 and 25 cm. An eyelid window present.
▪ *P. minor* FITZSIMONS, 1930. South Africa. About 20 cm. Very colorful.

Platysternidae: Big-headed Turtles. Monogeneric family of the Cryptodira. Southeast Asia. The conspicuously large head has a distinct hooked beak and can not be retracted into the carapace. The carapace is very flat. There are 3 rows of intermediate plates on each side of the bridge between the carapace and plastron. The tail is distinctly long, with large flat scales. Highly specialized for a life in shallow, cool, and rapidly flowing creeks.

Platysternon GRAY, 1831. Big-headed Turtles. Monotypic genus of the Platysternidae. Southeast Asia. Mainly in shallow mountain creeks. Carapace length to 20 cm. Head large, with an imposing hooked beak, and can not be retracted into carapace. Carapace distinctly flat, rigid. The relatively large plastron is connected to the carapace on both sides with 3 rows of intermediate plates. Tail about as long as carapace, covered with plate-like scales.

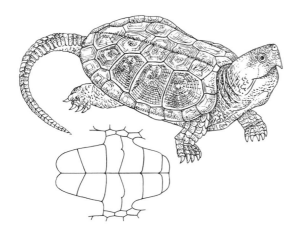

Platysternon megacephalum

Platysternon megacephalum megacephalum

Poor swimmers but excellent climbers. They feed mainly on molluscs. In captivity Chinese specimens should not be kept warmer than 20° C., while Burmese and Thai specimens prefer temperatures as high as 25° C. There is a possibility of animals drowning if the water bowl does not have easy egress. With gradual acclimation to temperate summer temperatures the animals can be kept outdoors during the summer. Acclimated specimens are hardy ter-

Platysternon megacephalum vogeli

rarium specimens. The climbing abilities of these turtles are excellent and must be kept in mind when building cages. They may inflict serious bites.
- *P. megacephalum* GRAY, 1831. Southern Burma to Thailand, southern China to Vietnam, and also found on Hainan. Several subspecies.

Plectrohyla BROCCHI, 1877. Genus of the Hylidae. Central America, Mexico to El Salvador. 10 species in mountain regions at 1000 to 3500 m elevation (high mountain meadows, coniferous forests, cloud forests). The skin in most species has scattered small wart-like protrusions. The snout is distinctly blunt, wide, and high. Webbing between fingers is barely indicated, but webbing is well-developed between the toes. The vocal sac in some species is absent, and these species presumably lack a voice. Males of some species have overdeveloped, strong front legs. Green, gray, or brown. Larvae (known for 6 species) with a very blunt tip of tail. Development occurs in flowing water.
- *P. avia* STUART, 1952. Mexico to Guatemala (1700 to 2000 m elevation). To 9 cm. Uniformly gray-green. Skin smooth. The largest species of the genus.
- *P. glandulosa* (BOULENGER, 1883). El Salvador, Guatemala (2400-3500 m). 5 cm. Gray-green, the sides, fingers, and toes reddish.
- *P. guatemalensis* BROCCHI, 1877. Mexico, Guatemala, El Salvador, Honduras (1000 to 2800 m). 8 cm. Dark green with washed-out brownish spots.

Plectrurus DUMERIL, 1851. Genus of the Uropeltidae. Southern India. 4 species. To 44 cm, only 9 to 10 mm thick. Characterized by the head lacking a temporal scale and the chin lacking a chin furrow. Tail compressed, the caudal scales distinctly keeled. Terminal scale small, its surface granular, terminating in a pair of thorns. Red-brown to brown-violet, often with darker spots or bars on the sides.
  Burrowing snakes.
- *P. perroteti* DUMERIL and BIBRON, 1854. Southern India, Nilgiri Mountains between 1300 and 1800 m elevation.

Plesiotypic: Original (primitive) character development, in contrast to apotypic character development. Mutual ple-siotypes, referred to as symplesiotypes, are of no value for the assessment of phylogenetic relationships.

Plethodon TSCHUDI, 1838. Woodland Salamanders. Ge-nus of the Plethodontidae. North America. 18 species, some polytypic. Some species have very large distributions while others have very restricted ranges. In coniferous,

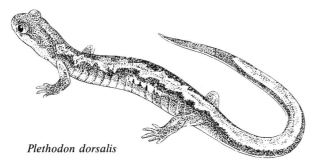

Plethodon dorsalis

Plethodon cinereus

Plethodon cinereus

mixed, and deciduous forests of the foothills and moun-tains. To about 18 cm. Elongated, limbs relatively weak. Tail long and more or less round. In contrast to similar-appearing *Desmognathus* species, the front and hind legs are of equal size. Sometimes a yellowish, reddish, or light brown dorsal band is present.

These salamanders are largely independent of water, and they lead a more or less cryptic life on and in the ground under bark, logs, rocks, and in crevices and similar hiding places. They only surface on dewy or rainy nights. Primary activity phases are in spring and fall rain periods. Southern populations may undergo only a brief winter dormancy period.

The diet is broad and includes (among other items) bee-tles, ants, and arthropods with foul-smelling, bad-tasting defensive secretions. Mating and egg deposition occur on land, the latter in burrows, damp moss, and other sites protected against desiccation. Newly metamorphosed sala-

Plethodon glutinosus

Plethodon glutinosus

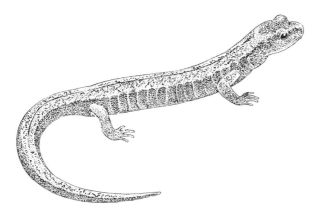

Plethodon vehiculum

Plethodon cinereus, lead-back phase

Plethodon richmondi

manders hatch directly from the eggs.

▪ *P. cinereus* (GREEN, 1818). Red-backed Salamander. Northeastern USA and southeastern Canada. 12 cm. Dark gray to black, usually with a red dorsal stripe.

▪ *P. dorsalis* BAIRD, 1889. Zigzag Salamander. Eastern central USA. 10 cm. Usually with a more or less distinct reddish zigzag dorsal stripe.

▪ *P. dunni* BISHOP, 1934. Dunn's Salamander. USA from southern Washington to Oregon. 13 cm. A yellow, red, or greenish yellow dorsal stripe extends to the tip of the tail.

▪ *P. elongatus* VAN DENBURGH, 1916. Del Norte Salamander. USA, border region of Oregon and California. 14 cm. Dark brown to black.

▪ *P. glutinosus* (GREEN, 1818). Slimy Salamander. Eastern USA. Wide distribution. 18 cm. Black with silvery white spots.

▪ *P. jordani* BLATCHLEY, 1901. Jordan's Salamander. Appalachian Mountains. 17 cm. Darkish with a marbled pattern; some forms have red spots or blotches on the legs and/or neck.

▪ *P. vehiculum* (COPER, 1860). Western Red-backed Salamander. Pacific coast from southern British Columbia to Oregon. 10 cm. Usually a pale dorsal line is present.

Plethodontidae: Lungless Salamanders. North America to central South America (the only salamanders that reach the Southern Hemisphere); some *Hydromantes* species occur in southern Europe. This family is a large one and presents a great diversity in form. General characteristics include the fact that all are without lungs, even terrestrial forms. A groove runs from the nostril to the margin of the upper lip and (in males) is often extended into a lobe. Males in many species have courtship glands on the head, body, and tail.

The most primitive species are found in montane creeks; others are blind, living in subterranean waters. Many species are terrestrial and even arboreal. Mode of reproduction is highly variable, involving spawning (often not for months after mating) in water, depositing the eggs in damp substrates followed by an aquatic larval stage, to having the eggs develop totally on land into young salamanders. The European *Hydromantes* species are live-bearers. Neoteny occurs in several species.

Systematic review:
• Subfamily Desmognathinae: genera *Desmognathus, Leurognathus, Phaeognathus.*
• Subfamily Plethodontinae:
Tribe Hemidactylini:
Eurycea, Gyrinophilus, Haideotriton, Hemidactylium, Pseudotriton, Stereochilus, Typhlomolge, Typhlotriton.
Tribe Plethodontini: *Aneides, Ensatina, Plethodon.*
Tribe Bolitoglossini: *Batrachoseps, Bolitoglossa, Chiropterotriton, Hydromantes, Lineatriton, Oedipina, Parvimolge, Pseudoeurycea, Thorius.*

Plethodontohyla BOULENGER, 1882. Genus of the Microhylidae. Madagascar. 7 species. In montane regions. Oval. Head wider than long, the snout very short. Pupil horizontal. Tympanum more or less indistinctly visible. Legs short. Fingers and toes free, the tips more or less thickened into adhesive discs.

Ground-dwellers. As far as is known they lack a freeswimming larval stage. Eggs are deposited in self-dug, small, damp cavities in the ground.
• *P. ocellata* NOBLE and PARKER, 1926. Eastern Madagascar, Marojezy Mountains. 5.5 cm. A large, round ocellus (eye-spot) with a light-colored margin in the inguinal region.
• *P. tuberata* (PETERS, 1883). Madagascar, Adringitra Mountains, 1500-2000 m. 4 cm. Skin with warts. Redbrown, the warts bright yellow-green.

Pletholax COPE, 1864. Monotypic genus of the Pygopodidae. Western Australia. In open, usually sandy habitats. The only genus in this family with keeled dorsal scales. Snout pointed but short.
• *P. gracilis* (SCHLEGEL, 1864). 25 to 35 cm. Light graybrownish with a dark longitudinal stripe. Burrower.

Pleurodeles MICHAHELLES, 1830. Ribbed Newts. Genus of the Salamandridae. Southwestern Palearctic. 2 species in warm standing waters (with ample underwater plant growth) of different types. 15-30 cm. Robust, with a flattened head, strong jaw musculature, and a laterally com-

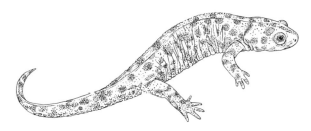

Pleurodeles waltl

Pleurodeles waltl

pressed, pointed tail. Sides with a row of wart-like elevations produced by the tips of the ribs; in *P. waltl* the skin is sometimes penetrated by the ribs without causing any harm to the animals. Males have a longer tail than females and during the breeding season they have nuptial pads along the inside of the arms and hands. The larvae are elongated; the dorsal tail crest starts on the neck.

Pleurodeles species lead a largely aquatic, crepuscular, predatory life and are active throughout the year. They rarely leave their hiding places during the day, and survive temporary drying up of their water habitats by burrowing under rocks.

Reproduction is not tied to a particular season, except under unfavorable climatic conditions. A male ready to mate crawls underneath a female, rubs her throat with his forehead, and grasps from below the arms of the female. By bending his body the male gives off a small, pointed spermatophore close to the female's mouth and then turns the female in such a manner that she can pick up the spermatophore with her cloaca. Older females can deposit up to 800 eggs per spawning, attaching them in clumps to water plants, submerged wood, and rocks.

Pleurodeles can be kept and bred for a decade or more. Therefore, they are often used as laboratory animals. They should be kept in spacious aquariums at room temperature set up with ample hiding places. Winter dormancy and a terrestrial mode of life during the summer are not required. They are very aggressive feeders; greedy feeding behavior can lead to the animals injuring each other. Consequently, only a few specimens can be kept in an aquarium.

▪ *P. poireti* (GERVAIS, 1835). Algerian Ribbed Newt. Northeastern Algeria and northern Tunisia. 15 cm (rarely to 20 cm); *P. p. hagenmulleri* reaches only 10 cm. Yellowish to light olive with darker spots or a marbled pattern.

▪ *P. waltl* MICHAHELLES, 1830. Spanish Ribbed Newt, Rough Spanish Newt. Southwestern half of the Iberian Peninsula and northwestern Morocco. To 30 cm (the largest European newt); specimens from African populations to 20 cm. Dark olive with indistinct rounded blackish spots; the rib warts are more or less light yellow.

Pleurodema TSCHUDI, 1838. Genus of the Leptodactylidae. In the High Andes (to 4,500 m elevation) of southern Peru to southern Chile and Argentina, in coastal regions of Uruguay and eastern Brasil, and in northern South America (Guyana, Surinam, French Guiana, Venezuela, Panama). 10 species, some requiring taxonomic revision. In areas with little tree growth, they are found mostly in grasslands (*puna, pampas*). Toad-like. Pupil horizontal. Tympanum more or less distinctly visible. Fingers and toes free (but in some species with lateral skin folds). Metatarsal tubercle more or less adapted as a digging spade. In the lateral sacral region in some species are paired ocelli (eyespots).

Ground-dwellers, not very agile and without real jumping capability. These animals survive dry periods and nocturnal cold spells by burrowing in the ground. The eggs are surrounded by foam and deposited in puddles or permanent standing waters.

The terrarium must be kept semimoist, with hiding places such as substrate, grass tussocks, and rocks. Animals from the Andes and from the southern extreme of the range do not require any additional heat. Open-air maintenance during the summer months is recommended.

▪ *P. bibroni* TSCHUDI, 1838. Four-eyed Toad. Chile, Argentina. To 1,500 m. 5.5 cm. Gray-brown with a darker marbled pattern and 4 eye-spots.

▪ *P. bufonia* BELL, 1843. Southern Chile, southern Argentina (Patagonian grasslands). 4.5 cm. Light gray with large black spots.

▪ *P. marmorata* (DUMERIL and BIBRON, 1841). Southern Peru, Bolivia, northwestern Argentina. High Andes to 4,500 m. Common. 3 cm. Olive to red-brown with a sparse pattern of dark spots.

Pleurodira: Side-neck Turtles. Suborder of the Testudines. South America, Australia, Africa, and Madagascar. Families: Pelomedusidae, Chelidae. The manner of hiding the head inside the caparace is characteristic for the Pleurodira: Due to the well-developed transverse processes of the neck vertebrae, the neck can only be partially withdrawn into the carapace or not at all and so is bent laterally underneath the front edge of the carapace. Pelvis solid, fused with carapace. Pleurodira can be easily recognized by the shield arrangement on the plastron: There is always an unpaired intermediate gular scute that either reaches the anterior margin of the plastron or is enclosed by the paired gular and pectoral shields.

Pleurodont: see Teeth.

Plica GRAY, 1831. Harlequin Racerunners. Genus of the Iguanidae. Northern South America in tropical rain forests. 2 species. To 40 cm. Slender, strongly flattened dorso-ventrally (*P. plica*) or cylindrical to slightly flattened (*P. umbra*). Head short, compact, the eyes placed high on the head and with large folds laterally. Tail easily twice snout-vent length. Limbs conspicuously long and thin. The unusually large hemipenes of the males play a role in Indian mythology.

Tree-dwellers with relatively low heat requirements. Prolonged exposure to sun is avoided. The diet consists mainly of arthropods, primarily ants. Reproduction occurs throughout the year; clutches with 2-4 eggs.

Plica should be kept in a moderately warm rain-forest terrarium with only slight temperature variations (day temperatures 25 to 28° C.). Spray regularly with water. Ants should be included in the diet if at all possible.

▪ *P. plica* (L., 1758). Northern South America east of the Andes, including Trinidad and Grenada. To 40 cm. Green with brown crossbands and a sprinkling of black dots.

▪ *P. umbra* (L., 1758). South America east of the Andes. About 30 cm. Green with black crossbands; throat in males yellow to orange. More common than the previous species.

Pliocercus COPE, 1860. Big-scaled False Corals. Genus of the Colubridae, Natricinae. Subfamily status questionable. Tropical Mexico through Central America southward to the Amazon Basin. 7 species in tropical lowland forests. 30 to 80 cm. Head only slightly set off, short-snouted, round. Colorfully banded with red-black-yellow (white) and thus frequently mistaken for the venomous *Micrurus*.

Pliocercus elapoides

Diurnal and nocturnal ground-dwelling snakes. They are found in the proximity of water, where they hunt for frogs and fish. Egg-layers.

These very attractive snakes should be kept in rain-forest terrariums with large water bowls. See Group 2 of the Natricinae.

▪ *P. elapoides* COPE, 1860. Mexico to Guatemala and Honduras.

▪ *P. euryzonus* COPE, 1862. Guatemala to western Amazon Basin (Brasil and Colombia).

Pneumonia: Inflammation of the lung tissue caused by a general infection (*Aeromonas, Salmonella*), a specific organ disease (as with *Pseudomonas* infection), or lungworm infestation. The most significant symptom of pneumonia is difficult breathing, which can be recognized by the increased respiratory movements of the body and breathing through an opened mouth. Close examination of the oral cavity often reveals the mucus forming bubbles coming out of the respiratory passages. The nostrils can be encrusted, and sometimes there is a pus-like discharge. In aquatic turtles pneumonia manifests itself in the inability of the affected animals to dive or (with singled-sided pneumonia) listing to one side. Convulsions indicate imminent death due to suffocation. In less acute cases death occurs after prolonged food refusal, loss of condition, and desiccation. Mouth rot can occur at the same time. In the majority of cases pneumonia is caused by bacterial infections, rarely by lungworm infestation, pentastomids, mycoses, or viral infections. Frequently one has to deal with a mixed infection within the framework of a complex of causes.

Therapy: Antibiotics or sulfonamide, which should be supported by vitamin supplements. Also recommended is the additional installation of an infrared radiator above the terrarium. It is best to go to an experienced veterinarian if your specimen seems to have pneumonia.

Prophylaxis: Avoidance of sudden temperature drops, drafts, and humidity too high. There must not be an overcrowded situation. Vitamins have to be sufficient.

Podarcis WAGLER, 1830. Wall Lizards. Genus of the Lacertidae. Predominantly Mediterranean. About 15 species in dry, warm habitats. Formerly included in *Lacerta* and externally rather similar to the rock lizard group, but there are substantial differences in hemipenis structure and skull morphology (*Podarcis* with a greater degree of ossification). Largely conforming to the "standard" lizard appearance. Snout-vent length 4.5 to 9.0 cm. Moderately flattened dorso-ventrally. Tail long. Dorsal scales often weakly keeled. Collar distinct, usually weakly serrated. Tail whorls, in contrast to *Lacerta* (*Zootoca*), of nearly equal length.

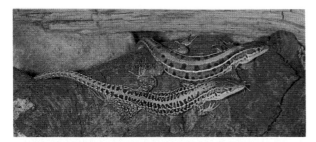

Podarcis taurica, male above, female below

Podarcis erhardi

Podarcis muralis

Primarily shades of brown and green, the markings consisting of light—rarely dark—longitudinal stripes and spots. Juvenile longitudinal stripes more distinctly retained by females, in males often completely broken into dots and vermiculate patterns. *P. melisellensis*, *P. taurica*, *P. sicula*, and others are "concolor" forms without any markings, and there are melanistic island forms (*P. lilfordi*, *P. sicula*, *P. pityusensis*). Sometimes even animals from adjacent islands differ so significantly that they have been described as species (*P. erhardi* and *P. pityusensis*, *P. sicula*).

Due to an apparent lack of animal food, some island populations of *Podarcis* also take some plant food (fruit, vegetables). Egg-layers, 1-3 clutches of 2-6 eggs per clutch per year. Incubation period 70-90 days.

For details on mode of life and care refer to *Lacerta*. Keeping several males together in the same indoor terrarium is not possible; ideally one male should be kept together with 2 or 3 females. However, mixing of different (not too similar) species of similar sizes (NOT *P. pityusensis*/*P. lilfordi*, *P. sicula*/*P. taurica*) is possible. Rearing the young is easier than for many of the other genera in this family.

• *P. dugesi* (MILNE-EDWARDS, 1829). Madeira Wall Lizard. Madeira, introduced to the Azores. In excess of 25 cm. Primarily brown, variable. Undemanding, but rather quar-

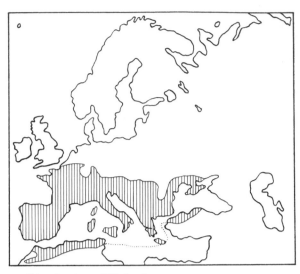

Distribution of *Podarcis*

relsome.

- *P. erhardi* (BEDRIAGA, 1882). Erhard's Wall Lizard, Aegean Lizard. Southern Balkans and Aegean Islands. More than 30 subspecies. Easily 20 cm. Variable. Abdominal region in males often red.
- *P. hispanica* (STEINDACHNER, 1870). Iberian or Spanish Wall Lizard. Iberian Peninsula and northwestern Africa. Usually in rocky habitats. 20 cm. Relatively inaggressive.
- *P. lilfordi* (GUENTHER, 1874). Lilford's Wall Lizard. Balearic Islands, not on Majorca and Minorca. Easily to 20 cm. The nominate subspecies is melanistic; there are also blue-green forms with stripes and spots. Undemanding, but quarrelsome.
- *P. melisellensis* (BRAUN, 1877). Dalmatian Wall Lizard. Eastern Adriatic region. Open forests. Barely 20 cm. Delicate. Dorsum often green; "concolor" form relatively frequent.
- *P. muralis* (LINNAEUS, 1768). Common Wall Lizard. Southern and central Europe, excluding the Iberian Peninsula. Rocky areas, walls. 20 cm. Some males have red abdomens.

- *P. peloponnesiaca* (BIBRON and BORY, 1833). Southern Greece. Meadows, open hill country, open forests. To easily 20 cm. Requires relatively great moisture. Somewhat sensitive.
- *P. pityusensis* (BOSCA, 1883). Ibiza Wall Lizard. Mediterranean islands off Spain. More than 30 subspecies. From barely 15 cm to more than 25 cm. Highly variable, some melanistic. Very incompatible, but otherwise undemanding.
- *P. sicula* (RAFINESQUE, 1810). Italian Wall Lizard. Corsica, Sardiania, Italy, and western Balkan Peninsula, southern Spain, Turkey. More than 40 subspecies. Often with green base coloration along the back; also melanistic forms. Rather adaptable. Easy to keep.
- *P. taurica* (PALLAS, 1814). Balkan Wall Lizard. Southeastern Europe. Grassy steppes, hardly ever in mountain regions. Barely 20 cm. At least central dorsal region green. Must not be kept too dry; somewhat sensitive.
- *P. tiliguerta* (GMELIN, 1789). Tyrrhenian Wall Lizard. Corsica and Sardinia. Rocky, dry regions. Barely 20 cm. Relatively undemanding.

Podocnemis WAGLER, 1830. American River Turtles, Arrau Turtles. Genus of the Pelomedusidae. Northern South America. 6 species. Other species formerly included in *Podocnemis* are now in *Peltocephalus* and *Erymnochelys*. In jungle rivers. Carapace to 80 cm. Characteristic longitudinal groove between the eyes. Front legs with 5 claws, hind legs with 4 claws.

Podocnemis unifilis

Podocnemis erythrocephala

Podarcis muralis brueggemanni

Podocnemis expansa, juv.

Podocnemis unifilis

Podocnemis expansa

Podocnemis unifilis, juv.

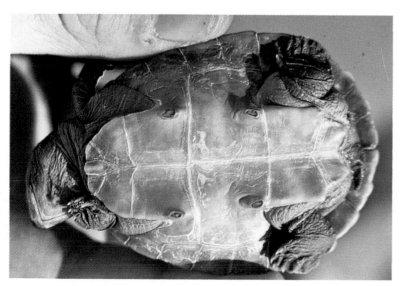

Podocnemis sextuberculata

Podocnemis erythrocephala

Podocnemis expansa

Podocnemis unifilis

Podocnemis unifilis, hatchlings

Podocnemis lewyana

Omnivorous, with substantial vegetarian component. They haul out on sand banks in large numbers to lay eggs. Strong hunting pressure (including egg collecting) has led to the rapid decline of some species. Only juveniles are suitable for terrarium maintenance. Adults require considerable swimming space. Must have a dry basking spot.
▪ *P. expansa* (SCHWEIGGER, 1812). Arrau Turtle. Orinoco and Amazon drainages. 80 cm, the largest species of the genus. Incubation takes 42 to 47 days.
▪ *P. unifilis* TROSCHEL, 1848. Yellow-spotted Amazon Turtle. Venezuela and Surinam to northern Brasil. To 45 cm. Distinct keel on carapace. Incubation takes 75 to 90 days.

Poikilothermic: Refers to animals in which the body temperature is subject to environmental temperature fluctuations; cold-blooded. Amphibians and all Recent reptiles are poikilothermic. (Reptiles, however, can maintain their body temperature to within certain limits by behavior.) Since they get their body heat from external sources, poikilothermic animals are also referred to as ectothermic animals. Homoiothermic or endothermic animals are the "opposite."

Poison glands: Glands giving off poisonous secretions (toxins). In many amphibians the skin mucus formed by numerous simple mucous glands contains toxic substances that can cause irritations of human eye and nose mucous membranes. In addition, there are also larger composite glands that are often concentrated on certain skin areas recognizable morphologically as glandular swellings or ridges (e. g., parotoid glands located behind the eyes in *Bufo* and *Salamandra*) and which secrete various poisonous substances (salamander toxins, frog toxins). These glands

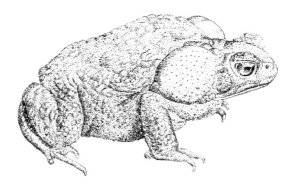

Poison glands: Enlarged parotoid glands of *Bufo marinus*

are often surrounded by muscles producing compression that then eject the toxic secretion. These glands function as defensive devices, since their poisons irritate mucous membranes.

In reptiles poison glands (more accurately venom glands) are found in beaded lizards (*Heloderma*) and numerous snakes. They are modified salivary glands, and their secretions (venom) are discharged into the oral cavity or are connected to special teeth (fangs) used to inject the venom. In snakes the poison glands have evolved from the upper salivary gland (*glandula labialis superior*) of nonvenomous

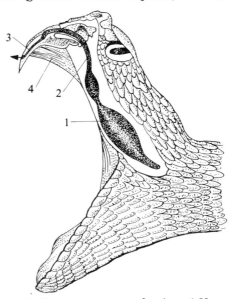

Poison glands: Venom apparatus of a viper. 1 Venom gland; 2 venom duct; 3 solenoglyph fang; 4 muscles for erection of fang

snakes, a mixed gland that produces mucoid substances (mucopolysaccharides) as well as proteins. In various members of the family Colubridae this gland is differentiated into two anatomically and physiologically different sections, the posterior section producing mainly poisonous and non-poisonous proteins and possessing a joint efferent duct that can be connected to a fang (as in the Boiginae). This section of the upper lip gland is then considered to be an independent gland, the Duvernoy gland (*glandula suspecta*). The most highly specialized glands (the *glandula venata*) occur in the true venomous snakes of the families Elapidae, Hydrophiidae, Viperidae, and Crotalidae. They become vastly extended in the genera *Maticora*, *Causus*, and *Atractaspis*, where they may reach all the way into the abdominal cavity or into the neck. Venom ejection can be controlled through muscles located in the connective tissue envelope and through accessory mucous glands on the efferent duct.

Poisoning: Despite various causes, poisoning symptoms are nearly always uniform. Effects on the central nervous system (trembling, cramps, uncoordinated head movements, atactic gait) resemble in part thiamine deficiency. Simultaneous respiratory difficulties increase any suspicion of poisoning. Many poisoning cases are due to overdoses or side-effects of medication. The effects of medication in poikilothermic animals often have not been fully tested. Chlorinated hydrocarbons, such as metronidazole (pure), chlorethylene, Peru balsam, and gentamycin, especially in prolonged treatments such as are used for the eradication of ectoparasites, are all potential poisoning agents. So are overdoses of vitamin A (leading to shedding problems) and vitamin D (leading to hardening of the blood vessels and internal organs). Poisoning can also be caused by food animals that have been fed on poisonous grain, by feeding poisonous salamanders to snakes, as well as by bites from venomous snakes.

Therapy: Specific antidotes for poisoning symptoms are virtually unknown, nor have any of them been tested on poikilothermic animals. Elimination of acute effects can sometimes be achieved by lowering the ambient temperature. In order to stimulate a more rapid excretion of a poison via the kidneys it is recommended to use 50 ml water per kg body weight or 50 ml 0.6% sodium chloride solution per animal subcutaneously.

Polemon JAN, 1858. Genus of the Colubridae, Aparallactinae. Tropical West Africa. 3 or 4 species. Closely related to and rather similar to *Miodon*. In tropical forests. 30 cm to 1 m.
  Nocturnal ground snakes that prey mainly on snakes (especially on blind worm snakes). Should be accommodated in a tropical forest terrarium with a deep substrate or in glass containers. Caution: Venomous bites are possible.
• *P. barthi* JAN, 1858. Ivory Coast to Cameroons. To 90 cm.
• *P. neuwiedi* (JAN, 1858). From Ghana to Benin. 30 cm.

Polychroides NOBLE, 1924. Monotypic genus of the Iguanidae. Northern Peru in forest-covered Andean valleys. Very closely related to and similar to *Polychrus*.
• *P. peruvianus* NOBLE, 1924.

Polychrus CUVIER, 1817. Genus of the Iguanidae. Tropical South and Central America. 5 species. Predominantly in semishaded outer forest zones or relatively open secondary forests. To 50 cm. Slender, laterally compressed. Head pointed. Tail 2 or 3 times snout-vent length. The forward-pointing eyes (lids fused except for a narrow opening), 1 or 2 toes moved to the inside of the foot and used just like the tail for grasping, and the rapid physiological color changes are all reminiscent of *Chamaeleo*. Primarily green with some irregular and indistinct, serrated, dark crossbands.
  Diurnal, strictly arboreal, not very agile. Eats arthropods, occasionally some fruit. Egg-layers, clutches usually with 7-8 eggs. For details of care refer to *Anolis*.
• *P. acutirostris* SPIX, 1825. Southern Brasil to Argentina.
• *P. marmoratus* (L., 1758). Many-colored Anole. Venezuela, Amazon Basin. To easily 30 cm.

Polychrus marmoratus

Polydaedalus, subgenus: see *Varanus*, genus.

Polypedates, genus: see *Rhacophorus*, genus.

Polyphyletic: Group of organisms derived from two (or more) different original species that have been artificially grouped together, possibly on the basis of similar external characteristics. Polyphyletic groups are justifiable really only in artificial systems such as keys. Also refer to monophyletic and paraphyletic.

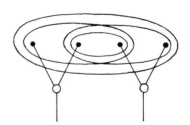

Schematic diagram of a polyphyletic group

Polyploidy: The presence of more than 2 sets of chromosomes in individual cells, tissues, or in the entire organism. Hybridization among amphibians, as within the genera *Ambystoma* and *Rana*, has produced forms with 3 sets of chromosomes (triploids). *Odontophrynus americanus* and *Hyla vesicolor* each possess a quadruple (tetraploid) set of chromosomes, and *Ceratophrys dorsata* even an octuplet (octoploid) set of chromosomes. Among reptiles triploid and tetraploid sets of chromosomes have only been found in the genera *Lacerta* (Caucasian rock lizards), *Leiolepis*, and *Cnemidophorus*. Polyploidy is considered to be an important mechanism in species formation.

Polytypic: Including several taxa: In reference to a species: development of subspecies; in reference to a genus: including at least 2 species. Opposite: monotypic.

Pond: Standing shallow body of water of any size that—in contrast to a pool—always contains water and in contrast to a lake has more or less complete light penetration due to its shallowness. This permits underwater plant growth in all regions. One of the largest ponds in the world is Lake Junin located high in the Peruvian Andes. This is habitat of the giant frogs of the genus *Batrachophrynus*.

Especially in subtropical and tropical climates, ponds provide optimum habitats for numerous frogs, water snakes, and turtles as well as for crocodilians. In the temperate latitudes of the Northern Hemisphere ponds are good habitat for many salamanders and newts.

Pool: Standing water, usually shallow, of relatively inconsequential size, which in contrast to a pond contains water on only a temporary basis, e. g., after snow has melted, after river flooding, or in arid climates following sporadic sudden downpours. One of the largest and most famous pools is Lake Eyre in the extremely arid interior of Australia, which carried water most recently in 1949 and 1964; at that time Lake Eyre was 145 km long and 45 km wide. Genuine pool inhabitants are more or less well adapted to the periodic drying up of the water. Many frogs and salamanders have short development periods of embryos and larvae and variable reproductive seasons triggered by sudden heavy rains. Amphibians and reptiles may have summer dormancy periods spent in permanently damp substrates (e. g., Pseudidae, *Cyclorana*, and *Crocodylus intermedius*).

Pope, Clifford H. (1899-1974): American herpetologist at the American Museum of Natural History and later the Field Museum in Chicago. *Reptiles of China* (1935), *Turtles of North America* (1939), *The Reptile World* (1956), *Giant Snakes* (1962).

Population: Collection of organisms of the same species that is more or less isolated from others of the same species. For instance, fire salamanders in a certain mountain stream valley, smooth snakes on sunny bush-covered slopes right in the middle of some agricultural land, or aquatic frogs in a pool. All members of a population produce among each other—at least potentially—fertile progeny and thus contribute to an unimpeded exchange of genetic material. However, such exchange with members of other populations would be difficult or sometimes even impossible due to distributional barriers. Such more or less strict genetic isolation of populations is particularly significant for evolution by natural selection and the resultant development of new species. Not only does the population interact with its environment, but also the individual members influence each other in many ways, such as through competition for food, sex partners, resting and brood sites, through mutual disturbances, and transmission of parasites and disease-causing organisms. Important parameters of a

population, such as its overall condition and mortality and reproductive rates (apart from factors independent of population density, such as climatic events), are therefore self-regulated via the population density.

Research on and description of the structure and dynamics of populations and ther interactions with the environment are research objectives of population ecology.

Population ecology: Subdiscipline of ecology with the objective to research the structure of populations (e. g., their age distribution, sex ratios, spacial distribution) and their dynamics (e. g., periodic density variations, gains and losses of population members). Also called biodemography.

Poromera BOULENGER, 1887. Monotypic genus of the Lacertidae. Tropical West Africa. Presumably related to *Bedriagaia*. Body moderately flattened dorso-ventrally. Tail more than twice snout-vent length. Hind legs long. Dorsal and ventral scales large, strongly keeled, with intermittent smaller scales. Caudal scales in unequal whorls, strongly keeled. Collar distinct. More than 10 femoral pores.

Mode of life similar to *Lacerta echinata*. Dendrophilic. Very rare.
- *P. fordi* (HALLOWELL, 1857). Tropical West Africa (Cameroons, Congo). Easily to 20 cm. Black-brown with 2 lighter lateral stripes on the anterior half of the body, appearing overall dark.

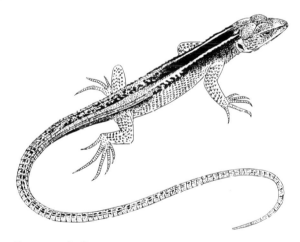

Poromera fordi

Potamal: Region with evenly flowing water with a medium or high dissolved oxygen content and high summer or seasonal temperatures. In temperate latitudes it corresponds to the lowland rivers, but also includes tropical streams in montane regions at moderate elevations. For terrarium hobbyists this does not necessarily mean that specimens that are ecologically tied to a "tropical creek" have to be maintained with state-of-the-art-technology like stream species from the temperate and high montane zones.

Pothos L. Genus of the Araceae. Mainly in Malaya. 47 species. Climbing semishrubs. Ideally suited for creeping along the back wall of a terrarium.
- *P. sandens* L. Leaves 6-8 cm.
- *P. loureirii* HOOK. and ARN. Resilient, with small leaves.

Potomotyphlus TAYLOR, 1968. Genus of the Typhlonecti-

dae. Tropical South America. 2 species. 50-70 cm. Body, in contrast to the other genera in this family, with a small head and a thin neck relative to the body diameter. 88-99 primary folds. Median skin fold posteriorly just as in the related genus *Typhlonectes*. Anal region of male cream-colored, a long deep groove with an extended copulatory organ.
▪ *P. kaupi* (BERTHOLD, 1859). To 70 cm. Dorsum gray-olive, head and neck lighter. Sides and abdomen yellow-olive.

Prairies: Form of vegetation of the eremial that occurs (or once occurred) over vast regions in eastern and central North America and has developed as grasslands analogous to the Euro-Siberian steppes. A temperature gradient (from south to north) and precipitation gradient (from east to west) necessitate many types of prairies. For herpetological purposes it suffices to subdivide the prairies into long

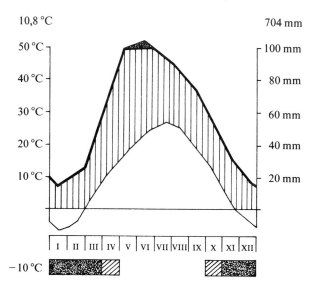

Climate diagram of prairies

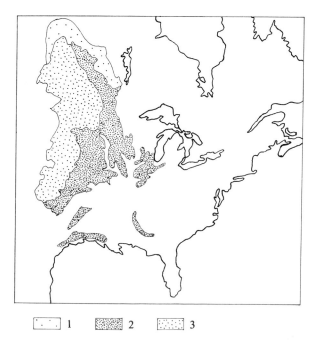

Prairies: 1 Northern; 2 long grass; 3 mixed grass and short grass

grass and short grass prairies. The eastern long grass prairies have—just as steppes—many flowering plants, but since there is no summer dry season flowers also occur in abundance into late summer and early fall. Since long grass prairies make excellent agricultural land there are now only remnants of this type of prairie left. The western short grass prairies are characterized by an arid climate and represent essentially grazing land with a poor flowering shrub fauna. Similar to steppes, prairies have a cold winter climate. Herpetological inhabitants of long grass prairies must not be kept too dry.

Prasinohaema GREER, 1974. Genus of the Scincidae, *Leiolopisma* Group. New Guinea and adjacent islands. 5 species. Related to *Scincella* and very similar. 15 to 25 cm. Tree-dwellers. Conspicuous green blood and various green tissues.
▪ *P. virens* PETERS, 1881.

Praslinia BOULENGER, 1909. Monotypic genus of the Caeciliidae. Seychelles. Relatively compact. Conspicuously small, rather numerous teeth, the anterior part of the upper jaw row with 85-95 teeth. Tentacle about 3 times as far from the nostril as from the eye. Skin with tiny calcareous scales.
▪ *P. cooperi* BOULENGER, 1909. To 23 cm. Uniformly black-brown.

Preanal pores: Skin glands in front of the cloacal region in various lizards that are very much better developed in males. They open to the outside on the upper sides of enlarged scales. The structure and secretion of these glands can be compared to femoral pores.

Predation: Feeding behavior directed toward feeding on animals. The vast majority of all reptiles and amphibians and many of their larvae and metamorphosed juveniles are predators.

Pregnancy: Condition of a female from fertilization of the eggs to the birth of the young or, in ovoviviparous animals, up to the laying of the egg membrane with the young. Duration of pregnancy is variable, depending upon species and upon environmental factors (temperature, moisture).

Prey capture: Predatory amphibians and reptiles can be categorized into two groups on the basis of the method employed to capture prey: active hunters that follow their anticipated prey, and those that lie passively in waiting for their prey to come within range accidentally. There are transitional forms between these two types. Some animals have specially developed adaptations to facilitate prey capture (e. g., *Chioglossa, Bufo, Macroclemys*, family Chamaeleonidae). Knowledge of the prey capture method used by various terrarium animals is important for hobbyists to be able to provide the correct type of food, especially during an acclimation period for newly arrived animals. For instance, an animal used to lying in wait may starve to death because it can not find the food available at the terrarium's feeding station or food container.

Prionodactylus O'SHAUGNESSY, 1881. Genus of the Teiidae. Panama to Bolivia. 4 species in tropical rain forests. To 15 cm, slender. Head pointed. Lower eyelid in some species with a semitransparent window. Dorsal scales large, keeled, not in regular longitudinal rows. Brown with conspicuous black lateral spots.

Ground-dwellers.

• *P. argulus* PETERS, 1862. Upper northern Amazon region, Orinoco. Easily 10 cm. White upper lips.

Priority: In nomenclature, the precedence of the oldest valid published scientific name for a particular taxon. The priority rule once was applied without exception, which led to instability of the nomenclature due to the frequent "uncovering" of always newer names which took precedence over established names. Nowadays the priority rule has been restricted; older synonyms must have been in use in the scientific literature for the preceding 50 years if they are to be considered valid. For certain long-established generic names there is even a list of *nomina conservanda*, names declared to be permanently valid even if older names are found.

Pristurus RUEPPEL, 1835. Genus of the Gekkonidae. Northeastern Africa to southwestern Asia. 7 species in dry, often rocky habitats. To 10 cm. Slender, cylindrical. Tail about snout-vent length, laterally compressed, and with distinctly protruding median keels above and below. Pupil round; lid swellings present around the eye. Brown to olive with darker spots.

Diurnal ground-dwellers. *Pristurus* species require more radiant heat than do most other gekkonids. For details of care refer to *Eremias*.

• *P. flavipunctatus* RUEPPEL, 1835. Arabia to Somalia. 8 cm.

• *P. rupestris* BLANFORD, 1874. Arabia to Pakistan. 7 cm. A reddish median stripe and lateral spots.

Proablepharus FUHN, 1969. Genus of the Scincidae. Australia. 3 species in arid regions. Barely to 10 cm. Eyes with transparent spectacles. Ear openings very small. Legs short. Only a few specimens known.

• *P. kinghorni* (COPLAND, 1947). New South Wales and Queensland. Formerly in *Notoscincus*.

Probreviceps PARKER, 1931. Genus of the Microhylidae. East Africa. 3 species. Closely related to *Breviceps*, similarly plump with conical skin warts. Pupil horizontal. Tympanum variably visible. Fingers and toes free and without adhesive discs. Inner metatarsal tubercle flat, large, oval; outer tubercle smaller, indistinctly developed.

Burrowing forest-dwellers. Eggs are deposited in damp hollows in the ground. Completely metamorphosed juvenile frogs hatch from the eggs.

Keep these frogs in a moderately damp terrarium setup with a thick layer of loose substrate and temperatures from 20 to 25° C. The diet should consist mainly of small insects (ants, wingless fruitflies) for best results.

• *P. macrodactylus* (NIEDEN, 1926). Rungwe, Uluguru, and Usambara Mountains, Tanzania. 3 subspecies. To 6 cm. Dorsally unicolored reddish brown, ventrally light brown with darker spots.

• *P. uluguruensis* (LOVERIDGE, 1925). Uluguru Mountains, Tanzania. 4.5 cm (females), 3 cm (males). Dorsally light brown, sides and belly reddish brown with a sparse pattern of lighter spots.

Proceratophrys MIRANDA-RIBEIRO, 1920. Smooth Horned Frogs. Genus of the Leptodactylidae. Brasil, Argentina. 4-8 species. Sometimes considered to be a synonym of *Ceratophrys*, but much more closely related to *Odontophrynus*. Compact. In contrast to *Odontophrynus*, always without parotoid glands and with free toes (lateral skin folds present). Some species have pointed upper eyelids as in *Ceratophrys*.

For details on mode of life and care refer to *Odontophrynus*.

• *P. boiei* (WIED, 1825). Upper eyelid lobate.

• *P. bigibbosa* (PETERS, 1872). Upper eyelid with a bump.

Proceratophrys boiei

Procinura COPE, 1879. Monotypic genus of the Colubridae, Boiginae. Mexico. Closely related to *Sonora* and now usually considered a synonym. In deserts and similar dry habitats in mountain regions to 2,800 m elevation. To 40 cm. Head not set off from body. Anal region and top of tail with extremely heavily keeled dorsal scales. Very irregularly and variably banded red-black on tan. Nocturnal burrowing snakes.

• *P. aemula* COPE, 1879.

Proctoporus TSCHUDI, 1845. Light Bulb Teiids. Genus of the Teiidae. Tropical South America. 15 species, some along the Andean slopes. 10-15 cm. Slender, with short, thin limbs. Primarily brown, the lower rows of lateral scales reflective, especially among males of some species. The light reflected is bright enough that light organs were once presumed to be present.

Crepuscular to nocturnal ground-dwellers found among fallen leaves.

• *P. shrevei* PARKER, 1935. Trinidad. Strong light reflecting ability.

• *P. bolivianus* WERNER, 1910. Peru to Bolivia, eastern Andean slopes.

Proctotretus DUMERIL and BIBRON, 1837. Genus of the Iguanidae. Central and southern South America east of the

Procinura aemula

Andes. 3 species. Easily to 20 cm. Weakly flattened. Similar to *Liolaemus*, but males without preanal pores. Tail about ½ snout-vent length. Dorsal crest weakly developed. Dorsal scales shingled and keeled, with a smooth transition between the lateral and ventral scales.

▪ *P. pectinatus* DUMERIL and BIBRON, 1837. Southern Brasil to central Argentina. Easily to 20 cm. Greenish to brown, sometimes with light-bordered spots and light longitudinal stripes.

Prolapse: Intestinal prolapse, cloacal prolapse. Protrusion of the end of the cloaca or intestine through the vent. Prolapse of the mucous membrane of the rectum and that of the cloaca as well as of the penis in males occurs predominantly in giant toads and salamanders but also in lizards, turtles, and snakes. Depending upon the duration of such prolapse the membrane is discolored bluish red, swollen, soiled, and not infrequently damaged.

Causes include a disturbed ion equilibrium, as with mineral or vitamin deficiency leading to an excessive relaxation of the tissue; constipation; and inflammatory irritation of the rectum or cloaca.

Therapy is more likely to be effective the sooner it is initiated. Depending upon the degree of injury and soiling there can either be a complete repositioning or there has to be a resection of the prolapsed tissue under local anesthesia. Following that the cloaca and rectum walls can be sewn together. Food should not be offered for the first 3 weeks after surgery. In most cases it will not be necessary to remove the catgut.

Prophylaxis: Measures that can be applied in order to avoid diseases. The peculiarities of diseases in poikilothermic animals (long incubation, frequent parasite infestation, and occurrence of clinical diseases following weakening of resistance, often subclinical disease progression) make pro-

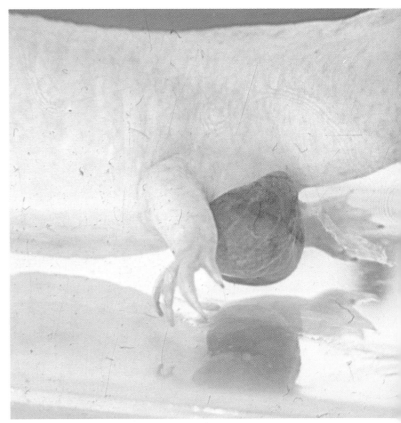

Cloacal prolapse in *Ambystoma mexicanum*

phylaxis one of the most important factors for treating diseases in terrarium animals. This includes optimum maintenance and nutrition (hiding places; bathing, climbing, and other facilities; assurance of correct temperature conditions; regular feeding; vitamin and mineral supplements) as well as a regular pathogen/parasite control through hygienic terrarium decoration and thorough cleaning, as well as frequent disinfection, frequent monitoring of the animals for abnormal behavior in order to be able to diagnose any occurring disease as quickly as possible, quarantine, and prophylactic treatment of those animals suspected to be disease or pathogen carriers.

Prosymma GRAY, 1849. Shovel-snouts. Genus of the Colubridae, Colubrinae, systematic position uncertain. Africa south of the Sahara, East Africa northeastward to Somalia. 12 species in steppes and savannahs, only *P. jani* and *P. ornatissima* also in evergreen forests; the other species prefer very dry habitats and also inhabit outer desert zones. From 30 to 40 cm. Cylindrical. Head barely set off. The large, projecting rostral, the fusion of some of the head scales into larger scales, and the strongly subterminal mouth are all features of the *Prosymma*. Scales smooth (only *P. jani* with keels). Tail short. Brown with various markings, such as neckbands and rows of spots, which are always conspicuous on the head; posteriorly the pattern tends to wash out into a unicolored appearance.

Burrowing snakes. During their subterranean activity inside the burrows in hard substrate they search mainly for eggs from various reptiles (gekkonids, agamids, skinks, snakes), for which they have become specialized. Egg-layers, 3-6 eggs.
• *P. sundevalli* (A. SMITH, 1849). Streaky Shovel-snout. Southern Africa. 2 subspecies. Row of dots along the vertebral column. Snout very pointed.

Protective adaptations: Special shapes, colorations, and types of behavior that can at least partially protect an animal against detrimental influences of other animals. While active protective adaptations become effective through actions on the part of the animals (such as the ability of venomous snakes to defend themselves with a venom bite), passive protective adaptations are always present, but they can be supported or activated only through particular behavior patterns.

A protective adaptation frequently present in amphibians and reptiles is protective coloration, e. g., the predominance of green or brown hues among tree-dwelling species that in combination with appropriate body shapes substantially enhance the camouflage effect. When other objects are imitated in color and form one refers to this as mimesis (e. g., certain frogs that may resemble leaves, while a particular gecko may look like the tree bark on which it spends much of its time). Another protective adaptation is disruptive coloration, which in normal surroundings breaks up body contours (somatolysis) but when viewed on its own the animal may be very conspicuous (e. g., Gaboon vipers, horned frogs).

An unusual form of protective adaptation is mimicry. This involves an imitation of an aggressively defensive, conspicuously colored animal by an essentially defenseless animal. Typical mimicry situations are the similarity between the typically colorfully ringed highly venomous coral snakes (*Micruroides, Micrurus*) and the harmless snakes of the genera *Lampropeltis, Erythrolamprus*, and others.

Behaviors associated with protective adaptations include catalepsy (a reflex triggering motionlessness and rigidity as a consequence of a long-lasting muscle contraction) and thanatosis (pretending to be dead, often observed in cer-

tain snakes where a total relaxation of the locomotory muscles occurs).

Protection is also afforded by various threat, fright, and warning types of behavior that frequently become effective in conjunction with certain colors and markings.

Proteidae: Olms and Waterdogs. Family of the Caudata. Holarctic. 2 genera (*Proteus* in Europe, *Necturus* in North America). Adult Proteidae always have a mixture of larval (permanently occurring gills and a high tail crest) and adult features (simple, sac-like lungs; lower jaw, intermaxillary, and palatine without teeth). The legs are relatively weak. Permanently aquatic, in contrast to *Ambystoma* the Proteidae can not be changed experimentally into land animals with thyroid extracts.

Proteroglyphic: see Teeth.

Proteus LAURENTI, 1768. Olms. Monotypic genus of the Proteidae. Northwestern Yugoslavia and near Trieste in subterranean limestone cave systems. Body very elongated, without pigment. Snout extended, duck-bill-like. Eyes small, lidless, covered by skin, vision poor. Legs frail, the front feet with 3 fingers, the hind feet with 2 toes. Larval stages have never been found in the wild, but are known through captive breeding. Eyes functional.

Proteus live in crystal-clear, substrate-filtered, practically germ-free, cool (6 to 12° C.), calcium-rich waters. Correct care requires complete compliance with optimal water conditions and a greatly reduced light level (electric illumination only for brief periods). The aquarium should be spacious and contain some large limestone rocks that serve as hiding places and a spawning substrate.

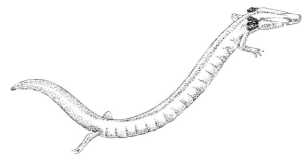

Proteus anguineus

With proper care *Proteus* will not only live for many years but will also breed regularly. Only during the breeding period does *Proteus* establish a territory that is defended against siblings. Under aquarium conditions *Proteus* can lay eggs (presumably the normal situation) or can give birth to live young. The eggs are yolk-rich, are deposited individually, and are guarded by the male. The incubation period depends upon the water temperature and generally takes several months. Larval size when hatching is 2 cm. Sexual maturity is reached after several years.
• *P. anguineus* LAURENTI, 1768. Olm. To 28 cm. Colorless. Gills red.

Protopipa: see *Pipa*, genus.

Protozoonosis: Protozoan infestations. Diseases caused by single-celled organisms and affecting mainly the mucous membranes of the digestive tract and the blood cells. The

Proteus anguineus

most important protozoan diseases include amoebic dysentery and coccidiosis, including infestations by hemogregarines. The flagellate genus *Leptomonas* in chameleons, *Hexamita* in turtles, and *Trichomonas* (which mainly parasitize the digestive tract of different reptiles but also move into the circulatory system) are all known to be pathogens. So far unresolved is the pathogenic significance of *Trypanosoma* that occur mainly in the blood of many reptiles. Leptomonads can cause a hemorrhaging intestinal inflammation; the host refuses to feed and regurgitates force-fed

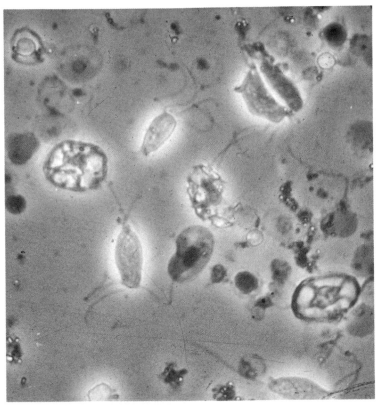

Protozoonosis: *Hexamita*

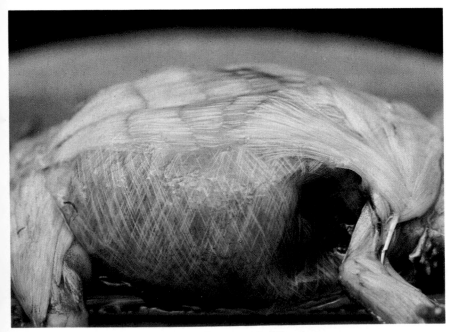

Protozoonosis: *Bufo bufo* with *Plistophora*

food. Diarrhea causes dehydration (the eyes suddenly sink in) and sudden death. *Hexamita* infection makes turtles apathetic; they lose weight and in advanced cases produce a slimy urine. Determination of parasite presence is by means of fecal sample checks. See your veterinarian for more details.

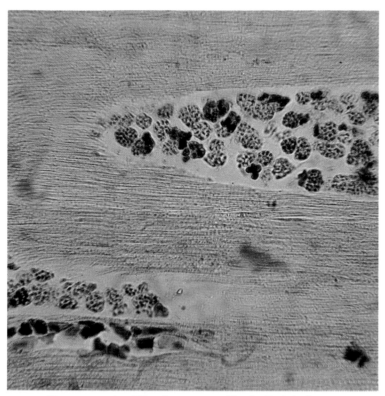

Protozoonosis: *Plistophora myotrophica* in *Bufo bufo*

Psammobates oculifer

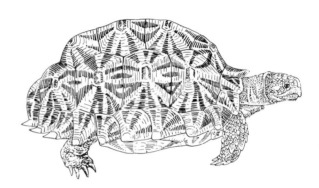

Psammobates oculifer

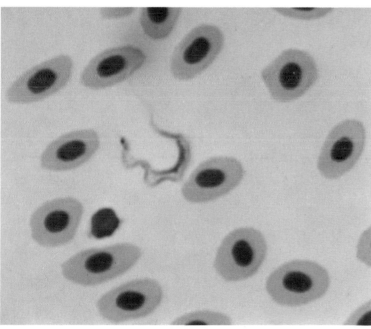

Protozoonosis: *Trypanosoma* in blood

Psammobates geometricus

Psammobates FITZINGER, 1835. Geometric Tortoises. Genus of the Testudinidae. Southern Africa. 3 species. In steppes and outer desert zones. 14 to 25 cm. Marked with yellow rays on the carapace shields; rare unicolored specimens are mutants.

These tortoises are specialized to feed on specific plants, and strict compliance with seasonal activity and rest periods is required. Populations of all species are seriously endangered.

▪ *P. geometricus* (L. 1758). Cape Geometric Tortoise. Southwestern Cape Province. The largest species. Margin of carapace smooth. Feeding specialist for certain sour grasses. Strictly protected. Most specimens are on a special reserve in southwestern Cape Province.

▪ *P. oculifer* (KUHL, 1820). Serrated Geometric Tortoise. Southwestern and southern Africa. Characteristic spine-like indentations on the marginal shields in the pelvic and neck region. Presumably feeds on various succulents. Virtually never lives more than 1 year in captivity.

▪ *P. tentorius* (BELL, 1828). Knobby Geometric Tortoise. Southern and southwestern Africa. 3 subspecies. Most

Psammobates tentorius verroxi

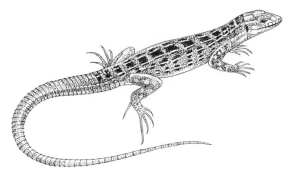

Psammodromus hispanicus

common species of this genus. Carapace scutes arched. Radiating marks, especially in *P. t. verroxi* (A. SMITH, 1839), strongly or completely reduced. With intensive efforts to supply a varied diet individual specimens have been kept for several years.

Psammodromus FITZINGER, 1826. Sand Lizards. Genus of the Lacertidae. Northwestern Africa and southwestern Europe. 4 species found in open sandy areas with little vegetation (frequently in dune areas); *P. algirus* frequently occurs in bushy steppes. Tail about twice snout-vent length. Dorsal scales large, rhombic, and keeled. Collar indistinct or absent. 10-21 femoral pores. Above mainly brown with light longitudinal stripes or spots. Abdomen or throat of males (*P. algirus*) orange to reddish during the breeding season.

Psammodromus algirus

Mating involves a neck bite. Egg-layers. They feed on various arthropods. Terrarium requirements are much as for *Eremias*, but less sensitive. A winter dormancy period of 2-3 months is recommended at least for European specimens. The smaller species are relatively compatible. Will breed readily.

▪ *P. algirus* (LINNAEUS, 1758). Algerian Sand Lizard. From southern France to Tunesia, Algeria, and Morocco. To 25 cm. Brown with 4 light lateral stripes; males with distinct ocelli behind bases of forelimbs; southern specimens with reddish throat. Largest species of the genus. Somewhat quarrelsome.

▪ *P. hispanicus* FITZINGER, 1826. Spanish Sand Lizard. Southern France and Iberian Peninsula. A social lizard occurring in small numbers in open, dry areas. 12 cm. Apart from light stripes, usually with light and dark rather regular spots; males with blue axillary and sometimes lateral spots. The similar *P. blanci* (LATASTE, 1880) and *P. microdactylus* (BOETTGER, 1881) occur in northwestern Africa.

Psammodynastes GUENTHER, 1859. Genus of the Colubridae, Boiginae. Eastern Himalayas through Indo-China, to southern China, Hainan, and Taiwan, southward through the Philippines and the Indo-Australian Archipelago. 2 species. In monsoon and montane forests, equally as common in lowlands as in mountain regions to nearly 2,000 m elevation. 50-65 cm. Slender, with an elongated head distinctly set off from the body, with a blunt snout and large eyes. Dorsal scales smooth. Coloration highly variable, but always with longitudinal stripes or rows of rhomboidal spots; a distinct pattern of 3 longitudinal stripes on top of the head in *P. pulverulentus*.

These snakes usually live in bushes and trees. The diet consists mainly of frogs and lizards, occasionally also other snakes. They give birth to 3-10 young. These snakes should be kept in a well-heated forest terrarium with ample climbing and hiding facilities. Caution: Venomous bites possible.

▪ *P. pulverulentus* (BOIE, 1827). Over entire generic range.

▪ *P. pictus* GUENTHER, 1858. Malaya, Sumatra, and some smaller islands.

Psammophilous: Preferring sandy substrates. Numerous reptiles and some amphibians with burrowing habits, forms such as *Breviceps, Cyclorana, Pelobates,* and *Scaphiopus,* are psammophilous.

Psammophilus FITZINGER, 1843. Genus of the Agamidae. Eastern India. 2 species. On rocky slopes to 2,000 m elevation. To 20 cm. Slender. Seldom available.

▪ *P. dorsalis* (GRAY, 1831). Southern India.

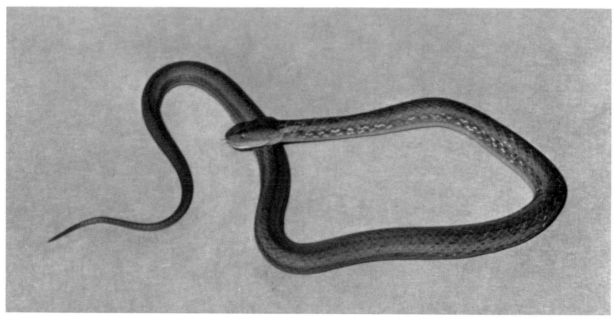

Psammodynastes pulverulentus

Psammophis BOIE, 1825. Sand Racers. Genus of the Colubridae, Boiginae. Africa and the Near East to central Asia. About 16 species in dry, hot habitats in thornbush steppes and deserts. About 70 cm to 1.7 m. Very slender, with a slender, long head only slightly set off from the body. Large eyes with round pupils, often protected by

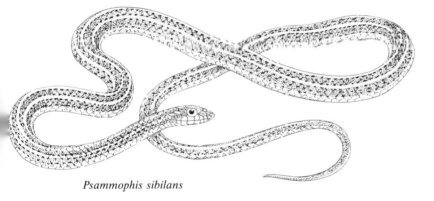

Psammophis sibilans

slightly arched supraorbital scales. Dorsal scales smooth, frequently shingled. Most species have longitudinal yellow to brown stripes; rarely unicolored (*P. s. sibilans*).

Diurnal ground snakes that are very agile hunters, mainly for lizards. When moving, often the anterior third of the body is slightly raised, to increase the field of vision. These snakes should be kept in a spacious, very well heated dry terrarium with lots of sun and a nocturnal temperature reduction. Resilient terrarium animals. Their food preference can sometimes be modified so they will accept mice as a substitute food. Caution: Venomous bites are possible. Serious bites have been attributed to *P. sibilans*.

▪ *P. sibilans* (LINNAEUS, 1758). Africa. 3 subspecies. Unicolored or striped. Largest species of the genus.

▪ *P. lineolatum* (BRANDT, 1838). Soviet Central Asia eastward to northwestern China and westward to Iran. Formerly contained in the monotypic genus *Taphrometopon*.

▪ *P. schokari* (FORSKAL, 1775). North Africa to the Arabian Peninsula and to southwestern Turkmenia (USSR). 2 subspecies.

Psammophis lineolatum

Psammophylax FITZINGER, 1843. African Grass Snakes. Genus of the Colubridae, Boiginae. Southern Africa. 2 species in steppes and savannahs. 80 cm to 1.1 m. Slender. Morphologically and biologically similar to *Psammophis*.

The diet consists mainly of lizards and small mammals, sometimes also frogs. Egg-layers, to 30 eggs. The venom of these snakes has a neurotoxic effect and is (at least in *P. rhombeatus*) rather dangerous to humans. For details on care refer to *Psammophis*.

▪ *P. rhombeatus* (LINNAEUS, 1758). Cape Province, eastward from South Africa to Transvaal. Back with rhomboidal spots.

▪ *P. tritaeniatus* (GUENTHER, 1868). Three-lined Grass Snake. Ethiopia to Republic of South Africa, in the west to Namibia. 2 subspecies. Attractive yellow-brown longitudinal stripes.

Psammosaurus, subgenus: see *Varanus*, genus.

Pseudablabes BOULENGER, 1896. Monotypic genus of the Colubridae, Boiginae; also included in the Natricinae or Xenodontinae by some systematists. Southern Brasil and Uruguay to northeastern Argentina. 40 cm. The head is small and indistinctly set off. Nocturnal burrowing snakes. Biological details are not available.
• *P. agassizi* (JAN, 1863).

Pseudacris FITZINGER, 1843. Chorus Frogs. Genus of the Hylidae. Nearctic. East of the Rocky Mountains from central Canada and all the USA southward to Florida and northeastern Mexico. 7 species, some polytypic. Usually in grasslands or swamps. 3-5 cm. Skin smooth. Fingers free, toes webbed over ⅔ of their length at the most. Adhesive discs barely wider than tips of fingers and toes. Yellow-brown or greenish with darker longitudinal stripes or rows of spots, a dark eyeband, and (in most species) a white upper lip.

These frogs are typical swamp and prairie species that may be common in some areas but generally lead a cryptic life outside the breeding season. During dry periods they remain in hiding. Loud, continuous, trilling calls during the mating season are triggered in northern populations by the onset of warm spring rains, but southern forms may breed during the winter months with cool rains. Brood waters are generally shallow ponds, flooded meadows, and similar habitats. These interesting little frogs should be kept in a swamp terrarium or an aqua-terrarium. Heating is not required. A winter dormancy period is not obligatory for southern forms.
• *P. clarki* (BAIRD, 1854). Spotted Chorus Frog. Kansas

Pseudacris ornata

Pseudacris clarki

Pseudacris triseriata

through Oklahoma and Texas to northeastern Mexico. 3 cm. Irregular green spots with black margins on a yellow-brown background. A triangular green spot on the forehead.
• *P. ornata* (HOLBROOK, 1836). Ornate Chorus Frog. Southeastern USA (North Carolina to Louisiana). 3.5 cm. Variably green to red brown with 2 brown longitudinal stripes or rows of spots. Large black, white-edged spots along the flanks.

Pseudaspis FITZINGER, 1843. Mole Snakes. Monotypic genus of the Colubridae, Colubrinae; systematic position uncertain. Africa from Angola and Kenya southward to Cape Province. One of the most common snakes in dry habitats in southern Africa. Found in rubble-covered mountain slopes as well as in sandy thornbush steppes. To 1.3 m. Massive and plump, with a small head not set off from the body and with normal head scales. The snout terminates in a pointed and small but distinctly projecting rostral scale. Juveniles are reddish brown with dark spots; adults are mostly unicolored darkish gray to black.

Burrowing snakes that feed mainly on small mammals plus lizards and reptile and bird eggs. Live-bearers, 30-50 young (a record of 95 young born at the London Zoo). For details on care refer to *Eryx*.
• *P. cana* (LINNAEUS, 1758).

Pseudechis WAGLER, 1830. Australian Black Snakes. Genus of the Elapidae. Australia and New Guinea. 4 species, some polytypic. *P. australis* and *P. colletti* occur in deserts

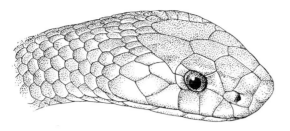

Pseudechis australis

and dry regions in tropical forests; *P. porphyriacus* is found in damp habitats (swamps and river and lake banks). 1.5 to 2 m. Robust. Similar to the closely related genus *Tropidechis*, but some subcaudals divided. A short, wide head. A strong tendency toward dark body colors and melanism.

Primarily diurnal venomous snakes that like to bathe (including species from dry regions), especially while hunting during warm nights. They prey on frogs, lizards, snakes, and small mammals. Live-bearers, 8 to 40 young. A characteristic threat behavior is the dorso-ventral flattening of the body, especially the widening of the neck region; a hood as in *Naja* and raising of the anterior part of the body do not occur.

Maintain in a well-heated terrarium with a large water bowl. Strict compliance with safety rules has to be assured, since the venom of these snakes is highly effective and they are quite aggressive. Some have been bred in captivity.
• *P. australis* (GRAY, 1842). Mulga, King Brown Snake. Australia except in extreme south and also in New Guinea. Usually solid brown.
• *P. porphyriacus* (SHAW, 1794). Red-bellied Black Snake. Eastern Australia. A shiny black back, the abdomen and flanks bright red.

Pseudemoia FUHN, 1969. Genus of the Scincidae. Systematic status uncertain. Southeastern Australia and Pedra Branca, a tiny rock island off the southern Tasmanian coast. 2 species. Often included in *Leiolopisma*. Found in damp montane forests (but Pedra Branca has no vegetation). 15 cm. Scales smooth to weakly keeled. Well-developed 5-toed limbs.

Ground-dwellers found under decaying wood and similar places. Ovoviviparous, 1-3 young.
• *P. spenceri* (LUCAS and FROST, 1894). Southeastern Australia. Dark brown to black with a lighter stripe and spot pattern.

Pseudemydura SIEBENROCK, 1901. Swamp Turtles. Monotypic genus of the Chelidae. Southwestern Australia. In swamps. Carapace 15 cm, flat. The very large intergular scute of the plastron completely separates the gular and pectoral scutes. Very short neck.

Carnivorous. Incubation under natural conditions takes about 180 days. Due to the very restricted range this is an endangered species and is strictly protected. Survival of the species through possible breeding in Australian zoos currently is being attempted.
• *P. umbrina* SIEBENROCK, 1901. Western Swamp Turtle. Swampy region near Perth, Western Australia.

Pseudemys: see *Chrysemys*, genus.

Pseudhymenochirus CHABANAUD, 1920. Monotypic ge-

Pseudemydura umbrina

nus of the Pipidae. Tropical West Africa. Together with closely related genus *Hymenochirus*, often referred to as dwarf clawed frogs. Both genera have the fingers and toes webbed. In contrast to *Hymenochirus*, *Pseudhymenochirus* has well-developed eyelids.

Aquatic. For details of care refer to *Hymenochirus*.
• *P. merlini* CHABANAUD, 1920. Guinea. To 4 cm.

Pseudidae: Harlequin Frogs, Shrinking Frogs. Family of the Salientia. South America. 2 genera (*Lysapsus, Pseudis*). 2 to 7.5 cm. Pupil horizontal. Tympanum visible. Hind legs conspicuously long and powerful. An extra bone is present in the fingers and toes as in Hylidae and Rhacophoridae. The thumb is opposable to the fingers. The larvae are extremely large in comparison to metamorphosed juvenile frogs, about 5 times as long as the juvenile frog.

Larvae and adults are aquatic.

Pseudis WAGLER, 1830. Common Shrinking Frogs. Genus of the Pseudidae. Tropical and subtropical South America east of the Andes. 3 partly polytypic species found in large standing waters in flood-prone areas of major rivers. 2-7.5 cm. Skin smooth. Snout pointed. Fingers free, the toes completely webbed. In contrast to the related genus *Lysapsus*, the palatine teeth are located between the choanal openings and the tips of the extremities are hardly enlarged. Larvae of *P. paradoxus* grow to 25 cm and are considered to be delicacies by the native population.

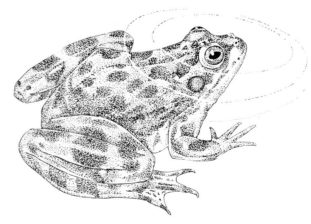

Pseudis paradoxus

Pseudis species are largely aquatic. If their habitat dries out temporarily they burrow in damp mud. These frogs lie in wait for their prey (flying insects) among floating plants at the surface but will also take fish eggs and even other frogs. In captivity they often take pieces of lean meat. *Pseudis* are surprisingly shy and will dive upon the slightest disturbance. They scatter their eggs at random among floating plants where they form foamy masses.

Pseudis should be kept in spacious, warm (about 25° C.) aquariums. Cover should be provided by robust floating water plants (*Pistia, Eichhornia*).
• *P. paradoxus* (LINNAEUS, 1758). From Guyana and Surinam to Argentina. 6 subspecies. To 7.5 cm, males smaller. Olive green to brownish, often with a darker pattern. Belly light, without spots.

Pseudoboa SCHNEIDER, 1801. Genus of the Colubridae, Boiginae. Panama through South America on both sides of the Andes Mountains. 4 species. Closely related to *Oxyrhopus*. Found in gallery forests and savannahs. About 1 m.

Ground snakes often living close to water. The main diet is lizards and small mammals. Egg-layers, 4-6 eggs.
• *P. coronata* SCHNEIDER, 1801. Amazon Basin and adjacent regions (Surinam and Guyana to Peru). Uniformly red with a black and yellow head.

Pseudoboa neuwiedii

Pseudobranchus GRAY, 1825. Dwarf Sirens. Monotypic genus of the Sirenidae. Southeastern USA. In varied but always shallow waters. To 21 cm. In contrast to the genus *Siren*, the hands have 3 fingers ending in horny claws and there is only 1 gill aperture.

Pseudobranchus have been helped by the introduction of the water hyacinth *Eichhornia*. They are able to find a lot of food and cover among the roots of these floating plants. In captivity dwarf sirens are hardy and interesting animals to observe. They should be kept in an aquarium with a low water level at subtropical temperatures (about 20° C.). It is advisable to cover the surface with floating plants, such as *Eichhornia* and *Pistia*, which reduce light levels, provide protection, and also counteract nutrient enrichment of the water.
• *P. striatus* (LE CONTE, 1824). Dwarf Siren. Florida and adjacent states. Polytypic, the 5 subspecies distinguished from each other mainly by details of their striped pattern.

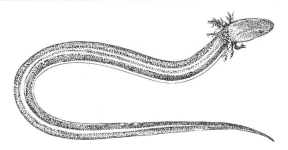

Pseudobranchus striatus

Back dark brown with 1 to 4 light stripes, the sides with 2 broader yellow longitudinal stripes.

Pseudobufo TSCHUDI, 1839. Monotypic genus of the Bufonidae. Tropical Southeast Asia in standing or slow-flowing waters very close to large lowland rivers. Massive, compact, and flattened. Tympanum clearly visible. Skin with warts, extremely rough. Limbs strong, the fingers and toes long and thin, webbed. Parotoid glands absent.

Aquatic, excellent swimmers and divers. Reproduction similar to *Bufo*; small pigmented eggs are deposited in large numbers. They should be kept in a spacious tropical aquarium with shallow water and a small land section (rocks, decorative cork island).
• *P. subasper* TSCHUDI, 1839. Sandpaper Toad. Malaya, eastern Sumatra, southern Kalimantan. 15 cm (females), 10 cm (males). Brown, often with oblique orange dorso-lateral stripes.

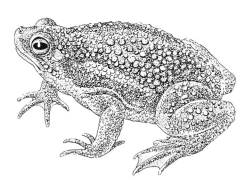

Pseudobufo subasper

Pseudoceramodactylus HAAS, 1957. Monotypic genus of the Gekkonidae. Arabia. Known only from the type locality.
• *P. khobarensis* HAAS, 1957.

Pseudocerastes BOULENGER, 1896. Asiatic Horned Vipers. Genus of the Viperidae, Viperinae. Near East. Systematics doubtful. Some systematists consider this genus monotypic (*P. persicus*); others distinguish 4 species. Possibly only a subgenus of *Daboia*. In deserts and rocky areas of desert-like character in mountain regions. About 1 m. Horny scales over the eyes. Dorsal scales with keels uniformly arranged in longitudinal rows in contrast to *Cerastes* and *Echis*. They move by sidewinding but do not rattle the scales. Cryptic coloration, sandy yellow to light olive with dark crossbands.

Nocturnal venomous snakes that prey on lizards (gekkonids) and small mammals. Only few young, 2 to 4.

Keep in a well-heated desert terrarium with large nightly temperature reductions. Adjustment to life in captivity is

Pseudocerastes persicus

often difficult, but adapted specimens are excellent display animals. Has occasionally been bred.

- *P. fieldi* SCHMIDT, 1930. Northern Arabia, Sinai Peninsula, Israel to Iraq.
- *P. latirostris* GUIBE, 1957. Iran.
- *P. persicus* (DUMERIL, BIBRON, and DUMERIL, 1854). Iran, Pakistan.

Pseudocordylus SMITH, 1838. False Girdled Lizards. Genus of the Cordylidae. Southern Africa. 4 species in rocky dry regions up to 2,000 m elevation. Over all very similar to *Cordylus*, but even more flattened dorso-ventrally and with only weakly spinous scales. Mainly shades of brown.

Mode of life and care as for *Cordylus*. Apart from various insects, they will also take leaves (such as lettuce and dandelions) and flowers. Ovoviviparous, usually 3 to 6 young.
- *P. microlepidotus* (CUVIER, 1829). To 32 cm. Spines on scales small. The largest species of the genus.

Pseudoeryx FITZINGER, 1826. Monotypic genus of the Colubridae, Natricinae. South America from Colombia and Guyana and Surinam to Argentina. In ponds and slow-flowing waters of tropical rain forests with dense vegetation. Males to 80 cm, females to 1.45 m. Head small, not set off from the body. Eyes small and turned upwards, as are the nostrils. Very wide, smooth dorsal scales. Back either uniformly brown or with two rows of blackish dots and longitudinal lateral bands.

Pseudoeryx lead an aquatic life. They hunt for relatively large fish and occasionally frogs during their nocturnal activity phase. Care as for Natricinae, Group 3.

- *P. plicatilis* (LINNAEUS, 1758).

Pseudoeurycea TAYLOR, 1944. Genus of the Plethodontidae. Northern Central America, mainly in the Mexican Highlands. About 25 species. Hard to distinguish on the basis of external features from the closely related genera *Bolitoglossa* and *Chiropterotriton*. The status of many species is uncertain.

As far as known, all species live more or less arboreally (some close to the ground in hollow tree stumps filled with decaying leaves, some in bromeliads) or strictly terrestrially in damp forests; some also follow human habitation in urban settlements, hiding during the day under flowerpots, damp lumber, decaying wood, and rocks. Species from arid regions require a dry dormancy period. They deposit a few (generally less than 25) large, unpigmented eggs in depressions, crevices, and similar damp sites, possibly also in epiphytes, and guard the clutch until the young, completely metamorphosed salamanders hatch, which usually takes place at the onset of the rainy season. Keep relatively

Pseudoeurycea belli

Pseudoeurycea scandens

cool (measured summer temperature 10.2° C. for a site of *P. juarezi*).

▪ *P. belli* (GRAY, 1849). Western and southwestern central Mexico. 12 cm. Back black with 2 rows of bright red spots.

▪ *P. juarezi* REGAL, 1966. Oaxaca, Mexico. 8 cm. Light brown with dark spots especially along the flanks.

▪ *P. nigromaculatus* (TAYLOR, 1941). Veracruz, Mexico. 11 cm. Brown with blackish spots.

Pseudoeurycea cephalica

Pseudoficimia BOCOURT, 1883. Genus of the Colubridae, Colubrinae. Western Mexico from southern Sonora to Guerrero. 2 species. To 30 cm. Burrowing snakes with a short shovel-like snout. Biology appears to be similar to that of *Ficimia*.

▪ *P. frontalis* (COPE, 1864). Brown with 3 longitudinal rows of black spots.

Pseudogekko TAYLOR, 1922. Genus of the Gekkonidae. Philippines and Solomon Islands. 2 species. Similar to *Gekko*, but smaller.

▪ *P. compressicorpus* (TAYLOR, 1915). Luzon, Philippines.

Pseudogonatodes RUTHVEN, 1915. Genus of the Gekkonidae. Northern and central South America in tropical forests. 4 species. About 5 to 6 cm. Similar to *Gonatodes*, but with retractile claws.

In part diurnal ground-dwellers.

▪ *P. furvus* RUTHVEN, 1915. Colombia.

Pseudohaje GUENTHER, 1858. Forest Cobras. Genus of the Elapidae. Central Africa. 2 species. In forests. 2 to 2.7 m. Conspicuously large eyes. Hood small. Dark.

Tree-dwellers feeding almost exclusively on frogs. They also enter water during their predominantly nocturnal activity phase and are agile swimmers. Due to their cryptic mode of life and rarity, their biology and venom potency are hardly known.

Maintenance requires a well-heated dry forest terrarium with a large water bowl. Nocturnal temperature reductions are easily tolerated.

▪ *P. goldii* (BOULENGER, 1895). Black Forest Cobra. Uganda to West Africa, Nigeria to Angola and Namibia.

Pseudohemisus MOCQUARD, 1895. Genus of the Microhylidae. Madagascar. 4 species (some of dubious taxonomic status). Compact. Pupil horizontal. Tympanum barely visible. Fingers free, the toes webbed at the base only and also with lateral skin folds. No distinct adhesive discs.

Presumably burrowing ground-dwellers.

▪ *P. madagascariensis* (BOULENGER, 1882). Adringitra Mountains. 5.5 cm. Gray-olive with large brown spots.

▪ *P. granulosus* GUIBE, 1952. Western Madagascar in forested areas. 2 cm. Brown with diffuse spots and a light dorsal stripe. Skin granular.

Pseudoleptodeira TAYLOR, 1938. Genus of the Colubridae, Boiginae. The Mexican Highlands between Michoacan and Oaxaca. 2 species. Related to *Leptodeira* and *Hypsiglena*. Found in dry habitats, thornbush steppes to cactus deserts. 40-60 cm. Distinctly set off head. Eye with a vertical pupil. The smooth-scaled back is brown with darker crossbands.

Nocturnal ground snakes that feed mainly on lizards. Maintain in a well-heated dry terrarium with a substantial nocturnal temperature reduction.

▪ *P. discolor* (GUENTHER, 1860). Central and southern Oaxaca. Crossbands dark with white edges, close together. This species is now placed in a monotypic genus, *Tantalophis* DUELLMAN, 1958.

▪ *P. latifasciata* (GUENTHER, 1894). Region of the Rio Balsas in western Mexico. Crossbands whitish, far apart.

Pseudomonad infection: Common bacterial infectious disease of reptiles, appearing mainly as stomatitis infectiosa, pneumonia, and diseases of the stomach and digestive tract (diarrhea). Abscesses are also frequently caused by pseudomonads. A general pseudomonad infection manifests itself through food refusal, regurgitation of partially digested food, and bloody discharges from various body openings. The pathogens *Pseudomonas aeruginosa* and *P. fluorescens* commonly occur in conjunction with other bacteria.

Therapy: Gentamycin, also sulfonamide. Required symptomatic measures depend upon the primary symptoms (diarrhea, pneumonia, stomatitis infectiosa).

Pseudonaja GUENTHER, 1858. Australian Brown Snakes. Genus of the Elapidae. Australia and New Guinea. Included in *Demansia* by some systematists. 6 species in deserts and savannah-like dry regions. 50 cm to 1.5 m. Slender, with a small head. Adult specimens are often unicolored and without markings. However, *P. modesta* and *P. guttata* have a more or less distinct neckband and crossbands on the body and tail. Coloration and markings show substantial intraspecific variations.

Pseudonaja species are partially diurnal (*P. modesta*, *P. textilis*) or crepuscular, very fast, venomous snakes. The diet consists mainly of lizards; small mammals are rarely taken. Egg-layers; 10 to 35 eggs. Maintain in a well-heated dry terrarium. *Pseudonaja* venom probably is not very dangerous to humans.

▪ *P. modesta* (GUENTHER, 1872). Ringed Brown Snake. Western and central Australia.

▪ *P. textilis* (DUMERIL and BIBRON, 1854). Eastern Brown Snake. Eastern Australia and New Guinea. 2-3 subspecies.

Pseudopaludicola MIRANDA-RIBEIRO, 1926. Genus of the Leptodactylidae. Coastal regions of Venezuela, Brasil, Argentina, Paraguay, eastern Bolivia, and Colombia (Sierra Nevada de Santa Marta, *llanos*). 6 species in swamps or close to stagnant waters. Snout-vent length a few centimeters. Elongated, long-snouted. Pupil horizontal. Tympanum not visible. Hind legs strong. Fingers and toes free and without skin folds. Vocal sac tends to be paired.

Semiaquatic, very agile, and excellent jumpers. Numerous small eggs are attached individually or in small clumps to underwater plants.

▪ *P. ameghini* (COPE, 1887). Brasil, sometimes very common. 1.5 cm. Earth colors with a darker pattern.

▪ *P. pusilla* (RUTHVEN, 1916) (= *P. boliviana* PARKER, 1927). Venezuela, Colombia, Bolivia. 1.5 cm.

Pseudophryne FITZINGER, 1843. Australian Toadlets. Genus of the Leptodactylidae. Australia. About 10 species. Found in various habitats (except in the extremely arid regions in the interior of Australia) and in mountains far above the tree line; *P. corroboree* occurs only at elevations above 1,500 m. Usually up to 3 cm. Compact, toad-like. Snout short. Pupil horizontal. Tympanum and middle ear structures absent. Parotoid glands in most species distinct. Limbs short and fragile. Fingers and toes free. Some species have a light dorsal pattern and all have characteristic black and white abdominal spots.

Ground-dwellers that usually remain hidden under rocks, logs, or in dense vegetation. Ponds serve as spawning grounds; some species deposit their eggs in small, damp crevices in the ground at the edge of swamps and moors.

These little frogs can be kept in small, slightly heated semimoist terrariums. Open-air maintenance is recom-

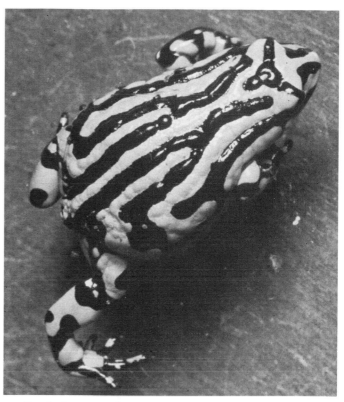

Pseudophryne corroboree

mended for the summer months.

▪ *P. australis* (GRAY, 1835). Red-crowned Toadlet. New South Wales, on the central coast. 3 cm. Dark brown to black, often with reddish spots and with a bright red triangular marking on top of the head.

▪ *P. bibroni* GUENTHER, 1858. Brown Toadlet. Southeastern Australia and Tasmania. 3 cm. Brown to black, with an orange or yellow pectoral spot. Widely distributed.

▪ *P. corroboree* MOORE, 1953. Corroboree Frog. Australian Alps of southeastern New South Wales. 3 cm. Very characteristic contrasting yellow and black stripes and spots. The most attractive species of the genus.

▪ *P. semimarmorata* LUCAS, 1892. Southern Toadlet. Southeastern tip of Australia and Tasmania. To 3 cm. Dark olive-green to brown with an irregular pattern of darker spots.

Pseudorhabdion JAN, 1862. Genus of the Colubridae, Calamarinae. Thailand southward through Malaya to Sumatra, Kalimantan, Sulawesi, and the Philippines. 2 species. 23 cm. Iridescent black-brown with a narrow yellow neckband.

Burrowing snakes.

▪ *P. longipes* (CANTOR, 1847). Over the entire generic range.

Pseudosiphonops TAYLOR, 1968. Monotypic genus of the Caeciliidae. Brasil. Elongated. Head somewhat wider than body. 89 primary folds (in type specimen), no secondary folds, without embedded scales. Only 1 row of teeth in the lower jaw. Tentacle located closer to nostril than to eye. Cloacal field extended, without furrows.

▪ *P. ptychodermis* TAYLOR, 1968. 26 cm. Brownish lilac with white rings.

Pseudotestudo LOVERIDGE and WILLIAMS, 1957. Genus of Testudinidae, usually considered a subgenus of *Testudo*.

Pseudophryne australis

Pseudotestudo kleinmanni

Northeastern Africa to western Asia in steppes and desert regions. To 12 cm. The carapace is light brownish with dark edges to the scutes. Posterior flap of plastron slightly movable.

Seasonally active. Due to its highly selective herbivorous diet, captive maintenance is rather difficult; different food plants may have to be tried. Rarely imported.
▪ *P. kleinmanni* (LORTET, 1883). Egyptian Tortoise. Eastern Libya through Egypt and the Sinai Peninsula to southern Israel.

Pseudothecadactylus BRONGERSMA, 1936. Genus of the Gekkonidae. 2 speces. Northern Australia and adjacent islands. 20 cm. Large, active geckos that are poorly known.
▪ *P. australis* (GUENTHER, 1887).

Pseudotomodon KOSLOWSKY, 1896. Monotypic genus of the Colubridae, Boiginae. South America. Possibly a synonym of the closely related genus *Tomodon*, as *P. trigonatus* is thought by some to be identical with *T. ocellatus*.

Pseudotriton TSCHUDI, 1838. Red Salamanders, Mud Salamanders. Genus of the Plethodontidae. Eastern North America. 2 polytypic species found in and close to small

Pseudotriton ruber schnecki

Pseudotomodon trigonatus

flowing waters of mountains and highlands and in swamps and bogs. 15 cm. Compact, the snout conspicuously short. Tail relatively short, heavy. Bright red, with increasing age becoming browner. Usually with round black dots or spots above.

Pseudotriton species as adults are more or less semi-aquatic, but during the summer they tend to frequent land more than at other seasons. The eggs are deposited from fall until spring, are without pigment, and are attached to leaves, the underside of flat rocks, and other suitable substrates in water, and then guarded by the female. These colorful salamanders should be kept in a cool aqua-terrarium with a large water bowl much like *Desmognathus* species. During the winter months they can live in an aquarium with a low water level at temperatures from 5 to 10° C. (possibly in a refrigerator).

• *P. montanus* BAIRD, 1849. Mud Salamander. Eastern USA southward to central Florida. 4 doubtful subspecies. Near and in muddy creeks. 15 cm. Iris brownish.

• *P. ruber* (SONNINI, 1802). Red Salamander. Eastern USA. 4 doubtful subspecies. In and near clear, cool creek with sandy bottom and in bogs. 15 cm. Iris yellow.

Pseudotriton ruber ruber

Pseudotyphlops SCHLEGEL, 1839. Monotypic genus of the Uropeltidae. Sri Lanka. 28 cm; 2.2 cm in diameter, which for Uropeltidae is rather thick. No chin furrows. Tail cylindrical, with smooth scales. Terminal caudal scale nearly circular, with radially arranged tubercles. Terminal spur absent. Burrowing snakes.

• *P. philippinus* SCHLEGEL, 1839. Sri Lanka. Lowlands.

Brown. The scientific name is in error, as the species does not occur in the Philippines.

Pseudoxenodon BOULENGER, 1890. Genus of the Colubridae, Natricinae. From Indo-China eastward to southeastern China and southward to Java. The center of diversity is this genus is in southeastern China, where more than half of all species occur. About 9 species in tropical monsoon forests, rain forests, and especially in montane rain forests (actually bamboo forests) to more than 2,000 m elevation. 0.5 to 1.2 m. Head distinctly set off from the body and with conspicuously large eyes. Dentition in upper jaw rather similar to that in *Rhabdophis*: the last two teeth are substantially enlarged and separated from the preceding one by a gap. Keeled scales. Coloration and markings highly variable and attractive, some species (*P. macrops* and others) with significant differences between juvenile and adult coloration.

Nocturnal. The diet consists mainly of toads, frogs, and lizards. They are capable of handling extremely large prey. Egg-layers. Excited specimens flatten their entire body and threaten with their mouth open. However, this is generally not accompanied by raising the anterior part of the body as in the closely related genus *Macropisthodon*. Care as for Natricinae, Group 1. Caution: Venomous bites possible; the venom is potent.

• *P. macrops* (BLYTH, 1854). From Nepal eastward to southern China and southward to the Malayan Peninsula; also on Hainan. In mountains to more than 2,000 m elevation.

• *P. jacobsoni* (VAN LIDTH DE JEUDE, 1922). Sumatra at elevations of about 800 m.

• *P. inornatus* (BOIE, 1827). Java.

• *P. karlschmidti* POPE, 1928. China (Fukien, Kwangsi, and Kwangtung) at elevations from 600 to 1200 m.

Pseudoxyrhopus GUENTHER, 1881. Genus of the Colubridae, Lycodontinae. Madagascar. 8 species. 35 cm to 1.1 m. The head is very distinct, elongated-oval, and has small upward-pointing eyes. Tail relatively short. Either solid brownish olive or with light and dark longitudinal bands.

Ecology and biology essentially unknown. Probably amphibious snakes of the tropical rain forest. Maintenance as for Natricinae, Groups 1 and 2.

• *P. quinquelineatus* (GUENTHER, 1881).

• *P. microps* (GUENTHER, 1881).

Pseustes FITZINGER, 1843. Genus of the Colubridae, Colubrinae. Neotropics from Mexico to southeastern Brasil. 4

Pseustes poecilonotus

Pseustes poecilonotus polylepis

Pseustes sulphureus

species inflate their throats and simultaneously vibrate their tails. Can be kept much as *Elaphe*, but in a well-heated terrarium.

• *P. poecilonotus* (GUENTHER, 1858). Mexico to the Amazon Basin.

• *P. sulphureus* (WAGLER, 1824). Amazon Basin to south-eastern Brasil.

Ptenopus GRAY, 1865. Genus of the Gekkonidae. Southern Africa. In deserts and semideserts (Kalahari). 2 species. To 10 cm. Tail clearly less than snout-vent length. The toes lack adhesive pads and serve as digging tools for which they are widened on top and have long claws. At dusk these geckos emit chirping sounds.

Nocturnal ground-dwellers that move relatively slowly. For maintenance refer to *Teratoscincus* (but without winter dormancy period).

• *P. garrulus* (SMITH, 1949). Whistling Gecko.

Pteris L. Border Ferns. Genus of the Filicatae. Tropics and subtropics, to the Mediterranean Region. 280 species. Robust ground ferns that require shade and even humidity and are relatively insensitive to temperature variations. 10° C. is sufficient during the winter.

• *P. argyraea* T. MOORE. Frequently cultured.

• *P. cretica* L. Leaves to 30 cm. Many cultured forms. Grows well.

• *P. umbrosa* R. BR. Undemanding, can take a lot of shade.

Pternohyla BOULENGER, 1882. Burrowing Treefrogs. Genus of the Hylidae. Southern Nearctic (southern Arizona, northern Mexico). 2 species. Closely related to *Smilisca*. Found in prairies to 1,500 m elevation. More than 5 cm. Head relatively small, distinctly narrower than body, with a fold of skin across the neck. Small adhesive discs on tips of fingers and toes. Fingers free, the toes webbed at base only. Males during the breeding season have laterally located horny growths on the throat and paired dark vocal sacs. Light brown with an irregular darker spotted pattern.

Pseustes shropshirei

species. Among the largest Neotropical colubrids, together with *Spilotes* and *Chironius*. In outer forest zones. To more than 2.8 m. Strongly built. Usually dark brown, often with yellow bands.

Diurnal and crepuscular semiarboreal snakes that feed preferentially on small mammals. When excited *Pseustes*

Pternohyla fodiens

Active during the rainy season (June to September), these frogs then stay close to ponds that serves as spawning grounds and larval rearing facilities. They burrow and estivate during the dry season.

• *P. fodiens* BOULENGER, 1882. Arizona and Pacific Mex-

ico. To 6.5 cm. Brown with an irregular pattern of dark spots.

Ptyas FITZINGER, 1843. Asian Rat Snakes. Genus of the Colubridae, Colubrinae. Central, eastern, and southeastern Asia. 3 species. In damp habitats such as river and lake banks in dry regions, but also in outer zones of monsoon forests and rain forests. To 3.6 m, among the largest of the Colubridae. Fairly massive. The head is more or less distinctly set off. Mostly unicolored dark brown to black; juveniles of some species (e. g., *P. korros*) have dark cross-bands on a light background.

Diurnal and crepuscular. The range of prey hunted includes toads and frogs, lizards, snakes, and mammals up to the size of rabbits. Egg-layers, 6-20 eggs.

Ptyas species usually do well in captivity, requiring a well-heated terrarium with bathing facilities. They quickly become tame. In their natural habitat they are often mistaken for dark cobras (*Naja*), with which they share the habitat and mode of life. Consequently they have become seriously decimated in some areas.

• *P. mucosus* (LINNAEUS, 1758). Dhaman. USSR to Afghanistan and Pakistan, eastward to southern China, southward to the Malaya Archipelago.

• *P. korros* (SCHLEGEL, 1837). Burma eastward to southern China, southward to the Indo-Australian Archipelago.

Ptyas mucosus

Ptyas korros

Ptyas korros

Ptychadena BOULENGER, 1920. Taxon of doubtful status within the Ranidae; considered to be either an independent genus or a subgenus or synonym of *Rana*. Africa and Madagascar. More than 12 species. Mostly in open areas such as savannahs and grasslands; in tropical West Africa also occurring in rain forests. Usually close to or in water. In shape, behavior, and mode of life reminiscent of *Rana*, but with longer and more pointed snouts.

Breeding occurs occurs during the rainy season. These frogs spawn mostly in shallow water with dense vegetation, such as flooded swamps and grasslands. They should be kept in spacious tropical, sunny aqua-terrariums. Outdoor maintenance is recommended during the summer months.
- *P. mascareniensis* (DUMERIL and BIBRON, 1841). Africa south of the Sahara and Madagascar. To 7 cm. Variable green to brown without spots and with a wide median dorsal band.

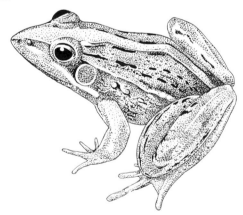

Ptychadena mascareniensis

- *P. oxyrhynchus* (SMITH, 1849). Tropical and southern Africa. To 7 cm. Variable gray to red-brown base, with a lighter triangular spot on the snout.
- *P. taeniosceles* LAURENT, 1954. Tropical and southern Africa. To 4.5 cm. 3 thin white dorsal stripes.

Ptychoglossus BOULENGER, 1890. Genus of the Teiidae. Costa Rica to northern South America east of the Andes.

7 species in tropical rain forests. 10 cm. Slender, with conspicuously large, very long, and overlapping but unkeeled dorsal scales. Brown.
Ground-dwellers.
- *P. festae* (PERACCA, 1896). Colombia, Panama.

Ptychohyla TAYLOR, 1944. Genus of the Hylidae. Central America. 8 species, some polytypic. In cloud forests and montane rain forests (350 to 2200 m elevation) in the proximity of fast-flowing water. Head rather large. One-third of the length of the fingers and ⅔ of the length of the toes with webbing. Males during the breeding season have 2 distinct, dark large gland fields in the breast region (the major difference from the genus *Hyla*). Brown to green above, with a more or less distinct dark pattern. Flanks whitish, in some species also with black spots. Abdomen white or yellowish, with or without dark dots. Iris red, copper, or bronze in color. Males give their mating calls from bushes and trees along the banks. The call consists of either a single long tone or a series of short ones.

These frogs are active throughout the year, and reproduction is not tied to a particular season. The larvae occupy flowing waters and remain in slow-flowing sections. Should be kept in a tropical rain-forest terarrarium with an evenly high humidity and a temperature from 23 to 27° C., at night slightly cooler. A water bowl must be present in the terrarium.
- *P. euthysanota* (KELLOGG, 1928). Central America (600 to 2,200 m elevation). Polytypic. To 4.5 cm. Brown with a darker pattern.
- *P. ignicolor* DUELLMAN, 1961. Mexico (1500 to 1850 m elevation). To 3 cm. Unicolored green.

Ptychophis GOMES, 1915. Monotypic genus of the Colubridae, Natricinae. Brasil, Santa Catarina and Parana States. Closely related to *Paraptychophis*. About 60 cm. Head distinctly set off, with well-developed opisthoglyphic fangs. Strongly keeled and shingled dorsal scales. Caution: Venomous bites possible.
- *P. flavovirgatus* GOMES, 1915.

Ptychozoon KUHL, 1822. Flying Geckos. Genus of the Gekkonidae. Southeast Asia and the islands of the Indo-Australian Archipelago in tropical rain forests. 5 species. To 20 cm. Slender, flattened dorso-ventrally. Tail barely snout-vent length. Pupil vertical. Toes with large adhesive lamellae without a central furrow. Wide skin folds along the sides of the head, flanks, tails, and legs serve as superb

Ptychozoon lionotum

Ptychozoon kuhli

Puna vegetation of the high Andes

camouflage against tree bark and also allow the lizard to glide from limb to limb.

Nocturnal tree-dwellers, primarily on stems and branches of older trees. Egg-layers, 2 eggs per clutch. These geckos require a terrarium that is heated to 25 to 30° C. during the day, dropping at night to about 22° C. The humidity must not be too low. Has been bred repeatedly.

• *P. kuhli* STEJNEGER, 1907. Malayan Peninsula, Sumatra, Kalimantan, Java,and other islands. To 20 cm. Tail fold large, vertical. Dorsal tubercles present.

• *P. lionotum* ANNANDALE, 1905. Burma, Thailand. Easily to 15 cm. Tail with a narrow skin fold situated posteriorly. Without dorsal tubercles.

Ptyctolaemus PETERS, 1864. Monotypic genus of the Agamidae. Southern Assam. Little known.

• *P. gularis* PETERS, 1864. About 20 cm.

Ptyodactylus GOLDFUSS, 1820. Fan-footed Geckos. Genus of the Gekkonidae. North Africa to southwestern Asia. 2 species, several subspecies. In dry, often rocky habitats; also follows human habitation. To 15 cm. Compact, flat-

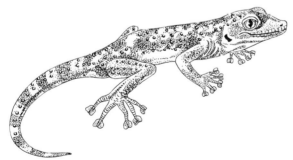

Ptyodactylus hasselquisti

tened dorso-ventrally. Tail shorter than snout-vent length. Tips of toes with substantially widened fan-shaped adhesive lamellae; claws retractile. Vertical pupil strongly lobate.

Diurnal and nocturnal, excellent climbers. Egg-layers, 4-5 clutches per year, each with 2 eggs. These geckos like to sunbathe. A winter dormancy period of about 4 to 8 weeks is recommended. For maintenance see *Cyrtodactylus*.

• *P. hasselquisti* (DONNDORF, 1798). Gray to yellow-brown with dark and light yellow spots.

Puna: Form of vegetation rich in grasses in the Peruvian and Bolivian Andes above 3,800 m, separated from the

edge of the eternal ice at 5,500 m by lichen-rich rocky deserts. The *puna* occupies vast areas on the Andean high plateau and is characteristically developed wherever the climate alternates from rainy season in November through April and the rest of the year dry, and where the climate is more or less even, with extremely high day-night variations (from -10° C. at night to 37° C. and higher during the day). Apart from *Bufo spinulosus*, the *puna* is inhabited mainly by Leptodactylidae and ground iguanas of several genera that all survive the nocturnal frost in hiding places under rocks, in burrows, or in rocky crevices.

Pygopodidae: Scaley-foots. Family of the Squamata, suborder Sauria. Australia and New Guinea plus some adjacent islands. Generaly subdivided into the following 8 genera: *Aclys*, *Aprasia*, *Delma*, *Lialis*, *Ophidiocephalus*, *Paradelma*, *Pletholax*, *Pygopus*. About 30 species in relatively dry to slightly moist habitats, semideserts, and open mountain forests. The only lizard family confined to Australasia. Systematic position not undisputed, but probably closely related to the Gekkonidae, with which they share several characters.

Distribution of the Pygopodidae

10 to 80 cm. Cylindrical, elongated. Head conical to very pointed, only weakly set off, with a few large scales. Tympanum visible or absent. Without movable eyelids, the lower transparent lid firmly fused with the upper one to produce spectacles. The eyes are regularly cleaned by licking with the fleshy tongue (not split). Generally the tail is

longer than the snout-vent length, but in some burrowing genera it is shorter (e. g., *Aprasia*), very brittle, and regenerates well but often very slowly. The anterior limbs are absent, the hind limbs rudimentary (at the most 1 cm long) and essentially useless for locomotion. Bones of the hind limbs are variably reduced; occasionally 4 toe bones are present (*Pygopus*). Hind limbs of the males are generally marginally larger than those of the female. Body scales small, in oblique rows, overlapping. Scaley-foots are capable of giving off weak squeaking or squawking noises. Predominantly shades of brown and gray, the markings if present consisting of spots or stripes.

Primarily nocturnal ground-dwellers that are more or less strong burrowers. Ecologically they can be placed (including transitional forms) into 2 morphologically distinct groups. The first group includes mainly those forms that live on the ground, have an externally visible tympanum, a long tail, and often a rather pointed head (e. g., *Pygopus*, *Delma*). This group also includes the large *Lialis* species with their long, sharp, posterior-pointing teeth. The second group contains those species that burrow more, often have very small eyes, the tympanum not visible, a conical head, strong reduced hind limbs, and—in part—a short tail (e. g., *Aprasia*).

Scaley-foots feed mainly on various insects; the larger species (*Lialis*) will also take small lizards. Little is known about their requirements in captivity. Usually they are kept in slightly damp terrariums with a thick bottom layer at temperatures from 25 to 30° C. with a nocturnal temperature reduction. It is reported that some specimens on occasion take some fruit. Generally rather undemanding, but apparently not yet bred in captivity.

Pygopus MERREM, 1820. Scaley-foots. Genus of the Pygopodidae. Australia and Tasmania. 2 species. To 70 cm. Slender. Tympanum externally visible. Tail usually longer than snout-vent length. Rudiments of hind limbs relatively long, the inner 4 toes identifiable. Dorsal scales keeled or smooth. Preanal pores present. Mainly brown with indistinct markings.

Diurnal or crepuscular ground-dwellers and only occasional burrowers or climbers. Details on captive maintenance (*P. lepidopodus*) have variously been reported. These animals should be kept in a relatively dry terrarium at day temperatures from 20 to 28° C. (locally higher) with a slight reduction at night. The diet should consist of arthropods and occasional pieces of banana. When threatened it assumes an S-shaped body position, inflating the body and hissing.

▪ *P. lepidopodus* (LACEPEDE, 1804). Common Scaley-foot. To 70 cm. Gray to reddish brown, occasionally with 3-5 rows of dark spots. Throat white, abdomen smoky gray.

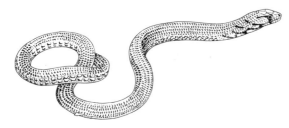

Pygopus lepidopodus

Scales keeled. Southern Australia.
▪ *P. nigriceps* FISCHER, 1882. Hooded or Western Scaley-foot. All of Australia except the South. To 60 cm. Collar-like black neck markings. Scales smooth.

Python DAUDIN, 1803. Pythons. Genus of the Boidae, subfamily Pythoninae. Africa and Southeast Asia including the Indonesian Islands. 7 species. The smallest species, *P. regius* and *P. anchietae*, are 1.2-2 m; the largest species, *P. reticulatus*, is in excess of 9 m; *P. molurus* reaches 8 m, *P. sebae* 7 m. Some *Python* species are distinctly slender (*P. reticulatus*, *P. sebae*, *P. timorensis*), others are massive (*P. molurus*), and in the extreme case short and plump (*P. curtus*). The head is large and distinctly set off from the body, with species-specific scalation and color patterns. The body may have attractive colors and markings (highly desired by snake leather merchants).

Mainly terrestrial (*P. curtus*, *P. molurus*, *P. reticulatus*, *P. sebae*, *P. timorensis*). Moisture requirements are highest

Python molurus bivittatus

Python curtus

Python anchietae

cludes mainly mammals and birds, rarely reptiles. Egg-layers, brood care provided.

Maintenance must be in relation to the size of species concerned. The giant species should really only be kept in zoological parks. When servicing or handling the very large *Python* species—particularly the always-aggressive *P. reticulatus* and *P. sebae*—proper safety precautions must prevail at all times: There should always be a second person present, and one should never work around these snakes in the evening or at night, their main activity period. The third giant species—*P. molurus*—often becomes very tame, but caution still should prevail at all times. Terrariums must be well-heated and adequately ventilated, with solidly anchored climbing branches, water bowls that can be easily cleaned, and a soft bottom substrate. Hiding places should be provided in the form of closable (for safety) boxes or hollow logs that provide pressure contact. Several species have been bred repeatedly (*P. reticulatus*, *P. molurus*, *P. regius*, *P. sebae*). Some species frequently provide some initial maintenance problems, especially *P. curtus* and *P. anchietae* (which feed on birds). Both species are often difficult to acclimate to life in captivity and usually live a relatively short period of time. The large species can obtain substantial longevities in captivity.

Python species are covered by import regulations and are therefore most often available as captive-bred specimens. Frightening numbers of these snakes have been killed for the leather trade, especially *P. sebae*, *P. reticulatus*, and *P. molurus*.

▪ *P. anchietae* BOCAGE, 1887. Angolan Python. Angola, Namibia. Semiarboreal. The smallest species of the genus.
▪ *P. curtus* SCHLEGEL, 1872. Blood Python, Short-tailed

for *P. reticulatus* and *P. curtus*. *P. sebae* and *P. molurus* also inhabit drier habitats (savannahs). Species of the tropical rain forest are *P. curtus*, *P. timorensis*, and *P. regius*, the latter with a primarily arboreal mode of life. The diet in-

Python molurus molurus

Python. Malaysia, Sumatra, Borneo. The most difficult species to keep.

▪ *P. molurus* (LINNAEUS, 1758). Asiatic Rock Python, Black-tailed Python. 2 subspecies: nominate form (arrow incomplete on head, light) from India, Sri Lanka; *P. m. bivittatus* (arrow complete on head, dark) from Indo-China, southern China, large areas of Indonesia. The most durable

Python sebae

and "trustworthy" species of this genus.

▪ *P. regius* (SHAW, 1802). Ball Python, Royal Python. Western and central Africa. Semiarboreal.

▪ *P. reticulatus* (SCHNEIDER, 1801). Reticulated Python. Indo-China, Indonesia, Philippines. Fast growing; apart from *Eunectes murinus*, the largest Recent snake.

▪ *P. sebae* (GMELIN, 1876). African Rock Python. Africa, except in the north.

▪ *P. timorensis* (PETERS, 1876). Timor Python. Flores, Timor.

Pythonodipsas GUENTHER, 1868. Monotypic genus of the Colubridae, Boiginae. Southwestern Africa in desert-like dry regions. 60 cm. Somewhat compact, adder-like. The very distinctly set off head has large eyes with vertical pupils. Scales smooth, strongly shingled. Dorsally light

Python reticulatus

Python regius

Python oenpelliensis

brown with large spots with light and dark edges.

Nocturnal ground snakes.

▪ *P. carinata* GUENTHER, 1868.

Pyxicephalus TSCHUDI, 1838. African Bullfrogs. Genus of the Ranidae. Sometimes considered a synonym of *Rana*. Tropical and southern Africa. Several in part polytypic species found in arid and semiarid regions such as semideserts, steppes, savannahs, and dry brushland. Stout, the body more or less inflated. Mouth large. The inner metatarsal tubercle is developed into a large, sharp, tough digging spade. Fingers free, toes more or less extensively webbed.

African bullfrogs lead a cryptic subterranean life during the dry season, appearing at the surface only after extensive rainfalls. At the onset of the rainy season they congregate in shallow regions of temporary or permanent bodies of water and spawn there. Clutches may have 4000 eggs. Should be kept in semi-moist, sunny terrarium at tropical temperatures.

These often fascinating frogs must be kept in a terrarium incorporating a deep loose substrate layer and a water bowl. In a terrarium these animals may spend days in water before they bury themselves again. Adult *P. adspersus*

Pyxicephalus delalandii

need large food animals, such as other frogs, mice, and even sparrows.

▪ *P. adspersus* TSCHUDI, 1838. African Bullfrog. Tropical Africa eastward and southward from Nigeria. Males 24 cm, females 12 cm (large males an exception in frogs). Olive-green with darker broken longitudinal skin ridges. Voice loud, a deep bellow. Highly aggressive, it can inflict serious bites with odontodes in the jaw. Considered to be a delicacy by the natives.

▪ *P. delalandii* TSCHUDI, 1838. Small African Bullfrog. Cape Province. 5.5 cm. Brownish with 3 longitudinal white stripes on the back. Often placed in *Tomopterna* (the type species of that generic name).

▪ *P. natalensis* SMITH, 1849. Cape Province, Natal, Zululand, and Transvaal. Plains and mountains. 4 cm. Green to red brown with dark spots. The most slender species in this genus. Often placed in *Tomopterna*.

Pyxidea GRAY, 1863. Indian Thorn Turtles. Monotypic genus of the Emydidae, often considered a synonym of *Cyclemys*. Southeast Asia in tropical forests, occasionally in temporary waters. To 20 cm. Carapace with 3 distinct

Pyxicephalus adspersus

Pyxicephalus adspersus

Pyxidea mouhoti

keels, the median keel distinctly flattened; posterior carapace margin distinctly serrated. Plastron with a slightly movable anterior hinge in fully mature specimens.

Remains buried in the ground during the day; nocturnal. Omnivorous, with a preference for plant material. Maintenance similar to *Terrapene*.

▪ *P. mouhoti* (GRAY, 1862). Eastern India, northern Thailand, North Vietnam, and the island of Hainan.

Pyxis BELL, 1827. Spider Tortoises. Genus of the Testudinidae. Southwestern Madagascar. 2 species in savannahs, steppes, and desert-like habitats. Barely more than 12 cm. Carapace strongly arched, elongated, with characteristic reticulated spider web markings radiating from the areole of each scute. The plastron in some adult *P. arachnoides* has a movable anterior flap.

Strongly seasonal, they survive prolonged dry periods buried in the ground. The diet is mainly succulent and bushy plants, fruit, and insect larvae. They reproduce by laying 1 to 3 eggs.

Pyxis arachnoides

Pyxis planicauda

Spider tortoises can be kept successfully in a terrarium, provided rest and activity periods are taken into account. Digging and burrowing opportunities must be provided, along with high daytime temperatures and substantial nocturnal temperature reductions.

▪ *P. arachnoides* BELL, 1827. Spider Tortoise. Southwestern Madagascar. Highly variable markings, but usually a yellow reticulated pattern on a black background, ranging to a complete reversal of the light and dark colors. Anterior flap of plastron in adult specimens in some subspecies movable (*P. a. arachnoides* BELL and *P. a. matzi* BOUR). Males easily recognizable by the tail ending in a spine.

▪ *P. planicauda* GRANDIDIER, 1867. Flatback Spider Tortoise. Western Madagascar (vicinity of Morondava). Markings and coloration similar to *P. arachnoides*. Carapace longer and characteristically flattened above. Plastron always rigid. Very rare in captivity. Until recently it was considered to belong to the monotypic genus *Acinixys* SIEBENROCK, 1902.

Quarantine: Housing for newly acquired specimens that is completely separated from that for other animals. For imported specimens the duration of quarantine is generally 4 weeks. During this time interval the animals have to be housed under proper conditions and their state of health observed. Particular emphasis is placed on a bacteriological and parasitological examination of fresh fecal samples, at least from cloacal smears. New arrivals have to be checked for ectoparasites. Snakes should be treated for mites. Due to stress and lack of suitable diet while in transit, new arrivals should be given a prophylactic vitamin treatment. If a particular therapy is required, the quarantine period must be extended accordingly.

Quedenfeldtia BOETTGER, 1883. Monotypic genus of the Gekkonidae. Morocco. Closely related to the *Gymnodactylus* Group. 10 cm. Found in mountain regions from 1600 to 3000 m elevation. Mainly brown.

Diurnal. Difficult to keep in a terrarium. It must be given radiant heat, ultraviolet radiation, and large nighttime temperature reductions, plus a winter dormancy period of about 6 to 8 weeks.

▪ *Q. trachyblepharus* (BOETTGER, 1874). Atlas Day Gecko.

Rafinesque, Constantine Fr. Schmalz (1783-1840): French-American zoologist and botanist. Author of various taxa of North American reptiles and amphibians.

Rain forests: Evergreen forests with great species diversity, found mostly in lowlands of the equatorial wet zone. The trees often have aerial roots or stilt roots, leaves with drop tips, and crowns at several levels (the highest at 50 m or higher). There is an abundance of lianas, but epiphytes are scarce. Light intensity at ground level is very low, the humidity high, but subject to larger variations than in montane rain forests. With increasing distance away from the Equator there is an increasing influence of a seasonal climate with dry and rainy seasons. In the transition area to temperate deciduous forests the upper tree crowns periodically lose their leaves, while the lower layers remain evergreen (a semi-evergreen rain forest). In the subtropics rain forests occur only in those areas that due to their location (e. g., within the barrier effect of mountains for pre-

Vegetation profile of a rain forest on Trindad

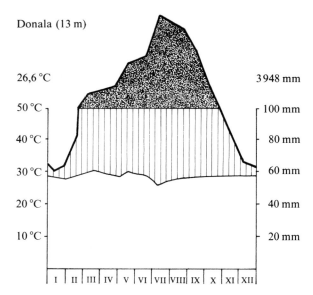

Climate diagram of a West African rain forest

cipitation-carrying winds) are perpetually wet, such as in southeastern Brasil.

As terrarium guidelines for most rain-forest displays one uses temperatures from 23 to 26° C. For Southeast Asian rain-forests, use temperatures to 29° C. (at night only marginally cooler) and humidities from 80 to 95%. Those animals requiring more light and heat should be provided with localized radiant heat.

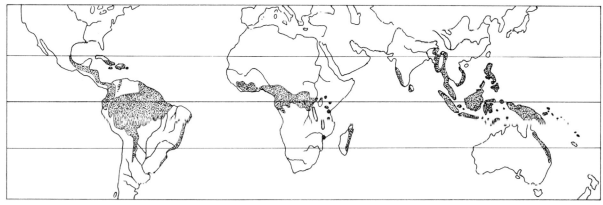

Distribution of rain forests

Rain-forest terrarium: Used for animals from rain forests and their peripheral zones. Due to the fact that rain-forest terrariums can have luxuriant plant growth that provides a high esthetic display value, rain-forest terrariums are the most popular type of indoor terrarium. The required climatic conditions can with adequate technical support be easily simulated. Many rain-forest animals are often easier to keep and breed than some desert animals.

The essential climatic requirements can be taken from the habitat description. Particular attention has to be paid to ventilation and humidity; an accumulation of excess wetness must be avoided.

The decorations of many rain-forest terrariums have so many epiphytes that they resemble more a mountain rain forest, which requires a substantial nocturnal temperature reduction and—most importantly—regular misting, which often inhibits direct solar radiation for prolonged periods of time. The following plants can be kept under conditions prevailing in a lowland rain forest:
▪ Plants from tropical climate regions of Australia and New Zealand: *Selaginella, Asplenium, Platycerium, Pteris,* Cyperaceae, *Ficus, Hoya,* Orchidaceae, Pandanaceae, *Piper.*
▪ From tropical regions of Asia: *Adiantum, Cyrtomium, Pla-*

tycerium, Selaginella, Pteris, Aglaonema, Araceae, in part also *Ceropegia, Codiaeum, Fatshedera, Fatsia, Ficus, Hemigraphis, Hoya, Ophiopogon,* Orchidaceae, *Pellionia, Perilepta, Pilea, Piper, Pothos, Rhaphiodophora, Reineckea, Scindapsus.*
▪ From tropical regions of Africa: *Asplenium, Platycerium, Clorophytum,* Commelinaceae, partly also *Dracaena, Kalanchoe,* Orchidaceae, Pandanaceae, *Rhipsalis, Sansevieria.*
▪ From tropical regions of America: *Selaginella, Nephrolepis, Psilotum, Polypodium, Anthurium,* Begoniaceae, Bromeliaceae, *Caladium, Calathea, Dieffenbachia, Episcia, Fittonia,* Marantaceae, *Monstera,* Orchidaceae, *Peperomia, Philodendron, Pilea, Piper, Rhipsalis, Ruellia, Syngonium, Tradescantia, Xantherantemun, Zebrina.*

Ramanella RAO and RAMANNA, 1925. Genus of the Microhylidae. Southern India, Sri Lanka. 8 species in tropical rain forests and cloud forests. Skin smooth to granular. Pupil horizontal. Tympanum not visible. Fingers and toes with distinct adhesive discs, the undersides with tubercles. Toes more or less webbed. In contrast to the related genus *Kaloula,* there are 2 metatarsal tubercles, the inner one large and not developed into a digging spade, the outer one small. Brown with a large dark, centrally constricted, dorsal spot. Larvae have a terminal mouth, contractile lower lip, and respiratory tube in a median location at the posterior part of body under a transparent skin fold.

Adults are ground-dwellers, although they can climb.

▪ *R. montana* (JERDON, 1854). Southwestern India, Sri Lanka (1200 to 2100 m elevation). 3.5 cm. Nearly smooth-skinned.

▪ *R. triangularis* (GUENTHER, 1875). Southwestern India (at about 2,000 m). 4 cm. Smooth-skinned, occasionally with some warts.

Rana LINNAEUS, 1758. Typical Frogs. Genus of the Ranidae, here treated in a restricted sense. The status of related taxa (*Abrana, Aubria, Conraua, Dicroglossus, Hildebrandtia, Hylarana, Ptychadena, Pyxicephalus, Tomopterna*) is still problematic, and a modern, complete revision is still wanting. Asia and the Indo-Australian Archipelago have about 140 species; Africa has about 40 species; North America some 17 species; Central America about 13 species; and Europe has about 11 species. Coming from the north, *R. palmipes* has penetrated into South America and *R. papua* into northeastern Australia. About 4 cm (*R. hascheana*) to 20 cm (*R. catesbeiana* and *R. tigrina*).

Rana boylei

Rana aurora

Rana catesbeiana, albino

Most *Rana* species can be divided into three groups:

▪ Green Frogs: Largely aquatic, possibly also over-wintering in water. Eyes pointing obliquely upwards, toes largely webbed. Usually green to dark olive. Including, among others, the European *R. esculenta, R. lessonae, R. ridibunda;* the North American *R. catesbeiana, R. clamitans, R. septentrionalis;* the Southeast Asian *R. tigrina, R. erythraea, R. hexadactyla*.

▪ Brown Frogs: Usually only breeding in water, occasionally also over-wintering in water, other than that often found away from water in swampy meadows and damp forests. Eyes occasionally located laterally, mostly covered by a dark brown temporal color band. Toes less webbed. Mostly brown or gray. This group includes, among others, the remaining European *Rana* species, the North American *R. pipiens* complex and *R. sylvatica*, and the Asiatic *R. chaochiaoensis, R. japonica, R. papua*.

Rana catesbeiana

▪ Stream Frogs: Plump, the skin with warts. Darkish frogs usually of considerable size found near or in clear, cool mountain streams and rivers. Among others it includes the Asiatic *R. boulengeri* and *R. phrynoides*, in New Guinea *R. jimiensis*, and in Africa *R. vertebralis*.

The pupil is horizontal in all *Rana* species. The tympanum in most cases is distinctly visible and large (in the males of some species larger than in females, e. g., in *R. clamitans*). Tongue deeply forked in back (in contrast to *Conraua*). Jaws and palatine with teeth; *R. macrodon* has 2 larger, fang-like odontodes on the lower jaw. Fingers free, the toes more or less widely webbed. Tips of fingers and toes—especially in Asiatic forms—may have distinct adhesive discs that can have a circular furrow (as in *Hylarana*). Males usually smaller than females. Vocal sac either paired and external (e. g., European green frogs, *R. hexadactyla*), a paired inner sac (e. g., *R. boulengeri*) or an unpaired sac (*R. catesbeiana*, *R. galamensis*); it may even be absent (*R. erythraea*, *R. hascheana*, *R. japonica*, *R. kuhli*). During the peak of the mating season there are usually horny nuptial pads on the fingers and hands of the males, also horny pectoral and abdominal spines (*R. boulengeri*, *R. phrynoides*). Vocalization ability in some species is considerable, particularly when in chorus. The larvae are of rather various sizes (in *R. boulengeri* up to 20 cm), and, in contrast to *Hylarana*, lack conspicuous glandular areas.

Usually *Rana* species are predominantly diurnal. In fact, the aquatic species love to bask, even when peak vocaliza-

Rana temporaria

Rana graeca

Rana lessonae

Rana (Hylarana) erythraea

Rana esculenta

Rana sylvatica

larvae undergo (similar to *Discodeles*) their entire development inside the eggs in damp ground. *Rana* species occupying the same area are biologically isolated either by different spawning seasons or by preferring different types of water. Yet, in spite of this hybridization does occur at times (*R. esculenta* is a stable hybrid of *R. ridibunda* X *lessonae*; similarly, forms of the *R. pipiens* Group hybridize with each other or with *R. palustris* in North America).

Several species follow human habitation quite exten-

tion occurs at night during the breeding season. A few species are strictly nocturnal, such as *R. andersoni* and *R. areolata*. It is known that some species establish territories that are defended by fighting (e. g., *R. catesbeiana*). Nearly all *Rana* species form more or less sizable breeding communities and spawn in sunny standing or slowly flowing water with dense aquatic vegetation. One female can lay several thousand eggs. In contrast to this, some mountain stream species attach their eggs to the underside of rocks in rapids (*R. boulengeri*) or to plants (*R. wagneri*).

The tendency toward water-independent reproduction is seen in some East Asian *Rana* species. *R. adenopleura* has reduced the number of eggs to 100 in favor of increased yolk volume and water content and spawns on land close to water, but it still has aquatic larvae. In *R. hascheana* the

Rana limnocharis greenii

sively, e. g., *R. cancrivora*, *R.erythraea*, and *R. limnocharis*, which inhabitat flooded rice paddies and water-filled roadside ditches. Others, such as *R. dalmatina* (preferentially in beech forests) and *R. kuhli* (along small, clear jungle streams) represent species that tend to flee from any human development. For same years now there has been a dramatic decline in central Europe of green and brown frogs due to causes that may be related to environmental pressures but which have not yet been fully explained.

Some *Rana* species are of considerable importance as laboratory and food animals, in Europe especially *R. esculenta* and *R. temporaria*, in North America *R. pipiens* and allies (which are often bred as laboratory strains). Similarly, skinned thighs of the some of the large *Rana* species are considered to be a great delicacy in North America, southern Europe, Southeast Asia, and also in Africa, so many *Rana* species are hunted commercially and even bred and fattened on special frog farms.

Most tropical *Rana* species are not particularly well suited for indoor terrarium maintenance. They are either excessively active and thus can injure themselves easily, or their ecological requirements are difficult to provide. Breeding under these conditions would only be an exception. In contrast, *Rana* species from the temperate and subtropical latitudes are excellent animals for suitably set up outdoor terrariums. Establishment of native frogs in a

Rana pipiens

sufficiently deep garden pond often occurs spontaneously, since these animals often are looking for a new breeding site.

▪ *R. adenopleura* BOULENGER, 1909. Southwestern China, Taiwan. Near or in standing mountain waters (about 1,100 m). To 5.5 cm. Olive-green with a light brown lateral stripe, the flanks with black spots.

▪ *R. andersoni* BOULENGER, 1882. Southwestern China. Near or in flowing mountain waters (1000 to 2500 m). To 10.5 cm. Distinct adhesive discs. Brown, the back with vermiform green spots and the thighs with golden-brown crossbands.

Rana clamitans clamitans

Rana clamitans melanota

▪ *R. angolensis* BOCAGE, 1866. Africa south of the Sahara to Cape Province. To 10 cm. Highly variable green to brown. Semiaquatic.

▪ *R. areolata* BAIRD and GIRARD, 1852. Gopher Frog. Central and southern USA. At the edge of water and in gopher tortoise and crawfish burrows. Dark round light-edged spots on a yellow-green or gray background.

▪ *R. arvalis* NILSSON, 1842. Swamp Frog. Central and northeastern Europe. 3 subspecies. To 8 cm. In contrast to *R. temporaria*, snout pointed and often with a light dorsal stripe present. Courting males have blue stripes.

▪ *R. boulengeri* GUENTHER, 1889. Western China. To 12.5 cm. Males larger than females. Compact, with warts. Blackish brown; in contrast to *R. phrynoides* the entire

Rana jerboa

chest and abdominal region of the male is covered with black spines.

• *R. cancrivora* GRAVENHORST, 1829. Malayan Peninsula to Philippines. 2 subspecies. To 8 cm. Gray-brown. Largely aquatic. In contrast to *R. limnocharis*, the snout is very pointed.

• *R. catesbeiana* SHAW, 1802. American Bullfrog. Widely distributed throughout the eastern USA, introduced in many other areas. To 20 cm. Tympanum very large. Olive-green with a gray to brown pattern; sometimes completely black.

• *R. clamitans* LATREILLE, 1802. American Green Frog. 10 cm. 2 subspecies. Eastern USA.

• *R. dalmatina* BONAPARTE, 1840. Spring Frog. Southern Europe (except Iberian Peninsula), enclaves in northern central Europe (Norway, East Germany, Sweden). To 9 cm. Legs very long, in contrast to *R. latastei*. Tympanum close behind eye. Brown.

• *R. erythraea* (SCHLEGEL, 1837). Red-eared Frog. Southeast Asia to Philippines. To 7.5 cm. Bright green with a yellow dorso-lateral skin fold. Abdomen white.

• *R. esculenta* LINNAEUS, 1758. Edible Frog. Central Europe. To 9 cm. A stable hybrid of *R. lessonae* and *R. ridibunda* with intermediate characteristics between both parent species. Dorsum green, thighs with yellow and black marbled pattern.

• *R. fasciata* DUMERIL and BIBRON, 1841. Striped Frog. South Africa. Grassland close to water. To 5.5 cm. Yellow and dark brown longitudinal stripes on a brown background.

• *R. galamensis* DUMERIL and BIBRON, 1841. Tropical Africa. 2 subspecies. Savannahs. Widely distributed. To 8.5 cm. Light dorso-lateral and flank stripes. Legs with marbled pattern.

• *R. graeca* BOULENGER, 1891. Stream Frog. Balkan Peninsula, Italy, and Greece. Mostly along flowing water. To 7

Rana ridibunda

cm. Legs very long. Tympanum indistinctly visible. Brown, the throat dark.

• *R. grayi* SMITH, 1849. Spotted Frog. South Africa. Grasslands and brushland close to water. To 6.5 cm. Light olive with large, roundish, dark brown spots and light dorsal stripes.

• *R. hascheana* (STOLIZKA, 1870). Southern and southeastern Asia. To 4 cm. Yellow-brown, variably spotted.

• *R. hexadactyla* LESSON, 1834. Southern India, Sri Lanka. To 14 cm. Dorsum green, ventral side yellow.

• *R. iberica* BOULENGER, 1879. Iberian Frog. Northwestern Iberian Peninsula. Very similar to *R. temporaria*, but dorso-lateral skin folds on shoulder not approaching each other.

• *R. japonica* GUENTHER, 1858. Agile Frog. China, Japan. To 7 cm. Similar to *R. temporaria*, but more slender.

• *R. jimiensis* TAYLOR, 1963. New Guinea. To 13 cm. Unicolored gray-black, with warts.

• *R. kuhli* DUMERIL and BIBRON, 1841. Southeast Asia and offshore islands. To 8 cm. Compact. Light brown with a darker pattern.

• *R. latastei* BOULENGER, 1879. Italian Agile Frog. Southern Alps below 800 m. Similar to *R. dalmatina*, but tympanum smaller and located away from eye.

• *R. lessonae* CAMERANO, 1882. Pool Frog. Central Europe and Italy into Asia. In contrast to *R. esculenta* and *R. ridibunda*, smaller and more yellow. Metatarsal tubercle very large.

• *R. limnocharis* WIEGMANN, 1835. Rice Frog. Asia south and east of the Himalayas, widely distributed (including adjacent islands). 6 subspecies. To 6 cm. Legs short. Back with irregular skin folds. Gray to brown with a darker pattern.

• *R. macrodon* DUMERIL and BIBRON, 1841. Toothed Frog. Southeast Asia and offshore islands. Mainly in flowing waters. To 12.5 cm. Compact. Limbs strong. Chocolate brown to red with indistinct darker spots.

Rana pustulosa

Rana nigromaculatus

- *R. nigromaculatus* HALLOWELL, 1860. Southern Siberia, China, Japan. Outside the breeding season cryptic close to water. To 8 cm. Dorsum green, gray, or brown, dorso-lateral skin folds and flanks light yellow-brown.
- *R. phrynoides* BOULENGER, 1917. Western China at 1500 to 2500 m elevation. To 11 cm. Very similar to *R. boulengeri*, the males lacking spines on the chest and in the center of the abdominal region.
- *R. papua* LESSON, 1830. Southeast Asia, New Guinea, northeastern Australia. 3 subspecies. To 7.5 cm. Snout pointed. Distinct dorso-lateral skin folds. Light gray-brown with an indistinct brown pattern.
- *R. pipiens* SCHREBER, 1782. Leopard Frog. Southern Canada to Mexico. A complex of about a dozen similar species. To 9 cm. Distinct dorso-lateral skin folds. Black rounded light-edged spots on a bright green to light brown background.
- *R. ridibunda* PALLAS, 1771. Marsh Frog. Southwestern and eastern Europe. 2 subspecies. To 17 cm (the largest European frog). Metatarsal tubercle small. Olive, in contrast to *R. esculenta* and *R. lessoneae* the thighs lacking any yellow. Vocal sac dark gray.
- *R. septentrionalis* BAIRD, 1854. Mink Frog. Canada west of the Great Lakes to the Atlantic. To 7 cm. Dark brown spots on a green background; in contrast to *R. clamitans*, the thighs lack crossbands.
- *R. sylvatica* LECONTE, 1825. Wood Frog. Canada, Alaska, northeastern USA. Forests and tundra. To 8 cm. Light gray-brown with darker markings and a dark brown mask behind the eyes.
- *R. temporaria* LINNAEUS, 1758. Eurasian Common Frog. Central and northern Europe, eastward to eastern Asia. 4 subspecies. To 10 cm. In contrast to *R. arvalis*, the snout is blunt and the back virtually never has light longitudinal stripes.

- *R. tigrina* DAUDIN, 1803. India, Sri Lanka, Southeast Asia, allochtonous on Madagascar. 3 subspecies. To 18 cm. Snout pointed. Green to olive, with darker markings and often with a light dorsal stripe.
- *R. vertebralis* HEWITT, 1927. South Africa. Very cold mountain streams. To 16 cm. Brown, olive, or gray with an irregular black pattern.
- *R. wagneri* POYNTON, 1963. Mountains of South Africa. Along clear creeks. To 5 cm. Highly varied, brown, green, or reddish with a darker temporal band.

Ranidae: True frogs. Family of the Salientia. Worldwide distribution except in large sections of South America, Australia, and New Zealand. Most species in Africa and southeastern Asia. Only the genus *Rana* occurs in the Holarctic. The Ranidae include very small scales as well as the very largest of recent frogs. Mode of life and type of reproduction vary considerably. Ranidae do not have—in contrast to Rhacophoridae—an additional bone in the digits. Compared to the Microhylidae they are distinguished by a wide mouth with teeth (except *Hemisus*), and the sacral vertebrae do not have enlarged transverse processes. The pupil is usually horizontal, but is vertical in the folowing genera: *Astylosternus, Nannobatrachus, Nyctibatrachus, Scotobleps*, and *Trichobatrachus*. Larvae have a left-sided spiracle and a median or right of median anal opening.

Just as in other large frog families, the Ranidae have also developed several special adaptations: burrowing (*Hemisus, Pyxicephalus*); tree-dwelling (*Platymantis*); and rock-dwelling (*Amolops, Natalobatrachus, Petropedetes, Staurios*). Many genera have development independent of the water: *Anhydrophryne, Arthroleptella, Arthroleptis, Batrachylodes, Discodeles, Platymantis, Sooglossus*, etc.

The systematic arrangement of the Ranidae is very uncertain and generic limits are especially subject to various

interpretations. The usual subfamilies are:
- Subfamily Arthroleptinae: Africa: *Anhydrophryne, Arthroleptella, Arthroleptis, Cardioglossa, Dendrobatorana, Natalobatrachus.*
- Subfamily Astylosterninae: Africa: *Astylosternus, Leptodactylodon, Scotobleps, Trichobatrachus.*
- Subfamily Hemisinae: Africa: *Hemisus.*
- Subfamily Petropedetinae (= Phrynobatrachinae): Africa: *Arthroleptides, Dimorphognathus, Petropedetes, Phrynobatrachus, Phrynodon.*
- Subfamily Platymantinae (= Cornuferinae): Africa and the Orient: *Hylarana.* Orient and northern Australasian (New Guinea, Solomon Islands): *Amolops, Batrachylodes, Ceratobatrachus, Discodeles, Micrixalus, Palmatorappia, Platymantis.*
- Subfamily Nyctibatrachinae: Orient: *Nannobatrachus, Nyctibatrachus.*
- Subfamily Ranidae: Widespread: *Rana.* Africa: *Abrana, Aubria, Cacosternum, Conraua, Dicroglossus, Hildebrandtia, Ptychadena, Pyxicephalus.* Orient: *Altirana, Microbatrachella, Nannophrys, Nanorana, Ooeidozyga.*

Additional genera (here not placed into a particular subfamily): *Elachyglossa, Nothophryne.*

Ranodon KESSLER, 1866. Siberian Salamanders. Genus of the Hynobiidae. Central Asia (Tsientchan to Tsinlingchan). 3 species in montane areas from 1300 m to the upper tree line and close to or in rocky streams (partially flowing underground). Due to the presence of palatine teeth and mode of reproduction, this genus is often considered to be representative of its own family (Ranodontidae). Snout short, protruding eyes, strong jaw musculature. Tail long, laterally flattened, spatulate. Larvae have relatively long gills and tiny horny nails on the tips of the fingers and toes.

Ranodon are less closely tied to cool temperatures than

Ranodon sibiricus

are other hynobiid genera (the upper water temperature limit under natural conditions is 19° C.). The breeding period is dependent upon altitude but is usually in late spring or the summer. The male initially deposits a spermatophore to which the female attaches the two egg sacs. The larvae of *R. sibiricus* hatch in 22 to 25 days at a water temperature of 8 to 12° C. They do not metamorphose until the third year. Sexual maturity is reached during the fifth year.

R. sibiricus (and possibly also the Chinese *Ranodon* species) do quite well in captivity. These salamanders should be kept in an aqaurium with clean water and a low water level; a land section is not required. Since they are light-sensitive, ample hiding places (rocks, etc.) must be available. Temperatures must not be much over 20° C., although *R. sibiricus* can tolerate up to 38° C. for a short period of time. Suitably small aquatic crustaceans, small earthworms, and various aquatic insect larvae are eaten.
- *R. sibiricus* KESSLER, 1866. Siberian Salamander. Western Tientchan (Alatau, Boro-choro-Mountains, Iran-Chbirga).

Detail of a rattle

Common. To 25 cm. Olive with some black dots, abdomen pink.

Rattle: A structure consisting of a series of horny rings loosely stacked inside each other at the tail end of rattlesnakes (*Crotalus* and *Sistrurus*). The rattling noise is caused by rapid vibrations of the tail and indicates a state of excitement. It has a warning effect. With each molt a new ring is formed. However, rattles rarely consist of more than 10 links, since the terminal pieces have a tendency to break off.

Ray, John (1627-1705): British anatomist and herpetologist. Worked mainly on the anatomy of the reptilian heart and described its differences from bird and mammal hearts in his *Synopsis Methodica Animalium Quadrupedum et Serpentini generis*. He was the first to describe exactly the tooth structure in nonvenomous and venomous snakes.

Red Data Book: Listing of endangered animal species. The *International Red Data Book* is published by the IUCN (International Union for the Conservation of Nature). National Red Books are published by national nature protection agencies. Amphibians and reptiles are dealt with in Volume III in the International Red Book. Among other things, the Red Books serve to determine the status of the species in Appendix I and II of the Washington Convention. The following 5 categories are distinguished in the International Red Book:

1 = Endangered. Survival of species or subspecies not likely or species or subspecies extinct. Reversal of survival-threatening factors (mainly environmental influences) have to be initiated without delay if the animals concerned are to be saved. Even collecting all remaining specimens and placing them in nature reserves or breeding institutions for selective breeding can bring positive results (e. g., Galapagos giant tortoises, geometric tortoise, Chinese alligator).

2 = Threatened. Species or subspecies exposed to threatening factors that affect the population detrimentally; up-grading to category 1 must be expected. Requires rapid elimination of the threats and the establishment of safe reserves.

3 = Rare. Species or subspecies living in very restricted areas that can be exposed to environmental changes (particularly during times of natural disaster). The danger to survival lies mainly in the smallness of the range. Reservations outside the normal area of distribution as backups (primarily in the form of maintenance breeding colonies in captivity) are possible.

4 = Out of danger. Species or subspecies that can be taken out of the emergency conditions 1 to 3 above. They were saved through positive human intervention and can currently be considered as relatively safe.

5 = Uncertain. Species or subspecies of unknown status due to insufficient information, but which probably belong in categories 1 through 3.

Red-leg: see *Aeromonas* infection.

Reflex: An unconscious reaction by an organism in response to a stimulus. Such a reaction occurs along a reflex arc that includes the receptor organ, nerve passages, and ganglia cells in the central nervous system, as well as the effector organ. Reflexes often have protective functions (e.

g., the toad reflex, autotomy of tails in many lizards) and have very short reaction times. A reaction delay occurs during prey capture in frogs and toads. While the tongue thrust of the snapping reflex is triggered by prey perception, it occurs with a minute delay. A directional adjustment of the tongue thrust is not possible once begun, so when the prey keeps moving the tongue misses its target.

Refuge: A retreat or survival region of animals and plants, especially during the Ice Ages, and therefore simultaneously also a distribution center following the Ice Ages. Important refuges in the Northern Hemisphere included the Mediterranean Sea, Black Sea, and Caspian Sea regions, Amur region, California, Mexico, and Florida, still recognizable by the abundance of species, especially endemic species.

Refuges in the modern sense are special areas set aside for such purposes, such as national parks that offer refuge for all those species with ecological requirements that can no longer be met on agricultural and settled land.

Regeneration: The ability of an organism to replace injured, dead, or lost parts of the body. This also includes the regular replacement of the upper epidermal layer in amphibians and reptiles during the molting process. In the strictest sense of the word regeneration refers to the replacement of large body parts or more or less complicated organs.

Salamanders and newts can replace completely lost limbs with identical replica organs. This regeneration capability is also known to occur in frog tadpoles, but it largely disappears with metamorphosis.

Regeneration is less developed in reptiles and is essentially restricted to formation of a new tail, which in part can be dropped by autotomy (well-developed in the families Gekkonidae, Lacertidae, Iguanidae, and Teiidae). However, tail regeneration to a variable degree is also known from other reptile groups (e. g., in the order Crocodylia, order Rhynchocephalia, Anguidae, and Agamidae). The carapace of turtles also possesses a considerable regeneration capacity, and where large sections are damaged they can be regrown.

Regenerated double tail of *Eumeces fasciatus*

Regina BAIRD and GIRARD, 1853. Crawfish Snakes. Genus of the Colubridae, Natricinae; status uncertain, very similar to *Nerodia*. Eastern North America from the Great Lakes to the Gulf Coast. 4 species. 35 to 80 cm. Strongly keeled dorsal scales except in *R. alleni*. Back usually dark brown with one or more yellow stripes. Belly usually with 1 or 2 rows of large black spots.

Aquatic snakes usually found in rivers and swamps, often preferring clean, flowing water. Their dietary requirements include significant amounts of crawfish plus some frogs and salamanders. 5 to 18 young. Maintenance as for Natricinae, Group 3, with flowing, clean water.
- *R. septemvittata* (SAY, 1825). Queen Snake. Central USA.
- *R. alleni* (GARMAN, 1874). Striped Swamp Snake. Florida. Formerly in *Liodytes*.
- *R. grahami* (BAIRD and GIRARD, 1853). Graham's Crawfish Snake. Central USA.
- *R. rigida* (SAY, 1825). Glossy Crawfish Snake. Southeastern USA, except Florida.

Reineckea KTH. Genus of the Liliaceae. *R. carnea* (ANDR.) KTH is the sole species. Japan, China. A low shrub with creeping ground shoots. Robust. Can be cultivated damp or dry, can take shade, and is not sensitive to temperature variations. A commonly cultured variety is one with yellow-striped leaves.

Relictivomer CARVALHO, 1954. Monotypic genus of the Microhylidae. Panama, Colombia. Plump, the body egg-shaped. Head very small, the snout pointed and conical, separated from the back by a neckfold. Tympanum not visible. Fingers and toes free.
- *R. pearsei* (RUTHVEN, 1914). 4 cm. Brown.

Relicts: From an evolutionary point of view, very old animal or plant groups that were only able to survive in a spacially more or less limited survival area (refuge). Such relicts include, for instance, olms (*Proteus*), tuataras (*Sphenodon*), earless monitors (*Lanthanotus*), and alligators. The term relict is also applied without age criteria to those species that occur only in a small area because as "cultural refugees" they can no longer exist in those landscapes imprinted and changed by man.

Reproduction: Development of new individuals from those present, primarily tied to an increase in the number of individuals. As in all other vertebrates, amphibians and reptiles reproduce only sexually; reproduction takes place

Sanzinia giving birth

through differentiated sex cells that join during the process of fertilization (exception: parthenogenesis). Fertilization leads to a new combination of parental genetic material. In order to facilitate fertilization of the female egg cell with the male sperm cell, both partners have to join in a mating process. This presupposes recognition of the respective partner and its readiness to mate. This process is facilitated through repeated, fixed reproductive periods where the respective sexual activities are matched with each other. Sexual recognition can be accomplished by means of various stimuli and mechanisms: smell (salamanders), vocalization (frogs), optical stimuli (lizards), or smell and tactile stimuli (snakes). Genetically fixed types of behavior also contribute to the recognition of a partner and its stimulation to mate; e. g., courtship in many newts and salamanders (genus *Triturus* and others) or males turtles (genus *Chrysemys* and others).

Reproduction in amphibians is tied mainly to water, where their gill-breathing larvae usually live. However, evolutionary processes have attempted to make amphibian reproduction independent of water (e. g., genera *Salamandra, Gastrotheca, Eleutherodactylus*, order Gymnophiona). Internal fertilization is typical for salamanders and newts and related forms. Here the fusion of egg and sperm cells occurs in the maternal body. Sperm enters the female by means of a spermatophore formed inside the cloaca of the male. In a few families (Hynobiidae, Cryptobranchidae, and Sirenidae) there is external fertilization, whereby the eggs and milt are given off simultaneously by both partners. This process also is characteristic of virtually all frogs (exceptions: genera *Ascaphus, Nectophrynoides*).

Reproduction in reptiles has become independent of water by the development of the amniote egg. In reptiles there is internal fertilization and the eggs are invariably deposited on land or they develop inside the maternal body (ovoviviparity or viviparity). A larval stage does not occur. Mating can occur in water (crocodilians, sea and freshwater turtles, sea snakes) or on land. Male reptiles possess copulatory organs (except in the order Rhynchocephalia).

Reproductive behavior: Includes the types of behavior involved in courtship (courtship behavior), in mating (mating behavior), and in brood care.

Reproductive period: Mating period when both males and females are sexually active. In amphibians and reptiles this is frequently restricted to certain seasons of the year (e. g., fixed breeding periods in many amphibians). However, a breeding period can also extend throughout the year, but then is usually of variable intensity. This occurs in many species from areas with a largely unchanging climate. Many species breed only once a year, while others may have several breeding periods in a single year. The triggering factors for breeding seem to be internal controlling mechanisms as well as environmental influences (temperature, light intensity, daylight period, humidity, and food supply), which are of substantial (but depending upon individual species also variable) importance.

Reptilia: Reptiles. Class of vertebrates (Vertebrata) in the usual sense. Occurring on all continents except in Antarctica, mainly in the tropics and subtropics. About 6,000 Recent species. Known since the Upper Carboniferous.

Within a phylogenetic system the "Reptilia" are a paraphyletic group; there are no synapotypes for reptiles that do not also include birds (Aves) and mammals (Mammalia) at the same time.

The reptiles include 4 Recent monophyletic orders: Testudines (also Testudinata, Chelonia), Rhynchocephalia, Squamata, and Crocodylia.

Reptiles are characterized by a yolk-rich amniote egg from which fully developed juvenile animals hatch, horny scales or plates, a conspicuous lack of skin glands, presence of osteoderms in many groups (Testudines, Crocodylia, some Sauria), and cold-bloodedness, which is related to the incomplete separation of heart chambers (except in Crocodylia) that gives rise to a partial mixing of arterial and venous blood. Body temperature is largely dependent upon the environment and can be actively modified only to a limited extent.

Nearly all environments have been invaded. Many species occupy fresh water and a few have entered the sea. Most reptiles are carnivorous. In addition to egg-laying species there are a number of ovoviviparous forms and a very few truly viviparous species. A few species practice brood care.

Respiration: Exchange of gases in organisms, where oxygen is taken in and carbon dioxide is given off. While the external respiration, breathing, between the environment and the circulatory fluid takes place within specific respiratory organs or along the body surface (skin surface respiration) internal respiration describes the gas exchange between tissues and the transport medium as well as the enzymatic oxidative processes within the cells. Through such biological oxidation—where hydrogen is derived from the reduction of food substances in conjunction with carbon dioxide with water being the result—the cells obtain the required energy for their various life-supporting processes. Respiratory intensity in poikilothermic amphibians and reptiles is largely dependent upon the environmental temperature. Among reptiles, particularly the turtles have the remarkable ability to survive without oxygen for several hours; they are apparently able to switch their metabolism to an anaerobic energy production system.

Respiratory organs:. Body parts facilitating external gas exchange. These organs are covered with strongly vascular, thin epithelial tissue that facilitates rapid diffusion of physically dissolved oxygen or carbon dioxide. In amphibians and reptiles the respiratory organs are lungs that develop from paired ventral protrusions of the embryonic foregut, to which they are still connected via the trachea (absent in frogs) and larynx. Lung capacity is dependent upon the surface area of the respiratory epithelium. The inclusion of numerous septa and splitting up of the bronchia can substantially increase lung capacity. The lungs are still of simple construction in amphibians, since a substantial amount of gas exchange takes place via the strongly vascularized skin, which is kept moist by numerous mucous glands (skin respiration). The richly chambered, often sponge-like lungs of reptiles are far more efficient (the often horny skin of reptiles largely inhibits skin respiration).

In amphibians, ventilation of the lungs occurs through suction-swallow movements of the throat, the bones and cartilages of the hyoid skeleton forming a pumping mechanism. On the other hand, the reptiles achieve lung ventilation through suction-pump respiration, where through movements of the rib cage and musculature the abdominal cavity in the region of the lungs becomes alternately enlarged and constricted. In crocodilians the muscular *septum posthepaticum* (a diaphragm-like partition that separates the lungs, heart, and liver from the remaining organs) plays an important role in respiration. Turtles, in which the rigid carapace excludes respiratory movements, ventilate their lungs—which are separated from the abdominal organs underneath by a horizontal diaphragm—with the aid of the pectoral girdle and pelvic musculature, as well as through hyoid bone pumps that produce regular changes of lung volume.

There are tendencies toward a reduction in the lungs in both reptiles and amphibians. There are numerous frogs and salamanders that have lost their lungs altogether. Here skin respiration has taken over, as in many of the lungless salamanders of the family Plethodontidae. Among amphibians, the caecilians have—as an adaptation to their elongated body—a regressed left lung. Among reptiles, the family Amphisbaenidae also has a regressed left lung, and the snakes as a rule have regressed left lungs. As a specialization in many snakes, the posterior lung sections are developed into the form of air sacs without respiratory epithelium. Air-sac-like formations are also found in the chameleons and some monitor lizards. Tracheal lungs, which occur in many of the more advanced snakes (Caenophidia), are characterized by the presence of respiratory epithelium in the dorsal region of the trachea. In aquatic soft-shelled turtles (family Trionychidae) gas exchange occurs in part through the leathery skin of the carapace and plastron, as well as through villi in the back of the throat that act like gills.

The gills in aquatic amphibian larvae develop from gill clefts in the foregut, where the walls of the gut grow outward into well vascularized lamellar skin folds. There are usually 3 pairs of these external gills (rarely 2 pairs), which are lost during the transition to terrestrial life at metamorphosis; however, neotenic species may retain these gills throughout their life. In tadpoles the external gills regress during their development to develop into internal gills that become overgrown by skin folds.

Rhabdophidium BOULENGER, 1894. Monotypic genus of the Colubridae, Calamarinae. Sulawesi. About 45 cm. Unicolor blackish above. The head terminates in a pointed rostral. Burrowing snakes.
- *R. forsteni* (DUMERIL and BIBRON, 1854).

Rhabdophis FITZINGER, 1848. Genus of the Colubridae, Natricinae. Sri Lanka through Indo-China and the Indo-Australian Archipelago to Japan, Korea, and the Far East. 12 species. To 1.4 m. More or less strongly keeled and shingled scales. Posterior part of upper jaw with two strongly enlarged teeth that can inject a quite dangerous venom into the circulatory system of prey (2 human fatalities are recorded from bites by *R. tigrinus*). However, compared to *Xenochrophis* these snakes are less aggressive. Coloration and markings highly variable, even within a species.

Rhabdophis swinhonis

Rhabdophis species are diurnal, with an amphibious mode of life. They prefer frogs over fish as food. Egg-layers, to 25 eggs. Care as for Natricinae, Group 2. They do well in captivity, and some have been bred. Caution is advised, as antivenin is hard or impossible to obtain.
- *R. chrysargus* (SCHLEGEL, 1837). Indo-China south of 19° north latitude, Sumatra, Java. In tropical highlands to 500 m elevation. Feeds on toads.
- *R. subminiatus* (SCHLEGEL, 1837). Burma and Thailand eastward to southern China and southward to Java. 2 subspecies. More inclined toward Natricinae, Group 1.
- *R. tigrinus* (BOIE, 1827). Asian Tiger Snake. From the Far East USSR to Korea and northeastern China, Japan, Taiwan, and Hainan. 2 subspecies. Very attractive color combinations of black, green, and red.

Rhabdophis tigrinus

Rhabdops BOULENGER, 1893. Genus of the Colubridae, Lycodontinae. Disjunctly distributed within the Orient. 2 species. 60-80 cm. Head broad, trapezoidal, the head scales largely fused, reduced in numbers, and similar to the closely related genus *Opisthotropis*.

Nocturnal ground snakes that hide during the day under rocks, logs, and similar places. The diet consists of worms and slugs. They should be kept in moderately heated terrarium set up for terrestrial Natricinae of Group 1.
- *R. olivaceus* (BEDDOME, 1863). Southern India (Wynaad). Olive-brown with 4 longitudinal rows of small black spots.
- *R. bicolor* (BLYTH, 1854). From Assam and Burma to southwestern China. Dark brown to black above, sharply delineated from the yellow-white ventral area along the flanks.

Rhachidelus BOULENGER, 1908. Monotypic genus of the Colubridae, Boiginae. Southern Brasil and adjacent region of northeastern Argentina.

Diurnal ground-dwellers. Omnivorous, but prefers to feed on birds. Egg-layers.
- *R. brazili* BOULENGER, 1908. Black-brown.

Rhacodactylus FITZINGER, 1843. Genus of the Gekkonidae. New Caledonia. 6 species in forests. From about 20 to 35 cm. Strongly built, stout. Head of most species with enlarged, very shiny granular scales anteriorly. Tail relatively short, used as a prehensile organ and with adhesive pads under the tip; unusual skin folds across the base. Fingers and toes webbed. 5-mm-wide skin folds on the head and sides of body. Mainly shades of brown with variable markings. Juveniles often very dark, the adults sometimes olive-green. Physiological color changes possible.

Nocturnal, arboreal geckos that generally hide in hollow trees and behind tree bark, although they are sometimes seen sunning themselves during the early morning hours. Primarily herbivorous, feeding on *Freycinetia* fruit. In captivity they will often accept bananas, also some arthropods and pink mice. Mainly egg-layers, but at least *R. trachyr-*

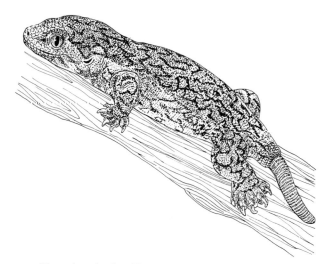

Rhacodactylus leachianus

hynchus is ovoviviparous. A diverse vocal repertoire. Rarely kept in terrariums, but should do well in captivity. Day temperatures 25 to 28° C., not much below 20° C. at night.
• *R. auriculatus* (BAVAY, 1869). 20 cm. Conspicuous small head bumps.
• *R. leachianus* (CUVIER, 1829). New Caledonian Giant Gecko. In excess of 35 cm. Mostly with large white lateral spots. Without conspicuous head scales. Cross folds at tail base particularly distinct.
• *R. trachyrhynchus* BOCAGE, 1873. 30 cm. Enlarged, shiny scales on front of head. Tail folds less conspicuous than in previous species. Ovoviviparous.

Rhacophoridae: Flying Frogs. Family of the Salientia, formerly referred to as Polypedatidae. Africa and Orient. In Africa and Southeast Asia representing the ecological equivalents of the (there absent) Hylidae, but more closely related to Ranidae and Microhylidae (vertebral column usually diplasiocoelic, rarely procoelic). Laurent broke up the Rhacophoridae, placing *Hyperolius* into a separate family and including the remaining genera in the Ranidae. Rhacophorids lack the anatomical characteristics of the Microhylidae, and in contrast to Ranidae they have an additional bone in the digits as in Hylidae and Pseudidae. Mostly bush and tree inhabitants. They generally spawn in foam nests outside of water.
Systematic zoogeographical review of the Rhacophoridae:
• Subfamily Rhacophorinae:
 Continental African genera: *Acanthixalus, Callixalus, Chiromantis, Chrysobatrachus, Cryptothylax, Kassina, Leptopelis, Opisthothylax, Phlyctimantis.*
 Genus with African-Madagascan distribution: *Afrixalus.*
 Genus from the Seychelles: *Megalixalus.*
 Genus with Madagascan-Oriental distribution: *Rhacophorus.*
 Genera of the Orient: *Philautus, Theloderma.*
• Subfamily Hyperoliinae: African-Madagascan distribution: *Hyperolius.*
• Subfamily Mantellinae: Madagascar: *Aglyptodactylus, Gephyromantis, Mantella, Mantidactylus, Trachymantis.*

Rhacophorus KUHL, 1827 (= *Polypedates* TSCHUDI, 1838). Flying Frogs. Genus of the Rhacophoridae. Sub-

tropical and tropical Asia to the Philippines, also Madagascar. More than 80 species. Mostly in brush or forest regions; some follow human habitation. To 10 cm. Treefroglike. Distinguished from closely related genera (*Philautus, Theloderma*) by possessing palatine teeth. The head in many species is distinctly flat, the eyes very large and protruding. Pupil horizontal. Tympanum usually clearly visible. Large adhesive discs present on fingers and toes. Fingers free, sometimes webbed basally or completely webbed; toes webbed to about half of their length. Males smaller than females, with an internal vocal sac and with thumb pads during the often extended breeding period.

Usually nocturnal, agile brush and tree inhabitants. Some species climb high into the tops of trees. These powerful jumpers can glide over distances of up to 15 meters. Other species remain close to the ground (e. g., *R. bambusicola, R. buergeri*) without having given up their adaptations for an arboreal life.

Rhacophorus leucomystax

Typically a *Rhacophorus* pair produces a foam nest during pectoral (axillary) amplexus, attaching it to leaves and on branches suspended above water. The female produces the secretions and eggs and the male sperm, which the female "whips" into a viscous, sticky foam mass. Up to 800 eggs are laid per spawning. One male may breed successively with many females during a breeding period (sexes are attracted by the vocalization of the males). The eggs or hatched larvae reach water during heavy rain and there continue to develop normally. The larvae of some species will actively seek water after they have fallen onto the ground. It is known that the larvae of some species develop in the nests and are independent of water (*R. microtympanum, R. schlegeli*). An exception within this genus is *R. buergeri*, which apparently spawns directly into cool, turbulent flowing waters. Species that penetrate into rice growing areas and even into cities tend to to use artificial water accumulations for their larval development (*R. leucomystax, R. schlegeli*). The bright green *R. nigropalmatus* is given religious status in some parts of Malaya.

Tree-dwelling species should be kept in a tall, well-planted tropical rain-forest terrarium with a water section. Ground-dwelling species that tend to follow human habitation should be provided with a moderately damp terrarium including rocks, tree bark, moss, and similar hiding places as well as a water section. Brown species have proven to be more durable in captivity than the rather sensitive pale green ones (e.g., *R. reinwardti* with essentially still unresolved captivity requirements). *R. buergeri*, which is tied to cool flowing waters, also demands considerable effort and attention. Diet similar to *Hyla*. Large species require a lot of food, have tendencies toward cannibalism, and will swallow even lizards (*Anolis* and geckos) that are longer than they are. *R. leucomystax* has been bred repeatedly. Most other species will probably require very large facilities such as greenhouses in order to breed in captivity.

- *R. albilabris* BOULENGER, 1888. Eastern Madagascar. 9.5 cm. Violet with a white upper lip.
- *R. bambusicola* (BARBOUR, 1920). Eastern Himalayas at 2400 to 3700 m elevation. Variably olive with red-brown, black-edged spots.
- *R. boettgeri* BOULENGER, 1882. Eastern Madagascar. 3.5 cm. Brown with a vermiculate dark pattern.
- *R. buergeri* (SCHLEGEL, 1838). Japanese Singing Frog. Japan to the Moluccas, Sumatra, and Java. 6 subspecies. *R. b. oxycephalus* BOULENGER, 1899, from Hainan, 7 cm, gray to olive with dark sprinkling.
- *R. leucomystax* (KUHL, 1829). White-bearded Flying Frog. China to the Greater Sunda Islands and the Philippines. 8 cm. Brown with a darker pattern.
- *R. nigropalmatus* BOULENGER, 1895. India, Thailand, Malaya, Sumatra. 5 subspecies. 10 cm. Bright green with white dots.
- *R. omeimontis* (STEJNEGER, 1924). Western China, 900 to 2000 m elevation. 8 cm. Brown with dark brown spots, sides with an irregular light and dark green marbled pattern.

- *R. pardalis* GUENTHER, 1858. Bornean Flying Frog. Sumatra, Borneo, Philippines. 5 subspecies. 7.5 cm. Light yellow-brown with cross-like dark dorsal markings.
- *R. reinwardti* (SCHLEGEL, 1840). Javan Flying Frog. Malaya, Sumatra, Java. 3 subspecies. 8 cm. Variably green, the webs of the limbs extensively black.
- *R. schlegeli* (GUENTHER, 1858). Japan, Sulawesi, and Java to Assam. 10 subspecies. 6 cm. Bright green covered sparingly with dark spots.
- *R. tephraeomystax* (DUMERIL, 1853). Eastern Madagascar. Frequent. 6 cm. Gray-brown with a darker marbled pattern.

Rhadinaea COPE, 1863. Genus of the Colubridae of uncertain subfamily (Xenodontinae or Boiginae). Southeastern USA, southward to northern Argentina and Uruguay. About 40 species. Found in highly variable habitats from swamps to rain forests and gallery forests, frequently also in plantations, especially where bananas are being grown; also montane deciduous forests and pine forests. 35 to 60 cm. Head slightly set off. Shades of brown, many species with longitudinal stripes.

Diurnal. The diet includes frogs, lizards, and small snakes. Should be kept in a well-heated terrarium with a water bowl.

- *R. flavilata* (COPE, 1871). Pine Woods Snake. Southeastern USA.
- *R. brevirostris* (PETERS, 1863). Amazon Basin.
- *R. poecilopogon* COPE, 1863. Southern Brasil, Uruguay, Argentina.

Rhadinella SMITH, 1941. Monotypic genus of the Colubridae, Xenodontinae or Boiginae. Eastern Mexico, foothills near Veracruz. Closely related to *Rhadinaea* and synonymized with it in the most recent revision.

- *R. schistosa* SMITH, 1941.

Rhamnophis: see *Thrasops*, genus.

Rhamphiophis PETERS, 1854. Beaked Snakes. Genus of the Colubridae, Boiginae. Tropical and southern Africa. 5 species in various dry habitats (savannahs, steppes, thornbush, and desert regions); *R. acutus* occurs in damp habitats (gallery forests, damp grasslands). 40 cm to 2.4 m. With large and distinct head. Recognized by the beak-like projecting rostral shield (often bent upward), thus the mouth is sub-terminal. Smooth dorsal scales. Brownish, sometimes unicolored (*R. oxyrhynchus*, *R. rubropunctatus*) or with a spotted pattern (*R. multimaculatus*).

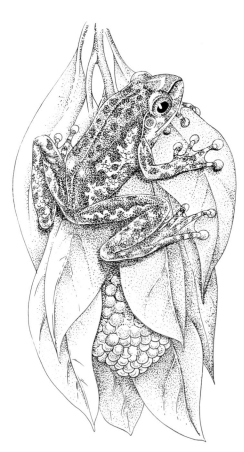

Rhacophorus omeimontis

Rhamphiophis oxyrhynchus

Diurnal ground snakes. Species found in dry habitats feed on a variety of prey, from frogs to reptiles and small mammals, while *R. acutus* prefers frogs. Egg-layers, 10-20 eggs. They should be kept in a dry terrarium that is well-heated and has adequate illumination, sunlight if possible (much as for *Coluber*).

▪ *R. oxyrhynchus* (BOULENGER, 1843). Rufous Beaked Snake. Central Africa to southeastern Africa. 2 subspecies. 1.3 m.

▪ *R. multimaculatus* (A. SMITH, 1847). Southern and southwestern Africa. 37 cm. The smallest species of the genus.

▪ *R. acutus* (GUENTHER, 1888). Central Africa. 1.1 m.

▪ *R. rubropunctatus* (FISCHER, 1884). East Africa. 2.4 m. The largest species of the genus.

Rhampholeon: see *Brookesia*, genus.

Rhamphotyphlops: see *Typhlina*, genus.

Rheobatrachus LIEM, 1973. Gastric Brooding Frogs. Monotypic genus of the Leptodactylidae. Eastern Australia (southeastern Queenland). In rocky mountain streams in seasonally wet forests. Robust. Eyes large, nostrils pointed upward, slightly raised. Pupil vertical. Tympanum not visible. Hind legs powerful. Fingers free, toes completely webbed.

Nocturnal aquatic frogs. Should be kept in an aquarium with a low water level and temperatures around 20° C. The tadpoles are brooded in the parents' stomach, the adult frog actually being able to prevent the flow of gastric juices.

▪ *R. silus* LIEM, 1973. 4 cm. Dark olive-brown with indistinct markings or uniformly black, the abdomen whitish. This species is believed to be extinct (at least it has not been found lately), but at least 1 more similar species is known.

Rheodytes LEGLER and CANN, 1980. Fitzroy Turtles. Monotypic genus of the Chelidae. Fitzroy River in Queensland, Australia. Flowing waters. Carapace to 25 cm. Morphology and biology very similar to *Elseya* and *Emydura*.

Up to 60 eggs in 2-3 clutches per year. Incubation in 47 days at 30° C.

▪ *R. leukops* LEGLER and CANN, 1980. The cloaca is able to pulse water in and out, creating a type of "jet propulsion" actually used for respiration.

Rhinatrema DUMERIL and BIBRON, 1841. Monotypic genus of the Ichthyophiidae. Northeastern South America. Tail very short. Teeth of uneven length. Body with 364-368 grooves. Tentacles tiny, located immediately in front of the eye (as in *Epicrionops*). Cloacal slit perpendicular (unique in this family).

▪ *R. bivittatum* (CUVIER, 1829). Guyana, Surinam. About 20 cm. Dorsum brown-violet, laterally with a wide yellow band. Abdomen light brown.

Rhineura COPE, 1861. Monotypic genus of the Amphisbaenia, family Amphisbaenidae. Florida. In dry, sandy habitats. Slender. Snout dorso-ventrally flattened, shovel-like. Head scales very horny. Tail flattened, dorsally with numerous tubercles. Reddish brown.

Its burrows can be closed off with the tail. Almost totally subterranean, feeding on worms, spiders, termites. Egg-layers.

▪ *R. floridana* (BAIRD, 1858). Florida Worm Lizard. Central and northern Florida. Generally to about 30 cm, rarely to 40 cm.

Rhinobotryum WAGLER, 1830. Genus of the Colubridae, Boiginae. Panama and Costa Rica southward to the Rio Paraguay. 2 species in tropical lowland forests. To 1.6 m. Head distinctly set off, with large eyes with vertical pupils

Rhinobotryum bovalli

and a very broad rostral scale. Body distinctly laterally compressed and covered with keeled scales. Brightly ringed or banded (*R. lentiginosum* often only red-black, *R. bovalli* red-yellow-black).

Tree snakes. Should be kept in a well-planted and heated rain-forest terrarium.

▪ *R. bovalli* ANDERSON, 1916. Honduras and Costa Rica southward to northwestern Colombia, Ecuador, and Venezuela.

▪ *R. lentiginosum* (SCOPOLI, 1785). Amazon Basin southward to the Rio Paraguay.

Rhinocephalus MUELLER, 1885. Monotypic genus of the Elapidae. Extreme southwestern Australia. To 40 cm. Unicolored olive-gray above, white below.

Rare venomous snakes. Biology and ecology hardly known. Probably feed on frogs.

▪ *R. bicolor* MUELLER, 1885.

Rhinocheilus BAIRD and GIRARD, 1853. Longnosed Snakes. Genus of the Colubridae, Colubrinae. Southwestern USA and Mexico. 2 species (often treated as subspecies). In prairies and deserts. About 1 m. Head hardly set off, with a projecting rounded rostral scale and subterminal mouth. Back with more or less distinct bands of red and black on tan to yellow.

Nocturnal, remaining buried in the ground during the day. The diet includes insects, lizards and their eggs, and small mammals. Can be kept in a desert terrarium.

▪ *R. lecontei* BAIRD and GIRARD, 1853.

Rhinocheilus lecontei "clarus"

Rhinocheilus lecontei lecontei

Rhinoclemmys FITZINGER, 1835 (= *Callopsis* GRAY, 1870). Painted Forest Turtles. Genus of the Emydidae. Central and South America. 6 species. In or near various bodies of water, often quite terrestrial. Carapace 25 cm. With a more or less developed longitudinal carapace keel that may become totally unrecognizable in old *R. rubida* specimens. The generic name is somewhat controversial; also spelled *Rhinoclemys* and formerly called *Callopsis*.

Rhinoclemmys punctularia

Rhinoclemmys pulcherrima manni

Rhinoclemmys pulcherrima incisa

Rhinoclemmys annulata

Rhinoclemmys rubida perixantha

Rhinoclemmys funerea

Some species are among the most colorful freshwater turtles. Primarily carnivorous, with only a small plant component. They are not uncommon in their native countries but are only infrequently imported. For details on care refer to *Chrysemys* and *Terrapene*. Egg incubation in *R. areolata* takes 67-120 days at 30° C. or 25° C. in an incubator; *R. funerea* takes 98-104 days in the wild.

▪ *R. pulcherrima* (GRAY, 1855). Mexican Forest Turtle. Mexico to Costa Rica, 3 subspecies. A very attractive species with variable markings on the carapace of yellow to reddish. The head and legs are also colorfully marked. Largely terrestrial.

▪ *R. punctularia* (DAUDIN, 1802). Tropical Forest Turtle. Colombia to northern Brasil, and on Trinidad. Head with contrasting yellow and red markings.

Rhinoclemmys melanosterna

Rhinoclemmys areolata

Rhinoderma DUMERIL and BIBRON, 1841. Darwin's Frogs. Genus of the Rhinodermatidae. 2 species. Southern Chile and Argentina. Found in damp, shady, cool valley forests close to flowing water. Snout extended into a narrow proboscis. Pupil horizontal. Tympanum small but clearly visible. Legs thin. Fingers free, the toes webbed at the base only. The voice resembles a soft, small bell.

During the southern winter these frogs withdraw under

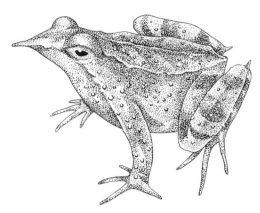

Rhinoderma darwini

rocks, decaying logs, and other protected hiding places. The diet consists of various insects and their larvae.

In *R. darwini* the female deposits on moist ground a clump of a few large, yolk-rich unpigmented eggs that are guarded by several males for 2 or 3 weeks. When the embryos move inside their egg membranes, each male takes a few eggs into its mouth and moves them into the vocal sac. The larvae will hatch there and undergo their entire development in the vocal sac, emerging as juvenile frogs. *R. rufum* males merely pick up the hatching eggs and move them to water.

Darwin's frogs should be kept at cool temperatures in shade and high humidity. A winter dormancy period of several months appears to be indicated.

▪ *R. darwini* DUMERIL and BIBRON, 1841. Darwin's Frog. Southern Chile and adjacent region in Argentina. 3 cm. Highly variable in color, all shades of green and brown, the belly black with white spots.

Rhinodermatidae: Family of the Salientia, suborder Procoela. Neotropics. One genus, *Rhinoderma*. Not particularly closely related to any South Amercian frog family, although once included in the Dendrobtidae, Leptodactylidae, or Microhylidae. Vertebrae procoelic. Mouth without teeth. Various facial bones absent. Shoulder girdle with characteristics of both the rigid and mobile types. Axillary amplexus. Development process and brood care complex.

Rhinoleptus OREJAS, ROUX-ESTEVE, and GUIBE, 1970. Monotypic genus of the Leptotyphlopidae. Africa. Hooklike, thorny, projecting rostral scale. To 50 cm, the largest species in the family.

▪ *R. koniagui* (VILLIERS, 1962). West Africa.

Rhinophis HEMPRICH, 1820. Genus of the Uropeltidae. Southern India and Sri Lanka. 10 species. 18-40 cm, 0.7 to 1 cm thick. The nostral shield projects strongly. Chin furrow absent. Tail cylindrical, terminating in a large scale that has elongated rows of tubercles extending to the tip. Terminal spine absent. Remainder of tail scales smooth. Blue-gray to red or dark brown with light or dark spots or washed-out crossbands.

Burrowing snakes.

▪ *R. drummondhayi* WALL, 1921. Sri Lanka. To 1200 m elevation.

▪ *R. travancoricus* BOULENGER, 1893. Southern India. Travancore Mountains to 1200 m elevation. Common.

• *R. trevelyanus* (KELAART, 1853). Sri Lanka, highlands at about 1200 m elevation.

• *R. oxyrhynchus* (SCHNEIDER, 1801). Sri Lanka, lowlands of the northern province. 58 cm (average about 40 cm), the largest species of the family. An enormous rostral shield.

• *R. sanguineus* (BEDDOME, 1863). Southern India. Particularly common in the Nilgiri Mountains.

Rhinophrynidae: Family of the Salientia, suborder Opisthocoela. Northern Neotropics. One genus: *Rhinophrynus*. Closer to the more primitive frog families (Pipidae, Discoglossidae) and has pelvic (inguinal) amplexus, but externally more similar to the Microhylidae. Without teeth. Tongue attached at rear of mouth, anteriorly free, protrusible. Vertebrae opisthocoelic. Breast bone and free trunk ribs not present. Larvae similar to *Xenopus*, with thread-like mouth barbels; horny ridges absent from around mouth.

Rhinophrynus DUMERIL and BIBRON, 1841. Cone-nosed Toads. Monotypic genus of the Rhinophrynidae. Coastal Mexico and northern Central America in grasslands and semideserts. Body flattened. Skin, especially along flanks, granular. Head and eyes small. Pupil vertical. Tympanum not visible. Forelimbs small, the fingers free. Hind legs powerful, the toes completely webbed. Metatarsal tubercle large, horny, shovel-like.

Ground-dwellers, excellent burrowers. Outside the breeding season they are found only occasionally at night on the surface. The diet consists mainly of termites. Heavy rainfalls or flooding triggers courtship behavior. Males congregate in temporary water holes and call for the females with loud, hoarse voices, the vocal sac an inflated ballon while vocalizing. The eggs are deposited in clumps that float at the surface but soon disintegrate. Captive maintenance is difficult since *Rhinophrynus* is a feeding specialist. Substitute foods (ants, wingless fruitflies) should be tried.

• *R. dorsalis* DUMERIL and BIBRON, 1841. Cone-nosed Toad, Mexican Burrowing Toad. Extreme southern Texas and coastally from Mexico to Honduras and Costa Rica. 9 cm. Olive-green to brown with a yellow to red middorsal stripe.

Rhinotyphlops FITZINGER, 1843. Genus of the Typhlopidae. Africa south of the Sahara. About 25 species. To 80 cm. Often with a pointed but always very large rostral scale.

• *R. lalandei* (SCHLEGEL, 1839). South Africa.

• *R. schlegeli* (BIANCONI, 1847). Eastern to southeastern Africa. 4 subspecies. *R. s. dinga* (PETERS, 1854) is the largest form in the family.

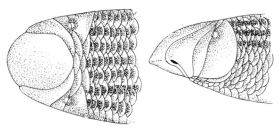

Rhinotyphlops schlegeli

Rhithral: Flowing water region with turbulent, perennially evenly cool, oxygen-supersaturated water. The rhithral corresponds to mountain streams of temperate latitudes, rivers in polar regions, streams at high elevations in the tropics.

Rhodona: see *Lerista*, genus

Rhombophryne BOETTGER, 1880. Monotypic genus of the Microhylidae. Madagascar and Reunion. Skin warty. Head very wide and short, the snout rather blunt. Mouth and eyes small. Pupil horizontal. Fingers and toes free. Tips of fingers slightly enlarged. Burrowing ground-dwellers.

• *R. testudo* BOETTGER, 1880. Nossi-Be, Marojezi Mountains, and Reunion. 4.5 cm. Red-brown with a darker, more or less vermiform pattern.

Rhinophrynus dorsalis

Rhoptropella HEWITT, 1937. Monotypic genus of the Gekkonidae. Southern Africa. Closely related to *Rhotropus*. Rock-dwellers. Little known.
- *R. ocellata* (BOULENGER, 1885).

Rhotropus PETERS, 1869. Genus of the Gekkonidae. Southern Africa. 5 species in dry, often stony or rocky habitats. Barely to 10 cm. Slender. Pupil vertical. Tail about snout-vent length. Toes narrow, of uneven length and with lamellae and small, retractile claws. Partially diurnal.
- *R. afer* PETERS, 1869. Southwestern Africa. Olive to gray-brown with numerous lighter spots; top of tail with bands.

Rhyacosiredon DUNN, 1928. Genus of the Ambystomatidae. Mexico. 4 species in clear, cold, oxygen-saturated mountain streams. Head large, broad, the body by comparison small. Tail long, basally rounded, flattened toward the tip. Mouth conspicuously small, delineated by upper lip lobes at eye level. Legs strong, fingers and toes long. Larvae with relatively small, dark green to yellowish gills.

Aquatic. Oxygen requirements are satisfied by means of skin respiration (generally not by gasping for atmospheric air). They press themselves flat against the bottom and push themselves slowly forward so as not to drift away in the current. Reproduction occurs during the winter. In contrast to the genus *Ambystoma*, the clutch consists of relatively few but large eggs generally attached under rocks in turbulent water. The larvae hatch in 30 to 40 days and metamorphose after about 7 months. Neoteny occurs rarely.

Rhyacosiredon species are difficult aquarium specimens as they must be kept in cold (maximum 15° C.), very clean water at low water levels, ideally inside a refrigerator or in a cool basement location. Even with natural food available (small freshwater crustaceans, various aquatic insects) these animals may still be very selective. Newly collected adult specimens or those caught on land will often refuse to feed. The egg masses must be constantly flushed with turbulent, flowing, oxygen-saturated water, otherwise fungus will develop.
- *R. altamirani* (DUGES, 1895). Sierra de las Cruces (2200 to 3100 m elevation). 24 cm. Olive-brown with black dots. The larvae have a marbled pattern.

Rhyacotriton DUNN, 1920. Olympic Salamanders. Monotypic genus of the Ambystomatidae. Pacific Coast of northwestern North America in clear, cold mountain streams in the middle of shady, humid coniferous forests, often together with *Ascaphus*. Tail short. Eyes large. 14 costal grooves. Tail rounded below, above (at least toward the tip) keeled. Male with conspicuously angular cloacal lobes. Lungless, respiration in adults only via the skin.

Largely aquatic; if on land, always within the splash zone. Should be kept in an aqua-terrarium (the land section to be kept small) preferably under semisterile conditions. Decorations can include a few dwarf ferns and some pieces of moss. Preferaby keep in a refrigerator or cool basement. The diet is mainly small freshwater crustaceans and aquatic insect larvae.
- *R. olympicus* (GAIGE, 1917). Olympic Salamander. 2 subspecies. To 11 cm. Brown, the abdomen yellow or greenish with some black dots.

Rhynchocalamus GUENTHER, 1864. Genus of the Colubridae, Lycodontinae. Arabian Peninsula northeastward to the Armenian Caucasus region (Arax Valley). 2 species in steppes and semideserts, in mountain regions to 1100 m. 40 cm. Very similar to the closely related genus *Oligodon*.

Nocturnal, usually hiding during the day under rocks.

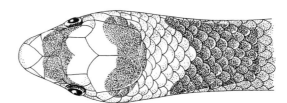

Rhynchocalamus melanocephalus satunini

Food mainly ant pupae, various arthropods, and small lizards (skinks, geckos, agamids). They should be kept in a well-heated dry terrarium with rocks to provide hiding places and large nocturnal temperature reductions.
- *R. melanocephalus* (JAN, 1862). Armenia USSR to Turkey and Iran, southward to Israel. Very attractive orange-red body with a black head (western nominate form) or with a black and white head (*R. m. satunini* NIKOLSKY, 1899, in the northeast).
- *R. arabicus* SCHMIDT, 1933. Arabian Peninsula.

Rhynchocephalia: Order of the Lepidosauria. Tuataras. Widely distributed during the Mesozoic, but only 1 living species. Characteristics include (among others) a diapsid skull and free abdominal ribs. Males without copulatory organs. These up to 4 m long herbivorous representatives of the suborder Rhynchosaurida (giant beaked lizards) have a beak-like extended, toothless upper jaw. *Sphenodon* is the only Recent form.

Rhynchoedura GUENTHER, 1867. Monotypic genus of the Gekkonidae. Australia in arid and semiarid habitats. To 8 cm. Slender. Tail barely snout-vent length, slightly thickened. Toes short and thick.

Nocturnal ground-dwellers found buried in sand during the day or under rocks. They feed on soft insects.
- *R. ornata* GUENTHER, 1867. Red-brown with a darker fine marbled pattern and large round yellow spots.

Rhynchophis MOCQUARD, 1897. Monotypic genus of the Colubridae, Colubrinae. Southeast Asia (North Vietnam, southwestern China). In mountain forests as well as in rocky areas. About 1.3 m. Slender, similar to *Ahaetulla*,

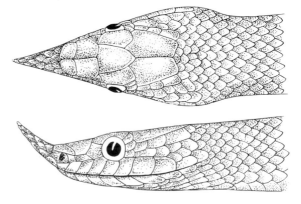

Rhynchophis boulengeri

with a distinctly set off head terminating in a point. However, in contrast to *Ahaetulla* the strongly elongated snout
is formed by a series of small scales inserted between the
internasal shields and the subterminal rostral. The extended tip of the snout is slightly turned upward. In contrast to *Ahaetulla* the large eye has a round pupil. Unicolored green.

Mode of life hardly known, presumably arboreal. Feeds
on lizards and frogs.
▪ *R. boulengeri* MOCQUARD, 1897.

Riopa GRAY, 1839. Genus of the Scincidae, subfamily Lygosominae. Africa through southern Asia to the Indonesian
islands. About 30 species. Found mostly in dry, steppe-like
habitats; *R. fernandi* is found in forests. To 35 cm. Slender,
elongated. Scales in some species weakly keeled (*R. fernandi*). Lower eyelid in some with a transparent window.
Distinguished from similar genera by the presence of su-
pranasals. Short, 5-toed limbs.

Predominantly diurnal ground-dwellers. The diet consists of arthropods and newborn mice. Some species are
ovoviviparous.
▪ *R. fernandi* (BURTON, 1836). Western Africa south to Angola. Damp forest habitats. To 35 cm. Dorsally red-brown,
the flanks bright red and black, posteriorly with white-
edged reddish bands. Ovoviviparous.
▪ *R. sundevalli* (SMITH, 1849). East Africa. 30 cm. Dry,
sandy habitats; burrower.

Riopa fernandi

Riparian: Living on the banks of a body of water.

Ristella GRAY, 1839. Cat Skinks. Genus of the Scincidae,
subfamily Lygosominae. Southern India. 4 species. To 15
cm. Slender, smooth-scaled. 4 fingers, 5 toes. These are
the only skinks that can retract their claws into a recess in
a large digital scale.

Partially arboreal. Little is known about their mode of
life.
▪ *R. rurkii* GRAY, 1839. Southern India.

Ritual combat: Innate intraspecific behavior patterns
that, in contrast to damaging fights, hardly ever result in
injuries since potentially dangerous weapons (such as the
venom apparatus in venomous snakes) are not used or
there are specific inhibiting mechanisms (e. g., submissive
behavior) developed. Simple ritualistic fights among the

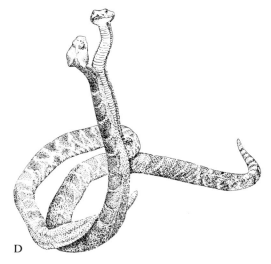

Ritual combat: A *Amblyrhynchus cristatus*; B *Varanus bengalensis*;
C *Elaphe longissima*; D *Crotalus atrox*

amphibians are known, for instance, in the family Dendrobatidae. Highly developed ritualistic fights are commonly observed among the males of various snakes, especially vipers and pit vipers, which become entwined around each other entirely or just with the anterior section of the body in a raised position and so attempt to press each other to the ground. The significance of such ritualistic fights is obscure. Ritual combat (sometimes even escalating into damaging fights) happens primarily among monitors, lacertids, chameleons, agamids, iguanids, and geckos, and then mainly during the mating season.

Ritualism: Behavioral changes for the purpose of creating signals. Ritualized types of behavior commonly occur, for instance, in the area of display behavior and courtship behavior as well as during ritualistic fights.

Roesel von Rosenhof, August Johann (1705-1759): German painter of miniatures and natural scientist. Apart from valuable entomological publications, his magnificently illustrated *Die natuerliche Historie der Froesche hiesigen Landes* (1753) with simultaneous Latin and German texts is still of significance to this day.

Romer, Alfred Sherwood (1884-1973): American paleontologist and anatomist. Contributed to the understanding of amphibians and reptiles. *Osteology of the Reptiles* (1956), *Vertebrate Paleontology* (1945, 1966).

Rooij, Nelly de (1883-1964): Dutch herpetologist, curator at the Zoological Museum of Amsterdam. *The Reptiles of the Indo-Australian Archipelago* (2 volumes, 1915 and 1917) is a standard faunal work.

Rotifers: Class Rotatoria of the phylum Nemathelminthes. Mostly microscopic aquatic species with a constantly whirling crown of cilia. Species belonging to the freshwater plankton are valuable food for very small amphibian larvae and are now readily available for culturing.

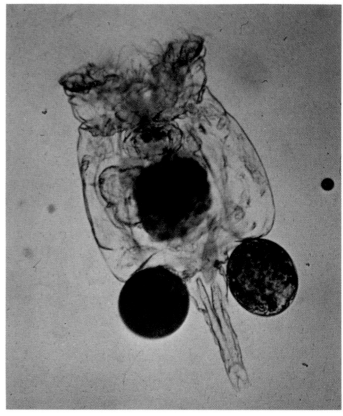

Rotifers: *Brachionus*

Ruellia L. Genus of the Acanthaceae. Predominantly in the tropics. 200 species. The weed-like species are important for terrarium use as bottom cover in rain-forest terrariums.
• *R. graecizans* BACKER. Leaves green.
• *R. portellae* HOOK. f. Low-growing, slightly hairy, richly branched. Leaves with white centers.

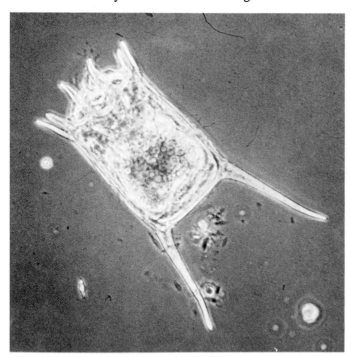

Rotifers: *Keratella*

Ruellia devosiana

Sacalia GRAY, 1870. Six-eyed Pond Turtles. Monotypic genus of the Emydidae. Southeast Asia in small bodies of water. To 16 cm. Carapace smooth. 2 pairs (occasionally 1) of characteristic yellowish eye-spots with dark centers along the posterior margin of head above and behind the eyes.
• *S. bealei* (GRAY, 1831). Southern China to eastern Indo-China, Hainan. Formerly included in *Clemmys*. Often flushed with pink, yellow, or red.

Saiphos GRAY, 1845. Monotypic genus of the Scincidae. Southeastern Australia in moderately dry rocky areas; in

Sacalia bealei

part following human habitation. Related to *Hemiergis*. To 15 cm. Elongated, cylindrical. In appearance reminiscent of *Chalcides*. Ear opening not visible. Limbs very short, 3-toed.

Ground-dwellers. Juveniles hatch from eggs within 1 to 3 weeks.

▪ *S. equalis* GRAY, 1845. Brown with small spots.

Salamander toxins: Secretions formed by poison glands in salamanders (especially newts) as a defense mechanism. They cause local skin irritations and hemolytic effects causing cramps.

Sacalia bealei

Sacalia bealei

Saiphos equalis

Salamandra LAURENTI, 1768. Fire Salamanders. Genus of the Salamandridae. Europe west of the Elbe and south of the Carpathian Mountains, southward to North Africa and southeastward to Iran. 2 species (some systematists include a third species, *Mertensiella luschani*, with *Salamandra*). Compact. Tail short and round. Parotoid glands large and clearly visible. Shiny black, sometimes with bright yellow spots. Larvae, if present, relatively short and high, with the dorsal skin fold starting at shoulder level; some populations live-bearers.

Terrestrial, typically crepuscular and nocturnal animals that may come out during the day only during dull, rainy weather. Although often found close to water (especially near fast-flowing valley streams), water is—at the most—entered for depositing larvae only. *S. atra* and some forms of *S. salamandra* even give birth to fully metamorphosed terrestrial young. Mating is dependent upon elevation, usually during summer or fall, and is identical to *Pleurodeles* but takes place on land. The male takes the female on his back and grasps her with a hook-like hold of the forearms. Readiness of the females to pick up spermatophores is achieved by the male stimulating the female by rubbing her throat and cloacal regions. The following year *S. sala-*

mandra deposits up to 70 larvae (with their legs fully developed) in slowly flowing reaches of streams or rarely in standing waters. *S. atra* gives birth to only 2 young salamanders after a development period of 2 to 4 years; their embryonic nutrition takes place in the oviduct and is at the expense of the other eggs and embryos. During the cold season fire salamanders often congregate in large numbers in frost-free locations (e. g., in caves, abandoned mine shafts, etc.) for a winter dormancy period.

Even with only marginally proper care *S. salamandra* has proved to be very durable, with longevities of up to 50 years. The terrarium should ideally be decorated with moss and flat stones on a layer of coarse gravel kept wet with some ground water and regular spraying with rain water. It should be located in a position without exposure to midday sun. Salamanders hide during the day in light-protected places; should they be seen walking around aimlessly then the terrarium is too dry. The diet consists of earthworms, slugs, waxmoth larvae, tubifex (placed on a flat feeding stone outside of water), spiders, and other slow-moving organisms; occasionally a few mealworms are acceptable. Rations have to be proportioned so that the salamanders do not become too fat. Following the winter dor-

Salamandra salamandra

Salamandra atra

mancy period pregnant females are transferred to an aqua-terrarium with a shallow water section. Rearing the larvae is easy. These salamanders should be over-wintered (cold but frost-free) in semimoist moss-lined containers from about October to March.

Somewhat more difficult is the maintenance and care of *S. atra* because this is a species from cool, more or less per-petually damp mountain regions, and as such it is sensitive to heat and dryness. Even its transport may present prob-lems. The terrarium should be set up with wet moss and limestone rocks and must be placed in a suitably cool area (refrigerator or basement) at 10-15° C.

• *S. atra* LAURENTI, 1768. Alpine Salamander. Alps and adjacent southeastern mountain regions of the western Bal-kan Peninsula, mostly between 800 and 2,000 m elevation. 13 cm. Solid shiny black.

• *S. salamandra* (LINNAEUS, 1758). Fire Salamander. Cen-tral and southern western Palearctic. Widely distributed and particularly common in highlands. 11 subspecies. The nominate form (with an irregular pattern of yellow spots) occurs in southeastern Europe and adjacent Asia Minor. Subspecies *terrestris* LACEPEDE, 1788 (more or less continu-ous yellow longitudinal stripes) occurs in western Europe. Further subspecies are on the Iberian Peninsula (4), Cor-sica (1), North Africa (1), Italy (1), and Asia Minor (2). 20-25 cm (maximum size 32 cm). Shiny black with a more or less extensive pattern of yellow or orange highly variable markings.

Salamandrella: see *Hynobius*, genus.

Salamandridae: Newts, Fire Salamanders, and allies. Family of the Caudata. Holarctic; in eastern Asia reaching tropical latitudes. Palatal dentition in the form of two sepa-rate, more or less arched longitudinal rows. The colloquial names newt and salamander refer to the two fundamental modes of life within the Salamandridae. The term newt ap-plies to those species that live aquatically at least during their breeding period and at that time have a laterally com-pressed paddle-like tail. In contrast, the salamanders lead a terrestrial life throughout the year and can be recognized by their more or less round tail in cross-section. Nearly all Salamandridae cannot take high air and water tempera-tures; only the genera *Cynops*, *Paramesotriton*, and *Pleuro-deles* contain species that are adapted to warmer temper-atures.

Mating behavior among the Salamandridae is rather vari-able. The most primitive type appears to be an amplexus-like contact between the partners, as it occurs in *Pleuro-deles*, *Tylototriton*, *Salamandra*, and *Mertensiella* (male grasps the female from below) or *Taricha* (male grasps the female from above). In *Euproctus* and *Notophthalmus* there is bodily contact between the partners that is moderately aggressive. Contact has been terminated altogether in *Cy-nops* and *Triturus*. Such variable mating behavior is fre-quently interpreted as an adaptation to particular types of water bodies, but there are no definitive correlations (com-pare this with the preferred bodies of water listed for par-ticular genera). Typically Salamandridae deposit their eggs in water (exception: *Salamandra*).

Generic review:
• Genera of the western Palearctic (Europe and Asia Mi-nor): *Chioglossa*, *Euproctus*, *Mertensiella*, *Neurergus*, *Pleuro-deles*, *Salamandra*, *Salamandrina*, *Triturus*.
• Genera of the eastern Palearctic (eastern and southeastern Asia): *Cynops*, *Hypselotriton*, *Pachytriton*, *Paramesotriton*, *Tylototriton*.
• Genera of the Nearctic (North America): *Notophthalmus*, *Taricha*.

Salamandrina FITZINGER, 1826. Monotypic genus of the Salamandridae. Italy, the western slopes of the Apennines. There mainly in forested, cool, damp stream valleys. Rib and vertebral processes externally not visible. Hands with 4 fingers, feet (in contrast to most other Caudata) with 4 toes. Tail long, rounded in cross-section, terminating in a point. The long tongue is attached only at the front and is used in a toad-like fashion for prey capture. When threat-ened they toss the tail forward over the body and pretend they are dead, displaying the warning coloration of the ventral side of the body.

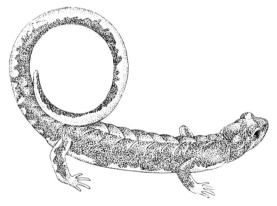

Salamandrina terdigitata

Largely nocturnal and terrestrial. Maintain winter and summer dormancy periods during the cold and hot seasons of the year. Skin respiration (the lungs are only 2 mm long). Spermatophore transfer apparently occurs on land. The females enter moderately flowing streams in March and attach their eggs in clumps to rocks. The larvae hatch in about 3 weeks.

Keeping these salamanders requires considerable effort due to their phlegmatic behavior and is best left to experi-enced specialist hobbyists. The preferred temperature is 13 to 15° C. during the activity phases; over-winter at 5° C., and 20° C. during summer dormancy. These temperature ranges have to be strictly complied with. The small terrarium should be set up with moss and flat stones and a very shallow water level (to provide for a high humidity). The diet must consist of small insects, whiteworms, and other small organisms.

▪ *S. terdigitata* (LACEPEDE, 1788). Spectacled Salamander. Italy, Liguria to Campania, particularly frequent around Genoa. 10 cm. Attractive, usually with brown spectacle-like markings between the eyes, the throat black, whitish toward the neck. Abdomen orange with an irregular pattern of black spots. Legs and tail bright red underneath.

Salamandrina terdigitata

Salea GRAY, 1845. Genus of the Agamidae. Asia Minor. 3 or 4 species. Easily to 20 cm. Slender. Distinguished from *Calotes* and others by the even larger, very strongly shingled dorsal scales and a rather high dorsal crest consisting of narrow, long scales.

▪ *S. horsfieldi* GRAY, 1845. Southern India in mountain forests to more than 2500 m elevation.

Salientia: Frogs. Also called Anura. Order of the Amphibia. Worldwide distribution with the exception of some oceanic islands and polar regions, the greatest species diversity in the tropics. Ecologically highly variable, found from rain forests to deserts, from lowlands to mountain regions in excess of 4000 m elevation, usually in highly variable inland waters and sometimes in areas far from water. In contrast to the Caudata, frogs are tailless upon completion of larval development; they have limbs, in contrast to the worm-like Gymnophiona. The body is compact and of such distinctive form that even highly adapted forms such as *Myobatrachus* can be recognized as frogs by any casual observer. Hind limbs always more strongly developed than the front limbs, which enables these animals to be such excellent jumpers. Hands with 4 fingers, feet with 5 toes (rare exceptions). Salientia have at the most 9 free presacral vertebrae (some Bufonidae), but mostly only 8, rarely 7 (*Mertensophryne*) or 6 (*Oreophrynella, Hymenochirus*), with individual shapes that are characteristic for particular suborders. True ribs occur only in the Discoglossidae; they are absent in other frogs but are not to be confused with the sometimes extended lateral processes of the vertebrae. The shoulder girdle can be rigidly connected in a ventral position (firmisternal) or movable and opposably displaceable (arciferal); both types as well as some transitional forms occur in some families.

Salientia are the first Tetrapoda with a middle ear closed off to the outside by a tympanum that is more or less easily visible, although sometimes indistinctly delineated or covered by skin. The tympanum and even the middle ear may be secondarily lost, as in some genera of the Bufonidae. In connection with the completion of hearing there is also the ability to vocalize usually for the purpose of finding a sex partner and for marking the territory. These sounds can be made visible by means of a sonagram and thus permit comparative studies that recently have allowed considerable scientific attention to the characterization and separation of closely related species.

For all Salientia the typical mating position is the amplexus. In contrast to some Caudata, the male frog always grasps the female from above. Nuptial pads present during the courtship season on the fingers, hands, and sometimes on other parts of the body facilitate grasping, especially in water. The most primitive form of amplexus is the pelvic or inguinal amplexus, as opposed to axillary or pectoral amplexus. Inguinal amplexus is typical for all primitive frogs but also occurs in some of the more advanced forms, such as among the Bufonidae and Leptodactylidae.

Following amplexus the eggs and sperm usually are released into the open water. This has been modified in numerous families, and in a few genera it has even been given up completely. Free-swimming larvae no longer occur in some genera of the Pipidae, Hylidae, Leptodactylidae, Bufonidae, and Ranidae, as well as the Leiopelmatidae. Modified larvae may develop in damp substrate within the egg membranes, in brood pouches, in the dorsal skin of the female, in the vocal sac of the male, or even in the stomach of the parent. *Nectophrynoides* is the only frog genus that is live-bearing. (Some *Eleutherodactylus* approach this condition also.) Internal fertilization occurs in *Nectophrynoides*, Ascaphidae, some genera of the Ranidae, and probably a few other scattered groups.

The larvae of the Salientia, tadpoles, are distinguished from those of the Caudata by the possession of a respiratory tube (spiracle). External gills are present only immediately after hatching. The hind legs are the first ones to break through (front legs in salamanders). Apart from the location of the spiracle and anal opening, considerable systematic significance is also given to the mouthparts, which usually are in the form of strongly keratinized lips, rows of horny teeth, and papillae. The larvae of most species are herbivorous, feeding on algae and similar items.

Many frog species are among the most suitable and most popular terrarium animals, but so far only a very small portion of their terrarium potential has been explored.

Schematic review of the Salientia:

▪ Suborder Amphicoela (vertebrae amphicoelic): Ascaphidae, Leiopelmatidae.

▪ Suborder Aglossa (vertebrae amphicoelic; tongue reduced; inguinal amplexus): Pipidae.

▪ Suborder Opisthocoela (vertebrae opisthocoelic; ribs can occur on the anterior vertebrae; arciferal pectoral girdle; inguinal amplexus): Discoglossidae, Rhinophrynidae.

▪ Suborder Anomocoela (vertebrae opisthocoelic or amphicoelic, in the latter case separated by free intervertebral discs; arciferal pectoral girdle; inguinal amplexus): Pelobatidae, Pelodytidae.

▪ Suborder Diplasiocoela (vertebrae 1-7 procoelic, vertebra 8 amphicoelic, rarely all vertebrae procoelic; usually with

opposable, displaceable pectoral girdle; mostly axillary amplexus): Dendrobatidae, Microhylidae, Phrynomeridae, Ranide, Rhacophoridae.
- Suborder Procoela (vertebrae procoelic; arciferal pectoral girdle; mostly with axillary amplexus): Atelopodidae, Bufonidae, Centrolenidae, Hylidae, Leptodactylidae, Pseudidae, Rhinodermatidae.

Salmonellosis: Second most common infectious bacterial disease in reptiles, the causative pathogen (*Salmonella*) often being carried by turtles without any external signs of a disease. The most important symptoms are a bloody diarrhea (in 60% of the cases) and/or symptoms of pneumonia, refusal to feed, lethargy, and unusual body positions. Juvenile snakes will die suddenly. About 190 different *Salmonella* serum types have been isolated from clinically healthy and diseased or dead reptiles. Triggering factors of salmonellosis are stress through overcrowding, transport, or unhealthy maintenance conditions, such as insufficient water for aquatic turtles. Unhealthy conditions can lead to massive population explosions of the causative pathogen and a subsequent increase of the danger of infection. Newly imported animals as well as the transfer of uneaten food can also lead to the introduction and further distribution of *Salmonella*. This can also take place through equipment transfer and free-moving insects.

Therapy: Ampicillin, chloramphenicol, chlortetracyclin, oxytetracyclin, and polymyxin B. Ideally these medications should be given orally or by means of intramuscular injections over 6 to 14 days. Supportive therapy in response to the most important disease symptoms (diarrhea, pneumonia). Therapy effectivness can be monitored by repeated (5-10 times) bacterial examinations of cloacal smears and/or fecal samples at intervals of 3 to 8 days.

Prophylaxis (including protection against transmission of pathogens to humans): General quarantine of all newly imported specimens and repeated bacterial checks of cloacal smears. It is suggested that turtles have 10 negative readings before quarantine is terminated. Clinical manifestations of the disease and the further distribution of the pathogens can be prevented through strict hygiene, including regular disinfection, frequent fecal examinations (especially in turtles), and strict separation in cases of proven salmonellosis.

Salomonelaps MCDOWELL, 1969. Monotypic genus of the Elapidae. Solomon Islands in forest regions. To 75 cm. Dorsally red-brown to dark brown with washed out, often almost unrecognizable darker crossbands. Head and snout lighter. Abdomen whitish.

These snakes prey on frogs and lizards. Their venom probably is dangerous to humans. Maintenance is similar to *Denisonia* and *Haplocephalus*.
- *S. par* (BOULENGER, 1894). Possibly 2 subspecies.

Salt glands: Glands used for osmoregulation, excreting excess salt. They occur in the mouth in marine snakes (Hydrophiidae, Acrochordidae). In other reptiles salt is also given off via the lacrimal glands (Cheloniidae, Dermochelyidae, *Malaclemys*) or via the nasal glands (*Amblyrhynchus*, *Iguana*, *Brachylophus*, *Dipsosaurus*, *Ctenosaura*, *Sauromalus*).

Salvadora BAIRD and GIRARD, 1853. Patchnosed Snakes. Genus of the Colubridae, Colubrinae. Southwestern USA extending into the dry regions of central Mexico. 8 species. In desert areas, mountain ranges (to 2400 m elevation), rubble fields, and cactus deserts. 50 cm to 1.2 m. Rostral scale huge, the edges free. In appearance similar to *Phyllorhynchus*, but with smooth scales, no suborbital scales, and a longitudinally striped pattern.

Salvadora hexalepis mojavensis

Salvadora hexalepis

Primarily diurnal. Will burrow when in danger. They prey on lizards and small mammals. Egg-layers, 5 to 12 eggs. Provide a desert terrarium with a substantial nocturnal temperature reduction.

- *S. hexalepis* (COPE, 1866). Western Patchnosed Snake. 5 subspecies. Southwestern USA and adjacent Mexico.
- *S. grahamiae* BAIRD and GIRARD, 1853. Mountain Patchnosed Snake. Southwestern USA to central Mexico.

Sanseveria THUNB. Genus of Agavaceae. Primarily found in tropical and southern Africa, also in tropical Asia. About 60 species. Shrubs with rough, stiff leaves. Used for landscaping terrariums featuring animals from African dry regions. They reproduce by means of rooted cuttings (about 5 cm long) under high soil temperature or through separation of shoots.

- *S. cylindrica* BOJ. Rounded leaves in excess of 50 cm. Ideally suited for semidesert terrariums. Robust, cannot be trampled down or climbed on by terrarium animals.
- *S. trifasciata* PRAIN. Bush with creeping rhizomes. Very resistant. The decorative form "Laurenti" has yellow leaf edges; "Hahnii" has a rosette or funnel-shaped growth form with 15 cm leaves.

Sanseveria

Sanzinia GRAY,1840. Madagascar Tree Boas. Monotypic genus of the Boidae, subfamily Boinae. Madagascar, in tropical rain forest or its outer zones. To 2.5 m. Olive-green with brown spots. Juveniles bright red-brown. Ecologically and morphologically similar to the Neotropical genus *Corallus*.

Arboreal, sometimes also on the forest floor and on plantations. Live-bearers. For details on care refer to *Corallus*. Tall tropical terrariums with adequate ventilation are required. The diet is mostly birds but small mammals are also taken. Has been bred repeatedly. Strictly protected, occasional specimens are available from captive-bred stock.

- *S. madagascariensis* (DUMERIL and BIBRON, 1844). Madagascar except in the southwestern part of the island.

Sator DICKERSON, 1919. Genus of the Iguanidae. Islands in the Gulf of California. 2 species. Closely related to *Sceloporus*, with a distinct gular fold or gular folds and the lateral scales of the rump granular.

- *S. angustus* DICKERSON, 1919. Santa Cruz Island, Gulf of California.

Sauresia GRAY, 1852. Monotypic genus of the Anguidae, subfamily Diploglossinae. Haiti. To 15 cm. Weakly developed limbs with only 4 toes. In contrast to *Wetmorena*, the tympanum is visible.

Ground-dwellers, probably burrowers. Very rare and very poorly known.

- *S. sepsoides* GRAY, 1852. Olive-brown with darker spots.

Sauria: Lizards. Suborder of the Squamata. Nearly worldwide. Lizards comprise about half of all Recent reptile species (about 3,000 species). Found in diverse habitats from deserts to rain forest, the majority in the tropics and subtropics. The position of the Amphisbaenia is under some debate, and these burrowing lizard-like animals may well fall into an independent group.

In contrast to snakes, lizards have the brain cavity incompletely ossified, have the primitive number of 24 vertebrae between the skull and the 2 pelvic vertebrae, often

Sanzinia madagascariensis

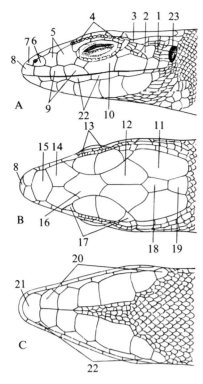

Scalation of a generalized lizard head: A lateral; B dorsal; C ventral
1 Temporals; 2 posttemporal or massetericum; 3 supratemporal; 4 ocular granules; 5 loreals; 6 postnasal; 7 supranasal; 8 rostral; 9 supralabials; 10 subocular; 11 parietal; 12 frontoparietal; 13 supraciliaries; 14 prefrontal; 15 frontonasal; 16 frontal; 17 supraoculars; 18 interparietal; 19 occipital; 20 submaxillaries; 21; mental or mentum; 22 sublabials; 23 ear opening

have preformed fracture lines in the tail (autotomy), and, in several families, have osteoderms. The tympanum may be externally invisible, windows and spectacles are occasionally present in the eyelids, and limb reductions or complete absence of limbs (with pelvic skeleton remnants present) may occur in burrowers of several families.

There are subterranean burrowing species as well as those that are strictly arboreal, of which some even have the ability to dive and glide. A few hunt in water or even catch their food in the sea. The majority are predators. With the exception of the Gekkonidae (where the eggs harden after laying, the eggs generally have parchment-like shells. A number of species are ovoviviparous; a few Scincidae are genuinely viviparous. Brood care (guarding the eggs) occurs occasionally. The majority of species can be kept rather well in a terrarium and even breeding them is often possible although seldom easy.

The systematics of the Sauria is not being handled uniformly by different authors. The basic system adopted here is one based on 4 large, possibly monophyletic groups:

1) Gekkota: Gekkonidae, Pygopodidae, Xanthusiidae.

2) Iguania: Iguanidae, Agamidae, Chamaeleonidae.

3) Scincomorpha: Dibamidae, Feyliniidae, Anelytropsidae, Scincidae, Cordylidae, Teiidae, Lacertidae.

4) Anguimorpha: Diploglossa—Anguidae, Anniellidae, Xenosauridae; Platynota—Helodermatidae, Lanthanotidae, Varanidae.

Saurodactylus FITZINGER, 1843. Lizardfinger Geckos. Genus of the Gekkonidae. Northwestern Africa. 2 species on rubble and rocky mountain slopes. To 6 cm. Slender, head large and high. Tail easily snout-vent length. Adhesive lamellae absent on digits. Pupil vertical. Brown to reddish brown with light spots, some with dark edges.

Crepuscular and nocturnal ground-dwellers that may occasionally also appear during the day. The diet consists mainly of small arthropods. Must not be kept too dry. They need hiding places.
- *S. mauritanicus* (DUMERIL and BIBRON, 1836).

Sauromalus DUMERIL, 1856. Chuckwallas. Genus of the Iguanidae. Southwestern USA and northern Mexico. 7 species, of which 5 are restricted to islands. Found in rocky semideserts and steppes. To 45 cm. Plump, strongly flattened dorso-ventrally, with skin folds along the sides. The tail is easily snout-vent length. Lacks the strongly keeled tail whorls and the dorsal crest of *Dipsosaurus*. Skin rough. Adult male with a dark brown to black head and anterior part of body, followed posteriorly by a variable pattern of reddish or yellowish spots on a slate or brown background. Tail in some specimens yellow or with yellow spots. Females similar to males. Juveniles lighter brown with dark brown crossbands.

Diurnal ground-dwellers that require lots of heat and feed mainly on plant matter such as fruit and soft leaves

Sauromalus obesus

Sauromalus obesus

Sauromalus varius

such as dandelion, lettuce, and cabbage. Egg-layers. For details of care refer to *Uromastyx*. Males very incompatible.
▪ *S. obesus* (BAIRD, 1858). Common Chuckwalla. Widely distributed in southwestern USA and northern Mexico. Several subspecies. The other species of the genus are sometimes lumped into 1 species, *S. ater* DUMERIL, 1856, a name that is older than *obesus*. If the authority recognizes only 1 species of chuckwalla, he may use the name *ater* for all chuckwallas.

Savannahs: Vegetation form of the eremial found in tropical and subtropical regions with a prevailing arid climate (short rainy season, long dry season). Savannahs are essentially grasslands with intermittent sparse tree and brush stands. Due to their wide distribution (especially in South America and Africa, also in Australia) they come in numerous types, such as wet savannahs, orchard savannahs, dry savannahs, thornbush savannahs, and *llanos*.

Wet savannahs along the outer tropical regions are particularly vast in Africa (as the Guinea savannah) and in Brazil (as the *campos cerados*). The amount of precipitation in these regions and the duration of the rainy season are great enough that dry forests had developed there. Following extensive clearing operations and utilization by man, wet savannahs have developed as their replacement.

Dry forests are succeeded by dry savannahs as soon as the climate becomes arid. A transitional form of character-

Savannah of northern Colombia with thornbush, cacti, and other vegetation

istic appearance is found especially in eastern Africa and eastern Peru as orchard savannahs, with tree stands resembling those of an orchard.

If the annual precipitation drops to 200-500 mm and the dry season lasts 8-10 months, then thornbush savannahs invariably develop; they are often referred to as *maturales* in Central America and in northeastern Brazil as the *caatinga*. In an even more arid climate thornbush savannahs change to semideserts.

Say, Thomas (1787-1834): American zoologist. Cofounder of the Academy of Natural Sciences in Philadelphia. Author of numerous taxa of North American amphibians and reptiles.

Scaphiodontophis TAYLOR and SMITH, 1943. American Many-toothed Snakes. Genus of the Colubridae, Sibynophinae. Central America in montane rain forests. About 5 variable species. To 70 cm. Usually more or less banded with black and white rings, sometimes with alternating reddish bands.

Nocturnal. The diet consists mainly of lizards, possibly also snakes and frogs. They should be kept in a moderately heated rain-forest terrarium.
▪ *S. annulatus* (DUMERIL, BIBRON, and DUMERIL, 1854). Yucatan Peninsula southward to Honduras.

Scaphiophis PETERS, 1870. Monotypic genus of the Colubridae, Colubrinae. Tropical Africa from Mali eastward to Tanzania in dry regions of savannahs. To 1.6 m. Compact, head not set off, with small eyes and a very large, strongly projecting rounded rostral scale. The mouth is subterminal. Back with smooth scales. Dirty brown with

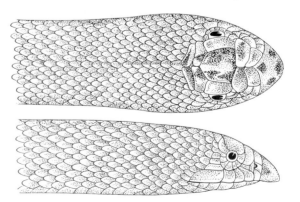

Scaphiophis albopunctatus

irregular blackish scales, white below.

Burrowing snakes that are quite capable of digging even into hard substrates. Often found in termite mounds. Stomach contents have revealed large numbers of insects (termites) as well as small mammals. Terrarium specimens have fed on live mice. Egg-layers, to 50 eggs. They should be kept in well-heated dry terrariums similar to *Eryx*.
▪ *S. albopunctatus* PETERS, 1870. 2 subspecies.

Scaphiophryne BOULENGER, 1882. Monotypic genus of the Microhylidae. Madagascar. In forest regions. Compact, flattened, with a small head. Pupil horizontal. Tympanum not visible. Fingers free, with large, wide adhesive discs. The toes have delicate webbing at the base only, with narrow lateral skin folds and small adhesive discs. Metatarsal tubercle large (outer one absent).

Presumably more or less arboreal at low levels in forests.
▪ *S. marmorata* BOULENGER, 1882. Eastern Madagascar. 5.5 cm. Olive with a darker pattern.

Scaphiopus HOLBROOK, 1836. American Spadefoot Toads. Genus of the Pelobatidae. North America and Mexico. 6 species, some polytypic. In appearance similar to the Palearctic genus *Pelobates*. Found in semiarid grasslands (prairies, semideserts) mostly west of the Mississippi; *S. holbrooki* occurs in sandy soils in the eastern USA. Stout, with a truncated nose. Eyes conspicuously large, protruding. Tympanum small, not very clearly visible. Parotoid glands weakly developed or absent. Metatarsal tubercle hard, black, sharply angular, forming a digging spade. Fingers webbed at base only, the toes more or less completely webbed. Skin smooth to granular, with scattered warts. The skin produces secretions that can cause irritations in humans.

Scaphiopus hammondi

Spadefoots survive dry periods buried in the soil. Activity is restricted to rainy nights during the warm season of the year. The breeding period is initiated by heavy precipitation during spring and late summer. Males congregate in rain puddles, ponds, and flooded areas, sometimes in flowing and artificial bodies of water, and loudly vocalize to attract females. The egg masses are attached to water plants and flooded grasses. Larvae are often small, and giant forms as known in *Pelobates* are absent; carnivorous larvae sometimes develop.

Scaphiopus holbrooki

Scaphiopus couchi

They should be kept in a moderately damp terrarium with a deep, loose substrate layer. If kept in open-air and outdoor terrariums during the summer months, the fencing must be deeply embedded to retain the deeply burrowing animals. For specimens from southern latitudes the winter dormancy period can be reduced or may even be omitted.
▪ *S. bombifrons* COPE, 1863. Plains Spadefoot. Central-western USA. 5.5 cm. Gray to earth colored. Forehead between eyes with a distinct boss (high bump).
▪ *S. couchi* BAIRD, 1854. Couch's Spadefoot. Southwestern USA and northern Mexico. 8 cm. Yellowish gray or light olive with blackish spots that become confluent into a reticulated pattern in females.
▪ *S. holbrooki* (HARLAN, 1835). Eastern Spadefoot. USA. Polytypic. 9 cm. Gray-brown to black-brown with 2 light dorsal bands forming a lyre figure.

Scapteira, subgenus: see *Eremias*, genus.

Scatopsidae: Fungus Gnats. Family of the Diptera, suborder Nematocera. About 100 species. Frequently found on decaying plant matter. About 2 mm. Large fungus gnats are suitable as food for small frogs. Breeding is easy. Some filter paper and a mixture of honey and yeast are added to a glass cylinder. A few small pieces of wood serve as resting places for the adult gnats. The generation time is little more than 2 weeks at 25° C. The gnats are strongly photopositive and thus can be concentrated at a certain part of the cylinder and from there easily collected.

Scelarcis: see *Podarcis,* genus.

Sceloporus WIEGMANN, 1829. Spiny Lizards, Fence Lizards. Genus of the Iguanidae. Southwestern Canada and most of USA south to Panama. Primarily in relatively dry areas, from deserts and rocky areas to agricultural plains; *S. undulatus* and *S. occidentalis* frequently are found very close to human habitation. Some species occur in mountains up to 4000 m in forest clearings. About 100 species. 10-30 cm. Strongly built; weakly flattened dorso-ventrally to nearly cylindrical. Wide, sometimes strongly flattened head. Limbs strong, hindlegs clearly longer. Dorsal scales conspicuously large, strongly keeled, and posteriorly terminating in a point, in regular oblique rows. Caudal scales slightly to strongly spinous, arranged in whorls. Femoral pores in males strongly developed. In contrast to related genera, always without a gular fold. Mostly brown or gray with darker crossbands or longitudinal bands; sometimes iridescent bronzy to green, some with a dark, light-edged neckband. Throat and abdomen or at least sides often bright blue, especially in males (sometimes also less developed in females).

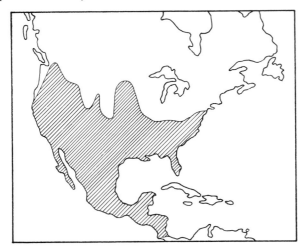

Distribution of *Sceloporus*

Sceloporus magister

Sceloporus graciosus

Sceloporus malachiticus

Sceloporus occidentalis, male

Preferred temperatures (at least for lowland species) from 35 to 40° C.; in *S. magister* it is alleged that digestion starts to work normally only at 37° C. Usually eats arthropods and occasionally newborn rodents; *S. poinsetti* has also been observed feeding on flowers and leaves. Mostly egg-layers, 1-3 (usually 2) clutches of 4-12 eggs each per year. The incubation period varies, depending upon the species and temperature, from 1 to 3 months; in *S. undulatus* it takes about 30 days at 35° C. and 60-70 days at 25° C. Some species, especially mountain inhabitants, are ovo-

Sceloporus magister

Sceloporus jarrovii

Sceloporus cyanogenes, ♂

Sceloporus virgatus

Sceloporus undulatus

viviparous with a gestation period of 7-10 months; mating occurs in fall.

Lowland species are best kept in a steppe terrarium with day temperatures from 30 to 40° C. under radiant heat (radiant heat is more suitable than bottom heat). Night temperatures can be about 20° C., and even lower values can be tolerated, especially by species from the USA. A 4-6 weeks winter dormancy period at about 10° C. may be tried. Mountain species such as *S. malachiticus* should be sprayed in the evening in order to maintain a high nighttime humidity. Juveniles of species from usually dry habitats also require additional moisture. Provide regular ultraviolet radiation and calcium and vitamin supplements. Some species have considerable longevities in captivity and repeated breeding successes.

▪ *S. clarki* BAIRD and GIRARD, 1852. Clark's Spiny Lizard. Southwestern USA (Arizona) to Mexico. Not too dry, low mountain slopes, also in trees. 32 cm. Gray-green with a darker shoulder spot; iridescent large scales.

▪ *S. cyanogenys* COPE, 1885. Blue Spiny Lizard. Southern

Sceloporus clarki

Sceloporus nelsoni

Texas to Mexico. Among rocks. Easily to 36 cm. Extremely large scales. Wide white-edged black neckband; back and tail of males bright blue on a brown base coloration; sides and throat blue. Ovoviviparous, 6-18 young.

• *S. jarrovi* COPE, 1875. Yarrow's Spiny Lizard. Southwestern USA and Mexico. Mountains, usually above 1500 m. To 22 cm. Gray-brown with small dark blue dots. Small scales. Ovoviviparous.

• *S. magister* HALLOWELL, 1854. Desert Spiny Lizard. Southwestern USA and northern Mexico. Deserts and semideserts. 22-35 cm. Very large scales. A dark shoulder spot; males with iridescent blue-violet center of back.

• *S. malachiticus* COPE, 1864. Green Spiny Lizard. Mexico to Panama. Mountain forests from 400 to 1500 m. 20 cm. Males bright iridescent green. Often on tree trunks. Ovoviviparous. Should not be kept too dry!

• *S. occidentalis* BAIRD and GIRARD, 1852. Western Fence Lizard. USA. Rocky steppes and fields. 23 cm.

• *S. orcutti* STEJNEGER, 1893. Granite Spiny Lizard. Rocky, dry mountain slopes and valleys to more than 2000 m. 20 to 28 cm. Males bluish green with violet center of the back.

• *S. poinsetti* BAIRD and GIRARD, 1852. Crevice Spiny Lizard. New Mexico and Texas and northern Mexico. Dry, rocky mountain slopes, in Mexico to 2500 m. Easily to 30 cm. Very large scales. White-edged dark neckband. Ovoviviparous, 5-16 young.

• *S. undulatus* DAUDIN, 1802. Eastern Fence Lizard. Southeastern and central USA to Texas. Frequently in fields, pine woods, and near human settlements. 15-20 cm. Very adaptable.

Scelotes FITZINGER, 1826. Genus of the Scincidae. Africa south of the Sahara and in Madagascar, in relatively moist habitats. Some 24 species. To 50 cm. Elongated. In contrast to similar genera such as *Acontia*, the pterygoid bones come together. Strongly reduced or absent limbs.

and fish. Ovoviviparous.
• *S. capensis* (SMITH, 1849). South Africa.

Schistometopum PARKER, 1941. Genus of the Caeciliidae. Tropical East Africa (1 species) and islands in the Gulf of Guinea, West Africa (3 species). 4 species. To about 36 cm. Tentacle closer to the eye than to nostril. Inner row of teeth in lower jaw with 18-20 teeth. 93-117 primary furrows, 16-55 secondary furrows. Tiny scales along posterior part of body. Cloacal slot perpendicular. Either uniformly olive or yellowish with brown spots.
• *S. gregorii* (BOULENGER, 1894). Tropical East Africa. To 36 cm. Dorsum olive or gray-olive, belly lighter.

Schmidt, Karl Patterson (1890-1957): American herpetologist and biologist at the American Museum of Natural History in New York. Founded the Herpetological Department at the Field Museum of Natural History in Chicago in 1922. Most notable among his herpetological publications are *Field Book of Snakes* (with Davis) (1941), the sixth edition of *A Check List of North American Amphibians and Reptiles* (1953), and (jointly with Inger) *Living Reptiles of the World* (1957).

Schoutedenella: see *Arthroleptis,* genus.

Schreiber, Egid (1836-1913): Austrian educator and herpetologist. Best known for his standard publication (revised twice) *Herpetologia Europaea* (1874, 1912), which was for decades the only handbook on the European herpetofauna.

Scincella MITTLEMAN, 1950. Ground Skinks. Genus of the Scincidae, *Leiolopisma* Group. Southeast Asia, southern India, and from Panama to the southeastern USA. 30-40 species found in various types of habitats that are not too dry and in mountain regions, some up to 4000 m elevation. Closely related and similar to *Ablepharus*, but the lower transparent eyelid is movable.

Ground-dwellers. Mostly egg-layers, some ovoviviparous. Care as for *Ablepharus*.

Scincella lateralis

▪ *S. himalayana* (GUENTHER, 1864). Himalayan Slender Skink. Himalayas Region to 4,000 m. Ovoviviparous.
▪ *S. silvicola* (TAYLOR, 1937). Mexico. To 15 cm. Ovoviviparous.
▪ *S. laterimaculata* (BOULENGER, 1887). Lateral-spot Slender Skink. Southern India. Juveniles with black tail.
▪ *S. sikkimensis* (BLYTH, 1854). Sikkim Slender Skink. Sikkim. To 3500 m. Juveniles with red tail. Egg-laying.
▪ *S. lateralis* (SAY, 1823). Ground Skink. Southern USA, 13 cm. Forest detritus, especially moist areas. Oviparous.

Scincidae: Skinks. Family of the Squamata. Tropics and warmer temperate zones, with distribution centers in Southeast Asia, Australia, and Africa. 700 to 800 species in more than 50 genera. With Teiidae, Lacertidae, and some smaller families it comprises the Scincomorpha. From barely 10 cm to 65 cm. Mainly slender, elongated, cylindrical lizards with long tails and more or less pointed heads, barely set off from the neck. The head is relatively large and massive, the cranial arch complete, with pleurodont teeth. The tongue is weakly forked anteriorly, freely movable, with scale papillae. External ear openings in many skinks are reduced or totally covered by scales. The eyes have variable lid development, from freely movable scaly lids to those that are firmly fused totally transparent "spectacles." Top of head with large, regularly arranged shields. Body scales smooth or weakly keeled (a few exceptions have spines), usually large, roundish, and shingled, frequently with a strong, in part iridescent, gloss. Osteoderms present. Femoral and preanal pores absent. Tail in nearly all species very brittle. There is a tendency toward limb reduction; apart from normally 5-toed representatives there are also transitional forms to completely legless forms.

The Scincidae are ground-dwellers, and some are burrowers. A few genera are distinctly arboreal (e. g., *Dasia*), and some genera are always found close to water (e. g., *Tropidophorus*). Several are predators, while *Corucia*, *Tiliqua*, and some other large types feed mainly on plants. A large proportion of the family (about ⅓) is ovoviviparous, and even in some egg-laying species the young hatch after a relatively short time. The females of some species provide brood care. A few species are genuinely viviparous,

their embryos developing without an eggshell (e. g., *Trachysaurus*, *Chalcides chalcides*).

The systematics of the family are very uncertain. Large genera such as *Lygosoma* and *Leiolopisma* have been split up recently, but the division is handled differently by different taxonomists. Frequently one distinguishes 3 subfamilies:
▪ Tiliquinae: Giant skinks and related forms. A group of genera possibly not closely related. Includes such very large and relatively primitive genera as *Corucia*, *Egernia*, *Macroscincus*, *Tiliqua*, and *Trachysaurus*.
▪ Scincinae: *Chalcides*, *Eumeces*, *Ophiomorus*, *Scincopus*, *Scincus*, and *Sphenops*.
▪ Lygosominae: Slender skinks and related forms. The largest subfamily, with many genera and species that are difficult to separate. Distinguished from the other subfamilies by the position of the pterygoid bones. Membership in this subfamily of some genera is questionable. Sometimes a subfamily Acontininae (*Acontias*) is split off. Typical members are the genera around *Lygosoma* and *Leiolopisma* (including all genera of uncertain status): *Ablepharus*, *Acontias*, *Afroablepharus*, *Anomalopus*, *Anotis*, *Barkudia*, *Brachymeles*, *Carlia*, *Cophoscincus*, *Cryptablepharus*, *Ctenotus*, *Dasia*, *Emoia*, *Eugongylus*, *Geomyersia*, *Hemiergis*, *Hemispaeriodon*, *Herpetoseps*, *Lampropholis*, *Lerista*, *Lipinia*, *Neoseps*, *Nessia*, *Notoscincus*, *Panaspis*, *Paratosaurus*, *Phoboscincus*, *Prasinohaema*, *Proablepharus*, *Pseudemoia*, *Riopa*, *Ristella*, *Saiphos*, *Scelotes*, *Scincella*, *Sepsina*, *Sepsophis*, *Sphenomorphus*, *Sphenops*, *Tachygia*, *Tribolonotus*, *Tropidophorus*, *Typhlacontias*, and *Typhlosaurus*.

Scincopus PETERS, 1864. Night Skinks. Monotypic genus of the Scincidae, subfamily Scincinae. North Africa in a few areas of the Sahara. Closely related to *Scincus*, but the ear openings are not as extensively covered. Head large, conical. Tail ½ snout-vent length. Dorsal scales keeled, with 2 enlarged central rows. Chromium yellow with 5 to 7 black crossbands and a black eyering.
Nocturnal, hiding during the day in sand.
▪ *S. fasciatus* PETERS, 1864.

Scincopus fasciatus

Scincus LAURENTI, 1768. Sand Skinks. Genus of Scincidae, subfamily Scincinae. Northern Africa to Iran in deserts. To about 20 cm. Strongly built, cylindrical. Head conical, with a chisel-like extended snout. Ear opening

Scincus scincus

nearly completely covered. Tail shorter than snout-vent length. Short, strong, 5-toed limbs with strongly flattened, widened fingers. Smooth scales. Yellowish to light brown, mostly with dark crossbands.

Diurnal ground-dwellers that disappear rapidly in loose sand when in danger. They prey on arthropods. Ovoviviparous.

Provide a dry terrarium with a deep sandy bottom, the lower layers kept slightly moist. Day temperatures of about 30° C. (under a localized basking light to 40° C.), with strong temperature reductions at night (15 to 20° C.) are fine. Give a 4-6 weeks winter dormancy period at 10° C. No water bowl (danger of drowning), occasional spraying is sufficient. Regular ultraviolet radiation and calcium and vitamin supplements should be given.

- *S. scincus* (L., 1758) (=*S. officinalis* LAURENTI, 1768). North Africa. Several subspecies.

Scindapsus SCHOTT. Pothos. Genus of the Araceae. Tropical Southeast Asia and eastern India. 20 species in rain forests. Popular climbing and hanging plants for rain-forest terrariums. For culturing details see *Philodendron*.

- *S. pictus* HASSK. Var. "Argyraeus" has silver-white spotted leaves.

Scolecomorphus BOULENGER, 1883. Genus of the Caeciliidae. Tropical Africa. 6 species. To 45 cm. In contrast to other caeciliid genera, characterized by a conspicuously large tentacle and a spinous penis. Eyes covered by orbital bones. Only 1 row of teeth in the lower jaw. Cloacal slit longitudinal. 104-154 primary folds, no secondary folds, no scales.

- *S. kirki* BOULENGER, 1883. Tropical East Africa. To 40 cm. Back and sides pale violet-olive, abdomen yellowish olive.
- *S. vittatus* (BOULENGER, 1895). Tanzania. To 35 cm. A wide chocolate brown band on the back, the sides and abdomen cream.

Scolecophidia: Blind Worm Snakes. Infraorder of the Serpentes. Circumtropical distribution. Families: Typhlopidae with about 4 genera and approximately 180 species; Anomalepidae with 4 genera and about 20 species; Leptotyphlopidae with 2 genera and about 40 species. In contrast to other snakes, the blind worm snakes have a compact skull, but the dentition and other details differ significantly from family to family. Rudimentary pelvic bones are present in most forms. Typhlopidae and Anomalepidae are closely related to each other, but they differ substantially from the Leptotyphlopidae and at the same time also from all other groups of snakes.

Primarily found in dry habitats, but also in rain forests and montane rain forests. To 70 cm, cylindrical, thin. The head is cylindrical and often has a wedge-like projecting rostral scale. The eyes are covered by ocular shields. Body scales smooth. Tail extremely short, frequently ending in a terminal spine. Brown or translucent, rarely any markings in the form of spots or stripes. Rarely any difference between dorsal and ventral coloration.

Subterranean burrowing snakes, often found in ant or termite mounds, in damp or dry substrates, and (exceptionally) even in epiphytes.

Blind worm snakes are of very little significance in terrarium keeping, although these snakes provide the possibility of many challenging observations that could be made on captive specimens.

Ideally these snakes are best kept in very high, long, but rather narrow glass terrariums where the burrows—by necessity—have to be established along a large glass side. The deep substrate layer (40 cm or more) must have proper drainage: the lowest layer can consist of coarse gravel, followed by medium size gravel, with loose sandy soil or humus on top. Ideally the bottom of the container should have a built-in drain. Ventilation of the bottom can be further enhanced by perforation of the bottom panel. Plants should be avoided; instead stones, pieces of bark, and similar items are useful. Spray thoroughly, preferably after dark when the snakes are induced to drink and to leave their burrows voluntarily. Usually they only come out at night. In order to provide better observation possibilities, the subterranean areas of the terrarium are covered with cardboard, so that with weak illumination (red light) the activities inside the burrows can be observed. Suitable ant species have to be tested as food and an adequate food organism breeding program or other food supplies (including laboratory termite strains) have to be established. For transport use cans with a foam rubber substrate. Apart from their possible role as interesting terrarium animals, they are also of significance as special food organisms for other snakes (e. g., for *Vermicella* and others).

Scolecophis FITZINGER, 1843. Monotypic genus of the Colubridae, Boiginae. Pacific coastal region from El Salvador to Costa Rica in tropical rain forests. About 40 cm. The head is slightly set off and round-snouted. Banded with black.

Nocturnal ground snakes. Biology hardly known.

- *S. atrocinctus* (SCHLEGEL, 1837).

Scolecosaurus: see *Bachia*, genus.

Scorpions: see Arachnida, class.

Scotobleps BOULENGER, 1900. Monotypic genus of the Ranidae. Nigeria and Cameroons. In flowing waters with dense vegetation along the banks, usually in the middle of tropical forests. Skin with warts. Pupil vertical. Short, bent claws on the toes, as in related genera *Astylosternum* and *Trichobatrachus*.

Nocturnal, largely aquatic. Keep in a spacious, densely planted aqua-terrarium.

- *S. gabonicus* BOULENGER, 1900. To 7 cm. Dark, iris gray.

Scutellation: see Pholidosis.

Scutiger THEOBALD, 1868 (=*Cophophryne* BOULENGER, 1887; *Aelurophryne* BOULENGER, 1919). Genus of the Pelobatidae. Himalayas. 7 species in high mountain ranges to 4,000 m. In contrast to the closely related genus *Oreolalax*, always without teeth and with ovally arched posterior tongue margin; males have a 2-part nuptial pad field on each side of the chest. Tympanum not visible. Fingers free, the toes webbed for about ⅔ of their length (completely webbed in *S. alticola*). Arms of courting males are strongly swollen and the first and second fingers in *S. breviceps* and *S. glandulatus* have black horny teeth; other than that, with colorless pads. Hands with warts. Larvae similar to *Pelobates*, but no giant forms present.

Lethargic ground-dwellers found in close proximity to their brood water (mountain creeks), usually hidden under rocks. Spawning as in *Oreolalax*. Maintain in a semisterile aqua-terrarium in a cool location in a refrigerator or cellar.
• *S. breviceps* (LIU, 1950). China, eastern Tibet. 7 cm. Light olive with a golden pattern.
• *S. mammatus* (GUENTHER, 1896). Sichuan, eastern Tibet. 7.5 cm. Dark black-brown with black warts.

Scythrophrys LYNCH, 1971. Monotypic genus of the Leptodactylidae. Southeastern Brazil. Originally included in *Zachaenus*. Pupil horizontal. Tympanum not visible. Fingers and toes without webbing, but with lateral skin folds. Thumbs very short.
• *S. sawayae* (COCHRAN, 1953). 2 cm.

Selaginella P. BEAUV. Moss Fern. Genus of the Lycopodiatae. Mainly in tropics. 700 species in rain forests. Hardy shrubs with low-lying, climbing, and creeping runners. They can take shade, like humidity, and are ideally suited for use in rain-forest terrariums to provide groundcover or as undergrowth.
• *S. serpens* (DESV. ex POIR.) SPRING. Lawn-forming.

Selaginella serving as an understory plant for *Saintpaulia* (blue flowers) and *Begonia* (white flowers)

Selva: Tropical rain forests in the Amazon region of 3 types: 1) the relatively dry *ete* forests in flood-free areas; 2) the *varzea*, open forests in the flood areas of white-water rivers, regularly flooded at high water; 3) the *igapo*, low, palm-rich swamp forests along the banks of black-water rivers, roots in part below mean water level. With the exception in the equatorial region, more or less well-defined

Selva of central Peru

rain and dry seasons occur in the *selva;* the annual precipitation is just sufficient to maintain the *ete* forest perpetually green, the tree tops (crowns) at various levels also benefitting from the strong evaporation-inhibiting effect.

Shade temperatures in *selvas* are 23 to 26° C.; a dry season of about 2-3 months exists, but apart from that there is evenly distributed substantial precipitation.

Semidesert: Vegetation form of the eremial, intermediate between grasslands and deserts, which during extensive drought periods have only some very sparse vegetation that are: 1) short-lived species with rapid growth; 2) bulbous species; 3) dry plants that can severely restrict their own water evaporation; 4) water-storing succulents (cacti, spurge); and 5) lower plant forms (blue-green algae, mosses, and lichens). Therefore, semideserts—in contrast to deserts—can have an extremely varied appearance, geographically as well as climatically. Following rainfalls semideserts can display virtual flower carpets. The fauna in such regions is surprisingly diverse since a large food spectrum is available.

From a herpetological point of view some of the most significant semideserts include the Karoo and Kalahari in Africa, the Sonoran in southwestern North America, the central Australian arid region, and central Asia.

Semidesert terrarium: Only the smallest number of terrarium animals from dry regions are true desert occupants. The vast majority occupy more or less dry semideserts, steppes, savannahs, or rocky areas. The common denominators are a well-defined day/night rhythm, relatively low humidity (at least during the day), and exposure to strong ultraviolet radiation. For details refer to habitat descriptions. In contrast to desert animals, those from semiarid regions can drink without difficulty from water containers without the danger of an accident.

Plants suitable for semidesert terrariums:
• Dry regions of South and East Africa: *Aloe, Caralluma, Crassula, Ceropegia, Euphorbia, Gasteria, Haworthia, Kalanchoe, Sansevieria.*
• Dry regions of America: *Agave, Aechmea,* some Cactaceae, *Dyckia, Echeveria, Furcraea, Tillandsia,* and some *Yucca.*
• Dry Mediterrenean region: *Hedera, Myrtus,* Myrtaceae, *Ruscus.*

▪ Subtropical regions of Australia: *Cissus, Hoycarnosa,* Myrtaceae.

Seminatrix COPE, 1895. Black Swamp Snakes. Monotypic genus of the Colubridae, Natricinae. Southeastern USA, with center of distribution in Florida. Formerly included in *Natrix.* They are common in cypress-beech swamp forests and water hyacinth carpets (*Eichhornia*). 25-35 cm. Scales smooth, in contrast to other North American water snakes. Back dark brown to black. Belly bright red, sometimes with black lines across scales.

Strongly aquatic water snakes (Natricinae, Group 3). They feed on worms, leeches, frogs and their larvae, as well as on aquatic salamanders.
▪ *S. pygaea* (COPE, 1871).

Semi-sterile maintenance: Often described erroneously as sterile maintenance. Reduction of terrarium decoration to a minimum and easily accessible corners, with no substrate or only a thin layer of sand, peat moss, wood shavings, or similar material, which must often be completely replaced. Plants are absent, and only a strong, easily cleanable climbing branch and a hiding box are placed inside the terrarium. These are optimal conditions for giant snakes, crocodilians, monitor lizards, and some tortoises, where large amounts of feces require frequent cleaning in order to maintain reasonably hygienic conditions and so reduce the risk of bacterial infection. Semi-sterile containers are also used for quarantine.

Sempervivum L. Houseleek. Genus of the Crassulaceae. Central Europe, Caucasus, highlands of Iran, North Africa. About 30 species in mountain regions. Rosette plants, often forming groups or growing like lawns due to the formation of short runners. Nearly always frost-resistant and therefore ideally suited for open-air terrariums, in rocky or dry sections. There is a great abundance of forms and varieties.
▪ *S. arachnoideum* L., Spiderweb Leek. Pads to 15 cm in diameter.
▪ *S. tectorum* L. Common Houseleek.

Sepsina BOCAGE, 1866. Genus of the Scincidae. Africa south of the Sahara and adjacent islands. Similar to *Scelotes.* Small, elongated, eyelids movable. Ear openings distinct. Short limbs present.

Burrowing ground-dwellers that prey on small arthropods.
▪ *S. splendidus.* Madagascar. Damp, in part sunny habitats. Barely to 25 cm.

Sepsophis BEDDOME, 1870. Monotypic genus of the Scincidae. India. In forests. Easily to 20 cm. Elongated. Lower eyelid with a transparent window. The ear opening in some species is covered. Rudimentary limbs are present.

Ground-dwellers. Little known.
▪ *S. punctatus* BEDDOME, 1870. Madras.

Serpentes: Ophidia. Snakes. Suborder of the Squamata. Worldwide in temperate and warm climatic regions of the world. Only a very few areas suitable climatically for snakes are actually free of snakes (Ireland, New Zealand, Oceanic Islands). 3 infraorders: Scolecophidia with 3 families; Henophidia with 5 families; and Caenophidia with 5

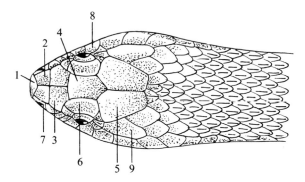

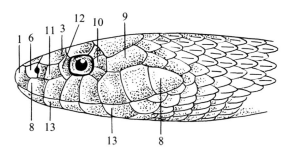

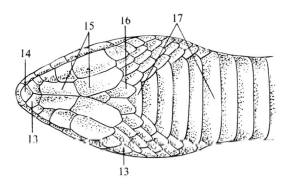

Head scalation of a generalized snake (dorsal, lateral, and ventral views). 1 Rostral; 2 internasal; 3 prefrontal; 4 frontal; 5 parietal; 6 supraocular; 7 nasal; 8 supralabial; 9 pretemporal; 10 postocular; 11 loreal; 12 preocular; 13 sublabial; 14 mental; 15 inframaxillaries; 16 gular; 17 ventrals

families. Altogether there are about 2500-2700 species in 414 genera. The oldest certain snake fossils are known from the Lower Cretaceous. The most diverse infraorder, the Caenophidia with the largest number of species of the Recent snake fauna, does not occur until the Tertiary, while the most highly specialized venomous snakes of the families Viperidae and Crotalidae probably have existed only since the Upper Tertiary. Without doubt the various groups of the Caenophidia are still actively evolving, while the Scolecophidia and Henophidia represent mainly primitive and conservative Serpentes that often possess relict characters.

Apart from the air, the Serpentes occupy all possible environments in favorable climates. There are numerous ecologically highly adaptable species that occupy a broad spectrum of different habitats and also many highly specialized forms. Ecological types include tree-dwellers, terrestrial and subterranean land snakes (subdivided into diurnal and nocturnal species), and aquatic snakes (in different inland and marine or brackish waters). Snakes do not have any functional limbs. Some representatives of primitive groups

(Scolecophidia and Henophidia) still have vestiges of pelvic bones, but the shoulder girdles and anterior limbs have been completely reduced. The rudiments of hind limbs occur in some Henophidia as clearly visible anal spurs. The vertebral column of snakes is characterized by its elasticity as well as the large number of vertebrae (160-435). The neck and trunk vertebrae usually have long ribs that terminate freely without a sternal connection. The caudal vertebrae in Serpentes are variably developed. Usually the tail is long. Climbing snakes possess either an extremely long or an extremely flexible tail used as a grasping organ. Burrowing snakes have short to very short tails with vertebrae that can be fused into a bony rod. A modified terminal tail scale in burrowing snakes may serve as an anchor during burrowing activity.

The enormous mobility of the tooth-carrying bones of the snake skull is conspicuous, as is the displacement of the mandibular joint behind the cranial capsule. Related to this is the loss of the zygomatic bone (cheek bone), which assures the firm connection of the upper jaw bone with the cranium in the normal reptile skull. Similarly, the two temporal bridges of the diapsid cranium have completely regressed. The tooth-carrying elements are held to other skull parts by tendons and bands of muscle. This assures the enomous elasticity of the jaws that enables the Serpentes to swallow whole prey as well as eggs.

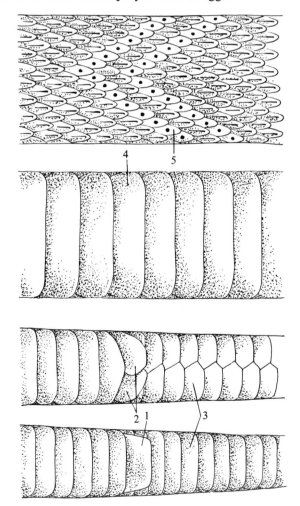

Body scalation of a generalized snake: Dorsal scalation, ventral scalation, and 2 views of the cloacal area. 1 Anal scale or plate (single); 2 divided anal scale; 3 subcaudals, single and divided; 4 ventral scales; 5 dorsal scales, showing method of counting scale rows

In burrowing snakes, especially in the Scolecophidia and some Henophidia, the upper jaw and palatine bones are still firmly connected to the cranium. Also in most burrowing snakes, including some from the Caenophidia, the nasal region of the cranium—used as a digging and burrowing tool—is formed very solidly and is rigidly fused with the cranial capsule. Even the vertebral column in burrowing snakes is usually more compact and rigidly developed in order to support the burrowing function of the head.

The teeth of most snakes are not highly differentiated. The primitive snakes have teeth of equal size distributed evenly over the upper jaw, the sphenoid, and the palatal bones as well as the lower jaw. Only members of the subfamily Pythoninae have additional teeth on the intermaxillary bone. The first major change led to differentiation of the teeth into large fangs and smaller grasping teeth on the upper and lower jaws (e. g., Lycodontinae and Xenodontinae). In the course of dental differentiation, individual teeth in the upper jaw of many Serpentes developed into venom teeth. This process is closely related to the transformation of the salivary glands into venom glands. The transformation of saliva into venom has to be understood as an increase in function of the digestive secretions: apart from the digestive function of saliva initiating the digestion of the food, there is then the added function of killing prey for food. The defensive function of the venomous bite is only a secondary characteristic. Various snakes of the family Colubridae have a more or less effective poisonous secretion from the posterior segment of their upper lip salivary glands (which are referred to as Duvernoy's gland) without actually possessing venom teeth. So far it has not yet been decided whether this phenomenon represents preliminary stages in the development of true venomous snakes or whether this represents regressive evolutionary tendencies. Numerous subfamilies of the Colubridae possess venom teeth (fangs) that are located more or less far posteriorly on the upper jaw, but in individual cases they have moved very forward or completely to the front and so essentially correspond to the fangs of true venomous snakes in some Xenodontinaè, some Natricinae, some Boiginae, Elachistodontinae, and Aparallactinae. The venom of these snakes is in many respects certainly not inferior to that of true venomous snakes (families Elapidae, Hydrophiidae, Viperidae, Cotalidae) and it has in fact led to fatal bites from the colubrid genera *Dispholidus*, *Thelotornis*, and *Rhabdophis*.

Another evolutionary trend has led to the reduction of teeth in the upper and/or lower jaws as observable in the almost toothless burrowing snakes of the Scolecophidia, the egg-eating snakes of the subfamilies Dasypeltinae and Elachistodontinae, as well as the ground vipers Aparallactinae and the true venomous snakes families. In various groups of the Serpentes, especially among the egg-eating species, the ventral process of the anterior vertebrae (the hypapophysis) extends into the pharynx. This process is sharply angular and covered with enamel so that the vertebrae become effective as a saw to cut through the hard eggshell of a bird egg being forced against them in the esophagus.

Scale patterns of snakes are group characteristics and so provide important and simple to handle aids for snake identification. Head scales are normally developed as large shields of constant shapes and patterns. Some derived forms show a tendency toward a transformation of large scales into small scales, while burrowing snakes often show a tendency toward fusing of the scales into larger units. Individual head scales are often characteristically modified. For instance, the anterior snout scale (the rostral) in burrowing snakes is often turned into a wedge-like, spade-like, or leaf-like digging tool. Ground-dwelling and tree-dwelling snakes sometimes have proboscis-like or elongated rostral scales. Nostril and eyelid horns are developed from several smaller scales in several venomous snakes. In sand-dwelling species these structures may function as an extension of touch perception, but they also prevent sand from entering the eyes and nose. There is even a pair of horizontal "feelers" in the strictly aquatic *Erpeton*. Sometimes unusual head extensions are sex-specific and probably do not represent functional organs (*Langaha*).

The relatively small dorsal scales, which are usually arranged in an overlapping manner in strictly defined rows, are rarely isolated or granular. Often the elongated dorsal scales overlap shingle-like. They can be smooth or keeled. Normally dorsal scale size is uniform, but sometimes the scales along the vertebral column are distinctly enlarged and shaped differently, while the scales along the flanks can be narrower or wider than other scales. The peak of their differentiation can be seen in the dorsal scales of some of the Xenoderminae, Boiginae, and Viperidae, where several scale types can occur side by side (*Xenodermus, Echis, Boiga*, and others). The number of scale rows around the body is just as characteristic of genera and species as are the number of ventral (abdominal) and subcaudal scales. The ventral scales in climbing snakes are particularly wide and laterally truncated, while in a few burrowing and aquatic snakes they may undergo a reduction to virtually rudimentary levels (Acrochordidae, Homalopsinae, Hydrophiidae). The totality of scale relationships qualitatively as well as quantitatively (pholidosis) represents in many respects the most important morphological identification feature of the snakes.

Sensory organs are variously developed. Scales on the head and back often show tiny pits that perhaps serve as tactile receptors. Skin glands in the form of neck glands and glands among the anterior abdominal shields occur in at least some species. Only the inner ear remains, the external parts (tympanum and middle ear) being absent. The preception of air-borne sound is strongly reduced, and the function of the ear as an equalibrium organ has taken on even more significance, particularly during the diverse, complicated locomotory seqences (sinusoidal movements, caterpillar-like crawling, side-winding, climbing, swimming, diving, jumping, and burrowing) and as a receptor for the perception of ground vibrations. The eye of snakes is different from that of lizards in details. The absence of movable eyelids (the lower lid has become transparent and is solidly fused to the scales around the eye as the spectacle or brille) gives snakes their staring look. Diurnal and many crepuscular and nocturnal Serpentes have effective eyes, while the Scolecophidia, many Henophidia, and also some Caenophiidia have reduced the eyes to the limit of functionality (some have become overgrown by head scales).

Another important sensory organ is the forked tongue, which is poked out regularly through a slot in the closed mouth with flicking motions. It serves as a tactile organ and for the transmission of aromatic substances, which are perceived by the Jacobson's organ located in a depression in the palatal roof at the level of the resting tip of the tongue. In addition, some boids also have sensory pits in the labial (lip) scales that house (just as does the pit organ located betweeen eye and nostril in the Crotalidae) highly developed temperature sensors. With these the snakes can distinguish dead or resting prey on the basis of its body temperature from other objects around them or find prey that has been killed by a venomous bite.

The internal organs of the Serpentes have been subject to modifications dictated by the elongated body structure. They are also more or less similarly elongated. Particularly interesting is the modification of paired organs. The lung consists of about equal-sized lobes only in a few primitive forms (e. g., Boinae); in most other forms there is usually a substantially shorter left lung lobe or it may be completely reduced. The right lobe extends in some Serpentes nearly to the anal region. However, in these cases the posterior section is not used in gas exchange and it lacks the extensive sacculation and vascularization of typical lung tissue. This "air sac" serves as an air reservoir. Terrestrial snakes use the stored air mainly for hissing, while in amphibious or aquatic snakes it serves as a diving and swimming aid. The air sac also enables snakes to become inflated, a common defensive reaction. Moreover, this stored air can be used to a limited extent in respiration when during the feeding process large prey has temporarily blocked the wind pipe.

Of the digestive organs it is particularly the stomach that is conspicuous due to its ability to become severely distended to receive large prey. Secretion of digestive juices, especially bile, is extremely intensive in order to assure sufficient reduction of prey in the stomach. In dead snakes secretions still present in the stomach will initiate self-digestion of the body that becomes visible within a few hours after death as a yellow-green discoloration of the belly and softening of the skin until the body breaks open at the level of the gall bladder.

The snakes are exclusively carnivorous, an unusual condition among the reptiles for such a comparatively large group of related forms. Arthropods and molluscs as well as all vertebrates serve as prey for snakes. Numerous snakes are closely imprinted upon particular prey or are highly specialized feeders (e. g., Leptotyphlopidae, which squeeze out the body juices of their prey—termites—and leave the body behind, or the egg-eating snakes of the subfamilies Dasypeltinae and Elachistodontinae, which regurgitate the eggshells after the content has been swallowed). Some snakes, on the other hand, have a very wide diet spectrum that enables them to utilize seasonally abundant food animals. Relatively many forms are more or less intensively ophiophagous, feeding mainly or exclusively on snakes.

The sex organs of the snakes correspond to those of all other Squamata. Characteristic of males are the paired hemipenes, the commonly spiny skin projections stabilized by bony supports facilitating solid attachment inside the female's cloaca. A further copulation aid in males of some snakes are particularly rough scales in the anal region, often easily recognizable sex characteristics in these species. The anal spurs also serve as copulation aids.

Courtship and mating often occur in the presence of a number of specimens. In some Viperidae and Crotalidae there are ritualized fights of a harmless nature among males. Courtship in snakes is generally simple and short. Following tongue-flicking between the partners, the male crawls over the female in search of cloacal contact. Actual copulation is often very long, lasting several hours. Females willing to mate react with an excited twitching in response to the courting male.

As in nearly all reptiles, the Serpentes reproduce by means of eggs that have a parchment-like shell. The number of eggs depends to some extent upon absolute and relative size of the female. Small species often produce only 2-4 eggs, while very large species may deposit up to 100 eggs per season. Incubation occurs either in a suitable substrate (heat-producing decay of plant matter or in sun-drenched incubation sites) or more or less inside the female's body (with only rather short incubation periods being observable). Ovoviviparity and sperm retention also occur in the Serpentes. Brood care, guarding of the clutch, is a rare exception in cobras (*Naja* and particularly *Ophiophagus*). Actual brooding of the eggs occurs in some giant snakes of the subfamily Pythoninae. Some species are capable of increasing their body temperature by muscle activity, thus increasing the incubation temperature of the eggs.

For terrarium purposes some ecological categorization can be made of the snakes, often on the basis of their shape, thus facilitating the most important prerequisites for the maintenance and care of most snakes. In view of the often insufficiently known biology of snakes, the snake keeper has to be able to rely on the recognition and applicability of such analogies.

The life of most snake species in temperate and tropical climates proceeds within seasonally oriented rhythms in annual cycles. The correct reproduction or simulation in a terrarium is a vital prerequisite, particularly if the animals are to be bred. While it is not difficult to duplicate the seasonal climate in temperate latitudes, the annual rhythm of tropical species often presents problems that can only be approximately resolved by complex studies of the geographic, climatic, and ecological conditions of the natural environment of a particular species. Thus the well-defined feeding rhythm (short intensive feeding periods followed by prolonged starvation periods) often represents a normal biological phenomenon. Distinguishing this normal behavior from fasting caused by disease, shock, or stress due to insufficient hiding places, particularly during the acclimation period, is often very difficult. Lack of knowledge of the ecological requirements and the normal food requirements make this task even more difficult. Only with the unmistakable occurrence of a loss of condition due to food refusal should force-feeding be attempted. Patience and cautious experimentation are often the better approach to such problems.

Serum institutes: These organizations are engaged in the production of antivenins against snake bites. They are usually combined with snake farms. The most famous serum institute was established by Brasil in Butantan near Sao Paulo. The Pasteur Institutes in former French colonies are well-known pharmacological centers where antivenins are also often produced.

The most important serum institutes include:
Algeria:
Institute Pasteur d'Algerie
Rue Docteur Laveran, Algiers
Argentina:
Instituto Nacional de Microbiologia Aveda
Velez Sarsfield 563, Buenos Aires
Australia:
Commonwealth Serum Laboratories
45 Popular Road
Parkville North 2
Melbourne, Victoria
Brasil:
Instituto Butantan
Caixa Postal 56, Sao Paulo

———

Instituto Pinheiros
1860 Rua Teodoro Sampaio, Sao Paulo
West Germany:
Behringwerke AG
Marsburg/Lahn
Burma:
Burma Pharmaceutical Industry
Rangoon
Great Britain:
L. Light and Co., Ltd.
Poyle Estate Colnbroock, Bucks.
France:
Institute Pasteur
36 rue Doctor-Roux, Paris XV
Guinea:
Institute Pasteur
Kindia
India:
Central Research Institute
P.O. Kasauli R.I., Punjab

———

Haffkine Institute
Parel Bombay 12
Indonesia:
Pasteur Institute
Dj. Pasteur 9
Kotak Pos. 47, Bandung
Iran:
Institute d'Etat des Serums et Vaccins Razi
Boite Postale 656, Teheran
Italy:
Istituto Sieroterapico e Vaccinogeno
1 Via Florentina, Siena
Yugoslavia:
Institute of Immunology
Rokkefellerova 2, Zagreb
Japan:
Institute for Infectious Diseases
University of Tokyo
Shiba Shirokane-Daimachi
Minato-Ku, Tokyo

˙*Colombia:*
Instituto Nacional de Salud
Calle 57, Bogota, D.E. Col.
Mexico:
Instituto Nacional Higiene Mexico
D.F. Laboratories
"MYN," 1707, av. Coyoacan
Mexico 12, D.F.
Philippines:
Bureau of Research and Laboratories
Department of Health, Manila
South Africa:
South African Institute for Medical Research
P.O. Box 1038
Johannesburg

FitzSimons Snake Laboratory
Box 1413, Durban, Natal
Switzerland:
Schweizerisches Serum- und Impfinstitut
Rehagstrasse 79, Bern
Soviet Union:
Taskind Institute
Minsitry of Health, Moscow
Thailand:
Queen Saorabba Memoral Institute
Thai Red Cross Society, Bangkok
USA:
Wyeth Laboratories
Philadelphia, Pennsylvania
Venezuela:
Laboratorio Behrens Aveda
Principal de Chapellin
Apartado 62, Caracas

Sex organs: All organs directly involved in reproduction. One distinguishes between the *internal sex organs*, which consist of the glands that produce the sex products and sex hormones and related duct systems, and the *external sex organs*, the mating and copulating organs with their support structures.

The relationship between sex organs and excretory organs is still clearly visible in amphibians (particularly among males), although in variable stages of development. In the most primitive case the primary urinary duct (Wolffian duct) passes sperm produced in the testes and urine from the kidneys jointly to the cloaca. Through the formation of a new secondary urinary duct (ureter), there occurs a separation into two partially or completely separated efferent ducts. In male reptiles the urinary and sperm ducts (the latter with its anterior section, the epididymis, strongly wound and serving to accumulate sperm) are completely separate or are joined into the urogenital papilla in the cloaca.

In females the eggs maturing in the two ovaries are discharged—through ovulation—initially directly into the abdominal cavity. There they are picked up by the funnel-shaped openings of the oviduct (a new formation designated as the Muellerian ducts) and are then lead to the cloaca. In amphibians the glands of the oviduct secrete the egg membranes; in reptiles similar glands produce the egg

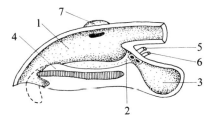

Sex organs: Cloacal region of a male turtle in cross-section. 1 Proctodeum; 2 urodeum; 3 urinary bladder; 4 penis with cavernous bodies; 5 urinary duct; 6 sperm duct; 7 cloacal sac

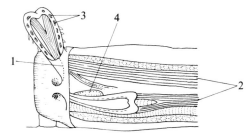

Sex organs: Cloacal region of a male snake in partial cross-section. 1 seminal groove; 2 retractor muscles of hemipenes; 3 cross-section of hemipene showing blood cavities; 4 anal scent gland

white and the egg shell. The terminal portion of the oviduct can be enlarged into a uterus, where the eggs are accumulated until they are extruded or where in ovoviviparous and viviparous species the embryos develop. In the oviduct there may be a seminal receptacle for sperm storage.

Special copulatory organs are absent in most amphibians (exceptions: *Ascaphus* and Gymnophiona). On the other hand, male reptiles (except *Sphenodon*) have special copulatory organs in the cloacal region. Turtles and crocodilians have in the ventral cloacal wall a penis that is erectile by means of two cavernous bodies that enclose the sperm groove in a tube. Homologous to the penis in males is the clitoris in females, which is substantially smaller. Copulatory organs in lizards and snakes are of a different structure. In these animals there are paired extrusible pockets of the posterior cloacal wall that are normally retracted into the base of the tail. They are referred to as hemipenes. During mating the hemipenis on one side is erected by special muscles that help extrude it and a circulatory blockage that allows the organ to swell up. The hemipene is pulled inside out like the finger of a glove. This places the sperm groove, normally located on the inside, on the outside. Frequently spines and hooks are present to anchor the hemipenis inside the cloaca. Due to their extremely variable but largely species-specific structure, knowledge of hemipene morphology is of systematic importance. Anal glands (anal sacs) present in both sexes sometimes produce rather foul-smelling secretions that are laid as scent trails to help sexually active animals meet.

Sexual dimorphism: Apart from primary sexual differences based on the sex organs, many amphibians and reptiles have also developed more or less conspicuous secondary sexual differences. These dimorphic characters play a role in mating or during courtship or display behaviors. Secondary sexual differences include different sizes for

Sexual dimorphism: Probing a male *Elaphe guttata* to determine
sex

Sexual dimorphism: Comparison of the tails of a male (bottom)
and female (top) *Elaphe guttata* to show dimorphism in relative
shape typical of many snakes

males and females of a species, different body proportions,
or different coloration, as well as special body appendages.

Knowledge of these sexual differences is of fundamental
importance to those terrarium hobbyists who may wish to
consider breeding their animals. While in many cases recognition of the sexes in adult specimens on the basis of
morphological differences is relatively simple (e. g., *Triturus*, tortoises, *Anolis, Lacerta*), the sex in numerous other
herptiles is more difficult and without comparison often is
not possible with any degree of certainty.

A relatively reliable method for the determination of the
sex in larger lizards or snakes is the method of probing. A
blunt probe of proper size is carefully inserted into the cloaca and into the base of the tail. In a male the probe can
be inserted much further since the withdrawn hemipenes
possess a tube-like cavity. Probing can injure a specimen

and should only be done by a practiced hand using the correct instruments.

Seychelles: Island group in the western Indian Ocean northeast of Madagascar. It is part of the Madagascan subregion of the Ethiopian, together with Madagascar and the Mascarenes as well as a few other island groups. The Seychelles consist of about 30 granite islands at a tropical latitude and surrounded by coral reefs. Due to high annual precipitation (to 400 cm) they were originally covered with tropical rain forests, but these have now been used largely as timber. Herpetologically they are of considerable signifi-

Seychelles

cance because of giant tortoises (*Megalochelys*), nesting areas for Cheloniidae and Dermochelyidae, and endemic Sooglossinae frogs. Also notable for the occurrence of several endemic genera of the Caeciliidae.

Shinisaurus AHL, 1930. Crocodile Lizards. Monotypic genus of the Xenosauridae. Southwestern China in damp forests. To 40 cm. Head relatively high and narrow. A characteristic double row of tubercles on the tail.

Ground-dwellers found close to water and occasionally climbing. They can be seen sunning themselves on branches above water and will jump into the water when in danger. The diet is presumably fish, small amphibians, and tadpoles. Very rare.
▪ *S. crocodilus* AHL, 1930. Dark brown.

Sibon FITZINGER, 1826. Genus of the Colubridae, Dipsadinae. Found from southern Mexico to northern South America. 9 species. Similar to *Dipsas* but with a chin fur-

Sibon sp.

row and a strongly enlarged sixth upper labial shield. To 80 cm.

Biology and care typical of the subfamily. The diet consists of snails, treefrogs, and possibly also small lizards.
▪ *S. annulata* (GUENTHER, 1872). Atlantic slopes of Costa Rica to Panama. Montane rain forests.
▪ *S. nebulata* (LINNAEUS, 1758). Southeastern Mexico to northwestern Ecuador. 4 subspecies. Tropical rain forest. Dark with a washed-out pattern of spots along the sides.

Sibynomorphus FITZINGER, 1843. Genus of the Colubridae, Dipsadinae. South America south of the Equator. 6 species. The most primitive genus of the subfamily, with the least degree of specialization as tree snakes. Underside of head without a chin furrow, yet body hardly compressed laterally. To 85 cm.

Presumably these snakes are more ground-dwellers than any of the other subfamily members.
▪ *S. mikani* (SCHLEGEL, 1837). Brasil. 2 subspecies. Rainforest regions and dry lowland forests.

Sibynomorphus ventrimaculatus

▪ *S. turgidus* (COPE, 1862). Southern Bolivia to northern Paraguay. Rain forests. Common in the Mato Grosso, Brasil.

Sibynophinae: Many-toothed Snakes. Subfamily of the Colubridae. Southeast Asia, Madagascar, Central America. 3 genera: *Sibynophis* with about 7 species, *Liophidum* and *Scaphiodontophis* with about 5 species. Found in tropical rain forests and montane rain forests. 30-80 cm. Head only slightly set off from the body, with a large number of narrow teeth on the jaws as well as on the palatine and sphenoid. There is also a very loose connection between the tooth-carrying dental and angular bones of the lower jaw. Presumably the dentition works in conjunction with the flexibility of the lower jaw in handling rather large prey. Dorsal scales with more or less developed tubercles extending onto the neck and dorsal side of the head, also extending to the tail.

Nocturnal ground-dwellers. Their diet consists mainly of lizards and snakes. Egg-layers, few eggs. They should be kept in a rain-forest terrarium with sufficient hiding places and should not be kept together with lizards and snakes of equal or smaller sizes.

Sibynophis: Asiatic Many-toothed Snakes. Genus of the Colubridae, Sibynophinae. Southeast Asia from the southern slopes of the Himalayas in India, Sri Lanka, and Indo-China eastward through southern China to Hainan and Taiwan and southward to the Malayan Peninsula. 7 species in monsoon forests, rain forests, and montane rain forests, including bamboo forests. *S. collaris* occurs in the eastern Himalayas and Assam to 3000 m. 30-80 cm. Of rather typical snake shape. Sometimes there is a dark neckband against a light brownish yellow background (*S. collaris, S. chinensis*) or there are dorsal rows of spots or stripes. The diet consists mainly of lizards and snakes. Egg-layers, 2-4 eggs. They should be kept in a weakly heated forest terrarium.

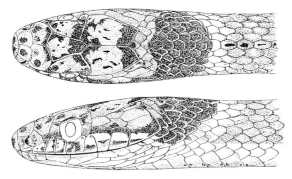

Sibynophis collaris

▪ *S. collaris* (GRAY, 1853). Indo-China to southern China and Malaya. Montane forests to 3,000 m.
▪ *S. subpunctatus* (DUMERIL and BIBRON, 1854). India, Sri Lanka. Monsoon forests.
▪ *S. chinensis* (GUENTHER, 1889). Southern China on Hainan and Taiwan, Vietnam. Rain forests and bamboo forests in lowlands.
▪ *S. geminatus* (BOIE, 1826). From Thailand to the Indo-Australian Archipelago. Montane rain forests to 1300 m. Red-brown with blackish crossbands and longitudinal bars.

Siebenrock, Friedrich (1853-1925): Austrian anatomist and herpetologist, Curator at the Imperial Vienese Museum. Research on the taxonomy of turtles. *Die Schildkroetenfamilie Cinosternidae* (1907), *Synopsis der rezenten Schildroeten* (1909), and others.

Siebenrockiella LINDHOLM, 1929. Fat-headed Turtles. Monotypic genus of the Emydidae. Indo-China to Sunda Archipelago. Carapace length to 20 cm. The relatively high carapace has a distinct keel. Unicolored black-brown, with whitish scribbles on the head.

Siebenrockiella crassicollis

Predominantly aquatic. Carnivorous. Due to their peaceful nature they are suitable for smaller aqua-terrariums and are compatible with other species.
▪ *S. crassicollis* (GRAY, 1831). Tenasserim to southern Indonesia through the Malayan Peninsula to Sumatra, Kalimantan, and Java.

Signals: All types of behavior that serve to transmit energy or convey information between different individuals or groups. Signals have often evolved through ritualization of other normal activities. In reptiles and amphibians signals can be of an optical, acoustical, chemical, or tactile nature. They play important roles in species recognition and in threat behavior, display behavior, and reproductive behavior.

Simophis PETERS, 1860. Genus of the Colubridae, Colubrinae. Brasil and Paraguay. 2 species in open areas (savannahs, steppes, peripheral forest areas). To 75 cm. Head only slightly set off from the body, with a conspicuous, pointed, up-turned horn-like snout similar to *Heterodon* and others.

Ground snakes feeding preferentially on small mammals. Egg-layers.
▪ *S. rhinostoma* (SCHLEGEL, 1837). Brasil.
▪ *S. rhodei* (BOETTGER, 1885). Paraguay.

Simoselaps JAN. 1858 (= *Brachyaspis* BOULENGER, 1896; *Rhynchoelaps* JAN, 1858). Australian Coral Snakes. Genus of the Elapidae. Australia. 6 species. Either in desert-like dry regions (*S. bertholdi, S. fasciolatus, S. incinctus*) or in deserts, savannahs, and tropical forests (*S. semifasciatus*), dry forests (*S. australis*), or exclusively in tropical forests (*S. warro*). About 60 cm. Usually dark-banded, all species have at least a wide dark crossband at eye level and frequently also a neckband; *S. warro* has only a neckband.

Snout more or less modified for a burrowing mode of life.

Terrestrial and nocturnal venomous snakes that can be found outside their hiding places on warm nights hunting for food (lizards and blind snakes).

- *S. australis* (KREFFT, 1864). Australian Coral Snake. New South Wales and Queensland.
- *S. bertholdi* (JAN, 1859). Desert Banded Snake. Western and central Australia. 2 subspecies.
- *S. fasciolatus* (GUENTHER, 1872). Narrow-banded Snake. Southwestern and central Australia.
- *S. incinctus* (STORR, 1967). Northern Territory and Queensland, Australia.
- *S. warro* (DE VIS, 1884). Orange Coral Snake. Eastern Queensland, Australia. Body bright orange above, with a reticulated appearance; broad blackish neckband.

Sinonatrix ROSSMAN and EBERLE, 1977. Asiatic Water Snakes. Genus of the Colubridae, Natricinae. Southeast Asia and China. 5 species.

Similar to European *Natrix*, they should be kept and bred accordingly.

- *S. aequifasciata* (BARBOUR, 1908). Southern China.
- *S. annularis* (HALLOWELL, 1856). Southern China.
- *S. percarinata* (BOULENGER, 1899). Central and southern China.
- *S. trianguligera* (BOIE, 1827). Malaya and the Indo-Australian Archipelago.

Siphlophis FITZINGER, 1843. Genus of the Colubridae, Boiginae. Neotropics from Panama southward to Brasil and Bolivia. 5 species. Closely related to *Leptodeira* and *Tripa-*

Sinonatrix suriki

Sinonatrix annularis

nurgos. 70 cm to 1 m. Slender. Markings consist of rows of spots along both flanks.

Nocturnal tree snakes that feed mainly on frogs and lizards. Caution: Venomous bites possible.
▪ *S. cervinus* (LAURENTI, 1768). Panama to central Bolivia, also on Trinidad.
▪ *S. longicaudatus* (ANDERSSON, 1907). Brasil from Espirito Santo to Rio Grande do Sul.
▪ *S. pulcher* (RADDI, 1820). Brasil, Guanabara, Minas Gerais to Rio Grande do Sul.

Siphonops WAGLER, 1839. Genus of the Caeciliidae. Tropical and subtropical South America. 6 species. Maximum size 48 cm. 78-146 primary folds, no secondary folds or tiny scales. Lower jaw with only 1 row of teeth. No rings around posterior part of body, including the cloaca.
▪ *S. annulatus* (MIKAN, 1820). Colombia to Argentina. To 41 cm. Dark ultramarine blue with narrow white rings.
▪ *S. paulensis* BOETTGER, 1892. Brasil, Paraguay, and Argentina. To 46 cm. Light slate gray, the eye, tentacle, nose, and cloacal regions yellowish.

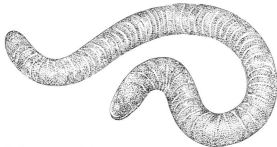

Siphonops annulatus

Siredon: see *Ambystoma*, genus.

Siren LINNAEUS, 1766. Sirens. Genus of the Sirenidae. Southern USA. 2 species, of these *S. intermedia* polytypic. Found in different types of water, but almost always in relatively shallow water. Elongated, eel-like. No hind legs. In contrast to the genus *Pseudobranchus*, *Siren* has 4 fingers on the front feet and 3 open gill apertures.

Droughts are easily survived for months by burying themselves in the mud. The gills are strongly reduced during such periods. The diet consists mainly of aquatic insect larvae, crustaceans, and small fish, but they will also swallow pieces of water plants with food organisms attached. The details of their reproduction are largely unknown, but the eggs are deposited individually or in clumps.

Sirens should be kept in spacious aquariums with low water levels and ample hiding places such as dense underwater plants, caves, and well-leached driftwood. The water must be free of chlorine, and frequent partial water changes are recommended. Animals of northern origin should be given a winter dormancy period of several months in cold water (refrigerated). Large specimens can bite.
▪ *S. intermedia* LE CONTE, 1827. Lesser Siren. Southern and central USA. 3 subspecies. 40-66 cm (over 40 cm only in southern Texas). Dark brown to blue-black or olive-green, with numerous fine washed-out black dots. Eastern subspecies (31-33 costal grooves) very hard to distinguish from *S. lacertina* (36-39 costal grooves).
▪ *S. lacertina* LINNAEUS, 1766. Greater Siren. Maryland to

Siren intermedia

Florida and Alabama. To 98 cm, mostly 51 to 76 cm. Olive to light gray, back darker than sides; sides and belly with greenish or yellowish dots. Sometimes also with black dots.

Sirenidae: Sirens. Family of the Caudata. Often considered as representative of its own order (Trachystomata). Southeastern Nearctic. Genera: *Siren* and *Pseudobranchus*. Eel-like, elongated, totally aquatic. Metamorphosis incomplete, external gills retained permanently. Anterior legs tiny, posterior legs absent. Jaws with horny cutting edges, toothless. Gill openings 3 (*Siren*) or 1 (*Pseudobranchus*). Lungs present. Males lack the cloacal glands that in other salamanders produce the envelope of the spermatophore. Mode of fertilization unknown, possibly external.

Sistrurus GARMAN, 1883. Pygmy Rattlesnakes. Genus of the Crotalidae (often considered as a subgenus of *Crotalus*). USA and Mexico. 3 partially polytypic species. *S. catenatus* occurs in damp outer forest regions on swampy meadows; *S. miliaris* often lives in dry habitats; *S. ravus* is found in

Sistrurus ravus

desert habitats. 50-90 cm. In contrast to *Crotalus*, the top of the head has the usual 9 large scales. Back with spots or chevrons against a lighter background.

Rather nocturnal compared to *Crotalus*. Prey normally hunted include arthropods and small vertebrates. Live-bearers, 4-10 young. Venom usually not fatal to adults in good health; *S. ravus* is said to be the most dangerous species. Often very hardy and durable. Have been bred re-

Sistrurus miliaris barbouri

Sistrurus catenatus

Sistrurus miliaris streckeri

peatedly.
▪ *S. catenatus* (RAFINESQUE, 1818). Massasauga. Great Lakes to northern Mexico. Feeds mainly on frogs and lizards, but also on small mammals.
▪ *S. ravus* (COPE, 1865). Mexican Pygmy Rattlesnake. Southern Mexican Highlands. The largest species. Requires more heat than the others, so maintenance more like *Crotalus*.

Sitana CUVIER, 1829). Sita Lizards. Monotypic genus of the Agamidae. India and Sri Lanka in hot lowland habitats. With the similar genus *Otocryptis* it forms the subfamily Sitaninae. Distinguished from *Otocryptis* by the absence of the fifth toe. There is a large gular pouch extending to the beginning of the abdomen. Mainly brown.

Diurnal ground-dwellers to semiarboreal. Insectivorous. Egg-layers.
▪ *S. ponticeriana* CUVIER, 1829. Sita Lizard. Easily to 20 cm. Tail longer than snout-vent length. Gular pouch brightly tricolored with large, high-keeled rows of scales.

Skeleton: Support elements of the vertebrate body. The skeleton serves as the attachment areas for the musculature and for protection of the internal organs. It consists of cartilaginous and osseous components. One distinguishes between the centrally located axial skeleton (vertebral column with ribs and sternum [breast bone]), the skull, and

Sistrurus miliaris miliaris

the limb skeleton (shoulder [pectoral] and hip [pelvic] girdles, arms and legs). The individual skeletal parts are differentially developed in amphibians and reptiles; some elements are present only in rudimentary form or are completely absent. Consequently in species with regressed legs (caecilians, various lizards, snakes) the corresponding skeletal parts including pectoral and pelvic girdles have also been lost or are regressed to a few remnants. The ribs have largely regressed in the Recent amphibians. A collarbone (clavicle) is generally absent in salamanders and crocodilians, and the breast bone (sternum) is not always present (caecilians, snakes, turtles). Substantial sections of the skeleton are cartilaginous, especially in salamanders but also in frogs. To a lesser degree this also applies to the skeleton of reptiles, where especially the sternum remains cartilaginous if present at all. The skeleton of turtles is also strongly modified; the vertebral column, ribs, and pectoral and pelvic girdles are connected to or in part integrated into the bony plates of the dermal carapace.

Skin diseases: Of particular significance as indicators of detrimental environmental influences such as extreme climatic conditions, pH value of water below 3 or above 9, secretion damage from strongly excreting amphibians such as salamanders or toads, excessive ultraviolet radiation, diet deficiencies, symptoms of diseases of other organs (kidney diseases), and infectious diseases.

Clinical symptoms range from molting problems, wounds, and localized abscesses to more or less characteristic changes associated with deficiencies and/or infections (newt plague, vitamin deficiencies, viral infections, mycoses, ecto- and endoparasitoses). Skin infections usually follow from mechanical skin damage.

Therapy: Depending upon locality, extent, and degree of skin damage, this can often be treated locally with powders, ointments, solutions, and sprays. Alternatively, a general treatment may be required involving antibiotics, sulfonamides, and/or vitamin preparations. Most suitable

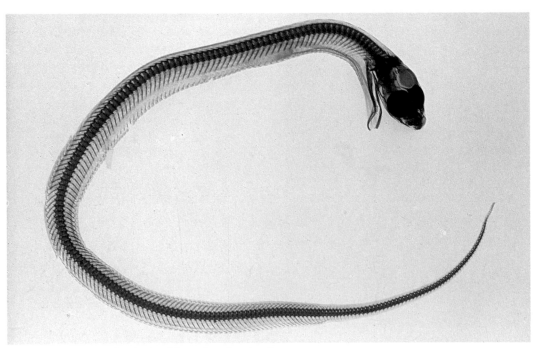

Skeleton of *Nerodia sipedon* (cleared and stained)

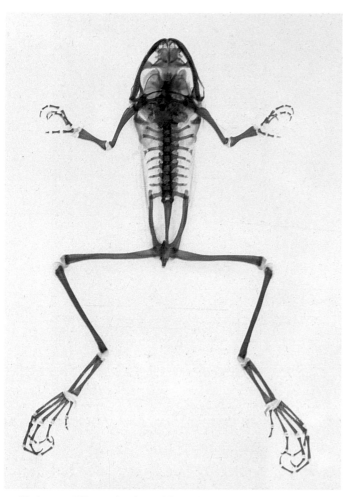

Skeleton of *Rana clamitans* (cleared and stained)

for localized applications are: sulfonamide in the form of solutions or sprays, antibiotic sprays, oily suspensions of vitamin A, chloramin solution 0.1%, sodium chloride solution 0.3%.

Skull: In vertebrates the brain case contains the brain as well as the eyes, inner ears, and the olfactory organ enclosed in the neurocranium and, located below, the facial skeleton (derived from the gill arch skeleton) with the upper and lower jaws and the hyoid bones. Both parts are made up of often partially fused bones that according to their origin are developed from cartilaginous elements or as membranous bone.

Among recent amphibians there is a conspicuous reduction in the bones of the skull roof, and the neurocranium remains largely cartilaginous. On the other hand, the skull

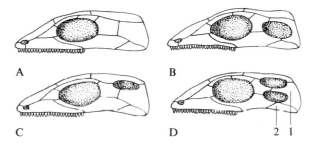

Development of temporal fenestra in reptile skulls:
A Anaspid type (stem reptiles, turtles)
B Synaspid type (mammal-like reptiles)
C Euryaspid type (fossils including plesiosaurs)
D Diapsid type (all living reptiles except turtles)
1 Squamosal; 2 quadratojugal

Skin diseases: Melanosarcoma in *Elaphe obsoleta*

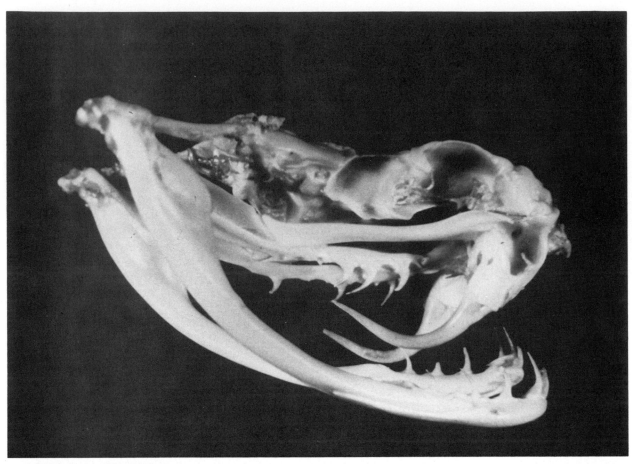

Skull of a pit viper, *Lachesis*

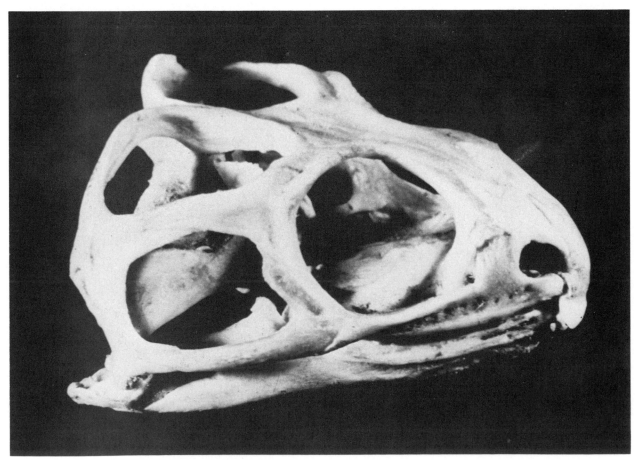

Skull of the tuatara, *Sphenodon punctatus*

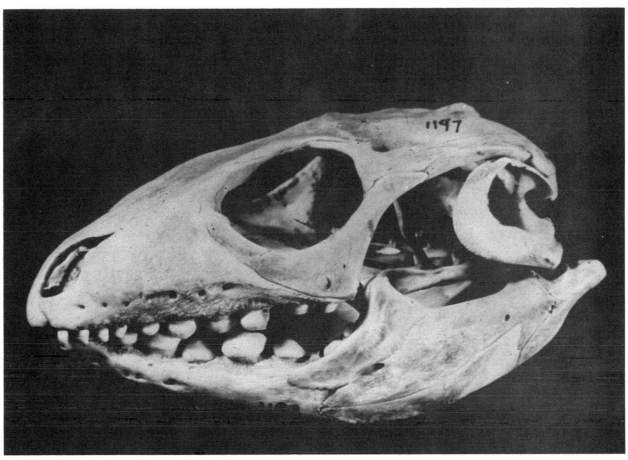

Skull of the caiman lizard, *Dracaena guianensis*

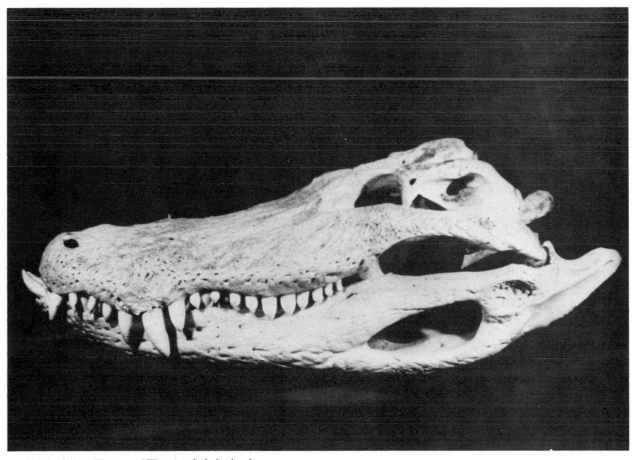

Skull of the alligator, *Alligator mississippiensis*

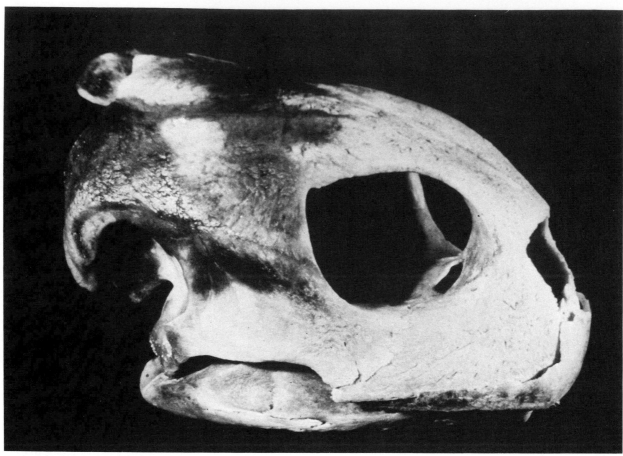

Skull of the green sea turtle, *Chelonia mydas*

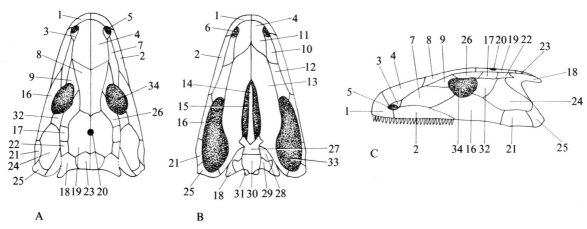

A   B   C

The skull bones of a generalized tetrapod: A Dorsal; B ventral; C lateral. 1 Premaxillary; 2 maxillary; 3 septomaxillary; 4 nasal; 5 nostril; 6 choanae; 7 lacrimal; 8 frontal; 9 prefrontal; 10 palatine; 11 vomer; 12 ectopterygoid; 13 pterygoid; 14 parasphenoid; 15 interpterygoid opening; 16 jugal; 17 intertemporal; 18 tabulare; 19 parietal; 20 parietal foramen; 21 quadratojugal; 22 supratemporal; 23 postparietal; 24 squamosal; 25 quadrate; 26 postfrontal; 27 basisphenoid; 28 prooticum; 29 opisthoticum; 30 basioccipital; 31 exoccipital; 32 postorbital; 33 masseter opening; 34 orbit

of reptiles is almost totally ossified. However, in the primitive, compact skull (*anapsid* type in extinct reptilian groups) there are 1 or 2 lateral openings, the temporal fenestrae. The remaining permanent bone connections are the zygomatic arches. Depending upon the arrangement and number of temporal openings one distinguishes different types of skulls in reptiles: a lower temporal opening (*synapsid* type, in extinct mammal-like reptiles); an upper temporal opening (*euryapsid* type, in some extinct saurians); two temporal openings (*diapsid* type, in beakheads

and crocodiles). Scaled reptiles were derived from diapsid ancestors, but they have lost one (lizards) or both (snakes, amphisbaenids) zygomatic arches. Because of that condition certain bones no longer have a firm connection to the skull, which now becomes substantially more flexible. Development has advanced furthest in snakes, enabling them to swallow very large prey.

Sleep: Condition of reduced activity occurring at certain (often connected with circadian rhythms) intervals, characterized by a relative insensitivity toward external stimuli and complete motor rest. Sleep preparations and positions are species-specific and certain protected sleeping sites are often utilized. Usually the eyes are closed by lids during sleep, but even in reptiles where the eyelids have fused into rigid spectacles (e. g., many geckos, snakes) sleep periods are known to occur.

Smilisca COPE, 1865. Genus of the Hylidae. Extreme southern Texas to Central America and northwestern South America (Colombia, Ecuador). 6 species in more or less perpetually moist tropical forests up to 2,000 m elevation; *S. baudinii* occurs in regions with prolonged dry periods. Characterized (together with the related genus *Pternohyla*) by paired darkly pigmented vocal sacs in the males during the breeding season. Fingers webbed at base only, toes webbed for ¾ of their length. Color variable, mostly with dark spots on a greenish or brownish background color; thighs of all species with crossbands.

Smilisca baudini

Most species are active more or less throughout the year. *S. baudinii* remains in tree holes, bromeliad funnels, and similar hiding places during the dry season. Larval development takes place in ponds (*S. baudinii*) or in rocky, moderately flowing waters (rain-forest species). Eggs are laid as a surface film, up to 2000 eggs/clutch. Maintenance as for arboreal *Hyla*.
▪ *S. baudinii* (DUMERIL and BIBRON, 1841). Mexican Smilisca. Southern Texas and both coasts of Mexico through Central America; one of the most frequent tropical frog species. To 9 cm (females), 7.5 cm (males). Highly variable irregular pattern of dark spots against a green or brown background; dark stripe from snout to tympanum.
▪ *S. sordida* (PETERS, 1863). Costa Rica, Panama. To 6.5 cm (females), 4.5 cm (males). Irregular dark spots against a brown background. Vocal sac not pigmented during breeding season (this is an exception in the *Smilisca*).

Sminthillus BARBOUR and NOBLE, 1920. Monotypic genus of the Leptodactylidae. Cuba. Closely related to *Eleutherodactylus*. Pupil horizontal. Tympanum clearly visible. Fingers and toes free.
    Terrestrial. A free-swimming larval stage is absent.
▪ *S. limbatus* (COPE, 1862). Cuban Dwarf Toadlet. To 1.5 cm.

Smith, Andrew (1797-1872): British physician and zoolo-

gist. Numerous early publications on the natural history of South Africa, including *Illustrations of the Zoology of South Africa, Pars Reptilia* (1849). Author of numerous taxa.

Smith, Malcolm Arthur (1875-1958): British physician and herpetologist. Investigated the herpetofauna in several countries in Southeast Asia. *Monograph of the Seasnakes* (1926), revised the Reptilia in the 2nd edition of *Fauna of British India* in 3 volumes (1931, 1935, 1943), *The British Amphibians and Reptiles* (1951).

Snake bite: Bites from venomous and rear-fanged snakes can lead in humans to more or less serious, possibly fatal, accidents. Various methods are employed in an attempt to remove the venom and to neutralize the remaining venom with the administration of antivenin. First aid measures often include the following steps, although all are controversial. (The publisher presents the following for information only; consult your physician for prevailing practice.)
    1) Apply a tourniquet between the bite and the heart. It is generally better in body and head bites to immediately make some cuts in the bite site with new razor blades or a quickly sterilized knife to cause strong bleeding. Even for bites where a tourniquet has been applied, cutting the wound should be quickly initiated. Bleeding the wound is further aided by massaging or actually evacuating the wound with a suction pump. Actual sucking out of the wound by mouth should be avoided due to possible mucous tissue wounds.
    2) Keep the affected part of the body still and immediately get the victim to a hospital. Tourniquets have to be loosened briefly every 30 minutes in order to avoid tissue necrosis (which can occur after about 2 to 2 ½ hours). Keeping the wound cool with ice is recommended by some experts.
    3) Administering alcohol as a circulatory support measure must be *avoided* under all circumstances. Coffee and tea can be given.
    Antivenin therapy must be administered by a medical practitioner so that possible complications (serum incompatibility of patient, serum shock) can be avoided. Clinical treatment of poisonous snake bites involves primarily the neutralization of the venom with an antivenin. This often requires considerable amounts of serum (in excess of 100 ml). This treatment can be further supported by blood transfusions. Of considerable significance is the use of medications to stabilize the cardiac and circulatory conditions, antishock treatment, and possibly artificial respiration on a respirator. The consequences of even successfully treated poisonous snake bites can include extensive tissue damage at the bite site (necrosis) that may make amputation necessary. Extensive kidney and liver damage may also occur.
    Secondary complications (even with bites from nonvenomous snakes) are abscesses following bacterial infections as well as gangrene and tetanus. Anyone who keeps nonvenomous but aggressive snakes and other reptiles should always be adequately immunized against tetanus and any bites should be promptly cleaned with iodine, alcohol, or similar disinfectants.

Snake farms: Serpentaria. In subtropical and tropical countries the keeping of mainly venomous snakes in out-

Snake farms serve the major purpose of keeping snakes for
"milking" of venom

door terrariums or in temperate climates in greenhouses in order to "milk" the snakes for their venom as the basis for antivenin production in serum laboratories or for the pharmacological industry (often combined with serum laboratories). Removal of venom is done by having a snake bite the edge of a glass beaker. By mechanically or electrically stimulating the venom gland the volume of venom given off can be increased. This sort of treatment tends to cause considerable mortality among the snakes within a short period of time, and they have to be continually replaced with freshly caught snakes. In this way snake farms and serum institutes have contributed significantly to the decimation (to complete extinction) of certain venomous snake species. In more recent times efforts are being made to introduce more effective husbandry measures and attempt whenever possible to breed the snakes.

The change in the character of snake farms from consumer to producer was initiated by North American and European institutions, while many tropical countries still believe they can utilize their venomous snake populations unimpeded. However, in more recent times even in these countries certain voices have been raised against the total exploitation of venomous snake species, in order to maintain these as part of the natural environment as well as keeping them as a scientific reserve.

Snake mites (blood mites): These minute animals are the cause of the most frequent and dreaded ectoparasitosis in snakes. The first symptoms are conspicuous restlessness, the snakes trying to rub the itching body parts, particularly the head; and rapid movements through the terrarium, types of behavior that normally are not observed. The mites tend to concentrate preferentially around the rims of the eyes, but they can also be observed all over the body,

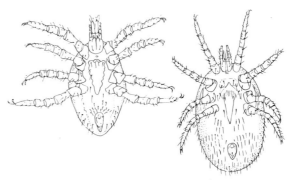

Snake mites, *Ophionyssus natricis*

especially under the scales. Mass infestation leads to a substantial loss of blood so that the snake rapidly loses condition and then stops feeding and eventually dies. Saliva given off by the mites while sucking blood tends to cause considerable tissue damage and thus can lead to secondary bacterial infections such as abscesses. The most common mite is *Ophionyssus natricis*.

Therapy and prophylaxis: Application of paradichorbenzol; castor oil; 90% alcohol mixed with water 1:1.

Snake venoms: Secretions produced in the venom glands of snakes, consisting of a white, yellow, or greenish viscous liquid. They represent a complicated mixture of substances with a water content of about 50-70%. The dried venom (which can be kept for years in this condition) consists of 90-95% various proteins with different toxicities and effectiveness, including non-toxic proteins and proteins with enzymatic characteristics. Moreover, snake venoms also often contain very small amounts of other organic compounds (free amino acids and small peptides, nucleotides, carbohydrates, lipids, and biogenic amines), as well as metals (e. g., calcium, zinc, manganese, sodium, potassium).

The effectiveness of the various snake venoms and venom components is in part highly variable and so far is not known in all details. Generally it is accepted (with many exceptions though) that the venom of snakes of the family Elapidae and sea snakes (family Hydrophiidae) contains a large amount of neurotoxins that affect the nervous system. Vipers (family Viperidae) and pit vipers (family Crotalidae) on the other hand have mainly cell-damaging (cytotoxic) and blood-clotting (hemotoxic) venoms. The following effects of snake venoms can be observed:
—damage to the nervous system
—damage of the heart muscle
—general tissue destruction
—muscle necrosis
—kidney necrosis
—destruction of capillary walls (hemorrhaging)
—destruction of red blood cells (haemolysis)
—inhibition of blood clotting mechanism
—triggering of blood clotting.
Various individual toxins and different factors are responsible for these effects; their presence and quantity in the higher groups of snakes as well as among closely related forms can be subject to large variations. Nearly all neurotoxins prevent transference of excitation from nerves to muscles; they block the synaptic transmission. This can occur in two ways. Some neurotoxins combine irreversibly

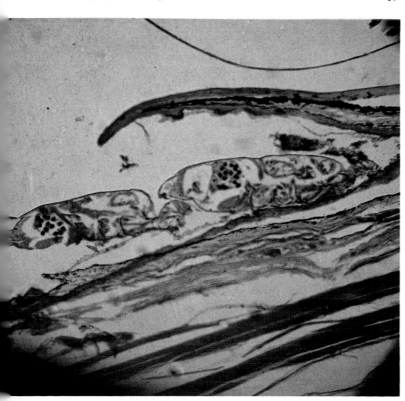

Snake mites: Cross-section through *Ophionyssus natricis* under the scales of *Thamnophis sirtalis*

Snake venoms: Drops of venom can be seen at the ends of the fangs of this *Dendroaspis angustatus*

venomous snakes cause direct damage to the heart as well as general cytotoxic and neurotoxic effects. The cytotoxins of vipers and pit vipers are high-molecular basic proteins that disperse slowly after the bite and destroy cell membranes.

Among the enzymes shown to be present in snake venoms are various esterases, proteases, and hydrolases. All snake venoms contain the enzyme hyaluronidase, which dissolves the hyaluronacid gel in the connective tissue of the skin, allowing the venom to enter the tissue easier. The enzyme phospholipase-A2 is indirectly responsible for the hemolytic venom effect, since it facilitates the transformation of lecithin into lysolecithin, which causes the hemolysis. Other factors, not specifically known, act directly to produce hemolytic and hemorrhagic (dissolution of blood capillaries, thus causing blood to enter the organs and body cavities) conditions and lead to muscle fiber or kidney tube necrosis. Several different factors, which can even occur within the same snake venom, influence blood clotting, either causing it or preventing it. Also shown to occur in snake venoms are various enzyme inhibitors as well as a nerve growth factor that induces the outgrowth of nerve fibers from ganglia cells.

Snake venoms can be obtained by massaging ("milking") or electrical stimulation of venom glands in venomous snakes. This is practiced on a large scale on snake farms. The venom collected is used in the production of antivenins, as well as in medical research. Snake venoms are also used for medical preparations for blood clotting or for inhibiting blood clotting. Moreover, snake venoms also find application in the treatment of leprosy and epileptic and rheumatic diseases.

Snares: Different sizes of snares are used depending upon the size of the animals that are to be caught. For small lizards horsehair snares are most effective. These snares are attached to the end of a handle not over 2 m long. Lizards do not seem to be afraid of these snares, and in fact they are often licked at in curiosity. The snare is gently moved over and past the head, and then suddenly the stick is jerked upward and the snare closes around the neck of the animal. The lizard must then be quickly removed from the snare. Since the snare does not pull very tightly there is little danger of injury to the animal.

Medium lizards that live in dense undergrowth are collected by means of a noose attached to the end of a stick. The free (leading) end of the string is carried along the

with the acetylcholines and excitation of the muscle becomes impossible (postsynaptic toxins: e. g., cobra neurotoxins, alpha-bungarotoxins). Other toxins inhibit the synaptic transmission on the nerve side, but the mechanism has not yet been determined (presynaptic toxins: e. g., beta-bungarotoxins). Moreover, they can prevent the transmission of impulses within the nerve. The cardiotoxins of

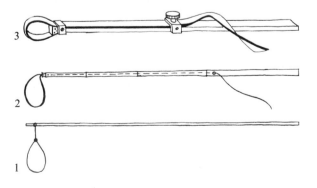

Common types of snares used in collecting snakes and lizards

stick to the upper end where it can be held by one hand. Fishing line of different strengths is very useful for such heavier snares. The noose is pulled tight around the neck of the animal. This requires some practice: if the pull is too light the lizard escapes, if the noose is pulled too heavily there is a danger of injuring the animal.

Snakes are collected with snares made from a leather strap that is moved about ⅓ over the snake and then pulled tight. The strap must not be directly over the neck of the snake because this would injure the snake, particularly since the snare has to be pulled fairly tightly to prevent the snake from winding its way out. Many snakes have very delicate neck vertebrae.

Sniffles: Nasal discharge due to inflammation of the mucous membranes of the upper respiratory passages. Sick animals usually have a watery, slightly bubbling secretion that rarely becomes pus. Encrustation of the nostrils together with whistling respiratory sounds are a further indication of obstructions of the upper respiratory passages. With serious respiratory difficulties, recognizable mainly by increased abdominal respiratory movements and more profound general disturbances, there is a simultaneous pneumonia.

Therapy: In mild cases without general disturbances a sulfonamide or antibiotic treatment can be omitted. However, an immediate bacteriological examination of the nasal secretion should be initiated. Other than that, treat as for pneumonia.

Social behavior: All types of behavior that serve to maintain and regulate the relationships between siblings. An important part of the social behavior is territorial behavior.

Soil moisture: Maintaining the correct soil moisture is an essential factor for the health and well-being of terrarium animals. For instance, the soil in a rain-forest terrarium must always be kept moist but not permitted to accumulate excess water. Often overlooked is the fact that the burrows of semidesert and desert animals are generally dug in areas that contain a certain residual moisture. It is imperative that this is kept in mind when such animals are kept in a terrarium. Selection of a suitable substrate depends upon the natural substrate the animals kept are used to and the degree of moisture that is to be maintained.

Soleirolia GAUD. (= *Helxine*). Genus of the Urticaceae. Sardinia, Corsica. Shrubs with thread-like, richly branching, creeping shoots covering the ground as a dense carpet. Hardy, they can take temperatures from 0 to 20° C. Reproduction is by means of small rooted branches. Only species: *S. soleirolii* (REQ.) DANDY.

Solenoglyphs: see Teeth.

Solomon Islands: Melanesian island group in the tropical Pacific, with New Guinea, the Fiji Islands, and other South Sea islands forming the Papuan-Polynesian subregion of the Australasian. Numerous mountain ranges (to 3050 m) with volcanos, high precipitation, and consequently with lush tropical vegetation (mountain rain forests). Herpetologically notable due to the presence of specialized Ranidae (e. g., *Discodeles*) and Scincidae (*Corucia*).

Sonora BAIRD and GIRARD, 1853. Ground Snakes. Genus of the Colubridae, Boiginae. Southwestern and central USA and Mexico. About 7 species, some polytypic; taxonomy very unstable. Found in desert and semideserts and in mountains up to almost 3,000 m elevation. To 50 cm. Slender, cylindrical, the head not set off from the body. Some *Sonora* have black and red bands on whitish tan, others have longitudinal markings or are uniformly orange-brown. These markings can occur in different populations of the same species. It has been suggested that there are only 1 or 2 very variable species in the genus.

Nocturnal ground snakes. Their main diet is spiders, scorpions, millipedes, crickets, and insect larvae. Maintain them in a well-heated desert terrarium with large nighttime temperature reductions.

• *S. episcopa* (KENNICOTT, 1859). Northeastern Mexico, Texas, and the southern Great Plains. Recently synonymized with the following species.

Sonora episcopa

• *S. semiannulata* BAIRD and GIRARD, 1853. Western Ground Snake. Western and northern Mexico.

Sooglossus BOULENGER, 1900. Seychelles Frogs. Genus of the Ranidae. Seychelle Islands. 2 species in mountain forests. Related to *Nesomantis*. Without adhesive discs and without webbing, externally similar to the genus *Arthroleptis*.

Ground-dwellers. A small number of eggs (large and yolk-rich) are deposited in moist, decaying material on the

ground. The male guards the clutch. At hatching time the young have only hind leg rudiments; they slide onto the back of the male, attach themselves, and remain there feeding on their yolk until metamorphosis. Due to their restricted distribution they are considered endangered.
- *S. gardineri* (BOULENGER, 1911). To 1.5 cm.
- *S. seychellensis* (BOETTGER, 1896). To 2.5 cm.

Sordellina PROCTER, 1923. Monotypic genus of the Colubridae, Xenodontinae. Eastern Brasil in tropical lowland forests. To 20 cm. Brown with black spots in longitudinal rows.

Ground snakes preferring the proximity of water. The prey is mainly frogs. Egg-layers.
- *S. punctata* (PETERS, 1880).

Spalerosophis JAN, 1865. Diadem Snakes. Genus of the Colubridae, Colubrinae. North Africa and the Near East to central Asia. 1-6 recognized species of uncertain taxonomic status. In extremely dry and hot habitats (desert to peripheral steppe areas) with large nocturnal temperature reductions. To 1.5 m. Distinctly set off head with large eyes. The anterior head shields are in part broken into several smaller shields. The dorsal scales are strongly shingled and in some species (particularly in older specimens) also distinctly keeled. Mostly brownish with squarish spots, but also with contrasting black and yellow coloration.

Ground snakes that still are active even during midday heat. Agile hunters of lizards, snakes, small mammals, and ground birds. Handled specimens tend to be very aggressive and will bite. Maintenance requires a well-heated sunny, dry terrarium with ample hiding places. They are often reluctant to feed when first in captivity, but once established they can reach substantial longevities. Diadem snakes rarely require drinking water.
- *S. diadema* (SCHLEGEL, 1837). North Africa, Arabia, and Near East to northern India, northeastward to Soviet Central Asia and southern Kasachstan. 3 or 4 subspecies.

Spalerosophis diadema

Spawn: Egg masses. Eggs from molluscs, fishes, and amphibians with shells that are membranous or gelatinous. Many amphibians produce their spawn in characteristic tubes or strings (e. g., *Andrias, Bufo*) or clumps (e. g., *Rana*), the gelatinous egg membranes swelling substantially in water to give rise to enormous masses of spawn. The tendency toward the development of spawning inde-

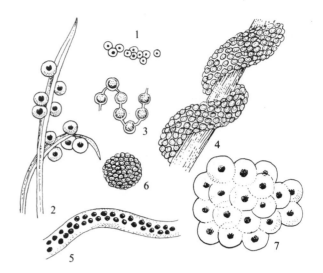

Spawn of various frogs: 1 *Discoglossus*; 2 *Bombina*; 3 *Alytes*; 4 *Pelobates*; 5 *Bufo*; 6 *Hyla*; 7 *Rana*

pendent of open water has lead in many amphibians toward specializations such as the terrestrial spawning of various salamanders (e. g., *Bolitoglossa*), the deposition of eggs inside brood pouches (e. g., *Flectonotus, Fritziana, Gastrotheca, Nototheca*), or the use of foam nests in some frogs (e. g., *Chiromantis, Philautus, Rhacophorus,* and *Theloderma*).

Masses of frog and toad eggs are often seen in the spring

Species: Scientific designation for a particular type of organism. In conjunction with adjectives used to designate species status, e.g.:
- *species nova (spec. nov., sp. n.):* new species;
- *species bona:* good (i. e., justified) species:
- *species dubia:* doubtful species.

Species concept: The species is the basic unit in systematics or taxonomy. In contrast to higher systematic categories it reflects to a high degree the objective reality of the organization of all living beings. Species are today defined as closed genetic systems (biological species concept). Each of these systems has a specific content of genetic properties (the gene pool) that retains its own characteristics through reproductive isolation from other species. It is only subject to change through evolutionary factors. Each species can be subdivided into populations and can be considered a continuum of those populations, which on the basis of their monophyletic orgins vary only to a degree in their genetic, physiological, ethological, ecological, and morphological characteristics to still enable individuals from the various populations to produce fertile progeny under natural conditions. "Super-species" are produced when members of adjacent populations interbreed to produce fertile progeny (prerequisite: only one species involved), while isolating mechanisms no longer allow successful reproduction between geographically remote populations.

While sympatric distributions of two taxa allow a taxonomist to reach a safe conclusion that the taxa are species, the delineation of species in taxa with allopatric distributions and when working with museum specimens is rather problematic. In these cases it is based almost exclusively on morphological differences. The term "morpho-species" means that the status of the species could only be assumed on morphological characters. Numerous reptile and amphibian species still have the uncertain status of morpho-species.

Not all species are monotypic. Most have developed, through isolation caused by more or less effective distribution barriers, geographical races—the subspecies. Such species are described as being polytypic.

Species recognition: The ability of members of a species to recognize each other through various mechanisms. Species recognition can be achieved visually through species-specific signals and types of behavior, as in numerous lizards (e. g., Agamidae, Iguanidae, Chamaeleonidae, Lacertidae). There are also acoustical forms of species recognition, such as the mating calls in frogs. Glandular secretions for chemical recognition also play a role in some species.

The ability to recognize conspecifics is of great importance during the mating season in order to avoid hybridization between similar species within the same habitat. While males of toads (genus *Bufo*) can not recognize their conspecific partners and thus attempt to mate with virtually anything of similar size that is moving, species recognition is highly developed in many lizards that have species-specific display behavior. Species recognition is also important in territorial species in order to be able to defend the territory against appropriate intruders.

Spelaeophryne AHL, 1924. Monotypic genus of the Microhylidae. East Africa. Closely related to *Breviceps* and *Probreviceps* and similarly plump. Skin smooth, very thick, with many glands. Pupil horizontal. Tympanum distinctly visible. No webbing or adhesive discs. Inner tubercle large and oval, outer one small and round. Mode of life and maintenance as for *Probreviceps*.
▪ *S. methneri* AHL, 1924. Uluguru Mountains and Matumbi (Tanzania). Easily to 5 cm. Reddish black with paired wide red head stripes.

Sphaenorhynchus TSCHUDI, 1838. Genus of the Hylidae. Tropical South America. About 9 species. From less than

2 cm to about 6 cm, more or less compact. Snout short. Vocal sacs of males when collapsed forming a longitudinal fold. Fingers webbed at base only, toes webbed up to adhesive discs. Hind legs of most species conspicuously strong for hylids. Yellowish to light green.

Largely aquatic. Maintain in a tropical aqua-terrarium with a large water bowl.
▪ *S. eurhostus* (RIVERO, 1969) (= *S. aurantiacus* (DAUDIN, 1803)). Amazon region. To 4 cm. Light green with a light yellow dorso-lateral stripe from the eye to the pelvic region. Thought to be a synonym of *S. lacteus* (DAUDIN, 1802) by some workers.
▪ *S. habrus* (GOIN, 1957). Amazon region near Leticia. To 1.5 cm. Light green with rust-red dorso-lateral stripes.

Sphaerodactylus WAGLER, 1830. Least Geckos, Reef Geckos. Genus of the Gekkonidae, subfamily Sphaerodactylinae. Tropical South America. More than 60 species in various not-too-dry habitats (coastal regions, forests, rocky steppes). Barely 4 to 8 cm. Slender. Tail about snout-vent length. Scales granular. Pupil round. Toes without distinct adhesive lamellae, the claws not retractable. Sexual dimorphism usually present. Coloration variable, mostly brown to red-brown with light dots and dark crossbands, these very distinct in juveniles and usually maintained as spots in females, in males often disappearing completely.

Sphaerodactylus cinereus

Sphaerodactylus sp.

Nocturnal, very fast dwellers on the ground and tree trunks. They prefer to remain—sometimes in groups—in moist areas such as under rocks, behind tree bark, and in bromeliads. Occasionally they come out to bask. The prey consists of very small arthropods, probably mainly springtails. Several clutches of only 1 egg each per year. They will feed in captivity on non-flying *Drosophila* and newly hatched crickets. Somewhat delicate.

▪ *S. argus* GOSSE, 1850. Ocellated Gecko. Antilles. Barely 6 cm.

▪ *S. cinereus* WAGLER, 1830. Ashy Gecko. Antilles, Florida (introduced). 7 cm.

Sphagnum L. Swamp Moss, Sphagnum Moss. Genus of the Bryophyta of worldwide distribution. About 300 species. A leafy moss with slightly branched main stems and short bushy side branches. Spongy in texture, with a seven-fold water storage capacity.

Sphargis: see *Dermochelys*, genus.

Sphenodon GRAY, 1831. Tuataras. Monotypic genus of the Rhynchocephalia. New Zealand. Strongly built, compact. Tail easily snout-vent length, with excellent regeneration capability. Neck, back, and tail with long flexible crests formed by vertical scales. Eyes large, with vertical pupil. Parietal eye present. Outer ear opening and inner auditory passage absent. Skull diapsid. Jaws weakly elongated, teeth acrodont, premaxillary with a pair of teeth, pterygoid teeth present. Vertebrae amphicoelic; ossified intermediate vertebral discs; free additional abdominal ribs. Copulatory organs absent, the cloacas pressed against each other during mating.

Crepuscular to nocturnal, hiding during the day in self-dug caves or in vacated seabird burrows, often cohabitating

Sphenodon punctatus

with the latter. Occasionally basks. Tuataras have the lowest optimal environmental temperature (about 12° C.) of all reptiles. Metabolism and growth rates are correspondingly slow; sexual maturity probably does not occur until about 20 years of age. Proven longevity of at least 77 years. The diet consists mainly of arthropods, earthworms, and snails, occasionally also bird eggs and juvenile birds; cannibalistic tendencies toward own young. Up to 17 eggs per clutch. The incubation period is 13 to 15 months, the development interrupted during the winter months.

Private ownership of these extremely rare, heavily protected animals should not be considered.

▪ *S. punctatus* (GRAY, 1842). Tuatara. Occurs on about 20 small islands in Cook Straits and offshore the northern

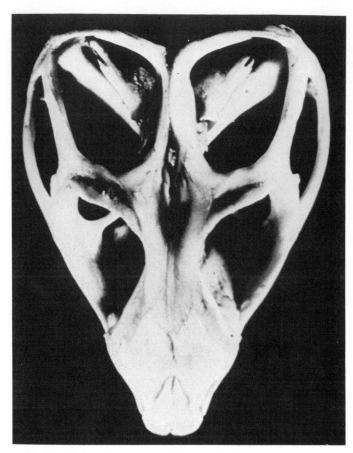

Skull of *Sphenodon punctatus* in ventral view

coastline of the South Island of New Zealand. Extinct on main islands. To 65 cm, females substantially smaller. Olive brown to gray, with distinct color change.

Sphenodontidae: Tuataras. Family of the Rhynchocephalia, suborder Sphenodontida. Only 1 recent genus, *Sphenodon*.

Sphenomorphus FITZINGER, 1843. Forest Skinks. Genus of the Scincidae, subfamily Lygosominae. India, Southeast Asia, Indonesia, and New Guinea to Australia. More than 150 species, some of uncertain taxonomic status; a systematic revision is urgently required. Found from tropical forests to dry sandy habitats. 15 to 25 cm. Slender, head deep, massive, with arched eye region. Lower lid movable, scaly. Ear opening large. Well-developed 5-toed limbs are present. Smooth-scaled, infrequently with weak keels. The long, strong tail is developed into a prehensile organ in *S. flavipes*. Highly variable in coloration and markings.

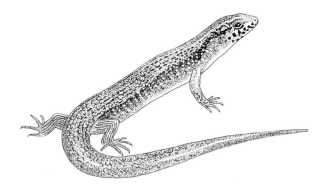

Sphenomorphus isolepis

Crepuscular ground-dwellers. Some remain close to water (*S. quoyi*), while others are largely arboreal (*S. flavipes*). The diet is mainly arthropods. Some are egg-layers, but the majority are ovoviviparous. Maintain in a moderately heated damp terrarium with relatively minor temperature gradients. Some Australian species should be kept dry and warm.

• *S. fasciolatus* (GUENTHER, 1867). Narrow-banded Sand Swimmer. Interior Australia, often in sandy, dry habitats. Easily to 20 cm. Tail keeled, highly flexible.
• *S. flavipes* (PARKER, 1936). New Guinea. 20 cm. Arboreal, with prehensile tail. Rare.
• *S. quoyi* (DUMERIL and BIBRON, 1839). Eastern Water Skink. Northeastern Australia. Close to water. 25 cm. Ovoviviparous.
• *S. richardsoni* (GRAY, 1845). Broad-banded Sand Swimmer. Western and central Australia. 25 cm.
• *S. tabrobanensis* KELAART, 1852. Sri Lanka. 20 cm. Forest floor.

Sphenophryne PETERS and DORIA, 1878. Genus of the Microhylidae. Tropical Southeast Asia and the Indo-Australian Archipelago to northern Australia, with the greatest species diversity in New Guinea. 15 species. In size, shape, and mode of life rather variable, only distinguishable by shoulder girdle characteristics from closely related genera (*Cophixalus*, *Oreophryne*). Pupil horizontal. Tympanum variously developed, in *S. palmipes* completely regressed. Mostly brown with a light or dark pattern.

Development as far as known occurs without an aquatic larval stage, embryonic and larval development passing within eggs deposited on land. *Sphenophryne* species with compact body structure and without adhesive discs are more or less skilled burrowers. Species with long legs and adhesive discs live in bushes and trees of rain-forests and cloud forests. Well developed webbing between the toes occurs only in *S. palmipes*, which leads a semiaquatic life on and in mountain waters.

Maintenance has to be adapted to the ecological requirements of the species. In most cases a suitably modified tropical rain-forest terrarium suffices. A water section is required only for *S. palmipes*.

• *S. cornuta* PETERS and DORIA, 1878. New Guinea. 4 cm. Upper eyelid lobate. Large adhesive discs.
• *S. palmipes* ZWEIFEL, 1956. New Guinea. To 4.5 cm.
• *S. rhododactyla* (BOULENGER, 1897). New Guinea. 6 cm. Fingers and toes red. Adhesive discs very small.
• *S. robusta* (FRY, 1912). Northeastern Australia. 3 cm. Adhesive discs on fingers smaller than on toes.

Sphenops WAGLER, 1830. Genus of the Scincidae, subfamily Scincinae. North Africa and Israel. Several species in dry, mostly sandy habitats. Related to *Chalcides*. To 17 cm. Slender, cylindrical. Snout wedge-shaped, the mouth conspicuously subterminal. Slit-like nostrils on upper side of head. Lower lid with a large window. Ear opening slit-like. Limbs very thin and short, number of toes partially reduced. Extremely smooth scales. Light brown to dirty yellow with dark longitudinal stripes.

In part burrowing ground-dwellers.
• *S. sepsoides* (AUDOUIN, 1829). Wedge-snout Skink. Egypt and Israel.

Spilotes WAGLER, 1830. Tropical Rat Snakes. Monotypic genus of the Colubridae, Colubrinae. Southern Mexico to northern Argentina in different habitats (gallery forests, secondary forests, and rain forests); also follows human habitation. To 2.5 m. Strong. One of the largest colubrids of the Neotropics. Head well set off, with yellowish white wide crossbands along the side of the head up to the occipital. Body with yellowish white crossbands in the neck region, becoming uniformly dark from the middle of the body back. Conspicuously large dorsal scales.

Ground snakes, sometimes also semiarboreal. They are also excellent swimmers. When excited they inflate the neck region and vibrate the tip of the tail. These large snakes feed exclusively on small mammals and birds. Egg-layers, 15 to 25 eggs. Will bite aggressively, but tend to tame down quickly. Maintain in a well-heated, spacious terrarium with bathing and climbing facilities, as for *Elaphe*.
• *S. pullatus* (LINNAEUS, 1758).

Spilotes pullatus mexicanus

Spilotes pullatus

Springs: Upper section of flowing water (stream, river, etc.) characterized by evenly (mostly cool) temperate water. A form of extreme habitat with only minimal production of biomass, springs are inhabitable only by a very few predators, such as *Desmognathus, Euproctus, Gyrinophilus,* and *Ascaphus*.

Springtails: Very small to minute insects of the order Collembola. Dozens of species and hundreds of individuals can be found in a handful of rich humus. Easily bred in the home (most feed on fungus spores and pollen in the litter) and make an excellent first food for many small lizards and salamanders.

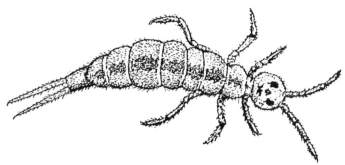

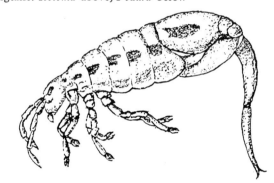

Springtails: *Isotoma* above, *Podura* below

Squamata: Scaled Reptiles. Largest, most comprehensive Recent order of the Reptilia, with worldwide distribution. About 5800 species, including the Sauria (lizards, amphisbaenids) and Serpentes (snakes). Conspicuous are the more or less regularly arranged horny scales that have to be shed periodically by molting. Unique among all vertebrates are the paired copulatory organs (hemipenes) of the males. The Jacobson's organ has special significance among the sensory organs.

The quadrate bone is attached movably to the skull, the frontal bone and parietal are nearly always unpaired, and free abdominal ribs are absent. The two temporal arches are reduced in the Squamata (the upper one usually present in Sauria).

Generally external identification characteristics between snakes and lizards are difficult to point out. Typical snake characteristics such as limblessness or the rigid lid spectacles can occasionally also be found in some lizard families as a convergent development. Differences do occur in skull anatomy, especially related to the loosely hinged lower jaw of snakes. In snakes the tympanum is also absent (not visible in all lizards), as well as the middle ear and urinary bladder, which are present in most lizards. Most Squamata lay soft, parchment-like eggs that harden secondarily only in the Gekkonidae. A few Squamata are ovoviviparous or viviparous.

Stapelia L. Carrion Flowers. Genus of the Asclepiadaceae. Primarily South Africa but also in East Africa and India. About 100 species in dry areas. Stem-forming succulent shrubs. The flowers should be removed before they open because of their unpleasant rotting meat odor. *Stapelia* can take prolonged dry periods, require a bright location, and can survive during winter at temperatures as low as 10° C. (with reduced water supply). Suitable for terrariums for animals from South African dry regions. The most frequently cultured species is *S. variegata* L.

Staurois COPE, 1865. Genus of Ranidae. Indo-Australian Archipelago. 3 species (other species here are included in *Amolops*) found in clear, fast-flowing waters in tropical rain forests. 4 to 6.5 cm, males smaller than females. Rough skin. Tympanum clearly visible. Large adhesive discs present on fingers and toes, with a ring furrow around the edges (in contrast to *Amolops*). Fingers free or with lateral skin folds. Toes completely webbed. Paired vocal sacs. During the courtship period males have pale nuptial pads on the hands. The larvae are adapted to flowing water and are elongated; the suction mouth is subterminal (but without a throat disc as in *Amolops*); tail paddle-like.

Staurois species are semiaquatic and prefer to sit on rocks surrounded by flowing water or in the splash zone along rocky banks. They should be kept in a spacious, suitably decorated rain-forest terrarium. The water section can have turbulence created by a circulating pump. The preferred diet is insects.
- *S. latopalmatus* (BOULENGER, 1887). Kalimantan. To 6.5 cm. Black with yellow dots.
- *S. natator* (GUENTHER, 1858). Kalimantan, Lesser Sunda Islands, Philippines. To 5.5 cm. Brown with black dots.

Staurotypus WAGLER, 1830. Giant Musk Turtles. Genus of the Kinosternidae. Central America. 2 species. 25-40 cm. Carapace always with 3 distinct keels; plastron very small, cross-shaped, rigid, and connected firmly to carapace.

Staurotypus triporcatus

Staurotypus salvini

Aquatic. Carnivorous. Has been bred occasionally. Incubation takes 207 to 230 days at 24-25° C. Caution: These turtles will bite.

- *S. salvini* GRAY, 1864. Southern Mexico to El Salvador in Pacific drainages. To 25 cm carapace length.
- *S. triporcatus* (WIEGMANN, 1828). Eastern Mexico, Belize, and Guatemala.

Stefania RIVERO, 1966. Genus of the Hylidae. Venezuela and Guyana. 4 species. Related to *Amphignathodon*, *Anotheca*, and *Fritziana*. Arboreal.
- *S. evansi* (BOULENGER, 1904).

Stegonotus DUMERIL and BIBRON, 1853. Genus of the Colubridae, Lycodontinae (included in the Natricine by some systematists). Philippines, Moluccas, New Guinea, northeastern Australia. 8-9 species. Montane rivers in New Guinea up to 1,000 m elevation (*S. modestus*). 60 cm to 1.4 m. Distinctly set off trapezoidal head with small eyes with vertical pupils. Body minimally laterally compressed. Dorsal scales smooth. More or less uniformly brown above or with darker spots.

Amphibious, crepuscular, ground snakes. The main diet is frogs, possibly also fish. They should be kept in a well-heated terrarium with a large water section as for Natricinae.
- *S. modestus* (SCHLEGEL, 1837). New Guinea. To 1.2 m.
- *S. batjanensis* (GUENTHER, 1865). Halmahera to Batjan. 1.5 m.
- *S. plumbeus* (MACLEAY, 1884). Southern New Guinea. 1.4 m.

Steindachner, Franz (1834-1919): Austrian zoologist, superintendent of Imperial Viennese Museum. Numerous ichthyological and herpetological publications.

Stejneger, Leonard (1851-1943): Norwegian zoologist and physician working at the Smithsonian Institution, Washington D. C. *The Poisonous Snakes of North America* (1895), *The Herpetology of Porto Rico* (1904), *Herpetology of Japan* (1907). Coauthorship with BARBOUR of *Check List of North American Amphibians and Reptiles* (1917).

Stenocercus DUMERIL and BIBRON, 1837. Genus of the Iguanidae. Ecuador, Peru, Bolivia. 7 to 14 species. Related to *Liolaemus* and very similar to them. Keeled scales. Very spiny scale whorls on the tail. Lateral skin folds present on neck. Primarily brown with variable patterns.

For mode of life and maintenance see *Liolaemus*.
- *S. crassicaudatus* TSCHUDI, 1845. Peru, eastern Andean slopes. 20 cm. Dark neckband.

Stenodactylus FITZINGER, 1826. Genus of the Gekkonidae, subfamily Gekkoninae. North Africa to southwestern Asia. 12 species in dry, often rocky habitats. About 10 cm. Slender. Tail about snout-vent length, without adhesive pads but with lateral serrations. Pupil vertical. Various tones of brown, usually with darker markings and rarely with lighter spots within the darker reticulated pattern.

Nocturnal ground-dwellers. Temperatures in terrarium should be from 28 to 30° C., at night 15 to 20° C. Also refer to *Cyrtodactylus*.
- *S. sthenodactylus* (LICHTENSTEIN, 1823). Dorsal scales unkeeled. Tail without an abrupt constriction behind the basal swelling.
- *S. petrii* ANDERSON, 1896. Israel to Algeria. Sharp constriction behind the basal tail enlargement.
- *S. grandiceps* HAAS, 1952. Southwestern Asia. Dorsal scales unkeeled.

Stenoglossa: see *Werneria*, genus.

Stenolepis BOULENGER, 1887. Monotypic genus of the Teiidae. Brasil. Small, inconspicuous ground-dwellers in tropical rain forests.

▪ *S. ridley* BOULENGER, 1887. Known only from the type locality, Pernambuco, Brasil.

Stenorrhina DUMERIL, 1853. Genus of the Colubridae, Boiginae. Tropical Mexico southward to Colombia, Venezuela, and the Pacific slopes of Ecuador. 2 species in damp lowland or mountain forests. To 75 cm. The small head is not set off from the body and has small eyes. Back gray to gray-brown with 5 distinct longitudinal bands (nominate subspecies of *S. degenhardti*) or unicolored.

Nocturnal ground snakes. Biology largely unknown.

▪ *S. freminvilli* DUMERIL, DUMERIL, and BIBRON, 1854. Mexico to Panama.

▪ *S. degenhardti* (BERTHOLD, 1846). Mexico to Ecuador.

Steppes: Grassy areas in the Eurosiberian steppe belt. In a larger sense also including prairies, *pampas*, and grasslands with sparse tree stands, such as savannahs and *llanos*. Today's vast Eurosiberian steppe regions represent in many areas vegetation forms created through agricultural and logging activities from areas that no doubt used to be extensively wooded forest steppes. Steppes and forest steppes are characterized by a blossom-rich spring and early summer aspect, while they become unicolored yellow-brown during later summer due to dried grasses from the prolonged drought and heat. During the winter steppes are exposed to long frost periods, but the steppe fauna and flora are protected by a thick snow cover. Steppes are mostly occupied by lizards and snakes, various tortoise species, and anurans, mainly *Pelobates* and *Bufo*.

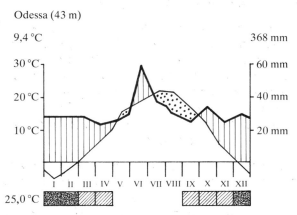

Climate diagram of the Eurosiberian steppe

Stereochilus COPE, 1869. Many-lined Salamanders. Monotypic genus of the Plethodontidae. Atlantic coast of the USA in standing waters and slow-flowing creeks and swampy forest areas. Head small, legs relatively weak and short. Tail flattened laterally. Head with conspicuous pores.

Aquatic, surviving short dry periods burrowed in the mud. Should be kept in an unheated or weakly heated aquarium with a low water level and hiding places (underwater plant thickets, driftwood, floating plants). Aeration not required. Should be kept under evenly cool conditions (10-15° C.) during the winter. Eats mainly mosquito larvae, large daphnia, and well rinsed tubifex worms.

▪ *S. marginatus* (HALLOWELL, 1857). Virginia to Georgia. 6 to 10 cm. Back dark yellowish brown, the lower sides with more or less distinctly defined yellow longitudinal stripe

Wooded steppe of southeastern Europe

(sometimes broken into series of spots). Abdomen yellow with dark dots.

Stereocyclops COPE, 1870. Monotypic genus of the Microhylidae. Southeastern Brasil. Plump, with a small head. Skin smooth, only slightly granular laterally. Tympanum indistinct, followed posteriorly by a skin fold extending toward the shoulder. Limbs frail. Fingers free, tubercles well developed. Toes webbed at base only, the inner and outer metatarsal tubercles long and large.

▪ *S. incrassatus* COPE, 1870. 4-6 cm. Earth-colored.

Sternotherus GRAY, 1825. Musk Turtles. Genus of the Kinosternidae. Eastern North America. 4 species in various types of water, including ditches and ponds. To 15 cm carapace length. The small plastron does not close off the openings of the shell. Cartilaginous connections of bony elements making up the plastron give it a certain flexibility, but the hinges are not formed.

Aquatic, crepuscular. Carnivorous. Specimens usually do well in captivity and have been bred repeatedly, some-

Sternotherus carinatus

Sternotherus minor minor

Sternotherus minor peltifer

Sternotherus (minor) depressus

Sternotherus odoratus

times for generations. The common names refer to the strong-smelling secretion that is given off when excited. This type of behavior is variously developed in the entire family Kinosternidae.

▪ *S. carinatus* (GRAY, 1856). Keel-backed Musk Turtle. Southern USA between Oklahoma and Texas to Mississippi. Carapace length about 15 cm, the largest species of the genus, the highly arched carapace has a sharp median keel and radiating markings. Incubation takes 93 to 104 days at 30° C. or 22° C., respectively.

▪ *S. minor* (AGASSIZ, 1857). Loggerhead Musk Turtle. Southeastern USA. 13 cm. Smallest species of the genus. Incubation takes 90 to 123 days at 30° C. or 22-25° C., respectively.

▪ *S. odoratus* (LATREILLE, 1801). Stinkpot, Common Musk Turtle. Southern Canada to southeastern Texas and Florida. 14 cm. Well suited for outdoor maintenance, but due to its crepuscular habits difficult to observe. Incubation 60 to 107 days at 29° C. or 25° C., respectively.

Stilosoma BROWN, 1890. Short-tailed Snakes. Monotypic genus of the Colubridae of uncertain subfamily status (Colubrinae or Lycodontinae). Central Florida in pine forests. To 60 cm.
- *S. extenuatum* BROWN, 1890.

Stimuli: Environmental factors that act upon an organism and trigger excitations in body cells. The ability to react to stimuli is a fundamental characteristic of live matter. Higher animals possess more or less sophisticated sensory organs for the uptake of stimuli, which can be of a mechanical, physical, or chemical nature. These receptor organs are developed for specific stimuli to which they respond at a relatively low stimulus threshold; that is, they change the stimulus to nervous excitation, which is then passed on to the central nervous system. On the other hand, inadequate stimuli for a sensory organ produce excitations only at a very high stimulus frequency and can also lead to permanent damage.

Stoliczkaia JERDON, 1870. Genus of the Colubridae, Xenoderminae. Southern Asia. 2 species in montane rain forests to 1200 m elevation. 50-70 cm. The distinctly set off narrow head has normal head scales. The dorsal scales are keeled, only the middorsal row in *S. borneensis* slightly enlarged. Abdominal scales large. Body slightly compressed. Tail long.

Ground snakes. Diet and mode of reproduction in nature unknown. They should be kept in a rain-forest terrarium (not too warm). Diet: frogs and earthworms, possibly small lizards.
- *S. borneensis* BOULENGER, 1899. Northern Kalimantan, Kinabalu (to 1200 m). Reddish above with blackish spots in 3 longitudinal rows.
- *S. khasiensis* JERDON, 1870. Khase Mountains, India. Back unicolored red-brown, belly and sides whitish.

Stomatitis infectiosa: Mouth rot. In snakes and lizards, usually a bacterial infection of the oral cavity. In early stages the only clinical signs are small bleeding areas and pustules, in snakes mainly in the area of the mucous membrane at the bases of the teeth; mucous membrane bluish to red and swollen. Food is refused. Later stages include pustular tissue changes and development of a thick coating. The tissue along the gums is frequently swollen so that the mouth can not be closed. There can also be symptoms of pneumonia and/or enteritis (diarrhea). If untreated or treated too late there is generally a further serious deterioration of the overall condition and other organs can be affected secondarily. Apart from inflammation of the respiratory and digestive organs there are in many cases penetration of the inflammation into the tissue of the cranial bones, which may lead to the development of a bone marrow infection.

Decisive causes of stomatitis infectiosa are resistance-lowering factors such as vitamin deficiency, insufficient metabolism under poor or incorrect captive maintenance conditions, exhaustion after prolonged transports, parasite infestations, general diseases, and wounds in the region of the gums as a result of trauma or infected teeth that can not be shed. In disease outbreaks where several animals in the same terrarium are affected, these can be infections caused by simultaneous excessive pathogen reproduction and by unphysiological or unhygienic maintenance conditions, respectively.

Therapy: Increase of general resistance level (vitamin deficiency diseases) and treatment of secondary infections. Apart from cleansing the oral mucous membrane of infectious matter with hydrogen peroxide and removal of necrotic material, disinfecting agents (Lugol's Solution, quaternary ammonia, silver nitrate 1%) as well as sulfonamide solutions and antibiotic sprays are also indicated. In order to support local regeneration processes vitamin A preparations and ascorbic acid (vitamin C) can also be dripped into the oral cavity.

Storeria BAIRD and GIRARD, 1853. Brown Snakes. Genus of the Colubridae, Natricinae. Eastern and central USA into Mexico. 3 species in different wet habitats. 20 to 40 cm. Weakly set off head. Body covered by keeled scales. Back gray to brown with pale continuous stripes (*S. occipitomaculata*) or rows of spots (*S. dekayi*). Back of head with half-moon-shaped occipital spots or a dark crossbar. Belly yellowish to red.

Nocturnal, terrestrial (group 1, Natricinae). Tend to follow human habitation, and often found in vacant lots. *S. dekayi* is often found in relatively moist habitats. Worms, arthropods, and frogs are eaten. Live-bearers.
- *S. dekayi* (HOLBROOK, 1842). Brown Snake. Eastern North America into coastal Mexico.
- *S. occipitomaculata* (STORER, 1839). Redbellied Snake. Eastern North America.

Storeria dekayi

Streptosaurus MITTLEMAN, 1942. Banded Rock Lizards. Genus of the Iguanidae. Southern California and Baja California. 2 species in rocky habitats. Sometimes included in *Petrosaurus*, but distinguished from it by large, spiny, tail and leg scales. Distinguished from the similar genus *Uta* by the presence of granular scales in the middle of the back. Gray to bright brown with numerous light, often bluish, dots and dark crossbands. A conspicuous narrow black neckband.

Agile climbers that feed on arthropods and also on flowers and buds. For details on maintenance see *Sceloporus*. At night do not drop temperatures much below 20° C. Should have plenty of rocks and basking areas.
- *S. mearnsi* (STEJNEGER, 1894). Banded Rock Lizard. Southern California and norther Baja California. 20 cm. Egg-layer.

Strobilurus WIEGMANN, 1834. Monotypic genus of the Iguanidae. Eastern Brasil. Related to *Uracentron*. In tropical forests. Easily to 10 cm. Tail spiny. Head with a conspicuously large interparietal. Presumably predominantly ground-dwellers.
- *S. torquatus* WIEGMANN, 1834.

Strongyloidea: Nematode worms frequently occurring in snakes. The larvae enter their host through the skin and travel through the circulatory system into the lung, or enter through the larynx and esophagus and travel into the digestive tract, where they reach sexual maturity. They damage the host through the removal of blood and can simultaneously cause a loss in iron, creating the symptoms of a characteristic anemia (hypochrome anemia).

Therapy: Broad-spectrum anthelmintics (e. g., Thiobendazole) repeated at intervals of 1 to 2 months assure successful treatment.

Struach, Alexander (1832-1893): German-Russian zoologist, director of Imperial Academy at St. Petersburg. Founder of Russian herpetology. *Die Schlangen des Russischen Reichs* (1873), publications on turtles (1862, 1865, 1890), salamandrids, gekkonids, crocodiles, viperids, *Essai d'une Erpetologie de l' Algerie* (1862).

Stumpffia BOETTGER, 1818. Genus of the Microhylidae. Madagascar. 4 species. Snout-vent length a few cm. Slender. Pupil horizontal. Tympanum variously developed. Fingers and toes free and without distinct adhesive discs. Middle finger and toes very long, inner and outer ones often shortened, stump-like. Presumably terrestrial.
- *S. grandis* GUIBE, 1974. 2. 5 cm. Gray with a black pattern.
- *S. psologlossa* BOETTGER, 1881. 1.5 cm. Gray with darker spots.

Submissive behavior: Intraspecific as well as interspecific behavior in which conflicts are avoided or ended by submission, thus avoiding a damaging fight. Typical submissive behavior is the treading of lizards or displaying of the belly by many animals.

Substitute activity: Mostly a consequence of a conflict between two opposing behavior patterns (conflict behavior) or the early termination of an ongoing action, in this context an alien behavioral element. Typical substitute actions can be seen, for instance, in the threatening behavior of the gecko *Teratoscincus scincus*: After raising the body and rattling the tail there occurs—with decreasing excitement—not the threatening behavior with the wide-open mouth and subsequent biting, but instead the substitute action of wiping the eyes from the area of comfort behavior, and subsequent turning away and fleeing.

Sulfonamide: Derivative of p-aminobenzoic acid that interferes with bacterial metabolism. Numerous commercial variants are available. Consult your veterinarian.

Suta WORRELL, 1961. Myalls, Curl Snakes. Monotypic genus of the Elapidae. Eastern and central Australia. Closely related to *Unechis*. 40 to 60 cm. Slender, with a narrow, pointed head distinctly set off from the body. Usually unicolored without markings, except for a distinct dark neckband.

Nocturnal venomous snakes that hide during the day under rocks, logs, and similar places. They hunt in open areas, mainly for geckos. The bite is moderately dangerous but very painful. Requires a well-heated dry terrarium.
- *S. suta* (PETERS, 1864).

Symbiosis: A temporary or permanent cohabitation between animals of different species for their mutual benefit. A special form is cleaning symbiosis, for instance that observed between birds and crocodiles. Some bird species pick parasites off the back of crocodiles without being driven off or attacked by them. It is also alleged that the birds even pick pieces of flesh and leeches out of the open mouth of crocodiles. Moreover, the birds—through their behavior—warn the crocodiles about approaching enemies. Cleaning symbiosis also exists between certain finches and the giant tortoises (*Chelonoidis elephantopus*) and iguanas (*Amblyrhynchus, Conolophus*) of the Galapagos Islands. The reptiles even take up special positions as cleaning invitations to the birds.

Sympatry: The occurrence of closely related taxa in the same area. Independent of the size of the area in common, a sympatric occurrence of similar forms (without intergradation) is considered proof that different species must be involved (e. g., *Testudo graeca* and *T. hermanni* on the Balkan Peninsula), since in such a case there is reproductive isolation. The same conclusion can not be drawn with allopatry.

Symphimus COPE, 1869. Monotypic genus of the Colubridae, probably Boiginae. Mexico (Isthmus of Tehuantepec) in dry habitats. To 80 cm.

Nocturnal burrowing snakes that feed on lizards.
- *S. leucostomus* COPE, 1869.

Sympholis COPE, 1861. Genus of the Colubridae, Boiginae. Mexico. Closely related to *Apostolepis* and *Stenorrhina*. To more than 50 cm. Snout round, head not set off. Dorsal scales very small, smooth. Yellow with black rings.

Burrowing snakes. Biology unknown.
- *S. lippiens* COPE, 1861. Western Mexico (Jalisco to Nayarit).

Synapturanus CARVALHO, 1954. Monotypic genus of the Microhylidae. Brasil, Guyana, and Surinam. In appearance

similar to *Myersiella*, but with distinct adhesive discs on tips of toes (except on inner toe).
▪ *S. microps* (DUMERIL and BIBRON, 1841).

Syncope WALKER, 1973. Genus of the Microhylidae. 2 species. Eastern Ecuador and Peru, in *selva*. Compact, very small. Tympanum clearly visible. Feet 4-toed (first toe missing). Fingers with lateral skin folds; toes without webbing, the tips enlarged into small adhesive discs. No vocalization ability.

Nocturnal, living on the ground or among low-lying plants. They feed mainly on ants and mites. Development presumably is terrestrial without a free-swimming larval stage.
▪ *S. antenori* WALKER, 1973. 1.2 cm (males), 1.4 cm (females). Dark brown, abdomen gray-brown with white spots.

Synecology: The reciprocal relationships between the links of a community and the reciprocal relationships between the community and the environment.

Syngonium SCHOTT. Genus of the Araceae. Tropics of Central and South America. 20 species. Climbing plants. For culture requirements refer to *Philodendron*, but more sensitive; temperature during the winter should not be below 14° C. All species have milky sap.

Synonym: Two or more scientific names for the same taxon. Synonyms develop through multiple descriptions of species, genera, families, etc. Each taxon can have only a single valid scientific name. Which of the synonyms is the valid one to be used is determined by the rules of nomenclature, especially priority. All other available names of a taxon are then younger synonyms.

Synophis PERACCA, 1896. Genus of the Colubridae of uncertain subfamily status (Natricinae or Xenodontinae). Upper Amazon Basin (Ecuador, Colombia). 3 species in standing and slowly flowing waters in tropical rain forests. To 75 cm. Head longish, distinctly set off. Head scales reduced, the anterior snout margin wide and straight. Teeth of almost equal size. Body covered with strongly keeled and shingled scales. Usually dark olive-brown.

Diet: Frogs and fish. For maintenance refer to Natricinae, groups 2 and 3.
▪ *S. bicolor* PERACCA, 1896. Ecuador. Back dark, belly light, sharply delineated.
▪ *S. lasallei* (NICEFORO MARIA, 1950). Colombia and Ecuador.

Syrrhophus COPE, 1878. Chirping Toadlets. Genus of the Leptodactylidae. Southern North America and Central America. 12 in part polytypic species. Related to *Eleutherodactylus* and *Tomodactylus*. Mainly in lowlands, but some mountain species occur to 2,000 m elevation; *S. cystignathoides* tends to follow human habitation. Snout-vent length only a few cm. Pupil horizontal. No obvious external distinguishing characteristics (tympanum visible or not, vocal sac present or absent, toes with or without lateral skin folds, tips of fingers and toes enlarged or not enlarged). If voice present, a chirping call.

Nocturnal ground-dwellers. Spawning occurs in a damp substrate, and there is no free-swimming larval stage.

Maintain in a semimoist terrarium with hiding places. A small container is sufficient. Open-air maintenance is recommended for the summer months.
▪ *S. cystignathoides* (COPE, 1877). Rio Grande Toadlet. Texas to Mexico. Common. 2.5 cm. Gray-brown with a dark eyeband. Legs with dark crossbands.
▪ *S. marnocki* COPE, 1878. Cliff Toadlet. Texas. 4 cm. Light green with irregular dark dots.

Systematics: Orderly form of depicting animal diversity. One distinguishes artificial, natural, and phylogenetic systems. Artificial systems are based on specific organizational principles and are useful for the identification of organisms, in the form of identification tables. By using systematic categories, natural systems reflect graduated similarities of groups of organisms based on numerous combinations of characteristics. In natural systems one distinguishes between monophyletic and polyphyletic, while paraphyletic (artificial) groups remain unrecognized. Phylogenetic systems are based on the genealogical relationships of organisms. These systems can only work with monophyletic groups. Whether a group is monophyletic can only be recognized by mutually derived characteristics, while parallelisms are of no value in the elucidation of the phylogenetic history.

Taxonomy is a part of systematics serving an organizational role by means of giving scientific names and by arranging the taxa into systematic categories.

Sequential steps of units or categories of taxa are arranged to form hierarchy. The essential systematic categories, arranged in declining ranks, are: kingdom; phylum; class; order; family; genus; species.

Through the addition of prefixes such as super- or sub- or with further systematic categories, such as division, cohort, or tribe, a comprehensive system can be established.

Tachygia MITTLEMAN, 1952. Monotypic genus of the Scincidae, *Leiolopisma* Group. Tongatapu, Tonga Islands. More than 40 cm. Ground-dwellers.
▪ *T. microlepis* (DUMERIL and BIBRON, 1839).

Tachymenis WIEGMANN, 1835. Genus of the Colubridae, Boiginae. South America along the Pacific coast from Peru to Chile, also in Amazon Basin of Peru, Bolivia, and eastward to Surinam. 6 species in various dry habitats from outer forest regions to rubble fields and semideserts, in mountain regions to 3,500 m elevation. About 60 cm. Slender, with distinctly set off head. Frequently with longitudinal stripes along the back.

Nocturnal ground snakes that feed mainly on lizards. Ovoviviparous. Maintenance depends upon origin of specimens. Usually can be kept in a dry terrarium with ample hiding places and a nocturnal temperature reduction appropriate to the habitats (high mountain species, desert species).
▪ *T. peruvianus* WIEGMANN, 1835. Coastal region between Peru and Chile, also in the Andes.

Tadpole: The aquatic larval form of frogs and toads. Characterized by an egg-shaped body and rudder-like tail equipped with skin crests, the presence of external gills that later change to internal gills by being covered by a skin fold. This resulting gill chamber has an opening, the respiratory aperture or spiracle, that leads to the outside and lateral line organs that monitor the water currents. Initially present are adhesive discs that produce sticky secretions; they are located below the mouth and serve to let the newly hatched larvae stick to solid objects.

At first tadpoles feed solely on very small plankton trapped by a mucous filter along the gill clefts. Later they start to feed actively. The diet consists of plant and animal detritus that is ground up with the aid of a horny beak and numerous horny teeth in the mouth and pharynx. The tadpoles of some species are predators. The mouth can also be modified into a large suction disc as an adaptation to rapidly flowing water. During the process of metamorphosis the tadpoles change to small frogs that usually become terrestrial.

Taiga: Boreal coniferous forests restricted to the Northern Hemisphere. There the boreal *taiga* extends in areas with warm summers and winters with prolonged frost and snow periods as a belt over the northern continents and extends over vast areas into permafrost ground. The *taiga* is herpetologically poor (in Europe, *Vipera berus, Lacerta vivipara, Rana arvalis,* and *R. temporaria;* in North America, *R. sylvatica* and *Bufo boreas*). Comparable but ecologically more diverse coniferous forest belts occur in the mountains of the Northern Hemisphere. These montane *taigas* accommodate a relatively rich amphibian and reptile fauna with many endemic forms in Pacific North America and eastern Asia.

Takydromus DAUDIN, 1802. Oriental Racers, Long-tailed Lizards. Genus of the Lacertidae. Amur region and Japan, throughout entire eastern Asia to Indonesia. *Platyplacopus* BOULENGER, 1918, from Taiwan, and *Apeltonotus* BOULENGER, 1918, from the Ryukyu Archipelago, should be considered as subgenera of *Takydromus.* Found in relatively damp forest habitats, also on rocks; the long-tailed species (especially *T. sexlineatus*) are found in relatively open grasslands. About 12 species. Extremely slender in appearance, tail about 2 to 5 times snout-vent length. Dorsal scales large, strongly keeled, the keels forming continuous longitudinal rows. Lateral scales small, granular. Ventral scales keeled at least along the sides. Toes with lamellae. Collar reduced, sometimes completely absent. Only 1 to 5 femoral pores. Mainly brown, mostly with light lateral stripes and dark spots.

Predominantly terrestrial, some are in part semiarboreal; the long-tailed species can move very rapidly, "running on top of the grass." Egg-layers, 1-10 eggs per clutch, up to 6 clutches per year; at least the southern species will breed throughout the year. The diet includes various arthropods. The terrarium must be spacious and relatively damp (but NOT wet). Depending upon origin, provide daytime tem-

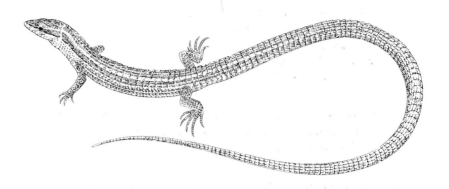

Takydromus sexlineatus

peratures from 22 to 30° C. with a basking area, slightly cooler at night. Overall somewhat difficult to keep and sensitive.
- *T. amurensis* PETERS, 1881. Amur region to Korea. Damp forests, river banks. 20 cm. Tail only twice snout-vent length. Brown to olive with dark spots and a lateral band. Maintenance similar to *Lacerta vivipara.*
- *T. sexlineatus* DAUDIN, 1802. Oriental Six-lined Runner. Southern China to Java, Kalimantan (southernmost species of the genus). Grasslands. To 36 cm, with the body only 6 cm. Olive-green to reddish brown above with light longitudinal stripes and sometimes spots; legs and tail often reddish.

Tantilla BAIRD and GIRARD, 1853. Flathead Snakes, Black-headed Snakes. Genus of the Colubridae, Boiginae. Southern USA, southward to Argentina. About 50 species found in various habitats from dry brush steppes and rubble fields in mountains to peripheral zones of rain forests and also in montane forests. 25 to 40 cm. 15 rows of smooth scales. Head indistinct, in many species black with a light nape marking contrasting with the uniformly tan body; sometimes with pale longitudinal stripes.

Nocturnal burrowers under rocks, logs, and similar items. Centipedes, insect larvae, and also small lizards are eaten. Maintain in a dry or forest terrarium as appropriate.

Tantilla nigriceps

Takydromus amurensis

• *T. coronata* BAIRD and GIRARD, 1853. Southeastern Crowned Snake. Southeastern USA.
• *T. gracilis* BAIRD and GIRARD, 1853. Flathead Snake. Texas to Missouri in the Plains.
• *T. melanocephala* (LINNAEUS, 1758). Central America to Argentina.

Tantillita SMITH, 1941. Monotypic genus of the Colubridae, Boiginae. Guatemala. Closely related to and rather similar to *Tantilla*.
• *T. lintoni* (SMITH, 1940).

Tarentola GRAY, 1825. Wall Geckos. Genus of the Gekkonidae. Mediterranean Region; also Cuba and Bahamas. 7 species in steppe-like and rocky habitats; some follow human habitation (*T. mauritanica*). To more than 15 cm. Strongly built, rather compact, flattened dorso-ventrally. Head very wide. Tail about snout-vent length. Toes with well-developed enlarged adhesive lamellae in a single row (without the median longitudinal furrow that occurs in many genera). Pupil vertical. Back with large, keeled scales in distinct rows. Ventral scales smooth. Tail scales arranged in whorls, spiny. Predominantly shades of brown.

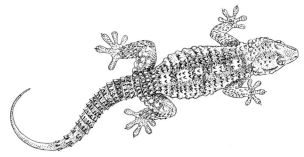

Tarentola mauritanica

Mostly crepuscular, but they like to sun themselves occasionally. Keep in a relatively dry terrarium with slightly damp hiding places at day temperatures of 22 to 28° C., at night 15 to 20° C. A winter dormancy period of about 8 weeks at 10° C. is recommended. It is also possible to keep these geckos running free in a heated room as long as a drinking bowl is provided and there is no possibility of escape. Males are very quarrelsome. *Tarentola* species are easy to keep and are known to have reached considerable longevities in captivity.
• *T. annularis* (GEOFFROY, 1823). Northeastern Africa, southwestern Asia. 15 cm. Tubercles in middle of back conspicuously low.
• *T. delalandi* (DUMERIL and BIBRON, 1836). Canary Islands and Cape Verde Islands. 12 cm. Gray to reddish brown, markings variable.
• *T. mauritanica* (L., 1758). Wall Gecko. Mediterranean Region, introduced elsewhere. 15 cm. Juveniles with dark wavy crossbands that become indistinct with increasing age.

Taricha GRAY, 1850. Western Newts. Genus of the Salamandridae. Pacific coastal North America from southern Alaska to northern Baja California. 3 species, in part polytypic. To 20 cm. Strongly built. Skin rough. Eyes large. Tail long. Unicolored dark brown above, ventral side bright orange to blood red. Mating males relatively smooth-skinned, without crests, but with nuptial pads on

Taricha granulosa

Taricha torosa, terrestrial stage

hands and feet.

These newts display a considerable homing instinct and return to their home pond to breed. The males appear first and wait for the females; males remain in the majority, because it seems that females are capable of breeding only every 2 or 3 years. During mating the male grasps the female from above and seeks to establish cloacal contact for spermatophore transfer. The eggs are attached individually (*T.*

Taricha torosa

granulosa) or in clumps (all remaining species) to a suitable substrate. *T. rivularis* is tied to small flowing waters. The females return to a terrestrial life immediately upon spawning, while the males usually remain in the water for some time. The larvae metamorphose at a size of about 7.5 cm; neoteny rarely occurs. *Taricha* species can reach considerable longevity. Sexual maturity is attained with the fifth year at the earliest.

These brilliantly colored newts should be kept in an aquarium or in a spacious aqua-terrarium with clear, cool, clean water during spring. The remainder of the time they do well in a damp terrarium. Food animals must be small, such as small earthworms, slugs, and similar organisms. Animals from northern populations require a winter dormancy period of several months; more southern forms need only 6 to 8 weeks at cool temperatures. Specimens not maintained optimally during the winter will often refuse to feed next spring, and it may be difficult to get them to go into water.

- *T. granulosa* (SKILTON, 1849). Rough-skinned Newt. Southern Alaska to California. Belly yellow to orange, lower eyelid dark.
- *T. rivularis* (TWITTY, 1935). Red-bellied Newt. Northern California. Belly bright red, black above. Lower eyelid dark.
- *T. torosa* (RATHKE, 1833). California Newt. Coastal California (*T. t. torosa*); *T. t. sierrae* along western slopes of the Sierra Nevada to 1250 m elevation. Belly orange, brown above. Lower eyelid orange.

Taudactylus STRAUGHAN and LEE, 1966. Australian Torrent Frogs. Genus of the Leptodactylidae. Eastern coastal Australia. 4 species with very small distributions. Near and in mountain streams in rain forests. Snout-vent length a few cm. Dorsal region more or less flattened, the head with a pointed snout. Related to *Crinia* and distinguished from it by anatomical differences of the finger and toe bones (in *Taudactylus* the distal phalanges are T-shaped). Tips of fingers and toes distinctly widened, fingers free; toes webbed at base only. An aquatic larval stage is present.
- *T. acutirostris* (ANDERSSON, 1916). Sharp-snouted Torrent Frog. Northeastern Queensland (Atherton Tableland). 3 cm. Fawn to olive-brown, flanks dark, distinctly set off from back by a distinct light yellow dorso-lateral stripe.

Tautonym: Exact repetition of a generic and specific name—*Natrix natrix* or *Bufo bufo*. Tautonyms are permitted only in zoological nomenclature but not in botanical nomenclature.

Taxon: A group with a valid or even invalid scientific name. For example, order Salientia, family Testudinidae, genus *Bufo*, species *Natrix natrix*. Plural, taxa.

Taxonomy: Subdivision of systematics that deals with the assignment of scientific names and places taxa into systematic categories; classification.

Taylor, Edward Harrison (1889-1978): American zoologist and herpetologist at the Museum of Natural History at the University of Kansas. *Herpetology of the Philippine Islands* (3 parts and supplements, 1921-1925), *The Caecilians of the World* (1968), numerous major works on Mexican and Costa Rican herpetofaunas.

Tectovaranus, subgenus: see *Varanus*, genus.

Teeth: In predatory animals such as amphibians and many reptiles, teeth serve primarily to grasp and hold the prey and also to partially macerate the food. Specialized teeth, the fangs or venom teeth, have taken over the role of transferring the venom in venomous lizards and snakes.

The teeth in recent amphibians consist of a cement-like socket and a crown made of dentine with a cap consisting of tooth enamel (or a similar substance). While both parts are separated by a fibrous ring in the salamanders and caecilians, this ring is hardened by the presence of a calcified dentine in the frogs. In amphibians the following bones can have teeth: premaxillary, upper jaw (maxillary), lower jaw (mandible), vomer, palatine, and pterygoid. The lower jaw (dentary) is nearly always toothless in frogs (exceptions: *Amphignathodon*, *Ceratobatrachus*). Teeth are completely absent in *Bufo*, *Pseudophryne*, most species in the family Dendrobatidae, and the family Microhylidae. Outgrowths from the jaws in the form of pseudoteeth or odontodes occur in a few genera.

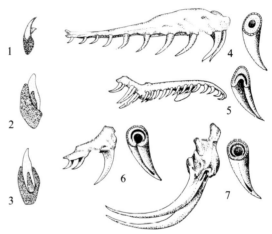

Types of reptilian teeth: 1 Acrodont; 2 pleurodont; 3 thecodont; 4 aglyphic; 5 opisthoglyphic; 6 proteroglyphic; 7 solenoglyphic

In reptiles there can be teeth on the palatine, premaxillary, pterygoid, and vomer, as well as the upper and lower jaws. Reptilian teeth can be highly variable: blunt and rounded, weak or strong, pointed backwards, serrated, large or small, as well as in different sizes.

Embryonically teeth develop from the dental ridge, which is formed from an indentation of the oral epithelium along the inside of the jaw bone. Depending upon the mode of attachment to the bone, one distinguishes:
- acrodont teeth positioned along the upper jaw margin (amphibians, some snakes and lizards, tuataras);
- pleurodont teeth positioned laterally along the edge of the jaw (many lizards and snakes);
- thecodont teeth located inside a bony socket (crocodilians). Turtles have become toothless secondarily and instead have sharp horny edges (rhamphotheca) on the jaws. Tooth replacement occurs by means of continuous new formation of teeth in the dental ridge, the older teeth (due to absorption and erosion processes) falling out at their bases. Since this change progresses in waves along the dental ridges, this always assures that usable teeth in different de-

velopmental stages are more or less evenly distributed over the tooth-carrying bone.

In snakes, the following types of teeth are distinguished:
• Aglyphic teeth: Solid teeth that do not have a venom transfer function.
• Opisthoglyphic teeth: Grooved venom teeth with the groove located anteriorly or posteriorly. This type of tooth occurs in boigine snakes, where the fangs are located in the posterior section of the mouth.
• Proteroglyphic teeth: Fangs where the groove is usually closed (families Elapidae, Hydrophiidae); the venom teeth are located in the anterior section of the mouth.
• Solenoglyphic teeth: Tubular venom teeth that function like a hypodermic needle (families Viperidae, Crotalidae).

Teiidae: Family of the Squamata, suborder Sauria, Scincomorpha. Americas. About 40 genera, approximately 200 species. From rain forests to deserts, in mountain regions to 4,000 m. Often considered as New World version of the Lacertidae, to which the teiids are indeed closely similar, with only minor morphological and anatomical differences. The head scales in teiids are not fused with the skull bones and the teeth are massive, i. e., not hollow at their base. All-in-all, the Teiidae have produced a greater species diversity than their Old World relatives. Certain smaller species resemble Scincidae but are without osteoderms. There is considerable size variation, from 10 cm to more than 1 m and almost monitor-like in appearance.

Body usually covered by variously large, granular, or shingled scales arranged in regular longitudinal, lateral, or oblique rows. The large ventral scales are particularly distinct. Some ground-dwelling or burrowing species have fused, transparent eyelids. No obvious crests or gular pouches. Usually with 4 well-developed limbs, but in some genera there is a tendency toward reduction. Femoral pores very often present.

The majority of teiids are predators feeding on insects and small vertebrates; a few are partially or totally herbivorous. Mating usually includes a neck bite. Egg-layers, as far as is known.

This family has up to now played only a minor role in terrarium husbandry, which is certainly not in line with its diversity. The following genera are here distinguished: *Alopoglossus, Ameiva, Anadia, Anotosaura, Argalia, Arthrosaura, Arthroseps, Bachia, Callopistes, Cercosaura, Cnemidophorus, Colobodactylus, Colobosaura, Crocodilurus, Dicrodon, Dracaena, Echinosaura, Ecpleopus, Euspondylus, Gymnophthalamus, Heterodactylus, Iphisa, Kentropyx, Leposoma, Macropholidus, Micrablepharus, Neusticurus, Ophiognomon, Opipeuter, Pantodactylus, Pholidobolus, Placosoma, Prionodactylus, Proctoporus, Ptychoglossus, Stenolepis, Teius, Tretioscincus,* and *Tupinambis.*

Teius MERREN, 1820. Monotypic genus of the Teiidae. Southeastern Brasil to northern Argentina in grasslands and brush steppes. 30 cm. Appearance similar to *Cnemidophorus,* but limbs with only 4 toes. Granular dorsal scales and large smooth ventral scales.

Ground-dwellers. Keep much like *Cnemidophorus.*
• *T. teyou* (DAUDIN, 1802). Four-toed Tegu. Bright green with yellow flanks.

Tejovaranus: see *Callopistes,* genus.

Telescopus WAGLER, 1830. Cat Snakes. Genus of the Colubridae, Boiginae. Southeastern Europe, southwestern Asia, and Africa. 11 species found in different dry habitats, marginal desert regions to savannahs. 80 cm to 1.3 m. Head distinctly set off. The large eyes have vertical pupils (thus the common name). Body slightly compressed laterally, covered with smooth scales. Brownish with darker crossbars or spots.

Telescopus fallax

Nocturnal ground snakes that prey mainly on lizards but also take small mammals and some ground-nesting birds and their eggs. Maintain in a well-heated dry terrarium with a nocturnal temperature reduction. Caution: Possibly dangerous bites.
• *T. fallax* (FLEISCHMANN, 1831). European Cat Snake. Southeastern Europe to the Caucasus and Asia Minor to Syria and Iran.
• *T. semiannulatus* A. SMITH, 1849. Central to South Africa.

Telescopus semiannulatus

Telmatobius WIEGMANN, 1835. Genus of the Leptodactylidae. High Andes (2000 to 4500 m) from southern Ecuador to Chile and Argentina; greatest species diversity in Peru. Depending upon individual systematists, 19 to 27 species, some polytypic; revision needed. Related to *Batrachophrynus, Telmatobufo,* and *Caudiverbera.* In and near creeks and streams (e. g., *T. peruvianus*), lakes (e. g., *T. culeus* and *T. marmoratus*). Body more or less egg-shaped. Pupil horizontal. Toes with webbing. Males without vocal sac.

Largely to completely aquatic, but some species also semiterrestrial (*T. jelski*). They remain in hiding during the day in water under rocks and among algae. The food consists mainly of small crustaceans, water insects, and small frogs and their larvae. Keep them in spacious, cool aquariums suitably set up with underwater rock caves and small land sections.

- *T. culeus* (GARMAN, 1875). Lake Titicaca. Lowland inhabitant. 10 cm and larger. Compact, eyes small. Respiration via skin only.
- *T. marmoratus* (DUMERIL and BIBRON, 1841). Lake Titicaca and other waters close by. 6 cm. Slender, with large, protruding eyes.
- *T. montanus* (PHILIPPI, 1902). Central Chile, Andean lakes. To 6 cm. Similar to *T. culeus*.
- *T. peruvianus* WIEGMANN, 1835. Southern Peru, northern Chile. To 5 cm. Slender.

Telmatobufo SCHMIDT, 1952. Monotypic genus of the Leptodactylidae. Central Chile. Related to *Batrachophrynus*, *Telmatobius*, and *Caudiverbera*. Shape toad-like. Skin with warts. Pupil vertical. Fingers free, toes webbed. Distinct parotoid glands. In contrast to related genera, largely terrestrial.
- *T. bullocki* SCHMIDT, 1952. Chilean Andes between Conception and Valdivia (1000 to 1200 m). 6.5 cm. Brown with a yellow pattern.

Temperature: This is one of the most important factors of the terrarium climate and also has diverse effects on other parameters (e. g., humidity). The highly variable requirements of individual species are discussed under the generic description and also under particular ecosystems.

Except for a few species, most herps require day temperatures between 18 and 35° C., with nightly temperature reduction from slight to substantial. The required temperatures are invariably achieved by means of heating. Cooling is required only in exceptional cases, such as amphibians from mountain creeks that must be kept in a refrigerator or cellar. A frequent mistake in terrarium maintenance is keeping the temperature too constant. This applies to daily as well as seasonal variations. Animals from the temperate regions often require a winter dormancy period with substantially reduced temperatures.

The daily temperature changes in rain forests (about 5 to 10° C., the latter especially for inhabitants of the treetops) are substantially smaller than in open habitats. Here it also has to be remembered that many desert occupants avoid temperature extremes by burrowing into the ground, where nocturnal reductions, depending upon depth, go down to 10 or 20° C. The temperature must not be constant throughout the terrarium. A gradient is invariably produced by a local heating source.

Finally, reference must be made to preferred natural temperatures that are frequently mentioned in the literature—under no circumstances must these be assumed to represent optimal terrarium temperatures. Preferred temperatures are invariably far too high and can only be a guideline for maximum temperatures under a local heating source. The preferred (optimal) natural temperatures listed in the literature are usually only of limited value to the terrarium enthusiast. They are commonly determined from

different temperature ranges that an animal selects in the wild and usually for only a short period of time. Other factors such as humidity commonly are not taken into consideration for the animal "preferring" a particular temperature at a given time. Usually preferred temperatures selected in this manner are critically close to the upper temperature limit survived by the animal and as terrarium temperatures they are often far too high. At best they can only be guidelines for temperatures at basking sites. The table below lists a few such values. Also refer to thermoregulation.

Agama stellio 45.6° C.
Lacerta agilis 38.0° C.
Lacerta vivipara 37.0° C.
Cyrtodactylus kotschyi 42.0° C.
Tarentola mauritanica 37.0° C.
Anolis carolinensis 38.6°C.
Phrynosoma cornutum 47.5°C.

Tenebrionidae: Black Beetles, Flour Beetles. Family of the Coleoptera. About 20,000 species. Many species are typical occupants of deserts and steppes, and some are worldwide pest species. Others play an important role as food organisms for terrarium animals. The best known species is the flour beetle (*Tenebrio molitor*). Its larvae are referred to as mealworms. These black-brown beetles are about 15 mm long; their yellow-brown larvae are about 30 mm. Egg development takes about 1 week at 25° C. Larval development occupies 4 to 6 months, then 1-2 weeks as pupae; egg-laying starts 1 week later. Mealworms are most

Flour beetles, *Tenebrio molitor*

suitably bred in plastic containers with an area of at least 30 x 20 cm and filled halfway with a mixture of wheat bran and oatmeal. Additional food should be provided occasionally in the form of fresh vegetables and small pieces of yeast, which leads to vitamin enrichment and increases the food value of mealworms. A calcium lactate supplement improves the calcium balance. This additional food is placed on top of a gauze frame or a flat piece of wood at the surface. The food must be changed regularly in order to avoid decay or mite infestations. Since these beetles can fly, the plastic container must be covered with a gauze lid. Preferably the pupae should be collected and transferred into a new breeding box where egg-laying can occur. The beetles must be given fresh, water-containing, but not moist, food.

Flour beetles and their larvae are eagerly eaten by virtu-

Mealworms, *Tenebrio molitor*

Teratoscincus scincus

ally all insectivorous terrarium animals of suitable size but must not be the main food item for prolonged periods of time.

Some other species of the genus *Tenebrio* will get larger than *T. molitor* and can be bred the same way, as can the about 7 mm long grain beetle *Alphitobius diaperinus*. Supplementary food can be in the form of crushed peanuts, ground carrots, and yeast. Under favorable conditions the generation time is less than 2 months.

Teratolepis GUENTHER, 1870. Monotypic genus of the Gekkonidae, subfamily Gekkoninae. Pakistan to Assam. To 8 cm. Relatively compact. Tail ⅔ snout-vent length, conspicuously enlarged.

Teratolepis fasciata

Nocturnal ground-dwellers in brushland.
• *T. fasciata* (BLYTH, 1853). Carrot-tailed Viper Gecko.

Teratoscincus STRAUCH, 1863. Wonder Geckos, Frog-eyed Geckos. Genus of the Gekkonidae. Southwestern to central Asia. 4 species in sandy or clay deserts and semi-deserts. To 20 cm. Cylindrical, the head large and high with protruding eyes. Pupil vertical. Tail strong, distinctly shorter than snout-vent length. Head scales fine (except snout scales), but the body scales are large to very large (*T. scincus*), semi-round, smooth, and shingled, but very loose (there is well-developed skin respiration); the caudal scales are the largest. Toes without adhesive lamellae, with lateral serrations. Sandy brown to pale reddish brown with dark, sometimes almost black, longitudinal stripes and/or spots; a light blue form of *T. scincus* exists.

Nocturnal, burrowing to 80 cm. Defensive behavior is particularly conspicuous: the geckos stand high on the

legs, form a regular arched "cat hump," and produce a rattling noise by rubbing the large tail scales together. They then move toward the opponent while emitting hissing noises, then suddenly turn around and flee. The female lays 2 eggs several times a year under rocks or in burrows.

Captive maintenance not easy. These geckos need a spacious terrarium with a very thick layer of sandy clay soil with the lower sections kept slightly moist. Suitable day temperatures are about 30° C. (local surface areas even higher), at night about 20° C. Winter rest period for about 6 weeks at 10 to 15° C. is suggested. Drinking water requirements are relatively large. Various arthropods are eaten, and the diet must be varied. Has been bred repeatedly recently.
• *T. scincus* (SCHLEGEL, 1858). Wonder Gecko. Iran, Kasachstan, western China. To 20 cm.

Teratoscincus scincus

Terentjev, Pavel Victorovich (1903-1970): Russian herpetologist, professor of vertebrate zoology at the University of Leningrad. Together with Cernov produced *Identification Key of Reptiles and Amphibians of the USSR* (1949 in Russian; English translation 1965). Also the monograph *The Frog* (1950, in Russian), as well as the textbook *Herpetologia* (1961, in Russian; English translation 1965). More than 150 scientific articles.

Teretrurus BEDDOME, 1886. Monotypic genus of the Uropeltidae. Southern India. 23 cm, 9 mm thick. Snout rounded, chin fold absent. Tail compressed, terminating (as in the closely related genus *Brachyophidium*) in a simple, compressed terminal scale with tiny tubercles and a terminal spine. Caudal scales of females only slightly roughened and with 2-3 low keels; males always with distinct, multiple-keeled caudal scales. Brown to purple-red, sometimes with black dots or spots.

Burrowing snakes.

▪ *T. sanguineus* (BEDDOME, 1867). Southern India. To 220 m elevation.

Terrapene MERREM, 1820. Box Turtles. Genus of the Emydidae. North America. 4 species in damp to dry habitats, largely independent of water. In mode of life close to tortoises, but most are still able to swim and dive. Feet without broad webs, relatively stumpy. Carapace to 18 cm, deep, arched, rounded. Carapace may have a more or less well-developed median keel. Plastron joined flexibly with carapace via connective tissue at the bridge; the anterior and posterior flaps are hinged to permit perfect closure of

Terrapene nelsoni

the carapace.

Omnivorous. The food eaten is dependent upon seasonal availability: worms and snails (following precipitation), ripe fruit, buds, berries, mushrooms, depending upon season. Box turtles should be kept in a terrarium rather than an aquarium. *T. carolina* is well-suited for outdoor maintenance throughout the year with proper winter protection. The terrarium should have a deep substrate for burrowing. Has been bred repeatedly.

▪ *T. carolina* (LINNAEUS, 1758). Eastern Box Turtle. Southern Canada and the eastern and central USA to southeastern Texas. Highly variable; rarely ever are two specimens from the same location completely identical. *T. carolina* prefers open forests with access to flowing or standing water. Incubation takes 50 to 90 days at 30° C. or

Terrapene carolina bauri

Terrapene carolina major

Terrapene coahuila

Terrapene carolina mexicana

Terrapene ornata ornata

22-25° C. in an incubator. Incubation under natural conditions (actually observed) takes 60-99 days.

▪ *T. ornata* (AGASSIZ, 1857). Western Box Turtle. Central (Great Plains) and southwestern USA to northern Mexico. Mostly in drier habitats than previous species. Plastron with yellow radiating markings against a black-brown background. Incubation takes 55 to 125 days at 30° C. or 23° C. in an incubator, under natural conditions 75 days.

Terrapene carolina carolina

Terrarium: Apart from accommodating various technical support materials, a terrarium serves to provide an environment that is as favorable as possible for the animals. Under no circumstances should one attempt to recreate a large segment of the natural habitat on a reduced scale. The terrarium setup is reduced to a minimum for semisterile maintenance. Special requirements have to be met for venomous snake care.

Everything that is to be placed inside the terrarium has to be thoroughly cleaned before use. One of the basic rules is never to transfer anything from one terrarium to another without first disinfecting it. The terrarium setup includes generally the substrate, hiding places, climbing facilities, frequently a specially constructed back wall, and usually also plants, as well as water and food containers.

The substrate can consist of various materials. For a dry terrarium one uses sand or a mixture of sand and soil. Some people also recommended the addition of sawdust, which contributes to an even dampness and prevents the substrate from becoming too hard. Careful selection of clay-free sand or fine gravel prevents hardening of the substrate after regular spraying, but it also stops burrowing animals from establishing permanent subterranean passages.

For damper terrariums one uses loose humus into which the pots for small plants are placed directly, or one uses various peat moss and soil mixtures (peat moss is relatively germ-free and can be further disinfected by boiling it).

The substrate should be at least 10 cm deep. The lower layers must be kept damp, even in a desert terrarium. In a dry terrarium the substrate can also include a box with a moderately damp substrate placed in one corner for depositing eggs. For special situations one can also use an artificial substrate such as foam rubber cubes (for Gymnophiona). Hiding places and climbing facilities are provided in the form of single rocks or rocky structures without sharp angular features. These can be used in the various, mostly more or less dry, terrariums but do not belong in a rainforest terrarium. Limestone, sandstone, granite, basalt, slate, and others are very useful. For esthetic reasons, it is advisable to always use the same type of rock in a particular terrarium. Rocks must never be piled loosely on top of each other in order to avoid injuries from collapsing structures. With large burrowing animals care has to be taken that small rocks are not thrown against the glass sides. Large rock formations should ideally be cemented together.

For ground-dwellers from damp forests one uses pieces of tree roots or small tree stumps. Every type of wood can be used in dry terrariums. Hiding places have to be accessible and placed in such a position that they can be closely monitored. Climbing branches are required by climbing animals. While the majority of arboreal species prefer thick, very rough branches covered by epiphytes for climbing, chameleons, for instance, prefer thin branches. One should only use completely dried branches. For climbing

A large bank of cages designed for breeding kingsnakes

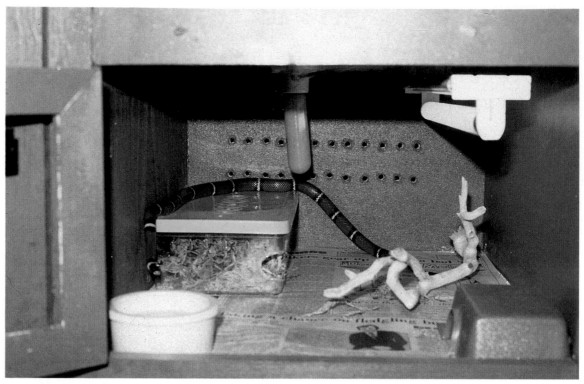

A fully furnished terrarium with lights, heat, hide boxes, etc.

A fancy display terrarium with heavy tropical vegetation

animals it is strongly recommended to decorate the back and side walls in some manner, which tends to enlarge the overall area usable by the animals considerably and also offers hiding places at the same time.

In dry terrariums rock back walls are usually constructed out of individual rocks that are cemented together. Artificial back walls can also be made out of various plastic or fiberglass materials, sprinkled with sand, and painted the color shade desired. Gypsum is another material that can be used for this and similar purposes. Usually these artificial media are applied to an uneven, rough, textured substrate (e. g., stryrofoam, chicken wire, etc.).

Damp, well-planted terrariums usually have back walls made up of joined pieces of cork or tree bark or even chicken wire covered with sphagnum moss and epiphytes.

Rapidly growing creeping plants, such as *Ficus pumila*, are also useful since they will cover the entire back wall quickly.

Back walls in small terrariums should not be permanently installed but only be put in place with a tight fit. This facilitates quick removal for cleaning and maintenance purposes.

If a small drinking container is insufficient and a water bowl for bathing has to be installed, a number of points have to be carefully considered. Not only the back wall but also all other items, including the substrate, should be removable since all of them will need to be cleaned regularly. Special attention has to be paid to providing a suitable feeding site inside the terrarium.

Setting up a terrarium has to take into account the lighting and heating, which must permit the animals to select sites with different temperatures, light intensities, and moisture. There must also be sufficient hiding places. Animals at the lower end of the hierarchy as well as females must have the opportunity to avoid sight contact with superior animals and be able to escape from them if need be.

Important factors of the terrarium climate are temperature, soil moisture, humidity, light, and ventilation. Apart from the macroclimate it takes detailed knowledge of the microclimate, which dominates the actual environment (niche) of the animals concerned and which can deviate quite substantially from the macroclimate, to be successful with terrarium maintenance. Invariably the animals avoid extremes of the macroclimate (e. g., excessive heat in the desert during the day or temperature reduction at night, frosts in temperate latitudes, extreme droughts). A specific, purposeful terrarium setup together with sensible terrarium techniques contributes quite significantly to establishing an optimum terrarium climate. One of the most common mistakes is to provide a constant temperature, while in nature there are always gradients and daily as well as annual rhythms.

A modern indoor terrarium could generally not function properly without various electrical support equipment; this includes heating, illumination, ventilators, and moisture and humidity generating devices and equipment. Connecting these components to an electrical timer, thermostat, and hygrostat permits semiautomatic operation by eliminating various manual service functions.

There are three basic types of terrarium: indoor terrariums, open-air terrariums, and outdoor terrariums. A special type of terrarium is the greenhouse terrarium, which can provide optimum conditions for many animals. There are different forms of indoor terrariums, depending upon construction and position, i. e., wall terrarium, table terrarium, window terrarium, etc.

There have been repeated attempts to categorize the indoor terrarium according to climate. In earlier categories one distinguished between unheated and heated terrariums, then dry, semimoist, and moist terrariums. There were further separations into aqua-terrariums and paludariums. However, even this diversity does not really reflect all possibilities or the actual ecological requirements. It would probably be more sensible (although not applicable in each case) to attempt a rough habitat classification that conveys essential requirements for setting up a particular type of terrarium and simultaneously describes the climatic conditions. This then provides for rain-forest terrariums, savannah, steppe, semidesert, and desert terrariums, rock terrariums, high-mountain terrariums, cool forest terrariums, and others. However, the variability even within these concepts is still so large that there are only very few extremely adaptable species that could simply be kept in any rain-forest or desert terrarium. Depending upon the geographic origin and habitat of a species to be kept, one has to establish on the basis of climate diagrams and habitat descriptions the terrarium conditions that have to be provided for that species.

Biologically correct terrariums should be set up so as to meet as closely as possible the exact climatic and ecological conditions for a particular species. Fortunately the plasticity of most species is such that they are able to adapt and in many cases are even able to reproduce.

The actual container used for the terrarium will vary with the animals to be kept. Commercially available aquariums used as terrariums are not recommended because of inadequate ventilation. Aquariums can sometimes be used for keeping various amphibians and some small reptiles when the entire top is covered with a screen lid and the container is not taller than 30 cm.

Many hobbyists may prefer to build their own terrarium to fit their particular needs in terms of size and shape. Most popular due to ease of construction are wooden frame structures into which glass side panels are fitted. However, even with proper installation and treatment of the wooden areas, this type of terrarium is not well suited for moist conditions. Recently the wooden frame type has been replaced more and more by light metal or hard plastic and fiberglass frames. The use of silicone cement now facilitates completely frameless terrariums, a tremendous advantage for small and medium containers. Glass is used for at least the front panel and may be also be used for the bottom, sides, and back wall. The latter is now often of some clear plastic material that permits perforation for ventilation and so eliminates the tedious gluing of gauze strips along the lower area of the back wall. While plexiglass has the advantage of ultraviolet penetration, due to its relative softness it becomes scratched fairly quickly by lizards. The bottom section should be at least 10 cm high (the door must not be set lower than that). The cover should be partially or completely made of gauze. Plastic gauze is adequate for small animals. With metal gauze or screening care has to be taken that there are no sharp wire ends projecting into the terrarium.

In order to assure adequate ventilation there must be (apart from a complete or partial gauze cover) a second gauze area or perforations in the lower section (side, front, or back panel) for air to enter. Large containers should be serviceable from the front or side either through a door or a sliding front glass panel; there may be the danger of substrate thrown about by burrowing animals becoming wedged into the sliding tract. Also useful are upwardly re-

A very simple terrarium suitable for temporarily keeping hardy specimens

movable front panels.

There are no firm standards for the shape of a terrarium. Even shallow coffee-table terrariums are being used. Shape and size depend mainly on the species to be kept. Tree-dwellers must be accommodated in tall containers, while ground-dwellers can easily live in suitable shallower and longer containers. Minimum dimensions (guidelines only) for 2 or 3 animals each follow (length x width x height, in cm):

Newts (e. g., *Triturus*): 40 x 30 x 20
Small treefrogs: 30 x 20 x 50
Swimming turtles (e. g., *Chrysemys*): 80 x 40 x 40

Emerald lizards (*Lacerta viridis*): 80 x 30 x 50
Wall lizards (*Podarcis*): 50 x 30 x 30
Small snakes (e. g., *Thamnophis*): 50 x 30 x 30
Boas (*Boa*): 120 x 80 x 100

Generally, relatively small containers will suffice for snakes, while lizards and especially turtles require more spacious facilities.

The technical equipment of a terrarium nearly always includes heating, illumination and ventilation. Automatic devices for spraying water are generally only used for larger facilities.

Territorial behavior: Types of behavior related to the possession or defense of a territory. The territory consists of a certain segment within the environment that is claimed by the territory's occupant and from which siblings or conspecifics are driven away. This is usually accomplished—accompanied by optical signals—through threat behavior, which can lead to ritualistic fights, and presupposes the ability of species recognition. The urgency to defend a territory decreases with increasing distance from the center of the territory, so that eventually flight behavior takes over and the territory's occupant withdraws to his territory.

The use and defense of territories (territoriality) is known, for instance, for Dendrobatidae, various species of turtles (Trionychidae), crocodiles, as well as from lizards (Gekkonidae, Iguanidae, Lacertidae, Teiidae, and Varanidae). If several specimens from these families are kept together it has to be remembered that due to the limited space available in a terrarium territorial aggression can easily lead to damaging fights. It is uncertain whether snakes establish territories.

Testudines: Turtles. Order of the Reptilia, often called Chelonia, distributed throughout all warm and most temperate zones. Two suborders, Cryptodira and Pleurodira, with about 75 living genera and 220 living species. Found in damp terrestrial habitats; dry, warm steppes and deserts; mountain streams; rivers and lakes; ponds and ditches; swamps; and brackish and marine habitats. The modern turtles first occurred during the Upper Cretaceous and have remained almost unchanged since then.

The turtles display a number of features that clearly separate them from the remainder of the reptiles. Characteristic is the bony carapace that is an inseparable component of the skeleton. Various carapace bone can easily be related to known skeletal elements (e. g., ribs, abdominal ribs, and parts of the shoulder girdle) of vertebrates, but others are additional bone formations. The head and neck, limbs, and tail can be more or less completely retracted into the carapace. The compact skull does not have temporal openings (anapsid type). This feature alone signifies the primitive state of the Testudines. However, in many groups the skull has become further characterized by secondary indentations. Only the leatherback and the other sea turtles among the Recent turtles have a closed skull, which has probably developed secondarily. Also notable are the quadrate being solidly fused with the other cranial bones and the absence of a nasal bone. The jaws in turtles do not carry any true teeth and instead have sometimes serrated horny shields (rhamphotheca) that may have rows of chew-

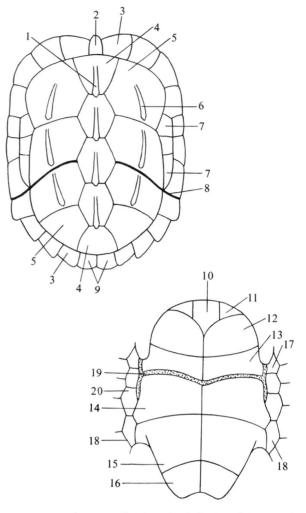

Plates or scutes of a generalized turtle shell, dorsal (carapace) and ventral (plastron). 1 Dorsal keel; 2 precentral or nuchal; 3 marginal; 4 central or vertebral; 5 lateral or costal; 4 + 5: central carapace field; 6 lateral keel; 7 supramarginal; 8 seam or hinge; 9 postcentral; 10 intergular; 11 gular; 12 humeral; 13 pectoral; 14 abdominal; 15 femoral; 16 anal; 17 inframarginal; 18 inguinal; 19 seam or hinge; 20 inframarginal

ing ridges, especially in herbivorous species.

The vertebral column has become largely fused with the carapace, and only the neck and tail regions are still freely movable.

The tail is relatively short and only rarely distinctly elongated (Chelydridae, Platysternidae). The number of caudal vertebrae ranges from 18 to 22. The tail can only be hidden when folded laterally under the carapace edge.

The shoulder girdle has become reduced in elements since it is involved in the carapace construction and both it and the pelvic girdle are inside the carapace, and thus they are inside the rib cage, a unique feature in living vertebrates.

The limbs are generally equipped with free, clawed toes that are often connected by webbing into fins. In tortoises and some other terrestrial species the toes have become fused into stumpy feet from which only the claws protrude. Strongly aquatic forms have paddle-like limbs with a reduced number of claws or no claws at all.

Of taxonomic significance and useful also as practical identification aids are the characteristic scale structures of the legs and tail; scales of the head are often hard to distinguish. Some turtles have spinous or wart-like scales on the thighs; the bases of these scales may even be ossified. Some turtles have dermal warts or barbels on the neck and chin and in extreme cases bizarre skin folds on the head (*Chelus*).

Respiration in turtles is peculiar because, due to the rigid carapace, normal respiratory rib movements are not possible. Therefore, certain muscles press the air out of the lungs and also assure refilling. This muscular action is supported by movements of the front limbs and the pumping action (lifting and lowering) of the hyoid (tongue) bone that can be seen in throat movements. Extraordinary also is the large amount of skin respiration in many aquatic forms, as well as gas exchange through the mucous membranes in the oral and cloacal cavities, most perfectly developed in the Trionychidae. In deep-diving turtles the lungs are located inside bony chambers as protection against water pressure.

Of the sensory organs, the eye is the most effective one in the Testudines. Form and color preception function well. The tear glands have taken over the function of a salt secreting organ in marine turtles. The well-developed sense of smell is of great importance for recognizing food and sibling species as well as sex partners. The hearing functions only in lower frequencies (100 to 700 Hz), and the seismic sense is better developed. Only a few species undergo a habitat change in the course of their life. Migrations to courtship and nesting sites or drinking and grazing areas display the well-developed sense of orientation in Testudines.

Many turtles have anal bladders in the form of intestinal appendages located in the vicinity of the cloaca. In tortoises they serve as water reservoirs (*Kinixys*), while in aquatic turtles these bladders are supplementary gas exchange organs or diving aids. Emptying the anal bladders is a common defense reaction when turtles are picked up.

The life of turtles progresses more or less rhythmically. Tortoises are mostly diurnal, while aquatic turtles are often crepuscular and nocturnal. Seasonal rhythms are found in tropical turtles (dry and rainy seasons) as well as in forms from temperate climates (winter dormancy).

Depending upon the species, turtles obtain ages generally from 50 to 150 years (these figures are mostly for tortoises—aquatic turtles probably live shorter lives). Sexual maturity occurs after 2 to 5 years in small species or 8 to 12 years in large species, growth proceeding rapidly up to that point but then slowing down considerably. Differences between juvenile and adult coloration are variably well-developed in turtles.

Turtles are herbivorous, carnivorous, or omnivorous. There are highly specialized mollusc-crackers and fish-catchers as well as succulent-feeders and grass-feeders. There are also many seasonal specialists among the plant-feeders. Some turtles also feed on carrion and on feces (for the intake of vitamins and protein). Many turtles also take in stones (lithophagy) that act as grinding aids for macerating the food or as roughage for the digestive process. Carnivorous species sometimes also take in indigestible plant matter as roughage material.

Dermal glands are absent in the Testudines, but there are potent musk glands in the cloacal region that serve to attract a sexual partner and/or as defensive mechanisms. The sex organ in males is a very large unpaired penis that can be extruded from the cloacal opening to extend along the body axis. External sex characteristics are often visible in the carapace shape: males may have a flatter carapace and a more or less strongly indented posterior plastral lobe, while females may have a highly arched carapace without an indentation on the plastron. The tail in males is often longer and equipped with a terminal spine; it is used to help insert the penis during mating. Further secondary sex characteristics can occur in the carapace scute arrangement, coloration and markings of carapace and soft parts, as well as eye color, and even in the development of extremely long claws in males. Also common is a distinct size and weight difference between the sexes in favor of the females. Some species, however, display hardly any external sexual characteristics and thus make sex determination difficult.

Copulation usually occurs after an extensive courtship. One of the best known behaviors in turtle courtship is ramming among tortoises. Through sperm storage the females can lay fertile eggs for up to 4 years without further matings. Reproduction is exclusively by means of eggs. Their numbers vary, depending upon the species, from 1 to more than 100. The eggs are relatively hard-shelled, spherical to elongated, and are buried by the female in loose soil or debris. Incubation takes from 2 to 3 months, in rare cases more than 1 year.

Keeping turtles is one of the most common branches of captive reptile maintenance and probably the oldest form of keeping reptiles. The diversity of these animals provides suitable representatives for all types of indoor and outdoor terrarium maintenance. Continuous breeding has so far been achieved from *Chelydra, Emys, Testudo, Chrysemys,* and a few others. Very difficult species, i. e., species that can not be kept for prolonged periods of time, include some of the sea turtles as well as some tortoises (*Psammobates, Homopus*) and a few freshwater turtles (*Malayemys, Notochelys*); with increasing knowledge about their ecology and biology the number of unkeepable species is declining. Due to their low fecundity and high degree of specialization, the turtles are the most endangered reptiles. Because of relentless hunting for food (sea and river turtles, giant tortoises) and tortoise shell (*Eretmochelys, Chelonia*) even once widely distributed species are now threatened with extinction or have indeed become extinct (such as the giant tortoises on various Indian Ocean islands). Populations of endemic species with small areas of distribution have become endangered through massive collecting efforts on behalf of the animal trade (*Asterochelys, Psammobates, Malacochersus, Testudo*). Therefore, many Testudines are now protected, and further measures cover the habitats of endangered species (egg laying sites), captive maintenance breeding programs (*Psammobates, Chelonoidis*), and other measures (Cheloniidae).

Testudinidae: Tortoises. Family of the Testudines, Cryptodira. Europe, Asia, Africa, and America, absent from

Australia. Genera: *Agrionemys, Asterochelys, Chelonoidis, Chersina, Geochelone, Gopherus, Homopus, Indotestudo, Kinixys, Malacochersus, Manouria, Megalochelys, Psammobates, Pseudotestudo, Pyxis,* and *Testudo.* Characteristics include a usually well-arched, massive carapace (flat in *Manouria, Malacochersus,* and a few others) and the always stump-footed legs without free fingers and toes but with claws. The carapace is mostly rigid, but in a few genera there is some flexibility in plastral flaps (*Pyxis*), the posterior carapace section (*Kinixys*), or the entire carapace (*Malacochersus*). Some Testudinidae have spur-like extended gular shields in males (used in tournament-like ramming bouts) or in both sexes (*Gopherus, Asterochelys, Chersina, Geochelone, Kinixys,* and others). Testudinidae is the best adapted family of the Testudines for a terrestrial life. The diet is mainly herbivorous, often with a supplementary animal tissue component.

These are the most seriously endangered Testudines because of their low fecundity, defenselessness, strong homing instinct, and popularity among terrarium hobbyists. Protection of all tortoises under various endangered species legislation restricts their use as terrarium animals and makes species maintenance breeding in terrariums that much more valuable.

Testudo LINNAEUS, 1758. European Tortoises. Genus of the Testudinidae. Southern Europe, northern Africa, and western Asia. 3 species in dry regions (steppes, dry forests). Formerly the name was used for nearly all tortoises, but now it is restricted to just a few species. Carapace length 35 cm. See also *Agrionemys* and *Pseudotestudo.*

Omnivorous with mainly herbivorous tendencies. Reproduction is by means of 8 to 15 eggs. Juveniles reach sexual maturity in 6 to 10 years. All species maintain some sort of winter dormancy period. Most are very good terrarium animals, although adult specimens are not always without problems. Species from northern latitudes or high altitudes are often well-suited for outdoor maintenance. *T. hermanni* is ideal for outdoor terrariums as it requires little heat. These tortoises can be overwintered outdoors if adequate frost protection is provided, otherwise allow cool overwintering in a basement. All species have been bred in captivity, some repeatedly. Incubation of eggs in an incubator at 22-28° C takes 60-90 days, in the wild 73-104 days. The proven longevity record in captivity is 115 years, and normal longevity in excess of 100 years is possible. Due to excessive hunting, populations over wide areas of southern Europe and North Africa are considerably reduced. Strictly protected in some Balkan countries such as

Testudo hermanni (top) compared to *Testudo graeca*

Testudo gracea

Testudo hermanni robertmertensi

Bulgaria.

• *T. gracea* LINNAEUS, 1758. Spur-thighed Mediterranean Tortoise, Iberian Tortoise. Southern Spain through North Africa to Asia Minor and the Balkan Peninsula. Supracaudal scute of the carapace undivided. Tail without a terminal spine, but spurs (groups of pointed scales) on thighs. Formerly but inappropriately called the Greek Tortoise (it does not occur in Greece).

• *T. hermanni* GMELIN, 1789. Greek Tortoise. Europe. 20 cm carapace length. Supracaudal scute divided. Tail with a terminal spine, spurs absent from upper thighs. Often sympatric with *T. graeca* in the Balkans.

• *T. marginata* SCHOEPFE, 1792. Margined Tortoise. Greece south of Mount Olympus, Sardinia. 35 cm carapace length, the largest species of the genus. Posterior margin of carapace characteristically wide and slightly bent upward (reverted). Melanistic forms not uncommon.

Testudo marginata

Tetradactylus MERREM, 1820. Whip Lizards. Genus of the Cordylidae, subfamily Gerrhosaurinae. Southern Africa. 6 species in dry grassy and brushy steppes. 20 to more than 30 cm. Body elongated, the tail long. Limbs reduced, the anterior ones in some species completely absent. Locomotion is exclusively through sinuous movements. In contrast to *Chamaesaura*, the scales are not conspicuously keeled. Lateral fold complete.

Diurnal ground-dwellers that prey on a variety of arthropods. Egg-layers. For details on care refer to *Chamaesaura*.

• *T. seps* (L., 1758). Five-toed Whip Lizard. Southern Africa. 20 cm. All limbs with 5 toes.

• *T. tetradactylus* (DAUDIN, 1802). Long-tailed Whip Lizard. South Africa. 28 cm. Limbs with 4 toes.

• *T. africanus* (GRAY, 1838). African Whip Lizard. South Africa. 30 cm. Anterior limbs tiny or completely absent. Hind limbs with 1 toe.

Tetralepis BOETTGER, 1892. Monotypic genus of the Col-

ubridae, placed either in Lycodontinae or Natricinae. Java. About 50 cm. Dark red-brown with a distinct dark middorsal stripe. Belly blue-gray or reddish gray with two brown spots on each ventral scale that form longitudinal lines.

Ecology and biology unknown. Apparently ground snakes in tropical rain forests at 1200 m elevation.

• *T. fruhstorferi* BOETTGER, 1892.

Tetrapoda: Monophyletic taxon that includes at least all originally 4-footed terrestrial vertebrates. The development of limbs represented substantial progress in evolution, allowing the invasion of the up to then unexploited land, while water was still essential for reproduction.

Tetraprion STEJNEGER and TEST, 1891. Monotypic genus of the Hylidae. Pacific coastal region from southern Colombia to northern Peru. Sometimes considered to be a synonym of *Trachycephalus* by some systematists. A large casque-headed treefrog distinguished from all other genera of the Hylidae on the basis of dentition. Fingers barely webbed; toes webbed for more than half of their length. Mode of life hardly known.

• *T. jordani* STEJNEGER and TEST, 1891. To 7.5 cm.

Thalassochelys: see *Caretta*, genus.

Thalassophis SCHMIDT, 1852. Ruddertails. Genus of the Hydrophiidae, Hydrophiinae. 2 species found from the Persian Gulf to southern China. They appear to prefer mangrove swamps. Hardly 1 m. Compact, stout, the blunt-snouted head not set off from the body. Body scales are placed side by side in a mosaic-like pattern, each with a spiny keel, giving a rough-skinned appearance. Back with dark crossbands or a spotted pattern against a blue-gray background.

• *T. viperinus* SCHMIDT, 1852. Viperine Ruddertail. From the Persian Gulf to Taiwan.

Thamnodynastes WAGLER, 1830. Genus of the Colubri-

Thamnodynastes strigatus

dae, Boiginae. Caribbean coastal region of South America southward to Argentina. About 5 species found in outer regions of lowland or secondary forests; only *T. strigilis* occurs in dry habitats (savannah to thornbush steppes); frequently following human habitation so found on plantations and in settlements. To 80 cm. Head well set off from body. Large eyes with vertically elliptical pupils. Dorsal scales in *T. strigatus and T. pallidus* smooth; keeled in other species, especially in *T. strigilis*. Brown with rows of spots or longitudinal stripes.

All species are semiarboreal to terrestrial snakes that feed mainly on lizards and small mammals.

• *T. strigatus* (GUENTHER, 1858). Southeastern Brasil, Paraguay, and northeastern Argentina.

• *T. strigilis* (THUNBERG, 1787). Northern South America.

• *T. pallidus* (LINNAEUS, 1758). Amazon Basin, especially along its northern perimeter.

Thamnophis FITZINGER, 1843. Garter Snakes, Ribbon Snakes. Genus of the Colubridae, Natricinae. North and Central America. About 22 species, some polytypic. Found in virtually all habitats, even close to human habitation and in city parks. 30 cm to 130 cm. Head more or less weakly set off from body. Dorsal scales shingled, keeled. Marked with a pattern of light longitudinal stripes (usually 1-3 stripes), usually yellow on black or greenish, often also with spots and crossbars.

Live-bearers. In terms of ecology and captive care *Thamnophis* conforms to the Natricinae, Group 1, partially Group 2. Several species have been bred over several gen-

Thamnophis elegans elegans

Thamnophis marcianus

Thamnophis cyrtopsis

Thamnophis proximus

erations. Due to their small size, bright coloration, hardiness, and the fact that these snakes will readily breed, they are very popular terrarium animals. The diet includes earthworms, fish, strips of raw beef, pink mice, and sometimes crickets.

▪ *T. sirtalis* (LINNAEUS, 1766). Common Garter Snake. Southern half of Canada over most of the USA except the southwestern deserts, barely entering Mexico. Exceedingly variable. 130 cm. The northernmost species of this genus.

Thamnophis sirtalis, albino

Thamnophis elegans vagrans

Thamnophis sirtalis concinnus

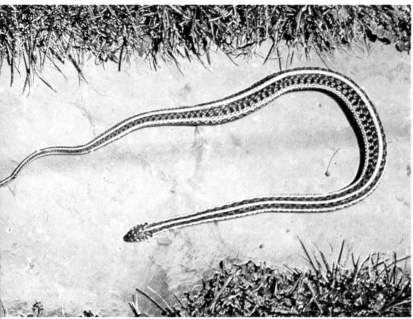

Thamnophis radix haydeni

Thamnophis sirtalis tetrataenia

• *T. marcianus* (BAIRD and GIRARD, 1853). Checkered Garter Snake. Southwestern USA to northern Costa Rica. 100 cm.

• *T. proximus* (SAY, 1823). Western Ribbon Snake. Central USA to Costa Rica. 120 cm.

• *T. elegans* (BAIRD and GIRARD, 1853). Western Terrestrial Garter Snake. Western North America into Mexico. 100 cm.

• *T. couchi* (KENNICOTT, 1859). Western Aquatic Garter Snake. Oregon and California coastal area and interior mountain ranges. 140 cm.

• *T. sauritus* (LINNAEUS, 1766). Eastern Ribbon Snake. United States and adjacent Canada east of the Mississippi River. 100 cm.

Thamnophis butleri, albino

Thamnophis sirtalis infernalis

Thamnophis sirtalis sirtalis

Thecadactylus GOLDFUSS, 1820. Monotypic genus of the Gekkonidae, subfamily Gekkoninae. Northern South America, Central America, Lesser Antilles. In tropical forests. To 20 cm. Dorso-ventrally flattened. Tail barely snout-vent length. Limbs relatively short and strong, with well-developed adhesive pads with a median longitudinal furrow. Pupil vertical. Scales fine. Brown to gray-brown with small whitish and black spots. Distinct light and dark color changes.

Nocturnal tree-dwellers that can occasionally be seen sunning themselves. Two eggs are laid, apparently at wide intervals.
• *T. rapicauda* (HOUTTUYN, 1782).

Thecodont: see Teeth.

Theloderma TSCHUDI, 1838. Insufficiently delineated genus of the Rhacophoridae, very close to *Philautus*. Tropical southern Asia (North Vietnam and Burma to Sumatra). 7 species in tropical rain forests and cloud forests. Treefrog-like in shape with numerous small and large, conical, ivory-colored warts. Tympanum very distinct. Large adhesive discs on fingers and toes. Fingers free or webbed at base only, the toes more or less completely webbed. Males without vocal sac or with an internal vocal sac.

Tree-dwellers that produce a few (often only 4 to 8) unpigmented eggs and deposit them (similar to *Rhacophorus*) in a foam nest above water accumulations in hollow trees. The spawn has to reach water (through the aid of rain) within a few days in order to be able to develop further. The larvae are free-swimming, with a strongly flattened dorsal region and protruding eyes. Care and breeding as for tree-dwelling *Rhacophorus*.
• *T. asperrima* (AHL, 1927). Burma, Thailand, Malaya (1100 to 1200 m). 3.5 cm. Blackish.
• *T. horrida* (BOULENGER, 1903). Thailand, Malaya, Mentawei Islands. 4 cm. Dark brown with a blackish pattern.
• *T. leporosa* MUELLER, 1838. Malaya and Sumatra (800 to 1400 m). 6.5 cm. Dark brown, ventral side of adhesive discs, fingers, and toes light red.

Thelotornis A. SMITH, 1849. Bird Snakes. Monotypic genus of the Colubridae, Boiginae. Central to South Africa. 1 polytypic species. Savannahs and gallery forests. To 1.3 m. Very slender, with a long, narrow head and large eyes, the pupil forming a resting figure "8". At eye level are very large opisthoglyphic fangs. The body is slightly later-

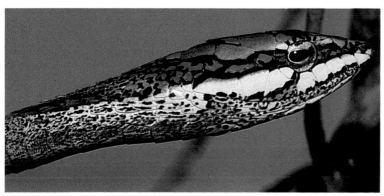

Thelotornis kirtlandi

ally compressed and has conspicuously narrowed scales along the sides that are only slightly keeled. Light gray to gray-green with a washed-out pattern of light crossbands and spots with dark edges.

Typical tree snakes that prey on lizards (mainly geckos and chameleons) but will also on occasion take snakes and frogs. Despite the colloquial name bird snakes, birds appear to be rarely—if ever—taken. Egg-layers, 6-10 large eggs. Excited specimens inflate their neck enormously (as in *Dispholidus*).

The venom of this snake is extremely potent and has caused human fatalities. In contrast to *Dispholidus*, an antivenin is not available. Maintenance as for *Dispholidus*.
• *T. kirtlandi* (HALLOWELL, 1844). 3 subspecies. *T. k. capensis* A. SMITH, 1849, is considered by some systematists to be a separate species.

Thermoregulation: Many poikilothermic amphibians and reptiles are capable of maintaining their body temperature more or less constant within a narrow range during periods of activity. The primary method is innate behavior where each species actively selects sites that conform to its genetically fixed preferred temperature. Amphibians generally prefer cooler locations, but reptiles demand higher temperatures (an exception is the tuatara, *Sphenodon punctatus*, with an activity temperature of only about 10° C.). Desert-dwelling reptiles, for instance, protect themselves against overheating and keep their body temperature within optimal limits by changing their position from basking in the sun to damp cool underground burrows. Basking with the body flattened is a characteristic behavior of many reptiles in temperate zones. Activity-induced changes of body colors can influence heat absorption.

To a lesser degree physiological thermoregulation is also possible through the circulatory system. Since blood takes over the task of heat distribution in the body, changes of heart beat frequency affecting blood circulation and thus the uptake or loss of heat can so be used to minimally affect thermoregulation.

Thorius COPE, 1869. Genus of the Plethodontidae, related to *Bolitoglossa* and *Parvimolge*. Southern Highlands of Mexico. 9 species. Mostly to 4 cm, rarely to 7 cm.
• *T. troglodytes* TAYLOR, 1941. Veracruz. To 6 cm. Dorsum light brown, flanks dark brown.
• *T. pennatulus* COPE, 1869. Veracruz. To 4 cm. Dorsum blue-black, belly dark gray with yellow spots.

Thoropa COPE, 1865. Genus of the Leptodactylidae. Southeastern Brasil. 3 species. Related to *Eupsophus*, *Batrachyla*, and *Hylorina*. In mountain ranges. Pupil horizontal. Tympanum visible. Fingers free, with skin folds; toes with enlarged tips.

These frogs deposit their few large eggs in fast-flowing, rocky creeks and streams. The larvae are exceptionally slender.
• *T. lutzi* COCHRAN, 1938.
• *T. miliaris* (SPIX, 1824).
• *T. petropolitanus* (WANDOLLECK, 1907).

Thrasops HALLOWELL, 1857. Black Tree Snakes. Genus of the Colubridae, Colubrinae. Tropical Africa. 3 or 4 species in tropical forests; in montain rain forests of East Af-

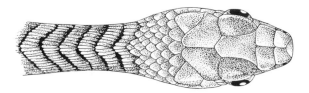

Thrasops jacksoni

Threat behavior: The coral snake *Micrurus frontalis* displaying the colorful underside of the tail

Thrasops jacksoni

Threat behavior: Collar display of the frilled lizard, *Chlamydosaurus kingi*

rica *T. jacksoni* occurs to 2,800 m elevation. 1.5 to 2.3 m. Distinctly set off head with large eyes. Body slightly laterally compressed. Keeled dorsal scales clearly enlarged along middle of the back, while the scales along the flanks are narrow and shingled, similar to *Dispholidus* and *Boiga* (*Thrasops* is sometimes mistaken for both). Ventral scales very large and wide. With the exception of *T. aethiopissa* (which is green), all adult specimens are shiny black.

Diurnal and crepuscular tree snakes that prey on vertebrates ranging from frogs and lizards to tree-dwelling small mammals and birds and their eggs. Egg-layers, 12-17 eggs. When excited *Thrasops* will flatten the neck region similar to cobras (*Naja*).

These large tree snakes should be kept in large, well-heated forest terrariums with ample climbing facilities, hiding places, and a water section for bathing.

• *T. jacksoni* GUENTHER, 1895. East Africa, Congo Basin.
• *T. aethiopissa* (GUENTHER, 1862). East and Central Africa. Considered to be a species of the monotypic genus *Rhamnophis* GUENTHER, 1862, by some systematists. A specialized frog-eater (treefrogs and toads). Green.
• *T. flavigularis* (HALLOWELL, 1852). Nigeria to Zaire.

Threat behavior: Behavior with aggressive motivation that includes intraspecific and interspecific fighting over food, sexual rivalry, repelling aggressors, and fights when specific individual distances and/or territorial borders are being violated. It is an innate behavior, species-specific, and always contains components of aggression and flight behavior. Often preceded by warning behavior, which warns an enemy or rival. Warning behavior is also de-

Threat behavior: Stiffening and display of the bright belly by the newt *Taricha torosa*

scribed as an aposematic behavior, where one distinguishes true (aposematic) warnings in defensive animals and nongenuine (pseudoaposematic) warnings in defenseless animals. However, these terms are not uniformly used. Mertens in 1946 divided aposematic behavior into threats always directed toward other species (antaposematic behavior) and threats against siblings (proaposematic behavior). Threat and warning behaviors usually consist of behavior expressions with optical and acoustic signals. Apart from that there are also chemical (glandular secretions) and mechanical (touching) processes employed in threat behavior.

Among the amphibians only the frogs have a substantial inventory of threat postures. Threat behavior in many species is expressed by inflating the body, raising the legs and simultaneously arching the back, accompanied by hissing and other sounds and biting. Newts may also curl over to display the bright belly colors.

Threat behavior: Spreading of the hood showing the bright ocelli in the spectacled cobra, *Naja naja naja*

Threat behavior: Arching of back into the rocker position by the common Eurasian toad, *Bufo bufo*

In reptiles threat behavior is very diverse, although in snakes and turtles this usually is only antaposematic behavior directed against other species. In lizards, especially, threat postures are often of ritualistic nature, often a com-

ponent of courtship behavior and as threat displays. Some of the typical types of behavior employed for threatening and warning by many lizards and snakes include inflating the throat or the entire body, the dorso-lateral and lateral widening of the neck, flattening of the body, raising of often conspicuously colored body appendages, display of consicuous body parts, opening of the mouth to show colored linings, swaying or swinging body motions, head nodding, various sounds (especially through skin structures such as rattling in rattlesnakes and scraping of lateral scales in *Echis* and *Dasypeltis*), discharge of foul-smelling glandular secretions, squirting blood from the eye (genus *Phrynosoma*), and pushing with the head.

Thyroid disease: Goiter. Usually iodine-related under-secretion of hormones with simultaneous thyroid gland enlargement. Goiter formation in reptiles leads to a knotty growth in the throat passage in the region of the neck and lower jaw. In turtles and snakes enlargements of the thyroid gland are not visible externally nor can they be felt due to the thyroid gland's location at the base of the heart. Thyroid diseases very often lack clinical symptoms. Prolonged conditions may lead to food refusal, lethargy, and loss of muscle tissue replaced with mucous connective tissue (myxoedema). Hypothyreosis can be expected in iodine-deficient regions ("endemic goiter"), in conjunction with extremely hard tap water, and also when feeding excessive amounts of certain vegetables (green cabbage, various other cabbages, soybean shoots, and others).

Therapy and prophylaxis: 0.2% potassium iodine solution, 1 ml/liter added to the bathing and drinking water.

Other thyroid diseases are pathogen-based strumitis and thyreoditis, tumors, and hard deposits visible only histologically.

Tiliqua GRAY, 1825. Blue-tongued Skinks. Genus of the Scincidae, subfamily Tiliquinae. Australia, Tasmania, New Guinea, and some Indonesian islands (1 species). 10 species in semideserts, brush steppes, and open forests. From 15 to 50 cm. Heavily built, cylindrical or flattened dorso-ventrally. Head large and deep, conical. The characteristic deep-blue tongue contrasts against the red oral cavity; *T. gerrardi* has a pink tongue. The limbs are well-developed and relatively short. Scales smooth.

Diurnal ground-dwellers that feed primarily on plant matter and some invertebrates. Ovoviviparous.

Blue-tongued skinks should be kept in a spacious, dry terrarium with slightly damp hiding places under rocks, roots, and similar items. Provide day temperatures of 28 to 32° C., locally under a radiant heat source up to 40° C. At night there should be a substantial temperature reduction to 18 to 20° C. A large water bowl must be available, since many specimens like to bathe. Apart from plant material they will also take arthropods, snails, and small pieces of meat. They should be given regular ultraviolet radiation and calcium and vitamin supplements. During the summer temporary outdoor maintenance is possible for adult animals in partially roofed enclosures providing rain protection.

• *T. gerrardi* (GRAY, 1845). Pink-tongued Skink, Snail-eating Skink. Eastern Australia. To 40 cm. Damper forest habitats that the other species of this genus. Gray-brown

Tiliqua scincoides

Tiliqua nigrolutea

with dark crossbands. Climbs occasionally. Prefers to feed on snails. Up to 30 young.

▪ *T. occipitalis* (PETERS, 1863). Western Blue-tongued Skink. Southwestern and central Australia. Dry habitats. 50 cm. Compact and with a short tail. Reddish brown with light crossbands.

▪ *T. nigrolutea* (GRAY, 1845). Blotched Blue-tongued Skink, Black and Yellow Blue-tongued Skink. Southern Australia and Tasmania. To 50 cm. Compact. Brown-black with a yellowish, irregularly spotted and striped pattern. Mostly 8 young.

▪ *T. scincoides* (SHAW, 1790). Common Blue-tongued Skink, Eastern Blue-tongued Skink. Semidesert to brush steppes, sometimes in agricultural areas. New Guinea and northern and eastern Australia. To 50 cm. Variable. 6 to 20 young.

Tillandsia L. Spanish Moss, Ball Moss. Genus of the Bromeliaceae. Southern states of the USA to Chile. About 500 species. Mostly on trees or rocks, in desert regions also found as rootless ground plants. The particular ecological requirements of these plants have to be taken into consideration when they are used for terrarium purposes. Epiphytes with green leaves, without scales, and with root formation (e. g., *T. anceps, T. brachycaulos, T. cyanea, T. lindeniana*) can also be cultured in pots. On the other hand, epiphytes that are densely covered with gray scales and are mostly without roots (e. g., *T. bulbosa, T. ionantha, T. usneoides*) can only be cultured on rought tree trunks or directly on epiphyte logs that are then suspended in the terrarium in a bright location.

▪ *T. anceps* LODD. Leaves about 20 cm, in delicate rosettes.
▪ *T. aeranthos* L. B. SMITH. Leaves rigid, with silver-gray scales.
▪ *T. brachycaulos* SCHLECHTEND. Rosette about 15 cm diameter.
▪ *T. bulbosa* HOOK. Grows downward from the base, at-

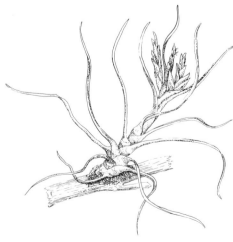

Tillandsia bulbosa

Tillandsia stricta

tached by a few clasping roots.
- *T. butzii* MEZ. Leaves to 30 cm. With a turnip-like water storage stem.
- *T. cyanea* LIND ex. K. KOCH. Leaves very narrow, with grooves.
- *T. ionantha* PLANCH. Small, stemless species ideal for very small terrariums.
- *T. lindenii* REGEL. With grass-like leaves, 20-30 cm, robust.
- *T. punctulata* CHAM. and SCHLECHTEND. Leaves about 20 cm.
- *T. stricta* SOLAND and SIMS. Rosettes about 20 cm tall. Leaves about 15 cm.
- *T. usneoides* (L.) L. Spanish Moss. Rootless aerial epiphyte resembling a beard lichen in appearance. Can be draped over an epiphyte stem without attachment. Requires frequent spraying with soft water.

Tillandsia cyanea (flowering) and *Tillandsia usneoides* (lower left)

Tofohr, Otto (?–1935): German animal dealer and terrarium hobbyist, owner of one of the best-known animal wholesales in Hamburg. Introduced substrate heating for terrariums, the so-called Tofohr-oven using petroleum lamps and later electric incandescent bulbs disguised as rocks or logs. Author of various articles and brochures in the popular series *Bibliothek fuer Aquarien- und Terrarienkunde* (1913).

Toluca KENNICOTT, 1859. Genus of the Colubridae, Boiginae. Southern Mexican Highlands. 3 species. About 50 cm. Ground snakes. Biology hardly known.
- *T. lineata* KENNICOTT, 1859.

Tomistoma MUELLER, 1846. False Gavials. Monotypic genus of the Crocodylidae. Tropical Indo-China and Sunda Archipelago in swampy freshwater habitats. The long, narrow snout reminiscent of *Gavialis* indicates it is a food specialist feeding on fish. To more than 5 m. In contrast to related genera (*Crocodylus, Osteolaemus*), the upper jaw has 20-21 teeth on each side, 19-20 teeth in the lower jaw. Head without or with only slight ornamentation and no ridges. Nuchal and dorsal bucklers not separated from each other. Occipital bucklers very small, located dorso-laterally and arranged in 2 irregular cross rows. As in *Crocodylus*, scale combs are present on limbs. Webbing only between toes of the hind limbs. Iris brownish.

Maintenance as for other Crocodylia. There is a tendency toward snout deformation in small terrariums because of calcium, vitamin, and ultraviolet radiation deficiencies. The diet consists of exclusively live fish.
- *T. schlegeli* (MUELLER, 1838). False Gavial, Sunda Crocodile. Malayan Peninsula, Sumatra, and Kalimantan. Dorsum olive-brown with a dark pattern.

Tomistoma schlegeli

Tomodactylus GUENTHER, 1901. Genus of the Leptodactylidae. Mexico. About 10 species. Closely related to *Eleutherodactylus* and *Syrrhophus*. In mountain ranges. 2-3 cm. Tympanum visible. Fingers and toes free. Tips more or less distinctly enlarged into adhesive discs. A large unpaired vocal sac.

No free-swimming larval stage. Terrestrial.
- *T. nitidus* (PETERS, 1869). Polytypic species.

Tomodon DUMERIL and BIBRON, 1853. Genus of the Colubridae, Boiginae. From the Mato Grosso, Brasil, to central Argentina. 2 species in dry tropical forest regions (savannah, outer secondary forests) as well as in *pampas*. 50-75 cm. Head distinctly set off. Upper jaw with 6 small anterior teeth followed by a pair of extremely large opisthoglyphic fangs. The body is covered by smooth scales. Dorsally brown with rows of dark spots.

Nocturnal ground snakes. Biology little known. They presumably feed primarily on lizards and should be kept in a well-heated dry terrarium with nighttime temperature

Tomodon ocellatus

reductions. Caution: Venomous bites possible.
▪ *T. dorsatus* DUMERIL, DUMERIL, and BIBRON, 1854. From central Brasil to Argentina.
▪ *T. ocellatus* DUMERIL, DUMERIL, and BIBRON, 1854. Southern Brasil, Paraguay, Uruguay, and Argentina.

Tomodon dorsatus

Tomopterna GUENTHER, 1858. Taxon of doubtful status within the Ranidae. Depending upon viewpoint either an independent genus or a subgenus or synonym of *Rana* or *Pyxicephalus*. Here considered a synonym of *Pyxicephalus*.

Tongue-flicking: Extending of the tongue in many lizards and snakes; in snakes it can occur with a closed mouth through a gap in the oral cleft. Monitors (family Varanidae) and most snakes flick their tongues quite often, actively moving it up and down. During tongue-flicking aromatic

Tongue-flicking by the garter snake *Thamnophis sirtalis*

substances are picked up by the moist upper side of the tongue and transported to the Jacobson's Organ for examination. The intensity of tongue-flicking is dependent upon activity and level of excitement. In addition, there is also a threatening type of tongue-flicking in various lizards (e. g., blue-tongue skinks, *Tiliqua*) and snakes (e. g., rattlesnakes, *Crotalus*).

Toxicalamus BOULENGER, 1896. Genus of the Elapidae. New Guinea and adjacent islands. About 9 species, some formerly considered as *Apistocalamus* and *Ultrocalamus*. Found in tropical forests, especially in mountain ranges. 35 cm to 100 cm. The short, rounded head is not set off from the body and has very small eyes. Body rounded. Tail conspicuously short, terminating in a more or less pointed, sometimes keeled, scale. Usually unicolored darkish, rarely interrupted by a light neckband (*T. stanleyanus*) or a light longitudinal stripe (*T. longissimus*).
   Nocturnal venomous snakes adapted to relatively low temperatures that are subject to only minor variations. Food and reproductive biology unknown. Maintenance similar to *Micrurus*.
▪ *T. longissimus* BOULENGER, 1896. New Guinea, Fergusson and Woodlark Islands.
▪ *T. grandis* BOULENGER, 1914. New Guinea. Lowlands. Nearly 1 m.

Tracheloptychus PETERS, 1854. Keeled Cordylids. Genus of the Cordylidae, subfamily Gerrhosaurinae. Madagascar. 2 species along river banks in tropical forests. Appearance similar to Lacertidae. About 20 cm. Lateral fold restricted to a short section of the neck. Dorsal scales strongly keeled and shingled. Ear opening closable with large movable scales.
   Little is known about their mode of life. Egg-layers.
▪ *T. madagascariensis* PETERS, 1854.

Trachischium GUENTHER, 1858. Genus of the Colubridae, Lycodontinae. Asia south of the Himalayan Mountains. 5 species in mountain forests from 100 to 2300 m elevation. 25 to 75 cm. Head barely set off from the body, which is covered by only 13-15 rows of smooth, shingled scales. In males of several species the scales along the sides of the posterior half of the body and on the tail are distinctly keeled; in females they are smooth or only have minimal keels. More or less dark brown with an iridescent effect.

Nocturnal ground snakes that hide during the day under rocks and logs. The main diet is worms and arthropods. Egg-layers, 3-6 eggs. Maintain like terrestrial Natricinae, Group 1.
▪ *T. monticola* (CANTOR, 1839). Assam, Bengal. Mountain regions. Common. 25 cm. A black longitudinal stripe on the back.
▪ *T. guentheri* BOULENGER, 1890. Sikkim and Bengal, particularly common in the Darjeeling Region. More than 40 cm.

Trachyboa PETERS, 1860. Rough Boas. Genus of the Boidae, subfamily Boinae (Tropidophiinae according to many systematists). Northwestern South America and Panama. 2 species in montane rain forests. 40 cm. Rough-scaled head and body. Related to *Tropidophis*.

Nocturnal or crepuscular ground snakes found close to water. Rarely kept in captivity. They should be kept in slightly heated habitat-correct planted terrariums. Bathing facilities must also be included. They feed almost exclusively on frogs in captivity.
▪ *T. gularis* PETERS, 1860. Ecuador.
▪ *T. boulengeri* PERACCA, 1910. Panama to Ecuador.

Trachycephalus TSCHUDI, 1838. Casque-headed Treefrogs. Genus of the Hylidae. Brasil. 2 species. Snout short. Tympanum distinctly visible. Fingers and toes flattened, with large adhesive discs. Fingers webbed at base only, the toes webbed for more than half of their length.

Nocturnal, arboreal. They have strong homing instincts and will always return to the same bromeliad funnel as a sleeping site. They feed on other arboreal frogs, nestling birds, and large insects. Spawning occurs in shallow standing water.
▪ *T. nigromaculatus* TSCHUDI, 1838. Eastern Brasil. Widely distributed and common in certain areas. To 10 cm. Olive with dark, black-edged spots, ventrally yellow-orange.

Trachydactylus HAAS and BATTERSBY, 1959. Monotypic genus of the Gekkonidae. Southwestern Arabia. Known only from the type locality.
▪ *T. jolensis* HAAS and BATTERSBY, 1959.

Trachydosaurus: see *Trachysaurus*, genus.

Trachymantis METHUEN, 1919. Genus of the Rhacophoridae. Madagascar. 3 species. Snout-vent length a few cm. Skin with warts. Head large, wide. Pupil horizontal. Fingers and toes free, the adhesive discs small. Presumed to be terrestrial.
▪ *T. horrida* (BOETTGER, 1880). Marojezi Mountains. 2 cm. Gray-black with 3 dark crossbands.

Trachyphrynus: see *Eleutherodactylus*, genus.

Trachysaurus GRAY, 1845. Shingle-back Skinks. Monotypic genus of the Scincidae. Southern Australia in dry habitats with sparse plant growth. Closely related to *Tiliqua* and sometimes included in that genus. 35 cm. Very heavily built, moderately flattened dorso-ventrally. Head large, triangular, distinctly set off from neck. Tail extremely short, thick. Limbs short but strong. Scales strongly enlarged, keeled, protruding, and not overlap-

Trachysaurus rugosus

ping. Dorsally brown with light spots or crossbands, ventrally lighter.

Diurnal ground-dwellers. Viviparous, the 2 embryos developing without egg shells and supplied from a placenta-like tissue. For details on maintenance refer to *Tiliqua*, but requires more animal food. Hardy.
▪ *T. rugosus* GRAY, 1845.

Tradescantia L. Tradescantias. Genus of the Commelinaceae. Tropical and subtropical America. More than 50 species. Erect or low-lying herbs or low shrubs with rooting shoot axis. Hardy, easy to culture from cuttings.
▪ *T. albiflora* KTH. and BRUECKN. White-flowering Tradescantia. Shoot axis low-lying to erect. Leaves green, about 4 cm. Takes temperatures between 5 and 25° C., sunny or shaded; requires sufficient water. Equally usable as a hanging or creeping plant.
▪ *T. blossfeldiana* MILDBR. To 20 cm high, growing erect.
▪ *T. fluminensis* VELL. and BRUECKN. Shoots and undersides of leaves reddish.
▪ *T. navicularis* ORTGIES. A succulent runner and carpet shrub. Takes temperatures between 10 and 20° C. Requires a bright and sunny location.

Tradescantia zebrina

Transport: Shipping or movement of the specimen should always be completed as quickly as possible. Nearly all amphibians and reptiles (except very small animals) easily sur-

vive 1 or 2 weeks without food, and large reptiles can endure even longer periods. Amphibians must always be kept
damp (not wet); reptiles are occasionally dampened or are
given water to drink. The animals should not be exposed
to the sun while being transported. With the exception of
rain-forest animals, the ideal transport temperature should
be about 15° C.; longer transport periods should be preceded by having the animals empty their bowels while
bathing in warm water.

Reptiles are generally transported in strong cotton bags
twice as long as wide. Turtles and tortoises are best packed
in solid boxes or, for short periods, their limbs are taped
against the carapace as firmly as possible (this is not possible for some groups, such as soft-shells). Geckos and anoles can easily be transported in plastic containers padded
with some damp foam rubber and having a perforated lid.
Chameleons and tree snakes require thin branches as hold-
fasts. As few animals as possible should be placed together
in the same container (this lessens any risk of injury). If
the animals have to be maintained under improvised conditions for a longer period of time (e. g., during a collecting
trip), the use of suspended gauze containers is especially
recommended for lizards. Amphibians are also generally
transported in plastic perforated containers. A damp substrate (moss, peat moss) is placed inside the container.
When transporting amphibians it has to be remembered
that many species give off poisonous skin secretions that
under confined conditions can be lethal for others. Here
too it is better to use several small containers rather than a
large one that holds several different species.

Upon arrival all animals must undergo quarantine and
then be gradually acclimated to their new surroundings.

Trematoda: Flukes. Parasitic worms that attach themselves to a host internally or externally by means of suction
discs and hook assemblies and are protected against digestive fluids by a thick cuticle. Trematodes occur inside the
urinary bladder, digestive tract, and other organs in amphibians and reptiles (especially in aquatic turtles). They
damage the host primarily by means of using food substances and also cause mechanical damage; especially the
blood parasites can cause blockages inside large blood vessels, particularly the mesenterial veins that can lead to a

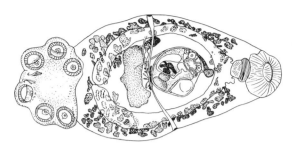

Trematoda (Monogenea) *(Polystomoidella oblonga)*

collapse of the system. Depending upon which organ is affected, there can occur—apart from a general weakening of
the body—pneumonia, kidney diseases (gout), anemia, and
others. In amphibians trematode larvae often cause inflammatory skin diseases in the form of tiny nodules and
pustules.

The life cycle of the digenetic trematodes includes several larval stages and at least one, usually two, intermediate hosts, so that the possibility of an infection in captivity
is small.

Therapy: 30-50 mg/kg body weight Chloroquinum orally
or intramuscular, twice.

Small flukes from the intestine of a snake

Trematoda: *Macrodera longicollis*

Tretanorhinus DUMERIL and BIBRON, 1854. Genus of the Colubridae, Xenodontinae. Disjunct distribution: Cuba, Isle of Pines, and Grand Cayman, as well as in southern Mexico southward to Colombia and Ecuador. 4 species.

Amphibious to aquatic water snakes that feed primarily on fish and frogs. For details on care refer to Natricinae, Groups 2-3.

▪ *T. variabilis* DUMERIL and BIBRON, 1854. Cuba, Cayman Islands, Isle of Pines.

▪ *T. nigroluteus* COPE, 1861. From Mexico to Panama and Costa Rica.

▪ *T. taeniatus* BOULENGER, 1903. Pacific lowlands of Colombia and Ecuador.

Tretanorhinus nigroluteus

Tretioscincus COPE, 1862 (= *Calliscincopus* RUTHVEN, 1916). Genus of the Teiidae. Northern South America. 2 species in tropical forests, in part following human habitation. About 15 cm. Cylindrical. Lower eyelid with a transparent window, the pupil with conspicuous indentations above and below. Tail about 1 ½ times snout-vent length. Limbs short but strong, inner toe rudimentary and clawless. All body scales of about equal size, semiround, smooth, shiny, strongly overlapping. Very colorful.

Ground-dwellers, but also in lower tree level. Diet: arthropods.

▪ *T. agilis* (RUTHVEN, 1916). Skink Tegu. Guyana, Surinam, northern Brasil. Easily to 15 cm. Red-brown with light longitudinal stripes that are yellow ocher anteriorly then greenish and blue on the tail; tip of tail blue. Belly blue-green.

Tribolonotus DUMERIL and BIBRON, 1839. Casque-headed Skinks. Genus of the Scincidae, subfamily Lygosominae. New Guinea, Solomon Islands, New Caledonia. 7 species found in shaded, damp mountain valleys close to water. To 20 cm. Head helmet-like, enlarged. Nuchal scales with spines. Body scales few, large, strongly keeled,

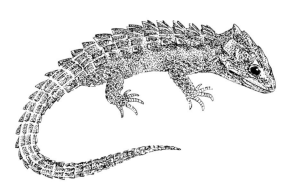

Tribolonotus novaeguineae

often spiny. The only known lizard with glands under the abdominal scales, as well as on surfaces of hands and undersides of feet. In females the left ovary and oviduct are regressed. Dark brown.

Crepuscular to nocturnal slow-moving ground-dwellers. The diet consists mainly of arthropods. *T. schmidti* is ovoviviparous but all other species are egg-layers. They should be kept in a damp terrarium at 25° C., at night about 20° C.

▪ *T. novaeguineae* (SCHLEGEL, 1834). Bush Crocodile. New Guinea.

Trichobatrachus BOULENGER, 1900. Hairy Frogs. Monotypic genus of the Ranidae. Tropical West Africa in rain forests. Body robust. Pupil vertical. The feet have sharp, pointed claws that are extendable. Males during the breeding season have peculiar shaggy, dense, hair-like skin growths on the flanks and thighs and also have serrated nuptial pads in 3 sections on the thumbs. Soft vocalization. Larvae to 9 cm, agile swimmers with large suction mouth.

Outside the breeding season these frogs lead a rather cryptic terrestrial life. During the breeding season (July to September) they move into creeks and streams where amplexus takes place and spawning occurs. The larvae are tied to flowing water habitats and presumably feed on microscopic plants and animals on rocks. Newly collected *Trichobatrachus* specimens initially act rather wildly but can be kept without difficulty in a spacious terrarium with a water section. The diet should be based on large earthworms and small frogs.

▪ *T. robustus* BOULENGER, 1900. Hairy Frog. Equatorial Guinea, Cameroons, and eastern Nigeria. Males to more than 13 cm, females smaller. Blackish, without distinct markings.

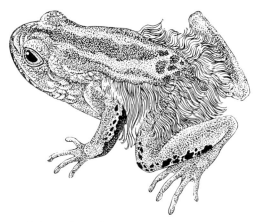

Trichobatrachus robustus

Trigonodactylus HAAS, 1957. Monotypic genus of the Gekkonidae. Arabia. Known only from the type locality.
▪ *T. arabicus* HAAS, 1957.

Trimeresurus LACEPEDE, 1804. Asian Lance-headed Vipers, Bamboo Vipers. Genus of the Crotalidae. According to some systematists, the species *chasemi*, *convictus*, *monticola*, *okinavensis*, and *tonkinensis* are considered to be part of the independent genus *Ovophis* BURGER, 1971, and *wagleri* belongs to the monotypic genus *Tropidolaemus* WAGLER, 1830. Southern Asia. About 32 species, some polytypic. Virtually inseparable from the American genus *Bothrops*. 70 cm to 1.6 m. Virtually all species have a triangular, markedly set off head with the upper side covered with small scales (except *T. macrolepis*).

Trimeresurus flavoviridis

Trimeresurus elegans

Trimeresurus purpureomaculatus

Trimeresurus mucrosquamatus

Trimeresurus gramineus

Trimeresurus stejnegeri

Trimeresurus (Ovophis) okinavensis

Trimeresurus tokarensis

On ecological and morphological grounds the species can be arranged into 2 groups (greatly simplified):

1) Ground-dwellers: Small mountain species from montane rain forests or dry forests, such as *T. malabaricus*, *monticola*, and *strigatus;* large species that occur in the outer zones of rain forests and monsoon forests, such as *T. macrolepis*, *mucrosquamatus*, *flavoviridis;* sometimes in semi-desert rocky areas, such as *T. purpureomaculatus.* Markings and coloration are mainly shades of brown with darker elements, rarely green.

2) Tree- and brush-dwellers: Found at various levels in rain forests, mountain rain forests, bamboo forests, and mangrove forests (*T. wagleri*). Most of the species in this genus belong here. Either they are more or less unicolored green (collective term "bamboo vipers"), e. g., *T. albolabris, flavomaculatus, gramineus, popeorum, sumatranus;* or they have camouflage markings and coloration with a large green component (e. g., *T. cantori, jerdoni, trigonocephalus, wagleri*). Arboreal species have more or less well-developed prehensile tails.

The diet consists mainly of frogs, lizards, small mammals, and birds. Females are often substantially larger than males, especially in the larger species. They are live-bearers, except *T. kaulbacki, mucrosquamatus,* and *monticola;* 6-35 young. It is reported that *T. monticola* and *T. kaulbacki* guard their egg clutches.

Potent venom is found in *T. mucrosquamatus* and *T. purpureomaculatus.* Fatal bites are known from *T. flavoviridis.* However, many species are not very aggressive (especially the arboreal species). *T. wagleri* is kept as a holy animal in Buddhist snake temples and is handled there without apparent caution. Yet the danger from the bite of these snakes must never be underestimated. Certain species are distinctly aggressive (e. g., *T. purpureomaculatus*).

Trimeresurus trigonocephalus

Trimeresurus wagleri

Maintenance should agree with the ecology in the wild. Group 2 in particular contains species that are popular and hardy terrarium animals that have been bred repeatedly. On the other hand, *T. wagleri* is a difficult species—adult specimens often stubbornly refuse to feed and may have to be force-fed. Group 1 contains tropical species with nonspecialized ecological requirements (such as *T. purpureomaculatus*) that are the easiest to keep. Montane species have

very high humidity requirements but must also be given a basking site with radiant heat.

▪ *T. albolabris* GRAY, 1842. White-lipped Tree Viper. Northern India and Nepal to southern China and Indo-China. Green. Group 2.

▪ *T. flavoviridis* (HALLOWELL, 1860). Okinawa Habu. Okinawa and Amami Islands. Pattern variable, rhomboids, spots, or longitudinal stripes in shades of brown and olive predominating. To 1.5 m. Group 1.

▪ *T. gramineus* (SHAW, 1802). Indian Green Tree Viper, Common Bamboo Viper. Pakistan, India, Indo-China. Group 2.

▪ *T. monticola* (GUENTHER, 1864). Chinese Mountain Viper. Nepal to southeastern China, southward to Malaya. Group 1.

▪ *T. macrolepis* BEDDOME, 1862. Southern India. Due to the large scales on top of the head and other morphological peculiarities, this species is sometimes referred to the monotypic genus *Peltopelor* GUENTHER, 1864. Mountains. Semiarboreal. In between Groups 1 and 2.

▪ *T. popeorum* SMITH, 1937. Pope's Tree Viper. Eastern Himalayas and Indo-China as well as Sumatra and Kalimantan. Green. Group 2.

▪ *T. purpureomaculatus* (GRAY, 1832). Mangrove Viper. Bengal and Indo-China and on many adjacent islands. To 1.6 m. Group 1.

▪ *T. stejnegeri* SCHMIDT, 1925. Chinese Green Tree Viper. Nepal to southern China, Taiwan, and Hainan. Green. Group 2. Hardy and has been bred repeatedly.

▪ *T. trigonocephalus* (SONNINI and LATREILLE, 1801). Sri Lanka. Apart from *T. wagleri,* the most colorful species of the genus, green with rhomboid markings. Group 2.

▪ *T. wagleri* (BOIE, 1827). Wagler's Palm Viper. Thailand and the Indo-Australian Archipelago, the Philippines.

Dark green to black with yellow and whitish rhomboid markings. Very attractive. Group 2.

Trimetopon COPE, 1885. Genus of the Colubridae, Natricinae. Southern Mexico to Guatemala and Panama. 10 doubtful species found in tropical rain forests. 30-40 cm.

Ground snakes. Biology largely unknown.

- *T. gracile* (GUENTHER, 1872). Costa Rica.
- *T. pliolepis* COPE, 1894. Costa Rica.

Trimorphodon COPE, 1861. Lyre Snakes. Genus of the Colubridae, Boiginae. Southwestern USA (California) to Costa Rica. 11 nominal species in pine forests, rocky areas, deserts, mountain regions to 3,500 m elevation; exceedingly variable, probably only 2 or 3 valid species. To 1 m. With markedly set off head that carries on its upper side a "V" pointing forward. The large eyes have vertical pupils. Usually marked with irregular rhomboids in shades of brown on pale brown.

Nocturnal ground snakes, good climbers. Egg-layers. The diet includes lizards and small mammals. They should be kept in a well-heated dry terrarium with ample hiding places and climbing facilities.

- *T. lambda* COPE, 1886. California to Mexico.
- *T. biscutatus* (DUMERIL and BIBRON, 1854). Mexico to Guatemala and Costa Rica.

Trionychidae: Soft shell Turtles. Family of the Cryptodira. Asia, Africa (except Madagascar), and North America. The subfamily Cyclanorbinae (hinged soft-shell turtles) contains *Cyclanorbis, Cycloderma*, and *Lissemys*. The sub-family Trionychinae (true soft-shell turtles) contains *Chitra, Pelochelys*, and *Trionyx*. Found mainly in freshwater, but some entering periodically in brackish water or even sea water (*Pelochelys*). Carapace length to 1 m. Soft-shells are characterized by the proboscis-like projecting nostrils and the leathery, scaleless carapace and plastron often of an elongated, oval shape; callosities (rough, thickened areas) may be present on the plastron. The marginal bones of the carapace are absent, and the carapace and plastron are connected only by straps. The upper surfaces of the plastral bones are deeply sculptured, an important distinguishing feature in Trionychidae. The skull is conspicuously elongated. The horny cutting edges of the jaws are covered by thick lips, and the anterior limbs have only 3 free claws.

Except when depositing their eggs, these turtles are strongly tied to the water, and a few species even enter brackish or sea water. A few species like to sunbathe, and some venture onto land at night. An estivation period is known for some species (e. g., of *Lissemys*) and is spent buried on land. Prolonged submerged periods are supported by well-developed respiratory action of the mucous membranes in the oral cavity and cloaca. Mainly carnivorous, with varying degrees of specialization. There are mollusc-eaters as well as those that feed on fish (*Chitra, Cycloderma*). Plant matter plays an insignificant part in the diet.

Maintenance requires a spacious aquarium with a soft substrate; heating and power filtration are prerequisites. These turtles are aggressive and are best kept individually, except for mating. Some species have been bred in captiv-

Trimorphodon lambda

ity and sometimes on a continuous basis in research laboratories as test animals. The delicate shells are very subject to fungal infections.

Trionyx GEOFFROY, 1809. Common Soft-shell Turtles. Genus of the Trionychidae. Africa, large areas of Asia, North America. 15 species found in various types of water, from large rivers and lakes to ponds and ditches. The oval leathery carapace reaches 90 cm. The head frequently is very pointed, terminating in a long rostrum. Plastron without skin flaps.

Purely carnivorous turtles, many species distinctly aggressive. They should be maintained in a well-filtered aquarium with a fine sand substrate. The aquarium heater and thermometer must be protected against bites from the animals. These soft-shells should be kept individually; multiple specimens must be closely monitored to prevent aggression. Some species have been bred. For egg deposition a land section or sand pit must be suspended above the water level inside the aquarium. Many species are only suitable for zoological parks because of their space requirements.

Trionyx ferox

Trionyx subplanus

Trionyx cartilagineus

Trionyx gangeticus, juvenile

Trionyx triunguis

- *T. cartilagineus* (BODDAERT, 1770). Cartilaginous Soft-shell Turtle. Indo-China, Sunda Archipelago. To 70 cm. Carapace with warts, unicolored brown.
- *T. euphraticus* (DAUDIN, 1802). Euphrates Soft-shell Turtle. Eastern Turkey to Iraq, Syria, and Israel. To 40 cm. Dark with numerous small light-colored spots on carapace.
- *T. gangeticus* CUVIER, 1825. Ganges Soft-shell Turtle. Northern India. To 70 cm. Juveniles have 4 or more eyespots on the carapace.
- *T. hurum* GRAY, 1831. Peacock Soft-shell Turtle. Eastern India. To 60 cm. Juveniles with 4 distinct eyespots on the carapace.
- *T. muticus* LE SEUR, 1827. Smooth Soft-shell Turtle. Central and southern USA. 2 subspecies. Incubation takes 59 to 102 days at 30 or 25° C., respectively. 35 cm.
- *T. sinensis* WIEGMANN, 1835. Chinese Soft-shell Turtle. USSR (Amur Region) and China, Korea, eastern Indo-China to Vietnam, Hainan, Taiwan, and Japan; introduced into Hawaii. To 25 cm. Suitable for outdoor maintenance during summer months. Incubation in the wild takes 28 to 83 days.
- *T. spiniferus* LE SEUR, 1827. Spiny Soft-shell Turtle. Southern Canada through eastern ⅔ of USA to northern Mexico. To 50 cm. Well-suited for outdoor maintenance during the summer months. Incubation takes 53 to 96 days at 31° C. or 25° C., respectively.
- *T. subplanus* GEOFFROY, 1809. Malayan Soft-shell Turtle. Indo-China, Sunda Archipelago, and Philippines. To 25 cm. Smallest species of this genus. Carapace distinctly elongated, the sides almost parallel. Conspicuously large head. It has been bred repeatedly. Often considered to be a species of the monotypic genus *Doguniu* GRAY, 1844.
- *T. triunguis* (FORSKAL, 1775). Nile Soft-shell Turtle. Africa, except in extreme northwest and south; also in Israel and southwestern Anatolia. To 90 cm. Carapace dark with small light-colored dots.

Tripanurgos FITZINGER, 1843. Monotypic genus of the Colubridae, Boiginae. Disjunct distribution in tropical America from Panama to the upper Amazon Region, Trinidad, and the coastal region of eastern Brazil (Rio de Janeiro). Tropical rain forests. About 75 cm. Very slender,

Trionyx hurum

Trionyx spiniferus asper

Trionyx muticus calvatus

Trionyx sinensis

with a large head distinctly set off from the long, thin neck. Long tail. The minimally compressed body has a middorsal row of enlarged scales. The head is dark brown, set off from the light brown body by a wide yellow collar. Body with dark brown spots grouped into crossbands.

Nocturnal tree snakes whose main diet is lizards and frogs. Keep in a rain-forest terrarium. Beware of possible venomous bites.
- *T. compressus* (DAUDIN, 1803).

Triprion COPE, 1865 (=*Diaglena* COPE, 1887). Casque-headed Treefrogs. Genus of the Hylidae. Mexico, Guatemala. 2 species closely related to *Smilisca* and *Pternohyla*. Found in grassland of the plains, with tree and brush stands. Head very characteristic, the snout beak-like, flat and extended; upper side of head with raised occipital edges, raised bony ridges and a concave, saddle-like appearance. Fingers free, the toes webbed for about half of their length. First finger and toe opposable to remaining digits. Gray or brown, with a dark pattern.

Nocturnal frogs that live in the protection of plants or in hollow trees and similar places during the long dry season. The activity phase is confined to the rainy season (June to September/October), when they are found in the proximity of ponds that also serve as spawning sites.
- *T. petasatus* (COPE, 1865). Mexico (Yucatan) to Guatemala. 7.5 cm (female), 6 cm (male). Compact snout, steep forehead. Paired vocal sacs.
- *T. spatulatus* GUENTHER, 1882. Mexico. To 10 cm (female), 8 cm (male). Snout flat and long. Unpaired vocal sac.

Trirhinopholis: see *Plagiopholis*, genus.

Triturus RAFINESQUE, 1815 (=*Triton* LAURENTI, 1768; *Molge* MERREM, 1820). European Newts. Genus of the Salamandridae. Western Palearctic southward to about Israel,

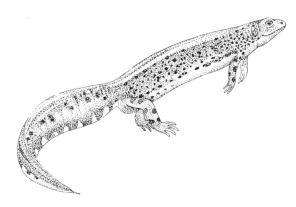

Triturus montandoni, ♂

eastward to the river system of the Ob and to the southeastern Caspian Sea region. 9 mostly polytypic species (with about 35 subspecies). 5 to 16 cm. In the terrestrial phase the tail is more or less cylindrical; during aquatic courtship both sexes (especially males) develop a high, laterally compressed paddle-like tail. Breeding aquatic males have a more or less well-developed dorsal crest and greatly heightened colors. Parotoid gland not visible externally. Larvae of still-water type, the dorsal crest starting at the neck.

According to external characteristics and more important internal characters, *Triturus* species can be categorized as follows:
- *Vulgaris* Group (with *T. boscai, T. helveticus, T. italicus, T. montandoni, T. vulgaris*): Small, tail often more or less terminating in a thread. Dorsal crest more or less developed, at most wavy but not comb-like, not constricted above base of tail.
- *Alpestris* Group (only *T. alpestris*): Medium size. Dorsal crest low. Tendency toward totally aquatic mode of life (comparable to *Euproctus*).

Triprion spatulatus

Triturus marmoratus

▪ *Cristatus* Group (with *T. cristatus*, *T. marmoratus*, and *T. vittatus*): Large. Dorsal crest comb-like, constricted above base of tail. Males during breeding season more or less strongly aggressive toward each other.

Occasional hybridization occurs naturally within these groups. Thus "*T. blasii* DE L'ISLE, 1862" is the hybrid between *T. cristatus* and *T. marmoratus*.

Triturus alpestris

Triturus helveticus

Triturus cristatus

Triturus cristatus

Following the winter dormancy period *Triturus* will seek out standing water in an open, usually sunny location and mate there. Mating behavior is similar in all species: the courting male examines the cloacal region of other newts to recognize species and sex. When the male has found a female of the same species, he positions himself obliquely to the female and fans toward her aromatic substances with powerful beats of his tail. This, as well as the sight of the species-specific tail coloration of the male and his peculiar shuffling gait, stimulates the female. She follows the male and after some brief mouth-tail pushing picks up the spermatophore dropped by the male with strong jerking move-

ments. Egg-laying can extend over months. During this period the female attaches a total of several hundred eggs individually on small water plant leaves and bends the leaf into a protective cover around the sticky egg with her hind legs. Depending on species and temperature, the larvae hatch in 2 to 3 weeks and metamorphose that same summer. After the breeding season the animals generally return to land and will even drown if prevented from doing so. Certain exceptions occur in *T. alpestris* and *T. vittatus*, which frequently stay in water during the entire plant growing period and more rarely are completely aquatic. Neoteny occurs occasionally, especially in *T. alpestris*.

During spring *Triturus* is best kept in an aquarium or aqua-terrarium with a spacious water section. The remainder of the time the animals can be kept in a damp terrarium with hiding places. High temperatures must be avoided (thus the terrariums cannot be placed at a window with southern exposure and, in fact, windows are not suited for *Triturus* containers). Winter dormancy is passed in semimoist moss containers. Some *T. alpestris* and *T. vittatus* can be carefully adapted to permanently living in water (kept very low during the summer).

Successful breeding requires strict compliance with hygenic measures (*Triturus* larvae are often particularly susceptible to skin diseases), optimal feeding, and cool overwintering. An alternative is to in spring obtain males in breeding condition or females that are already fertilized. Unfortunately, however, the most attractive species (*Cristatus* Group) are often rather sensitive toward habitat changes and commonly will react by losing their breeding stimulus and appearance within hours after capture.

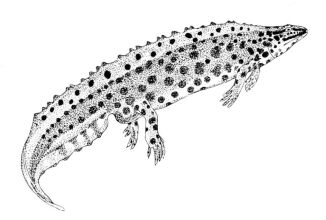

Triturus vulgaris, ♂

- *T. alpestris* (LAURENTI, 1768). Alpine Newt. Central, western, and southeastern Europe. 9 subspecies. Particularly in mountain regions. 10-12 cm. Bluish black, the abdomen bright orange, laterally light blue sharply delineated and with dark dots.
Dorsal crest with yellow and black oblique bands.
- *T. boscai* (LATASTE, 1879). Western Iberian Peninsula. 7-10 cm. Light gray-brown, abdomen orange, laterally white. Dark dots present especially along the flanks.
- *T. cristatus* (LAURENTI, 1768). Northern Crested Newt. Most of Europe (except the southwest and north), also in northern Anatolia and the Caucasus region. 4 subspecies. 16 cm (rarely larger). Gray-black above, orange below. Round black spots on sides, with white dots during mating.
- *T. helveticus* (RAZOUMOWSKY, 1789). Palmate Newt. Great Britain and western Europe. 2 subspecies. 9 cm. Yellowish to gray-brown, abdomen yellow, whitish along flanks, with a dark dotted pattern.
- *T. italicus* (PERACCA, 1898). Italian Newt. Central and southern Italy. 5 to 7.5 cm. Gray-brown, ventrally light yellow, the throat orange. With a variable pattern of dark

dots.
- *T. marmoratus* (LATREILLE, 1800). Marbled Newt. Southwestern France and Iberian Peninsula. 2 subspecies. 14 cm (rarely larger). Green and black marbled pattern above, abdomen gray and white marbled; a thin yellow dorsal line.
- *T. montandoni* (BOULENGER, 1880). Carpathian Newt. Carpathia. 8 to 10 cm. Coloration similar to *T. helveticus,* but lower edge of tail bright yellow.
- *T. vittatus* (GRAY, 1835). Banded Newt. Western Caucasus and Anatolia to Israel. 5 subspecies. Usually at elevations from 1000 to 1600 m. 15 cm (rarely larger). Yellow-brown with a dense pattern of black dots. Lower flanks with silvery white to yellow, dark-edged longitudinal band. Abdomen yellow to orange. The most colorful subspecies, with superb crest development, is *T. v. ophryticus* (BERTHOLD, 1846).
- *T. vulgaris* (LINNAEUS, 1758). Smooth Newt, Common Newt. Western Eurasia northward to central Sweden. 10 subspecies. 8 to 11 cm. Yellow-gray to gray-brown, ventrally orange, the sides cream-colored. Dark circular spots. Largest dorsal crest within the *Vulgaris* Group.

Trivial name: Popular (colloquial) name, which in contrast to the scientific name is not obligatory and therefore neither specific nor has international uniformity.

Trogonophidae: Family of the Amphisbaenia. Old World. 4 genera, 6 species. Relatively primitive. Found in more or less dry areas. To 20 cm. Relatively compact, the head short, with a rounded-off snout. The tail is pointed, bent downward, and is oval to nearly triangular in cross-section. At least partially ovoviviparous. Genera: *Agamodon, Diplometopon, Pachycalamus,* and *Trogonophis.*

Trogonophis KAUP, 1830. Checkerboard Snake Lizards. Monotypic genus of the Amphisbaenia, family Trogonophidae. Northwestern Africa in various habitats from open steppes to rocky slopes and forests. Easily 20 cm. Bright whitish yellow with dark brown to black spots.

Triturus vulgaris, female

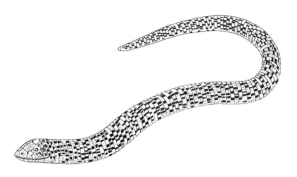

Trogonophis wiegmanni

Found more often at the surface than other snake lizards, where they also catch some of their food. They have even been observed basking, the head and posterior part of body hidden in the ground. Ovoviviparous, 2-5 young born mostly in September. The terrarium must contain some flat rocks. Food in the wild is mostly ants and termites, but neither is essential. A winter dormancy period of 4 to 6 weeks at about 10° C. is recommended.
- *T. wiegmanni* KAUP, 1830. Checkerboard Snake Lizard. Morocco to Tunesia. 22 cm.

Tropidechis GUENTHER, 1863. Rough-scaled Snakes. Monotypic genus of the Elapidae. Eastern Australia in forests. 75 cm. Strongly built, with a cobra-like head. Dorsal scales strongly keeled. Dirty brown with washed-out, partially broken dark crossbands. Very old specimens are usually unicolored.

Diurnal and nocturnal terrestrial venomous snakes that prefer the proximity of water and feed on frogs, reptiles, and small mammals. Very aggressive when disturbed, highly venomous, and potentially deadly to humans.

Maintain in a well-heated dry terrarium with bathing facilities. A hiding box should be in the terrarium.
- *T. carinata* (KREFFT, 1863). Coastal areas of Queensland and New South Wales.

Tropidoclonion COPE, 1860. Lined Snakes. Monotypic genus of the Colubridae, Natricinae. South Dakota to Texas. Closely related to *Thamnophis*, with similar longitudinal stripes and with keeled dorsal scales. Belly with 2 central rows of black half-moon-shaped spots.

Mode of life and care as for *Thamnophis*.
- *T. lineatum* (HALLOWELL, 1856). 53 cm.

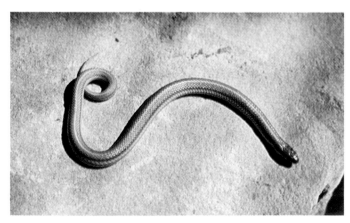

Tropidoclonion lineatum

Tropidodactylus BOULENGER, 1885. Monotypic genus of the Iguanidae. Northern Venezuela. Easily to 20 cm. Slender. In appearance and mode of life reminiscent of *Anolis*, but without adhesive lamellae on toes. Tree-dwellers.
- *T. onca* (O'SHAUGHNESSY, 1875).

Tropidodipsas GUENTHER, 1858. Genus of the Colubridae, Lycodontinae. Tropical Central America, Mexico to Guatemala. 10 species in forest regions of the lowlands. 30 to 65 cm. Slender, head distinctly set off from body. Large eyes with vertical pupils. Body round or minimally compressed laterally. Dorsal scales smooth or slightly keeled. Most species have dark spots or crossbands on a light background.

Nocturnal, terrestrial or semiarboreal. Biology unknown.
- *T. fasciata* GUENTHER, 1858. Mexico to Guatemala. 3 subspecies.
- *T. philippi* (JAN, 1863). Mexico.
- *T. sartorii* COPE, 1863. Mexico to Guatemala. 3 subspecies.

Tropidonotus: see *Natrix*, genus.

Tropidophis BIBRON, 1843. Wood Snakes, Dwarf Boas. Genus of the Boidae, subfamily Boinae (Tropidophiinae according to many). Antilles and northern South America. About 15 species. To 1 m. Scales in few rows. Head scales and general appearance as in colubrid snakes. Browns and grays.

Ground-dwellers that are often seen climbing but usually hide under rocks, tree stumps, in epiphyte roots, and similar places. They prefer some dampness in their hiding

Tropidophis haetianus

Tropidophis greenwayi

Tropidophis semicinctus

Tropidophis melanurus

places as well as the proximity of water. These snakes prey preferably on frogs and toads, less frequently on lizards and small mammals. Live-bearers.

Keep in a moderately tropical terrarium with sufficiently deep substrate (moss, wood shavings, peat moss, and similar items). Hiding places must be damp, and climbing facilities must be present. Some species (*T. melanurus, T. canus*) have been bred repeatedly. Hardy terrarium animals. Endangered or threatened, only rarely available.

- *T. canus* (COPE, 1868). Bahamas.
- *T. caymanensis* BATTERSBY, 1838. Cayman Islands.
- *T. haetianus* (COPE, 1879). Cuba, Jamaica, and Haiti.
- *T. maculatus* (BIBRON, 1843). Western Cuba, Isle of Pines.
- *T. melanurus* (SCHLEGEL, 1837). Cuba, Isle of Pines, Navassa Island.
- *T. pardalis* (GUNDLACH, 1840). Cuba, Isle of Pines.
- *T. taczanowskyi* (STEINDACHNER, 1880). Peru, Ecuador, Amazon Region.

Tropidophorus DUMERIL and BIBRON, 1839. Keeled Skinks. Genus of the Scincidae, subfamily Lygosominae. Southern China to northern Australia. About 20 species in tropical forests close to water. 15-30 cm. Lids movable. Ear openings large. Conspicuously keeled scales. Well developed limbs. Mostly darkish.

Primarily crepuscular. When in danger they will invariably flee into water, where some of their prey (crustaceans) is hunted. Other dietary items include arthropods and earthworms. At least partially ovoviviparous (6-9 young).

Maintain in a slightly heated, moist terrarium with a larger water bowl.
- *T. brookei* (GRAY, 1845). Southeast Asia.

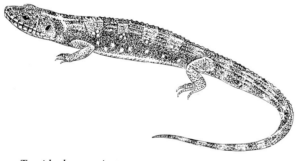

Tropidophorus scincus

Tropidosaura FITZINGER, 1826. Genus of the Lacertidae. Southern Africa (Cape Province and Lesotho). 5 species found in open grassy or rocky steppes, partially in mountain regions. Body not flattened, snout blunt, limbs short, tail to twice snout-vent length. Dorsal scales large, strongly keeled, and shingled like roof tiles. Collar completely absent. Femoral pores present. Dorsally mostly brown with a dark vertebral stripe and light lateral stripes.

Diurnal ground-dwellers. Feed on various arthropods. Egg-layers. Maintenance similar to European species of the genus *Lacerta*, but without a winter dormancy period.
- *T. montana* (GRAY, 1831). Cape Province. Mountain regions between 1000 and 2000 m elevation. To 18 cm. Care as for *Lacerta vivipara*.

Tropidurus WIED, 1824. Lava Lizards. Genus of the Iguanidae. Galapagos Islands (8 species) and tropical South America. About 20 species in dry, sunny, very rough habitats. 35 cm. Appearance similar to *Sceloporus*, but far less spiny and without femoral pores. Anterior margin of the large ear opening covered by a strongly serrated scale margin. Dorsal scales small, at least toward the flanks arranged into regular transverse rows. Caudal scales relatively large, slightly spiny. Mainly shades of brown with variable markings, belly light. Males with dark markings, especially on throat and on upper thighs.

Tropidurus sp., Galapagos, female

Tropidurus sp., Galapagos, male

Tropidurus torquatus

Tropidurus semitaeniatus

Lava lizards prefer elevated basking and observation sites, where they remain for hours head-down and bent forward. The diet consists mainly of arthropods, young lizards, and occasionally plant matter. Males very quarrelsome, with ritualistic fighting and strong tail lashing, at least among Galapagos species. As far as known they are egg-layers; in *T. torquatus* from Venezuela the young hatch after two days. For maintenance see *Sceloporus*, but without pronounced seasonal variation.

- *T. grayi* (BELL, 1843). Galapagos Islands. Barely to 20 cm.
- *T. occipitalis* PETERS, 1871. Peru and Ecuador from the coast to western Andean slopes. Brushland. 20 cm. Tail about twice snout-vent length.
- *T. peruvianus* (LESSON, 1826). Ecuador to northern Chile, west of the Andes. Sandy and rocky semideserts. Easily to 35 cm.
- *T. torquatus* (WIED, 1820). Amazon Basin. Forest clearings close to settlements, not directly in shaded forests. About 25 cm. Often found sunning themselves on lower sections of tree trunks.

Tropiocolotes PETERS, 1880. Genus of the Gekkonidae. Northern Africa to southwestern Asia. 4 species in dry, mostly sandy, habitats. To 10 cm. Slender. Tail easily snout-vent length. Toes cylindrical, without enlarged adhesive lamellae. Pupil vertical. Dorsal scales large and overlapping. Mainly light brown with dark spots.

Nocturnal ground-dwellers that occasionally climb. Keep at day temperatures of about 30° C., at night 20° C.

Tropiocolotes sp.

- *T. steudneri* (PETERS, 1869). Algeria to outer southwestern Asia. 9 cm. Ventral scales smooth.
- *T. tripolitanus* PETERS, 1880. North Africa. About 10 cm. Ventral scales strongly keeled.

Tschudi, Johann Jakob von (1818-1889): Swiss physician, diplomat, cultural and natural scientist of universal character. *Monographie der schweizerischen Eidechsen* (1837), *Clasification der Batrachier* (1838), *Fauna Peruana* (1846) (an evaluation of his South America excursions).

Tuberculosis: Infectious bacterial disease that is not transmissible from cold-blooded to warm-blooded animals. Tuberculosis in poikilothermic animals is relatively rare, but it does cause severe pathological changes, mainly in the lungs, in those animals that are affected. In aquatic species this may lead to pneumonia, diarrhea, formation of nodules (granulomas) under the skin, and general metabolic disturbances. Reptiles are greatly adversely affected by tuberculosis, and those that are suspected to have the disease in an advanced stage should be destroyed.

Tubificidae: Tubifex Worms. Family of the Annelida, class Oligochaeta. Mainly inhabitants of mud. The best known genus is *Tubifex*. These reddish, 8 cm, slender worms often occur in masses along the bottom in polluted water. Widely used by aquarists as fish food and also quite suitable for many amphibians and their larvae.

Tubifex worms, Tubificidae

Tumors: Tissue growth due to uncontrollable, irreversible reproduction of cells from a starting tissue. May be harmless (benign) or cancerous (malignant). Malignant tumors, such as black melanosarcoma, plate epithelial carcinoma especially on the head, osteochondromas of bone and cartilaginous tissue, and thyroid carcinoma, are rare. Surgical

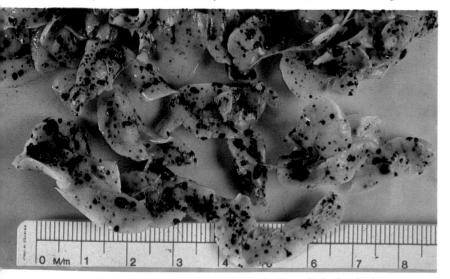

Tumors: Melanosarcoma in fat bodies of *Elaphe obsoleta*

removal can be attempted, and in all cases the removed tissue should be histologically examined. While a prognosis is usually good for benign tumors of the skin and subcutis, it is generally recommended that animals with proven malignant tumors be destroyed.

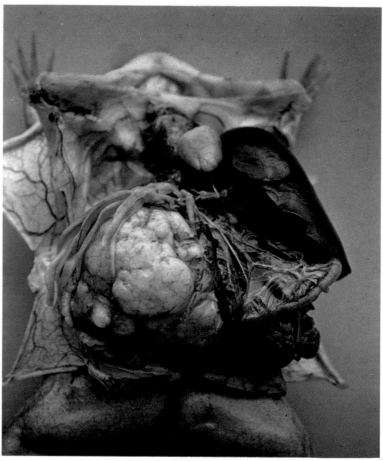

Tumors: Renal carcinoma in *Xenopus*

Tundra: Forest-free zone in regions close to the pole, caused by the prevailing climate, whereby the perma-frost thaws out only at the surface during the brief polar summer and so only permits the growth of mosses and dwarf heather shrubs. There are no true tundra inhabitants among the amphibians and reptiles.

Tupinambis DAUDIN, 1803. Tegus. Genus of the Teiidae. South America east of the Andes, southward to northern Argentina. 2 species in forests, somewhat following human habitation. To 140 cm. Strongly built. Head pointed. Tongue retractile into a basal sheath. Tail twice snout-vent length. Dorsal scales small, granular; ventral scales distinctly larger, but in comparison to many other genera in this family still small, in 22 to 27 longitudinal rows.

Ground-dwellers (mainly in forest clearings) that dig their own burrows. They are also agile climbers and swimmers. Small vertebrates and large arthropods are eaten; they also like to feed on eggs and occasionally on sweet fruit and other plant parts, especially blossoms. Egg-layers, clutches of 4-8 eggs deposited in termite mounds, then cemented in by the termites. Upon hatching the young will break open the termite mound.

Due to their size, tegus require spacious terrariums. The substrate should consist of sand, which must always be

Tupinambis teguixin

Tupinambis teguixin (top) and *Varanus exanthematicus*

somewhat damp. If the digging behavior of large specimens can not be catered to, there must at least be adequate hiding places under rocks, tree stumps, and similar items. They must be given drinking and bathing facilities. The terrarium should also contain a few strong branches for climbing. Day temperatures of 25 to 30° C., up to 40° C. under basking lights, are best, reduced at night by about 5 to 10° C. (but never below 20° C.). The diet in captivity can include young mice, frogs, fish, arthropods, heart, and lean beef. Occasionally eggs (broken) and some fruit should also be given. Regular ultraviolet radiation is essential. Food must be offered in moderation, since these animals have a tendency toward obesity. They should only be kept together with lizards of equal size. Somewhat difficult to keep, but once established they can obtain longevities in excess of 10 years.

• *T. rufescens* (GUENTHER, 1871). Red or Golden Tegu. Northern Argentina. To 1.2 m. Reddish brown with indistinct wide dark crossbands.

• *T. teguixin* (LINNAEUS, 1758). Common or Black Tegu, Banded Tegu. Eastern and central South America. To 1.4 m. Black with 9-10 groups of whitish yellow spots arranged in crossbands. Has a strong tendency to follow human habitation. Also included here recently is *T. t. nigropunctatus* SPIX, 1825, the Northern Tegu or Jacuaru, from northern South America to central Brasil; to 1.2 m; black with numerous yellow spots and bluish dots along the lower sides.

Tylototriton ANDERSON, 1871. Crocodile Newts. Genus of the Salamandridae. Eastern Palearctic (China, northern Southeast Asia, Japan). 6 species in damp forests in mountain regions to 3,000 m elevation. During the Miocene the genus also was found in central Europe. Closely related to *Pleurodeles* and *Salamandra*. Compact, strongly built. Skin rough, appearing to be armored due to conspicuous warts and bony ridges (thus the colloquial name). Head large, triangular when viewed from above. Tail in cross-section roundish or laterally compressed. Legs strong. The species are hard to distinguish on the basis of coloration alone.

Cryptic ground-dwellers spending the often extended reproductive period in stagnant water, there spawning relatively large eggs (6 to 10 mm). Activity phases are confined to the monsoon season; the rest of the year is spent in dry dormancy periods.

Due to their apathetic behavior, these animals are only recommended for specialists. They should be kept in a damp container with ample hiding and bathing facilities in a cool location. For breeding purposes transfer them in the spring to an aqua-terrarium with low water level.

• *T. andersoni* BOULENGER, 1892. Ryukyu Islands. To 16 cm.

• *T. asperrimus* UNTERSTEIN, 1930. Southern China. 13 cm.

• *T. verrucosus* ANDERSON, 1871. Western Yunnan, northern India, northern Thailand, North Vietnam. 16 cm.

Tympanocryptis PETERS, 1863. Australian Earless Lizards. Genus of the Agamidae. Australia, except in the northeastern and southwestern regions. About 5 species in steppes and deserts. Barely to 15 cm. Strongly reminiscent of *Phrynocephalus*, but distinguished from this genus by the preanal pores of the males and the smooth toe scales. The tail is short, thickened and turnip-like at the base (a fat reservoir?). Mainly brown and gray.

The diet appears to include mostly ants and termites. Maintenance presumably is similar to *Phrynocephalus*.

• *T. cephalus* GUENTHER, 1864. Central and western Australia. 12 cm.

Type locality: Place of origin of the type specimen used when establishing a new taxon. The specimens of a species taken at its type locality are referred to as topotypic specimens or topotypes.

Type specimen: The single specimen on which a species-level taxon is based.

Typhlacontias BOCAGE, 1873. Genus of the Scincidae Southern Africa. 6 species. Legless burrowers of arid areas. Related to *Scelotes*.

• *T. punctatissimus* BOCAGE, 1783.
Closely related to *Acontias* and very similar to it.

Typhlina WAGLER, 1830. Blind Worm Snakes. Genus of the Typhlopidae. Central America, Africa, Southeast Asia, Australia. About 30 species. To 40 cm. Recently split from *Typhlops* on reproductive characters.

• *T. bramina* (DAUDIN, 1803). Brahminy Worm Snake, Flowerpot Snake. Circumtropical distribution from East Africa and Madagascar, Southeast Asia, Indo-Australian Archipelago, to Central America and Florida (widely introduced). To 17 cm. Parthenogenic.

• *T. nigrescens* (GRAY, 1859). Australia.

Tylototriton verrucosus

Typhlina bramina

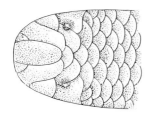

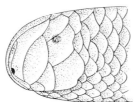

Typhlina bramina

Typhlogeophis GUENTHER, 1879. Monotypic genus of the Colubridae, Calamarinae; considered by some systematists to be a member of the Natricinae. Philippines. About 35 cm. With pointed head and extremely short tail.
Burrowing snakes. Biology unknown.
• *T. brevis* GUENTHER, 1879.

Typhlomolge STEJNEGER, 1896. Texas Blind Salamanders. Genus of the Plethodontidae, closely related to *Eurycea* and synonymized with it by some authorities. Cave systems of the Edward Plateau, Texas. 2 species. To 11 cm. Externally distinguishable from *Haideotriton* by a more or less indented forehead profile, smaller gills, and extremely thin, long limbs; from *Eurycea* by a smaller number of costal grooves (11-12). Neotenic and largely albinistic (pinkish in life). Mode of life and care as for other blind salamanders. Endangered.
• *T. rathbuni* STEJNEGER, 1896. San Marcos Blind Salamander. Snout long. Forehead profile grotesquely indented.

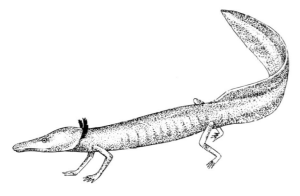

Typhlomolge rathbuni

Typhlonectes PETERS, 1879. Aquatic Caecilians. Genus of the Typhlonectidae. Tropical South America. 6 species. About 40-70 cm, worm-like. 80-95 primary folds. Posterior section of body with a median skin fold (as in *Potomotyphlus*). Mostly darkish gray to olive or black; anal region often whitish.
• *T. natans* PETERS, 1879. Rivers in northwestern Colombia. 50 cm. Dark olive.
• *T. compressicaudus* (DUMERIL and BIBRON, 1841). Guyana and Amazon region. More than 50 cm. Black, white above the eyes.

Typhlonectidae. Aquatic Caecilians. Family of the Gymnophiona. Tropical and subtropical South America, southward to Buenos Aires, in standing and flowing waters, also in damp ground close to water. Tailless, the cloaca subterminal on the ventral side of the body. The skin usually is smooth. Embedded scales and secondary furrows absent. Primary furrows often difficult to distinguish. Tentacle

Typhlonectes natans

Typhlonectes natans

very small, disguised, its position characteristic of the genera. Anal region of male characteristically formed, usually more or less round and with radial furrows, used as a suction disc for adhering to the female during copulation; in *Potomotyphlus* there are even prehensile structures to grasp the female. Oviparous or ovoviviparous. Larvae during the embryonic stage (at least in *Typhlonectes*) have giant, lobate external gills that regress completely prior to birth; then the gill openings are also closed. The larval median skin fold on the posterior part of the body is partially retained in the adults.

There is little known about the care of these animals. Because of their uncertain mode of life, they should be kept in a spacious aqua-terrarium at temperatures of about 25° C. where they can have a choice between land and water. The land section must permit the animals to burrow. The water section should also contain hiding places (water plants, flat rocks, leeched driftwood, soft substrate). Captive *Chthonerpeton* were reported to, when maintained in an aqua-terrarium, occupy the land section above the water line during the day and venture into the water at night in search of food. They feed on waxmoth larvae, the larvae and adults of aquatic insects, crustaceans, worms, and small fish.

Genera: *Chthonerpeton, Nectocaecilia, Potomotyphlus,* and *Typhlonectes*. Beyond that, *Copeotyphlinus* perhaps should be removed from the family Caeciliidae and placed in the Typhlonectidae.

Typhlophis FITZINGER, 1843. Monotypic genus of the Anomalepidae. Northeastern South America, Trinidad. To 30 cm. Scales generally small, but equal over the entire upper side of the head. Teeth absent from dentary.
- *T. squamosus* (SCHLEGEL, 1839).

Typhlopidae: Common Blind Worm Snakes. Family of the Scolecophidia. Found in all warm regions of the world, most diversely represented in Africa and Asia; only 1 species in southeastern Europe. 180 species. Many herpetologists place all the species into 1 genus (*Typhlops*), but arrangement into several genera on the basis of anatomical, morphological, and zoogeographical characters appears justified: *Typhlops, Typhlina, Rhamphotyphlops, Rhinotyphlops*. However, the relationships are not yet sufficiently researched. Closely related to Anomalepidae, but not to Leptotyphlopidae. To 80 cm, with evenly pencil- to finger-thick body. Head not set off from the body, its dorsal side covered with large scales; frequently the rostral scale is substantially larger than all other ones, often projecting and spine-like, the mouth subterminal. Upper jaw with movable teeth placed perpendicular to body axis. Lower jaw without teeth. Tail very short, wider than long, with horny terminal spine for anchorage inside burrows. Pelvic girdle reduced to some cartilaginous remnants. Body scales numerous, very small, in many rows, not differentiated between dorsal and ventral region (usually 20 to 40 rows of scales around the middle of the body). Coloration mostly uniformly brown, sometimes dark above and light below; some species have irregular light and dark spotted patterns.

Subterranean, burrowing under rocks and similar places, hiding in narrow passages. Many live in ant and termite nests, feeding on the pupae. Some typhlopids appear to merely squeeze out the fluids of their prey and do not swallow the hard shell. The absolutely smooth skin protects them against attacks from their prey. At night and after rains these snakes can be found on the surface.

Mostly egg-layers (4-10 eggs), but a few species are livebearers (*T. diardi*). Best kept in tall glass containers with a deep substrate layer (adequate drainage is important!) and flat rocks, tiles, or branches. The diet should consist of ant and termite pupae.

The Typhlopidae offer many observation tasks since mating behavior, feeding and feeding behavior, daily rhythms, and other facets are virtually unknown. These animals must be transported in plastic containers and similar solid containers. They will quickly penetrate cotton cloth bags.

Typhlops OPPEL, 1811. Common Blind Worm Snakes. Genus of the Typhlopidae. Worldwide except in Australia (where replaced by a related genus). About 180 species, some polytypic. 10-70 cm. The rostral is the largest scale on the dorsal side of the head, often substantially projecting.
- *T. diardi* SCHLEGEL, 1839. Diard's Blind Snake. From Bengal to Indo-China and Malaya. 2 subspecies. 45 cm.

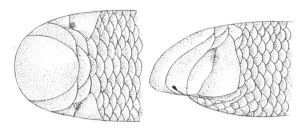

Typhlops lineolatus

Back dark, belly light, sometimes sharply delineated. Livebearer (up to 14 young).
- *T. lumbricalis* (LINNAEUS, 1758). Earthworm Blind Snake. Cuba and Bahamas. 40 cm. Outer forest regions and agricultural land.
- *T. punctatus* (LEACH, 1819). Tropical Africa. 3 subspecies. In savannahs and outer rain-forest areas. At 65 cm, one of the largest species of the genus. Spotted.
- *T. reuteri* (BOETTGER, 1881). Reuter's Blind Snake. Madagascar. 10 cm. Smallest species of the genus.
- *T. vermicularis* MERREM, 1820. Eurasian Worm Snake. Southeastern Europe (Balkan Peninsula) through the Near East to central Asia. To 30 cm. Egg-layer, 4 eggs.

Typhlops vermicularis

Typhlosaurus WIEGMANN, 1834. African Blind Skinks. Genus of the Scincidae. Southern Africa. 7 species. Taxonomic position uncertain; related to *Acontias*. Barely 10 cm. Eyes covered over by scales. Limbless.

Burrowing ground-dwellers.
- *T. lineatus* BOULENGER, 1887. Southwest Africa.

Typhlotriton STEJNEGER, 1892. Grotto Salamander. Monotypic genus of the Plethodontidae. Ozark and Ouachita Mountains, central USA. The larvae are found in mountain streams and springs, rarely in cave waters. Meta-

Typhlotriton spelaeus

morphosis occurs in subterranean habitats (grottos, caves). Elongated, slender. In contrast to the other blind salamanders, there is complete metamorphosis. Adults lack gills and the tail is more or less round in cross-section. Eyes in adults are very small, overgrown by skin. Albinistic. Larvae are similar to *Eurycea* larvae and are pigmented, with functional eyes.

Adults should be kept in a cool, dark location (refrigerator or basement).

• *T. spelaeus* STEJNEGER, 1892. Southern Missouri, northern Arkansas, and adjacent regions of Oklahoma. 8 to 12 cm. Larvae brownish; adults without pigmentation, pinkish white.

Ultraviolet light: UV radiation is the best and most natural substitute for direct sunlight. Many tropical and subtropical reptiles can be kept temporarily outside during the summer in outdoor terrariums or open-air terrariums, or at least they can be given some sun exposure for a few hours (beware of the danger of overheating; some shade must always be accessible to the animals). While normal glass almost completely absorbs ultraviolet radiation, plexiglass and other clear acrylics are relatively permeable (at 3 mm thick they still transmit about 70% of the UV). If direct sun exposure is not possible, there has to be a regular

course (1-2 times weekly) of ultraviolet radiation exposure for a few minutes from a commercially available ultraviolet lamp. Since the amount of ultraviolet radiation varies from 1 type of lamp to the next, it is difficult to provide a specific exposure time. The minimum distance from lamp to animal must be 50 cm. If the animals have an opportunity to avoid the radiation they will do it on their own before they are injured. In rare cases there can be mild inflammations of the eyes that usually heal themselves within a short period. Caution must be exercised with young animals; they should be exposed to ultraviolet radiation for shorter periods of time, but possibly at more frequent intervals. The growth of animals is especially supported by regular ultraviolet radiation in conjunction with calcium and vitamin supplements, prophylactic treatment against rickets.

More recently fluorescent light tubes have become available that have an ultraviolet component of a measured intensity that allows permanent exposure. In any event, it has to be checked in each case that the tubes primarily emit the relatively long-wave UV-A radiation and not the short-wave, health-damaging UV-C and UV-B radiation.

Ultraviolet exposure is essential for nearly all reptiles except some burrowing and nocturnal types. Even some amphibians like to sun themselves. Desert and steppe species have the largest demand for ultraviolet, while occupants of the lower regions of tropical rain forests have relatively small requirements for ultraviolet rays. Ultraviolet rays stimulate the metabolism and sex glands (one can often observe an increase in intensity of coloration within a few minutes after the onset of exposure to ultraviolet rays) and change provitamin D into the effective vitamin D, which is absolutely essential for the bone structure. Therefore, many reptiles have to receive ultraviolet rays at regular intervals.

Uma BAIRD, 1858. Fringe-toed Lizards. Genus of the Iguanidae. Southwestern USA and Mexico, 4 species in deserts and semideserts. About 20 cm. Slender. Superbly adapted to a life on loose sand, with wide toe fringes and closable nostrils and ear openings. Yellowish to gray-brown with dark spots or a reticulated pattern. Particularly characteristic are a black spot on each side of the abdomen and black and white crossbands on the distal half of the underside of the tail. The throat has a species-specific dark banded pattern. Markings in females less pronounced.

Diurnal ground-dwellers capable of burrowing themselves into the sand with lightning speed. They can also

Uma notata

move along under the sand surface and can detect their prey—small arthropods—when they are below the surface. Egg-layers, 1-3 clutches per year with 1-6 eggs each.

These lizards should be kept in a spacious, dry terrarium with a thick layer of sand as the substrate (lower layers to be kept moist at all times). Day temperatures can range from 30 to 40° C., with a basking light. At night 15-20° C. is satisfactory. Regular ultraviolet radiation is particularly important (also refer to *Sceloporus*). Not easy to keep and rather delicate (temperature variations must be observed).
▪ *U. notata* BAIRD, 1853. Desert Fringe-toed Lizard. Southern California, northern Lower California. To 20 cm.

Umbrivaga ROZE, 1964. Genus of the Colubridae, Xenodontinae. Venezuela, Colombia, Ecuador. 3 species. Closely related to *Leimadophis*. In tropical forests. 30-40 cm.

Ground-dwelling snakes.
▪ *U. mertensi* ROZE, 1964. Venezuela.
▪ *U. pygmaeus* (COPE, 1868). Upper Amazon Basin (Colombia, Ecuador).

Underwoodisaurus WERMUTH, 1965. Genus of the Gekkonidae. Eastern and southern Australia. 2 species. *Gymnodactylus* Group, but also included in *Phyllurus* by some authors. To 17 cm. Pupil vertical, lobate. Tail easily ½ snout-vent length, enlarged and turnip-like. Reddish brown with numerous enlarged granular scales, some yellowish.

Crepuscular to nocturnal ground-dwellers found during the day under rocks or behind bark. For details on care refer to *Cyrtodactylus*.
▪ *U. mili* (BORY, 1825). Turnip-tailed Gecko, Thick-tailed Bark Gecko. Eastern and southern Australia.

Unechis WORREL, 1961. Genus of the Elapidae. Australia. About 6 species. Closely related to *Suta* and not recognized as distinct by some systematists or placed with *Denisonia*. In deserts, savannahs, and tropical forests. To 50 cm. More or less slender, with a narrow, elongated head more or less distinctly set off from the body. Mostly unicolored, but some species with a wide dark neckband or a dark dorsal stripe.

Nocturnal, terrestrial venomous snakes found under rocks, logs, and similar hiding places. They feed exclusively on lizards. *U. flagellum* is a live-bearer; the mode of reproduction of the other species is not known.
▪ *U. carpentariae* (MACLEAY, 1888). Carpentaria Whip Snake. Eastern Queensland. Savannahs. 45 cm.
▪ *U. gouldi* (GRAY, 1841). Black-headed Snake. Southern Australia. Deserts and thornbush steppes. Head black. 40 cm.

Ungaliophis MUELLER, 1880. Dwarf Boas, Banana Boas. Genus of the Boidae, subfamily Boinae (or Tropidophinae). Southern Mexico to Colombia. 2 species in montane rain forests. To 75 cm. Closely related to *Trachyboa* and *Tropidophis* and ecologically also rather similar. With a complex spotted or rhomboidal pattern, very attractively marked and colored. Terrestrial or semiarboreal, often close to water. The diet is presumably frogs, lizards, and small mammals. Few experiences related to captive maintenance.

▪ *T. continentalis* MUELLER, 1880. Mexico to Honduras.
▪ *T. panamensis* SCHMIDT, 1933. Southern Nicaragua to western Colombia.

Ungaliophis panamanensis

Uperodon DUMERIL and BIBRON, 1841 (= *Cacopus* GUENTHER, 1864). Genus of the Microhylidae. India. 2 species. Related to *Glyphoglossus*. 5 to 8 cm. Externally reminiscent of the African *Breviceps*. Head disproportionately small relative to egg-shaped bloated body. Skin smooth. Eyes small, slightly protruding. Pupil triangular (pointing downward), round when enlarged. Tympanum not visible. Limbs short. Fingers free, toes webbed at base only. 2 shovel-like metatarsal tubercles, the inner one very large.

Burrowing ground-dwellers that feed mainly on ants and termites. Spawning occurs during the monsoon season in still water. The males vocalize with characteristic calls to attract females. Eggs are numerous, small, and drift on the surface in clumps. Captive care is presumably difficult because of their food restrictions, and due to their cryptic mode of life they are only of interest to specialized hobbyists. It is important to provide a thick, loose, slightly damp substrate layer and a local heat source (infrared lamp).
▪ *U. globulosum* (GUENTHER, 1864). Tamil Nadu, central India, Bengal. 8 cm. Brown, ventrally whitish.
▪ *U. systoma* (SCHNEIDER, 1799). Southern and eastern India, Sri Lanka. 5.5 cm. Olive with dark vermiform spots. Ventral region white.

Uperoleia GRAY, 1841. Genus of the Leptodactylidae. Australia. 2 species. Found in various types of habitats. Very similar to *Pseudophryne* and *Glauertia*. In contrast to *Pseudophryne*, there are well-developed parotoid glands. Distinguished from *Glauertia* by the presence of free toes and the 2 metatarsal tubercles on the same level. Bright red or orange dots on the throat. Pond spawners.

• *U. marmorata* GRAY, 1841. Yellow-spotted Toadlet. Southeastern and northwestern Australia. 3 cm. Similar to *U. rugosa*, but maxillary teeth present and metatarsal tubercles not compressed.

• *U. rugosa* (ANDERSSON, 1916). Red-groined Toadlet. Australia. 3 cm. Highly variable, mostly gray to dark brown with an irregular dark pattern. Maxillary teeth absent, metatarsal tubercles compressed.

Uracentron KAUP, 1826. Spiny-tailed Iguanids. Genus of the Iguanidae. Northern South America, Amazon Basin. 4 species in tropical rain forests. About 15 cm. Stout, with a blunt snout. Tail easily ½ snout-vent length and with very large, spiny scales. Other scales small.

Partially arboreal. Stomach analysis indicates the main food to be ants.

• *U. azureum* (L., 1758). Guyana, Surinam, northern Brasil. To 14 cm. Bright green with wide dark crossbands on the body.

Uracentron azureum

Uraeotyphlus PETERS, 1879. Genus of the Gymnophiona of uncertain family status, usually placed with Caeciliidae but should possibly be included in the family Ichthyophiidae. India. 4 species. A distinct but short tail present, the cloacal slit longitudinal. Tentacle located underneath nostril. 90 to 100 primary folds, secondary folds present. Egg-layers.

• *U. malabaricus* (BEDDOME, 1870). Malabar. To 24 cm. Violet, ventral side lighter.

• *U. oxyurus* (DUMERIL and BIBRON, 1841). Southern India and along the Malabar Coast. To 30 cm. Dark brown, the grooves more or less yellowish.

Uranoscodon KAUP, 1825. Mop-headed Iguanids. Monotypic genus of the Iguanidae. Northeastern South America in tropical rain forests. To 45 cm. Somewhat compressed laterally. Head short and high, the eyes strongly pointed upward, area between them deeply indented. Tail about twice snout-vent length. Low dorsal and caudal crests.

Diurnal, slow-moving ground-dwellers found along the wooded banks of rivers. When in danger they will often flee into the water. Avoid prolonged, direct sun exposure. The diet consists mainly of insects and earthworms. They will still feed at 15° C. Water is thought to be taken up through the skin. Egg-layers, 3-12 eggs deposited in hollow decaying logs.

• *U. superciliosa* (L., 1758). To 45 cm. Olive-green to brown with small yellowish spots and an indistinct light lateral band.

Uranoscodon superciliosa

Uromacer DUMERIL and BIBRON, 1853. Genus of the Colubridae, Xenodontinae. Haiti and adjacent small islands. 4 species in dry forests. 1.2 to almost 2 m. Slender, the head pointed to very pointed (*U. oxyrhynchus*), distinctly set off from the slender body.

Diurnal, more or less arboreal; *U. oxyrhynchus* is most strongly adapted to life in trees. Dorsally bright breen to blue-green. These snakes prey mainly on lizards (*Anolis*), but will also take frogs. Egg-layers, 5-12 eggs per clutch. Should be kept in a well-heated forest terrarium that must not be too damp. Beware of possible venomous bites.

• *U. catesbyi* (SCHLEGEL, 1837).

• *U. oxyrhynchus* DUMERIL and BIBRON, 1854.

Uromacerina AMARAL, 1929. Monotypic genus of the Colubridae, Xenodontinae. Southeastern Brasil (State of Sao Paulo). In appearance and mode of life similar to *Uromacer*.

• *U. ricardinii* (PERACCA, 1897).

Uromastyx MERREM, 1820 (=*Aporoscelis* BOULENGER, 1885). Spiny-tailed Agamids. Genus of the Agamidae. Northwestern Africa to southwestern Asia. At least 10 species in dry, often desert-like or rocky habitats. To 45 cm. Strongly flattened dorso-ventrally. Head distinctly set off, with lateral swellings on the occiput. The anterior upper jaw teeth are replaced by a sharp-edged projection of the intermaxillary bone; the anterior lower jaw teeth are fused

Uromastyx acanthinurus

to each other. Tail short, club-like, with large, strong, keeled and pointed scales arranged in whorls.

Often misspelled *Uromastix*. Diurnal ground-dwellers that dig long, deep tunnels where they stay during the hottest midday hours and at night. The coloration becomes distinctly lighter when the animals are warmed up. Temperatures in excess of 30° C. are preferred, while temperatures in excess of 42° C. increase respiration with the mouth open. Water requirements are extremely minimal. Most of the water in the urine is resorbed. Salt is given off during hot periods by means of glands along the nasal passages without any significant loss of water. One then finds regular salt crusts in the nostrils. During periods of extreme drought and lack of food, the water gained from burning the fat reserves in the tail is sufficient. Primarily phytophagous, according to their habitat feeding mainly on hard shrubs (e. g., *Artemisia*). Sometimes large insects are also taken, especially by younger animals. Egg-layers, up to 20 eggs, usually fewer. Juveniles 6-10 cm.

Uromastyx require spacious terrariums with a very deep substrate layer and sufficient hiding places. It is even more advantageous to place earthenware pipes obliquely into the substrate. Day temperatures between 30 and 35° C., locally along the bottom up to 40° C.; prefers a nocturnal reduction to about 20° C. Minimal water requirements. The diet should be composed of lettuce, clover, dandelions (especially the yellow blossoms), various types of cabbage, grain (especially corn, possibly water-soaked), or even rodent pellets. Larger insects should also be offered occasionally. Regular ultraviolet radiation and basking are required. It is recommended that specimens from more northern origin be given a cool winter dormancy period at 10-15° C. *U. acanthinurus* has been kept outdoors during the summer for years in central Europe. More recently breeding has occa-

sionally been successful, but this generally remains problematic. *Uromastyx* species are rather quarrelsome among each other, but they do become tame quickly and can often be hand-fed.

▪ *U. acanthinurus* BELL, 1825. African Spiny-tailed Agamid. Northern Africa, Senegal to Egypt. To 40 cm. Head often nearly black. Coloration highly variable, gray-brown, reddish, greenish, or yellowish with dark, mostly reticulated, scribbly markings. Tail whorls strong.

▪ *U. aegypticus* (FORSKAL, 1775). Egyptian Spiny-tailed Agamid. Northeastern Africa. More than 40 cm. Light beige to almost black.

▪ *U. hardwicki* GRAY, 1877. Indian Spiny-tailed Agamid. Northwestern India. About 35 cm. Smaller tail spines than the previous species, each whorl of 2-3 rows of smaller scales. Sandy yellow to light gray with dark markings. Requires a substantial amount of heat and will take grains, even dry rice.

Uropeltidae: Shield-tailed Snakes. Family of the Henophidia. Southern India and Sri Lanka. 8 genera: *Brachyophidium*, *Melanophidium*, *Platyplectrurus*, *Plectrurus*, *Pseudotyphlops*, *Rhinophis*, *Teretrurus*, and *Uropeltis*; 44 species found in monsoon forests, rain forests, and montane forests. Often up to 2,000 m elevation in mountain regions. 10-58 cm. Body cylindrical, of even thickness, the head not set off, mostly wedge-shaped and terminating in a point. The projecting rostral scale makes the mouth subterminal. The upper side of the head is covered with more or less normal head scales. The eyes are covered by ocular scales (except in *Platyplectrurus*) and are largely nonfunctional. The dorsal body scales are relatively large and smooth, the ventral scales small. The skeleton of Uropeltidae retains the rudiments of a pelvic girdle, but externally visible anal spurs are absent.

Uromastyx hardwicki

The characteristic short tail in the most modified genera terminates in a large, flat scale that looks like it is obliquely cut. This scale is covered with spiny tubercles and in the genus *Rhinophis* it is formed into a tube-like structure covered by rough warts. Primitive genera only have the scale at the end of the tail ending in a two-pointed structure. Frequently the other tail scales have strong keels and also give a rough appearance (*Plectrurus* and others). The function of this terminal tail scale is comparable to that of the terminal spine in Typlopidae: it is used for anchoring inside the burrow. Moreover, the Uropeltidae also use their tails for burrowing.

The diet consists of earthworms and small arthropods and their larvae that accumulate inside the burrows. Livebearers, 3-14 young that are sometimes quite large.

These snakes have rarely been kept in captivity. A tall glass container appears to be quite suitable if it has a deep, well-drained substrate with loose flat rocks or pieces of tree bark. The container must be tightly covered, especially when the sides are lower than the longest specimen inside. So that the burrows will pass next to the glass walls, it is recommended that all walls be darkened by removable coverings. With weak illumination (red light) the covers can be removed at night to observe and study the behavior of the animals inside their burrows.

Uropeltis CUVIER, 1829. Genus of the Uropeltidae. Southern India, Sri Lanka. About 22 species. 19-54 cm long, 1.2 to 1.7 cm in diameter. Head pointed, wedge-shaped, flattened. Chin furrow absent. Tail cylindrical. Scales in sloping region of upper side of tail repeatedly shingled. Actual terminal scale small, ending in 2 spines. Highly variable in coloration and markings. Uniformly brown, blackish, or reddish; some species with incomplete dark crossbands or rows of spots along the flanks. Burrowing snakes.
- *U. beddomei* GUENTHER, 1862. Southern India, Anamalai Hills.
- *U. ceylanicus* COCTEAU, 1833. Southern India, but not Sri Lanka. The most common species in the Travancore Anamalai Hills.
- *U. ocellatus* (BEDDOME, 1863). Southern India south of Goa, frequently in Nilgiris and Anamalai Hills.
- *U. melanogaster* (GRAY, 1858). Sri Lanka, mountains of the Central Province. Dark brown with irregular yellow stripes or rows of dots along flanks.
- *U. woodmasoni* (THEOBALD, 1876). Southern India. Palni Mountains at 1,800 m elevation.

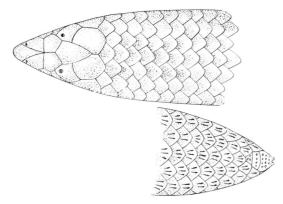

Uropeltis smithi

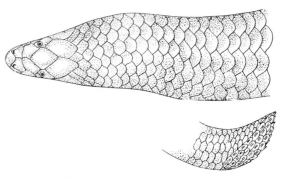

Uropeltis ceylanicus

Uroplatus DUMERIL, 1805. Flat-tailed Geckos. Genus of the Gekkonidae. Madagascar and adjacent islands. 6 species in tropical rain forests. To barely 25 cm. Strongly flattened dorso-ventrally. Tail barely ½ snout-vent length, extremely flat and substantially widened, constricted at base. Adhesive toe lamellae well developed. Eyes strongly protruding, with vertical pupils. Dorsal scales heterogenous, with a serrated margin along the sides of the body and the limbs formed by scales. Brown to gray-brown with irregular spots. Physiological color changes possible.

Relatively slow, primarily nocturnal tree-dwellers that can remain motionless head down on a tree trunk for hours. Captive specimens require high humidity and daytime temperatures between 25 and 28° C., at night about 20° C., possibly slightly warmer, but never below 20° C.
- *U. fimbriatus* (SCHNEIDER, 1797). Flat-tailed Gecko.

Uroplatus fimbriatus

Urosaurus HALLOWELL, 1854. Tree Lizards. Genus of the Iguanidae. Southwestern USA and Mexico. Closely related to *Sceloporus* and *Uta*. 10 species in dry habitats. 15-20 cm. Slender. A distinct gular fold. Lateral scales small, granular. Central dorsal region with large, keeled dorsal scales. Inconspicuous gray-brown with dark spots, some species with longitudinal stripes. Sides of abdomen of males with pale blue spots. Throat light blue, reddish, orange, or yellow.

Diurnal; *U. ornatus* is mainly arboreal. Egg-layers, sometimes 2 clutches of 3 to 15 eggs. For details on care refer to *Sceloporus*. Climbing branches must be present. Watch for moisture. Eat small arthropods. Delicate.
- *U. ornatus* (BAIRD and GIRARD, 1852). Tree Lizard. Texas to Arizona and Mexico. 12 to 15 cm. Requires lots of heat. Quarrelsome
- *U. graciosus* HALLOWELL, 1854. Brush Lizard. Nevada to California and northwestern Mexico. Semideserts with

brush stands. To 15 cm. Less tree-dwelling than previous species.

Urosaurus ornatus

Urostrophus DUMERIL and BIBRON, 1837. Genus of the Iguanidae of uncertain taxonomic status. South America. 3 species in steppes to semideserts. 20-25 cm. Slender. Tail easily 1 ½ times snout-vent length.

Agile ground-dwellers. Maintenance similar to *Liolaemus*.

• *U. vautieri* DUMERIL and BIBRON, 1837. Brasil.

Uta BAIRD and GIRARD, 1852. Side-blotched Lizards. Genus of the Iguanidae. Southwestern USA, Mexico. Closely related to *Sceloporus* and *Urosaurus*. 7-9 species in dry, open habitats. 12-15 cm. Slender. Distinct gular fold. No body fold as in *Urosaurus*. Tail about twice snout-vent length. Lateral scales small. Median dorsal scales large, keeled. Gray-brown with a pattern of dark spots and characteristic blue to black spots in front limb axilla. Females also have light longitudinal stripes. Males have a pale bluish throat and sides.

Diurnal ground-dwellers often found on rocks, rarely on trees. Natural longevity rarely more than 1 year. Egg-layers. For maintenance see *Sceloporus*. These lizards need to be kept very warm and are very quarrelsome among each other (best kept in pairs only).

• *U. stansburiana* BAIRD and GIRARD, 1852. Side-blotched Lizard. Southwestern USA, northern Mexico. About 14 cm.

Uta stansburiana

Varanidae: Monitors. Family of the Platynota, Squamata. Africa, southern Asia, and Australia. They form—together with the extinct Aigialosauridae, Dolichosauridae, and Mosasauridae and the still living Lanthanotidae—a sister group to the Serpentes. Known as fossils since the Upper Cretaceous, during the Pleistocene they were also found in southern Europe. As in snakes, the cranium of the Varanidae is completely ossified and so is protected from below against the pressure caused by swallowing large pieces of food. Through spreading of the hyoid apparatus the pharynx can be enlarged. Varanids have carnassial (tearing) teeth, and the food is swallowed whole or in large pieces. The shape of the vertebrae, chamber arrangement of the heart, and absence of a urinary bladder are similar to the Boidae, but they also share more primitive features with the Diploglossa, especially with the Xenosauridae, such as the spiny scales along the sides of the cloacal slit (not in all species) and the basic color pattern. Only Recent genus: *Varanus*.

Varanus MERREM, 1820. Monitors. Only living genus of the Varanidae. Africa, southern Asia, and Australia (more than 50% of the species); absent from Madagascar, Tasmania, and New Zealand. More than 30 species in 10 subgenera found in many different habitats. 20 cm to 3 m, 20 g to 150 kg. Most species are relatively massive, with strong 5-toed, claw-equipped limbs. The head is large, pointed, and mostly carried erect. The neck is elongated. The eyes have round pupils. The nasal openings are circular or slits and are of variable shape and position important in subgeneric classification. Ear opening distinct. Teeth strong, slightly bent backward. The long tongue is deeply forked. The tail is long, very strong, either round or slightly laterally compressed in cross-section and keeled on top, nearly always more than twice snout-vent length. Body scales are small, not shingled or overlapping, in some instances keeled. Enlarged buckler-like scales are most likely in the neck region if they occur. Occasionally there are spiny

Varanus flavescens

Varanus griseus caspius, juvenile

Varanus gouldi

Varanus exanthematicus

Varanus griseus

Varanus storri

scales on the tail. Spiny scales along the cloacal slit are characteristic for species of the subgenus *Odatria*.

Most varanids are equally agile on land and in water. A more or less aquatic mode of life is lead by *V. niloticus, V. salvator, V. indicus,* and *V. mertensi. V. niloticus* can dive for up to 1 hour. Amphibious varanids have laterally compressed tails used as a rudder while swimming. Inhabitants of deserts and dry steppes are, among others, *V. giganteus, V. griseus, V. gouldi,* and *V. flavescens*. Those from open forests and savannahs include *V. exanthematicus* and *V. komodoensis. V. prasinus* and *V. gilleni* live arboreally.

Diurnal predators that feed, depending on their size, on insects (*V. brevicauda, V. caudolineatus*) and up to medium-size vertebrates (*V. niloticus, V. exanthematicus, V. varius, V. giganteus, V. bengalensis, V. komodoensis*). It has been observed that predatory varanids also lick up the contents of the digestive tract of their herbivorous prey, presumably to satisfy their vitamin requirements. They will also feed on eggs, and carrion is also generally taken.

During ritualistic fights the males stand on their hind legs—opposing each other—and try to push over the opponent. There is rarely any biting involved. Sexual maturity occurs between the third and fifth years, in captivity sometimes even earlier. During mating the male grasps the hind legs of the female and with its tongue flicks at the neck region of the female. An actual neck bite is not obligatory. Egg-layers, clutches with 7-60 eggs. Sometimes the eggs are laid in hollow trees or termite mounds.

Monitors are generally easy to keep in a terrarium, but they do require spacious containers. For larger specimens one usually prefers semisterile maintenance without a substrate. Terrarium plants really only make sense for small species. Hiding places, climbing branches, and a large water bowl should be provided even for species that prefer dry habitats. Day temperatures from 25° C. to 30° C. are typical. For inhabitants of open plains there should also be a heat lamp for basking; for these a nocturnal temperature reduction by about 10° C. is satisfactory, and for forest species only about 5° C. Regular ultraviolet radiation and vitamin supplements (and for insectivorous species also calcium supplements) should be provided in order to avoid nutritional deficiencies. All varanids have a tendency toward obesity.

Varanus niloticus

Varanus salvator

Varanus niloticus, juvenile

Except in their native countries where they are often kept and bred in larger outdoor enclosures, captive breeding of varanids is still problematic. The following species (among others) have been bred in captivity: *V. timorensis, V. brevicauda, V. mertensi, V. komodoensis, V. niloticus, V. salvator, V. varius, V. exanthematicus, V. spenceri.* Incubation periods vary from 70 to 327 days (usually 130-220 days) at temperatures from 28 to 32° C.

All varanids are quite capable of defending themselves, and when handling large specimens (even those that are allegedly "tame") considerable caution has to be exercised. Not only do they have powerful bites, but with their strong tails they can administer painful lashes that can cause bone fractures. Keeping monitors can today only be justified for experienced hobbyists and then only under exceptional circumstances. Many are threatened by habitat loss and hunting pressure.

The Recent varanid species are placed into 10 subgenera. Subgenera are indicated in the following species listing:

Varanus varius

Varanus rudicollis

Varanus komodoensis

- *V. (Indovaranus* MERTENS, 1942) *bengalensis* (DAUDIN, 1802). Bengal Monitor. Sri Lanka and southeastern India to Java. Rocky dry regions. To 2 m.
- *V. (Odatria* GRAY, 1838) *caudolineatus* BOULENGER, 1885. Stripe-tail Monitor. Western Australia. Steppe regions. Maximum size 28 cm.
- *V. (Tectovaranus* MERTENS, 1942) *dumerili* (SCHLEGEL, 1839). Dumeril's Monitor. Indonesia. Damp forests along river banks. To 1.3 m. Often climbs.
- *V. (Empagusia* GRAY, 1838) *exanthematicus* (BOSC, 1792). Savannah Monitor. Western and central Africa southward to Zaire and northern Angola. Rocky savannah regions. Easily to 1.5 m. Tolerates large temperature variations.
- *V. (E.) flavescens* (HARDWICKE and GRAY, 1827). Yellow Monitor. Northern India and Indo-China. Steppes and open forests. Easily to 1 m.
- *V (V.) gouldi* (GRAY, 1838). Gould's Monitor. Australia. Semideserts to damp forests (not common there). 1.5 m. Variable.
- *V. (O.) gilleni* LUCAS and FROST, 1895. Gillen's Dwarf Monitor. Central Australia. Dry forests. To 35 cm.
- *V. (Psammosaurus* FITZINGER, 1826) *griseus* (DAUDIN, 1803). Desert Monitor. Northwestern Africa to southwestern Asia. Often in rocky deserts and savannahs. 1.5 m. A short winter dormancy is recommended. Tolerates large temperature variations.
- *V. (V.) indicus* (DAUDIN, 1802). Pacific Monitor. South-

Varanus timorensis similis

ern Asia to northern Australia along damp river banks and in coastal forests. Easily to 1.5 m. Spends much time in water, even seawater.

- *V. (V.) komodoensis* OUWEN, 1912. Komodo Dragon. Restricted to a few Indonesian islands (Komodo, Flores, Rindja). Open forests but also an excellent swimmer. To 3 m. Largest of all Recent lizards.
- *V. (Polydaedalus* WAGLER, 1830) *niloticus* (L., 1758). Nile Monitor. Africa with the exception of the northwest. It has disappeared from many areas or strongly declined in numbers. Closely tied to water. To 2 m.
- *V. (O.) prasinus* (SCHLEGEL, 1839). Emerald Monitor. New Guinea in rain forests. To 80 cm. Bright green. Will occasionally take fruit.
- *V. (Dendrovaranus* MERTENS, 1942) *rudicollis* (GRAY, 1845). Rough-neck Monitor. Malaya, Sumatra, and Kalimantan. About 1.2 m. Arboreal.
- *V. (V.) salvator* (LAURENTI, 1768). Water Monitor, Two-banded Monitor. Southeast Asia. More than 2 m. Semi-aquatic, but also an agile climber.
- *V. (O.) timorensis* (GRAY, 1831). Timor Monitor. Timor and adjacent islands, New Guinea, and large areas of northern Australia. To 60 cm. In part arboreal, but also commonly on the forest floor.
- *V. (V.) varius* SHAW, 1790. Variegated Monitor. Australia. Forest regions. 2 m. Adults mainly on the ground.

Variety: Group of organisms within a species with a distinctive morphological feature that, in contrast to a subspecies, is not restricted in geographical distribution. A variety is not a systematic category and is not subject to nomenclatural rules.

Venomous snake care: Apart from specific husbandry conditions based on the ecological requirements of the snake species, there are also a number of general prerequisites that must be met when venomous snakes are kept.

1) Keeping venomous snakes must always remain an exceptional terrarium experience. The only acceptable motive is a deep-seated scientific interest to research the biology of venomous snakes. The relevant laws applicable to your particular area (city, state, county, country) must be complied with.

2) Only those who have many years of experience in keeping and handling nonvenomous snakes are sufficiently suited to keep venomous snakes. Adequate health (no heart or circulatory diseases, no allergies) reduces the risk should a bite accident occur.

3) Considerations to protect the keeper and those around him are essential. Venomous snakes must always be housed in absolutely secure escape-proof terrariums (heavy security glass, safety locks, anchored so can not be knocked over). Unauthorized persons (children, family members) must not be able to have access to the snakes. Ideally a venomous snake terrarium should be located in a separate room that can be locked and has adequately protected (burglar-proof) windows.

4) The correct antivenin (and in ample quantities) must be kept on hand in case of a venomous bite. Apart from the serum, also required for first aid are a sterile hypodermic and the correct needle, sterile razor blades, and bandages. More recently very effective venom extraction apparatuses of simple construction have become available and are particularly useful when antivenin is not at hand or there is serum incompatibility. Such kits should be part of the obligatory first aid equipment kept by anyone who keeps venomous snakes.

5) Since most snake bite accidents happen when a terrarium is being serviced, there should be adequate lock-up facilities (with sliding doors) for the snake. All specimens must be accounted for (inside lock-up boxes) BEFORE service is performed. Specially-designed venomous snake forceps as well as plastic slip tubes are also essential accessories when venomous snakes are handled, particularly for transfers, transport, or special handling requirements (to aid in molting, remove parasites, etc.).

6) Through educational efforts from hobbyist organizations and community control of those who keep venomous snakes, any risks for the population and environment should be eliminated. This demand includes compliance with relevant government controls placed on the commercial trade of venomous snakes.

7) Liability and accident insurance should be taken out by any responsible venomous snake keeper. It is also the responsibility of any law-abiding person to assure that other venomous snake keepers comply with these basic prerequisites; they should report violations to the authorities.

8) Should a venomous snake escape from a terrarium or even out of a special terrarium room, the first rule is to destroy the animal if it cannot be caught. An escaped venomous snake can cause severe panic among the general public, require expensive police action, and lead to judicial action against the snake's keeper. Accidents to third parties (including family members) could be treated as negligent bodily injury or negligent homicide.

Venomous snakes: Collective term for all snakes of the families Viperidae (true adders), Crotalidae (pit vipers), Elapidae (cobras), Hydrophiidae (sea snakes), and the colubrid subfamily Aparallactinae (ground vipers).

True venomous snakes have venom glands that produce venoms and fangs that, as the anterior-most teeth of the upper jaw, are connected to the venom glands through venom ducts. Several groups of colubrid snakes also have venom glands with toxic secretions that are connected by means of venom ducts to special fangs, but these fangs, however, are located among the posterior teeth of the up-

Venomous snakes: The fangs of a puff adder, *Bitis*

per jaw (Boiginae, Homalopsinae, various genera of the Natricinae, and others). The fangs of these "rear-fanged" snakes are of a more primitive structure than those of truly venomous species and possess an open venom groove. Among the Natricinae there are also genera with powerful venoms that are freely discharged into the pharynx. The Boiginae and all other venomous representatives of the Colubridae are generally not considered to be true venomous snakes, although at least the genera *Dispholidus*, *Thelotornis*, and *Rhabdophis* can administer bites that may be fatal to humans. Therefore, in terrarium practice these and all unknown snakes must always be treated as being venomous.

Ventilation: A sufficient supply of fresh air is essential for the terrarium. Usually this involves more (with the exception for extremely shallow containers) than the use of gauze covers. An adequate fresh air supply should enter the terrarium through a slot at the lower section of the container. This slot can be covered with gauze or perforated aluminum. From the entry port the air should circulate upward and exit there. This flow-through process is further enhanced by radiant light sources, which then continuously draw in fresh air because of convection currents produced. Problems arise if there is a substantial temperature gradient between the room and the inside of the terrarium, which may well lead to cold-related respiratory problems. Should this situation exist, the incoming air must be preheated in a separate chamber equipped with a heater before it enters the terrarium.

In a rain-forest terrarium the entering fresh air may lower the humidity. This may be corrected by passing the entering fresh air over a large, shallow bowl filled with water. Here the effect is enhanced when a low wattage aquarium heater is placed in the water bowl. Generally speaking, preheating the incoming fresh air may not be necessary because a small temperature difference of about 5° C. does not have any detrimental effect on the animals.

Large terrariums can effectively be equipped with a small fan. Such a fan ventilator is then installed in the lid

or upper part of the terrarium and should preferably be equipped with a thermostat in order to adjust the flow. For very large terrariums a fan can also be placed inside the container (protected with suitable fine wire mesh) and so produce better air circulation. Drafts must be avoided. The leaves of delicate plants inside the container should barely be moved by the air flow.

Fresh air must be clean—it must not be contaminated with tobacco smoke.

Vermicella GUENTHER, 1858. Bandy-bandies. Genus of the Elapidae. Australia. 2 species in extreme desert regions as well as in dry forest regions. 50 cm. The round, blunt head is simulated by the short, truncated tail. Strongly banded black and white.

Nocturnal, largely burrowing venomous snakes that prey mainly on blind snakes (Typhlopidae). Probably egg-layers.

▪ *V. annulata* (GRAY, 1841). Bandy-bandy. Australia except in extreme northwest, southwest, and southeast of the continent.

Vertebral column: Together with the ribs and the sternum (breast bone) the vertebral column forms the axial skeleton of vertebrate animals. It replaces the primitive and embryonically always present older support organ, the notochord, whose remnants are still present to a variable extent in the vertebral discs or in the center of the vertebrae. The vertebral column, consisting of successively arranged individual vertebrae, is linked anteriorly via a joint to the cranial skeleton and it extends posteriorly to the tip of the tail. Each vertebra consists of a vertebral body and various projections that form the dorsal spinal canal (neural arches) and ventrally enclose the dorsal aorta (hemal arches). The laterally projecting processes provide additional points of attachment for muscles. They are completely fused with the ribs in most anurans, and in most amphibians they remain extremely short. Ribs can be attached to nearly all the trunk vertebrae (as in snakes), usually by joints.

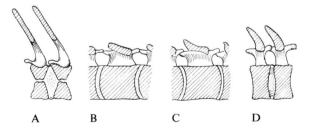

Vertebrae: A Amphicoelic; B opisthocoelic; C procoelic; D acoelic or biplanar

The number of vertebrae is highly variable in amphibians and reptiles, and it is somewhat related to the length of the body. While most salamanders have 15-20 trunk and 25-30 caudal vertebrae, the number of vertebrae in the tailless frogs is reduced to only 6-9; the posterior vertebrae (12 or more) have become fused into a single solid bone, the urostyle. In reptiles the number of vertebrae can be very much higher due to the sometimes extremely long tail. The maximum number is reached in the snakes, specifically in the genus *Python* with 435 vertebrae.

Depending upon the development of the anterior and posterior faces of the trunk vertebra, one distinguishes amphicoelic vertebrae (both areas deeply concave), opisthocoelic vertebrae (anteriorly convex and posteriorly concave), and procoelic vertebrae (concave anteriorly and convex posteriorly). In addition to the large ball joints of vertebral bodies there are neural arch articulating projections (zygapophyses) that prevent the vertebral column from twisting, thus improving stability. Snakes and some lizards also possess 2 additional articulatory projections, zygosphene and zygantrum, that serve as joints to provide further support to the vertebral column.

Vibrissaphora LIU, 1945. Genus of the Pelobatidae. Himalayas. 2 species. Males larger than females. Eyes large, the pupil vertical. Tympanum not visible. Spinous skin processes sometimes present on upper lip (well developed in males, only indicated in females). Males have heavy arms. Fingers free, toes webbed at base only, tips of fingers and toes thickened and knob-like. 2 metatarsal tubercles, inner 1 oval. Movement rather spider-like, the abdomen raised off the ground.

Outside the breeding season these frogs are rather cryptic in dry regions and are found at the surface only during rainy nights. Mating usually occurs in standing water; details are not known. Keep much as *Scaphiopus* and *Pelobates* in a slightly moist, unheated terrarium.
▪ *V. boringi* LIU, 1945. China, Sichuan, Omei Mountain (1000 to 1400 m). 8 cm. Dark brown, dorsal skin reticulated.

Vicariance: Reciprocal representation, either spacially (local or geographical vicariance) or in time. Spacial vicariance exists, for instance, among subspecies, among the large crocodilian species (probably for reasons of competition for food), and among taxa distributed along the various types of flowing water from headwaters to mouth. One refers to a vicariance in time mainly with different species that have a similar food spectrum or similar developmental requirements (e. g., different breeding periods of frogs or salamanders in the same spawning pool).

Vipera LAURENTI, 1768. Eurasian Adders or True Vipers. Genus of the Viperidae, Viperinae. Western Palearctic. The species range from cold-adapted species (*V. berus, V. ursinii*) to those living in tundras and in subalpine mountain zones. Some species also occur on dry, warm rubble fields, rocky slopes, and in nearly subtropical lowlands (*V. ammodytes, V. latastii*). 50 cm to 1 m.

2 subgenera, 6 species:
▪ Subgenus *Vipera*: *V. berus, V. kaznakovi,* and *V. ursinii*. Large scales of the top of the head still largely present, the small scales are not keeled. Snout sharp-edged, nostril horns absent. Head narrow and elongated. Body with 19-21 rows of keeled scales along center of body. Markings are a zig-zag band, rarely dissolved into crossbands (*V. berus bosniensis*) or into longitudinal stripes (*V. kaznakovi, V. berus seoanei*). 50 to 80 cm.

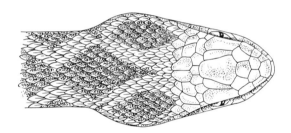

Vipera ursinii

Vipera aspis

Vipera berus

• Subgenus *Rhinaspis* BONAPARTE, 1834; *V. aspis*, *V. am-modytes*, and *V. latastii*. Large head scales always reduced to small scales and more or less distinctly keeled (as an ata-vism there are occasionally large scale remnants). Tip of snout turned up (*V. aspis*) or with a nasal horn (*V. ammo-dytes*, *V. latastii*). Head compact. 21 rows of scales around middle of body. Markings are a zig-zag or rhomboid band, rarely crossbands (*V. aspis*). *V. aspis* is the most primitive species of this subgenus, with many transitional forms to the first subgenus. To 1 m (*V. aspis*, *V. ammodytes*, and *V. latastii*).

All other species formerly included in *Vipera* have now been placed with the genus *Daboia*.

Ritualistic fights are typical among males. Ovovivipa-rous. Maintenance of *V. ammodytes* and *V. latastii* requires a heated dry terrarium with nocturnal temperature reduc-tion. Diet: Mice. Some species have been bred in captivity over several generations. *V. aspis* require more moisture than the others. Maintenance of *V. berus* and *V. ursinii* most ideally is in an open-air terrarium with supplemen-tary heat, nocturnal temperature reduction, and damp hid-ing places. Refusal to feed is often a response to brutal col-lecting methods and incorrect accommodation (too damp and cold or too dry and warm). *V. berus* sometimes is im-printed on brown frogs or lizards as preferred food. *V. ur-sinii* often feeds exclusively on lizards or crickets, and a change-over to laboratory mice is often unsuccessful. Keeping *V. berus* and *V. ursinii* is recommended only for advanced hobbyists. *V. kaznakovi* has similar requirements for moisture as the two previously mentioned species but needs more heat. *V. berus* and *V. ursinii* have occasionally been bred, and *V. kaznakovi* has been bred over several generations and has also been hybridized with *V. berus*.

• *V. ammodytes* (LINNAEUS, 1758). Sand Viper, Nose-horned Viper. Southeastern Europe and western Asia. 4 subspecies. Most easily kept species of this genus.

• *V. aspis* (LINNAEUS, 1758). Asp Viper. Southwestern Eu-

Vipera kaznakovi, juvenile

Vipera kaznakovi

rope. 4-6 subspecies. Pronounced tendency toward the development of blackish specimens without markings (melanistic).

▪ *V. berus* (LINNAEUS, 1758). Common Adder. From Spain to Sachalin, over the entire Palearctic, reaching the Polar Circle in Scandinavia and found at higher elevations in southern Europe. About 4 subspecies. Unicolored, melanistic, and red-brown mutants not too uncommon. *V. b. seoanei* LATASTE, 1879, from Spain is considered to be a valid species by some systematists.

▪ *V. kaznakovi* NIKOLSKY, 1909. Caucasus Viper. Western Caucasus and northeastern Anatolia. Does well in captivity. Hardy.

Vipera ursinii

Vipera ammodytes transcaucasiana

▪ *V. latastii* BOSCA, 1878. Lataste's Viper. Iberian Peninsula and northwestern Africa. 2 subspecies.

▪ *V. ursinii* (BONAPARTE, 1835). Orsini's Viper. Southern France to Altei in the east, southward to Elbrus Mountains in Iran. 4-5 subspecies, disjunct. Difficult to keep.

Viperidae: Vipers or Adders. Family of the Caenophidia. Europe, Asia, and Africa in tropical to temperate or cool climates (*Vipera berus* penetrating to the Polar Circle in Europe), but with greatest diversity in tropical regions. Found mainly in dry habitats, some genera show adaptations to extreme desert conditions (*Echis*, some *Bitis*, some *Daboia*, *Eristicophis*, *Pseudocerastes*) and to a life on or in the ground; other genera are found in tropical forests (some *Bitis*, *Causus*, *Atheris*, and some *Daboia*). Some *Vipera* species live in damp forests of temperate zones, such as *Vipera kaznakovi* in beech tree forests in the Asia Minor-Caucasus-Black Sea area and *V. berus* at the northern edge of its range preferably in high moors. Most *Vipera* species are nocturnal predators and can be seen sunning themselves and looking for mates during the day. The main diet consists of small mammals, but some species also take birds, lizards, and arthropods. Following the venomous bite the prey is let go and the snake will then look for it, the sense of smell playing an important role in the search.

Egg-layers (usually with a very short incubation period of 8 to 14 days), ovoviviparous, also frequently viviparous. These transitional stages between egg-laying and live-bearing can even be found within the same species (*Daboia lebetina*). Some species have been bred in captivity over several generations, while other species remain problematic in regard to captive breeding since some of their ecological requirements are not yet fully known (some miniature forms of *Bitis*, *Eristicophis*) or rearing of the very small young presents insurmountable food and feeding problems (*Echis*, *Atheris*).

3 subfamilies:

▪ Subfamily Azemiophinae: Fea vipers. Only 1 genus: *Azemiops*, found in southern Asia.

▪ Subfamily Viperinae: Adders, vipers. *Adenorhinos, Atheris, Bitis, Cerastes, Daboia, Echis, Eristicophis, Pseudocerastes, Vipera.*

▪ Subfamily Causinae: Toad vipers. Only 1 genus: *Causus*, only in Africa.

Viperinae: Subfamily of the Viperidae. 9 genera, 3 restricted to Africa, the remainder Palearctic. Characterized by the triangular head and a reduction in size of the scales on top of the head, except for some members of the genus *Vipera*. Dorsal scales more or less strongly keeled. Pattern variable, often consisting of zig-zag lines, rhomboid bands, or crossbars; a few species are unicolored, without markings.

Virginia BAIRD and GIRARD, 1853 (=*Haldea* BAIRD and GIRARD). Earth Snakes. Genus of the Colubridae, Natricinae. Eastern and central USA except in Florida. 2 species found in various damp habitats (grasslands to forests), frequently following human habitation even into yards and city parks. To 40 cm. Unicolored brownish gray to reddish brown, sometimes yellow below.

Found on the ground underneath rocks and similar places. The diet consists mainly of earthworms, arthro-

Virginia valeriae

pods, and small salamanders, frogs, and lizards. Live-bearers, 6-18 young. Care as for Natricinae, Group 1.
- *V. striatula* (LINNAEUS, 1766). Rough Earth Snake. Dorsal scales keeled.
- *V. valeriae* (BAIRD and GIRARD, 1853). Smooth Earth Snake. 3 subspecies. Dorsal scales almost smooth.

Virus infections: Diseases caused by viruses (strictly intracellular potentially pathogenic elementary bodies), usually with symptoms of a general infection (apparent tiredness, refusal to feed, general apathy) or skin growths. Secondary bacterial infections (*Aeromonas, Pseudomonas*) will then in most cases cause changes that are significant for the further progress of the disease.

Therapy: Treatment can be directed only against secondary bacterial pathogens (antibiotics, sulfonamide) and should be supported by symptomatic measures for diarrhea, liver diseases, pneumonia, or stomatitis infectiosa as appropriate.

Prophylaxis: Daily changes of drinking water, ultraviolet radiation, eradication of cockroaches, quarantine of any terrarium with diseased animals.

Vitamin A deficiency: Diseases of the eye glands in various reptiles and white spot disease in turtles are considered to be specific vitamin A deficiency diseases. White spot disease is characterized by the replacement of the normal plastron markings with white spots; white pieces of tissue come off the neck region, the extremities, and the scutes of the carapace. The animal rests apathetically under water and refuses to feed.

In all skin diseases of the visible mucous membranes (yellow coating of the tongue in turtles, stomatitis infectiosa) as well as the clouding of the cornea of the eye (ceratitis), vitamin A deficiency should be considered. An exact differentiation from other vitamin deficiency syndromes is usually not possible. Even cases of diarrhea and diseases of the respiratory organs (pneumonia) may be traced to vitamin A deficiency. The most rapid development of vitamin A deficiency occurs in those species with a diet that consists of raw meat for prolonged period of time without supplements, as well as herbivores with a carotine-deficient winter diet for several months.

Therapy: 60-120,000 IU of vitamin A per kg body weight twice at an interval of 3 weeks.

Vitamin deficiency: Avitaminosis, hypovitaminosis. This develops in amphibians and reptiles due to maintenance conditions that do not completely meet their requirements. Least affected are those animals that are fed live food organisms if this meets with their normal nutritional requirements. Juveniles—due to their higher nutritional requirements—are usually the first ones to be affected by a vitamin deficiency. Deficiencies—often of several different vitamins—are now known to be associated with many general diseases of amphibians and reptiles (newt plague, pseudomonad infections, stomatitis infectiosa, tuberculosis). It is the lessened resistance due to lack of vitamins that permits the massive spread of pathogens and their penetration into lower layers of the skin and mucous membranes.

Specific diseases of particular organs or tissues (eye diseases, gout, skin diseases, metabolic disturbances in bones) indicate the presence of a specific vitamin deficiency. Although not every disease has been sufficiently researched and documented, the following appear to be related to vitamin deficiencies: diseases of the eye glands and white spot disease in turtles (presumably vitamin A deficiency); specific central nervous system symptoms in fish-feeding species (vitamin B deficiency); bone or carapace softness (vitamin D deficiency, often in combination with a lack of calcium. Symptoms of vitamin E deficiency occur after feeding fatty fish or fat laboratory rats (steatitis). Vitamin K deficiency causes gum bleeding in crocodilians.

Due to resorption disturbances in enteritis or increased metabolic demands during the course of infectious diseases, there often develops a secondary vitamin deficiency.

Therapy: Multivitamin preparations. Application can be by injection or, in animals that are still feeding and drinking, via the drinking water. The largest doses are required by chameleons (1 ml aqueous multiple vitamin solution per 20 ml drinking water); for other animals it is sufficient to give much lower dosages. Animals below 500 g body weight should receive the lowest possible dose by injection (e. g., 0.01 ml) of a multivitamin preparation. Consult your veterinarian.

Hypervitaminosis is mainly due to high levels of vitamin D3 (metabolic disturbances of bones and bone structures) and vitamin A supplements (molting problems).

Viviparity: Form of reproduction where the female gives birth to live young. A clear delineation from ovoviviparity is not possible. Strictly speaking, viviparity presupposes nutrition of the embryo inside the maternal body via a placenta by means of the maternal circulatory system, as is characteristic of mammals. In many live-bearing reptiles there are placenta-like formations of variable development and functional ability that in highly evolved forms can include a partial supply of the embryo with nutritive substances. This situation occurs, for instance, in Australian skinks of the genera *Lygosoma* and *Trachysaurus*, which have eggs containing very little yolk. Also refer to oviparity, ovoviviparity.

Vocalization: Using the voice to transmit information and so facilitate intra- and interspecific communication. This can express, among other things, territorial delineation and

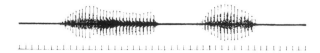

Vocalization: Sonogram of the call of *Rana temporaria*

can promote the meeting between sexual partners during the breeding season. It can also play a role in intraspecific conflicts and warn or deter enemies. The most familiar herptile vocalizations are the mating calls of frogs and toads. Many other amphibians and reptiles are able to produce a variety of sounds with the aid of their lungs and larynx, which in some species can produce loud sounds (families Testudinidae, Lacertidae, Gekkonidae, suborder Serpentes). Rattlesnakes, saw-scaled vipers, and African egg-eating snakes can produce rattling noises with a rattle or specialized scales along the flanks. Electronic recordings of vocalization and their depictions as sonograms offer opportunities for graphic evaluation. Today this method is commonly used with frogs to resolve taxonomic problems.

Vocal sac: Thin-walled, elastic pouches on the floor of the mouth in many male frogs. They produce sounds (vocalization) and are resonating organs. They become visible in an inflated condition while being used, and may be simple or paired. In addition to these basic types there are also some abdominal and thoracic vocal sacs (e. g., genus *Physalaemus*).

Vocal sac: Fully inflated single median sac of *Bufo*

Vriesea LINDL. Genus of the Bromeliaceae. Brasil to Central America. About 200 species mainly in tropical rain forests. Most are epiphytes, some rock-dwellers. Rosette plants. Many cultured varieties, such as "Chantieri," "Favorite," and "Flame," can be used just as the wild species. They require ample humidity and shade, with temperatures even at night not below 20° C.
- *V. carinata* WAWRA. Rosette 25 cm high.
- *V. guttata* LIND. and ANDRE. Leaves to 30 cm. Grows very large, but slow growing.

Vriesea scalaris

- *V. hieroglyphica* (CARR.) E. MORR. Leaves to 60 cm. One of the most attractive bromeliads with colorful leaves.
- *V. racinae* L. B. SMITH. Small, about fist-size rosette. Leaves with brown spots on the underside.
- *V. saundersii* (CARR.) E. MORR. ex MEZ. Leaves 25 cm, with white dots on the underside.
- *V. scalaris* E. MORR. Leaves to 35 cm. One of the most attractive species. Frequently cultured. To be used only for large terrariums.

Wagler, Johann Georg (1800-1832): German physician and zoologist. Author of several taxa, especially in *Naturliches System der Amphibien* (1830).

Waglerophis: see *Xenodon*, genus.

Wallacea: Transitional area between the Oriental and Australian Regions, including the Lesser Sunda Islands (except Lom, Bok, and Bali), Sulawesi (Celebes), and the Moluccas. Herpetofaunistically it is poorly defined since many Oriental herps penetrate well into New Guinea in the Australian Region.

Wallsaurus UNDERWOOD, 1954. Genus of the Gekkonidae, subfamily Gekkoninae. Central South America. 2 species. Formerly included in *Gymnodactylus* but distinguishable from it by the lobate pupil. More recently sometimes included in *Homonota*.
- *W. horridus* (BURMEISTER, 1861). Bolivia to northern Argentina.

Walterinnesia LATASTE, 1887. Desert Cobras. Monotypic genus of the Elapidae. Egypt and the Arabian Peninsula to Lebanon and Iran in desert regions. Easily to 1 m. Unicolored dark, adults shiny black.
   Ability to produce a hood almost completely absent. The typical cobra warning behavior has also largely been lost. Instead, specimens encountered during the day will attempt to press their head down onto the ground and hide

it under the coiled body.

Nocturnal venomous snakes adapted to substantial temperature reduction at night and still active at 10-12° C. Prey consists mainly of toads and geckos. Sleeping diurnal lizards are detected in their hiding places by means of the heat-sensing ability of these snakes.

Maintain in a desert terrarium with strong nocturnal temperature reduction.
- *W. aegyptia* LATASTE, 1887.

Washington Convention: An agreement on international trade of endangered species of animals and plants signed on 3 March 1973 in Washington, D.C., and registered with the U.N. According to this Convention the import and export of certain animals and plants require a permit by the signing countries of the Convention that is issued by the respective national authorities. The restrictions upon trade are based on Appendices I and II of the Convention, which list the species involved. Appendix I contains the seriously endangered species, appendix II the less endangered species. Both appendices are subject to constant revisions through additions and deletions of species and their rearrangement depending upon their changed status.

Water: The majority of terrarium animals must drink regularly in order to satisfy their water requirements. Amphibians particularly, but also some reptiles, can take up water through the skin. Only a few desert animals receive enough water from the food they eat, and here it has to be remembered that the soil in their often deep burrows is perpetually damp. In a terrarium the animals usually drink from a water dish. Cleanliness is important and the water must be changed daily, particularly in larger bowls that are also used for bathing.

Some arboreal species never adapt to water dishes on the bottom, and bromeliad funnels are often a satisfactory solution. Sprayed droplets of water are also often eagerly licked up.

Drop dispensers are quite useful for arboreal species. For this purpose one uses a closed container with a small hole drilled in the bottom. The container is filled with water and is then attached above or inside the upper section of the terrarium. In addition, a piece of string serving as a wick can be threaded through the small hole. A suitable drop speed (about 1 to 2 drops per minute) can be adjusted by means of the bore diameter or thickness of the wick. The wicks have to be replaced frequently to prevent bacterial growth. If the tap water is very hard, "dew-drinking" small animals should get some of the tap water diluted with distilled water. Rain water can only be used in areas without air pollution.

Problems can also occur when watering desert animals. Generally spraying is sufficient, and the animals can meet their requirement by licking up the droplets. Water can also be offered by means of a pipette that offers good control (excessive drinking is often a sign of disease, except in newly arrived, partially dehydrated animals). Drinking water is also an excellent medium to administer measured doses of calcium and vitamin supplements. Extreme caution has to be exercised with small desert animals (e. g., *Phrynocephalus*) and the use of open water dishes. Since these animals do not know open water, accidents can happen because they may try to "burrow" in water and easily drown.

Waxmoths: Members of the Lepidoptera, family Pyralidae. Easily bred, the larvae and adults eagerly eaten by many terrarium animals, especially by small lizards and amphibians.

The large waxmoth (*Galleria melonella*) is widely used as a food organism for terrarium animals. The moth reaches a wingspan of about 35 mm. Its development in the wild occurs exclusively in bee hives, where they feed on honey combs and are considered to be a serious pest. One female can lay up to 1,000 eggs. At a temperature of about 30° C. the whitish gray larvae will hatch in about 1 week. These pupate in 4 to 6 weeks, the adult moth emerging in 1 to 2 weeks. The next egg-laying period starts in about 1 to 2 days. An important element in breeding waxmoths is a sufficiently high temperature (about 30° C.). In a well-stocked container waxmoths generate an additional amount of heat of their own. Development stagnates at temperatures below 20° C.

Waxmoth, *Galleria*

Brood containers can be made of various materials (glass, plastic, metal cans) with a volume of about 2 liters. These containers are filled about halfway with old honey combs and a few caterpillars or moths are added before it is covered with gauze. In order to avoid a massive mite infestation (which would destroy the entire culture), the gauze cover can be impregnated with an acaride. If honey combs are not available, an artificial food mixture can also be used: 500 g corn meal, 500 g chicken meal or dry dog food, 125 g dry yeast, 75 g wheat germ (ground), 125 g honey, and 125 g glycerin. After the dry components have been thoroughly mixed, the honey and glycerin are added. A different composition is: 500 g honey, 500 g glycerin, 100 g dry yeast, 200 g bran, 200 g skimmed milk powder, 200 g whole milk powder, and 400 g semolina or maize. A few added drops of a multivitamin solution will further enhance this mixture. Ideally, the medium is shaped into individual small balls that are placed on crinkled paper or corrugated cardboard.

Obviously, large numbers of waxmoths are hard to digest, especially by smaller terrarium animals such as young chameleons.

Similar to its larger cousin is the small waxmoth (*Achroea grisella*), which reaches a wingspan of only 15 mm.

This species requires a little bit more heat. In contrast to the larvae of the preceding larger species that may be permitted to crawl about in the terrarium, the larvae of *A. grisella* will immediately go into hiding. Both species will utilize cardboard for pupation, so one can easily take a strip of this material covered with cocoons and place it into the terrarium in a somewhat disguised location. The moths will then immediately be eaten when they hatch. If any moths of either species should accidentally escape they will cause practically no damage and can not breed in an apartment or house.

On the other hand, a serious pest species is the flour moth *Anagasta kuehniella*, which develops in stored grain and grain products. When this animal is bred caution must be exercised. Breeding can be done with the same procedures described for waxmoths. Suitable food items include flour, black bread, oatmeal, yeast, or the artificial diets described above for waxmoths. Generation period is 6 to 8 weeks at 25° C.

Werner, Franz (1867-1939): Austrian zoologist and herpetologist. Oriented the Viennese herpetological school toward the herpetofauna of the Aegean region and the Near East, as well as toward the Balkan countries, which at that time were administered by the Austro-Hungarian government. Apart from his excellent popular revision of the amphibians and reptiles in the fourth volume of Brehm's *Tierleben* (1912, 1913), he produced many papers on snake systematics (1912, 1924, 1929) and an abundance of other papers.

Werneria POECHE, 1903 (=*Stenoglossa* ANDERSSON, 1903). Monotypic genus of the Bufonidae. Tropical West Africa in mountain regions near and in streams. Tympanum not visible. Tongue very small. Fingers and toes long, webbed at base and up to half way along the digits.
▪ *W. fulva* (ANDERSSON, 1903). Cameroons. 3.5 cm. Olive-brown, the legs with small black crossbands.

Wetmorena COCHRAN, 1927. Monotypic genus of the Anguidae, subfamily Diploglossinae. Haiti. To 15 cm. Weakly developed limbs with only 4 toes. In contrast to the similar *Sauresia* the tympanum is not visible.
Ground-dwellers, presumably burrowing.
▪ *W. haetiana* COCHRAN, 1927. Haiti. Olive-gray with a pattern of dark dots.

Wettstein-Westerheimb, Otto von (1892-1967): Austrian herpetologist who continued Werner's research on the Aegean herpetofauna. *Herpetologica Aegaea* (1953).

Whiteworms: Family Enchytraeidae of the Annelida. Small, mostly whitish or semitransparent species that live in moist soil or small water accumulations. Some species, such as the common whiteworm (*Enchytraeus albidus*) and the 1 cm long Grindalworm or microworm (*Enchytraeus buchholtzi*), are easily bred and useful as food organisms for many amphibians and their larvae. The whitish, up to more than 3 cm long, *E. albidus* is most suitably bred in wooden boxes about 20 x 30 x 15 cm filled with a mixture of humus topsoil, sand, and peat moss at temperatures between 15 and 20° C. A starter culture and then some food is placed in a depression at the top of the soil mixture, which is then covered with a sheet of glass. It is important that

Whiteworms, *Enchytraeus albidus*

excessive wetness is avoided, as it often gives rise to mildew and thus destroys the culture. Decaying excess food must be removed. A suitable diet consists of a mixture of boiled oats (oatmeal), milk, egg yolk, leftover vegetables, and similar items. Soaked white bread and mashed potatoes are also useful as food. The nutritional value of whiteworms is further enhanced if they are given some calcium and/or vitamin supplements shortly before they are used as food.

Wiegmann, Arend Friedrich August (1802-1841): German zoologist. Evaluated collections for the Natural History Museum in Berlin. His *Herpetologia Mexicana* (1834) is the first standard publication on the herpetofauna of that region.

Window terrarium: A flower window sill, glassed over on the outside and inside, with limited use as a terrarium, especially for smaller arboreal forest-dwellers. Care has to be taken that during full exposure to the sun the window terrarium does not overheat. Shaded places must always be available for the animals. Windows facing east or west are the most suitable. Ventilation is often a problem with window terrariums.

Winter dormancy: Winter rest periods essential for well-being of many amphibians and reptiles from temperate climatic zones. Such rest periods can also be very stimulating for the following reproductive and mating periods for animals of subtropical origin. Juvenile specimens usually can do without such winter rest since they may not have sufficient energy reserves. In animals from temperate climates the resting temperature should be about 4 to 6° C. For subtropical specimens usually 10° C. is sufficient, and in many cases even the mere turning off of terrarium heating is enough. Healthy specimens can easily undergo a winter dormancy of 3 to 4 months, but generally 1 or 2 months are sufficient. Specimens from the Southern Hemisphere may require only about 4 to 6 weeks. An ideal location for the winter dormancy period is a cool basement room; in a centrally heated building a refrigerator may have to be used (beware of the danger of desiccation). The animals can be over-wintered in either a small terrarium, a wooden box, or an all-glass aquarium that is filled ⅔ with a damp (not wet) substrate. For instance, oak leaves over a layer of sand or wood shavings have proven to be satisfactory, as is moss for amphibians. A few amphibian species over-winter on the bottom of ponds, lakes, and rivers. If such under-water over-wintering is attempted, provisions should be made to also offer these animals an opportunity to leave the water.

If subtropical species are being over-wintered in their terrarium simply by turning off the heating, special care has to be taken that there is sufficient dampness, since the animals do not drink during their winter dormancy. The temperature is lowered gradually. It is sufficient to start out by adjusting the heating and lighting cycles gradually to shorter periods. Just before the winter dormancy period the animals should have one last good feeding, but then must not be given any food for several days so that their digestive tract is completely devoid of food. Otherwise decomposition can occur in the intestinal tract, which can easily lead to the death of the animal (usually shortly after the winter dormancy has been completed). During the winter rest the animals should be checked every 2 to 4 weeks without actually disturbing them. Specimens found on top of the substrate are usually sick and must be removed. If there is any danger of a brief warm period, a drinking container with water must be available to the animals. If need be, the winter dormancy should be terminated at that point. Temperature increases at the end of the winter dormancy period must again be gradual over 1 to 2 days. Subsequently the animals should first be bathed (especially turtles) and then given drinking water. Food is offered from the second day on.

Wolterstorff, Willy (1864-1943): German zoologist and herpetologist at the Museum of Magdeburg. He started there a significant special collection of newts and salamanders, which unfortunately was destroyed during WW II. Author of numerous herpetological articles, especially on newts. Terrarium science is particularly indebted to him for his experience in systematic breeding of newts as well as for his activities in *Salamandra*, the first German terrarium and herpetological association.

Wolterstorffina MERTENS, 1939. Monotypic genus of the Bufonidae. Tropical West Africa, so far only found on Mount Cameroon at 920 to 1800 m elevation and on the Obudu Plateau, Nigeria, at 1700 m. Compact, with a conspicuous constriction behind the head.

Good climbers. Hardy and durable in captivity. They hide during the day on the ground and climb about actively at night. The diet is small insects.
• *W. parvipalmata* (WERNER, 1898). Cameroons, Nigeria. 3.5 cm. Dorsum blackish, violet toward the posterior part of the body.

Wounds: Traumatically induced separations of skin or mucous membranes, including also the lower-lying tissues. Depending upon the cause, there are bites, burns, cuts, stings, scrapes, tears, and crush wounds. Additional complications occur with simultaneous bone fractures, especially of the carapace of turtles, and from secondary infections. Fresh wounds can be surgically treated; deep wound require anesthesia. Internal wounds due to injuries from foreign bodies require X-ray examinations and possibly surgery as well as the general administration of antibiotics. Older wounds that may be infected, as well as skin lesions, are treated solely with medication. Amphibians and rep-

tiles have excellent healing tendencies.

Wright, Albert Hazen (1879-1970): American herpetologist. Together with his wife Anna Allen Wright, authored *Handbook of Frogs and Toads of the United States and Canada* (1949) and the 2-volume *Handbook of Snakes of the United States and Canada* (1957). Many important early papers on frog development and distribution.

Xanthusia BAIRD, 1859. Night Lizards. Genus of the Xanthusiidae. Southwestern USA and northern Mexico. 3 species primarily in rocky arid or semiarid habitats. 9 to 15 cm. Relatively flat with a broad head. The dorsal scales are small and smooth. Femoral pores of males are larger than in females. These lizards have the ability to undergo physiological light/dark color changes; during the day they generally are darker.

Crepuscular and nocturnal, hiding during the day under rocks or decaying logs; *X. vigilis* appears to prefer to hide under decaying stems of *Yucca arborescens*. The prey includes small arthropods; termites that live in yucca stems are sometimes significant. Occasionally some plant material is taken.

Xanthusia henshawi

Live-bearers, 1-3 (mostly 2) young. Gestation period about 4 months. All species usually do well in a terrarium at temperatures between 22 and 32° C. with a distinct nocturnal temperature reduction. The terrarium should only be slightly damp but must have ample hiding places. Termites and ants are not absolutely essential as food. These animals will now and then drink some water. They have been bred repeatedly.
• *X. henshawi* STEJNEGER, 1893. Granite Night Lizard. Southern California and adjacent Baja California; Durango, Mexico. Easily to 12 cm. Prefers rocky, more shaded slopes or the proximity of water. Whitish gray to yellowish with large dark brown or black spots.
• *X. vigilis* BAIRD, 1858. Desert Night Lizard. Southwestern USA and northwestern Mexico, from the coast to more than 3,000 m. About 10-14 cm. Olive, gray, or dark brown with numerous black dots; normally a light dark-bordered stripe from eye to shoulder.

Xanthusiidae: Night Lizards. Family of the Squamata, suborder Sauria. Southwestern USA to Panama and Cuba. 12 Recent species in 4 genera: *Cricosaura, Klauberina, Lepidophyma,* and *Xanthusia*. Only sparse fossil records from the Middle Eocene have been found in North America. Systematic position uncertain, although closely related to the Gekkonidae (family series Gekkota), with which they share some characters. Other features of this generally primitive group point toward the Scincomorpha. They are found in arid regions, tropical coastlands, or coniferous forests in Central American montane regions. In appearance some are strongly reminiscent of *Lacerta vivipara*. The head is relatively blunt and covered with large scales. Just as do geckos, they have lid spectacles, the lower transparent eyelid window solidly fused to the upper eye margin. These lizards also clean their spectacles occasionally with their tongue as do geckos. Dorsal scales (at least in the center) are small, flat, and smooth. Ventral scales are large and angular. The tail is round in cross-section and

Xanthusia vigilis

generally at least snout-vent length; it has excellent regeneration capability. A gular fold and a small lateral fold are present, and at least males have femoral pores.

In regard to vertebral structure and certain skull features they are similar to geckos, but in contrast to these the upper temporal arch is structured normally. The temporal window is covered by the parietal bone. Peculiarities also occur in the musculature and in the structure of the hyoid bone.

Night lizards hide under rocks, in rocky crevices, decaying wood, and fallen leaves. At night they prey on various small arthropods. *Klauberina* is also partially herbivorous. All species are ovoviviparous (as far as is known), with generally 2 (rarely 1) or several young.

Various night lizards make good terrarium animals. Maintenance conditions vary according to origin of the species and specimens. Some have been bred in captivity.

Xenelaphis GUENTHER, 1864. Genus of the Colubridae, Natricinae. Southeast Asia to the Indo-Australian Archipelago and southward to Java. 2 species found near standing or flowing waters. 1.6 to 2 m. Dorsal scales smooth, more or less elongate, sexagonal. Back with light and dark wide brown longitudinal stripes.

Amphibious. The diet consists mainly of frogs. For care see Natricinae, Group 2.
- *X. hexagonotus* (CANTOR, 1847). Thailand and South Vietnam southward to Kalimantan and Java.
- *X. ellipsifer* BOULENGER, 1900. Kalimantan.

Xenobatrachus PETERS and DORIA, 1878. Genus of the Microhylidae. New Guinea. 7 species in lowland rain forests and mountain regions (to 2,500 m). Skin usually smooth. Pupil horizontal. Tympanum rather indistinct, as large as the eye or smaller. 1 or 2 pairs of large fang-like projections in the anterior oral cavity roof. Most *Xenobatrachus* have an arch-like descending skin fold from the ear region to the shoulder. Fingers and toes are free. Adhesive discs are very small or absent. The metatarsal tubercles are indistinct. Brown.

Mode of life insufficiently known, but presumably ground-dwellers. Eggs large, small in number; development occurs without an aquatic larval stage. See also *Genyophryne* and *Asterophrys*.
- *X. bidens* (VAN KAMPEN, 1909). 3 cm. 1 pair of fangs. Without a skin fold in the ear region.
- *X. giganteus* (VAN KAMPEN, 1915). 9 cm. 2 pairs of fangs.
- *X. rostratus* (MEHELY, 1898). 5 cm. 1 pair of fangs. Snout pointed.

Xenoboa HOGE, 1953. Monotypic genus of the Boidae. Brasil. Closely related to *Epicrates*. About 1 m. Only a few specimens have been found.

Ground snakes, possibly even burrowers.
- *X. cropanii* HOGE, 1953. Sao Paulo, coastal region.

Xenocalamus GUENTHER, 1868. Quill-nosed Snakes. Genus of the Colubridae, Boiginae. Tropical western Africa to central South Africa. 4 partially polytypic species found mainly in dry habitats. 40 to 60 cm. Head not set off and with reduced head scales. Rostral scale projecting far forward and terminating in a point, therefore mouth strongly subterminal. Eyes small. Unicolored or with longitudinal bands or rows of spots in shades of brown.

Burrowers. The diet consists mainly of *Calamelaps*. Egg-layers. These sharp-headed snakes should be transported only in solid containers, not in cloth bags.

Xenoboa cropanii

• *X. bicolor* GUENTHER, 1868. Slender Quill-nosed Snake. Eastern Africa.
• *X. mechovi* NIEDEN, 1913. Zaire and Angola to Republic of South Africa.

Xenochrophis GUENTHER, 1864. Striped Water Snakes. Genus of the Colubridae, Natricinae. Southeast Asia to Pakistan and China. About 5 species. To 1.3 m. Head distinctly set off. Back with strongly keeled and shingled scales. Upper jaw teeth not as clearly differentiated as in *Amphiesma* or even *Rhabdophis*, but very large.

In part amphibious, some species almost aquatic (Groups 2 and 3 of the Natricinae). The preferred food is fish. All species are very aggressive when handled. Egg-layers, up to 20 eggs. *X. piscator* has been bred repeatedly.
• *X. cerasogaster* (CANTOR, 1839). Pakistan and northern India. 75 cm. Longitudinally striped pattern. Keep as Natricinae, Group 3; strongly aquatic.
• *X. piscator* (SCHNEIDER, 1799). Fish Snake. Pakistan eastward to southern China, southward to the Indo-Australian Archipelago. 2 subspecies. The nominate subspecies has ir-

Xenochrophis piscator

Xenochrophis piscator

regular spots, while the Indo-Australian subspecies *X. p. melanozostus* (GRAVENHORST, 1807) has a longitudinally striped pattern.
• *X. vittata* (LINNAEUS, 1758). Sumatra, Java, Sulawesi. Dark brown longitudinal stripes on a lighter background. Natricinae, Groups 2 and 3.

Xenoderminae: Odd-scaled Snakes. Subfamily of the Colubridae. Disjunct, in the Orient and Neotropics. Found in damp habitats (swamps, ground zones of rain forests). Characteristic are the vertebrae, which have enlarged flat-topped lateral projections (particularly well developed in *Xenodermus*, *Cercaspis*, *Xenopholis*, and *Nothopsis*). In many genera there are also conspicuous modifications of the lip scales, which are either covered with small bumps (*Achalis*) or may show a strongly rimmed posterior margin (*Fimbrios*). In *Stoliczkaia* the chin shields are covered with bumps. The head scales are largely normally developed, but in *Xenodermus* they are strongly reduced. The dorsal scales may be strongly differentiated. Most genera have markedly keeled, rather uniform dorsal scales. In *Stoliczkaia* the central scales along the vertebral column are enlarged. This tendency reaches its apex in the unique differentiation into 4 groups of scales in *Xenodermus*. On the other hand, *Nothopsis* displays a modification of the keeled dorsal scales into rough granular scales. In general, this subfamily is rather variable. Without doubt, the representatives of the Xenoderminae are a primitive and at the same time highly specialized branch of colubrid evolution. Keeping these snakes in terrariums can provide potentially major contributions to the rather limited biological knowledge about them.

The diet consists mostly of earthworms, slugs, and frogs. Terrarium maintenance can be as for those Natricinae species that prefer higher temperatures and are less tied to water (e. g., southern *Thamnophis* or *Amphiesma* species). This is most suitable for *Achalinus, Fimbrios, Stoliczkaia, Cercaspis, Nothopsis,* and *Xenopholis; Xenodermus* should be kept the same as the strongly aquatic Natricinae of Group 2.

Systematic-zoogeographic summary:
• 5 Oriental genera: *Achalinus, Cercaspis, Fimbrios, Stoliczkaia, Xenodermus.*
• 2 Neotropical genera: *Nothopsis, Xenopholis.*

Xenodermus REINHARDT, 1836. Strange-scaled Snakes. Monotypic genus of the Colubridae, Xenoderminae. Malaya to Sumatra, Java, and Kalimantan in swamps in tropical forests to 1100 m; also tends to follow human habitation (rice fields). To 65 cm. Unique differentiation of dorsal scales: Along the vertebral column there is a chain consisting of groups of 3 strongly enlarged, keeled scales surrounding a smaller keeled scale. On each side of these there is a wide field of small, irregular mosaic scales crossed by a longitudinal row of larger isolated scales. The sides have normal rows of large, keeled scales. The rounded, distinctly set off head is covered by small mosaic scales; only the very large nasal scales, the following pair of scales, and a small rostral scale remain of the head scales. There are a large number of lip scales, 20 on each side. The back is unicolored dark brown, ventrally slightly lighter.

Amphibious. The diet consisting mainly of frogs. Egg-layers, 2-4 eggs. Maintenance as for Natricinae, Groups 2-3.
• *X. javanicus* REINHARDT, 1836.

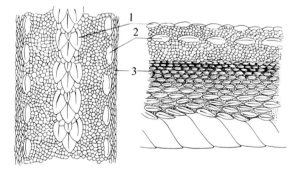

Xenodermus javanicus

Xenodon BOIE, 1827. Genus of the Xenodontinae. Neotropics, Mexico southward to Argentina; in South America only east of the Andes. 7-8 species in tropical forests. To 1.4 m. Massive, with a large head barely set off from the body, flattened. Body wide and flat. Juveniles have dark crossbands on a lighter background; adults are mostly uniform darkish.

Diurnal and nocturnal snakes found on the ground in damp areas, preferring the proximity of water. The diet includes large frogs and toads as well as small mammals and birds. Egg-layers, 15-25 eggs. Disturbed, excited specimens will flatten the body, especially in the neck region, and threaten with loud hissing and fake attacks. Beware of

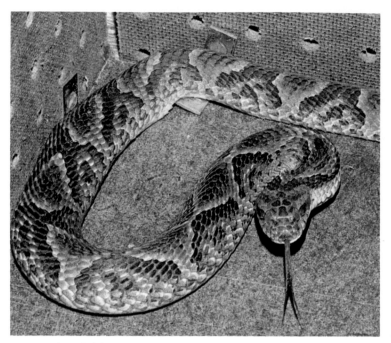

Xenodon rhabdocephalus

Xenodon merremi

bites: venom is presumed to be present although the large posterior upper jaw teeth are without venom grooves.

Maintenance of *Xenodon* should be in well-heated, damp forest terrariums as for large Natricinae, Group 1 (similar to *Macropisthodon, Pseudoxenodon,* and others).
• *X. merremi* (WAGLER, 1824). Sapera, False Yarara. From Guyana and Surinam to northern Argentina. Often placed in the genus *Waglerophis*.
• *X. rhabdocephalus* (WIED, 1824). Mexico to Bolivia. 2 subspecies.
• *X. severus* (LINNAEUS, 1758). Amazon Basin.

Xenodontinae: Odd-toothed Snakes. Subfamily of the Colubridae. Americas. 27 genera. Small to medium-size (rarely very large) snakes that possess in part rather well-developed opisthoglyphic venom teeth located far in the

Xenodon severus

Xenodon suspectus

back of the upper jaw. The always heterogenous dentition resembles that of the Lycodontinae. The group includes several morphologically and ecologically rather variable types. Most typical is a group of thick, plump ground snakes (*Cyclagras, Heterodon, Lystrophis, Platynion,* and *Xenodon*) that live in damp as well as dry habitats. Another small group developed into amphibious water snakes (*Synophis, Tretanorhinus*). There are a large number of ground-dwelling species that live in damp habitats and prey mainly on frogs: *Antillophis, Arrhyton, Darlingtonia, Dromicus, Leimadophis, Liophis, Lygophis, Rhadinaea,* and *Umbrivaga*. A few genera prefer drier habitats, where they prey mainly on lizards: *Alsophis, Conophis*. On the other hand, some species have developed into more or less arboreal snakes: *Philodryas, Ditaxodon;* more perfectly arboreal are the genera *Uromacer* and *Uromacerina*.

Caution is advised when any of these snakes are being handled, especially since in some genera the venom teeth are placed rather far forward (under the eyes), as in *Ialtris, Platynion,* and *Uromacer*. Large genera without venom teeth can inflict painful bites: *Cyclagras, Xenodon*. Very excited or alarmed specimens may play "dead" during the last phase of their defense, a behavior most commonly seen in *Heterodon* and *Xenodon*. All genera appear to be egg-layers.

Systematic review: 27 genera: *Alsophis, Antillophis, Arr-*

hyton, Conophis, Cyclagras, Darlingtonia, Ditaxodon, Dromicus, Heterodon, Hypsyrhynchus, Ialtris, Leimadophis, Liophis, Lioheterophis, Lygophis, Paroxyrhopus, Philodryas, Platynion, Rhadinaea, Rhadinella, Sordellina, Synophis, Tretanorhinus, Umbrivaga, Uromacer, Uromacerina, Xenodon.

Xenopeltidae: Sunbeam Snakes. Monogeneric family of the Henophidia. Indo-China from Burma to southern China, southward to the Indo-Australian Archipelago, but not in New Guinea and Australia. Found in monsoon forests and at the edge of rain forests. About 1 m. The round body is covered by very large scales that are iridescent in sunlight. The belly is covered by wide ventral scales. The head is barely set off from the body and is covered with large head scales; the snout is blunt and wide. The tail is short (only 10% of the total length). Sunbeam snakes have teeth on the intermaxillary bone, distinctive skull characteristics, and two functional lungs, all primitive characters.

Ground-dwellers but not true burrowing snakes. They will not avoid swampy terrain during nocturnal hunting for frogs, lizards, and small mammals, occasionally also other snakes. Live-bearers. They should be kept in a well-heated terrarium with ample hiding places and bathing facilities. Sunbeams will readily accept food in captivity, and rearing of imported juvenile specimens is without difficulties, with rapid growth.

Xenopeltis REINWARDT, 1827. Sunbeam Snakes. Monotypic genus of the Xenopeltidae. Southeast Asia. Juvenile specimens have a dark to black-brown body set off from the dark tip of the head by a very wide, clearly delineated, yellow neckband that extends to the middle of the head. Adults are unicolored medium to light brown with characteristic iridescent gloss. Excited specimens will vibrate the tip of their tail.
▪ *X. unicolor* REINWARDT, 1827.

Xenopholis PETERS, 1869. Monotypic genus of the Colubridae, Xenoderminae. Amazon Basin (Peru, Bolivia,

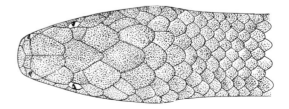

Xenopeltes unicolor

Xenopeltis unicolor

Ecuador, and Brasil) in tropical rain forests.

Small ground snakes, their biology and ecology practically unknown.

▪ *X. scalaris* (WUCHERER, 1861).

Xenopus WAGLER, 1827. African Clawed Frogs, Underwater Frogs. Genus of the Pipidae. Africa south of the Sahara. 6 to 14 (most separable only by chromosomes) species in muddy standing or slowly flowing water. Body more or less egg-shaped, flattened. Skin smooth, with whitish fringing mucous canals (skin sensory organs) along the sides. A more or less distinctly developed tentacle is lo-

Xenopus laevis

cated close to the eye. The head is relatively small, the eyes are turned obliquely upward, and eyelids are present although only weakly developed. The front legs are weak, with free fingers. The back legs are large and muscular. The toes are long, webbed, the inner three toes with black horny claws. Males during the breeding season have ridge-like nuptial pads on fingers and occasionally on the sides of the arms; females can be recognized by a cloaca with three papillae. Males are capable of emitting trill-like sounds. The larvae have 2 long, catfish-like barbels.

Primarily crepuscular and aquatic, but during the rainy season *Xenopus* can undertake extensive land migrations. When the water dries up temporarily *Xenopus* will survive buried in the wet mud. They are capable of swimming forward and backward with equal ease. Usually they stay close to the lower water layer, surfacing only briefly for breathing. Carnivorous, they will eat anything of bite size. Feeding takes place extremely fast and is assisted by the front legs. Well-defined cannibalism is a limiting factor in population size. The large *Xenopus* species are very aggressive and competitive feeders, especially *X. laevis*, and when introduced into a new area can adversely affect aquatic communities, as has happened in California.

Xenopus laevis, tadpole

X. laevis used to be important as a laboratory animal, since young females were used in pregnancy tests (the Hobgen test). They react to the hormones contained in urine from pregnant women by spawning spontaneously within 6-10 hours after having a urine sample injected into the dorsal lymph sac.

Clawed frogs should be kept in a spacious, shallow aquarium at water temperatures from 20 to 27° C.; they can also take temperatures above and below this range for short periods. The water level is kept low so *Xenopus* can breathe from the bottom in an oblique position. Underwater plants are not advisable, since these frogs tend to destroy them with their burrowing and swimming. Hiding places can consist of leached driftwood, rocks, and flowerpot halves. During the summer these frogs can also be kept temporarily outdoors, and they may even breed there. They may even survive a mild winter outdoors if temperatures do not drop below 10 to 15° C. The diet should be varied, and can include earthworms, tubifex, fish, tadpoles, water insects, and crustaceans. They can often be changed over to dead foods, such as strips of lean beef and liver.

For details on reproduction refer to Pipidae. *Xenopus* will sometimes spawn spontaneously, but spawning can be induced by the injection of hormones into the dorsal lymph sac of both sexes and keeping the animals in darkness for 4 hours; this is followed by courtship, and after 8 hours the eggs and sperm are produced. A large female can lay up to 2,000 eggs. Under confined conditions in captivity the spawn is usually eaten without delay (spawning grates can be used or the adults can be removed immediately after

Xenopus laevis

spawning). The larvae will hatch in 2 days at temperatures higher than 20° C. Initially they can eat only very small particles; food that is too large can cause blockages of their filter apparatus and thus lead to death. The most suitable rearing food is a suspension of finely ground nettle power that has been pressed through a piece of cotton cloth; to this one can add similarly treated algae, boiled eggs, and occasionally a supplement of infusoria. Metamorphosis starts on the 40th day and sexual maturity is reached at about the 10th month. One of the small *Xenopus* species, *X. gilli*, is endangered.

▪ *X. laevis* (DAUDIN, 1802). Smooth Clawed Toad, Platanna. Angola, East Africa, southern Africa. To 13 cm (females), males smaller. Variable, back with a dark irregularly spotted pattern on a yellow to gray-brown background. Sometimes almost totally gray-black; belly whitish, in part with brown spots.

▪ *X. muelleri* (PETERS, 1844). Central and southern Africa. To 9 cm. Colored like *X. laevis*, but abdomen yellowish. Eye tentacle long. Well-developed cone-shaped metatarsal tubercle without a horny cover.

▪ *X. tropicalis* (GRAY, 1864). Tropical West Africa. A horny metatarsal tubercle present. Eye tentacle long. Dorsal region without distinct pattern.

Xenosauridae: Knob-scale Lizards. Family of the Squamata, suborder Sauria. Disjunct distribution: Mexico to Guatemala, China. 2 genera, about 4 Recent species. Certainly related to the Diploglossa, although some features also relate them to the Platynota. Xenosaurs occur in the fossil record since the Upper Cretaceous and are known from Europe. 20 to 40 cm. Massive deep head with conspicuously strong temporal arches. Jaws with numerous teeth, palatine without teeth. Tympanum covered by scales. Well-developed limbs.

Ground-dwellers with a cryptic mode of life, often found close to water; they like to bathe.

Genera: *Shinisaurus* and *Xenosaurus*.

Xenosaurus PETERS, 1861. American Knob-scale Lizards. Genus of the Xenosauridae. 3 species. Central America and Mexico. Easily to 20 cm. Slightly flattened dorso-ventrally, the head also relatively flat. Brown with yellow crossbands, very distinct along tail. Characteristic black salivary membranes.

Crepuscular ground-dwellers that like to bathe. The diet is mainly termites and ants. Ovoviviparous, 2 to 4 young.

▪ *X. grandis* (GRAY, 1856). Mexico (Veracruz, Oaxaca).

▪ *X. rackhami* STUART, 1941. Guatemala and Mexico (Chiapas).

Xenosaurus grandis

Xerobates: see *Gopherus*, genus.

Xiphicercus, subgenus: see *Anolis*, genus.

Xylophis BEDDOME, 1878. Genus of the Colubridae, Lycodontinae. Southern India. 2 species. In mountains. 25 to 60 cm. Head pointed, not set off from the body. Back dark brown, either uniform or with longitudinal stripes or rows of spots arranged longitudinally.

▪ *X. perroteti* (DUMERIL and BIBRON, 1854). To 60 cm.

▪ *X. stenorhynchus* (GUENTHER, 1875). To 25 cm.

Yucca L. Yuccas. Genus of the Agavaceae. Southern USA, California, Texas, Arizona, and adjacent Mexico to Central America. 35 species in semiarid regions. Hardy stemless or stem-forming species. Young plants of all species are suitable for terrariums containing animals from the semidesert regions of North and Central America. Some *Yucca* species are frost-resistant and can be used in open-air terrariums.

▪ *Y. glauca* NUTT. ex. FRAS. Stemless. Leaves 60 to 90 cm.

▪ *Y. gloriosa* L. Leaves to 50 cm. Almost frost-resistant, requiring protection only in very exposed cold areas.

▪ *Y. filamentosa* L. Base of stem buried; carpet-forming in later stages. Leaves to 60 cm.

Zachaenus COPE, 1866 (=*Craspedoglossa* MUELLER, 1922). Genus of the Leptodactylidae. South America. About 5 species. 2 to 7 cm. Egg-shaped. Skin smooth.

Eyes slightly protruding. Pupil horizontal. Tympanum not visible. Tips of fingers and toes not enlarged, not webbed.

Ground-dwellers that deposit a few large eggs in damp substrate, where the larvae—surrounded by gelatinous egg remnants—undergo development to metamorphosis.
▪ *Z. stejnegeri* (NOBLE, 1924). Southeastern Brasil in montane regions, about 100 to 1500 m. To 4.7 cm.
▪ *Z. parvulus* (GIRARD, 1853). Distribution as for *Z. stejnegeri*. 2 cm.

Zaocys COPE, 1860. Asian Rat Snakes. Genus of the Colubridae, Colubrinae. Indo-China and southern China through large sections of the Indo-Australian Archipelago to the Philippines. 6 species in dry, warm areas along the banks of lakes, pools, rivers, and canals. *Z. nigromarginatus* occurs in mountain regions up to 2400 m in the eastern Himalayas. Easily to 3 m (almost ⅓ of it tail). Strong but slender, the largest snakes of the subfamily. The elongated head is distinctly set off and has large eyes. The dorsal scales are either all smooth or the central 4 to 6 rows are keeled (*Z. carinatus, Z. nigromarginatus*). Colorations and markings often notably different from juvenile to adult: juveniles have yellow spots on a light brown background, crossbands and black-brown longitudinal stripes, or a reticulated pattern. Adults often have darker colors, often becoming melanistic.

These rat snakes have a substantial flight distance and usually flee into the water; they are excellent swimmers and divers. The main diet consists of frogs, but other vertebrates are also taken. Reproduction is by means of advanced eggs. Care is as for the Natricinae, Group 2. A well-heated, dry sunning site and dry sleeping place must be available. They will readily tame and take food directly from the hand, largely losing the flight reflex. They should be permitted to adapt to new surroundings undisturbed.

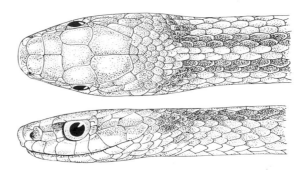

Zaocys dhumnades

▪ *Z. carinatus* (GUENTHER, 1858). From Tenasserim and Burma to Malaya and Sumatra, Kalimantan, Java. In excess of 3 m. The largest species of the genus.
▪ *Z. dhumnades* (CANTOR, 1842). Big-eye Snake. China, frequently along the upper reaches of the Yangtsekiang. 2 subspecies. Barely to 2 m.
▪ *Z. nigromarginatus* (BLYTH, 1854). Nepal, Sikkim, and Burma to western China. In mountain regions. 2.2 m.

Zebrina SCHNIZL. Zebra Tradescantia. Genus of the Commelinaceae. Central America. Low-lying shrubs. Similar in appearance to *Tradescantia*.
▪ *Z. pendula* SCHNIZL. Can be used as hanging or ground-covering plants. Will not take temperatures below 12° C.

Zonosaurus BOULENGER, 1887. Girdled Lizards. Genus of the Cordylidae, subfamily Gerrhosaurinae. Madagascar. 3 species found along rivers in tropical rain forests. In appearance similar to *Gerrhosaurus*. 20 to 60 cm. Strongly built. The head is only slightly set off. The tail is barely twice the snout-vent length. A lateral fold is well-developed. Dorsal scales are "ribbed," the initially strong median keel disappearing in older specimens. In contrast to

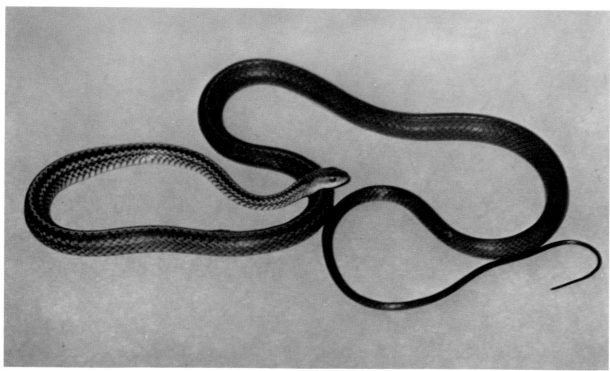

Zaocys dhumnades

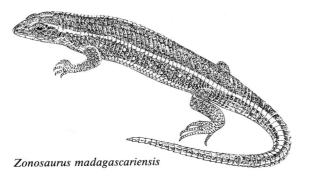

Zonosaurus madagascariensis

Gerrhosaurus, the ventral scales are strongly overlapping and the nostrils are restricted by an anterior snout scale.

Zonosaurus species are diurnal. The diet consists of various small animals and also some fruit. Egg-layers. They should be kept in a spacious, damp terrarium with a large water dish and sufficient hiding places. Provide day temperatures from 25 to 32° C. with a weak basking light. Do not allow the temperature to fall below 20° C. at night.
▪ *Z. madagascariensis* (GRAY, 1831). Madagascar. Barely to 40 cm. Red-brown to black with light yellow spots and 2 longitudinal bands. Head mainly light colored.

Zonuridae: see Cordylidae, family.

Zonurus: see *Cordylus*, genus.

Zoogeographical regions: Division of the earth according to criteria of animal distribution. Within a zoogeographical region numerous distribution areas overlap, yet between 2 adjacent zoogeographical regions there is comparatively little overlap. Therefore, a particular zoogeographical region is characterized by its typical animal groups. Since the distribution of animals is not only dependent upon geographical features but also upon ecological and geological factors, the borders of zoogeographical zones do not necessarily coincide with geographical borders. Similarly, zoogeographical regions are also not comparable with botanical geographical regions.

The largest zoogeographical regions are the faunal kingdoms (Holarctic, Ethiopian, Oriental, Neotropic, Australasian, Antarctic), which are subdivided into subregions, which can also be further divided into yet smaller regions.

Zoogeography: Part of biogeography that deals with the geographical distribution of animals and its fundamental causes.

Zoological nomenclature: Establishing scientific names for all animals. For reasons of clarity and international understanding, each taxon has a Latin or Latinized name. Formation and use of these names within the species, genus, and family realm (systematic categories) have to be in conformity with the International Code of Zoological Nomenclature.

Zoological Record: Important reference publication that provides annual reviews on a worldwide basis of all zoological papers and books published since 1864. It contains exact reference sources for all new taxa of amphibians and reptiles established during a particular year.

Zootoca: see *Lacerta*, genus.

Zygaspis COPE, 1885. Monotypic genus of the Amphisbaenia. Tropical Africa. Similar to *Amphisbaena* and often included in it.
▪ *Z. quadrifrons* (PETERS, 1862). Cape Province to southern Congo.

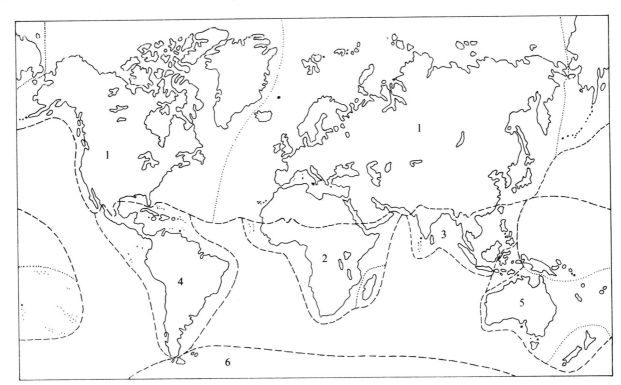

Zoogeographical regions: 1 Holarctic; 2 Ethiopian; 3 Oriental; 4 Neotropic; 5 Australasian; 6 Antarctic

Many photographers, both professional and amateur, have contributed to the spectacular collection of photographs assembled here. The following photographers produced or allowed the use of color photographs added to the English-language edition:

Federico Achaval; Dr. Gerald R. Allen; American Museum of Natural History; Robert Anderson; Robert W. Applegate; M. Auber-Thomay; G. S. Axelrod; Dr. Herbert R. Axelrod; R. W. Barbour; G. Baumgart; Bertrand E. Baur; R. Bechter; V. Bels; W. Bischoff; W. Boehme; M. Bonnetier; R. Bour; W. R. Branch; Jim Bridges; Robert L. Brown; Patrick Burchfield; Dr. Warren E. Burgess.

Tom Caravaglia; Dr. Bruce Carlson; Chester Zoo; Dr. J. C. Chubb; Coffey and Bloxam; J. T. Collins; Cotswold Wildlife Park; Sorin Damian; Walter Deas; George Dibley; Dr. Guido Dingerkus; F. J. Dodd, Jr.; John Dommers.

Dr. E. Elkans; P. van den Elzen; P. A. Federsoni; Wade Ferrar; Lyle Flesher; Isabelle Francais; Stanislav Frank; H. Frauca; Dr. Marcos Freiberg; J. Fretey; Frickhinger; U. Erich Friese; Jeff Gee; Keith Gillett; Michael Gilroy; Bob Gossington; A. I. Grasso; Dr. Harry Greir; Rogelio Gutierrez.

Richard Haas; H. Hansen; J. D. Hardy, Jr.; Dr. Nelson Herwig; Richard L. Holland; Stephan Holley; R. T. Hoser; Ray E. Hunziker; Peter Irtz; Dr. P. Juster; Burkhard Kahl; John T. Kellnhauser; Alex Kerstitch; D. Kiehlmann; Otto Klee; K. Knaack; Sergei Kochetov; R. E. Kuntz.

J. K. Langhammer; Larry Lantz; Dr. M. Leach; J. Lescure; F. Letellier; London Zoo; L. M. Lozzia; Ken Lucas, Steinhart Aquarium; S. McKeown; G. Marcuse; C. O. Masters; Sven Mathiason; John M. Mehrtens; Dr. R. Mertens; Dr. Sherman A. Minton; Russell Mittermeier; David R. Moenich; W. Mudrack.

National Museum of Natural History; K. T. Nemuras; A. van den Nieuwenhuizen; Aaron Norman; Peter Parks; Parrots of the World; Alcide Perucca; Hans Peter; Hector Piacentini; D. Poisson; Cl. Poivre; Louis Porras; Allan Power; Dr. Peter C. H. Pritchard.

Elaine Radford; Dwayne Reed; Dr. H. Reichenbach-Klinke; Mervin F. Roberts; W. Sachsse; Ivan Sazima; Harald Schultz; Peter Scott; G. Scrocchi; R. S. Simmons; P. J. Stafford; Rainer Stawikowski; J. P. Swaak.

Dr. Dennis Terver, Nancy Aquarium, France; W. Tomey; Dr. M. A. del Toro; R. G. Tuck, Jr.; Ch. Vaucher; N. Viloteau; John Visser; Uwe Werner; L. C. de Zolessi; Ruda Zukal.

The following photographers were represented in the original German edition:

Bischoff, Bonn; Boehme, Bonn; Foekema, Amsterdam; Foerster, Leipzig; Fritsche, Dresden; Hallmann, Zepernick; Jacob, Dresden-Hellerau; Kaden, Halle; Kahl, Stuttgart; Kratzer, Zurich; Kretz, Bern; Langerwerf, Waspik; Mueller, Halle; Obst, Dresden; Pelz, Merseburg; Richter, Waldsteinberg; Rudloff, Berlin; Schaarschmidt, Hamburg; Schmidt, Schoenow; Schroeter, Karl-Marx-Stadt; Sochurek, Vienna; Trutnau, Altrich; Wiesner, Berlin; Winkler, Rostock.

GUIDELINES FOR USE OF LIVE AMPHIBIANS AND REPTILES IN FIELD RESEARCH

*American Society of Ichthyologists
and Herpetologists (ASIH)
The Herpetologists' League (HL)
Society for the Study of Amphibians
and Reptiles (SSAR)*

[The following guidelines for captive and field studies involving reptiles and amphibians are the result of a joint effort by the major herpetological societies of the U.S.A. to provide a basic framework for modern studies. Although some parts are not especially pertinent to terrarium studies, all parts are of some interest to herpetologists in general. With the growing body of restrictive regulations being imposed on herp care by many local and national agencies, the terrarium keeper can no longer exist in a vacuum and must become aware that his hobby is of concern to many people and groups that he may never directly contact. Perusal of these guidelines may not only help keep you out of trouble but will probably give you some good ideas to make your collecting and terrarium care easier and more productive...ED.]

INTRODUCTION

Consistent with our long standing interests in conservation, education, research and the general well-being of amphibians and reptiles, the ASIH, HL and SSAR support the following guidelines and principles for scientists conducting field research on these animals. As professional biologists specializing in herpetology and concerned with the welfare of these animals, we recognize that guidelines for the laboratory care and use of domesticated stocks of amphibians and reptiles are frequently impossible to apply without endangering the well-being of wild-caught animals. Such guidelines may also preclude techniques or types of investigations known to have minimal adverse effects on individuals or populations (1, 20), and which are necessary for the acquisition of new knowledge.

The humane treatment of wild vertebrates in field research is both an ethical and a scientific necessity. Traumatized animals may exhibit abnormal physiological, behavioral and ecological responses that defeat the purposes of the investigation (21, 25). It is of particular importance that animals which are captured and marked be returned to the wild without impairment to resuming their normal activities, and that habitats essential for these activities not be rendered unsuitable in the course of capture efforts.

Due to the very considerable range of adaptive diversity represented by the over 8,000 species of amphibians and reptiles, no concise or specific compendium of approved methods for field research is practical or desirable. Rather, the guidelines presented below build on the most current information to advise the investigator, who will often be an authority on the biology of the species under study, as to techniques that are known to be humane and effective in the conduct of field research. Ultimate responsibility for the ethical and scientific validity of an investigation and the methods employed must rest with the investigator. To those who adhere to the principles of careful field research these guidelines will simply be a formal statement of precautions already in place.

GENERAL CONSIDERATIONS

Each investigator should provide written assurance in applications and proposals that field research with amphibians and reptiles will meet the following criteria:

a. Procedures should avoid or minimize distress to the animals consistent with sound research design.

b. Procedures that may cause more than momentary or slight distress to the animals should be performed with appropriate sedation, analgesia, or anesthesia, except when justified for scientific reasons by the investigator.

c. Animals that would otherwise experience severe or chronic distress that cannot be relieved will be euthanized at the end of the procedure or, if appropriate, during the procedure.

d. Methods of euthanasia will be consistent with recommendations of the American Veterinary Medical Association (AVMA) Panel on Euthanasia (13) unless deviation is justified for scientific reasons by the investigator. The AVMA recommendations cannot be taken rigidly for ectotherms; the methods suggested for endotherms are often not applicable to ectotherms with significant anaerobic capacities.

e. The living conditions of animals held in captivity at field sites should be appropriate for that species and contribute to their health and well-being. The housing, feeding, and nonmedical care of the animals will be directed by a scientist (generally the investigator) trained and experienced in the proper care, handling, and use of the species being maintained or studied. Some experiments (e.g., competition studies) will require the housing of mixed species, possibly in the same enclosure. Mixed housing is also appropriate for holding or displaying certain species.

Additional general considerations that should be incorporated into any research design using wild amphibians or reptiles include the following:

f. The investigator must have knowledge of all regulations pertaining to the animals under study, and must obtain all permits necessary for carrying out proposed studies. (Most applicable regulations are referenced in publications of the Association of Systematics Collections [2,3,4].) Researchers working outside the United States should ensure that they comply with all wildlife regulations of the country in which the research is being performed. Work with many species is regulated by the provisions of the Convention on International Trade in Endangered Species of Wild Flora and Fauna (CITES; see "CITES" references in 2, 3). Regulations affecting a single species may vary with country. Local regulations may also apply.

g. Individuals of endangered or threatened taxa should neither be removed from the wild (except in collaboration with conservation efforts), nor imported or exported, except in compliance with applicable regulations.

h. Before initiating field research, investigators must be familiar with the target species and its response to disturbance, sensitivity to capture and restraint and, if necessary, requirements for captive maintenance to the extent that these factors are known and applicable to a particular study. Special concern should be shown for species known to remain with nests or young in certain seasons. Removal from the wild of potentially tending individuals of species known to tend nests should, as a general principle, be avoided during the nesting season unless justified for scientific reasons.

i. Every effort should be made prior to removal of animals (if any) to understand the population status (abundant, threatened, rare, etc.) of the taxa to be studied, and the numbers of animals removed from the wild must be kept to the minimum the investigator determined is necessary to accomplish the goals of the study. This statement should not be interpreted as proscribing study and/or collection of uncommon species. Indeed, collection for scientific study can be crucial to understanding why a species is uncommonly observed.

j. The numbers of specimens required for an investigation will vary greatly, depending upon the questions being explored. As discussed later in these guidelines, certain kinds of investigations require collection of relatively large numbers of specimens, though the actual percent of any population taken will generally be very small. Studies should use the fewest animals necessary to answer reliably the questions posed. Use of adequate numbers to assure reliability is essential, as inadequate studies will ultimately require repetition, thus wasting any benefit derived from any animal distress necessarily incurred during the study.

Numerous publications exist that will assist investigators and animal care committees in implementing these general guidelines; a number of such journals, monographs, etc., are listed in Additional References.

ROLE OF THE INSTITUTIONAL ANIMAL CARE AND USE COMMITTEE (IACUC)

Field resources for the care and use of wild vertebrates are very different from laboratory resources, and the role of the IACUC necessarily is limited to considerations that are practical for implementation at locations where field research is to be conducted. Prevailing conditions may prevent investigators from following these guidelines to the letter at all times. Investigators must, however, make every effort to follow the spirit of these guidelines. The omission from these guidelines of a specific research or husbandry technique should not be interpreted as proscription of the technique.

The IACUC must be aware that whereas vertebrates typically used in laboratory research represent a small number of species with well understood husbandry requirements, the classes Amphibia and Reptilia contain at least 8,000 distinct species with very diverse and often poorly known behavioral, physiological and ecological characteristics. This diversity, coupled with the diversity of field research situations, requires that each project be judged on its own merits. Techniques that are useful and fitting for one taxon, experiment, or field situation may, in another time, place or design be counter-productive. Therefore, ". . . in most cases, it is impossible to generate specific guidelines for groups larger than a few closely related species. Indeed, the premature stipulation of specific guidelines would severely inhibit humane care as well as research" (23). The IACUC must note the frequent use of the word "should" throughout these guidelines, and be aware that this is in deliberate recognition of the diversity of animals and situations covered by the guidelines. Investigators, on the other hand, must be aware that the use of the word "should" denotes the ethical obligation to follow these guidelines when realistically possible.

Field investigations very commonly involve studies of interactions among many related or sympatric species, of which a large proportion may be very poorly known. There is sound scientific merit in exploratory work, and ample reason for investigators to propose studies of a rather general nature, where opportunity and the flexibility to pursue unanticipated observations may become crucial to the success of the undertaking. New species continue to be discovered in this fashion, and the discovery of novel attributes of known species is to be expected as a consequence of the investigation. The IACUC should recognize that the acquisition of such new knowledge constitutes a major justification for any investigation, and that a corollary of this approach is that protocols may list a large number of individual species, or may refer to taxa above the species level.

When field studies on wild vertebrates are to be reviewed, the IACUC must include personnel who can provide an understanding of the nature and impact of the proposed field investigation, the housing of the species to be studied, and knowledge concerning the risks associated with maintaining certain species of wild vertebrates in captivity. Each IACUC should therefore include at least one institution-appointed member who is experienced in zoological field investigations. Such personnel may be appointed to the committee on an *ad hoc* basis to provide necessary expertise. When sufficient personnel with the necessary expertise in this area are not available within an institution, this *ad hoc* representative may be a qualified member from another institution.

Field research on native amphibians and reptiles usually requires permits from state and/or federal wildlife agencies. These agencies review applications for their scientific merit and their potential impact on native populations, and issue permits that authorize the taking of specified numbers of individuals, the taxa and methods allowed, the period of study, and often other restrictions which are designed to minimize the likelihood that an investigation will have deleterious effects. Permission to conduct field research rests with these agencies by law, and the IACUC should seek to avoid infringement on their authority to control the use of wildlife species.

If manipulation of parameters of the natural environment (daylength, etc.) is not part of the research protocol, field housing for wild vertebrates being held for an extended period of time should approximate natural conditions as closely as possible while adhering to appropriate standards of care (e.g., 16, 17, 28). Caging and maintenance should provide for the safety and wellbeing of the animal, while adequately allowing for the objectives of the study.

FIELD ACTIVITIES WITH WILD AMPHIBIANS AND REPTILES

1. Collecting

Field research with amphibians and reptiles frequently involves capture of specimens, whether for preservation, data recording, marking, temporary confinement, or relocation. While certain of these activities are treated separately below, they form a continuum of potential field uses of amphibians and reptiles.

The collection of samples for museum preparation from natural populations is critical to: 1) understanding the biology of animals throughout their ranges and over time; 2) recording the biotic diversity, over time and/or in different habitats; and 3) establishing and maintaining taxonomic reference material essential to understanding the evolution and phylogenetic relationships of amphibians and reptiles. The number of specimens collected should be kept to the minimum the investigator determines necessary to accomplish the goal of a study. Some studies (e.g., diversity over geographic range or delineation of variation of new species) require relatively ˜re samples.

Museum Specimens and Other Killed Specimens

The collection of live animals and their preparation as museum specimens is necessary for research and teaching activities in systematic zoology, and for many other types of studies. Such collections should further our understanding of these animals in their natural state and not serve merely as tools for teaching specimen preparation techniques. Herpetological collecting techniques and representative practices of collection management have been compiled (5), as have references to field techniques (32). Whenever amphibians or reptiles are collected for museum deposition, specimens should be fixed and preserved according to accepted methods (6, 7) to assure the maximum utility of each animal and to minimize the need for duplicate collecting. In principle, each animal collected should serve as a source of information on many levels of organization from behavior to DNA sequence. Whenever practical, blood and other tissues should be collected for karyotypic and molecular study prior to formalin fixation of the specimen.

Formalin fixation of dead specimens is acceptable practice; however, killing unanesthetized specimens by immersion in a formalin solution is unacceptable, unless justified for scientific reasons. Formalin immersion of unanesthetized animals may, however, be the only way to adequately fix certain details of morphology critical to the successful completion of research. Adult amphibians (A) and reptiles (R) may be painlessly killed by use of a chemical anesthetic such as sodium pentobarbitol (R), hydrous chlorobutanol (A), MS-222 (A) (Tricaine methane sulfonate, marketed as Finquel by Ayerst, Inc.), urethane-ethyl-carbamate (A) (referred to hereafter as urethane), 10% ethanol (A) or similar anesthetics. The euthanasia agent T-61 (National Laboratories) is very effective on reptiles (27). Use of such chemicals requires little additional time and effort, adds little to the bulk or weight of collecting equipment, and allows for preparation of better quality specimens. Urethane is carcinogenic, and caution should be observed with its use and field disposal. Other anesthetics may also be acceptable, especially since new agents are frequently developed. Gunshot is an acceptable and often necessary collecting technique, and is also recognized for euthanasia (13).

When special circumstances require that specimens (very small or larval animals, for example) be formalin-fixed without prior anesthetic killing, prior light anesthetization with an anesthetic such as MS-222 is recommended (31).

Live Capture

Investigators should be familiar with herpetological capture techniques (5) and should choose a method suited to both the species and the study. Live-capture techniques should prevent or minimize damage to the animal.

Trapping

Traps of various kinds are often necessary to obtain unbiased samples of secretive, nocturnal or infrequently active species. The interval between visits to traps should be as short as possible, although it may vary with species, weather, objectives of the study, and the type of trap. Traps should be checked at least daily when weather conditions threaten survival of trapped animals. Investigators must make every effort to prevent trap deaths from exposure, drowning, cardiogenic shock, or capture myopathy (1). Traps should be sheltered from direct sunlight, and care should be taken to reduce predation in pitfall traps (29). Pitfall traps set during extremely dry periods should have some moisture provided to prevent desiccation of captured amphibians. Traps should be tightly covered between sampling periods and removed at conclusion of a study.

Habitat and Population Considerations

Whether collecting for future release or for museum preparation, each investigator should observe and pass on to students and co-workers a strict ethic of habitat conservation. Because many essential details of life history will remain unknown until a study is well along, collecting always should be conducted so as to leave habitat as undisturbed as possible. Permanent removal of more than 50% of the animals from any breeding or hibernation aggregation should be avoided unless justified in writing for scientific reasons by the investigator. Similarly, relatively large collections of gravid females from any population

for destructive sampling should be avoided unless justified for scientific reasons. When permanent, destructive human alteration of habitat is imminent (construction, water impoundment, etc.), removal of entire populations may be justified. Systematists should investigate extant collections for suitable specimens before conducting field work.

2. Restraint and Handling

General Principles

The decision to use physical or chemical restraint of wild amphibians or reptiles should be based upon design of the experiment, knowledge of behavior of the animals, and availability of facilities. Investigators should determine and use the least amount of restraint necessary to do the job in a humane manner. Because amphibians or reptiles, especially venomous species (including those with toxic skin secretions), may be capable of inflicting serious injury either on themselves or those handling them, some form of restraint often is prudent. Species should not be confined with others (other than food prey) that they may injure. The well-being of the animal under study is of paramount importance; improper restraint, especially of frightened animals, can lead to major physiological disturbances that can result in deleterious or even fatal consequences.

Animals are best handled quietly and with the minimum personnel necessary. Darkened conditions tend to alleviate stress and quiet the animals and are recommended whenever appropriate. When handling large reptiles, netting, or maneuvering or dropping them into a bag via hook, tongs, etc., is preferable inasmuch as they may suffer disproportionately great damage during struggling.

Administration of a tranquilizer to an animal that is restrained in a body squeeze may prevent injury to the animal and/or persons working with it. A brief review of restraint techniques for venomous snakes is available (15). Techniques often vary with size and species of the animal being handled.

In some cases, administration of general anesthesia for restraint in the field may be advisable. If so, the anesthetic chosen should be a low-risk one that permits rapid return to normal physiological and behavioral state. The animal must be kept under observation until complete recovery occurs. The relatively unpredictable and potentially delayed response of some ectotherms to immobilants or anesthetics may contraindicate use of these chemicals under field conditions. Investigators must understand the specific action of restraint chemicals on the taxa studied.

Hazardous Species

Venomous snakes and lizards, certain large non-venomous lizards and snakes, some colubrid snakes (35), highly poisonous frogs, crocodilians, and some large turtles potentially are dangerous, and require special methods of restraint as a compromise between potential injury to handlers and injurious restraint of the animal. The particular method chosen will vary with species and the purpose of the project. Adherence to the following general guidelines is recommended when working with hazardous species (36):

a. Procedures chosen should minimize the amount of handling time required, and reduce or eliminate contact between handler and animal.

b. Those handling venomous snakes or lizards should be knowledgeable concerning the proper method of handling those animals. They should be aware of emergency procedures to be instituted in case of accidental envenomation. Location of a reasonably nearby supply of antivenin and of a physician with knowledge of envenomation treatment should be ascertained in advance.

c. One should avoid working alone. A second person, knowledgeable of capture/handling techniques and emergency measures, should be present whenever possible.

d. Prior consultation with workers experienced with these species, and review of the relevant literature, is of particular importance here since much of the information on handling dangerous species is not published, but is passed simply from one investigator to another.

Chemical Restraint

Many chemicals used for restraint or immobilization of amphibians or reptiles are controlled by the Federal Bureau of Narcotics and Dangerous Drugs/Drug Enforcement Administration (DEA). A DEA permit is required for purchase or use of these chemicals. Extensive information on these substances and their use is available (8-10), and permit application procedures are available from regional DEA offices.

The potent drugs available for wildlife immobilization when properly used are, with the exception of succinylcholine, safe for target animals but can be extremely dangerous if accidentally administered to humans. The degree of danger varies according to the drug, and users must be aware of the appropriate action to take in the event of accident (11). Neuromuscular blocking agents do not render animals unconscious, and subsequent handling may be traumatic. More effective chemicals are available for immobilizing most amphibians and reptiles (9). Several common local anesthetics (e.g., Tetracaine, Lidocaine, Piperocaine, etc.) have temporary, but severe, myotoxic effects on mammals (34). Their effect on ectotherms is unknown, but animals treated with these should be observed before release to the wild to be certain that behavior approximates normal. Investigators should choose the chemical for immobilization with consideration of the effects of that chemical on the target organism. Because of the uncertainty of chemical actions on ectotherms, certain minor procedures may in the long run be less traumatic to animals when anesthetics are not used.

Certain chemicals produce initial excitement before anesthesia, suggesting their use in conjunction with tranquilizers. An increasing body of knowledge (e.g., 33) indicates that pain perception of the many species of vertebrates is not uniform over the various homologous portions of their bodies. Therefore, broad extrapolation of pain perception across taxonomic lines should be avoided. What causes pain and distress to a mammal does not necessarily affect a reptile or amphibian equivalently.

3. Animal Marking

Marking animals for field recognition is an essential technique in biological research. Important considerations in choosing a marking technique concern effects on behavior, physiology, and survival of the animal. The utility of any technique varies with the species under study; tissue-removal techniques may pose less long-term survival threat to some species than certain tagging methods. Marking techniques for amphibians and reptiles have been reviewed extensively (12). Although field observation indicates that individual wild animals can survive extensive tissue damage from natural causes (30), the effect of most tissue-removal marking techniques on survival and fitness is not adequately known and is a topic worth investigating.

When choosing an acceptable marking technique, investigators must consider the nature and duration of restraint, the amount of tissue affected, whether pain is momentary or prolonged, whether the animal will be at greater than normal predation risk, whether the animal's ability to mate is reduced, and whether the risk of infection is minimal. Careful testing of marking techniques on captive animals before use on free-ranging animals may reveal potential problems and is recommended. It may be desirable to use redundant techniques to assure accuracy during a study.

Toe Clipping

Toe clipping should be used only for general marking of free-ranging animals when toe removal is not judged (by observation of captives or of a closely-related species) to impair the normal activities of the marked animal. Toes essential to animals for activities such as burrowing, climbing, amplexus, or nest excavation, should never be removed. No more than two non-adjacent toes per foot should ever be removed. If behavior or survival of the animal is likely to be seriously impaired, alternate marking techniques should be used. Clarke (24) reported adverse effect of toe-clipping on survival of *Bufo woodhousei*. Critical study of the effects of this technique on fitness would be a valuable contribution.

Scale Clipping/Branding

Removal of subcaudal or ventral scutes according to a standardized numerical code provides a good permanent marking system for snakes which does not appear to increase mortality or impair locomotion (26). The scute is removed with small surgical scissors, or by rapid cauterization; healing usually is rapid, and infec-

tion is rare. Electrocauterization of a number or letter on the skin, in which deep layers of skin are cauterized to prevent regeneration, is comparable. Brand marks may not be visible in amphibians after a few months. The use of a local anesthetic (aerosols containing benzocaine, such as Cetacaine, may be applied) is urged with branding or electrocauterization. The less permeable skin of reptiles reduces the effectiveness of topical products.

Tattoos and Dye Markers

Tattooing has been used with success on both amphibians and reptiles. Two potential problems should be resolved prior to tattooing: 1) selection of a dye which will contrast with the normal skin pigmentation; and 2) loss of legibility due to diffusion or ultraviolet degradation of the dye.

Paint should not be used to mark the moist and permeable skin of amphibians. Various vital stains are more suitable. Reptile skin permeability is quite variable, and paint or paint solvents may be absorbed and cause death of the animal. Paints with non-toxic pigments, bases, and solvents must be used. When toxicity is unknown, laboratory trials, even if limited, should be done before field use. Very tenacious paints may, if applied across shell sutures, severely distort the normal shell growth of turtles, especially subadults. Paint should not be applied to sutures of turtle shells.

Banding and Tagging

The size, shape and placement of tags should be appropriate to permit normal behavior of the animal marked. Bands and tags projecting from the body may produce physical impairment or enhance the risk of entanglement in undergrowth or aquatic cover. Brightly colored tags also may compromise an animal's camouflage. Raney and Lachner (21) documented growth cessation in jaw-tagged toads. Graham (19) cautioned that Petersen discs may cause mortality when used on freshwater turtles; they therefore must be used with great care in this application. Their use on marine turtles less exposed to the hazards cited by Graham may be less risky. Colored mylar ribbon tags 1–2″ long may prove an acceptable alternative for freshwater turtles. Colored discs and tags conceivably could function as predator attractants.

Shell Marking

In most species of turtles, the bony shell can be marked by cutting notches or small holes in the marginal scutes of the carapace. In addition, disc-type tags and clamp-on ear-type tags (see cautionary remarks above) have been applied to those softshelled turtles that lack bony scutes and to sea turtles.

Radiotelemetry

Radiotelemetry is a specialized form of animal marking, and the same general caveats apply. Transmission is regulated by the Federal Communications Commission, and investigators should inquire about the availability of the frequencies they plan to use. General telemetry techniques are summarized in (14), and new ones are continuously becoming available.

There are differences of opinion regarding maximum recommended ratios for transmitter weight to animal weight. Most agreement seems to settle around 10%, and most of this weight will be battery where long transmitter life is necessary; in practice, component miniaturization allows ratios of about 6% for many applications. Smaller (and hence shorter-lived) batteries presently are the only means of achieving these ratios with small animals. Researchers intending to use radiotelemetry on amphibian or reptilian species should consider the following guidelines and comments:

a. Force-Fed and Implanted Transmitters

Force-fed packages should be small enough to pass through the gut without greatly impairing the passage of food. Force-fed or implanted packages should be coated with an impervious, biologically inert material before use. Force-fed packages should not be secured within the animal by suturing the gut. If secured within the animal via body-band, the band should be removed periodically to allow resumption of feeding.

The size and placement of implanted transmitters should not interfere with the function(s)

of the organs surrounding them or with normal behavior. For intracoelomic or subcutaneous implants, suturing the transmitter package in place may be necessary to prevent its movement or interference with vital organs. Implants should be done in aseptic conditions.

b. Externally Attached Transmitters

Consideration must be given to the effect of the package on behavioral interactions between tagged animals and other individuals. For example, the transmitter should neither conceal nor enhance the appearance of behaviorally important dorsal crests or gular flaps. Transmitters should be shaped and attached so as to eliminate or minimize the risk of entanglement with vegetation or other obstructions. Transmitter attachments that can be expected to greatly impair reproduction, locomotion or other normal activity of the animal should be avoided.

Most amphibians and reptiles, including adults, may continue to grow throughout life. External transmitters must be removed or designed to be lost after a time, or they may constrict or irritate the animals. External transmitters can be attached to crocodilians and turtles by collars, clamps, or adhesives. Rigid adhesives and paints extensively applied across sutures of shells of young turtles may impair normal growth if left in place over several years. Special consideration must be given to softshelled species to prevent abrasion (18).

Radioisotopes

The use of radioisotopes as markers in natural systems is valuable, and may be the only means of adequately gathering data on movements of very small species; the technique, however, should be undertaken with caution. Special training and precautions are required of researchers by federal and, frequently, state law (22). A license, which specifies safety procedures for laboratory use, is required for release of isotopes into natural systems and for disposal of waste material. The pros and cons of using strong emitters must be assessed in terms of possible deleterious effects on the animal, to predators that might ingest isotope-labelled animals, and potential hazard to the public.

HOUSING AND MAINTENANCE AT FIELD SITES

Because the biological needs of each species and the nature of individual projects vary widely, only the most general recommendations on housing wild vertebrates in the field can be made. When dealing with unfamiliar species, testing and comparing several methods of housing to find the method most appropriate for the needs of the animal and the purposes of the study may be necessary. Restraint and ease of maintenance by animal keepers should not be the prime determinant of housing conditions. Normal field maintenance should incorporate, as far as possible, those aspects of natural habitat deemed important to the survival and well-being of the animal. Adequacy of maintenance can be judged, relative to the natural environment, by monitoring a combination of factors such as changes in growth and weight, survival rates, breeding success, activity levels, general behavior, and appearance. Consideration should be given to providing an environment that includes features such as natural materials, refuges, perches, and water baths. Natural foods should be duplicated as closely as possible, as should natural light and temperature conditions unless alterations of these are factors under investigation.

Frequency of cage cleaning should represent a compromise between the level of cleanliness necessary to prevent disease, and the amount of stress imposed by frequent handling and exposure to unfamiliar surroundings and bedding. Applied knowledge of animal ethology can assist the investigator to provide optimum care and housing.

DISPOSITION FOLLOWING STUDIES

Upon completion of studies, researchers should release field-trapped specimens whenever this is practical and ecologically appropriate. Exceptions are: if national, state or local laws prohibit release, or if release might be detrimental to the existing gene pools in a specific geographic area. Obviously, some specimens will be deposited as voucher specimens in an appropriate reference collection to document that the identification was appropriate and to provide a basis for comparison among studies.

As a general rule, field-trapped animals should be released only:

a. At the original site of capture, unless conservation efforts or safety considerations dictate otherwise. For these latter exceptional circumstances, prior approval of relocation should be obtained from appropriate state and/or federal agencies, and approved relocations should be noted in subsequent publication of research results.

b. If their ability to survive in nature has not been irreversibly impaired.

c. Where there is reasonable expectation that the released animal will reestablish its former social status.

d. When local and seasonal conditions are conducive to survival.

Captive animals that cannot be released should be disposed of properly, either by distribution to colleagues for further study, or by preservation and deposition as teaching or voucher specimens in research collections.

In both the field and laboratory, the investigator must be careful to ensure that animals subjected to euthanasia procedure are dead before disposal. In those rare instances where specimens are unacceptable for deposition as vouchers or teaching purposes, disposal of carcasses must be in accordance with acceptable practices as required by applicable regulations. Animals containing administered toxic substances or drugs (including euthanasia agents like T-61) must not be disposed of in areas where they may become part of the natural food web.

PREPARATION AND REVISIONS OF THESE GUIDELINES

The initial draft of these guidelines was prepared by George R. Pisani (SSAR), Stephen D. Busack (HL) and Herbert C. Dessauer (ASIH). Victor H. Hutchison prepared the final copy and Gary D. Schnell the camera-ready copy. The final product represents the collective efforts of over 60 persons and the societies extend sincere thanks to all participants.

Periodic revision of these guidelines is expected. Investigators are encouraged to send constructive criticisms or applicable new information to officers of the societies.

REFERENCES   (1987)

1. Young, E. (editor). 1975. The Capture and Care of Wild Animals. Ralph Curtis Books.P. O. Box 183, Sanibel, FL 33957.

2. Estes, Carol and K. W. Sessions (compilers). 1984. Controlled Wildlife, vol. 1: Federal Permit Procedures. ISBN 0-942924-05-3. 304 pp. Association of Systematics Collections, Museum of Natural History, Univ. Kansas, Lawrence, KS 66045.

3. ibid. 1983. Controlled Wildlife, vol. 2: Federally Controlled Species. ISBN 0-942924-06-1. 327 pp. (as above).

4. King, Steven T. and R S. Schrock. 1985. Controlled Wildlife, vol. 3: State Regulations. ISBN 0-942924-07X. 315 pp. (as above).

5. Simmons, John. (in press). Herpetological Collecting and Collections Management. ca. 225 pp. To appear 1987, Herpetological Circulars. Society for the Study of Amphibians and Reptiles, Dept. Zoology (D. Taylor), Miami Univ., Oxford, OH 45056.

6. Pisani, George R. 1973. A Guide to Preservation Techniques for Amphibians and Reptiles. 22 pp. Herpetological Circulars No. 1. Society for the Study of Amphibians and Reptiles (as above).

7. Pisani, George R. and Jaime Villa. 1974. Guia de Tecnicas de Preservacion por Anfibios y Reptiles. 28 pp. Herpetological Circulars No. 2. Society for the Study of Amphibians and Reptiles (as above).

8. Code of Federal Regulations 21: Food and Drugs, Part 1300 to End. April 1, 1980. Superintendent of Documents, U. S. Government Printing Office, Washington, DC 20402.

9. Wallach, J. D. and W. J. Boever. 1983. Diseases of Exotic Animals: Medical and Surgical Management. 1159 pp. W. B. Saunders Co., Philadelphia.

10. Marcus, Leonard C. 1981. Veterinary Biology and Medicine of Captive Amphibians and Reptiles. Lea & Febiger, Philadelphia.

11. Parker, J. L.and H. R. Adams. 1978. The influence of chemical restraining agents on cardio-vascular function: A review. Lab. Anim. Sci. 28:575.

12. Ferner, John W. 1979. A Review of Marking Techniques for Amphibians and Reptiles. Herpetological Circulars No. 9. 42 pp. Society for the Study of Amphibians and Reptiles, Dept. Zoology (D. Taylor), Miami Univ., Oxford, OH 45056.

13. Smith, A. W., et al. 1986. Report of the AVMA Panel on Euthanasia. Journal AVMA 188(13):252-268

14. Amlaner, C. J., Jr. and D. W. MacDonald (editors). 1980. A Handbook on Biotelemetry and Radio Tracking. Pergamon Press, Oxford, England.

15. Gillingham, J. C., et al. 1983. Venomous snake immobilization: A new technique. Herp. Review 14(2):40.

16. National Institutes of Health Guide for Grants and Contracts. Special Edition: Laboratory Animal Welfare. 14(3):1-30, June 25, 1985. Superintendent of Documents, U. S. Government Printing Office, Washington, DC 20402.

17. ibid. Supplement. 14(8): 1-82, June 25, 1985.

18. Eckert, S. A. and K. L. Eckert. 1986. Harnessing leatherbacks. Marine Turtle Newsletter No. 371-3.

19. Graham, T. E. 1986. A warning against the use of Petersen disc tags in turtle studies. Herp. Review 17(2):42-43.

20. Guide to the Care and Use of Experimental Animals, vols. 1 (120 pp.) and 2 (208 pp.). Canadian Council on Animal Care, 1105-151 Slater, Ottawa, Ontario K1P 5H3, Canada.

21. Raney, E. C. and E. A. Lachner. 1947. Studies on the growth of tagged toads (*Bufo terrestris americanus* Holbrook). Copeia (2):113-116.

22. Code of Federal Regulations Title 10, Part 20. 1984. Standards for Protection Against Radiation. Superintendent of Documents, U. S. Government Printing Office, Washington, DC 20402. (Other information is available from: U. S. Atomic Energy Commission, Oak Ridge, TN 37831.)

23. Guidelines for the Care and Use of Lower Vertebrates. September 17, 1986. 8 pp. Committee for the Protection of Animal Subjects, Univ. California, Berkeley, CA 94720.

24. Clarke, R. D. 1972. The effect of toe-clipping on survival in Fowler's toad, *Bufo woodhousei fowleri*. Copeia 1972(1):182-185.

25. Pritchard, P. C. H., et al. 1982. Sea turtle manual of research and conservation techniques. 95 pp. Western Atlantic Turtle Symposium, San Jose, Costa Rica.

26. Blanchard, F. N. and E. B. Finster. 1933. A method of marking living snakes for future recognition, with a discussion of some problems and results. Ecology 14(4):334.

27. Johnson, J. Pers. comm. Manuscript in preparation.

28. Nace, G. W., et al. 1974. Amphibians: Guidelines for the breeding, care and management of laboratory animals. I. L. A. R. (HAS/NRC). ISBN 0-309-00210-X. 150 pp. National Academy of Sciences, 2101 Constitution Ave. NW, Washington, DC 29418.

29. Gibbons, J. W. and R. Semlitsch. 1981. Terrestrial drift fences with pitfall traps: an effective technique for quantitative sampling of animal populations. Brimleyana No. 7:1-16.

30. Brunson, K. 1986. Some unusual injuries to snakes. Kansas Herpetological Society Newsl. No. 65: 13-14.

31. Fowler, M. E. (editor). 1986. Zoo and Wild Animal Medicine. W. B. Saunders Co., Toronto.

32. Thomas, R. A. 1977. Selected bibliography of certain vertebrate techniques. USDI/BLM Tech. Note (306): 1-88.

33. Green, C. J. 1979. Animal Anesthesia Handbook 8. Lab. Anim. Ltd., London.

34. Carlson, B. M. and E. A. Rainer. 1985. Rat extraocular muscle regeneration. Arch. Ophthalmol. 103:1372-1377.

35. McKinstry, D. M. 1983. Morphologic evidence of toxic saliva in colubrid snakes: a checklist of world genera. Herp. Review 14(1):12-15.

36. Gans, C. and A. M. Taub. 1964. Precautions for keeping poisonous snakes in captivity. Curator 7(3):196-205.

ADDITIONAL REFERENCES

Canadian Journal of Zoology. National Research Council of Canada, Ottawa, Ontario K1A 0R6, Canada.

Canadian Veterinary Journal. 339 Booth St., Ottawa, Ontario K1R 7K1, Canada.

Copeia. American Society of Ichthyologists and Herpetologists, Florida State Museum, Univ. Florida, Gainesville, FL 32611.

Directory, Resources of Biomedical and Zoological Specimens. 1981. Registry of Comparative Pathology, Washington, DC 20306.

Guidelines and Procedures for Radioisotope Licensing. U. S. Atomic Energy Commissions, Isotopes Branch - Division of Materials Licensing, Washington, DC 20545.

Herpetologica. The Herpetologists League, Dept. Biology, Univ. Richmond, Richmond, VA 23173.

Herpetological Review. Society for the Study of Amphibians and Reptiles, Dept. Zoology, Ohio Univ., Athens, OH 45701.

International Species Inventory. World Geographic and Zoological Institute. Minneapolis Zoo, Minneapolis, MN.

Journal of Herpetology. Society for the Study of Amphibians and Reptiles, Dept. Zoology, Ohio Univ., Athens, OH 45701.

Journal of the American Veterinary Medicine Association. 930 N. Meacham Rd., Schaumburg, IL 60196.

Journal of Wildlife Diseases. Wildlife Diseases Association. Box 886, Ames, IA 50010.

Veterinary Anesthesia, 2nd Edition. 1984. W.V. Lumb and E. W. Jones. 693 pp. Lea & Febiger, Philadelphia, PA.

INDEX TO COMMON NAMES

Atlas agamas: *Agama*
Aubry's soft-shells: *Cycloderma*
Aurora house snakes: *Lamprophis*
Australasian treefrogs: *Litoria*
Australian barred frogs: *Mixophyes*
Australian black-naped snakes: *Neelaps*
Australian black snakes: *Pseudechis*
Australian brown-headed snakes: *Glyphodon*
Australian brown snakes: *Pseudonaja*
Australian copperheads: *Austrelaps*
Australian coral snakes: *Simoselaps*
Australian crocodiles: *Crocodylus*
Australian crowned snakes: *Cacophis*
Australian crowned snakes: *Drysdalia*
Australian earless lizards: *Tympanocryptis*
Australian froglets: *Crinia*
Australian house geckos: *Gehyra*
Australian short-necked turtles: *Emydura*
Australian snake-neck turtles: *Chelodina*
Australian swamp frogs: *Limnodynastes*
Australian toadlets: *Pseudophryne*
Australian torrent frogs: *Taudactylus*
Australian whip snakes: *Demansia*
Austral river turtles: *Elseya*
Axolotl: *Ambystoma*

B

Baja rock lizards: *Petrosaurus*
Balkan emerald lizards: *Lacerta*
Balkan wall lizards: *Podarcis*
Ball pythons: *Calabaria*
Ball pythons: *Python*
Bamboo vipers: *Trimeresurus*
Banana boas: *Ungaliophis*
Banana frogs: *Afrixalus*
Banded basilisks: *Basiliscus*
Banded geckos: *Coleonyx*
Banded kraits: *Bungarus*
Banded newts: *Triturus*
Banded rock lizards: *Streptosaurus*
Banded sand snakes: *Chilomeniscus*
Banded sea snakes: *Hydrophis*
Banded tegus: *Tupinambis*
Banded tree skinks: *Dasia*
Bandy-bandies: *Vermicella*
Bardicks: *Echiopsis*
Barking toads: *Hylactophryne*
Bark lizards: *Lepidophyma*
Bark snakes: *Hemirhagerrhis*
Barrel skinks: *Chalcides*
Basilisk rattlesnakes: *Crotalus*
Basilisks: *Basiliscus*
Batagur turtles: *Batagur*
Beaded geckos: *Lucasium*
Beaded lizards: *Heloderma*
Beaked snakes: *Rhamphiophis*
Bearded dragons: *Amphibolurus*
Bearded snakes: *Fimbrios*
Bearded toad-heads: *Phrynocephalus*
Bedriaga's rock lizards: *Lacerta*
Bell's hinged tortoises: *Kinixys*

Bengal monitors: *Varanus*
Berber skinks: *Eumeces*
Berber toads: *Bufo*
Bigheaded anoles: *Anolis*
Big-headed mud turtles: *Claudius*
Big-headed turtles: *Platysternon*
Big-scaled false corals: *Pliocercus*
Big-tooth snakes: *Dinodon*
Bird snakes: *Thelotornis*
Black agamas: *Agama*
Black and yellow blue-tongued skinks: *Tiliqua*
Black-backed whistling frogs: *Leptodactylus*
Black-banded sea kraits: *Laticauda*
Black-bellied notched turtles: *Geoemyda*
Black-bellied salamanders: *Desmognathus*
Black-bellied terrapins: *Melanochelys*
Black caimans: *Melanosuchus*
Black forest cobras: *Pseudohaje*
Black-headed centipede-eaters: *Aparallactus*
Black-headed pythons: *Aspidites*
Black-headed snakes: *Tantilla*
Black-headed snakes: *Unechis*
Black iguanas: *Ctenosaura*
Black-lined plated lizards: *Gerrhosaurus*
Black-lipped cobras: *Naja*
Black mambas: *Dendroaspis*
Black pond turtles: *Geoclemys*
Black salamanders: *Aneides*
Black-spined toads: *Bufo*
Black-spotted newts: *Notophthalmus*
Black-striped snakes: *Coniophanes*
Black swamp snakes: *Seminatrix*
Black-tailed pythons: *Python*
Blacktail rattlesnakes: *Crotalus*
Black tiger snakes: *Notechis*
Black tree snakes: *Thrasops*
Blanding's turtles: *Emydoidea*
Bleating treefrogs: *Litoria*
Blind salamanders: *Haideotriton*
Blind salamanders: *Typhlomolge*
Blind salamanders: *Typhlotriton*
Blind snakes: Leptotyphlopidae
Blind snakes, slender: *Leptotyphlops*
Blind snakes: Typhlopidae
Blind worm snakes: *Typhlina*
Blood pythons: *Python*
Blood-suckers: *Calotes*
Blotched blue-tongued skinks: *Tiliqua*
Blue-banded sea snakes: *Hydrophis*
Blue-black plated lizards: *Cordylosaurus*
Blue spiny lizards: *Sceloporus*
Blue-tailed day geckos: *Phelsuma*
Blue-tailed skinks: *Eumeces*
Blue-tailed slender skinks: *Emoia*
Blue-throated agamas: *Agama*
Blue-throated keeled lizards: *Algyroides*
Blue-tongued skinks: *Tiliqua*
Blunt-headed tree snakes: *Imantodes*
Bluntnosed leopard lizards: *Gambelia*
Blunt-nosed vipers: *Daboia*
Blunt-tailed scaley-foots: *Aprasia*

Boa constrictors: *Boa*
Boas: Boidae
Bog turtles: *Clemmys*
Bolson tortoises: *Gopherus*
Boomslangs: *Dispholidus*
Bornean earless monitors: *Lanthanotus*
Bornean flying frogs: *Rhacophorus*
Bornean river turtles: *Orlitia*
Bow-finger geckos: *Cyrtodactylus*
Bow-sprit tortoises: *Chersina*
Box turtles, Asian: *Cuora*
Box turtles: *Terrapene*
Brahminy river turtles: *Hardella*
Brahminy worm snakes: *Typhlina*
Brasilian chameleons: *Enyalius*
Brasilian snake-neck turtles: *Hydromedusa*
Brasilian water-cobras: *Cyclagras*
Bridled soft-shells: *Cycloderma*
Broad-banded sand swimmers: *Sphenomorphus*
Broad-headed skinks: *Eumeces*
Broad-snouted spectacled caimans: *Caiman*
Bromeliad alligator lizards: *Abronia*
Bronzy tree snakes: *Dendrelaphis*
Brown anoles: *Anolis*
Brown pricklenapes: *Acanthosaura*
Brown sand boas: *Eryx*
Brown sea snakes: *Aipysurus*
Brown snakes: *Storeria*
Brown-striped frogs: *Limnodynastes*
Brown toadlets: *Pseudophryne*
Brown tortoises: *Manouria*
Brown water dragons: *Physignathus*
Brown water pythons: *Liasis*
Brown water snakes: *Lycodonomorphus*
Brush lizards: *Urosaurus*
Bull snakes: *Pituophis*
Burmese tortoises: *Geochelone*
Burrowing treefrogs: *Pternohyla*
Burrowing vipers: *Atractaspis*
Burton's snake-lizards: *Lialis*
Bush crocodiles: *Tribolonotus*
Bushmasters: *Lachesis*
Bush snakes: *Meizodon*
Bush vipers: *Atheris*
Butterfly lizards: *Leiolepis*
Butterfly runners: *Leiolepis*
Bynoe's geckos: *Heteronotia*

C
Caecilians: Gymnophiona
Caicaca: *Bothrops*
Caiman lizards: *Dracaena*
Caimans: Alligatoridae
California legless lizards: *Anniella*
California mountain kingsnakes: *Lampropeltis*
California slender salamanders: *Batrachoseps*
Callagur turtles: *Callagur*
Canary Island lizards: *Gallotia*
Canebrake rattlesnakes: *Crotalus*
Cantils: *Agkistrodon*
Canyon treefrogs: *Hyla*

Cape cobras: *Naja*
Cape file snakes: *Mehelya*
Cape geometric tortoises: *Psammobates*
Cape many-spotted snakes: *Amplorhinus*
Cape snake lizards: *Chamaesaura*
Cape toads: *Bufo*
Cape Verde giant skinks: *Macroscincus*
Carpathian newts: *Triturus*
Carpentaria whip snakes: *Unechis*
Carpet pythons: *Morelia*
Carrot-tailed viper geckos: *Teratolepis*
Cartilaginous soft-shell turtles: *Trionyx*
Cascaval: *Crotalus*
Caspian even-fingered geckos: *Alsophylax*
Caspian naked-finger geckos: *Cyrtodactylus*
Caspian pond turtles: *Mauremys*
Caspian whip snakes: *Coluber*
Casque-headed horned treefrogs: *Hemiphractus*
Casque-headed iguanas: *Laemanctus*
Casque-headed skinks: *Tribolonotus*
Casque-headed treefrogs: *Aparasphenodon*
Casque-headed treefrogs: *Osteocephalus*
Casque-headed treefrogs: *Tetraprion*
Casque-headed treefrogs: *Trachycephalus*
Casque-headed treefrogs: *Triprion*
Catalina rattlesnakes: *Crotalus*
Cat-eyed snakes: *Leptodeira*
Cat geckos: *Aeluroscalabotes*
Cat skinks: *Ristella*
Cat snakes: *Telescopus*
Caucasian agamas: *Agama*
Caucasus adders: *Daboia*
Caucasus emerald lizards: *Lacerta*
Caucasus mud divers: *Pelodytes*
Caucasus parsley frogs: *Pelodytes*
Caucasus rock lizards: *Lacerta*
Caucasus salamanders: *Mertensiella*
Caucasus vipers: *Vipera*
Cave anoles: *Anolis*
Cave salamanders: *Eurycea*
Centipede-eaters: *Aparallactus*
Central African egg-eating snakes: *Dasypeltis*
Central American night lizards: *Lepidophyma*
Central American river turtles: *Dermatemys*
Central Asian cobras: *Naja*
Ceylonese hump-nosed vipers: *Hypnale*
Ceylonese pipe snakes: *Cylindrophis*
Ceylonese tree skinks: *Dasia*
Chaco twist-neck turtles: *Platemys*
Chameleons: *Brookesia*
Chameleons: *Chamaeleo*
Checkerboard snake lizards: *Trogonophis*
Checkered garter snakes: *Thamnophis*
Chicken turtles: *Deirochelys*
Chinese alligators: *Alligator*
Chinese copperheads: *Agkistrodon*
Chinese crested newts: *Hypselotriton*
Chinese dwarf newts: *Cynops*
Chinese giant salamanders: *Andrias*
Chinese green tree vipers: *Trimeresurus*
Chinese mountain vipers: *Trimeresurus*

Chinese redneck turtles: *Chinemys*
Chinese soft-shell turtles: *Trionyx*
Chinese striped turtles: *Ocadia*
Chinese swamp turtles: *Chinemys*
Chinese warty newts: *Paramesotriton*
Chirping toadlets: *Syrrhophus*
Chorus frogs: *Pseudacris*
Chuckwallas: *Sauromalus*
Clark's spiny lizards: *Sceloporus*
Clawed frogs, dwarf African: *Hymenochirus*
Clawed frogs: Pipidae
Clawed geckos: *Coleonyx*
Clawed salamanders: *Onychodactylus*
Cliff toadlets: *Syrrhophus*
Climbing rat snakes: *Gonyosoma*
Climbing salamanders: *Aneides*
Clouded salamanders: *Aneides*
Cloud-forest agamids: *Japalura*
Coachwhips: *Masticophis*
Coastal rosy boas: *Lichanura*
Coastal slender skinks: *Emoia*
Coast horned lizards: *Phrynosoma*
Cobras: *Naja*
Cogwheel turtles: *Heosemys*
Collared dwarf snakes: *Eirenis*
Collared lizards: *Crotaphytus*
Colombian giant toads: *Bufo*
Colorado checkered whiptails: *Cnemidophorus*
Common adders: *Vipera*
Common agamas: *Agama*
Common bamboo vipers: *Trimeresurus*
Common basilisks: *Basiliscus*
Common blind worm snakes: *Typhlops*
Common blue-tongued skinks: *Tiliqua*
Common Cape toads: *Bufo*
Common chameleons: *Chamaeleo*
Common chuckwallas: *Sauromalus*
Common dwarf geckos: *Lygodactylus*
Common eastern froglets: *Crinia*
Common egg-eating snakes: *Dasypeltis*
Common Eurasian lizards: *Lacerta*
Common flying dragons: *Draco*
Common frogs: *Rana*
Common garter snakes: *Thamnophis*
Common girdled lizards: *Cordylus*
Common horned frogs: *Ceratophrys*
Common iguanas: *Iguana*
Common lanceheads: *Bothrops*
Common Madagascar day geckos: *Phelsuma*
Common mambas: *Dendroaspis*
Common musk turtles: *Sternotherus*
Common newts: *Triturus*
Common parsley frogs: *Pelodytes*
Common sand vipers: *Cerastes*
Common scaley-foots: *Pygopus*
Common shrinking frogs: *Pseudis*
Common soft-shell turtles: *Trionyx*
Common spadefoots: *Pelobates*
Common tegus: *Tupinambis*
Common wall lizards: *Podarcis*
Common water snakes: *Nerodia*

Cone-nosed toads: *Rhinophrynus*
Congo eels: *Amphiuma*
Cooters: *Chrysemys*
Copperheads: *Agkistrodon*
Copper-tailed skinks: *Ctenotus*
Coral pipe snakes: *Anilius*
Coral snakes, American: *Micrurus*
Coral snakes, Arizona: *Micruroides*
Coral snakes, Australian: *Simoselaps*
Coral snakes, long-glanded: *Maticora*
Coral snakes, Pacific: *Micropechis*
Corn snakes: *Elaphe*
Corroboree frogs: *Pseudophryne*
Corsican mountain salamanders: *Euproctus*
Cottonmouths: *Agkistrodon*
Couch's spadefoots: *Scaphiopus*
Crawfish snakes: *Regina*
Creeping frogs: *Phrynomerus*
Crested anoles: *Chamaeleolis*
Crested newts, northern: *Triturus*
Crevice spiny lizards: *Sceloporus*
Cricket frogs: *Acris*
Crocodile lizards: *Shinisaurus*
Crocodile newts: *Tylototriton*
Crocodiles: *Crocodylus*
Crocodile tegus: *Crocodilurus*
Crucifix toads: *Notaden*
Cuban boas: *Epicrates*
Cuban crocodiles: *Crocodylus*
Cuban curly-tails: *Leiocephalus*
Cuban dwarf toads: *Sminthillus*
Cuban giant toads: *Bufo*
Cuban grass anoles: *Anolis*
Cuban night lizards: *Cricosaura*
Cuban toads: *Bufo*
Cuban treefrogs: *Hyla*
Cunningham's skinks: *Egernia*
Curl snakes: *Suta*
Curly-tailed lizards: *Leiocephalus*

D

Dakota toads: *Bufo*
D'Albert's pythons: *Liasis*
Dalmatian lance-headed lizards: *Lacerta*
Dalmatian wall lizards: *Podarcis*
Danford's lizards: *Lacerta*
Dark toad-headed turtles: *Phrynops*
Darwin's frogs: *Rhinoderma*
Darwin's iguanas: *Diplolaemus*
Death adders: *Acanthophis*
Del Norte salamanders: *Plethodon*
Desert agamas: *Agama*
Desert banded snakes: *Simoselaps*
Desert boas: *Eryx*
Desert cobras: *Walterinnesia*
Desert fringe-toed lizards: *Uma*
Desert iguanas: *Dipsosaurus*
Desert lacertids: *Eremias*
Desert monitors: *Varanus*
Desert night lzards: *Xanthusia*
Desert spiny lizards: *Sceloporus*

Desert tegus: *Dicrodon*
Desert tortoises: *Gopherus*
Desert treefrogs: *Litoria*
DeVis's banded snakes: *Denisonia*
Dhaman: *Ptyas*
Diadem snakes: *Spalerosophis*
Diamondback terrapins: *Malaclemys*
Diamond-back water snakes: *Nerodia*
Diamond pythons: *Morelia*
Diard's blind worm snakes: *Typhlops*
Dibamids: *Dibamus*
Dice snakes: *Natrix*
Dish-backed treefrogs: *Fritziana*
Dog-faced watersnakes: *Cerberus*
Dog-toothed mangrove snakes: *Boiga*
Donner-weer tortoises: *Homopus*
Dotted African soft-shell turtles: *Cycloderma*
Dotted racerunners: *Cnemidophorus*
Double-banded chameleons: *Chamaeleo*
Double-crested basilisks: *Basiliscus*
Dumeril's helmeted turtles: *Peltocephalus*
Dumeril's Madagascar boas: *Acrantophis*
Dumeril's monitors: *Varanus*
Dunn's salamanders: *Plethodon*
Dusky salamanders: *Desmognathus*
Dwarf African clawed frogs: *Hymenochirus*
Dwarf barking frogs: *Eleutherodactylus*
Dwarf boas: *Tropidophis*
Dwarf boas: *Ungaliophis*
Dwarf caimans: *Paleosuchus*
Dwarf chameleons: *Chamaeleo*
Dwarf crowned snakes: *Cacophis*
Dwarf geckos: *Lygodactylus*
Dwarf lizards: *Lacerta*
Dwarf puff adders: *Bitis*
Dwarf reed frogs: *Hyperolius*
Dwarf rocket frogs: *Litoria*
Dwarf salamanders: *Eurycea*
Dwarf sirens: *Pseudobranchus*
Dwarf snakes: *Calamaria*
Dwarf snakes: *Eirenis*
Dwarf toads: *Bufo*
Dwarf waterdogs: *Necturus*

E
Earless agamas: *Cophotis*
Earless lizards: *Holbrookia*
Earless monitors: Lanthanotidae
Earth snakes: *Virginia*
Earthworm blind snakes: *Typhlops*
East African black turtles: *Pelusios*
Eastern blue-tongued skinks: *Tiliqua*
Eastern box turtles: *Terrapene*
Eastern brown snakes: *Pseudonaja*
Eastern diamondback rattlesnakes: *Crotalus*
Eastern fence lizards: *Sceloporus*
Eastern glass lizards: *Ophisaurus*
Eastern hog-nosed snakes: *Heterodon*
Eastern kingsnakes: *Lampropeltis*
Eastern mud turtles: *Kinosternon*
Eastern narrow-mouthed toads: *Gastrophryne*

Eastern newts: *Notophthalmus*
Eastern ribbon snakes: *Thamnophis*
Eastern ringnecked snakes: *Diadophis*
Eastern small-eyed snakes: *Cryptophis*
Eastern spadefoots: *Pelobates*
Eastern spadefoots: *Scaphiopus*
Eastern water skinks: *Sphenomorphus*
Edible frogs: *Rana*
Eel newts: *Amphiuma*
Egg-eating snakes, African: *Dasypeltis*
Egg-eating snakes, Indian: *Elachistodon*
Egyptian cobras: *Naja*
Egyptian spiny-tailed agamids: *Uromastyx*
Egyptian tortoises: *Pseudotestudo*
Elephant trunk snakes: Acrochordidae
Elongate tortoises: *Indotestudo*
Emerald geckos: *Gekko*
Emerald lizards: *Lacerta*
Emerald monitors: *Varanus*
Emerald skinks: *Dasia*
Emerald tree boas: *Corallus*
Ensatina salamanders: *Ensatina*
Ensatinas: *Ensatina*
Eremias: *Eremias*
Erhard's wall lizards: *Podarcis*
Euphrates soft-shell turtles: *Trionyx*
Eurasian adders: *Vipera*
Eurasian common frogs: *Rana*
Eurasian common toads: *Bufo*
Eurasian grass snakes: *Natrix*
Eurasian pond turtles: *Mauremys*
Eurasian spadefoot toads: *Pelobates*
Eurasian water snakes: *Natrix*
Eurasian worm snakes: *Typhlops*
European brook salamanders: *Euproctus*
European cat snakes: *Telescopus*
European fringe-fingers: *Acanthodactylus*
European leaf-finger: *Phyllodactylus*
European mountain salamanders: *Euproctus*
European naked-finger geckos: *Cyrtodactylus*
European newts: *Triturus*
European pond turtles: *Emys*
European snake-eyes: *Ophisops*
European tortoises: *Testudo*
European treefrogs: *Hyla*
Even-fingered geckos: *Alsophylax*
Eyed lizards: *Lacerta*
Eyelash lanceheads: *Bothrops*

F
Faded snakes: *Arizona*
False coral snakes: *Erythrolamprus*
False gavials: *Tomistoma*
False girdled lizards: *Pseudocordylus*
False map turtles: *Graptemys*
False smooth snakes: *Macroprotodon*
False water snakes: *Enhydris*
False yarara: *Xenodon*
Fan-footed geckos: *Ptyodactylus*
Fat-headed anoles: *Enyalius*
Fat-headed turtles: *Siebenrockiella*

Fat-tailed geckos: *Eublepharis*
Fat-tailed geckos: *Hemitheconyx*
Fea's vipers: *Azemiops*
Fence lizards: *Sceloporus*
Fierce snakes: *Parademansia*
Fijian snakes: *Ogmodon*
Fiji iguanas: *Brachylophus*
File snakes: Acrochordidae
File snakes: *Mehelya*
Fire-bellied newts: *Cynops*
Fire-bellied toads: *Bombina*
Fire salamanders: *Salamandra*
Firetail skinks: *Morethia*
Fischer's boas: *Epicrates*
Fischer's chameleons: *Chamaeleo*
Fish snakes: *Xenochrophis*
Fitzroy turtles: *Rheodytes*
Five-lined skinks: *Eumeces*
Five-striped mabuyas: *Mabuya*
Five-toed whip lizards: *Tetradactylus*
Flatback spider tortoises: *Pyxis*
Flatback turtles: *Chelonia*
Flat-back turtles: *Notochelys*
Flathead snakes: *Tantilla*
Flat lizards: *Platysaurus*
Flat-tailed geckos: *Uroplatus*
Fletcher's frogs: *Lechriodus*
Florida sand skinks: *Neoseps*
Florida worm lizards: *Rhineura*
Flowerpot snakes: *Typhlina*
Flower snakes: *Elaphe*
Flying dragons: *Draco*
Flying frogs: *Rhacophorus*
Flying geckos: *Ptychozoon*
Flying tree snakes: *Chrysopelea*
Forest cobras: *Pseudohaje*
Forest skinks: *Sphenomorphus*
Forest treefrogs: *Leptopelis*
Four-eyed toads: *Pleurodema*
Four-lined rat snakes: *Elaphe*
Four-toed salamanders: *Hemidactylium*
Four-toed tegus: *Teius*
Four-toed tortoises: *Agrionemys*
Fowler's toads: *Bufo*
Fox snakes: *Elaphe*
Fraser's Scaleyfoots: *Delma*
Freshwater turtles: Emydidae
Frilled lizards: *Chlamydosaurus*
Fringe-finger lizards: *Acanthodactylus*
Fringe-toed lizards: *Uma*
Frog-eyed geckos: *Teratoscincus*
Frog-headed turtles: *Phrynops*
Frogs: Salientia

G
Gaboon vipers: *Bitis*
Galapagos giant tortoises: *Chelonoidis*
Galapagos land iguanas: *Conolophus*
Galliwasps: *Diploglossus*
Ganges soft-shell turtles: *Trionyx*
Garden tree boas: *Corallus*

Garlic toads: *Pelobates*
Garter snakes: *Thamnophis*
Garter snakes, venomous: *Elapsoidea*
Gastric brooding frogs: *Rheobatrachus*
Gavials: *Gavialis*
Geckos: Gekkonidae
Geometric tortoises: *Psammobates*
Georgia blind salamanders: *Haideotriton*
Gharials: *Gavialis*
Giant African frogs: *Conraua*
Giant barred frogs: *Mixophyes*
Giant burrowing frogs: *Heleioporus*
Giant coral snakes: *Micrurus*
Giant emerald lizards: *Lacerta*
Giant fire-bellied toads: *Bombina*
Giant glass frogs: *Centrolene*
Giant marsupial frogs: *Gastrotheca*
Giant musk turtles: *Staurotypus*
Giant plated lizards: *Gerrhosaurus*
Giant salamanders: Cryptobranchidae
Giant salamanders: *Dicamptodon*
Giant snakes: Boidae
Giant soft-shell turtles: *Pelochelys*
Giant toads: *Bufo*
Giant treefrogs: *Litoria*
Gidgee skinks: *Egernia*
Gila monsters: *Heloderma*
Gillen's dwarf monitors: *Varanus*
Girdled lizards: *Zonosaurus*
Girdle-tailed lizards: *Cordylus*
Gironde smooth snakes: *Coronella*
Glass frogs: *Centrolenella*
Glass lizards: *Ophisaurus*
Glossy crawfish snakes: *Regina*
Golddust day geckos: *Phelsuma*
Golden crowned snakes: *Cacophis*
Golden frogs: *Mantella*
Gold-striped salamanders: *Chioglossa*
Goliath frogs: *Conraua*
Gopher frogs: *Rana*
Gopher snakes: *Pituophis*
Gopher tortoises: *Gopherus*
Gould's monitors: *Varanus*
Graham's crawfish snakes: *Regina*
Granite night lizards: *Xanthusia*
Granite spiny lizards: *Sceloporus*
Grasping frogs: *Phyllomedusa*
Grass anoles: *Anolis*
Grass snakes: *Natrix*
Gray foam-nest treefrogs: *Chiromantis*
Great barred frogs: *Mixophyes*
Greater earless lizards: *Holbrookia*
Greater flat lizards: *Platysaurus*
Greater sirens: *Siren*
Great Plains skinks: *Eumeces*
Great Plains toads: *Bufo*
Greek keeled lizards: *Algyroides*
Greek rock lizards: *Lacerta*
Greek snake skinks: *Ophiomorus*
Greek tortoises: *Testudo*
Green and gold bell frogs: *Litoria*

Green anoles: *Anolis*
Green bush snakes: *Philothamnus*
Green iguanas: *Iguana*
Green jararaca: *Bothrops*
Green lizards: *Lacerta*
Green mambas: *Dendroaspis*
Green night adders: *Causus*
Green poison arrow frogs: *Dendrobates*
Green pricklenapes: *Acanthosaura*
Green salamanders: *Aneides*
Green snakes: *Opheodrys*
Green snakes, South American: *Philodryas*
Green spiny lizards: *Sceloporus*
Green toads: *Bufo*
Green treefrogs: *Hyla*
Green tree geckos: *Naultinus*
Green tree pythons: *Chondropython*
Green tree snakes: *Boiga*
Green turtles: *Chelonia*
Green vine snakes: *Oxybelis*
Green water dragons: *Physignathus*
Green water snakes: *Nerodia*
Grotto salamanders: *Hydromantes*
Grotto salamanders: *Typhlotriton*
Ground skinks: *Scincella*
Ground snakes: *Sonora*
Ground vipers: Aparallactinae
Gulf Coast waterdogs: *Necturus*
Gypsy geckos: *Hemiphyllodactylus*

H

Habus: *Trimeresurus*
Hairy frogs: *Trichobatrachus*
Haitian giant anoles: *Anolis*
Halfmoon lanceheads: *Bothrops*
Halys's vipers: *Agkistrodon*
Hamadryads: *Ophiophagus*
Hardun: *Agama*
Harlequin frogs: Pseudidae
Harlequin racerunners: *Plica*
Hawksbill turtles: *Eretmochelys*
Headband dwarf snakes: *Eirenis*
Hediger's snakes: *Parapistocalamus*
Hellbenders: *Cryptobranchus*
Helmeted chameleons: *Chamaeleo*
Helmeted iguanas: *Corytophanes*
Helmeted side-necks: Pelomedusidae
Helmeted terrapins: *Pelomedusa*
Helmeted water toads: *Caudiverbera*
Hermann's tortoises: *Testudo*
High-mountain lizards: *Phymaturus*
Himalayan slender skink: *Scincella*
Hinge-back tortoises: *Kinixys*
Hog-nosed snakes: *Heterodon*
Home's hinged tortoises: *Kinixys*
Hong Kong warty newts: *Paramesotriton*
Hooded keelbacks: *Macropisthodon*
Hooded scaley-foots: *Pygopus*
Hooded snakes: *Macroprotodon*
Horned agamas: *Ceratophora*
Horned frogs, Asian: *Megoprhys*

Horned frogs: *Ceratophrys*
Horned lizards: *Phrynosoma*
Horned puff adders: *Bitis*
Horned toads: *Phrynosoma*
Horned vipers: *Cerastes*
Horseshoe snakes: *Coluber*
House geckos: *Hemidactylus*
House skinks: *Mabuya*
House snakes: *Boaedon*
Humpback toad-headed turtles: *Phrynops*
Hump-headed dragons: *Gonocephalus*
Hump-nosed vipers: *Hypnale*
Hynobid salamanders: Hynobiidae

I

Iberian emerald lizards: *Lacerta*
Iberian frogs: *Rana*
Iberian pond turtles: *Mauremys*
Iberian tortoises: *Testudo*
Iberian wall lizards: *Podarcis*
Ibiboboca: *Micrurus*
Ibiza wall lizards: *Podarcis*
Iguanas: *Iguana*
Ikaheka snakes: *Micropechis*
Indian cobras: *Naja*
Indian egg-eating snakes: *Elachistodon*
Indian flap-shelled turtles: *Lissemys*
Indian green tree vipers: *Trimeresurus*
Indian hump-nosed vipers: *Hypnale*
Indian kraits: *Bungarus*
Indian roof turtles: *Kachuga*
Indian spiny-tailed agamids: *Uromastyx*
Indian star tortoises: *Geochelone*
Indian terrapins: *Melanochelys*
Indian thorn turtles: *Pyxidea*
Indian wart snakes: *Chersydrus*
Indigo snakes: *Drymarchon*
Indo-Australian rock pythons: *Liasis*
Indo-Chinese tortoises: *Manouria*
Indonesian snake skinks: *Ophioscincus*
Indonesian spitting cobras: *Naja*
Island iguanas: *Cyclura*
Island lanceheads: *Bothrops*
Island night lizards: *Klauberina*
Italian agile frogs: *Rana*
Italian newts: *Triturus*
Italian wall lizards: *Podarcis*

J

Jacuaru: *Tupinambis*
Jacuruxy: *Dracaena*
Jamaican crested anoles: *Anolis*
Japanese fire-bellied newts: *Cynops*
Japanese geckos: *Gekko*
Japanese giant salamanders: *Andrias*
Japanese pond turtles: *Mauremys*
Japanese singing frogs: *Rhacophorus*
Jararaca: *Bothrops*
Jararaca pintada: *Bothrops*
Javan flying frogs: *Rhacophorus*
Java wart snakes: *Acrochordus*

Javelin sand boas: *Eryx*
Jeweled lizards: *Lacerta*
Jordan's salamanders: *Plethodon*
Jungle runners: *Ameiva*
Juniper skinks: *Ablepharus*

K
Karroo toads: *Bufo*
Karroo tortoises: *Homopus*
Keeled cordylids: *Tracheloptychus*
Keeled lizards: *Algyroides*
Keeled skinks: *Tropidophorus*
Keeled tegus: *Kentropyx*
Keeled water snakes: *Amphiesma*
Kemp's ridleys: *Lepidochelys*
King brown snakes: *Pseudechis*
King cobras: *Ophiophagus*
King's alligator lizards: *Gerrhonotus*
Kingsnakes: *Lampropeltis*
Knight anoles: *Anolis*
Knobby geometric tortoises: *Psammobates*
Knob-scale lizards: Xenosauridae
Knob-tail geckos: *Nephrurus*
Koelliker's glass lizards: *Ophisaurus*
Komodo dragons: *Varanus*
Kraits: *Bungarus*

L
Ladder snakes: *Elaphe*
Lanceheads, American: *Bothrops*
Lanceheads, Asian: *Trimeresurus*
Lance skinks: *Acontias*
Large-scale snake lizards: *Chamaesaura*
Lataste's vipers: *Vipera*
Lateral fold lizards: Anguidae
Lateral-spot slender skinks: *Scincella*
Lava lizards: *Tropidurus*
Leaf anoles: *Anolis*
Leaf chameleons: *Brookesia*
Leaf-fingered geckos: *Phyllodactylus*
Leafnosed snakes: *Phyllorhynchus*
Leafnose snakes: *Langaha*
Leaf-tailed geckos: *Phyllurus*
Leaf toads: *Nectophryne*
Leaf-toed geckos: *Hemidactylus*
Least geckos: *Sphaerodactylus*
Least grassfrogs: *Limnaeodus*
Leatherback turtles: *Dermochelys*
Legless lizards: *Anniella*
Lemur frogs: *Phyllomedusa*
Leopard frogs: *Rana*
Leopard geckos: *Eublepharis*
Leopard lizards: *Gambelia*
Leopard snakes: *Elaphe*
Leopard tortoises: *Geochelone*
Lesser earless lizards: *Holbrookia*
Lesser sirens: *Siren*
Lesueur's velvet geckos: *Oedura*
Levantine adders: *Daboia*
Light bulb teiids: *Proctoporus*
Lilford's wall lizards: *Podarcis*

Lined snakes: *Tropidoclonion*
Little brown snakes: *Elapognathus*
Livebearing toads: *Nectophrynoides*
Lizardfinger geckos: *Saurodactylus*
Lizards: Sauria
Lobed chameleons: *Chamaeleo*
Loggerhead musk turtles: *Sternotherus*
Loggerhead turtles: *Caretta*
Long-fingered frogs: *Cardioglossa*
Long-glanded coral snakes: *Maticora*
Long-headed scaley-foots: *Lialis*
Longnosed leopard lizards: *Gambelia*
Long-nosed reed frogs: *Hyperolius*
Long-nosed sand snakes: *Lytorhynchus*
Longnosed snakes: *Rhinocheilus*
Long-tailed lizards: *Takydromus*
Long-tailed salamanders: *Eurycea*
Long-tailed whip lizards: *Tetradactylus*
Lungless salamanders: Plethodontidae
Luschan's salamanders: *Mertensiella*
Lyre-headed agamids: *Lyriocephalus*
Lyre snakes: *Trimorphodon*

M
Mabuyas: *Mabuya*
McMahon's vipers: *Eristicophis*
Madagascan boas: *Acrantophis*
Madagascan swifts: *Oplurus*
Madagascar day geckos: *Phelsuma*
Madagascar river turtles: *Erymnochelys*
Madagascar tree boas: *Sanzinia*
Madeira wall lizards: *Podarcis*
Mainland tiger snakes: *Notechis*
Malayan box turtles: *Cuora*
Malayan moccasins: *Agkistrodon*
Malayan narrow-mouthed toads: *Kaloula*
Malayan snail-eating turtles: *Malayemys*
Malayan soft-shell turtles: *Trionyx*
Mambas: *Dendroaspis*
Mamushi: *Agkistrodon*
Mandarin rat snakes: *Elaphe*
Mangrove skinks: *Emoia*
Mangrove snakes: *Boiga*
Mangrove vipers: *Trimeresurus*
Many-colored anoles: *Polychrus*
Many-lined salamanders: *Stereochilus*
Many-ribbed salamanders: *Eurycea*
Many-striped mabuyas: *Mabuya*
Many-toothed snakes: Sibynophinae
Map turtles: *Graptemys*
Marbled newts: *Triturus*
Marbled salamanders: *Ambystoma*
Marbled shovel-nosed frogs: *Hemisus*
Marbled toads: *Bufo*
Marbled velvet geckos: *Oedura*
Margined tortoises: *Testudo*
Marine iguanas: *Amblyrhynchus*
Marine toads: *Bufo*
Marsh frogs: *Rana*
Marsupial frogs: *Gastrotheca*
Masked curly-tails: *Leiocephalus*

Massasaugas: *Sistrurus*
Matamatas: *Chelus*
Meadow lizards: *Lacerta*
Mediterranean geckos: *Hemidactylus*
Mediterranean worm lizards: *Blanus*
Meller's chameleons: *Chamaeleo*
Mexican beaded lizards: *Heloderma*
Mexican burrowing pythons: *Loxocemus*
Mexican dwarf boas: *Exiliboa*
Mexican forest turtles: *Rhinoclemmys*
Mexican hook-nosed snakes: *Ficimia*
Mexican horned lizards: *Phrynosoma*
Mexican moccasins: *Agkistrodon*
Mexican newts: *Notophthalmus*
Mexican pygmy rattlesnakes: *Sistrurus*
Mexican rosy boas: *Lichanura*
Mexican smiliscas: *Smilisca*
Mexican vine snakes: *Oxybelis*
Mexican white-lipped frogs: *Leptodactylus*
Midwife toads: *Alytes*
Milk snakes: *Lampropeltis*
Mink frogs: *Rana*
Mississippi alligators: *Alligator*
Mississippi map turtles: *Graptemys*
Moaning frogs: *Heleioporus*
Moccasins: *Agkistrodon*
Mole salamanders: *Ambystoma*
Mole snakes: *Pseudaspis*
Mole vipers: *Atractaspis*
Moloch: *Moloch*
Monitors: *Varanus*
Monitor tegus: *Callopistes*
Monkey frogs: *Phyllomedusa*
Monocled cobras: *Naja*
Montpellier snakes: *Malpolon*
Mop-headed iguanids: *Uranoscodon*
Moroccan spadefoots: *Pelobates*
Mountain adders: *Bitis*
Mountain adders: *Daboia*
Mountain chameleons: *Chamaeleo*
Mountain dusky salamanders: *Desmognathus*
Mountain lizards: *Japalura*
Mountain patchnosed snakes: *Salvadora*
Mountain treefrogs: *Hyla*
Mount Lyell salamanders: *Hydromantes*
Mourning geckos: *Lepidodactylus*
Mudpuppies: *Necturus*
Mud salamanders: *Pseudotriton*
Mud snakes: *Farancia*
Mud turtles: *Kinosternon*
Muhlenberg's turtles: *Clemmys*
Mulgas: *Pseudechis*
Murray River turtles: *Emydura*
Musk turtles: *Sternotherus*
Mussuranas: *Clelia*
Myalls: *Suta*

N

Naked-finger geckos: *Cyrtodactylus*
Namib sanddivers: *Aporosaura*
Namib sand geckos: *Palmatogecko*

Narrow-banded sand swimmers: *Sphenomorphus*
Narrow-banded snakes: *Simoselaps*
Narrow-headed soft-shell turtles: *Chitra*
Narrow-mouthed toads: *Gastrophryne*
Narrow-mouthed toads: Microhylidae
Narrow-snouted spectacled caimans: *Caiman*
Natal black snakes: *Macrelaps*
Natterjack toads: *Bufo*
Near Eastern newts: *Neurergus*
Netted dragons: *Amphibolurus*
New Guinea crocodiles: *Crocodylus*
New Guinea dwarf pythons: *Bothrochilus*
New Guinea short-necked turtles: *Emydura*
New Guinea snake-lizards: *Lialis*
New Guinea snake-neck turtles: *Chelodina*
New Guinea snappers: *Elseya*
New Guinea soft-shelled turtles: *Carettochelys*
Newts, European: *Triturus*
Newts, red-spotted: *Notophthalmus*
Newts: Salamandridae
Newts, western: *Taricha*
New Zealand frogs: *Leiopelma*
Nicholl's toadlets: *Metacrinia*
Night adders: *Causus*
Night lizards: *Xanthusia*
Night lizards: Xanthusiidae
Night skinks: *Egernia*
Night skinks: *Scincopus*
Night snakes: *Hypsiglena*
Nile crocodiles: *Crocodylus*
Nile monitors: *Varanus*
Nile soft-shell turtles: *Trionyx*
Northern alligator lizards: *Gerrhonotus*
Northern coral snakes: *Micrurus*
Northern crested newts: *Triturus*
Northern dtella: *Gehyra*
Northern dusky salamanders: *Desmognathus*
Northern dwarf treefrogs: *Litoria*
Northern leaf-tailed geckos: *Phyllurus*
Northern mudpuppies: *Necturus*
Northern tegus: *Tupinambis*
Nose-horned vipers: *Vipera*
Nubian soft-shell turtles: *Cyclanorbis*

O

Oak toads: *Bufo*
Ocellated barrel skinks: *Chalcides*
Ocellated bullfrogs: *Leptodactylus*
Ocellated geckos: *Sphaerodactylus*
Ocellated lizards: *Lacerta*
Ocellated peacock turtles: *Morenia*
Ocellated skinks: *Ablepharus*
Odd-scaled snakes: Xenoderminae
Odd-toothed snakes: Xenodontinae
Okinawa habus: *Trimeresurus*
Old World racerunners: *Eremias*
Olive pythons: *Liasis*
Olive ridleys: *Lepidochelys*
Olms: *Proteus*
Olympic salamanders: *Rhyacotriton*
One-lined dragons: *Diporiphora*

One-toed amphiumas: *Amphiuma*
Orange coral snakes: *Simoselaps*
Orange-thighed narrow-mouthed toads: *Microhyla*
Oregon slender salamanders: *Batrachoseps*
Oriental adders: *Daboia*
Oriental coral snakes: *Calliophis*
Oriental fire-bellied toads: *Bombina*
Oriental hellbenders: *Andrias*
Oriental pipe snakes: *Cylindrophis*
Oriental racers: *Takydromus*
Oriental six-lined runners: *Takydromus*
Orinoco crocodiles: *Crocodylus*
Ornamental snakes: *Denisonia*
Ornate burrowing frogs: *Limnodynastes*
Ornate chorus frogs: *Pseudacris*
Ornate flying snakes: *Chrysopelea*
Ornate frogs: *Hildebrandtia*
Ornate horned frogs: *ceratophrys*
Orsini's vipers: *Vipera*

P
Pacific coral snakes: *Micropechis*
Pacific geckos: *Gehyra*
Pacific giant salamanders: *Dicamptodon*
Pacific Island boas: *Candoia*
Pacific monitors: *Varanus*
Pacific ridleys: *Lepidochelys*
Pacific slender salamanders: *Batrachoseps*
Pacific treefrogs: *Hyla*
Paddy frogs: *Ooeidozyga*
Painted dragons: *Amphibolurus*
Painted dwarf geckos: *Lygodactylus*
Painted forest turtles: *Rhinoclemmys*
Painted frogs: *Discoglossus*
Painted turtles: *Chrysemys*
Pale-headed snakes: *Hoplocephalus*
Palestinian vipers: *Daboia*
Palmate newts: *Triturus*
Panama golden stub-footed toads: *Atelopus*
Pancake tortoises: *Malacochersus*
Panther toads: *Bufo*
Panzer crocodiles: *Crocodylus*
Paradise flying snakes: *Chrysopelea*
Paraguay anacondas: *Eunectes*
Parrot-beaked tortoises: *Homopus*
Parrot snakes: *Leptophis*
Parsley frogs: *Pelodytes*
Patchnosed snakes: *Salvadora*
Peacock day geckos: *Phelsuma*
Peacock soft-shell turtles: *Trionyx*
Peacock turtles: *Morenia*
Pelagic sea snakes: *Pelamis*
Peron's treefrogs: *Litoria*
Peter's peacock turtles: *Morenia*
Phelsumas: *Phelsuma*
Pine Barrens treefrogs: *Hyla*
Pine snakes: *Pituophis*
Pine woods snakes: *Rhadinaea*
Pink-tongued skinks: *Tiliqua*
Pipe snakes: Aniliidae
Pit vipers: Crotalidae

Plains spadefoots: *Scaphiopus*
Platannas: *Xenopus*
Plated lizards: *Gerrhosaurus*
Plump sea snakes: *Lapemis*
Poison arrow frogs: *Dendrobates*
Poison arrow frogs: *Phyllobates*
Poison dart frogs: *Dendrobates*
Poisonous treefrogs: *Phrynohyas*
Pond turtles: *Clemmys*
Pope's tree vipers: *Trimeresurus*
Pouched frogs: *Assa*
Prairie rattlesnakes: *Crotalus*
Pricklenapes: *Acanthosaura*
Prickle-tailed iguanas: *Hoplocercus*
Puerto Rican boas: *Epicrates*
Puff adders: *Bitis*
Pygmy rattlesnakes: *Sistrurus*
Pygmy salamanders: *Desmognathus*
Pygmy spiny-tailed skinks: *Egernia*
Pythons: Boidae
Pythons: *Python*

Q
Queen snakes: *Regina*
Quill-nosed snakes: *Xenocalamus*

R
Racers: *Coluber*
Racers, Oriental: *Takydromus*
Racerunners: *Cnemidophorus*
Racerunners: *Eremias*
Radiated tortoises: *Asterochelys*
Rainbow boas: *Epicrates*
Rainbow rock skinks: *Mabuya*
Rainbow snakes: *Farancia*
Ramsay's pythons: *Aspidites*
Rat snakes: *Elaphe*
Rattlesnakes: *Crotalus*
Rattlesnakes, pygmy: *Sistrurus*
Rear-fanged snakes: Boiginae
Red-backed salamanders: *Plethodon*
Red-banded crevice creepers: *Phrynomerus*
Red banded snakes: *Dinodon*
Red-bellied black snakes: *Pseudechis*
Red-bellied newts: *Taricha*
Redbellied snakes: *Storeria*
Red-bellied turtles: *Chrysemys*
Red-bellied water snakes: *Nerodia*
Red-cheeked mud turtles: *Kinosternon*
Red-crowned toadlets: *Pseudophryne*
Red-eared frogs: *Rana*
Red-eared sliders: *Chrysemys*
Red-eyed Australian treefrogs: *Litoria*
Red-eyed treefrogs: *Agalychnis*
Red-groined toadlets: *Uperoleia*
Red-headed kraits: *Bungarus*
Red Hills salamanders: *Phaeognathus*
Red-legged tortoises: *Chelonoidis*
Red-naped snakes: *Furina*
Red pipe snakes: *Cylindrophis*
Red salamanders: *Pseudotriton*

Red-sided curly-tails: *Leiocephalus*
Red-spotted newts: *Notophthalmus*
Red-spotted toads: *Bufo*
Red-tailed rat snakes: *Gonyosoma*
Red tegus: *Tupinambis*
Red-throated anoles: *Anolis*
Red toads: *Bufo*
Red worm lizards: *Amphisbaena*
Reed frogs: *Hyperolius*
Reef geckos: *Sphaerodactylus*
Reeves's turtles: *Chinemys*
Reticulate collared lizards: *Crotaphytus*
Reticulated pythons: *Python*
Reticulated toads: *Bufo*
Reuter's blind snakes: *Typhlops*
Rhinoceros agamas: *Ceratophora*
Rhinoceros iguanas: *Cyclura*
Rhinoceros lanceheads: *Bothrops*
Rhinoceros vipers: *Bitis*
Ribbed newts: *Pleurodeles*
Ribbon snakes: *Thamnophis*
Rice frogs: *Rana*
Ridley turtles: *Lepidochelys*
Ringed brown snakes: *Pseudonaja*
Ringed cobras: *Hemachatus*
Ringed map turtles: *Graptemys*
Ringed salamanders: *Ambystoma*
Ringed snakes: *Natrix*
Ringed tree boas: *Corallus*
Ringhals: *Hemachatus*
Ringnecked coffee snakes: *Ninia*
Ringnecked snakes: *Diadophis*
Rio Grande toadlets: *Syrrhophus*
River cooters: *Chrysemys*
River snappers: *Elseya*
Rock agamas: *Agama*
Rocket frogs: *Litoria*
Rock geckos: *Afroedura*
Rock rattlesnakes: *Crotalus*
Rococo toads: *Bufo*
Roof turtles: *Kachuga*
Rosy boas: *Lichanura*
Rough boas: *Trachyboa*
Rough earth snakes: *Virginia*
Rough green snakes: *Opheodrys*
Rough-neck monitors: *Varanus*
Rough sand boas: *Eryx*
Rough-scaled bush vipers: *Atheris*
Rough-scaled sand lizards: *Ichnotropis*
Rough-scaled snakes: *Tropidechis*
Rough-sided snakes: *Aspidura*
Rough-skinned foam-nest treefrogs: *Chiromantis*
Rough-skinned newts: *Taricha*
Rough Spanish newts: *Pleurodeles*
Rough teiids: *Echinosaura*
Round Island burrowing boas: *Bolyeria*
Round Island ground boas: *Casarea*
Roundtailed horned lizards: *Phrynosoma*
Royal pythons: *Python*
Rubber boas: *Charina*
Rudder-tailed sea snakes: Hydrophiinae

Ruddertails: *Thalassophis*
Rufous beaked snakes: *Rhamphiophis*
Running frogs: *Kassina*
Russell's vipers: *Daboia*

S
Sacramento Mountain salamanders: *Aneides*
Saddle-back toads: *Brachycephalus*
Sailfin dragons: *Hydrosaurus*
Salamanders: Caudata
Saltwater crocodiles: *Crocodylus*
Sand boas: *Eryx*
Sand dune plated lizards: *Angolosaurus*
Sand geckos: *Chondrodactylus*
Sand lizards: *Lacerta*
Sand lizards: *Psammodromus*
Sandpaper toads: *Pseudobufo*
Sand racers: *Psammophis*
Sand skinks: *Scincus*
Sand swimmers: *Sphenomorphus*
Sand toads: *Bufo*
Sand vipers: *Vipera*
San Marcos blind salamanders: *Typhlomolge*
Sapera: *Xenodon*
Sardinian mountain salamanders: *Euproctus*
Savannah monitors: *Varanus*
Sawback agamids: *Calotes*
Saw-scaled vipers: *Echis*
Saw-shelled snappers: *Elseya*
Sawtailed lizards: *Holaspis*
Scaly-foots: Pygopodidae
Scaley-foots: *Pygopus*
Scarlet snakes: *Cemophora*
Schneider's skinks: *Eumeces*
Schreiber's green lizards: *Lacerta*
Schweigger's hinge-back tortoises: *Kinixys*
Scorpion mud turtles: *Kinosternon*
Sea kraits: *Laticauda*
Seal salamanders: *Desmognathus*
Sea snakes: Hydrophiidae
Sea turtles: Cheloniidae
Seepage salamanders: *Desmognathus*
Senegal kassinas: *Kassina*
Senegal running frogs: *Kassina*
Senegal soft-shell turtles: *Cyclanorbis*
Serrated geometric tortoises: *Psammobates*
Serrated turtles: *Pelusios*
Seven-pacers: *Daboia*
Seychelles frogs: *Sooglossus*
Seychelles giant tortoises: *Megalochelys*
Sharp-nosed copperheads: *Agkistrodon*
Sharp-nosed mud turtles: *Kinosternon*
Sharp-snouted rock lizards: *Lacerta*
Sharp-snouted torrent frogs: *Taudactylus*
Sharptail snakes: *Contia*
Sheep toads: *Hypopachus*
Sheltopusik: *Ophisaurus*
Shield-nosed cobras: *Aspidelaps*
Shield-tailed snakes: Uropeltidae
Shingle-back skinks: *Trachysaurus*
Shiny skinks: *Mabuya*

Short-headed frogs: *Breviceps*
Short-horned horned frogs: *Ceratophrys*
Short-horned lizards: *Phrynosoma*
Short-nosed rock lizards: *Petrosaurus*
Short-tailed pythons: *Python*
Short-tailed snakes: *Stilosoma*
Shovel-nosed frogs: *Hemisus*
Shovel-nosed salamanders: *Leurognathus*
Shovelnosed snakes: *Chionactis*
Shovel-snouts: *Prosymma*
Shrinking frogs: Pseudidae
Siamese crocodiles: *Crocodylus*
Siberian salamanders: *Ranodon*
Side-blotched lizards: *Uta*
Sidewinders: *Crotalus*
Sikkim slender skinks: *Scincella*
Singalese skinks: *Nessia*
Sipos: *Chironius*
Sirens: *Siren*
Sita lizards: *Sitana*
Six-eyed pond turtles: *Sacalia*
Six-lined racerunners: *Cnemidophorus*
Skinks: Scincidae
Skink tegus: *Tretioscincus*
Slender agamas: *Agama*
Slender blind snakes: *Leptotyphlops*
Slender boas: *Epicrates*
Slender coral snakes: *Leptomicrurus*
Slender glass lizards: *Ophisaurus*
Slender quill-nosed snakes: *Xenocalamus*
Slender racers: *Coluber*
Slender salamanders: *Batrachoseps*
Sliders: *Chrysemys*
Slimy salamanders: *Plethodon*
Slow worms: *Anguis*
Small African bullfrogs: *Pyxicephalus*
Small-eyed snakes: *Cryptophis*
Small flat lizards: *Platysaurus*
Small-headed worm lizards: *Leposternon*
Smooth clawed frogs: *Xenopus*
Smooth earth snakes: *Virginia*
Smooth-fronted caimans: *Paleosuchus*
Smooth green snakes: *Opheodrys*
Smooth-headed helmeted iguanas: *Corytophanes*
Smooth horned frogs: *Proceratophrys*
Smooth knob-tail geckos: *Nephrurus*
Smooth newts: *Triturus*
Smooth-scaled scaleyfoots: *Delma*
Smooth snake-neck turtles: *Chelodina*
Smooth snakes: *Coronella*
Smooth soft-shell turtles: *Trionyx*
Smooth-throated swifts: *Liolaemus*
Snail-eating skinks: *Tiliqua*
Snake-eyed lacertids: *Ophisops*
Snake-necked frogs: *Phrynomerus*
Snake-neck turtles: Chelidae
Snake skinks: *Ophiomorus*
Snake teiids: *Ophiognomon*
Snapping turtles: *Chelydra*
Soa soas: *Hydrosaurus*
Soft-shell turtles: Trionychidae

Solomons tree skinks: *Corucia*
Sonoran green toads: *Bufo*
Sonoran mountain kingsnakes: *Lampropeltis*
Sonoran shovelnosed snakes: *Chionactis*
South African house snakes: *Lamprophis*
South African sand lizards: *Meroles*
South African snake lizards: *Chamaesaura*
South American bullfrogs: *Leptodactylus*
South American green snakes: *Philodryas*
South American hog-nosed snakes: *Lystrophis*
South American rattlesnakes: *Crotalus*
South American snake-neck turtles: *Hydromedusa*
South American swifts: *Liolaemus*
South American water snakes: *Helicops*
South American worm lizards: *Amphisbaena*
South American worm lizards: *Ophiodes*
Southeastern crowned snakes: *Tantilla*
Southern alligator lizards: *Gerrhonotus*
Southern leaf-tailed geckos: *Phyllurus*
Southern toadlets: *Pseudophryne*
Spadefoot toads: Pelobatidae
Spanish barrel skinks: *Chalcides*
Spanish keeled lizards: *Algyroides*
Spanish ribbed newts: *Pleurodeles*
Spanish sand lizards: *Psammodromus*
Spanish wall lizards: *Podarcis*
Speckled racers: *Drymobius*
Speckled tortoises: *Homopus*
Speckled worm lizards: *Amphisbaena*
Spectacled caimans: *Caiman*
Spectacled cobras: *Naja*
Spectacled salamanders: *Salamandrina*
Spectacled tegus: *Gymnophthalamus*
Spider geckos: *Agamura*
Spider tortoises: *Pyxis*
Spine-tail salamanders: *Mertensiella*
Spiny agamas: *Agama*
Spiny chameleons: *Brookesia*
Spiny lizards: *Sceloporus*
Spiny soft-shell turtles: *Trionyx*
Spiny-tailed agamids: *Uromastyx*
Spiny-tailed iguanas: *Ctenosaura*
Spiny-tailed iguanids: *Uracentron*
Spiny-tailed lizards: *Lacerta*
Spiny-tailed skinks: *Egernia*
Spiny-tailed swifts: *Enyaliosaurus*
Spiny toad-heads: *Phrynocephalus*
Spiny toads: *Bufo*
Spiny tree skinks: *Egernia*
Spiny turtles: *Heosemys*
Spitting cobras: *Hemachatus*
Spitting cobras: *Naja*
Splendid keeled lizards: *Algyroides*
Spotted chorus frogs: *Pseudacris*
Spotted frogs: *Rana*
Spotted grass frogs: *Limnodynastes*
Spotted monitor tegus: *Callopistes*
Spotted racerunners: *Cnemidophorus*
Spotted salamanders: *Ambystoma*
Spotted sand snakes: *Chilomeniscus*
Spotted shovel-nosed frogs: *Hemisus*

Spotted toads: *Bufo*
Spotted turtles: *Clemmys*
Spring frogs: *Rana*
Spring peepers: *Hyla*
Spring salamanders: *Gyrinophilus*
Spurred tortoises: *Geochelone*
Spur-thighed Mediterranean tortoises: *Testudo*
Steppe rat snakes: *Elaphe*
Steppe tortoises: *Agrionemys*
Stinkpots: *Sternotherus*
Strange-scaled snakes: *Xenodermus*
Strawberry poison arrow frogs: *Dendrobates*
Streaky shovel-snouts: *Prosymma*
Stream frogs: *Rana*
Stream toads: *Ansonia*
Striped day geckos: *Phelsuma*
Striped frogs: *Rana*
Striped mud turtles: *Kinosternon*
Striped newts: *Notophthalmus*
Striped swamp snakes: *Regina*
Stripe-footed anoles: *Anolis*
Stripe-tail monitors: *Varanus*
Stub-footed toads: *Atelopus*
Stub-tailed chameleons: *Brookesia*
Sunbeam snakes: *Xenopeltis*
Sunda crocodiles: *Tomistoma*
Sun-gazers: *Cordylus*
Sun-gazing agamids: *Phrynocephalus*
Surinam toads: *Pipa*
Surucucu: *Lachesis*
Swamp crocodiles: *Crocodylus*
Swamp frogs: *Rana*
Swamp turtles: *Pseudemydura*
Swordtail newts: *Cynops*
Syrian spadefoots: *Pelobates*

T
Tailed toads: *Ascaphus*
Tail rollers: *Phrynocephalus*
Taipans: *Oxyuranus*
Tartar sand boas: *Eryx*
Tawny plated lizards: *Gerrhosaurus*
Tegus: Teiidae
Tegus: *Tupinambis*
Temple turtles: *Hieremys*
Tennessee cave salamanders: *Gyrinophilus*
Tentacled snakes: *Erpeton*
Texas blind salamanders: *Typhlomolge*
Texas blind snakes: *Leptotyphlops*
Texas horned lizards: *Phrynosoma*
Texas tortoises: *Gopherus*
Thick-tailed bark geckos: *Underwoodisaurus*
Thick-toed geckos: *Pachydactylus*
Thorny devils: *Moloch*
Three-horned chameleons: *Chamaeleo*
Three-keeled box turtles: *Cuora*
Three-keeled Indian terrapins: *Melanochelys*
Three-keeled pond turtles: *Mauremys*
Three-lined emerald lizards: *Lacerta*
Three-lined grass snakes: *Psammophylax*
Three-toed amphiumas: *Amphiuma*

Three-toed skinks: *Chalcides*
Three-toed snake skinks: *Ophiomorus*
Tibetan toads: *Bufo*
Tiger lizards: *Nucras*
Tiger salamanders: *Ambystoma*
Tiger snakes: *Notechis*
Timber rattlesnakes: *Crotalus*
Timor monitors: *Varanus*
Timor pythons: *Python*
Toad adders: *Causus*
Toad-headed agamas: *Phrynocephalus*
Toad-headed turtles: *Phrynops*
Tokay geckos: *Gekko*
Tomato frogs: *Dyscophus*
Tongueless frogs: Pipidae
Toothed frogs: *Rana*
Tortoises: Testudinidae
Trans-Pecos snakes: *Elaphe*
Transvaal snake lizards: *Chamaesaura*
Travancore tortoises: *Indotestudo*
Tree boas: *Corallus*
Treefrogs: *Hyla*
Treefrogs: Hylidae
Tree lizards: *Urosaurus*
Tree pythons: *Chondropython*
Tree salamanders: *Aneides*
Tree skinks: *Corucia*
Tree skinks: *Dasia*
Tree snakes: *Boiga*
Tree vipers: *Trimeresurus*
Trilling frogs: *Neobatrachus*
Tropical bullfrogs: *Leptodactylus*
Tropical forest turtles: *Rhinoclemmys*
Tropical geckos: *Hemidactylus*
Tropical lungless salamanders: *Bolitoglossa*
Tropical racers: *Drymobius*
Tropical racers: *Mastigodryas*
Tropical rat snakes: *Spilotes*
Tropical sliders: *Chrysemys*
Tropical worm salamanders: *Oedipina*
True toads: *Bufo*
True vipers: *Vipera*
Tuataras: *Sphenodon*
Turkish geckos: *Hemidactylus*
Turkmenian agamas: *Agama*
Turnip-tailed geckos: *Underwoodisaurus*
Turtle frogs: *Myobatrachus*
Turtle-headed sea snakes: *Emydocephalus*
Turtles: Testudines
Tusked frogs: *Adelotus*
Twist-neck turtles: *Platemys*
Two-banded monitors: *Varanus*
Two-legged worm lizards: *Bipes*
Two-lined salamanders: *Eurycea*
Two-toed amphiumas: *Amphiuma*
Tyrrhenian mountain lizards: *Lacerta*
Tyrrhenian wall lizards: *Podarcis*

U
Underwater frogs: *Xenopus*
Urutu: *Bothrops*

V

Varied lizards: *Calotes*
Variegated monitors: *Varanus*
Variegated racers: *Coluber*
Velvet geckos: *Oedura*
Velvety geckos: *Homopholis*
Venomous garter snakes: *Elapsoidea*
Vietnamese warty newts: *Paramesotriton*
Vine snakes: *Oxybelis*
Viperine ruddertails: *Thalassophis*
Viperine water snakes: *Natrix*
Vipers: Viperidae
Viviparous lizards: *Lacerta*

W

Wagler's palm vipers: *Trimeresurus*
Wahlberg's velvety geckos: *Homopholis*
Wall geckos: *Tarentola*
Wall lizards: *Podarcis*
Warren's girdled lizards: *Cordylus*
Wart snakes: Acrochordidae
Warty newts: *Paramesotriton*
Water anoles: *Anolis*
Water cobras: *Boulengerina*
Waterdogs: *Necturus*
Water dragons: *Physignathus*
Water-holding frogs: *Cyclorana*
Water moccasins: *Agkistrodon*
Water monitors: *Varanus*
Water snakes, American: *Nerodia*
Water snakes: Natricinae
Water tegus: *Neusticurus*
Web-toed salamanders: *Hydromantes*
Wedge-headed treefrogs: *Aparasphenodon*
Wedge-snouted amphisbaenids: *Monopeltis*
Wedge-snout skinks: *Sphenops*
West African black turtles: *Pelusios*
Western aquatic garter snakes: *Thamnophis*
Western banded geckos: *Coleonyx*
Western banjo frogs: *Limnodynastes*
Western blind snakes: *Leptotyphlops*
Western blue-tongued skinks: *Tiliqua*
Western box turtles: *Terrapene*
Western diamondback rattlesnakes: *Crotalus*
Western fence lizards: *Sceloporus*
Western ground snakes: *Sonora*
Western hog-nosed snakes: *Heterodon*
Western hook-nosed snakes: *Gyalopion*
Western mud divers: *Pelodytes*
Western narrow-mouthed toads: *Gastrophryne*
Western newts: *Taricha*
Western patchnosed snakes: *Salvadora*
Western pond turtles: *Clemmys*
Western rattlesnakes: *Crotalus*
Western red-backed salamanders: *Plethodon*
Western ribbon snakes: *Thamnophis*
Western ringnecked snakes: *Diadophis*
Western scaley-foots: *Pygopus*
Western shovelnosed snakes: *Chionactis*
Western snake-eyes: *Ophisops*

Western spadefoots: *Pelobates*
Western swamp turtles: *Pseudemydura*
Western terrestrial garter snakes: *Thamnophis*
Western toads: *Bufo*
Whip lizards: *Tetradactylus*
Whipsnakes: *Masticophis*
Whiptails: *Cnemidophorus*
Whistling geckos: *Ptenopus*
White-bearded flying frogs: *Rhacophorus*
White-bellied water snakes: *Fordonia*
White-fronted box turtles: *Cuora*
White-lipped frogs: *Leptodactylus*
White-lipped mud turtles: *Kinosternon*
White-lipped pythons: *Liasis*
White-lipped snakes: *Crotaphopeltis*
White-lipped snakes: *Drysdalia*
White-lipped tree vipers: *Trimeresurus*
White-lipped water snakes: *Lycodonomorphus*
White's skinks: *Egernia*
White's treefrogs: *Litoria*
White-throated geckos: *Gonatodes*
Wolf snakes: Lycodontinae
Wolf snakes: *Lycophidion*
Woma: *Aspidites*
Wonder geckos: *Teratoscincus*
Wood frogs: *Rana*
Wood geckos: *Diplodactylus*
Woodhouse's toads: *Bufo*
Woodland salamanders: *Plethodon*
Wood snakes: *Tropidophis*
Wood turtles: *Clemmys*
Worm lizards: Amphisbaenia
Worm snakes: *Carphophis*
Wrinkled ground frogs: *Platymantis*

Y

Yararanata: *Bothrops*
Yarrow's spiny lizards: *Sceloporus*
Yellow anacondas: *Eunectes*
Yellow-bellied sea snakes: *Pelamis*
Yellow-bellied toads: *Bombina*
Yellow-faced whip snakes: *Demansia*
Yellow-footed tortoises: *Chelonoidis*
Yellow-green leaf-toed geckos: *Hemidactylus*
Yellow-green racers: *Coluber*
Yellow-headed geckos: *Gonatodes*
Yellow-headed tortoises: *Indotestudo*
Yellow-lipped sea kraits: *Laticauda*
Yellow-margined box turtles: *Cuora*
Yellow monitors: *Varanus*
Yellow mud turtles: *Kinosternon*
Yellow-spotted Amazon turtles: *Podocnemis*
Yellow-spotted monitor tegus: *Callopistes*
Yellow-spotted toadlets: *Uperoleia*
Yellow-throated plated lizards: *Gerrhosaurus*

Z

Zanzibar day geckos: *Phelsuma*
Zebra-tailed lizards: *Callisaurus*
Zigzag salamanders: *Plethodon*

Measurement Conversion Factors

When you know—	Multiply by—	To find—
Length:		
Millimeters (mm)	0.04	inches (in)
Centimeters (cm)	0.4	inches (in)
Meters (m)	3.3	feet (ft)
Meters (m)	1.1	yards (yd)
Kilometers (km)	0.6	miles (mi)
Inches (in)	2.54	centimeters (cm)
Feet (ft)	30	centimeters (cm)
Yards (yd)	0.9	meters (m)
Miles (mi)	1.6	kilometers (km)
Area:		
Square centimeters (cm^2)	0.16	square inches (sq in)
Square meters (m^2)	1.2	square yards (sq yd)
Square kilometers (km^2)	0.4	square miles (sq mi)
Hectares (ha)	2.5	acres
Square inches (sq in)	6.5	square centimeters (cm^2)
Square feet (sq ft)	0.09	square meters (m^2)
Square yards (sq yd)	0.8	square meters (m^2)
Square miles (sq mi)	1.2	square kilometers (km^2)
Acres	0.4	hectares (ha)
Mass (Weight):		
Grams (g)	0.035	ounces (oz)
Kilograms (kg)	2.2	pounds (lb)
Ounces (oz)	28	grams (g)
Pounds (lb)	0.45	kilograms (kg)
Volume:		
Milliliters (ml)	0.03	fluid ounces (fl oz)
Liters (L)	2.1	pints (pt)
Liters (L)	1.06	quarts (qt)
Liters (L)	0.26	U.S. gallons (gal)
Liters (L)	0.22	Imperial gallons (gal)
Cubic centimeters (cc)	16.387	cubic inches (cu in)
Cubic meters (cm^3)	35	cubic feet (cu ft)
Cubic meters (cm^3)	1.3	cubic yards (cu yd)
Teaspoons (tsp)	5	millimeters (ml)
Tablespoons (tbsp)	15	millimeters (ml)
Fluid ounces (fl oz)	30	millimeters (ml)
Cups (c)	0.24	liters (L)
Pints (pt)	0.47	liters (L)
Quarts (qt)	0.95	liters (L)
U.S. gallons (gal)	3.8	liters (L)
U.S. gallons (gal)	231	cubic inches (cu in)
Imperial gallons (gal)	4.5	liters (L)
Imperial gallons (gal)	277.42	cubic inches (cu in)
Cubic inches (cu in)	0.061	cubic centimeters (cc)
Cubic feet (cu ft)	0.028	cubic meters (m^3)
Cubic yards (cu yd)	0.76	cubic meters (m^3)
Temperature:		
Celsius (°C)	multiply by 1.8, add 32	Fahrenheit (°F)
Fahrenheit (°F)	subtract 32, multiply by 0.555	Celsius (°C)